16th Edition
2007 North American
Coins & Prices
A GUIDE TO U.S., CANADIAN AND MEXICAN COINS

Edited by David C. Harper, editor of Numismatic News,
World Coin News and Bank Note Reporter

©2006 KP Books

Published by

krause publications

An Imprint of F+W Publications

700 East State Street • Iola, WI 54990-0001
715-445-2214 • 888-457-2873

Our toll-free number to place an order or obtain
a free catalog is (800) 258-0929.

Library of Congress Catalog Number: 9465-0597

ISBN-13: 978-0-89689-380-1
ISBN-10 : 0-89689-380-4

Edited by David C. Harper
Designed by Sally Olson

Printed in United States of America

Contents

Preface

Providing coin collectors with accurate, independently produced pricing information on collectible coins has become a trademark of F+W Publications' numismatic division in its 50 years of publishing. Visit our Web site at www.collect.com for more information about us. We employ a full-time staff of market analysts who monitor auction results, trading on the Internet and trading at major shows.

This information is compiled by our analysts and they determine what price most accurately reflects the trading that has occurred for each date and mintmark in each grade listed in *North American Coins & Prices*. By studying this information and referring back to it repeatedly, a collector can arm himself with the necessary knowledge to go out in the market and make wise purchasing decisions. It must be remembered that these prices are intended solely as a guide. They are neither offers to buy or sell. Because prices do fluctuate, those that appear in this book may be in some cases obsolete by the time of publication. By checking the more than 40 price charts in the U.S. section, you can get a feel as to how price swings have occurred since 1972.

U.S. coins are the most popularly collected issues in the world. This is attributable in part to the popularity of coin collecting in the United States, but collectors in many other countries also covet collectible U.S. coins. After collecting U.S. coins for a while, many collectors in the United States branch out into issues of Canada and Mexico. These coins also enjoy a popular following in their countries of origin.

Thus, *North American Coins & Prices* brings together pricing information on all three of these countries. But this book also takes the price-guide concept a step further by providing information on the nuts and bolts of collecting coins: acquiring coins, grading them, organizing them into a collection, storing them properly and much more. Novice collectors can gain the necessary knowledge to collect coins enjoyably; veterans can pick up some pointers to add to their knowledge.

1

'A small beginning'
The U.S. Mint grew from a modest start

By Robert R. Van Ryzin

It was a "small beginning" but a significant one. In July 1792, a site for the new U.S. Mint not yet having been secured, 1,500 silver half dismes were struck on a small screw press nestled in the cellar of a Philadelphia building owned by sawmaker John Harper. Though some have since categorized these early emissions of the fledgling U.S. Mint as patterns, it is clear that first President George Washington – who is said to have deposited the silver from which the coins were struck – considered this small batch of half dismes the first official U.S. coins.

It is true that this limited coinage, the first since passage of the act establishing the Mint on April 2, 1792, pales by comparison to modern U.S. Mint presses. Today's machines can churn out up to 750 coins a minute, striking as many as four coins at a time and boasting yearly mintages in the billions. But it is also true that these first small pieces – struck from silver and stamped with a plump Liberty on the obverse and a scrawny eagle in flight on the reverse – have tremendous historical importance.

For within what Washington would declare in his 1792 address to Congress as a "small beginning" were the seeds of a monetary system that has lasted more than 200 years and has become the study and admiration of many.

Before the U.S. Mint

Collectors today can trace much of the nation's development and learn of its struggles and growth through its coinage: from a cumbersome system first proposed by Robert Morris, a Revolutionary War financier and first superintendent of finance, to the refinements tendered by Thomas Jefferson and Alexander Hamilton, which firmly placed the nation on an easily understood decimal system of coinage.

At first there was little coinage in circulation, except for foreign coins that arrived through trade or in the purses of the first settlers. Despite a dire need for coinage in the Colonies, Great Britain considered it a royal right and granted franchises sparingly. Much of the Colonial economy, therefore, revolved around barter, with food staples, crops, and goods serving as currency. Indian waupum or bead money also was used, first in the fur trade and later as a form of money for Colonial use.

Copper pieces were produced around 1616 for the Sommer Islands (now Bermuda), but coinage within the American Colonies apparently didn't begin until 1652, when John Hull struck silver threepence, sixpence and shillings under authority of the General Court of Massachusetts. This coinage continued, with design changes (willow, oak and pine trees), through 1682. Most of the coins were dated 1652, apparently to avoid problems with England.

In 1658 Cecil Calvert, second Lord Baltimore, commissioned coins to be struck in England for use in Maryland. Other authorized and unauthorized coinages – including those of Mark Newby, John Holt, William Wood, and Dr. Samuel Higley – all became part of the landscape of circulating coins. In the 1780s this hodgepodge of coinage was augmented by influxes of counterfeit British halfpenny coins and various state coinages.

In terms of the latter, the Articles of Confederation had granted individual states the right to produce copper coins. Many states found this to be appealing, and merchants in the mid-1780s traded copper coins of Vermont, Connecticut, Massachusetts, New Jersey, and New York. Not all were legal issues; various entrepreneurs used this as an invitation to strike imitation state coppers and British halfpence. Mutilated and worn foreign coins also circulated in abundance. Included among these were coins of Portugal, Great Britain and France, with the large majority of the silver arriving from Spain.

The accounting system used by the states was derived from the British system of pounds, shillings and pence. Each state was allowed to set its own rates at which foreign gold and silver coins would trade in relation to the British pound.

In 1782 Robert Morris, newly named superintendent of finance, was appointed to head a committee to determine the values and weights of the gold and silver coins in circulation. Asked simply to draw up a table of values, Morris took the opportunity to propose the establishment of a federal mint. In his Jan. 15, 1782, report (largely prepared by his assistant, Gouverneur Morris), Morris noted that the exchange rates between the states were complicated.

He observed that a farmer in New Hampshire would be hard-pressed if asked to determine the value of a bushel of wheat in South Carolina. Morris recorded that an amount of wheat worth four shillings in his home state of New Hampshire would be worth 21 shillings and eightpence under the accounting system used in South Carolina.

Morris claimed these difficulties plagued not only farmers, but that "they are perplexing to most Men and troublesome to all." Morris further pressed for the adoption of an American coin to solve the problems of the need for small change and debased foreign coinages in circulation.

In essence, what he was advocating was a monometallic system based on silver. He said that gold and silver had fluctuated throughout history. Because these fluctuations resulted in the more valuable metal leaving the country, any nation that adopted a bimetallic coinage was doomed to have its gold or silver coins disappear from circulation.

Robert Morris devised a complicated plan for a national coinage based on a common denominator of 1,440.

Gouverneur Morris calculated the rate at which the Spanish dollar traded to the British pound in the various states. Leaving out South Carolina, because it threw off his calculations, Gouverneur Morris arrived at a common denominator of 1,440. Robert Morris, therefore, recommended a unit of value of 1/1,440, equivalent to a quarter grain of silver. He suggested the striking of a silver 100-unit coin, or cent; a silver 500-unit coin, or quint; a silver 1,000-unit coin, or mark; and two copper coins, one of eight units and the other of five units.

On Feb. 21, 1782, the Grand Committee of Congress approved the proposal and directed Morris to press forward and report with a plan to establish a mint. Morris had already done so. Apparently feeling confident that Congress would like his coinage ideas, Morris (as shown by his diary) began efforts at the physical establishment prior to his January 1782 report. He had already engaged Benjamin Dudley to acquire necessary equipment for the mint and hoped to have sample coins available to submit with his original report to Congress.

Things went awry, however.

By Dec. 12, 1782, 10 months after Congress had approved his plan, Morris still could not show any samples of his coins. He was forced, ironically, to suggest that Congress draw up a table of rates for foreign coins to be used until his report was ready. It was not until April 2, 1783, that Morris was able to note in his diary that the first of his pattern coins were being struck.

"I sent for Mr. Dudley who delivered me a piece of Silver Coin," he wrote, "being the first that has been struck as an American Coin."

He also recorded that he had urged Dudley to go ahead with production of the silver patterns.

It wasn't until April 23, 1783, that Morris was able to send his Nova Constellatio patterns to Congress and suggest that he was ready to report on establishing a mint. Apparently nothing came of Morris' efforts. Several committees looked into the matter, but nothing was accomplished. Dudley was eventually discharged as Morris' hopes dimmed.

Thomas Jefferson was the next to offer a major plan. Jefferson liked the idea of a decimal system of coinage, but disliked Morris' basic unit of value. As chairman of the Currency Committee, Jefferson reviewed Morris' plan and formulated his own ideas.

To test public reaction, Jefferson gave his "Notes on Coinage" to *The Providence Gazette*, and *Country Journal,* which published his plan in its July 24, 1784, issue. Jefferson disagreed with Morris' suggestion for a 1/1,440 unit of value and instead proposed a decimal coinage based on the dollar, with the lowest unit of account being the mil, or 1/1,000.

"The most easy ratio of multiplication and division is that by ten," Jefferson wrote. "Every one knows the facility of Decimal Arithmetic."

Jefferson argued that although Morris' unit would have eliminated the unwanted fraction that occurred when merchants converted British farthings to dollars, this was of little significance. After all, the original idea of establishing a mint was to get rid of foreign currencies.

Morris' unit, Jefferson said, was too cumbersome for use in normal business transactions. According to Jefferson, under Morris' plan a horse valued at 80 Spanish dollars would require a notation of six figures and would be shown as 115,200 units.

Jefferson' coinage plan suggested the striking of a dollar, or unit; half dollar, or five-tenths; a double tenth, or fifth of a dollar, equivalent to a pistereen; a tenth, equivalent to a Spanish bit; and a one-fifth copper coin, relating to the British farthing. He also wanted a gold coin of $10, corresponding to the British double guinea; and a copper one-hundredth coin, relating to the British halfpence.

In reference to his coinage denominations, Jefferson said, it was important that the coins "coincide in value with some of the known coins so nearly, that the people may by quick reference in the mind, estimate their value."

More than a year, however, passed without any further action on his plan or that proposed by Morris. In a letter to William Grayson, a member of the Continental Congress, Washington expressed concern for the establishment of a national coinage system, terming it "indispensably necessary." Washington also complained of the coinage in circulation: "A man must travel with a pair of scales in his pocket, or run the risk of receiving gold at one-fourth less than it counts."

A plan at last

On May 13, 1785, the 13-member Grand Committee, to whom Jefferson's plan had been submitted, filed its report, generally favoring Jefferson's coinage system. The committee did, however, make slight alterations, including the elimination of the gold $10 coin, the addition of a gold $5 coin, and the dropping of Jefferson's double

Thomas Jefferson proposed that the United States adopt a decimal system of coinage.

tenth, which it replaced with a quarter dollar. The committee also added a coin equal to 1/200th of a dollar (half cent). On July 6, 1785, Congress unanimously approved the Grand Committee's plan. It failed, however, to set a standard weight for the silver dollar or to order plans drawn up for a mint. These two factors led to new proposals.

On April 8, 1786, the Board of Treasury, which had been reinstated after Morris' resignation as superintendent of finance two years prior, tendered three distinct coinage proposals based on varying weights and bimetallic ratios for the silver dollar. The first of these three plans (the one passed by Congress on Aug. 8, 1786) required the silver dollar to contain 375.64 grains of pure silver. The board's proposal varied from earlier coinage plans in that it advocated a higher bimetallic ratio of 15.256-to-1 and differing charges to depositors for coining of gold and silver. It called for minting of gold $5 and $10 coins, and silver denominations of the dime, double dime, half dollar, and dollar. In copper were a cent and half cent. The proposal came during the peak of state coinages and influxes of debased coppers, which, as the board reported, were being "Imported into or manufactured in the Several States."

Concerned over the need to control state coinages and foreign coppers, the board suggested that, within nine months of passage of its proposal, the legal-tender status of all foreign coppers be repealed and that values be set at which the state coppers would circulate. The board obviously expected immediate action and ordered a supply of copper that was being stored in Boston to be brought to New York in the hope that it might soon be coined. Their hopes, however, rested on the positive and quick action of Congress, something that hadn't occurred with the other proposals and would not occur this time.

Opposition to the mint was beginning to surface. Several members of Congress expressed their belief that the supply of foreign gold and silver coins in circulation was sufficient to preclude any need for a mint. They also argued that the problem with debased coppers could be solved by contracting with private individuals to strike the nation's cents and half cents.

Several proposals were offered for a contract coinage. On April 21, 1787, the board accepted a proposal by James Jarvis to strike 300 tons of copper coin at the federal standard. Jarvis, however, delivered slightly less than 9,000 pounds of his contract. The contract was voided the following year for his failure to meet scheduled delivery times, but helped to delay further action on a mint. Concerted action on a coinage system and a mint would wait until the formation of the new government.

Alexander Hamilton, named in September 1789 to head the new Treasury, offered three different methods by which the new nation could achieve economic stability, including the funding of the national debt, establishment of the Bank of North America, and the founding of the U.S. Mint. On Jan. 21, 1791, Hamilton submitted to Congress a "Report on the Establishment of a Mint." It was compiled through his study of European economic theories and the earlier works of Morris and Jefferson, along with the 1786 report of the Board of Treasury.

Hamilton agreed with Jefferson that the dollar seemed to be best suited to serve as the basic unit, but believed it necessary to establish a proper weight and fineness for the new coin. To do so, Hamilton had several Spanish coins assayed to determine the fine weight of the Spanish dollar. He also watched the rate at which Spanish dollars traded for fine gold (24 3/4 grains per dollar) on the world market.

From his assays and observations he determined that the Spanish dollar contained 371 grains of silver. He then multiplied 24 3/4 by 15 (the gold value of silver times his suggested bimetallic ratio) and arrived at 371 1/4 as the proper fine silver weight for the new silver dollar.

In regard to his findings, Hamilton admitted that Morris had made similar assays and had arrived at a weight of 373 grains for the Spanish dollar. Hamilton attributed the discrepancy to the differing equipment used in making the assays. He failed, however, to observe that silver coins were traded in the world market at actual weight rather than the weight at time of issue. The Spanish dollar contained 376 grains of pure silver when new, 4 3/4 grains more than Hamilton's proposed silver dollar.

Hamilton also wanted a bimetallic ratio of 15-to-1, in contrast to the Board of Treasury's 15.6-to-1 ratio. Hamilton said his ratio was closer to Great Britain's, which would be important for trade, and Holland's, which would be important for repaying loans from that country.

His report suggested the striking of a gold $10; gold dollar; silver dollar; silver tenth, or disme; and copper one-hundredth and half-hundredth. Hamilton felt the last of these, the half cent, was necessary because it would enable merchants to lower their prices, which would help the poor.

Congress passed the act establishing the U.S. Mint in April 1792. It reinstated several coin denominations left out by Hamilton and dropped his gold dollar. In gold, the act authorized at $10 coin, or "eagle"; a $5 coin, or "half eagle"; and a $2.50 coin, or "quarter eagle." In silver were to be a dollar, half dollar, quarter dollar, disme, and half disme, and in copper a cent and half cent.

Though it established a sound system of U.S. coinage, the act failed to address the problem of foreign coins in circulation. It was amended in February 1793 to cancel their legal-tender status within three years of the Mint's opening.

Coinage begins

Coinage totals at the first mint were understandably low. Skilled coiners, assayers and others who could handle the mint's daily operations were in short supply in the United States. Also in want were adequate equipment and supplies of metal for coinage. Much of the former had to be built or imported. Much of the latter was also imported or salvaged from various domestic sources, including previously struck tokens and coins, and scrap metal.

Coinage began in earnest in 1793 with the striking of half cents and cents at the new mint located at Seventh Street between Market and Arch streets in Philadelphia. Silver coinage followed in 1794, with half dimes, half dollars and dollars. Gold coinage did not begin until 1795 with the minting of the first $5 and $10 coins. Silver dimes and quarters and gold $2.50 coins did not appear until 1796.

Under the bimetallic system of coinage by which gold and silver served as equal representations of the unit of value, much of the success and failure of the nation's coinage to enter and remain in circulation revolved around the supply and valuation of precious metals. One need only to gain a cursory knowledge of such movements to understand what role precious metals played in development of U.S. coinage. That role, to a large extent, determined why some coins today are rare and why some passed down from generation to generation are still plentiful and of lower value to collectors.

From the Mint's beginning, slight miscalculations in the proper weight for the silver dollar and a proper bimetallic ratio led gold and silver to disappear from circulation. The U.S. silver dollar traded at par with Spanish and Mexican dollars, but because the U.S. coin was lighter, it was doomed to export.

A depositor at the first mint could make a profit at the mint's expense by sending the coins to the West Indies. There they could be traded at par for the heavier Spanish or Mexican eight reales, which were then shipped back to the United States for recoinage. As a result, few early silver dollars entered domestic circulation; most failed to escape the melting pots.

Gold fared no better. Calculations of the bimetallic ratio by which silver traded for gold on the world market were also askew at first and were always subject to fluctuations. Gold coins either disappeared quickly after minting or never entered circulation, languishing in bank vaults. These problems led President Jefferson to halt coinage of the gold $10 and silver dollar.

Production at the first U.S. mint, in Philadelphia, was minuscule by today's standards.

The gold $10 reappeared in 1838 at a new, lower-weight standard. The silver dollar, not coined for circulation since 1803, returned in 1836 with a limited mintage. Full-scale coinage waited until 1840.

Nor was the coinage of copper an easy matter for the first mint. Severe shortages of the metal led the Mint to explore various avenues of obtaining sufficient supplies for striking cents and half cents.

Witness, for example, the half-cent issues of 1795 and 1797 struck over privately issued tokens of the New York firm of Talbot, Allum & Lee because of a shortage of copper for the federal issue. Rising copper prices and continued shortages forced the Mint to lower the cent's weight from 208 grains to 168 grains in 1795.

By that same year Congress had begun to investigate the Mint. Complaints about high costs and low production had been raised. Suggestions that a contract coinage might be more suitable for the new nation surfaced again, despite bad experiences with previous attempts.

The Mint survived this and another investigation, but the problems of fluctuating metal supplies continued to plague the nation. In 1798, because of the coinage shortage, the legal-tender status of foreign coins was restored. Several more extensions were given during the 1800s, ending with the withdrawal of legal-tender status for Spanish coins in 1857.

In the 1830s great influxes of silver from foreign mints raised the value of gold in relation to silver, which made it necessary for the Mint to lower the standard weight of all gold coins in 1834. It also led to the melting of great numbers of gold coins of the old specifications.

By the 1850s discovery of gold in California had again made silver the dearer metal. All silver quickly disappeared from circulation. Congress reacted in 1853 by lowering the weight of the silver half dime, dime, quarter, and half dollar, hoping to keep silver in circulation. A new gold coin of $20 value was introduced to absorb a great amount of the gold from Western mines.

Not long after, silver was discovered in Nevada. By the mid-1870s the various mines that made up what was known as the Comstock Lode (after its colorful early proprietor, Henry P. Comstock) had hit the mother lode. Large supplies of silver from the Comstock, combined with European demonetization, caused a severe drop in its value, which continued through the close of the 19th century.

It was believed that the introduction of a heavier, 420-grain silver dollar in 1873, known as the Trade dollar, would create a market for much of the Comstock silver, bolster its price, and at the same time wrest control from Great Britain of lucrative trade with the Orient. It didn't. Large numbers of Trade dollars eventually flooded back into the United States, where they were, ironically, accepted only at a discount to the lesser-weight Morgan dollars.

The latter had been introduced in 1878 as a panacea to the severe economic problems following the Civil War. Those who proudly carried the banner of free silver contended that by taking the rich output of the Comstock mines and turning it into silver dollars, a cheaper, more plentiful form of money would become available. In its wake, they believed, would be a much needed economic recovery.

The Free Silver Movement gained its greatest support during the late 19th century when William Jennings Bryan attempted to gain the White House on a plank largely based on restoration of the free and unlimited coinage of the standard 412.5-grain silver dollar. He failed. Silver failed. Shortly thereafter the United States officially adopted a gold standard.

Silver continued to be a primary coinage metal until 1964, when rising prices led the Mint to remove it from the dime and quarter. Mintage of the silver dollar had ended in 1935. The half dollar continued to be coined through 1970 with a 40-percent-silver composition. It, too, was then debased.

Gold coinage ended in 1933 and exists today only in commemorative issues and American Eagle bullion coins with fictive face values. A clad composition of copper and nickel is now the primary coinage metal. Even the cent is no longer all copper; a copper-coated zinc composition has been used since 1982.

Precious-metal supplies were also linked to the opening of additional mints, which served the parent facility in Philadelphia. The impact of gold discoveries in the 1820s in the southern Appalachian Mountains was directly tied to the construction of branch mints in Dahlonega, Ga., and Charlotte, N.C., in 1838. These new mints struck only gold coins. New Orleans also became the site of a branch mint in the same year as Dahlonega and Charlotte. It took in some of the outflow of gold from Southern mines, but also struck silver coins.

Discovery of gold in California in the late 1840s created a gold rush, and from it sprang a great western migration. Private issues of gold coinage, often of debased quality, were prevalent, and the cost of shipping the metal eastward for coinage at Philadelphia was high. A call for an official branch mint was soon heard and heeded in 1852 with the authorization of the San Francisco Mint, which began taking deposits in 1854.

The discovery of silver in the Comstock Lode led to yet another mint. Located only a short distance via Virginia & Truckee Railroad from the fabulous Comstock Lode, the Carson City mint began receiving bullion in early 1870. It struck only silver coins during its tenure.

Denver, also located in a mineral-rich region, became the site of an assay office in 1863 when the government purchased the Clark, Gruber & Co. private mint. It became a U.S. branch mint in 1906. In addition to the Denver and Philadelphia mints, San Francisco and a facility in West Point, N.Y., continue to serve as U.S. mints, but the others have left behind a rich legacy.

The collector taking a more extended journey into the history of U.S. coinage can find plenty of interesting tales – some as tall as the day is long and others factually based – all of which are part of the rich and ever-changing panoply of U.S. coinage history. There are stories of denominations that failed, great discoveries, great rarities, great collectors, and, for those with an artistic bent, a rich field of pattern coins to be explored and a wealth of much-heralded designs by famous sculptors such as Augustus Saint-Gaudens, Adolph Weinman, James Earle Fraser, and others.

For those who are drawn to the hobby by the allure of age-old relics of days gone by, or by coins handed down through the family, or even by dreams of great wealth, coin collecting has much to offer. The history of the U.S. Mint, with its small but ever so important beginning, is the starting point.

2

Making money
How coins are manufactured

By Alan Herbert

Just as printing is the process by which paper money is made, so is minting the method of manufacturing coins. The two are often confused by the public, but they are completely different.

The history of minting goes back several centuries before the birth of Christ. The Lydians are credited with making the first crude coins in the Middle East about 700 B.C., although the Chinese and Koreans trace their coinage back even further.

Some early coins were cast. That process continued in China into the 1900s, but only for low-value pieces. Here again the average person often assumes that all coins are cast, but as you will see, only a tiny fraction of a percent are – or were – actually made that way.

The methods developed by the Greeks and Romans centered on making dies that could be hammered by hand into the surface of a lump of metal, flattening it and impressing a design. Hammered coinage continued until after the end of the Middle Ages, about 1500. After that the first machines that could strike coins were invented. Today their successors can pound out 750 or more coins a minute.

From the early days when the fixed die was driven into a stump or a hole drilled in a rock, through fixing it in an anvil (the fixed die is still called the anvil die), to today's modern coin presses, the process is much the same. Force is applied to devices that impress or apply a design to a piece of material, which is transformed into a coin.

Early dies were made of wood. Then came copper, bronze, and finally iron as technology advanced. Today dies are made from exotic steels with special qualities that make them ideal for striking coins.

The history of coinage is fascinating. Interwoven into it are several familiar names: Leonardo da Vinci is credited with inventing one of the first coin presses. James Watt, English inventor of the steam engine, was the first to incorporate steam power to drive the coin presses that earlier had depended on horses or human arms.

Whether the power comes from a hand holding a hammer or a mechanical ram, and whether it comes from above, below, or the side, the process is called "striking" a coin. Modern coin presses use a variety of methods in applying brute force to a piece of metal to turn it into a coin.

Another fable that traces to casting coins is the common belief that coins are made from liquid metal or at the least are red hot when they are struck. Neither is true. A coin's design is formed by the pressure that causes the metal to cold-flow into the pattern that you see on the coins in your pocket.

There are three basic parts of the minting process: (1) the making of the planchet, which is divided into the selection and processing of the metal and the preparation of the planchets, (2) the making of the dies, and (3) the use of the dies to strike the planchets. To help you remember these three parts, think of "P," "D" and "S" for planchet, die and striking.

Choosing a metal

Many different metals have and are being used for coins. The most popular coinage metals are those commonly found and relatively cheap, so they can be used for striking low-value coins. Precious metals – like silver, gold and platinum – are still used for commemorative coins.

A good coinage metal requires certain properties. The metal must be soft enough to be easily worked yet hard enough to withstand the wear and tear of a thousand pockets, a hundred thousand transactions. Few metals have all the right properties, so coin metals usually are an alloy, or mixture of two or more metals.

Copper is a favorite coin metal, either by itself or in an alloy. Zinc, nickel, iron, and aluminum are also found in coins struck by the United States and other countries. Silver and gold have to be alloyed with some metal, usually copper, to be hard enough to withstand commercial life. The so-called "pure" coins of silver or gold are known as "bullion coins," bought and sold primarily for their precious-metal content.

The metals chosen for a coin are melted and mixed together, and either poured into ingots or blocks, or extruded from furnaces that continuously cast a long strip of the metal. The ingots are passed several times between the big rolls in a rolling mill to reduce the ingot to the thickness of the blanks needed.

Once the strip is rolled to the correct thickness, it is sent to a blanking press. A gang of blunt-end punches are driven through the sheet, producing a dozen or more blanks with each stroke. The rough blanks are then ready to be processed.

Making the 'blanks'

The piece of metal (occasionally some other material, so it isn't always metal) that becomes a coin is known as a "blank." This is a usually round, flat piece that usually has been punched or cut from a sheet or strip of coin metal.

Strips of coin metal stand ready to be cut into "blanks."

A binful of blanks are ready for the coin press.

Before a blank can become a coin it has to be processed, cleaned, softened, and given what is known as an "upset edge" – a raised ridge or rim around both sides. The blank then becomes a "planchet" and is ready to be struck into a coin by the dies.

First they go through what looks like a monstrous cement mixer. A huge cylinder revolves slowly as the planchets are fed in at one end and spiral their way through. This is an annealing oven, which heats the planchets to soften them. When they come out the end, they fall into a bath where they are cleaned with a diluted acid or soap solution.

As the final step, they go through the upsetting mill, the machine that puts the raised rim on the blank and turns it into a planchet, ready to be struck. In a different department the process of making the dies used to strike the coins has already begun.

Preparing the dies

For those who haven't studied metallurgy, the concept of hard metal flowing about is pretty hard to swallow, but this is actually what happens. It is basically the same process as the one used in an auto plant to turn a flat sheet of steel into a fender with multiple curves and sharp bends. The cold metal is moved about by the pressure applied.

To make the metal move into the desired design, there has to be a die. Actually there has to be two dies, because one of the laws of physics is that for every action there has to be an equal and opposite reaction. You cannot hold a piece of metal in midair and strike one side of it. Instead you make two dies, fix one, and drive the other one against it – with a piece of metal in between to accept the design from each die.

A die is a piece of hard metal, like steel, with a design on its face that helps to form a mirror image on the struck coin. Early dies were made by hand. Engravers used hand tools to laboriously cut each letter, each digit, and each owl or eagle or whatever design was being used into the face of the die. Notice that this is "into" the surface of the die. Each part of the die design is a hole or cavity of varying shape and depth.

This is because we want a mirror image on the coin, but we want it raised, or in "relief." To make a relief image on a coin, the image on the die has to be into the face of the die, or "incuse." Of course, if we want an incuse image on the coin, such as the gold $2.50 and $5 coins of 1908-1929, the design on the die face would have to be in relief.

To fully understand this, take a coin from your pocket and a piece of aluminum foil. Press the foil down over the coin design and rub it with an eraser. When you take the foil off and look at the side that was in contact with the coin, you have a perfect copy of a die. Everywhere there is a relief design on the coin there is an incuse design on your foil "die."

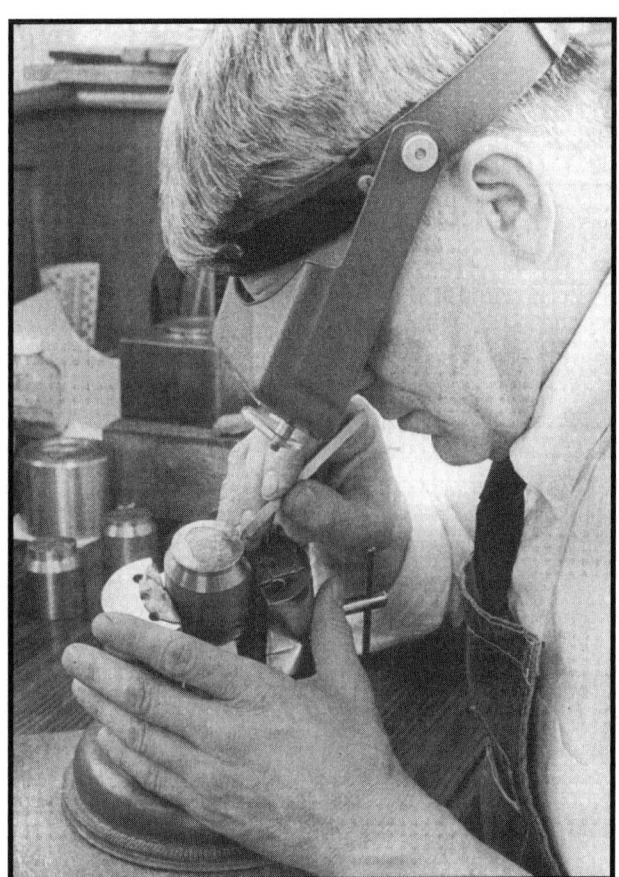

An engraver at the U.S. Mint puts the finishing touches on a die.

A galvano goes on the reducing lathe.

From sketchbook to coin

The design process begins with an artist's sketch. This is translated into a three-dimensional relief design that is hand-carved from plaster or, in recent years, from a form of plastic.

The plaster or plastic design is then transformed into a "galvano," which is an exact copy of the design that has been plated with a thin layer of copper. This is used as a template or pattern in a reducing lathe, which cuts the design into a die blank.

This die becomes the master die, from which all of the following steps descend. The process can be reversed so that the designs will be cut in relief, forming a tool called a "hub," which is simply a piece of steel with the design in relief, exactly the same as the relief design on the intended coin.

To make working dies, pieces of special steel are prepared, with one end shaped with a slight cone. The die blank is softened by heating it. Then the hub is forced into the face of the die, forming the incuse, mirror-image design in the face of the die.

The process usually has to be repeated because the die metal will harden from the pressure. The die is removed, softened, and returned to the hubbing press for a second impression from the hub. As you can imagine, it takes several hundred tons per square inch to force the hub into the die. Logically, this process is called "hubbing" a die.

The advantage of hubbing a die is that thousands of working dies can be made from a single hub, each one for all practical purposes as identical as the proverbial peas in a pod. This enables, for example, U.S. mints to strike billions of one-cent coins each year, each with the identical design.

Die making has come a long way from the early days when it took a skilled engraver a full day to carve a single letter into a die. The use of punches with the digits, letters or even parts of the design on the end reduced the amount of time required for the process. Today, thanks to the use of hubs, a complete die can be finished in a matter of hours.

Striking the coin

Yesterday's die might strike only a few hundred coins. Today it is not unusual for a die to strike well over a million coins.

The coin press used to strike modern coins is a complicated piece of equipment that consists basically of a feed system to place the planchets in position for the stroke of the hammer die to form a coin. This process takes only a fraction of a second, so the press has to operate precisely to spew out the hundreds of coins that are struck every minute.

The end of the early hammered coinage came with the introduction of the collar, which often is called the "third" die. The collar is nothing more than a steel plate with a hole in it. This hole is the exact diameter of the intended coin and often is lined with carbide to prolong its life. It surrounds the lower, or fixed, die. Its sole

Rows of modern coin presses at the Philadelphia Mint turn out billions of coins a year.

A hopper is full of shiny new one-cent coins ready for shipment.

purpose is to contain the coin metal to keep it from spreading sideways under the force of the strike.

If the intended coin has serrations, or "reeds," on the edge, then the collar has the matching design. The strike forces the coin metal against the serrations in the collar, forming the reeded edge at the same time that the two dies form the front and back, or obverse and reverse, of the coin.

Lettered-edge coins are produced usually by running the planchets through an edge-lettering die, or by using a segmented collar that is forced against the edge of the planchet during the strike by hydraulic pressure.

Several hundred tons were required to drive a hub into a die. Not as much but still significant amounts of force are needed to strike coins. A cent, for example, requires about 30 tons per square inch. One of the silver dollars took 150 tons. The other denominations fall in between.

Modern coin presses apply pressure in a variety of ways. A ram, carrying the moving or "hammer" die, is forced against the planchet. Most commonly this is with the mechanical advantage of a "knuckle" or connected pieces to which pressure is applied from the side. When the joint straightens – like straightening your finger – the ram at the end of the piece is driven into the planchet.

Once the strike is complete, at the final impact of the die pair, the coin has been produced. It is officially a coin now, and it's complete and ready to be spent.

The making of proof coins

While the high-speed coining presses are turning out billions of coins for commerce, there are other presses working at much slower speeds to produce collector coins, such as "proof" coins.

Proof coins started out as special presentation pieces. They were and still are struck on specially prepared planchets with specially prepared dies. Today the definition of a proof coin also requires that it be struck two or more times.

To make a proof coin, the planchets go through much the same process, but with some special care and some extra steps. Currently all proof versions of circulating U.S. coins are struck at the San Francisco Mint, but some of the proof commemorative coins have been struck at the other mints, including West Point.

After the proof blanks are punched from the strip, they go through the annealing oven, but on a conveyor belt rather than being tumbled in the revolving drum. After cleaning and upsetting they go into a huge vibrating machine where they are mixed with steel pellets that look like tiny footballs. The movement of the steel pellets against the planchets burnishes, or smooths, the surface so any scratches and gouges the planchets pick up during processing are smoothed over.

Proof dies get an extra polishing before the hubbing process. Like all other dies, they are made at Philadelphia and shipped to the branch mints.

When the proof dies arrive at San Francisco, they are worked on by a team of specialists who use diamond dust and other polishing agents to turn the fields of the proof dies into mirrorlike surfaces. The incuse design is sandblasted to make the surface rough, producing what is known as a "frosted" design.

Because collectors like the frosted proofs, the design is periodically swabbed with acid to keep the surface rough and increase the number of frosted proofs from each die. This is a relatively recent improvement, so frosted examples of earlier proofs are considerably scarcer.

The presses that strike proof coins usually are hand-operated rather than automatic. Some of the newer presses use equipment such as vacuum suction devices to pick up the planchets, place them in the coining chamber, and then remove the struck coins. This avoids handling the pieces any more than necessary.

On a hand-operated press, the operator takes a freshly washed and dried planchet and, using tongs, places it in the collar. The ram with the die descends two or more times before the finished coin is removed from the collar and carefully stored in a box for transport to storage or the packaging line. After each strike the operator wipes the dies to make sure that lint or other particles don't stick to the dies and damage the coins as they are struck.

Proof dies are used for only a short time before being discarded. Maximum die life is usually less than 10,000 coins, varying with the size of the coin and the alloy being struck.

Keeping up with demand

The minting process has come a long way from the first metal pellets that are barely recognizable as coins. Companies that manufacture equipment used in the world's mints are constantly researching to develop new methods of producing coins.

The purpose is to strike coins at as low a cost as possible and still retain the desired beauty in the design. Modern machines and new methods help the mints keep up with demand for coins.

The important point to remember is that the coins in your pocket are made no differently from the coins in the pocket of an English schoolchild or a Spanish police officer or an Italian opera singer. Mints around the world use the same methods, same equipment, and same common coin metals, with few if any variations from the basic methods. The minting process was shrouded in secrecy for centuries, but now has become common knowledge.

For the collector, knowing exactly how coins are minted can be some of the most valuable knowledge that can be learned. It often will make the difference between accepting a coin as a valuable addition to a collection or spotting it as a fake, counterfeit, or altered coin.

Because of the improvements in the making of coins, collecting the rare misstrikes and defective coins that escape quality control has become an important segment of the numismatic hobby. For a detailed description of over 400 categories of minting varieties, see the "U.S. Minting Varieties and Errors" section in this book.

3

The thrill of the hunt
How to acquire coins for your collection

By Al Doyle

Among the many pleasures coin collecting offers is the satisfaction of acquiring that long-sought piece that fills an important hole in a set or completes a collection. Many collectors say half the fun of pursuing the hobby is the thrill of the hunt — trying to find that needed coin in the condition desired and for a good price. Following are the main sources from which collectors acquire coins.

Circulation finds

Once the most popular method of building a collection, hunting through pocket change has declined substantially since 1965, when silver dimes and quarters were replaced by clad (base-metal) coinage.

Most collectors from 1935 into the 1960s got started in numismatics by searching through circulating coinage. It was worth the effort, as scarce and interesting coins such as the 1909-S VDB and 1914-D Lincoln cents, Liberty and Buffalo nickels, 1916-D and 1921 Mercury dimes, and Barber and Standing Liberty quarters were often found. Hobbyists who searched bank rolls and bags obtained at face value had no downside risk, and entire date collections of Lincoln cents were obtained in this manner.

Other denominations were also pursued in the treasure hunt. One Midwestern dealer found dozens of 1939-D Jefferson nickels (worth $1 to $30 each at the time, depending on condition) by searching through change obtained from parking meters of a nearby city. Another well-known numismatist put together a complete date and mintmark set of Walking Liberty half dollars in one afternoon by searching through coins obtained at his bank. Needless to say, those days are gone forever.

What is available to pocket-change searchers today? Even the pre-1959 cents, with the Wheat-Ears reverse, are rare sights, but some interesting coins remain undiscovered.

It's still possible to find collectible coins by searching large quantities of change, such as rolls.

Jefferson nickels can provide plenty of collecting enjoyment for virtually no financial commitment. A recent sampling of five rolls (200 coins, or $10) turned up 58 different date and mintmark combinations. Some of the highlights were a 1938-S (mintage 4.1 million) in grade fine, a 1947 in very fine, and a 1953-S. Looking through Jeffersons on a regular basis should lead to building the better part of a date and mintmark set.

Washington quarters experienced a circulation finds rebirth of sorts when the 50-state commemorative program began in 1999. Millions of Americans who had never collected coins before joined the hunt to acquire each of the new state designs as they were released at the rate of five per year.

Half dollars in your area may be another relatively untapped area in modern coinage. The 40-percent-silver pieces of 1965 to 1969 can sometimes be found in bank rolls. Half dollars seldom circulate, which means that older coins may be gathering dust in your local bank vault at this very moment.

Collecting Lincoln cents with the Memorial reverse, from 1959 to date, makes an excellent starter set. Many of the dates can be found in circulation.

What else might turn up in pocket change? Modern proofs enter circulation from time to time, and foreign coins are found occasionally. Canadian and U.S. coins frequently cross their respective borders.

Collectors of error coins sometimes find unusual pieces in circulation. What may be scorned as a reject by the average person is a valuable item to the error and variety specialist.

Start examining your pocket change. It's an inexpensive and pleasant way to get involved in the coin hobby.

Coin shops

Most medium-sized or larger cities and suburbs have at least one coin shop within driving distance, and a surprising number of small towns also boast of having a store that caters to local numismatists. Living in or near a metropolitan area is an advantage for the coin-shop enthusiast. For example, more than 15 dealers live in or near

Cincinnati, and southern California and the New York area are home to hundreds of numismatic firms.

In some ways, a coin shop is similar to a small museum. All kinds of items from early coppers to gold coinage and other collectibles such as paper currency, stock certificates, and historic curiosities can be seen. A visit to a well-stocked shop is a visual treat.

It is likely that some of those coins in the display cases will appeal to you, and that means some comparison shopping and determining the value of your favorite coin are desirable. Prices do fluctuate, although collector-oriented coins tend to maintain steadier values than coins sought by investors.

If you are a casual collector, consider a subscription to *Coins* magazine. A monthly publication, *Coins* offers articles on a wide range of topics as well as a Coin Value Guide of retail prices for U.S. coins in most grades.

Serious collectors and others who want more frequent information will find *Numismatic News* to be a timely source of knowledge. Published weekly, the *News* includes coverage of recent market trends and reports from major coin conventions. *World Coin News* is published monthly and covers non-U.S. issues. All three publications also carry display advertisements from dozens of coin dealers.

Prices are determined by supply and demand as well as the grade, or state of preservation. Grading is often described as a subjective art rather than an exact science, and it does take some study and experience to become a competent grader (see Chapter 4).

Numismatic education is a never-ending process. Getting to know an experienced dealer who is enthusiastic about his product will certainly increase your knowledge of coins. Most shops carry a wide assortment of items, but dealers (like anyone else) have their personal favorites. If you find a dealer who is especially knowledgeable about a certain series, it could be to your advantage to do business with him or her if that also happens to be your favorite area too.

Strangely enough, doing business with a dealer who does not share your particular interest could work in your favor. Learning about collectible coins is a massive undertaking, and no one knows everything. Collectors of large cents and Bust half dollars are willing to pay substantial premiums for coins that have minor differences from other specimens struck during the same year, and specialists in those areas frequently "cherrypick" rare varieties that are offered at common-date prices.

Never be embarrassed to ask questions about coins or the dealer's experience in the hobby. As the old saying goes, "There is no such thing as a dumb question." A question asked at the right time could save you plenty of grief and money.

Mail order

This is one area that generates a fair amount of emotion among collectors. Many hobbyists swear by the convenience of shopping at home; others swear at mail-order firms that send overgraded and overpriced coins. Common sense and the same guidelines that apply to shopping for any other item should be used in selecting a mail-order coin dealer.

Look for someone who has a fair amount of experience in coins as well as enthu-

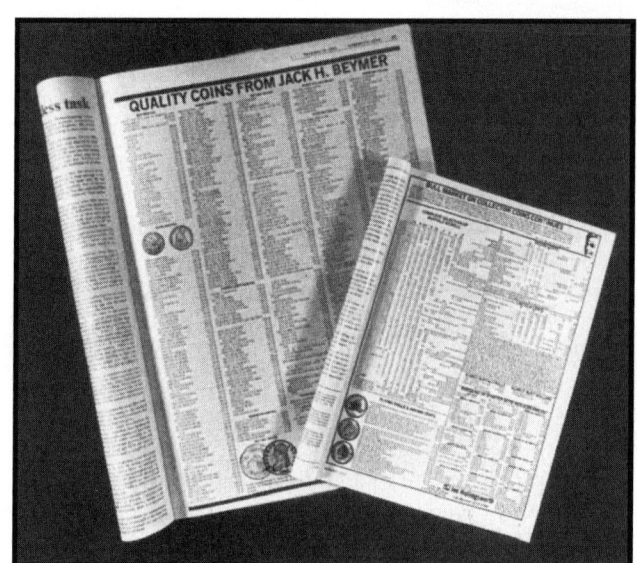

Advertisements in numismatic publications provide the convenience of shopping at home.

siasm for the hobby. Reputable dealers are willing to answer questions about their numismatic backgrounds and business practices. Word of mouth is often said to be one of the most effective forms of advertising, and it pays to ask other collectors about their favorite mail-order companies.

If several people agree that a firm provides accurately graded coins at fair prices, chances are excellent that you will also be a satisfied customer. How do you avoid being cheated? Collectors can be their own worst enemies and are often victimized by their own greed.

Take a coin that has a retail value in the $100 range in a particular grade. If that same coin is advertised at the same grade for $49.95, the savvy collector should immediately become suspicious. When a coin is offered at a price far under the going rate, remember these two sayings: "If it sounds too good to be true, it usually is," and "there is no Santa Claus in numismatics."

A dealer will generally pay $70 to $80 to acquire a popular coin with a retail value of $100. With that in mind, how can someone offer the same coin in the same grade at far less than wholesale cost? Wouldn't it be much easier to sell those coins to other dealers at a higher price and save on advertising expenses?

Obviously, the "underpriced" coins are not the same quality as their properly graded counterparts. It pays to keep up with current prices and grading standards. It is possible to find good deals at less than full retail cost, but don't expect to purchase decent coins for half price.

Does that mean all coins sold at real market prices are properly graded? Don't get complacent; overgraded coins are sometimes sold at full retail. But not everyone who sells an overgraded coin is intentionally fraudulent.

Grading standards are not carved in stone, which means that one person's MS-63 can be someone else's MS-64. Even though most dealers are extremely knowledgeable about coins, they can be fooled at times. The altered coin that a dealer bought as problem-free may be passed on to a collector in good faith, with no intention of deceit.

There is one important means of protection for consumers who buy through the mail: the return policy. Reputable firms allow buyers to return any unsatisfactory item for a full refund. The time allowed for returns varies widely from three working days to a month, but seven to ten days seems to be the most popular policy among mail-order dealers.

Look for "terms of sale" in dealer ads. Always read them before placing your order.

If you don't like coins received through the mail for any reason, send them back within the alloted time for a full refund. Companies might extend the deadline by a day or two if you call and ask for extra time.

What happens if you don't receive a refund or cannot satisfactorily resolve a problem with a mail-order dealer? There are several options:

The first step is to file a written complaint with the advertising department of any publication in which the dealer advertises. Include copies of invoices and other documentation. The publication cannot act on verbal complaints.

Written complaints can also be filed with a local or state chapter of the Better Business Bureau as well as any hobby-related organizations (the American Numismatic Association, Professional Numismatists Guild, and so on) in which the dealer holds membership. If you do business with a reputable dealer, it is unlikely that you will ever have to endure such a drawn-out complaint process, but be ready to take the proper steps if necessary.

For those who live in rural areas or prefer to shop at home, buying coins through the mail can be a rewarding experience and a convenient way to build a collection.

Coin shows

Dozens of shows are held every weekend across the nation. These events range from simple one-day shows with 10 to 20 tables to nationally known events such as the annual American Numismatic Association convention, Florida United Numismatists convention, the three-times-a-year shows held in Long Beach, Calif., and the Central States Numismatic Society convention.

Admission to club-sponsored shows is usually free. Commercially sponsored shows oftentimes charge a small admission fee.

Somewhere between the show at the local VFW hall and Long Beach are state and regional conventions. Often sponsored by a club, these shows will have 40 to 150 dealer tables as compared to the 400 to 600 tables at a major convention. Tables at local and some regional conventions are often manned by part-time, or "vest pocket," dealers. Smaller shows tend to feature less expensive items; the larger shows will have a greater variety of scarce and expensive coins in addition to the more affordable pieces.

Major conventions will have a stunning array of merchandise ranging from coins of ancient Greece to major U.S. rarities. Even if you can't afford the expensive items, it doesn't cost anything to stroll the aisles and see some historic coins.

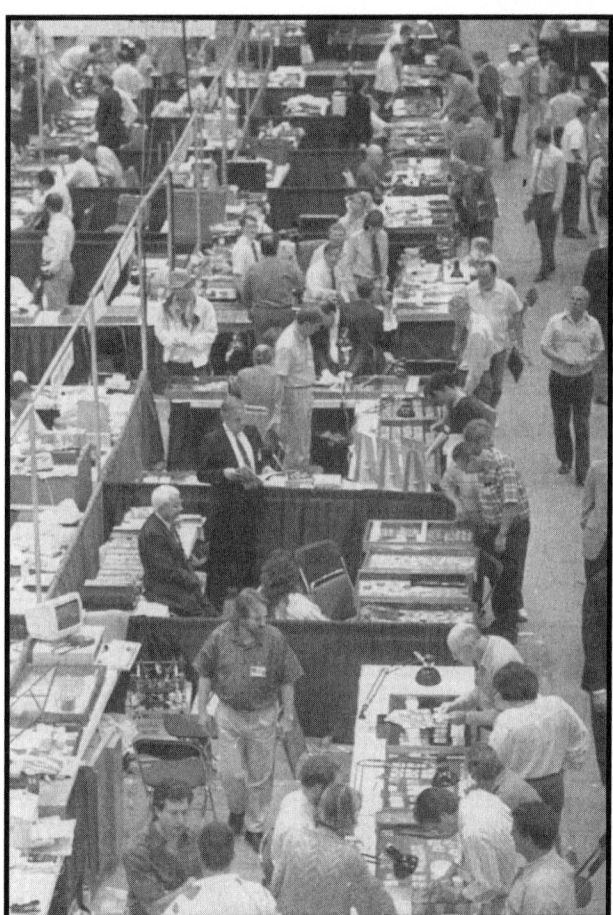

Shows big and small are held across the nation every weekend.

The big-ticket items are just part of the action at regional and major shows. A large assortment of affordable coins are available, and prices are often lower than at coin shops.

Dealers buy and sell thousands of coins among themselves at shows, and new purchases can often be had for a small markup. Good buys can sometimes be found later in the show when dealers are preparing to return home. A reasonable offer will often result in a new addition to your collection.

Speaking of offers, negotiating and dickering are as much a part of coin shows as silver dollars, but be reasonable. Tossing out an offer of $50 on a $200 coin is not shrewd; it's insulting.

If you make an offer on a coin and it is accepted, the coin is yours. Backing out of a deal is considered bad form. The coin business tends to be informal, and verbal offers carry serious weight. Your word is your bond on the bourse floor.

Purchases at a coin show do not carry a return policy. Unlike a mail-order transaction, you have ample opportunity to carefully examine the coin firsthand before making a financial commitment.

Why attend a show when you can acquire coins through the mail or from a local shop? There are many reasons to give the show circuit a try:

Conventions are an educational experience. Touring the bourse floor and talking to dealers and other collectors will increase your knowledge of numismatics, but there are other learning opportunities as well.

Many shows offer educational forums featuring speakers and presentations on various topics. These seminars cover everything from little-known specialties to advice on obtaining the best buys in a particular area of numismatics.

Exhibits will also add to your knowledge. Most medium-sized and major shows reserve a section of the bourse for collectors to display some of their holdings and compete for awards based on the educational value of their exhibit. The exhibit section offers an excellent opportunity to view something new and different.

You might be motivated to put together an exhibit yourself after a visit to a show. Keep in mind that it does not require a major collection to create a decent exhibit. Some of the most interesting displays incorporate low-priced coins and other collectibles.

Shows are excellent places to search for key-date coins and other material that may not be in stock at your local shop. Dealers do much of their shopping at shows, which should tell you something about the opportunities at a good-sized convention.

Want to introduce a friend or relative to coin collecting? Take them to a show and let them look around. Chances are excellent that the newcomer will become a fellow collector.

Looking for something different to collect? Paper money, world coins, tokens, medals, and medieval coins are often found at shows. You could find a new area of interest, and shows provide collectors with a chance to meet dealers and well-known hobbyists from across the country.

Have a game plan when you attend a show. Decide beforehand what you want to buy and how much money you plan to spend. Buying whatever looks nice will soon deplete your funds.

Coin shows offer something for everyone, so consider bringing the family. Jewelry (usually for much less than jewelry-store prices), baseball cards, antiques, and arts and crafts are also sometimes found at bourse tables.

One final note on coin-show etiquette: If you don't agree with a dealer's prices or grading, do not tell him that you can buy the same coin for less at another table or call him a crook. Just move on to the next table, and enjoy the rest of the show.

Information on upcoming shows in your area can be found in *Coins* and *Numismatic News*. Shows that feature a significant number of world coins are also listed in *World Coin News*. Coin-show advertising sometimes appears in local newspapers during the week prior to a show or in the paper's free listings of community events.

Auctions

Public auctions play an important role in the coin business. Prices realized at major auctions can indicate where the coin market is headed, as price fluctuations are a fact of life in numismatics. Important collections with major rarities are usually

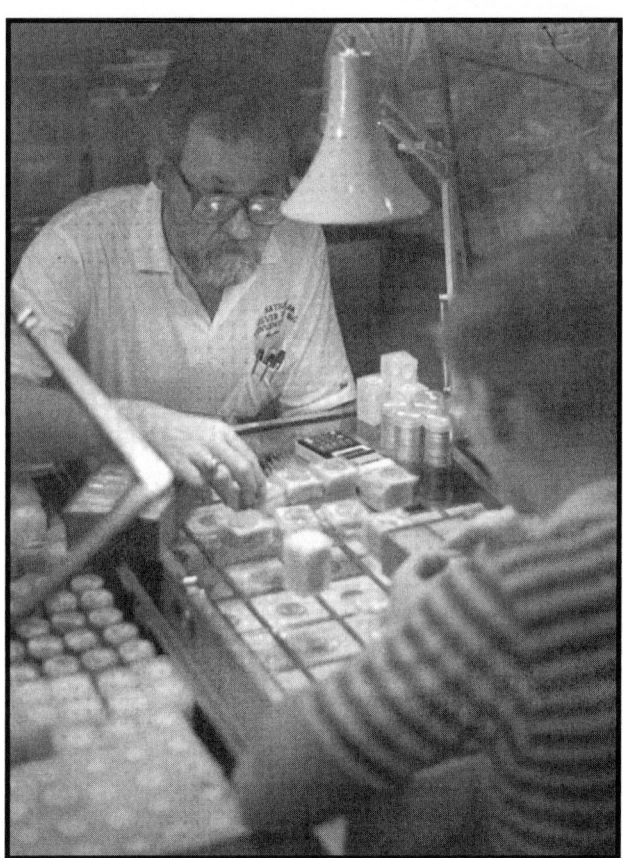

It's OK to bargain with a dealer at a show or shop, but collectors should be reasonable with their offers.

sold at a public auction. These sales are often held in conjunction with major shows.

However, affordable coins are often sold along with the rarities. A typical sale for a major auction firm will contain 1,000 to 6,000 lots, and most of those coins are not of the headline-grabbing variety. The larger the sale, the greater the likelihood that it will be broken into sessions conducted over a number of days.

The vast number of coins offered at a typical coin auction can work in favor of the collector who has a limited budget. Typical low- to medium-priced coins are often overlooked, as dealers and collectors focus on the trophy items. That may allow you to pick up some coins at reasonable prices. Internet auctions are another venue for lower priced items (See Chapter 13 for Web addresses and information.)

How can you participate in a public auction that is being held thousands of miles from your home? Catalogs are produced by auction companies for each sale, and mail, telephone and Internet bids are encouraged.

A typical auction catalog is illustrated with black and white as well as color photos of hundreds of coins. Descriptions of each lot give you an idea of the appearance of any coins that might be of interest. Many major firms post their catalogs on their Internet Web site.

If you are located near an auction site, it pays to examine your potential purchases

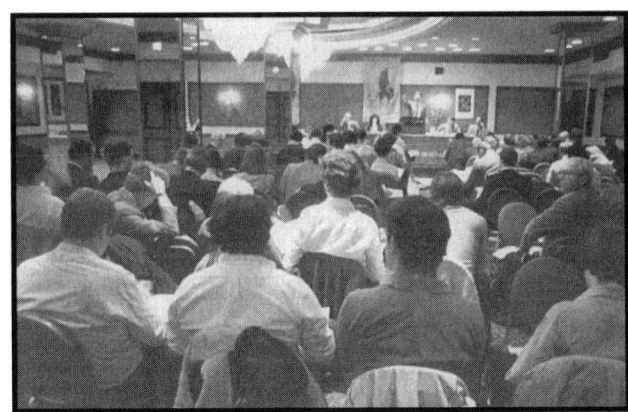

A collector doesn't have to actually attend an auction to participate in it.

at the pre-auction viewing session. The process is simple: Just visit the auction location (usually a major hotel or convention center) prior to the sale. The auction company sets up a room where the lots can be viewed. Long rows of tables with good lighting are provided. All you have to do is tell one of the attendants the lot numbers of the coins you want to view.

You can place written bids before you leave the premises, but it might pay to hang around for the auction and bid on coins in person. The action can be fast and furious at a major auction. Bidding increments of thousands of dollars are the rule when an expensive coin is being sold. It's an unforgettable sight to watch five or six serious competitors run up the price on a truly rare coin.

Keep several things in mind before you get involved in buying through auctions:

■ You are legally responsible to honor all winning bids placed, so plan accordingly. It is unlikely that you will win every coin on which you bid, but placing too many bids could be hazardous to your financial health.

■ Return policies vary among the major firms. Generally, floor bidders (those who personally attend the sale) do not have return privileges, as it is assumed that an adequate opportunity was provided to examine coins during the pre-auction viewing session.

One auction house does not allow any returns by mail bidders on certified coins, which are independently graded and encapsulated in a protective holder by an outside grading service. However, return privileges are the rule for all coins graded by the auction company's staff.

■ Winning bids are generally subject to a 15 percent premium, or buyer's fee. If you successfully bid $300 on a coin, your final cost will be $345 plus postage and handling. Consider the buyer's fee when deciding on bids.

Getting started in buying through auctions requires a catalog of an upcoming sale. Typically priced at $10 to $25, auction catalogs can be excellent buys even if you don't participate in the sale, as they provide a wealth of numismatic information.

Following are six major U.S. auction houses:

■ American Numismatic Rarities, LLC, P.O. Box 1804, Wolfeboro, NH 03894.

■ Bowers and Merena Galleries, 18022 Cowan, Suite 200D. Irvine, CA 92614.

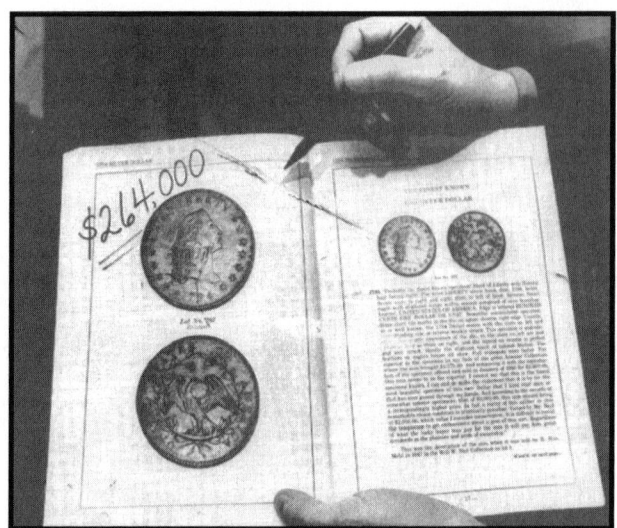

An auction catalog describes each lot offered.

■ Ira and Larry Goldberg Coins and Collectibles, Inc., 350 S. Beverly Drive, Suite 350, Beverly Hills, CA 90212.

■ Heritage Numismatic Auctions, 3500 Maple Ave., 17th Floor, Dallas, TX 75219-3941.

■ Stack's, 123 W. 57th St., New York, NY 10019.

■ Superior Galleries, 9478 W Olympic Blvd., Beverly Hills, CA 90212-4246.

Smaller auctions will allow you to test the bidding process before you compete at a major sale. Local firms concentrate on less expensive coins, and a typical sale for these companies ranges from 250 to 1,000 lots. Catalogs are less elaborate, but they are also inexpensive. Prices range from free to $3, and mail bids are accepted.

Among the dozens of local companies that conduct coin auctions are the following:

■ Michael Aron, P.O. Box 4388, San Clemente, CA 92674.

■ Sonny Henry's Auction Service, 1510 Illinois Ave., Mendota, IL 61342.

Where to write for more information

Coins Magazine: 700 E. State St, Iola, WI 54990.
Numismatic News: 700 E. State St., Iola, WI 54990.
World Coin News: 700 E. State St., Iola, WI 54990.
American Numismatic Association: 818 N. Cascade Ave., Colorado Springs, CO 80903-3279. Web address is http://www.money.org

Visit the Krause Publications Web site
http://www.collect.com

4

The grading factor
How to classify a coin's condition

By Arlyn G. Sieber

Grading is one of the most important factors in buying and selling coins as collectibles. Unfortunately, it's also one of the most controversial. Since the early days of coin collecting in the United States, buying through the mail has been a convenient way for collectors to acquire coins. As a result, there has always been a need in numismatics for a concise way to classify the amount of wear on a coin and its condition in general.

A look back

In September 1888, Dr. George Heath, a physician in Monroe, Mich., published a four-page pamphlet titled *The American Numismatist*. Publication of subsequent issues led to the founding of the American Numismatic Association, and *The Numismatist*, as it's known today, is the association's official journal. Heath's first issues were largely devoted to selling world coins from his collection. There were no formal grades listed with the coins and their prices, but the following statement by Heath indicates that condition was a consideration for early collectors:

"The coins are in above average condition," Heath wrote, "and so confident am I that they will give satisfaction, that I agree to refund the money in any unsatisfactory sales on the return of the coins."

As coin collecting became more popular and *The Numismatist* started accepting paid advertising from others, grading became more formal. The February 1892 issue listed seven "classes" for the condition of coins (from worst to best): mutilated, poor, fair, good, fine, uncirculated, and proof. Through the years, the hobby has struggled with developing a grading system that would be accepted by all and could apply to all coins. The hobby's growth was accompanied by a desire for more grades, or classifications, to more precisely define a coin's condition. The desire for more precision, however, was at odds with the basic concept of grading: to provide a concise method for classifying a coin's condition.

For example, even the conservatively few classifications of 1892 included fudge factors.

"To give flexibility to this classification," *The Numismatist* said, "such modification of fine, good and fair, as 'extremely,' 'very,' 'almost,' etc., are used to express slight variations from the general condition."

The debate over grading continued for decades in *The Numismatist*. A number of articles and letters prodded the ANA to write grading guidelines and endorse them as the association's official standards. Some submitted specific suggestions for terminology and accompanying standards for each grade. But grading remained a process of "instinct" gained through years of collecting or dealing experience.

A formal grading guide in book form finally appeared in 1958, but it was the work of two individuals rather than the ANA, *A Guide to the Grading of United States Coins* by Martin R. Brown and John W. Dunn was a break-through in the great grading debate. Now collectors had a reference that gave them specific guidelines for specific coins and could be studied and restudied at home.

The first editions of Brown and Dunn carried text only, no illustrations. For the fourth edition, in 1964, publication was assumed by Whitman Publishing Co. of Racine, Wis., and line drawings were added to illustrate the text.

The fourth edition listed six principal categories for circulated coins (from worst to best): good, very good, fine, very fine, extremely fine, and about uncirculated. But again, the desire for more precise categories were evidenced. In the book's introduction, Brown and Dunn wrote, "Dealers will sometimes advertise coins that are graded G-VG, VG-F, F-VF, VF-XF. Or the description may be ABT. G. or VG plus, etc. This means that the coin in question more than meets minimum standards for the lower grade but is not quite good enough for the higher grade."

When the fifth edition appeared, in 1969, the "New B & D Grading System" was introduced. The six principal categories for circulated coins were still intact, but variances within those categories were now designated by up to four letters: "A," "B," "C" or "D." For example, an EF-A coin was "almost about uncirculated." An EF-B was "normal extra fine" within the B & D standards. EF-C had a "normal extra fine" obverse, but the reverse was "obviously not as nice as obverse due to poor strike or excessive wear." EF-D had a "normal extra fine" reverse but a problem obverse.

But that wasn't the end. Brown and Dunn further listed 29 problem points that could appear on a coin – from No. 1 for an "edge bump" to No. 29 for "attempted re-engraving outside of the Mint." The number could be followed by the letter "O" or "R" to designate whether the problem appeared on the obverse or reverse and a Roman numeral corresponding to a clock face to designate where the problem appears on the obverse or reverse. For example, a coin described as "VG-B-9-O-X" would grade "VG-B"; the "9" designated a "single rim nick"; the "O" indicated the nick was on the obverse; and the "X" indicated it appeared at the 10 o'clock position, or upper left, of the obverse.

The author's goal was noble – to create the perfect grading system. They again, however, fell victim to the age-old grading-system problem: Precision comes at the expense of brevity. Dealer Kurt Krueger wrote in the January 1976 issue of *The Numismatist*, "Under the new B & D system, the numismatist must contend with a minimum of 43,152 different grading combinations! Accuracy is apparent, but simplicity has been lost." As a result, the "New B & D Grading System" never caught on in the marketplace.

The 1970s saw two important grading guides make their debut. The first was *Photograde* by James F. Ruddy. As the title implies, Ruddy uses photographs instead of line drawings to show how coins look in the various circulated grades. Simplicity is also a virtue of Ruddy's book. Only seven circulated grades are listed (about good, good, very good, fine, very fine, extremely fine, and about uncirculated), and the designations stop there.

In 1977 the longtime call for the ANA to issue grading standards was met with the release of *Official A.N.A. Grading Standards for United States Coins*. Like Brown and Dunn, the first edition of the ANA guide used line drawings to illustrate coins in various states of wear. But instead of using adjectival descriptions, the ANA guide adopted a numerical system for designating grades.

The numerical designations were based on a system used by Dr. William H. Sheldon in his book *Early American Cents*, first published in 1949. He used a scale of 1 to 70 to designate the grades of large cents.

"On this scale," Sheldon wrote, "1 means that the coin is identifiable and not mutilated – no more than that. A 70-coin is one in flawless Mint State, exactly as it left the dies, with perfect mint color and without a blemish or nick."

(Sheldon's scale also had its pragmatic side. At the time, a No. 2 large cent was worth about twice a No. 1 coin; a No. 4 was worth about twice a No. 2, and so on up the scale.)

With the first edition of its grading guide, the ANA adopted the 70-point scale for grading all U.S. coins. It designated 10 categories of circulated grades: AG-3, G-4, VG-8, F-12, VF-20, VF-30, EF-40, EF-45, AU-50, and AU-55. The third edition, released in 1987, replaced the line drawings with photographs, and another circulated grade was added: AU-58. A fourth edition was released in 1991.

Grading circulated U.S. coins

Dealers today generally use either the ANA guide or Photograde when grading circulated coins for their inventories. (Brown and Dunn is now out of print.) Many local coin shops sell both books. Advertisers in *Numismatic News*, *Coins* Magazine, and *Coin Prices* must indicate which standards they are using in grading their coins. If the standards are not listed, they must conform to ANA standards.

Following are some general guidelines, accompanied by photos, for grading circulated U.S. coins. Grading even circulated pieces can be subjective, particularly when attempting to draw the fine line between, for example, AU-55 and AU-58. Two longtime collectors or dealers can disagree in such a case.

But by studying some combination of the following guidelines, the ANA guide, and *Photograde*, and by looking at a lot of coins at shops and shows, collectors can gain enough grading knowledge to buy circulated coins confidently from dealers and other collectors. The more you study, the more knowledge and confidence you will gain. When you decide which series of coins you want to collect, focus on the guidelines for that particular series. Read them, reread them, and then refer back to them again and again.

AU-50

Indian cent   Lincoln cent

Buffalo nickel   Jefferson nickel

Mercury dime

Standing Liberty quarter

Washington quarter

Walking Liberty half dollar

Morgan dollar

Barber coins

AU-50 (about uncirculated): Just a slight trace of wear, result of brief exposure to circulation or light rubbing from mishandling, may be evident on elevated design areas. These imperfections may appear as scratches or dull spots, along with bag marks or edge nicks. At least half of the original mint luster generally is still evident.

XF-40

Indian cent

Lincoln cent

Buffalo nickel

Jefferson nickel

Mercury dime

Standing Liberty quarter

Washington quarter

Walking Liberty half dollar

Morgan dollar

Barber coins

XF-40 (extremely fine): The coin must show only slight evidence of wear on the highest points of the design, particularly in the hair lines of the portrait on the obverse. The same may be said for the eagle's feathers and wreath leaves on the reverse of most U.S. coins. A trace of mint luster may still show in protected areas of the coin's surface.

VF-20

Indian cent

Lincoln cent

Buffalo nickel

Jefferson nickel

Mercury dime

Standing Liberty quarter

Washington quarter

Walking Liberty half dollar

Morgan dollar

Barber coins

VF-20 (very fine): The coin will show light wear at the fine points in the design, though they may remain sharp overall. Although the details may be slightly smoothed, all lettering and major features must remain sharp.

Indian cent: All letters in "Liberty" are complete but worn. Headdress shows considerable flatness, with flat spots on the tips of the feathers.

Lincoln cent: Hair, cheek, jaw, and bow-tie details will be worn but clearly separated, and wheat stalks on the reverse will be full with no weak spots.

Buffalo nickel: High spots on hair braid and cheek will be flat but show some detail, and a full horn will remain on the buffalo.

Jefferson nickel: Well over half of the major hair detail will remain, and the pillars on Monticello will remain well defined, with the triangular roof partially visible.

Mercury dime: Hair braid will show some detail, and three-quarters of the detail will remain in the feathers. The two diagonal bands on the fasces will show completely but will be worn smooth at the middle, with the vertical lines sharp.

Standing Liberty quarter: Rounded contour of Liberty's right leg will be flattened, as will the high point of the shield.

Washington quarter: There will be considerable wear on the hair curls, with feathers on the right and left of the eagle's breast showing clearly.

Walking Liberty half dollar: All lines of the skirt will show but will be worn on the high points. Over half the feathers on the eagle will show.

Morgan dollar: Two-thirds of the hair lines from the forehead to the ear must show. Ear should be well defined. Feathers on the eagle's breast may be worn smooth.

Barber coins: All seven letters of "Liberty" on the headband must stand out sharply. Head wreath will be well outlined from top to bottom.

F-12

Indian cent

Lincoln cent

Buffalo nickel

Jefferson nickel

Mercury dime   Standing Liberty quarter

Washington quarter   Walking Liberty half dollar

Morgan dollar   Barber coins

F-12 (fine): Coins show evidence of moderate to considerable but generally even wear on all high points, though all elements of the design and lettering remain bold. Where the word "Liberty" appears in a headband, it must be fully visible. On 20th century coins, the rim must be fully raised and sharp.

VG-8

Indian cent

Lincoln cent

Buffalo nickel

Jefferson nickel

Mercury dime

Standing Liberty quarter

Washington quarter

Walking Liberty half dollar

Morgan dollar

Barber coins

VG-8 (very good): The coin will show considerable wear, with most detail points worn nearly smooth. Where the word "Liberty" appears in a headband, at least three letters must show. On 20th century coins, the rim will start to merge with the lettering.

SELL YOUR COINS TO AN EXPERT!
Gary Adkins

Gary Adkins Associates, Inc. is one of the premier numismatic firms in the country. Our goal is to be the best company in the rare coin business. Not the biggest, but the best! We do that by providing personalized service and attention to every customer. Gary Adkins, our senior numismatist, has over 40 years in the business. As a board member of the Professional Numismatic Guild, he brings qualifications and credentials that insure our most important goal ... your complete satisfaction. We are proud to have a staff of very experienced numismatists who are qualified to help you with your coin purchases or sales, find coins that you need to complete your collection, and answer any of your numismatic questions.

We work with clients to provide whatever is best for each individual and we never lose sight of the fact that coins are not a necessity of life. They are a luxury meant to be enjoyed as objects of beauty, history, and pride of ownership. You can be assured that we will make every effort to give you the finest quality coins at the best possible price level for the grade you select. Our desire is to assist you in obtaining your objectives, both in portfolio selection and in the purchase or sale of your coins. Our company "motto" is "If we wouldn't put it in our collection, we wouldn't ask you to put it in yours." We are here to build long-term relationships and help you enjoy your collecting to the fullest.

TEAR OUT AND MAIL IN TODAY

FREE INFORMATION! FREE APPRAISALS!*

Yes, I would like to know more about:

_____ Collecting rare coins

_____ Investing in rare coins

_____ Monthly collecting plans

_____ Having my coins appraised

_____ Selling my coins

Please send me your free information on the items checked above. I understand that I am under no obligation and that any information I provide will remain strictly confidential.

NAME _____

ADDRESS _____

CITY _____ ST ____ ZIP _____

DAYTIME PHONE _____

EVENING PHONE _____

E-MAIL _____

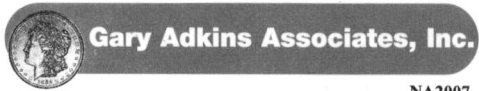

NA2007

*Free appraisals are limited phone consultation or 1/2 hour off of billing for a formal written appraisal.

G-4

Indian cent

Lincoln cent

Buffalo nickel

Jefferson nickel

Mercury dime

Standing Liberty quarter

Washington quarter

Walking Liberty half dollar

Morgan dollar

Barber coins

G-4 (good): Only the basic design remains distinguishable in outline form, will all points of detail worn smooth. The word "Liberty" has disappeared, and the rims are almost merging with the lettering.

About good or fair: The coin will be identifiable by date and mint but otherwise badly worn, with only parts of the lettering showing. Such coins are of value only as fillers in a collection until a better example of the date and mintmark can be obtained. The only exceptions would be rare coins

Grading uncirculated U.S. coins

The subjectivity of grading and the trend toward more classifications becomes more acute when venturing into uncirculated, or mint-state, coins. A minute differ-

Collectors have a variety of grading services to choose from. This set of Arkansas half dollars that appeared in an Early American History Auctions sale used two of the services.

ence between one or two grade points can mean a difference in value of hundreds or even thousands of dollars. In addition, the standards are more difficult to articulate in writing and illustrate through drawings or photographs. Thus, the possibilities for differences of opinion on one or two grade points increase in uncirculated coins.

Back in Dr. George Heath's day and continuing through the 1960s, a coin was either uncirculated or it wasn't. Little distinction was made between uncirculated coins of varying condition, largely because there was little if any difference in value. When *Numismatic News* introduced its value guide in 1962 (the forerunner of today's Coin Market section in the *News*), it listed only one grade of uncirculated for Morgan dollars.

But as collectible coins increased in value and buyers of uncirculated coins became more picky, distinctions within uncirculated grade started to surface. In 1975 *Numismatic News* still listed only one uncirculated grade in Coin Market, but added this note: "Uncirculated and proof specimens in especially choice condition will also command proportionately higher premiums than these listed."

The first edition of the ANA guide listed two grades of uncirculated, MS-60 and MS-65, in addition to the theoretical but non-existent MS-70 (a flawless coin). MS-60 was described as "typical uncirculated" and MS-65 as "choice uncirculated." *Numismatic News* adopted both designations for Coin Market. In 1981, when the second edition of the ANA grading guide was released, MS-67 and MS-63 were added. In 1985 *Numismatic News* started listing six grades of uncirculated for Morgan dollars: MS-60, MS-63, MS-65, MS-65+, and MS-63 prooflike.

Then in 1986, a new entity appeared that changed the nature of grading and trading uncirculated coins ever since. A group of dealers led by David Hall of Newport Beach, Calif., formed the Professional Coin Grading Service. For a fee, collectors could submit a coin through an authorized PCGS dealer and receive back a professional opinion of its grade.

The concept was not new; the ANA had operated an authentication service since 1972 and a grading service since 1979. A collector or dealer could submit a coin directly to the service and receive a certificate giving the service's opinion on authenticity and grade. The grading service was the source of near constant debate among dealers and ANA officials. Dealers charged that ANA graders were too young and inexperienced, and that their grading was inconsistent.

Grading stability was a problem throughout the coin business in the early 1980s, not just with the ANA service. Standards among uncirculated grades would tighten during a bear market and loosen during a bull market. As a result, a coin graded MS-65 in a bull market may have commanded only MS-63 during a bear market.

PCGS created several innovations in the grading business in response to these problems:

1. Coins could be submitted through PCGS-authorized dealers only.

2. Each coin would be graded by at least three members of a panel of "top graders," all prominent dealers in the business. (Since then, however, PCGS does not allow its graders to also deal in coins.)

3. After grading, the coin would be encapsulated in an inert, hard-plastic holder with a serial number and the grade indicated on the holder.

4. PCGS-member dealers pledged to make a market in PCGS-graded coins and honor the grades assigned.

5. In one of the most far-reaching moves, PCGS said it would use all 11 increments of uncirculated on the 70-point numerical scale: MS-60, MS-61, MS-62, MS-63, MS-64, MS-65, MS-66, MS-67, MS-68, MS-69, and MS-70.

The evolution of more uncirculated grades had reached another milestone.

Purists bemoaned the entombment of classic coins in the plastic holders and denounced the 11 uncirculated grades as implausible. Nevertheless, PCGS was an immediate commercial success. The plastic holders were nicknamed "slabs," and dealers couldn't get coins through the system fast enough.

In subsequent years, a number of similar services have appeared. Among them, one of the original PCGS "top graders," John Albanese, left PCGS to found the Numismatic Guaranty Corp. The ANA grading service succumbed to "slab mania" and introduced its own encapsulated product.

There now are numerous other reputable private third-party grading services. PCGS and NGC are the oldest and remain the leaders. In 1990 the ANA sold its grading service to a private company. It operates under the ANACS acronym.

How should a collector approach the buying and grading of uncirculated coins? Collecting uncirculated coins worth thousands of dollars implies a higher level of numismatic expertise by the buyer. Those buyers without that level of expertise should cut their teeth on more inexpensive coins, just as today's experienced collectors did. Inexperienced collectors can start toward that level by studying the guidelines for mint-state coins in the ANA grading guide and looking at lots of coins at shows and shops.

Study the condition and eye appeal of a coin and compare it to other coins of the same series. Then compare prices. Do the more expensive coins look better? If so, why? Start to make your own judgments concerning relationships between condition and value.

According to numismatic legend, a collector walked up to a crusty old dealer at a show one time and asked the dealer to grade a coin the collector had with him. The dealer looked at the coin and said, "I grade it a hundred dollars." Such is the bottom line to coin grading.

Grading U.S. proof coins

Because proof coins are struck by a special process using polished blanks, they receive their own grading designation. A coin does not start out being a proof and then become mint state if it becomes worn. Once a proof coin, always a proof coin.

In the ANA system, proof grades use the same numbers as circulated and uncirculated grades, and the amount of wear on the coin corresponds to those grades. But the number is preceded by the word "proof." For example, Proof-65, Proof-55, Proof-45, and so on. In addition, the ANA says a proof coin with many marks, scratches or other defects should be called an "impaired proof."

Grading world coins

The state of grading non-U.S. issues is similar to U.S. coin grading before Brown and Dunn. There is no detailed, illustrated guide that covers the enormous scope and variety of world coins; collectors and dealers rely on their experience in the field and knowledge of the marketplace.

The *Standard Catalog of World Coins* gives the following guidelines for grading world coins, which apply to the Canadian and Mexican value listings in this book:

In grading world coins, there are two elements to look for: (1) overall wear and (2) loss of design details, such as strands of hair, feathers on eagles, designs on coats of arms, and so on. Grade each coin by the weaker of the two sides. Age, rarity or type of coin should not be considered in grading.

Grade by the amount of overall wear and loss of detail evident in the main design on each side. On coins with a moderately small design element that is prone to early wear, grade by that design alone.

In the marketplace, adjectival grades are still used for Mexican coins. The numerical system for Canadian coins is now commonplace:

Uncirculated, MS-60: No visible signs of wear or handling, even under a 30X microscope. Bag marks may be present.

Almost uncirculated, AU-50: All detail will be visible. There will be wear on only the highest points of the coin. There will often be half or more of the original mint luster present.

Extremely fine, XF-40: About 95 percent of the original detail will be visible. Or, on a coin with a design that has no inner detail to wear down, there will be light wear over nearly the entire coin. If a small design is used as the grading area, about 90 percent of the original detail will be visible. This latter rule stems from the logic that a smaller amount of detail needs to be present because a small area is being used to grade the whole coin.

Very fine, VF-20: About 75 percent of the original detail will be visible. Or, on a coin with no inner detail, there will be moderate wear over the entire coin. Corners of letters and numbers may be weak. A small grading area will have about 60 percent of the original detail.

Fine, F-12: About 50 percent of the original detail will be visible. Or, on a coin with no inner detail, there will be fairly heavy wear over the entire coin. Sides of letters will be weak. A typically uncleaned coin will often appear dirty or dull. A small grading area will have just under 50 percent of the original detail.

Very good, VG-8: About 25 percent of the original detail will be visible. There will be heavy wear on the entire coin.

Good, G-4: Design will be clearly outlined but with substantial wear. Some of the larger detail may be visible. The rim may have a few weak spots of wear.

About good, AG-3: Typically only a silhouette of a large design will be visible. The rim will be worn down into the letters, if any.

Where to write for more information

American Numismatic Association: 818 N. Cascade Ave., Colorado Springs, CO 80903-3279.

Independent Coin Grading Co.: 7901 E. Belleview Ave., Suite 50, Englewood, CO 80111.

Numismatic Guaranty Corp: P.O. Box 4776, Sarasota, FL 34230.

NTC (Numistrust Corp.): 2500 N. Military Trail, Suite 210, Boca Raton, FL 33431.

PCI, Inc.: P.O. Box 486, Rossville, GA 30741.

Professional Coin Grading Service: P.O. Box 9458, Newport Beach, CA 92658.

Sovereign Entities Grading Service: 401 Chestnut St., Suite 103, Chattanooga, TN 37402-4924.

Visit the Krause Publications Web site
http://www.collect.com

5

Get a map
How to organize a collection

By David C. Harper

Do you have a jar full of old coins? Did a favorite relative give you a few silver dollars over the years? Or did you just come across something unusual that you set aside?

All three circumstances make good beginnings for collecting coins. It may surprise you, but this is how just about everybody starts in the hobby. It is a rare collector who decides to start down the hobby road without first having come into a few coins one way or another.

What these random groupings lack is organization. It is organization that makes a collection. But think about it another way: Organization is the map that tells you where you can go in coin collecting and how you can get there.

Have you ever been at a large fair or a huge office building and seen the maps that say "you are here"? Did you ever consider that, over time, thousands of other people have stood on the same spot? This is true in numismatics also. Figuratively, you are standing on the same spot on which the writers of this book stood at some point in their lives.

At a fair, the map helps you consider various ways of seeing all the sights. In coin collecting, too, there are different ways to organize a collection. The method you choose helps you see the hobby sights you want to see.

It should be something that suits you. Remember, do what you want to do. See what you want to see. But don't be afraid to make a mistake; there aren't any. Just as one can easily retrace steps at a fair, one can turn around and head in another direction in the coin-collecting hobby. Besides, when you start off for any given point, often you see something along the way that was unplanned but more interesting. That's numismatics.

There are two major ways to organize a collection: by type, and by date and mint-mark. These approaches work in basically the same fashion for coins of the United States, Canada and Mexico. Naturally, there are differences. But to establish the concepts, let's focus first on U.S. coins.

United States

Let's take collecting by type first. Look at your jar of coins, or take the change out of your pocket. You find Abraham Lincoln and the Lincoln Memorial on current cents. You find Thomas Jefferson and his home, Monticello, on the nickel. Franklin D. Roosevelt and a torch share the dime. George Washington and an eagle (or since 1999, designs honoring states) appear on the quarter. John F. Kennedy and the presidential seal are featured on the half dollar. Sacagawea and an eagle are on the dollar.

Each design is called a "type." If you took one of each and put the five coins in a holder, you would have a type set of the coins that are currently being produced for circulation by the U.S. Mint.

With just these six coins, you can study various metallic compositions. You can evaluate their states of preservation and assign a grade to each. You can learn about the artists who designed the coins, and you can learn of the times in which these designs were created.

As you might have guessed, many different coin types have been used in the United States over the years. You may remember seeing some of them circulating. These designs reflect the hopes and aspirations of people over time. Putting all of them together forms a wonderful numismatic mosaic of American history.

George Washington did not mandate that his image appear on the quarter. Quite the contrary. He would have been horrified. When he was president, he headed off those individuals in Congress who thought the leader of the country should have his image on its coins. Washington said it smacked of monarchy and would have nothing of it.

Almost a century and a half later, during the bicentennial of Washington's birth in 1932, a nation searching for its roots during troubled economic times decided that it needed his portrait on its coins as a reminder of his great accomplishments and as reassurance that this nation was the same place it had been in more prosperous days.

In its broadest definition, collecting coins by type requires that you obtain an example of every design that was struck by the U.S. Mint since it was founded in 1792. That's a tall order. You would be looking for denominations like the half cent, two-cent piece, three-cent piece, and 20-cent piece, which have not been produced in over a century. You would be looking for gold coins ranging in face value from $1 to $50.

But even more important than odd-sounding denominations or high face values is the question of rarity. Some of the pieces in this multi-century type set are rare and expensive. That's why type collectors often divide the challenge into more digestible units.

Type collecting can be divided into 18th, 19th, 20th and 21st century units. Obviously, a 21st century set is a short one. Just pull the change out of your pocket and ask the local bank for the half and dollar. Starting type collectors can focus on 20th century coin designs, which are easily obtainable. The fun and satisfaction of putting the 20th century set together then creates the momentum to continue backward in time.

In the process of putting a 20th century type set together, one is also learning how to grade, learning hobby jargon, and discovering how to obtain coins from dealers, the U.S. Mint, and other collectors. All of this knowledge is then refined as the collector increases the challenge to himself.

This book is designed to help. How many dollar types were struck in the 20th century? Turn to the U.S. price-guide section and check it out. We see the Morgan dollar, Peace dollar, Eisenhower dollar, and Anthony dollar. Hobbyists could also add the Ike dollar with the Bicentennial design of 1976 and the silver American Eagle bullion coin struck since 1986. One can also find out their approximate retail prices from the listings.

The beauty of type collecting is that one can choose the most inexpensive example of each type. There is no need to select a 1903-O Morgan when the 1921 will do just as well. With the 20th century type set, hobbyists can dodge some truly big-league prices.

As a collector's hobby confidence grows, he can tailor goals to fit his desires. He can take the road less traveled if that is what suits him. Type sets can be divided by denomination. You can choose over two centuries of one-cent coins. You can take just obsolete denominations or copper, silver or gold denominations.

You can even collect by size. Perhaps you would like to collect all coin types larger than 30 millimeters or all coins smaller than 20 millimeters. Many find this freedom of choice stimulating.

Type collecting has proven itself to be enduringly popular over the years. It provides a maximum amount of design variety while allowing collectors to set their own level of challenge.

The second popular method of collecting is by date and mintmark. What this means, quite simply, is that a collector picks a given type – Jefferson nickels, for example – and then goes after an example of every year, every mintmark, and every type of manufacture that was used with the Jefferson design.

Looking at this method of collecting brings up the subject of mintmarks. The "U.S. Mint" is about as specific as most non-collectors get in describing the government agency that provides everyday coins. Behind that label are the various production facilities that actually do the work.

In the more than two centuries of U.S. coinage, there have been eight such facilities. Four are still in operation. Those eight in alphabetical order are Carson City, Nev., which used a "CC" mintmark to identify its work; Charlotte, N.C. ("C"); Dahlonega, Ga. ("D"); Denver (also uses a "D," but it opened long after the Dahlonega Mint closed, so there was never any confusion); New Orleans ("O"); Philadelphia (because it was the primary mint, it used no mintmark for much of its history, but currently uses a "P"); San Francisco ("S"); and West Point, N.Y. ("W").

A person contemplating the collecting of Jefferson nickels by date and mintmark will find that three mints produced them: San Francisco, Denver and Philadelphia. Because of first two are branch mints serving smaller populations, their output has tended over time to be smaller than that of Philadelphia. This fact, repeated in other series, has helped give mintmarks quite an allure to collectors. It provides one of the major attractions in collecting coins by date and mintmark.

The key date for Jeffersons is the 1950-D when using mintages as a guide. In that year, production was just 2.6 million pieces. Because collectors of the time were aware of the coin's low mintage, many examples were saved. As a result, prices are

A basic type set of 20th century dollar coins would consist of (from top) a Morgan type, Peace type, Eisenhower type and Anthony type.

reasonable.

The Depression-era 1939-D comes in as the most valuable regular-issue Jefferson nickel despite a mintage of 3.5 million – almost 1 million more than the 1950-D. The reason: Fewer were saved for later generations of coin collectors.

Date and mintmark collecting teaches hobbyists to use mintage figures as a guide but to take them with a grain of salt. Rarity, after all, is determined by the number of surviving coins, not the number initially created.

The Jefferson series is a good one to collect by date and mintmark, because the mintmarks have moved around, grown in size, and expanded in number.

When the series was first introduced, the Jefferson nickel was produced at the three mints previously mentioned. In 1942, because of a diversion of certain metals to wartime use, the coin's alloy of 75 percent copper and 25 percent nickel was

Jefferson nickels have been produced at the (from top) Philadephia, Denver and San Francisco Mints. Note the Denver and San Francisco mintmarks to the right of Monticello.

The wartime nickels of 1942-1945 marked the first time a "P" mintmark, for Philadelphia, was used.

changed. The new alloy was 35 percent silver, 56 percent copper, and 9 percent manganese.

To denote the change, the mintmarks were moved and greatly enlarged. The pre-1942 mintmarks were small and located to the right of Monticello; the wartime mintmarks were enlarged and placed over the dome. What's more, for the first time in American history, the Philadelphia Mint used a mintmark ("P").

The war's end restored the alloy and mintmarks to their previous status. The "P" disappeared. This lasted until the 1960s, when a national coin shortage saw all mintmarks removed for three years (1965-1967) and then returned, but in a different location. Mintmarks were placed on the obverse, to the right of Jefferson's portrait near the date in 1968. In 1980 the "P" came back in a smaller form and is still used.

Another consideration arises with date and mintmark collecting: Should the hobbyist include proof coins in the set? This can be argued both ways. Suffice to say that anyone who has the desire to add proof coins to the set will have a larger one. It is not necessary nor is it discouraged.

Some of the first proof coins to carry mintmarks were Jefferson nickels. When proof coins were made in 1968 after lapsing from 1965 to 1967, production occurred at San Francisco instead of Philadelphia. The "S" mintmark was placed on the proof coins of that year, including the Jefferson nickel, to denote the change. Since that time, mintmarks used on proof examples of various denominations have included the "P", "D", "S", and "W".

For all of the mintmark history that is embodied in the Jefferson series, prices are reasonable. For a first attempt at collecting coins by date and mintmark, it provides excellent background for going on to the more expensive and difficult types. After all, if you are ever going to get used to the proper handling of a coin, it is far better to experiment on a low-cost coin than a high-value rarity.

As one progresses in date and mintmark collecting and type collecting, it is important to remember that all of the coins should be of similar states of preservation. Sets look slapdash if one coin is VG and another is MS-65 and still another is VF. Take a look at the prices of all the coins in the series before you get too far, figure out what you can afford, and then stick to that grade or range of grades.

Sure, there is a time-honored practice of filling a spot with any old example until a better one comes along. That is how we got the term "filler." But if you get a few placeholders, don't stop there. By assembling a set of uniform quality, you end up

In 1968 the mintmarks reappeared on U.S. coins and production of proof coins resumed, this time at the San Francisco Mint. On the nickels, the mintmark moved from the reverse to the obverse below the date.

with a more aesthetically pleasing collection.

The date and mintmark method used to be the overwhelmingly dominant form of collecting. It still has many adherents. Give it a try if you think it sounds right for you.

Before we leave the discussion of collecting U.S. coins, it should be pointed out that the two major methods of organizing a collection are simply guidelines. They are not hard-and-fast rules that must be followed without questions. Collecting should be satisfying to the hobbyist. It should never be just one more item in the daily grind. Take the elements of these collecting approaches that you like or invent your own.

It should also be pointed out that U.S. coinage history does not start with 1792 nor do all of the coins struck since that time conform precisely to the two major organizational approaches. But these two areas are good places to start.

There are coins and tokens from the American Colonial period (1607-1776) that are just as fascinating and collectible as regular U.S. Mint issues. There are federal issues struck before the Mint was actually established. See the Colonial price-guide section in this book.

There are special coins called commemoratives, which have been struck by the U.S. Mint since 1892 to celebrate some aspect of American history or a contemporary event. They are not intended for circulation. There was a long interruption between 1954 and 1982, but currently annual commemoratives are being offered for sale directly to collectors by the Mint.

Collecting commemoratives has always been considered something separate from collecting regular U.S. coinage. It is, however, organized the same way. Commemoratives can be collected by date and mintmark or by type.

Current commemoratives can be purchased from the U.S. Mint. To get on its mailing list, write U.S. Mint, Customer Care Center, 801 Ninth St., N.W., Washington, D.C. 20220. Check the U.S. Mint Web site at www.usmint.gov. Once on the list, hobbyists will get the various solicitations for not only commemoratives, but regular proof sets and mint sets and proof American Eagle bullion coins. Hobbyists who order from the U.S. Mint's Web site receive notices of product availability by e-mail.

Buying coins from the Mint can be considered a hobby pursuit in its own right. Some collectors let the Mint organize their holdings for them. They buy complete sets and put them away. They never buy anything from anywhere else.

Admittedly, this is a passive form of collecting, but there are individuals around the world who enjoy collecting at this level without ever really going any deeper. They like acquiring every new issue as it comes off the Mint's presses.

Once done, there is a certain knowledge that one has all the examples of the current year. Obviously, too, collectors by date and mintmark of the current types would have to buy the new coins each year, but, of course, they do not stop there.

Varieties and errors make up another area. Under this heading come the coins the Mint did not intend to make. There are all kinds of errors. Many of them are inexpensive. Check out the U.S. Minting Varieties and Errors section in the price guide. If you want to pursue it further, there are specialty books that deal with the topic in more detail.

Canada

Starting point for the national coinage of Canada is popularly fixed at 1858. In that year a large cent was first produced for use in Upper and Lower Canada (Ontario and Quebec). These prices were intended to supplant local copper coinage, which in turn had been attempts to give various regions a medium of exchange.

What was circulating in Canada at the time was a hodgepodge of world issues. The large cent predates a unified national government by nine years, but it is considered the beginning of national issues nevertheless.

There are many similarities between the United States and Canada and their respective monetary systems. Both continent-sized nations thought in terms of taming the frontier, new settlements, and growth. Both came to use the dollar as the unit of account because of the pervasiveness of the Spanish milled dollar in trade. For each, the dollar divides into 100 cents.

However, Canada had a far longer colonial history. Many of its residents resisted the tide that carried the United States to independence and worked to preserve their loyalties to the British crown. As a result, Canada was firmly a part of the British Empire. So even today with its constitution (the British North America Act transferred from Westminster to Ottawa in 1982), parliamentary democracy, and a national consciousness perhaps best symbolized by the maple leaf, Canada retains a loyalty to the crown in the person of Queen Elizabeth II of the United Kingdom. Canada is a member of the British Commonwealth of Nations.

The effect of this on coins is obvious. Current issues carry the queen's effigy. How Canada got its coins in the past was also influenced. The fledgling U.S. government set about creating its own mint as one of its earliest goals, despite that better-quality pieces could be purchased abroad at lower cost. Canada found that ties to mints located in England were logical and comfortable.

The Royal Canadian Mint was not established until 1908, when it was called the Ottawa branch of the British Royal Mint, and it was not given its present name until 1931. Both events are within living memory. Canadian coins, therefore, have a unique mixture of qualities. They are tantalizingly familiar to U.S. citizens yet distinctly different.

The coinage of a monarchy brings its own logic to the organization of a collec-

Canadian coins have depicted (from top) Queen Victoria, King Edward VII, King George V, King George VI and Queen Elizabeth II.

tion. Type collecting is delineated by the monarch. United Canada has had six. The first was Queen Victoria, whose image appeared on those large cents of 1858. Her reign began in 1837 and lasted until 1901.

She was followed by Edward VII, 1901-1910; George V, 1910-1936; Edward VII, 1936; George VI, 1936-1952; and Queen Elizabeth II, 1952-present. All but Edward VIII had coins struck for circulation in Canada. The collectible monarchs, therefore, number five, but the longer reigns inspired changes of portraits over time to show the aging process at work. Legends also changed. When George VI ceased being emperor of India, Canada's coins were modified to recognize the change.

Like U.S. coins, sizes and alloys were altered to meet new demands placed on the coinage. However, the separateness of each nation might best be summed up this way: Though the United States abolished its large cent in 1857, Canada's was just getting under way in 1858. The United States put an end to the silver dollar in 1935, the very year Canada finally got its series going.

And Canada, the nickel-mining giant, used a small-sized silver five-cent coin until 1921, almost 50 years after the half dime was abolished in the United States. But whereas the Civil War was the major cause of the emergence of modern U.S. coinage as specified by the Coinage Act of 1873, World War I influenced the alterations that made Canada's coins what they are today.

It might be assumed that change in the monarch also signaled a change in the reverse designs of the various denominations. A check of the Canadian price guide section shows this is not necessarily the case. Current designs paired with Queen Elizabeth II basically date back to the beginning of her father's reign. The familiar maple-leaf cent, beaver five-cent piece, schooner 10-cent, caribou 25-cent, and coat-of-arms 50-cent have been running for over 50 years. Significant changes were made to the 50-cent coin in 1959, but the reverse design remains the coat of arms.

So where does that leave type collectors? It puts them in a situation similar to categorizing the various eagles on U.S. coins. They can be universalists and accept the broadest definitions of type, or they can narrow the bands to whatever degree suits them best.

By checking the price-guide section, date and mintmark collectors will quickly note that their method of organization more or less turns into collecting by date. Though currently there are three mints in Canada – Hull, Quebec; Ottawa, Ontario; and Winnipeg, Manitoba – they don't use mintmarks. Historically, few mintmarks were employed.

Ottawa used a "C" on gold sovereigns of 1908-1919 and on some exported colonial issues. The private Heaton Mint in Birmingham, England, used an "H" on coins it supplied to Canada from 1871 to 1907.

But the coins supplied to Canada by the British Royal Mint and later by its Ottawa branch did not carry any identifying mark. Collectors who confine their activities to the more recent issues need never think about a mintmark.

It would be easy to slant a presentation on Canadian issues to stress similarities or differences to U.S. issues. One should remember that the monetary structures of each evolved independently, but each was always having an impact on the other.

Common events, such as World War II, had a similar impact. For example, the Canadian five-cent coin changed in much the same way as the U.S. nickel. In

Canada, nickel was removed and replaced first by a tombac (brass) alloy and then by chromium-plated steel. Peace brought with it a return to the prewar composition.

To see an example of differences between the United States and Canada, take the Canadian approach to the worldwide trend of removing silver from coinage. Canada made its move in 1968, three years after the United States. Instead of choosing a copper-nickel alloy as a substitute for silver, Canada looked to its own vast natural resources and employed pure nickel.

Canada also seems more comfortable with its coinage than the United States. Whereas the United States often feared confusion and counterfeiting from making the least little changes in its coins, Canada has long embraced coinage to communicate national events, celebrations and culture. Its silver-dollar series actually began as a celebration of George V's 25 years on the throne.

Succeeding years saw additional commemorative $1 designs interspersed with the regular Voyageur design. When the centennial of national confederation was observed in 1967, all of the denominations were altered for one year. The United States only reluctantly tried out the idea on three of its denominations for the nation's Bicentennial.

Ultimately, Canada began an annual commemorative dollar series in 1971. It issued coins for the 1976 Montreal Olympic Games and again in 1988 for the Calgary Olympic Games. Bullion coins were created to market its gold, silver and platinum output. A commemorative series of gold $100 coins was also undertaken. Canada, too, issues special proof, prooflike and specimen sets, similar to the United States.

Hobbyists who would like to be informed of new issues should write Royal Canadian Mint, P.O. Box 457, Station A, Ontario K1A 8V5, Canada. The mint also maintains special toll-free lines. In the United States, hobbyists may telephone the Royal Canadian Mint at 1-800-268-6468. In Canada, the number is 1-800-267-1871. You can get on the mailing list by using these numbers and you can buy currently available coins. (See Chapter 6 for Web information.)

When collecting Canada, another thing to remember is the importance varieties play in the nation's various series. Certainly, a type collector has no need to dwell on this information, but the date and mintmark collector may puzzle over the many extra identifying abbreviations in the price guide for certain coins. These varieties should not be confused with the U.S. variety-and-error category.

Here the varieties are not mistakes; they are deliberately created and issued variations of the standard design. We see Voyageur dollars on which the number of water lines changes. Other dollars count the number of beads.

These differences are minor. Though they were deliberately done to meet varying mint needs, they were not intended to be set apart in the public mind. The hobby, however, likes to look at things under a microscope.

Some varieties were indeed intended to be deliberately and noticeably different. An example of this occurs with 1947-dated issues. A maple leaf was placed on the 1947-dated cent through 50-cent issues. This indicated the coin was struck after George VI lost his title of emperor of India, as proclaimed in the Latin legend, but that the design had not yet been altered to reflect this. All of these varieties are considered integral parts of the Canadian series, and they are listed as such.

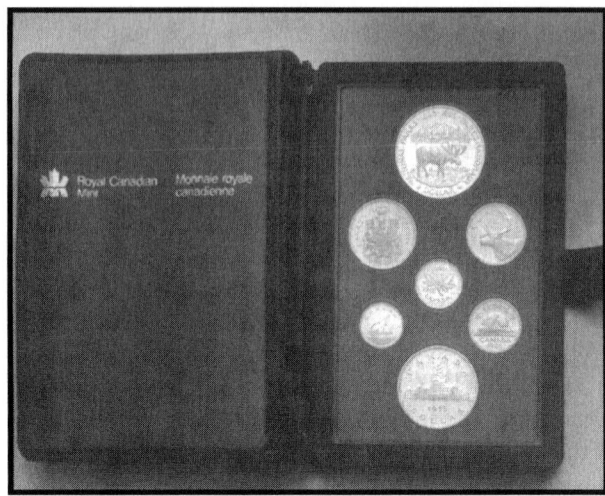

Like the U.S. Mint, the Royal Canadian Mint offers sets of coins in a variety of finishes to the collector market.

Do not construe any of this to mean there is no collecting of varieties and errors of the type common in the United States. There is. Collecting Royal Canadian Mint mistakes is just as active, just as interesting, and just as rewarding. After all, mint errors are universal. The methods of manufacture are the same. So the mistakes can be classified in the same manner.

Canada's numismatic listings also include items from various provinces issued before they were part of the confederation. The largest portion of this section is devoted to Newfoundland, because it retained a separate status far longer than the other provinces – until 1949 in fact.

Advice given to collectors of U.S. coins also applies to collectors of Canadian coins: Do what interests you. Do what you can afford. Create sets of uniform grade.

The rules of rarity transcend national boundaries. The only thing to keep in mind is the relative size of the collecting population. Because Canada has only a tenth of the U.S. population, it stands to reason that the number of collectors in that nation is but a fraction of the U.S. number. A mintage that seems to indicate scarcity for U.S. coin, therefore, could indicate something quite common in Canada. Don't forget that mintage is just a guide. The same factors that caused loss of available specimens or preserved unusually large quantities were at work in Canada, too.

Mexico

Coinage produced in Mexico dates to the establishment of a mint in Mexico City in 1536, over 250 years before a federal mint was set up in the United States and more than 300 years before Canada circulated its own coins. The output of those extra centuries alone would make organizing a Mexican coin collection more challenging than a collection of U.S. or Canadian coins. But there are numerous other factors involved.

You say you like the kings and queens on Canada's coins? Mexico has kings, too

– nearly 300 years' worth, plus a couple of emperors. You say the ideals of liberty embodied by the great men and women on U.S. coins is more your cup of tea? Mexico's coins also feature men and women committed to liberty.

In addition, Mexico is the crossroads of civilizations and empires. The great pyramid-building society of southern Mexico and Central America met its end at the hands of the Spanish conquistadors led initially by Hernando Cortez. The great Aztec empire was looted and overturned in 1519-1521 in the name of Spain.

The great natural resources of the area then supported successive Spanish kings in their grand dreams of dominating Europe. Through the doors of the Mexico City Mint and later facilities scattered about the country passed legendary quantities of silver. Even today the country ranks at the top of the list of silver producers.

But while Spain could dominate Mexico for a long time, the basic ideals of liberty and human dignity eventually motivated the people to throw off the foreign yoke. Unfortunately, victory was often neither complete nor wisely led. And in more recent years, the scourge of inflation had exacted a high toll on the currency itself. The numismatic consequences of a long history punctuated by periods of turmoil are an abundance of denominations, metals and types.

It is tempting for a would-be collector of Mexican coins to forget about anything that happened in the country prior to its monetary reform of 1905. By starting at that point, a hobbyist can happily overlook anything other than a decimal monetary system in which 100 centavos equal 1 peso. That system is as modern as any. The coins' striking quality is high. Legends are easy to read and understand, and the variety of issues is wide but not overwhelming.

There always is a certain logic to begin the collecting of any country with recent issues. The costs of learning are minimized, and as one becomes comfortable, a level of confidence can be built up sufficient to prompt diving further into the past.

The issues of 1905 to date also more easily fit into the mold of type collecting and collecting by date and mintmark. To take type collecting, for example, let's look at the peso. In 1905 it was a silver-dollar-sized coin with a silver-dollar-sized quantity of bullion in it, 0.786 ounces. In 1918 it was reduced to 0.4663 ounces; in 1920, 0.3856 ounces; in 1947, 0.2250 ounces; 1950, 0.1285 ounces; 1957, 0.0514 ounces; and in 1970 silver was eliminated completely in favor of a copper-nickel alloy.

At almost every one of those steps, the design changed, too. After sinking to 3,300 to the U.S. dollar, monetary reform dropped three zeroes in 1993. The new peso, equal to 1,000 old ones, is now 10 to the U.S. dollar.

By beginning with 1905, a date and mintmark collector misses out on issues of the various branch mints that were located around the country. Regular issues were all struck in Mexico City. Yearly output was reasonably regular for the various denominations, so date sets are extensive.

There have been rumblings since the early 1980s that Mexico would abandon the peso because of its greatly reduced value. The government, however, has been working hard to retain it since the monetary reform. So far it has succeeded.

One thing the government cannot do, however, is turn the clock back to a time when the fractional denominations of 1, 2, 5, 10, 20, 25, and 50 centavos were relatively high face values. However, it is stimulating to assemble sets because they offer a range of rarities. They are neither so expensive that it would prevent a collector

One thousand of these equaled one new peso as 1993 began.

from acquiring them at some point, but neither are they so common that you can walk into a shop, write a check, and come away with all of the 20th century sets complete. Check out the price guide section and see.

Gold in the post-1905 era is basically so much bullion. There are some scarcer pieces and some strikingly beautiful designs, such as the Centenario, a gold 50-peso coin containing 1.2 ounces of bullion. It was first struck in 1921 to mark 100 years of independence. Because Mexico actively restruck its gold coins, however, it is virtually impossible to tell an original issue from the newer version.

The result is a retail price structure based on metallic content. Gold, however, does not conjure up the images that silver does. Silver is the magic word for Mexico. That, of course, means the peso.

The modern Mexico City Mint also strikes commemoratives and collector sets from time to time. These are generally marketed to collectors through private firms, details of which are published in hobby newspapers like *World Coin News*. Mexico, like the United States and Canada, also issues gold and silver bullion coins.

These also are marketed through arrangements with private firms. Interestingly, Mexico's many gold-coin restrikes were the bullion coins of their day. They had the advantage of ready identification, and they were legally tradable according to gold-coin regulations that existed in the United States from 1933 through 1974.

It is appropriate that we conclude discussion of the modern period on the concept of bullion, because bullion is at the root of Mexico's numismatic history. That is a period to which we now turn.

When Cortez toppled the Aztec Empire, for a time the wealth returning to Spain was merely that taken by the victors from the vanquished. But the business of permanently administering a vast area in the name of the Spanish king, exploiting its natural resources, and funneling the proceeds to Spain quite soon involved the establishment of a mint in Mexico City. This was undertaken in 1536, just 15 years after the end of Aztec dominion.

At first, the authorized coins were low denominations: silver quarter, half, 1, 2, 3, and 4 reales, and copper 2 and 4 maravedis. To understand their face values and how they related to each other, let's take the common reference point of a silver dollar. The silver dollar is 8 reales, and you might recognize the nickname for the denomination of "piece of eight" from pirate lore. The eighth part, the silver real, was divided into 34 copper maravedis. That means the 8 reales was worth 272 copper maravedis.

Mexico also strikes commemorative coins for the collector market. They are available through private firms in the United States.

The copper coinage was hated and soon abolished, not to reappear until 1814. The silver coins were fine as far as they went. When the mines of Mexico began producing undreamed of quantities of metal, however, it was the 8 reales that took center stage. This occurred after 1572. The piece of eight became the standard form for shipping silver back to Spain.

Mexico City's output was prodigious. Minting standards were crude. All denominations produced are called "cobs," because they are basically little more than irregular-looking lumps of metal on which bits and pieces of design can be seen. The only constant was weight, fineness, and the appearance of assayer's initials (which guaranteed the weight and fineness). Not showing those initials was cause for severe punishment.

Designs showed the arms of the monarch on one side, a cross on the other, appropriate legends, and an indication of denomination. The period of cob issues lasted until 1732. Rulers of the period start with Charles and Johanna, 1516-1556; Philip II, 1556-1598; Philip III, 1598-1621; Philip IV, 1621-1665; Charles II, 1665-1700; Philip V, 1700-1724 and 1724-1746; and Luis I, 1724.

Modern mint machinery began turning out coins in 1732. Quality was similar to today. The arms design was continued. It was not until 1772 that the monarch's portrait began appearing. The honor of this numismatic debut belongs to Charles III. Kings of this period are Ferdinand VI, 1746-1759; Charles III, 1760-1788; Charles IV, 1788-1808; and Ferdinand VII, 1808-1821. *The Standard Catalog of Mexican Coins* by Colin R. Bruce II and Dr. George W. Vogt is recommended to those who want to study this period in greater depth.

The revolutionary period begins in 1810, when a parish priest, Miguel Hidalgo y Costilla, issued the call for independence. The first attempts to achieve this were violently suppressed. Hidalgo was executed, but independence did come in 1821.

With revolt against central authority came a dispersal of the right to strike coins. Mexico City continued as the major facility, but other operations began. The list of these over the next century is lengthy. Mintmarks and assayer initials proliferated.

The old colonial coinage standard survived the period. The 8 reales and its parts carried on. A slight reduction in bullion content had been ordered by the king in 1760, but otherwise things continued as they were. Gold was coined during the colonial period beginning in 1679 based on an 8-escudo piece, which divided into eighths just like the 8 reales. Gold, however, was not as important as silver.

Mexico's first emperor came shortly after independence. He was a leader in the struggle that set Mexico free from Spain. Augustin de Iturbide, originally an officer in the service of Spain, was proclaimed emperor in 1822. He abdicated in 1823 and was executed in 1824.

The second emperor had a reign almost as short as the first. Maximilian I, emperor only because he had a French army to secure the throne, reigned from 1863 to 1867. He was shot by a firing squad when the French left.

He is remembered numismatically because he decided to decimalize the coinage. The centavo and peso were born. Soon afterward, the republic was re-established. Further monetary changes were minor thereafter until 1905.

Collectors focusing on Mexico can devote much time to the study of the quasi-official issues of rebels during the periods of instability. They can look at hacienda tokens, which were issued by large farms or ranches that employed hundreds or thousands of people. Or they can pick whichever period in Mexico's history that fascinates them most. Whatever collectors of Mexico eventually settle on, they will find it rewarding.

Where to write for more information

World Coin News: 700 E. State St., Iola, WI 54990.

Better than map

Three mints have Web sites

By David C. Kranz

Here's a handy electronic means of finding North American coinage.

The U.S. Mint's Web site, www.usmint.gov, has been most active, making several limited, exclusively online offers. These have involved small bags of the nation's 50 states quarter issues as well as numismatic-philatelic covers and Sacagawea dollars. The U.S. Mint also sells its traditional annual products such as mint sets and proof sets on the Web, along with commemorative coins and other Mint sales catalog items.

Online orders can be more convenient for many hobbyists. Shipping charges are currently the same between sets ordered online or by mail.

Canadian gold and silver, annual sets and commemoratives are available for purchase on the Royal Canadian Mint's site, www.mint.ca. Both French and English language versions of the RCM site are available. The site is set up for online orders (placed from Canada and the United States only), and the mint accepts Visa, Mastercard and American Express.

At the site of the Mexican Mint, www.cmonedam.com.mx/cmm, you can learn that it was the first mint in America, and that it has served without interruption since its inception by Spanish decree. The Mexican Mint site has Spanish and English language versions, with coinage history, current news, sales and promotions Web pages as well as technical information about the circulating coinage of Mexico. Telephone, fax, mail and e-mail information is provided for placing orders.

The fourth component of the North American continent, Greenland, has no mint within its borders and uses coins of Denmark in commerce. For more on these coins, see the *Standard Catalog of World Coins*, published by F+W Publications (www.collect.com).

For a quick introduction to these countries' latest coinage, their Web sites can't be beat.

7

Caring for coins
How to store and preserve your collection

By Alan Herbert

From the day you acquire your first collectible coin, you have to consider where and how to store your collection. Often a shoebox or a small cardboard or plastic box of some kind will be the principal storage point as you start to gather coins, even before they can be considered a collection. Sooner or later you will outgrow that first box and need to think seriously about what to do with your coins to protect and preserve them.

All too often security takes precedence over preservation. We're more worried that the kids will dip into the coins for candy or ice cream or that burglars will somehow learn about your "valuable" collection and pay a visit. It often isn't until years later when you suddenly notice that your once beautiful coins are now dingy and dull, with spots and fingerprints all over them, that preservation becomes a primary consideration.

Learning good storage habits should be one of the first things to do right along with acquiring those first coins. There are a multitude of storage products on the market that are intended for more or less specific situations, so learning which to use and how to use them is vital to the health of your collection. Most if not all of the products mentioned here should be available at your nearest coin shop or hobby store.

Safe storage methods

The common impulse is to use what's available around the house; never allow that impulse to control your collecting. Plastic wrap, aluminum foil, cardboard, stationery envelopes, and other common household products are not designed for coin storage and never should be used for your collection. The same goes for soaps and cleansers found around the home.

There are specific products that have been designed, tested and found safe to use for coins. These are the media your collection deserves. The slight added expense

Two-by-two cardboard holders are a common form of short-term, inexpensive coin storage.

Many dealers sell coins in 2-by-2 plastic "flips," but these should not be used for long-term storage.

will pay a thousand dividends years from now when you sell you collection or pass it on to your heirs.

The most common storage media are 2-inch by 2-inch cardboard holders with Mylar windows, 2-by-2 plastic "flips," coin tubes, hard-plastic holders, coin boards, and coin albums.

The 2-by-2 cardboard holders are the cheapest and most commonly used storage method. They are usually folded and stapled around the coin. They are intended for short-term general storage. They are not airtight or watertight, and staples driven too close to the coin can ruin it.

The 2-by-2 plastic flips come in good and bad varieties. The old, usually soft flips are made of plastics that contain polyvinyl chloride, a chemical found in many plastics. Over time it breaks down into substances that put a green slime on your coins, which attacks the surface and ruins them.

The good flips are made of Mylar, but they are brittle and prone to splitting. So they should not be used to mail coins or when the coins are moved about frequently. Mylar flips, too, are for short-term general storage.

Often you will find coins in PVC holders when you buy them from a dealer. Remove them immediately and put them in some better storage medium.

Coin tubes come in clear and cloudy, or translucent, plastic. These are made of an inert plastic that will not harm your coins. Tubes are intended for bulk, medium- to long-term storage, with one caution: Use care when inserting the coins. Merely

Coin tubes are often used for bulk storage, but there is a proper technique to placing the coins in the tube.

dropping one coin onto another in a tube can damage both coins. The best technique is to make a stack or pile of the coins, then slide the pile carefully into the tube while holding it at an angle.

Hard-plastic holders are the elite items for storing your collection. There are a number of varieties, some of which come in three parts that are screwed together. Some come in two pieces that fit together. Some of these are airtight and watertight. They are more expensive, but they deserve to be used for any really valuable coins in your collection.

Coins processed by the third-party grading services come in hard-plastic holders, most of which are at least semi-airtight. The hard-plastic holders used by the U.S. Mint for proof sets since 1968 are not airtight, so coins should be watched carefully for signs of problems. In recent years these holders have been improved, but you should check your proof sets periodically.

Any stored coins should be checked regularly, at least twice a year. Check coins for signs of spotting or discoloration. Check the storage media for any signs of deterioration, rust, mildew, or other problems.

The older mint sets and proof sets – issued from 1955 to 1964 – come in soft-plastic envelopes that are not intended for long-term storage. Coins in these envelopes should be put in better storage media for the long term. In recent years the Mint has switched to an inert, stiffer plastic for the mint sets. This plastic is safe.

A coin folder is frequently the first piece of equipment the beginning collector buys. It is simply a piece of cardboard with holes to hold the coins. The holder folds up for storage. It is intended for inexpensive circulated coins only.

They give no protection from contamination or fingerprints. Worn coins will often fall out of the holes, which leads some novice collectors to tape the coins in the

Hard-plastic holders are the top of the line in coin storage.

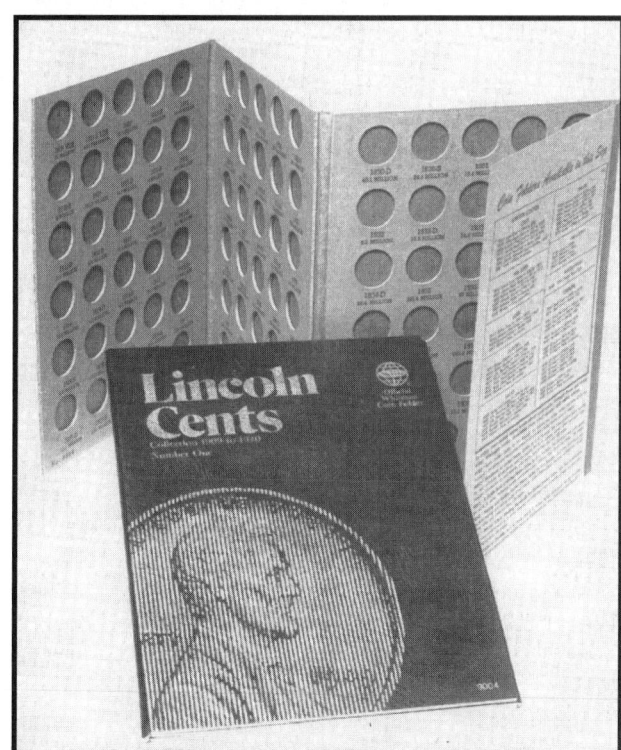

Coin folders are a low-cost and attractive way to store inexpensive circulated coins.

album. This is another example of misuse of a household product; tape can permanently damage a coin's surface.

Pride of ownership and the desire to show off a collection are the moving forces behind the sale of thousands of coin albums. They should also be used for inexpensive circulated coins only, with a couple of exceptions.

Some albums are merely coin boards mounted between covers. Others have pages with sliding plastic strips on both sides of the page so both sides of the coin can be seen.

The open-face albums are subject to fingerprints and contamination. Sneezing on your coins can do as much damage as gouging them with a knife. The slides will rub

Coin albums also provide attractive storage for inexpensive circulated coins.

on your coins, damaging the high points of the design over time. These two types of albums should never be used for expensive uncirculated or proof coins, although they are fine for circulated coins that you want to display.

Fairly new on the market are albums designed for coins in inert, airtight holders. This allows you to display your coins and still keep them safe from handling and contact with the atmosphere.

One more storage medium that deserves mention is the clear-plastic notebook page that has pockets for 2-by-2 holders or flips. Here again there are good and bad. Most old pocket sheets contain PVC, so they cannot be used to hold coins in non-airtight holders because the gases will migrate into the holders and damage the coins. The newer Mylar pages are brittle but will not generate damaging gases or liquids.

When buying storage media, make sure the dealer guarantees that his products are safe for coins. Many of the old albums, flips and pocket pages are still around, especially at flea markets. If you are in doubt, don't buy.

There are also thin, two-piece, inert plastic holders that many collectors use to protect coins put in flips or 2-by-2 cardboard holders, especially to protect them from moving about against the holder and getting scratched. They are virtually airtight, so they do offer some protection.

Coins need to be protected from burglars. A box under the bed or in the closet offers no protection. If you must keep coins at home, a good, fireproof safe is a must. Otherwise, rent a safe-deposit box at a bank, but read the fine print on your box contract to make sure a coin collection is covered.

Most homeowner's insurance policies will not cover a coin collection or will cover only a fraction of its value. Special riders are expensive, but if you keep most of your coins at the bank, this will cut costs. For details, consult your insurance agent. The American Numismatic Association also offers collection insurance.

Where to store coins is often a problem. The commonest solution is to put them in the attic or basement. Those are the two worst places for your collection. Attics are notoriously hot. Heat can damage almost any storage media, and if there is the slightest hint of PVC, you've got trouble.

Basements are equally bad. They can flood, and humidity is high. Mildew can attack holders and other material stored with your coins.

So what's left? Ideally coins should be treated like a family member. They should be stored in some part of the house where temperature and humidity are relatively constant year round. If it's comfortable for you, it's probably much more comfortable for your coins than the basement or attic.

Protecting coins from humidity is always a good idea, even in areas where it is not a major health problem. For your coins, too much dampness can become a serious problem, often before you realize it. A good solution is to get several good-sized packets of silica gel and store them with your coins in your safe or a container of some kind that will isolate them from the general climate in the home.

To clean or not to clean

Before you store your coins, you should be aware that coins are like dishes: They should never be put away dirty. Ah, but you've probably already heard or read that you should never clean a coin. If you haven't, I'll say it now: Never clean a coin.

OK, so there are exceptions, but be careful of those exceptions and for good reason. Ignoring the exception can be excruciatingly and embarrassingly expensive.

Coins get dirty, just like anything else. The impulse is to shine them up – polish them to a brilliance that will dazzle the viewer. If you've already succumbed to the temptation to clean even a single coin, stand up, kick yourself, then sit back down and read on. The one exception is loose dirt, grease, oil, or something similar, and there are even exceptions to that rule.

Use a neutral solvent to dissolve the grease and oils that usually coat uncirculated coins as they come from the mint. Follow the instructions on the container exactly, and if the directions say to use the product outdoors, they mean it.

For circulated coins, lighter fluid will often dissolve the accumulated "gunk" that sticks to them, but I don't recommend it for uncirculated coins, especially copper alloy coins. Air dry the coins; don't rub or wipe them. Even the softest cloth or paper towel can pick up sharp-edged particles that will ruin a coin's surface. Proof coins are clean when they are packaged, so this should not be necessary and should be done only as a last resort if they have somehow picked up oil in handling.

Using dips, household cleansers, metal polish, and even soap can permanently damage a coin. Avoid acid-based cleaners at all costs. They work by eating away the coin's surface to remove the embedded dirt or discoloration. Cleaning a coin with any of these products will sharply reduce its collectible value. To put it simply, collectors do not want cleaned coins, so they are heavily discounted.

One of the reasons for this is that once a coin has been cleaned, it will discolor much more quickly, requiring fresh cleaning. Each time it is cleaned, the surface is further dulled, reducing the coin's appeal and reducing its value.

Obviously this advice applies especially to uncirculated and proof coins, but it applies to any coin that is or has the potential to become valuable. But if you clean it, its career ends right there.

There are products specifically designed for removing the green PVC slime from coins. They do not contain acid, so they are safe. They will stop but cannot reverse the damage that the PVC has already done to the coin. Read the label, and use exactly as directed.

I frequently am asked about ultrasonic cleaners. They fall under the same heading as the various cleaning products I've described. In other words, the apparatus should not be used for uncirculated, proof, or other valuable coins. If you do use one, do one coin at a time so there is no chance for the vibration to rub two coins together. Change or filter the cleaning solution frequently to keep abrasive particles from coming in contact with the vibrating coin.

Like anything else, cleaning can be carried to an extreme, so I'll give you one horror story and just such a mistake: Years ago I had a collector fly several hundred miles to bring his collection for me to sell for him. When he laid out the coins on the table, I was shocked to discover that the hundreds of coins had all been harshly cleaned.

When I questioned him he calmly recounted that he had decided that the coins needed cleaning, so he dumped them all into a rock tumbler and left it on for several hours. It ruined all his coins, reducing them to face value. With his passion for cleanliness he had destroyed several thousand dollars worth of collectible value, plus air fare, a rental car, and a motel bill.

The key to a long-term collection that might appreciate in value is to learn what not to do to your coins and what care they need to survive years of waiting in the wings. Learning to protect your coins with the best available storage methods and media is a key first step toward enjoying your collection for years to come.

A private firm, Numismatic Conservation Services, LLC, will clean coins that need it for a fee. The firm's Web site address is www.ncscoin.com.

Where to write for more information

American Numismatic Association: 818 N. Cascade Ave., Colorado Springs, CO 80903-3279. Web address is http://www.money.org.

8

Join the club
Coin collecting has lots of organizations

By David C. Harper

More than 160 years ago, Alexis de Tocqueville noted in his *Democracy in America* the penchant of people in the United States to create and voluntarily join public groups for a multitude of purposes. This urge to join carries over into coin collecting.

Whether it be a national organization or local coin club, groups have been organized in the United States, Canada and Mexico to help collectors enhance their hobby knowledge and enjoyment. They serve as clearinghouses for new information, maintain libraries, and bring collectors together in meetings to share their hobby experiences with each other. Clubs are so well defined that collectors can find one to serve any activity level and any degree of personal interaction with other collectors.

At the extreme, you can join a national organization by mail, spend a hobby lifetime utilizing its services, and yet never leave the privacy and comfort of home. At the other end, some areas offer such a multitude of clubs that you can find a meeting to attend on many nights of the week.

There are many ways to find a club. Some hobbyists inquire at the local coin shop to identify the organization nearest them. *Numismatic News* publishes news about clubs. Also, watch your local newspaper for listings of community events.

How does a collector match his needs with an appropriate club? The closest thing to a one-stop shopping place for an answer is the American Numismatic Association.

It is the United States' national coin-collecting organization and was granted a perpetual charter by Congress with a mission of education. It can be reached at 818 N. Cascade Ave., Colorado Springs, CO 80903-3279. Its Web address is www.money.org. It offers a wide array of personal hobby services, and its benefits cross national boundaries. In fact, when it was founded in 1891, it was expected that Canadians and Mexicans would be just as likely to join as U.S. citizens.

The most obvious benefit to an ANA member is a subscription to *The Numismatist*, the association's monthly magazine. In it you find news, historical features, membership information, and advertisements placed by dealers who are ready to fill every collector's want list.

More than 30,000 titles are available in the ANA library, and you don't have to walk into the ANA building to check them out. Any member anywhere can do that by mail. The ANA has called upon renowned numismatic authorities to create a correspondence course, which distills into 29 separate readings information that has taken many people a lifetime to learn. There are ANA educational seminars held in Colorado Springs and other sites across the United States.

The ANA sponsors two conventions annually. The early spring convention is usually held in March at locations across the country, selected and announced well in advance. The summer convention, which is so huge that it's billed as the "World's Fair of Money," is a tradition that dates back almost to the organization's founding.

Members also are offered a variety of optional services, ranging from coin-collection insurance to credit cards and car rental discounts. And if you do go to Colorado Springs, the ANA maintains its Money Museum at its headquarters. In it are some of the rarest and most famous coins in history.

Joining the ANA is easy. The membership fee is $39 the first year and $33 thereafter. Members over 65 years old get a $4 discount, and junior members (those under 18) are charged $15.

Beyond simply belonging to the ANA, though, are the doors that open to members. If you want to find a regional, state or local club, you can get help from the ANA. The important thing to remember is that you set your own level of involvement. If your profession is so hectic that you don't need another meeting to go to, the ANA is the place for you. If your hours are so regular that joining in the fun and camaraderie of a local club is just what you are looking for, the ANA can help you find that, too.

And just because the American Numismatic Association has "American" in its name, it doesn't mean that members are focused only on U.S. coins. Far from it. It is more accurate to say that if a coin was struck at any time anywhere in the world in the last 2,600 years, there are ANA members who collect it.

The ANA, if it connotes any exclusivity at all, is basically a regional designation based on where its members live. The farther one gets from the United States, the longer correspondence takes and the greater the possibility of a language barrier between the ANA staff and a potential member. It is therefore not surprising to find that 29,000 members are predominantly located in the United States.

The Canadian Numismatic Association dates to 1950. It publishes *The Canadian Numismatic Journal*, published 11 times a year, and it also sponsors an annual convention. Membership is considerably smaller than the ANA's, in line with the population difference between the United States and Canada. Membership fee is $33 a year. The mailing address is Executive Secretary, Canadian Numismatic Association, P.O. Box 226, Barrie, Ontario L4M 4T2, Canada.

The Sociedad Numismatica de Mexico A.C. was established in 1952. Basically, it oversees an annual convention in Mexico City. It may be contacted through its U.S. representative, Don Bailey, at PMB #139, 250 "D" South Lyon Ave., Hemet, CA 92543. A related group at the same address is the U.S. Mexican Numismatic Society.

That covers the national hobby umbrella groups. There are many more organizations of a national character that have somewhat narrower poses. Among these is the American Numismatic Society in New York City. It is older than the ANA, having been established in 1858. It also maintains a superb museum of U.S. and world coins, and a world-class library. Emphasis in the ANS is on scholarly research.

Numismatics would be nothing if it were not for its research pioneers. If that is what appeals to you, you can write the ANS at Broadway and 155th St., New York, NY 10032, for information regarding its structure and various classes of membership.

Other national organizations focus on specific collectible areas, such as Seated Liberty coinage or tokens and medals. These are popular and active. Many are member organizations of the ANA and hold meetings in conjunction with the ANA's conventions.

Coin dealers have organizations of their own. The Professional Numismatists Guild Inc. maintains high standards of membership qualification and conduct. Members are a who's who of the commercial sector of the hobby. All are ready to serve you in furthering your collecting goals. For a membership roster, contact Robert Brueggeman, Executive Director, 3950 Concordia Lane, Fallbrook, CA 92028.

This brief review merely puts you on the threshold of the organized numismatic world. It is up to you to open that door or walk away. Over the years, many collectors have found membership to be the most rewarding aspect of the hobby. They have benefited from working with others with a common interest to further their own knowledge and advance their collecting goals in an environment of mutual support and friendship.

9

New American Buffalo
Gold bullion coin stampedes to market

By David C. Harper

Take a look. Take a good look. You know you like it. That's the point. Few designs are as popular as James Earle Fraser's Buffalo nickel design. That's why the Mint has "borrowed" it for a new gold bullion coin. It is the first new American gold bullion coin in 20 years and the Mint doesn't want to take any chances. The nickel was popular. A Buffalo commemorative silver dollar in 2001 using the same design was also popular. It sold out its 500,000 mintage in just two weeks during June 2001. The Mint likes sellouts. They build confidence. They build a sense of daring. They build a "can do' attitude in a governing bureaucracy that is not known for its bravery. It also doesn't hurt that congressional supporters of the new gold coin decided to tell the Mint to use it rather than simply hope that the Mint would find it.

The American Buffalo gold bullion coin was born officially at a first-strike ceremony in West Point, N.Y., June 20, 2006. The deputy Mint director, pushed a button and a coin was struck. Many more followed. On June 22, coin collectors were given the opportunity to begin buying the proof version. This part of the story is pretty routine to collectors who watch new commemoratives get introduced. But we haven't seen the introduction of a new gold bullion coin since 1986 when the very concept was born in the United States. It was in that year that the American Eagle gold bullion coin was authorized by Congress and then produced. It has been very successful. It is the largest selling gold bullion coin in the United States. Some might wonder why in light of its great success would we need to have another gold bullion coin. Good question. To answer that, we need to look beyond American borders.

The fact is, buyers in East Asia (here read China) like to buy the purest gold obtainable. They want 24-karat gold coins. Expressed another way, they want gold coins that are .9999 fine. The United States was not able to meet this demand with

Will a beloved American coin design help sell gold to the Chinese?

the American Eagle. It has a fineness of only .9167, or 22 karat. That's not bad, but for Chinese buyers and others, it is not good enough. So, the popular gold bullion coins in East Asia are made in Canada. There, the Royal Canadian Mint strikes gold Maple Leaf coins in .9999 fine gold. Canada eats our lunch with the Maple Leaf in East Asia. There are other gold coins. The Austrian Philharmonic is .9999 fine. Australia has the Nugget. They do quite well in the East Asian market. America wants a piece of this action. Yes, it has taken 20 years to take steps to tackle this market, but better late than never. Besides, gold is eternal. Gold's value glistens no matter what, but it doesn't hurt to pick a new uptrend in gold pricing to help focus people's desire on the precious yellow metal. Hence the American Buffalo was born to high hopes.

Will the American Buffalo succeed where the American Eagle has failed? We don't know. Collectors who know history can tell you that American created another coin in an attempt to crack the Chinese market. It was called the Trade dollar. Now it is avidly collected. Back in 1873 when it was created, it was a dismal failure. The irony in this failure was that the Trade dollar was a bullion coin of its day. Chinese merchants liked silver. They particularly liked the Mexican 8-reales and peso silver coins. These weighed more than a U.S. dollar. When a Chinese merchant had the choice, he wanted the heavier Mexican pieces. No U.S. silver dollars for him. The Trade dollar tried to correct this by being just as heavy as the Mexican coin. The silver was just as good, but the coin's image apparently wasn't. The Chinese merchants stayed loyal to Mexico. The Trade dollar mintages dribbled down quickly, but the coin did not reach its final end until 1885, 12 years after its ill-fated start.

Not surprisingly, the Mint doesn't want to go down that road again. They don't want to make collectors in 2140 smile. They want gold buyers to smile here and now. They want the buyers' hard cash for a hard asset. Enter the Buffalo. Will it appeal to the newly rich in China who want to diversify assets into gold? Will the new Buffalo be distinctive enough, appealing enough to persuade Chinese buyers to forsake the Maple Leaf, Philharmonic or Nugget? They might remain as loyal to these familiar .9999 fine gold coins as their ancestors did to the Mexican Trade dollar.

Hoping to get the new coin launched properly, the Mint limited the mintage of the proof collector version of the American Buffalo to 300,000. Officials hoped to build a buzz of excitement among hobby buyers in hopes that their enthusiasm would be contagious and spread. For a day, they seemed right. The Mint's Web site was overwhelmed with would-be buyers on the first day. The Mint's telephone lines were backed up to near infinity. For six hours it was a fight for anyone to get through. In the first 24 hours, the Mint sold 50,000 of the new proof American Buffalo coins. But then the orders started slowing down. In the first five days, total orders were 75,000. After 10 days, orders stood at 100,000. This book will go to press before the coin likely sells out. It is possible that it won't. Does that mean something went wrong? Perhaps. 300,000 doesn't sound like much when compared to the 500,000 Buffalo silver dollars, but that doesn't take into account the fact that gold is so much more expensive. To sell out the silver dollar, the hobby only had to come up with less than $20 million. To buy all the proof American Buffalo gold coins, the hobby will have to come up with $240 million. That's almost one-quarter of a billion dollars. That's big bucks. They might be too big even for a booming American hobby. There are an awful lot of collectors who will think they can spend $800 better on something besides a new proof one-ounce gold coin. Sure, gold might rise and bail them out, but if they want to be a gold speculator, why not spend $150 less per ounce and just get an American Eagle? Any savvy gold buyer would rather get a coin at the closest to melt value that he can. That way, he has more ounces of gold for his money and a great shot at making a profit every time gold bullion goes up on the international market.

So, what do you think? Will the Buffalo gold coin win a respected place in the East Asian market, or will it follow the road the Trade dollar did? It is hard to know so early in the process. Give it a year or two and we will have a better idea. After all, the logic of the Trade dollar still seems reasonable today. Why shouldn't the same weight of silver be given equal treatment? We might learn the answer when we find out if the same weight of pure gold in the American Buffalo gold coin is given equal treatment as the other coins.

In the meantime, look forward to the introduction of fractional sizes in the American Buffalo gold coin family. The half ounce, quarter ounce and the tenth ounce will come in a year or two, just like the pattern set by the American Eagle family of sizes. That will raise the same question for American collectors as Chinese gold buyers. Just how many proof gold bullion coins do we want? The four-coin set of American Eagles is expensive enough without adding four more Buffalo coins to the mix.

Watching the market settle down will be very interesting. The Mint picked a good time to introduce a new gold coin. Anything made of gold is hot. See Chapter 11 for a rundown of the excitement.

10

State quarters stay hot
Clock ticking toward end of program

By David C. Harper

There is nothing worse in numismatics than a collector with regrets. I remember when brilliant uncirculated 1963 Franklin half dollar rolls were $12 each. That's just $2 over face value. Even though it was a common coin almost 40 years ago, it still did well since then. I wish I had a truckload of the rolls now. Perhaps I would have found the mother lode of MS-67, -68 and -69 pieces. I remember when brilliant uncirculated Mercury dimes could be purchased for $1. Sure, they were the war years, but how many of those might have been full-split bands? I can go on and on. No I don't cry over 1913 Liberty Head nickels, which I couldn't afford 40 years ago, either, but my point is there is huge opportunity abounding in the state quarter series right now. Don't miss it. They might seem common. Some certainly are. However, time is running out. The clock is ticking. In 2007, the state quarters will be in their ninth year of a 10-year set. That means there isn't much time to take advantage of

The first two   coins of 2006 were the Nevada   and Nebraska issues. In 2007, the first two will be Montana and Washington.

current availability. Coins that seem very common now won't stay that way. Coins that are starting to be scarce now will be even harder to get in 10 or 20 years. Truly scarce error coins like the Wisconsin extra leaf varieties might be unobtainable.

The first thing to do when approaching state quarters is take a look at the U.S. Mint Web site. See what is currently available right now as you read this. Take advantage of buying the current coins at issue price. Go to www.usmint.gov to see what is there.

Check current sets. State quarters have had a tremendous impact on ongoing values of proof sets and mint sets. What do I mean? Well, as this is written, the 2006 10-coin clad proof set is being sold by the Mint for $22.95 each. In addition to the five state quarters, the set also contains the cent, nickel, dime, half dollar and dollar coins.

Since the beginning of the state quarter program, values of proof sets on the secondary market have done wonderful things as newcomers to the hobby find that in order to put a state quarter set together, they have to get the coins from the sets from the first year of issue, 1999, right down to the present. The 1999 proof set, which was sold to collectors for $19.95 will now set you back $72.50 on the secondary market. That's a nice profit and a strong indication of just what this extra state quarter demand is doing to prices of proof sets. The 1999 set is good, but the truly great performer is the 2001 set. Care to guess how expensive it is? Try $119. Its price has shot up in five years faster than gold bullion. Other years haven't done as spectacularly, but they will all cost you more now than they would have had you bought them directly from the Mint.

Silver proof sets are the same story. These sets include silver dimes, quarters and half dollars rather than clad composition. Issue price is higher at $37.95 currently, but even with the higher initial cost, the secondary market has seen wondrous

Colorado, then North and South Dakota round out 2006. Idaho, Wyoming and Utah are the 2007 final three.

things. What do you think the 1999 silver proof set has done? It is now $395. That's more than 10 times its initial price. Say thanks to new state quarter collectors for that. The 2001 set isn't bad either, but the $145 price seems low when compared to the 1999 set's price. Again, other years have done less well, but most of them are still above issue price on the secondary market.

A similar tale is told by U.S. Mint Uncirculated Coin Sets. These sets are popularly referred to as mint sets. Current price of a set, which includes one of each denomination and design from each mint, is $16.95. Remember, since there are two mints, there are 10 state quarters per set. Now look at the 2004 set on the secondary market. It is priced at $79. Why? Its that state quarter demand manifesting itself again and again across the broad range of U.S. Mint products.

You can also buy individual coins, rolls and bags. The table at right will give you some sense of relative scarcity of the quarters struck for release into circulation. But you know what? Trying to make sense of pricing on the secondary market with the mintage figures just doesn't cut it. Somehow or other, collector behavior has had a stronger impact on values. Otherwise, how can you explain the fact that an uncirculated roll of Tennessee Philadelphia quarters has, at $44, the highest price of any roll of state quarters minted to date? But that is part of the fun. Get state quarters now before they become even harder to get and higher priced. If this sounds appealing act now. Don't be a collector with regrets in 10 or 20 years' time.

State Quarter Production

States	Philadelphia	Denver
Delaware (1999)	373,400,000	401,424,000
Pennsylvania	349,000,000	358,332,000
New Jersey	363,200,000	299,028,000
Georgia	451,188,000	488,744,000
Connecticut	688,744,000	657,880,000
Massachusetts (2000)	628,600,000	535,184,000
Maryland	678,200,000	556,532,000
South Carolina	742,576,000	566,208,000
New Hampshire	673,040,000	495,976,000
Virginia	943,000,000	651,616,000
New York (2001)	655,400,000	619,640,000
North Carolina	627,600,000	427,876,000
Rhode Island	423,000,000	447,100,000
Vermont	423,400,000	459,404,000
Kentucky	353,000,000	370,564,000
Tennessee (2002)	361,600,000	286,468,000
Ohio	217,200,000	414,832,000
Louisiana	362,000,000	402,204,000
Indiana	362,600,000	327,200,000
Mississippi	290,000,000	289,600,000
Illinois (2003)	225,800,000	237,400,000
Alabama	225,000,000	232,400,000
Maine	217,400,000	231,400,000
Missouri	225,000,000	228,200,000
Arkansas	228,000,000	229,800,000
Michigan (2004)	233,800,000	225,800,000
Florida	240,200,000	241,600,000
Texas	278,800,000	263,000,000
Iowa	213,800,000	251,800,000
Wisconsin	226,400,000	226,800,000
California (2005)	257,200,000	263,200,000
Minnesota	239,600,000	248,400,000
Oregon	316,200,000	
404,000,000		
300,000,000	Kansas	263,400,000
West Virginia	365,400,000	356,200,000
Nevada	277,000,000	312,800,000
Nebraska	318,000,000	273,000,000
Colorado	NA	NA
North Dakota	NA	NA

11

Gold and silver soar
Party like it's 1980

By David C. Harper

If Rip Van Winkle had gone to sleep in early 1980 and awakened in 2006, checking the gold market each time, he would conclude that things were deadly dull, with hardly any movement at all. Nothing could be further from the truth as those of us who have been awake all those years can attest. Gold had a merry run to 1980 and then spent most of the next 25 years giving up much of what it had gained. But for those who missed the first gold party, never fear. The second gold party is now under way. The only question is how high it will go in this upturn.

As this is written, gold recovered nearly all of the ground it lost from its record $850 price set in January of 1980. On May 11, 2006, it closed trading at $719.80. It was only 18 percent away from regaining the mountain top that it had sat on oh so briefly Jan. 21, 1980. Many investors in 2006 did not participate in the market peak in 1980, so have no memory of it. For them, gold instead of being dull, is a frisky thing that seems to have nowhere to go but up. After all, it began trading in 2006 at $517.10. To jump to $719.80 in less than five months is stellar. That $202.70 gain, or almost 40 percent, was fueled by all the old fears hauled out and dusted off from 1980. Inflation was a worry. The federal government was spending too much and taking in too little, leaving a huge budget deficit. The balance of trade was hugely in favor of foreign countries, undermining confidence in the U.S. dollar. With all this being true, where else could gold go but up? As clear-cut as it might seem, nothing ever is so obvious. When gold touched its most recent lows, $255.10 on Feb. 15, 2001, the opposite seemed true. Gold had been declining for 21 years. Inflation was low. The Federal Reserve board was even fretting about deflation. The federal budget was in surplus. None of this was expected to change. But it did. The terror attacks on Sept. 11, 2001, changed the world forever. The beneficiary was gold and the other precious metals. Gold was up 282 percent from its bottom. That kind of investment return beat out just about any alternatives, even house prices. But to have gotten in at the bottom would have required an ability to think independently. Outside of an occasional article in *Numismatic News* pointing out that the time had come to buy cheap gold collector coins, there was little out there that didn't seem like the same information simply rehashed. Those pioneer investors are feeling mighty good today. But what comes next? With investment newsletters sprouting up shouting that gold will be at $1,000, $2,000, even $10,000 not all that long into the future, what should a collector do now? The lesson of 1980 is that no matter how certain things seem to be, they can change on a dime. If you collect gold coins, enjoy your profits and continue to build your sets. Now is not the time to bet the ranch on a market fluctuation. Then again, now is not the time to ignore gold either. If you don't own any gold coins, now might be the time to buy a gold $20 or two before prices rise. If gold goes back to sleep, use the opportunity to build a type set. Both Liberty Head $20s of the late 19th century and the Saint-Gaudens $20s of the early 20th century can be obtained at prices hardly more than the value of the precious metal in them. If you like the experience, go after other denominations. A type set is a challenge, but it is not an overwhelming one. You can have collecting fun and all the while you will be taking a position in a precious metal that could continue to rise in value.

And while you are doing that, don't forget silver. This metal means more to average collectors because they tend to own it. A rise in silver delivers profits to most numismatists. In the time gold was rising 282 percent, silver was jumping from $4.51 to $14.85, or 329 percent. That's great for the average hobbyist. It is a bigger jump for the little guy. Can silver go higher? Back in 1980, it reached $50. If it does that again, there will be a lot of collectors retiring to a tropical beach in a nice sunny country. But just as is the case with gold, react to the market-bestowed riches by continuing to do what has made you successful in the first place: collect. If you collect Morgan dollars, try Peace dollars. If you collect Barber halves, jump forward to Walking Liberty halves. If Mercury dimes are your thing, give Seated Liberty dimes a shot. There are a lot of silver coins to choose from. Naturally, the rarer the coins, the portion of value derived from bullion is small. However, it is the swings in price that tend to influence the value of the scarcer coins. When speculators are making money in bullion, the cash flow tends too make everyone in numismatics a little better off. They use that money to bid up prices of collector coins. That being the case, you can use bullion prices as a yardstick to collector coin values. It is not exact. It can't be. The tie isn't even absolute. Morgans had a heck of a run higher in the 1980s when silver was washing out from $50 to $5.

So party like its in 1980, but don't get carried away and don't lose sight of the fact that you are in it as a collector, not a bullion speculator. That makes the rewards even sweeter and takes the sting out of any declines along the way.

12

What's hot in 2007?
If you want it, others will, too!

By David C. Harper

In 1924, the presidential slogan of the winning candidate was, "Keep cool with Coolidge." Let's borrow that and adjust it for conditions in 2007 and say, "Keep cool with numismatics." It is not catchy like the presidential slogan, but it does have meaning, two meanings actually. For the first time since the 1950s it is cool to be a coin collector again. Newspapers write stories about us. The Mint wants to sell more and more coins to us. And, eBay built a business with our help. But what popular culture bestows, it also takes away. Coin collectors find that they are more often the objects of ridicule in their lifetimes than persons who are envied. That has made them internally directed. They collect through thick and thin and they don't need anybody else to tell them what to do, thank you very much.

Worse, not only are coin collectors currently popular, the prices of precious metals are soaring, making it seem that we are people with the golden touch. Buy anything of precious metals, stand back and watch it fly higher and higher. Well, anyone in the field for any length of time knows it isn't that easy.

What do you do then when you are looking to spot some undervalued coin that may become a hot item when the rest of the world catches up to us? The first thing to remember is that collectors appreciate rarity and condition. And of the two, rarity always eventually has its day. Condition is a little more iffy in a field that now has numerous MS-70 items offered for sale and Registry Sets are all the rage with competitive coin collectors. But that very competition is a sign of our temporary coolness, or prestige. When it goes, we don't want to go with it. We simply want to get on with our collecting lives.

So what is hot in 2007? Perhaps we should say, what should be hot in 2007? Lincoln cents are our theme this year. They are not made of precious metals and therefore are not participating in the boom inspired by the rise of precious metals. They rise only from increasing collector demand. That increased demand is coming. It is coming because 2009 is the Bicentennial of the birth of Abraham Lincoln and the 100th anniversary of the Lincoln cent. The United States will issue five

**New
interest
in the 1909-S**

commemorative   cents in 2009 to mark the occasion. Four   designs will be representative of various stages of Lincoln's life, birth in Kentucky, growing up in Indiana, Illinois lawyer and his White House years. A fifth design might just be the key. This one has to be the identical design to the 1909 issue, portrait on obverse, Wheat Ears on reverse, and it must be made of the bronze alloy of that first cent. Who is to say that this mandate cannot take the form of a 2009-S VDB cent. It meets all the requirements and it will call enormous attention to the key to the Lincoln series, the 1909-S VDB. Other key dates will benefit also.

Consider adding the 1909-S VDB to your collection before the spotlight hits it. It has been rising in value in recent years and is currently $1,050 in VF-20, $1,500 in MS-60 and $7,500 in MS-65. When the whole world is focused on Lincoln, how high can this go?

The other keys will benefit also.

First stop, the 1909-S. It is a product of the same year and same mint as the famous coin, but it is not as scarce. It is priced at $1,500 in MS-60.

Take a look at the 1911-S. It might have eluded you in your circulation finds youth, or you might never have looked for it. It is a hard one to find and a current price of $160 in MS-60 makes it look far easier than veteran cent collectors would admit.

Then there is the 1914-D. This was always right behind the 1909-S VDB in desirability. In MS-60, it is $1,900 now.

The error 1922 plain was always a hard one, but because it is an error, it gets bursts of interest. Current MS-60 price of $9,600 shows how hard it is to get one in top condition, so you probably should look in circulated grades. Even a G-4 is $525.

The 1931-S has a mintage of just 866,000, but its MS-60 price of $120 shows that much of the mintage was saved by collectors for future generations. Take advantage of it and get one.

Then jump forward to the 1955 doubled die. It was a product of the last time it was cool to be collectors. It is $1,425 in XF-40, a pleasing circulated grade, but soars to $37,500 in MS-65.

These and other Lincolns all stand to benefit from the attention that will be focused on them when 2009 arrives. It should pay well to be early.

13

Internet now standard
Collectors take online use to new heights

By Ray Sidman

Everywhere you look, everything you read, the Internet has permeated our culture. Whether promoting a business or a personal Web site, "www" has become a common word at all levels of our culture, and "dot-com" – no longer vast enough to cover it all – has been joined by "dot-net," "dot-org" and many other extensions.

Coin collectors congregate online in chatrooms, dealers operate solely from their online sites. Libraries and other public facilities and even private enterprises offer Internet access services for individuals who don't have a home computer.

Week by week the level of person-to-person interaction and business growth increases with this technology. Don't be left in the cold. See what's available to you.

Grading Services
ANACS
www.anacs.com
Currency Grading & Certification
www.currencygradingcertification. com
Digital Coin Grading Service
www.digitalcoingrading.com
Global Certification Services
www.globalcertified.com
Independent Coin Grading Company
www.icgcoin.com
Numismatic Guaranty Corporation of America
www.ngccoin.com
Numistrust
www.numistrust.com
PCI Coin Grading Services
www.chattanooga.net/pci
Professional Coin Grading Service
www.pcgs.com

Sovereign Entities Grading Service
www.segsgrading.com

Auction Firms
America West Archives
www.americawestarchives.com
American Numismatic Rarities
www.anrcoins.com
Best Collectors
www.bestcollectors.com
BidXS.com
www.bidxs.com
Bowers & Merena Galleries
www.bowersandmerena.com
Centennial Auctions
www.centennialauctions.com
Certified Coin Auction
www.cce-auction.com
Collector Online
www.collectoronline.com

Currency Auctions of America
www.currencyauction.com
Gary Duskie Rare Coins
www.coinmall.com/duskie
eBay
www.ebay.com
E-Bid
www.ebid.com.au
Early American History Auctions
www.earlyamerican.com
El Mundo de la Moneda
www.elmundodelamoneda.com
Jean Elsen s.a.
www.elsen.be
eWanted
www.ewanted.com
Ira & Larry Goldberg Coins &
    Collectibles
www.goldbergcoins.com
Heritage Auction Galleries
www.HA.com
Jeffrey Hoare Auctions
www.jeffreyhoare.on.ca
Fred Holabird Americana
www.holabird.org
Jackson's
www.jacksonsauction.com
Lyn Knight Currency Auctions
www.lynknight.com
Lone Star Auctioneers
www.lonestarauctioneers.com

Malter Galleries
www.maltergalleries.com
Greg Manning Auctions
www.gregmanning.com
MastroNet
www.mastronet.com
Ponterio & Associates
www.ponterio.com
Roxbury's Auction House
www.roxburys.com
Smythe
www.smytheonline.com
Sotheby's
www.sothebys.com
Spink & Son Ltd
www.spink-online.com
Stack's
www.stacks.com
Superior Galleries
www.superiorgalleries.com
Surpluzz.com
www.surpluzz.com
Tangible Asset Galleries
www.tagz.com
Teletrade Auctions
www.teletrade.com
Whyte's
www.whytes.ie

Numismatic Dealers
A-Mark Precious Metals
www.amark.com
Abbott's Corporation
www.abbottscorp.com
Alaska Mint
www.akmint.com
Albanese Rare Coins
www.coinace.com
All American Coin Company
www.aacoinco.com
American Gold Exchange
www.amergold.com
American Heritage Mint
www.mtnhighcoin.com
American Rare Coin Supply
www.rarecoinsupply.com
American Rarities
www.americanrarities.com
Amphora Coins
www.amphoracoins.com
Joel Anderson
www.joelscoins.com

Please Note

Web sites often incorporate capital letters as part or all of their addresses. This is not always necessary. Please note that capital letters found in the addresses shown in this directory are ones necessary in order to arrive at the correct Web site.

Also, the prefix "www." is not always needed, and often it is necessary to leave it off. Please note that when a Web address listed here does not start with "www." that address will only work without this prefix.

Antique Carta
www.antiquecarta.com
Aspen Coins
www.aspencoins.com
Aspen Park Rare Coins
www.aprci.com
ATSnotes.com
www.atsnotes.com
Austin Rare Coins & Bullion
www.austincoins.com
Lois & Don Bailey Numismatic
   Services
www.donbailey-mexico.com
Bank Note Reporter
www.banknotereporter.com
BankNote1 Currency
www.banknote1.com
Ken Barr Numismatics
www.kenbarr.com
Alexander Basok
www.rustypennies.com
Harlan J. Berk, Ltd.
www.harlanjberk.com
Allen G. Berman
www.bermania.com
Blanchard and Company
www.blanchardonline.com
Bob's Coins & Collectibles
www.bobscoins.com

Bob's Coins, Collectibles and More
biblecom.tripod.com/aa-index.html
Bonavita Ltd.
www.eligi.ca/bonavita
Brooklyn Gallery Coins & Stamps
www.brooklyngallery.com
Byers Numismatic Corporation
www.byersnc.com
C & D Gale
www.cdgale.com/default.htm
Calgary Coin & Antique
www.calgarycoin.com
California Numismatic Investments
www.golddealer.com
Camco
www.camcocoin.com
Cameo CC
www.cameocc.com
Canadian Coinoisseur
www.coinoisseur.com
Cape Mint
www.exinet.co.za/pagliari/index.htm
Capital Collectors Plastics
www.capitalplastics.com/nnn
Carat-Coin-Collectibles
www.caratcoin.com
Carolina Gold & Silver
www.carolinacoin.com
CDA Bullion Precious Metals
www.cdabullion.com
Tom Cederlind Numismatics & Antiq-
   uities
www.tomcederlind.com
Centerville Coin & Jewelry
www.centercoin.com
CH Coins
www.chcoins.com
Robert Charles Coin Company
www.robertcharlescoins.com
Cheap Slab Store
www.cheapslabs.com
Chicago Coin Company
www.chicagocoin.com
David F. Cieniewicz
www.banknotestore.com
Civil War Tokens
www.civilwartokens.com
Cline's Rare Coins
www.slqs.com
Coast to Coast Coins
www.coastcoin.com

Want the eNewsletter?

Subscribe to the FREE *Numismatic eNewsletter.*

Enjoy the latest news and information about the coin and paper money hobby delivered electronically.

Simply sign up at the *Numismatic News* Web site www.numismaticnews.net to become a registered user of the site and begin receiving the biweekly *Numismatic eNewsletter*!

Cochran's Coins
www.cochran14k.com
The Coin and Currency Institute
www.coin-currency.com
Coincraft
www.coincraft.com
CoinCrazy.com
www.coincrazy.com
Coin Dealer Newsletter
www.greysheet.com
CoinFacts.com
www.coinfacts.com
Coin Gallery Online
www.coin-gallery.com
TheCoinGuy.com
www.thecoinguy.com
CoinIndex.com
www.coinindex.com
Coin Prices
www.coinpricesmagazine.net
Coin Restoration Service
www.crs-stockton.com
CoinScape
www.coinscape.com
Coin Shop
www.coin-shop.com
Coins International
www.coinsinternational.com
Coins Magazine
www.coinsmagazine.net
CoinsOfTheUSA.com
www.coinsoftheusa.com
Coin Webstore
www.coinwebstore.com
Coinwire.com
www.coinwire.com
Collectors Universe
www.collectors.com
Colonial Acres Coins
www.colonialacres.com
Compu-Quote
www.compu-quote.net
Continental Coin Investors
www.internet4coins.com
Corrosion Free Coin Supply, LLC
www.coinshield.com
Cybercoins
www.cybercoins.net
D & M Coins
www.dmcoins.com
Chuck D'Ambra Coins
www.telesphere.com/ts/coins

Dallas Gold & Silver Exchange
www.dgse.com
David Hall Rare Coins
www.davidhall.com
Denly's of Boston
www.denlys.com
Distinctive Coins
www.distinctivecoins.com
DistinctiveGiftware.com
www.distinctivegiftware.com
Michael Dixon Rare Coins
www.michaeldixonrarecoins.com
Dolphin Coins and Medals Ltd.
www.dolphincoins.com
Downies Ltd.
www.downies.com
Eagle Coin Supplies
www.eaglecoinholders.com
Eagle Eye Rare Coins
www.indiancent.com
Eagle Numismatics
www.coinmaven.com
Eureka Trading System
www.eurekatrading.com
Educational Coin Company
www.educationalcoin.com
Eligi Consultants
www.eligi.ca
Ellesmere Numismatics
www.ellesmerecoin.com
Elusive Spondulix
www.rarecoin.com
Estate Wholesalers
www.estatewholesaler.com
Steve Estes, P.N.
www.steveestes.com
Euro Collections International
www.eurocollections.com
Steve Eyer
www.eyersworld.com
Florida Coin & Jewelry
www.floridacoin.com
The Franklin Mint
www.franklinmint.com
Gaithersburg Coin Exchange
www.gaithersburgcoin.com
Gallery Mint Museum
www.gallerymint.com
Gatewest Coin Ltd.
www.gatewestcoin.com
Ronald J. Gillio
www.gillio.com

Goldline International
www.goldline.com
Gold Rarities Gallery
www.goldrarities.com
Graded Currency
www.gradedcurrency.com
Orville J. Grady
www.gradybooks.com
Great Lakes Coin Company
www.greatlakescoin.com
Hallenbeck Coin Gallery
www.hallenbeck-coins.com
Hancock & Harwell
www.raregold.com
H.E. Harris & Co.
www.heharris.com
Hans W. Hercher Munzen GmbH
www.herchercoins.com
Wayne Herndon Rare Coins
www.wayneherndon.com
Hobby Coin Exchange
www.hobbycoinexchange.com
Hoffman Mint
www.hoffmanmint.com
Richard Hokanson Rare Coin Investments
www.hokanson-coins.com
Randall P. Holder Rare Coins
www.rpholdercoins.bigstep.com
Horwedel's Currency
www.horwedelscurrency.com
House of Coins
www.houseofcoins.com
Hudson Rare Coins
www.hudsonrarecoins.com
International Coins & Currency
www.iccoin.com
J & J Coins
www.jjcoins.com
J & M Coin
www.jandm.com
Eric Jackson
www.ericjackson.com
Jake's Marketplace
www.jakesmp.net
Jamestown Stamp Company
www.jamestownstamp.com
Jefferson Coin & Bullion
www.jeffinc.com

Jencius Coins
www.vaticancoins.com
J.G.M. Numismatics
www.jgmnumismatics.com
Jim's Stamp & Coin Shop
www.thepilot.com/busdir/jimsstamp
Glen Johnson Rare U.S. Currency
www.uspapermoney.com
Kagin's
www.kagins.com
The Kanawha Coin Shop
www.kanawhacoin.com
Kelgory Coin and Currency Supply
www.kelgory.com
Don C. Kelly
www.donckelly.com
Jonathan K. Kern Company
www.jkerncoins.com
Keshequa Coins
www.keshequacoins.com
Jeff Kierstead Rare Coins
www.jkrarecoin.com
King of Carson City
www.carsoncityking.com
Kitco
www.kitco.com
Knight Coin
www.knightcoin.com
George Frederick Kolbe
www.numislit.com
Bill Kracov
www.choiceworldbanknotes.com
Krause Publications
www.collect.com
www.krause.com
www.coincollecting.net
Tim Kyzivat
www.kyzivatcurrency.com
George H. LaBarre Galleries
www.glabarre.com
Harry Laibstain Rare Coins
www.hlrc.com
David Lawrence Rare Coins
www.davidlawrence.com
Legend Numismatics
www.legendcoin.com
Julian M. Leidman
www.juliancoin.com
Bret Leifer Numismatics
www.coinguy.com

Liberty Coin Service
www.libertycoinservice.com
Libnick's Coins and Currency
www.libnick.com
Limited Editions
www.limitededitionsinc.org
Littleton Coin Company
www.littletoncoin.com
Lone Star Coins & Collectibles
www.lonestarcoins.com
Lone Star Mint
www.lsmint.com
Louisiana Gold & Gems
www.louisianagold.com
Luck 'E' Penny
www.wcmassey.com/lep/index.htm
Marc One Numismatics
www.marconenumismatics.com
Mark Johnson Coins & Supplies
www.mjcoins.com
Mayer Mint GmbH Germany
www.mayermint.com
McKinn's Coins
www.mckinn.com
McQueeney Coins
www.mcqueeneycoins.com
Mexican Coin Company
www.mexicancoincompany.com
Midwest Estate Buyers
www.midwest-estate-buyers.com
Mietens & Partner
www.mietens.de
Miller's Mint Ltd.
www.millersmint.com
Minneapolis Gold, Silver and Numis-
    matic Services
www.coindeals.com
Mintmark Numismatics
www.mintmark.com
Money-Changers
www.home.earthlink.
    net/~moneychanger/index.html
Mountain High Coins & Collectibles
www.mtnhighcoin.com
Mount Vernon Coin Company
www.mtvcoins.com
The Naples Bank Note Company
www.banknotables.com
Colin Narbeth & Son
www.colin-narbeth.com
National Collectors Mint
www.ncmint.com

National Gold Exchange
www.ngegold.com
New World Rarities Ltd.
www.nwrarities.com
North American Certified Trading
www.natcoin.com
Northeast Numismatics
www.northeastcoin.com
www.foreigncoin.com
Nostomania
www.nostomania.com
NumisAd
www.numisgroup.com
Numismatic Assets
www.numismaticassets.com
Numismatic News
www.numismaticnews.net
NumisMedia
www.numismedia.com
Numis-Phil Pte. Ltd.
www.worldcurrency.com
Old Coin Shop
www.oldcoinshop.com
Olde Towne Coin Company
www.oldetownecoin.com
Old Pueblo Coin
www.oldpueblocoin.com
Original Weather Coin Company
www.weathercoin.com
Pacific Atlantic Coin Company
www.pacoin.com
PandaAmerica
www.pandaamerica.com
PaperMoneyFacts.com
www.papermoneyfacts.com
Paradise Coin & Gift
www.paradisecoin.com
Park Avenue Numismatics
www.parkavenumis.com
Jay Parrino's The Mint LLC
www.jp-themint.com
Penny Farmer
www.pennyfarmer.com
Perth Numismatics
www.perthmoney.com
Pinnacle Rarities
www.pinnaclerarities.com
Tony Pisciotta
www.banknotesoftheworld.com
Ken Potter
koinpro.tripod.com

Premier Precious Metals
www.premierpreciousmetals.com
Tim Prusmack
www.money-art.com
Puro's Coins and Jewelry
www.vtcoins.com
R & I Coins
www.ricoins.com
Rare Coin Company of America
www.coinsthatmatter.com
RareCurrency.com
www.rarecurrency.com
Hans & Beate Rauch
www.apcpapercollect.com
Richard J. Reed World Paper Money
www.misterbanknote.com
James J. Reeves
www.jamesjreeves.com
Regency Coins
www.rgncycoin.com
Bob Reis' Anything Anywhere
www.anythinganywhere.com
Joel D. Rettew
www.fastcoin.com
Roy Reynolds Coins
*www.geocities.com/rodeodrive/7533/
    royhomepage.html*
River City Coins & Jewelry
www.rivercitycoins.com
Frank S. Robinson
www.albany.net/~fr/index.html
RR Rare Coins and Currency
www.rrcoins.net
Sahara Coins LLC
www.saharacoins.com
San Joaquin Valley Rare Coins
goldcoin.dds-tech.net
Wayne G. Sayles
www.ancientcoins.ac
Jim Sazama
www.jimsazama.com
Rich Schemmer
www.richerrors.com
Reinhard Schimmer GmbH
www.schimmer.de
Scotsman Coin and Currency
www.scoins.com
Daniel Frank Sedwick
www.sedwickcoins.com
David Seelye
www.thempcman.net

Shawnee Coin Company
www.shawneecoin.com
Showcase Coins
www.showcasecoins.com
Showgard
www.showgard.com
Sigma Ancient Coins
www.sigmacoins.com
Silver State Coin & Bullion
www.silverstatecoin.com
SilverTowne
www.silvertowne.com
Slater Numismatics
www.slatercoins.com
Sam Sloat Coins
sloat.coinnet.com
Southern Coin Investments
www.southerncoin.com
Southern Coins and Precious Metals
www.scpm.com
Spectrum Numismatics
www.spectrumnumismatics.com
Stanton Books & Supplies
www.stantonbooks.com
Steinberg's
www.steinbergs.com
Sunshine Rarities
www.sunshinerarities.com
Anthony J. Swiatek Numismatics
www.anthonyjswiatek.com
Swiss America Trading Corporation
www.swissamerica.com
M. Louis Teller Numismatic Company
www.tellercoins.com
G.R. Tiso Numismatics
www.grtiso.com
Tiitus Syngraphics
www.syngraphics.net/imbl
Token Publishing
www.medal-news.com
Scott Travers Rare Coin Galleries
www.inch.com/~travers/travers3.htm
Trove Software
www.trovesoftware.com
The Tulving Company
www.tulving.com
UBS Gold & Numismatics
*www.ubs.com/e/pb/solutions/numis-
    matics.html*

USA Rare
www.usarare.com
USCents.com
www.uscents.com
U.S. Currency Online
www.uscurrencyonline.com
USMintQuarters.com
www.usmintquarters.com
U.S. State Quarters.com
www.usstatequarters.com
Valley View Coins & Collectibles
www.valleyviewcoins.com
Edward J. Waddell, Ltd.
www.coin.com
Washington Mint
www.washingtonmint.com
Washington Square Coin Exchange
www.wscoin.com
Fred Weinberg & Co.
www.fredweinberg.com
West Bay Trading Company
www.westbaytrading.com
Pam West British Bank Notes
www.west-banknotes.co.uk
Scott J. Winslow Associates
www.scottwinslow.com
Douglas Winter Numismatics
www.raregoldcoins.com
Charles W. Woodruff Rare Coins & Currency
www.cwwoodruff.com
The Working Man's Rare Coins
www.workingmancoins.com
World Coin News
www.worldcoinnews.net
World Exonumia
www.exonumia.com
WorldWide Coins
www.wwc.coins.ru
WVW Classics
www.wvwclassics.com
William Youngerman
www.williamyoungerman.com
Jeffrey S. Zarit
www.klippes.com

Numismatic Organizations
Albuquerque Coin Club
www.albuquerquecoinclub.org
Alexandria Coin Club
www.members.cox.net/alexandriacoinclub

American Israel Numismatic Association
www.amerisrael.com
American Medallic Sculpture Association
www.amsamedals.org
American Numismatic Association
www.money.org
American Numismatic Society
www.amnumsoc.org
www.numismatics.org
American Play Money Society
www.members.tripod.com/playmoneytoo/apms/home.html
American Society of Check Collectors
members.aol.com/asccinfo
Americans for Common Cents
www.pennies.org
APL Coin Club
www.money.org/clubs/apl_index.html
Atlantic Provinces Numismatic Association
www.nunetcan.net/apna.htm
Baltimore Coin Club
www.money.org/club_bcc.html
Bexley Coin Club
www.bexleycoinclub.org.uk
Big Island Coin Club
www.collectibleshawaii.com
Blue Ridge Numismatic Association
www.brna.org
British Association of Numismatic Societies
www.coinclubs.freeserve.co.uk
Calgary Numismatic Society
www.ucalgary.ca/~cns
California State Numismatic Association
www.coinmall.com/CSNA
Canadian Association of Numismatic Dealers
www.nunetcan.net/cand.htm
Canadian Association of Token Collectors
www.nunetcan.net/catc.htm
Canadian Association of Wooden Money Collectors
www.nunetcan.net/cawmc.htm
Canadian Numismatic Association
www.canadian-numismatic.org

Canadian Numismatic Research Society
www.nunetcan.net/cnrs.htm
Canadian Paper Money Society
www.nunetcan.net/cpms.htm
Casino Chips and Gaming Tokens Collectors Club
www.ccgtcc.com
Central Florida Coin Club
www.centralfloridacoinclub.org
Central States Numismatic Society
www.centralstates.info
Chicago Coin Club
www.chicagocoinclub.org
Chippewa Valley Coin Club
www.54701.com/clubs/cvcc/index.htm
Civil War Token Society
www.cwtsociety.com
Classical & Medieval Numismatic Society
www.nunetcan.net/cmns.htm
Clements High School Coin Club
www.fortbendisd.com/ campuses/chs/ActivityDetail. cfm?activityIndex=10067
Coin Master's Online Coin Club
www.coinmasters.org
Columbus Numismatic Society/ Central Ohio International Numismatic Society
www.cnscoins.com
Combined Organization of Numismatic Error Collectors of America
www.conecaonline.org
CopperCoins.com
www.coppercoins.com
Crescent City Coin Club
www.money.org/clubs/cccc_index.html
Croatian Philatelic Society
www.croatianmall.com/cps/index.htm
CSA Collectors Page
www.csacurrency.com
Denver Coin Club
www.telesphere.com/ts/dcc
Early American Coppers
www.eacs.org
Edmonton Numismatic Society
www.edmontoncoinclub.com
Elgin Coin Club
www.prairienet.com/coins/ecc
The Elongated Collectors
www.tecnews.org

Florida United Numismatists
www.funtopics.com
Fox Valley Coin Club
www.prairienet.com/coins/fvcc
Fractional Currency Collectors Board
www.fractionalcurrency.org
Full Horn Buffalo Nickel Club
www.geocities.com/RodeoDrive/4044/ fullhorn.html
Garden State Numismatic Association
www.gsna.org
Glendale Coin Club
www.glencoin.com
Greater Houston Coin Club
www.money.org/sum-ross.html
Greater Jacksonville Coin Club
www.angelfire.com/fl/gjccweb
Hawaii State Numismatic Association
www.hawaiicollectibles.org
Illinois Numismatic Association
www.ilnaclub.org
International Association of Professional Numismatists
www.iapn.ch/iapn
International Bank Note Society
www.ibns.it
International Bond & Share Society
www.scripophily.org
International Numismatic Commission
www.amnumsoc.org/inc
Islamic Coins Group
www.islamiccoinsgroup.50g.com
John Reich Collectors Society
www.jrcs.org
Johnson County Numismatic Society
www.money.org/club_jcns.html
Liberty Seated Collectors Club
www.numismalink.com/lscc.html
Lincoln Coin Club
www.geocities.com/jb91437/Lincoln-CoinClub.html
Lower Cape Fear Coin Club
www.money.org/clubs/lcfcc.html
Marion Coin Club
www.members.tripod.com/marioncoinclub
Maryland State Numismatic Association
www.money.org/club_msna.html

Maryland Token and Medal Society
www.money.org/clubs/mdtams/
mdtams.html
Metropolitan Coin Club of Atlanta
www.mccatl.org
Model City Coin Club
home.tricon.net/alanphil/mccc.html
Montgomery County Coin Club
www.money.org/club_mccc.html
Mount Vernon Numismatic Society
www.money.org/clubs/mvns_main.htm
National Collectors Association of Die
  Doubling
www.geocities.com/ResearchTriangle/
Facility/4968/NCADD.html
National Token Collectors Association
home.pacbell.net/tokenbob
North Carolina Numismatic Associa-
  tion
www.ncnaonline.org
Numismatic Association of Southern
  California
www.nasc.net
Numismatic Bibliomania Society
www.coinbooks.org
Numismatic Literary Guild
www.numismaticliteraryguild.org
Numismatic Network Canada
www.nunetcan.net
Oak Park Coin Club
www.oakparkcoinclub.com
Ontario Numismatic Society
www.nunetcan.net/ona.htm
Oriental Numismatic Society
www.onsnumis.org
Original Hobo Nickel Society
www.hobonickels.org
Oslo Numismatic Society
www.mynter.org/onf
Pacific Coast Numismatic Society
www.pcns.org
Pacific County Friends of Lewis and
  Clark
www.lewisandclarkingot.com
Pacific Northwest Numismatic Association
www.pnna.org
Peninsula Coin Club
www.stanford.edu/~clint/pcc
Pennsylvania Association of Numismatists
www.money.org/club_pan.html

Pensacola Numismatic Association
coinclub.freeyellow.com
Prince Edward Island Numismatic
  Association
www.angelfire.com/art/peina
Professional Numismatists Guild
www.pngdealers.com
Raleigh Coin Club
www.raleighcoinclub.org
Rockford Area Coin Club
www.exonumia.com/racc.htm
Roxbury Coin Club
www.ledgewood.net/rcc
Royal Numismatic Society
www.rns.dircon.co.uk
Royal Numismatic Society of New
  Zealand
www.geocities.com/rnsnz
San Jose Coin Club
www.sanjosecoinclub.org
Society for U.S. Commemorative
  Coins
www.money.org/clubs/suscc.html
Society of Paper Money Collectors
www.spmc.org
Society of Philatelists and Numismatists
span.atsecure.net
Society of U.S. Pattern Collectors
www.uspatterns.com
Stanislaus County Coin Club
www.stancocoinclub.com
Swedish Numismatic Society
www.users.wineasy.se/snf
Tasmanian Numismatic Society
www.vision.net.au/~pwood/tns.html
Tennessee State Numismatic Society
www.tsns.org
Texas Numismatic Association
www.tna.org
Token and Medal Society
www.money.org/clubs/tams/index.html
U.S. Mexican Numismatic Association
www.grasshoppernet.com/walrafen/
usmexna.html
Victoria Numismatic Society
www.victoria.tc.ca/Recreation/VNS
Washington Historical Autograph and
  Certificate Organization
www.whaco.com

Washington Numismatic Society
www.money.org/clubs/wns/wns_index.
   html
Waterloo Coin Society
www.angelfire.com/tx/wcshomepage
Willamette Coin Club
www.pdxcoinclub.org
Wilmington Coin Club
www.money.org/clubs/wcc.html
Women In Numismatics
www.money.org/sum-baber.html
Wooden Nickel Collector's Organization
www.wooden-nickel.org
Worldwide Bi-Metallic Collectors
   Club
www.wbcc-online.com
Young Numismatists of America
www.ynaclub.org

Miscellaneous Related Sites

American Bankers Association
www.abacoins.com
Art in the Hand Gallery
www.artinthehand.com
Asset Strategies International
www.assetstrategies.com
Bank for International Settlements
   – Central Bank Web sites
www.bis.org/cbanks1.htm
The Harry Bass Research Foundation
www.hbrf.org
Bestcoins.com
bestcoins.com
Bick International
www.bick.net
The British Museum
www.thebritishmuseum.ac.uk
Bureau of Engraving and Printing
www.moneyfactory.com
www.bep.treas.gov
California Gold Marketing Group
www.sscentralamerica.com
Canadian Coin Reference Site
www.canadiancoin.com
Canadian Numismatic Bibliography
   Project
www.julaine.ca/canbiblio
Carlisle Development Corporation
www.carlisledevelopment.com
CCE and FACTS

www.certifiedcoinexchange.com
www.cce-auction.com
CNN Financial Network
cnnfn.cnn.com
CoinClubs.com
www.coinclubs.com
Coin Coalition
www.coincoalition.org
CoinGrading.com
www.coingrading.com
CoinLink
www.coinlink.com
Coin Optics
www.coinoptics.com
CoinResource.com
www.coinresource.com
Coinsheet Numismatic Directory
www.coinsheetlinks.com
Coinstar
www.coinstar.com
Coin Today
www.goldstockcenter.com/index2.htm
Collectify
www.collectify.com
Collectorama Show
www.hometown.aol.com/collectora-
   mashow/index.html
Collectors Software
www.vpackrat.com
U.S. Commission of Fine Arts
www.cfa.gov
Congressional Medal of Honor Society
www.cmohs.org
Enroute.ca
www.enroute.ca
Federal Reserve Bank of Richmond
   Money Museum
www.rich.frb.org/econed/museum/
   index.html
Forrest's Token Page
users.pullman.com/fjstevens/tokens/
   index.html
GFMS Ltd.
www.gfms.co.uk
Gold Institute
www.goldinstitute.org
Gold Rush Gallery
www.goldrushgallery.com
Goldsheet Numismatic Web Page
www.goldsheetlinks.com/index.htm

Industry Council for Tangible Assets
www.ictaonline.org
International Collectible Expo
www.collectibleshow.com
Jewish-American Hall of Fame
www.amuseum.org/jahf
Johnson Matthey
www.johnsonmatthey.com
Krause Publications
www.collect.com
www.krause.com
www.coincollecting.net
Londoh.com
www.londoh.com
London Banknote and Monetary
    Research Centre Ltd.
www.lbmrc.co.uk
Long Beach Coin, Stamp & Collect-
    ibles Expo
www.longbeachshow.com
MonsterCoin.com
www.monstercoin.com
Museum of American Financial
    History
www.financialhistory.org
National Numismatic Collection
*www.americanhistory.si.edu/csr/
    cadnnc.htm*
National Trust for Historic Preserva-
    tion
www.nationaltrust.org
Norfed
www.norfed.org
Numismatica
www.limunltd.com/numismatica
Numismaticards
www.cointradingcards.com
Platinum Guild International
www.platinumguild.org
Saint-Gaudens National Historic Site
www.sgnhs.org
Santa Clara Coin, Stamp & Collect-
    ibles Expo
www.santaclarashow.com
Silver Institute
www.silverinstitute.org
Smithsonian Institute
www.si.edu
Southeast Asian Treasury
www.seasiantreasury.com
Stonewalls Civil War Currency
www.home.earthlink.net/~icepick119

Trade Token Tales
*members.fortunecity.com/tokenguy/
    tokentales*
U.S. Secret Service
www.treas.gov/usss
U.S. Treasury
www.ustreas.gov
U.S. Treasury – Office of the Inspec-
    tor General
www.ustreas.gov/oig
Universal Currency Converter
www.xe.net/ucc
University of Notre Dame – Coin and
    Currency Collections
www.coins.nd.edu
Vendio
www.vendio.com
Where's George?
www.wheresgeorge.com
Where's Willy?
www.whereswilly.com
World Gold Council
www.gold.org

World Mint Sites

Austrian Mint
www.austrian-mint.com
    Austria's North American rep.
        www.eurocollections.com
Bermuda Monetary Authority
www.bma.bm
British Royal Mint
www.royalmint.com
Czech Mint
www.bcm.cz
The French Mint
www.monnaiedeparis.com
Israel Government Coins and Medals
    Corp. Ltd.
www.coins.co.il
Mexican Mint
www.cmonedam.com.mx
The Mint Bureau (Japan)
www.mint.go.jp
Mint of Finland
www.mint.fi
Perth Mint
www.perthmint.com.au
Pobjoy Mint Ltd.
www.pobjoy.com

Polish State Mint
www.mennica.com.pl
Royal Australian Mint
www.ramint.gov.au
Royal Canadian Mint
www.mint.ca
www.monnaie.ca
Royal Norwegian Mint
www.dkm.no
San Marino Mint
www.aasfn.sm
Singapore Mint
www.singaporemint.com.sg
South African Mint
www.samint.co.za
Spanish Mint
www.fnmt.es
Turkish State Mint
www.mint.gov.tr/english.htm
U.S. Mint
www.usmint.gov

U.S. Federal Reserve Banks
Atlanta, Ga.
www.atl.frb.org
Board of Governors of the Federal
    Reserve System
www.federalreserve.gov
Boston, Mass.
www.bos.frb.org
Chicago, Ill.
www.chicagofed.org
Cleveland, Ohio
www.clevelandfed.org
Dallas, Texas

www.dallasfed.org
Kansas City, Kan.
www.kc.frb.org
Minneapolis, Minn.
www.minneapolisfed.org
New York, N.Y.
www.ny.frb.org
Philadelphia, Pa.
www.phil.frb.org
Richmond, Va.
www.rich.frb.org
San Francisco, Calif.
www.sf.frb.org
St. Louis, Mo.
www.stls.frb.org

Theft Reporting Sites
CoinFacts.com
*www.coinfacts.com/Administrative/
    stolen_coin_reports.htm*
World Exonumia
www.exonumia.com/stolen.htm

Euro Sites
Euro Bill Tracker
www.eurobilltracker.com
Euro Issues
home.hetnet.nl/~asliesem
European Union
www.europa.eu.int/euro
Euro-sceptic Web Resource
www.euro-sceptic.org
Microsoft Windows – Euro Support
www.microsoft.com/windows/euro.asp

Newsgroups

For those who wish to communicate with other collectors more directly, there are newsgroups.

*search.mailgate.org/rec/rec.
collecting.coins
    search.mailgate.org/rec/rec.
collecting.paper-money
    groups.google.com*

Missing?

If your group or organization's Internet address has never appeared in our Web directory, let us know and we'll put it in a future edition.

Just contact us by writing to *North American Coins & Prices*, Krause Publications, 700 E. State St., Iola, WI 54990 or send e-mail to david. harper@fwpubs.com.

Glossary of coin terms

Adjustment marks: Marks made by use of a file to correct the weight of over-weight coinage planchets prior to striking. Adjusting the weight of planchets was a common practice at the first U.S. Mint in Philadelphia and was often carried out by women hired to weigh planchets and do any necessary filing of the metal.

Altered coin: A coin that has been changed after it left the mint. Such changes are often to the date or mintmark of a common coin in an attempt to increase its value by passing to an unsuspecting buyer as a rare date or mint.

Alloy: A metal or mixture of metals added to the primary metal in the coinage composition, often as a means of facilitating hardness during striking. For example, most U.S. silver coins contain an alloy of 10 percent copper.

Anneal: To heat in order to soften. In the minting process planchets are annealed prior to striking.

Authentication: The act of determining whether a coin, medal, token or other related item is a genuine product of the issuing authority.

Bag marks: Scrapes and impairments to a coin's surface obtained after minting by contact with other coins. The term originates from the storage of coins in bags, but such marks can occur as coins leave the presses and enter hoppers. A larger coin is more susceptible to marks, which affect its grade and, therefore, its value.

Base metal: A metal with low intrinsic value.

Beading: A form of design around the edge of a coin. Beading once served a functional purpose of deterring clipping or shaving parts of the metal by those looking to make a profit and then return the debased coin to circulation.

Blank: Often used in reference to the coinage planchet or disc of metal from which the actual coin is struck. Planchets or blanks are punched out of a sheet of metal by what is known as a blanking press.

Business strike: A coin produced for circulation.

Beading ➤

Cast copy: A copy of a coin or medal made by a casting process in which molds are used to produce the finished product. Casting imparts a different surface texture to the finished product than striking and often leaves traces of a seam where the molds came together.

Center dot: A raised dot at the center of a coin caused by use of a compass to aid the engraver in the circular positioning of die devices, such as stars, letters, and dates. Center dots are prevalent on early U.S. coinage.

Chop mark ➤

Chop mark: A mark used by Oriental merchants as a means of guaranteeing the silver content of coins paid out. The merchants' chop marks, or stamped insignia, often obliterated the original design of the host coin. U.S. Trade dollars, struck from 1873 through 1878 and intended for use in trade with China, are sometimes found bearing multiple marks.

Clash marks: Marks impressed in the coinage dies when they come together without a planchet between them. Such marks will affect coins struck subsequently by causing portions of the obverse design to appear in raised form on the reverse, and vice versa.

Clipping: The practice of shaving or cutting small pieces of metal from a coin in circulation. Clipping was prevalent in Colonial times as a means of surreptitiously extracting precious metal from a coin before placing it back into circulation. The introduction of beading and a raised border helped to alleviate the problem.

Coin alignment: U.S. coins are normally struck with an alignment by which, when a coin is held by the top and bottom edge and rotated from side-to-side, the reverse will appear upside down.

Collar: A ring-shaped die between which the obverse and reverse coinage dies are held during striking. The collar contains the outward flow during striking and can be used to produce edge reeding.

Commemorative: A coin issued to honor a special event or person. United States commemorative coins have historically been produced for sale to collectors and not placed in circulation, though the 50-states quarters are circulating commemoratives.

Copy: A replica of an original issue. Copies often vary in quality and metallic composition from the original. Since passage of the Hobby Protection Act (Public Law 93-167) of Nov. 29, 1973, it has been illegal to produce or import copies of coins or other numismatic items that are not clearly and permanently marked with the word "Copy."

Counterfeit: A coin or medal or other numismatic item made fraudulently, either for entry into circulation or sale to collectors.

Denticles: The toothlike pattern found around a coin's obverse or reverse border.

Die: A cylindrical piece of metal containing an incuse image that imparts a raised image when stamped into a planchet.

Die crack: A crack that develops in a coinage die after extensive usage, or if the die is defective or is used to strike harder metals. Die cracks, which often run through border lettering, appear as raised lines on the finished coin.

Device: The principal design element.

Double eagle: Name adopted by the Act of March 3, 1849, for the gold coin valued at 20 units or $20.

Rim

Field

Mintmark

Exergue

Obverse

Legend

Reverse

Eagle: Name adopted by the Coinage Act of 1792 for a gold coin valued at 10 units or $10. Also a name used to refer to gold, silver, and platinum coins of the American Eagle bullion coinage program begun in 1986.

Edge: The cylindrical surface of a coin between the two sides. The edge can be plain, reeded, ornamented, or lettered.

Electrotype: A copy of a coin, medal, or token made by electroplating.

Exergue: The lower segment of a coin, below the main design, generally separated by a line and often containing the date, designer initials, and mintmark.

Face value: The nominal legal-tender value assigned to a given coin by the governing authority.

Fasces: A Roman symbol of authority consisting of a bound bundle of rods and an axe.

Field: The flat area of a coin's obverse or reverse, devoid of devices or inscriptions.

Galvano: A reproduction of a proposed design from an artist's original model produced in plaster or other substance and then electroplated with metal. The galvano is then used in a reducing lathe to make a die or hub.

Glory: A heraldic term for stars, rays or other devices placed as if in the sky or luminous.

Grading: The largely subjective practice of providing a numerical or adjectival ranking of the condition of a coin, token, or medal. The grade is often a major determinant of value.

Gresham's law: The name for the observation made by Sir Thomas Gresham, 16th century English financier, that when two coins with the same face value but different intrinsic values are in circulation at the same time, the one with the lesser intrinsic value will remain in circulation while the other is hoarded.

Half eagle: Name adopted by the Coinage Act of 1792 for a gold coin valued at five units or $5.

Hub: A piece of die steel showing the coinage devices in relief. The hub is used to produce a die that, in contrast, has the relief details incuse. The die is then used to produce the final coin, which looks much the same as the hub. Hubs may be reused to make new dies.

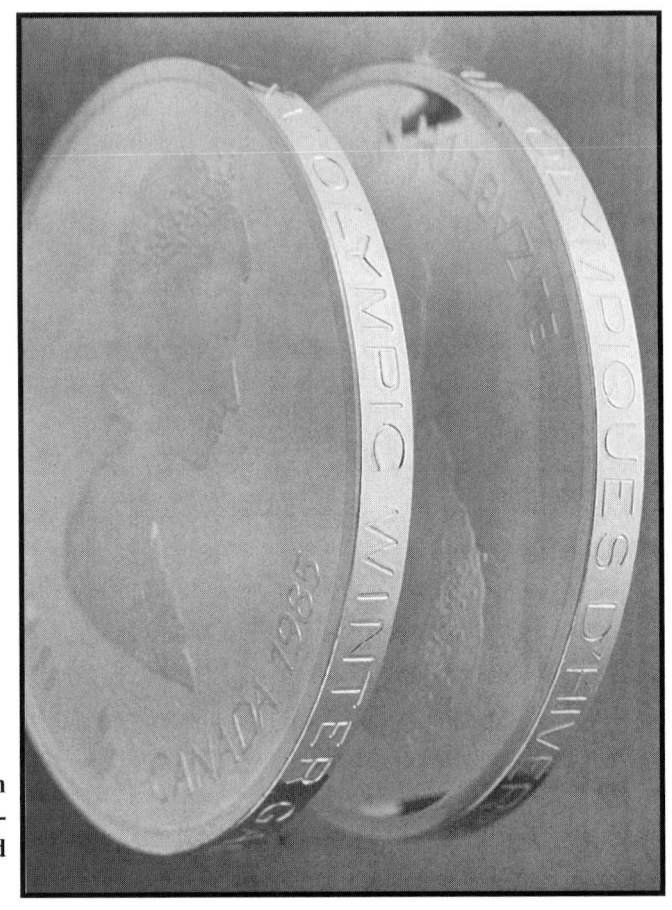

These Canadian Olympic commemoratives have lettered edges.

Legend: A coin's principal lettering, generally shown along its outer perimeter.

Lettered edge: Incuse or raised lettering on a coin's edge.

Matte proof: A proof coin on which the surface is granular or dull. On U.S. coins this type of surface was used on proofs of the early 20th century. The process has since been abandoned.

Magician's coin: A term sometimes used to describe a coin with two heads or two tails. Such a coin is considered impossible in normal production due to physical differences in obverse and reverse die mountings, though as of 2001 two have been certified as genuine by professional coin authenticators. The vast majority are products made outside the Mint as novelty pieces.

Medal: Made to commemorate an event or person. Medals differ from coins in that a medal is not legal tender and, in general, is not produced with the intent of circulating as money.

A medal usually commemorates an event but has no monetary value. It can be issued by a private entity or a government.

Medal alignment: Medals are generally struck with the coinage dies facing the same direction during striking. When held by the top and bottom edge and rotated from side-to-side, a piece struck in this manner will show both the obverse and reverse right side up.

Mintage: The total number of coins struck during a given time frame, generally one year.

Mintmark: A letter or other marking on a coin's surface to identify the mint at which the coin was struck.

Mule: The combination of two coinage dies not intended for use together.

Numismatics: The science, study or collecting of coins, tokens, medals, paper money, and related items.

Obverse: The front or "heads" side of a coin, medal, or token.

Overdate: Variety produced when one or more digits of the date are repunched over an old date on a die at the Mint, generally to save on dies or correct an error. Portions of the old date can still be seen under the new one.

Overmintmark: Variety created at the Mint when a different mintmark is punched over an already existing mintmark, generally done to make a coinage die already punched for one mint usable at another. Portions of the old mintmark can still be seen under the new one.

Overstrike: A coin, token or medal struck over another coin, token, or medal.

Pattern: A trial strike of a proposed coin design, issued by the Mint or authorized agent of a governing authority. Patterns can be in a variety of metals, thicknesses, and sizes.

**This U.S. Trade dollar
has a reeded edge.**

Phrygian cap: A close-fitting, egg-shell-shaped hat placed on the head of a freed slave when Rome was in its ascendancy. Hung from a pole, it was a popular symbol of freedom during the French Revolution and in 18th century United States.

Planchet: A disc of metal or other material on which the image of the dies are impressed, resulting in a finished coin. Also sometimes called a blank.

Proof: A coin struck twice or more from specially polished dies and polished planchets. Modern proofs are prepared with a mirror finish. Early 20th century proofs were prepared with a matte surface.

Prooflike: A prooflike coin exhibits some of the characteristics of a proof despite having been struck by regular production processes. Many Morgan dollars are found with prooflike surfaces. The field will have a mirror background similar to that of a proof, and design details are frosted like some proofs.

Quarter eagle: Name adopted by the Coinage Act of 1792 for a gold coin valued at 2.5 units or $2.50.

Reeding: Serrated (toothlike) ornamentation applied to the coin's edge during striking.

Relief: The portion of a design raised above the surface of a coin, medal, or token.

A token is issued by a private entity and can be redeemed for its face value in trade or service.

Restrike: A coin, medal or token produced from original dies at a later date, often with the purpose of sale to collectors.

Reverse: The backside or "tails" side of a coin, medal or token, opposite from the principal figure of the design or obverse.

Rim: The raised area bordering the edge and surrounding the field.

Series: The complete group of coins of the same denomination and design and representing all issuing mints.

Token: A privately issued piece, generally in metal, with a represented value in trade or offer of service. Tokens are also produced for advertising purposes.

Type coin: A coin from a given series representing the basic design. A type coin is collected as an example of a particular design rather than for its date and mint-mark.

Variety: Any coin noticeably different in dies from another of the same design, date and mint. Overdate and overmintmarks are examples of varieties.

Wire edge: Created when coinage metal flows between the coinage die and collar, producing a thin flange of coin metal at the outside edge or edges of a coin.

Introduction to pricing

The following value guide is divided into six sections:
1. U.S. minting varieties and errors.
2. Colonial coins, issued prior to the establishment of the United States
3. U.S. issues of 1792.
4. U.S. issues of 1793-present.
5. Canadian coins.
6. Mexican coins.

Value listings

Values listed in the following price guide are average retail prices. These are the approximate prices collectors can expect to pay when purchasing coins from dealers. They are not offers to buy or sell. The pricing section should be considered a guide only; actual selling prices will vary.

The values were compiled by Krause Publications' independent staff of market analysts. They derived the values listed by monitoring auction results, business on electronic dealer trading networks, and business at major shows, and in consultation with a panel of dealers. For rare coins, when only a few specimens of a particular date and mintmark are known, a confirmed transaction may occur only once every several years. In those instances, the most recent auction result is listed.

Grading

Values are listed for coins in various states of preservation, or grades. Standards used in determining grades for U.S. coins are those set by the American Numismatic Association. See Chapter 4 for more on grading.

Dates and mintmarks

The dates listed are the individual dates that appear on each coin. The letter that follows the date is the mintmark and indicates where the coin was struck: "C" — Charlotte, N.C. (1838-1861); "CC" — Carson City, Nev. (1870-1893); "D" — Dahlonega, Ga. (1838-1861), and Denver (1906-present); "O" New Orleans (1838-1909); "P" — Philadelphia (1793-present); "S" San Francisco (1854-present); and "W" — West Point, N.Y. (1984-present). Coins without mintmarks were struck at Philadelphia.

A slash mark in a date indicates an overdate. This means a new date was engraved on a die over an old date. For example, if the date is listed as "1899/8," an 1898 die had a 9 engraved over the last 8 in the date. Portions of the old numeral are still visible on the coin.

A slash mark in a mintmark listing indicates an overmintmark (example: "1922-P/D"). The same process as above occurred, but this time a new mintmark was engraved over an old.

See the "U.S. Minting Varieties and Errors" section for more information on overdates and overmintmarks.

Price charts

Pricing data for the selected charts in the U.S. section were taken from the January issues of "Coin Prices" for the years indicated.

Mexican coin mintages

Quantities minted of each date are indicated when that information is available, generally stated in millions and rounded off to the nearest 10,000 pieces. The following mintage conversion formulas are used:

10,000,000 —10.000.
1,000,000 — 1,000.
100,000 — 100.
10,000 — .010.
9,999 — 9,999.
1,000 — 1,000.
842 — 842 pcs. (pieces).
27 — 27 pcs.

Precious-metal content

Throughout this book precious-metal content is indicated in troy ounces. One troy ounce equals 480 grains, or 31.103 grams.

Abbreviations

AGW. Actual gold weight.

APW. Actual platinum weight.

ASW. Actual silver weight.

BV. Bullion value. This indicates the coin's current value is based on the amount of its precious-metal content and the current price for that metal.

Est. Indicates the exact mintage is not known and the figure listed is an estimate.

G. Grams.

Inc. Abv. Indicates the mintage for the date and mintmark listed is included in the previous listing.

KM#. In the Canadian and Mexican price sections, indicates "Krause-Mishler number." This sequential cataloging numbering system originated with the *Standard Catalog of World Coins* by Chester L. Krause and Clifford Mishler, and provides collectors with a means for identifying world issues.

Leg. Legend.

Mkt value. Market value.

MM. Millimeters.

Obv. Obverse.

P/L. Indicates "prooflike," a type of finish used on some Canadian coins.

Rev. Reverse.

Spec. Indicates "specimen," a type of finish used on some Canadian coins.

PRICING
SECTION

U.S. Minting Varieties and Errors

Introduction

By Alan Herbert

The P.D.S. cataloging system used here to list minting varieties was originally compiled by Alan Herbert in 1971. PDS stands for the three main divisions of the minting process, "planchet," "die" and "striking." Two more divisions cover collectible modifications after the strike, as well as non-collectible alterations, counterfeits and damaged coins.

This listing includes 445 classes, each a distinct part of the minting process or from a specific non-mint change in the coin. Classes from like causes are grouped together. The PDS system applies to coins of the world, but is based on U.S. coinage with added classes for certain foreign minting practices.

Price ranges are based on a U.S. coin in MS-60 grade (uncirculated.) The ranges may be applied in general to foreign coins of similar size or value although collector values are not usually as high as for U.S. coins. Prices are only a guide as the ultimate price is determined by a willing buyer and seller.

To define minting varieties, "A coin which exhibits a variation of any kind from the normal, as a result of any portion of the minting process, whether at the planchet stage, as a result of a change or modification of the die, or during the striking process. It includes those classes considered to be intentional changes, as well as those caused by normal wear and tear on the dies or other minting equipment and classes deemed to be "errors."

The three causes are represented as follows:
1. (I) = Intentional Changes
2. (W) = Wear and Tear
3. (E) = Errors
Note: A class may show more than one cause and could be listed as (IWE).

Rarity level

The rarity ratings are based on the following scale:
1 - Very Common. Ranges from every coin struck down to 1,000,000.
2 - Common. From 1,000,000 down to 100,000.
3 - Scarce. From 100,000 down to 10,000.

4 - Very Scarce. From 10,000 down to 1,000.
5 - Rare. From 1,000 down to 100.
6 - Very Rare. From 100 down to 10.
7 - Extremely Rare. From 10 down to 1.

Unknown: If there is no confirmed report of a piece fitting a particular class, it is listed as Unknown. Reports of finds by readers would be appreciated in order to update future presentations.

An Unknown does not mean that your piece automatically is very valuable. Even a Rarity 7 piece, extremely rare, even unique, may have a very low collector value because of a lack of demand or interest in that particular class.

Classes, definitions and price ranges are based on material previously offered in Alan Herbert's book, *The Official Price Guide to Minting Varieties and Errors* and in *Coin Prices* Magazine.

Pricing information has also been provided by John A. Wexler and Ken Potter, with special pricing and technical advice from Del Romines.

Also recommended is the *Cherrypicker's Guide to Rare Die Varieties* by Bill Fivaz and J.T. Stanton. Check your favorite coin shop, numismatic library or book seller for availability of the latest edition.

For help with your coin questions, to report significant new finds and for authentication of your minting varieties, include a loose first class stamp and write to Alan Herbert, 700 E. State St., Iola, WI 54990-0001. Don't include any numismatic material until you have received specific mailing instructions from me.

Quick check index

If you have a coin and are not sure where to look for the possible variety:

If your coin shows doubling, first check V-B-I.

Then try II-A, II-B, II-C, II-I (4 & 5), III-J, III-L, or IV-C.

If part of the coin is missing, check III-B, III-C, or III-D.

If there is a raised line of coin metal, check II-D, II-G.

If there is a raised area of coin metal, check II-E, II-F, or III-F.

If the coin is out of round, and too thin, check III-G.

If coin appears to be the wrong metal, check III-A, III-E, III-F-3 and III-G.

If the die appears to have been damaged, check II-E, II-G. (Damage to the coin itself usually is not a minting variety.)

If the coin shows incomplete or missing design, check II-A, II-E, III-B-3, III-B-5 or III-D.

If only part of the planchet was struck, check III-M.

If something was struck into the coin, check III-J and III-K.

If something has happened to the edge of the coin, check II-D-6, II-E-10, III-I, III-M and III-O.

If your coin shows other than the normal design, check II-A or II-C.

If a layer of the coin metal is missing, or a clad layer is missing, check III-B and III-D.

If you have an unstruck blank, or planchet, check I-G.

If your coin may be a restrike, check IV-C.

If your coin has a counterstamp, countermark, additional engraving or apparent official modifications, check IV-B and V-A-8.

Do not depend on the naked eye to examine your coins. Use a magnifying lens whenever possible, as circulation damage, wear and alterations frequently can be mistaken for legitimate minting varieties.

Division I: planchet varieties

The first division of the PDS System includes those minting varieties that occur in the manufacture of the planchet upon which the coins will ultimately be struck and includes classes resulting from faulty metallurgy, mechanical damage, faulty processing, or equipment or human malfunction prior to the actual coin striking.

Planchet alloy mix (I-A)

This section includes those classes pertaining to mixing and processing the various metals which will be used to make a coin alloy.

I-A-1 Improper Alloy Mix (WE), Rarity Level: 3-4, Values: $5 to $10.

I-A-2 Slag Inclusion Planchet (WE), Rarity Level: 5-6, Values: $25 up.

Damaged and defective planchets (I-B)

To be a class in this section the blank, or planchet, must for some reason not meet the normal standards or must have been damaged in processing. The classes cover the areas of defects in the melting, rolling, punching and processing of the planchets up to the point where they are sent to the coin presses to be struck.

I-B-1 Defective Planchet (WE), Rarity Level: 6, Values: $25 up.

I-B-2 Mechanically Damaged Planchet (WE), Rarity Level: –, Values: No Value. (See values for the coin struck on a mechanically damaged planchet.)

I-B-3 Rolled Thin Planchet (WE), Rarity Level: 6 - (Less rare on half cents of 1795, 1797 and restrikes of 1831-52.) Values: $10 up.

I-B-4 Rolled Thick Planchet (WE), Rarity Level: 7 - (Less rare in Colonial copper coins. Notable examples occur on the restrike half cents of 1840-52.) Values: $125 up.

I-B-5 Tapered Planchet (WE), Rarity Level: 7, Values: $25 up.

I-B-6 Partially Unplated Planchet (WE), Rarity Level: 6, Values: $15 up.

I-B-7 Unplated Planchet (WE), Rarity Level: 6-7, Values: $50 up.

I-B-8 Bubbled Plating Planchet (WE), Rarity Level: 1, Values: No Value.

I-B-9 Included Gas Bubble Planchet (WE), Rarity Level: 6-7, Values: $50 up.

I-B-10 Partially Unclad Planchet (WE), Rarity Level: 6, Values: $20 up.

I-B-11 Unclad Planchet (WE), Rarity Level: 6-7, Values: $50 up.

I-B-12 Undersize Planchet (WE), Rarity Level: 7, Values: $250 up.

I-B-13 Oversize Planchet (WE), Rarity Level: 7, Values: $250 up.

I-B-14 Improperly Prepared Proof Planchet (WE), Rarity Level: 7, Values: $100 up.

I-B-15 Improperly Annealed Planchet (WE), Rarity Level: - , Values: No Value.

I-B-16 Faulty Upset Edge Planchet (WE), Rarity Level: 5-6, Values: $10 up.

I-B-17 Rolled-In Metal Planchet (WE), Rarity Level: 6-7, Values: $50 up.

I-B-18 Weld Area Planchet (WE), Rarity Level: Unknown, Values: No Value Established. (See values for the coins struck on weld area planchets.)

I-B-19 Strike Clip Planchet (WE), Rarity Level: 7, Values: $150 up.

I-B-20 Unpunched Center-Hole Planchet (WE), Rarity Level: 5-7, Values: $5 and up.

I-B-21 Incompletely Punched Center-Hole Planchet (WE), Rarity Level: 6-7, Values: $15 up.

I-B-22 Uncentered Center-Hole Planchet (WE), Rarity Level: 6-7, Values: $10 up.

I-B-23 Multiple Punched Center-Hole Planchet (WE), Rarity Level: 7, Values: $35 up.

I-B-24 Unintended Center-Hole Planchet (WE), Rarity Level: Unknown, Values: -.

I-B-25 Wrong Size or Shape Center-Hole Planchet (IWE), Rarity Level: 5-7, Values: $10 up.

Clipped planchets (I-C)

Clipped blanks, or planchets, occur when the strip of coin metal fails to move forward between successive strokes of the gang punch to clear the previously punched holes, in the same manner as a cookie cutter overlapping a previously cut hole in the dough. The size of the clip is a function of the amount of overlap of the next punch.

The overlapping round punches produce a missing arc with curve matching the outside circumference of the blanking punch. Straight clips occur when the punch overlaps the beginning or end of a strip which has had the end sheared or sawed off. Ragged clips occur in the same manner when the ends of the strip have been left as they were rolled out.

The term "clip" as used here should not be confused with the practice of clipping or shaving small pieces of metal from a bullion coin after it is in circulation.

I-C-1 Disc Clip Planchet (WE), Rarity Level: 3-5, Values: $5 up.

I-C-2 Curved Clip Planchet - (To 5%) (WE), Rarity Level: 5-6, Values: $5 up.

I-C-3 Curved Clip Planchet - (6 to 10%) (WE), Rarity Level: 6, Values: $10 up.

I-C-4 Curved Clip Planchet - (11 to 25%) (WE), Rarity Level: 5-6, Values: $15 up.

I-C-5 Curved Clip Planchet - (26 to 60%) (WE), Rarity Level: 6-7, Values: $25 up.

I-C-6 Double Curved Clip Planchet (WE), Rarity Level: 6, Values: $10 up.

I-C-7 Triple Curved Clip Planchet (WE), Rarity Level: 5-6, Values: $25 up.

I-C-8 Multiple Curved Clip Planchet (WE), Rarity Level: 6-7, Values: $35 up.

I-C-9 Overlapping Curved Clipped Planchet (WE), Rarity Level: 6-7, Values: $50 up.

I-C-10 Incompletely Punched Curved Clip Planchet (WE), Rarity Level: 6, Values: $35 up.

I-C-11 Oval Curved Clip Planchet (WE), Rarity Level: 6-7, Values: $50 up.

I-C-12 Crescent Clip Planchet - (61% or more) (WE), Rarity Level: 7, Values: $200 up.

I-C-13 Straight Clip Planchet (WE), Rarity Level: 6, Values: $30 up.

I-C-14 Incompletely Sheared Straight Clip Planchet (WE), Rarity Level: 6, Values: $50 up.

I-C-15 Ragged Clip Planchet (WE), Rarity Level: 6-7, Values: $35 up.

I-C-16 Outside Corner Clip Planchet (E), Rarity Level: -, Values: No Value.

I-C-17 Inside Corner Clip Planchet (E), Rarity Level: -, Values: No Value.

I-C-18 Irregularly Clipped Planchet (E) Rarity Level: -, Values: Value not established.

I-C-19 Incompletely Punched Scalloped or Multi-Sided Planchet (E), Rarity Level: 7, Values: $25 up.

Laminated, split, or broken planchet (I-D)

For a variety of reasons the coin metal may split into thin layers (delaminate) and either split completely off the coin, or be retained. Common causes are included gas or alloy mix problems. Lamination cracks usually enter the surface of the planchet at a very shallow angle or are at right angles to the edge. The resulting layers differ from slag in that they appear as normal metal.

Lamination cracks and missing metal of any size below a split planchet are too common in the 35 percent silver 1942-1945 nickels to be collectible or have any significant value.

I-D-1 Small Lamination Crack Planchet (W), Rarity Level: 4-5, Values: $1 up.

I-D-2 Large Lamination Crack Planchet (W), Rarity Level: 3-4, Values: $5 up.

I-D-3 Split Planchet (W), Rarity Level: 5-6, Values: $15 up.

I-D-4 Hinged Split Planchet (W), Rarity Level: 6-7, Values: $75 up.

I-D-5 Clad Planchet With a Clad Layer Missing (W), Rarity Level: 5-6, Values: $35 up.

I-D-6 Clad Planchet With Both Clad Layers Missing (W), Rarity Level: 6-7, Values: $75 up.

I-D-7 Separated Clad Layer (W), Rarity Level: 5, Values: $25 up.

I-D-8 Broken Planchet (WE), Rarity Level: 3-4, Values: $5 up.

Wrong stock planchet (I-E)

The following classes cover those cases where the wrong coin metal stock was run through the blanking press, making blanks of the correct diameter, but of the wrong thickness, alloy or metal or a combination of the wrong thickness and the wrong metal.

I-E-1 Half Cent Stock Planchet (IE), Rarity Level: Unknown, Values: No Value Established.

I-E-2 Cent Stock Planchet (IE), Rarity Level: Unknown, Values: No Value Established.

I-E-3 Two Cent Stock Planchet (E), Rarity Level: Unknown, Values: No Value Established.

I-E-4 Three Cent Silver Stock Planchet (E), Rarity Level: Unknown, Values: No Value Established.

I-E-5 Three Cent Nickel Stock Planchet (E), Rarity Level: Unknown, Values: No Value Established.

I-E-6 Half Dime Stock Planchet (E), Rarity Level: Unknown, Values: No Value Established.

I-E-7 Dime Stock Planchet (E), Rarity Level: 7, Values: $200 up.

I-E-8 Twenty Cent Stock Planchet (E), Rarity Level: Unknown, Values: No Value Established.

I-E-9 Quarter Stock Planchet (E), Rarity Level: Unknown, Values: No Value Established.

I-E-10 Half Dollar Stock Planchet (E), Rarity Level: Unknown, Values: No Value Established.

I-E-11 Dollar Stock Planchet (E), Rarity Level: 7, Values: $300 up.

I-E-12 Token or Medal Stock Planchet (E), Rarity Level: Unknown, Values: No Value Established.

I-E-13 Wrong Thickness Spoiled Planchet (IWE), Rarity Level: Unknown, Values: No Value Established.

I-E-14 Correct Thickness Spoiled Planchet (IWE), Rarity Level: Unknown, Values: No Value Established.

I-E-15 Cut Down Struck Token Planchet (IWE), Rarity Level: Unknown, Values: No Value Established.

I-E-16 Experimental or Pattern Stock Planchet (IE), Rarity Level: Unknown, Values: No Value Established.

I-E-17 Proof Stock Planchet (IE), Rarity Level: Unknown, Values: No Value Established.

I-E-18 Adjusted Specification Stock Planchet (IE), Rarity Level: 7, Values: $25 up.

I-E-19 Trial Strike Stock Planchet (IE), Rarity Level: Unknown, Values: No Value Established.

I-E-20 U.S. Punched Foreign Stock Planchet (E), Rarity Level: 7, Values: $75 up.

I-E-21 Foreign Punched Foreign Stock Planchet (E), Rarity Level: 7, Values: $75 up.

I-E-22 Non-Standard Coin Alloy Planchet (IE), Rarity Level: 7, Values: Unknown.

Extra metal on a blank, or planchet (I-F)

True extra metal is only added to the blank during the blanking operation. This occurs as metal is scraped off the sides of the blanks as they are driven down through the thimble, or lower die in the blanking press. The metal is eventually picked up by a blank passing through, welded to it by the heat of friction.

A second form of extra metal has been moved to this section, the sintered coating planchet, the metal deposited on the planchet in the form of dust during the annealing operation.

I-F-1 Extra Metal on a Type 1 Blank (W), Rarity Level: 7, Values: $50 up.

I-F-2 Extra Metal on a Type 2 Planchet (W), Rarity Level: 6-7, Values: $75 up.

I-F-3 Sintered Coating Planchet (W), Rarity Level: 7, Values: $75 up.

Normal or abnormal planchets (I-G)

This section consists of the two principal forms – the blank as it comes from the blanking press – and in the form of a planchet after it has passed through the upsetting mill. It also includes a class for purchased planchets and one for planchets produced by the mint.

I-G-1 Type I Blank (IWE), Rarity Level: 3-5, Values: $2 up.
I-G-2 Type II Planchet (IWE), Rarity Level: 3-4, Values: 50 up.
I-G-3 Purchased Planchet (I), Rarity Level: 1, Values: No Value.
I-G-4 Mint Made Planchet (I), Rarity Level: 1, Values: No Value.
I-G-5 Adjustment-Marked Planchet (I), Rarity Level: Unknown, Values: No Value.
I-G-6 Hardness Test-Marked Planchet (I), Rarity Level: -, Values: No Value Established.
Note: There are no classes between I-G-6 and I-G-23
I-G-23 Proof Planchet (IE), Rarity Level: 6-7, Values: $1 up.

Coin metal strip (I-H)

When the coin metal strip passes through the blanking press it goes directly to a chopper. This cuts the remaining web into small pieces to be sent back to the melting furnace. Pieces of the web or the chopped up web may escape into the hands of collectors.

I-H-1 Punched Coin Metal Strip (IWE), Rarity Level: 4-6, Values: $5 up, depending on size, denomination and number of holes showing.
I-H-2 Chopped Coin Metal Strip (IE), Rarity Level: 3-5, Values: $5 up.

The die varieties
Division II

Die varieties may be unique to a given die, but will repeat for the full life of the die unless a further change occurs. Anything that happens to the die will affect the appearance of the struck coin. This includes all the steps of the die making:

● Cutting a die blank from a tool steel bar.
● Making the design.
● Transferring it to a model.
● Transferring it to the master die or hub.
● The hubbing process of making the die.
● Punching in the mintmark.
● Heat treating of the die.

The completed dies are also subject to damage in numerous forms, plus wear and tear during the striking process and repair work done with abrasives. All of these factors can affect how the struck coin looks.

Engraving varieties (II-A)

In all cases in this section where a master die, or master hub is affected by the class, the class will affect all the working hubs and all working dies descending from it.

Identification as being on a master die or hub depends on it being traced to two or more of the working hubs descended from the same master tools.

II-A-1 Overdate (IE), Rarity Level: 1-7, Values: $1 up.
II-A-2 Doubled Date (IE), Rarity Level: 1-7, Values: $1 up.
II-A-3 Small Date (IE), Rarity Level: 2-5, Values: $1 up.
II-A-4 Large Date (IE), Rarity Level: 2-5, Values: $1 up.
II-A-5 Small Over Large Date (IE), Rarity Level: 4-6, Values: $15 up.
II-A-6 Large Over Small Date (IE), Rarity Level: 3-5, Values: $10 up.
II-A-7 Blundered Date (E), Rarity Level: 6-7, Values: $50 up.
II-A-8 Corrected Blundered Date (IE), Rarity Level: 3-5, Values: $5 up.
II-A-9 Wrong Font Date Digit (IE), Rarity Level: 5-6, Values: Minimal.
II-A-10 Worn, Broken or Damaged Punch (IWE), Rarity Level: 5-6, Values: $5 up.
II-A-11 Expedient Punch (IWE), Rarity Level: 5-6, Values: $10 up.
II-A-12 Blundered Digit (E), Rarity Level: 4-5, Values: $50 up.
II-A-13 Corrected Blundered Digit (IE), Rarity Level: 3-6, Values: $10 up.

II-A-14 Doubled Digit (IWE), Rarity Level: 2-6, Values: $2 up.
II-A-15 Wrong Style or Font Letter or Digit (IE), Rarity Level: 3-5, Values: Minimal.
II-A-16 One Style or Font Over Another (IE), Rarity Level: 4-6, Values: $10 up.
II-A-17 Letter Over Digit (E), Rarity Level: 6-7, Values: $25 up.
II-A-18 Digit Over Letter (E), Rarity Level: 6-7, Values: $25 up.
II-A-19 Omitted Letter or Digit (IWE), Rarity Level: 4-6, Values: $5 up.
II-A-20 Blundered Letter (E), Rarity Level: 6-7, Values: $50 up.
II-A-21 Corrected Blundered Letter (IE), Rarity Level: 1-3, Values: $10 up.
II-A-22 Doubled Letter (IWE), Rarity Level: 2-6, Values: $2 up.
II-A-23 Blundered Design Element (IE), Rarity Level: 6-7, Values: $50 up.
II-A-24 Corrected Blundered Design Element (IE), Rarity Level: 3-5, Values: $10 up.
II-A-25 Large Over Small Design Element (IE), Rarity Level: 4-6, Values: $2 up.
II-A-26 Omitted Design Element (IWE), Rarity Level: 5-7, Values: $10 up.
II-A-27 Doubled Design Element (IWE), Rarity Level: 2-6, Values: $2 up.
II-A-28 One Design Element Over Another (IE), Rarity Level: 3-6, Values: $5 up.
II-A-29 Reducing Lathe Doubling (WE), Rarity Level: 6-7, Values: $50 up.
II-A-30 Extra Design Element (IE), Rarity Level: 3-5, Values: $10 up.
II-A-31 Modified Design (IWE), Rarity Level: 1-5, Values: No Value up.
II-A-32 Normal Design (I), Rarity Level: 1, Values: No Extra Value.
II-A-33 Design Mistake (IE), Rarity Level: 2-6, Values: $1 up.
II-A-34 Defective Die Design (IWE), Rarity Level: 1, Values: No Value.
II-A-35 Pattern (I), Rarity Level: 6-7, Values: $100 up.
II-A-36 Trial Design (I), Rarity Level: 5-7, Values: $100 up.
II-A-37 Omitted Designer's Initial (IWE), Rarity Level: 3-7, Values: $1 up.
II-A-38 Layout Mark (IE), Rarity Level: 5-7, Values: Minimal.
II-A-39 Abnormal Reeding (IWE), Rarity Level: 2-5, Values: $1 up.
II-A-40 Modified Die or Hub (IWE), Rarity Level: 1-5, Values: No Value up.
II-A-41 Numbered Die (I), Rarity Level: 3-5, Values: $5 up.
II-A-42 Plugged Die (IW), Rarity Level: 5-6, Values: Minimal.
II-A-43 Cancelled Die (IE), Rarity Level: 3-6, Values: No Value up.
II-A-44 Hardness Test Marked Die (IE), Rarity Level: 7, Values: $100 up.
II-A-45 Coin Simulation (IE), Rarity Level: 6-7, Values: $100 up, but may be illegal to own.
II-A-46 Punching Mistake (IE), Rarity Level: 2-6, Values: $1 up.
II-A-47 Small Over Large Design (IE), Rarity Level: 4-6, Values: $5 up.
II-A-48 Doubled Punch (IE), Rarity Level: 5-7, Values: $5 up.
II-A-49 Mint Display Sample (I) Rarity Level: 7, Values not established.
II-A-50 Center Dot, Stud or Circle (IE) Rarity Level: 7, much more common on early cents, Values not established

Hub doubling varieties (II-B)

Rotated hub doubling   **Hub break**

This section includes eight classes of hub doubling. Each class is from a different cause, described by the title of the class. At the latest count over 2,500 doubled dies have been reported in the U.S. coinage, the most famous being examples of the 1955, 1969-S and 1972 cent dies.
II-B-I Rotated Hub Doubling (WE), Rarity Level: 3-6, Values: $1 up
II-B-II Distorted Hub Doubling (WE), Rarity Level: 3-6, Values: $1 up.
II-B-III Design Hub Doubling (IWE), Rarity Level: 3-6, Values: $1 up to five figure amounts.

II-B-IV Offset Hub Doubling (WE), Rarity Level: 4-6, Values: $15 up.
II-B-V Pivoted Hub Doubling (WE), Rarity Level: 3-6, Values: $10 up.
II-B-VI Distended Hub Doubling (WE), Rarity Level: 2-5, Values: $1 up.
II-B-VII Modified Hub Doubling (IWE), Rarity Level: 2-5, Values: $1 up.
II-B-VIII Tilted Hub Doubling (WE), Rarity Level: 4-6, Values: $5 up.

Mintmark varieties (II-C)

Double   **Triple**

Mintmarks are punched into U.S. coin dies by hand (Up to 1985 for proof coins, to 1990 for cents and nickels and 1991 for other denominations). Variations resulting from mistakes in the punching are listed in this section. Unless exceptionally mispunched, values are usually estimated at 150 percent of numismatic value. Slightly tilted or displaced mintmarks have no value.

II-C-1 Doubled Mintmark (IE), Rarity Level: 2-6, Values: 50 cents up.
II-C-2 Separated Doubled Mintmark (IE), Rarity Level: 5-6, Values: $15 up.
II-C-3 Over Mintmark (IE), Rarity Level: 3-6, Values: $2 up.
II-C-4 Tripled Mintmark (IE), Rarity Level: 3-5, Values: 50 up.
II-C-5 Quadrupled Mintmark (IE), Rarity Level: 4-6, Values: $1 up.
II-C-6 Small Mintmark (IE), Rarity Level: 2-5, Values: No Extra Value up.
II-C-7 Large Mintmark (IE), Rarity Level: 2-5, Values: No Extra Value up.
II-C-8 Large Over Small Mintmark (IE), Rarity Level: 2-5, Values: $2 up.
II-C-9 Small Over Large Mintmark (IE), Rarity Level: 3-6, Values: $5 up.
II-C-10 Broken Mintmark Punch (W), Rarity Level: 5-6, Values: $5 up.
II-C-11 Omitted Mintmark (IWE), Rarity Level: 4-7, Values: $125 up.
II-C-12 Tilted Mintmark (IE), Rarity Level: 5-7, Values: $5 up.
II-C-13 Blundered Mintmark (E), Rarity Level: 4-6, Values: $5 up.
II-C-14 Corrected Horizontal Mintmark (IE), Rarity Level: 4-6, Values: $5 up.
II-C-15 Corrected Upside Down Mintmark (IE), Rarity Level: 4-6, Values: $5 up.
II-C-16 Displaced Mintmark (IE), Rarity Level: 4-6, Values: $5 to $10.
II-C-17 Modified Mintmark (IWE), Rarity Level: 1-4, Values: No Extra Value up.
II-C-18 Normal Mintmark (I), Rarity Level: 1, Values: No Extra Value.
II-C-19 Doubled Mintmark Punch (I), Rarity Level: 6-7, Values: No Extra Value up.
II-C-20 Upside Down Mintmark (E) Rarity Level 6-7, Values: $5 up.
II-C-21 Horizontal Mintmark (E) Rarity Level 6-7, Values: $5 up.
II-C-22 Wrong Mintmark (E) Rarity Level 6-7, Values $15 up. (Example has a D mintmark in the date, but was used at Philadelphia.)

Die, collar and hub cracks (II-D)

Die cracks

Cracks in the surface of the die allow coin metal to be forced into the crack during the strike, resulting in raised irregular lines of coin metal above the normal surface of the coin. These are one of the commonest forms of die damage and wear, making them easily collectible.

Collar cracks and hub cracks are added to this section because the causes and effects are similar or closely associated.

Die cracks, collar cracks and hub cracks are the result of wear and tear on the tools, with intentional use assumed for all classes.

II-D-1 Die Crack (W), Rarity Level: 1-3, Values: 10 to $1, $25 up on a proof coin with a rarity level of 6-7.

II-D-2 Multiple Die Cracks (W), Rarity Level: 1-3, Values: 25 cents to $2.

II-D-3 Head-To-Rim Die Crack (Lincoln Cent) (W), Rarity Level: 2-6, Values: 25 to $10 for multiple die cracks.

II-D-4 Split Die (W), Rarity Level: 5-6, Values: $10 up.

II-D-5 Rim-To-Rim Die Crack (W), Rarity Level: 2-5, Values: $1 up.

II-D-6 Collar Crack (W), Rarity Level: 4-6, Values: $10 up.

II-D-7 Hub Crack (W), Rarity Level: 3-5, Values: $1-$2.

Small die break II-E-2   Clogged letter II-E-1

Major die break, date missing, II-E-5   Rim die break II-E-4

Die breaks (II-E)

Breaks in the surface of the die allow coin metal to squeeze into the resulting holes, causing raised irregular areas above the normal surface of the coin. Die chips and small die breaks are nearly as common as the die cracks, but major die breaks, which extend in from the edge of the coin, are quite rare on the larger coins.

If the broken piece of the die is retained, the resulting design will be above or below the level of the rest of the surface.

II-E-1 Die Chip (W), Rarity Level: 1-2, Values: 10 to $1.

II-E-2 Small Die Break (W), Rarity Level: 1-3, Values: 10 to $2.

II-E-3 Large Die Break (W), Rarity Level: 3-5, Values: $1 to $50 and up.

II-E-4 Rim Die Break (W), Rarity Level: 2-3, Values: 25 cents to $5.

II-E-5 Major Die Break (WE), Rarity Level: 3-6, Values: $5 to $100 and up.

II-E-6 Retained Broken Die (W), Rarity Level: 3-5, Values: $1 to $10 and up.

II-E-7 Retained Broken Center of the Die (W), Rarity Level: 6-7, Values: $100 up.

II-E-8 Laminated Die (W), Rarity Level: 3-5, Values: 10 cents to $5.

II-E-9 Chipped Chrome Plating (W), Rarity Level: 4-5, Values: $10 to $25 on proofs.

II-E-10 Collar Break (W), Rarity Level: 4-6, Values: $5 to $25 and up.

II-E-11 Broken Letter or Digit on an Edge Die (W), Rarity Level: 4-6, Values: Minimal.

II-E-12 "Bar" Die Break (W), Rarity Level: 3-5, Values: 25 to $20.

II-E-13 Hub Break (W), Rarity Level: 4-6, Values: 50 to $10 and up.

"BIE" varieties (II-F)

A series of small die breaks or die chips in the letters of "LIBERTY" mostly on the wheat-reverse Lincoln cent are actively collected. The name results from the resemblance to an "I" between the "B" and "E" on many of the dies, but they are found between all of the letters in different cases. Well over 1,500 dies are known and cataloged. Numerous more recent examples are known.

II-F-1 ILI Die Variety (W), Rarity Level: 4-5, Values: 25 cents to $10.

II-F-2 LII Die Variety (W), Rarity Level: 3-5, Values: 50 cents to $15.

II-F-3 IIB Die Variety (W), Rarity Level: 3-5, Values: 50 cents to $15.

BIE variety II-F-4

II-F-4 BIE Die Variety (W), Rarity Level: 3-5, Values: $1 to $20.
II-F-5 EIR Die Variety (W), Rarity Level: 3-5, Values: 50 to $15.
II-F-6 RIT Die Variety (W), Rarity Level: 4-5, Values: $2 to $25.
II-F-7 TIY Die Variety (W), Rarity Level: 4-5, Values: $5 to $30.
II-F-8 TYI Die Variety (W), Rarity Level: 4-5, Values: $2 to $25.

Worn and damaged dies, collars and hubs (II-G)

Die clashes and design transfer

Many dies are continued deliberately in service after they have been damaged, dented, clashed or show design transfer, since none of these classes actually affect anything but the appearance ofthe coin. The root cause is wear, but intent or mistakes may enter the picture.

II-G-1 Dented Die, Collar or Hub (IWE), Rarity Level: 3-5, Values: 25 to $5.

II-G-2 Damaged Die, Collar or Hub (IWE), Rarity Level: 3-5, Values: 25 to $5.

II-G-3 Worn Die, Collar or Hub (IWE), Rarity Level: 2-3, Values: No Extra Value to Minimal Value.

II-G-4 Pitted or Rusted Die, Collar or Hub (IWE), Rarity Level: 3-4, Values:No Extra Value, marker only.

II-G-5 Heavy Die Clash (IWE), Rarity Level: 4-5, Values: $1 to $10 and up.

II-G-6 Heavy Collar Clash (IWE), Rarity Level: 3-4, Values: $1 to $5 and up.

II-G-7 Heavy Design Transfer (IWE), Rarity Level: 3-4, Values: 10 cents to $1.

Die progressions (II-H)

The progression section consists of three classes. These are useful as cataloging tools for many different die varieties, but especially the die cracks and die breaks which may enlarge, lengthen or increase in number.

II-H-1 Progression (W), Rarity Level: 3-5, Values: $1 up.

II-H-2 Die Substitution (IW), Rarity Level: 2-4, Values: No Extra Value to Minimal Value.

II-H-3 Die Repeat (I), Rarity Level: 2-4, Values: No Extra Value to Minimal Value.

Die scratches, polished and abraded dies (II-I)

Die scratches II-I-1

This section consists of those classes having to do with the use of an abrasive in some form to intentionally polish proof dies, or repair the circulating die surface. Several classes which previously were referred to as "polished" now are listed as "abraded."

II-I-1 Die Scratch (IW), Rarity Level: 1-2, Values: No Extra Value to 10 cents to 25 cents, as a marker.

II-I-2 Polished (proof) Die (IW), Rarity Level: 1, Values: No Extra Value.

II-I-3 Abraded (Circulation) Die (IW), Rarity Level: 1-2, Values: No Extra Value up to $10.

II-I-4 Inside Abraded Die Doubling (IW), Rarity Level: 1-3, Values: No Extra Value to $1.
II-I-5 Outside Abraded Die Doubling (IW), Rarity Level: 1-3, Values: No Extra Value to $1.
II-I-6 Lathe Marks (IW), Rarity Level: 5-7, Values: No Extra Value, marker only.

Striking varieties
Division III

Once the dies are made and the planchets have been prepared, they are struck by a pair of dies and become a coin. In this division, we list the misstrikes resulting from human or mechanical malfunction in the striking process. These are one-of-a-kind varieties, but there may be many similar coins that fall in a given class.

Multiples and combinations of classes must be considered on a case by case basis. The first several sections match the planchet sections indicated in the title.

Struck on defective alloy mix planchets (III-A)

This section includes those classes of coins struck on planchets that were made from a defective alloy.
III-A-1 Struck on an Improper Alloy Mix Planchet (IE), Rarity Level: 2-3, Values: 10 cents to $2.
III-A-2 Struck on a Planchet With Slag Inclusions(IE), Rarity Level: 5-6, Values: $10 up.

Struck on damaged, defective or abnormal planchet (III-B)

Struck on a defective planchet III-B-1   **Struck on a tapered planchet III-B-5**

Coins get struck on many strange objects. The more common of course are planchets which have been damaged in some way in the production process. In most of the classes in this section intent is at least presumed, if not specifically listed as a cause.

III-B-1 Struck on a Defective Planchet (IWE), Rarity Level: 4-6, Values: $5 to $10 and up.
III-B-2 Struck on a Mechanically Damaged Planchet (IWE), Rarity Level: 5-6, Values: $10 to $20 and up.
III-B-3 Struck on a Rolled Thin Planchet (IWE), Rarity Level: 5-6, Values: $2 to $5 and up.
III-B-4 Struck on a Rolled Thick Planchet (IWE), Rarity Level: 5-6, Values: $35 to $50 and up.
III-B-5 Struck on a Tapered Planchet (WE), Rarity Level: 4-6, Values: $2 to $5 and up.
III-B-6 Struck on a Partially Unplated Planchet (WE), Rarity Level: 5, Values: $10 up.
III-B-7 Struck on an Unplated Planchet (WE), Rarity Level: 6-7, Values: $100 up.
III-B-8 Struck on a Bubbled Plating Planchet (IWE), Rarity Level: 1, Values: No Value.
III-B-9 Struck on an Included Gas Bubble Planchet (WE), Rarity Level: 5-6, Values: $5 up.
III-B-10 Struck on a Partially Unclad Planchet (WE), Rarity Level: 5-6, Values: $5 up.
III-B-11 Struck on an Unclad Planchet (WE), Rarity Level: 4-5, Values: $5 and up.
III-B-12 Struck on an Undersize Planchet (WE), Rarity Level: 4-6, Values: Minimal.
III-B-13 Struck on an Oversize Planchet (WE), Rarity Level: 6-7, Values: Minimal.
III-B-14 Struck on an Improperly Prepared Proof Planchet (IWE), Rarity Level: 3-5, Values: $5 up.
III-B-15 Struck on an Improperly Annealed Planchet (IWE), Rarity Level: 4-5, Values: $5 up.
III-B-16 Struck on a Faulty Upset Edge Planchet (IWE), Rarity Level: 4-5, Values: $1 to $2.
III-B-17 Struck on a Rolled In Metal Planchet (WE), Rarity Level: 4-6, Values: $2 up.
III-B-18 Struck on a Weld Area Planchet (WE), Rarity Level: 6, Values: $25 to $50.
III-B-19 Struck on a Strike Clip Planchet (W), Rarity Level: 6-7, Values: $25 up.
III-B-20 Struck on an Unpunched Center Hole Planchet (WE), Rarity Level: 4-6, Values: $1 and up.
III-B-21 Struck on an Incompletely Punched Center Hole Planchet (WE), Rarity Level: 6-7, Values: $5 up.

III-B-22 Struck on an Uncentered Center Hole Planchet (WE), Rarity Level: 6-7, Values: $10 up.

III-B-23 Struck on a Multiple Punched Center Hole Planchet (WE), Rarity Level: 7, Values: $25 up.

III-B-24 Struck on an Unintended Center Hole Planchet (WE), Rarity Level: 6-7, Values: $25 and up.

III-B-25 Struck on a Wrong Size or Shape Center Hole Planchet (WE), Rarity Level: 5-7, Values: $5 up.

III-B-26 Struck on Scrap Coin Metal (E), Rarity Level: 4-6, Values: $10 up.

III-B-27 Struck on Junk Non Coin Metal (E), Rarity Level: 4-6, Values: $15 up.

III-B-28 Struck on a False Planchet (E), Rarity Level: 3-5, Values: $35 up.

III-B-29 Struck on Bonded Planchets (E), Rarity Level: 6-7, Values: $50 up.

Struck on a clipped planchet (III-C)

Ragged edge clip III-C-15

Multiple clip III-C-8   **Incomplete curved clip III-C-10**

Coins struck on clipped blanks, or planchets, exhibit the same missing areas as they did before striking, modified by the metal flow from the strike which rounds the edges and tends to move metal into the missing areas. Values for blanks will run higher than planchets with similar clips.

III-C-1 Struck on a Disc Clip Planchet (WE), Rarity Level: 4-5, Values: $1 on regular coins, $20 and up for clad coins.

III-C-2 Struck on a Curved Clip Planchet - to 5% (WE), Rarity Level: 3-5, Values: 50 cents up.

III-C-3 Struck on a Curved Clip Planchet - (6 to 10%) (WE), Rarity Level: 4-5, Values: $1 up.

III-C-4 Struck on a Curved Clip Planchet - (11 to 25%) (WE), Rarity Level: 4-5, Values: $2 up.

III-C-5 Struck on a Curved Clip Planchet - (26 to 60%) (WE), Rarity Level: 4-6, Values: $10 up.

III-C-6 Struck on a Double Curved Clip Planchet (WE), Rarity Level: 3-4, Values: $2 up.

III-C-7 Struck on a Triple Curved Clip Planchet (WE), Rarity Level: 4-5, Values: $5 up.

III-C-8 Struck on a Multiple Curved Clip Planchet (WE), Rarity Level: 4-6, Values: $5 up.

III-C-9 Struck on an Overlapping Curved Clipped Planchet (WE), Rarity Level: 5-6, Values: $15 up.

III-C-10 Struck on an Incomplete Curved Clip Planchet (WE), Rarity Level: 4-5, Values: $10 up.

III-C-11 Struck on an Oval Clip Planchet (WE), Rarity Level: 5-6, Values: $20 up.

III-C-12 Struck on a Crescent Clip Planchet - (61% or more) (WE), Rarity Level: 6-7, Values: $100 up.

III-C-13 Struck on a Straight Clip Planchet (E), Rarity Level: 4-6, Values: $10 up.

III-C-14 Struck on an Incomplete Straight Clip Planchet (WE), Rarity Level: 5-6, Values: $20 up.

III-C-15 Struck on a Ragged Clip Planchet (E), Rarity Level: 4-6, Values: $15 up.

III-C-16 Struck on an Outside Corner Clip Planchet (E), Rarity Level: 7, Values: $100 up.

III-C-17 Struck on an Inside Corner Clip Planchet (E), Rarity Level: Unknown outside mint., Values: -.

III-C-18 Struck on an Irregularly Clipped Planchet (E), Rarity Level: 6-7, Values: $20 up.

III-C-19 Struck on an Incompletely Punched Scalloped or Multi-Sided Planchet (E), Rarity Level: 7, Values: $20 up.

Struck on a laminated, split or broken planchet (III-D)

This section has to do with the splitting, cracking or breaking of a coin parallel to the faces of the coin, or at least very nearly parallel, or breaks at right angles to the faces of the coin.

| Lamination crack III-D-1 | Layer peeled off III-D-2 | Split planchet III-D-3 |

Lamination cracks and missing metal of any size below a split planchet are too common in the 35-percent silver 1942-1945 nickels to be collectible or have any significant value.

III-D-1 Struck on a Small Lamination Crack Planchet (W), Rarity Level: 3-4, Values: 10 up.

III-D-2 Struck on a Large Lamination Crack Planchet (W), Rarity Level: 3-6, Values: $1 up.

III-D-3 Struck on a Split Planchet (W), Rarity Level: 4-6, Values: $5 up.

III-D-4 Struck on a Hinged Split Planchet (W), Rarity Level: 5-6, Values: $35 up.

III-D-5 Struck on a Planchet With a Clad Layer Missing (W), Rarity Level: 4-5, Values: $15 up.

III-D-6 Struck on a Planchet With Both Clad Layers Missing (W), Rarity Level: 4-5, Values: $25 up.

III-D-7 Struck on a Separated Clad Layer or Lamination (W), Rarity Level: 6-7, Values: $75 up.

III-D-8 Struck on a Broken Planchet Before the Strike (W), Rarity Level: 3-5, Values: $10 up.

III-D-9 Broken Coin During or After the Strike (W), Rarity Level: 4-6, Values: $20 up.

III-D-10 Struck Coin Fragment Split or Broken During or After the Strike (W), Rarity Level: 3-5, Values: $5 up.

III-D-11 Reedless Coin Broken During or After the Strike (W), Rarity Level: Unknown, Values: -.

Struck on wrong stock planchets (III-E)

**Quarter on dime stock
III-E-7 (lower coin edge)**

These classes cover those cases where the wrong stock was run through the blanking press, making planchets of the correct diameter, but of the wrong thickness, alloy or metal or a combination of incorrect thickness and metal.

III-E-1 Struck on a Half Cent-Stock Planchet (IE), Rarity Level: Unknown, Values: No Value Established.

III-E-2 Struck on a Cent-Stock Planchet (IE), Rarity Level: Unknown, Values: No Value Established.

III-E-3 Struck on a Two-Cent-Stock Planchet (E), Rarity Level: Unknown, Values: -.

III-E-4 Struck on a Three-Cent-Silver Stock Planchet (E), Rarity Level: Unknown, Values: -.

III-E-5 Struck on a Three-Cent-Nickel Stock Planchet (E), Rarity Level: Unknown, Values: -.

III-E-6 Struck on a Half Dime-Stock Planchet (E), Rarity Level: Unknown, Values: -.

III-E-7 Struck on a Dime-Stock Planchet (E), Rarity Level: 5-6, Values: $20 up.

III-E-8 Struck on a Twenty-Cent-Stock Planchet (E), Rarity Level: Unknown, Values: -.

III-E-9 Struck on a Quarter-Stock Planchet (E), Rarity Level: 6, Values: $50 up.

III-E-10 Struck on a Half Dollar-Stock Planchet (E), Rarity Level: 6-7, Values: $100 up.

III-E-11 Struck on a Dollar-Stock Planchet (E), Rarity Level: 6-7, Values: $300 up.

III-E-12 Struck on a Token/Medal-Stock Planchet (E), Rarity Level: 7, Values: No Value Established.

III-E-13 Struck on a Wrong Thickness Spoiled Planchet (IWE), Rarity Level: 7, Values: $50 up.

III-E-14 Struck on a Correct Thickness Spoiled Planchet (IWE), Rarity Level: Unknown, Values: No Value Established.

III-E-15 Struck on a Cut Down Struck Token (IWE), Rarity Level: 6-7, Values: $50 up.

III-E-16 Struck on an Experimental or Pattern-Stock Planchet (IE), Rarity Level: 7, Values: $50 up.

III-E-17 Struck on a Proof-Stock Planchet (IE), Rarity Level: 7, Values: $100 up.

III-E-18 Struck on an Adjusted Specification-Stock Planchet (IE), Rarity Level: 3-7, Values: No Value to $5 and up.

III-E-19 Struck on a Trial Strike-Stock Planchet (IE), Rarity Level: Unknown, Values: No Value Established.

III-E-20 U.S. Coin Struck on a Foreign-Stock Planchet. (E), Rarity Level: 5, Values: $35 up.

III-E-21 Foreign Coin Struck on a Foreign-Stock Planchet (E), Rarity Level: 5-6, Values: $25 up.

III-E-22 Struck on a Non-Standard Coin Alloy (IE), Rarity Level: 4-7, Values: $20 up.

Extra metal (III-F)

**Extra metal on a
struck coin (III-F-2)**

Sintered coating III-F-3

The term "extra metal" for the purpose of this section includes both extra metal added to the blank during the blanking operation and metal powder added to the planchet during the annealing operation.

III-F-1 Struck on a Type 1 Blank With Extra Metal (W), Rarity Level: Unknown, Values: -.

III-F-2 Struck on a Type 2 Planchet With Extra Metal (W), Rarity Level: 4-5, Values: $10 up.

III-F-3 Struck on a Sintered Coating Planchet (W), Rarity Level: 6-7, Values: $35 up.

Struck on normal or abnormal blanks, or planchets (III-G)

Cent on dime planchet III-G-10

Half on dime planchet III-G-10

Half on quarter planchet III-G-11

This section includes coins struck on either a blank, as it comes from the blanking press, or as a planchet that has passed through the upsetting mill. Added to this section are those planchets which are normal until they are struck by the wrong dies. These differ from the wrong stock planchets because the wrong stock planchets are already a variety before they are struck.

III-G-1 Struck on a Type 1 Blank (IWE), Rarity Level: 1, Values: $10 up.

III-G-2 Struck on a Type 2 Planchet (I), Rarity Level: 1, Values: No Extra Value.

III-G-3 Struck on a Purchased Planchet (I), Rarity Level: 1, Values: No Extra Value.

III-G-4 Struck on a Mint-Made Planchet (I), Rarity Level: 1, Values: No Extra Value.

III-G-5 Struck on an Adjustment-Marked Planchet (I), Rarity Level: 4-7, Values: Minimal, and may reduce value of coin in some cases.

III-G-6 Struck on a Hardness Test-Marked Planchet (I), Rarity Level: 6-7, Values: $10 up.

III-G-7 Wrong Planchet or Metal on a Half Cent Planchet (IE), Rarity Level: 5-7, Values: $100 up.

III-G-8 Wrong Planchet or Metal on a Cent Planchet (IE), Rarity Level: 3-6, Values: $25 up.

III-G-9 Wrong Planchet or Metal on a Nickel Planchet (E), Rarity Level: 4-6, Values: $35 up

III-G-10 Wrong Planchet or Metal on a Dime Planchet (E), Rarity Level: 4-6, Values: $50 up.

III-G-11 Wrong Planchet or Metal on a Quarter Planchet (E), Rarity Level: 4-6. Values: $100 up.

III-G-12 Wrong Planchet or Metal on a Half Dollar Planchet (E), Rarity Level: 6-7, Values: $500 up.

III-G-13 Wrong Planchet or Metal on a Dollar Planchet (E), Rarity Level: 7, Values: $500 up.

III-G-14 Wrong Planchet or Metal on a Gold Planchet (E), Rarity Level: 7, Values: $1000 up.

III-G-15 Struck on a Wrong Series Planchet (IE), Rarity Level: 6-7, Values: $1500 up.

III-G-16 U.S. Coin Struck on a Foreign Planchet (E), Rarity Level: 5-7, Values: $35 up.

III-G-17 Foreign Coin Struck on a U.S. Planchet (E), Rarity Level: 6-7, Values: $50 up.

III-G-18 Foreign Coin Struck on a Wrong Foreign Planchet (E), Rarity Level: 6-7, Values: $50 up.

III-G-19 Struck on a Medal Planchet (E), Rarity Level: 6-7, Values: $100 up.

III-G-20 Medal Struck on a Coin Planchet (IE), Rarity Level: 3-5, Values: $10 up.

III-G-21 Struck on an Official Sample Planchet (IE), Rarity Level: Unknown, Values: No Value Established.

III-G-22 Struck Intentionally on a Wrong Planchet (I), Rarity Level: 6-7, Values: Mainly struck as Presentation Pieces, full numismatic value.

III-G-23 Non-Proof Struck on a Proof Planchet (IE), Rarity Level: 6-7, Values: $500 up.

Struck on coin metal strip (III-H)

Pieces of the coin metal strip do manage at times to escape into the coin press.

III-H-1 (See I-H-1 Punched Coin Metal Strip), Rarity Level: Impossible, Values: -.

III-H-2 Struck on Chopped Coin Metal Strip (E), Rarity Level: 6-7, Values: $25 up.

Die adjustment strikes (III-I)

As the dies are set up and adjusted in the coin press, variations in the strike occur until the dies are properly set. Test strikes are normally scrapped, but on occasion reach circulation.

III-I-1 Die Adjustment Strike (IE), Rarity Level: 5-6, Values: $35 up.

III-I-2 Edge Strike (E), Rarity Level: 5-6, Values: $10 to $20 and up.

III-I-3 Weak Strike (W), Rarity Level: 1, Values: No Extra Value.

III-I-4 Strong Strike (IWE), Rarity Level: 1, Values: No value except for the premium that might be paid for a well struck coin.

III-I-5 Jam Strike (IE), Rarity Level: 7, Values: $50 up.

III-I-6 Trial Piece Strike (I), Rarity Level: 6-7, Values: $100 up.

III-I-7 Edge-Die Adjustment Strike (I), Rarity Level: 5-7, Values: $5 up.

III-I-8 Uniface Strike (I), Rarity Level 7, Values: $50 up.

Indented, brockage and counter-brockage strikes (III-J)

Indented strike III-J-1   **Counter-brockage strike III-J-11**   **Capped die strike III-J-15**

Indented and uniface strikes involve an extra unstruck planchet between one of the dies and the planchet being struck. Brockage strikes involve a struck coin between one of the dies and the planchet and a counter-brockage requires a brockage coin between one of the dies and the planchet.

A cap, or capped die strike results when a coin sticks to the die and is squeezed around it in the shape of a bottle cap.

III-J-1 Indented Strike (W), Rarity Level: 3-6, Values: $5 up.

III-J-2 Uniface Strike (W), Rarity Level: 3-5, Values: $15 up.

III-J-3 Indented Strike By a Smaller Planchet (WE), Rarity Level: 5-7, Values: $100 up.

III-J-4 Indented Second Strike (W), Rarity Level: 3-5, Values: $10 up, about the same as a regular double strike of comparable size.

III-J-5 Partial Brockage Strike (W), Rarity Level: 3-6, Values: $15 up.

III-J-6 Full Brockage Strike (W), Rarity Level: 3-6, Values: $5 up.

III-J-7 Brockage Strike of a Smaller Coin (WE), Rarity Level: 6-7, Values: $200 up.

III-J-8 Brockage Strike of a Struck Coin Fragment (WE), Rarity Level: 4-6, Values: $5 up.

III-J-9 Brockage Second Strike (WE), Rarity Level: 3-5, Values: $5 up.

III-J-10 Partial Counter-Brockage Strike (WE), Rarity Level: 3-5, Values: $10 up.

III-J-11 Full Counter-Brockage Strike (WE), Rarity Level: 5-7, Values: $100 up.

III-J-12 Counter-Brockage Second Strike (WE), Rarity Level: 4-6, Values: $10 up.

III-J-13 Full Brockage-Counter-Brockage Strike (WE), Rarity Level: 6-7, Values: $150 up.

III-J-14 Multiple Brockage or Counter-Brockage Strike (WE), Rarity Level: 5-7, Values: $100 up.

III-J-15 Capped Die Strike (WE), Rarity Level: 6-7, Values: $500 up.

III-J-16 Reversed Capped Die Strike (WE), Rarity Level: 7, Values: $1,000 up.

Struck through abnormal objects (III-K)

Struck through cloth III-K-1

**Struck through a
filled die III-K-4**

**Struck through a
dropped filling III-K-5**

This section covers most of the objects or materials which might come between the planchet and the die and be struck into the surface of the coin. Unless noted, the materials - even the soft ones - are driven into the surface of the coin.

III-K-1 Struck Through Cloth (IWE), Rarity Level: 3-6, Values: $35 up.

III-K-2 Struck Through Wire (IWE), Rarity Level: 3-6, Values: $5 up.

III-K-3 Struck Through Thread (IWE), Rarity Level: 3-6, Values: $5 up.

III-K-4 Struck Through Dirt-and-Grease-Filled Die (IWE), Rarity Level: 1-4, Values: 10 cents to 25 cents up, but no value on a worn or circulated coin.

III-K-5 Struck Through a Dropped Filling (IWE), Rarity Level: 5-6, Values: $10 up.

III-K-6 Struck Through Wrong Metal Fragments (IWE), Rarity Level: 4-6, Values: $1 up.

III-K-7 Struck Through an Unstruck Planchet Fragment (IWE), Rarity Level: 3-5, Values: $1 up.

III-K-8 Struck Through a Rim Burr (IWE), Rarity Level: 3-5, Values: $1 to $2 and up.

III-K-9 Struck Through plit-Off Reeding (IWE), Rarity Level: 5-6, Values: $25 up.

III-K-10 Struck Through a Feed Finger (IWE), Rarity Level: 5-7, Values: $25 to $50 and up.

III-K-11 Struck Through Miscellaneous Objects (IWE), Rarity Level: 4-6, Values: $1 up.

III-K-12 Struck Through Progression (IWE), Rarity Level: 4-6, Values: $1 up.

Note: Some 1987 through 1994 quarters are found without mintmarks, classed as III-K-4, a Filled Die. Values depend on market conditions. Filled dies have value ONLY on current, uncirculated grade coins.

Double strikes (III-L)

Only coins which receive two or more strikes by the die pair fall in this section and are identified by the fact that both sides of the coin are affected. Unless some object interferes, an equal area of both sides of the coin will be equally doubled.

The exception is the second strike with a loose die, which will double only one side of a coin, but is a rare form usually occurring only on proofs. A similar effect is flat field doubling from die chatter.

III-L-1 Close Centered Double Strike (WE), Rarity Level: 4-6, Values: $15 up.

III-L-2 Rotated Second Strike Over a Centered First Strike (WE), Rarity Level: 4-6, Values: $15 up.

III-L-3 Off-Center Second Strike Over a Centered First Strike (WE), Rarity Level: 4-6, Values: $15 up.

III-L-4 Off-Center Second Strike Over an Off-Center First Strike (WE), Rarity Level: 4-6, Values: $10 up.

III-L-5 Off-Center Second Strike Over a Broadstrike (WE), Rarity Level: 5-6, Values: $20 up.

III-L-6 Centered Second Strike Over an Off-Center First Strike (WE), Rarity Level: 5-6, Values: $50 up.

III-L-7 Obverse Struck Over Reverse (WE), Rarity Level: 5-6, Values: $25 up.

III-L-8 Nonoverlapping Double Strike (WE), Rarity Level: 5-6 Values: $20 up.

III-L-9 Struck Over a Different Denomination or Series (WE), Rarity Level: 6, Values: $300 and up.

III-L-10 Chain Strike (WE), Rarity Level: 6, Values: $300 up for the pair of coins that were struck together.

Off-center second strike over centered first strike III-L-3

Non-overlapping double strike III-L-8

Multiple strike III-L-16

Chain strike III-L-10

III-L-11 Second-Strike Doubling From a Loose Die (W), Rarity Level: 6-7, Values: $200 up.

III-L-12 Second-Strike Doubling From a Loose Screw Press Die (W), Rarity Level: 5-6, Values: $100 up.

III-L-13 Second Strike on an Edge Strike (WE), Rarity Level: 5-6, Values: $20 up.

III-L-14 Folded Planchet Strike (WE), Rarity Level: 5-7, Values: $100 up.

III-L-15 Triple Strike (WE), Rarity Level: 6-7, Values: $100 up.

III-L-16 Multiple Strike (WE), Rarity Level: 6-7, Values: $200 up.

III-L-17 U.S. Coin Struck Over a Struck Foreign Coin (WE), Rarity Level: 6-7, Values: $300 up.

III-L-18 Foreign Coin Struck Over a Struck U.S. Coin (WE), Rarity Level: 6-7, Values: $400 up.

III-L-19 Foreign Coin Struck Over a Struck Foreign Coin (WE), Rarity Level: 7, Values: $500 up.

III-L-20 Double Strike on Scrap or Junk (E), Rarity Level: 6, Values: $50 up.

III-L-21 Struck on a Struck Token or Medal (E), Rarity Level: 5-6, Values: $100 up.

III-L-22 Double-Struck Edge Motto or Design (E), Rarity Level: 6-7, Values: $200 up.

III-L-23 One Edge Motto or Design Struck Over Another (E), Rarity Level: 7, Values: $300 up.

III-L-24 Flat Field Doubling (W), Rarity Level: 2-3, Values: $1 to $5.

III-L-25 Territorial Struck over Struck U.S. Coin: (I) Rarity Level: 6-7, Values: $200 up.

III-L-26 Pattern Struck over Struck U.S. Coin: (I) Rarity Level: 6-7, Values: $200 up.

III-L-27 Pattern Struck over Struck Pattern:(I) Rarity Level 6-7, Values: $200 up.

III-L-28 Pattern Struck Over Foreign Coin:(I) Rarity Level 6-7, Values - $200 up.

Collar striking varieties (III-M)

The collar is often referred to as the "Third Die," and is involved in a number of forms of misstrikes. The collar normally rises around the planchet, preventing it from squeezing sideways between the dies and at the same time forming the reeding on reeded coins.

If the collar is out of position or tilted, a partial collar strike results; if completely missing, it causes a broadstrike; if the planchet is not entirely between the dies, an off-center strike.

III-M-1 Flanged Partial Collar Strike (WE), Rarity Level: 5-6, Values: $20 up.

III-M-2 Reversed Flanged Partial Collar Strike (WE), Rarity Level: 6-7, Values: $35 up.

III-M-3 Tilted Partial Collar Strike (WE), Rarity Level: 5-6, Values: $20 up.

III-M-4 Centered Broadstrike (WE), Rarity Level: 5-6, Values: $5 up.

III-M-5 Uncentered Broadstrike (WE), Rarity Level: 5, Values: $3 up.

III-M-6 Reversed Broadstrike (WE), Rarity Level: 6, Values: $10 up.

III-M-7 Struck Off-Center 10-30% (W), Rarity Level: 3-6, Values: $3 up.

Flanged partial collar III-M-1

Struck off center	**Struck off center**	**Struck off center**
10 to 30 percent III-M-7	**31 to 70 percent III-M-8**	**71 percent or more**
		III-M-9

III-M-8 Struck Off-Center 31-70% (W), Rarity Level: 4-6, Values: $5 up.
III-M-9 Struck Off-Center 71% or More (W), Rarity Level: 3-5, Values: $2 up.
III-M-10 Rotated Multi-sided Planchet Strike (W), Rarity Level: 5-6, Values: $10 up.
III-M-11 Wire Edge Strike (IWE), Rarity Level: 1-2, Values: No Extra Value.
III-M-12 Struck With the Collar Too High (WE), Rarity Level: 6-7, Values: $20 up.
III-M-13 Off-Center Slide Strike (W), Rarity Level:3-6 $4 up.

Misaligned and rotated (die) strike varieties (III-N)

Misaligned die III-N-1

Normal rotation	**90 degrees**	**180 degrees**

One (rarely both) of the dies may be Offset Misaligned, off to one side, or may be tilted (Vertically Misaligned). One die may either have been installed so that it is turned in relation to the other die, or may turn in the holder, or the shank may break allowing the die face to rotate in relation to the opposing die.

Vertical misaligned dies are rarely found, and like rotated dies, find only limited collector interest. Ninety and 180 degree rotations are the most popular. Rotations of 14 degrees or less have no value. The 1989-D Congress dollar is found with a nearly 180 degree rotated reverse, currently retailing for around $2,000. Only about 30 have been reported to date.

III-N-1 Offset Die Misalignment Strike (WE), Rarity Level: 3-5, Values: $2 up.
III-N-2 Vertical Die Misalignment Strike (WE), Rarity Level: 4-6, Values: $1 up.
III-N-3 Rotated Die Strike - 15 to 45 Degrees (IWE), Rarity Level: 4-6, Values: $2 up.
III-N-4 Rotated Die Strike - 46 to 135 Degrees (IWE), Rarity Level: 5-6, Values: $10 up.
III-N-5 Rotated Die Strike - 136 to 180 Degrees (IWE), Rarity Level: 5-6, Values: $25 up.

Lettered and design edge strike varieties (III-O)

Early U.S. coins and a number of foreign coins have either lettered edges, or designs on the edge of the coin. Malfunctions of the application of the motto or design to the edge fall in this section.

Overlapping edge letters III-O-1

III-O-1 Overlapping Edge Motto or Design (WE), Rarity Level: 3-4, Values: $5 to $10 and up.
III-O-2 Wrong Edge Motto or Design (WE), Rarity Level: 5-6-7, Values: $50 up.
III-O-3 Missing Edge Motto, Design or Security Edge (IWE), Rarity Level: 5-6-7, Values: $50 up.
III-O-4 Jammed Edge Die Strike (W), Rarity Level: 6, Values: $10 up.
III-O-5 Misplaced Segment of an Edge Die (E), Rarity Level: 4-7, Values: $25 up.
III-O-6 Reeded Edge Struck Over a Lettered Edge (IE), Rarity Level: 3-6, Values: No Extra Value up.

Defective strikes and mismatched dies (III-P)

The final section of the Striking Division covers coins which are not properly struck for reasons other than those in previous classes, such as coins struck with mismatched (muled) dies. The mismatched die varieties must be taken on a case by case basis, while the otherclasses presently have little collector demand or premium.

III-P-1 Defective Strike (WE), Rarity Level: 1, Values: No Extra Value.
III-P-2 Mismatched Die Strike (E), Rarity Level: 4-7, Values: $25 up.
III-P-3 Single-Strike Proof (WE), Rarity Level: 4-5, Values: Minimal.
III-P-4 Single Die-Proof Strike (IE), Rarity Level: 5-6, Values: $100 up.
III-P-5 Reversed Die Strike (I), Rarity Level: 4-5, Values: No Extra Value to Minimal.

Official Mint modifications
Division IV

Several mint produced varieties occur after the coin has been struck, resulting in the addition of the fourth division to my PDS System. Since most of these coins are either unique or are special varieties, each one must be taken on a case by case basis. All classes listed here are by definition intentional.

I have not listed values as the coins falling in these classes which are sold through regular numismatic channels, are cataloged with the regular issues or are covered in specialized catalogs in their particular area.

Matte proofs (IV-A)

**Matte proofs
IV-A-1**

Matte proofs as a section include several of the forms of proof coins which have the striking characteristics of a mirror proof but have been treated AFTER striking to give them a grainy, non-reflective surface.

IV-A-1 Matte Proof (I), Rarity Level: 3-5, Values: Normal Numismatic Value.
IV-A-2 Matte Proof on One Side (I), Rarity Level: 7, Values: Normal Numismatic Value.
IV-A-3 Sandblast Proof (I), Rarity Level: 4-6, Values: Normal Numismatic Value.

Additional engraving (IV-B)

Counterstamp IV-B-3

This section includes any added markings which are placed on the struck coin and struck coins which later were cut into pieces for various purposes. The warning is repeated: Anything done to a coin after the strike is extremely difficult to authenticate and is much easier to fake than a die struck coin.

IV-B-1 Counterstamp and Countermark (I), Rarity Level: 3-6, Values: Normal Numismatic Value.
IV-B-2 Perforated and Cut Coins (I), Rarity Level: 4-6, Values: Normal Numismatic Value.

Restrikes (IV-C)

Restrike with new dies IV-C-7

Restrikes cover a complicated mixture of official use of dies from a variety of sources. Whether or not some were officially sanctioned is always a problem for the collector.

IV-C-1) Restrike on the Same Denomination Planchet (I), Rarity Level: 4-6, Values: Normal Numismatic Value.
IV-C-2 Restrike on a Different Denomination or Series Planchet (I), Rarity Level: 4-6, Values: Normal Numismatic Value.
IV-C-3 Restrike on a Foreign Coin (I), Rarity Level: 6-7, Values: Normal Numismatic Value.
IV-C-4 Restrike on a Token or Medal (I), Rarity Level: 5-6, Values: Normal Numismatic Value.
IV-C-5 Restruck With the Original Dies (I), Rarity Level: 4-6, Values: Normal Numismatic Value.
IV-C-6 Restruck With Mismatched Dies (I), Rarity Level: 4-6, Values: Normal Numismatic Value.
IV-C-7 Copy Strike With New Dies (I), Rarity Level: 3-5, Values: Normal Numismatic Value.
IV-C-8 Fantasy Strike (I), Rarity Level: 4-6, Values: Normal Numismatic Value.

After strike modifications
Division V

This division includes both modifications that have value to collectors – and those that don't. I needed a couple of divisions to cover other things that happen to coins to aid in cataloging them. This avoids the false conclusion that an unlisted coin is quite rare, when the exact opposite is more likely to be the case.

Collectible modifications after strike (V-A)

Mint modification V-A-8

This section includes those classes having to do with deliberate modifications of the coin done with a specific purpose or intent which makes them of some value to collectors. Quite often these pieces were made specifically to sell to collectors, or at least to the public under the guise of being collectible.

V-A-1 Screw Thaler, Rarity Level: 5-6, Values: Normal Numismatic Value.
V-A-2 Love Token, Rarity Level: 3-6, Values: $10 up.
V-A-3 Satirical or Primitive Engraving, Rarity Level: 6-7, Values: $5 up.
V-A-4 Elongated Coin, Rarity Level: 2-7, Values: 50 cents to $1 and up.
V-A-5 Coin Jewelry, Rarity Level: 2-5, Values: $1 up.
V-A-6 Novelty Coin, Rarity Level: 1-3, Values: No Value up to $5 to $10.
V-A-7 Toning, Rarity Level: 3-6, Values: No value up, depending on coloration. Easily faked.
V-A-8 Mint Modification, Rarity Level: 4-7, Values: $5 up. Easily faked.
V-A-9 Mint Packaging Mistake, Rarity Level: 5-7, Values: Nominal $1. Very easily faked.

Alterations and damage after the strike (V-B)

Machine doubling damage V-B-1

This section includes those changes in a coin which have no collector value. In most cases their effect on the coin is to reduce or entirely eliminate any collector value - and in the case of counterfeits they are actually illegal to even own.

V-B-1 Machine Doubling Damage: NOTE: Machine doubling damage is defined as: "Damage to a coin after the strike, due to die bounce or chatter or die displacement, showing on the struck coin as scrapes on the sides of the design elements, with portions of the coin metal in the relief elements either displaced sideways or downward, depending on the direction of movement of the loose die." Machine doubling damage, or MDD, is by far the most common form of doubling found on almost any coin in the world. Rarity Level: 0, Values: Reduces the coin's value.

V-B-2 Accidental or Deliberate Damage, Rarity Level: 0, Values: Reduces the coin's value.

V-B-3 Test Cut or Mark, Rarity Level: 0, Values: Reduces value of coin to face or bullion value.

V-B-4 Alteration, Rarity Level: 0, Values: Reduces value to face or bullion value.

V-B-5 Whizzing, Rarity Level: 0, Values: Reduces value sharply and may reduce it to face or bullion value.

V-B-6 Counterfeit, Copy, Facsimile, Forgery or Fake, Rarity Level: 0, Values: No Value and may be illegal to own.

V-B-7 Planchet Deterioration. Very common on copper-plated zinc cents. Rarity level: 0, Values: No Value.

COLONIAL AMERICA

COLONIAL COINAGE

MARYLAND
Lord Baltimore

PENNY (DENARIUM)

KM# 1 • Copper •

Date	AG	Good	VG	Fine	VF	XF	Unc
(1659) 4 known	—	—	—	—	—	—	—

4 PENCE (GROAT)

KM# 2 • Silver • Obv: Large bust Rev: Large shield

Date	AG	Good	VG	Fine	VF	XF	Unc
(1659)	750	1,250	2,500	4,500	8,500	15,000	—

KM# 3 • Silver • Obv: Small bust Rev: Small shield

Date	AG	Good	VG	Fine	VF	XF	Unc
(1659) unique	—	—	—	—	—	—	—

Note: Norweb $26,400

6 PENCE

KM# 4 • Silver • Obv: Small bust Note: Known in two other rare small-bust varieties and two rare large-bust varieties.

Date	AG	Good	VG	Fine	VF	XF	Unc
(1659)	450	950	1,750	3,500	6,750	12,500	—

SHILLING

KM# 6 • Silver • Note: Varieties exist; one is very rare.

Date	AG	Good	VG	Fine	VF	XF	Unc
(1659)	500	1,000	2,000	4,000	8,000	14,500	—

MASSACHUSETTS
New England

3 PENCE

KM# 1 • Silver • Obv: NE Rev: III

Date	AG	Good	VG	Fine	VF	XF	Unc
(1652) 2 known	—	—	—	—	—	—	—

6 PENCE

KM# 2 • Silver • Obv: NE Rev: VI

Date	AG	Good	VG	Fine	VF	XF	Unc
(1652) 8 known	—	—	—	—	—	—	—

Note: Garrett $75,000

SHILLING

KM# 3 • Silver • Obv: NE Rev: XII

Date	AG	Good	VG	Fine	VF	XF	Unc
(1652)	2,000	4,500	7,500	15,000	35,000	—	—

Oak Tree

2 PENCE

KM# 7 • Silver •

Date	AG	Good	VG	Fine	VF	XF	Unc
1662	150	300	550	850	2,150	—	—

3 PENCE

KM# 8 • Silver • Note: Two types of legends.

Date	AG	Good	VG	Fine	VF	XF	Unc
1652	200	400	650	1,000	2,600	—	—

6 PENCE

KM# 9 • Silver • Note: Three types of legends.

Date	AG	Good	VG	Fine	VF	XF	Unc
1652	250	450	750	1,250	3,000	—	—

SHILLING

KM# 10 • Silver • Note: Two types of legends.

Date	AG	Good	VG	Fine	VF	XF	Unc
1652	175	300	650	1,150	2,850	—	—

Pine Tree

3 PENCE

KM# 11 • Silver • Obv: Tree without berries

Date	AG	Good	VG	Fine	VF	XF	Unc
1652	150	300	450	750	1,600		

KM# 12 • Silver • Obv: Tree with berries

Date	AG	Good	VG	Fine	VF	XF	Unc
1652	165	325	500	850	1,850	—	—

6 PENCE

KM# 13 • Silver • Obv: Tree without berries; "spiney tree"

Date	AG	Good	VG	Fine	VF	XF	Unc
1652	525	950	1,650	2,000	3,000	—	—

KM# 14 • Silver • Obv: Tree with berries

Date	AG	Good	VG	Fine	VF	XF	Unc
1652	150	300	575	1,150	2,100	—	—

SHILLING

KM# 15 • Silver • Note: Large planchet. Many varieties exist; some are very rare.

Date	AG	Good	VG	Fine	VF	XF	Unc
1652	200	425	775	1,350	2,650	—	—

KM# 16 • Silver • Note: Small planchet; large dies. All examples are thought to be contemporary fabrications.

Date	AG	Good	VG	Fine	VF	XF	Unc
1652	—	—	—	—	—	—	—

KM# 17 • Silver • Note: Small planchet; small dies. Many varieties exist; some are very rare.

Date	AG	Good	VG	Fine	VF	XF	Unc
1652	150	300	575	1,250	2,300	—	—

Willow Tree

3 PENCE

KM# 4 • Silver •

Date	AG	Good	VG	Fine	VF	XF	Unc
1652	3 known	—	—	—	—	—	—

6 PENCE

KM# 5 • Silver •

Date	AG	Good	VG	Fine	VF	XF	Unc
1652	3,500	7,500	10,000	18,000	35,000	—	—

SHILLING

KM# 6 • Silver •

Date	AG	Good	VG	Fine	VF	XF	Unc
1652	4,000	10,000	12,500	20,000	36,500	—	—

NEW JERSEY
St. Patrick or Mark Newby

FARTHING

KM# 1 • Copper •

Date	AG	Good	VG	Fine	VF	XF	Unc
(1682)	20.00	40.00	80.00	200	425	—	—

KM# 1a • Silver •

Date	AG	Good	VG	Fine	VF	XF	Unc
(1682)	350	550	1,150	1,650	2,750	—	—

HALFPENNY

KM# 2 • Copper •

Date	AG	Good	VG	Fine	VF	XF	Unc
(1682)	50.00	100.00	200	400	900	—	—

EARLY AMERICAN TOKENS
American Plantations

1/24 REAL

KM# Tn5.1 • Tin • Obv. Legend: ET HIB REX

Date	AG	Good	VG	Fine	VF	XF	Unc
(1688)	65.00	125	165	210	285	450	—

KM# Tn5.3 • Tin • Rev: Horizontal 4

Date	AG	Good	VG	Fine	VF	XF	Unc
(1688)	175	300	400	500	650	1,350	—

KM# Tn5.4 • Tin • Obv. Legend: ET HIB REX

Date	AG	Good	VG	Fine	VF	XF	Unc
(1688)	—	—	—	—	—	—	6,000

KM# Tn6 • Tin • Rev: Arms of Scotland left, Ireland right

Date	AG	Good	VG	Fine	VF	XF	Unc
(1688)	450	750	1,250	2,000	2,500	—	—

KM# Tn5.2 • Tin • Obv: Rider's head left of "B" in legend **Note:** Restrikes made in 1828 from two obverse dies.

Date	AG	Good	VG	Fine	VF	XF	Unc
(1828)	35.00	65.00	100.00	150	225	325	—

Elephant

KM# Tn1.1 • 15.5500 g., Copper • Note: Thick planchet.

Date	AG	Good	VG	Fine	VF	XF	Unc
(1664)	60.00	100.00	150	250	450	850	—

KM# Tn1.2 • Copper • Note: Thin planchet.

Date	AG	Good	VG	Fine	VF	XF	Unc
(1664)	80.00	150	200	350	600	1,250	—

KM# Tn2 • Copper • Rev: Diagonals tie shield

Date	AG	Good	VG	Fine	VF	XF	Unc
(1664)	120	185	225	400	700	1,450	—

KM# Tn3 • Copper • Rev: Sword right side of shield

Date	AG	Good	VG	Fine	VF	XF	Unc
(1664) 3 known	—	—	—	—	—	—	—

Note: Norweb $1,320

KM# Tn4 • Copper • Rev. Legend: LON DON

Date	AG	Good	VG	Fine	VF	XF	Unc
(1684)	175	300	500	1,000	1,850	3,750	—

KM# Tn7 • Copper • Rev. Legend: NEW ENGLAND

Date	AG	Good	VG	Fine	VF	XF	Unc
(1694) 2 known	—	—	—	—	—	—	—

Note: Norweb $25,300

KM# Tn8.1 • Copper • Rev. Legend: CAROLINA (PROPRIETORS)

Date	AG	Good	VG	Fine	VF	XF	Unc
(1694) 5 known	—	—	—	—	—	—	—

Note: Norweb $35,200

KM# Tn8.2 • Copper • Rev. Legend: CAROLINA (PROPRIETORS, O over E)

Date	AG	Good	VG	Fine	VF	XF	Unc
1694	700	1,100	1,700	2,750	5,750	11,000	—

Note: Norweb $17,600

Gloucester

KM# Tn15 • Copper •

Date	AG	Good	VG	Fine	VF	XF	Unc
(1714) 2 known	—	—	—	—	—	—	—

Note: Garrett $36,000

Hibernia-Voce Populi

FARTHING

KM# Tn21.1 • Copper • Note: Large letters

Date	AG	Good	VG	Fine	VF	XF	Unc
1760	90.00	150	275	450	750	1,550	—

KM# Tn21.2 • Copper • Note: Small letters

Date	AG	Good	VG	Fine	VF	XF	Unc
1760 extremely rare	—	—	—	—	—	—	—

Note: Norweb $5,940.

HALFPENNY

KM# Tn22 • Copper •

Date	AG	Good	VG	Fine	VF	XF	Unc
1700 date is error, extremely rare	—	—	—	—	—	—	—

Note: ex-Roper $575. Norweb $577.50. Stack's Americana, VF, $2,900

Date	AG	Good	VG	Fine	VF	XF	Unc
1760 varieties	10.00	30.00	50.00	100.00	185	350	—
1760 legend VOOE POPULI	20.00	35.00	60.00	110	200	400	—

Higley or Granby

KM# Tn16 • Copper • Obv. Legend: CONNECTICVT **Note:** THE VALVE OF THREE PENCE.

Date	AG	Good	VG	Fine	VF	XF	Unc
1737	—	—	—	—	—	—	—

Note: Garrett $16,000

KM# Tn17 • Copper • Obv. Legend: THE VALVE OF THREE PENCE **Rev. Legend:** I AM GOOD COPPER

Date	AG	Good	VG	Fine	VF	XF	Unc
1737 2 known	—	—	—	—	—	—	—

Note: ex-Norweb $6,875

KM# Tn18.1 • Copper • Obv. Legend: VALUE ME AS YOU PLEASE **Rev. Legend:** I AM GOOD COPPER

Date	AG	Good	VG	Fine	VF	XF	Unc
1737	6,500	8,500	10,500	14,500	25,000	—	—

KM# Tn18.2 • Copper • Obv. Legend: VALVE ME AS YOU PLEASE. **Rev. Legend:** I AM GOOD COPPER.

Date	AG	Good	VG	Fine	VF	XF	Unc
1737 2 known	—	—	—	—	—	—	—

KM# Tn19 • Copper • Rev: Broad axe

Date	AG	Good	VG	Fine	VF	XF	Unc
(1737)	—	—	—	—	—	—	—

Note: Garrett $45,000

Date	AG	Good	VG	Fine	VF	XF	Unc
1739 5 known	—	—	—	—	—	—	—

Note: Eliasberg $12,650. Oechsner $9,900. Steinberg (holed) $4,400.

Date	AG	Good	VG	Fine	VF	XF	Unc
1739 5 known	—	—	—	—	—	—	—

Note: Eliasberg $12,650. Oechsner $9,900. Steinberg (holed) $4,400.

KM# Tn20 • Copper • Obv. Legend: THE WHEELE GOES ROUND **Rev:** J CUT MY WAY THROUGH

Date	AG	Good	VG	Fine	VF	XF	Unc
(1737) unique	—	—	—	—	—	—	—

Note: Roper $60,500

New Yorke

KM# Tn9 • Brass • Note: The 1700 date is circa.

Date	AG	Good	VG	Fine	VF	XF	Unc
1700		650	1,250	2,850	4,500	7,500	—

KM# Tn9a • White Metal •

Date	AG	Good	VG	Fine	VF	XF	Unc
1700 4 known	—	—	—	—	—	—	—

Pitt

FARTHING

KM# Tn23 • Copper •

Date	AG	Good	VG	Fine	VF	XF	Unc
1766	—	—	—	1,350	2,850	6,000	—

HALFPENNY

KM# Tn24 • Copper •

Date	AG	Good	VG	Fine	VF	XF	Unc
1766	45.00	85.00	175	350	700	1,500	—

ROYAL PATENT COINAGE

Hibernia

FARTHING

KM# 20 • Copper • Note: Pattern.

Date	AG	Good	VG	Fine	VF	XF	Unc
1722	25.00	50.00	125	220	325	700	—

KM# 24 • Copper • Obv: 1722 obverse **Obv. Legend:** ...D:G:REX.

Date	AG	Good	VG	Fine	VF	XF	Unc
1723	20.00	40.00	60.00	90.00	150	350	—

KM# 25 • Copper • Obv. Legend: DEI • GRATIA • REX •

Date	AG	Good	VG	Fine	VF	XF	Unc
1723	10.00	20.00	40.00	65.00	90.00	200	—

KM# 25a • Silver •

Date	Good	VG	Fine	VF	XF	Unc	Proof
1723	—	—	—	800	1,600	—	2,700
1724	45.00	75.00	125	250	485	—	—

HALFPENNY

KM# 21 • **Copper** • **Rev:** Harp left, head right

Date	AG	Good	VG	Fine	VF	XF	Unc
1722	—	15.00	35.00	65.00	135	350	—

KM# 22 • **Copper** • **Obv:** Harp left, head right
Note: Pattern.

Date	AG	Good	VG	Fine	VF	XF	Unc
1722	7.00	—	—	1,150	1,750	3,000	—

KM# 23.1 • **Copper** • **Rev:** Harp right

Date	AG	Good	VG	Fine	VF	XF	Unc
1722	2.00	15.00	35.00	60.00	125	250	—
1723	7.00	15.00	25.00	40.00	80.00	175	—
1723/22	10.00	20.00	45.00	90.00	185	375	—
1724	7.00	15.00	35.00	60.00	125	265	—

KM# 23.2 • **Copper** • **Obv:** DEII error in legend

Date	AG	Good	VG	Fine	VF	XF	Unc
1722	40.00	90.00	180	300	500	750	—

KM# 26 • **Copper** • **Rev:** Large head **Note:**
Rare. Generally mint state only. Probably a pattern.

Date	AG	Good	VG	Fine	VF	XF	Unc
1723	—	—	—	—	—	—	—

KM# 27 • **Copper** • **Rev:** Continuous legend
over head

Date	AG	Good	VG	Fine	VF	XF	Unc
1724	30.00	65.00	150	300	475	750	—

Rosa Americana

HALFPENNY

KM# 1 • **Copper** • **Obv. Legend:** D • G • REX •

Date	AG	Good	VG	Fine	VF	XF	Unc
1722	20.00	40.00	60.00	100.00	220	475	—

KM# 2 • **Copper** • **Obv:** Uncrowned rose **Obv. Legend:** DEI GRATIA REX. **Note:** Several varieties exist.

Date	AG	Good	VG	Fine	VF	XF	Unc
1722	18.00	35.00	55.00	100.00	200	475	—
1723	285	525	750	1,350	2,250	—	—

KM# 3 • **Copper** • **Rev. Legend:** VTILE DVLCI

Date	AG	Good	VG	Fine	VF	XF	Unc
1722	250	450	650	1,100	—	—	—

KM# 9 • **Copper** • **Rev:** Crowned rose

Date	AG	Good	VG	Fine	VF	XF	Unc
1723	18.00	35.00	55.00	100.00	200	450	—

PENNY

KM# 4 • **Copper** • **Rev. Legend:** UTILE DULCI
Note: Several varieties exist.

Date	AG	Good	VG	Fine	VF	XF	Unc
1722	18.00	35.00	55.00	100.00	175	385	—

KM# 5 • **Copper** • **Note:** Several varieties exist. Also known in two rare pattern types with long hair ribbons, one with V's for U's on the obverse.

Date	AG	Good	VG	Fine	VF	XF	Unc
1722	18.00	35.00	55.00	100.00	220	475	—

KM# 10 • **Copper** • **Note:** Several varieties exist.

Date	AG	Good	VG	Fine	VF	XF	Unc
1723	18.00	35.00	55.00	100.00	200	420	—

KM# 12 • **Copper** • **Note:** Pattern.

Date	AG	Good	VG	Fine	VF	XF	Unc
1724 2 known	—	—	—	—	—	—	—

KM# 13 • **Copper** •

Date	AG	Good	VG	Fine	VF	XF	Unc
(1724) 5 known	—	—	—	—	—	—	—

Note: Norweb $2,035

KM# 14 • **Copper** • **Obv:** George II **Note:** Pattern.

Date	AG	Good	VG	Fine	VF	XF	Unc
1727 2 known	—	—	—	—	—	—	—

2 PENCE

KM# 6 • **Copper** • **Rev:** Motto with scroll

Date	AG	Good	VG	Fine	VF	XF	Unc
(1722)	35.00	60.00	110	200	350	700	—

KM# 7 • **Copper** • **Rev:** Motto without scroll

Date	AG	Good	VG	Fine	VF	XF	Unc
(1722) 3 known	—	—	—	—	—	—	—

KM# 8.1 • **Copper** • **Obv:** Period after REX **Rev:** Dated

Date	AG	Good	VG	Fine	VF	XF	Unc
1722	25.00	40.00	70.00	125	265	500	—

KM# 8.2 • **Copper** • **Obv:** Without period after REX

Date	AG	Good	VG	Fine	VF	XF	Unc
1722	22.00	40.00	70.00	125	275	525	—

KM# 11 • **Copper** • **Obv:** No stop after REX **Rev:** Stop after 1723 **Note:** Several varieties exist.

Date	AG	Good	VG	Fine	VF	XF	Unc
1723	25.00	45.00	75.00	140	285	550	—

KM# 15 • Copper • Note: Pattern. Two varieties exist; both extremely rare.

Date	AG	Good	VG	Fine	VF	XF	Unc
1724	—	—	—	—	—	—	—

Note: ex-Garrett $5,775. Stack's Americana, XF, $10,925

KM# 16 • Copper • Note: Pattern.

Date	AG	Good	VG	Fine	VF	XF	Unc
1733 4 known	—	—	—	—	—	—	—

Note: Norweb $19,800

Virginia Halfpenny

KM# Tn25.1 • Copper • Rev: Small 7s in date.
Note: Struck on Irish halfpenny planchets.

Date	Good	VG	Fine	VF	XF	Unc	Proof
1773	—	—	—	—	—	—	3,500

KM# Tn25.2 • Copper • Obv: Period after GEORGIVS **Rev:** Varieties with 7 or 8 strings in harp

Date	AG	Good	VG	Fine	VF	XF	Unc
1773	6.00	12.00	25.00	50.00	100.00	250	465

KM# Tn25.3 • Copper • Obv: Without period after GEORGIVS **Rev:** Varieties with 6, 7 or 8 strings in harp

Date	AG	Good	VG	Fine	VF	XF	Unc
1773	7.00	15.00	30.00	60.00	135	275	525

KM# Tn25.4 • Copper • Obv: Without period after GEORGIVS **Rev:** 8 harp strings, dot on cross

Date	AG	Good	VG	Fine	VF	XF	Unc
1773	—	—	—	—	—	—	—

Note: ex-Steinberg $2,600
KM# Tn26 • Silver • Note: So-called "shilling" silver proofs.

Date	AG	Good	VG	Fine	VF	XF	Unc
1774 6 known	—	—	—	—	—	—	—

Note: Garrett $23,000

UNITED STATES

REVOLUTIONARY COINAGE

Continental "Dollar".

KM# EA1 • Pewter • Obv. Legend: CURRENCY.

Date	AG	Good	VG	Fine	VF	XF	Unc
1776	—	—	1,850	3,000	4,750	8,750	18,500

KM# EA2 • Pewter • Obv. Legend: CURRENCY, EG FECIT.

Date	AG	Good	VG	Fine	VF	XF	Unc
1776	—	—	1,750	2,850	4,250	7,750	16,000

KM# EA2a • Silver • Obv. Legend: CURRENCY, EG FECIT.

Date	AG	Good	VG	Fine	VF	XF	Unc
1776 2 known	—	—	—	—	—	—	—

KM# EA3 • Pewter • Obv. Legend: CURRENCY.

Date	AG	Good	VG	Fine	VF	XF	Unc
1776 extremely rare	—	—	—	—	—	—	—

KM# EA4 • Pewter • Obv. Legend: CURRENCY. **Rev:** Floral cross.

Date	AG	Good	VG	Fine	VF	XF	Unc
1776 3 recorded	—	—	—	—	—	—	—

Note: Norweb $50,600. Johnson $25,300

KM# EA5 • Pewter • Obv. Legend: CURENCY.

Date	AG	Good	VG	Fine	VF	XF	Unc
1776	—	—	1,650	2,750	4,000	8,000	16,000

KM# EA5a • Brass • Obv. Legend: CURENCY. **Note:** Two varieties exist.

Date	AG	Good	VG	Fine	VF	XF	Unc
1776	—	—	—	—	13,500	17,500	—

KM# EA5b • Silver • Obv. Legend: CURENCY.

Date	AG	Good	VG	Fine	VF	XF	Unc
1776 unique	—	—	—	—	—	—	—

Note: Romano $99,000

STATE COINAGE
CONNECTICUT

KM# 1 • Copper • Obv: Bust facing right.

Date	AG	Good	VG	Fine	VF	XF	Unc
1785	20.00	30.00	50.00	85.00	190	450	—

KM# 2 • Copper • Obv: "African head."

Date	AG	Good	VG	Fine	VF	XF	Unc
1785	25.00	45.00	85.00	200	450	1,500	—

KM# 3.1 • Copper • Obv: Bust facing left.

Date	AG	Good	VG	Fine	VF	XF	Unc
1785	60.00	100.00	150	275	400	750	—

Date	AG	Good	VG	Fine	VF	XF	Unc
1786	20.00	30.00	50.00	90.00	185	465	—
1787	22.00	35.00	60.00	110	125	350	—
1788	20.00	30.00	50.00	100.00	220	500	—

KM# 4 • Copper • Obv: Small mailed bust facing left. **Rev. Legend:** ETLIB INDE.

Date	AG	Good	VG	Fine	VF	XF	Unc
1786	22.00	35.00	55.00	85.00	165	400	—

KM# 5 • Copper • Obv: Small mailed bust facing right. **Rev. Legend:** INDE ET LIB.

Date	AG	Good	VG	Fine	VF	XF	Unc
1786	30.00	55.00	75.00	115	225	475	—

KM# 6 • Copper • Obv: Large mailed bust facing right.

Date	AG	Good	VG	Fine	VF	XF	Unc
1786	30.00	50.00	90.00	165	350	850	—

KM# 7 • Copper • Obv: "Hercules head."

Date	AG	Good	VG	Fine	VF	XF	Unc
1786	25.00	40.00	75.00	135	300	700	—

KM# 8.1 • Copper • Obv: Draped bust.

Date	AG	Good	VG	Fine	VF	XF	Unc
1786	22.00	35.00	65.00	120	275	600	—

KM# 9 • Copper • Obv: Small head. **Rev. Legend:** ETLIB INDE.

Date	AG	Good	VG	Fine	VF	XF	Unc
1787	25.00	40.00	90.00	150	350	800	—

KM# 10 • Copper • Obv: Small head. **Rev. Legend:** INDE ET LIB.

Date	AG	Good	VG	Fine	VF	XF	Unc
1787	75.00	135	175	275	450	950	—

KM# 11 • Copper • Obv: Medium bust. **Note:** Two reverse legend types exist.

Date	AG	Good	VG	Fine	VF	XF	Unc
1787	50.00	80.00	140	200	325	625	—

KM# 12 • Copper • Obv: "Muttonhead" variety. **Note:** Extremely rare with legend INDE ET LIB.

Date	AG	Good	VG	Fine	VF	XF	Unc
1787	30.00	50.00	120	250	650	1,500	—

KM# 3.3 • Copper • Obv: Perfect date. **Rev. Legend:** IN DE ET.

Date	AG	Good	VG	Fine	VF	XF	Unc
1787	35.00	65.00	85.00	135	250	600	—

KM# 13 • Copper • Obv: "Laughing head"

Date	AG	Good	VG	Fine	VF	XF	Unc
1787	22.00	35.00	60.00	110	250	700	—

KM# 14 • Copper • Obv: "Horned head"

Date	AG	Good	VG	Fine	VF	XF	Unc
1787	15.00	25.00	40.00	70.00	175	475	—

KM# 15 • Copper • Rev. Legend: IND ET LIB

Date	AG	Good	VG	Fine	VF	XF	Unc
1787/8	25.00	40.00	75.00	130	250	650	—
1787/1887	20.00	30.00	50.00	90.00	200	520	—

KM# 16 • Copper • Obv. Legend: CONNECT. **Rev. Legend:** INDE ET LIB. **Note:** Two additional scarce reverse legend types exist.

Date	AG	Good	VG	Fine	VF	XF	Unc
1787	22.00	37.50	60.00	115	220	550	—

KM# 8.2 • Copper • Obv: Draped bust. **Note:** Many varieties.

Date	AG	Good	VG	Fine	VF	XF	Unc
1787	12.00	20.00	40.00	80.00	135	275	—

KM# 8.3 • Copper • Obv. Legend: AUCIORI.

Date	AG	Good	VG	Fine	VF	XF	Unc
1787	15.00	25.00	50.00	110	250	600	—

KM# 8.4 • Copper • Obv. Legend: AUCTOPI.

Date	AG	Good	VG	Fine	VF	XF	Unc
1787	20.00	30.00	60.00	125	265	650	—

KM# 8.5 • Copper • Obv. Legend: AUCTOBI.

Date	AG	Good	VG	Fine	VF	XF	Unc
1787	15.00	25.00	50.00	110	225	550	—

KM# 8.6 • Copper • Obv. Legend: CONNFC.

Date	AG	Good	VG	Fine	VF	XF	Unc
1787	12.00	20.00	40.00	85.00	200	525	—

KM# 8.7 • Copper • Obv. Legend: CONNLC.

Date	AG	Good	VG	Fine	VF	XF	Unc
1787	—	30.00	60.00	125	265	650	—

KM# 8.8 • Copper • Rev. Legend: FNDE.

Date	AG	Good	VG	Fine	VF	XF	Unc
1787	15.00	25.00	45.00	90.00	210	535	—

KM# 8.9 • Copper • Rev. Legend: ETLIR.

Date	AG	Good	VG	Fine	VF	XF	Unc
1787	15.00	25.00	45.00	90.00	210	535	—

KM# 8.10 • Copper • Rev. Legend: ETIIB.

Date	AG	Good	VG	Fine	VF	XF	Unc
1787	20.00	30.00	50.00	100.00	225	550	—

KM# 20 • Copper • Obv: Mailed bust facing right.

Date	AG	Good	VG	Fine	VF	XF	Unc
1788	15.00	25.00	45.00	90.00	200	425	—

KM# 21 • Copper • Obv: Small mailed bust facing right.

Date	AG	Good	VG	Fine	VF	XF	Unc
1788	75.00	150	285	550	1,100	2,500	—

KM# 3.4 • Copper • Obv. Legend: CONNLC.

Date	AG	Good	VG	Fine	VF	XF	Unc
1788	15.00	25.00	40.00	80.00	175	400	—

KM# 22.1 • Copper • Obv: Draped bust facing left. **Rev. Legend:** INDE ET LIB.

Date	AG	Good	VG	Fine	VF	XF	Unc
1788	12.00	20.00	35.00	55.00	135	375	—

KM# 22.2 • Copper • Rev. Legend: INDLET LIB.

Date	AG	Good	VG	Fine	VF	XF	Unc
1788	20.00	30.00	55.00	90.00	185	400	—

KM# 22.3 • Copper • Obv. Legend: CONNEC. Rev. Legend: INDE ET LIB.

Date	AG	Good	VG	Fine	VF	XF	Unc
1788	22.00	35.00	60.00	100.00	200	425	—

KM# 22.4 • Copper • Obv. Legend: CONNEC. Rev. Legend: INDL ET LIB.

Date	AG	Good	VG	Fine	VF	XF	Unc
1788	22.00	35.00	60.00	100.00	200	425	—

MASSACHUSETTS

HALFPENNY

KM# 17 • Copper •

Date	AG	Good	VG	Fine	VF	XF	Unc
1776 unique	—	—	—	—	—	—	—

Note: Garrett $40,000

PENNY

KM# 18 • Copper •

Date	AG	Good	VG	Fine	VF	XF	Unc
1776 unique	—	—	—	—	—	—	—

HALF CENT

KM# 19 • Copper • Note: Varieties exist; some are rare.

Date	AG	Good	VG	Fine	VF	XF	Unc
1787	30.00	50.00	90.00	175	350	800	—
1788	35.00	55.00	100.00	185	375	850	—

CENT

KM# 20.1 • Copper • Rev: Arrows in right talon

Date	AG	Good	VG	Fine	VF	XF	Unc
1787 7 known	—	—	—	—	—	—	—

Note: Ex-Bushnell-Brand $8,800. Garrett $5,500

KM# 20.2 • Copper • Rev: Arrows in left talon

Date	AG	Good	VG	Fine	VF	XF	Unc
1787	25.00	40.00	65.00	120	285	785	—

KM# 20.3 • Copper • Rev: "Horned eagle" die break

Date	AG	Good	VG	Fine	VF	XF	Unc
1787	28.00	45.00	70.00	130	300	785	—

KM# 20.4 • Copper • Rev: Without period after Massachusetts

Date	AG	Good	VG	Fine	VF	XF	Unc
1788	28.00	45.00	70.00	135	320	850	—

KM# 20.5 • Copper • Rev: Period after Massachusetts, normal S's

Date	AG	Good	VG	Fine	VF	XF	Unc
1788	28.00	45.00	70.00	120	275	775	—

KM# 20.6 • Copper • Rev: Period after Massachusetts, S's like 8's

Date	AG	Good	VG	Fine	VF	XF	Unc
1788	22.00	35.00	60.00	120	275	775	—

NEW HAMPSHIRE

KM# 1 • Copper •

Date	AG	Good	VG	Fine	VF	XF	Unc
1776 extremely rare	—	—	—	—	—	—	—

Note: Garrett $13,000

NEW JERSEY

KM# 8 • Copper • Obv: Date below draw bar.

Date	AG	Good	VG	Fine	VF	XF	Unc
1786 extremely rare	—	—	—	—	—	—	—

Note: Garrett $52,000

KM# 9 • Copper • Obv: Large horse head, date below plow, no coulter on plow.

Date	AG	Good	VG	Fine	VF	XF	Unc
1786	75.00	150	285	550	1,450	5,500	—

KM# 10 • Copper • Rev: Narrow shield, straight beam.

Date	AG	Good	VG	Fine	VF	XF	Unc
1786	25.00	40.00	65.00	150	350	975	—

KM# 11.1 • Copper • Rev: Wide shield, curved beam. **Note:** Varieties exist.

Date	AG	Good	VG	Fine	VF	XF	Unc
1786	28.00	45.00	85.00	180	425	1,000	—

KM# 11.2 • Copper • Obv: Bridle variety (die break). **Note:** Reverse varieties exist.

Date	AG	Good	VG	Fine	VF	XF	Unc
1786	30.00	50.00	90.00	185	425	1,000	—

KM# 12.1 • Copper • Rev: Plain shield. **Note:** Small planchet. Varieties exist.

Date	AG	Good	VG	Fine	VF	XF	Unc
1787	20.00	30.00	60.00	100.00	200	675	—

KM# 12.2 • Copper • Rev: Shield heavily outlined. **Note:** Small planchet.

Date	AG	Good	VG	Fine	VF	XF	Unc
1787	22.00	35.00	75.00	125	285	800	—

KM# 13 • Copper • Obv: "Serpent head."

Date	AG	Good	VG	Fine	VF	XF	Unc
1787	40.00	60.00	120	285	700	1,275	—

KM# 14 • Copper • Rev: Plain shield. **Note:** Large planchet. Varieties exist.

Date	AG	Good	VG	Fine	VF	XF	Unc
1787	22.00	35.00	75.00	135	300	850	—

KM# 15 • Copper • Rev. Legend: PLURIBS.

Date	AG	Good	VG	Fine	VF	XF	Unc
1787	30.00	50.00	100.00	225	600	1,100	—

KM# 16 • Copper • Obv: Horse's head facing right. **Note:** Varieties exist.

Date	AG	Good	VG	Fine	VF	XF	Unc
1788	20.00	30.00	65.00	125	375	750	—

KM# 17 • Copper • Rev: Fox before legend. **Note:** Varieties exist.

Date	AG	Good	VG	Fine	VF	XF	Unc
1788	—	55.00	110	275	725	1,550	—

KM# 18 • Copper • Obv: Horse's head facing left. **Note:** Varieties exist.

Date	AG	Good	VG	Fine	VF	XF	Unc
1788	65.00	125	285	575	1,150	3,000	—

NEW YORK

KM# 1 • Copper • Obv. Legend: NON VI VIRTUTE VICI.

Date	AG	Good	VG	Fine	VF	XF	Unc
1786	1,200	2,200	3,750	6,000	11,500	—	—

KM# 2 • Copper • Obv: Eagle on globe facing right.

Date	AG	Good	VG	Fine	VF	XF	Unc
1787	175	750	1,250	3,500	6,500	12,750	—

KM# 3 • Copper • Obv: Eagle on globe facing left.

Date	AG	Good	VG	Fine	VF	XF	Unc
1787	350	700	1,200	3,250	6,000	12,000	—

KM# 4 • Copper • Rev: Large eagle, arrows in right talon.

Date	AG	Good	VG	Fine	VF	XF	Unc
1787 2 known	—	—	—	—	—	—	—

Note: Norweb $18,700

KM# 5 • Copper • Obv: George Clinton.

Date	AG	Good	VG	Fine	VF	XF	Unc
1787	2,250	4,000	5,500	9,500	20,000	—	—

KM# 6 • Copper • Obv: Indian. **Rev:** New York arms.

Date	AG	Good	VG	Fine	VF	XF	Unc
1787	1,000	2,000	4,000	6,500	10,500	25,000	—

KM# 7 • Copper • Obv: Indian. **Rev:** Eagle on globe.

Date	AG	Good	VG	Fine	VF	XF	Unc
1787	1,650	3,000	6,500	11,500	23,500	35,000	—

KM# 8 • Copper • Obv: Indian. **Rev:** George III.

Date	AG	Good	VG	Fine	VF	XF	Unc
1787	125	200	350	650	1,350	4,200	—

Nova Eboracs

KM# 9 • Copper • Obv. Legend: NOVA EBORAC. **Rev:** Figure seated right.

Date	AG	Good	VG	Fine	VF	XF	Unc
1787	40.00	75.00	125	260	525	1,100	—

KM# 10 • Copper • Rev: Figure seated left.

Date	AG	Good	VG	Fine	VF	XF	Unc
1787	35.00	55.00	110	225	500	1,000	—

KM# 11 • Copper • Obv: Small head, star above. **Obv. Legend:** NOVA EBORAC.

Date	AG	Good	VG	Fine	VF	XF	Unc
1787	300	600	1,750	3,000	4,500	6,500	—

KM# 12 • Copper • Obv: Large head, two quatrefoils left. **Obv. Legend:** NOVA EBORAC.

Date	AG	Good	VG	Fine	VF	XF	Unc
1787	200	300	400	650	1,150	2,500	—

Machin Mill

KM# 13 • Copper • Note: Crude, lightweight imitations of the British Halfpenny were struck at Machin's Mill in large quantities bearing the obverse legends: GEORGIVS II REX, GEORGIVS III REX, and GEORGIUS III REX, with the BRITANNIA reverse. There are many different mulings. These pieces, which have plain crosses in the shield of Britannia, are not to be confused with the very common British made imitations, which usually have outlined crosses in the shield. Some varieties are very rare.

Date	AG	Good	VG	Fine	VF	XF	Unc
(1747-1788)	—	—	—	—	—	—	—

Note: Examples are dated: 1747, 1771, 1772, 1774, 1775, 1776, 1777, 1778, 1784, 1785, 1786, 1787 and 1788. Other dates may exist

VERMONT

KM# 1 • Copper • Rev. Legend: IMMUNE COLUMBIA.

Date	AG	Good	VG	Fine	VF	XF	Unc
(1785)	1,250	2,000	3,000	5,000	9,000	—	—

KM# 2 • Copper • Obv. Legend: VERMONTIS.

Date	AG	Good	VG	Fine	VF	XF	Unc
1785	120	200	300	600	1,150	—	—

KM# 3 • Copper • Obv. Legend: VERMONTS.

Date	AG	Good	VG	Fine	VF	XF	Unc
1785	85.00	150	225	450	900	3,200	—

KM# 4 • Copper • Obv. Legend: VERMONT-ENSIUM.

Date	AG	Good	VG	Fine	VF	XF	Unc
1786	75.00	125	200	450	950	3,250	—

KM# 5 • Copper • Obv: "Baby head." **Rev:** AUCTORI: VERMONS.

Date	AG	Good	VG	Fine	VF	XF	Unc
1786	120	200	300	550	1,150	4,500	—

KM# 6 • Copper • Obv: Bust facing left. **Obv. Legend:** VERMON: AUCTORI:.

Date	AG	Good	VG	Fine	VF	XF	Unc
1786	60.00	100.00	185	300	750	2,250	—
1787 extremely rare	—	—	—	—	—	—	—

KM# 7 • Copper • Obv: Bust facing right. **Note:** Varieties exist.

Date	AG	Good	VG	Fine	VF	XF	Unc
1787	—	—	—	—	—	—	—

KM# 8 • Copper • Note: Britannia mule.

Date	AG	Good	VG	Fine	VF	XF	Unc
1787	25.00	40.00	65.00	140	285	950	—

KM# 9.1 • Copper • Rev. Legend: INDE ET LIB. **Note:** Varieties exist.

Date	AG	Good	VG	Fine	VF	XF	Unc
1788	40.00	65.00	120	220	550	1,850	—

KM# 9.2 • Copper • Obv: "C" backward in AUCTORI.

Date	AG	Good	VG	Fine	VF	XF	Unc
1788 extremely rare	—	—	—	—	—	—	—

Note: Stack's Americana, Fine, $9,775

KM# 10 • Copper • Rev. Legend: ET LIB INDE.

Date	AG	Good	VG	Fine	VF	XF	Unc
1788	75.00	125	300	600	1,100	—	—

KM# 11 • Copper • Note: George III Rex mule.

Date	AG	Good	VG	Fine	VF	XF	Unc
1788	85.00	145	325	650	1,250	2,750	—

EARLY AMERICAN TOKENS

Albany Church "Penny"

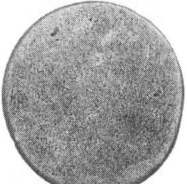

KM# Tn54.1 • Copper • Obv: Without "D" above church. **Note:** Uniface.

Date	AG	Good	VG	Fine	VF	XF	Unc
5 known	—	—	3,500	7,000	14,000	—	—

KM# Tn54.2 • Copper • Obv: With "D" above church. **Note:** Uniface.

Date	AG	Good	VG	Fine	VF	XF	Unc
rare	—	—	3,000	5,000	10,000	—	—

Auctori Plebis

KM# Tn50 • Copper •

Date	AG	Good	VG	Fine	VF	XF	Unc
1787	20.00	45.00	90.00	150	300	600	—

Bar "Cent"

KM# Tn49 • Copper •

Date	AG	Good	VG	Fine	VF	XF	Unc
(1785)	85.00	150	275	675	1,200	2,500	—

Castorland "Half Dollar"

KM# Tn87.1 • Silver • Edge: Reeded.

Date	AG	Good	VG	Fine	VF	XF	Unc
1796	—	—	—	—	—	3,550	—

KM# Tn87.1a • Copper • Edge: Reeded.

Date	AG	Good	VG	Fine	VF	XF	Unc
1796 3 known	—	—	—	—	—	1,650	—

KM# Tn87.1b • Brass • Edge: Reeded.

Date	AG	Good	VG	Fine	VF	XF	Unc
1796 unique	—	—	—	—	—	—	—

KM# Tn87.2 • Copper • Edge: Plain. **Note:** Thin planchet.

Date	AG	Good	VG	Fine	VF	XF	Unc
1796 unique	—	—	—	—	—	—	—

KM# Tn87.3 • Silver • Edge: Reeded. **Note:** Thin planchet. Restrike.

Date	Good	VG	Fine	VF	XF	Unc	Proof
1796	—	—	—	—	—	325	—

KM# Tn87.4 • Silver • Edge: Lettered. **Edge Lettering:** ARGENT. **Note:** Thin planchet. Restrike.

Date	Good	VG	Fine	VF	XF	Unc	Proof
1796	—	—	—	—	—	60.00	—

KM# Tn87.3a • Copper • Edge: Reeded. **Note:** Thin planchet. Restrike.

Date	Good	VG	Fine	VF	XF	Unc	Proof
1796	—	—	—	—	—	285	—

KM# Tn87.5 • Copper • Edge: Lettered. **Edge Lettering:** CUIVRE. **Note:** Thin planchet. Restrike.

Date	Good	VG	Fine	VF	XF	Unc	Proof
1796	—	—	—	—	—	40.00	—

Chalmers

3 PENCE

KM# Tn45 • Silver •

Date	AG	Good	VG	Fine	VF	XF	Unc
1783	250	500	1,000	1,500	2,650	5,500	—

6 PENCE

KM# Tn46.1 • Silver • Rev: Small date

Date	AG	Good	VG	Fine	VF	XF	Unc
1783	350	700	1,500	2,250	5,500	12,000	—

KM# Tn46.2 • Silver • Rev: Large date

Date	AG	Good	VG	Fine	VF	XF	Unc
1783	300	600	1,300	2,000	4,000	10,000	—

SHILLING

KM# Tn47.1 • Silver • Rev: Birds with long worm

Date	AG	Good	VG	Fine	VF	XF	Unc
1783	180	300	500	1,000	2,000	4,500	—

KM# Tn47.2 • Silver • Rev: Birds with short worm

Date	AG	Good	VG	Fine	VF	XF	Unc
1783	150	250	475	900	1,850	4,500	—

KM# Tn48 • Silver • Rev: Rings and stars

Date	AG	Good	VG	Fine	VF	XF	Unc
1783 4 known	—	—	—	—	—	—	—

Note: Garrett $75,000

Copper Company of Upper Canada

HALFPENNY

KM# Tn86 • Copper •

Date	Good	VG	Fine	VF	XF	Unc	Proof
1796	—	—	—	—	—	—	3,750

Franklin Press

KM# Tn73 • Copper • Edge: Plain.

Date	AG	Good	VG	Fine	VF	XF	Unc
1794	18.00	35.00	55.00	85.00	175	300	600

Kentucky Token

KM# Tn70.1 • **Copper** • **Edge:** Plain. **Note:** 1793 date is circa.

Date	AG	Good	VG	Fine	VF	XF	Unc
ND(1793)	12.00	25.00	40.00	60.00	100.00	265	575

KM# Tn70.2 • **Copper** • **Edge:** Engrailed.

Date	AG	Good	VG	Fine	VF	XF	Unc
ND(1793)	35.00	75.00	125	200	350	950	1,850

KM# Tn70.3 • **Copper** • **Edge:** Lettered. **Edge Lettering:** PAYABLE AT BEDWORTH.

Date	AG	Good	VG	Fine	VF	XF	Unc
ND(1793)unique	—	—	—	—	—	1,980	—

KM# Tn70.4 • **Copper** • **Edge:** Lettered. **Edge Lettering:** PAYABLE AT LANCASTER.

Date	AG	Good	VG	Fine	VF	XF	Unc
ND(1793)	14.00	28.00	45.00	65.00	110	285	725

KM# Tn70.5 • **Copper** • **Edge:** Lettered. **Edge Lettering:** PAYABLE AT I.FIELDING.

Date	AG	Good	VG	Fine	VF	XF	Unc
ND(1793)unique							

KM# Tn70.6 • **Copper** • **Edge:** Lettered. **Edge Lettering:** PAYABLE AT W. PARKERS.

Date	AG	Good	VG	Fine	VF	XF	Unc
ND(1793)unique	—	—	—	—	1,800	—	—

KM# Tn70.7 • **Copper** • **Edge:** Ornamented branch with two leaves.

Date	AG	Good	VG	Fine	VF	XF	Unc
ND(1793)unique	—	—	—	—	—	—	—

Mott Token

KM# Tn52.1 • **Copper** • **Note:** Thin planchet.

Date	AG	Good	VG	Fine	VF	XF	Unc
1789	30.00	60.00	120	220	350	850	—

KM# Tn52.2 • **Copper** • **Note:** Thick planchet. Weight generally about 170 grams.

Date	AG	Good	VG	Fine	VF	XF	Unc
1789		100.0					
	25.00	50.00	0	175	300	700	—

KM# Tn52.3 • **Copper** • **Edge:** Fully engrailed. **Note:** Specimens struck with perfect dies are scarcer and generally command higher prices.

Date	AG	Good	VG	Fine	VF	XF	Unc
1789	40.00	85.00	175	350	600	1,250	—

Myddelton Token

KM# Tn85 • **Copper** •

Date	Good	VG	Fine	VF	XF	Unc	Proof
1796	—	—	—	—	—	—	6,500

KM# Tn85a • **Silver** •

Date	Good	VG	Fine	VF	XF	Unc	Proof
1796	—	—	—	—	—	—	5,500

New York Theatre

KM# Tn90 • **Copper** • **Note:** 1796 date is circa.

Date	AG	Good	VG	Fine	VF	XF	Unc
1796	—	—	300	900	2,000	3,250	8,000

North American

KM# Tn30 • **Copper** •

Date	AG	Good	VG	Fine	VF	XF	Unc
1781	6.50	12.50	25.00	75.00	135	365	750

Rhode Island Ship

KM# Tn27a • **Brass** • **Obv:** Without wreath below ship.

Date	AG	Good	VG	Fine	VF	XF	Unc
1779	50.00	100.00	175	275	500	1,000	2,000

KM# Tn27b • **Pewter** • **Obv:** Without wreath below ship.

Date	AG	Good	VG	Fine	VF	XF	Unc
1779	—	—	—	—	1,250	2,500	5,500

KM# Tn28a • Brass • Obv: Wreath below ship.

Date	AG	Good	VG	Fine	VF	XF	Unc
1779	60.00	120	200	325	600	1,150	2,200

KM# Tn28b • Pewter • Obv: Wreath below ship.

Date	AG	Good	VG	Fine	VF	XF	Unc
1779	—	—	—	—	1,500	3,000	6,500

KM# Tn29 • Brass • Obv: VLUGTENDE below ship

Date	AG	Good	VG	Fine	VF	XF	Unc
1779 unique	—	—	—	—	—	—	—

Note: Garrett $16,000

Standish Barry

3 PENCE

KM# Tn55 • Silver •

Date	AG	Good	VG	Fine	VF	XF	Unc
1790		850	1,350	2,000	3,000	6,500	12,000	—

Talbot, Allum & Lee

CENT

KM# Tn71.1 • Copper • Rev: NEW YORK above ship **Edge:** Lettered. **Edge Lettering:** PAYABLE AT THE STORE OF

Date	AG	Good	VG	Fine	VF	XF	Unc
1794	12.00	25.00	45.00	90.00	175	300	925

KM# Tn71.2 • Copper • Rev: NEW YORK above ship **Edge:** Plain. **Note:** Size of ampersand varies on obverse and reverse dies.

Date	AG	Good	VG	Fine	VF	XF	Unc
1794 4 known	—	—	—	—	2,350	3,000	—

KM# Tn72.3 • Copper • Edge: Lettered. **Edge Lettering:** CURRENT EVERYWHERE.

Date	AG	Good	VG	Fine	VF	XF	Unc
1795 unique	—	—	—	—	—	—	—

KM# Tn72.4 • Copper • Edge: Olive leaf.

Date	AG	Good	VG	Fine	VF	XF	Unc
1795 unique	—	—	—	—	—	—	—

Note: Norweb $4,400

KM# Tn72.5 • Copper • Edge: Plain.

Date	AG	Good	VG	Fine	VF	XF	Unc
1795 plain edge, 2 known	—	—	—	—	—	—	—
1795 edge: Cambridge Bedford Huntington. X.X., unique	—	—	—	—	—	—	—

Note: Norweb, $3,960

Washington Pieces

KM# Tn35 • Copper • Obv. Legend: GEORGIVS TRIUMPHO.

Date	AG	Good	VG	Fine	VF	XF	Unc
1783	25.00	40.00	65.00	150	325	750	—

KM# Tn36 • Copper • Obv: Large military bust. **Note:** Varieties exist.

Date	AG	Good	VG	Fine	VF	XF	Unc
1783	8.00	15.00	25.00	50.00	110	280	—

KM# Tn37.1 • Copper • Obv: Small military bust. **Edge:** Plain.

Date	AG	Good	VG	Fine	VF	XF	Unc
1783	10.00	20.00	35.00	65.00	125	300	—

Note: One proof example is known. Value: $12,500

KM# Tn37.2 • Copper • Obv: Small military bust. **Edge:** Engrailed.

Date	AG	Good	VG	Fine	VF	XF	Unc
1783	18.00	35.00	50.00	80.00	175	345	—

KM# Tn38.1 • Copper • Obv: Draped bust, no button on drapery, small letter.

Date	AG	Good	VG	Fine	VF	XF	Unc
1783	10.00	20.00	35.00	65.00	125	285	—

KM# Tn38.2 • Copper • Obv: Draped bust, button on drapery, large letter.

Date	AG	Good	VG	Fine	VF	XF	Unc
1783	25.00	40.00	60.00	100.00	200	350	—

KM# Tn38.4 • Copper • Edge: Engrailed. **Note:** Restrike.

Date	Good	VG	Fine	VF	XF	Unc	Proof
1783	—	—	—	—	—	—	400

KM# Tn38.4a • Copper • Note: Bronzed. Restrike.

Date	Good	VG	Fine	VF	XF	Unc	Proof
1783	—	—	—	—	—	—	—

KM# Tn83.3 • Copper • Obv: Large modern lettering. **Edge:** Plain. **Note:** Restrike.

Date	Good	VG	Fine	VF	XF	Unc	Proof
1783	—	—	—	—	—	—	500

KM# Tn83.4b • Silver • Note: Restrike.

Date	Good	VG	Fine	VF	XF	Unc	Proof
1783	—	—	—	—	—	—	1,000

KM# Tn83.4c • Gold • Note: Restrike.

Date	AG	Good	VG	Fine	VF	XF	Unc
1783 2 known	—	—	—	—	—	—	—

KM# Tn60.1 • Copper • Obv. Legend: WASHINGTON PRESIDENT. **Edge:** Plain.

Date	AG	Good	VG	Fine	VF	XF	Unc
1792	850	1,450	3,250	5,000	7,500	—	—

Note: Steinberg $12,650. Garrett $15,500

KM# Tn60.2 • Copper • Obv. Legend: WASHINGTON PRESIDENT. **Edge:** Lettered. **Edge Lettering:** UNITED STATES OF AMERICA.

Date	AG	Good	VG	Fine	VF	XF	Unc
1792	1,350	2,250	4,500	7,500	12,500	—	—

KM# Tn61.1 • Copper • Obv. Legend: BORN VIRGINIA. **Note:** Varieties exist.

Date	AG	Good	VG	Fine	VF	XF	Unc
ND	250	500	1,000	2,200	3,750	7,500	—

KM# Tn61.2 • Silver • Edge: Lettered. **Edge Lettering:** UNITED STATES OF AMERICA.

Date	AG	Good	VG	Fine	VF	XF	Unc
ND 2 known	—	—	—	—	—	—	—

KM# Tn61.1a • Silver • Edge: Plain.

Date	AG	Good	VG	Fine	VF	XF	Unc
ND 4 known	—	—	—	—	—	—	—

Note: Roper $16,500

KM# Tn62 • Silver • Rev: Heraldic eagle. 1792 half dollar. **Note:** Mule.

Date	AG	Good	VG	Fine	VF	XF	Unc
3 known	—	—	—	—	—	—	—

KM# Tn77.1 • Copper • Obv. Legend: LIBERTY AND SECURITY. **Edge:** Lettered. **Note:** "Penny."

Date	AG	Good	VG	Fine	VF	XF	Unc
(1795)	25.00	40.00	75.00	135	275	625	2,000

KM# Tn77.2 • Copper • Edge: Plain. **Note:** "Penny."

Date	AG	Good	VG	Fine	VF	XF	Unc
(1795) extremely rare	—	—	—	—	—	—	—

KM# Tn77.3 • Copper • Note: "Penny." Engine-turned borders.

Date	AG	Good	VG	Fine	VF	XF	Unc
(1975) 12 known	—	—	—	—	—	—	3,750

KM# Tn78 • Copper • Note: Similar to "Halfpenny" with date on reverse.

Date	AG	Good	VG	Fine	VF	XF	Unc
1795 very rare	—	—	—	—	—	—	—

Note: Roper $6,600

KM# Tn81.2 • Copper • Rev. Legend: NORTH WALES **Edge:** Lettered.

Date	AG	Good	VG	Fine	VF	XF	Unc
(1975)	120	250	400	600	950	2,000	4,500

HALFPENNY

KM# Tn56 • Copper • Obv. Legend: LIVERPOOL HALFPENNY

Date	AG	Good	VG	Fine	VF	XF	Unc
1791	300	450	550	850	1,650	2,350	—

KM# Tn66.1 • **Copper** • **Rev:** Ship **Edge:** Lettered.

Date	AG	Good	VG	Fine	VF	XF	Unc
1793	20.00	30.00	60.00	110	235	500	—

KM# Tn66.2 • **Copper** • **Rev:** Ship **Edge:** Plain.

Date	AG	Good	VG	Fine	VF	XF	Unc
1793 5 known	—	—	—	— 2,000	—	—

KM# Tn75.1 • **Copper** • **Obv:** Large coat buttons **Rev:** Grate **Edge:** Reeded.

Date	AG	Good	VG	Fine	VF	XF	Unc
1795	12.00	20.00	30.00	60.00	120	265	575

KM# Tn75.2 • **Copper** • **Rev:** Grate **Edge:** Lettered.

Date	AG	Good	VG	Fine	VF	XF	Unc
1795	45.00	85.00	165	225	300	625	1,200

KM# Tn75.3 • **Copper** • **Obv:** Small coat buttons **Rev:** Grate **Edge:** Reeded.

Date	AG	Good	VG	Fine	VF	XF	Unc
1795	10.00	35.00	60.00	100.00	175	375	850

KM# Tn76.1 • **Copper** • **Obv. Legend:** LIBERTY AND SECURITY. **Edge:** Plain.

Date	AG	Good	VG	Fine	VF	XF	Unc
1795	18.00	35.00	60.00	100.00	175	435	975

KM# Tn76.2 • **Copper** • **Edge:** Lettered. **Edge Lettering:** PAYABLE AT LONDON ...

Date	AG	Good	VG	Fine	VF	XF	Unc
1795	12.00	20.00	30.00	60.00	125	375	800

KM# Tn76.3 • **Copper** • **Edge:** Lettered. **Edge Lettering:** BIRMINGHAM ...

Date	AG	Good	VG	Fine	VF	XF	Unc
1795	14.00	22.00	35.00	70.00	150	425	950

KM# Tn76.4 • **Copper** • **Edge:** Lettered. **Edge Lettering:** AN ASYLUM ...

Date	AG	Good	VG	Fine	VF	XF	Unc
1795	18.00	35.00	60.00	100.00	225	450	1,000

KM# Tn76.5 • **Copper** • **Edge:** Lettered. **Edge Lettering:** PAYABLE AT LIVERPOOL ...

Date	AG	Good	VG	Fine	VF	XF	Unc
1795 unique	—	—	—	—	—	—	—

KM# Tn76.6 • **Copper** • **Edge:** Lettered. **Edge Lettering:** PAYABLE AT LONDON-LIVERPOOL.

Date	AG	Good	VG	Fine	VF	XF	Unc
1795 unique	—	—	—	—	—	—	—

KM# Tn81.1 • **Copper** • **Rev. Legend:** NORTH WALES **Edge:** Plain.

Date	AG	Good	VG	Fine	VF	XF	Unc
(ca.1795)	25.00	45.00	85.00	145	250	550	1,450

KM# Tn82 • **Copper** • **Rev:** Four stars at bottom **Rev. Legend:** NORTH WALES

Date	AG	Good	VG	Fine	VF	XF	Unc
(1795)	200	400	700	1,500	2,850	5,500	—

CENT

KM# Tn39 • **Copper** • **Obv. Legend:** UNITY STATES

Date	AG	Good	VG	Fine	VF	XF	Unc
1783	12.00	22.00	40.00	70.00	160	325	—

KM# Tn40 • **Copper** • **Note:** Double head.

Date	AG	Good	VG	Fine	VF	XF	Unc
(1783)	10.00	20.00	35.00	65.00	135	300	—

KM# Tn41 • Copper • Obv: "Ugly head." **Note:** 3 known in copper, 1 in white metal.

Date	AG	Good	VG	Fine	VF	XF	Unc
1784	—	—	—	—	—	—	—

Note: Roper $14,850

KM# Tn57 • Copper • Rev: Small eagle

Date	AG	Good	VG	Fine	VF	XF	Unc
1791	30.00	60.00	125	250	335	675	—

KM# Tn58 • Copper • Rev: Large eagle

Date	AG	Good	VG	Fine	VF	XF	Unc
1791	35.00	65.00	145	275	375	725	—

KM# Tn65 • Copper • Obv: "Roman" head

Date	Good	VG	Fine	VF	XF	Unc	Proof
1792	—	—	—	—	—	—	17,600

HALF DOLLAR

KM# Tn59.1 • Copper • Edge: Lettered. **Edge Lettering:** UNITED STATES OF AMERICA

Date	AG	Good	VG	Fine	VF	XF	Unc
1792 2 known	—	—	—	—	—	—	—

Note: Roper $2,860. Benson, EF, $48,300

KM# Tn59.2 • Copper • Edge: Plain.

Date	AG	Good	VG	Fine	VF	XF	Unc
1792 3 known	—	—	—	—	—	—	—

KM# Tn59.1a • Silver • Edge: Lettered. **Edge Lettering:** UNITED STATES OF AMERICA

Date	AG	Good	VG	Fine	VF	XF	Unc
1792 rare	—	—	—	—	—	—	—

Note: Roper $35,200

KM# Tn59.2a • Silver • Edge: Plain.

Date	AG	Good	VG	Fine	VF	XF	Unc
1792 rare	—	—	—	—	—	—	—

KM# Tn59.1b • Gold • Edge: Lettered. **Edge Lettering:** UNITED STATES OF AMERICA

Date	AG	Good	VG	Fine	VF	XF	Unc
1792 unique	—	—	—	—	—	—	—

KM# Tn63.1 • Silver • Rev: Small eagle **Edge:** Plain.

Date	AG	Good	VG	Fine	VF	XF	Unc
1792				12,50	20,00	37,50	
	4,500	7,000	9,000	0	0	0	—

KM# Tn63.2 • Silver • Edge: Ornamented, circles and squares.

Date	AG	Good	VG	Fine	VF	XF	Unc
1792 5 known	—	—	—	—	—	—	—

KM# Tn63.1a • Copper • Edge: Plain.

Date	AG	Good	VG	Fine	VF	XF	Unc
1792	750	1,500	3,500	5,750	8,500	—	—

Note: Garrett $32,000

KM# Tn63.3 • Silver • Edge: Two olive leaves.

Date	AG	Good	VG	Fine	VF	XF	Unc
1792 unique	—	—	—	—	—	—	—

KM# Tn64 • Silver • Rev: Large heraldic eagle

Date	AG	Good	VG	Fine	VF	XF	Unc
1792 unique	—	—	—	—	—	—	—

Note: Garrett $16,500

EARLY AMERICAN PATTERNS

Confederatio

KM# EA22 • Copper • Rev: Small circle of stars.

Date	AG	Good	VG	Fine	VF	XF	Unc
1785	—	—	—	—	8,800	16,500	—

KM# EA23 • **Copper** • **Rev:** Large circle of stars. **Note:** The Confederatio dies were struck in combination with 13 other dies of the period. All surviving examples of these combinations are extremely rare.

Date	AG Good	VG	Fine	VF	XF	Unc
1785 extremely rare	—	—	—	—	—	—

Immune Columbia

KM# EA20 • **Copper** • **Obv:** George III.

Date	AG	Good	VG	Fine	VF	XF	Unc
1785		750	1,250	1,850	2,250	5,000	9,000	—

KM# EA21 • **Copper** • **Obv:** Vermon.

Date	AG	Good	VG	Fine	VF	XF	Unc
1785		600	1,000	1,650	2,000	4,750	8,500	—

KM# EA17a • **Silver** • **Rev. Legend:** CONSTELLATIO.

Date	AG	Good	VG	Fine	VF	XF	Unc
1785	—	—	—	—	—	20,700	—

KM# EA19a • **Gold** • **Rev. Legend:** CONSTELATIO.

Date	AG	Good	VG	Fine	VF	XF	Unc
1785 unique	—	—	—	—	—	—	—

KM# EA17 • **Copper** • **Rev. Legend:** CONSTELLATIO.

Date	AG	Good	VG	Fine	VF	XF	Unc
1785	—	—	—	—	—14,375	—

KM# EA18 • **Copper** • **Obv. Legend:** Extra star in border. **Rev. Legend:** CONSTELLATIO.

Date	AG	Good	VG	Fine	VF	XF	Unc
1785	—	—	—	—	—	—	—

Note: Caldwell $4,675

KM# EA19 • **Copper** • **Rev:** Blunt rays.

Date	AG	Good	VG	Fine	VF	XF	Unc
1785 2 known	—	—	—	—	—	—

Note: Norweb $22,000

KM# EA28 • **Copper** • **Obv. Legend:** IMMUNIS COLUMBIA. **Rev:** Eagle.

Date	AG	Good	VG	Fine	VF	XF	Unc
1786 3 known	—	—	—	—	—	—

KM# EA24 • **Copper** • **Obv:** Washington.

Date	AG	Good	VG	Fine	VF	XF	Unc
1786 3 known	—	—	—	—	—	—

Note: Garrett $50,000. Steinberg $12,650

KM# EA25 • **Copper** • **Obv:** Eagle.

Date	AG	Good	VG	Fine	VF	XF	Unc
1786 unique	—	—	—	—	—	—

Note: Garrett $37,500

KM# EA26 • **Copper** • **Obv:** Washington. **Rev:** Eagle.

Date	AG	Good	VG	Fine	VF	XF	Unc
1786 2 known	—	—	—	—	—	—

KM# EA27 • **Copper** • **Obv. Legend:** IMMUNIS COLUMBIA.

Date	AG	Good	VG	Fine	VF	XF	Unc
1786 extremely rare	—	—	—	—	—	—

Note: Rescigno, AU, $33,000. Steinberg, VF, $11,000

Nova Constellatio

KM# EA6.1 • Copper • Obv: Pointed rays. **Obv. Legend:** CONSTELLATIO. **Rev:** Small "US".

Date	AG	Good	VG	Fine	VF	XF	Unc
1783	20.00	35.00	65.00	125	255	585	—

KM# EA6.2 • Copper • Obv: Pointed rays. **Obv. Legend:** CONSTELLATIO. **Rev:** Large "US".

Date	AG	Good	VG	Fine	VF	XF	Unc
1783	20.00	35.00	70.00	140	285	650	—

KM# EA7 • Copper • Obv: Blunt rays. **Obv. Legend:** CONSTELATIO.

Date	AG	Good	VG	Fine	VF	XF	Unc
1783	22.00	40.00	80.00	150	350	750	—

KM# EA8 • Copper • Obv: Blunt rays. **Obv. Legend:** CONSTELATIO.

Date	AG	Good	VG	Fine	VF	XF	Unc
1785	22.00	40.00	80.00	160	375	775	—

KM# EA9 • Copper • Obv: Pointed rays. **Obv. Legend:** CONSTELLATIO.

Date	AG	Good	VG	Fine	VF	XF	Unc
1785	20.00	35.00	70.00	140	285	650	—

KM# EA10 • Copper • Note: Contemporary circulating counterfeit. Similar to previously listed coin.

Date	AG	Good	VG	Fine	VF	XF	Unc
1786 extremely rare	—	—	—	—	—	—	—

5 UNITS

KM# EA12 • Copper •

Date	AG	Good	VG	Fine	VF	XF	Unc
1783 unique	—	—	—	—	—	—	—

100 (BIT)

KM# EA13.1 • Silver • Edge: Leaf.

Date	AG	Good	VG	Fine	VF	XF	Unc
1783 2 known	—	—	—	—	—	—	—

Note: Garrett $97,500. Stack's auction, May 1991, $72,500

KM# EA13.2 • Silver • Edge: Plain.

Date	AG	Good	VG	Fine	VF	XF	Unc
1783 unique	—	—	—	—	—	—	—

500 (QUINT)

KM# EA14 • Silver • Obv. Legend: NOVA CONSTELLATIO

Date	AG	Good	VG	Fine	VF	XF	Unc
1783 unique	—	—	—	—	—	—	—

Note: Garrett $165,000

KM# EA15 • Silver • Obv: Without legend

Date	AG	Good	VG	Fine	VF	XF	Unc
1783 unique	—	—	—	—	—	—	—

Note: Garrett $55,000

1000 (MARK)

KM# EA16 • Silver •

Date	AG	Good	VG	Fine	VF	XF	Unc
1783 unique	—	—	—	—	—	—	—

Note: Garrett $190,000

EARLY FEDERAL COINAGE

Brasher

KM# Tn51.1 • Gold • Obv: Sunrise over mountains. **Rev:** Displayed eagle with shield on breast, EB counterstamp on wing.

Date	AG	Good	VG	Fine	VF	XF	Unc
1787 6 known	—	—	—	—	—	—	—

Note: Heritage FUN Sale, January 2005, AU-55, $2.415 million.

KM# Tn51.2 • Gold • Obv: Sun rise over mountains **Rev:** Displayed eagle with sheild on breast. EB counterstamp on breast.

Date	AG	Good	VG	Fine	VF	XF	Unc
1787 unique	—	—	—	—	—	—	—

Note: Heritage FUN Sale, January 2005, XF-45, $2.99 million

Fugio "Cent"

KM# EA30.1 • Copper • Obv: Club rays, round ends.

Date	AG	Good	VG	Fine	VF	XF	Unc
1787	40.00	75.00	150	375	850	1,600	—

KM# EA30.2 • Copper • Obv: Club rays, concave ends.

Date	AG	Good	VG	Fine	VF	XF	Unc
1787	250	700	1,800	2,750	5,000	—	—

KM# EA30.3 • Copper • Obv. Legend: FUCIO.

Date	AG	Good	VG	Fine	VF	XF	Unc
1787	—	750	1,850	2,850	55,000	—	—

KM# EA31.1 • Copper • Obv: Pointed rays. **Rev:** UNITED above, STATES below.

Date	AG	Good	VG	Fine	VF	XF	Unc
1787	100.00	250	550	1,000	1,500	3,500	—

KM# EA31.2 • Copper • Rev: UNITED STATES at sides of ring.

Date	AG	Good	VG	Fine	VF	XF	Unc
1787	20.00	45.00	90.00	175	300	650	—

KM# EA31.3 • Copper • Rev: STATES UNITED at sides of ring.

Date	AG	Good	VG	Fine	VF	XF	Unc
1787	25.00	55.00	110	220	350	700	—

KM# EA31.4 • Copper • Rev: Eight-pointed stars on ring.

Date	AG	Good	VG	Fine	VF	XF	Unc
1787	30.00	65.00	120	250	400	800	—

KM# EA31.5 • **Copper** • **Rev:** Raised rims on ring, large lettering in center.

Date	AG	Good	VG	Fine	VF	XF	Unc
1787	35.00	75.00	135	275	450	950	—

KM# EA32.1 • **Copper** • **Obv:** No cinquefoils, cross after date. **Obv. Legend:** UNITED STATES.

Date	AG	Good	VG	Fine	VF	XF	Unc
1787	50.00	110	250	425	650	1,250	—

KM# EA32.2 • **Copper** • **Obv:** No cinquefoils, cross after date. **Obv. Legend:** STATES UNITED.

Date	AG	Good	VG	Fine	VF	XF	Unc
1787	60.00	110	250	425	650	1,250	—

KM# EA32.3 • **Copper** • **Obv:** No cinquefoils, cross after date. **Rev:** Raised rims on ring.

Date	AG	Good	VG	Fine	VF	XF	Unc
1787	—	—	—	—	2,600	—	—

KM# EA33 • **Copper** • **Obv:** No cinquefoils, cross after date. **Rev:** With rays. **Rev. Legend:** AMERICAN CONGRESS.

Date	AG	Good	VG	Fine	VF	XF	Unc
1787 extremely rare	—	—	—	—	—	—	—

Note: Norweb $63,800

KM# EA34 • **Brass** • **Note:** New Haven restrike.

Date	AG	Good	VG	Fine	VF	XF	Unc
1787	—	—	—	—	—	—	500

KM# EA34a • **Copper** • **Note:** New Haven restrike.

Date	AG	Good	VG	Fine	VF	XF	Unc
1787	—	—	—	—	—	500	—

KM# EA34b • **Silver** • **Note:** New Haven restrike.

Date	AG	Good	VG	Fine	VF	XF	Unc
1787	—	—	—	—	—	—	1,850

KM# EA34c • **Gold** • **Note:** New Haven restrike.

Date	AG	Good	VG	Fine	VF	XF	Unc
1787 2 known	—	—	—	—	—	—	—

Note: Norweb (holed) $1,430

ISSUES OF 1792

CENT

KM# PnE1 • **Copper Around Silver** • **Note:** Silver plug in center.

Date	AG	Good	VG	Fine	VF	XF	Unc
1792 12 known	—	—	—	—	—	—	—

Note: Norweb, MS-60, $143,000

KM# PnF1 • **Copper** • **Note:** No silver center.

Date	AG	Good	VG	Fine	VF	XF	Unc
1792 8 known	—	—	—	—	—	—	—

Note: Norweb, EF-40, $35,200; Benson, VG-10, $57,500

KM# PnG1 • **Copper** • **Edge:** Plain **Note:** Commonly called "Birch cent."

Date	AG	Good	VG	Fine	VF	XF	Unc
1792 unique	—	—	—	—	—	—	—

KM# PnH1 • **Copper** • **Obv:** One star in edge legend **Note:** Commonly called "Birch cent."

Date	AG	Good	VG	Fine	VF	XF	Unc
1792 2 known	—	—	—	—	—	—	—

Note: Norweb, EF-40, $59,400

KM# PnI1 • **Copper** • **Obv:** Two stars in edge legend **Note:** Commonly called "Birch cent."

Date	AG	Good	VG	Fine	VF	XF	Unc
1792 6 known	—	—	—	—	—	—	—

Note: Hawn, strong VF, $57,750

KM# PnJ1 • **White Metal** • **Rev:** "G.W.Pt." below wreath tie **Note:** Commonly called "Birch cent."

Date	AG	Good	VG	Fine	VF	XF	Unc
1792 unique	—	—	—	—	—	—	—

Note: Garrett, $90,000

HALF DISME

KM# 5 • Silver •

Date	AG	Good	VG	Fine	VF	XF	Unc
1792	1,250	—	3,500	6,500	8,500	16,500	—

KM# PnA1 • Copper •

Date	AG	Good	VG	Fine	VF	XF	Unc
1792	unique	—	—	—	—	—	—

DISME

KM# PnB1 • Silver •

Date	AG	Good	VG	Fine	VF	XF	Unc
1792	3 known	—	—	—	—	—	—

Note: Norweb, EF-40, $28,600

KM# PnC1 • Copper • Edge: Reeded

Date	AG	Good	VG	Fine	VF	XF	Unc
1792	14 known	—	—	—	—	—	—

Note: Hawn, VF, $30,800; Benson, EF-45, $109,250

KM# PnD1 • Copper • Edge: Plain

Date	AG	Good	VG	Fine	VF	XF	Unc
1792	2 known	—	—	—	—	—	—

Note: Garrett, $45,000

QUARTER

KM# PnK1 • Copper • Edge: Reeded **Note:** Commonly called "Wright quarter."

Date	AG	Good	VG	Fine	VF	XF	Unc
1792	2 known	—	—	—	—	—	—

KM# PnL1 • White Metal • Edge: Plain **Note:** Commonly called "Wright quarter."

Date	AG	Good	VG	Fine	VF	XF	Unc
1792	2 known	—	—	—	—	—	—

Note: Norweb, VF-30 to EF-40, $28,600

KM# PnM1 • White Metal • Note: Commonly called "Wright quarter."

Date	AG	Good	VG	Fine	VF	XF	Unc
1792	die trial	—	—	—	—	—	—

Note: Garrett, $12,000

UNITED STATES

CIRCULATION COINAGE

HALF CENT

Liberty Cap
Head facing left obverse

KM# 10 • 6.7400 g., **Copper**, 22 mm. • **Designer:** Henry Voigt

Date	Mintage	G-4	VG-8	F-12	VF-20	XF-40	MS-60
1793	35,334	2,000	2,750	4,200	6,000	12,500	35,000

Head facing right obverse

KM# 14 • **Copper**, 6.74 g. (1794-95) and 5.44 g. (1795-97), 23.5 mm. • **Designer:** Robert Scot (1794) and John Smith Gardner (1795) **Notes:** The "lettered edge" varieties have "Two Hundred for a Dollar" inscribed around the edge. The "pole" varieties have a pole upon which the cap is hanging, resting on Liberty's shoulder. The "punctuated date" varieties have a comma after the 1 in the date. The 1797 "1 above 1" variety has a second 1 above the 1 in the date.

Date	Mintage	G-4	VG-8	F-12	VF-20	XF-40	MS-60
1794	81,600	400	650	900	1,600	3,500	18,000
1795 lettered edge, pole	25,600	450	700	950	1,500	4,250	17,500
1795 plain edge, no pole	109,000	375	475	800	1,400	3,500	16,000
1795 lettered edge, punctuated date	Inc. above	475	700	1,000	1,600	3,750	20,000
1795 plain edge, punctuated date	Inc. above	350	450	750	1,200	3,000	27,500
1796 pole	5,090	16,000	20,000	23,500	30,000	35,000	—
1796 no pole	1,390	27,000	32,500	47,500	90,000	—	—
1797 plain edge	119,215	400	575	950	1,900	6,000	27,500
1797 lettered edge	Inc. above	1,700	2,700	4,000	8,000	25,000	—
1797 1 above 1	Inc. above	375	475	950	1,600	3,250	20,000
1797 gripped edge	Inc. above	16,000	37,500	48,000	60,000	70,000	—

Draped Bust Half Cent

Stemless   Stems

KM# 33 • 5.4400 g., **Copper**, 23.5 mm. • **Designer:** Robert Scot **Notes:** The wreath on the reverse was redesigned slightly in 1802, resulting in "reverse of 1800" and "reverse of 1802" varieties. The "stems" varieties have stems extending from the wreath above and on both sides of the fraction on the reverse. On the 1804 "crosslet 4" variety, a serif appears at the far right of the crossbar on the 4 in the date. The "spiked chin" variety appears to have a spike extending from Liberty's chin, the result of a damaged die. Varieties of the 1805 strikes are distinguished by the size of the 5 in the date. Varieties of the 1806 strikes are distinguished by the size of the 6 in the date.

Date	Mintage	G-4	VG-8	F-12	VF-20	XF-40	MS-60
1800	211,530	50.00	75.00	100.00	200	500	2,500
1802/0 rev. 1800	14,366	15,000	22,000	30,000	—	—	—
1802/0 rev. 1802	Inc. above	800	1,400	2,750	6,500	17,000	—

Date	Mintage	G-4	VG-8	F-12	VF-20	XF-40	MS-60
1803	97,900	45.00	70.00	125	275	950	7,000
1804 plain 4, stemless wreath	1,055,312	50.00	60.00	85.00	130	250	1,400
1804 plain 4, stems	Inc. above	45.00	75.00	125	250	1,500	12,000
1804 crosslet 4, stemless	Inc. above	50.00	75.00	85.00	125	250	1,350
1804 crosslet 4, stems	Inc. above	47.00	75.00	110	175	300	1,200
1804 spiked chin	Inc. above	60.00	90.00	125	175	325	1,200
1805 small 5, stemless	814,464	50.00	75.00	90.00	135	400	3,500
1805 small 5, stems	Inc. above	800	1,200	2,400	4,500	8,000	—
1805 large 5, stems	Inc. above	49.00	65.00	85.00	125	400	3,000
1806 small 6, stems	356,000	200	325	600	1,000	2,750	—
1806 small 6, stemless	Inc. above	50.00	65.00	85.00	125	235	1,350
1806 large 6, stems	Inc. above	50.00	65.00	85.00	125	250	1,200
1807	476,000	50.00	80.00	120	175	300	1,400
1808/7	400,000	300	400	600	1,200	6,000	27,500
1808	Inc. above	50.00	65.00	90.00	135	350	5,000

Classic Head Half Cent

KM# 41 • 5.4400 g., **Copper**, 23.5 mm. • **Designer:** John Reich **Notes:** Restrikes listed were produced privately in the mid-1800s. The 1831 restrikes have two varieties with different-size berries in the wreath on the reverse. The 1828 strikes have either 12 or 13 stars on the obverse.

Date	Mintage	G-4	VG-8	F-12	VF-20	XF-40	MS-60
1809/6	1,154,572	60.00	80.00	110	150	215	1,000
1809	Inc. above	32.00	40.00	55.00	80.00	215	800
1809 circle in 0	—	35.00	45.00	60.00	110	250	2,100
1810	215,000	45.00	60.00	120	200	600	3,250
1811	63,140	225	375	750	1,800	4,000	—
1811 restrike, reverse of 1802, uncirculated	—	—	—	—	—	—	27,500
1825	63,000	45.00	60.00	75.00	110	200	950
1826	234,000	40.00	55.00	75.00	90.00	200	750

1825 Half Cent
Grade F-12

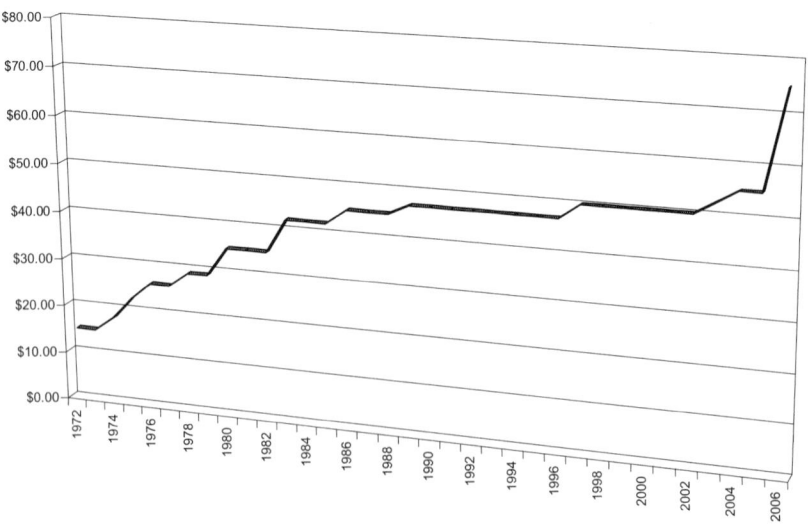

Retail Price

Date	Mintage	G-4	VG-8	F-12	VF-20	XF-40	MS-60
1828 13 stars	606,000	40.00	60.00	75.00	85.00	110	300
1828 12 stars	Inc. above	50.00	80.00	120	175	250	850
1829	487,000	40.00	55.00	70.00	100.00	150	500
1831 original	2,200	5,500	7,500	11,000	16,500	22,500	—
1831 1st restrike, lg. berries, reverse of 1836	—	—	—	—	—	—	6,500
1831 2nd restrike, sm. berries, reverse of 1840, proof	—	—	—	—	—	—	25,000
1832	154,000	39.00	50.00	70.00	95.00	130	350
1833	120,000	39.00	50.00	70.00	95.00	130	350
1834	141,000	39.00	50.00	70.00	95.00	130	350
1835	398,000	39.00	50.00	70.00	95.00	130	350
1836 original, proof	—	—	—	—	—	—	6,000
1836 restrike, reverse of 1840, proof	—	—	—	—	—	—	20,000

Braided Hair Half Cent

KM# 70 • 5.4400 g., **Copper**, 23 mm. • **Designer:** Christian Gobrecht **Notes:** 1840-1849 and 1852 strikes, both originals and restrikes, are known in proof only; mintages are unknown. The small-date varieties of 1849, both originals and restrikes are known in proof only. The Restrikes were produced clandestinely by Philadelphia Mint personnel in the mid-1800s.

Date	Mintage	G-4	VG-8	F-12	VF-20	XF-40	MS-60	Prf-60
1840 original	—	1,000	1,200	1,500	2,000	3,000	—	5,500
1840 1st restrike	—	1,000	1,200	1,500	2,000	3,000	—	6,500
1840 2nd restrike	—	1,000	1,200	1,500	2,000	3,000	—	5,500
1841 original	—	1,000	1,200	1,500	2,000	3,000	—	5,500
1841 1st restrike	—	1,000	1,200	1,500	2,000	3,000	—	6,500
1841 2nd restrike	—	1,000	1,200	1,500	2,000	3,000	—	6,000
1842 original	—	1,000	1,200	1,500	2,000	3,000	—	6,000
1842 1st restrike	—	1,000	1,200	1,500	2,000	3,000	—	6,000
1842 2nd restrike	—	1,000	1,200	1,500	2,000	3,000	—	6,000
1843 original	—	1,000	1,200	1,500	2,000	3,000	—	6,500
1843 1st restrike	—	1,000	1,200	1,500	2,000	3,000	—	6,000
1843 2nd restrike	—	1,000	1,200	1,500	2,000	3,000	—	6,500
1844 original	—	1,000	1,200	1,500	2,000	3,000	—	6,000
1844 1st restrike	—	1,000	1,200	1,500	2,000	3,000	—	6,000
1844 2nd restrike	—	1,000	1,200	1,500	2,000	3,000	—	6,000
1845 original	—	1,000	1,200	1,500	2,000	3,000	—	6,000
1845 1st restrike	—	1,000	1,200	1,500	2,000	3,000	—	6,000
1845 2nd restrike	—	1,000	1,200	1,500	2,000	3,000	—	6,000
1846 original	—	1,000	1,200	1,500	2,000	3,000	—	6,000
1846 1st restrike	—	1,000	1,200	1,500	2,000	3,000	—	6,500
1846 2nd restrike	—	1,000	1,200	1,500	2,000	3,000	—	6,000
1847 original	—	1,000	1,200	1,500	2,000	3,000	—	6,000
1847 1st restrike	—	3,000	4,000	4,500	5,000	5,500	—	8,000
1847 2nd restrike	—	1,000	1,200	1,500	2,000	3,000	—	6,000
1848 original	—	1,000	1,200	1,500	2,000	3,000	—	6,000
1848 1st restrike	—	1,000	1,200	1,500	2,000	3,000	—	6,000
1848 2nd restrike	—	1,000	1,200	1,500	2,000	3,000	—	6,000
1849 original, small date	—	1,000	1,200	1,500	2,000	3,000	—	6,500
1849 1st restrike small date	—	1,000	1,200	1,500	2,000	3,000	—	6,000
1849 large date	39,864	50.00	70.00	90.00	125	175	325	—
1850	39,812	45.00	60.00	90.00	150	200	400	—
1851	147,672	45.00	60.00	75.00	90.00	120	175	—
1852 original	—	12,000	25,000	30,000	35,000	40,000	—	90,000
1852 1st restrike	—	1,000	1,200	1,500	2,000	3,000	—	5,000
1852 2nd restrike	—	1,000	1,200	1,500	2,000	3,000	—	7,000
1853	129,694	50.00	75.00	90.00	125	160	300	—
1854	55,358	50.00	75.00	90.00	125	160	300	—
1855	56,500	50.00	75.00	90.00	125	160	300	—
1856	40,430	50.00	75.00	90.00	125	160	300	—
1857	35,180	80.00	100.00	200	250	300	500	—

CENT
Flowing Hair Cent
Chain reverse

KM# 11 • 13.4800 g., **Copper**, 26-27 mm. • **Designer:** Henry Voigt

Date	Mintage	G-4	VG-8	F-12	VF-20	XF-40	MS-60
1793	36,103	7,750	11,000	15,000	23,000	33,000	135,000

Wreath reverse

KM# 12 • 13.4800 g., **Copper**, 26-28 mm. • **Designer:** Henry Voigt

Date	Mintage	G-4	VG-8	F-12	VF-20	XF-40	MS-60
1793	63,353	1,700	2,500	4,000	8,000	12,000	30,000

Liberty Cap Cent
Thick Planchet

KM# 13 • Copper, 13.48 g. (1793-95) and 10.89 g. (1795-96), 29 mm. • **Designer:** Joseph Wright (1793-1795) and John Smith Gardner (1795-1796) **Notes:** The heavier pieces were struck on a thicker planchet. The Liberty design on the obverse was revised slightly in 1794, but the 1793 design was used on some 1794 strikes. A 1795 "lettered edge" variety has "One Hundred for a Dollar" and a leaf inscribed on the edge.

Date	Mintage	G-4	VG-8	F-12	VF-20	XF-40	MS-60
1793 cap	11,056	5,000	6,000	9,000	20,000	26,000	—
1794	918,521	350	485	750	1,200	3,750	9,000
1794 head '93	Inc. above	1,500	2,600	4,000	7,900	12,000	—
1795	501,500	350	485	650	1,000	2,000	4,750

Thin Planchet

KM# 13a • 10.8900 g., **Copper**, 29 mm. • **Designer:** Joseph Wright (1793-1795) and John Smith Gardner (1795-1796)

Date	Mintage	G-4	VG-8	F-12	VF-20	XF-40	MS-60
1795 lettered edge, "One Cent" high in wreath	37,000	400	550	900	1,750	4,000	15,000

Date				Mintage	G-4	VG-8	F-12	VF-20	XF-40	MS-60
1796				109,825	350	500	800	1,400	3,750	21,000

Draped Bust Cent

Stemless   Stems

KM# 22 • 10.9800 g., **Copper**, 29 mm. • **Designer:** Robert Scot **Notes:** The "stemless" variety does not have stems extending from the wreath above and on both sides of the fraction on the reverse. The 1801 "3 errors" variety has the fraction on the reverse reading "1/000," has only one stem extending from the wreath above and on both sides of the fraction on the reverse, and "United" in "United States of America" appears as "linited."

Date	Mintage	G-4	VG-8	F-12	VF-20	XF-40	MS-60
1796	363,375	350	600	850	1,800	3,400	—
1797	897,510	130	175	250	335	1,150	3,300
1797 stemless	Inc. above	300	495	600	910	3,200	—
1798	1,841,745	90.00	130	200	350	1,300	3,100
1798/7	Inc. above	200	300	375	1,200	3,900	—
1799	42,540	3,500	5,000	8,500	16,000	35,000	—
1800	2,822,175	50.00	95.00	200	400	1,750	—
1801	1,362,837	60.00	87.00	180	325	1,000	—
1801 3 errors	Inc. above	225	500	925	1,750	5,500	—
1802	3,435,100	50.00	75.00	150	250	775	2,250
1803	2,471,353	50.00	80.00	150	250	775	2,250
1804	96,500	1,400	2,000	2,600	3,200	7,000	—
1804 Restrike of 1860	—	400	500	700	900	1,100	1,500
1805	941,116	60.00	90.00	160	300	875	2,450
1806	348,000	70.00	100.00	150	375	1,100	4,700
1807	727,221	60.00	80.00	160	300	800	2,250
1807/6 large 7/6	—	60.00	80.00	160	350	1,275	—
1807/6 small 7/6	—	1,900	2,900	4,200	6,000	19,000	—

1804 Cent
Grade F-12

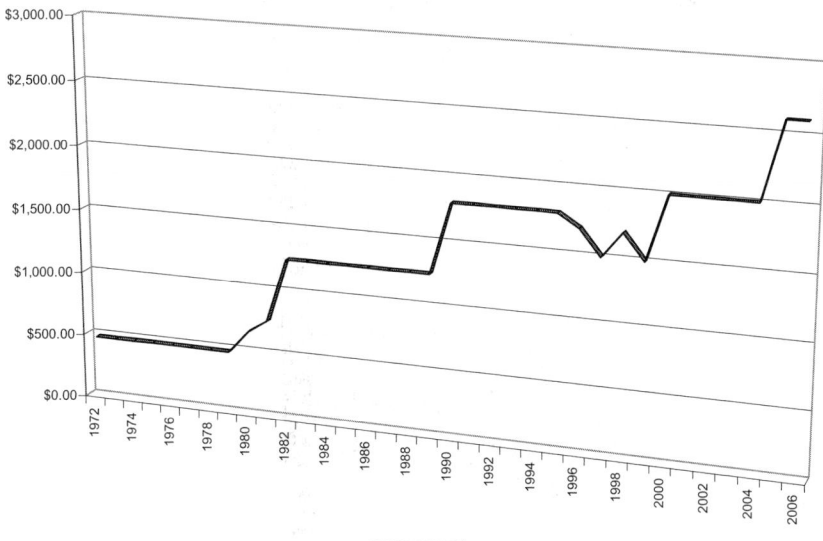

■ Retail Price

Classic Head Cent

KM# 39 • 10.8900 g., Copper, 29 mm. • Designer: John Reich

Date	Mintage	G-4	VG-8	F-12	VF-20	XF-40	MS-60
1808	1,109,000	125	200	325	575	1,200	3,600
1809	222,867	250	350	600	1,200	2,650	6,300
1810	1,458,500	75.00	95.00	210	550	1,100	3,850
1811	218,025	110	175	400	1,000	1,500	7,000
1811/10	Inc. above	130	200	440	1,200	2,200	—
1812	1,075,500	48.00	83.00	200	525	975	2,800
1813	418,000	60.00	175	400	800	1,200	—
1814	357,830	45.00	80.00	200	530	975	2,800

Coronet Cent

KM# 45 • 10.8900 g., Copper, 28-29 mm. • Designer: John Reich **Notes:** The 1817 strikes have either 13 or 15 stars on the obverse.

Date	Mintage	G-4	VG-8	F-12	VF-20	XF-40	MS-60
1816	2,820,982	25.00	35.00	50.00	100.00	175	420
1817 13 stars	3,948,400	25.00	35.00	45.00	75.00	145	500
1817 15 stars	Inc. above	35.00	50.00	90.00	225	500	1,600
1818	3,167,000	25.00	30.00	35.00	60.00	125	270
1819	2,671,000	25.00	30.00	35.00	63.00	120	285
1820	4,407,550	25.00	30.00	35.00	65.00	120	300
1821	389,000	40.00	75.00	250	400	1,500	6,000
1822	2,072,339	25.00	35.00	50.00	100.00	195	750
1823 Included in 1824 mintage	—	90.00	200	310	690	2,750	—
1823/22 Included in 1824 mintage	—	80.00	110	300	675	2,450	—
1823 Restrike	—	600	750	850	1,000	1,200	2,000
1824	1,262,000	25.00	26.00	38.00	160	350	950
1824/22	Inc. above	35.00	45.00	100.00	400	975	3,600
1825	1,461,100	25.00	35.00	50.00	110	300	960
1826	1,517,425	25.00	35.00	40.00	84.00	175	750
1826/25	Inc. above	30.00	40.00	75.00	175	600	2,000
1827	2,357,732	25.00	35.00	40.00	75.00	160	750
1828	2,260,624	25.00	35.00	40.00	90.00	175	450
1829	1,414,500	25.00	35.00	40.00	90.00	175	475
1830	1,711,500	25.00	35.00	40.00	90.00	175	400
1831	3,359,260	25.00	35.00	40.00	80.00	175	315
1832	2,362,000	25.00	35.00	40.00	80.00	175	380
1833	2,739,000	25.00	35.00	40.00	80.00	175	300
1834	1,855,100	25.00	35.00	40.00	80.00	175	375
1835	3,878,400	25.00	35.00	40.00	80.00	200	300
1836	2,111,000	25.00	35.00	40.00	80.00	175	350
1837	5,558,300	25.00	30.00	40.00	80.00	175	300
1838	6,370,200	25.00	30.00	45.00	80.00	175	300
1839	3,128,661	30.00	40.00	65.00	90.00	175	350
1839/36	Inc. above	425	700	850	1,500	3,900	—

Braided Hair Cent

KM# 67 • 10.8900 g., **Copper**, 27.5 mm. • **Designer:** Christian Gobrecht **Notes:** 1840 and 1842 strikes are known with both small and large dates, with little difference in value. 1855 and 1856 strikes are known with both slanting and upright 5s in the date, with little difference in value. A slightly larger Liberty head and larger reverse lettering were used beginning in 1843. One 1843 variety uses the old obverse with the new reverse.

Date	Mintage	G-4	VG-8	F-12	VF-20	XF-40	MS-60
1840	2,462,700	20.00	30.00	40.00	50.00	70.00	475
1841	1,597,367	20.00	30.00	40.00	50.00	80.00	440
1842	2,383,390	20.00	30.00	40.00	50.00	70.00	425
1843	2,425,342	20.00	30.00	40.00	50.00	75.00	445
1843 obverse 1842 with reverse of 1844	Inc. above	20.00	30.00	40.00	50.00	80.00	400
1844	2,398,752	20.00	30.00	40.00	50.00	75.00	300
1844/81	Inc. above	65.00	125	225	300	400	850
1845	3,894,804	20.00	30.00	40.00	50.00	75.00	250
1846	4,120,800	20.00	30.00	40.00	50.00	75.00	250
1847	6,183,669	20.00	30.00	40.00	50.00	75.00	250
1848	6,415,799	20.00	30.00	40.00	50.00	75.00	250
1849	4,178,500	20.00	30.00	40.00	50.00	75.00	325
1850	4,426,844	20.00	30.00	40.00	50.00	75.00	250
1851	9,889,707	20.00	30.00	40.00	50.00	75.00	200
1851/81	Inc. above	50.00	75.00	125	175	290	600
1852	5,063,094	20.00	30.00	40.00	50.00	75.00	200
1853	6,641,131	20.00	30.00	40.00	50.00	75.00	200
1854	4,236,156	20.00	30.00	40.00	50.00	75.00	200
1855	1,574,829	20.00	30.00	40.00	50.00	75.00	200
1856	2,690,463	20.00	30.00	40.00	50.00	75.00	200
1857	333,456	150	175	200	225	300	600

1857 Cent
Grade XF-40

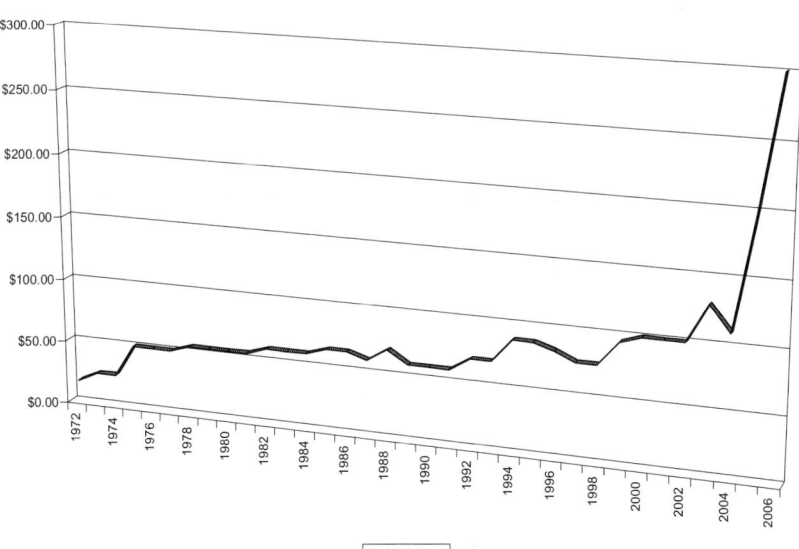

Retail Price

Flying Eagle Cent

   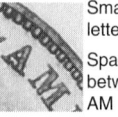

Large letters

AM touch at bottom

Small letters

Space between AM

KM# 85 • 4.6700 g., **Copper-Nickel**, 19 mm. • **Designer:** James B. Longacre **Notes:** On the large-letter variety of 1858, the "A" and "M" in "America" are connected at their bases; on the small-letter variety, the two letters are separated.

Date	Mintage	G-4	VG-8	F-12	VF-20	XF-40	AU-50	MS-60	MS-65	Prf-65
1856	Est. 2,500	6,250	7,250	9,000	12,500	14,000	13,500	17,500	62,500	30,000
1857	17,450,000	21.00	32.50	35.00	45.00	130	165	320	3,750	31,000
1858/7	—	65.00	92.50	180	400	790	1,500	3,400	60,000	—
1858 large letters	24,600,000	21.00	35.00	39.00	57.50	150	225	350	3,950	25,500
1858 small letters	Inc. above	21.00	32.50	35.00	45.00	130	175	320	3,700	31,000

Indian Head Cent

KM# 87 • 4.6700 g., **Copper-Nickel**, 19 mm. • **Designer:** James B. Longacre

Date	Mintage	G-4	VG-8	F-12	VF-20	XF-40	AU-50	MS-60	MS-65	Prf-65
1859	36,400,000	12.50	15.00	22.50	47.50	100.00	175	215	3,200	5,000

Shield added at top of wreath reverse

KM# 90 • 4.6700 g., **Copper-Nickel**, 19 mm. • **Designer:** James B. Longacre

Date	Mintage	G-4	VG-8	F-12	VF-20	XF-40	AU-50	MS-60	MS-65	Prf-65
1860	20,566,000(1,000)	11.00	15.00	22.00	34.00	70.00	100.00	200	1,000	3,900
1861	10,100,000	20.00	30.00	41.00	60.00	90.00	160	180	1,000	7,500
1862	28,075,000	7.50	9.00	10.00	14.50	27.50	55.00	80.00	1,000	2,400
1863	49,840,000	7.50	9.00	10.00	11.00	24.00	54.00	72.50	1,000	3,500
1864	13,740,000	15.00	20.00	34.00	52.50	73.50	99.00	150	1,250	3,250

1864-L Indian Cent
Grade F-12

Indian Head Cent

1864 "L"

KM# 90a • 3.1100 g., **Bronze**, 19 mm. • **Designer:** James B. Longacre **Notes:** The 1864 "L" variety has the designer's initial in Liberty's hair to the right of her neck.

Date	Mintage	G-4	VG-8	F-12	VF-20	XF-40	AU-50	MS-60	MS-65	Prf-65
1864	39,233,714	6.50	12.50	22.00	37.50	60.00	75.00	90.00	325	4,300
1864 L	Inc. above	52.50	65.00	130	175	275	310	400	1,650	110,000
1865	35,429,286	6.00	10.00	17.50	23.00	35.00	50.00	80.00	450	1,550
1866	9,826,500	40.00	56.00	75.00	110	180	215	250	1,250	950
1867	9,821,000	50.00	60.00	85.00	110	175	210	265	1,250	1,050
1868	10,266,500	37.50	40.00	65.00	110	160	190	220	1,000	985
1869/9	6,420,000	110	170	350	495	670	750	775	1,900	—
1869	Inc. above	72.50	100.00	220	325	400	475	510	1,650	950
1870	5,275,000	55.00	90.00	200	285	375	440	515	1,600	1,075
1871	3,929,500	77.50	100.00	300	350	450	500	425	2,550	1,100
1872	4,042,000	90.00	160	375	440	575	700	775	4,100	1,100
1873	11,676,500	21.00	30.00	46.00	80.00	150	190	215	1,300	850
1874	14,187,500	15.00	22.00	35.00	57.50	100.00	125	170	700	800
1875	13,528,000	15.00	27.50	53.50	70.00	110	150	175	800	1,500
1876	7,944,000	27.00	35.00	70.00	130	210	265	315	1,100	925
1877	852,500	750	900	1,350	1,900	2,500	3,250	3,750	9,350	6,750
1878	5,799,850	26.00	35.00	65.00	135	225	265	315	900	490
1879	16,231,200	7.00	10.00	16.00	33.00	65.00	72.50	75.00	350	450
1880	38,964,955	4.00	6.00	8.00	11.00	25.00	37.50	60.00	350	435
1881	39,211,575	4.00	5.00	7.00	10.00	18.00	30.00	40.00	330	425
1882	38,581,100	4.00	6.00	8.00	11.00	18.00	30.00	37.50	330	425
1883	45,589,109	3.00	4.50	7.00	10.00	16.00	24.00	38.50	330	425
1884	23,261,742	4.00	6.00	8.00	14.00	27.00	38.00	65.00	500	425
1885	11,765,384	6.00	8.00	15.00	29.00	54.00	65.00	95.00	750	425
1886	17,654,290	4.00	6.00	19.00	55.00	120	150	160	1,250	500
1887	45,226,483	2.00	3.00	4.00	6.00	15.00	28.00	50.00	395	475
1888	37,494,414	2.00	2.50	4.00	7.00	20.00	28.00	42.00	950	525
1889	48,869,361	1.75	2.20	2.50	4.00	10.00	27.00	35.00	395	450
1890	57,182,854	1.50	2.00	2.50	4.00	10.00	22.00	35.00	395	500
1891	47,072,350	1.70	2.25	3.00	4.50	10.00	22.00	35.00	400	520
1892	37,649,832	2.00	2.25	3.00	5.00	16.00	20.00	34.00	395	525
1893	46,642,195	1.85	2.75	3.00	5.00	10.00	22.00	30.00	340	540
1894	16,752,132	3.50	5.00	10.00	20.00	45.00	55.00	70.00	375	525
1895	38,343,636	1.75	2.20	3.00	6.00	12.00	22.00	32.00	200	475
1896	39,057,293	1.50	2.20	2.75	5.00	10.00	21.00	33.00	230	425
1897	50,466,330	1.50	2.00	2.25	4.00	10.00	20.00	30.00	200	425
1898	49,823,079	1.50	2.20	2.25	3.00	10.00	20.00	30.00	200	425
1899	53,600,031	1.50	2.00	2.20	3.00	10.00	18.00	27.50	140	415
1900	66,833,764	1.40	2.00	2.20	4.00	12.00	20.00	25.00	175	425
1901	79,611,143	1.35	2.00	2.20	3.00	7.50	17.00	25.00	140	425
1902	87,376,722	1.35	2.00	2.20	3.00	7.00	17.00	25.00	140	425
1903	85,094,493	1.35	2.00	2.20	3.00	7.00	17.00	25.00	140	425
1904	61,328,015	1.35	2.00	2.20	3.00	7.00	17.00	25.00	140	475
1905	80,719,163	1.35	2.00	2.20	3.00	7.00	17.00	25.00	140	475
1906	96,022,255	1.35	2.00	2.20	3.00	7.00	17.00	25.00	140	395
1907	108,138,618	1.35	2.00	2.20	3.00	7.00	17.00	25.00	145	485
1908	32,327,987	1.60	2.00	2.25	3.00	7.50	18.00	26.00	145	395
1908S	1,115,000	62.50	65.00	75.00	88.00	150	185	275	650	—
1909	14,370,645	4.75	5.25	5.60	5.95	15.00	22.50	30.00	150	400
1909S	309,000	425	450	480	525	625	700	750	1,500	—

Lincoln Cent
Wheat Ears reverse

1955
Double die

KM# 132 • 3.1100 g., **Bronze**, 19 mm. • **Designer:** Victor D. Brenner **Notes:** The 1909 "VDB" varieties have the designer's initials inscribed at the 6 o'clock position on the reverse. The initials were removed until 1918, when they were restored on the obverse.

Date	Mintage	G-4	VG-8	F-12	VF-20	XF-40	AU-50	MS-60	MS-65	Prf-65
1909	72,702,618	1.50	1.85	2.30	2.80	4.40	10.00	15.00	80.00	520

Date	Mintage	G-4	VG-8	F-12	VF-20	XF-40	AU-50	MS-60	MS-65	Prf-65
1909 VDB	27,995,000	7.00	7.50	7.75	8.00	8.25	10.50	11.00	100.00	6,000
1909S	1,825,000	68.50	75.00	95.00	140	195	225	285	1,300	—
1909S VDB	484,000	750	578	825	960	1,150	1,250	1,500	7,500	—
1910	146,801,218	.25	.30	.40	.50	3.75	8.00	17.50	250	700
1910S	6,045,000	7.50	9.50	11.00	13.50	28.50	60.00	65.00	800	—
1911	101,177,787	.40	.50	1.50	2.15	4.00	8.00	19.00	375	600
1911D	12,672,000	5.00	5.75	9.50	15.00	40.00	65.00	80.00	1,350	—
1911S	4,026,000	16.00	20.00	23.50	30.00	47.50	90.00	150	3,300	—
1912	68,153,060	1.25	1.75	2.20	5.50	11.00	20.00	30.00	550	950
1912D	10,411,000	6.75	7.75	9.50	22.00	50.00	85.00	150	2,800	—
1912S	4,431,000	14.00	16.75	20.00	25.00	55.00	85.00	130	4,400	—
1913	76,532,352	.65	.75	1.40	3.00	13.50	20.00	33.50	415	550
1913D	15,804,000	2.75	3.00	3.50	10.50	30.00	61.00	90.00	2,100	—
1913S	6,101,000	6.50	7.75	9.00	14.00	33.50	75.00	150	5,500	—
1914	75,238,432	.45	.70	2.00	5.25	13.50	32.50	47.50	415	600
1914D	1,193,000	150	200	350	415	650	1,300	1,900	22,000	—
1914S	4,137,000	13.00	15.00	17.00	27.00	60.00	150	285	10,000	—
1915	29,092,120	1.35	1.75	3.50	12.50	41.50	67.50	80.00	1,150	600
1915D	22,050,000	1.50	1.90	3.00	5.50	19.00	41.50	67.50	1,250	—
1915S	4,833,000	8.00	10.00	13.00	22.00	45.00	75.00	160	4,800	—
1916	131,833,677	.20	.25	.80	2.15	5.00	10.00	18.00	415	1,650
1916D	35,956,000	1.00	1.85	2.80	5.50	12.50	27.50	65.00	3,000	—
1916S	22,510,000	1.60	3.15	4.35	6.75	16.50	35.00	71.00	8,500	—
1917	196,429,785	.20	.25	.30	1.85	4.00	9.50	16.00	450	—
1917D	55,120,000	1.00—	1.25	2.50	5.30	16.00	30.00	60.00	3,000	—
1917S	32,620,000	.50	.80	1.25	2.15	9.50	21.50	58.50	7,200	—
1918	288,104,634	.20	.25	.30	.80	3.75	7.50	12.50	415	—
1918D	47,830,000	.80	1.30	2.20	4.00	12.50	26.00	70.00	3,550	—
1918S	34,680,000	.30	.75	1.00	2.75	8.50	30.00	61.00	7,800	—
1919	392,021,000	.20	.25	.30	.50	1.35	4.00	8.00	100.00	—
1919D	57,154,000	.80	1.00	1.25	2.75	7.00	30.00	50.00	2,700	—
1919S	139,760,000	.25	.40	1.40	2.50	4.50	16.00	41.50	4,300	—
1920	310,165,000	.20	.25	.55	1.05	2.80	6.25	13.50	205	—
1920D	49,280,000	.80	1.35	2.80	5.30	16.00	31.00	62.50	2,750	—
1920S	46,220,000	.60	.65	1.50	2.15	8.50	32.50	90.00	9,000	—
1921	39,157,000	.40	.65	.95	2.80	9.00	20.00	41.50	375	—
1921S	15,274,000	1.50	1.95	2.50	4.40	25.00	67.00	100.00	6,700	—
1922D	7,160,000	12.50	13.50	14.00	20.00	27.50	55.00	90.00	2,350	—
1922 No D-T.2	Inc. above	525	700	1,150	1,700	3,550	7,000	9,600	180,000	—
1923	74,723,000	.35	.45	.65	.90	3.40	8.00	13.50	480	—
1923S	8,700,000	2.50	3.50	4.40	7.75	30.00	80.00	195	15,000	—

1914-D Cent
Grade F-12

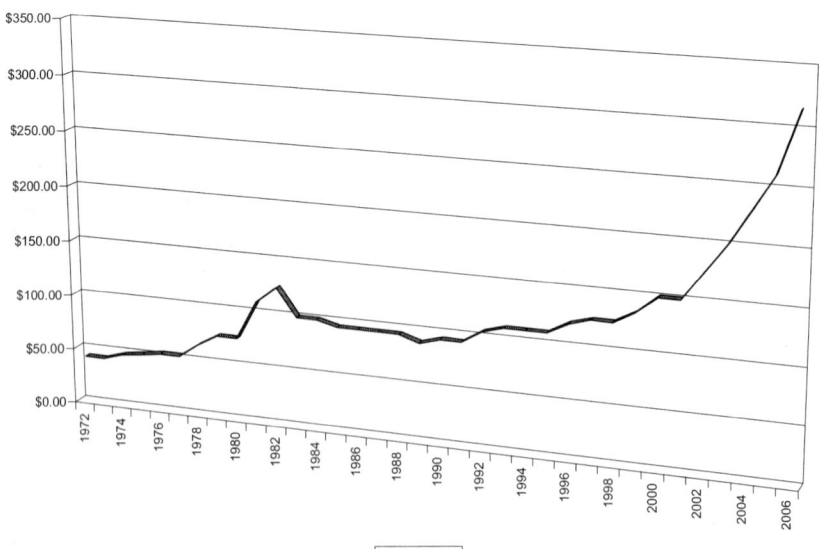

Retail Price

Date	Mintage	G-4	VG-8	F-12	VF-20	XF-40	AU-50	MS-60	MS-65	Prf-65
1924	75,178,000	.20	.30	.40	.60	3.00	8.00	20.00	390	—
1924D	2,520,000	16.75	21.00	25.00	35.00	85.00	150	235	8,500	—
1924S	11,696,000	1.50	1.50	2.80	5.00	17.00	62.50	115	11,000	—
1925	139,949,000	.20	.25	.30	.50	2.50	6.00	8.50	100.00	—
1925D	22,580,000	.90	1.70	2.80	5.00	15.00	27.50	60.00	5,000	—
1925S	26,380,000	.75	1.00	1.85	2.60	11.00	30.00	80.00	9,000	—
1926	157,088,000	.15	.20	.25	.50	1.35	4.00	7.00	66.00	—
1926D	28,020,000	1.05	1.35	2.80	4.15	12.50	32.50	80.00	4,350	—
1926S	4,550,000	5.00	6.00	8.00	11.00	20.00	56.00	110	10,500	—
1927	144,440,000	.15	.20	.25	.50	1.35	3.25	7.00	6,000	—
1927D	27,170,000	1.05	1.40	2.20	3.15	7.00	23.00	58.50	1,850	—
1927S	14,276,000	1.25	1.85	3.00	4.65	11.00	32.50	62.50	6,000	—
1928	134,116,000	.15	.20	.25	.45	1.10	3.00	7.50	90.00	—
1928D	31,170,000	.80	1.05	1.85	2.80	5.60	13.50	34.00	1,100	—
1928S	17,266,000	.90	1.40	2.50	3.45	8.00	25.00	71.50	4,800	—
1929	185,262,000	.15	.20	.25	.40	.70	4.25	6.00	85.00	—
1929D	41,730,000	.40	.80	1.10	2.15	4.65	11.00	21.50	550	—
1929S	50,148,000	.50	.85	1.50	2.15	4.00	6.75	17.50	415	—
1930	157,415,000	.15	.20	.25	.40	1.10	2.25	3.75	32.50	—
1930D	40,100,000	.20	.25	.40	.55	1.95	4.00	10.50	95.00	—
1930S	24,286,000	.25	.35	.50	.65	1.50	6.50	10.00	50.00	—
1931	19,396,000	.45	.50	.80	1.85	2.50	8.00	19.00	130	—
1931D	4,480,000	3.75	4.40	5.00	6.25	11.00	37.50	52.00	815	—
1931S	866,000	64.00	67.00	75.00	80.00	85.00	100.00	120	750	—
1932	9,062,000	1.35	1.75	2.75	3.25	4.25	11.50	19.00	83.50	—
1932D	10,500,000	1.10	1.85	2.35	2.75	4.15	9.60	17.50	96.00	—
1933	14,360,000	1.10	1.65	2.35	2.75	4.00	8.50	17.50	80.00	—
1933D	6,200,000	3.25	4.00	4.75	6.25	10.00	16.00	23.00	100.00	—
1934	219,080,000	—	.15	.20	.25	.75	1.50	4.00	28.50	—
1934D	28,446,000	.15	.20	.25	.45	1.50	5.00	16.50	52.00	—
1935	245,338,000	—	.10	.15	.25	.75	1.00	2.50	13.00	—
1935D	47,000,000	—	.15	.20	.30	.95	2.50	5.50	9.50	—
1935S	38,702,000	.10	.20	.30	.40	1.00	3.00	12.00	52.50	—
1936	309,637,569	—	.10	.15	.25	.75	1.00	2.00	6.00	1,200
1936D	40,620,000	—	.10	.15	.25	.75	1.50	2.75	11.00	—
1936S	29,130,000	.10	.15	.25	.35	.85	1.75	2.75	13.50	—
1937	309,179,320	—	.10	.15	.20	.70	.90	1.75	7.00	125
1937D	50,430,000	—	.10	.15	.25	.70	1.00	2.50	11.00	—
1937S	34,500,000	—	.10	.15	.25	.60	1.25	3.00	9.50	—
1938	156,696,734	—	.10	.15	.20	.50	1.00	2.00	8.00	85.00
1938D	20,010,000	.20	.25	.35	.45	.75	1.50	3.50	13.50	—
1938S	15,180,000	.30	.40	.50	.70	1.00	2.00	2.80	9.50	—
1939	316,479,520	—	.10	.15	.20	.30	.50	1.00	5.75	78.00
1939D	15,160,000	.35	.45	.35	.60	.85	1.90	2.25	9.50	—
1939S	52,070,000	—	.15	.20	.25	.45	.90	1.35	13.50	—
1940	586,825,872	—	.15	.20	.25	.30	.45	1.00	5.75	70.00
1940D	81,390,000	—	.15	.20	.25	.35	.50	1.20	9.50	—
1940S	112,940,000	—	.15	.20	.25	.30	.75	1.25	7.50	—
1941	887,039,100	—	—	.10	.15	.25	.40	.85	5.75	65.00
1941D	128,700,000	—	—	.15	.20	.25	1.00	2.00	8.50	—
1941S	92,360,000	—	—	.15	.20	.25	1.25	2.25	12.50	—
1942	657,828,600	—	—	.10	.15	.20	.25	.50	4.00	78.00
1942D	206,698,000	—	—	.10	.15	.20	.30	.50	7.50	—
1942S	85,590,000	—	—	.10	.20	.30	1.50	3.50	19.00	—

WWII Steel Cents

KM# 132a • 2.7000 g., **Zinc Coated Steel**, 19 mm. • **Designer:** Victor D. Brenner

Date	Mintage	G-4	VG-8	F-12	VF-20	XF-40	AU-50	MS-60	MS-65	Prf-65
1943	684,628,670	—	—	.25	.30	.50	.70	1.00	4.75	—
1943D	217,660,000	—	—	.25	.35	.60	.65	1.25	8.50	—
1943S	191,550,000	—	.30	.35	.40	.70	1.00	3.00	13.50	—

Wheat Ears reverse

KM# A132 • 3.1100 g., **Copper-Zinc**, 19 mm. • **Designer:** Victor D. Brenner **Notes:** KM#132 design and composition resumed.

Date	Mintage	XF-40	MS-65	Prf-65		Date	Mintage	XF-40	MS-65	Prf-65
1944	1,435,400,000	.20	2.00	—		1945	1,040,515,000	.20	2.00	—
1944D	430,578,000	.20	2.00	—		1945D	226,268,000	.20	2.00	—
1944D/S	—	180	1,700	—		1945S	181,770,000	.20	5.50	—
1944S	282,760,000	.20	5.50	—		1946	991,655,000	.20	2.00	—

Date	Mintage	XF-40	MS-65	Prf-65	Date	Mintage	XF-40	MS-65	Prf-65
1946D	315,690,000	.20	4.50	—	1952S	137,800,004	.15	5.00	—
1946S	198,100,000	.20	4.60	—	1953	256,883,800	.10	1.25	28.00
1947	190,555,000	.20	2.25	—	1953D	700,515,000	.10	1.25	—
1947D	194,750,000	.20	2.00	—	1953S	181,835,000	.15	1.75	—
1947S	99,000,000	.20	5.50	—	1954	71,873,350	.15	1.25	9.00
1948	317,570,000	.20	2.00	—	1954D	251,552,500	.10	.50	—
1948D	172,637,000	.20	2.25	—	1954S	96,190,000	.15	.75	—
1948S	81,735,000	.20	5.50	—	1955	330,958,000	.10	.75	13.00
1949	217,775,000	.20	3.50	—	1955 doubled die	—	1,425	37,500	—
1949D	153,132,000	.20	3.50	—	**Note:** The 1955 "doubled die" has distinct doubling of the				
1949S	64,290,000	.25	6.00	—	date and lettering on the obverse.				
1950	272,686,386	.20	1.75	40.00	1955D	563,257,500	.10	.75	—
1950D	334,950,000	.20	1.50	—	1955S	44,610,000	.25	1.00	—
1950S	118,505,000	.20	2.50	—	1956	421,414,384	—	.50	3.00
1951	295,633,500	.20	2.00	40.00	1956D	1,098,201,100	—	.50	—
1951D	625,355,000	.10	1.65	—	1957	283,787,952	—	.50	2.00
1951S	136,010,000	.15	3.00	—	1957D	1,051,342,000	—	.50	—
1952	186,856,980	.15	3.00	34.00	1958	253,400,652	—	.50	3.00
1952D	746,130,000	.10	1.60	—	1958D	800,953,300	—	.50	—

Lincoln Memorial reverse

1972
Double die

Large
date

Small
date

Small
date

Large
date

KM# 201 • 3.1100 g., **Copper-Zinc** • **Rev. Designer:** Frank Gasparro **Notes:** The dates were modified in 1960, 1970 and 1982, resulting in large-date and small-date varieties for those years. The 1972 "doubled die" shows doubling of "In God We Trust." The 1979-S and 1981-S Type II proofs have a clearer mint mark than the Type I proofs of those years. Some 1982 cents have the predominantly copper composition; others have the predominantly zinc composition. They can be distinguished by weight.

Date	Mintage	XF-40	MS-65	Prf-65	Date	Mintage	XF-40	MS-65	Prf-65
1959	610,864,291	—	.50	1.50	1970	1,898,315,000	—	.40	—
1959D	1,279,760,000	—	.50	—	1970D	2,891,438,900	—	.40	—
1960 small date	588,096,602	2.10	7.00	16.00	1970S	693,192,814	—	.40	1.20
1960 large date	Inc. above	—	.30	1.25	1970S small date	Inc. above	—	55.00	60.00
1960D small date	1,580,884,000	—	.30	—	1971	1,919,490,000	—	.35	—
1960D large date	Inc. above	—	.30	—	1971D	2,911,045,600	—	.40	—
1961	756,373,244	—	.30	1.00	1971S	528,354,192	—	.25	1.20
1961D	1,753,266,700	—	.30	—	1972	2,933,255,000	—	.25	—
1962	609,263,019	—	.30	1.00	1972 doubled die	—	285	800	—
1962D	1,793,148,400	—	.30	—	1972D	2,665,071,400	—	.25	—
1963	757,185,645	—	.30	1.00	1972S	380,200,104	—	.25	1.15
1963D	1,774,020,400	—	.30	—	1973	3,728,245,000	—	.25	—
1964	2,652,525,762	—	.30	1.00	1973D	3,549,576,588	—	.25	—
1964D	3,799,071,500	—	.30	—	1973S	319,937,634	—	.25	0.80
1965	1,497,224,900	—	.30	—	1974	4,232,140,523	—	.25	—
1966	2,188,147,783	—	.30	—	1974D	4,235,098,000	—	.25	—
1967	3,048,667,100	—	.50	—	1974S	412,039,228	—	.25	0.75
1968	1,707,880,970	—	.30	—	1975	5,451,476,142	—	.25	—
1968D	2,886,269,600	—	.40	—	1975D	4,505,245,300	—	.25	—
1968S	261,311,510	—	.40	1.00	1975S	(2,845,450)	—	—	5.50
1969	1,136,910,000	—	.60	—	1976	4,674,292,426	—	.25	—
1969D	4,002,832,200	—	.40	—	1976D	4,221,592,455	—	.25	—
1969S	547,309,631	—	.40	1.10	1976S	(4,149,730)	—	—	5.00

Date	Mintage	XF-40	MS-65	Prf-65
1977	4,469,930,000	—	.25	—
1977D	4,149,062,300	—	.25	—
1977S	(3,251,152)	—	—	3.00
1978	5,558,605,000	—	.25	—
1978D	4,280,233,400	—	.25	—
1978S	(3,127,781)	—	—	3.50
1979	6,018,515,000	—	.25	—
1979D	4,139,357,254	—	.25	—
1979S type I, proof	(3,677,175)	—	—	4.00
1979S type II, proof	Inc. above	—	—	4.25
1980	7,414,705,000	—	.25	—
1980D	5,140,098,660	—	.25	—
1980S	(3,554,806)	—	—	2.25
1981	7,491,750,000	—	.25	—
1981S type II, proof	Inc. above	—	—	60.00
1981D	5,373,235,677	—	.25	—
1981S type I, proof	(4,063,083)	—	—	3.50
1982 large date	10,712,525,000	—	.25	—
1982 small date	—	—	.25	—
1982D large date	6,012,979,368	—	.25	—

Lincoln Memorial reverse
KM# 201a • 2.5000 g., **Copper Plated Zinc**, 19 mm. •

Date	Mintage	XF-40	MS-65	Prf-65
1982 large date	—	—	.50	—
1982 small date	—	—	2.00	—
1982D large date	—	—	.30	—
1982D small date	—	—	.25	—

Lincoln Memorial reverse

KM# 201b • **Copper Plated Zinc**, 19 mm. •
Notes: The 1983 "doubled die reverse" shows doubling of "United States of America." The 1984 "doubled die" shows doubling of Lincoln's ear on the obverse.

Date	Mintage	XF-40	MS-65	Prf-65
1982S	(3,857,479)	—	—	3.00
1983	7,752,355,000	—	.25	—
1983 doubled die	—	—	400	—
1983D	6,467,199,428	—	.50	—
1983S	(3,279,126)	—	—	4.00
1984	8,151,079,000	—	.25	—
1984 doubled die	—	—	275	—
1984D	5,569,238,906	—	.75	—
1984S	(3,065,110)	—	—	4.50
1985	5,648,489,887	—	.25	—
1985D	5,287,399,926	—	.25	—
1985S	(3,362,821)	—	—	6.00
1986	4,491,395,493	—	1.50	—
1986D	4,442,866,698	—	1.25	—
1986S	(3,010,497)	—	—	7.50
1987	4,682,466,931	—	.25	—
1987D	4,879,389,514	—	.25	—
1987S	(4,227,728)	—	—	5.00
1988	6,092,810,000	—	.25	—
1988D	5,253,740,443	—	.25	—
1988S	(3,262,948)	—	—	4.00
1989	7,261,535,000	—	.25	—
1989D	5,345,467,111	—	.25	—
1989S	(3,220,194)	—	—	6.00
1990	6,851,765,000	—	.25	—
1990D	4,922,894,533	—	.25	—
1990S	(3,299,559)	—	—	5.00
1990 no S	—	—	—	2,750
1991	5,165,940,000	—	.25	—
1991D	4,158,442,076	—	.25	—
1991S	(2,867,787)	—	—	5.00
1992	4,648,905,000	—	.25	—
1992D	4,448,673,300	—	.25	—
1992S	(4,176,560)	—	—	5.00
1993	5,684,705,000	—	.25	—
1993D	6,426,650,571	—	.25	—
1993S	(3,394,792)	—	—	7.00
1994	6,500,850,000	—	.25	—
1994D	7,131,765,000	—	.25	—
1994S	(3,269,923)	—	—	4.00
1995	6,411,440,000	—	.25	—
1995 doubled die	—	20.00	50.00	—
1995D	7,128,560,000	—	.25	—
1995S	(2,707,481)	—	—	9.50
1996	6,612,465,000	—	.25	—
1996D	6,510,795,000	—	.25	—
1996S	(2,915,212)	—	—	6.50
1997	4,622,800,000	—	.25	—
1997D	4,576,555,000	—	.25	—
1997S	(2,796,678)	—	—	11.50
1998	5,032,155,000	—	.25	—
1998D	5,255,353,500	—	.25	—
1998S	(2,957,286)	—	—	9.50
1999	5,237,600,000	—	.25	—
1999D	6,360,065,000	—	.25	—
1999S	(3,362,462)	—	—	5.00
2000	5,503,200,000	—	.25	—
2000D	8,774,220,000	—	.25	—
2000S	(4,063,361)	—	—	4.00
2001P	4,959,600,000	—	.25	—
2001D	5,374,990,000	—	.25	—
2001S	(3,099,096)	—	—	4.00
2002P	3,260,800,000	—	.25	—
2002D	4,028,055,000	—	.25	—
2002S	(3,157,739)	—	—	4.00
2003P	—	—	.25	—
2003D	—	—	.25	—
2003S	(3,116,590)	—	—	4.00
2004P	—	—	.25	—
2004D	—	—	.25	—
2004S	—	—	—	4.00
2005P	—	—	.25	—
2005D	—	—	.25	—
2005S	—	—	—	4.00
2006P	—	—	.25	—
2006D	—	—	.25	—
2006S	—	—	—	4.00

2 CENTS

Small motto   Large motto

KM# 94 • 6.2200 g., **Copper-Tin-Zinc**, 23 mm. • **Designer:** James B. Longacre **Notes:** The motto "In God We Trust" was modified in 1864, resulting in small-motto and large-motto varieties for that year.

Date	Mintage	G-4	VG-8	F-12	VF-20	XF-40	AU-50	MS-60	MS-65	Prf-65
1864 small motto	19,847,500	125	185	265	400	595	675	900	3,000	45,000

Date	Mintage	G-4	VG-8	F-12	VF-20	XF-40	AU-50	MS-60	MS-65	Prf-65
1864 large motto	Inc. above	15.00	16.00	22.00	28.50	38.50	67.50	85.00	520	1,400
1865	13,640,000	15.00	16.00	22.00	28.50	38.50	67.50	85.00	520	850
1866	3,177,000	15.00	19.00	23.00	28.50	38.50	67.50	85.00	660	850
1867	2,938,750	17.50	22.00	36.00	46.00	60.00	96.00	130	550	850
1868	2,803,750	17.50	22.00	37.50	47.50	62.50	100.00	145	625	850
1869	1,546,000	18.50	23.00	40.00	50.00	71.00	120	160	650	850
1870	861,250	25.00	32.50	46.00	65.00	115	160	255	775	850
1871	721,250	34.00	41.50	55.00	82.50	130	195	270	750	850
1872	65,000	325	375	470	650	850	960	1,350	4,300	900
1873 proof	Est. 1,100	1,250	1,350	1,500	1,600	1,750	2,000	—	—	4,350

SILVER 3 CENTS

Type 1
No outlines in star obverse

KM# 75 • 0.8000 g., 0.7500 **Silver**, 0.0193 oz. ASW, 14 mm. • **Designer:** James B. Longacre

Date	Mintage	G-4	VG-8	F-12	VF-20	XF-40	AU-50	MS-60	MS-65	Prf-65
1851	5,447,400	25.00	41.50	42.50	45.00	65.00	155	185	975	—
1851O	720,000	38.50	47.50	55.00	100.00	160	250	340	2,600	—
1852	18,663,500	25.00	41.50	42.50	45.00	65.00	155	180	975	—
1853	11,400,000	25.00	41.50	42.50	45.00	65.00	155	180	975	—

Type 2
Three outlines in star obverse

KM# 80 • 0.7500 g., 0.9000 **Silver**, 0.0218 oz. ASW, 14 mm. • **Designer:** James B. Longacre

Date	Mintage	G-4	VG-8	F-12	VF-20	XF-40	AU-50	MS-60	MS-65	Prf-65
1854	671,000	26.00	42.50	44.00	50.00	105	230	350	3,450	33,500
1855	139,000	44.00	57.50	75.00	125	205	340	550	8,500	15,000
1856	1,458,000	30.00	45.00	46.00	65.00	125	205	275	4,500	15,500
1857	1,042,000	28.50	42.50	45.00	62.50	130	240	300	3,300	13,500
1858	1,604,000	27.50	42.50	44.00	55.00	110	200	240	3,300	6,400

1851-O Silver Three-Cent Piece
Grade XF-40

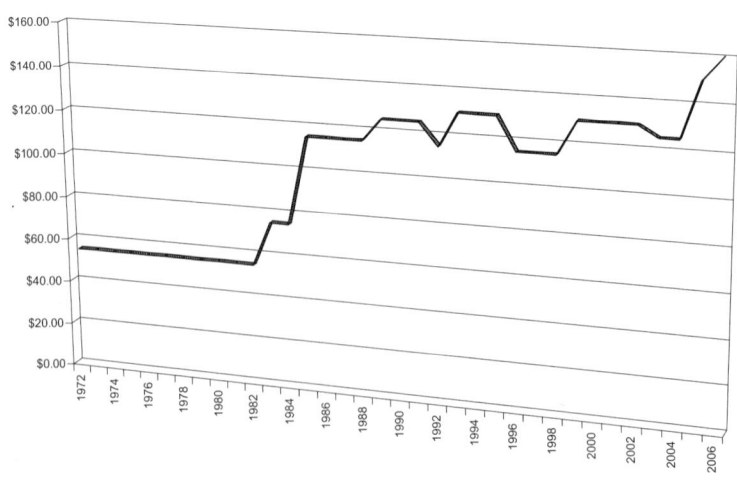

Retail Price

Type 3
Two outlines in star obverse

KM# 88 • 0.7500 g., 0.9000 **Silver**, 0.0218 oz. ASW, 14 mm. • **Designer:** James B. Longacre

Date	Mintage	G-4	VG-8	F-12	VF-20	XF-40	AU-50	MS-60	MS-65	Prf-65
1859	365,000	30.00	44.00	50.00	62.50	82.50	170	195	975	2,150
1860	287,000	30.00	44.00	45.00	60.00	80.00	170	195	975	4,000
1861	498,000	30.00	44.00	45.00	60.00	80.00	170	195	975	1,800
1862	343,550	38.50	51.00	50.00	70.00	82.50	195	230	975	1,400
1863	21,460	340	375	400	445	480	625	780	2,250	1,350
1863/62 proof only; Rare	Inc. above	470	480	575	600	650	700	—	—	5,400
1864	12,470	340	375	400	445	480	625	780	1,700	1,350
1865	8,500	400	440	475	520	550	600	750	1,700	1,350
1866	22,725	340	375	400	445	495	550	650	1,900	1,325
1867	4,625	400	440	475	520	550	600	720	2,750	1,300
1868	4,100	400	445	480	520	575	625	740	5,750	1,400
1869	5,100	400	445	480	520	575	625	720	2,350	1,400
1869/68 proof only; Rare	Inc. above	—	—	—	—	—	—	—	—	—
1870	4,000	420	450	495	550	595	670	900	5,500	1,350
1871	4,360	400	440	480	520	575	625	750	1,700	1,450
1872	1,950	420	450	495	550	595	675	795	5,500	1,350
1873 proof only	600	650	685	730	800	890	980	—	—	2,350

NICKEL 3 CENTS

KM# 95 • 1.9400 g., **Copper-Nickel**, 17.9 mm. • **Designer:** James B. Longacre

Date	Mintage	G-4	VG-8	F-12	VF-20	XF-40	AU-50	MS-60	MS-65	Prf-65
1865	11,382,000	15.00	16.00	17.50	24.50	35.00	57.50	105	700	6,500
1866	4,801,000	15.00	16.00	17.50	24.50	35.00	57.50	105	700	1,725
1867	3,915,000	15.00	16.00	17.50	24.50	35.00	57.50	105	750	1,575
1868	3,252,000	15.00	16.00	17.50	24.50	35.00	57.50	105	700	1,400
1869	1,604,000	16.00	17.50	19.00	26.00	37.50	62.50	120	775	1,000
1870	1,335,000	17.50	18.50	20.50	28.50	40.00	65.00	135	825	2,300
1871	604,000	17.50	19.00	22.50	30.00	41.50	70.00	150	850	1,200
1872	862,000	19.00	22.50	25.00	32.50	44.00	75.00	170	1,100	880
1873	1,173,000	16.00	18.50	22.50	27.50	40.00	65.00	140	1,400	1,050
1874	790,000	17.50	20.50	22.50	30.00	41.50	72.50	155	1,050	950
1875	228,000	19.00	22.50	26.00	34.00	48.50	90.00	190	850	1,700
1876	162,000	20.50	23.50	28.50	38.50	52.50	105	220	1,700	1,000
1877 proof	Est. 900	1,100	1,150	1,175	1,250	1,300	1,350	—	—	3,750
1878 proof	2,350	615	645	720	770	795	825	—	—	1,200
1879	41,200	65.00	75.00	96.00	105	115	170	320	850	580
1880	24,955	100.00	115	130	155	185	230	375	800	630
1881	1,080,575	15.00	16.00	19.00	25.00	37.50	60.00	100.00	715	580
1882	25,300	130	150	180	205	250	200	425	1,100	625
1883	10,609	200	225	260	305	355	415	480	4,350	580
1884	5,642	415	445	550	595	645	730	800	5,800	600
1885	4,790	470	520	645	700	745	790	900	2,300	650
1886 proof	4,290	320	330	345	385	385	415	—	—	700
1887/6 proof	7,961	350	390	415	450	460	515	—	—	975
1887	Inc. above	305	355	395	430	455	495	540	1,350	1,350
1888	41,083	52.50	62.50	715	825	100.00	170	315	725	580
1889	21,561	90.00	115	140	180	215	250	320	800	580

HALF DIME
Flowing Hair Half Dime

KM# 15 • 1.3500 g., 0.8920 **Silver**, 0.0388 oz. ASW, 16.5 mm. • **Designer:** Robert Scot

Date	Mintage	G-4	VG-8	F-12	VF-20	XF-40	MS-60
1794	86,416	1,000	1,250	1,750	2,700	4,800	13,500
1795	Inc. above	700	900	1,350	2,000	4,000	9,500

Draped Bust Half Dime
Small eagle reverse

KM# 23 • 1.3500 g., 0.8920 **Silver**, 0.0388 oz. ASW, 16.5 mm. • **Designer:** Robert Scot **Notes:** Some 1796 strikes have "Liberty" spelled as "Likerty." The 1797 strikes have either 13, 15 or 16 stars on the obverse.

Date	Mintage	G-4	VG-8	F-12	VF-20	XF-40	MS-60
1796	10,230	1,000	1,350	2,000	3,500	6,000	13,500
1796 "Likerty"	Inc. above	1,100	1,400	2,100	3,750	6,250	14,500
1796/5	Inc. above	1,000	1,350	2,200	4,000	7,000	25,000
1797 13 stars	44,527	1,750	2,300	3,000	5,500	9,000	25,000
1797 15 stars	Inc. above	1,000	1,250	1,900	3,250	5,750	12,500
1797 16 stars	Inc. above	1,050	1,350	2,100	3,650	6,250	13,750

1802 Half Dime
Grade F-12

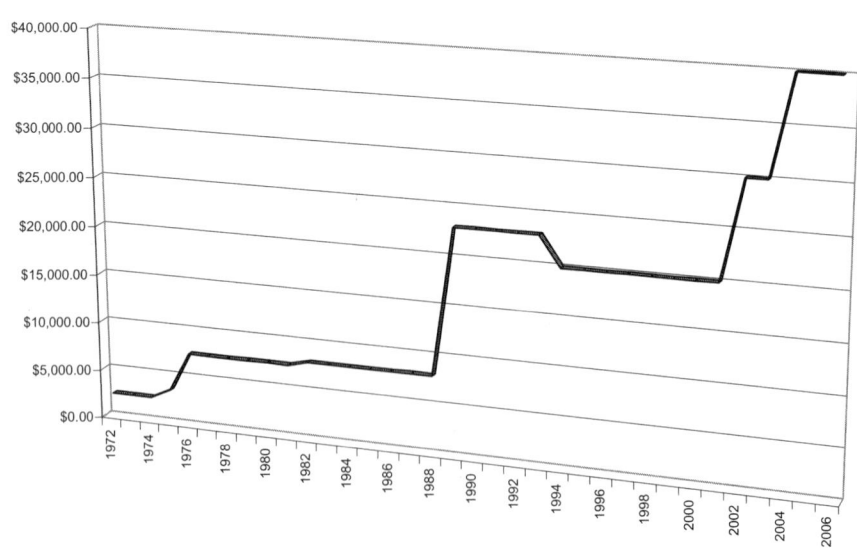

Retail Price

Heraldic eagle reverse

KM# 34 • 1.3500 g., 0.8920 **Silver**, 0.0388 oz. ASW, 16.5 mm. • **Designer:** Robert Scot **Notes:** Some 1800 strikes have "Liberty" spelled as "Libekty."

Date	Mintage	G-4	VG-8	F-12	VF-20	XF-40	MS-60
1800	24,000	575	750	1,500	2,500	4,250	9,000
1800 "Libekty"	Inc. above	600	800	1,575	2,650	4,400	9,300
1801	33,910	775	1,150	1,600	2,800	5,000	15,000
1802	13,010	17,500	25,000	40,000	65,000	85,000	185,000
1803 Large 8	37,850	750	950	1,300	2,000	4,000	9,000
1803 Small 8	Inc. above	950	1,400	1,900	3,000	5,500	11,500
1805	15,600	900	1,250	1,650	2,500	5,500	27,500

Liberty Cap Half Dime

KM# 47 • 1.3500 g., 0.8920 **Silver**, 0.0388 oz. ASW, 15.5 mm. • **Designer:** William Kneass **Notes:** Design modifications in 1835, 1836 and 1837 resulted in variety combinations with large and small dates, and large and small "5C." inscriptions on the reverse.

Date	Mintage	G-4	VG-8	F-12	VF-20	XF-40	AU-50	MS-60	MS-65
1829	1,230,000	27.50	36.00	48.00	80.00	140	250	350	2,650
1830	1,240,000	25.00	36.00	48.00	75.00	140	250	350	2,650
1831	1,242,700	25.00	36.00	48.00	75.00	140	250	350	2,600
1832	965,000	25.00	36.00	48.00	75.00	140	250	350	2,600
1833	1,370,000	25.00	36.00	48.00	75.00	140	250	350	2,650
1834	1,480,000	25.00	36.00	48.00	75.00	140	250	350	2,600
1835 lg. dt., lg. 5C.	2,760,000	25.00	36.00	48.00	75.00	140	250	350	2,600
1835 lg. dt., sm. 5C	Inc. above	25.00	36.00	48.00	75.00	140	250	350	2,600
1835 sm. dt., lg. 5C	Inc. above	25.00	36.00	48.00	75.00	140	250	350	2,600
1835 sm. dt., sm. 5C	Inc. above	25.00	36.00	48.00	75.00	140	250	350	2,600
1836 lg. 5C.	1,900,000	25.00	36.00	48.00	75.00	140	250	350	2,600
1836 sm. 5C.	Inc. above	25.00	36.00	48.00	75.00	140	250	350	2,600
1837 lg. 5C.	2,276,000	27.50	36.00	48.00	80.00	140	250	350	3,500
1837 sm. 5C.	Inc. above	33.00	40.00	55.00	100.00	200	450	950	8,750

Seated Liberty Half Dime
No stars around rim obverse

KM# 60 • 1.3400 g., 0.9000 **Silver**, 0.0388 oz. ASW, 15.5 mm. • **Designer:** Christian Gobrecht **Notes:** A design modification in 1837 resulted in small-date and large-date varieties for that year.

Date	Mintage	G-4	VG-8	F-12	VF-20	XF-40	AU-50	MS-60	MS-65
1837 small date	Inc. above	30.00	42.00	62.50	115	190	485	800	3,900
1837 large date	Inc. above	34.00	46.00	70.00	125	200	375	625	3,250
1838O	70,000	80.00	125	225	400	750	1,450	2,000	25,000

Stars around rim. No drapery obverse

KM# 62.1 • 1.3400 g., 0.9000 **Silver**, 0.0388 oz. ASW, 15.5 mm. • **Designer:** Christian Gobrecht **Notes:** The two varieties of 1838 are distinguished by the size of the stars on the obverse. The 1839-O with reverse of 1838-O was struck from rusted reverse dies. The result is a bumpy surface on this variety's reverse.

Date	Mintage	G-4	VG-8	F-12	VF-20	XF-40	AU-50	MS-60	MS-65
1838 large stars	2,255,000	15.00	17.50	20.00	27.50	70.00	150	250	2,250
1838 small stars	Inc. above	18.00	27.50	45.00	100.00	175	315	650	3,850
1839	1,069,150	16.00	18.50	21.00	30.00	75.00	160	250	2,500
1839O	1,034,039	17.50	20.00	25.00	35.00	93.50	185	550	5,500

Date	Mintage	G-4	VG-8	F-12	VF-20	XF-40	AU-50	MS-60	MS-65
1839O reverse 1838O	—	375	575	750	1,200	2,250	3,500	—	—
1840	1,344,085	16.00	18.50	21.00	30.00	75.00	160	250	2,100
1840O	935,000	17.50	20.00	23.50	40.00	80.00	215	700	17,000

Drapery added to Liberty's left elbow obverse

KM# 62.2 • 1.3400 g., 0.9000 **Silver**, 0.0388 oz. ASW, 15.5 mm. • **Designer:** Christian Gobrecht **Notes:** In 1840 drapery was added to Liberty's left elbow. Varieties for the 1848 Philadelphia strikes are distinguished by the size of the numerals in the date.

Date	Mintage	G-4	VG-8	F-12	VF-20	XF-40	AU-50	MS-60	MS-65
1840	Inc. above	25.00	40.00	75.00	125	225	350	450	300
1840O	Inc. above	35.00	60.00	115	190	450	1,250	6,500	—
1841	1,150,000	15.00	17.50	21.00	28.50	56.00	115	160	1,250
1841O	815,000	17.50	20.00	25.00	43.50	110	280	650	6,500
1842	815,000	15.00	17.50	20.00	27.50	55.00	115	160	1,750
1842O	350,000	30.00	45.00	75.00	225	500	1,250	2,500	—
1843	1,165,000	15.00	17.50	20.00	27.50	55.00	110	160	1,350
1844	430,000	17.50	20.00	22.50	31.50	56.00	115	175	1,150
1844O	220,000	75.00	105	175	450	1,000	2,250	5,400	25,000
1845	1,564,000	15.00	17.50	20.00	33.50	56.00	110	160	1,150
1845/1845	Inc. above	16.00	20.00	22.50	35.00	60.00	115	160	1,200
1846	27,000	325	500	850	1,250	2,250	3,600	8,500	—
1847	1,274,000	15.00	17.50	20.00	27.50	55.00	110	160	1,150
1848 medium date	668,000	17.50	20.00	23.50	30.00	57.50	125	230	2,850
1848 large date	Inc. above	22.50	30.00	45.00	65.00	135	275	450	4,000
1848O	600,000	19.00	25.00	33.00	50.00	110	265	400	1,950
1849/8	1,309,000	28.50	35.00	47.50	62.50	125	250	625	2,600
1849/6	Inc. above	20.00	26.00	30.00	52.50	105	200	400	2,500
1849	Inc. above	16.00	18.50	27.50	50.00	65.00	125	180	1,700
1849O	140,000	29.00	40.00	95.00	225	475	975	1,950	14,000
1850	955,000	17.50	20.00	23.50	31.50	60.00	115	165	1,400
1850O	690,000	18.50	22.50	30.00	56.00	125	280	675	4,250
1851	781,000	15.00	17.50	20.00	27.50	56.00	110	160	1,500
1851O	860,000	17.50	20.00	25.00	41.50	110	220	500	4,350
1852	1,000,500	15.00	17.50	20.00	27.50	56.00	110	160	1,150
1852O	260,000	23.00	32.00	65.00	135	275	475	750	10,000
1853	135,000	35.00	50.00	75.00	135	220	385	750	3,000
1853O	160,000	250	325	450	800	1,800	2,750	500	25,000

1846 Half Dime Grade XF-40

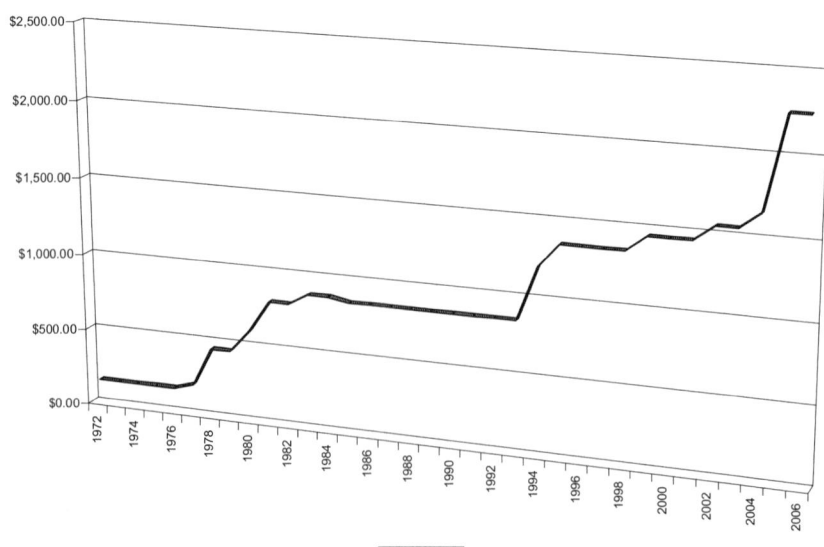

Retail Price

Arrows at date obverse

KM# 76 • 1.2400 g., 0.9000 **Silver**, 0.0362 oz. ASW • **Designer:** Christian Gobrecht

Date	Mintage	G-4	VG-8	F-12	VF-20	XF-40	AU-50	MS-60	MS-65	Prf-65
1853	13,210,020	13.50	16.00	17.50	21.00	50.00	120	190	1,850	35,000
1853O	2,200,000	13.50	16.00	17.50	21.00	65.00	135	275	3,500	—
1854	5,740,000	13.50	16.00	17.50	21.00	45.00	110	185	1,850	16,000
1854O	1,560,000	13.50	16.00	17.50	21.00	60.00	145	250	4,250	—
1855	1,750,000	13.50	16.00	17.50	21.00	47.00	115	190	1,950	18,000
1855O	600,000	15.00	20.00	30.00	55.00	135	235	600	4,000	—

Arrows at date removed obverse

KM# A62.2 • 1.2400 g., 0.9000 **Silver**, 0.0362 oz. ASW • **Designer:** Christian Gobrecht **Notes:** On the 1858/inverted date variety, the date was engraved into the die upside down and then re-engraved right side up. Another 1858 variety has the date doubled.

Date	Mintage	G-4	VG-8	F-12	VF-20	XF-40	AU-50	MS-60	MS-65	Prf-65
1856	4,880,000	13.50	16.00	17.50	23.50	50.00	115	170	1,650	15,000
1856O	1,100,000	16.00	18.50	20.00	46.00	95.00	250	550	2,000	—
1857	7,280,000	13.50	16.00	17.50	23.50	50.00	110	170	1,550	5,500
1857O	1,380,000	15.00	16.00	18.50	37.50	60.00	185	325	1,800	—
1858	3,500,000	13.50	16.00	17.50	23.50	55.00	175	300	1,700	5,500
1858 inverted date	Inc. above	30.00	43.50	62.50	90.00	185	275	675	3,000	—
1858 double date	Inc. above	45.00	60.00	90.00	175	285	425	700	—	—
1858O	1,660,000	15.00	16.00	20.00	42.50	75.00	135	265	1,600	—
1859	340,000	16.00	17.50	21.50	34.00	70.00	135	225	1,550	4,000
1859O	560,000	17.50	20.00	28.50	43.50	115	200	260	1,850	—

"United States of America" replaced stars

KM# 91 • 1.2400 g., 0.9000 **Silver**, 0.0362 oz. ASW • **Designer:** Christian Gobrecht **Notes:** In 1860 the legend "United States of America" replaced the stars on the obverse.

Date	Mintage	G-4	VG-8	F-12	VF-20	XF-40	AU-50	MS-60	MS-65	Prf-65
1860	799,000	13.50	16.00	17.50	21.00	40.00	72.50	125	1,150	1,850
1860O	1,060,000	13.50	16.00	18.50	25.00	43.50	93.50	180	1,450	—
1861	3,361,000	13.50	16.00	17.50	21.00	40.00	72.50	125	1,175	2,500
1861/0	Inc. above	25.00	32.50	59.00	125	260	435	560	4,000	—
1862	1,492,550	20.00	25.00	33.50	43.50	55.00	93.50	160	1,150	1,650
1863	18,460	200	250	300	375	475	550	700	1,650	1,700
1863S	100,000	25.00	35.00	50.00	75.00	150	295	700	2,500	—
1864	48,470	350	425	500	650	850	1,000	1,250	2,250	1,750
1864S	90,000	50.00	65.00	100.00	150	250	450	700	3,750	—
1865	13,500	350	425	500	650	8,580	975	1,000	1,950	1,750
1865S	120,000	25.00	35.00	50.00	75.00	135	375	800	—	—
1866	10,725	375	475	550	700	875	1,000	1,250	2,550	1,700
1866S	120,000	25.00	35.00	50.00	75.00	135	285	450	5,000	—
1867	8,625	500	600	750	900	1,000	1,200	1,400	2,250	1,750
1867S	120,000	25.00	35.00	50.00	80.00	150	325	550	3,850	—
1868	89,200	65.00	80.00	135	190	285	375	570	2,400	1,750
1868S	280,000	20.00	25.00	30.00	40.00	55.00	125	300	3,250	—
1869	208,600	20.00	25.00	30.00	40.00	55.00	125	235	1,500	1,750
1869S	230,000	18.00	22.00	29.00	35.00	50.00	115	325	4,000	—
1870	536,600	18.00	22.00	29.00	35.00	50.00	125	175	1,200	1,650
1870S unique	—	—	—	—	—	—	—	—	—	—

Note: 1870S, Superior Galleries, July 1986, brilliant uncirculated, $253,000.

Date	Mintage	G-4	VG-8	F-12	VF-20	XF-40	AU-50	MS-60	MS-65	Prf-65
1871	1,873,960	14.00	16.00	17.50	21.00	37.50	75.00	125	1,250	1,650
1871S	161,000	25.00	30.00	45.00	60.00	85.00	175	250	2,450	—
1872	2,947,950	14.00	16.00	17.50	21.00	37.50	75.00	125	1,200	1,650
1872S mint mark in wreath	837,000	14.00	16.00	17.50	21.00	37.50	75.00	125	1,200	—
1872S mint mark below wreath	Inc. above	14.00	16.00	17.50	21.00	37.50	75.00	125	1,200	—
1873	712,600	14.00	16.00	17.50	21.00	37.50	75.00	125	1,300	1,750
1873S	324,000	20.00	25.00	30.00	39.00	50.00	90.00	150	1,350	—

5 CENTS

Shield Nickel

Rays between stars reverse

KM# 96 • 5.0000 g., **Copper-Nickel**, 20.5 mm. • **Designer:** James B. Longacre

Date	Mintage	G-4	VG-8	F-12	VF-20	XF-40	AU-50	MS-60	MS-65	Prf-65
1866	14,742,500	27.50	38.50	50.00	75.00	155	235	260	2,700	3,850
1867	2,019,000	37.50	50.00	67.50	100.00	200	295	350	4,150	75,000

No rays between stars reverse

KM# 97 • 5.0000 g., **Copper-Nickel** •

Date	Mintage	G-4	VG-8	F-12	VF-20	XF-40	AU-50	MS-60	MS-65	Prf-65
1867	28,890,500	16.00	19.00	25.00	32.50	50.00	105	135	950	3,450
1868	28,817,000	16.00	19.00	25.00	32.50	50.00	105	135	1,000	1,500
1869	16,395,000	16.00	19.00	25.00	32.50	50.00	105	135	775	1,000
1870	4,806,000	25.00	30.00	49.00	60.00	80.00	130	195	1,650	1,250
1871	561,000	65.00	85.00	120	155	230	275	345	2,200	1,100
1872	6,036,000	30.00	39.00	62.50	75.00	96.00	130	215	1,350	820
1873	4,550,000	26.00	32.50	49.00	60.00	75.00	120	190	2,400	840
1874	3,538,000	27.50	39.00	65.00	80.00	96.00	130	200	1,500	1,000
1875	2,097,000	37.50	49.00	80.00	100.00	130	170	230	2,000	1,650
1876	2,530,000	34.00	46.00	70.00	96.00	125	155	220	1,950	900
1877 proof	Est. 900	1,500	1,650	1,750	2,000	2,100	2,250	—	—	4,300
1878 proof	2,350	800	1,000	1,000	1,100	1,400	1,500	—	—	2,150

1884 Nickel Five-Cent
Grade F-12

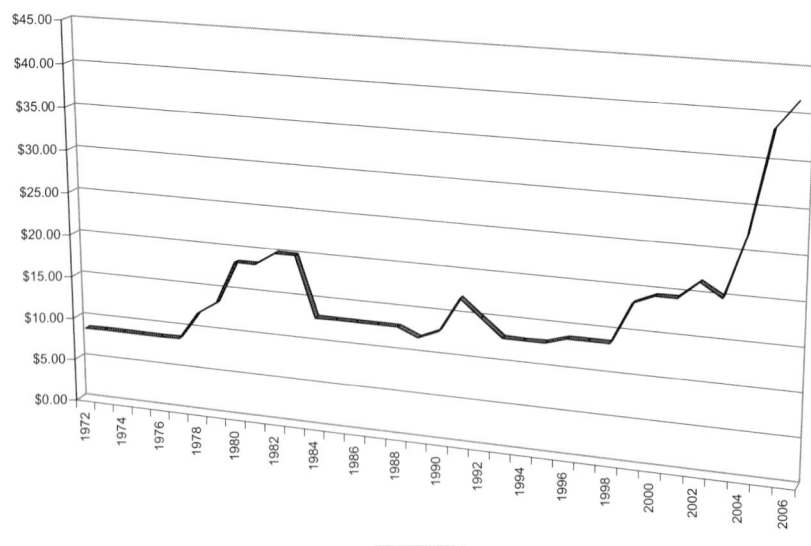

Retail Price

Date	Mintage	G-4	VG-8	F-12	VF-20	XF-40	AU-50	MS-60	MS-65	Prf-65
1879	29,100	415	520	625	675	730	800	970	2,000	840
1880	19,995	650	700	850	1,000	1,400	2,000	3,450	40,000	670
1881	72,375	270	340	445	500	600	730	800	1,900	660
1882	11,476,600	16.00	19.50	25.00	32.50	50.00	105	135	750	660
1883	1,456,919	18.00	21.00	32.00	37.50	60.00	105	140	750	660
1883/2	—	190	260	335	395	650	850	1,050	3,800	—

Liberty Nickel
Without "Cents" below "V" reverse

KM# 111 • 5.0000 g., Copper-Nickel, 21.2 mm. • Designer: Charles E. Barber

Date	Mintage	G-4	VG-8	F-12	VF-20	XF-40	AU-50	MS-60	MS-65	Prf-65
1883	5,479,519	5.50	6.75	7.00	7.50	8.25	11.50	24.00	275	1,100

"Cents" below "V" reverse

KM# 112 • 5.0000 g., Copper-Nickel •

Date	Mintage	G-4	VG-8	F-12	VF-20	XF-40	AU-50	MS-60	MS-65	Prf-65
1883	16,032,983	13.50	22.00	41.50	57.50	85.00	110	160	720	550
1884	11,273,942	19.50	30.00	41.50	60.00	93.50	135	200	2,000	575
1885	1,476,490	550	625	900	1,100	1,350	1,700	2,000	8,400	1,500
1886	3,330,290	225	260	415	520	715	850	1,000	9,000	850
1887	15,263,652	11.00	16.00	32.50	45.00	82.50	110	150	1,400	570
1888	10,720,483	28.50	42.50	70.00	130	185	240	305	2,000	570
1889	15,881,361	7.50	11.00	30.00	48.50	75.00	110	150	1,000	570
1890	16,259,272	7.00	16.00	27.50	41.50	68.50	115	170	1,950	650
1891	16,834,350	6.00	8.00	22.00	38.50	62.50	110	160	1,000	570
1892	11,699,642	7.00	8.00	23.00	41.50	65.00	125	160	1,500	570
1893	13,370,195	5.50	8.00	25.00	38.50	62.50	115	155	1,650	570
1894	5,413,132	14.00	29.00	110	160	240	315	360	1,500	570
1895	9,979,884	4.00	6.75	25.00	47.50	70.00	110	150	2,800	650
1896	8,842,920	8.00	18.00	41.50	68.50	96.00	150	215	2,500	620
1897	20,428,735	3.00	4.50	12.50	27.50	41.50	68.50	100.00	1,250	600
1898	12,532,087	2.00	3.75	11.00	23.50	41.50	71.50	140	1,250	500
1899	26,029,031	1.70	2.00	8.50	20.00	34.00	65.00	96.00	725	560
1900	27,255,995	1.70	2.00	8.50	19.50	35.00	70.00	90.00	725	560
1901	26,480,213	1.70	2.50	7.00	15.00	32.50	60.00	75.00	720	560
1902	31,480,579	1.70	2.50	4.00	15.00	30.00	60.00	77.50	720	560
1903	28,006,725	1.70	2.50	5.00	15.00	30.00	57.50	80.00	725	560
1904	21,404,984	1.70	2.50	5.00	11.00	27.50	55.00	72.50	750	725
1905	29,827,276	1.70	2.00	4.00	11.00	27.50	55.00	72.50	720	560
1906	38,613,725	1.70	2.00	4.00	11.00	27.50	55.00	70.00	950	560
1907	39,214,800	1.70	2.00	4.00	11.00	27.50	55.00	72.50	1,400	625
1908	22,686,177	1.70	2.00	4.00	11.00	27.50	55.00	72.50	1,250	560
1909	11,590,526	2.50	3.00	5.00	12.50	30.00	62.50	82.50	1,300	560
1910	30,169,353	1.70	2.00	4.00	10.00	27.50	48.50	65.00	750	560
1911	39,559,372	1.70	2.00	4.00	10.00	27.50	48.50	65.00	720	560
1912	26,236,714	1.70	2.00	4.00	10.00	27.50	48.50	65.00	720	575
1912D	8,474,000	2.50	4.00	10.00	35.00	68.50	150	290	2,500	—
1912S	238,000	150	200	300	500	850	1,350	1,500	7,500	—
1913 5 known	—	—	—	—	—	—	—	—	—	—

Note: 1913, Superior Sale, March 2001, Proof, $1,840,000.

Buffalo Nickel
Buffalo standing on a mound reverse

KM# 133 • 5.0000 g., **Copper-Nickel**, 21.2 mm. • **Designer:** James Earle Fraser

Date	Mintage	G-4	VG-8	F-12	VF-20	XF-40	AU-50	MS-60	MS-65	Prf-65
1913	30,993,520	8.00	11.00	11.25	12.00	18.50	23.50	32.50	185	3,500
1913D	5,337,000	12.50	15.00	19.00	25.00	35.00	50.00	62.50	330	—
1913S	2,105,000	35.00	42.00	50.00	60.00	75.00	92.50	125	700	—

Buffalo standing on a line reverse

1918/17D   1937D 3-legged

KM# 134 • 5.0000 g., **Copper-Nickel**, 21.2 mm. • **Designer:** James Earle Fraser **Notes:** In 1913 the reverse design was modified so the ground under the buffalo was represented as a line rather than a mound. On the 1937D 3-legged variety, the buffalo's right front leg is missing, the result of a damaged die.

Date	Mintage	G-4	VG-8	F-12	VF-20	XF-40	AU-50	MS-60	MS-65	Prf-65
1913	29,858,700	8.00	11.00	11.50	12.50	18.50	25.00	34.00	375	2,600
1913D	4,156,000	110	140	155	170	195	225	285	1,575	—
1913S	1,209,000	310	375	415	475	570	650	850	4,300	—
1914	20,665,738	15.00	17.50	19.00	21.50	27.50	37.50	49.00	450	2,350
1914D	3,912,000	80.00	110	155	220	315	395	450	1,850	—
1914S	3,470,000	23.50	33.50	45.00	62.50	90.00	135	150	2,350	—
1915	20,987,270	4.75	5.50	6.75	11.00	21.50	38.50	50.00	325	2,100
1915D	7,569,500	16.00	25.00	41.50	66.00	115	150	225	2,500	—
1915S	1,505,000	40.00	60.00	90.00	185	320	490	625	3,400	—
1916	63,498,066	4.00	5.25	6.00	7.50	13.50	22.50	43.50	350	3,850
1916/16	Inc. above	2,000	4,250	8,000	12,000	17,000	38,000	55,000	395,000	—
1916D	13,333,000	12.00	18.50	25.00	38.50	82.50	110	150	2,500	—
1916S	11,860,000	11.00	13.50	20.00	35.00	75.00	115	175	2,650	—
1917	51,424,029	4.00	5.25	6.25	975	15.00	32.50	60.00	580	—
1917D	9,910,800	16.00	23.00	47.50	80.00	135	255	345	4,400	—
1917S	4,193,000	23.00	35.00	70.00	110	180	285	395	5,250	—
1918	32,086,314	4.00	5.25	6.75	15.00	31.00	48.50	110	1,700	—
1918/17D	8,362,314	1,050	1,550	2,850	6,250	10,000	11,500	28,500	285,000	—
1918D	Inc. above	18.50	32.50	50.00	130	220	330	430	5,000	—
1918S	4,882,000	14.00	27.50	47.50	100.00	175	300	495	32,500	—
1919	60,868,000	1.75	2.75	3.25	7.00	15.00	30.00	60.00	595	—
1919D	8,006,000	12.50	23.50	57.50	115	235	335	570	8,000	—
1919S	7,521,000	8.00	20.00	50.00	110	225	360	540	19,000	—
1920	63,093,000	1.35	2.10	3.00	7.50	15.00	30.00	59.00	850	—
1920D	9,418,000	8.50	15.00	35.00	125	275	340	555	7,800	—
1920S	9,689,000	4.50	10.00	30.00	100.00	200	300	525	28,500	—
1921	10,663,000	3.75	6.25	8.50	25.00	53.50	70.00	125	850	—
1921S	1,557,000	67.50	110	200	545	845	1,100	1,500	8,000	—
1923	35,715,000	1.70	3.00	4.25	7.00	13.50	37.50	60.00	750	—
1923S	6,142,000	7.50	10.00	25.00	125	260	335	595	12,500	—
1924	21,620,000	1.00	2.10	4.15	9.60	19.00	41.00	73.50	950	—
1924D	5,258,000	7.50	11.00	30.00	85.00	215	315	375	5,600	—
1924S	1,437,000	18.00	34.00	96.00	470	1,100	1,700	2,300	12,000	—
1925	35,565,100	2.00	2.50	3.75	8.50	17.50	30.00	44.00	525	—
1925D	4,450,000	8.00	16.00	40.00	80.00	160	240	380	6,600	—
1925S	6,256,000	4.50	9.00	17.50	77.50	170	240	445	45,000	—
1926	44,693,000	.90	1.10	2.80	5.40	11.50	20.00	31.50	185	—
1926D	5,638,000	7.50	13.50	28.50	100.00	170	295	315	6,400	—
1926S	970,000	20.00	35.00	85.00	465	915	2,850	5,250	115,000	—
1927	37,981,000	.90	1.10	2.15	4.15	12.50	20.00	35.00	300	—
1927D	5,730,000	2.00	4.00	5.50	27.50	75.00	110	150	9,000	—
1927S	3,430,000	2.00	3.00	6.00	31.00	80.00	160	485	22,500	—
1928	23,411,000	.85	1.10	2.20	4.15	12.50	23.00	32.50	325	—
1928D	6,436,000	1.20	2.10	3.45	15.00	40.00	45.00	50.00	1,000	—
1928S	6,936,000	1.35	1.50	2.20	11.50	27.50	100.00	215	5,500	—
1929	36,446,000	.90	1.10	2.15	4.15	12.50	20.00	35.00	375	—
1929D	8,370,000	1.00	1.25	3.00	6.75	32.50	42.50	55.00	2,000	—
1929S	7,754,000	.90	1.25	2.25	5.00	11.50	25.00	47.50	525	—

Date	Mintage	G-4	VG-8	F-12	VF-20	XF-40	AU-50	MS-60	MS-65	Prf-65
1930	22,849,000	.90	1.40	2.15	4.15	11.50	20.00	32.50	250	—
1930S	5,435,000	1.00	1.40	2.75	4.25	15.00	34.00	52.50	500	—
1931S	1,200,000	16.00	18.00	20.00	22.00	33.00	50.00	65.00	315	—
1934	20,213,003	.90	1.40	2.15	4.15	10.00	19.00	48.50	440	—
1934D	7,480,000	1.75	2.75	4.40	9.60	22.00	50.00	82.50	1,000	—
1935	58,264,000	.90	1.00	1.10	1.40	2.75	8.50	20.00	135	—
1935D	12,092,000	1.35	2.20	2.80	8.00	20.00	46.00	75.00	540	—
1935S	10,300,000	.90	1.00	1.10	1.50	3.15	16.00	50.00	260	—
1936	119,001,420	.90	1.00	1.10	1.40	2.00	6.50	15.00	100.00	1,100
1936D	24,814,000	.90	1.00	1.10	1.85	3.85	11.50	35.00	110	—
1936S	14,930,000	.90	1.00	1.10	1.50	3.15	10.00	35.00	110	—
1937	79,485,769	.90	1.00	1.10	1.40	2.00	6.50	14.50	70.00	850
1937D	17,826,000	.90	1.00	1.10	1.50	3.15	9.00	30.00	75.00	—
1937D 3-legged	Inc. above	550	600	850	1,000	1,200	1,450	2,700	29,500	—
1937S	5,635,000	.90	1.20	1.40	1.80	4.00	11.00	27.50	67.50	—
1938D	7,020,000	3.50	3.75	3.90	4.00	4.25	8.00	20.00	70.00	—
1938D/D	—	2.50	4.50	6.00	8.00	10.00	17.00	20.00	52.50	—
1938D/S	Inc. above	4.50	6.75	9.00	12.50	19.00	32.50	50.00	185	—

Jefferson Nickel
Monticello, mintmark to right side reverse

KM# 192 • 5.0000 g., **Copper-Nickel**, 21.2 mm. • **Designer:** Felix Schlag **Notes:** Some 1939 strikes have doubling of the word "Monticello" on the reverse.

Date	Mintage	VG-8	F-12	VF-20	XF-40	MS-60	MS-65	-65FS	Prf-65
1938	19,515,365	.30	.50	.80	1.25	4.00	8.50	125	130
1938D	5,376,000	.90	1.00	1.25	1.75	3.50	8.00	95.00	—
1938S	4,105,000	1.75	2.00	2.50	3.00	4.75	8.50	165	—
1939 T I	—	—	—	—	—	—	—	300	70.00
1939 T II	120,627,535	—	.20	.25	.30	1.75	3.50	40.00	130
1939 doubled Monticello T II	—	30.00	50.00	80.00	140	250	750	900	—
1939D T I	—	—	—	—	—	—	—	275	—
1939D T II	3,514,000	3.50	4.00	5.00	10.00	42.00	125	250	—
1939S T I	—	—	—	—	—	—	—	250	—

1921-S Nickel
Grade F-12

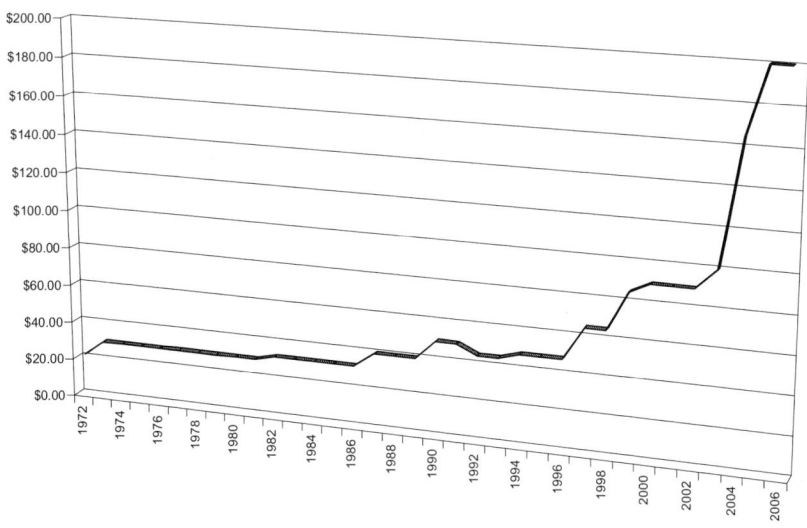

Retail Price

Date	Mintage	VG-8	F-12	VF-20	XF-40	MS-60	MS-65	-65FS	Prf-65
1939S T II	6,630,000	.45	.60	1.50	2.75	15.00	45.00	275	—
1940	176,499,158	—	—	—	.25	1.00	3.00	35.00	135
1940D	43,540,000	—	.20	.30	.40	1.50	2.75	25.00	—
1940S	39,690,000	—	.20	.25	.50	2.50	6.00	45.00	—
1941	203,283,720	—	—	—	.20	.75	2.50	40.00	130
1941D	53,432,000	—	.20	.30	.50	2.50	6.00	25.00	—
1941S	43,445,000	—	.20	.30	.50	3.75	6.75	60.00	—
1942	49,818,600	—	—	—	.40	5.00	8.50	75.00	115
1942D	13,938,000	.30	.40	1.00	2.00	27.00	60.00	70.00	—

Note: Fully Struck Full Step nickels command higher prices. Bright, Fully Struck coins command even higher prices. 1938 thru 1989 - 5 Full Steps. 1990 to date - 6 Full Steps. Without bag marks or nicks on steps.

Monticello, mint mark above reverse

1943/2 P

KM# 192a • **Copper-Silver-Manganese**, 0 oz., 21.2 mm. • **Designer:** Felix Schlag **Notes:** War-time composition nickels have the mint mark above Monticello on the reverse. Composition: 0.350 Silver, .0563 oz. ASW.

Date	Mintage	VG-8	F-12	VF-20	XF-40	MS-60	MS-65	-65FS	Prf-65
1942P	57,900,600	.65	.85	1.00	1.75	6.00	22.50	70.00	205
1942S	32,900,000	.70	1.00	1.10	1.75	6.00	20.00	125	—
1943P	271,165,000	.50	.85	1.00	1.50	2.75	15.00	35.00	—
1943/2P	Inc. above	35.00	50.00	75.00	110	250	650	1,000	—
1943D	15,294,000	.90	1.20	1.50	1.75	4.00	13.00	30.00	—
1943S	104,060,000	.55	.70	1.00	1.50	3.00	13.00	55.00	—
1944P	119,150,000	.50	.70	1.00	1.50	4.00	22.50	100.00	—
1944D	32,309,000	.60	.80	1.00	1.75	6.50	17.50	30.00	—
1944S	21,640,000	.70	1.00	1.25	2.00	3.50	14.00	185	—
1945P	119,408,100	.50	.70	1.00	1.50	3.50	13.50	125	—
1945D	37,158,000	.55	.75	1.00	1.50	3.50	13.00	40.00	—
1945S	58,939,000	.50	.70	.80	.90	3.00	14.00	250	—

Note: Fully Struck Full Step nickels command higher prices. Bright, Fully Struck coins command even higher prices. 1938 thru 1989 - 5 Full Steps. 1990 to date - 6 Full Steps. Without bag marks or nicks on steps.

Pre-war design resumed reverse

KM# A192 • 5.0000 g., **Copper-Nickel**, 21.2 mm. • **Designer:** Felix Schlag **Notes:** KM#192 design and composition resumed. The 1979-S and 1981-S Type II proofs have clearer mint marks than the Type I proofs of those years.

Date	Mintage	VG-8	F-12	VF-20	XF-40	MS-60	MS-65	-65FS	Prf-65
1946	161,116,000	—	—	.20	.25	.80	3.50	40.00	—
1946D	45,292,200	—	—	.25	.35	.95	3.50	30.00	—
1946S	13,560,000	—	—	.30	.40	.50	2.00	45.00	—
1947	95,000,000	—	—	.20	.25	.75	2.00	30.00	—
1947D	37,822,000	—	—	.20	.30	.90	2.50	30.00	—
1947S	24,720,000	—	—	.20	.25	1.00	2.25	55.00	—
1948	89,348,000	—	—	.20	.25	.50	2.50	60.00	—
1948D	44,734,000	—	—	.25	.35	1.20	4.50	30.00	—
1948S	11,300,000	—	—	.25	.50	1.20	3.50	45.00	—
1949	60,652,000	—	—	.25	.30	2.25	6.00	200	—
1949D	36,498,000	—	—	.30	.40	1.25	5.00	75.00	—
1949D/S	Inc. above	—	35.00	40.00	65.00	170	325	1,750	—
1949S	9,716,000	.25	.35	.45	.90	1.50	3.50	145	—
1950	9,847,386	.20	.30	.35	.75	1.50	4.75	150	70.00
1950D	2,630,030	11.00	11.50	12.00	12.50	22.00	30.00	45.00	—
1951	28,609,500	—	—	.40	.50	1.50	9.00	90.00	70.00
1951D	20,460,000	.25	.30	.40	.50	3.00	10.00	45.00	—
1951S	7,776,000	.30	.40	.50	1.10	1.75	5.00	150	—
1952	64,069,980	—	—	.20	.25	.85	4.50	125	37.50
1952D	30,638,000	—	—	.30	.45	2.00	7.00	65.00	—
1952S	20,572,000	—	—	.20	.25	.75	3.50	195	—
1953	46,772,800	—	—	.20	.25	.40	1.50	200	37.50
1953D	59,878,600	—	—	.20	.25	.40	1.50	100.00	—
1953S	19,210,900	—	—	.20	.25	.60	2.50	1,750	—

Date	Mintage	VG-8	F-12	VF-20	XF-40	MS-60	MS-65	-65FS	Prf-65
1954	47,917,350	—	—	—	—	.60	2.00	95.00	20.00
1954D	117,136,560	—	—	—	—	.35	2.00	175	—
1954S	29,384,000	—	—	—	.20	1.00	3.00	1,000	—
1954S/D	Inc. above	—	6.00	9.00	13.00	22.00	65.00	—	—
1955	8,266,200	.25	.35	.40	.45	.75	2.00	85.00	13.50
1955D	74,464,100	—	—	—	—	.20	1.00	150	—
1955D/S	Inc. above	—	5.00	8.50	13.00	33.00	75.00	—	—
1956	35,885,384	—	—	—	—	.30	.70	35.00	2.50
1956D	67,222,940	—	—	—	—	.25	.60	90.00	—
1957	39,655,952	—	—	—	—	.25	.60	40.00	1.50
1957D	136,828,900	—	—	—	—	.25	.60	55.00	—
1958	17,963,652	—	—	.15	.20	.30	.65	80.00	7.00
1958D	168,249,120	—	—	—	—	.25	.60	30.00	—

Note: Fully Struck Full Step nickels command higher prices. Bright, Fully Struck coins command even higher prices. 1938 thru 1989 - 5 Full Steps. 1990 to date - 6 Full Steps. Without bag marks or nicks on steps.

KM# A192 • 5.0000 g., Copper-Nickel, 21.2 mm. • Designer: Felix Schlag Notes: KM#192 design and composition resumed. The 1979-S and 1981-S Type II proofs have clearer mint marks than the Type I proofs of those years.

Date	Mintage	MS-65	MS-65FS	Prf-65	Date	Mintage	MS-65	MS-65FS	Prf-65
1959	28,397,291	.65	30.00	1.25	1982D	373,726,544	3.50	45.00	—
1959D	160,738,240	.55	45.00	—	1982S	(3,857,479)	—	—	3.50
1960	57,107,602	2.00	60.00	1.00	1983P	561,615,000	4.00	45.00	—
1960D	192,582,180	.55	650	—	1983D	536,726,276	2.50	35.00	—
1961	76,668,244	.55	100.00	1.00	1983S	(3,279,126)	—	—	4.00
1961D	229,342,760	.55	800	—	1984P	746,769,000	3.00	65.00	—
1962	100,602,019	1.50	75.00	1.00	1984D	517,675,146	.85	30.00	—
1962D	280,195,720	.55	600	—	1984S	(3,065,110)	—	—	5.00
1963	178,851,645	.55	45.00	1.00	1985P	647,114,962	.75	60.00	—
1963D	276,829,460	.55	650	—	1985D	459,747,446	.75	35.00	—
1964	1,028,622,762	.55	55.00	1.00	1985S	(3,362,821)	—	—	4.00
1964D	1,787,297,160	.50	500	—	1986P	536,883,483	1.00	70.00	—
1965	136,131,380	.50	225	—	1986D	361,819,140	2.00	60.00	—
1966	156,208,283	.50	350	—	1986S	(3,010,497)	—	—	7.00
1967	107,325,800	.50	275	—	1987P	371,499,481	.75	30.00	—
1968 none minted	—	—	—	—	1987D	410,590,604	.75	25.00	—
1968D	91,227,880	.50	750	—	1987S	(4,227,728)	—	—	3.50
1968S	103,437,510	.50	300	0.75	1988P	771,360,000	.75	30.00	—
1969 none minted	—	—	—	—	1988D	663,771,652	.75	25.00	—
1969D	202,807,500	.50	—	—	1988S	(3,262,948)	—	—	6.50
1969S	123,099,631	.50	450	0.75	1989P	898,812,000	.75	75.00	—
1970 none minted	—	—	—	—	1989D	570,842,474	.75	25.00	—
1970D	515,485,380	.50	500	—	1989S	(3,220,194)	—	—	5.50
1970S	241,464,814	.50	125	0.75	1990P	661,636,000	.75	25.00	—
1971	106,884,000	2.00	35.00	—	1990D	663,938,503	.75	25.00	—
1971D	316,144,800	.50	25.00	—	1990S	(3,299,559)	—	—	5.50
1971S	(3,220,733)	—	—	2.00	1991P	614,104,000	.75	25.00	—
1972	202,036,000	.50	35.00	—	1991D	436,496,678	.75	25.00	—
1972D	351,694,600	.50	25.00	—	1991S	(2,867,787)	—	—	5.00
1972S	(3,260,996)	—	—	2.00	1992P	399,552,000	2.00	25.00	—
1973	384,396,000	.50	20.00	—	1992D	450,565,113	.75	25.00	—
1973D	261,405,000	.50	20.00	—	1992S	(4,176,560)	—	—	4.00
1973S	(2,760,339)	—	—	1.75	1993P	412,076,000	.75	25.00	—
1974	601,752,000	.50	75.00	—	1993D	406,084,135	.75	25.00	—
1974D	277,373,000	.50	50.00	—	1993S	(3,394,792)	—	—	4.50
1974S	(2,612,568)	—	—	2.00	1994P	722,160,000	.75	25.00	—
1975	181,772,000	.75	65.00	—	1994P matte proof	(167,703)	—	—	75.00
1975D	401,875,300	.50	60.00	—	1994D	715,762,110	.75	25.00	—
1975S	(2,845,450)	—	—	2.25	1994S	(3,269,923)	—	—	4.00
1976	367,124,000	.75	150	—	1995P	774,156,000	.75	25.00	—
1976D	563,964,147	.60	55.00	—	1995D	888,112,000	.85	25.00	—
1976S	(4,149,730)	—	—	2.00	1995S	(2,707,481)	—	—	7.50
1977	585,376,000	.40	65.00	—	1996P	829,332,000	.75	25.00	—
1977D	297,313,460	.55	35.00	—	1996D	817,736,000	.75	25.00	—
1977S	(3,251,152)	—	—	1.75	1996S	(2,915,212)	—	—	4.00
1978	391,308,000	.40	40.00	—	1997P	470,972,000	.75	25.00	—
1978D	313,092,780	.40	35.00	—	1997P matte proof	(25,000)	—	—	200
1978S	(3,127,781)	—	—	1.75	1997D	466,640,000	2.00	25.00	—
1979	463,188,000	.40	95.00	—	1997S	(1,975,000)	—	—	5.00
1979D	325,867,672	.40	35.00	—	1998P	688,272,000	.80	25.00	—
1979S type I, proof	(3,677,175)	—	—	1.50	1998D	635,360,000	.80	25.00	—
1979S type II, proof	Inc. above	—	—	1.75	1998S	(2,957,286)	—	—	4.50
1980P	593,004,000	.40	30.00	—	1999P	1,212,000,000	.80	20.00	—
1980D	502,323,448	.40	25.00	—	1999D	1,066,720,000	.80	20.00	—
1980S	(3,554,806)	—	—	1.50	1999S	(3,362,462)	—	—	3.50
1981P	657,504,000	.40	70.00	—	2000P	846,240,000	.80	20.00	—
1981D	364,801,843	.40	40.00	—	2000D	1,509,520,000	.80	20.00	—
1981S type I, proof	(4,063,083)	—	—	2.00	2000S	(4,063,361)	—	—	2.00
1981S type II, proof	Inc. above	—	—	2.50	2001P	675,704,000	.50	20.00	—
1982P	292,355,000	12.50	80.00	—	2001D	627,680,000	.50	20.00	—

Date	Mintage	MS-65	MS-65FS	Prf-65
2001S	(3,099,096)	—	—	2.00
2002P	539,280,000	.50	—	—
2002D	691,200,000	.50	—	—
2002S	(3,157,739)	—	—	2.00
2003P	441,840,000	.50	—	—
2003D	383,040,000	.50	—	—
2003S	(3,116,590)	—	—	2.00

Jefferson - Peace Reverse

KM# 360 • 5.0000 g., **Copper Nickel**, 21.2 mm.
• **Rev. Designer:** Norman E. Nemeth

Date	Mintage	MS-65	Prf-65
2004P	361,440,000	.50	—
2004D	372,000,000	.50	—
2004S	—	—	12.50

Jefferson - Keelboat Reverse

KM# 361 • 5.0000 g., **Copper Nickel**, 21.2 mm. •
Rev. Designer: Al Maletsky

Date	Mintage	MS-65	Prf-65
2004P	366,720,000	.50	—
2004D	344,880,000	.50	—
2004S	—	—	12.50

Jefferson large profile - Bison Reverse

KM# 368   • **Copper Nickel**, 0 oz., 21.2 mm. •
Obv. Designer: Joe Fitzgerald and Don Everhart
Rev. Designer: Jamie Franki and Norman E.
Nemeth

Date	Mintage	MS-65	Prf-65
2005P	448,320,000	.50	—
2005D	487,680,000	.50	—
2005S	—	—	2.00

Jefferson - Pacific Coastline

KM# 369   • 0.5000 g., **Copper Nickel**, 0 oz. •
Obv. Designer: Joe Fitzgerald and Don Everhart
Rev. Designer: Joe Fitzgerald and Donna Weaver

Date	Mintage	MS-65	Prf-65
2005P	—	.50	—
2005D	—	.50	—
2005S	—	—	2.00

Jefferson large facing portrait - Enhanced Monticello Reverse

KM# 381   • 5.0000 g., **Copper-Nickel**, 0 oz.,
21 mm. • **Obv. Designer:** Jamie N. Franki and
Donna Weaver **Rev. Designer:** Felix Schlag and
John Mercanti

Date	Mintage	MS-65	Prf-65
2006	—	—	—
2006D	—	—	—
2006S	—	—	—

DIME

Draped Bust Dime
Small eagle reverse

KM# 24 • 2.7000 g., 0.8920 **Silver**, 0.0775 oz. ASW, 19 mm. • **Designer:** Robert Scot **Notes:** 1797 strikes have either 13 or 16 stars on the obverse.

Date	Mintage	G-4	VG-8	F-12	VF-20	XF-40	MS-60
1796	22,135	1,300	1,950	2,250	3,250	5,000	12,000
1797 13 stars	25,261	1,500	2,000	2,500	3,500	6,000	12,000
1797 16 stars	Inc. above	1,500	2,000	2,500	3,500	6,000	12,000

Heraldic eagle reverse

KM# 31 • 2.7000 g., 0.8920 **Silver**, 0.0775 oz. ASW, 19 mm. • **Designer:** Robert Scot **Notes:** The 1798 overdates have either 13 or 16 stars on the obverse. Varieties of the regular 1798 strikes are distinguished by the size of the 8 in the date. The 1805 strikes have either 4 or 5 berries on the olive branch held by the eagle.

Date	Mintage	G-4	VG-8	F-12	VF-20	XF-40	MS-60
1798	27,550	650	800	1,000	1,500	2,750	6,500
1798/97 13 stars	Inc. above	2,000	3,000	4,500	7,000	11,000	—
1798/97 16 stars	Inc. above	675	800	1,050	1,500	2,500	5,500
1798 small 8	Inc. above	900	1,150	1,700	2,400	3,600	9,500
1800	21,760	600	800	1,100	1,600	2,750	—
1801	34,640	650	850	1,300	2,500	4,500	—
1802	10,975	950	1,400	2,000	3,000	6,000	17,500
1803	33,040	550	700	950	1,500	3,600	—
1804 13 stars	8,265	1,400	1,900	2,650	5,500	13,500	—
1804 14 stars	Inc. above	1,600	2,100	3,000	6,000	15,000	—
1805 4 berries	120,780	450	650	800	1,050	2,100	5,000
1805 5 berries	Inc. above	700	1,000	1,300	1,800	2,700	5,250
1807	165,000	450	650	800	1,050	2,100	5,000

1809 Dime
Grade F-12

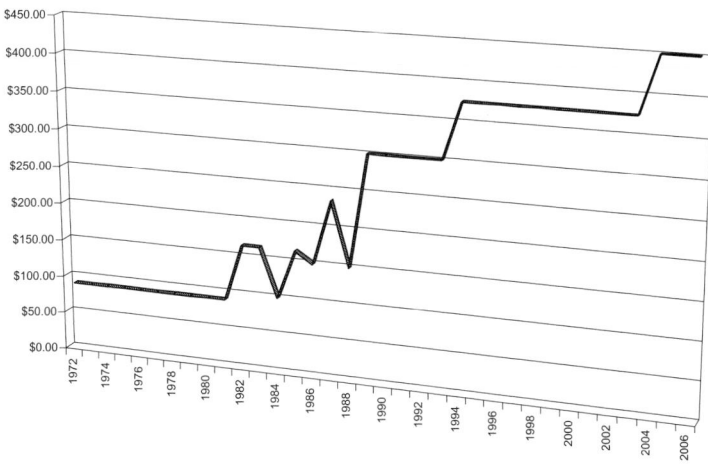

Retail Price

Liberty Cap Dime

KM# 42 • 2.7000 g., 0.8920 **Silver**, .0775 oz. ASW, 18.8 mm. • **Designer:** John Reich **Notes:** Varieties of the 1814, 1821 and 1828 strikes are distinguished by the size of the numerals in the dates. The 1820 varieties are distinguished by the size of the 0 in the date. The 1823 overdates have either large E's or small E's in "United States of America" on the reverse.

Date	Mintage	G-4	VG-8	F-12	VF-20	XF-40	AU-50	MS-60	MS-65
1809	51,065	150	250	450	800	1,400	3,000	4,500	22,500
1811/9	65,180	90.00	165	275	650	1,100	2,000	4,000	22,500
1814 small date	421,500	60.00	70.00	120	475	700	1,000	2,000	8,000
1814 large date	Inc. above	29.00	35.00	55.00	200	400	800	1,100	8,000
1820 large O	942,587	26.00	33.00	55.00	150	375	750	1,050	8,000
1820 small O	Inc. above	26.00	33.00	55.00	175	425	750	1,050	8,000
1821 large date	1,186,512	26.00	33.00	60.00	150	375	750	1,050	8,000
1821 small date	Inc. above	26.00	33.00	55.00	175	400	750	1,050	8,000
1822	100,000	425	600	1,100	1,700	3,000	6,000	10,000	—
1823/22 large E's	440,000	26.00	33.00	50.00	150	375	750	1,050	8,000
1823/22 small E's	Inc. above	26.00	33.00	50.00	150	375	750	1,050	8,000
1824/22 mintage undetermined	—	30.00	50.00	150	400	750	1,500	2,500	—
1825	510,000	26.00	33.00	50.00	150	450	900	1,250	8,000
1827	1,215,000	26.00	33.00	50.00	140	375	775	1,050	8,000
1828 large date	125,000	80.00	110	175	375	750	1,275	3,000	—

KM# 48 • **Silver**, 18.5 mm. • **Designer:** John Reich **Notes:** The three varieties of 1829 strikes and two varieties of 1830 strikes are distinguished by the size of "10C." on the reverse. On the 1833 "high 3" variety, the last 3 in the date is higher than the first 3. The two varieties of the 1834 strikes are distinguished by the size of the 4 in the date.

Date	Mintage	G-4	VG-8	F-12	VF-20	XF-40	AU-50	MS-60	MS-65
1828 small date	Inc. above	30.00	45.00	75.00	195	475	775	1,750	—
1829 very large 10C.	770,000	35.00	45.00	85.00	150	375	600	1,500	—
1829 large 10C.	—	26.00	30.00	40.00	75.00	270	400	725	8,000
1829 medium 10C.	Inc. above	26.00	30.00	40.00	70.00	270	400	725	8,000
1829 small 10C.	Inc. above	26.00	30.00	40.00	70.00	270	400	725	8,000
1829 curl base 2	—	3,200	5,000	7,500	—	—	—	—	—
1830 large 10C.	510,000	26.00	30.00	38.00	65.00	260	375	675	8,000
1830 small 10C.	Inc. above	26.00	30.00	38.00	65.00	260	375	675	8,000
1830/29	Inc. above	35.00	60.00	115	250	500	775	1,500	—
1831	771,350	26.00	30.00	38.00	65.00	260	375	675	6,000
1832	522,500	26.00	30.00	38.00	65.00	260	375	675	6,500
1833	485,000	26.00	30.00	38.00	65.00	260	375	675	6,700
1834	635,000	26.00	30.00	38.00	65.00	260	375	675	6,500
1835	1,410,000	26.00	30.00	38.00	65.00	260	375	675	6,500
1836	1,190,000	26.00	30.00	38.00	65.00	260	375	675	6,500
1837	1,042,000	26.00	30.00	38.00	65.00	260	375	675	6,600

Seated Liberty Dime
No stars around rim obverse

KM# 61 • 2.6700 g., 0.9000 **Silver**, 0.0773 oz. ASW, 17.9 mm. • **Designer:** Christian Gobrecht **Notes:** The two 1837 varieties are distinguished by the size of the numerals in the date.

Date	Mintage	G-4	VG-8	F-12	VF-20	XF-40	AU-50	MS-60	MS-65
1837 small date	Inc. above	40.00	50.00	85.00	290	550	750	1,100	6,500
1837 large date	Inc. above	32.50	43.50	75.00	275	550	750	1,100	6,500
1838O	406,034	40.00	60.00	110	375	725	1,250	3,500	21,000

Stars around rim. No drapery obverse

No drapery at elbow

KM# 63.1 • 2.6700 g., 0.9000 **Silver**, 0.0773 oz. ASW, 17.9 mm. • **Obv. Designer:** Christian Gobrecht
Notes: The two 1838 varieties are distinguished by the size of the stars on the obverse. The 1838 "partial drapery" variety has drapery on Liberty's left elbow. The 1839-O with reverse of 1838-O variety was struck from rusted dies. This variety has a bumpy surface on the reverse.

Date	Mintage	G-4	VG-8	F-12	VF-20	XF-40	AU-50	MS-60	MS-65
1838 small stars	1,992,500	25.00	30.00	50.00	80.00	165	350	600	—
1838 large stars	Inc. above	17.50	20.00	30.00	37.50	110	215	280	8,500
1838 partial drapery	Inc. above	30.00	45.00	65.00	125	195	325	550	—
1839	1,053,115	16.00	18.50	25.00	35.00	105	195	280	3,000
1839O	1,323,000	18.50	22.50	31.50	45.00	115	365	1,250	6,000
1839O reverse 1838O	—	145	200	350	550	1,150	—	—	—
1840	1,358,580	16.00	18.50	25.00	35.00	105	195	300	4,000
1840O	1,175,000	18.50	22.50	40.00	70.00	125	295	975	6,500

Drapery added to Liberty's left elbow obverse

Drapery at elbow

KM# 63.2 • 2.6700 g., 0.9000 **Silver**, 0.0773 oz. ASW, 17.9 mm. • **Designer:** Christian Gobrecht

Date	Mintage	G-4	VG-8	F-12	VF-20	XF-40	AU-50	MS-60	MS-65
1840	Inc. above	35.00	50.00	95.00	185	350	1,250	—	—
1841	1,622,500	16.00	18.50	21.50	27.50	50.00	175	260	2,700
1841O	2,007,500	18.50	22.50	28.50	42.50	75.00	250	1,500	5,000
1841O large O	Inc. above	600	900	1,200	2,500	—	—	—	—
1842	1,887,500	15.00	17.50	21.50	26.00	45.00	175	260	2,700
1842O	2,020,000	18.50	23.50	30.00	75.00	225	1,350	2,900	—
1843	1,370,000	15.00	17.50	21.50	26.00	45.00	175	260	3,000
1843/1843	—	16.00	18.50	22.50	30.00	75.00	200	295	—
1843O	150,000	40.00	75.00	135	300	1,100	2,250	—	—
1844	72,500	275	350	550	800	1,450	2,200	3,000	—
1845	1,755,000	16.00	18.50	21.50	27.50	45.00	120	260	2,600
1845/1845	Inc. above	17.00	20.00	35.00	55.00	100.00	175	—	—
1845O	230,000	22.00	35.00	80.00	250	750	1,750	—	—
1846	31,300	200	225	300	400	950	2,250	5,500	—
1847	245,000	19.00	25.00	40.00	75.00	150	350	950	9,000
1848	451,500	18.50	21.50	25.00	45.00	85.00	185	750	7,000
1849	839,000	17.50	19.50	23.50	33.50	60.00	140	500	4,000
1849O	300,000	21.50	30.00	45.00	120	275	750	2,200	—
1850	1,931,500	17.50	19.50	23.50	32.50	55.00	120	260	5,900
1850O	510,000	21.50	25.00	40.00	80.00	175	475	1,250	—
1851	1,026,500	17.50	20.00	22.50	30.00	60.00	120	325	5,000
1851O	400,000	21.50	25.00	40.00	85.00	175	500	1,850	—
1852	1,535,500	15.00	16.00	18.50	23.50	50.00	120	290	2,550
1852O	430,000	22.50	30.00	45.00	125	235	550	1,800	—
1853	95,000	80.00	100.00	130	200	300	475	800	—

Arrows at date obverse

KM# 77 • 2.4900 g., 0.9000 **Silver**, 0.0721 oz. ASW • **Designer:** Christian Gobrecht

Date	Mintage	G-4	VG-8	F-12	VF-20	XF-40	AU-50	MS-60	MS-65	Prf-65
1853	12,078,010	8.00	9.00	10.00	14.00	45.00	125	330	2,500	31,500
1853O	1,100,000	11.00	14.00	20.00	45.00	145	400	900	—	—
1854	4,470,000	8.75	9.25	10.00	15.00	45.00	125	330	2,500	31,500
1854O	1,770,000	10.00	11.00	14.00	25.00	75.00	175	600	—	—
1855	2,075,000	8.75	9.25	14.00	20.00	55.00	150	350	3,800	31,500

Arrows at date removed obverse

KM# A63.2 • 2.4900 g., 0.9000 **Silver**, 0.0721 oz. ASW • **Designer:** Christian Gobrecht **Notes:** The two 1856 varieties are distinguished by the size of the numerals in the date.

Date	Mintage	G-4	VG-8	F-12	VF-20	XF-40	AU-50	MS-60	MS-65	Prf-65
1856 small date	5,780,000	14.00	15.00	18.00	22.00	37.50	115	250	7,050	38,000
1856 large date	Inc. above	16.00	18.50	19.50	25.00	65.00	175	475	—	—
1856O	1,180,000	16.00	18.50	19.50	35.00	85.00	215	625	5,250	—
1856S	70,000	160	225	325	500	1,200	1,750	—	—	—
1857	5,580,000	14.00	15.50	16.50	22.50	37.50	110	260	2,600	3,400
1857O	1,540,000	14.00	16.00	18.50	25.00	65.00	200	375	2,600	—
1858	1,540,000	14.00	15.50	16.50	22.50	55.00	145	260	2,600	3,400
1858O	290,000	19.00	25.00	40.00	85.00	165	280	800	5,000	—
1858S	60,000	135	200	300	425	975	1,400	—	—	—
1859	430,000	16.00	20.00	25.00	45.00	70.00	140	350	—	3,400
1859O	480,000	16.00	20.00	25.00	45.00	80.00	225	550	—	—
1859S	60,000	150	225	325	500	1,350	3,000	—	—	—
1860S	140,000	30.00	40.00	55.00	135	300	800	—	—	—

"United States of America" replaced stars obverse

KM# 92 • 2.4900 g., 0.9000 **Silver**, 0.0721 oz. ASW • **Obv. Designer:** Christian Gobrecht **Notes:** The 1873 "closed-3" and "open-3" varieties are distinguished by the amount of space between the upper left and lower left serifs of the 3 in the date.

Date	Mintage	G-4	VG-8	F-12	VF-20	XF-40	AU-50	MS-60	MS-65	Prf-65
1860	607,000	15.00	22.00	29.00	31.00	55.00	125	275	1,350	1,400
1860O	40,000	400	500	975	1,750	3,500	5,500	8,500	—	—
1861	1,884,000	12.50	15.00	17.00	20.00	35.00	72.50	135	1,250	1,400
1861S	172,500	55.00	90.00	165	275	400	900	1,400	—	—
1862	847,550	16.00	17.50	19.50	25.00	45.00	77.50	165	1,250	1,400

1866-S Dime
Grade F-12

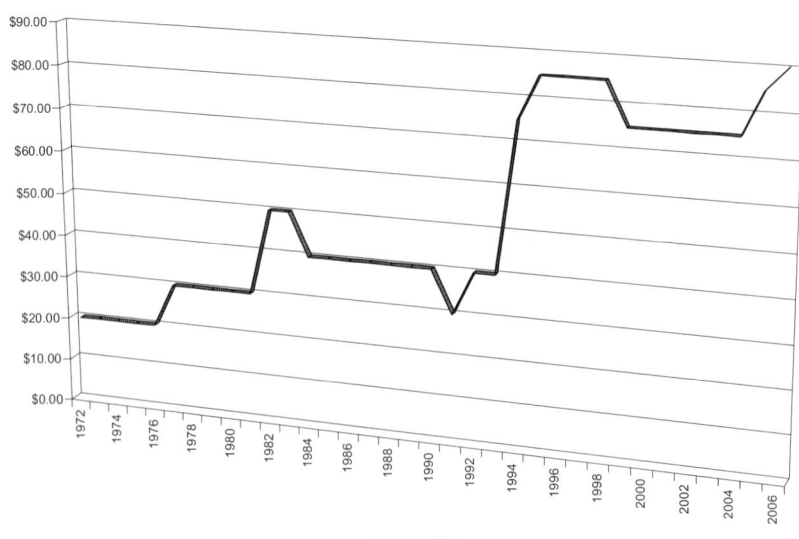

Retail Price

Date	Mintage	G-4	VG-8	F-12	VF-20	XF-40	AU-50	MS-60	MS-65	Prf-65
1862S	180,750	45.00	65.00	95.00	185	375	775	1,000	—	—
1863	14,460	400	475	600	700	875	1,100	1,300	—	1,400
1863S	157,500	34.00	44.00	75.00	125	275	550	1,200	—	—
1864	11,470	400	475	600	700	875	1,000	1,200	—	1,400
1864S	230,000	35.00	45.00	75.00	110	225	425	1,200	—	—
1865	10,500	450	525	650	750	900	1,100	1,250	—	1,400
1865S	175,000	45.00	55.00	85.00	125	325	850	—	—	—
1866	8,725	500	600	750	900	1,000	1,200	1,800	—	1,750
1866S	135,000	50.00	60.00	90.00	150	325	700	1,900	—	—
1867	6,625	600	700	950	1,100	1,450	1,600	1,800	—	1,750
1867S	140,000	50.00	60.00	90.00	150	325	700	1,200	—	—
1868	464,000	18.00	22.00	29.00	39.00	85.00	175	300	—	1,400
1868S	260,000	30.00	35.00	50.00	85.00	165	300	600	—	—
1869	256,600	25.00	35.00	45.00	80.00	135	250	600	—	1,400
1869S	450,000	25.00	30.00	40.00	55.00	85.00	175	400	—	—
1870	471,000	18.00	22.00	30.00	40.00	50.00	80.00	150	—	1,400
1870S	50,000	300	375	500	600	750	950	2,000	—	—
1871	907,710	16.00	20.00	25.00	33.00	55.00	175	300	—	1,400
1871CC	20,100	1,800	2,250	3,250	5,000	8,500	—	—	—	—
1871S	320,000	35.00	55.00	75.00	130	195	350	900	—	—
1872	2,396,450	12.00	15.00	17.00	20.00	31.00	95.00	175	—	1,400
1872CC	35,480	575	875	1,350	2,750	6,500	—	—	—	—
1872S	190,000	40.00	60.00	80.00	150	235	450	1,100	—	—
1873 closed 3	1,568,600	12.50	15.00	18.00	22.00	50.00	100.00	200	—	1,400
1873 open 3	Inc. above	22.00	30.00	40.00	60.00	110	225	650	—	—
1873CC	12,400	—	—	—	—	—	—	—	—	—

Note: 1873-CC, Heritage Sale, April 1999, MS-64, $632,500.

Arrows at date obverse

KM# 105 • 2.5000 g., 0.9000 **Silver**, 0.0724 oz. ASW • **Designer:** Christian Gobrecht

Date	Mintage	G-4	VG-8	F-12	VF-20	XF-40	AU-50	MS-60	MS-65	Prf-65
1873	2,378,500	15.00	18.50	25.00	55.00	150	350	500	4,500	4,500
1873CC	18,791	1,800	2,250	3,250	5,000	9,500	—	—	—	—
1873S	455,000	20.00	30.00	40.00	70.00	190	400	1,500	—	—
1874	2,940,700	13.50	17.50	22.50	50.00	150	315	500	4,500	4,500
1874CC	10,817	4,200	5,500	8,000	12,500	25,000	—	—	—	—
1874S	240,000	60.00	75.00	100.00	160	250	450	1,500	—	—

Arrows at date removed obverse

KM# A92 • 2.5000 g., 0.9000 **Silver**, 0.0724 oz. ASW • **Designer:** Christian Gobrecht **Notes:** On the 1876-CC doubled-obverse variety, doubling appears in the words "of America" in the legend.

Date	Mintage	G-4	VG-8	F-12	VF-20	XF-40	AU-50	MS-60	MS-65	Prf-65
1875	10,350,700	12.50	15.00	17.00	20.00	27.50	72.50	125	2,250	4,600
1875CC mint mark in wreath	4,645,000	15.00	16.00	18.50	26.00	42.50	90.00	190	2,700	—
1875CC mint mark under wreath	Inc. above	15.00	16.00	22.50	37.50	65.00	165	235	3,000	—
1875S mint mark in wreath	9,070,000	20.00	25.00	30.00	43.00	65.00	125	225	3,100	—
1875S mint mark under wreath	Inc. above	12.50	15.50	17.50	20.00	27.50	72.50	125	1,100	—
1876	11,461,150	12.00	15.00	17.00	20.00	24.00	72.50	125	1,100	1,200
1876CC	8,270,000	15.00	16.00	18.50	26.00	42.50	82.50	180	—	—
1876CC doubled obverse	Inc. above	16.00	20.00	30.00	80.00	135	300	500	—	—
1876S	10,420,000	12.50	15.00	17.00	20.00	35.00	72.50	125	1,750	—
1877	7,310,510	12.00	15.00	17.00	20.00	27.50	72.50	125	1,100	1,200
1877CC	7,700,000	15.00	16.00	18.50	26.00	42.50	82.50	180	1,100	—
1877S	2,340,000	14.00	18.00	20.00	30.00	50.00	105	225	—	—
1878	1,678,800	12.50	15.00	17.00	20.00	36.00	72.50	125	1,500	1,200
1878CC	200,000	60.00	85.00	135	225	325	475	775	3,900	—
1879	15,100	225	250	300	350	425	525	675	1,750	1,500
1880	37,335	185	215	250	300	350	400	500	1,750	1,500
1881	24,975	200	225	275	325	400	500	650	2,500	1,600

Date	Mintage	G-4	VG-8	F-12	VF-20	XF-40	AU-50	MS-60	MS-65	Prf-65
1882	3,911,100	12.50	15.00	17.00	20.00	27.50	72.50	125	1,100	1,200
1883	7,675,712	12.50	15.00	17.00	20.00	27.50	72.50	125	1,100	1,200
1884	3,366,380	12.50	15.00	17.00	20.00	27.50	72.50	125	1,100	1,200
1884S	564,969	30.00	35.00	45.00	55.00	125	280	650	—	—
1885	2,533,427	12.50	15.00	17.00	20.00	27.50	72.50	125	1,100	1,200
1885S	43,690	375	525	725	1,450	2,200	3,600	5,000	—	—
1886	6,377,570	12.50	15.00	17.00	20.00	27.50	72.50	125	1,100	1,200
1886S	206,524	50.00	70.00	80.00	125	175	280	600	—	—
1887	11,283,939	12.50	15.00	17.00	20.00	27.50	72.50	125	1,100	1,200
1887S	4,454,450	12.50	15.00	17.00	20.00	38.00	80.00	125	1,100	
1888	5,496,487	12.50	15.00	17.00	20.00	27.50	72.50	125	1,100	1,200
1888S	1,720,000	12.50	15.00	17.00	25.00	40.00	95.00	200	—	—
1889	7,380,711	12.50	15.00	17.00	20.00	27.50	72.50	125	1,100	1,200
1889S	972,678	14.00	18.00	25.00	45.00	70.00	150	475	4,500	
1890	9,911,541	12.50	15.00	17.00	20.00	27.50	72.50	125	1,100	1,200
1890S	1,423,076	14.00	15.00	22.50	50.00	85.00	155	400	4,900	
1891	15,310,600	12.50	15.00	17.00	20.00	27.50	72.50	125	1,100	1,200
1891O	4,540,000	12.50	15.00	17.00	20.00	27.50	72.50	175	1,750	—
1891O /horizontal O	Inc. above	65.00	95.00	125	175	225	400	—	—	—
1891S	3,196,116	13.50	15.00	17.50	20.00	30.00	75.00	225	1,650	—
1891S/S	Inc. above	25.00	30.00	40.00	85.00	135	250	—	—	—

Barber Dime

KM# 113 • 2.5000 g., 0.9000 **Silver**, 0.0724 oz. ASW, 17.9 mm. • **Designer:** Charles E. Barber

Date	Mintage	G-4	VG-8	F-12	VF-20	XF-40	AU-50	MS-60	MS-65	Prf-65
1892	12,121,245	5.00	6.25	16.00	23.50	27.50	70.00	110	750	1,450
1892O	3,841,700	11.00	15.00	32.50	54.00	75.00	96.00	160	1,275	—
1892S	990,710	66.00	115	200	235	285	335	425	4,000	—
1893	3,340,792	8.25	12.50	20.00	30.00	46.00	82.50	160	1,000	1,450
1893O	1,760,000	31.00	45.00	115	150	190	250	330	3,250	—
1893S	2,491,401	14.00	25.00	37.50	45.00	85.00	155	300	4,350	—
1894	1,330,972	25.00	45.00	115	155	190	235	320	1,200	1,450
1894O	720,000	70.00	105	205	275	445	650	1,550	14,500	—
1894S	24	—	—	—	—	—	—	—	1,300,000	—

Note: 1894S, Eliasberg Sale, May 1996, Prf-64, $451,000.

Date	Mintage	G-4	VG-8	F-12	VF-20	XF-40	AU-50	MS-60	MS-65	Prf-65
1895	690,880	85.00	180	345	480	575	650	775	2,800	2,000
1895O	440,000	385	575	880	1,250	2,500	3,800	6,000	19,500	—
1895S	1,120,000	43.50	60.00	130	185	240	320	500	7,800	—
1896	2,000,762	11.50	23.00	55.00	90.00	100.00	120	160	1,500	1,450
1896O	610,000	80.00	155	295	375	480	715	1,000	9,400	—
1896S	575,056	85.00	160	280	325	400	525	770	4,600	—
1897	10,869,264	2.50	3.45	8.00	15.00	32.50	76.00	130	700	1,450
1897O	666,000	69.50	115	280	375	480	615	975	4,700	—
1897S	1,342,844	21.00	45.00	96.00	125	185	275	450	4,250	—
1898	16,320,735	2.50	3.45	8.00	15.00	32.50	76.00	130	720	1,450
1898O	2,130,000	13.00	27.50	85.00	140	205	285	450	4,150	—
1898S	1,702,507	8.50	15.00	32.50	47.50	80.00	160	370	3,850	—
1899	19,580,846	2.50	2.80	7.50	11.50	26.00	70.00	115	700	1,450
1899O	2,650,000	9.75	19.50	70.00	100.00	150	230	415	4,850	—
1899S	1,867,493	8.50	16.00	26.00	34.00	47.50	110	300	4,600	—
1900	17,600,912	2.80	4.00	7.00	11.00	27.50	780	100.00	825	1,450
1900O	2,010,000	19.50	38.50	110	150	225	355	595	6,000	—
1900S	5,168,270	4.75	6.25	12.50	19.50	31.50	75.00	155	1,900	—
1901	18,860,478	2.50	3.75	6.50	10.00	27.50	65.00	110	850	1,450
1901O	5,620,000	3.75	5.25	16.00	27.50	67.50	180	450	4,500	—
1901S	593,022	80.00	150	360	450	520	675	1,000	5,500	—
1902	21,380,777	3.00	3.75	5.50	8.00	23.00	65.00	100.00	700	1,450
1902O	4,500,000	3.45	5.25	15.00	32.50	62.50	130	125	4,650	—
1902S	2,070,000	8.00	21.00	55.00	85.00	135	200	385	4,000	—
1903	19,500,755	2.50	3.75	4.40	8.00	25.00	65.00	110	1,150	1,450
1903O	8,180,000	3.50	5.00	13.50	23.50	50.00	110	250	5,100	—
1903S	613,300	84.00	130	340	490	770	845	1,150	3,750	—
1904	14,601,027	2.50	3.75	6.25	9.50	25.00	65.00	110	1,950	1,450
1904S	800,000	45.00	75.00	160	240	345	480	750	4,500	—
1905	14,552,350	2.80	3.45	5.60	8.00	25.00	65.00	110	700	1,450
1905O	3,400,000	4.00	10.00	34.00	57.50	96.00	155	285	1,900	—
1905S	6,855,199	3.50	3.85	9.00	18.50	45.00	100.00	220	800	—
1906	19,958,406	1.75	2.20	3.75	6.75	22.00	62.50	100.00	700	1,450
1906D	4,060,000	2.75	3.85	7.00	15.00	36.00	80.00	175	1,600	—
1906O	2,610,000	5.50	13.00	47.50	75.00	100.00	135	200	1,300	—
1906S	3,136,640	2.80	5.25	12.50	22.00	46.00	115	240	1,300	—

1901-S Dime
Grade F-12

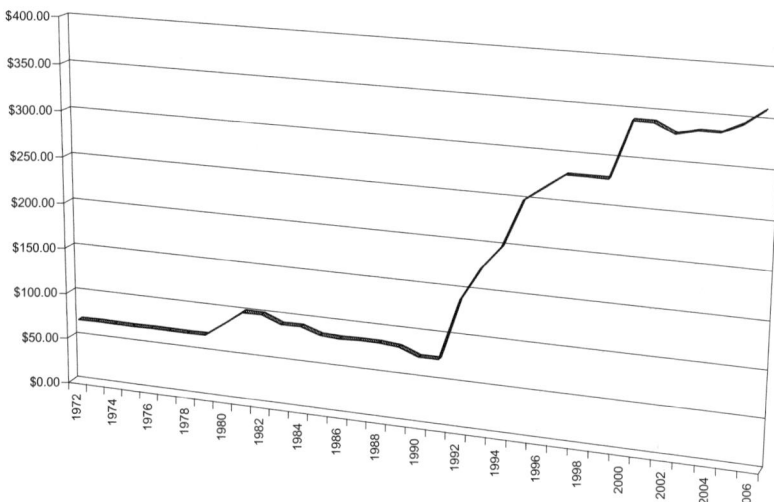

Date	Mintage	G-4	VG-8	F-12	VF-20	XF-40	AU-50	MS-60	MS-65	Prf-65
1907	22,220,575	1.75	2.20	3.40	6.75	22.00	62.50	110	700	1,450
1907D	4,080,000	2.50	4.00	8.50	17.50	45.00	115	280	4,600	—
1907O	5,058,000	3.45	6.75	31.50	47.50	62.50	110	210	1,350	—
1907S	3,178,470	3.45	5.50	16.00	27.50	67.50	150	420	2,500	—
1908	10,600,545	2.20	2.50	3.40	6.75	22.00	62.50	110	700	1,450
1908D	7,490,000	2.15	2.50	4.65	9.50	30.00	62.50	130	1,150	—
1908O	1,789,000	5.00	11.00	42.50	61.00	96.00	150	300	1,700	—
1908S	3,220,000	3.45	5.25	11.50	22.00	47.50	175	325	2,750	—
1909	10,240,650	2.20	2.50	3.40	6.75	22.00	62.50	110	700	1,700
1909D	954,000	7.50	19.50	60.00	96.00	135	230	500	3,600	—
1909O	2,287,000	4.00	7.50	12.50	22.00	50.00	96.00	190	2,000	—
1909S	1,000,000	9.00	20.00	85.00	125	190	330	535	3,200	—
1910	11,520,551	1.85	2.20	3.40	9.50	23.00	62.50	110	700	1,450
1910D	3,490,000	2.50	4.00	8.50	19.50	47.50	110	220	1,550	—
1910S	1,240,000	5.25	10.00	50.00	71.00	110	200	435	2,600	—
1911	18,870,543	1.75	2.10	3.40	6.75	22.00	62.50	110	700	1,700
1911D	11,209,000	1.75	2.10	3.40	6.75	25.00	62.50	110	750	—
1911S	3,520,000	2.80	3.75	8.50	19.00	41.50	110	200	1,300	—
1912	19,350,700	1.75	2.10	3.40	6.75	22.00	62.50	110	700	1,700
1912D	11,760,000	1.75	2.10	3.75	6.75	22.00	62.50	110	700	—
1912S	3,420,000	2.20	2.75	5.60	12.50	34.00	96.00	160	850	—
1913	19,760,622	1.75	2.10	3.00	6.50	22.00	62.50	110	700	1,450
1913S	510,000	35.00	45.00	100.00	160	250	330	500	1,450	—
1914	17,360,655	1.75	2.10	3.00	6.50	22.00	62.50	110	700	1,700
1914D	11,908,000	1.75	2.10	3.40	6.50	22.00	62.50	110	700	—
1914S	2,100,000	3.00	4.00	8.00	17.50	41.50	80.00	150	1,350	—
1915	5,620,450	2.20	2.50	3.00	7.00	22.00	62.50	110	700	2,000
1915S	960,000	7.00	12.00	32.50	47.50	70.00	135	250	1,600	—
1916	18,490,000	1.75	2.15	3.40	8.00	22.00	62.50	110	700	—
1916S	5,820,000	1.75	2.65	4.00	8.00	23.50	65.00	110	850	—

Mercury Dime

Mint mark   1942/41

KM# 140 • 2.5000 g., 0.9000 **Silver**, 0.0724 oz. ASW, 17.9 mm. • **Designer:** Adolph A. Weinman **Notes:** All specimens listed as -65FSB are for fully struck MS-65 coins with fully split and rounded horizontal bands on the fasces.

Date	Mintage	G-4	VG-8	F-12	VF-20	XF-40	MS-60	MS-65	Prf-65	-65FSB
1916	22,180,080	3.45	4.70	6.25	7.00	10.00	30.00	90.00	—	120

Date	Mintage	G-4	VG-8	F-12	VF-20	XF-40	MS-60	MS-65	Prf-65	-65FSB
1916D	264,000	795	1,400	2,500	3,850	6,200	9,350	22,500	—	44,500
1916S	10,450,000	4.00	4.75	9.75	12.50	20.00	35.00	155	—	600
1917	55,230,000	1.85	2.00	2.50	5.00	7.50	30.00	155	—	400
1917D	9,402,000	4.00	5.00	10.00	21.50	42.00	120	1,100	—	6,000
1917S	27,330,000	1.80	2.00	3.50	5.75	10.00	62.00	470	—	1,150
1918	26,680,000	2.25	2.75	5.50	10.00	25.00	70.00	420	—	1,150
1918D	22,674,800	2.65	3.00	4.50	10.00	21.50	105	600	—	33,500
1918S	19,300,000	2.40	2.75	3.50	8.50	16.00	90.00	660	—	6,600
1919	35,740,000	1.90	2.00	3.00	5.00	10.00	37.00	320	—	700
1919D	9,939,000	3.35	6.00	11.00	21.50	35.00	175	1,400	—	38,500
1919S	8,850,000	2.75	3.00	8.00	15.00	31.00	175	1,000	—	13,000
1920	59,030,000	1.35	1.45	2.00	3.50	6.50	27.50	235	—	515
1920D	19,171,000	2.40	2.75	4.00	7.00	18.00	105	750	—	4,000
1920S	13,820,000	2.40	2.75	4.00	7.50	15.00	110	1,300	—	8,000
1921	1,230,000	43.50	75.00	125	275	565	1,000	3,200	—	4,400
1921D	1,080,000	62.50	115	205	385	700	1,150	3,200	—	5,600
1923	50,130,000	1.35	1.60	2.00	3.50	6.00	27.50	110	—	295
1923S	6,440,000	2.40	2.75	7.00	12.50	65.00	160	1,150	—	6,900
1924	24,010,000	1.35	1.60	2.50	4.25	12.00	42.00	175	—	520
1924D	6,810,000	2.75	4.00	6.00	16.00	49.00	160	950	—	1,400
1924S	7,120,000	2.75	3.50	4.00	8.75	44.00	170	1,100	—	14,000
1925	25,610,000	1.35	1.45	2.00	3.75	7.50	27.00	195	—	1,000
1925D	5,117,000	4.00	4.25	11.50	38.00	110	350	1,750	—	3,500
1925S	5,850,000	2.40	2.75	7.00	12.50	65.00	175	1,400	—	4,400
1926	32,160,000	1.35	1.45	1.70	2.75	4.25	25.00	240	—	525
1926D	6,828,000	2.75	4.00	4.50	8.50	24.00	125	550	—	2,650
1926S	1,520,000	9.00	11.00	25.00	55.00	225	900	3,000	—	6,500
1927	28,080,000	1.35	1.45	1.75	3.50	4.50	26.00	125	—	400
1927D	4,812,000	2.75	5.00	7.25	18.50	65.00	175	1,200	—	8,500
1927S	4,770,000	2.10	3.50	4.75	8.00	23.00	280	1,400	—	7,700
1928	19,480,000	1.35	1.45	1.75	3.50	4.00	27.50	110	—	300
1928D	4,161,000	3.75	4.00	8.00	18.50	44.00	170	875	—	2,500
1928S	7,400,000	1.80	2.10	2.75	5.50	16.00	125	425	—	1,900
1929	25,970,000	1.35	1.60	1.95	2.75	4.00	20.00	60.00	—	265
1929D	5,034,000	1.80	3.00	3.50	6.25	14.50	25.00	70.00	—	225
1929S	4,730,000	1.35	1.60	2.00	4.00	7.00	32.50	120	—	525
1930	6,770,000	1.35	1.50	2.00	3.50	7.00	26.00	115	—	525
1930S	1,843,000	2.50	3.50	4.80	6.25	15.00	75.00	200	—	565
1931	3,150,000	2.10	2.50	2.75	4.25	8.75	35.00	135	—	725
1931D	1,260,000	9.00	11.00	15.00	18.00	32.50	85.00	225	—	350
1931S	1,800,000	3.00	3.50	5.00	9.00	16.00	85.00	225	—	2,100
1934	24,080,000	—	1.45	1.75	3.00	5.00	21.50	40.00	—	150
1934D	6,772,000	1.60	2.10	2.75	4.00	8.00	50.00	72.00	—	360
1935	58,830,000	—	—	1.50	2.15	4.25	8.00	30.00	—	70.00

1916-D Dime
Grade F-12

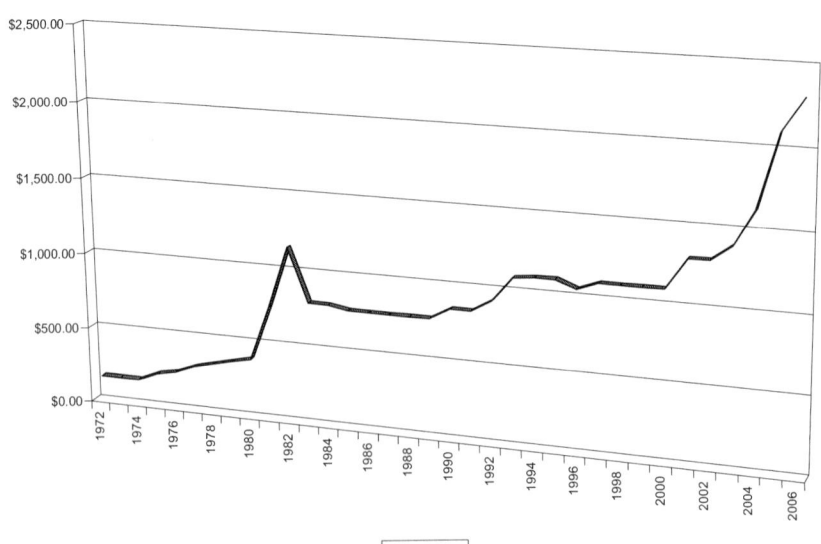

Retail Price

Date	Mintage	G-4	VG-8	F-12	VF-20	XF-40	MS-60	MS-65	Prf-65	-65FSB
1935D	10,477,000	1.25	1.75	2.50	3.75	7.50	34.00	72.00	—	600
1935S	15,840,000	1.00	1.50	1.75	3.00	5.50	24.00	31.50	—	500
1936	87,504,130	—	—	1.50	2.25	3.50	8.00	25.00	2,000	90.00
1936D	16,132,000	—	1.25	1.50	3.00	6.50	26.00	42.00	—	295
1936S	9,210,000	—	1.25	1.50	2.50	3.00	20.00	31.50	—	85.00
1937	56,865,756	—	—	1.50	2.00	3.25	8.00	23.00	800	42.00
1937D	14,146,000	—	1.25	1.50	3.00	5.50	21.00	43.00	—	100.00
1937S	9,740,000	—	1.25	1.50	3.00	5.50	24.00	34.00	—	195
1938	22,198,728	—	—	1.50	2.25	3.50	13.00	27.50	450	80.00
1938D	5,537,000	1.50	1.75	2.00	3.50	6.00	16.00	28.00	—	65.00
1938S	8,090,000	1.35	1.55	1.75	2.35	3.75	20.00	35.00	—	135
1939	67,749,321	—	—	1.50	2.00	3.25	8.50	25.00	425	170
1939D	24,394,000	—	1.25	1.50	2.00	3.50	7.50	26.00	—	45.00
1939S	10,540,000	1.25	1.50	2.00	2.50	4.25	21.00	35.00	—	750
1940	65,361,827	—	—	—	1.10	2.50	6.00	26.00	385	57.50
1940D	21,198,000	—	—	—	1.10	1.50	8.00	30.00	—	55.00
1940S	21,560,000	—	—	—	1.10	1.50	8.50	30.00	—	95.00
1941	175,106,557	—	—	—	1.10	1.50	5.00	30.00	385	42.00
1941D	45,634,000	—	—	—	1.10	1.50	8.00	23.00	—	40.00
1941S	43,090,000	—	—	—	1.10	1.50	7.00	30.00	—	50.00
1942	205,432,329	—	—	—	1.10	1.50	5.50	24.00	385	52.50
1942/41	Inc. above	525	525	625	715	835	1,900	12,500	—	38,500
1942D	60,740,000	—	—	—	1.10	1.50	8.00	27.50	—	40.00
1942/41D	Inc. above	500	595	650	780	920	2,250	5,600	—	19,500
1942S	49,300,000	—	—	—	1.10	1.50	9.50	24.00	—	140
1943	191,710,000	—	—	—	1.10	1.50	5.50	30.00	—	50.00
1943D	71,949,000	—	—	—	1.10	1.50	7.50	27.50	—	40.00
1943S	60,400,000	—	—	—	1.10	1.50	8.25	25.00	—	66.00
1944	231,410,000	—	—	—	1.10	1.50	5.50	23.00	—	80.00
1944D	62,224,000	—	—	—	1.10	1.50	6.50	23.00	—	40.00
1944S	49,490,000	—	—	—	1.10	1.50	6.50	30.00	—	50.00
1945	159,130,000	—	—	—	1.10	1.50	5.50	23.00	—	8,000
1945D	40,245,000	—	—	—	1.10	1.50	6.00	24.00	—	40.00
1945S	41,920,000	—	—	—	1.10	1.50	6.50	24.00	—	135
1945S micro S	Inc. above	1.00	1.25	1.50	3.00	4.25	26.00	85.00	—	650

Roosevelt Dime

  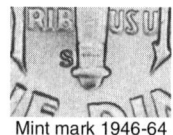

Mint mark 1946-64

KM# 195 • 2.5000 g., 0.9000 **Silver**, 0.0724 oz. ASW, 17.9 mm. • **Designer:** John R. Sinnock

Date	Mintage	G-4	VG-8	F-12	VF-20	XF-40	AU-50	MS-60	MS-65	Prf-65
1946	225,250,000	—	—	—	—	—	.95	3.10	9.00	—
1946D	61,043,500	—	—	—	—	—	1.10	4.00	10.00	—
1946S	27,900,000	—	—	—	—	—	.90	4.00	11.00	—
1947	121,520,000	—	—	—	—	—	.95	6.00	15.00	—
1947D	46,835,000	—	—	—	—	.95	1.50	8.50	17.00	—
1947S	34,840,000	—	—	—	—	.95	1.25	5.00	16.00	—
1948	74,950,000	—	—	—	—	.95	1.50	5.00	14.00	—
1948D	52,841,000	—	—	—	—	1.20	2.00	6.00	14.00	—
1948S	35,520,000	—	—	—	—	.95	1.10	5.00	12.00	—
1949	30,940,000	—	—	—	1.00	1.50	4.00	29.00	50.00	—
1949D	26,034,000	—	—	.60	.80	1.25	2.00	14.00	30.00	—
1949S	13,510,000	—	1.00	1.25	1.50	2.75	6.00	45.00	65.00	—
1950	50,181,500	—	—	—	—	.95	1.35	14.00	25.00	55.00
1950D	46,803,000	—	—	—	—	—	1.60	6.00	10.00	—
1950S	20,440,000	—	.85	1.00	1.10	1.25	6.00	40.00	55.00	—
1951	102,937,602	—	—	—	—	—	1.00	3.00	6.00	65.00
1951D	56,529,000	—	—	—	—	—	.95	2.00	5.00	—
1951S	31,630,000	—	—	—	.75	1.05	3.25	15.00	26.00	—
1952	99,122,073	—	—	—	—	—	1.15	2.50	6.00	40.00
1952D	122,100,000	—	—	—	—	—	.95	2.75	7.00	—
1952S	44,419,500	—	—	—	.75	1.05	1.50	6.00	15.00	—
1953	53,618,920	—	—	—	—	—	1.00	3.00	6.00	45.00
1953D	136,433,000	—	—	—	—	—	.95	3.00	6.00	—
1953S	39,180,000	—	—	—	—	—	—	1.50	5.00	—
1954	114,243,503	—	—	—	—	—	—	1.50	5.00	22.00
1954D	106,397,000	—	—	—	—	—	—	1.50	5.00	—
1954S	22,860,000	—	—	—	—	—	—	1.00	3.15	—
1955	12,828,381	—	—	—	.70	—	—	1.00	3.15	20.00
1955D	13,959,000	—	—	—	—	—	—	1.00	3.15	—
1955S	18,510,000	—	—	—	—	—	—	1.00	3.15	—
1956	109,309,384	—	—	—	—	—	—	1.00	3.00	8.00
1956D	108,015,100	—	—	—	—	—	—	1.00	3.00	—

Date	Mintage	G-4	VG-8	F-12	VF-20	XF-40	AU-50	MS-60	MS-65	Prf-65
1957	161,407,952	—	—	—	—	—	—	1.00	3.00	4.00
1957D	113,354,330	—	—	—	—	—	—	1.25	4.00	—
1958	32,785,652	—	—	—	—	—	—	1.00	3.00	6.00
1958D	136,564,600	—	—	—	—	—	—	1.00	3.00	—
1959	86,929,291	—	—	—	—	—	—	1.00	3.00	2.50
1959D	164,919,790	—	—	—	—	—	—	1.00	3.00	—
1960	72,081,602	—	—	—	—	—	—	1.00	3.00	2.50
1960D	200,160,400	—	—	—	—	—	—	1.00	3.00	—
1961	96,758,244	—	—	—	—	—	—	1.00	3.00	2.00
1961D	209,146,550	—	—	—	—	—	—	1.00	3.00	—
1962	75,668,019	—	—	—	—	—	—	1.00	3.00	2.00
1962D	334,948,380	—	—	—	—	—	—	1.00	3.00	—
1963	126,725,645	—	—	—	—	—	—	1.00	3.00	2.00
1963D	421,476,530	—	—	—	—	—	—	1.00	3.00	—
1964	933,310,762	—	—	—	—	—	—	1.00	3.00	2.00
1964D	1,357,517,180	—	—	—	—	—	—	1.00	3.00	—

Roosevelt Dime

1982 No mint mark

Mint Mark
1968-present

KM# 195a • 2.2700 g., **Copper-Nickel Clad Copper**, 17.9 mm. • **Designer:** John R. Sinnock **Notes:** The 1979-S and 1981-S Type II proofs have clearer mint marks than the Type I proofs of those years. On the 1982 no-mint-mark variety, the mint mark was inadvertently left off.

Date	Mintage	MS-65	Prf-65	Date	Mintage	MS-65	Prf-65
1965	1,652,140,570	1.00	—	1981S type I	—	—	1.00
1966	1,382,734,540	1.00	—	1981S type II	—	—	2.00
1967	2,244,007,320	1.50	—	1982P	519,475,000	8.50	—
1968	424,470,000	1.00	—	1982 no mint mark	—	—	225
1968D	480,748,280	1.00	—	1982D	542,713,584	3.00	—
1968S	(3,041,506)	—	1.00	1982S	(3,857,479)	—	2.00
1969	145,790,000	3.00	—	1983P	647,025,000	7.00	—
1969D	563,323,870	1.00	—	1983D	730,129,224	2.50	—
1969S	(2,934,631)	—	0.80	1983S	(3,279,126)	—	2.00
1970	345,570,000	1.00	—	1984P	856,669,000	1.00	—
1970D	754,942,100	1.00	—	1984D	704,803,976	2.00	—
1970S	(2,632,810)	—	1.00	1984S	(3,065,110)	—	2.00
1971	162,690,000	2.00	—	1985P	705,200,962	1.00	—
1971D	377,914,240	1.00	—	1985D	587,979,970	1.00	—
1971S	(3,220,733)	—	1.00	1985S	(3,362,821)	—	1.00
1972	431,540,000	1.00	—	1986P	682,649,693	2.00	—
1972D	330,290,000	1.00	—	1986D	473,326,970	2.00	—
1972S	(3,260,996)	—	1.00	1986S	(3,010,497)	—	2.75
1973	315,670,000	1.00	—	1987P	762,709,481	1.00	—
1973D	455,032,426	1.00	—	1987D	653,203,402	1.00	—
1973S	(2,760,339)	—	1.00	1987S	(4,227,728)	—	1.00
1974	470,248,000	1.00	—	1988P	1,030,550,000	1.00	—
1974D	571,083,000	1.00	—	1988D	962,385,488	1.00	—
1974S	(2,612,568)	—	1.00	1988S	(3,262,948)	—	3.00
1975	585,673,900	1.00	—	1989P	1,298,400,000	1.00	—
1975D	313,705,300	1.00	—	1989D	896,535,597	1.00	—
1975S	(2,845,450)	—	2.00	1989S	(3,220,194)	—	4.00
1976	568,760,000	1.50	—	1990P	1,034,340,000	1.00	—
1976D	695,222,774	1.00	—	1990D	839,995,824	1.00	—
1976S	(4,149,730)	—	1.00	1990S	(3,299,559)	—	2.00
1977	796,930,000	1.00	—	1991P	927,220,000	1.00	—
1977D	376,607,228	1.00	—	1991D	601,241,114	1.00	—
1977S	(3,251,152)	—	2.00	1991S	(2,867,787)	—	3.00
1978	663,980,000	1.00	—	1992P	593,500,000	1.00	—
1978D	282,847,540	1.00	—	1992D	616,273,932	1.00	—
1978S	(3,127,781)	—	1.00	1992S	(2,858,981)	—	4.00
1979	315,440,000	1.00	—	1993P	766,180,000	1.00	—
1979D	390,921,184	1.00	—	1993D	750,110,166	1.50	—
1979 type I	—	—	1.00	1993S	(2,633,439)	—	7.00
1979S type I	(3,677,175)	—	1.00	1994P	1,189,000,000	1.00	—
1979S type II	Inc. above	—	2.00	1994D	1,303,268,110	1.00	—
1980P	735,170,000	1.00	—	1994S	(2,484,594)	—	5.00
1980D	719,354,321	.70	—	1995P	1,125,500,000	1.50	—
1980S	(3,554,806)	—	1.00	1995D	1,274,890,000	2.00	—
1981P	676,650,000	1.00	—	1995S	(2,010,384)	—	20.00
1981D	712,284,143	1.00	—	1996P	1,421,163,000	1.00	—

Date	Mintage	MS-65	Prf-65
1996D	1,400,300,000	1.00	—
1996W	1,457,949	25.00	—
1996S	(2,085,191)	—	2.50
1997P	991,640,000	2.00	—
1997D	979,810,000	1.00	—
1997S	(1,975,000)	—	11.00
1998P	1,163,000,000	1.00	—
1998D	1,172,250,000	1.25	—
1998S	(2,078,494)	—	4.00
1999P	2,164,000,000	1.00	—
1999D	1,397,750,000	1.00	—
1999S	(2,557,897)	—	4.00
2000P	1,842,500,000	1.00	—
2000D	1,818,700,000	1.00	—
2000S	(3,097,440)	—	1.00
2001P	1,369,590,000	1.00	—
2001D	1,412,800,000	1.00	—
2001S	(2,249,496)	—	1.00
2002P	1,187,500,000	1.00	—
2002D	1,379,500,000	1.00	—
2002S	(2,268,913)	—	2.00
2003P	1,085,500,000	1.00	—
2003D	986,500,000	1.00	—
2003S	(2,076,165)	—	2.00
2004P	1,328,000,000	1.00	—

Date	Mintage	MS-65	Prf-65
2004D	1,159,500,000	1.00	—
2004S	(1,804,396)	—	4.75
2005P	1,412,000,000	1.00	—
2005D	1,423,500,000	1.00	—
2005S	—	—	2.25
2006P	—	1.00	—
2006D	—	1.00	—
2006S	—	—	2.25

KM# A195 • Silver •

Date	Mintage	Prf-65
1992S	(1,317,579)	5.00
1993S	(761,353)	9.00
1994S	(785,329)	9.00
1995S	(838,953)	25.00
1996S	(830,021)	9.00
1997S	(821,678)	25.00
1998S	(878,792)	9.00
1999S	(804,565)	6.50
2000S	(965,921)	4.00
2001S	(849,600)	5.00
2002S	(888,826)	5.00
2003S	(1,090,425)	4.00
2004S	—	4.50
2005S	—	3.50
2006S	—	—

20 CENTS

KM# 109 • 5.0000 g., 0.9000 **Silver**, 0.1447 oz. ASW, 22 mm. • **Designer:** William Barber

Date	Mintage	G-4	VG-8	F-12	VF-20	XF-40	AU-50	MS-60	MS-65	Prf-65
1875	39,700	110	125	175	215	280	440	650	5,500	9,500
1875S	1,155,000	85.00	92.50	105	135	175	295	470	5,000	—
1875CC	133,290	160	185	250	315	400	580	850	10,000	—
1876	15,900	200	250	300	350	450	600	800	5,200	9,500
1876CC	10,000	—	—	—	—	—	—	—	—	—

Note: 1876CC, Eliasberg Sale, April 1997, MS-65, $148,500. Heritage 1999 ANA, MS-63, $86,500.

Date	Mintage	G-4	VG-8	F-12	VF-20	XF-40	AU-50	MS-60	MS-65	Prf-65
1877 proof only	510	1,600	1,800	2,250	2,600	2,800	3,150	—	—	10,500
1878 proof only	600	1,350	1,525	1,850	2,000	2,300	2,600	—	—	9,700

QUARTER

Draped Bust Quarter
Small eagle reverse

KM# 25 • 6.7400 g., 0.8920 **Silver**, 0.1935 oz. ASW, 27.5 mm. • **Designer:** Robert Scot

Date	Mintage	G-4	VG-8	F-12	VF-20	XF-40	AU-50	MS-60	MS-65
1796	6,146	9,000	14,000	27,500	36,500	41,500	72,000	82,500	150,000

1876 20-Cent
Grade F-12

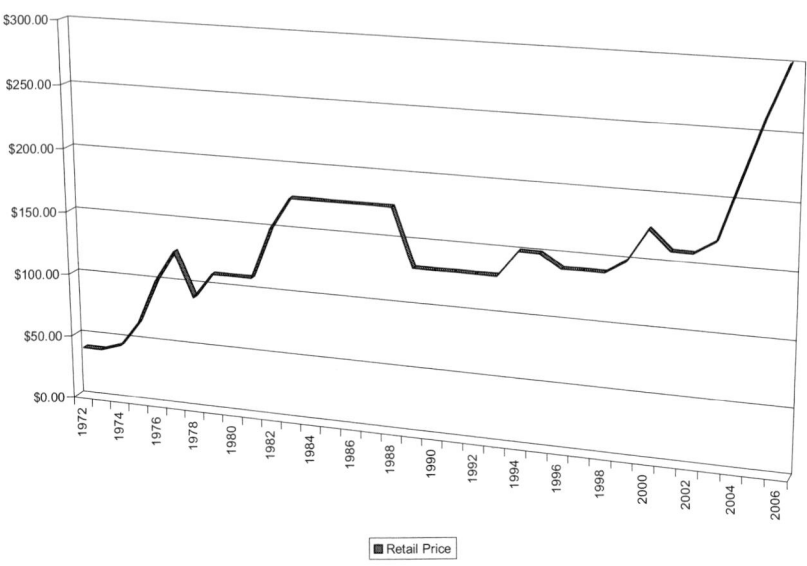

■ Retail Price

1804 Quarter
Grade XF-40

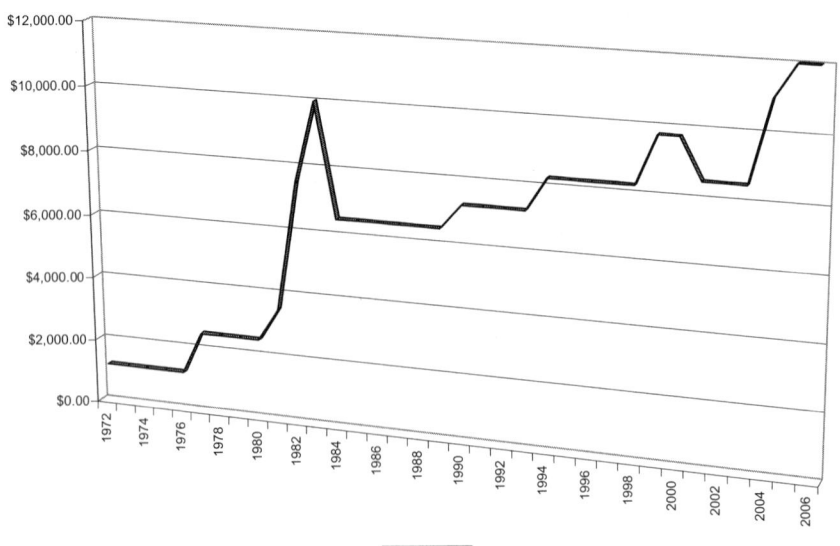

■ Retail Price

Heraldic eagle reverse

KM# 36 • 6.7400 g., 0.8920 **Silver**, .1935 oz. ASW, 27.5 mm. • **Designer:** Robert Scot

Date	Mintage	G-4	VG-8	F-12	VF-20	XF-40	AU-50	MS-60	MS-65
1804	6,738	2,750	3,300	4,750	6,000	12,000	23,000	45,000	120,000
1805	121,394	220	275	500	950	1,700	3,500	5,850	62,000
1806	206,124	220	275	500	900	1,650	3,300	5,300	46,500
1806/5	Inc. above	250	375	650	1,400	2,700	4,000	6,500	62,500
1807	220,643	220	275	500	925	1,650	3,400	5,300	48,500

Liberty Cap Quarter
"E Pluribus Unum" above eagle reverse

KM# 44 • 6.7400 g., 0.8920 **Silver**, 0.1935 oz. ASW, 27 mm. • **Designer:** John Reich **Notes:** Varieties of the 1819 strikes are distinguished by the size of the 9 in the date. Varieties of the 1820 strikes are distinguished by the size of the 0 in the date. One 1822 variety and one 1828 variety have "25" engraved over "50" in the denomination. The 1827 restrikes were produced privately using dies sold as scrap by the U.S. Mint.

Date	Mintage	G-4	VG-8	F-12	VF-20	XF-40	AU-50	MS-60	MS-65
1815	89,235	90.00	110	175	400	1,200	1,700	3,000	25,000
1818	361,174	80.00	100.00	150	375	1,100	1,500	2,750	16,000
1818/15	Inc. above	82.50	110	175	425	1,200	1,700	3,200	20,000
1819 small 9	144,000	80.00	100.00	150	375	1,100	1,500	2,900	22,000
1819 large 9	Inc. above	80.00	100.00	150	375	1,100	1,500	2,900	22,000
1820 small O	127,444	80.00	100.00	150	375	1,100	1,500	2,750	28,000
1820 large O	Inc. above	80.00	100.00	150	375	1,100	1,500	2,750	25,000
1821	216,851	92.50	110	160	385	1,175	1,700	2,700	16,500
1822	64,080	96.00	115	175	400	1,125	2,700	4,000	—
1822 25/50C.	Inc. above	1,500	3,000	4,600	6,500	12,500	20,000	—	—
1823/22	17,800	14,000	16,500	22,000	31,000	41,500	75,000	—	—

Note: 1823/22, Superior, Aug. 1990, Proof, $62,500.

Date	Mintage	G-4	VG-8	F-12	VF-20	XF-40	AU-50	MS-60	MS-65
1824/2 mintage unrecorded	—	170	240	350	750	2,000	3,900	7,500	—
1825/22	168,000	92.50	115	200	425	1,100	1,900	3,000	22,500
1825/23	Inc. above	82.50	110	165	375	11,000	1,650	2,750	16,500
1825/24	Inc. above	82.50	110	165	375	1,100	1,650	2,750	16,500
1827 original	4,000	—	—	—	70,000	75,000	80,000	85,000	—

Note: 1827 original, Eliasberg, April 1997, VF-20, $39,600.

Date	Mintage	G-4	VG-8	F-12	VF-20	XF-40	AU-50	MS-60	MS-65
1827 restrike	Inc. above	—	—	—	—	—	—	—	—

Note: 1827 restrike, Eliasberg, April 1997, Prf-65, $77,000.

Date	Mintage	G-4	VG-8	F-12	VF-20	XF-40	AU-50	MS-60	MS-65
1828	102,000	75.00	100.00	150	350	1,000	1,600	3,000	19,500
1828 25/50C.	Inc. above	125	250	475	1,100	1,925	3,500	8,500	—

"E Pluribus Unum" removed from above eagle reverse

KM# 55 • 0.8920 **Silver**, 24.3 mm. • **Designer:** William Kneass **Notes:** Varieties of the 1831 strikes are distinguished by the size of the lettering on the reverse.

Date	Mintage	G-4	VG-8	F-12	VF-20	XF-40	AU-50	MS-60	MS-65
1831 small letter	398,000	65.00	72.50	92.50	140	350	850	1,100	13,500

Date	Mintage	G-4	VG-8	F-12	VF-20	XF-40	AU-50	MS-60	MS-65
1831 large letter	Inc. above	65.00	72.50	92.50	140	350	850	1,100	18,500
1832	320,000	65.00	72.50	92.50	140	350	850	1,100	16,000
1833	156,000	67.50	77.50	100.00	165	400	925	1,400	13,500
1834	286,000	65.00	72.50	92.50	140	350	850	1,100	13,500
1835	1,952,000	65.00	72.50	92.50	140	350	850	1,100	13,500
1836	472,000	65.00	72.50	92.50	140	350	850	1,100	14,500
1837	252,400	65.00	72.50	92.50	140	350	850	1,100	13,500
1838	832,000	65.00	72.50	92.50	140	350	850	1,100	14,750

Seated Liberty Quarter
No drapery obverse

KM# 64.1 • 6.6800 g., 0.9000 **Silver**, 0.1934 oz. ASW, 24.3 mm. • **Designer:** Christian Gobrecht

Date	Mintage	G-4	VG-8	F-12	VF-20	XF-40	AU-50	MS-60	MS-65
1838	Inc. above	26.00	30.00	46.00	85.00	350	550	1,250	30,000
1839	491,146	25.00	29.00	44.00	75.00	350	550	1,250	34,000
1840O	425,200	28.50	35.00	60.00	400	375	575	1,350	38,500

Drapery added to Liberty's left elbow obverse

KM# 64.2 • 6.6800 g., 0.9000 **Silver**, 0.1934 oz. ASW, 24.3 mm. • **Designer:** Christian Gobrecht **Notes:** Two varieties for 1842 and 1842-O are distinguished by the size of the numerals in the date. 1852 obverse dies were used to strike the 1853 no-arrows variety, with the 2 being recut to form a 3.

Date	Mintage	G-4	VG-8	F-12	VF-20	XF-40	AU-50	MS-60	MS-65
1840	188,127	30.00	55.00	80.00	125	225	350	950	12,000
1840O	Inc. above	29.00	39.00	70.00	115	250	450	1,000	—
1841	120,000	75.00	90.00	120	185	300	385	750	11,000
1841O	452,000	21.50	27.50	50.00	85.00	165	350	700	10,000
1842 small date	88,000	—	—	—	—	—	—	—	—
Note: 1842 small date, Eliasberg, April 1997, Prf-63, $66,000.									
1842 large date	Inc. above	85.00	120	170	275	350	800	1,250	—
1842O small date	769,000	425	650	1,100	1,850	4,000	—	—	—
1842O large date	Inc. above	22.50	27.50	37.50	50.00	125	300	900	4,000
1843	645,600	20.00	25.00	31.50	40.00	70.00	150	400	6,750
1843O	968,000	25.00	31.50	47.50	100.00	250	750	2,000	11,000
1844	421,200	20.00	25.00	31.50	41.50	70.00	160	450	5,500
1844O	740,000	25.00	28.50	40.00	75.00	140	280	1,000	6,000
1845	922,000	20.00	25.00	31.50	40.00	70.00	150	465	5,000
1846	510,000	20.00	25.00	36.50	50.00	75.00	160	475	6,000
1847	734,000	20.00	25.00	31.50	40.00	70.00	150	450	5,000
1847O	368,000	27.50	40.00	60.00	120	275	700	1,900	—
1848	146,000	40.00	60.00	110	185	225	375	1,000	10,000
1849	340,000	20.00	25.00	36.00	65.00	125	275	750	9,000
1849O mintage unrecorded	—	475	600	1,000	1,700	2,900	5,750	—	—
1850	190,800	40.00	50.00	80.00	125	175	275	800	—
1850O	412,000	20.00	30.00	50.00	100.00	150	450	1,300	—
1851	160,000	60.00	75.00	125	225	285	400	850	8,500
1851O	88,000	150	265	375	575	1,000	2,250	4,000	—
1852	177,060	50.00	60.00	100.00	185	225	350	500	4,800
1852O	96,000	185	250	400	675	1,200	3,500	8,000	—
1853 recut date	44,200	400	600	800	950	1,350	1,600	2,600	9,000

Arrows at date obverse   Rays around eagle reverse

KM# 78 • 6.2200 g., 0.9000 **Silver**, 0.1800 oz. ASW, 24.3 mm. • **Designer:** Christian Gobrecht

Date	Mintage	G-4	VG-8	F-12	VF-20	XF-40	AU-50	MS-60	MS-65	Prf-65
1853	15,210,020	15.00	20.00	27.50	45.00	150	275	950	19,000	90,000
1853/4	Inc. above	40.00	65.00	100.00	200	275	750	1,750	—	—
1853O	1,332,000	18.00	35.00	50.00	100.00	275	1,100	2,750	—	—

Rays around eagle removed reverse

KM# 81 • 6.6800 g., 0.9000 **Silver**, .1934 oz. ASW, 24.3 mm. • **Designer:** Christian Gobrecht **Notes:** The 1854-O "huge O" variety has an oversized mint mark.

Date	Mintage	G-4	VG-8	F-12	VF-20	XF-40	AU-50	MS-60	MS-65	Prf-65
1854	12,380,000	15.00	20.00	27.50	35.00	75.00	225	440	7,500	17,500
1854O	1,484,000	17.00	24.00	35.00	60.00	125	300	1,750	—	—
1854O huge O	Inc. above	—	—	—	—	—	—	—	—	—
1855	2,857,000	15.00	20.00	27.50	35.00	75.00	225	440	8,500	18,500
1855O	176,000	50.00	75.00	110	240	475	950	2,750	—	—
1855S	396,400	40.00	60.00	80.00	225	500	1,250	2,000	—	—

Arrows at date removed obverse

KM# A64.2 • 6.2200 g., 0.9000 **Silver**, 0.1800 oz. ASW, 24.3 mm. • **Designer:** Christian Gobrecht

Date	Mintage	G-4	VG-8	F-12	VF-20	XF-40	AU-50	MS-60	MS-65	Prf-65
1856	7,264,000	15.00	20.00	27.50	35.00	60.00	145	290	4,250	15,000
1856O	968,000	20.00	30.00	40.00	60.00	110	250	1,000	8,500	—
1856S	286,000	45.00	65.00	110	250	450	900	2,200	—	—
1856S/S	Inc. above	70.00	100.00	185	375	875	1,250	—	—	—
1857	9,644,000	15.00	20.00	27.50	35.00	60.00	145	290	4,000	9,500
1857O	1,180,000	15.00	20.00	29.00	40.00	80.00	275	975	—	—
1857S	82,000	100.00	145	250	400	600	950	2,750	—	—
1858	7,368,000	15.00	20.00	27.50	35.00	60.00	160	300	4,000	6,500
1858O	520,000	25.00	30.00	45.00	70.00	135	360	1,350	—	—
1858S	121,000	60.00	100.00	175	275	650	1,250	—	—	—
1859	1,344,000	17.00	24.00	30.00	40.00	75.00	175	375	6,000	7,000
1859O	260,000	25.00	30.00	50.00	80.00	150	400	1,000	15,000	—
1859S	80,000	100.00	135	225	450	1,350	2,500	—	—	—
1860	805,400	18.00	22.00	28.00	33.00	60.00	160	500	—	5,250
1860O	388,000	20.00	30.00	40.00	55.00	100.00	275	1,200	—	—
1860S	56,000	175	325	575	900	3,500	6,000	—	—	—
1861	4,854,600	16.00	19.00	27.00	32.00	55.00	150	290	4,200	5,500
1861S	96,000	80.00	125	235	400	1,250	2,750	—	—	—
1862	932,550	18.00	22.00	33.00	40.00	65.00	165	300	4,350	5,350
1862S	67,000	80.00	125	200	300	700	1,600	2,750	—	—
1863	192,060	30.00	45.00	60.00	120	185	300	650	4,350	5,500
1864	94,070	75.00	100.00	135	200	300	400	650	5,000	5,500
1864S	20,000	375	575	875	1,250	2,350	3,750	7,000	—	—
1865	59,300	75.00	100.00	150	200	290	375	875	9,500	5,500
1865S	41,000	100.00	135	200	350	650	1,250	2,350	11,500	—
1866 unique	—	—	—	—	—	—	—	—	—	—

1856-S Quarter
Grade F-12

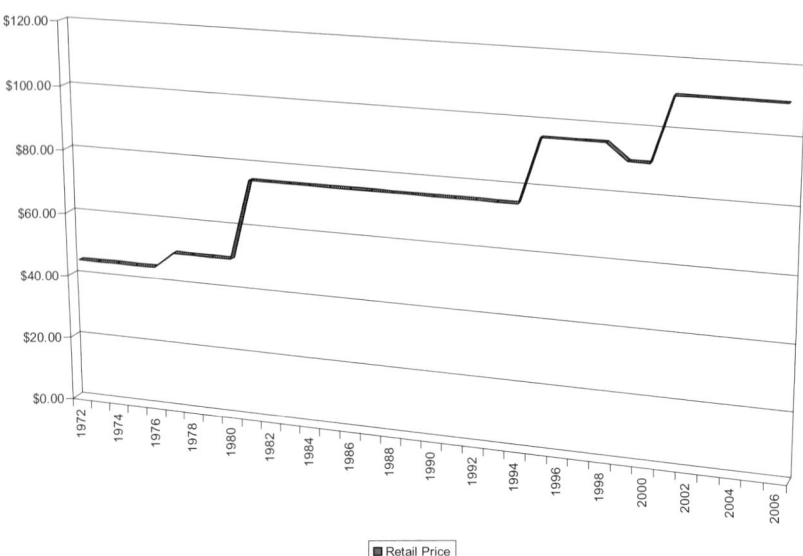

Retail Price

"In God We Trust" above eagle reverse

KM# 98 • 6.2200 g., 0.9000 **Silver**, 0.1800 oz. ASW, 24.3 mm. • **Designer:** Christian Gobrecht **Notes:** The 1873 closed-3 and open-3 varieties are distinguished by the amount of space between the upper left and lower left serifs in the 3.

Date	Mintage	G-4	VG-8	F-12	VF-20	XF-40	AU-50	MS-60	MS-65	Prf-65
1866	17,525	475	600	750	1,000	1,200	1,500	2,250	7,500	3,000
1866S	28,000	275	325	625	975	1,450	2,000	3,000	—	—
1867	20,625	225	325	500	675	800	975	1,200	—	2,450
1867S	48,000	275	385	600	900	1,350	1,700	—	—	—
1868	30,000	200	250	325	400	500	650	900	7,000	3,450
1868S	96,000	95.00	110	195	300	625	1,350	2,000	—	—
1869	16,600	350	450	575	750	850	975	1,275	—	2,500
1869S	76,000	110	135	225	375	700	1,400	2,400	16,000	—
1870	87,400	55.00	80.00	125	200	285	375	850	6,000	2,750
1870CC	8,340	4,000	6,000	9,000	15,000	—	—	—	—	—
1871	119,160	40.00	65.00	75.00	150	195	350	650	6,000	2,500
1871CC	10,890	3,000	4,000	6,500	12,500	18,000	—	—	—	—
1871S	30,900	350	475	600	850	1,100	1,850	3,000	10,000	—
1872	182,950	30.00	40.00	80.00	110	155	300	600	6,500	2,500
1872CC	22,850	700	950	1,650	3,250	6,500	7,500	14,000	—	—
1872S	83,000	900	1,250	1,650	2,100	3,500	4,500	7,500	—	—
1873 closed 3	212,600	150	225	325	525	600	1,000	2,000	—	2,600
1873 open 3	Inc. above	30.00	42.50	80.00	120	175	250	450	5,000	—
1873CC 6 known	4,000	—	75,000	—	—	—	—	—	—	—

Note: 1873CC, Heritage, April 1999, MS-62, $106,375.

Arrows at date obverse

KM# 106 • 6.2500 g., 0.9000 **Silver**, 0.1808 oz. ASW, 24.3 mm. • **Designer:** Christian Gobrecht

Date	Mintage	G-4	VG-8	F-12	VF-20	XF-40	AU-50	MS-60	MS-65	Prf-65
1873	1,271,700	16.00	23.00	30.00	60.00	200	400	775	4,250	8,000
1873CC	12,462	2,250	3,500	5,250	8,500	14,500	18,000	35,000	—	—
1873S	156,000	25.00	40.00	85.00	140	275	550	1,200	8,000	—
1874	471,900	20.00	26.00	40.00	70.00	220	420	850	4,000	6,750
1874S	392,000	23.00	30.00	50.00	110	240	425	900	4,500	—

Arrows at date removed obverse

KM# A98 • 6.2500 g., 0.9000 **Silver**, 0.1808 oz. ASW, 24.3 mm. • **Designer:** Christian Gobrecht **Notes:** The 1876-CC fine-reeding variety has a more finely reeded edge.

Date	Mintage	G-4	VG-8	F-12	VF-20	XF-40	AU-50	MS-60	MS-65	Prf-65
1875	4,293,500	14.00	17.00	25.00	30.00	50.00	135	225	1,600	2,300
1875CC	140,000	60.00	90.00	175	300	550	850	1,600	15,000	—
1875S	680,000	25.00	36.00	67.00	110	175	275	575	3,200	—
1876	17,817,150	14.00	17.00	25.00	30.00	50.00	135	225	1,600	2,250
1876CC	4,944,000	25.00	30.00	40.00	50.00	70.00	150	325	3,600	—
1876CC fine reeding	Inc. above	25.00	30.00	40.00	50.00	70.00	150	325	3,600	—
1876S	8,596,000	16.00	19.00	25.00	30.00	50.00	135	225	2,000	—
1877	10,911,710	14.00	17.00	25.00	30.00	50.00	135	225	1,600	2,250
1877CC	4,192,000	25.00	30.00	40.00	50.00	75.00	150	325	2,000	—
1877S	8,996,000	14.00	17.00	25.00	30.00	50.00	135	225	1,600	—
1877S /horizontal S	Inc. above	32.00	48.00	85.00	150	250	375	650	—	—
1878	2,260,800	16.00	18.00	28.00	34.00	55.00	145	250	2,750	2,300
1878CC	996,000	19.00	29.00	45.00	85.00	110	150	450	3,500	—
1878S	140,000	165	200	300	400	650	875	1,450	—	—
1879	14,700	190	235	285	325	400	485	575	1,700	2,250
1880	14,955	190	235	285	325	400	485	575	1,600	2,250
1881	12,975	200	250	300	350	425	500	600	1,650	2,200
1882	16,300	200	250	300	350	425	500	600	1,850	2,200
1883	15,439	210	265	315	365	435	525	625	2,450	2,200
1884	8,875	325	400	485	585	675	750	850	1,900	2,200
1885	14,530	210	265	315	365	435	525	625	2,600	2,200
1886	5,886	500	600	700	800	900	1,000	1,250	2,600	2,400
1887	10,710	300	350	400	485	585	625	750	2,350	2,200
1888	10,833	250	300	350	400	475	550	650	2,000	2,350
1888S	1,216,000	15.00	20.00	27.50	30.00	60.00	160	245	2,450	—
1889	12,711	225	285	325	385	450	500	625	1,750	2,350
1890	80,590	65.00	85.00	100.00	125	200	300	425	—	2,350
1891	3,920,600	15.00	20.00	27.50	30.00	60.00	160	245	1,750	2,350
1891O	68,000	150	225	325	550	950	1,250	3,000	14,500	—
1891S	2,216,000	16.00	22.00	29.00	65.00	52.50	185	275	2,400	—

Barber Quarter

KM# 114 • 6.2500 g., 0.9000 **Silver**, 0.1809 oz. ASW, 24.3 mm. • **Designer:** Charles E. Barber

Date	Mintage	G-4	VG-8	F-12	VF-20	XF-40	AU-50	MS-60	MS-65	Prf-65
1892	8,237,245	5.25	8.50	25.00	46.00	75.00	120	220	1,300	2,000

Date	Mintage	G-4	VG-8	F-12	VF-20	XF-40	AU-50	MS-60	MS-65	Prf-65
1892O	2,640,000	13.50	21.50	41.50	55.00	96.00	150	300	1,650	—
1892S	964,079	30.00	50.00	80.00	125	190	300	480	4,850	—
1893	5,484,838	6.25	8.50	27.50	41.50	75.00	120	210	1,750	2,000
1893O	3,396,000	8.00	13.50	30.00	55.00	100.00	160	275	1,900	—
1893S	1,454,535	18.00	34.00	62.50	110	160	300	480	8,400	—
1894	3,432,972	5.50	9.50	34.00	50.00	93.50	150	250	1,550	2,000
1894O	2,852,000	8.50	16.00	41.50	67.50	125	225	340	3,000	—
1894S	2,648,821	8.25	12.50	38.00	62.50	115	205	315	3,000	—
1895	4,440,880	6.00	9.00	31.50	41.50	80.00	135	230	1,900	2,000
1895O	2,816,000	11.00	18.00	46.00	75.00	135	225	400	2,750	—
1895S	1,764,681	18.00	27.50	60.00	100.00	150	285	445	4,150	—
1896	3,874,762	5.00	7.00	25.00	41.50	80.00	135	235	1,600	2,000
1896O	1,484,000	26.00	48.50	115	250	425	750	850	7,750	—
1896S	188,039	690	1,100	1,800	2,750	4,300	5,500	800	54,000	—
1897	8,140,731	5.00	6.25	21.50	33.50	75.00	120	220	1,300	2,000
1897O	1,414,800	18.00	38.50	115	235	395	640	1,000	4,150	—
1897S	542,229	85.00	120	275	300	440	700	1,000	7,000	—
1898	11,100,735	5.00	6.25	22.50	33.50	75.00	120	220	1,300	2,000
1898O	1,868,000	13.00	27.50	75.00	150	295	435	650	10,000	—
1898S	1,020,592	12.00	18.50	47.50	65.00	96.00	210	400	7,200	—
1899	12,624,846	5.00	6.25	22.50	33.50	75.00	120	215	1,300	2,000
1899O	2,644,000	11.00	19.00	35.00	60.00	130	275	415	3,400	—
1899S	708,000	17.00	28.50	70.00	85.00	135	275	440	3,800	—
1900	10,016,912	6.00	8.00	21.50	35.00	71.50	135	215	1,300	2,000
1900O	3,416,000	11.00	25.00	62.50	100.00	150	345	585	3,800	—
1900S	1,858,585	8.00	15.00	38.00	55.00	80.00	135	385	5,400	—
1901	8,892,813	11.00	13.00	25.00	41.50	80.00	135	215	2,250	2,200
1901O	1,612,000	40.00	60.00	135	275	470	685	900	6,000	—
1901S	72,664	6,500	12,000	16,000	18,500	22,500	27,500	37,000	62,500	—
1902	12,197,744	6.00	8.00	19.50	33.50	70.00	125	220	1,300	2,100
1902O	4,748,000	8.50	16.00	52.50	82.50	150	245	485	5,000	—
1902S	1,524,612	13.50	22.00	55.00	95.00	170	260	540	3,600	—
1903	9,670,064	6.75	8.00	19.00	33.50	66.00	115	215	2,600	2,000
1903O	3,500,000	8.00	12.50	41.50	65.00	125	260	450	5,800	—
1903S	1,036,000	15.50	25.00	46.00	80.00	145	285	450	2,900	—
1904	9,588,813	8.00	9.75	20.00	36.00	72.50	125	225	1,475	2,000
1904O	2,456,000	11.00	21.50	62.50	100.00	225	460	850	3,250	—
1905	4,968,250	11.00	13.00	27.50	41.50	75.00	125	215	1,650	2,000
1905O	1,230,000	18.50	32.50	82.50	160	260	375	515	6,600	—
1905S	1,884,000	9.00	15.00	43.50	66.00	115	225	350	3,650	—
1906	3,656,435	6.75	8.00	19.00	33.50	70.00	115	215	1,300	2,000
1906D	3,280,000	7.00	8.00	25.00	42.50	71.50	155	220	2,200	—
1906O	2,056,000	7.00	9.00	41.50	60.00	105	200	300	1,400	—
1907	7,192,575	5.25	8.00	17.50	33.50	66.00	115	215	1,300	2,000
1907D	2,484,000	6.00	9.00	29.00	52.50	80.00	180	250	2,750	—

1896-S Quarter
Grade F-12

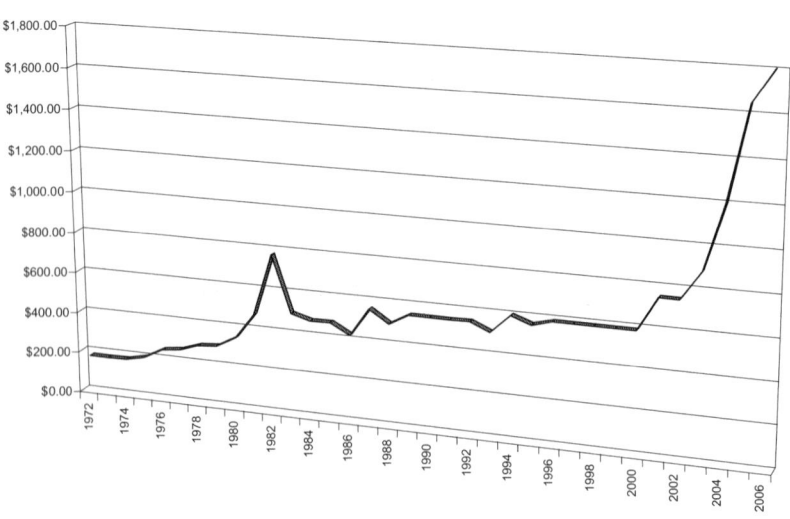

■ Retail Price

Date	Mintage	G-4	VG-8	F-12	VF-20	XF-40	AU-50	MS-60	MS-65	Prf-65
1907O	4,560,000	5.25	8.00	19.00	38.50	70.00	135	220	2,600	—
1907S	1,360,000	10.00	18.50	47.50	75.00	135	275	480	3,500	—
1908	4,232,545	5.00	6.25	18.50	33.50	70.00	115	215	1,300	2,200
1908D	5,788,000	5.00	6.25	17.50	32.50	70.00	120	250	1,750	—
1908O	6,244,000	5.00	8.50	17.50	38.50	75.00	125	215	1,300	—
1908S	784,000	20.00	40.00	92.50	160	320	520	775	5,100	—
1909	9,268,650	5.00	6.25	17.50	33.50	66.00	115	215	1,300	2,000
1909D	5,114,000	6.25	8.00	22.00	41.50	90.00	160	215	2,350	—
1909O	712,000	25.00	60.00	175	400	900	1,250	1,700	9,000	—
1909S	1,348,000	8.00	11.00	37.50	57.50	96.00	200	300	2,400	—
1910	2,244,551	7.75	10.00	30.00	46.00	80.00	140	215	1,300	2,000
1910D	1,500,000	8.00	11.00	47.50	75.00	130	260	375	2,250	—
1911	3,720,543	5.25	8.00	17.50	33.50	72.50	125	215	1,300	2,000
1911D	933,600	8.00	19.00	95.00	215	330	500	700	6,250	—
1911S	988,000	7.00	12.00	51.50	80.00	160	300	400	1,500	—
1912	4,400,700	5.75	8.00	17.50	33.50	70.00	115	215	1,300	2,000
1912S	708,000	10.00	13.00	46.00	77.50	125	230	390	2,750	—
1913	484,613	15.00	25.00	75.00	185	415	535	960	5,000	2,200
1913D	1,450,800	12.50	13.50	38.50	58.50	94.00	185	275	1,400	—
1913S	40,000	1,300	2,000	3,800	5,600	6,500	7,000	9,000	24,000	—
1914	6,244,610	5.00	6.25	17.50	30.00	57.50	115	215	1,300	2,200
1914D	3,046,000	5.00	6.25	17.50	30.00	57.50	115	215	1,300	—
1914S	264,000	70.00	105	200	315	520	700	940	3,550	—
1915	3,480,450	5.00	6.25	17.50	30.00	66.00	115	215	1,300	2,200
1915D	3,694,000	5.00	6.25	17.50	30.00	66.00	115	215	1,300	—
1915S	704,000	9.00	13.00	35.00	57.50	110	220	285	1,300	—
1916	1,788,000	5.00	9.50	17.50	27.50	57.50	115	215	1,300	—
1916D	6,540,800	5.00	6.25	17.50	30.00	57.50	115	215	1,300	—

Standing Liberty Quarter
Right breast exposed; Type 1 obverse

Right breast exposed

KM# 141 • 6.2500 g., 0.9000 **Silver**, 0.1809 oz. ASW, 24.3 mm. • **Designer:** Hermon A. MacNeil

Date	Mintage	G-4	VG-8	F-12	VF-20	XF-40	AU-50	MS-60	MS-65	-65FH
1916	52,000	3,500	6,350	9,500	13,000	14,500	16,500	18,500	30,000	37,500
1917	8,792,000	25.00	40.00	50.00	65.00	95.00	185	250	1,000	1,650

1913-S Quarter
Grade XF-40

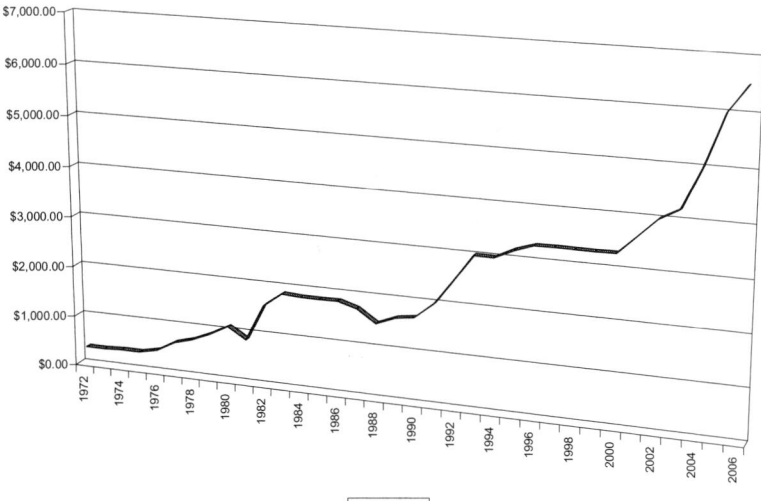

Retail Price

Date	Mintage	G-4	VG-8	F-12	VF-20	XF-40	AU-50	MS-60	MS-65	-65FH
1917D	1,509,200	28.00	40.00	55.00	75.00	125	195	300	1,100	2,800
1917S	1,952,000	30.00	40.00	60.00	80.00	160	220	450	1,800	4,100

Right breast covered; Type 2 obverse   Three stars below eagle reverse

Right breast covered   Mint mark

KM# 145 • 6.2500 g., 0.9000 Silver, 0.1809 oz. ASW, 24.3 mm. • Designer: Hermon A. MacNeil

Date	Mintage	G-4	VG-8	F-12	VF-20	XF-40	AU-50	MS-60	MS-65	-65FH
1917	13,880,000	22.00	27.00	35.00	40.00	55.00	92.50	200	750	1,350
1917D	6,224,400	40.00	50.00	85.00	95.00	100.00	160	295	1,550	4,100
1917S	5,522,000	45.00	55.00	80.00	85.00	100.00	155	300	1,600	4,600
1918	14,240,000	18.50	22.00	30.00	38.00	50.00	95.00	200	750	2,200
1918D	7,380,000	28.00	38.00	55.00	70.00	97.50	160	400	1,750	6,250
1918S	11,072,000	19.00	27.00	38.00	50.00	66.00	135	350	1,750	17,500
1918/17S	Inc. above	1,900	2,750	4,500	6,000	8,500	16,000	20,000	110,000	375,000
1919	11,324,000	35.00	58.00	60.00	65.00	77.50	110	250	825	2,100
1919D	1,944,000	100.00	145	185	300	550	670	1,000	3,800	39,000
1919S	1,836,000	100.00	200	250	325	600	725	1,400	5,000	39,500
1920	27,860,000	16.00	21.00	30.00	37.00	49.00	80.00	250	800	2,400
1920D	3,586,400	60.00	70.00	88.00	120	160	200	500	2,950	8,500
1920S	6,380,000	22.00	30.00	39.00	45.00	66.00	140	400	3,300	36,000
1921	1,916,000	185	240	350	480	550	750	1,000	3,000	6,000
1923	9,716,000	15.00	21.00	35.00	45.00	55.00	75.00	200	800	4,900
1923S	1,360,000	375	475	675	850	1,250	1,600	2,300	3,950	6,500
1924	10,920,000	16.00	20.00	28.00	34.00	39.00	80.00	300	650	2,100
1924D	3,112,000	60.00	80.00	100.00	140	185	220	400	750	5,500
1924S	2,860,000	30.00	40.00	45.00	55.00	105	220	425	2,250	6,750
1925	12,280,000	2.50	4.00	7.00	15.00	35.00	80.00	250	600	1,900
1926	11,316,000	2.50	4.00	7.00	14.00	35.00	75.00	250	650	2,600
1926D	1,716,000	8.00	10.00	19.00	36.00	65.00	105	225	600	30,000
1926S	2,700,000	2.75	5.00	14.00	30.00	110	275	500	2,500	35,000
1927	11,912,000	2.50	4.00	6.00	16.00	40.00	80.00	250	600	1,400
1927D	976,400	14.00	19.00	27.50	65.00	135	200	250	750	3,300
1927S	396,000	35.00	45.00	90.00	350	1,250	3,100	4,750	17,000	210,000
1928	6,336,000	2.50	4.00	5.00	15.00	37.00	85.00	200	650	2,800
1928D	1,627,600	3.50	6.00	8.00	22.50	42.50	105	300	600	6,500
1928S	2,644,000	3.00	5.00	6.00	15.00	38.00	79.00	200	600	1,200
1929	11,140,000	2.50	4.00	6.00	12.00	36.00	75.00	200	600	1,200
1929D	1,358,000	3.25	6.00	10.00	18.00	38.50	79.00	200	600	6,900
1929S	1,764,000	3.25	4.00	6.00	15.00	36.00	79.00	200	600	1,200
1930	5,632,000	2.50	4.00	5.00	12.50	35.00	75.00	200	600	1,200
1930S	1,556,000	3.25	7.00	10.00	15.00	39.00	95.00	200	700	1,600

Washington Quarter

Mint mark
1932-64

KM# 164 • 6.2500 g., 0.9000 Silver, 0.1809 oz. ASW, 24.3 mm. • Designer: John Flanagan

Date	Mintage	G-4	VG-8	F-12	VF-20	XF-40	AU-50	MS-60	MS-65	Prf-65
1932	5,404,000	4.00	5.50	6.25	7.50	9.75	15.00	26.00	450	—
1932D	436,800	175	195	215	240	315	550	1,000	26,500	—
1932S	408,000	175	185	202.5	215	260	260	500	7,700	—
1934	31,912,052	3.00	3.20	3.30	3.50	4.40	9.25	27.50	110	—
1934D	3,527,200	4.40	6.25	7.50	12.50	23.50	90.00	250	1,550	—
1935	32,484,000	3.00	3.20	3.30	3.50	3.50	8.00	21.50	130	—
1935D	5,780,000	3.00	3.75	7.00	13.50	30.00	130	260	975	, —
1935S	5,660,000	3.00	3.75	4.80	6.50	15.00	38.50	100.00	370	—
1936	41,303,837	3.00	3.20	3.30	3.50	3.25	8.50	21.50	110	1,050
1936D	5,374,000	4.50	5.25	7.00	22.00	55.00	275	625	1,900	—
1936S	3,828,000	3.00	3.75	4.40	6.25	13.50	52.50	115	4.40	—
1937	19,701,542	3.00	3.20	3.30	3.50	4.50	16.00	23.50	94.00	380
1937D	7,189,600	3.00	3.20	3.75	6.25	13.50	34.00	70.00	175	—
1937S	1,652,000	4.00	5.00	7.00	15.00	34.00	100.00	170	415	—

1932-D Quarter
Grade F-12

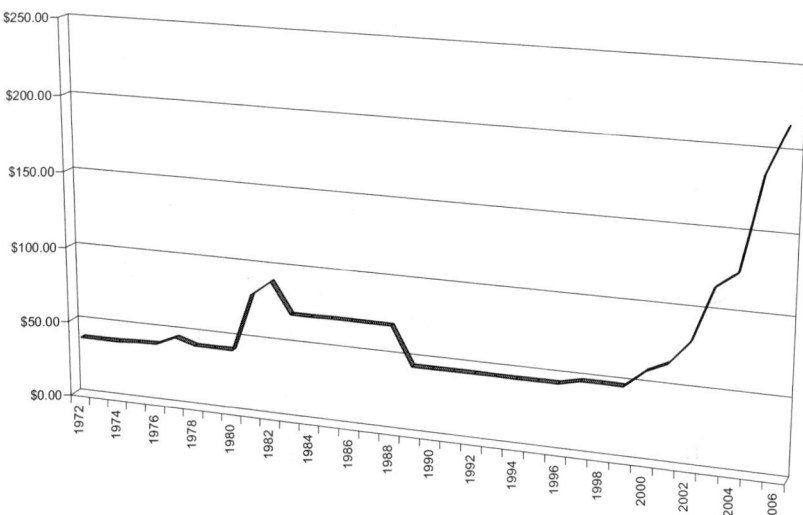

■ Retail Price

Date	Mintage	G-4	VG-8	F-12	VF-20	XF-40	AU-50	MS-60	MS-65	Prf-65
1938	9,480,045	4.00	4.75	5.25	6.25	16.00	46.00	96.00	250	225
1938S	2,832,000	4.75	5.25	6.00	9.75	22.50	57.50	115	300	—
1939	33,548,795	3.00	3.20	3.30	3.50	3.25	7.00	16.00	56.00	150
1939D	7,092,000	3.00	3.20	3.50	5.25	11.00	20.00	45.00	125	—
1939S	2,628,000	4.00	4.40	5.25	9.00	22.00	60.00	110	375	—
1940	35,715,246	3.00	3.20	3.30	3.50	3.25	5.50	18.50	57.50	150
1940D	2,797,600	3.25	3.75	7.00	12.50	27.50	70.00	135	350	—
1940S	8,244,000	3.00	3.20	5.00	6.50	9.00	18.00	25.00	62.50	—
1941	79,047,287	—	—	—	—	3.00	4.40	9.75	45.00	110
1941D	16,714,800	—	—	—	3.00	4.50	15.00	35.00	70.00	—
1941S	16,080,000	—	—	—	2.50	3.50	12.50	31.00	70.00	—
1942	102,117,123	—	—	—	—	3.00	3.50	5.50	37.50	110
1942D	17,487,200	—	—	—	2.50	3.75	11.00	19.00	45.00	—
1942S	19,384,000	—	—	—	3.00	5.00	24.00	80.00	180	—
1943	99,700,000	—	—	—	—	3.00	3.25	5.00	44.00	—
1943D	16,095,600	—	—	—	3.50	6.00	16.50	31.00	52.50	—
1943S	21,700,000	—	—	3.00	5.00	7.50	15.00	28.00	55.00	—
1944	104,956,000	—	—	—	—	3.00	3.25	5.00	37.50	—
1944D	14,600,800	—	—	—	—	3.75	10.00	20.00	37.50	—
1944S	12,560,000	—	—	—	3.00	4.00	9.00	15.00	37.50	—
1945	74,372,000	—	—	—	—	3.00	3.25	5.00	45.00	—
1945D	12,341,600	—	—	—	3.50	6.50	11.50	19.00	47.50	—
1945S	17,004,001	—	—	—	3.00	3.50	6.00	9.00	38.50	—
1946	53,436,000	—	—	—	—	3.00	3.50	5.00	47.50	—
1946D	9,072,800	—	—	—	—	2.50	5.25	10.00	47.50	—
1946S	4,204,000	—	—	—	3.00	4.00	5.00	9.00	50.00	—
1947	22,556,000	—	—	—	—	3.00	5.00	11.50	47.50	—
1947D	15,338,400	—	—	—	—	3.00	4.50	11.00	44.00	—
1947S	5,532,000	—	—	—	—	3.00	4.50	10.00	40.00	—
1948	35,196,000	—	—	—	—	3.00	4.00	5.50	45.00	—
1948D	16,766,800	—	—	—	—	3.00	7.00	13.50	62.50	—
1948S	15,960,000	—	—	—	—	3.00	5.00	8.00	50.00	—
1949	9,312,000	—	—	—	3.00	6.50	15.00	38.50	65.00	—
1949D	10,068,400	—	—	—	3.00	5.00	10.00	18.00	50.00	—
1950	24,971,512	—	—	—	—	2.25	3.00	5.50	30.00	55.00
1950D	21,075,600	—	—	—	—	2.50	3.00	5.00	32.00	—
1950D/S	Inc. above	30.00	33.00	40.00	60.00	140	215	275	2,250	—
1950S	10,284,004	—	—	—	—	3.25	4.50	9.00	40.00	—
1950S/D	Inc. above	32.00	36.00	44.00	70.00	180	315	400	850	—
1951	43,505,602	—	—	—	—	2.25	3.50	6.00	32.00	40.00
1951D	35,354,800	—	—	—	—	2.50	3.50	7.00	38.00	—
1951S	9,048,000	—	—	3.00	4.50	6.00	9.00	24.00	52.00	—
1952	38,862,073	—	—	—	—	2.75	3.50	5.50	35.00	37.00
1952D	49,795,200	—	—	—	—	2.75	3.25	5.00	32.00	—

Date	Mintage	G-4	VG-8	F-12	VF-20	XF-40	AU-50	MS-60	MS-65	Prf-65
1952S	13,707,800	—	—	—	4.00	6.00	9.00	21.00	42.00	—
1953	18,664,920	—	—	—	—	—	3.00	5.50	30.00	25.00
1953D	56,112,400	—	—	—	—	—	2.75	4.25	29.00	—
1953S	14,016,000	—	—	—	—	2.25	2.75	5.00	30.00	—
1954	54,645,503	—	—	—	—	—	2.75	5.00	30.00	13.00
1954D	42,305,500	—	—	—	—	—	2.75	4.75	30.00	—
1954S	11,834,722	—	—	—	—	—	2.75	4.00	25.00	—
1955	18,558,381	—	—	—	—	—	2.75	3.50	25.00	14.00
1955D	3,182,400	—	—	—	—	2.50	2.75	3.25	45.00	—
1956	44,813,384	—	—	—	—	—	2.75	4.00	22.00	4.00
1956D	32,334,500	—	—	—	—	—	2.50	3.00	26.00	—
1957	47,779,952	—	—	—	—	—	2.25	3.50	23.00	4.00
1957D	77,924,160	—	—	—	—	—	2.25	2.25	26.00	—
1958	7,235,652	—	—	—	—	2.25	2.50	2.75	20.00	6.00
1958D	78,124,900	—	—	—	—	—	2.25	2.50	20.00	—
1959	25,533,291	—	—	—	—	—	2.25	2.75	20.00	4.25
1959D	62,054,232	—	—	—	—	—	2.25	2.75	25.00	—
1960	30,855,602	—	—	—	—	—	2.25	2.50	17.00	3.75
1960D	63,000,324	—	—	—	—	—	2.25	2.50	17.00	—
1961	40,064,244	—	—	—	—	—	2.25	2.75	19.00	3.50
1961D	83,656,928	—	—	—	—	—	2.25	2.50	16.00	—
1962	39,374,019	—	—	—	—	—	2.25	2.50	18.00	3.50
1962D	127,554,756	—	—	—	—	—	2.25	2.50	16.00	—
1963	77,391,645	—	—	—	—	—	2.25	2.50	15.00	3.50
1963D	135,288,184	—	—	—	—	—	2.25	2.50	15.00	—
1964	564,341,347	—	—	—	—	—	2.25	2.50	15.00	3.50
1964D	704,135,528	—	—	—	1.50	—	2.25	2.50	15.00	—

KM# 164a • 5.6700 g., Copper-Nickel Clad Copper, 24.3 mm. • Designer: John Flanagan

Date	Mintage	MS-65	Prf-65	Date	Mintage	MS-65	Prf-65
1965	1,819,717,540	8.00	—	1971S	(3,220,733)	—	3.00
1966	821,101,500	4.50	—	1972	215,048,000	4.00	—
1967	1,524,031,848	6.50	—	1972D	311,067,732	5.50	—
1968	220,731,500	7.50	—	1972S	(3,260,996)	—	3.00
1968D	101,534,000	5.00	—	1973	346,924,000	7.00	—
1968S	(3,041,506)	—	3.50	1973D	232,977,400	9.00	—
1969	176,212,000	7.50	—	1973S	(2,760,339)	—	3.00
1969D	114,372,000	6.50	—	1974	801,456,000	6.50	—
1969S	(2,934,631)	—	3.50	1974D	353,160,300	10.00	—
1970	136,420,000	6.50	—	1974S	(2,612,568)	—	3.00
1970D	417,341,364	6.00	—	1975 none minted	—	—	—
1970S	(2,632,810)	—	3.00	1975D none minted	—	—	—
1971	109,284,000	6.00	—	1975S none minted	—	—	—
1971D	258,634,428	· 2.50	—				

Bicentennial design, drummer boy reverse

Mint Mark
1968-present

KM# 204 • 5.6700 g., Copper-Nickel Clad Copper, 24.3 mm. • Rev. Designer: Jack L. Ahr

Date	Mintage	G-4	VG-8	F-12	VF-20	XF-40	MS-60	MS-65	Prf-65
1976	809,784,016	—	—	—	—	—	.60	3.50	—
1976D	860,118,839	—	—	—	—	—	.60	4.00	—
1976S	(4,149,730)	—	—	—	—	—	—	—	3.00

Bicentennial design, drummer boy reverse

KM# 204a • 5.7500 g., Silver Clad, 0.074 oz., 24.3 mm. • Rev. Designer: Jack L. Ahr

Date	Mintage	G-4	VG-8	F-12	VF-20	XF-40	MS-60	MS-65	Prf-65
1976S	4,908,319(3,998,621)	—	—	—	—	—	1.25	3.00	3.00

Regular design resumed reverse

KM# A164a • 5.6700 g., Copper-Nickel Clad Copper, 24.3 mm. • Notes: KM#164 design and composition resumed. The 1979-S and 1981 Type II proofs have clearer mint marks than the Type I proofs for those years.

Date	Mintage	MS-65	Prf-65	Date	Mintage	MS-65	Prf-65
1977	468,556,000	6.50	—	1979S T-I	—	—	2.00
1977D	256,524,978	4.00	—	1979S T-II	—	—	3.00
1977S	(3,251,152)	—	1.50	1980P	635,832,000	5.00	—
1978	521,452,000	6.00	—	1980D	518,327,487	4.75	—
1978D	287,373,152	8.00	—	1980S	(3,554,806)	—	2.00
1978S	(3,127,781)	—	3.00	1981P	601,716,000	6.00	—
1979	515,708,000	6.00	—	1981D	575,722,833	4.00	—
1979D	489,789,780	4.00	—	1981S T-I	—	—	1.75

Date	Mintage	MS-65	Prf-65
1981S T-II	—	—	5.00
1982P	500,931,000	18.50	—
1982D	480,042,788	10.00	—
1982S	(3,857,479)	—	2.75
1983P	673,535,000	45.00	—
1983D	617,806,446	30.00	—
1983S	(3,279,126)	—	2.75
1984P	676,545,000	10.00	—
1984D	546,483,064	7.00	—
1984S	(3,065,110)	—	2.75
1985P	775,818,962	10.00	—
1985D	519,962,888	6.00	—
1985S	(3,362,821)	5.00	1.75
1986P	551,199,333	7.00	—
1986D	504,298,660	10.00	—
1986S	(3,010,497)	—	3.00
1987P	582,499,481	7.00	—
1987D	655,594,696	5.00	—
1987S	(4,227,728)	—	1.75
1988P	562,052,000	9.00	—
1988D	596,810,688	8.00	—
1988S	(3,262,948)	—	2.25
1989P	512,868,000	9.00	—
1989D	896,535,597	3.00	—
1989S	(3,220,194)	—	2.25
1990P	613,792,000	9.00	—
1990D	927,638,181	3.00	—
1990S	(3,299,559)	—	6.00
1991P	570,968,000	8.00	—
1991D	630,966,693	7.00	—
1991S	(2,867,787)	—	2.50

Date	Mintage	MS-65	Prf-65
1992P	384,764,000	12.00	—
1992D	389,777,107	15.00	—
1992S	(2,858,981)	—	3.00
1993P	639,276,000	6.00	—
1993D	645,476,128	7.50	—
1993S	(2,633,439)	—	4.50
1994P	825,600,000	12.00	—
1994D	880,034,110	7.00	—
1994S	(2,484,594)	—	4.00
1995P	1,004,336,000	10.00	—
1995D	1,103,216,000	9.00	—
1995S	(2,010,384)	—	16.50
1996P	925,040,000	5.00	—
1996D	906,868,000	5.00	—
1996S	—	—	4.00
1997P	595,740,000	4.00	—
1997D	599,680,000	4.00	—
1997S	(1,975,000)	—	9.50
1998P	896,268,000	4.00	—
1998D	821,000,000	4.00	—
1998S	—	—	11.00

KM# A164b • **Silver** • **Notes:** Resumption of silver.

Date	Mintage	Prf-65
1992S	(1,317,579)	3.50
1993S	(761,353)	6.50
1994S	(785,329)	12.50
1995S	(838,953)	18.00
1996S	—	11.50
1997S	—	19.00
1998S	—	10.00

50 State Quarters

Connecticut

KM# 297 • **Copper-Nickel Clad Copper** •

Date	Mintage	MS-63	MS-65	Prf-65
1999P	688,744,000	.75	.75	—
1999D	657,480,000	.75	.75	—
1999S	(3,713,359)	—	—	10.00

KM# 297a • **0.9000 Silver** •

Date	Mintage	MS-63	MS-65	Prf-65
1999S	(804,565)	—	—	40.00

Delaware

KM# 293 • 5.6700 g., **Copper-Nickel Clad Copper**, 24.3 mm. •

Date	Mintage	MS-63	MS-65	Prf-65
1999P	373,400,000	1.25	1.25	—
1999D	401,424,000	1.25	1.25	—
1999S	(3,713,359)	—	—	10.00

KM# 293a • **0.9000 Silver** •

Date	Mintage	MS-63	MS-65	Prf-65
1999S	(804,565)	—	—	40.00

Georgia

KM# 296 • **Copper-Nickel Clad Copper** •

Date	Mintage	MS-63	MS-65	Prf-65
1999P	451,188,000	.75	.75	—
1999D	488,744,000	.75	.75	—
1999S	(3,713,359)	—	—	10.00

KM# 296a • **0.9000 Silver** •

Date	Mintage	MS-63	MS-65	Prf-65
1999S	(804,565)	—	—	40.00

New Jersey

KM# 295 • **Copper-Nickel Clad Copper** •

Date	Mintage	MS-63	MS-65	Prf-65
1999P	363,200,000	1.00	1.00	—
1999D	299,028,000	1.00	1.00	—
1999S	(3,713,359)	—	—	10.00

KM# 295a • **0.9000 Silver** •

Date	Mintage	MS-63	MS-65	Prf-65
1999S	(804,565)	—	—	40.00

Pennsylvania

KM# 294 • 5.6700 g., **Copper-Nickel Clad Copper, 24.3 mm.** •

Date	Mintage	MS-63	MS-65	Prf-65
1999P	349,000,000	1.50	1.50	—
1999D	358,332,000	1.25	1.25	—
1999S	(3,713,359)	—	—	10.00

KM# 294a • **0.9000 Silver** •

Date	Mintage	MS-63	MS-65	Prf-65
1999S	(804,565)	—	—	40.00

Maryland

KM# 306 • **Copper-Nickel Clad Copper** •

Date	Mintage	MS-63	MS-65	Prf-65
2000P	678,200,000	.75	.75	—
2000D	556,526,000	.75	.75	—
2000S	(4,078,747)	—	—	5.00

KM# 306a • **0.9000 Silver** •

Date	Mintage	MS-63	MS-65	Prf-65
2000S	(965,921)	—	—	7.50

Massachusetts

KM# 305 • **Copper-Nickel Clad Copper** •

Date	Mintage	MS-63	MS-65	Prf-65
2000P	629,800,000	.75	.75	—
2000D	535,184,000	.75	.75	—
2000S	(4,078,747)	—	—	5.00

KM# 305a • **0.9000 Silver** •

Date	Mintage	MS-63	MS-65	Prf-65
2000S	(965,921)	—	—	7.50

New Hampshire

KM# 308 • **Copper-Nickel Clad Copper** •

Date	Mintage	MS-63	MS-65	Prf-65
2000P	673,040,000	.75	.75	—
2000D	495,976,000	.75	.75	—
2000S	(4,078,747)	—	—	5.00

KM# 308a • **0.9000 Silver** •

Date	Mintage	MS-63	MS-65	Prf-65
2000S	(965,921)	—	—	7.50

South Carolina

KM# 307 • **Copper-Nickel Clad Copper** •

Date	Mintage	MS-63	MS-65	Prf-65
2000P	742,756,000	.75	.75	—
2000D	566,208,000	.75	.75	—
2000S	(4,078,747)	—	—	5.00

KM# 307a • **0.9000 Silver** •

Date	Mintage	MS-63	MS-65	Prf-65
2000S	(965,921)	—	—	7.50

Virginia

KM# 309 • **Copper-Nickel Clad Copper** •

Date	Mintage	MS-63	MS-65	Prf-65
2000P	943,000,000	.75	.75	—
2000D	651,616,000	.75	.75	—
2000S	(4,078,747)	—	—	5.00

KM# 309a • **0.9000 Silver** •

Date	Mintage	MS-63	MS-65	Prf-65
2000S	(965,921)	—	—	7.50

Kentucky

KM# 322 • **Copper-Nickel Clad Copper** •

Date	Mintage	MS-63	MS-65	Prf-65
2001P	353,000,000	.75	.75	—
2001D	370,564,000	.75	.75	—
2001S	(3,009,800)	—	—	6.50

KM# 322a • **0.9000 Silver** •

Date	Mintage	MS-63	MS-65	Prf-65
2001S	(849,500)	—	—	22.50

KM# • **Copper-Nickel Clad Copper, 0 oz.** •

Date	Mintage	MS-63	MS-65	Prf-65
2001P	353,000,000	.75	1.00	—
2001D	370,564,000	.75	1.00	—
2001S	(3,009,800)	—	—	6.50

New York

KM# 318 • Copper-Nickel Clad Copper •

Date	Mintage	MS-63	MS-65	Prf-65
2001P	655,400,000	.75	.75	—
2001D	619,640,000	.75	.75	—
2001S	(3,009,800)	—	—	6.50

KM# 318a • 0.9000 Silver •

Date	Mintage	MS-63	MS-65	Prf-65
2001S	(849,600)	—	—	22.50

North Carolina

KM# 319 • Copper-Nickel Clad Copper •

Date	Mintage	MS-63	MS-65	Prf-65
2001P	627,600,000	.75	.75	—
2001D	427,876,000	.75	.75	—
2001S	(3,009,800)	—	—	6.50

KM# 319a • 0.9000 Silver •

Date	Mintage	MS-63	MS-65	Prf-65
2001S	(849,600)	—	—	22.50

Rhode Island

KM# 320 • Copper-Nickel Clad Copper •

Date	Mintage	MS-63	MS-65	Prf-65
2001P	423,000,000	.75	.75	—
2001D	447,100,000	.75	.75	—
2001S	(3,009,800)	—	—	6.50

KM# 320a • 0.9000 Silver •

Date	Mintage	MS-63	MS-65	Prf-65
2001S	(849,600)	—	—	22.50

Vermont

KM# 321 • Copper-Nickel Clad Copper •

Date	Mintage	MS-63	MS-65	Prf-65
2001P	423,400,000	.75	.75	—
2001D	459,404,000	.75	.75	—
2001S	(3,009,800)	—	—	6.50

KM# 321a • 0.9000 Silver •

Date	Mintage	MS-63	MS-65	Prf-65
2001S	(849,600)	—	—	22.50

Indiana

KM# 334 • Copper-Nickel Clad Copper •

Date	Mintage	MS-63	MS-65	Prf-65
2002P	362,600,000	.75	.75	—
2002D	327,200,000	.75	.75	—
2002S	(3,084,185)	—	—	6.00

KM# 334a • 0.9000 Silver •

Date	Mintage	MS-63	MS-65	Prf-65
2002S	(892,229)	—	—	18.00

Louisiana

KM# 333 • Copper-Nickel Clad Copper •

Date	Mintage	MS-63	MS-65	Prf-65
2002P	362,000,000	.75	.75	—
2002D	402,204,000	.75	.75	—
2002S	(3,084,185)	—	—	6.00

KM# 333a • 0.9000 Silver •

Date	Mintage	MS-63	MS-65	Prf-65
2002S	(892,229)	—	—	18.00

Mississippi

KM# 335 • Copper-Nickel Clad Copper •

Date	Mintage	MS-63	MS-65	Prf-65
2002P	290,000,000	.75	.75	—
2002D	289,600,000	.75	.75	—
2002S	(3,084,185)	—	—	6.00

KM# 335a • 0.9000 Silver •

Date	Mintage	MS-63	MS-65	Prf-65
2002S	(892,229)	—	—	18.00

Ohio

KM# 332 • Copper-Nickel Clad Copper •

Date	Mintage	MS-63	MS-65	Prf-65
2002P	217,200,000	.75	.75	—
2002D	414,832,000	.75	.75	—
2002S	(3,084,185)	—	—	6.00

KM# 332a • 0.9000 Silver •

Date	Mintage	MS-63	MS-65	Prf-65
2002S	(892,229)	—	—	18.00

Tennessee

KM# 331 • Copper-Nickel Clad Copper •

Date	Mintage	MS-63	MS-65	Prf-65
2002P	361,600,000	1.25	1.25	—
2002D	286,468,000	.85	.85	—
2002S	(3,084,185)	—	—	6.00

KM# 331a • 0.9000 Silver •

Date	Mintage	MS-63	MS-65	Prf-65
2002S	(892,229)	—	—	18.00

Alabama

KM# 344 • Copper-Nickel Clad Copper •

Date	Mintage	MS-63	MS-65	Prf-65
2003P	225,000,000	.75	.75	—
2003D	232,400,000	.75	.75	—
2003S	(3,270,603)	—	—	5.00

KM# 344a • 0.9000 Silver •

Date	Mintage	MS-63	MS-65	Prf-65
2003S	—	—	—	9.00

Arkansas

KM# 347 • Copper-Nickel Clad Copper •

Date	Mintage	MS-63	MS-65	Prf-65
2003P	228,000,000	.75	.75	—
2003D	229,800,000	.75	.75	—
2003S	(3,270,603)	—	—	5.00

KM# 347a • 0.9000 Silver •

Date	Mintage	MS-63	MS-65	Prf-65
2003S	—	—	—	9.00

Illinois

KM# 343 • Copper-Nickel Clad Copper •

Date	Mintage	MS-63	MS-65	Prf-65
2003P	225,800,000	.75	.75	—
2003D	237,400,000	.75	.75	—
2003S	(3,270,603)	—	—	5.00

KM# 343a • 0.9000 Silver •

Date	Mintage	MS-63	MS-65	Prf-65
2003S	—	—	—	9.00

Maine

KM# 345 • Copper-Nickel Clad Copper •

Date	Mintage	MS-63	MS-65	Prf-65
2003P	217,400,000	.75	.75	—
2003D	213,400,000	.75	.75	—
2003S	(3,270,603)	—	—	5.00

KM# 345a • 0.9000 Silver •

Date	Mintage	MS-63	MS-65	Prf-65
2003S	—	—	—	9.00

Missouri

KM# 346 • Copper-Nickel Clad Copper •

Date	Mintage	MS-63	MS-65	Prf-65
2003P	225,000,000	.75	.75	—
2003D	228,200,000	.75	.75	—
2003S	(3,270,603)	—	—	5.00

KM# 346a • 0.9000 Silver •

Date	Mintage	MS-63	MS-65	Prf-65
2003S	—	—	—	9.00

Florida

KM# 356	•	Copper-Nickel Clad Copper	•	
Date	Mintage	MS-63	MS-65	Prf-65
2004P	240,200,000	.75	.75	—
2004D	241,600,000	.75	.75	—
2004S	—	—	—	5.00

KM# 356a	•	0.9000 Silver	•	
Date	Mintage	MS-63	MS-65	Prf-65
2004S	—	—	—	9.00

Iowa

KM# 358	•	Copper-Nickel Clad Copper	•	
Date	Mintage	MS-63	MS-65	Prf-65
2004P	213,800,000	.75	.75	—
2004D	251,800,000	.75	.75	—
2004S	—	—	—	5.00

KM# 358a	•	0.9000 Silver	•	
Date	Mintage	MS-63	MS-65	Prf-65
2004S	—	—	—	9.00

Michigan

KM# 355	•	Copper-Nickel Clad Copper	•	
Date	Mintage	MS-63	MS-65	Prf-65
2004P	233,800,000	.75	.75	—
2004D	225,800,000	.75	.75	—
2004S	—	—	—	5.00

KM# 355a	•	0.9000 Silver	•	
Date	Mintage	MS-63	MS-65	Prf-65
2004S	—	—	—	9.00

Texas

KM# 357	•	Copper-Nickel Clad Copper	•	
Date	Mintage	MS-63	MS-65	Prf-65
2004P	278,800,000	.75	.75	—
2004D	263,000,000	.75	.75	—
2004S	—	—	—	5.00

KM# 357a	•	0.9000 Silver	•	
Date	Mintage	MS-63	MS-65	Prf-65
2004S	—	—	—	9.00

Wisconsin

KM# 359	•	Copper-Nickel Clad Copper	•	
Date	Mintage	MS-63	MS-65	Prf-65
2004P	226,400,000	.75	.75	—
2004D	226,800,000	.75	.75	—
2004D Extra Leaf Low	Est. 9,000	250	800	—
2004D Extra Leaf High	Est. 3,000	400	1,000	—
2004S	—	—	—	5.00

KM# 359a	•	0.9000 Silver	•	
Date	Mintage	MS-63	MS-65	Prf-65
2004S	—	—	—	9.00

California

KM# 370	•	Copper-Nickel Clad Copper	•	
Date	Mintage	MS-63	MS-65	Prf-65
2005P	257,200,000	.75	.75	—
2005D	263,200,000	.75	.75	—
2005S	—	—	—	5.00

KM# 370a	•	6.2500 g., 0.9000 Silver, 0.1808 oz. ASW	•	
Date	Mintage	MS-63	MS-65	Prf-65
2005S	—	—	—	9.00

Kansas

KM# 373	•	Copper-Nickel Clad Copper	•	
Date	Mintage	MS-63	MS-65	Prf-65
2005P	263,400,000	.75	.75	—
2005D	300,000,000	.75	.75	—
2005S	—	—	—	9.00

KM# 373a	•	6.2500 g., 0.9000 Silver, 0.1808 oz. ASW	•	
Date	Mintage	MS-63	MS-65	Prf-65
2005S	—	—	—	9.00

Minnesota

KM# 371   • **Copper-Nickel Clad Copper** •

Date	Mintage	MS-63	MS-65	Prf-65
2005P	226,400,000	.75	.75	—
2005D	226,800,000	.75	.75	—
2005S	—	—	—	5.00

KM# 371a   • 6.2500 g., 0.9000 **Silver**, 0.1808 oz. ASW •

Date	Mintage	MS-63	MS-65	Prf-65
2005S	—	—	—	9.00

Oregon

KM# 372   • **Copper-Nickel Clad Copper** •

Date	Mintage	MS-63	MS-65	Prf-65
2005P	316,200,000	.75	.75	—
2005D	404,000,000	.75	.75	—
2005S	—	—	—	5.00

KM# 372a   • 6.2500 g., 0.9000 **Silver**, 0.1808 oz. ASW •

Date	Mintage	MS-63	MS-65	Prf-65
2005S	—	—	—	9.00

West Virginia

KM# 374   • **Copper-Nickel Clad Copper** •

Date	Mintage	MS-63	MS-65	Prf-65
2005P	365,400,000	.75	.75	—
2005D	356,200,000	.75	.75	—
2005S	—	—	—	5.00

KM# 374a   • 6.2500 g., 0.9000 **Silver**, 0.1808 oz. ASW •

Date	Mintage	MS-63	MS-65	Prf-65
2005S	—	—	—	9.00

Colorado

KM# 384   • **Copper-Nickel Clad Copper** •

Date	Mintage	MS-63	MS-65	Prf-65
2006P	—	.75	.75	—
2006D	—	.75	.75	—
2006S	—	—	—	5.00

KM# 384a   • 6.2500 g., 0.9000 **Silver**, 0.1808 oz. ASW •

Date	Mintage	MS-63	MS-65	Prf-65
2006S	—	—	—	9.00

Nebraska

KM# 383   • **Copper-Nickel Clad Copper** •

Date	Mintage	MS-63	MS-65	Prf-65
2006P	—	.75	.75	—
2006D	—	.75	.75	—
2006S	—	—	—	5.00

KM# 383a   • 6.2500 g., 0.9000 **Silver**, 0.1808 oz. ASW •

Date	Mintage	MS-63	MS-65	Prf-65
2006	—	—	—	9.00

Nevada

KM# 382   • **Copper-Nickel Clad Copper** •

Date	Mintage	MS-63	MS-65	Prf-65
2006P	—	.75	.75	—
2006D	—	.75	.75	—
2006S	—	—	—	5.00

KM# 382a   • 6.2500 g., 0.9000 **Silver**, 0.1808 oz. ASW •

Date	Mintage	MS-63	MS-65	Prf-65
2006S	—	—	—	9.00

North Dakota

KM# 385   • **Copper-Nickel Clad Copper** •

Date	Mintage	MS-63	MS-65	Prf-65
2006P	—	.75	.75	—
2006D	—	.75	.75	—
2006S	—	—	—	5.00

KM# 385a   • 6.2500 g., 0.9000 **Silver**, 0.1808 oz. ASW •

Date	Mintage	MS-63	MS-65	Prf-65
2006S	—	—	—	9.00

South Dakota

KM# 386   • **Copper-Nickel Clad Copper** •

Date	Mintage	MS-63	MS-65	Prf-65
2006P	—	.75	.75	—
2006D	—	.75	.75	—
2006S	—	—	—	5.00

KM# 386a   • 6.2500 g., 0.9000 **Silver**, 0.1808 oz. ASW •

Date	Mintage	MS-63	MS-65	Prf-65
2006S	—	—	—	9.00

HALF DOLLAR

Flowing Hair Half Dollar

KM# 16 • 13.4800 g., 0.8920 **Silver**, 0.3869 oz. ASW, 32.5 mm. • **Designer:** Robert Scot **Notes:** The 1795 "recut date" variety had the date cut into the dies twice, so both sets of numbers are visible on the coin. The 1795 "3 leaves" variety has three leaves under each of the eagle's wings on the reverse.

Date	Mintage	G-4	VG-8	F-12	VF-20	XF-40	MS-60
1794	23,464	2,400	4,000	6,000	13,000	20,000	90,000
1795	299,680	650	900	1,700	3,500	7,500	22,000
1795 recut date	Inc. above	700	950	1,750	3,750	7,750	25,000
1795 3 leaves	Inc. above	1,050	1,800	3,000	6,000	12,500	—

Draped Bust Half Dollar
Small eagle reverse

KM# 26 • 13.4800 g., 0.8920 **Silver**, 0.3869 oz. ASW, 32.5 mm. • **Designer:** Robert Scot **Notes:** The 1796 strikes have either 15 or 16 stars on the obverse.

1797 Half Dollar
Grade F-12

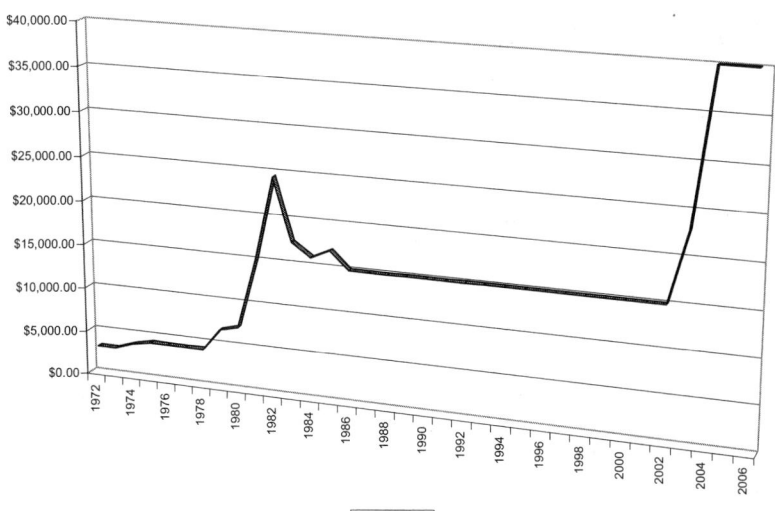

Retail Price

Date	Mintage	G-4	VG-8	F-12	VF-20	XF-40	MS-60
1796 15 stars	3,918	29,000	35,000	40,000	55,000	80,000	175,000
1796 16 stars	Inc. above	30,000	36,000	42,000	60,000	85,000	200,000
1797	Inc. above	29,000	35,000	40,000	55,000	80,000	175,000

Heraldic eagle reverse

KM# 35 • 13.4800 g., 0.8920 **Silver**, 0.3869 oz. ASW, 32.5 mm. • **Designer:** Robert Scot **Notes:** The two varieties of the 1803 strikes are distinguished by the size of the 3 in the date. The several varieties of the 1806 strikes are distinguished by the style of 6 in the date, size of the stars on the obverse, and whether the stem of the olive branch held by the reverse eagle extends through the claw.

Date	Mintage	G-4	VG-8	F-12	VF-20	XF-40	MS-60
1801	30,289	225	300	700	1,500	5,000	35,000
1802	29,890	225	300	700	1,500	4,500	40,000
1803 small 3	188,234	150	170	300	600	1,500	8,500
1803 large 3	Inc. above	125	150	250	500	1,000	9,000
1805	211,722	125	150	250	550	1,050	9,000
1805/4	Inc. above	190	300	500	1,000	2,500	26,000
1806 round-top 6, large stars	839,576	125	150	190	450	1,100	6,000
1806 round-top 6, small stars	Inc. above	125	140	180	450	1,100	6,250
1806 knobbed 6, stem not through claw	—	—	35,000	40,000	50,000	65,000	—
1806 pointed-top 6, stem not through claw	Inc. above	115	130	250	340	1,000	5,750
1806 pointed-top 6, stem through claw	Inc. above	120	150	250	340	1,000	5,750
1806/5	Inc. above	125	160	275	500	1,400	8,000
1806 /inverted 6	Inc. above	200	350	600	1,200	2,100	15,000
1807	301,076	120	150	250	340	1,000	5,750

Bust Half Dollar
"50 C." below eagle reverse

KM# 37 • 13.4800 g., 0.8920 **Silver**, 0.3869 oz. ASW, 32.5 mm. • **Designer:** John Reich **Notes:** There are three varieties of the 1807 strikes. Two are distinguished by the size of the stars on the obverse. The third was struck from a reverse die that had a 5 cut over a 2 in the "50C" denomination. Two varieties of the 1811 are distinguished by the size of the 8 in the date. A third has a period between the 8 and second 1 in the date. One variety of the 1817 has a period between the 1 and 7 in the date. Two varieties of the 1819/18 overdate are distinguished by the size of the 9 in the date. Two varieties of the 1820 are distinguished by the size of the date. On the 1823 varieties, the "broken 3" appears to be almost separated in the middle of the 3 in the date; the "patched 3" has the error repaired; the "ugly 3" has portions of its detail missing. The 1827 "curled-2" and "square-2" varieties are distinguished by the numeral's base -- either curled or square. Among the 1828 varieties, "knobbed 2" and "no knob" refers to whether the upper left serif of the digit is rounded. The 1830 varieties are distinguished by the size of the 0 in the date. The four 1834 varieties are distinguished by the sizes of the stars, date and letters in the inscriptions. The 1836 "50/00" variety was struck from a reverse die that had "50" recut over "00" in the denomination.

Date	Mintage	G-4	VG-8	F-12	VF-20	XF-40	AU-50	MS-60	MS-65
1807 small stars	750,500	65.00	105	200	475	800	3,500	5,900	35,000
1807 large stars	Inc. above	60.00	100.00	180	475	800	3,500	5,500	—
1807 50/20 C.	Inc. above	55.00	92.50	140	250	500	2,100	4,000	30,000
1807 bearded goddess	—	300	500	900	1,500	2,750	7,500	—	—
1808	1,368,600	50.00	57.50	65.00	100.00	260	600	1,800	15,000
1808/7	Inc. above	52.50	62.50	92.50	160	330	900	1,850	17,500
1809	1,405,810	50.00	57.50	65.00	100.00	210	525	1,600	15,000
1810	1,276,276	52.50	57.50	66.00	100.00	175	475	1,550	13,000

Date	Mintage	G-4	VG-8	F-12	VF-20	XF-40	AU-50	MS-60	MS-65
1811 small 8	1,203,644	52.50	60.00	65.00	100.00	140	375	800	7,500
1811 large 8	Inc. above	50.00	57.50	62.50	95.00	150	500	1,000	8,500
1811 dated 18.11	Inc. above	55.00	60.00	80.00	150	300	800	2,100	12,000
1812	1,628,059	52.50	60.00	65.00	100.00	150	340	775	7,500
1812/1 small 8	Inc. above	53.50	61.00	90.00	160	250	700	2,000	12,000
1812/1 large 8	Inc. above	1,350	1,900	3,500	4,850	7,500	15,500	—	—
1813	1,241,903	52.50	60.00	65.00	100.00	165	500	1,250	11,000
1813 50/UNI reverse	1,241,903	55.00	62.50	92.50	135	300	900	1,900	12,000
1814	1,039,075	52.50	60.00	66.00	100.00	165	500	1,350	9,800
1814/3	Inc. above	62.50	75.00	110	150	275	850	2,000	16,500
1815/2	47,150	840	1,150	1,550	1,900	3,000	4,750	11,000	60,000
1817	1,215,567	52.50	60.00	66.00	90.00	160	385	900	10,000
1817/3	Inc. above	80.00	125	175	385	800	1,800	3,750	43,500
1817/4	—	50,000	60,000	115,000	145,000	190,000	240,000	—	—
1817 dated 181.7	Inc. above	54.00	62.50	70.00	100.00	175	650	1,500	12,500
1818	1,960,322	52.50	60.00	66.00	85.00	135	375	900	8,500
1818/7	Inc. above	60.00	72.50	85.00	105	160	700	1,500	11,000
1819	2,208,000	52.50	60.00	66.00	85.00	125	375	900	9,000
1819/8 small 9	Inc. above	57.50	62.50	75.00	100.00	200	550	1,300	1,150
1819/8 large 9	Inc. above	57.50	62.50	75.00	100.00	200	550	1,300	11,500
1820 small date	751,122	53.50	61.00	75.00	145	260	650	1,500	12,500
1820 large date	Inc. above	53.50	61.00	75.00	125	250	660	1,350	12,000
1820/19	Inc. above	62.50	75.00	85.00	150	300	900	2,000	15,000
1821	1,305,797	52.50	60.00	66.00	80.00	140	525	1,200	9,750
1822	1,559,573	52.50	60.00	66.00	85.00	125	300	750	7,700
1822/1	Inc. above	60.00	68.50	92.50	150	250	800	1,750	11,000
1823	1,694,200	47.50	52.50	57.50	66.00	110	300	825	7,500
1823 broken 3	Inc. above	55.00	66.00	92.50	140	360	900	1,750	12,000
1823 patched 3	Inc. above	52.50	62.50	85.00	115	225	400	1,300	13,500
1823 ugly 3	Inc. above	53.50	67.50	88.00	135	235	900	1,700	14,000
1824	3,504,954	47.50	52.50	66.00	75.00	110	260	650	7,500
1824/21	Inc. above	52.50	60.00	66.00	85.00	150	400	1,000	8,000
1824 1824/various dates	Inc. above	52.50	60.00	70.00	125	200	750	1,750	12,000
1825	2,943,166	47.50	52.50	66.00	75.00	110	260	550	7,000
1826	4,004,180	47.50	52.50	66.00	75.00	110	260	550	7,000
1827 curled 2	5,493,400	47.50	52.50	66.00	100.00	130	345	900	8,500
1827 square 2	Inc. above	47.50	52.50	60.00	75.00	110	260	650	7,500
1827/6	Inc. above	57.50	68.50	80.00	100.00	150	375	975	9,000
1828 curled-base 2, no knob	3,075,200	47.50	52.50	66.00	75.00	110	260	650	7,000
1828 curled-base 2, knobbed 2	Inc. above	47.50	52.50	66.00	85.00	120	270	700	7,250
1828 small 8s, square-base 2, large letters	Inc. above	47.50	52.50	66.00	75.00	110	260	550	6,250
1828 small 8s, square-base 2, small letters	Inc. above	52.50	70.00	95.00	135	220	720	1,200	9,500
1828 large 8s, square-base 2	Inc. above	48.50	52.50	66.00	75.00	110	260	750	9,000
1829	3,712,156	45.00	50.00	53.50	60.00	100.00	250	600	9,000
1829/7	Inc. above	47.50	57.50	67.50	85.00	165	330	925	11,750
1830 small letter rev.	4,764,800	45.00	50.00	53.50	60.00	100.00	250	500	7,000
1830 large letter rev.	Inc. above	1,250	1,850	2,250	3,300	4,500	7,500	—	—
1831	5,873,660	45.00	50.00	53.50	60.00	100.00	250	500	7,000
1832 small letters	4,797,000	45.00	50.00	53.50	60.00	100.00	250	575	7,000
1832 large letters	Inc. above	45.00	50.00	64.00	90.00	155	315	700	7,500
1833	5,206,000	45.00	50.00	53.50	60.00	100.00	250	575	7,000
1834 small date, large stars, small letters	6,412,004	45.00	50.00	53.50	60.00	100.00	250	575	7,000
1834 small date, small stars, small letters	Inc. above	45.00	50.00	53.50	60.00	100.00	250	575	7,000
1834 large date, small letters	Inc. above	45.00	50.00	53.50	60.00	100.00	250	575	7,000
1834 large date, large letters	Inc. above	45.00	50.00	53.50	60.00	100.00	250	575	7,000
1835	5,352,006	45.00	50.00	53.50	60.00	100.00	275	600	9,000
1836	6,545,000	45.00	50.00	53.50	60.00	100.00	250	500	7,000
1836 50/00	Inc. above	55.00	80.00	100.00	185	300	800	1,750	10,000

"50 Cents" below eagle reverse

KM# 58 • 13.3600 g., 0.9000 **Silver**, 0.3867 oz. ASW, 30 mm. • **Designer:** Christian Gobrecht **Edge Desc:** Reeded.

Date	Mintage	G-4	VG-8	F-12	VF-20	XF-40	AU-50	MS-60	MS-65
1836	1,200	700	1,000	1,200	1,500	2,250	3,200	6,000	40,000
1837	3,629,820	50.00	60.00	75.00	110	165	325	750	12,500

"Half Dol." below eagle reverse

KM# 65 • 13.3600 g., 0.9000 **Silver**, 0.3867 oz. ASW, 30 mm. • **Designer:** Christian Gobrecht

Date	Mintage	G-4	VG-8	F-12	VF-20	XF-40	AU-50	MS-60	MS-65
1838	3,546,000	50.00	60.00	75.00	110	165	475	825	17,000
1838O proof only	Est. 20	85,000	105,000	115,000	125,000	150,000	180,000	—	—
1839	1,392,976	56.00	66.00	82.50	115	185	375	990	30,000
1839O	178,976	135	215	300	400	675	1,200	2,500	45,000

Seated Liberty Half Dollar

KM# 68 • 13.3600 g., 0.9000 **Silver**, .3867 oz. ASW, 30.6 mm. • **Designer:** Christian Gobrecht **Notes:** The 1839 varieties are distinguished by whether there's drapery extending from Liberty's left elbow. One variety of the 1840 strikes has smaller lettering; another used the old reverse of 1838. Varieties of 1842 and 1846 are distinguished by the size of the numerals in the date.

Date	Mintage	G-4	VG-8	F-12	VF-20	XF-40	AU-50	MS-60	MS-65
1839 no drapery from elbow	Inc. above	38.00	65.00	110	315	725	1,650	4,500	150,000
1839 drapery	Inc. above	20.00	30.00	50.00	75.00	145	265	450	—
1840 small letters	1,435,008	23.00	32.00	47.50	67.00	110	350	575	8,250
1840 reverse 1838	Inc. above	150	200	275	350	650	1,100	2,900	12,000
1840O	855,100	23.00	28.00	45.00	80.00	125	275	430	—
1841	310,000	40.00	50.00	90.00	150	225	300	1,100	5,700
1841O	401,000	19.00	28.00	44.00	75.00	125	250	550	5,900
1842 small date	2,012,764	35.00	42.00	60.00	110	185	325	1,300	12,000
1842 large date	Inc. above	18.00	28.00	43.00	52.00	100.00	175	1,250	12,000
1842O small date	957,000	650	850	1,400	2,250	4,000	—	—	—
1842O large date	Inc. above	22.00	29.00	48.00	115	225	750	1,750	—
1843	3,844,000	17.00	28.00	43.00	52.00	100.00	180	350	4,500
1843O	2,268,000	17.00	28.00	43.00	60.00	115	250	550	—
1844	1,766,000	17.00	28.00	43.00	52.00	100.00	210	350	4,500
1844O	2,005,000	18.00	28.00	43.00	52.00	100.00	225	525	—
1844/1844O	Inc. above	500	775	1,000	1,375	2,300	4,900	—	—
1845	589,000	35.00	45.00	70.00	125	225	375	900	—
1845O	2,094,000	18.00	28.00	43.00	52.00	125	240	550	—
1845O no drapery	Inc. above	25.00	35.00	65.00	115	185	375	750	—
1846 medium date	2,210,000	18.00	28.00	43.00	52.00	100.00	200	500	9,000
1846 tall date	Inc. above	22.00	30.00	60.00	85.00	145	250	650	12,000
1846 /horizontal 6	Inc. above	175	235	300	400	575	1,000	2,500	—
1846O medium date	2,304,000	18.00	28.00	43.00	52.00	100.00	225	550	12,000
1846O tall date	Inc. above	135	245	325	575	950	2,000	3,600	—
1847/1846	1,156,000	2,250	3,000	3,750	5,200	7,500	—	—	—
1847	Inc. above	25.00	35.00	55.00	70.00	115	250	480	9,000
1847O	2,584,000	18.00	28.00	43.00	52.00	95.00	250	640	7,000
1848	580,000	40.00	60.00	85.00	170	265	475	1,000	9,000
1848O	3,180,000	18.00	28.00	43.00	52.00	110	285	750	9,000
1849	1,252,000	26.00	40.00	55.00	90.00	150	365	1,250	9,000
1849O	2,310,000	17.00	28.00	43.00	60.00	110	250	650	9,000
1850	227,000	275	325	400	500	675	1,000	1,500	—
1850O	2,456,000	20.00	28.00	45.00	80.00	135	275	650	9,000
1851	200,750	450	500	700	950	1,100	1,350	1,950	—
1851O	402,000	40.00	50.00	75.00	105	175	300	700	9,000
1852	77,130	400	500	700	875	1,100	1,350	1,700	—
1852O	144,000	100.00	125	200	350	600	1,050	1,850	—

Date	Mintage	G-4	VG-8	F-12	VF-20	XF-40	AU-50	MS-60	MS-65
1853O mintage unrecorded	—	—	—	—	—	—	—	—	—,

Note: 1853O, Eliasberg Sale, 1997, VG-8, $154,000.

Seated Liberty Half Dollar
Arrows at date obverse   Rays around eagle reverse

KM# 79 • 12.4400 g., **0.9000 Silver**, 0.3600 oz. ASW • **Designer:** Christian Gobrecht

Date	Mintage	G-4	VG-8	F-12	VF-20	XF-40	AU-50	MS-60	MS-65	Prf-65
1853	3,532,708	17.00	27.00	40.00	90.00	250	505	1,700	21,500	—
1853O	1,328,000	21.00	32.00	50.00	125	290	700	2,100	21,500	—

Seated Liberty Half Dollar
Rays around eagle removed reverse

KM# 82 • 12.4400 g., **0.9000 Silver**, 0.3600 oz. ASW • **Designer:** Christian Gobrecht

Date	Mintage	G-4	VG-8	F-12	VF-20	XF-40	AU-50	MS-60	MS-65	Prf-65
1854	2,982,000	17.00	28.00	43.00	55.00	100.00	270	675	8,000	—
1854O	5,240,000	17.00	28.00	43.00	55.00	100.00	270	600	8,000	—
1855	759,500	23.00	33.00	45.00	75.00	150	325	1,200	8,000	22,500
1855/4	Inc. above	35.00	60.00	80.00	125	225	400	1,500	—	—
1855O	3,688,000	17.00	28.00	43.00	55.00	100.00	270	650	8,000	—
1855S	129,950	350	475	850	1,400	2,400	6,000	—	—	—

Arrows at date removed obverse

KM# A68 • 12.4400 g., **0.9000 Silver**, 0.3600 oz. ASW • **Designer:** Christian Gobrecht

Date	Mintage	G-4	VG-8	F-12	VF-20	XF-40	AU-50	MS-60	MS-65	Prf-65
1856	938,000	19.00	31.00	43.00	55.00	90.00	195	425	6,500	12,500
1856O	2,658,000	17.00	28.00	43.00	52.00	90.00	190	385	12,500	—
1856S	211,000	85.00	120	160	260	475	1,250	3,500	19,000	—
1857	1,988,000	17.00	28.00	43.00	52.00	90.00	190	385	5,150	12,500
1857O	818,000	21.00	31.00	43.00	75.00	125	275	885	12,500	—
1857S	158,000	100.00	120	145	285	575	975	3,500	19,000	—
1858	4,226,000	17.00	28.00	43.00	52.00	90.00	190	385	6,500	12,500
1858O	7,294,000	17.00	28.00	43.00	52.00	90.00	190	385	12,500	—
1858S	476,000	25.00	35.00	50.00	95.00	185	400	950	12,500	—
1859	748,000	17.00	28.00	43.00	60.00	110	200	650	6,600	5,500
1859O	2,834,000	17.00	28.00	43.00	50.00	90.00	190	450	6,500	—
1859S	566,000	25.00	38.00	55.00	85.00	215	375	750	12,500	—

Date	Mintage	G-4	VG-8	F-12	VF-20	XF-40	AU-50	MS-60	MS-65	Prf-65
1860	303,700	25.00	35.00	47.50	85.00	125	350	1,000	6,500	5,500
1860O	1,290,000	17.00	28.00	43.00	52.00	90.00	190	450	5,150	—
1860S	472,000	20.00	30.00	50.00	75.00	130	245	850	12,500	—
1861	2,888,400	17.00	28.00	43.00	52.00	90.00	190	440	5,150	5,500
1861O	2,532,633	18.00	29.00	50.00	65.00	100.00	190	450	5,150	—
1861S	939,500	18.00	29.00	43.00	65.00	110	195	975	9,500	—
1862	253,550	28.00	40.00	55.00	100.00	185	285	750	5,150	5,500
1862S	1,352,000	18.00	29.00	43.00	65.00	110	195	460	9,000	—
1863	503,660	20.00	32.00	43.00	75.00	130	250	750	5,150	5,500
1863S	916,000	18.00	29.00	43.00	65.00	110	195	460	9,000	—
1864	379,570	29.00	35.00	60.00	95.00	175	250	750	5,150	5,500
1864S	658,000	18.00	28.00	45.00	65.00	115	215	675	9,000	—
1865	511,900	28.00	37.00	55.00	85.00	135	275	750	5,150	5,500
1865S	675,000	18.00	29.00	43.00	65.00	110	235	500	9,000	—
1866 proof, unique	—	—	—	—	—	—	—	—	—	—
1866S	60,000	175	250	400	600	1,100	1,500	5,000	—	—

"In God We Trust" above eagle reverse

KM# 99 • 12.4400 g., 0.9000 **Silver**, 0.3600 oz. ASW • **Designer:** Christian Gobrecht **Notes:** In 1866 the motto "In God We Trust" was added to the reverse. The "closed-3" and "open-3" varieties are distinguished by the amount of space between the upper and lower left serifs of the 3.

Date	Mintage	G-4	VG-8	F-12	VF-20	XF-40	AU-50	MS-60	MS-65	Prf-65
1866	745,625	18.00	27.00	45.00	70.00	120	225	350	4,800	3,750
1866S	994,000	19.00	29.00	45.00	65.00	110	275	650	5,000	—
1867	449,925	25.00	35.00	55.00	100.00	150	250	350	4,800	3,750
1867S	1,196,000	19.00	29.00	40.00	65.00	110	250	350	7,000	—
1868	418,200	35.00	49.00	80.00	135	225	300	525	7,100	3,750
1868S	1,160,000	19.00	29.00	41.00	60.00	110	250	350	7,000	—
1869	795,900	19.00	29.00	41.00	60.00	110	190	385	4,600	3,750
1869S	656,000	20.00	29.00	41.00	60.00	120	265	600	7,000	—
1870	634,900	21.00	31.00	42.00	70.00	125	250	475	7,000	3,750

1855-S Half Dollar
Grade XF-40

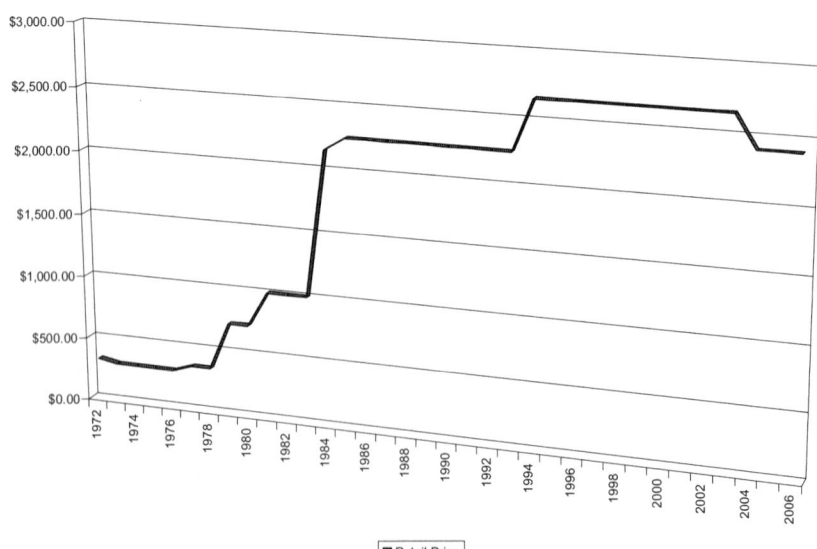

Retail Price

Date	Mintage	G-4	VG-8	F-12	VF-20	XF-40	AU-50	MS-60	MS-65	Prf-65
1870CC	54,617	800	1,200	1,750	2,900	10,000	—	—	—	—
1870S	1,004,000	19.00	31.00	45.00	70.00	125	275	575	7,000	—
1871	1,204,560	18.00	29.00	41.00	60.00	110	165	350	7,000	3,750
1871CC	153,950	225	325	600	1,200	1,950	10,000	15,000	—	—
1871S	2,178,000	18.00	29.00	41.00	65.00	110	215	400	7,000	—
1872	881,550	18.00	29.00	40.00	65.00	110	195	430	2,850	3,750
1872CC	272,000	80.00	115	235	350	1,500	4,000	8,000	50,000	—
1872S	580,000	28.00	33.00	60.00	110	185	375	975	7,000	—
1873 closed 3	801,800	23.00	30.00	50.00	90.00	135	250	500	4,500	3,750
1873 open 3	Inc. above	2,200	2,700	4,100	5,500	7,500	—	—	—	—
1873CC	122,500	170	225	325	800	1,500	2,500	4,100	9,000	3,750
1873S no arrows	5,000	—	—	—	—	—	—	—	—	—

Note: 1873S no arrows, no specimens known to survive.

Arrows at date obverse

KM# 107 • 12.5000 g., 0.9000 **Silver**, 0.3618 oz. ASW • **Designer:** Christian Gobrecht

Date	Mintage	G-4	VG-8	F-12	VF-20	XF-40	AU-50	MS-60	MS-65	Prf-65
1873	1,815,700	18.00	27.00	40.00	85.00	210	400	850	17,500	9,000
1873CC	214,560	115	220	335	725	1,700	2,400	5,700	42,000	—
1873S	233,000	55.00	75.00	125	225	375	675	2,200	40,000	—
1874	2,360,300	18.00	27.00	40.00	85.00	210	400	850	12,750	9,000
1874CC	59,000	400	550	950	1,500	2,500	4,500	8,000	—	—
1874S	394,000	35.00	65.00	85.00	175	315	600	1,600	—	—

Arrows at date removed obverse

KM# A99 • 12.5000 g., 0.9000 **Silver**, 0.3618 oz. ASW • **Designer:** Christian Gobrecht

Date	Mintage	G-4	VG-8	F-12	VF-20	XF-40	AU-50	MS-60	MS-65	Prf-65
1875	6,027,500	17.00	25.00	39.00	47.00	70.00	160	425	3,500	3,200
1875CC	1,008,000	20.00	34.00	53.00	95.00	185	300	540	5,450	—
1875S	3,200,000	17.00	26.00	40.00	47.00	80.00	165	340	2,700	—
1876	8,419,150	17.00	25.00	39.00	45.00	70.00	160	340	5,300	3,200
1876CC	1,956,000	18.00	30.00	48.00	85.00	175	275	560	4,200	—
1876S	4,528,000	17.00	25.00	39.00	45.00	70.00	160	340	2,700	—
1877	8,304,510	17.00	25.00	39.00	45.00	70.00	160	340	2,700	3,750
1877CC	1,420,000	18.00	33.00	43.00	75.00	145	275	630	3,250	—
1877S	5,356,000	17.00	25.00	39.00	45.00	70.00	160	340	2,700	—
1878	1,378,400	20.00	28.00	36.00	55.00	115	170	425	3,650	3,200
1878CC	62,000	375	525	875	1,250	2,750	5,000	7,000	42,500	—
1878S	12,000	15,000	17,500	22,000	27,500	33,000	40,000	52,500	125,000	—
1879	5,900	295	325	375	425	525	600	825	2,900	3,250
1880	9,755	275	310	365	415	500	575	800	2,900	3,250
1881	10,975	275	300	350	400	485	550	800	2,900	3,250
1882	5,500	350	400	425	500	585	650	850	3,600	3,250
1883	9,039	275	310	365	415	500	575	800	2,900	3,250
1884	5,275	375	425	450	550	600	675	825	2,900	3,250
1885	6,130	350	400	425	500	585	650	800	2,900	3,250
1886	5,886	375	425	475	575	625	700	850	4,800	3,250
1887	5,710	450	500	575	650	750	800	900	2,900	3,250
1888	12,833	280	310	365	400	485	550	800	2,900	3,250
1889	12,711	275	300	350	400	485	550	800	2,900	3,250
1890	12,590	285	310	365	415	500	550	800	3,250	3,250
1891	200,600	50.00	60.00	80.00	115	165	290	500	3,250	3,250

1878-S Half Dollar
Grade F-12

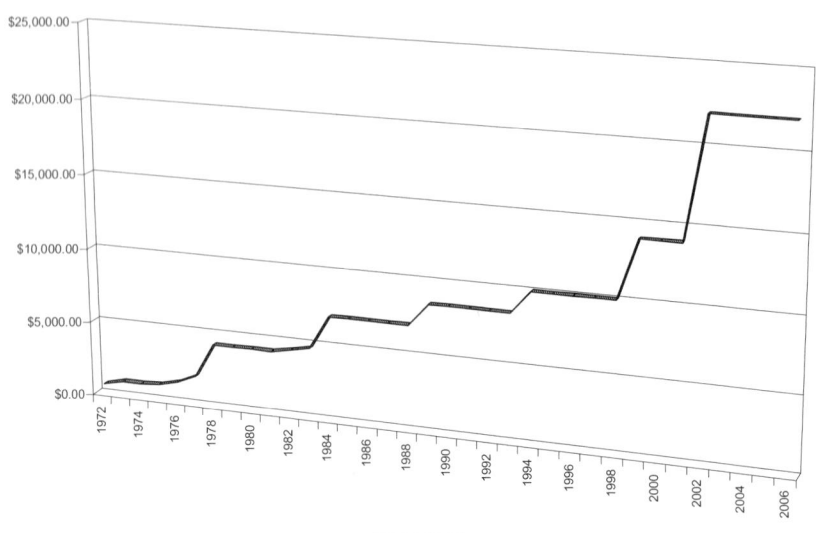

Retail Price

Barber Half Dollar

Mint mark

KM# 116 • 12.5000 g., 0.9000 **Silver**, 0.3618 oz. ASW, 30.6 mm. • **Designer:** Charles E. Barber

Date	Mintage	G-4	VG-8	F-12	VF-20	XF-40	AU-50	MS-60	MS-65	Prf-65
1892	935,245	28.50	41.50	65.00	125	190	295	475	3,600	3,300
1892O	390,000	325	415	525	590	640	725	850	4,750	—
1892O micro O	—	2,000	3,750	4,500	7,000	10,000	17,500	—	55,000	—
1892S	1,029,028	250	340	425	540	615	720	975	5,500	—
1893	1,826,792	20.00	30.00	75.00	135	205	325	535	5,500	3,300
1893O	1,389,000	36.00	62.50	125	220	360	450	650	10,500	—
1893S	740,000	200	230	300	550	700	800	1,400	30,000	—
1894	1,148,972	32.50	50.00	110	190	290	380	500	4,000	3,300
1894O	2,138,000	22.00	31.00	90.00	170	275	345	525	7,250	—
1894S	4,048,690	17.50	27.50	70.00	125	220	350	500	12,250	—
1895	1,835,218	17.50	25.00	71.00	150	200	325	595	3,800	3,300
1895O	1,766,000	22.50	37.50	125	230	300	415	595	7,850	—
1895S	1,108,086	35.00	55.00	130	220	285	385	575	9,000	—
1896	950,762	20.00	27.50	85.00	155	250	340	565	6,000	3,400
1896O	924,000	41.50	55.00	175	285	475	750	1,500	15,500	—
1896S	1,140,948	92.50	135	200	350	495	750	1,400	11,750	—
1897	2,480,731	12.50	15.00	47.50	100.00	160	325	485	4,300	3,300
1897O	632,000	170	230	495	850	1,100	1,350	1,700	10,000	—
1897S	933,900	150	205	385	550	840	1,050	1,500	8,500	—
1898	2,956,735	12.50	15.00	38.50	96.00	160	325	485	4,000	3,300
1898O	874,000	36.00	75.00	225	355	500	625	1,250	12,000	—
1898S	2,358,550	27.50	50.00	85.00	165	300	425	970	10,500	—
1899	5,538,846	13.50	15.00	38.50	100.00	155	310	485	4,800	3,900
1899O	1,724,000	25.00	36.00	80.00	160	285	400	675	8,500	—
1899S	1,686,411	22.00	32.50	72.50	135	225	360	660	7,000	—
1900	4,762,912	13.50	15.50	37.50	96.00	155	310	485	4,300	3,300
1900O	2,744,000	17.50	22.50	60.00	165	285	375	850	16,500	—
1900S	2,560,322	15.00	18.50	47.50	100.00	205	320	650	12,500	—

Date	Mintage	G-4	VG-8	F-12	VF-20	XF-40	AU-50	MS-60	MS-65	Prf-65
1901	4,268,813	13.50	16.00	38.50	96.00	180	300	510	4,500	3,500
1901O	1,124,000	16.50	27.50	80.00	205	350	475	1,350	17,000	—
1901S	847,044	34.00	55.00	160	355	625	1,050	1,850	20,000	—
1902	4,922,777	12.50	13.50	32.50	85.00	210	295	485	4,250	3,700
1902O	2,526,000	13.50	17.00	52.50	105	225	360	725	14,000	—
1902S	1,460,670	16.00	19.00	62.50	150	250	430	750	9,350	—
1903	2,278,755	13.50	16.00	47.50	100.00	205	340	500	11,000	3,825
1903O	2,100,000	13.00	17.00	55.00	115	215	345	680	10,000	—
1903S	1,920,772	15.00	18.00	55.00	125	235	380	610	5,750	—
1904	2,992,670	12.00	13.50	34.00	85.00	155	310	1,300	6,600	4,100
1904O	1,117,600	20.00	32.50	80.00	220	400	600	1,100	13,300	—
1904S	553,038	38.50	70.00	260	550	1,075	1,800	6,250	37,500	—
1905	662,727	22.50	27.50	95.00	180	270	345	575	8,250	3,900
1905O	505,000	30.00	50.00	125	235	340	440	760	5,250	—
1905S	2,494,000	15.50	16.50	50.00	125	235	380	565	9,800	—
1906	2,638,675	12.00	16.00	31.00	85.00	170	300	485	3,800	3,300
1906D	4,028,000	12.00	13.50	34.00	93.50	160	300	485	4,700	—
1906O	2,446,000	12.00	13.50	44.00	100.00	180	325	625	3,750	—
1906S	1,740,154	13.00	16.00	57.50	110	220	310	610	3,800	—
1907	2,598,575	12.00	13.50	30.00	85.00	155	300	485	4,000	4,000
1907D	3,856,000	12.00	13.50	30.00	78.50	155	300	485	3,400	—
1907O	3,946,000	12.00	13.50	31.00	93.50	155	325	595	3,700	—
1907S	1,250,000	16.00	22.00	80.00	170	325	650	1,275	13,500	—
1908	1,354,545	12.00	13.50	30.00	85.00	155	295	485	4,500	4,000
1908D	3,280,000	12.00	13.50	30.00	85.00	155	295	485	3,800	—
1908O	5,360,000	12.00	13.50	30.00	93.50	155	325	550	3,800	—
1908S	1,644,828	18.00	25.00	75.00	160	285	435	850	6,850	—
1909	2,368,650	12.50	16.00	32.50	85.00	160	295	485	3,800	4,000
1909O	925,400	16.00	23.00	60.00	140	300	525	775	3,800	—
1909S	1,764,000	12.00	13.50	38.50	100.00	200	350	595	5,000	—
1910	418,551	20.00	28.50	90.00	170	330	420	625	4,000	4,250
1910S	1,948,000	13.50	17.00	37.50	100.00	190	350	650	6,850	—
1911	1,406,543	12.00	13.50	30.00	85.00	155	300	485	3,800	3,300
1911D	695,080	14.00	16.00	41.00	96.00	200	295	575	3,800	—
1911S	1,272,000	13.50	17.00	41.00	100.00	180	330	580	6,250	—
1912	1,550,700	12.00	13.50	30.00	85.00	160	300	485	4,200	4,000
1912D	2,300,800	13.00	13.50	30.00	85.00	155	325	485	3,800	—
1912S	1,370,000	15.00	20.00	41.50	100.00	200	340	550	6,000	—
1913	188,627	70.00	90.00	220	420	600	850	1,150	4,850	3,800
1913D	534,000	17.00	21.00	46.00	100.00	200	315	500	5,250	—
1913S	604,000	22.00	26.00	55.00	110	230	375	625	5,250	—
1914	124,610	150	170	325	550	775	1,025	1,400	7,500	4,300
1914S	992,000	15.00	19.00	41.00	100.00	190	315	580	5,000	—
1915	138,450	95.00	135	255	380	575	900	1,250	6,500	4,250
1915D	1,170,400	12.00	13.50	30.00	78.50	155	295	485	3,800	—
1915S	1,604,000	15.00	20.00	41.50	99.00	170	295	485	3,800	—

Walking Liberty Half Dollar

Obverse
mint mark

Reverse
mint mard

KM# 142 • 12.5000 g., 0.9000 **Silver**, 0.3618 oz. ASW, 30.6 mm. • **Designer:** Adolph A. Weinman **Notes:** The mint mark appears on the obverse below the word "Trust" on 1916 and some 1917 issues. Starting with some 1917 issues and continuing through the remainder of the series, the mint mark was changed to the reverse, at about the 8 o'clock position near the rim.

Date	Mintage	G-4	VG-8	F-12	VF-20	XF-40	AU-50	MS-60	MS-65	Prf-65
1916	608,000	45.00	52.50	100.00	180	250	285	350	1,800	—
1916D	1,014,400	45.00	52.50	80.00	140	225	265	375	2,400	—
1916S	508,000	110	130	285	470	650	750	1,100	6,250	—
1917D obv.	765,400	22.00	31.50	80.00	160	235	350	640	8,000	—
1917S obv.	952,000	27.50	44.00	135	375	720	1,225	2,300	19,500	—
1917	12,292,000	7.00	7.25	9.00	20.00	44.00	75.00	135	1,000	—
1917D rev.	1,940,000	10.00	16.50	45.00	135	275	575	975	18,500	—
1917S rev.	5,554,000	7.00	8.00	16.50	33.00	65.00	160	345	13,000	—
1918	6,634,000	7.00	7.25	16.00	70.00	160	275	580	3,800	—
1918D	3,853,040	8.00	13.00	36.00	96.00	235	500	1,350	25,000	—
1918S	10,282,000	7.00	7.25	15.00	35.00	65.00	200	525	18,000	—
1919	962,000	19.00	32.50	78.50	275	550	920	1,350	7,500	—
1919D	1,165,000	18.00	38.50	100.00	325	765	1,550	6,250	130,000	—

1923-S Half Dollar
Grade XF-40

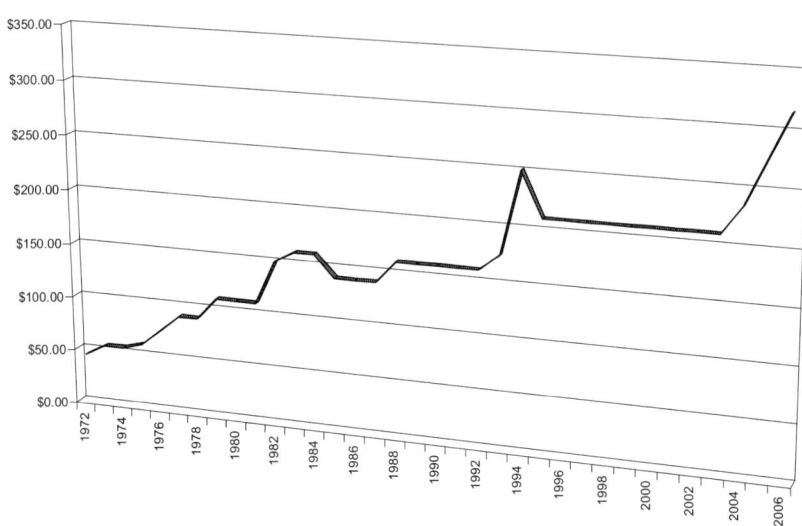

Retail Price

Date	Mintage	G-4	VG-8	F-12	VF-20	XF-40	AU-50	MS-60	MS-65	Prf-65
1919S	1,552,000	17.50	30.00	75.00	325	850	1,800	3,450	20,500	—
1920	6,372,000	7.00	7.25	16.00	44.00	75.00	160	350	5,250	—
1920D	1,551,000	12.00	20.00	70.00	250	475	960	1,550	12,000	—
1920S	4,624,000	7.00	7.50	20.00	80.00	235	520	850	12,500	—
1921	246,000	175	220	350	780	1,550	2,750	4,350	18,000	—
1921D	208,000	285	360	550	940	2,200	3,400	5,300	27,500	—
1921S	548,000	46.00	70.00	220	750	4,800	8,600	14,000	105,000	—
1923S	2,178,000	8.50	11.50	27.50	115	315	700	1,400	15,000	—
1927S	2,392,000	7.00	7.50	13.50	47.50	160	415	1,050	10,000	—
1928S	1,940,000	7.00	7.50	15.00	70.00	200	480	1,050	10,500	—
1929D	1,001,200	8.00	12.00	19.00	60.00	110	210	415	3,500	—
1929S	1,902,000	7.00	7.50	12.50	28.50	115	230	425	3,550	—
1933S	1,786,000	8.50	11.00	12.50	20.00	60.00	260	625	4,500	—
1934	6,964,000	7.00	7.25	7.50	7.00	11.00	26.00	85.00	625	—
1934D	2,361,400	7.00	7.50	8.00	10.00	29.00	90.00	155	1,700	—
1934S	3,652,000	7.00	7.50	8.00	8.50	27.00	105	395	5,200	—
1935	9,162,000	7.00	7.25	7.50	8.00	8.50	22.50	45.00	585	—
1935D	3,003,800	7.00	7.50	8.00	10.00	32.50	70.00	140	3,150	—
1935S	3,854,000	7.00	7.50	8.00	8.50	29.00	100.00	295	3,700	—
1936	12,617,901	7.00	7.25	7.50	8.00	8.50	21.50	38.50	300	6,600
1936D	4,252,400	7.00	7.50	8.00	8.50	20.00	55.00	80.00	700	—
1936S	3,884,000	7.00	7.50	8.00	8.50	21.50	62.50	135	1,050	—
1937	9,527,728	7.00	7.00	7.50	8.00	8.50	22.50	40.00	335	1,700
1937D	1,676,000	7.00	7.75	8.50	14.00	33.50	110	225	850	—
1937S	2,090,000	7.00	7.50	8.00	8.50	25.50	65.00	175	850	—
1938	4,118,152	7.00	7.50	8.00	8.50	9.50	41.50	70.00	550	1,275
1938D	491,600	125	135	155	175	220	260	525	1,550	—
1939	6,820,808	7.00	7.25	7.50	8.00	8.50	22.50	42.50	230	1,150
1939D	4,267,800	7.00	7.25	7.50	8.00	8.50	26.00	47.50	275	—
1939S	2,552,000	7.00	7.50	8.00	9.00	25.00	80.00	150	370	—
1940	9,167,279	7.00	7.25	7.50	8.00	8.50	11.00	30.00	200	1,000
1940S	4,550,000	7.00	7.25	7.50	8.00	11.00	22.00	52.50	450	—
1941	24,207,412	7.00	7.25	7.50	8.00	8.50	11.00	32.50	160	850
1941D	11,248,400	7.00	7.25	7.50	8.00	8.50	18.00	38.50	275	—
1941S	8,098,000	7.00	7.25	7.50	8.00	8.50	27.50	75.00	1,300	—
1942	47,839,120	7.00	7.25	7.50	8.00	8.50	11.00	32.50	150	850
1942D	10,973,800	7.00	7.25	7.50	8.00	8.50	19.00	38.50	345	—
1942S	12,708,000	7.00	7.25	7.50	8.00	8.50	17.50	38.50	700	—
1943	53,190,000	7.00	7.25	7.50	8.00	8.50	11.00	33.50	150	—
1943D	11,346,000	7.00	7.25	7.50	8.00	8.50	25.00	43.50	310	—
1943S	13,450,000	7.00	7.25	7.50	8.00	8.50	18.50	43.50	495	—
1944	28,206,000	7.00	7.25	7.50	8.00	8.50	11.00	33.50	165	—
1944D	9,769,000	7.00	7.25	7.50	8.00	8.50	20.00	37.50	195	—
1944S	8,904,000	7.00	7.25	7.50	8.00	8.50	16.00	38.50	600	—

Date	Mintage	G-4	VG-8	F-12	VF-20	XF-40	AU-50	MS-60	MS-65	Prf-65
1945	31,502,000	7.00	7.25	7.50	8.00	8.50	11.00	32.50	160	—
1945D	9,966,800	7.00	7.25	7.50	8.00	8.50	19.00	34.00	160	—
1945S	10,156,000	7.00	7.25	7.50	8.00	8.50	17.50	35.00	220	—
1946	12,118,000	7.00	7.25	7.50	8.00	8.50	11.00	32.50	250	—
1946D	2,151,000	7.00	7.25	7.50	8.00	25.50	38.50	50.00	150	—
1946S	3,724,000	7.00	7.25	7.50	8.00	8.50	19.00	43.50	165	—
1947	4,094,000	7.00	6.25	7.50	8.00	9.50	22.00	52.50	230	—
1947D	3,900,600	7.00	7.25	7.50	8.00	12.50	31.50	52.50	150	—

Franklin Half Dollar

Mint mark

KM# 199 • 12.5000 g., 0.9000 **Silver**, 0.3618 oz. ASW, 30.6 mm. • **Designer:** John R. Sinnock

Date	Mintage	G-4	VG-8	F-12	VF-20	XF-40	AU-50	MS-60	MS-65	-65FBL	-65CAM
1948	3,006,814	—	—	—	—	6.50	10.00	15.00	80.00	200	—
1948D	4,028,600	—	—	—	—	6.00	11.00	15.00	130	200	—
1949	5,614,000	—	—	—	—	6.00	12.00	38.50	145	300	—
1949D	4,120,600	—	—	—	—	8.00	25.00	43.50	900	1,750	—
1949S	3,744,000	—	—	—	7.00	11.00	30.00	62.50	155	650	—
1950	7,793,509	—	—	—	—	6.00	10.00	26.00	110	250	3,700
1950D	8,031,600	—	—	—	—	7.50	11.50	22.00	425	1,150	—
1951	16,859,602	—	—	—	—	—	6.50	11.00	75.00	235	2,200
1951D	9,475,200	—	—	—	—	7.50	17.50	26.00	170	525	—
1951S	13,696,000	—	—	—	—	—	15.00	23.50	125	775	—
1952	21,274,073	—	—	—	—	—	6.50	8.50	80.00	200	1,100
1952D	25,395,600	—	—	—	—	—	6.50	7.75	135	450	—
1952S	5,526,000	—	—	—	—	—	28.50	46.00	75.00	1,250	—
1953	2,796,920	—	—	—	—	6.00	15.00	23.50	125	850	475
1953D	20,900,400	—	—	—	—	—	6.50	8.00	160	400	—
1953S	4,148,000	—	—	—	—	—	15.00	25.00	65.00	16,000	—
1954	13,421,503	—	—	—	—	—	6.50	7.00	80.00	250	250
1954D	25,445,580	—	—	—	—	—	6.50	7.00	110	200	—
1954S	4,993,400	—	—	—	—	—	8.50	13.50	105	425	—

1953 Half Dollar
Grade MS-60

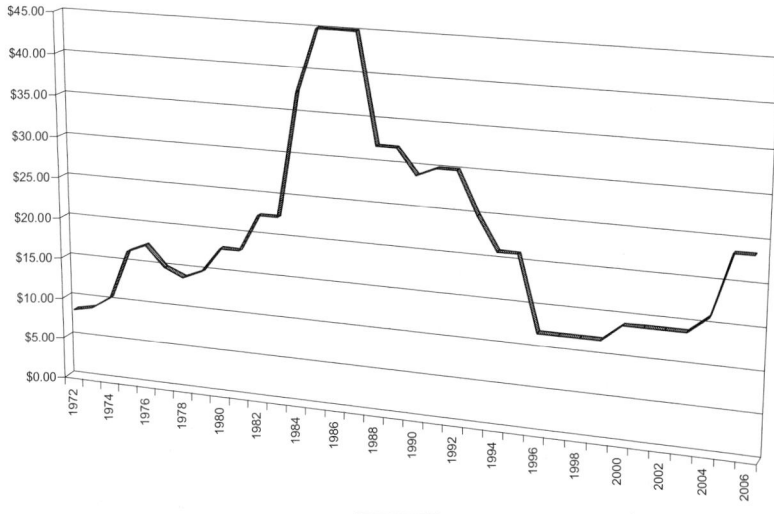

Retail Price

Date	Mintage	G-4	VG-8	F-12	VF-20	XF-40	AU-50	MS-60	MS-65	-65FBL	-65CAM
1955	2,876,381	20.00	21.00	22.00	23.00	24.00	25.00	26.00	72.50	185	195
1955 Bugs Bunny	—	20.00	21.00	22.00	23.00	24.00	26.00	27.00	100.00	750	—
1956	4,701,384	—	7.00	7.50	8.00	8.50	9.00	11.00	58.50	95.00	75.00
1957	6,361,952	—	—	—	—	—	6.50	7.00	62.50	95.00	135
1957D	19,966,850	—	—	—	—	—	6.50	7.00	70.00	65.00	—
1958	4,917,652	—	—	—	—	—	6.50	7.00	60.00	100.00	250
1958D	23,962,412	—	—	—	—	—	6.50	7.00	62.50	75.00	—
1959	7,349,291	—	—	—	—	—	6.50	7.00	105	250	475
1959D	13,053,750	—	—	—	—	—	6.50	7.00	135	190	—
1960	7,715,602	—	—	—	—	—	6.50	7.00	135	350	75.00
1960D	18,215,812	—	—	—	—	—	6.50	7.00	475	1,250	—
1961	11,318,244	—	—	—	—	—	6.50	7.00	145	1,750	75.00
1961D	20,276,442	—	—	—	—	—	6.50	7.00	200	875	—
1962	12,932,019	—	—	—	—	—	6.50	7.00	160	1,850	50.00
1962D	35,473,281	—	—	—	—	—	6.50	7.00	225	775	—
1963	25,239,645	—	—	—	—	—	6.50	7.00	55.00	775	50.00
1963D	67,069,292	—	—	—	—	—	6.50	7.00	70.00	125	—

Kennedy Half Dollar

Mint mark 1964

KM# 202 • 12.5000 g., 0.9000 **Silver**, 0.3618 oz. ASW, 30.6 mm. • **Obv. Designer:** Gilroy Roberts **Rev. Designer:** Frank Gasparro

Date	Mintage	G-4	VG-8	F-12	VF-20	XF-40	MS-60	MS-65	Prf-65
1964	277,254,766	—	—	—	—	—	3.00	9.00	10.00
1964D	156,205,446	—	—	—	—	—	3.50	12.00	—

Mint mark
1968-present

KM# 202a • 11.5000 g., 0.4000 **Silver**, 0.1480 oz. ASW, 30.6 mm. • **Obv. Designer:** Gilroy Roberts **Rev. Designer:** Frank Gasparro

Date	Mintage	G-4	VG-8	F-12	VF-20	XF-40	MS-60	MS-65	Prf-65
1965	65,879,366	—	—	—	—	—	1.25	9.50	—
1965 SMS	2,360,000	—	—	—	—	—	—	9.50	—
1966	108,984,932	—	—	—	—	—	1.40	11.00	—
1966 SMS	2,261,583	—	—	—	—	—	—	11.00	—
1967	295,046,978	—	—	—	—	—	1.50	9.50	—
1967 SMS	18,633,440	—	—	—	—	—	—	9.50	—
1968D	246,951,930	—	—	—	—	—	1.25	9.00	—
1968S	3,041,506	—	—	—	—	—	—	—	5.00
1969D	129,881,800	—	—	—	—	—	1.25	7.50	—
1969S	2,934,631	—	—	—	—	—	—	—	5.00
1970D	2,150,000	—	—	—	—	—	10.00	32.00	—
1970S	2,632,810	—	—	—	—	—	—	—	10.00

KM# 202b • 11.3400 g., **Copper-Nickel Clad Copper**, 30.6 mm. • **Obv. Designer:** Gilroy Roberts **Rev. Designer:** Frank Gasparro

Date	Mintage	G-4	VG-8	F-12	VF-20	XF-40	MS-60	MS-65	Prf-65
1971	155,640,000	—	—	—	—	—	1.50	12.00	—
1971D	302,097,424	—	—	—	—	—	1.00	5.00	—
1971S	3,244,183	—	—	—	—	—	—	—	3.00
1972	153,180,000	—	—	—	—	—	1.00	9.00	—
1972D	141,890,000	—	—	—	—	—	1.00	6.00	—
1972S	3,267,667	—	—	—	—	—	—	—	2.50
1973	64,964,000	—	—	—	—	—	1.00	6.00	—
1973D	83,171,400	—	—	—	—	—	—	5.50	—
1973S	(2,769,624)	—	—	—	—	—	—	—	2.50
1974	201,596,000	—	—	—	—	—	1.00	5.00	—
1974D	79,066,300	—	—	—	—	—	1.00	6.00	—
1974S	(2,617,350)	—	—	—	—	—	—	—	3.00
1975 none minted	—	—	—	—	—	—	—	—	—
1975D none minted	—	—	—	—	—	—	—	—	—
1975S none minted	—	—	—	—	—	—	—	—	—

Bicentennial design, Independence Hall reverse

KM# 205 • Copper-Nickel Clad Copper • Rev. Designer: Seth Huntington

Date	Mintage	G-4	VG-8	F-12	VF-20	XF-40	MS-60	MS-65	Prf-65
1976	234,308,000	—	—	—	—	—	1.00	10.00	—
1976D	287,565,248	—	—	—	—	—	1.00	7.00	—
1976S	(7,059,099)	—	—	—	—	—	—	—	2.00

Bicentennial design, Independence Hall reverse

KM# 205a • 11.5000 g., 0.4000 Silver, 0.1480 oz. ASW • Rev. Designer: Seth Huntington

Date	Mintage	G-4	VG-8	F-12	VF-20	XF-40	MS-60	MS-65	Prf-65
1976S	4,908,319(3,998,621)	—	—	—	—	—	—	13.00	5.00

Regular design resumed reverse

KM# A202b • 11.3400 g., Copper-Nickel Clad Copper, 30.6 mm. • Notes: KM#202b design and composition resumed. The 1979-S and 1981-S Type II proofs have clearer mint marks than the Type I proofs of those years.

Date	Mintage	MS-65	Prf-65	Date	Mintage	MS-65	Prf-65
1977	43,598,000	6.50	—	1988S	(3,262,948)	—	7.00
1977D	31,449,106	6.00	—	1989P	24,542,000	10.00	—
1977S	(3,251,152)	—	2.00	1989D	23,000,216	8.00	—
1978	14,350,000	6.50	—	1989S	(3,220,194)	—	7.00
1978D	13,765,799	6.50	—	1990P	22,780,000	15.00	—
1978S	(3,127,788)	—	2.00	1990D	20,096,242	15.00	—
1979	68,312,000	5.50	—	1990S	(3,299,559)	—	5.00
1979D	15,815,422	6.00	—	1991P	14,874,000	10.00	—
1979S type I, proof	(3,677,175)	—	2.00	1991D	15,054,678	12.00	—
1979S type II, proof	Inc. above	—	18.00	1991S	(2,867,787)	—	11.50
1980P	44,134,000	5.00	—	1992P	17,628,000	7.00	—
1980D	33,456,449	4.50	—	1992D	17,000,106	8.00	—
1980S	(3,547,030)	—	2.00	1992S	(2,858,981)	—	10.00
1981P	29,544,000	6.00	—	1993P	15,510,000	8.00	—
1981D	27,839,533	5.50	—	1993D	15,000,006	12.00	—
1981S type I, proof	(4,063,083)	—	2.00	1993S	(2,633,439)	—	14.00
1981S type II, proof	Inc. above	—	14.50	1994P	23,718,000	6.00	—
1982P	10,819,000	5.00	—	1994D	23,828,110	6.00	—
1982D	13,140,102	7.00	—	1994S	(2,484,594)	—	8.00
1982S	(38,957,479)	—	3.50	1995P	26,496,000	6.00	—
1983P	34,139,000	10.00	—	1995D	26,288,000	6.00	—
1983D	32,472,244	10.00	—	1995S	(2,010,384)	—	47.50
1983S	(3,279,126)	—	3.00	1996P	24,442,000	6.00	—
1984P	26,029,000	6.50	—	1996D	24,744,000	6.00	—
1984D	26,262,158	7.00	—	1996S	(2,085,191)	—	10.00
1984S	(3,065,110)	—	4.00	1997P	20,882,000	7.00	—
1985P	18,706,962	10.00	—	1997D	19,876,000	6.00	—
1985D	19,814,034	12.00	—	1997S	(1,975,000)	—	25.00
1985S	(3,962,138)	—	4.50	1998P	15,646,000	9.00	—
1986P	13,107,633	16.00	—	1998D	15,064,000	8.00	—
1986D	15,336,145	12.00	—	1998S	(2,078,494)	—	14.00
1986S	(2,411,180)	—	7.50	1999P	8,900,000	6.00	—
1987P	2,890,758	12.00	—	1999D	10,682,000	6.00	—
1987D	2,890,758	10.00	—	1999S	(2,557,897)	—	10.00
1987S	(4,407,728)	—	3.50	2000P	22,600,000	6.00	—
1988P	13,626,000	10.00	—	2000D	19,466,000	6.00	—
1988D	12,000,096	10.00	—	2000S	(3,082,944)	—	4.50

Date	Mintage	MS-65	Prf-65
2001P	21,200,000	6.00	—
2001D	19,504,000	6.00	—
2001S	(2,235,000)	—	10.00
2002P	3,100,000	15.00	—
2002D	2,500,000	10.00	—
2002S	(2,268,913)	—	7.00
2003P	2,500,000	10.00	—
2003D	2,500,000	10.00	—
2003S	(2,076,165)	—	7.00
2004P	2,900,000	10.00	—
2004D	2,900,000	10.00	—
2004S	—	—	7.00
2005P	3,800,000	10.00	—
2005D	3,500,000	10.00	—
2005S	—	—	7.00
2006P	—	10.00	—
2006D	—	10.00	—
2006S	—	—	7.00

KM# B202b • Silver • .900.

Date	Mintage	Prf-65
1992S	(1,317,579)	15.00
1993S	(761,353)	25.00
1994S	(785,329)	35.00
1995S	(838,953)	100.00
1996S	(830,021)	50.00
1997S	(821,678)	100.00
1998S	(878,792)	30.00
1998S Matte Proof	(62,350)	400
1999S	(804,565)	15.00
2000S	(965,921)	12.50
2001S	(849,600)	12.50
2002S	(888,816)	12.50
2003S	(1,040,425)	12.50
2004S	—	12.50
2005S	—	12.50
2006S	—	12.50

1794 Silver Dollar
Grade XF-40

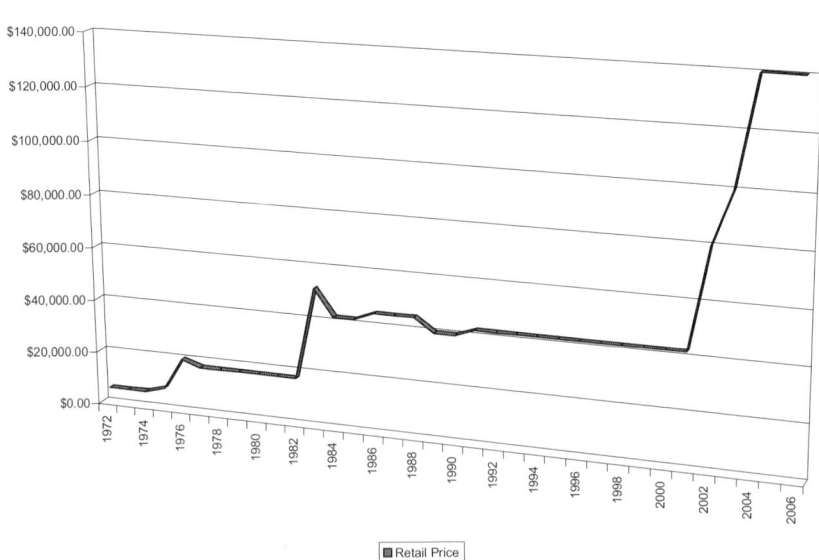

Retail Price

DOLLAR

Flowing Hair Dollar

KM# 17 • 26.9600 g., 0.8920 **Silver**, 0.7737 oz. ASW, 39-40 mm. • **Designer:** Robert Scot **Notes:** The two 1795 varieties have either two or three leaves under each of the eagle's wings on the reverse.

Date	Mintage	F-12	VF-20	XF-40	AU-50	MS-60	MS-63
1794	1,758	45,000	80,000	140,000	250,000	—	—
1795 2 leaves	203,033	3,250	5,750	10,000	17,000	38,000	58,000
1795 3 leaves	Inc. above	3,000	5,500	9,500	15,000	34,000	55,000

Draped Bust Dollar
Small eagle reverse

KM# 18 • 26.9600 g., 0.8920 **Silver**, 0.7737 oz. ASW, 39-40 mm. • **Designer:** Robert Scot **Notes:** The 1796 varieties are distinguished by the size of the numerals in the date and letters in "United States of America." The 1797 varieties are distinguished by the number of stars to the left and right of the word "Liberty" and by the size of the letters in "United States of America." The 1798 varieties have either 13 or 15 stars on the obverse.

Date	Mintage	F-12	VF-20	XF-40	AU-50	MS-60	MS-63
1795	Inc. above	2,000	3,300	5,900	7,800	24,500	57,500
1796 small date, small letters	72,920	2,000	3,300	5,900	7,800	24,500	—
1796 small date, large letters	Inc. above	2,050	11,350	6,000	8,000	25,500	—
1796 large date, small letters	Inc. above	1,975	3,250	5,850	7,750	27,000	65,000
1797 9 stars left, 7 stars right, small letters	7,776	3,000	4,800	9,000	16,500	42,500	70,000
1797 9 stars left, 7 stars right, large letters	Inc. above	2,050	3,350	6,000	7,750	28,500	60,000
1797 10 stars left, 6 stars right	Inc. above	1,975	3,250	5,850	7,750	24,500	60,000
1798 13 stars	327,536	1,875	3,350	6,250	9,500	28,500	—
1798 15 stars	Inc. above	2,350	3,800	8,000	12,500	33,500	—

Heraldic eagle reverse

KM# 32 • 26.9600 g., 0.8920 **Silver**, 0.7737 oz. ASW, 39-40 mm. • **Designer:** Robert Scot **Notes:** The 1798 "knob 9" variety has a serif on the lower left of the 9 in the date. The 1798 varieties are distinguished by the number of arrows held by the eagle on the reverse and the number of berries on the olive branch. On the 1798 "high-8" variety, the 8 in the date is higher than the other numerals. The 1799 varieties are distinguished by the number and positioning of the stars on the obverse and by the size of the berries in the olive branch on the reverse. On the 1700 "irregular date" variety, the first 9 in the date is smaller than the other numerals. Some varieties of the 1800 strikes had letters in the legend cut twice into the dies; as the dies became worn, the letters were touched up. On the 1800 "very wide date, low 8" variety, the spacing between the numerals in the date are wider than other varieties and the 8 is lower than the other numerals. The 1800 "small berries" variety refers to the size of the berries in the olive branch on the reverse. The 1800 "12 arrows" and "10 arrows" varieties refer to the number of arrows held by the eagle. The 1800 "Americai" variety appears to have the faint outline of an "I" after "America" in the reverse legend. The "close" and "wide" varieties of 1802 refer to the amount of space between the numerals in the date. The 1800 large-3 and small-3 varieties are distinguished by the size of the 3 in the date.

Date	Mintage	F-12	VF-20	XF-40	AU-50	MS-60	MS-63
1798 knob 9	Inc. above	1,125	1,775	2,850	4,200	16,750	34,500
1798 10 arrows	Inc. above	1,125	1,775	2,850	4,200	16,750	34,500
1798 4 berries	Inc. above	1,125	1,775	2,850	4,200	16,750	34,500
1798 5 berries, 12 arrows	Inc. above	1,125	1,775	2,850	4,200	16,750	34,500
1798 high 8	Inc. above	1,125	1,775	2,850	7,200	16,750	34,500
1798 13 arrows	Inc. above	1,125	1,775	2,850	4,200	16,750	34,500
1799/98 13-star reverse	423,515	1,350	2,050	3,300	6,000	18,500	36,000
1799/98 15-star reverse	Inc. above	1,225	1,825	3,000	6,200	19,500	36,000
1799 irregular date, 13-star reverse	Inc. above	1,200	1,850	2,900	4,650	18,500	38,500
1799 irregular date, 15-star reverse	Inc. above	1,175	1,825	2,850	4,600	16,500	36,000
1799 perfect date, 7- and 6-star obverse, no berries	Inc. above	1,100	1,750	2,750	• 4,800	13,500	33,500
1799 perfect date, 7- and 6-star obverse, small berries	Inc. above	1,100	1,350	2,750	4,200	13,500	33,500
1799 perfect date, 7- and 6-star obverse, medium large berries	Inc. above	1,125	1,350	2,750	4,200	13,500	33,500
1799 perfect date, 7- and 6-star obverse, extra large berries	Inc. above	1,125	1,350	2,750	4,200	13,500	33,500
1799 8 stars left, 5 stars right on obverse	Inc. above	1,200	1,850	2,900	4,650	19,000	42,500
1800 "R" in "Liberty" double cut	220,920	1,175	1,825	2,850	4,600	16,500	36,000
1800 first "T" in "States" double cut	Inc. above	1,175	1,825	2,850	4,600	16,500	36,000
1800 both letters double cut	Inc. above	1,175	1,825	2,850	4,600	16,500	36,000
1800 "T" in "United" double cut	Inc. above	1,175	1,825	2,850	4,600	16,500	36,000
1800 very wide date, low 8	Inc. above	1,175	1,825	2,850	4,600	16,500	36,000
1800 small berries	Inc. above	1,200	1,850	2,900	4,650	17,000	—
1800 dot date	Inc. above	1,350	2,050	3,300	6,000	16,500	39,500
1800 12 arrows	Inc. above	1,175	1,825	2,850	4,600	16,500	36,000
1800 10 arrows	Inc. above	1,175	1,825	2,850	4,600	16,500	36,000
1800 "Americai"	Inc. above	1,350	2,050	3,300	6,000	16,500	39,500
1801	54,454	1,300	2,100	3,000	4,600	20,000	40,000
1801 proof restrike	—	—	—	—	—	—	—
1802/1 close	Inc. above	1,350	2,050	3,300	6,000	15,500	—
1802/1 wide	Inc. above	1,350	2,050	3,300	6,000	15,500	—
1802 close, perfect date	Inc. above	1,200	1,850	2,900	4,650	15,500	—
1802 wide, perfect date	Inc. above	1,175	1,825	2,850	4,600	16,500	—
1802 proof restrike, mintage unrecorded	—	—	—	—	—	—	—
1803 large 3	85,634	1,225	1,925	3,000	5,400	15,500	37,500
1803 small 3	Inc. above	1,350	2,050	3,300	6,000	16,500	38,500
1803 proof restrike, mintage unrecorded	—	—	—	—	—	—	—
1804 15 known	—	—	—	— 1,000,000	—	—	—

Note: 1804, Childs Sale, Aug. 1999, Prf-68, $4,140,000.

Gobrecht Dollar

"C. Gobrecht F." below base obverse Eagle flying left amid stars reverse

KM# 59.1 • 26.7300 g., 0.9000 **Silver**, 0.7736 oz. ASW, 38.1 mm. • **Obv. Designer:** Christian Gobrecht **Edge Desc:** Plain.

Date	Mintage	VF-20	XF-40	AU-50	Prf-60
1836	1,000	3,750	4,750	—	12,500

"C. Gobrecht F." below base obverse Eagle flying in plain field reverse

KM# 59.2 • 26.7300 g., 0.9000 **Silver**, 0.7736 oz. ASW, 38.1 mm. • **Obv. Designer:** Christian Gobrecht. **Edge Desc:** Plain.

Date	Mintage	VF-20	XF-40	AU-50	Prf-60
1836 Restrike	—	—	—	—	—

"C. Gobrecht F." on base obverse

KM# 59a.1 • 26.7300 g., 0.9000 **Silver**, 0.7736 oz. ASW, 38.1 mm. • **Obv. Legend**Eagle flying left amid stars. **Edge Desc:** Plain.

Date	Mintage	VF-20	XF-40	AU-50	Prf-60
1836	600	—	—	—	—

"C. Gobrecht F." on base obverse Eagle flying left amid stars reverse

KM# 59a.2 • 26.7300 g., 0.9000 **Silver**, 0.7736 oz. ASW, 38.1 mm. • **Edge Desc:** Reeded.

Date	Mintage	VF-20	XF-40	AU-50	Prf-60
1836 Restrike	—	—	—	—	—

Designer's name omitted obverse Eagle in plain field reverse

KM# 59a.3 • 26.7300 g., 0.9000 **Silver**, 0.7736 oz. ASW, 38.1 mm. • **Edge Desc:** Reeded.

Date	Mintage	VF-20	XF-40	AU-50	Prf-60
1839	300	—	—	—	—

KM# 59a.4 • 26.7300 g., 0.9000 **Silver**, .7734 oz. ASW, 38.1 mm. •

Date	Mintage	VF-20	XF-40	AU-50	Prf-60
1839 Restrike	—	—	—	—	—

Note: All other combinations are restrikes of the late 1850's.

Seated Liberty Dollar

No motto above eagle reverse

KM# 71 • 26.7300 g., 0.9000 **Silver**, 0.7736 oz. ASW, 38.1 mm. • **Designer:** Christian Gobrecht

Date	Mintage	G-4	VG-8	F-12	VF-20	XF-40	AU-50	MS-60	MS-63	MS-65	Prf-65
1840	61,005	225	250	295	360	525	750	1,850	13,500	—	62,500
1841	173,000	190	210	240	320	400	625	1,500	3,500	44,000	—
1842	184,618	190	210	240	320	400	600	1,250	3,800	—	90,000
1843	165,100	190	210	240	320	400	625	1,600	5,000	—	—
1844	20,000	220	240	300	395	535	840	2,500	11,000	47,000	—
1845	24,500	275	305	360	420	575	840	5,500	17,500	—	70,000
1846	110,600	205	230	275	350	480	600	1,600	5,300	—	85,000

Date	Mintage	G-4	VG-8	F-12	VF-20	XF-40	AU-50	MS-60	MS-63	MS-65	Prf-65
1846O	59,000	215	250	315	400	560	1,000	5,250	15,000	37,500	—
1847	140,750	190	210	245	320	395	625	1,250	3,850	27,500	44,000
1848	15,000	285	350	480	590	800	1,250	3,000	7,800	40,000	96,000
1849	62,600	205	220	260	340	460	675	1,850	5,150	32,500	120,000
1850	7,500	360	475	650	800	1,100	1,800	5,000	13,000	50,000	46,000
1850O	40,000	295	450	450	670	1,125	3,550	11,500	20,500	60,000	—
1851	1,300	3,150	4,000	5,000	7,000	13,500	22,000	34,500	50,000	75,000	62,500
1852	1,100	2,700	3,300	4,500	6,200	12,500	21,500	30,000	49,000	71,500	62,500
1853	46,110	280	325	470	550	740	1,075	2,250	7,000	28,000	75,000
1854	33,140	1,000	1,300	1,850	2,600	3,750	4,950	7,600	10,000	2,800	47,500
1855	26,000	900	1,150	1,350	2,000	2,950	3,850	7,000	15,500	—	38,000
1856	63,500	345	425	600	650	1,050	1,900	3,700	7,500	—	27,000
1857	94,000	385	475	550	700	1,100	1,300	2,250	5,300	28,500	29,500
1858 proof only	Est. 800	3,000	3,400	3,850	4,600	5,500	7,300	9,000	12,000	—	27,000
Note: Proof Only restruck in later years.											
1859	256,500	240	280	360	480	550	700	1,650	5,100	—	13,000
1859O	360,000	190	205	240	320	395	600	1,100	3,100	32,500	—
1859S	20,000	280	330	445	600	1,250	3,000	13,500	35,000	62,500	—
1860	218,930	220	240	330	460	550	600	1,100	3,400	27,500	13,500
1860O	515,000	190	205	240	320	395	595	1,050	3,000	16,500	—
1861	78,500	515	675	800	950	1,200	1,550	2,600	4,900	25,000	13,500
1862	12,090	395	525	775	925	1,100	1,450	2,500	5,100	37,500	13,500
1863	27,660	325	440	500	600	700	1,100	2,200	4,900	23,500	20,000
1864	31,170	295	325	420	530	640	1,050	2,150	4,900	22,000	13,000
1865	47,000	260	300	345	500	625	1,000	1,850	4,750	35,000	13,000
1866 2 known without motto	—	—	—	—	—	—	—	—	—	—	—

"In God We Trust" above eagle reverse

KM# 100 • 26.7300 g., 0.9000 **Silver**, 0.7736 oz. ASW, 38.1 mm. • **Designer:** Christian Gobrecht **Notes:** In 1866 the motto "In God We Trust" was added to the reverse above the eagle.

Date	Mintage	G-4	VG-8	F-12	VF-20	XF-40	AU-50	MS-60	MS-63	MS-65	Prf-65
1866	49,625	250	280	345	485	560	900	1,650	3,150	25,500	12,500
1867	47,525	230	260	325	430	525	875	1,500	3,250	27,500	11,000
1868	162,700	225	250	315	405	475	850	1,600	6,600	35,000	12,500
1869	424,300	230	240	295	395	450	650	1,450	3,550	32,500	11,000
1870	416,000	200	215	245	320	440	600	1,400	3,250	25,500	12,500
1870CC	12,462	420	500	720	1,050	1,700	3,000	10,250	20,500	42,500	—
1870S 12-15 known	—	50,000	44,000	65,000	125,000	250,000	500,000	750,000	1,250,000	—	—
Note: 1870S, Eliasberg Sale, April 1997, EF-45 to AU-50, $264,000.											
1871	1,074,760	190	205	240	340	425	600	1,100	3,000	25,500	11,000
1871CC	1,376	2,000	2,750	4,000	6,000	9,750	18,500	50,000	175,000	300,000	—
1872	1,106,450	190	205	250	340	425	600	1,100	2,950	25,500	11,000
1872CC	3,150	900	1,300	2,200	3,250	5,300	10,000	19,000	47,500	—	—
1872S	9,000	250	325	450	650	1,100	2,750	8,500	23,500	62,500	—
1873	293,600	220	240	285	360	475	700	1,250	3,150	31,500	11,500
1873CC	2,300	3,450	4,750	6,500	9,000	16,000	30,000	70,000	110,000	—	—
1873S none known	700	—	—	—	—	—	—	—	—	—	—

Trade Dollar

KM# 108 • 27.2200 g., 0.9000 **Silver**, 0.7878 oz. ASW, 38.1 mm. • **Designer:** William Barber

Date	Mintage	G-4	VG-8	F-12	VF-20	XF-40	AU-50	MS-60	MS-65	Prf-65
1873	397,500	100.00	110	125	165	250	325	1,000	12,000	12,000
1873CC	124,500	200	250	300	450	700	1,200	2,100	80,000	—
1873S	703,000	130	145	160	220	280	400	1,200	25,000	—
1874	987,800	120	130	150	185	240	340	700	15,000	12,000
1874CC	1,373,200	80.00	90.00	105	165	240	350	1,000	40,000	—
1874S	2,549,000	70.00	80.00	95.00	120	165	250	675	30,000	—
1875	218,900	260	350	425	525	675	800	1,850	13,000	6,500
1875CC	1,573,700	80.00	90.00	105	130	200	375	900	40,000	—
1875S	4,487,000	60.00	70.00	85.00	100.00	120	210	500	7,000	—
1875S/CC	Inc. above	275	325	400	525	695	1,100	1,900	—	—
1876	456,150	70.00	80.00	100.00	125	165	400	675	7,500	6,500
1876CC	509,000	200	240	300	325	400	500	2,100	75,000	—
1876S	5,227,000	60.00	70.00	85.00	100.00	120	210	475	10,000	—
1877	3,039,710	60.00	70.00	85.00	105	130	210	525	16,000	19,000
1877CC	534,000	150	175	210	290	400	600	1,275	70,000	—
1877S	9,519,000	60.00	70.00	85.00	100.00	120	210	475	8,000	—
1878 proof only	900	—	—	—	1,100	1,300	1,500	—	—	22,000
1878CC	97,000	425	525	675	850	1,750	2,100	5,500	67,500	—
1878S	4,162,000	60.00	70.00	85.00	100.00	120	210	475	7,000	—
1879 proof only	1,541	—	—	—	900	950	1,100	—	—	22,000
1880 proof only	1,987	—	—	—	900	950	1,100	—	—	19,500
1881 proof only	960	—	—	—	1,000	1,100	1,250	—	—	20,000
1882 proof only	1,097	—	—	—	950	1,000	1,250	—	—	20,000
1883 proof only	979	—	—	—	1,100	1,200	1,400	—	—	20,000

1875 Trade Dollar
Grade F-12

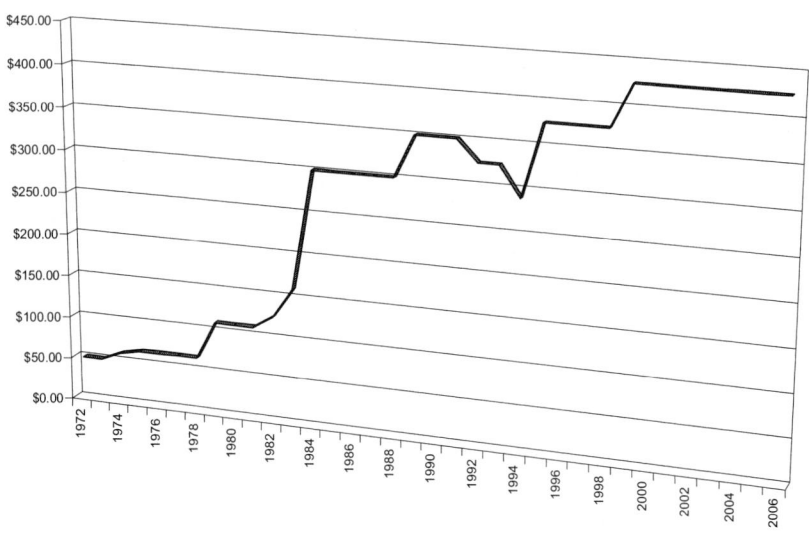

Retail Price

Date	Mintage	G-4	VG-8	F-12	VF-20	XF-40	AU-50	MS-60	MS-65	Prf-65
1884 proof only	10	—	—	—	—	—	—	—	—	—
Note: 1884, Eliasberg Sale, April 1997, Prf-66, $396,000.										
1885 proof only	5	—	—	—	—	—	—	—	—	—
Note: 1885, Eliasberg Sale, April 1997, Prf-65, $907,500.										

Morgan Dollar

8 tail feathers   7 tail feathers   7/8 tail feathers

KM# 110 • 26.7300 g., 0.9000 **Silver**, 0.7736 oz. ASW, 38.1 mm. • **Designer:** George T. Morgan **Notes:** "65DMPL" values are for coins grading MS-65 deep-mirror prooflike. The 1878 "8 tail feathers" and "7 tail feathers" varieties are distinguished by the number of feathers in the eagle's tail. On the "reverse of 1878" varieties, the top of the top feather in the arrows held by the eagle is straight across and the eagle's breast is concave. On the "reverse of 1879 varieties," the top feather in the arrows held by the eagle is slanted and the eagle's breast is convex. The 1890-CC "tail-bar variety has a bar extending from the arrow feathers to the wreath on the reverse, the result of a die gouge.

Date	Mintage	VG-8	F-12	VF-20	XF-40	AU-50	MS-60	MS-63	MS-64	MS-65	65DMPL	Prf-65
1878 8 tail feathers	750,000	27.50	30.00	37.50	46.00	73.50	125	170	400	1,300	6,300	7,500
1878 7 tail feathers, reverse of 1878	Inc. above	20.00	21.00	22.50	24.00	40.00	56.00	105	280	1,375	6,300	—
1878 7 tail feathers, reverse of 1879	Inc. above	20.00	21.00	24.00	26.00	43.50	75.00	150	550	2,600	8,800	9,000
1878 7 over 8 tail feathers	9,759,550	20.00	24.00	27.50	41.50	75.00	150	350	525	2,600	14,500	—
1878CC	2,212,000	98.50	100.00	105	125	130	230	400	590	2,000	3,450	—
1878S	9,744,000	20.00	21.00	22.50	24.00	34.00	47.50	62.50	105	270	2,250	—
1879	14,807,100	18.00	18.50	19.00	20.00	22.50	32.50	56.00	130	1,100	6,950	6,000
1879CC	756,000	120	130	200	630	1,350	3,400	7,000	10,500	29,500	65,000	—
1879O	2,887,000	19.00	20.00	20.50	21.50	22.00	75.00	185	450	3,400	16,500	—
1879S reverse of 1878	9,110,000	20.00	22.00	25.00	30.00	47.50	120	415	1,450	7,600	22,000	—
1879S reverse of 1879	9,110,000	18.00	18.50	19.00	19.50	22.00	41.50	17.50	60.00	175	450	—
1880	12,601,335	17.00	18.50	19.00	20.50	22.50	33.50	50.00	120	715	3,450	5,900
1880CC reverse of 1878	591,000	110	130	150	205	260	550	640	1,225	3,125	11,000	—
1880CC reverse of 1879	591,000	115	150	170	225	300	535	550	750	1,450	3,650	—
1880O	5,305,000	17.50	18.50	19.00	20.50	22.50	62.50	385	1,750	24,500	70,000	—
1880S	8,900,000	17.50	18.50	19.00	20.50	22.50	33.50	20.00	68.50	205	450	—
1881	9,163,975	17.50	18.50	19.00	20.50	22.50	33.50	50.00	130	840	13,750	6,250
1881CC	296,000	350	365	375	400	450	555	575	650	1,000	1,450	—
1881O	5,708,000	17.50	18.50	19.00	20.50	22.50	37.50	50.00	180	1,675	15,000	—
1881S	12,760,000	17.50	18.50	19.00	20.50	22.50	33.50	50.00	68.50	205	450	—
1882	11,101,100	17.50	18.50	19.00	20.50	22.50	33.50	50.00	68.50	460	4,100	5,900
1882CC	1,133,000	98.50	100.00	105	125	130	230	245	275	545	725	—
1882O	6,090,000	17.50	18.50	19.00	20.50	22.50	33.50	50.00	75.00	850	4,200	—
1882S	9,250,000	17.50	18.50	19.00	20.50	26.00	33.50	50.00	68.50	205	1,100	—
1883	12,291,039	17.50	18.50	19.00	20.50	22.50	33.50	50.00	68.50	205	760	5,900
1883CC	1,204,000	98.50	100.00	105	125	130	220	230	270	465	830	—
1883O	8,725,000	17.50	18.50	19.00	20.50	22.50	33.50	50.00	68.50	205	575	—
1883S	6,250,000	17.50	18.50	19.00	33.50	150	660	2,800	4,400	22,500	94,500	—
1884	14,070,875	17.50	18.50	19.00	20.50	22.50	33.50	50.00	68.50	255	2,200	5,900
1884CC	1,136,000	115	135	160	175	180	220	230	260	460	600	—
1884O	9,730,000	17.50	18.50	19.00	20.50	22.50	33.50	50.00	68.50	205	670	—
1884S	3,200,000	17.50	18.50	20.00	42.50	280	6,000	31,500	110,000	205,000	220,000	—
1885	17,787,767	17.50	18.50	19.00	20.50	22.50	33.50	50.00	68.50	205	570	5,900
1885CC	228,000	550	585	600	630	635	720	725	740	1,600	1,450	—
1885O	9,185,000	17.50	18.50	19.00	20.50	22.50	33.50	50.00	68.50	205	490	—
1885S	1,497,000	22.00	28.50	41.50	66.00	135	240	325	650	1,900	16,500	—
1886	19,963,886	17.50	18.50	19.00	20.50	80.00	685	3,850	10,500	220,000	283,500	—
1886O	10,710,000	17.50	18.50	19.00	20.50							

Date	Mintage	VG-8	F-12	VF-20	XF-40	AU-50	MS-60	MS-63	MS-64	MS-65	65DMPL	Prf-65
1886S	750,000	47.50	62.50	85.00	90.00	180	320	465	730	3,250	16,500	—
1887	20,290,710	17.50	18.50	19.00	20.50	22.50	33.50	50.00	68.50	205	530	5,900
1887O	11,550,000	17.50	18.50	19.00	20.50	22.50	54.00	110	415	3,300	8,500	—
1887S	1,771,000	19.00	20.50	22.00	23.00	45.00	115	285	700	3,500	27,000	—
1888	19,183,833	17.50	18.50	19.00	20.50	22.50	33.50	50.00	68.50	205	2,350	6,000
1888O	12,150,000	17.50	18.50	19.00	20.50	23.50	33.50	50.00	68.50	470	1,600	—
1888S	657,000	100.00	190	220	225	275	300	480	850	3,450	10,500	—
1889	21,726,811	17.50	18.50	19.00	20.50	22.50	33.50	50.00	68.50	325	2,950	5,900
1889CC	350,000	625	900	1,600	3,800	7,500	22,500	44,000	55,000	315,000	285,000	—
1889O	11,875,000	17.50	18.50	19.00	20.50	31.50	140	425	720	4,800	14,500	—
1889S	700,000	37.50	60.00	65.00	85.00	125	215	445	550	2,050	7,550	—
1890	16,802,590	17.50	18.50	19.00	20.50	22.50	33.50	50.00	118.5	2,050	12,500	5,900
1890CC	2,309,041	98.50	100.00	105	160	215	415	1,050	2,800	7,300	9,750	—
1890CC tail bar	Inc. above	135	145	180	500	900	1,600	4,000	8,500	—	9,800	—
1890O	10,701,000	17.50	18.50	19.00	20.50	25.00	57.50	110	370	1,500	7,500	—
1890S	8,230,373	17.50	18.50	19.00	20.50	25.00	57.50	105	260	900	8,200	—
1891	8,694,206	17.50	18.50	19.00	20.50	27.50	52.50	185	595	7,000	25,000	5,900
1891CC	1,618,000	98.50	100.00	105	160	215	360	920	1,475	5,300	20,000	—
1891O	7,954,529	17.50	18.50	19.00	20.50	35.00	135	350	800	7,500	21,500	—
1891S	5,296,000	17.50	18.50	19.00	20.50	25.00	57.50	135	275	1,250	7,250	—
1892	1,037,245	20.50	22.00	23.00	34.00	75.00	155	420	960	4,000	15,750	5,900
1892CC	1,352,000	150	175	260	480	825	1,400	2,600	3,850	11,000	27,000	—
1892O	2,744,000	18.00	19.50	20.00	34.00	62.50	160	325	720	5,000	27,000	—
1892S	1,200,000	23.00	34.00	82.50	237.5	1,850	35,500	65,000	10,500	175,000	170,000	—
1893	378,792	235	250	255	285	400	770	1,400	2,700	7,500	38,000	5,900
1893CC	677,000	215	280	580	1,750	2,400	3,800	7,800	15,000	55,000	85,000	—
1893O	300,000	205	260	395	650	1,050	1,850	7,500	22,500	220,000	201,500	—
1893S	100,000	3,000	4,400	6,750	11,500	27,500	85,000	150,000	250,000	415,000	380,000	—
1894	110,972	1,400	1,550	1,850	2,500	3,350	5,250	7,250	12,000	47,000	44,000	6,500
1894O	1,723,000	62.50	65.00	70.00	110	325	580	4,000	11,000	55,000	56,500	—
1894S	1,260,000	62.50	65.00	110	150	525	720	1,150	2,000	6,850	19,000	—
1895 proof only	12,880	21,500	27,500	29,000	33,500	37,500	—	—	—	—	—	79,000
1895O	450,000	350	450	625	880	1,500	18,000	57,500	100,000	225,000		—
1895S	400,000	415	480	495	925	1,850	4,150	6,500	8,500	21,500	40,500	—
1896	9,967,762	17.50	18.50	19.00	20.50	22.50	33.50	50.00	71.00	205	975	5,900
1896O	4,900,000	17.50	18.50	19.00	20.50	185	1,100	8,000	47,500	185,000	170,000	—
1896S	5,000,000	22.00	34.00	60.00	235	895	1,625	3,500	4,800	16,000	25,000	—
1897	2,822,731	17.50	18.50	19.00	20.50	22.50	33.50	50.00	71.00	277.5	2,900	5,900
1897O	4,004,000	17.50	18.50	19.00	25.00	110	750	5,125	15,500	52,000	56,500	—
1897S	5,825,000	17.50	18.50	19.00	20.50	25.00	60.00	120	160	615	1,700	—
1898	5,884,735	18.00	18.50	19.00	20.50	22.50	33.50	50.00	68.50	285	1,075	5,900
1898O	4,440,000	20.50	22.00	23.00	25.00	25.50	32.50	47.50	61.50	175	510	—
1898S	4,102,000	20.00	25.00	35.00	55.00	105	260	475	895	2,300	11,250	—

1889-O Silver Dollar
Grade F-12

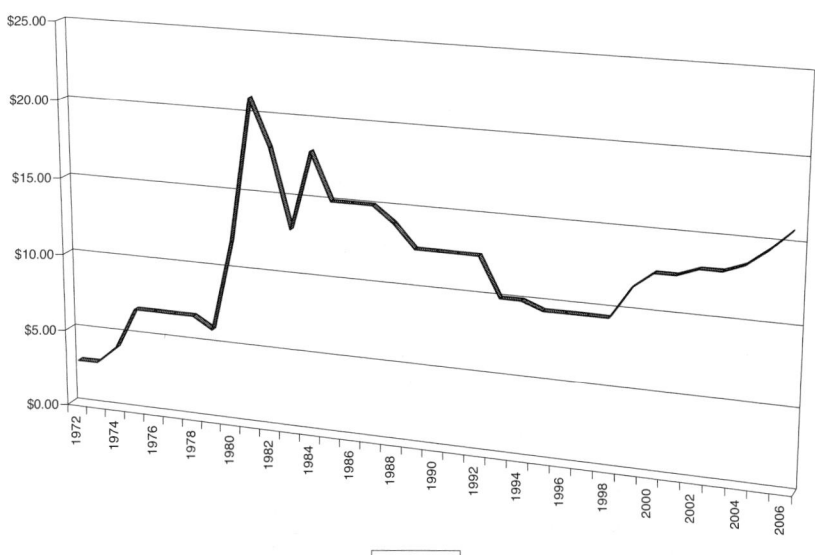

Retail Price

1903-O Dollar
Grade MS-60

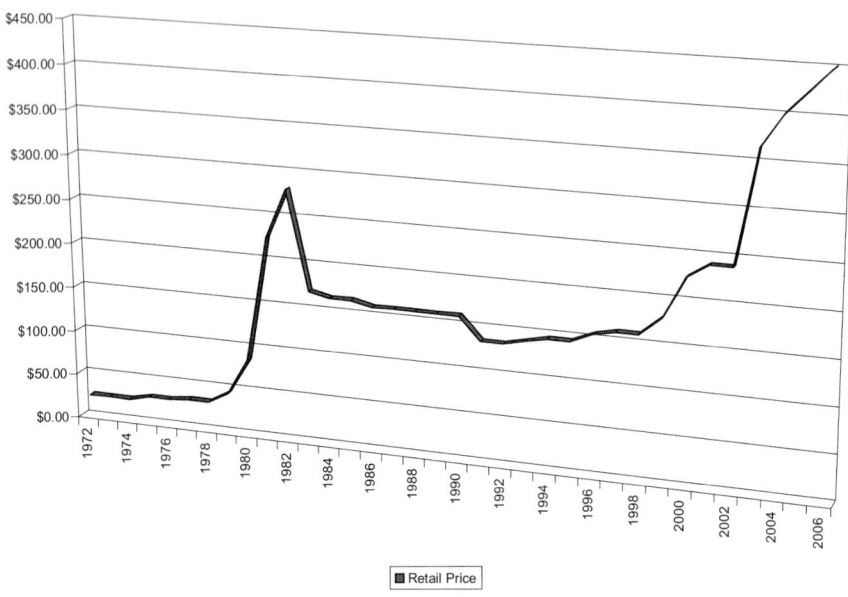

1897-O Dollar
Grade MS-60

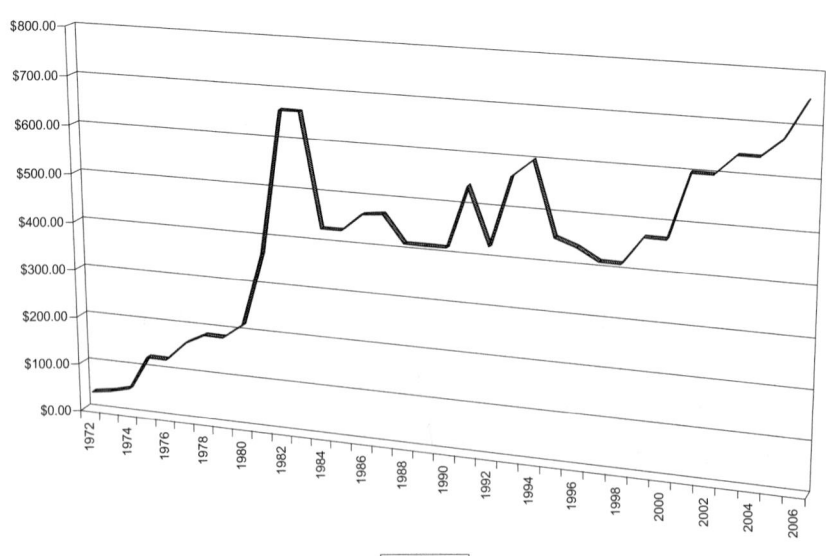

1921 Silver Dollar
Grade MS-60

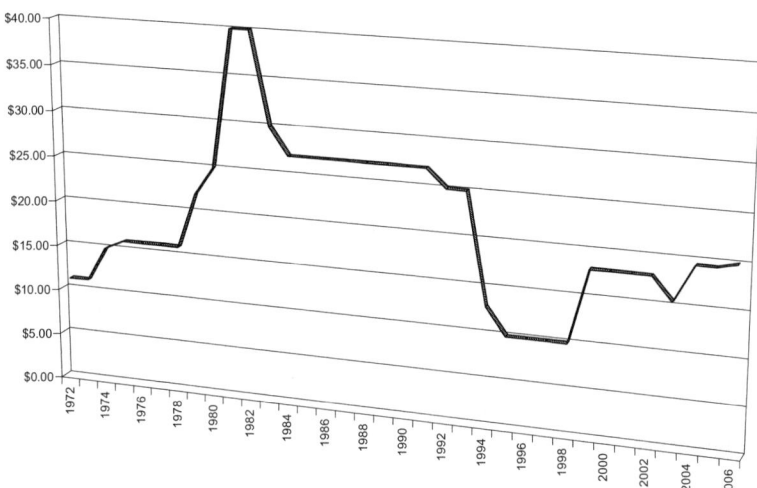

Date	Mintage	VG-8	F-12	VF-20	XF-40	AU-50	MS-60	MS-63	MS-64	MS-65	65DMPL	Prf-65
1899	330,846	140	155	185	220	275	340	425	560	900	2,250	6,000
1899O	12,290,000	18.00	18.50	23.00	23.50	24.50	33.50	50.00	68.50	205	825	—
1899S	2,562,000	22.00	26.00	37.50	62.50	125	330	480	800	1,850	8,600	—
1900	8,880,938	17.50	18.50	19.00	20.50	22.50	33.50	50.00	68.50	220	11,000	5,900
1900O	12,590,000	17.50	18.50	19.00	20.50	25.00	33.50	50.00	68.50	205	3,000	—
1900O/CC	Inc. above	37.50	47.50	62.50	100.00	190	350	960	1,500	3,500	19,000	—
1900S	3,540,000	17.50	18.50	20.00	37.50	85.00	340	420	540	1,500	9,450	—
1901	6,962,813	27.50	36.00	57.50	110	375	2,150	17,000	56,000	220,000	220,000	6,500
1901O	13,320,000	18.00	18.50	19.00	21.50	22.50	33.50	47.50	71.00	220	3,800	—
1901S	2,284,000	18.00	20.50	31.50	46.00	220	470	700	1,000	4,100	12,500	—
1902	7,994,777	18.00	18.50	20.00	21.50	23.50	44.00	100.00	150	475	15,750	5,900
1902O	8,636,000	18.00	18.50	20.00	21.50	22.50	32.50	47.50	61.50	185	3,600	—
1902S	1,530,000	62.50	85.00	150	220	315	425	625	1,050	2,900	15,000	—
1903	4,652,755	50.00	52.50	53.50	60.00	65.00	77.50	93.50	130	280	9,150	5,900
1903O	4,450,000	350	375	400	425	440	450	475	500	700	4,650	—
1903S	1,241,000	55.00	82.50	155	335	1,800	4,250	7,000	8,450	10,500	40,000	—
1904	2,788,650	24.00	25.00	26.00	27.50	34.00	82.50	270	715	4,200	38,000	5,900
1904O	3,720,000	24.00	25.00	26.00	27.50	28.00	35.00	47.50	67.50	175	550	—
1904S	2,304,000	35.00	47.50	85.00	230	560	1,150	3,600	5,500	8,000	19,000	—
1921	44,690,000	16.00	16.25	16.50	17.00	18.00	21.00	35.00	42.00	175	8,800	—
1921D	20,345,000	16.00	16.25	16.50	17.00	18.00	44.00	60.00	135	300	15,000	—
1921S	21,695,000	16.00	16.25	16.50	17.00	18.00	31.00	66.00	160	950	22,000	—

Peace Dollar

Mint mark

KM# 150 • 26.7300 g., 0.9000 **Silver**, 0.7736 oz. ASW, 38.1 mm. • **Designer:** Anthony DeFrancisci
Notes: Commonly called Peace dollars.

Date	Mintage	G-4	VG-8	F-12	VF-20	XF-40	AU-50	MS-60	MS-63	MS-64	MS-65
1921	1,006,473	70.00	130	135	140	150	170	245	460	850	2,500
1922	51,737,000	8.00	16.00	16.25	16.50	17.00	17.50	18.00	33.50	60.00	225

1927-S Dollar
Grade MS-60

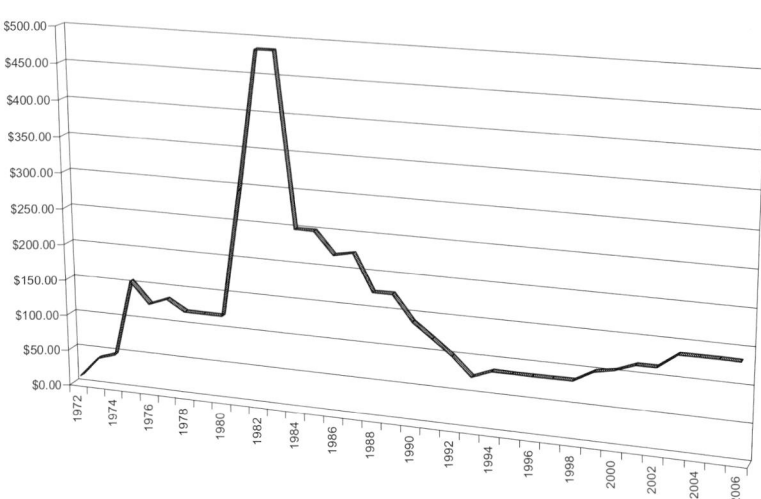

Retail Price

Date	Mintage	G-4	VG-8	F-12	VF-20	XF-40	AU-50	MS-60	MS-63	MS-64	MS-65
1922D	15,063,000	8.00	16.00	16.25	16.50	17.00	17.50	26.50	48.00	92.50	350
1922S	17,475,000	8.00	16.00	16.25	16.50	17.00	17.50	26.50	66.00	240	2,300
1923	30,800,000	8.00	16.00	16.25	16.50	17.00	17.50	18.50	33.50	60.00	225
1923D	6,811,000	8.00	16.00	16.25	16.50	17.00	18.00	55.00	120	250	925
1923S	19,020,000	8.00	16.00	16.25	16.50	17.00	17.50	28.00	70.00	260	5,850
1924	11,811,000	8.00	16.00	16.25	16.50	17.00	17.50	18.50	33.50	60.00	225
1924S	1,728,000	12.00	25.00	27.50	34.00	44.00	68.50	200	625	1,350	9,500
1925	10,198,000	8.00	16.00	16.25	16.50	17.00	17.50	18.50	32.50	60.00	225
1925S	1,610,000	10.00	17.50	19.00	25.00	30.00	47.50	75.00	185	715	21,000
1926	1,939,000	9.00	17.00	17.25	17.50	18.50	23.00	41.50	78.50	120	375
1926D	2,348,700	8.00	17.00	17.50	18.00	22.00	32.50	66.00	150	300	600
1926S	6,980,000	8.00	16.00	16.25	16.50	18.00	19.00	41.50	90.00	255	860
1927	848,000	15.00	26.00	30.00	31.50	32.50	55.00	70.00	165	360	2,600
1927D	1,268,900	12.00	26.00	27.50	28.50	29.00	84.00	150	340	860	5,000
1927S	866,000	16.00	26.00	28.50	30.00	32.50	80.00	135	425	1,300	11,700
1928	360,649	300	450	470	480	495	500	525	850	1,350	4,500
1928S	1,632,000	16.00	33.50	35.00	38.50	45.00	67.50	155	580	1,500	19,500
1934	954,057	14.00	20.50	21.50	22.00	22.50	47.50	120	245	435	800
1934D	1,569,500	11.00	20.00	20.50	21.50	22.00	47.50	135	450	600	1,950
1934S	1,011,000	12.00	34.00	45.00	85.00	200	500	1,800	4,000	6,250	8,500
1935	1,576,000	11.00	17.50	20.00	21.50	22.00	30.00	62.50	100.00	190	640
1935S	1,964,000	11.00	17.50	18.50	19.00	23.00	96.00	250	385	595	1,250

Eisenhower Dollar

KM# 203 • 22.6800 g., **Copper-Nickel Clad Copper**, 38.1 mm. • **Designer:** Frank Gasparro

Date	Mintage	Proof	MS-63	Prf-65	Date	Mintage	Proof	MS-63	Prf-65
1971	47,799,000	—	3.75	—	1972D	92,548,511	—	2.25	—
1971D	68,587,424	—	2.00	—	1973	2,000,056	—	11.00	—
1972	75,890,000	—	2.75	—	1973D	2,000,000	—	11.00	—

Date	Mintage	Proof	MS-63	Prf-65
1973S	—	(2,769,624)	—	11.00
1974	27,366,000	—	3.00	—
1974D	35,466,000	—	2.75	—
1974S	—	(2,617,350)	—	6.50

KM# 203a • 24.5900 g., **Silver**, 38.1 mm. • **Designer:** Frank Gasparro

Date	Mintage	Proof	MS-63	Prf-65
1971S	6,868,530	(4,265,234)	6.00	7.50
1972S	2,193,056	(1,811,631)	7.50	8.50
1973S	1,833,140	(1,005,617)	8.50	25.00
1974S	1,720,000	(1,306,579)	7.50	18.00

Bicentennial design, moon behind Liberty Bell reverse

Type I   Type II

KM# 206 • 22.6800 g., **Copper-Nickel Clad Copper**, 38.1 mm. • **Rev. Designer:** Dennis R. Williams **Notes:** In 1976 the lettering on the reverse was changed to thinner letters, resulting in the Type II variety for that year. The Type I variety was minted 1975 and dated 1976.

Date	Mintage	Proof	MS-63	Prf-65
1976 type I	117,337,000	—	4.00	—
1976 type II	Inc. above	—	2.00	—
1976D type I	103,228,274	—	3.25	—
1976D type II	Inc. above	—	2.00	—
1976S type I	—	(2,909,369)	—	5.75
1976S type II	—	(4,149,730)	—	5.75

Bicentennial design, moon behind Liberty Bell reverse

KM# 206a • 24.5900 g., 0.4000 **Silver**, 0.3162 oz. ASW • **Rev. Designer:** Dennis R. Williams

Date	Mintage	Proof	MS-63	Prf-65
1976S	4,908,319	(3,998,621)	14.00	12.50

Regular design resumed reverse

KM# A203 • Copper-Nickel Clad Copper, 38.1 mm. •

Date	Mintage	Proof	MS-63	Prf-65
1977	12,596,000	—	4.25	—
1977D	32,983,006	—	3.25	—
1977S	—	(3,251,152)	—	8.00
1978	25,702,000	—	2.75	—
1978D	33,012,890	—	3.00	—
1978S	—	(3,127,788)	—	10.00

Susan B. Anthony Dollar

Susan B. Anthony bust right. Obverse Eagle landing on moon, symbolic of Apollo manned moon landing. reverse

KM# 207 • 8.1000 g., **Copper-Nickel Clad Copper**, 0 oz., 26.5 mm. • **Designer:** Frank Gasparro **Edge Desc:** Reeded **Notes:** The 1979-S and 1981-S Type II coins have a clearer mint mark than the Type I varieties for those years.

Date	Mintage	MS-63	Prf-65
1979P	360,222,000	2.00	—
1979P Near date	Inc. above	12.00	—
1979D	288,015,744	1.75	—
1979S	109,576,000	2.00	—
1979S Proof, Type I	(3,677,175)	—	8.00
1979S Proof, Type II	Inc. above	—	110
1980P	27,610,000	2.00	—
1980D	41,628,708	2.00	—
1980S	20,422,000	2.00	—
1980S Proof	3,547,030	—	8.00
1981P	3,000,000	5.75	—
1981D	3,250,000	5.75	—
1981S	3,492,000	6.00	—
1981S Proof, Type I	4,063,083	—	8.00
1981S Proof, Type II	Inc. above	—	230
1999P	29,592,000	1.50	—
1999D	11,776,000	1.75	—
1999P Proof; *maximum mintage	(750,000)	—	25.00

Sacagawea Dollar

Sacagawea bust right, with baby on back obverse Eagle in flight left reverse

KM# 310 • 8.0700 g., **Copper-Zinc-Manganese-Nickel Clad Copper**, 26.4 mm. •

Date	Mintage	MS-63	Prf-65
2000P	767,140,000	2.00	—
2000D	518,916,000	2.00	—
2000S	(4,048,865)	—	10.00
2001P	62,468,000	4.00	—
2001D	70,909,500	4.00	—
2001S	(3,084,600)	—	100.00
2002P	3,865,610	2.00	—
2002D	3,732,000	2.00	—
2002S	(3,157,739)	—	28.50
2003P	3,090,000	2.50	—
2003D	3,090,000	2.50	—
2003S	(3,116,590)	—	20.00
2004P	2,660,000	2.50	—
2004D	2,660,000	2.50	—
2004S	—	—	22.50
2005P	2,520,000	2.50	—
2005D	2,520,000	2.50	—
2005S	—	—	22.50
2006P	—	2.50	—
2006D	—	2.50	—
2006S	—	—	22.50

ONE DOLLAR GOLD
Liberty Head - Type 1

KM# 73 • 1.6720 g., 0.9000 **Gold**, 0.0484 oz. AGW, 13 mm. • **Designer:** James B. Longacre **Notes:** On the "closed wreath" varieties of 1849, the wreath on the reverse extends closer to the numeral 1.

Date	Mintage	F-12	VF-20	XF-40	AU-50	MS-60
1849 open wreath	688,567	110	140	200	235	425
1849 closed wreath	Inc. above	110	135	190	220	365
1849C closed wreath	11,634	800	950	1,250	1,900	8,000
1849C open wreath	Inc. above	—	—	—	—	—
1849D open wreath	21,588	950	1,300	1,800	2,350	7,000
1849O open wreath	215,000	125	175	240	325	1,000
1850	481,953	110	145	200	215	360
1850C	6,966	900	1,150	1,600	2,300	9,000
1850D	8,382	975	1,250	1,650	2,800	10,000
1850O	14,000	185	275	375	850	3,600
1851	3,317,671	110	145	190	215	315
1851C	41,267	840	1,150	1,500	1,950	4,900
1851D	9,882	950	1,200	1,600	2,500	5,650
1851O	290,000	135	175	225	265	750
1852	2,045,351	110	145	200	215	330
1852C	9,434	800	1,150	1,400	1,700	5,100
1852D	6,360	950	1,250	1,600	2,300	10,000
1852O	140,000	125	165	230	385	1,500
1853	4,076,051	110	135	190	200	245
1853C	11,515	900	1,100	1,400	1,750	6,200
1853D	6,583	975	1,150	1,600	2,400	9,700
1853O	290,000	135	160	235	270	665
1854	736,709	110	145	200	230	335
1854D	2,935	990	1,400	2,350	6,000	13,000
1854S	14,632	245	360	525	840	2,450

Indian Head - Type 2

KM# 83 • 1.6720 g., 0.9000 **Gold**, 0.0484 oz. AGW, 15 mm. • **Designer:** James B. Longacre

Date	Mintage	F-12	VF-20	XF-40	AU-50	MS-60
1854	902,736	210	315	440	650	3,600
1855	758,269	210	315	440	650	3,600
1855C	9,803	975	1,450	3,500	11,000	33,000
1855D	1,811	3,000	4,750	9,800	22,000	48,000
1855O	55,000	345	475	700	1,400	7,800
1856S	24,600	575	900	1,400	2,300	8,500

Indian Head - Type 3

KM# 86 • 1.6720 g., 0.9000 **Gold**, 0.0484 oz. AGW, 15 mm. • **Designer:** James B. Longacre **Notes:** The 1856 varieties are distinguished by whether the 5 in the date is slanted or upright. The 1873 varieties are distinguished by the amount of space between the upper left and lower left serifs in the 3.

Date	Mintage	F-12	VF-20	XF-40	AU-50	MS-60	Prf-65
1856 upright 5	1,762,936	135	170	210	275	575	—
1856 slanted 5	Inc. above	140	160	195	250	400	50,000
1856D	1,460	2,950	3,800	5,800	8,000	32,000	—
1857	774,789	130	166	200	215	290	31,000
1857C	13,280	900	1,150	1,750	3,750	14,000	—
1857D	3,533	1,000	1,300	2,300	4,400	11,000	—
1857S	10,000	250	500	615	1,300	5,800	—
1858	117,995	135	160	200	220	325	27,500
1858D	3,477	925	1,250	1,600	2,750	10,000	—
1858S	10,000	300	400	575	1,300	5,500	—
1859	168,244	145	170	200	215	260	17,000

Date	Mintage	F-12	VF-20	XF-40	AU-50	MS-60	Prf-65
1859C	5,235	885	1,050	1,700	4,000	15,000	—
1859D	4,952	1,000	1,400	1,800	3,100	11,000	—
1859S	15,000	185	225	480	1,050	5,000	—
1860	36,668	135	170	190	240	400	14,500
1860D	1,566	2,000	2,800	3,800	7,000	23,000	—
1860S	13,000	280	380	480	750	2,300	—
1861	527,499	140	155	190	215	325	14,000
1861D mintage unrecorded	—	4,600	7,000	10,000	18,000	47,500	—
1862	1,361,390	130	150	200	240	325	15,000
1863	6,250	370	500	925	2,100	3,750	18,000
1864	5,950	270	350	440	750	950	18,000
1865	3,725	270	350	570	750	1,600	18,000
1866	7,130	275	360	470	670	950	18,000
1867	5,250	300	400	515	675	1,100	17,500
1868	10,525	265	290	415	490	950	19,000
1869	5,925	315	335	530	800	1,300	17,000
1870	6,335	245	285	400	480	850	16,000
1870S	3,000	290	475	750	1,150	2,300	—
1871	3,930	250	285	380	470	750	18,000
1872	3,530	245	275	400	480	975	18,000
1873 closed 3	125,125	300	425	800	950	1,600	—
1873 open 3	Inc. above	130	160	200	250	325	—
1874	198,820	130	160	200	245	340	18,000
1875	420	1,600	2,350	3,850	4,700	340	32,500
1876	3,245	220	275	345	475	650	16,750
1877	3,920	145	190	345	450	800	18,000
1878	3,020	180	250	350	465	675	15,500
1879	3,030	170	225	325	350	525	14,000
1880	1,636	150	180	200	240	440	14,000
1881	7,707	150	175	200	250	550	11,500
1882	5,125	160	180	200	265	600	9,500
1883	11,007	150	175	200	275	600	9,400
1884	6,236	140	155	200	260	550	9,400
1885	12,261	140	165	215	265	585	9,400
1886	6,016	150	175	215	285	550	9,400
1887	8,543	145	170	200	260	550	9,400
1888	16,580	145	170	200	250	550	9,400
1889	30,729	150	180	200	240	400	9,000

$2.50 (QUARTER EAGLE)

GOLD

Liberty Cap

KM# 27 • 4.3700 g., 0.9160 **Gold**, 0.1289 oz. AGW, 20 mm. • **Designer:** Robert Scot **Notes:** The 1796 "no stars" variety does not have stars on the obverse. The 1804 varieties are distinguished by the number of stars on the obverse.

Date	Mintage	F-12	VF-20	XF-40	MS-60
1796 no stars	963	30,000	42,000	70,000	165,000
1796 stars	432	28,000	40,000	63,000	140,000
1797	427	17,000	23,000	27,500	120,000
1798	1,094	4,750	10,000	12,500	55,000
1802/1	3,035	4,400	8,000	9,500	32,000
1804 13-star reverse	3,327	23,500	36,500	72,000	200,000
1804 14-star reverse	Inc. above	4,800	7,400	9,000	27,500
1805	1,781	6,000	7,500	9,000	21,000
1806/4	1,616	5,750	8,000	9,500	23,000
1806/5	Inc. above	6,000	8,000	18,000	77,000
1807	6,812	5,500	7,000	9.00	21,000

Turban Head

KM# 40 • 4.3700 g., 0.9160 **Gold**, 0.1289 oz. AGW, 20 mm. • **Designer:** John Reich

Date	Mintage	F-12	VF-20	XF-40	MS-60
1808	2,710	22,500	31,000	45,000	125,000

KM# 46 • 4.3700 g., 0.9160 **Gold**, 0.1289 oz. AGW, 18.5 mm. • **Designer:** John Reich

Date	Mintage	F-12	VF-20	XF-40	MS-60
1821	6,448	5,500	6,250	7,500	23,000
1824/21	2,600	5,500	6,250	7,250	22,000
1825	4,434	5,500	6,500	7,800	21,000
1826/25	760	6,000	7,000	8,500	36,000
1827	2,800	5,500	7,500	9,000	22,500

KM# 49 • 4.3700 g., 0.9160 **Gold**, 0.1289 oz. AGW, 18.2 mm. • **Designer:** John Reich

Date	Mintage	F-12	VF-20	XF-40	MS-60
1829	3,403	4,900	5,850	6,700	12,500
1830	4,540	4,950	5,850	6,700	12,500
1831	4,520	4,950	5,850	6,700	12,500
1832	4,400	4,950	5,850	6,700	12,500
1833	4,160	4,950	5,850	6,800	12,750
1834	4,000	8,800	12,000	16,000	36,000

Classic Head

KM# 56 • 4.1800 g., 0.8990 **Gold**, 0.1209 oz. AGW, 18.2 mm. • **Designer:** William Kneass

Date	Mintage	VF-20	XF-40	AU-50	MS-60	MS-65
1834	112,234	475	675	965	3,300	27,000
1835	131,402	475	675	950	3,200	32,000
1836	547,986	475	675	940	3,100	29,000
1837	45,080	500	800	1,500	4,000	35,000
1838	47,030	500	625	1,100	3,200	30,000
1838C	7,880	1,700	3,000	8,000	27,000	55,000
1839	27,021	500	900	1,900	5,500	—
1839C	18,140	1,500	2,650	4,500	26,500	—
1839D	13,674	1,750	3,450	8,000	24,000	—
1839O	17,781	700	1,100	2,500	7,250	—

Coronet Head

1848 'Cal.' reverse

KM# 72 • 4.1800 g., 0.9000 **Gold**, 0.121 oz. AGW, 18 mm. • **Designer:** Christian Gobrecht **Notes:** Varieties for 1843 are distinguished by the size of the numerals in the date. One 1848 variety has "Cal." inscribed on the reverse, indicating it was made from California gold. The 1873 "closed-3" and "open-3" varieties are distinguished by the amount of space between the upper left and lower left serifs in the 3 in the date.

Date	Mintage	F-12	VF-20	XF-40	AU-50	MS-60	Prf-65
1840	18,859	160	190	900	2,950	6,000	—
1840C	12,822	975	1,400	1,600	6,000	13,000	—
1840D	3,532	2,000	3,200	8,700	15,500	35,000	—
1840O	33,580	250	400	825	2,100	11,000	—
1841	—	—	48,000	85,000	96,000	—	—
1841C	10,281	750	1,500	2,000	3,500	18,500	—
1841D	4,164	950	2,100	4,750	11,000	25,000	—
1842	2,823	500	900	2,600	6,500	20,000	140,000
1842C	6,729	700	1,700	3,500	8,000	27,000	—
1842D	4,643	900	2,100	4,000	11,750	38,000	—
1842O	19,800	240	370	1,200	2,500	14,000	—
1843	100,546	160	180	450	915	3,000	140,000
1843C small date	26,064	1,500	2,400	5,500	9,000	29,000	—
1843C large date	Inc. above	800	1,600	2,200	3,500	8,800	—
1843D small date	36,209	920	1,800	2,350	3,250	10,500	—
1843O small date	288,002	165	190	250	350	1,700	—
1843O large date	76,000	210	260	465	1,600	8,000	—
1844	6,784	225	365	850	2,000	7,500	140,000
1844C	11,622	700	1,600	2,600	7,000	20,000	—
1844D	17,332	785	1,650	2,200	3,200	7,800	—
1845	91,051	190	250	350	600	1,275	140,000
1845D	19,460	950	1,900	2,600	3,900	15,000	—
1845O	4,000	550	1,050	2,300	9,000	20,000	—
1846	21,598	200	275	500	950	6,000	140,000
1846C	4,808	725	1,575	3,500	9,250	18,750	—
1846D	19,303	800	1,400	2,000	3,000	12,000	—
1846O	66,000	170	280	400	1,150	6,500	—
1847	29,814	140	220	360	825	3,800	—
1847C	23,226	900	1,800	2,300	3,500	7,250	—
1847D	15,784	800	1,650	2,250	3,250	10,500	—
1847O	124,000	160	240	400	1,000	4,000	—
1848	7,497	315	500	850	2,400	7,000	125,000
1848 "Cal."	1,389	8,000	15,000	26,000	36,000	50,000	—
1848C	16,788	800	1,600	2,100	3,800	14,000	—
1848D	13,771	1,000	2,000	2,500	4,500	12,000	—
1849	23,294	180	275	475	1,000	2,600	—
1849C	10,220	800	1,475	2,150	5,150	23,500	—
1849D	10,945	950	2,000	2,500	4,500	18,000	—
1850	252,923	160	180	275	350	1,100	—
1850C	9,148	800	1,500	2,100	3,400	17,500	—
1850D	12,148	950	1,800	2,500	4,000	15,000	—
1850O	84,000	170	225	450	1,200	4,900	—
1851	1,372,748	145	180	200	225	325	—
1851C	14,923	900	1,750	2,300	4,800	13,000	—
1851D	11,264	950	1,700	2,600	4,200	13,000	—
1851O	148,000	160	200	220	1,000	4,650	—
1852	1,159,681	150	175	200	250	325	—
1852C	9,772	675	1,500	2,100	4,250	18,000	—
1852D	4,078	840	1,600	2,800	7,250	17,000	—
1852O	140,000	160	190	300	950	5,000	—
1853	1,404,668	150	180	200	225	350	—
1853D	3,178	950	2,100	3,400	4,900	18,000	—
1854	596,258	150	180	215	240	350	—
1854C	7,295	800	1,500	2,400	5,000	14,750	—
1854D	1,760	1,750	2,900	6,950	12,000	27,500	—
1854O	153,000	150	185	240	425	1,600	—
1854S	246	32,500	70,000	115,000	215,000	300,000	—
1855	235,480	145	180	225	250	360	—
1855C	3,677	800	1,675	3,300	6,500	25,000	—
1855D	1,123	1,750	3,250	7,500	24,000	46,000	—
1856	384,240	145	175	210	250	390	75,000
1856C	7,913	650	1,150	2,200	4,400	15,500	—
1856D	874	3,500	6,700	12,500	30,000	72,500	—
1856O	21,100	180	240	750	1,500	8,000	—
1856S	71,120	160	250	375	950	4,500	—
1857	214,130	150	190	205	230	380	75,000
1857D	2,364	875	1,750	2,900	3,850	13,000	—
1857O	34,000	155	210	350	1,100	4,600	—
1857S	69,200	160	210	340	900	5,500	—
1858	47,377	150	200	250	360	1,350	59,000
1858C	9,056	825	1,500	2,100	3,350	9,250	—
1859	39,444	150	185	265	400	1,250	61,000
1859D	2,244	1,000	1,900	3,300	4,900	20,000	—
1859S	15,200	200	350	1,000	2,800	7,000	—
1860	22,675	150	200	265	470	1,300	58,000
1860C	7,469	815	1,550	2,200	3,950	21,000	—
1860S	35,600	170	250	675	1,200	4,000	—
1861	1,283,878	150	180	210	230	325	31,500
1861S	24,000	200	400	1,000	3,700	7,400	—

Date	Mintage	F-12	VF-20	XF-40	AU-50	MS-60	Prf-65
1862	98,543	160	200	300	520	1,375	32,500
1862/1	Inc. above	450	950	2,000	4,000	8,000	—
1862S	8,000	500	1,000	2,100	4,500	17,000	—
1863	30	—	—	—	—	—	95,000
1863S	10,800	250	500	1,500	3,200	13,500	—
1864	2,874	2,500	5,500	8,800	21,500	37,500	27,000
1865	1,545	2,400	6,000	8,000	19,000	38,000	30,000
1865S	23,376	160	225	650	1,650	5,000	—
1866	3,110	650	1,300	3,500	6,000	11,500	25,000
1866S	38,960	180	300	650	1,600	6,250	—
1867	3,250	190	385	900	1,250	4,800	27,000
1867S	28,000	170	250	625	1,750	4,000	—
1868	3,625	170	235	400	675	1,600	27,000
1868S	34,000	150	200	300	1,100	4,000	—
1869	4,345	170	250	450	715	3,000	24,500
1869S	29,500	160	240	440	775	5,000	—
1870	4,555	165	225	425	740	3,800	22,750
1870S	16,000	155	215	400	800	4,900	—
1871	5,350	160	230	325	600	2,200	24,000
1871S	22,000	150	185	280	530	2,200	—
1872	3,030	200	400	750	1,100	4,650	22,000
1872S	18,000	155	225	415	900	4,500	—
1873 closed 3	178,025	155	170	210	260	535	22,500
1873 open 3	Inc. above	155	165	195	250	300	—
1873S	27,000	160	225	425	900	2,800	—
1874	3,940	170	240	380	720	2,100	32,000
1875	420	1,750	3,500	5,000	11,000	21,500	32,500
1875S	11,600	150	200	300	850	4,500	—
1876	4,221	170	275	675	925	3,200	22,000
1876S	5,000	170	225	525	980	3,300	—
1877	1,652	275	400	800	1,100	3,250	22,000
1877S	35,400	150	160	200	230	635	—
1878	286,260	150	160	200	225	275	26,000
1878S	178,000	150	160	200	235	340	—
1879	88,990	150	160	195	235	300	26,000
1879S	43,500	155	200	300	550	2,150	—
1880	2,996	170	210	335	600	1,300	20,250
1881	691	900	2,200	3,400	5,000	10,000	19,000
1882	4,067	160	210	290	400	700	15,000
1883	2,002	175	220	440	1,000	2,600	15,500
1884	2,023	175	225	420	600	1,600	16,000
1885	887	400	715	1,800	2,500	4,400	15,000
1886	4,088	170	190	270	425	1,100	16,500
1887	6,282	175	200	245	325	700	16,500
1888	16,098	160	180	240	285	340	15,000
1889	17,648	155	180	230	250	325	17,000
1890	8,813	170	190	240	280	500	13,750
1891	11,040	165	175	215	230	400	14,000
1892	2,545	170	180	250	325	765	15,000
1893	30,106	165	175	200	240	300	14,000
1894	4,122	170	180	225	325	800	13,500
1895	6,199	150	175	225	275	395	12,500
1896	19,202	150	175	225	235	285	12,500
1897	29,904	150	175	210	235	285	12,500
1898	24,165	150	175	210	235	285	12,500
1899	27,350	150	175	210	235	300	12,500
1900	67,205	150	175	240	320	415	12,500
1901	91,322	150	175	200	235	275	12,500
1902	133,733	150	170	200	235	275	12,500
1903	201,257	150	170	200	235	275	13,000
1904	160,960	150	170	200	240	275	12,500
1905	217,944	150	170	200	240	275	12,500
1906	176,490	150	170	200	240	275	12,500
1907	336,448	150	170	200	240	275	12,500

Indian Head

KM# 128 • 4.1800 g., 0.9000 **Gold**, 0.121 oz. AGW, 18 mm. • **Designer:** Bela Lyon Pratt

Date	Mintage	VF-20	XF-40	AU-50	MS-60	MS-63	MS-65	Prf-65
1908	565,057	165	220	230	275	1,800	8,500	16,000
1909	441,899	175	220	230	275	2,600	11,000	30,000
1910	492,682	175	220	230	275	2,600	12,500	18,000

1911-D $2.50 Gold
Grade MS-60

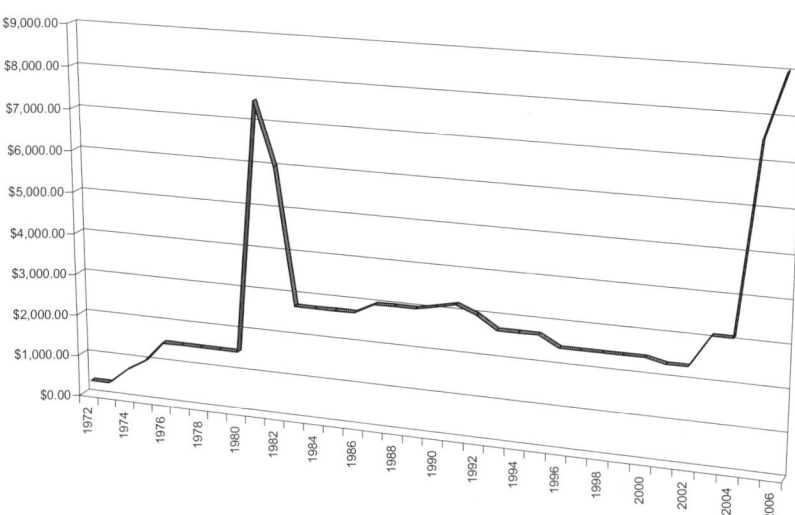

Date	Mintage	VF-20	XF-40	AU-50	MS-60	MS-63	MS-65	Prf-65
1911	704,191	175	220	230	280	1,600	12,500	16,000
1911D	55,680	2,200	2,900	4,000	9,000	28,000	110,000	16,000
1912	616,197	175	220	230	275	2,800	16,000	16,000
1913	722,165	175	220	230	280	1,725	14,000	16,500
1914	240,117	175	235	260	480	8,500	34,000	16,500
1914D	448,000	175	220	230	300	2,650	40,000	23,000
1915	606,100	175	220	230	275	1,650	13,500	15,250
1925D	578,000	175	220	230	275	1,450	7,000	—
1926	446,000	175	220	230	275	1,450	7,000	—
1927	388,000	175	220	230	275	1,450	7,000	—
1928	416,000	175	220	230	275	1,450	7,000	—
1929	532,000	180	230	250	340	1,600	10,000	—

GOLD

KM# 84 • 5.0150 g., 0.9000 Gold, 0.1452 oz. AGW, 20.5 mm. • **Designer:** James B. Longacre **Notes:** The 1873 "closed-3" and "open-3" varieties are distinguished by the amount of space between the upper left and lower left serifs of the 3 in the date.

Date	Mintage	VF-20	XF-40	AU-50	MS-60	MS-65	Prf-65
1854	138,618	850	1,100	2,000	3,400	18,000	125,000
1854D	1,120	8,300	15,000	29,000	65,000	—	—
1854O	24,000	1,000	2,000	4,000	20,000	—	—
1855	50,555	900	1,100	2,000	3,300	32,000	120,000
1855S	6,600	1,025	2,150	5,700	25,000	—	—
1856	26,010	880	1,100	2,150	3,500	27,000	—
1856S	34,500	900	1,500	2,350	10,000	—	—
1857	20,891	900	1,100	2,100	3,500	—	62,500
1857S	14,000	950	2,200	5,500	18,000	—	—
1858	2,133	950	1,800	3,000	9,000	—	62,500
1859	15,638	900	1,800	1,800	3,000	—	60,000
1860	7,155	900	1,600	2,000	3,600	21,000	46,000
1860S	7,000	950	2,000	7,000	17,000	—	—
1861	6,072	925	1,500	2,200	3,600	27,000	46,000
1862	5,785	925	1,850	2,200	3,600	28,000	46,500
1863	5,039	900	1,450	2,200	3,600	20,000	43,000
1864	2,680	950	1,500	2,300	3,600	29,000	42,000

Date	Mintage	VF-20	XF-40	AU-50	MS-60	MS-65	Prf-65
1865	1,165	1,350	2,500	6,000	10,000	39,000	40,000
1866	4,030	970	1,100	2,000	3,600	27,500	42,000
1867	2,650	950	1,100	2,400	4,000	28,000	41,500
1868	4,875	740	1,100	2,100·	3,000	22,000	42,000
1869	2,525	1,150	2,200	2,600	4,000	—	46,000
1870	3,535	1,000	1,500	2,400	5,000	—	47,000
1870S unique	—	—	—	—	—	—	—
Note: Est. value, $1.25 million, AU50 cleaned, Bass Collection.							
1871	1,330	1,000	1,500	2,000	4,000	27,500	47,000
1872	2,030	900	1,800	2,250	3,600	—	33,000
1873 open 3, proof only	25	3,300	5,000	8,700	—	—	—
1873 closed 3, mintage unknown	—	4,000	6,000	10,000	—	—	42,000
1874	41,820	800	1,300	1,900	3,000	16,000	42,000
1875 proof only	20	20,000	28,000	47,500	—	—	175,000
1876	45	6,000	10,000	16,500	—	—	60,000
1877	1,488	1,200	2,900	5,200	12,000	60,000	43,500
1878	82,324	800	1,300	1,900	3,000	16,000	43,000
1879	3,030	850	1,300	2,000	2,650	19,000	32,000
1880	1,036	850	1,700	3,000	4,000	20,000	29,500
1881	554	1,400	2,750	5,500	8,000	24,000	25,000
1882	1,576	925	1,400	2,000	3,500	22,000	25,000
1883	989	1,000	1,600	3,500	3,600	24,000	25,000
1884	1,106	1,250	1,700	2,200	3,600	24,000	24,000
1885	910	1,300	1,800	2,850	3,900	24,000	25,000
1886	1,142	1,250	1,800	3,000	4,000	20,000	24,000
1887	6,160	900	1,300	2,000	3,000	18,000	21,000
1888	5,291	950	1,500	2,000	3,300	20,000	23,000
1889	2,429	925	1,300	1,700	3,100	18,000	22,000

$5 (HALF EAGLE) GOLD

Liberty Cap

KM# 19 • 8.7500 g., 0.9160 **Gold**, 0.258 oz. AGW, 25 mm. • **Designer:** Robert Scot **Notes:** From 1795 through 1798, varieties exist with either a "small eagle" or a "large (heraldic) eagle" on the reverse. After 1798, only the heraldic eagle was used. Two 1797 varieties are distinguished by the size of the 8 in the date. 1806 varieties are distinguished by whether the top of the 6 has a serif.

Date	Mintage	F-12	VF-20	XF-40	MS-60
1795 small eagle	8,707	11,500	17,000	19,000	47,000
1795 large eagle	Inc. above	8,800	14,000	20,000	75,000
1796/95 small eagle	6,196	12,000	17,500	24,000	75,000
1797/95 large eagle	3,609	8,600	14,000	22,000	150,000
1797 15 stars, small eagle	Inc. above	14,000	21,000	35,000	150,000
1797 16 stars, small eagle	Inc. above	13,000	17,500	34,000	145,000
1798 small eagle	—	90,000	155,000	275,000	—
1798 large eagle, small 8	24,867	3,300	4,500	6,000	21,000
1798 large eagle, large 8, 13-star reverse	Inc. above	3,000	3,700	4,500	17,500
1798 large eagle, large 8, 14-star reverse	Inc. above	3,000	4,200	7,000	35,000
1799	7,451	3,000	3,800	5,300	16,500
1800	37,628	3,000	3,800	5,000	8,800
1802/1	53,176	3,000	4,000	4,300	8,900
1803/2	33,506	3,000	3,800	4,300	8,700
1804 small 8	30,475	3,000	3,800	4,300	8,700
1804 large 8	Inc. above	3,000	3,800	4,300	9,600
1805	33,183	3,000	3,800	4,300	8,600
1806 pointed 6	64,093	3,200	3,700	4,300	9,000
1806 round 6	Inc. above	3,000	3,700	4,300	8,600
1807	32,488	3,000	3,800	4,300	8,700

Turban Head
Capped draped bust obverse

KM# 38 • 8.7500 g., 0.9160 **Gold**, 0.258 oz. AGW, 25 mm. • **Designer:** John Reich **Notes:** The 1810 varieties are distinguished by the size of the numerals in the date and the size of the 5 in the "5D." on the reverse. The 1811 varieties are distinguished by the size of the 5 in the "5D." on the reverse.

Date	Mintage	F-12	VF-20	XF-40	MS-60
1807	51,605	2,400	3,000	4,300	8,400
1808	55,578	2,400	3,000	4,300	8,250
1808/7	Inc. above	3,000	3,800	4,500	13,000
1809/8	33,875	2,500	3,000	3,750	8,500
1810 small date, small 5	100,287	9,600	22,500	32,000	95,000
1810 small date, large 5	Inc. above	2,300	3,000	3,800	8,500
1810 large date, small 5	Inc. above	13,500	24,000	32,000	115
1810 large date, large 5	Inc. above	2,600	3,000	3,750	8,500
1811 small 5	99,581	2,600	3,000	3,750	8,500
1811 large 5	Inc. above	2,500	2,900	38,000	9,000
1812	58,087	2,400	2,850	4,000	8,000

Capped head obverse

KM# 43 • 8.7500 g., 0.9160 **Gold**, 0.258 oz. AGW, 25 mm. • **Designer:** John Reich **Notes:** 1820 varieties are distinguished by whether the 2 in the date has a curved base or square base and by the size of the letters in the reverse inscriptions. 1832 varieties are distinguished by whether the 2 in the date has a curved base or square base and by the number of stars on the reverse. 1834 varieties are distinguished by whether the 4 has a serif at its far right.

Date	Mintage	F-12	VF-20	XF-40	MS-60
1813	95,428	2,400	2,750	3,800	7,800
1814/13	15,454	2,500	2,800	3,500	10,000
1815	635	27,000	33,000	70,000	—
Note: 1815, private sale, Jan. 1994, MS-61, $150,000.					
1818	48,588	2,475	3,100	4,000	8,250
1819	51,723	9,600	16,500	275,000	62,000
1820 curved-base 2, small letters	263,806	2,600	3,000	4,500	11,000
1820 curved-base 2, large letters	Inc. above	2,600	3,000	4,150	20,000
1820 square-base 2	Inc. above	2,600	3,000	3,800	14,000
1821	34,641	7,000	15,000	23,000	70,000
1822 3 known	—	—	—	—	1,000,000
Note: 1822, private sale, 1993, VF-30, $1,000,000.					
1823	14,485	2,500	3,400	5,000	16,000
1824	17,340	5,000	10,000	16,000	38,000
1825/21	29,060	5,150	9,500	12,000	38,000
1825/24	Inc. above	—	—	250,000	350,000
Note: 1825/4, Bowers & Merena, March 1989, XF, $148,500.					
1826	18,069	4,000	7,500	9,300	32,000
1827	24,913	6,000	10,000	12,250	34,000
1828/7	28,029	15,000	27,500	41,000	125,000
Note: 1828/7, Bowers & Merena, June 1989, XF, $20,900.					
1828	Inc. above	6,000	13,000	21,000	7,000
1829 large planchet	57,442	15,000	27,500	50,000	135,000
Note: 1829 large planchet, Superior, July 1985, MS-65, $104,500.					
1829 small planchet	Inc. above	37,500	50,000	82,500	140,000
Note: 1829 small planchet, private sale, 1992 (XF-45), $89,000.					
1830 small "5D."	126,351	14,500	17,500	21,000	40,000
1830 large "5D."	Inc. above	14,500	17,500	21,000	40,000
1831	140,594	14,500	17,500	21,000	42,500
1832 curved-base 2, 12 stars	157,487	50,000	80,000	135,000	—
1832 square-base 2, 13 stars	Inc. above	14,500	17,500	21,000	40,000
1833	193,630	14,500	17,500	21,000	40,000

Date	Mintage	F-12	VF-20	XF-40	MS-60
1834 plain 4	50,141	14,500	17,500	21,000	40,000
1834 crosslet 4	Inc. above	14,500	17,500	21,000	40,000

Classic Head

KM# 57 • 8.3600 g., 0.8990 **Gold**, 0.2418 oz. AGW, 22.5 mm. • **Designer:** William Kneass **Notes:** 1834 varieties are distinguished by whether the 4 has a serif at its far right.

Date	Mintage	VF-20	XF-40	AU-50	MS-60	MS-65
1834 plain 4	658,028	390	550	950	3,000	48,000
1834 crosslet 4	Inc. above	1,650	2,900	6,000	20,000	—
1835	371,534	390	560	1,000	3,150	70,000
1836	553,147	390	550	1,000	2,950	70,000
1837	207,121	390	585	1,200	3,500	75,000
1838	286,588	390	5,500	1,000	3,700	58,000
1838C	17,179	2,200	4,000	13,000	38,500	—
1838D	20,583	2,000	3,850	9,000	25,000	—

Coronet Head
No motto above eagle reverse

KM# 69 • 8.3590 g., 0.9000 **Gold**, 0.242 oz. AGW, 21.6 mm. • **Designer:** Christian Gobrecht **Notes:** Varieties for the 1842 Philadelphia strikes are distinguished by the size of the letters in the reverse inscriptions. Varieties for the 1842-C and -D strikes are distinguished by the size of the numerals in the date. Varieties for the 1843-O strikes are distinguished by the size of the letters in the reverse inscriptions.

Date	Mintage	F-12	VF-20	XF-40	MS-60	Prf-65
1839	118,143	250	275	480	4,000	—
1839/8 curved date	Inc. above	275	325	700	2,250	—
1839C	17,205	1,250	2,300	2,900	24,000	—
1839D	18,939	1,125	2,200	3,200	22,000	—
1840	137,382	200	230	360	3,700	—
1840C	18,992	1,200	2,200	3,000	26,000	—
1840D	22,896	1,200	2,200	3,000	16,000	—
1840O	40,120	200	365	875	11,000	—
1841	15,833	200	400	875	5,500	—
1841C	21,467	1,200	1,850	2,400	20,000	—
1841D	30,495	1,400	1,800	2,350	15,000	—
1841O 2 known	50	—	—	—	—	—
1842 small letters	27,578	2,000	345	1,100	—	—
1842 large letters	Inc. above	350	750	2,000	11,000	—
1842C small date	28,184	4,500	10,000	23,000	110,000	—
1842C large date	Inc. above	900	1,800	2,200	18,000	—
1842D small date	59,608	1,000	2,000	2,300	15,000	—
1842D large date	Inc. above	1,400	2,350	6,500	48,000	—
1842O	16,400	550	1,000	3,400	22,000	—
1843	611,205	200	230	330	1,850	—
1843C	44,201	1,250	1,850	2,500	14,000	—
1843D	98,452	1,250	1,950	2,600	13,000	—
1843O small letters	19,075	300	660	1,700	26,000	—
1843O large letters	82,000	200	265	1,175	12,000	—
1844	340,330	200	230	330	2,000	—
1844C	23,631	1,300	1,900	3,000	24,000	—
1844D	88,982	1,500	1,950	2,400	12,000	—
1844O	364,600	220	250	375	4,700	—
1845	417,099	200	235	260	2,000	—
1845D	90,629	1,300	1,900	2,400	12,500	—
1845O	41,000	235	415	800	9,900	—
1846	395,942	200	230	330	2,400	—
1846C	12,995	1,350	1,900	3,000	24,000	—
1846D	80,294	1,250	1,800	2,400	13,000	—
1846O	58,000	215	375	1,000	11,500	—

Date	Mintage	F-12	VF-20	XF-40	MS-60	Prf-65
1847	915,981	200	230	250	1,650	—
1847C	84,151	1,350	1,800	2,400	13,000	—
1847D	64,405	1,400	2,000	2,000	10,000	—
1847O	12,000	550	2,200	6,750	28,000	—
1848	260,775	200	230	275	1,500	—
1848C	64,472	1,400	1,900	2,250	19,250	—
1848D	47,465	1,450	2,000	2,350	14,500	—
1849	133,070	200	230	280	2,800	—
1849C	64,823	1,500	1,900	2,400	14,000	—
1849D	39,036	1,550	2,000	2,600	16,500	—
1850	64,491	200	300	625	4,250	—
1850C	63,591	1,350	1,850	2,300	14,000	—
1850D	43,984	1,450	1,950	2,500	33,000	—
1851	377,505	200	230	250	2,800	—
1851C	49,176	1,300	1,900	2,350	17,500	—
1851D	62,710	1,400	1,950	2,400	15,000	—
1851O	41,000	280	590	1,500	13,000	—
1852	573,901	200	230	260	1,400	—
1852C	72,574	1,350	1,900	2,450	7,750	—
1852D	91,584	1,450	2,000	2,450	13,000	—
1853	305,770	200	230	250	1,400	—
1853C	65,571	1,500	1,950	2,350	8,500	—
1853D	89,678	1,550	2,000	2,500	11,000	—
1854	160,675	200	230	260	2,000	—
1854C	39,283	1,400	1,900	2,300	14,000	—
1854D	56,413	1,400	1,875	2,200	11,500	—
1854O	46,000	225	300	525	8,250	—
1854S	268	—	—	—	—	—
Note: 1854S, Bowers & Merena, Oct. 1982, AU-55, $170,000.						
1855	117,098	200	230	250	1,800	—
1855C	39,788	1,400	1,900	2,300	16,000	—
1855D	22,432	1,500	1,950	2,400	19,000	—
1855O	11,100	315	675	2,100	20,000	—
1855S	61,000	200	390	1,000	15,500	—
1856	197,990	200	230	240	2,300	—
1856C	28,457	1,450	1,875	2,400	20,000	—
1856D	19,786	1,475	1,950	2,600	15,000	—
1856O	10,000	370	650	1,600	14,000	—
1856S	105,100	200	300	700	6,750	—
1857	98,188	200	230	260	1,600	123,500
1857C	31,360	1,400	1,900	2,500	9,500	—
1857D	17,046	1,500	2,000	2,650	14,500	—
1857O	13,000	340	640	1,400	15,000	—
1857S	87,000	200	300	700	11,000	—
1858	15,136	200	240	550	3,850	190,000
1858C	38,856	1,400	1,900	2,350	11,000	—
1858D	15,362	1,500	2,000	2,450	12,500	—

1852-C $5 Gold
Grade MS-60

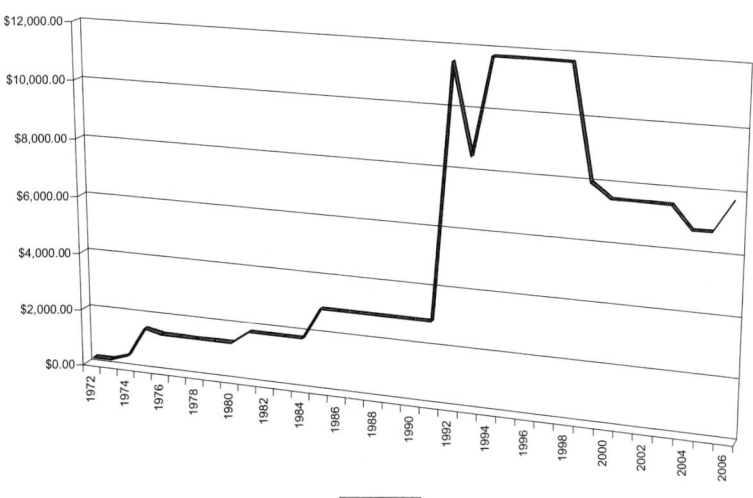

Retail Price

Date	Mintage	F-12	VF-20	XF-40	MS-60	Prf-65
1858S	18,600	400	825	2,350	31,000	—
1859	16,814	200	325	625	7,000	—
1859C	31,847	1,400	1,900	2,450	16,000	—
1859D	10,366	1,600	2,150	2,600	16,000	—
1859S	13,220	615	1,800	4,150	30,000	—
1860	19,825	200	280	575	3,500	100,000
1860C	14,813	1,500	2,100	3,000	15,000	—
1860D	14,635	1,500	1,900	2,600	15,000	—
1860S	21,200	500	1,100	2,100	27,000	—
1861	688,150	200	230	245	1,450	100,000
1861C	6,879	1,500	2,400	3,900	25,000	—
1861D	1,597	3,000	4,700	7,000	50,000	—
1861S	18,000	500	1,100	4,500	36,500	—
1862	4,465	400	800	1,850	20,000	96,000
1862S	9,500	1,500	3,000	6,000	62,000	—
1863	2,472	450	1,200	3,750	27,500	90,000
1863S	17,000	600	1,450	4,100	35,500	—
1864	4,220	350	650	1,850	15,000	72,000
1864S	3,888	2,300	4,750	16,000	55,000	—
1865	1,295	500	1,450	4,100	20,000	82,500
1865S	27,612	475	1,400	2,400	20,000	—
1866S	9,000	750	1,750	4,000	40,000	—

"In God We Trust" above eagle reverse

KM# 101 • 8.3590 g., 0.9000 **Gold**, 0.242 oz. AGW, 21.6 mm. • **Designer:** Christian Gobrecht **Notes:** The 1873 "closed-3" and "open-3" varieties are known and are distinguished by the amount of space between the upper left and lower left serifs of the 3 in the date.

Date	Mintage	VF-20	XF-40	AU-50	MS-60	MS-63	MS-65	Prf-65
1866	6,730	800	1,650	3,500	16,500	—	—	70,000
1866S	34,920	900	2,600	8,800	25,000	—	—	—
1867	6,920	500	1,500	3,300	11,500	—	—	70,000
1867S	29,000	1,400	2,900	8,000	34,500	—	—	—
1868	5,725	650	1,000	3,500	11,500	—	—	70,000
1868S	52,000	400	1,550	4,000	20,000	—	—	—
1869	1,785	925	2,400	3,500	17,500	34,000	—	65,000
1869S	31,000	500	1,750	4,000	26,000	—	—	—
1870	4,035	800	2,000	2,850	18,000	—	—	75,000
1870CC	7,675	5,250	15,000	30,000	110,000	137,500	200,000	—
1870S	17,000	950	2,600	8,250	29,000	—	—	—
1871	3,230	900	1,700	3,300	12,500	—	—	70,000
1871CC	20,770	1,250	3,000	12,000	60,000	—	—	—
1871S	25,000	500	950	2,950	13,000	—	—	—
1872	1,690	850	1,925	3,000	15,000	18,000	—	60,000
1872CC	16,980	1,250	5,000	20,000	60,000	—	—	—
1872S	36,400	460	800	3,400	13,500	—	—	—
1873 closed 3	49,305	215	225	440	1,200	6,500	24,000	70,000
1873 open 3	63,200	215	220	350	850	3,650	—	—
1873CC	7,416	2,600	12,500	27,500	60,000	—	—	—
1873S	31,000	525	1,400	3,250	21,000	—	—	—
1874	3,508	660	1,675	2,500	13,000	26,000	—	66,000
1874CC	21,198	850	1,700	9,500	36,000	—	—	—
1874S	16,000	640	2,100	4,800	22,500	—	—	—
1875	220	34,000	45,000	60,000	190,000	—	—	185,000
1875CC	11,828	1,400	4,500	11,500	52,000	—	—	—
1875S	9,000	715	2,250	5,000	16,500	32,500	—	—
1876	1,477	1,100	2,500	4,125	11,000	14,500	55,000	60,000
1876CC	6,887	1,450	5,000	14,000	46,500	82,500	165,000	—
1876S	4,000	2,000	3,600	9,500	30,000	—	—	—
1877	1,152	900	2,750	4,000	13,750	29,000	—	75,000
1877CC	8,680	1,000	3,300	11,000	52,500	—	—	—
1877S	26,700	400	650	1,400	9,200	—	—	—
1878	131,740	215	220	240	425	2,000	—	50,000
1878CC	9,054	3,100	7,200	20,000	60,000	—	—	—
1878S	144,700	215	220	3,000	675	4,250	—	—
1879	301,950	215	220	225	400	2,000	12,000	55,000
1879CC	17,281	575	1,500	3,150	22,000	—	—	—
1879S	426,200	215	225	240	950	3,300	—	—
1880	3,166,436	215	225	225	235	840	7,500	54,000
1880CC	51,017	425	815	1,375	9,900	—	—	—
1880S	1,348,900	215	220	225	235	800	5,750	—

Date	Mintage	VF-20	XF-40	AU-50	MS-60	MS-63	MS-65	Prf-65
1881	5,708,802	215	220	225	235	775	4,800	54,000
1881/80	Inc. above	330	600	750	1,500	4,500	—	—
1881CC	13,886	550	1,500	7,000	22,500	60,000	—	—
1881S	969,000	215	220	225	235	775	7,150	—
1882	2,514,568	215	220	225	235	800	6,150	54,000
1882CC	82,817	415	625	900	7,500	40,000	—	—
1882S	969,000	215	220	225	235	800	4,500	—
1883	233,461	215	220	225	260	1,200	—	40,000
1883CC	12,958	460	1,100	3,200	18,000	—	—	—
1883S	83,200	215	240	315	1,000	2,950	—	—
1884	191,078	215	220	225	650	2,250	—	35,000
1884CC	16,402	550	975	3,000	17,000	—	—	—
1884S	177,000	215	220	225	345	2,000	—	—
1885	601,506	215	220	225	260	825	4,800	35,000
1885S	1,211,500	215	220	225	235	790	4,000	—
1886	388,432	215	220	225	235	1,125	5,600	44,000
1886S	3,268,000	215	220	225	235	815	4,500	—
1887	87	—	14,500	20,000	—	—	—	120,000
1887S	1,912,000	215	220	225	235	800	4,800	—
1888	18,296	215	230	300	550	1,500	—	29,000
1888S	293,900	215	220	320	1,200	4,000	—	—
1889	7,565	350	440	515	1,150	2,400	—	30,000
1890	4,328	400	475	550	2,200	6,500	—	27,000
1890CC	53,800	330	460	615	1,600	8,000	55,000	—
1891	61,413	215	220	230	450	1,900	5,400	29,000
1891CC	208,000	315	415	525	750	3,150	31,500	—
1892	753,572	215	220	225	235	880	7,000	30,000
1892CC	82,968	315	400	575	1,500	6,000	33,500	—
1892O	10,000	515	1,000	1,375	3,300	—	—	—
1892S	298,400	215	220	225	525	3,300	—	—
1893	1,528,197	215	220	225	235	800	3,900	34,000
1893CC	60,000	345	465	770	1,400	6,350	—	—
1893O	110,000	225	315	480	950	6,500	—	—
1893S	224,000	215	220	225	245	825	9,000	—
1894	957,955	215	220	225	235	800	2,600	35,000
1894O	16,600	200	360	570	1,300	5,500	—	—
1894S	55,900	240	375	575	2,900	10,000	—	—
1895	1,345,936	215	220	225	235	800	4,500	29,000
1895S	112,000	215	275	400	3,150	6,500	26,000	—
1896	59,063	215	220	225	235	9,750	4,500	30,000
1896S	155,400	215	240	300	1,150	6,000	24,500	—
1897	867,883	215	220	225	235	825	4,500	35,000
1897S	354,000	215	220	235	865	5,150	—	—
1898	633,495	215	220	225	235	885	6,000	30,000
1898S	1,397,400	215	220	225	230	950	—	—
1899	1,710,729	215	220	225	235	730	3,600	30,000
1899S	1,545,000	215	220	225	235	1,000	9,600	—
1900	1,405,730	215	220	225	235	790	3,600	30,000
1900S	329,000	215	220	230	245	900	14,000	—
1901	616,040	215	220	225	235	750	3,650	27,000
1901S	3,648,000	215	220	225	235	730	3,600	—
1902	172,562	215	220	225	235	730	4,400	27,000
1902S	939,000	215	220	225	235	730	3,600	—
1903	227,024	215	220	225	235	730	4,000	27,000
1903S	1,855,000	215	220	225	235	730	3,600	—
1904	392,136	215	220	225	235	730	3,600	27,000
1904S	97,000	215	240	285	900	3,850	9,600	—
1905	302,308	215	220	225	235	740	4,000	27,000
1905S	880,700	215	225	250	235	1,500	9,600	—
1906	348,820	215	220	225	235	745	3,600	26,000
1906D	320,000	215	220	225	235	930	3,200	—
1906S	598,000	215	220	230	240	900	4,400	—
1907	626,192	215	220	225	235	730	3,400	23,000
1907D	888,000	215	220	225	235	730	3,400	—
1908	421,874	215	220	225	235	730	3,400	—

Indian Head

KM# 129 • 8.3590 g., 0.9000 **Gold**, .2420 oz. AGW, 21.6 mm. • **Designer:** Bela Lyon Pratt

Date	Mintage	VF-20	XF-40	AU-50	MS-60	MS-63	MS-65	Prf-65
1908	578,012	330	355	385	460	4,350	25,000	25,500

Date	Mintage	VF-20	XF-40	AU-50	MS-60	MS-63	MS-65	Prf-65
1908D	148,000	330	355	385	460	4,350	27,500	—
1908S	82,000	330	415	430	1,275	4,350	24,000	—
1909	627,138	330	355	385	460	4,350	25,000	36,000
1909D	3,423,560	330	355	385	460	4,350	25,000	—
1909O	34,200	2,000	3,400	6,000	21,000	66,000	260,000	—
1909S	297,200	330	355	385	1,400	11,000	45,000	—
1910	604,250	330	355	385	460	4,350	25,000	37,000
1910D	193,600	330	355	385	460	4,350	42,500	—
1910S	770,200	330	355	385	1,000	6,000	44,000	—
1911	915,139	330	355	385	460	4,350	25,000	28,500
1911D	72,500	475	535	515	4,500	37,000	200,000	—
1911S	1,416,000	340	355	385	560	4,350	41,500	—
1912	790,144	330	355	385	460	4,350	25,000	28,500
1912S	392,000	330	365	400	1,700	13,500	93,500	—
1913	916,099	330	355	385	460	4,350	25,000	28,000
1913S	408,000	340	350	385	1,400	11,500	120,000	—
1914	247,125	330	355	385	460	4,350	25,000	28,500
1914D	247,000	335	355	385	460	4,350	26,000	—
1914S	263,000	340	365	400	1,375	13,500	100,000	—
1915	588,075	330	355	385	460	4,350	25,000	39,000
1915S	164,000	340	400	385	2,000	17,000	110,000	—
1916S	240,000	330	355	385	560	4,350	25,000	—
1929	662,000	4,200	9,600	10,500	13,250	17,500	45,000	—

$10 (EAGLE) GOLD

Liberty Cap
Small eagle reverse

KM# 21 • 17.5000 g., 0.9160 **Gold**, 0.5159 oz. AGW, 33 mm. • **Designer:** Robert Scot

Date	Mintage	F-12	VF-20	XF-40	MS-60
1795 13 leaves	5,583	18,000	24,000	33,000	70,000
1795 9 leaves	Inc. above	26,000	40,000	60,000	230,000
1796	4,146	23,000	27,500	38,000	80,000
1797 small eagle	3,615	30,000	38,000	45,000	185,000

Heraldic eagle reverse

KM# 30 • 17.5000 g., 0.9160 **Gold**, 0.5159 oz. AGW, 33 mm. • **Designer:** Robert Scot **Notes:** The 1798/97 varieties are distinguished by the positioning of the stars on the obverse.

Date	Mintage	F-12	VF-20	XF-40	MS-60
1797 large eagle	10,940	9,000	11,000	14,000	40,000
1798/97 9 stars left, 4 right	900	11,000	19,000	29,000	100,000
1798/97 7 stars left, 6 right	842	23,000	30,000	65,000	—
1799	37,449	8,000	10,000	12,500	31,000
1800	5,999	8,200	11,000	12,000	33,000
1801	44,344	8,200	11,000	12,000	29,000
1803	15,017	8,200	11,000	12,000	32,000
1804	3,757	9,500	11,500	14,000	38,000

Coronet Head
Old-style head obverse   No motto above eagle reverse

KM# 66.1 • 16.7180 g., 0.9000 **Gold**, 0.4839 oz. AGW, 27 mm. • **Designer:** Christian Gobrecht

Date	Mintage	F-12	VF-20	XF-40	MS-60	Prf-65
1838	7,200	800	1,200	2,900	35,500	—
1839 large letters	38,248	800	1,150	1,950	32,000	—

New-style head obverse   No motto above eagle reverse

KM# 66.2 • 16.7180 g., 0.9000 **Gold**, 0.4839 oz. AGW, 27 mm. • **Designer:** Christian Gobrecht **Notes:** The 1842 varieties are distinguished by the size of the numerals in the date.

Date	Mintage	F-12	VF-20	XF-40	MS-60	Prf-65
1839 small letters	Inc. above	825	1,600	3,500	30,000	—
1840	47,338	410	435	650	10,500	—
1841	63,131	410	435	500	9,500	—
1841O	2,500	1,400	2,400	5,000	30,000	—
1842 small date	81,507	410	435	650	16,500	—
1842 large date	Inc. above	410	435	475	9,500	—
1842O	27,400	410	450	500	22,500	—
1843	75,462	410	435	500	19,000	—
1843O	175,162	410	435	475	12,000	—

1853 $10 Gold
Grade XF-40

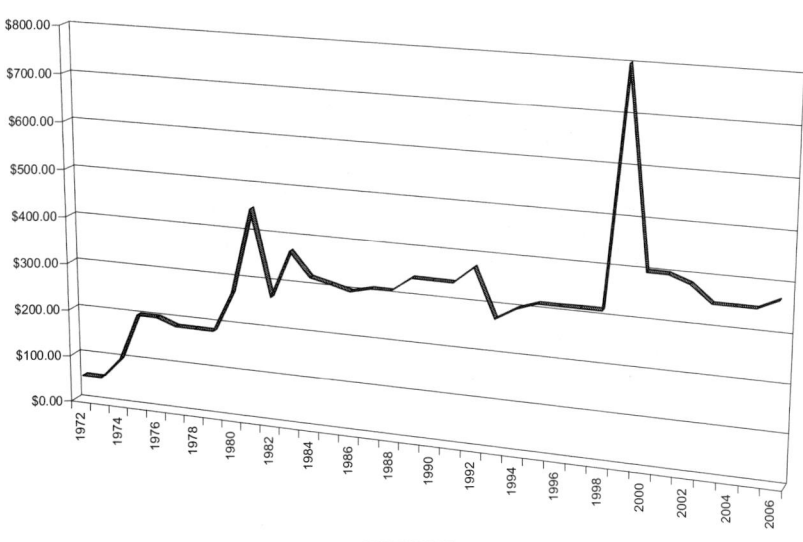

■ Retail Price

Date	Mintage	F-12	VF-20	XF-40	MS-60	Prf-65
1844	6,361	800	1,350	2,900	16,750	—
1844O	118,700	410	435	475	15,000	—
1845	26,153	410	600	775	14,000	—
1845O	47,500	410	435	700	16,500	—
1846	20,095	435	625	900	20,000	—
1846O	81,780	410	435	770	14,750	—
1847	862,258	410	435	380	3,000	—
1847O	571,500	410	435	450	4,850	—
1848	145,484	410	435	450	4,300	—
1848O	38,850	410	525	1,050	14,000	—
1849	653,618	410	435	450	3,400	—
1849O	23,900	425	710	2,100	25,000	—
1850	291,451	410	435	450	3,600	—
1850O	57,500	410	440	880	—	—
1851	176,328	410	435	500	5,150	—
1851O	263,000	410	435	450	5,750	—
1852	263,106	410	435	370	5,000	—
1852O	18,000	425	650	1,100	19,000	—
1853	201,253	410	435	450	3,500	—
1853O	51,000	410	435	500	13,000	—
1854	54,250	410	435	450	6,000	—
1854O small date	52,500	410	435	675	11,000	—
1854O large date	Inc. above	420	475	875	—	—
1854S	123,826	410	435	450	5,500	—
1855	121,701	410	435	450	4,150	—
1855O	18,000	415	435	1,250	20,000	—
1855S	9,000	800	1,500	2,500	29,500	—
1856	60,490	410	435	450	4,500	—
1856O	14,500	425	725	1,250	10,000	—
1856S	68,000	410	435	515	8,500	—
1857	16,606	410	515	850	12,000	—
1857O	5,500	600	1,000	1,850	20,000	—
1857S	26,000	410	450	1,000	10,000	—
1858	2,521	3,000	5,200	8,200	35,000	—
1858O	20,000	410	460	750	10,000	—
1858S	11,800	900	1,600	3,100	34,000	—
1859	16,093	410	435	800	10,500	—
1859O	2,300	2,000	4,000	8,200	47,500	—
1859S	7,000	1,200	1,800	4,500	40,000	—
1860	15,105	410	475	800	8,000	—
1860O	11,100	425	600	1,300	8,250	—
1860S	5,000	1,400	3,250	6,100	40,500	—
1861	113,233	410	435	450	4,000	—
1861S	15,500	690	1,600	2,950	32,500	—
1862	10,995	410	550	1,200	13,500	—
1862S	12,500	700	2,000	3,000	37,000	—
1863	1,248	2,400	3,650	10,000	42,500	—
1863S	10,000	700	1,600	3,350	24,000	—
1864	3,580	775	1,600	4,500	18,000	—
1864S	2,500	2,600	5,100	13,000	50,000	—
1865	4,005	900	1,950	3,500	32,000	—
1865S	16,700	1,700	5,500	12,000	45,000	—
1865S /inverted 186	—	1,300	3,000	6,100	50,000	—
1866S	8,500	1,000	2,800	3,800	44,000	—

New-style head obverse   "In God We Trust" above eagle reverse

KM# 102 • 16.7180 g., 0.9000 **Gold**, 0.4839 oz. AGW, 27 mm. • **Designer:** Christian Gobrecht **Notes:** The 1873 "closed-3" and "open-3" varieties are distinguished by the amount of space between the upper left and lower left serifs of the 3 in the date.

Date	Mintage	VF-20	XF-40	AU-50	MS-60	MS-63	MS-65	Prf-65
1866	3,780	850	1,800	5,000	17,000	—	—	75,000
1866S	11,500	1,550	4,000	8,000	26,000	—	—	—
1867	3,140	1,500	2,600	6,000	26,000	—	—	75,000
1867S	9,000	2,000	6,000	12,000	40,000	—	—	—
1868	10,655	550	800	2,000	18,000	—	—	60,000
1868S	13,500	1,300	2,600	4,000	24,000	—	—	—
1869	1,855	1,600	3,000	6,000	36,000	—	—	—

Date	Mintage	VF-20	XF-40	AU-50	MS-60	MS-63	MS-65	Prf-65
1869S	6,430	1,600	2,700	6,250	25,000	—	—	—
1870	4,025	850	1,500	2,500	18,000	—	—	60,000
1870CC	5,908	10,000	22,000	42,000	90,000	—	—	—
1870S	8,000	1,300	3,000	7,000	34,000	—	—	—
1871	1,820	1,600	3,000	5,000	25,000	—	—	75,000
1871CC	8,085	2,600	6,000	21,000	60,000	—	—	—
1871S	16,500	1,300	1,700	6,000	30,000	—	—	—
1872	1,650	2,400	3,600	11,000	18,000	33,000	—	60,000
1872CC	4,600	3,150	11,000	24,000	60,000	—	—	—
1872S	17,300	550	950	1,800	22,000	—	—	—
1873 closed 3	825	5,000	1,000	17,500	55,000	—	—	60,000
1873CC	4,543	6,000	12,500	28,000	58,000	—	—	—
1873S	12,000	950	2,350	5,100	25,000	—	—	—
1874	53,160	290	425	450	2,100	8,750	—	60,000
1874CC	16,767	950	3,100	10,500	40,000	—	—	—
1874S	10,000	1,150	3,250	7,250	4,000	—	—	—
1875	120	40,000	59,000	80,000	95,000	—	—	185,000

Note: 1875, Akers, Aug. 1990, Proof, $115,000.

Date	Mintage	VF-20	XF-40	AU-50	MS-60	MS-63	MS-65	Prf-65
1875CC	7,715	4,250	11,000	25,000	65,000	—	—	—
1876	732	3,500	6,250	17,000	55,000	—	—	60,000
1876CC	4,696	2,400	7,950	23,000	50,000	—	—	—
1876S	5,000	1,475	2,000	6,500	40,000	—	—	—
1877	817	2,650	5,750	9,250	—	—	—	—
1877CC	3,332	2,600	6,400	15,000	48,000	—	—	—
1877S	17,000	500	850	2,200	23,000	—	—	—
1878	73,800	420	425	450	1,000	5,000	—	60,000
1878CC	3,244	4,000	10,000	16,000	47,000	—	—	—
1878S	26,100	475	615	2,150	16,000	—	—	—
1879	384,770	420	425	450	665	2,850	—	50,000
1879/78	Inc. above	420	450	800	1,250	2,000	—	—
1879CC	1,762	9,500	15,000	26,000	60,000	—	—	—
1879O	1,500	2,300	3,750	10,000	28,750	—	—	—
1879S	224,000	420	425	450	1,100	7,750	—	—
1880	1,644,876	420	425	450	465	2,250	—	45,000
1880CC	11,190	590	900	1,800	14,500	—	—	—
1880O	9,200	450	800	1,400	13,000	—	—	—
1880S	506,250	420	425	450	465	3,300	—	—
1881	3,877,260	420	425	450	465	1,200	—	45,000
1881CC	24,015	515	800	950	7,000	20,000	—	—
1881O	8,350	550	820	1,600	6,750	—	—	—
1881S	970,000	420	425	450	465	—	—	—
1882	2,324,480	420	425	450	465	1,200	—	42,000
1882CC	6,764	950	1,300	3,000	13,000	35,000	—	—
1882O	10,820	420	575	1,200	7,700	16,750	—	—
1882S	132,000	420	425	450	465	4,200	—	—
1883	208,740	420	425	450	465	2,400	—	42,000
1883CC	12,000	575	915	2,600	14,000	35,000	—	—
1883O	800	3,300	7,200	10,500	33,500	—	—	—
1883S	38,000	420	425	450	1,350	13,000	—	—
1884	76,905	420	425	450	750	4,000	—	46,000
1884CC	9,925	600	1,100	2,250	13,000	35,000	—	—
1884S	124,250	420	425	450	575	6,500	—	—
1885	253,527	420	425	450	465	4,200	—	43,000
1885S	228,000	420	425	450	465	4,300	22,000	—
1886	236,160	420	425	450	465	1,800	—	41,000
1886S	826,000	420	425	450	465	1,500	—	—
1887	53,680	420	425	450	800	4,750	—	37,000
1887S	817,000	420	425	450	465	1,950	—	—
1888	132,996	420	425	450	850	5,700	—	38,500
1888O	21,335	420	425	450	675	4,500	—	—
1888S	648,700	420	425	450	465	2,700	—	—
1889	4,485	600	700	1,100	2,700	7,200	—	43,000
1889S	425,400	420	425	450	465	1,500	22,000	—
1890	58,043	420	425	450	825	5,200	22,000	37,500
1890CC	17,500	420	450	650	2,000	13,500	—	—
1891	91,868	420	425	450	465	1,900	—	32,500
1891CC	103,732	515	575	770	2,400	6,000	—	—
1892	797,552	420	425	450	465	1,300	13,000	38,000
1892CC	40,000	475	600	825	3,800	9,000	22,000	—
1892O	28,688	420	425	450	465	6,000	—	—
1892S	115,500	420	425	450	465	4,500	—	—
1893	1,840,895	420	425	450	465	850	—	36,000
1893CC	14,000	550	900	1,800	8,500	18,000	—	—
1893O	17,000	420	425	450	625	5,300	—	—
1893S	141,350	420	425	450	500	4,400	—	—
1894	2,470,778	420	425	450	465	1,400	22,000	35,000
1894O	107,500	420	425	475	1,200	5,250	—	—
1894S	25,000	420	450	900	3,500	8,800	—	—
1895	567,826	420	425	450	465	1,400	22,000	33,000

Date	Mintage	VF-20	XF-40	AU-50	MS-60	MS-63	MS-65	Prf-65
1895O	98,000	420	425	475	525	4,800	—	—
1895S	49,000	420	425	700	2,250	9,500	—	—
1896	76,348	420	425	450	465	2,100	—	31,500
1896S	123,750	420	425	485	2,500	11,000	—	—
1897	1,000,159	420	425	450	465	1,400	22,000	35,000
1897O	42,500	420	425	450	750	4,200	—	—
1897S	234,750	420	425	450	870	5,000	—	—
1898	812,197	420	425	450	465	1,450	22,000	35,000
1898S	473,600	420	425	450	465	4,250	—	—
1899	1,262,305	420	425	450	465	1,400	22,000	31,000
1899O	37,047	420	425	450	550	4,750	—	—
1899S	841,000	420	425	450	465	3,250	—	—
1900	293,960	420	425	450	465	1,400	22,000	30,500
1900S	81,000	420	425	450	850	5,200	—	—
1901	1,718,825	420	425	450	465	1,400	22,000	30,500
1901O	72,041	420	425	450	465	3,700	—	—
1901S	2,812,750	420	425	450	465	1,400	22,000	—
1902	82,513	420	425	450	465	2,450	—	30,500
1902S	469,500	420	425	450	465	1,400	22,000	—
1903	125,926	420	425	450	465	2,500	—	30,000
1903O	112,771	420	425	450	465	3,250	—	—
1903S	538,000	420	425	450	465	1,400	22,000	—
1904	162,038	420	425	450	465	2,400	—	31,500
1904O	108,950	420	425	450	465	3,700	—	—
1905	201,078	420	425	450	465	1,450	22,000	30,000
1905S	369,250	420	425	450	1,100	4,500	—	—
1906	165,497	420	425	450	465	2,275	22,000	30,000
1906D	981,000	420	425	450	465	1,450	22,000	—
1906O	86,895	420	425	450	470	3,400	—	—
1906S	457,000	420	425	450	515	4,400	22,000	—
1907	1,203,973	420	425	450	465	1,400	—	30,000
1907D	1,030,000	420	425	450	465	1,400	—	—
1907S	210,500	420	425	450	600	4,650	—	—

Indian Head
No motto next to eagle reverse

KM# 125 • 16.7180 g., 0.9000 **Gold**, 0.4839 oz. AGW, 27 mm. • **Designer:** Augustus Saint-Gaudens
Notes: 1907 varieties are distinguished by whether the edge is rolled or wired, and whether the legend "E Pluribus Unum" has periods between each word.

Date	Mintage	VF-20	XF-40	AU-50	MS-60	MS-63	MS-65	Prf-65
1907 wire edge, periods before and after legend	500	7,500	12,000	13,500	18,000	31,500	47,000	—
1907 same, without stars on edge, unique	—	—	—	—	—	—	—	—
1907 rolled edge, periods	42	15,000	35,000	42,500	65,000	90,000	95,000	—
1907 without periods	239,406	425	550	595	625	2,750	7,200	—
1908 without motto	33,500	425	550	595	850	4,000	14,000	—
1908D without motto	210,000	440	550	595	715	6,400	40,000	—

"In God We Trust" left of eagle reverse

KM# 130 • 16.7180 g., 0.9000 **Gold**, 0.4839 oz. AGW, 27 mm. • **Designer:** Augustus Saint-Gaudens

Date	Mintage	VF-20	XF-40	AU-50	MS-60	MS-63	MS-65	Prf-65
1908	341,486	425	550	595	625	2,100	8,000	37,000
1908D	836,500	425	550	595	770	7,000	30,000	—
1908S	59,850	475	550	595	2,700	9,500	24,000	—

1933 $10 Gold
Grade MS-60

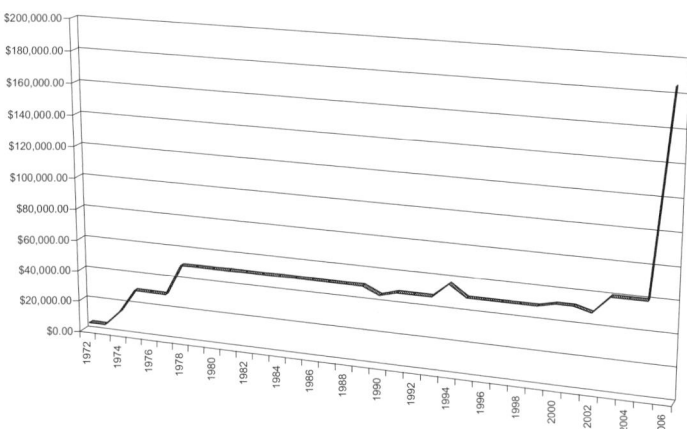

Date	Mintage	VF-20	XF-40	AU-50	MS-60	MS-63	MS-65	Prf-65
1909	184,863	425	550	595	625	2,300	10,000	43,500
1909D	121,540	425	550	595	680	3,850	44,000	—
1909S	292,350	425	550	595	690	4,350	13,500	—
1910	318,704	425	550	595	625	2,100	8,000	43,500
1910D	2,356,640	425	550	595	625	2,100	8,000	—
1910S	811,000	425	550	595	625	7,000	55,000	—
1911	505,595	425	550	595	625	2,100	7,000	37,500
1911D	30,100	575	800	950	4,000	19,000	120,000	—
1911S	51,000	425	600	650	1,300	8,200	13,000	—
1912	405,083	425	550	595	625	2,100	8,500	37,500
1912S	300,000	425	550	595	715	5,300	48,500	—
1913	442,071	425	550	595	625	2,100	8,000	37,500
1913S	66,000	600	725	595	4,000	27,500	100,000	—
1914	151,050	425	550	595	625	2,100	9,000	37,500
1914D	343,500	425	550	595	625	2,100	13,000	—
1914S	208,000	425	550	595	750	7,000	39,000	—
1915	351,075	425	550	595	625	2,100	8,000	45,000
1915S	59,000	575	725	1,000	3,300	12,000	65,000	—
1916S	138,500	425	550	595	900	4,400	19,000	—
1920S	126,500	6,000	7,500	9,000	19,000	6,500	275,000	—
1926	1,014,000	425	550	595	600	2,100	8,000	—
1930S	96,000	6,000	7,000	9,000	12,000	28,000	60,000	—
1932	4,463,000	425	550	595	6,235	2,100	8,000	—
1933	312,500	18,000	140,000	150,000	185,000	230,000	650,000	—

$20 (DOUBLE EAGLE) GOLD
Liberty
"Twenty D." below eagle. No motto above eagle reverse

KM# 74.1 • 33.4360 g., 0.9000 **Gold**, 0.9677 oz. AGW, 34 mm. • **Designer:** James B. Longacre

Date	Mintage	VF-20	XF-40	AU-50	MS-60	MS-63	MS-65	Prf-65
1849 unique, in Smithsonian collection	1	—	—	—	—	—	—	—
1850	1,170,261	850	1,150	3,000	7,000	46,000	—	—
1850O	141,000	1,000	2,400	7,600	36,000	—	—	—
1851	2,087,155	850	865	970	3,600	23,000	—	—

Date	Mintage	VF-20	XF-40	AU-50	MS-60	MS-63	MS-65	Prf-65
1851O	315,000	850	1,400	2,600	26,000	—	—	—
1852	2,053,026	850	865	1,000	3,650	14,000	—	—
1852O	190,000	900	1,100	3,800	19,000	—	—	—
1853	1,261,326	850	875	1,000	5,000	24,000	—	—
1853O	71,000	875	2,200	3,600	36,000	—	—	—
1854	757,899	850	865	1,050	6,000	24,000	—	—
1854O	3,250	45,000	70,000	165,000	350,000	—	—	—
1854S	141,468	850	900	1,500	5,000	13,000	44,000	—
1855	364,666	850	900	1,450	10,000	—	—	—
1855O	8,000	3,400	9,500	23,000	88,000	—	—	—
1855S	879,675	850	900	1,500	7,200	17,000	—	—
1856	329,878	850	865	1,200	8,900	30,000	—	—
1856O	2,250	70,000	90,000	200,000	425,000	—	—	—
1856S	1,189,750	850	865	1,300	5,500	14,000	35,000	—
1857	439,375	850	865	975	3,400	30,000	—	—
1857O	30,000	1,300	2,650	4,800	30,000	130,000	—	—
1857S	970,500	850	865	1,200	4,800	8,000	—	—
1858	211,714	875	1,000	1,500	5,800	40,000	—	—
1858O	35,250	1,750	2,600	7,600	29,000	—	—	—
1858S	846,710	850	875	1,700	10,500	—	—	—
1859	43,597	1,100	2,450	4,400	32,000	—	—	—
1859O	9,100	4,700	9,000	22,000	85,000	—	—	—
1859S	636,445	850	865	1,800	5,000	—	—	—
1860	577,670	850	865	1,000	4,400	23,000	—	—
1860O	6,600	4,650	9,000	23,000	89,000	—	—	—
1860S	544,950	850	865	1,000	6,400	23,000	—	—
1861	2,976,453	850	865	1,000	3,000	11,000	40,000	—
1861O	17,741	3,300	6,500	23,000	88,000	—	—	—
1861S	768,000	900	950	2,450	11,000	35,000	—	—

Paquet design reverse

KM# 93 • 33.4360 g., 0.9000 **Gold**, 0.9677 oz. AGW • **Notes:** In 1861 the reverse was redesigned by Anthony C. Paquet, but it was withdrawn soon after its release. The letters in the inscriptions on the Paquet-reverse variety are taller than on the regular reverse.

Date	Mintage	VF-20	XF-40	AU-50	MS-60	MS-63	MS-65	Prf-65
1861 2 Known	—	—	—	—	—	—	—	—

Note: 1861 Paquet reverse, Bowers & Merena, Nov. 1988, MS-67, $660,000.

1861S	—	12,000	24,000	52,000	185,000	—	—	—

Note: Included in mintage of 1861S, KM#74.1

Longacre design resumed reverse

KM# A74.1 • 33.4360 g., 0.9000 **Gold**, 0.9677 oz. AGW •

Date	Mintage	VF-20	XF-40	AU-50	MS-60	MS-63	MS-65	Prf-65
1862	92,133	1,000	1,600	4,000	15,500	34,000	—	—
1862S	854,173	850	1,500	2,100	13,000	—	—	—
1863	142,790	900	1,450	2,600	17,000	38,000	—	—
1863S	966,570	850	1,400	1,950	16,000	34,000	—	—
1864	204,285	875	1,000	1,750	14,000	—	—	—
1864S	793,660	850	865	1,700	6,600	—	—	—
1865	351,200	850	865	1,000	6,000	29,500	—	—
1865S	1,042,500	850	865	1,000	4,000	7,850	18,000	—
1866S	Inc. below	2,800	2,850	11,000	60,000	—	—	—

"Twenty D." below eagle. "In God We Trust" above eagle reverse

KM# 74.2 • 33.4360 g., 0.9000 **Gold**, 0.9677 oz. AGW, 34 mm. • **Designer:** James B. Longacre **Notes:** The 1873 "closed-3" and "open-3" varieties are known and are distinguished by the amount of space between the upper left and lower left serif in the 3 in the date.

Date	Mintage	VF-20	XF-40	AU-50	MS-60	MS-63	MS-65	Prf-65
1866	698,775	845	900	2,100	6,000	32,000	—	—
1866S	842,250	845	850	2,000	16,000	—	—	—
1867	251,065	845	850	925	2,400	23,000	—	—
1867S	920,750	845	850	1,600	15,000	—	—	—
1868	98,600	845	950	2,000	10,000	44,000	—	—
1868S	837,500	845	850	1,900	9,500	—	—	—
1869	175,155	845	850	1,250	6,000	24,000	—	—
1869S	686,750	845	850	1,100	5,300	33,000	—	—
1870	155,185	845	1,000	1,750	10,000	—	—	—
1870CC	3,789	100,000	150,000	260,000	700,000	—	—	—
1870S	982,000	845	850	860	5,300	27,000	—	—
1871	80,150	845	850	1,500	4,500	30,000	—	—
1871CC	17,387	6,750	11,000	27,000	45,000	—	—	—
1871S	928,000	845	850	860	4,400	22,000	—	—
1872	251,880	845	850	860	3,000	25,000	—	—
1872CC	26,900	2,200	2,500	7,000	33,000	—	—	—
1872S	780,000	845	850	860	3,000	24,000	—	—
1873 closed 3	Est. 208,925	845	850	1,100	2,600	—	—	—
1873 open 3	Est. 1,500,900	845	850	860	990	12,000	—	—
1873CC	22,410	2,600	4,750	8,000	36,000	100,000	—	—
1873S	1,040,600	845	850	860	1,800	23,000	—	—
1874	366,800	845	850	860	1,400	22,000	—	—
1874CC	115,085	1,500	1,900	2,650	9,200	—	—	—
1874S	1,214,000	845	850	860	1,700	28,000	—	—
1875	295,740	845	850	860	1,000	13,000	—	—
1875CC	111,151	1,300	1,500	1,850	3,000	19,000	—	—
1875S	1,230,000	845	850	860	1,100	18,000	—	—
1876	583,905	845	850	860	1,000	13,000	—	—
1876CC	138,441	1,300	1,500	1,900	5,750	37,000	—	—
1876S	1,597,000	845	850	860	990	12,000	—	—

"Twenty Dollars" below eagle reverse

KM# 74.3 • 33.4360 g., 0.9000 **Gold**, 0.9677 oz. AGW •

Date	Mintage	VF-20	XF-40	AU-50	MS-60	MS-63	MS-65	Prf-65
1877	397,670	825	830	840	850	5,250	—	—
1877CC	42,565	1,500	1,900	2,600	17,500	—	—	—
1877S	1,735,000	825	830	840	875	12,500	—	—
1878	543,645	825	830	840	850	5,600	—	—
1878CC	13,180	2,200	3,000	6,000	26,000	—	—	—
1878S	1,739,000	825	830	840	850	22,000	—	—
1879	207,630	825	830	840	1,000	14,000	—	—
1879CC	10,708	2,000	4,000	7,000	34,000	—	—	—
1879O	2,325	7,000	9,000	24,000	75,000	120,000	—	—
1879S	1,223,800	825	830	840	1,200	—	—	—
1880	51,456	825	830	840	3,000	16,500	—	—

Date	Mintage	VF-20	XF-40	AU-50	MS-60	MS-63	MS-65	Prf-65
1880S	836,000	825	830	840	950	16,000	—	—
1881	2,260	4,500	6,750	13,750	52,000	—	—	105,000
1881S	727,000	825	830	840	900	17,500	—	—
1882	630	8,000	22,000	35,000	80,000	135,000	—	—
1882CC	39,140	1,200	1,500	2,200	7,000	—	—	—
1882S	1,125,000	825	830	840	850	16,000	—	—
1883 proof only	92	—	—	14,000	—	—	—	—
1883CC	59,962	1,350	1,600	2,000	4,800	21,500	—	—
1883S	1,189,000	825	830	840	850	9,000	—	—
1884 proof only	71	—	—	15,000	—	—	—	150,000
1884CC	81,139	1,250	1,550	1,900	3,100	—	—	—
1884S	916,000	825	830	840	850	7,000	—	—
1885	828	7,000	8,500	12,000	35,000	—	—	—
1885CC	9,450	3,000	4,000	6,000	13,000	—	—	—
1885S	683,500	825	830	840	850	7,000	—	—
1886	1,106	9,500	12,000	33,000	45,000	57,500	—	67,000
1887	121	—	—	8,000	—	—	—	85,000
1887S	283,000	825	830	840	850	14,000	—	—
1888	226,266	825	830	840	850	4,500	32,000	—
1888S	859,600	825	8,300	840	850	5,500	—	—
1889	44,111	835	860	875	850	11,000	—	57,500
1889CC	30,945	1,500	1,600	2,200	4,700	17,500	—	—
1889S	774,700	825	830	840	850	7,250	—	—
1890	75,995	825	860	840	850	6,500	—	27,000
1890CC	91,209	1,250	1,600	2,000	4,750	22,000	—	—
1890S	802,750	825	830	840	850	8,800	—	—
1891	1,442	3,500	5,000	9,500	40,000	—	—	62,500
1891CC	5,000	3,500	7,250	9,500	20,000	45,000	—	—
1891S	1,288,125	825	830	840	850	3,500	—	—
1892	4,523	1,300	2,000	2,600	6,000	20,000	—	55,000
1892CC	27,265	1,300	1,600	2,200	5,000	31,000	—	—
1892S	930,150	825	830	840	850	4,000	—	—
1893	344,339	825	830	840	850	2,600	—	60,000
1893CC	18,402	1,600	1,900	2,500	5,000	18,000	—	—
1893S	996,175	825	830	840	850	4,000	—	—
1894	1,368,990	825	830	840	850	1,700	—	55,000
1894S	1,048,550	825	830	840	850	2,600	—	—
1895	1,114,656	825	830	840	850	1,300	13,000	54,000
1895S	1,143,500	825	830	840	850	2,500	15,000	—
1896	792,663	825	830	840	850	2,000	13,000	49,000
1896S	1,403,925	825	830	840	850	2,400	—	—
1897	1,383,261	825	830	840	850	1,350	—	55,000
1897S	1,470,250	825	830	840	850	1,400	14,000	—
1898	170,470	825	830	840	850	5,250	—	49,000
1898S	2,575,175	825	830	840	850	1,300	11,000	—
1899	1,669,384	825	830	840	850	1,050	8,500	49,000
1899S	2,010,300	825	830	840	850	1,900	12,500	—
1900	1,874,584	825	830	840	850	1,000	6,000	49,000
1900S	2,459,500	825	830	840	850	2,300	—	—
1901	111,526	825	830	840	850	1,000	6,500	—
1901S	1,596,000	825	830	840	850	3,850	—	—
1902	31,254	825	830	840	850	10,000	—	—
1902S	1,753,625	825	830	840	850	4,000	—	—
1903	287,428	825	830	840	850	1,000	6,000	51,500
1903S	954,000	825	830	840	850	1,800	12,000	—
1904	6,256,797	825	830	840	850	1,000	5,000	50,000
1904S	5,134,175	825	830	840	850	1,000	6,600	—
1905	59,011	825	830	840	850	15,000	—	—
1905S	1,813,000	825	830	840	850	3,850	16,500	—
1906	69,690	825	830	840	850	6,600	15,000	52,500
1906D	620,250	825	830	840	850	2,350	15,000	—
1906S	2,065,750	825	830	840	850	2,300	19,000	—
1907	1,451,864	825	830	840	850	1,000	7,500	—
1907D	842,250	825	830	840	850	2,350	7,000	—
1907S	2,165,800	825	830	840	850	2,400	17,000	—

1907-S $20 Gold
Grade VF-20

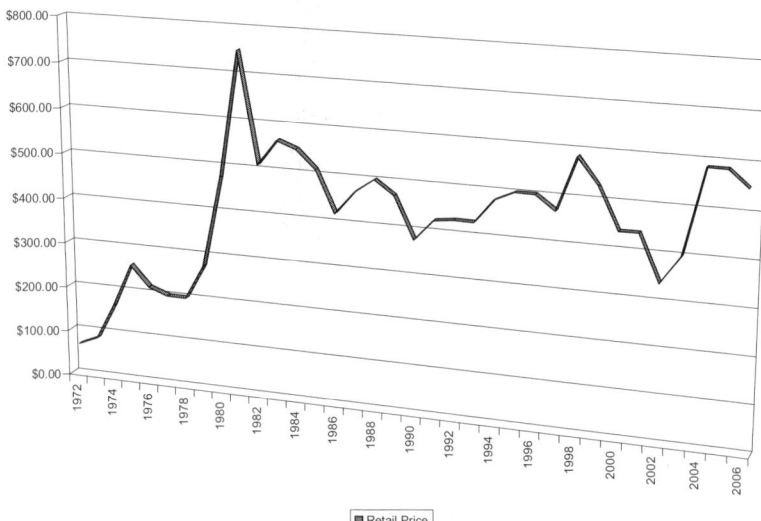

Retail Price

Saint-Gaudens
Roman numerals in date obverse   No motto below eagle reverse

KM# 126 • 33.4360 g., 0.9000 **Gold**, 0.9677 oz. AGW, 34 mm. • **Designer:** Augustus Saint-Gaudens
Edge Desc: Plain.

Date	Mintage	VF-20	XF-40	AU-50	MS-60	MS-63	MS-65	Prf-65
MCMVII (1907) high relief, unique, AU-55, $150,000	—	—	—	—	—	—	—	—
MCMVII (1907) high relief, wire rim	11,250	7,000	10,000	11,000	16,500	29,000	54,500	—
MCMVII (1907) high relief, flat rim	Inc. above	7,250	10,500	11,500	17,000	29,500	55,000	—

Arabic numerals in date obverse   No motto below eagle reverse

KM# 127 • 33.4360 g., 0.9000 **Gold**, 0.9677 oz. AGW, 34 mm. • **Designer:** Augustus Saint-Gaudens
Edge Desc: Lettered; large letters.

Date	Mintage	VF-20	XF-40	AU-50	MS-60	MS-63	MS-65	Prf-65
1907 large letters on edge, unique	—	—	—	—	—	—	—	—
1907 small letters on edge	361,667	835	845	850	905	1,100	3,400	—

Date	Mintage	VF-20	XF-40	AU-50	MS-60	MS-63	MS-65	Prf-65
1908	4,271,551	835	845	850	875	1,000	1,950	—
1908D	663,750	835	845	850	910	1,075	10,500	—

Roman numerals in date obverse   No motto below eagle reverse

KM# Pn1874 • 33.4360 g., 0.9000 **Gold**, 0.9677 oz. AGW, 34 mm. • **Designer:** Augustus Saint-Gaudens
Edge Desc: Plain. **Notes:** The "Roman numerals" varieties for 1907 use Roman numerals for the date instead of Arabic numerals. The lettered-edge varieties have "E Pluribus Unum" on the edge, with stars between the words.

Date	Mintage	VF-20	XF-40	AU-50	MS-60	MS-63	MS-65	Prf-65
1907 extremely high relief, unique	—	—	—	—	—	—	—	—
1907 extremely high relief, lettered edge	—	—	—	—	—	—	—	—

Note: 1907 extremely high relief, lettered edge, Prf-68, private sale, 1990, $1,500,000.

"In God We Trust" below eagle reverse

KM# 131 • 33.4360 g., 0.9000 **Gold**, 0.9677 oz. AGW, 34 mm. • **Designer:** Augustus Saint-Gaudens

Date	Mintage	VF-20	XF-40	AU-50	MS-60	MS-63	MS-65	Prf-65
1908	156,359	835	845	850	870	1,800	23,500	49,500
1908D	349,500	835	845	850	870	1,300	5,600	—
1908S	22,000	1,100	1,800	2,100	7,000	17,500	43,000	—
1909/8	161,282	850	900	950	1,300	6,000	35,000	—
1909	Inc. above	840	850	875	925	3,450	41,000	49,000
1909D	52,500	835	845	850	1,750	8,250	37,500	—
1909S	2,774,925	835	845	850	870	1,000	6,250	—
1910	482,167	835	845	850	870	1,000	8,600	49,000
1910D	429,000	835	845	850	870	1,100	3,100	—
1910S	2,128,250	835	845	850	870	1,000	10,000	—
1911	197,350	835	845	850	870	2,100	15,500	39,500
1911D	846,500	835	845	850	870	1,000	1,980	—
1911S	775,750	835	845	850	870	1,000	6,200	—
1912	149,824	835	845	850	870	1,800	19,500	44,000
1913	168,838	835	845	850	870	3,000	34,000	44,000

1908-D $20 Gold
Grade MS-60

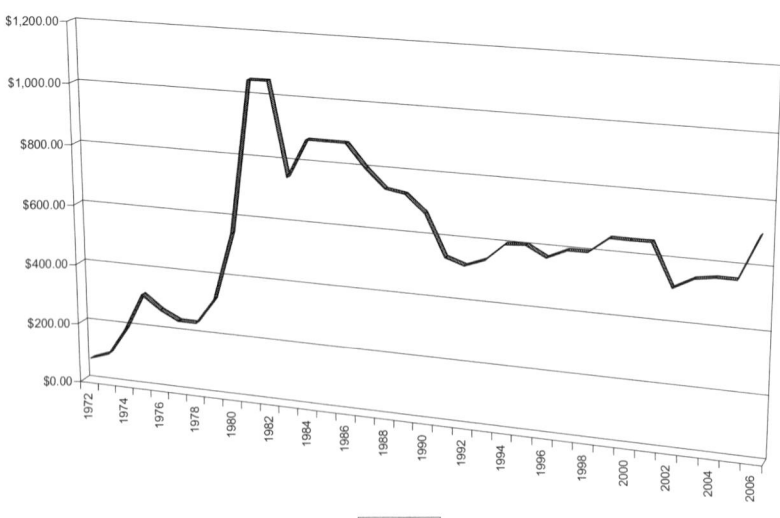

Date	Mintage	VF-20	XF-40	AU-50	MS-60	MS-63	MS-65	Prf-65
1913D	393,500	835	845	850	870	1,100	6,500	—
1913S	34,000	900	950	1,000	1,350	4,200	42,500	—
1914	95,320	835	845	850	870	3,100	23,000	41,500
1914D	453,000	835	845	850	870	1,000	3,250	—
1914S	1,498,000	835	845	850	870	1,000	2,000	—
1915	152,050	835	845	850	870	2,100	28,000	47,500
1915S	567,500	835	845	850	870	1,000	2,000	—
1916S	796,000	835	845	850	870	1,000	3,200	—
1920	228,250	835	845	850	870	1,000	62,500	—
1920S	558,000	7,500	14,000	21,000	41,000	95,000	210,000	—
1921	528,500	12,000	23,000	30,000	90,000	200,000	950,000	—
1922	1,375,500	835	845	850	870	1,000	3,600	—
1922S	2,658,000	835	845	850	2,200	4,500	43,000	—
1923	566,000	850	875	900	870	1,000	6,350	—
1923D	1,702,250	835	845	850	870	1,000	1,980	—
1924	4,323,500	835	845	850	870	1,000	1,980	—
1924D	3,049,500	950	1,500	1,700	2,800	8,250	75,000	—
1924S	2,927,500	900	1,500	1,750	3,000	8,000	47,500	—
1925	2,831,750	835	845	850	870	1,000	1,980	—
1925D	2,938,500	1,200	2,100	2,300	3,800	10,000	96,000	—
1925S	3,776,500	1,150	1,900	2,700	8,500	26,000	96,000	—
1926	816,750	835	845	850	870	1,000	1,980	—
1926D	481,000	2,000	6,000	7,000	15,500	34,000	115,000	—
1926S	2,041,500	900	1,500	1,650	2,200	4,800	36,000	—
1927	2,946,750	835	845	850	870	1,000	1,980	—
1927D	180,000	100,000	210,000	265,000	340,000	1,600,000	2,100,000	—
1927S	3,107,000	4,000	7,000	7,000	15,000	57,500	115,000	—
1928	8,816,000	835	845	850	870	1,000	1,980	—
1929	1,779,750	4,750	8,000	10,000	13,500	26,000	70,000	—
1930S	74,000	8,000	20,000	22,000	28,000	130,000	150,000	—
1931	2,938,250	6,000	12,000	15,000	20,000	45,000	75,000	—
1931D	106,500	7,000	12,000	20,000	30,000	47,500	80,000	—
1932	1,101,750	8,000	13,500	15,000	21,000	34,000	70,000	—
1933 Sotheby/Stack Sale, July 2002	445,500	—	—	—	—	—	7,590,000	—

MINT SETS

Mint, or uncirculated, sets contain one uncirculated coin of each denomination from each mint produced for circulation that year. Values listed here are only for those sets sold by the U.S. Mint. Sets were not offered in years not listed. In years when the Mint did not offer the sets, some private companies compiled and marketed uncirculated sets. Mint sets from 1947 through 1958 contained two examples of each coin mounted in cardboard holders, which caused the coins to tarnish. Beginning in 1959, the sets have been packaged in sealed Pliofilm packets and include only one specimen of each coin struck for that year (both P & D mints). Listings for 1965, 1966 and 1967 are for "special mint sets," which were of higher quality than regular mint sets and were prooflike. They were packaged in plastic cases. The 1970 large-date and small-date varieties are distinguished by the size of the date on the coin. The 1976 three-piece set contains the quarter, half dollar and dollar with the Bicentennial design. The 1971 and 1972 sets do not include a dollar coin; the 1979 set does not include an S-mint-marked dollar.

Date	Sets Sold	Issue Price	Value	Date	Sets Sold	Issue Price	Value
1947 Est. 5,000	—	4.87	1,400	1976	1,892,513	6.00	7.50
1948 Est. 6,000	—	4.92	650	1977	2,006,869	7.00	9.50
1949 Est. 5,200	—	5.45	900	1978	2,162,609	7.00	10.50
1950 None issued	—	—	—	1979	2,526,000	8.00	7.25
1951	8,654	6.75	1,000	1980	2,815,066	9.00	7.50
1952	11,499	6.14	900	1981	2,908,145	11.00	14.50
1953	15,538	6.14	560	1982 & 1983 None issued	—	—	—
1954	25,599	6.19	295	1984	1,832,857	7.00	6.50
1955	49,656	3.57	175	1985	1,710,571	7.00	7.50
1956	45,475	3.34	165	1986	1,153,536	7.00	17.25
1957	32,324	4.40	285	1987	2,890,758	7.00	8.50
1958	50,314	4.43	160	1988	1,646,204	7.00	8.50
1959	187,000	2.40	62.50	1989	1,987,915	7.00	6.00
1960	260,485	2.40	35.00	1990	1,809,184	7.00	7.00
1961	223,704	2.40	51.25	1991	1,352,101	7.00	10.50
1962	385,285	2.40	19.00	1992	1,500,143	7.00	6.50
1963	606,612	2.40	17.00	1993	1,297,094	8.00	8.50
1964	1,008,108	2.40	17.00	1994	1,234,813	8.00	9.00
1965 Special Mint Set	2,360,000	4.00	10.25	1995	1,038,787	8.00	22.00
1966 Special Mint Set	2,261,583	4.00	10.50	1996	1,457,949	8.00	28.00
1967 Special Mint Set	1,863,344	4.00	20.00	1997	950,473	8.00	30.00
1968	2,105,128	2.50	6.00	1998	1,187,325	8.00	9.50
1969	1,817,392	2.50	9.25	1999	1,421,625	14.95	29.25
1970 large date	2,038,134	2.50	19.00	2000	1,490,160	14.95	12.25
1970 small date	Inc. above	2.50	60.00	2001	1,066,900	14.95	18.50
1971	2,193,396	3.50	7.50	2002	1,139,388	14.95	13.75
1972	2,750,000	3.50	7.75	2003	1,002,555	14.95	23.75
1973	1,767,691	6.00	22.00	2004	1,160,000	16.95	83.50
1974	1,975,981	6.00	8.00	2005	—	16.95	26.00
1975	1,921,488	6.00	10.50	2006	—	16.95	—
1976 3 coins	4,908,319	9.00	15.00				

PROOF SETS

Proof coins are produced through a special process involving specially selected, highly polished planchets and dies. They usually receive two strikings from the coin press at increased pressure. The result is a coin with mirrorlike surfaces and, in recent years, a cameo effect on its raised design surfaces. Proof sets have been sold off and on by the U.S. Mint since 1858. Listings here are for sets from what is commonly called the modern era, since 1936. Values for earlier proofs are included in regular date listings. Sets were not offered in years not listed. Since 1968, proof sets have been produced at the San Francisco Mint; before that they were produced at the Philadelphia Mint. In 1942 the five-cent coin was struck in two compositions. Some proof sets for that year contain only one type (five-coin set); others contain both types. Two types of packaging were used in 1955 -- a box and a flat, plastic holder. The 1960 large-date and small-date sets are distinguished by the size of the date on the cent. Some 1968 sets are missing the mint mark on the dime, the result of an error in the preparation of an obverse die. The 1970 large-date and small-date sets are distinguished by the size of the date on the cent. Some 1970 sets are missing the mint mark on the dime, the result of an error in the preparation of an obverse die. Some 1971 sets are missing the mint mark on the five-cent piece, the result of an error in the preparation of an obverse die. The 1976 three-piece set contains the quarter, half dollar and dollar with the Bicentennial designs. The 1979 and 1981 Type II sets have clearer mint marks than the Type I sets for those years. Some 1983 sets are missing the mint mark on the dime, the result of an error in the preparation of an obverse die. Prestige sets contain the five regular-issue coins plus a commemorative silver dollar from that year.

Date	Sets Sold	Issue Price	Value	Date	Sets Sold	Issue Price	Value
1936	3,837	1.89	8,000	1951	57,500	2.10	685
1937	5,542	1.89	4,400	1952	81,980	2.10	380
1938	8,045	1.89	2,000	1953	128,800	2.10	335
1939	8,795	1.89	1,850	1954	233,300	2.10	175
1940	11,246	1.89	1,550	1955 box	378,200	2.10	150
1941	15,287	1.89	1,550	1955 flat pack	Inc. above	2.10	160
1942 6 coins	21,120	1.89	1,550	1956	669,384	2.10	65.00
1942 5 coins	Inc. above	1.89	1,400	1957	1,247,952	2.10	28.50
1950	51,386	2.10	800	1958	875,652	2.10	65.00

Date	Sets Sold	Issue Price	Value	Date	Sets Sold	Issue Price	Value
1959	1,149,291	2.10	26.00	1992S Silver	1,009,585	21.00	18.00
1960 large date	1,691,602	2.10	22.50	1992S Silver premier	308,055	37.00	18.00
1960 small date	Inc. above	2.10	36.00	1993S	2,337,819	12.50	13.50
1961	3,028,244	2.10	12.00	1993S Prestige Set	224,045	57.00	45.00
1962	3,218,019	2.10	12.00	1993S Silver	570,213	21.00	41.50
1963	3,075,645	2.10	15.50	1993S Silver premier	191,140	37.00	41.50
1964	3,950,762	2.10	12.00	1994S	2,308,701	13.00	14.00
1968S	3,041,509	5.00	8.00	1994S Prestige Set	175,893	57.00	55.00
1968S no mint mark dime	Inc. above	5.00	11,000	1994S Silver	636,009	21.00	49.00
1969S	2,934,631	5.00	8.00	1994S Silver premier	149,320	37.50	49.00
1970S large date	2,632,810	5.00	13.00	1995S	2,010,384	12.50	51.25
1970S small date	Inc. above	5.00	100.00	1995S Prestige Set	107,112	57.00	205
1970S no mint mark dime	Inc. above	5.00	1,350	1995S Silver	549,878	21.00	110
1971S	3,224,138	5.00	6.25	1995S Silver premier	130,107	37.50	110
1971S no mint mark nickel				1996S	2,085,191	16.00	18.50
Est. 1,655	1,655	5.00	1,350	1996S Prestige Set	55,000	57.00	650
1972S	3,267,667	5.50	6.00	1996S Silver	623,655	21.00	53.50
1973S	2,769,624	7.00	10.50	1996S Silver premier	151,366	37.50	53.50
1974S	2,617,350	7.00	9.00	1997S	1,975,000	12.50	42.50
1975S	2,909,369	7.00	13.00	1997S Prestige Set	80,000	57.00	230
1975S no mint mark dime	Inc. above	7.00	50,000	1997S Silver	605,473	21.00	91.00
1976S 3 coins	3,998,621	12.00	20.50	1997S Silver premier	136,205	37.50	91.00
1976S	4,149,730	7.00	12.50	1998S	2,078,494	12.50	27.00
1977S	3,251,152	9.00	8.50	1998S Silver	638,134	21.00	39.50
1978S	3,127,788	9.00	9.50	1998S Silver premier	240,658	37.50	39.50
1979S Type I	3,677,175	9.00	9.00	1999S	2,557,899	19.95	85.00
1979S Type II	Inc. above	9.00	135	1999S 5 quarter set	1,169,958	13.95	77.50
1980S	3,547,030	10.00	8.50	1999S Silver	804,565	31.95	425
1981S Type I	4,063,083	11.00	9.00	2000S	3,097,442	19.95	25.00
1981S Type II	Inc. above	11.00	440	2000S 5 quarter set	995,803	13.95	13.00
1982S	3,857,479	11.00	6.00	2000S Silver	965,421	31.95	37.50
1983S	3,138,765	11.00	6.50	2001S	2,249,498	19.95	135
1983S Prestige Set	140,361	59.00	110	2001S 5 quarter set	774,800	13.95	61.00
1983S no mint mark dime	Inc. above	11.00	1,000	2001S Silver	849,600	31.95	170
1984S	2,748,430	11.00	8.00	2002S	2,319,766	19.95	38.50
1984S Prestige Set	316,680	59.00	29.25	2002S 5 quarter set	764,419	13.95	23.50
1985S	3,362,821	11.00	7.00	2002S Silver	892,229	31.95	67.50
1986S	2,411,180	11.00	13.00	2003 X#207, 208, 209.2	—	44.00	28.75
1986S Prestige Set	599,317	48.50	42.50	2003S	2,175,684	19.95	25.50
1987S	3,972,233	11.00	7.00	2003S 5 quarter set	1,225,507	13.95	20.00
1987S Prestige Set	435,495	45.00	27.50	2003S Silver	1,142,858	31.95	32.50
1988S	3,031,287	11.00	8.00	2004S 11 pieces	2,275,000	22.95	63.50
1988S Prestige Set	231,661	45.00	40.00	2004S 5 quarter set	987,960	15.95	30.00
1989S	3,009,107	11.00	8.00	2004S Silver 11 pieces	1,187,673	37.95	50.00
1989S Prestige Set	211,087	45.00	47.50	2004S Silver 5 quarter set	594,137	23.95	30.00
1990S	2,793,433	11.00	8.50	2005S 11 Pieces	—	22.95	28.00
1990S no S 1¢	3,555	11.00	7,500	2005S 5 quarter set	—	15.95	20.00
1990S Prestige Set	506,126	45.00	28.00	2005S Silver 11 pieces	—	37.95	28.50
1990S Prestige Set, no S 1¢	Inc. above	45.00	8,000	2005S Silver 5 quarter set	—	23.95	—
1991S	2,610,833	11.00	13.50	2006S 10 pieces clad	—	22.95	—
1991S Prestige Set	256,954	59.00	76.00	2006S 5 quarter set	—	15.95	—
1992S	2,675,618	12.00	8.50	2006S Silver 10 pieces	—	37.95	—
1992S Prestige Set	183,285	59.00	100.00	2006S Silver 5 quarter set	—	23.95	—

1952 Proof Set

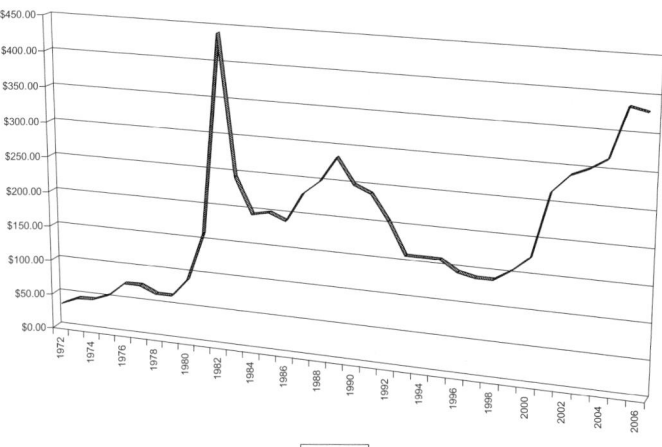

Retail Price

UNCIRCULATED ROLLS

Listings are for rolls containing uncirculated coins. Large date and small date varieties for 1960 and 1970 apply to the one cent coins.

Date	Cents	Nickels	Dimes	Quarters	Halves
1938	400	260	1,050	3,300	1,900
1938D	475	250	900	—	—
1938S	425	360	1,250	3,500	—
1939	130	80.00	600	1,000	1,250
1939D	265	3,600	550	1,850	2,000
1939S	205	1,200	1,500	3,300	2,400
1940	165	130	500	1,700	1,000
1940D	185	110	640	4,500	—
1940S	180	200	650	1,300	1,200
1941	115	92.00	390	800	750
1941D	215	180	650	2,950	1,200
1941S	375	180	415	2,500	3,250
1942	70.00	260	400	440	700
1942P	—	500	—	—	—
1942D	50.00	1,700	590	1,000	1,300
1942S	675	480	900	5,500	1,400
1943	130	270	400	425	700
1943D	200	280	485	2,250	1,800
1943S	500	280	580	2,000	1,400
1944	40.00	660	400	425	700
1944D	40.00	520	515	800	1,250
1944S	45.00	360	415	850	1,300
1945	50.00	300	400	380	700
1945D	60.00	280	415	1,100	1,050
1945S	38.00	270	400	650	950
1946	30.00	92.00	155	440	1,050
1946D	32.00	96.00	180	440	850
1946S	40.00	42.00	200	415	900
1947	150	48.00	290	850	1,000
1947D	30.00	60.00	340	750	950
1947S	155	60.00	180	660	—
1948	40.00	60.00	190	300	500
1948D	60.00	110	300	675	375
1948S	140	90.00	190	470	—
1949	128	180	1,400	2,250	1,750
1949D	100.00	160	550	1,650	1,440
1949S	200	92.00	2,200	—	2,500
1950	50.00	120	460	385	960
1950D	40.00	600	230	360	960
1950S	60.00	—	1,800	530	—
1951	65.00	220	130	460	430
1951D	25.00	360	100.00	440	850
1951S	61.00	160	550	1,300	800
1952	135	120	110	440	420
1952D	25.00	240	115	370	265
1952S	175	48.00	275	1,100	875
1953	30.00	20.00	140	575	400
1953D	25.00	18.00	140	240	200
1953S	42.00	60.00	60.00	350	750
1954	20.00	50.00	55.00	350	250
1954D	20.00	30.00	48.50	350	180
1954S	25.00	72.00	37.50	200	490
1955	22.00	30.00	40.00	150	500
1955D	20.00	11.00	40.00	100.00	—
1955S	25.00	—	35.00	—	—
1956	12.00	8.40	35.00	225	340
1956D	12.00	8.00	35.00	170	—
1957	12.00	12.00	36.00	140	175
1957D	12.00	6.00	41.50	85.00	175
1958	12.00	10.00	35.00	70.00	140
1958D	12.00	4.50	35.00	70.00	140
1959	2.00	7.00	35.00	72.50	135
1959D	2.00	7.00	35.00	70.00	160
1960 large date	2.00	7.00	35.00	70.00	135
1960 small date	240	—	—	—	—
1960D large date	2.00	7.00	35.00	70.00	135
1960D small date	2.50	—	—	—	—
1961	2.00	7.00	35.00	70.00	140
1961D	2.00	7.00	35.00	75.00	125
1962	2.00	6.00	35.00	75.00	120
1962D	2.00	7.00	35.00	70.00	105
1963	2.00	5.25	35.00	70.00	110
1963D	2.00	5.50	35.00	75.00	110
1964	2.00	4.50	35.00	66.00	75.00

Date	Cents	Nickels	Dimes	Quarters	Halves
1964D	2.00	4.50	35.00	66.00	75.00
1965	3.00	5.75	8.50	30.00	30.00
1966	6.00	5.00	11.00	28.00	30.00
1967	12.00	10.00	16.00	27.00	30.00
1968	5.00	—	8.50	40.00	—
1968D	3.00	7.00	10.00	35.00	28.00
1968S	4.00	6.25	—	—	—
1969	10.00	—	44.00	110	—
1969D	2.00	5.50	15.00	60.00	28.00
1969S	4.00	5.25	—	—	—
1970	5.00	—	8.00	30.00	—
1970D	4.00	4.50	8.50	16.00	375
1970S	4.00	4.50	—	—	—
1970S small date	2,500	—	—	—	—
1971	8.00	30.00	16.00	42.50	30.00
1971D	8.00	6.00	9.50	22.50	19.00
1971S	6.00	—	—	—	—
1972	3.00	6.00	10.00	25.00	38.00
1972D	3.00	4.50	11.00	22.50	32.00
1972S	4.00	—	—	—	—
1973	2.00	4.50	11.50	25.00	40.00
1973D	2.00	6.00	12.00	27.00	26.00
1973S	4.00	—	—	—	—
1974	1.50	4.50	8.50	22.00	22.00
1974D	1.50	6.00	10.00	18.00	24.00
1974S	4.00	—	—	—	—
1975	2.00	11.00	14.00	—	—
1975D	2.00	4.50	12.50	—	—
1976	2.00	15.00	20.00	22.50	22.00
1976D	5.00	14.00	19.00	23.00	22.00
1977	2.00	4.50	12.50	17.00	30.00
1977D	2.00	6.00	8.50	18.50	36.00
1978	3.00	4.50	10.00	16.00	48.00
1978D	3.00	5.00	8.00	17.00	90.00
1979	2.00	5.00	8.50	17.00	30.00
1979D	2.00	5.50	8.00	24.00	32.00
1980	2.00	4.50	10.00	17.00	22.00
1980D	2.00	4.50	8.00	19.00	23.00
1981	2.00	4.50	10.00	19.00	33.00
1981D	2.00	4.50	10.00	19.00	28.00
1982	2.00	275	250	220	85.00
1982D	2.00	76.00	60.00	90.00	60.00
1983	6.00	85.00	240	1,500	80.00
1983D	18.00	36.00	45.00	480	80.00
1984	8.00	34.00	10.00	20.00	40.00
1984D	25.00	5.00	25.00	30.00	52.00
1985	10.00	10.00	11.00	40.00	80.00
1985D	6.00	8.00	9.50	24.00	75.00
1986	40.00	8.00	27.50	125	145
1986D	50.00	42.00	26.00	275	115
1987	5.00	6.00	10.00	19.00	95.00
1987D	6.00	4.50	10.00	19.00	95.00
1988	9.00	5.50	10.25	41.50	98.00
1988D	9.00	8.00	9.50	24.00	63.00
1989	4.00	5.50	20.00	22.50	63.00
1989D	4.00	8.00	13.50	21.00	46.00
1990	3.00	10.00	15.00	29.00	56.00
1990D	3.00	11.00	12.50	30.00	76.00
1991	3.00	12.50	15.00	35.00	80.00
1991D	3.00	12.50	20.00	35.00	120
1992	3.00	48.00	10.00	26.00	36.00
1992D	5.00	8.50	10.00	34.00	65.00
1993	4.00	11.50	9.50	45.00	50.00
1993D	4.50	12.50	15.00	37.50	65.00
1994	3.00	7.00	12.50	45.00	18.00
1994D	3.00	6.00	12.50	45.00	32.50
1995	2.25	7.50	17.50	45.00	18.00
1995D	2.25	20.00	21.00	45.00	13.00
1996	2.00	5.50	11.00	22.00	15.00
1996D	2.50	7.50	11.50	28.00	20.00
1997	2.00	13.50	31.00	24.00	20.00
1997D	2.00	32.50	8.50	40.00	14.50
1998	2.25	12.50	10.50	30.00	14.50
1998D	2.25	13.50	9.00	24.00	15.00
1999P	2.50	6.00	25.00	—	18.00
1999D	2.50	5.50	12.00	—	17.50
2000P	2.00	6.00	10.00	—	14.50
2000D	2.00	3.50	10.00	—	20.00
2001P	2.00	6.00	10.00	—	18.00

Date	Cents	Nickels	Dimes	Quarters	Halves
2001D	2.00	4.50	10.00	—	15.00
2002P	2.00	3.40	10.00	—	28.00
2002D	2.00	3.40	8.00	—	32.00
2003P	2.00	3.50	8.00	—	35.00
2003D	2.00	3.50	8.00	—	35.00
2004P Peace	1.50	25.00	8.00	—	20.00
2004D Peace	1.50	9.50	8.00	—	20.00
2004P Keelboat	1.50	7.50	8.00	—	20.00
2004D Keelboat	1.50	6.00	8.50	—	20.00
2005P Buffalo	1.50	6.00	8.00	—	20.00
2005D Buffalo	1.50	5.50	8.00	—	20.00
2005P Ocean	1.50	5.50	8.00	—	20.00
2005D Ocean	1.50	5.50	8.00	—	20.00

COMMEMORATIVE COINAGE

All commemorative half dollars of 1892-1954 have the following specifications: diameter -- 30.6 millimeters; weight -- 12.5000 grams; composition -- 0.9000 silver, 0.3617 ounces actual silver weight. Values for PDS sets contain one example each from the Philadelphia, Denver and San Francisco mints. Type coin prices are the most inexpensive single coin available from the date and mint-mark combinations listed.

QUARTER

KM# 115 COLUMBIAN EXPOSITION Weight: 6.2500 g. **Composition:** 0.9000 Silver, 0.1808 oz. ASW **Diameter:** 24.3mm. **Obv:** Queen Isabella

Date	Mintage	AU-50	MS-60	MS-63	MS-64	MS-65
1893	24,214	640	720	960	1,400	3,800

HALF DOLLAR

KM# 117 COLUMBIAN EXPOSITION Obv. Designer: Charles E. Barber **Rev. Designer:** George T. Morgan

Date	Mintage	AU-50	MS-60	MS-63	MS-64	MS-65
1892	950,000	19.00	30.00	80.00	200	825
1893	1,550,405	16.00	30.00	80.00	215	1,000

KM# 135 PANAMA-PACIFIC EXPOSITION Designer: Charles E. Barber

Date	Mintage	AU-50	MS-60	MS-63	MS-64	MS-65
1915S	27,134	495	570	860	1,700	1,925

KM# 143 LINCOLN-ILLINOIS Obv. Designer: George T. Morgan **Rev. Designer:** John R. Sinnock

Date	Mintage	AU-50	MS-60	MS-63	MS-64	MS-65
1918	100,058	145	160	175	265	525

KM# 146 MAINE CENTENNIAL Designer: Anthony de Francisci

Date	Mintage	AU-50	MS-60	MS-63	MS-64	MS-65
1920	50,028	140	175	225	330	615

KM# 147.1 PILGRIM TERCENTENARY Designer: Cyrus E. Dallin

Date	Mintage	AU-50	MS-60	MS-63	MS-64	MS-65
1920	152,112	92.50	115	130	160	550

1892 Columbian Expo Half
Grade MS-60

■ Retail Price

KM# 147.2 PILGRIM TERCENTENARY Obv:
1921 date next to Pilgrim **Designer:** Cyrus E. Dallin

Date	Mintage	AU-50	MS-60	MS-63	MS-64	MS-65
1921	20,053	185	220	235	285	600

KM# 148.2 ALABAMA CENTENNIAL Obv.
Designer: Laura G. Fraser

Date	Mintage	AU-50	MS-60	MS-63	MS-64	MS-65
1921	59,038	220	225	550	825	2,400

KM# 149.1 MISSOURI CENTENNIAL Designer:
Robert Aitken

Date	Mintage	AU-50	MS-60	MS-63	MS-64	MS-65
1921	15,428	430	750	1,000	1,850	6,250

2x2

KM# 148.1 ALABAMA CENTENNIAL Obv: "2x2"
at right above stars **Designer:** Laura G. Fraser

Date	Mintage	AU-50	MS-60	MS-63	MS-64	MS-65
1921	6,006	330	340	630	1,000	2,600

2x4

KM# 149.2 MISSOURI CENTENNIAL Obv: 2 star 4 in field at left **Designer:** Robert Aitken

Date	Mintage	AU-50	MS-60	MS-63	MS-64	MS-65
1921	5,000	680	840	1,180	2,100	5,850

KM# 151.1 GRANT MEMORIAL Designer: Laura G. Fraser

Date	Mintage	AU-50	MS-60	MS-63	MS-64	MS-65
1922	67,405	125	135	170	325	850

KM# 151.2 GRANT MEMORIAL Obv: Star above the word "Grant" **Designer:** Laura G. Fraser

Date	Mintage	AU-50	MS-60	MS-63	MS-64	MS-65
1922	4,256	1,000	1,350	2,200	3,150	8,250

KM# 153 MONROE DOCTRINE CENTENNIAL Designer: Chester Beach

Date	Mintage	AU-50	MS-60	MS-63	MS-64	MS-65
1923S	274,077	62.50	80.00	155	570	3,750

KM# 154 HUGUENOT-WALLOON TERCENTENARY Obv: Huguenot leader Gaspard de Coligny and William I of Orange **Designer:** George T. Morgan

Date	Mintage	AU-50	MS-60	MS-63	MS-64	MS-65
1924	142,080	150	160	185	260	475

KM# 155 CALIFORNIA DIAMOND JUBILEE Designer: Jo Mora

Date	Mintage	AU-50	MS-60	MS-63	MS-64	MS-65
1925S	86,594	200	230	275	500	1,225

KM# 158 FORT VANCOUVER CENTENNIAL Designer: Laura G. Fraser

Date	Mintage	AU-50	MS-60	MS-63	MS-64	MS-65
1925	14,994	345	445	450	625	1,500

KM# 156 LEXINGTON-CONCORD SESQUICENTENNIAL Designer: Chester Beach

Date	Mintage	AU-50	MS-60	MS-63	MS-64	MS-65
1925	162,013	96.00	115	130	200	640

KM# 157.1 STONE MOUNTAIN MEMORIAL
Designer: Gutzon Borglum

Date	Mintage	AU-50	MS-60	MS-63	MS-64	MS-65
1925	1,314,7					
	09	72.50	80.00	90.00	92.50	285

KM# 159 OREGON TRAIL MEMORIAL
Designer: James E. and Laura G. Fraser

Date	Mintage	AU-50	MS-60	MS-63	MS-64	MS-65
1926	47,955	150	180	190	210	350
1926S	83,055	150	180	190	210	320
1928	6,028	230	260	295	300	390
1933D	5,008	400	415	425	430	580
1934D	7,006	210	230	245	250	345
1936	10,006	168	200	215	220	320

Date	Mintage	AU-50	MS-60	MS-63	MS-64	MS-65
1936S	5,006	180	200	225	230	375
1937D	12,008	190	215	223	225	320
1938 PDS set	6,005	515	560	675	700	960
1939 PDS set	3,004	1,665	1,875	1,900	1,910	2,300

KM# 160 U.S. SESQUICENTENNIAL   Designer:
John R. Sinnock

Date	Mintage	AU-50	MS-60	MS-63	MS-64	MS-65
1926	141,120	98.00	115	160	615	5,500

KM# 162 VERMONT SESQUICENTENNIAL
Obv. Designer: Charles Keck

Date	Mintage	AU-50	MS-60	MS-63	MS-64	MS-65
1927	28,142	280	300	315	350	1,100

1926 Oregon Trail Half
Grade MS-60

Retail Price

KM# 163 HAWAIIAN SESQUICENTENNIAL
Designer: Juliette M. Fraser

Date	Mintage	AU-50	MS-60	MS-63	MS-64	MS-65
1928	10,008	1,825	2,750	3,450	4,200	7,000

KM# 165.1 DANIEL BOONE BICENTENNIAL
Designer: Augustus Lukeman

Date	Mintage	AU-50	MS-60	MS-63	MS-64	MS-65
1934	10,007	130	135	145	150	240
1935 PDS set	2,003	960	1,040	1,050	1,150	2,150

KM# 165.2 DANIEL BOONE BICENTENNIAL
Rev: "1934" added above the word "Pioneer."
Designer: Augustus Lukeman

Date	Mintage	AU-50	MS-60	MS-63	MS-64	MS-65
1935 PDS set	5,005	400	415	440	460	735
Type coin	—	130	135	145	150	240
1936 PDS set	5,005	400	415	440	460	735
1937 PDS set	2,506	860	965	975	980	1,400
1938 PDS set	2,100	1,150	1,250	1,275	1,290	1,825

KM# 166 MARYLAND TERCENTENARY
Designer: Hans Schuler

Date	Mintage	AU-50	MS-60	MS-63	MS-64	MS-65
1934	25,015	168	185	195	220	400

KM# 167 TEXAS CENTENNIAL Designer:
Pompeo Coppini

Date	Mintage	AU-50	MS-60	MS-63	MS-64	MS-65
1934	61,463	145	158	163	165	260
Type coin	—	145	158	163	165	260

Date	Mintage	AU-50	MS-60	MS-63	MS-64	MS-65
1935 PDS set	9,994	435	475	495	500	790
1936 PDS set	8,911	435	475	495	500	790
1937 PDS set	6,571	435	475	495	500	790
1938 PDS set	3,775	750	840	960	960	1,575

KM# 168 ARKANSAS CENTENNIAL Designer:
Edward E. Burr

Date	Mintage	AU-50	MS-60	MS-63	MS-64	MS-65
Type coin	—	110	115	125	130	210
1935 PDS set	5,505	335	350	380	405	825
1936 PDS set	9,600	335	350	380	405	850
1937 PDS set	5,505	335	350	380	415	1,050
1938 PDS set	3,155	510	590	610	625	2,000
1939 PDS set	—	1,000	1,200	1,300	1,315	3,500

KM# 169 CONNECTICUT TERCENTENARY
Designer: Henry Kreiss

Date	Mintage	AU-50	MS-60	MS-63	MS-64	MS-65
1935	25,018	260	305	315	385	645

KM# 170 HUDSON, N.Y., SESQUICENTENNIAL
Designer: Chester Beach

Date	Mintage	AU-50	MS-60	MS-63	MS-64	MS-65
1935	10,008	770	960	1,200	1,550	2,200

KM# 172 OLD SPANISH TRAIL Designer: L.W.
Hoffecker

Date	Mintage	AU-50	MS-60	MS-63	MS-64	MS-65
1935	10,008	1,250	1,400	1,550	1,600	2,000

KM# 171 SAN DIEGO, CALIFORNIA - PACIFIC EXPOSITION **Designer:** Robert Aitken

Date	Mintage	AU-50	MS-60	MS-63	MS-64	MS-65
1935S	70,132	105	140	150	153	180
1936D	30,092	105	150	155	160	185

KM# 173 ALBANY, N.Y., CHARTER ANNIVERSARY **Designer:** Gertrude K. Lathrop

Date	Mintage	AU-50	MS-60	MS-63	MS-64	MS-65
1936	17,671	340	350	380	375	430

KM# 187 ARKANSAS CENTENNIAL **Obv:** Sen. Joseph T. Robinson **Obv. Designer:** Henry Kreiss **Rev. Designer:** Edward E. Burr

Date	Mintage	AU-50	MS-60	MS-63	MS-64	MS-65
1936	25,265	155	165	175	178	450

KM# 181 BATTLE OF GETTYSBURG 75TH ANNIVERSARY **Designer:** Frank Vittor

Date	Mintage	AU-50	MS-60	MS-63	MS-64	MS-65
1936	26,928	435	475	505	525	775

KM# 175 BRIDGEPORT, CONN., CENTENNIAL **Designer:** Henry Kreiss

Date	Mintage	AU-50	MS-60	MS-63	MS-64	MS-65
1936	25,015	180	185	210	220	315

KM# 176 CINCINNATI MUSIC CENTER **Designer:** Constance Ortmayer

Date	Mintage	AU-50	MS-60	MS-63	MS-64	MS-65
Type coin	—	335	345	375	560	700
1936 PDS set	5,005	1,000	1,025	1,125	1,700	2,850

KM# 177 CLEVELAND-GREAT LAKES EXPOSITION **Designer:** Brenda Putnam

Date	Mintage	AU-50	MS-60	MS-63	MS-64	MS-65
1936	50,030	143	145	160	165	268

KM# 178 COLUMBIA, S.C., SESQUICENTENNIAL **Designer:** A. Wolfe Davidson

Date	Mintage	AU-50	MS-60	MS-63	MS-64	MS-65
1936 PDS set	9,007	785	800	880	900	920
Type coin	—	280	290	330	335	385

KM# 179 DELAWARE TERCENTENARY
Designer: Carl L. Schmitz

Date	Mintage	AU-50	MS-60	MS-63	MS-64	MS-65
1936	20,993	340	360	385	395	500

KM# 180 ELGIN, ILL., CENTENNIAL Designer:
Trygve Rovelstad

Date	Mintage	AU-50	MS-60	MS-63	MS-64	MS-65
1936	20,015	245	275	290	300	340

KM# 182 LONG ISLAND TERCENTENARY
Designer: Howard K. Weinman

Date	Mintage	AU-50	MS-60	MS-63	MS-64	MS-65
1936	81,826	96.00	103	115	125	450

KM# 183 LYNCHBURG, VA.,
SESQUICENTENNIAL **Designer:** Charles Keck

Date	Mintage	AU-50	MS-60	MS-63	MS-64	MS-65
1936	20,013	255	285	295	298	375

KM# 184 NORFOLK, VA., BICENTENNIAL
Designer: William M. and Marjorie E. Simpson

Date	Mintage	AU-50	MS-60	MS-63	MS-64	MS-65
1936	16,936	555	575	615	625	650

KM# 185 RHODE ISLAND TERCENTENARY
Designer: Arthur G. Carey and John H. Benson

Date	Mintage	AU-50	MS-60	MS-63	MS-64	MS-65
1936 PDS set	15,010	320	335	375	385	870
Type coin	—	105	110	125	128	290

KM# 174 SAN FRANCISCO-OAKLAND BAY
BRIDGE **Designer:** Jacques Schnier

Date	Mintage	AU-50	MS-60	MS-63	MS-64	MS-65
1936	71,424	180	185	220	225	360

KM# 188 WISCONSIN TERRITORIAL
CENTENNIAL **Designer:** David Parsons

Date	Mintage	AU-50	MS-60	MS-63	MS-64	MS-65
1936	25,015	250	270	295	325	420

KM# 189 YORK COUNTY, MAINE, TERCENTENARY Designer: Walter H. Rich

Date	Mintage	AU-50	MS-60	MS-63	MS-64	MS-65
1936	25,015	235	250	270	280	350

KM# 190 BATTLE OF ANTIETAM 75TH ANNIVERSARY Designer: William M. Simpson

Date	Mintage	AU-50	MS-60	MS-63	MS-64	MS-65
1937	18,028	750	775	800	830	940

KM# 186 ROANOKE ISLAND, N.C. Designer: William M. Simpson

Date	Mintage	AU-50	MS-60	MS-63	MS-64	MS-65
1937	29,030	265	310	325	330	375

KM# 191 NEW ROCHELLE, N.Y. Designer: Gertrude K. Lathrop

Date	Mintage	AU-50	MS-60	MS-63	MS-64	MS-65
1938	15,266	430	450	470	475	585

KM# 198 BOOKER T. WASHINGTON Designer: Isaac S. Hathaway

Date	Mintage	AU-50	MS-60	MS-63	MS-64	MS-65
1946 PDS set	200,113	45.00	50.00	70.00	75.00	160
Type coin	—	15.00	16.00	17.50	18.50	56.00
1947 PDS set	100,017	52.50	75.00	85.00	120	300
1948 PDS set	8,005	85.00	150	160	165	225
1949 PDS set	6,004	160	230	245	250	355
1950 PDS set	6,004	75.00	135	140	150	250
1951 PDS set	7,004	84.00	115	155	160	225

KM# 197 IOWA STATEHOOD CENTENNIAL Designer: Adam Pietz

Date	Mintage	AU-50	MS-60	MS-63	MS-64	MS-65
1946	100,057	115	125	134	135	240

KM# 200 BOOKER T. WASHINGTON AND GEORGE WASHINGTON CARVER Designer: Isaac S. Hathaway

Date	Mintage	AU-50	MS-60	MS-63	MS-64	MS-65
1951 PDS set	10,004	70.00	85.00	105	125	585
Type coin	—	14.00	16.00	18.50	20.00	52.50
1952 PDS set	8,006	58.50	82.50	110	135	600
1953 PDS set	8,003	58.50	82.50	110	135	600
1954 PDS set	12,006	55.00	80.00	105	125	445

DOLLAR

KM# 118 LAFAYETTE Weight: 26.7300 g.
Composition: 0.9000 Silver, 0.7736 oz. ASW
Diameter: 38.1mm. **Designer:** Charles E. Barber

Date	Mintage	AU-50	MS-60	MS-63	MS-64	MS-65
1900	36,026	675	1,025	2,400	4,600	11,250

KM# 120 LOUISIANA PURCHASE EXPOSITION
Weight: 1.6720 g. **Composition:** 0.9000 Gold,
0.0484 oz. AGW **Diameter:** 15mm. **Obv:** William
McKinley **Obv. Designer:** Charles E. Barber

Date	Mintage	AU-50	MS-60	MS-63	MS-64	MS-65
1903	17,500	730	780	975	2,450	3,600

KM# 119 LOUISIANA PURCHASE EXPOSITION
Weight: 1.6720 g. **Composition:** 0.9000 Gold,
0.0484 oz. AGW **Diameter:** 15mm. **Obv:** Jefferson
Designer: Charles E. Barber

Date	Mintage	AU-50	MS-60	MS-63	MS-64	MS-65
1903	17,500	725	780	1,100	2,600	3,800

KM# 121 LEWIS AND CLARK EXPOSITION
Weight: 1.6720 g. **Composition:** 0.9000 Gold,
0.7736 oz. AGW **Diameter:** 15mm. **Obv.**
Designer: Charles E. Barber

Date	Mintage	AU-50	MS-60	MS-63	MS-64	MS-65
1904	10,025	1,075	1,125	2,300	6,400	12,250
1905	10,041	1,300	1,550	2,800	8,000	18,500

KM# 136 PANAMA-PACIFIC EXPOSITION
Weight: 1.6720 g. **Composition:** 0.9000 Gold,
0.0484 oz. AGW **Diameter:** 15mm. **Obv.**
Designer: Charles Keck

Date	Mintage	AU-50	MS-60	MS-63	MS-64	MS-65
1915S	15,000	675	770	950	1,600	3,000

KM# 144 MCKINLEY MEMORIAL Weight:
1.6720 g. **Composition:** 0.9000 Gold, 0.0484 oz.
AGW **Diameter:** 15mm. **Obv. Designer:** Charles
E. Barber **Rev. Designer:** George T. Morgan

Date	Mintage	AU-50	MS-60	MS-63	MS-64	MS-65
1916	9,977	650	705	850	1,550	3,000
1917	10,000	800	850	1,200	2,700	4,250

KM# 152.1 GRANT MEMORIAL Weight: 1.6720
g. **Composition:** 0.9000 Gold, 0.0484 oz. AGW
Diameter: 15mm. **Obv. Designer:** Laura G. Fraser
Notes: Without an incuse "star" above the word
GRANT on the obverse.

Date	Mintage	AU-50	MS-60	MS-63	MS-64	MS-65
1922	5,016	1,800	1,900	2,400	4,200	5,000

  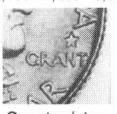

Grant w/star

KM# 152.2 GRANT MEMORIAL Weight: 1.6720
g. **Composition:** 0.9000 Gold, 0.0484 oz. AGW
Diameter: 15mm. **Obv. Designer:** Laura G. Fraser
Notes: Variety with an incuse "star" above the word
GRANT on the obverse.

Date	Mintage	AU-50	MS-60	MS-63	MS-64	MS-65
1922	5,000	1,900	2,000	2,300	3,500	4,250

$2.50 (QUARTER EAGLE)

KM# 137 PANAMA-PACIFIC EXPOSITION
Weight: 4.1800 g. **Composition:** 0.9000 Gold,
0.121 oz. AGW **Diameter:** 18mm. **Obv. Designer:**
Charles E. Barber **Rev. Designer:** George T.
Morgan

Date	Mintage	AU-50	MS-60	MS-63	MS-64	MS-65
1915S	6,749	1,750	2,100	4,200	6,300	8,000

KM# 161 PHILADELPHIA SESQUICENTENNIAL
Weight: 4.1800 g. **Composition:** 0.9000 Gold,
0.121 oz. AGW **Diameter:** 18mm. **Obv. Designer:**
John R. Sinnock

Date	Mintage	AU-50	MS-60	MS-63	MS-64	MS-65
1926	46,019	585	600	900	1,600	4,850

$50

KM# 138 PANAMA-PACIFIC EXPOSITION
Weight: 83.5900 g. **Composition:** 0.9000 Gold,
2.419 oz. AGW **Diameter:** 44mm. **Obv. Designer:**
Robert Aitken

Date	Mintage	AU-50	MS-60	MS-63	MS-64	MS-65
1915S	483	41,500	52,500	78,000	95,000	155,000

KM# 139 PANAMA-PACIFIC EXPOSITION
Weight: 83.5900 g. **Composition:** 0.9000 Gold,
2.419 oz. AGW **Diameter:** 44mm. **Obv. Designer:**
Robert Aitken

Date	Mintage	AU-50	MS-60	MS-63	MS-64	MS-65
1915S	645	39,500	50,000	69,000	90,000	140,000

COMMEMORATIVE COINAGE

All commemorative silver dollar coins of 1982-present have the following specifications: diameter -- 38.1 millimeters; weight -- 26.7300 grams; composition -- 0.9000 silver, 0.7736 ounces actual silver weight. All commemorative $5 coins of 1982-present have the following specificiations: diameter -- 21.6 millimeters; weight -- 8.3590 grams; composition: 0.9000 gold, 0.242 ounces actual gold weight.

Note: In 1982, after a hiatus of nearly 20 years, coinage of commemorative half dollars resumed. Those designated with a 'W' were struck at the West Point Mint. Some issues were struck in copper--nickel. Those struck in silver have the same size, weight and composition as the prior commemorative half--dollar series.

HALF DOLLAR

**KM# 208 GEORGE WASHINGTON, 250TH
BIRTH ANNIVERSARY Weight:** 12.5000 g.
Composition: 0.9000 Silver, 0.3618 oz. ASW
Diameter: 30.6mm. **Obv. Designer:** Elizabeth Jones

Date	Mintage	Proof	MS-65	Prf-65
1982D	2,210,458	—	5.50	—
1982S	—	(4,894,044)	—	5.75

KM# 212 STATUE OF LIBERTY CENTENNIAL
Weight: 11.3400 g. **Composition:** Copper-Nickel
Clad Copper **Obv. Designer:** Edgar Z. Steever
Rev. Designer: Sherl Joseph Winter

Date	Mintage	Proof	MS-65	Prf-65
1986D	928,008	—	6.75	—
1986S	—	(6,925,627)	—	6.50

KM# 224 BICENTENNIAL OF THE CONGRESS
Weight: 11.3400 g. **Composition:** Copper-Nickel Clad Copper **Obv. Designer:** Patricia L. Verani **Rev. Designer:** William Woodward and Edgar Z. Steever

Date	Mintage	Proof	MS-65	Prf-65
1989D	163,753	—	8.00	—
1989S	—	—	—	8.00

KM# 228 MOUNT RUSHMORE 50TH ANNIVERSARY
Weight: 11.3400 g. **Composition:** Copper-Nickel Clad Copper **Obv. Designer:** Marcel Jovine **Rev. Designer:** T. James Ferrell

Date	Mintage	Proof	MS-65	Prf-65
1991D	172,754	—	21.50	—
1991S	—	—	—	22.00

KM# 233 1992 OLYMPICS
Weight: 11.3400 g. **Composition:** Copper-Nickel Clad Copper **Obv. Designer:** William Cousins **Rev. Designer:** Steven M. Bieda

Date	Mintage	Proof	MS-65	Prf-65
1992P	161,607	—	8.50	—
1992S	—	(519,645)	—	8.50

KM# 237 500TH ANNIVERSARY OF COLUMBUS DISCOVERY
Weight: 11.3400 g. **Composition:** Copper-Nickel Clad Copper **Designer:** T. James Ferrell

Date	Mintage	Proof	MS-65	Prf-65
1992D	135,702	—	11.50	—

Date	Mintage	Proof	MS-65	Prf-65
1992S	—	(390,154)	—	11.50

KM# 240 JAMES MADISON AND BILL OF RIGHTS
Weight: 12.5000 g. **Composition:** 0.9000 Silver, 0.3618 oz. ASW **Obv. Designer:** T. James Ferrell **Rev. Designer:** Dean McMullen

Date	Mintage	Proof	MS-65	Prf-65
1993W	173,224	—	20.50	—
1993S	—	(559,758)	—	16.50

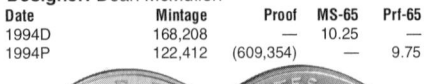

KM# 243 WORLD WAR II 50TH ANNIVERSARY
Weight: 11.3400 g. **Composition:** Copper-Nickel Clad Copper **Obv. Designer:** George Klauba **Rev. Designer:** William J. Leftwich

Date	Mintage	Proof	MS-65	Prf-65
(1993)P	192,968	(290,343)	38.50	37.50

KM# 246 1994 WORLD CUP SOCCER
Weight: 11.3400 g. **Composition:** Copper-Nickel Clad Copper **Obv. Designer:** Richard T. LaRoche **Rev. Designer:** Dean McMullen

Date	Mintage	Proof	MS-65	Prf-65
1994D	168,208	—	10.25	—
1994P	122,412	(609,354)	—	9.75

KM# 257 ATLANTA OLYMPICS
Weight: 11.3400 g. **Composition:** Copper-Nickel Clad Copper **Obv:** Basketball

Date	Mintage	Proof	MS-65	Prf-65
1995S	171,001	(169,655)	22.50	18.50

KM# 262 ATLANTA OLYMPICS Weight:
11.3400 g. **Composition:** Copper-Nickel Clad
Copper **Obv:** Baseball **Obv. Designer:** Edgar Z.
Steever

Date	Mintage	Proof	MS-65	Prf-65
1995S	164,605	(118,087)	23.50	19.00

KM# 254 CIVIL WAR Weight: 11.3400 g.
Composition: Copper-Nickel Clad Copper **Obv.
Designer:** Don Troiani **Rev. Designer:** T. James
Ferrell

Date	Mintage	Proof	MS-65	Prf-65
1995S	119,510	(330,099)	47.50	43.50

KM# 271 ATLANTA OLYMPICS Weight:
11.3400 g. **Composition:** Copper-Nickel Clad
Copper **Obv:** Soccer

Date	Mintage	Proof	MS-65	Prf-65
1996S	52,836	(122,412)	90.00	105

KM# 267 ATLANTA OLYMPICS Weight:
11.3400 g. **Composition:** Copper-Nickel Clad
Copper **Obv:** Swimming

Date	Mintage	Proof	MS-65	Prf-65
1996S	49,533	(114,315)	170	37.50

KM# 323   U. S. CAPITOL VISITOR CENTER
Weight: 11.3400 g. **Composition:** Copper-Nickel
Clad Copper, 0 oz. **Obv. Designer:** Dean
McMullen **Rev. Designer:** Alex Shagin and Marcel
Jovine

Date	Mintage	Proof	MS-65	Prf-65
2001	99,157	(77,962)	13.50	18.00

KM# U. S. CAPITOL VISITOR CENTER
Weight: 11.3400 g. **Composition:** Copper-Nickel
Clad Copper **Obv. Designer:** Dean McMullen **Rev.
Designer:** Alex Shagin and Marcel Jovine

Date	Mintage	Proof	MS-65	Prf-65
2001	99,157	(77,962)	13.50	18.00

KM# 348   FIRST FLIGHT CENTENNIAL
Weight: 11.3400 g. **Composition:** Copper-Nickel
Clad Copper **Obv. Designer:** John Mercanti **Rev.
Designer:** Donna Weaver

Date	Mintage	Proof	MS-65	Prf-65
2003P	—	—	16.00	18.00

DOLLAR

**KM# 209 LOS ANGELES XXIII OLYMPIAD Obv.
Designer:** Elizabeth Jones

Date	Mintage	Proof	MS-65	Prf-65
1983P	294,543	—	11.50	—
1983D	174,014	—	12.00	—
1983S	174,014	(1,577,025)	11.50	13.00

KM# 220 CONSTITUTION BICENTENNIAL Obv.
Designer: Patricia L. Verani

Date	Mintage	Proof	MS-65	Prf-65
1987P	451,629	—	11.00	—
1987S	—	(2,747,116)	—	11.00

KM# 210 LOS ANGELES XXIII OLYMPIAD Obv.
Designer: Robert Graham

Date	Mintage	Proof	MS-65	Prf-65
1984P	217,954	—	13.50	—
1984D	116,675	—	18.00	—
1984S	116,675	(1,801,210)	19.00	13.00

KM# 214 STATUE OF LIBERTY CENTENNIAL
Obv. Designer: John Mercanti **Rev. Designer:**
John Mercanti and Matthew Peloso

Date	Mintage	Proof	MS-65	Prf-65
1986P	723,635	—	15.00	—
1986S	—	(6,414,638)	—	15.50

KM# 222 OLYMPICS Obv. Designer: Patricia L.
Verani **Rev. Designer:** Sherl Joseph Winter

Date	Mintage	Proof	MS-65	Prf-65
1988D	191,368	—	11.50	—
1988S	—	(1,359,366)	—	11.50

KM# 225 BICENTENNIAL OF THE CONGRESS
Designer: William Woodward and Chester Y. Martin

Date	Mintage	Proof	MS-65	Prf-65
1989D	135,203	—	16.00	—
1989S	—	(762,198)	—	21.50

KM# 231 KOREAN WAR Obv. Designer: John
Mercanti **Rev. Designer:** T. James Ferrell

Date	Mintage	Proof	MS-65	Prf-65
1991D	213,049	—	16.00	—
1991P	—	(618,488)	—	19.00

KM# 227 EISENHOWER CENTENNIAL Obv.
Designer: John Mercanti **Rev. Designer:** Marcel
Jovine and John Mercanti

Date	Mintage	Proof	MS-65	Prf-65
1990W	241,669	—	18.00	—
1990P	—	(638,335)	—	22.50

KM# 229 MOUNT RUSHMORE GOLDEN
ANNIVERSARY Obv. Designer: Marika Somogyi
Rev. Designer: Frank Gasparro

Date	Mintage	Proof	MS-65	Prf-65
1991P	133,139	—	34.00	—
1991S	—	(738,419)	—	41.50

**KM# 232 USO 50TH ANNIVERSARY   Obv.
Designer:** Robert Lamb **Rev. Designer:** John
Mercanti

Date	Mintage	Proof	MS-65	Prf-65
1991D	124,958	—	16.00	—
1991S	—	(321,275)	—	22.50

KM# 234 OLYMPICS   Obv. Designer: John R.
Deecken and Chester Y. Martin **Rev. Designer:**
Marcel Jovine

Date	Mintage	Proof	MS-65	Prf-65
1992D	187,552	—	26.00	—
1992S	—	(504,505)	—	28.50

**KM# 238 COLUMBUS QUINCENTENARY   Obv.
Designer:** John Mercanti **Rev. Designer:** Thomas
D. Rogers, Sr.

Date	Mintage	Proof	MS-65	Prf-65
1992D	106,949	—	31.00	—
1992P	—	(385,241)	—	46.00

**KM# 236 WHITE HOUSE BICENTENNIAL   Obv.
Designer:** Edgar Z. Steever **Rev. Designer:**
Chester Y. Martin

Date	Mintage	Proof	MS-65	Prf-65
1992D	123,803	—	38.50	—
1992W	—	(375,851)	—	46.00

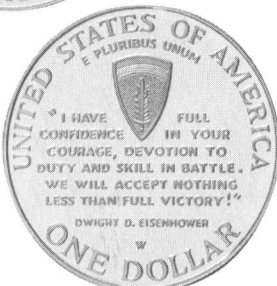

KM# 241 JAMES MADISON AND BILL OF RIGHTS
Obv. Designer: William Krawczewicz and Thomas D. Rogers, Sr. **Rev. Designer:** Dean McMullen and Thomas D. Rogers, Sr.

Date	Mintage	Proof	MS-65	Prf-65
1993D	98,383	—	21.00	—
1993S	—	(534,001)	—	22.00

KM# 244 WORLD WAR II 50TH ANNIVERSARY
Designer: Thomas D. Rogers, Sr.

Date	Mintage	Proof	MS-65	Prf-65
1993D	94,708	—	35.00	—
1993W	—	(322,422)	—	42.50

KM# 249 THOMAS JEFFERSON 250TH BIRTH ANNIVERSARY
Designer: T. James Ferrell

Date	Mintage	Proof	MS-65	Prf-65
1993P	266,927	—	27.50	—
1993S	—	(332,891)	—	31.00

KM# 251 NATIONAL PRISONER OF WAR MUSEUM
Obv. Designer: Thomas Nielson and Alfred Maletsky **Rev. Designer:** Edgar Z. Steever

Date	Mintage	Proof	MS-65	Prf-65
1994W	54,790	—	96.00	—
1994P	—	(220,100)	—	80.00

KM# 253 U.S. CAPITOL BICENTENNIAL

Date	Mintage	Proof	MS-65	Prf-65
1994D	68,352	—	23.00	—
1994S	—	(279,416)	—	30.00

KM# 250 VIETNAM VETERANS MEMORIAL
Obv. Designer: John Mercanti **Rev. Designer:** Thomas D. Rogers, Sr.

Date	Mintage	Proof	MS-65	Prf-65
1994W	57,317	—	85.00	—
1994P	—	(226,262)	—	100.00

KM# 252 WOMEN IN MILITARY SERVICE
MEMORIAL **Obv. Designer:** T. James Ferrell
Rev. Designer: Thomas D. Rogers, Sr.

Date	Mintage	Proof	MS-65	Prf-65
1994W	53,054	—	62.50	—
1994P	—	(213,201)	—	59.00

KM# 247 WORLD CUP SOCCER **Obv.**
Designer: Dean McMullen and T. James Ferrell

Date	Mintage	Proof	MS-65	Prf-65
1994D	81,698	—	27.50	—
1994S	—	(576,978)	—	31.00

KM# 260 ATLANTA OLYMPICS Obv: Gymnastics

Date	Mintage	Proof	MS-65	Prf-65
1995D	42,497	—	77.50	—
1995P	—	(182,676)	—	62.50

KM# 263 ATLANTA OLYMPICS Obv: Cycling **Obv. Designer:** John Mercanti

Date	Mintage	Proof	MS-65	Prf-65
1995D	19,662	—	150	—
1995P	—	(118,795)	—	47.50

KM# 264 ATLANTA OLYMPICS Obv: Track and field **Obv. Designer:** John Mercanti

Date	Mintage	Proof	MS-65	Prf-65
1995D	24,796	—	96.00	—
1995P	—	(136,935)	—	57.50

KM# 259 ATLANTA OLYMPICS, PARALYMPICS Obv: Blind runner

Date	Mintage	Proof	MS-65	Prf-65
1995D	28,649	—	97.50	—
1995P	—	(138,337)	—	66.00

KM# 255 CIVIL WAR Obv. Designer: Don
Troiani and Edgar Z. Steever **Rev. Designer:** John
Mercanti

Date	Mintage	Proof	MS-65	Prf-65
1995P	45,866	—	77.50	—
1995S	—	(437,114)	—	90.00

**KM# 266 SPECIAL OLYMPICS WORLD GAMES
Obv. Designer:** Jamie Wyeth and T. James Ferrell
Rev. Designer: Thomas D. Rogers, Sr.

Date	Mintage	Proof	MS-65	Prf-65
1995W	89,301	—	25.00	—
1995P	—	(351,764)	—	27.50

KM# 272A ATLANTA OLYMPICS Obv: High
jumper **Rev. Designer:** Thomas D. Rogers, Sr.

Date	Mintage	Proof	MS-65	Prf-65
1996D	15,697	—	415	—
1996P	—	(124,502)	—	62.50

KM# 269 ATLANTA OLYMPICS Obv: Tennis
Rev. Designer: Thomas D. Rogers, Sr.

Date	Mintage	Proof	MS-65	Prf-65
1996D	15,983	—	330	—
1996P	—	(92,016)	—	96.00

KM# 272 ATLANTA OLYMPICS   Obv: Rowing
Rev. Designer: Thomas D. Rogers, Sr.

Date	Mintage	Proof	MS-65	Prf-65
1996D	16,258	—	360	—
1996P	—	(151,890)	—	75.00

KM# 268 ATLANTA OLYMPICS, PARALYMPICS
Obv: Wheelchair racer **Rev. Designer:** Thomas D.
Rogers, Sr.

Date	Mintage	Proof	MS-65	Prf-65
1996D	14,497	—	415	—
1996P	—	(84,280)	—	90.00

KM# 275 NATIONAL COMMUNITY SERVICE
Obv. Designer: Thomas D. Rogers, Sr. **Rev.**
Designer: William C. Cousins

Date	Mintage	Proof	MS-65	Prf-65
1996S	23,500	(101,543)	285	96.00

KM# 276 SMITHSONIAN INSTITUTION 150TH
ANNIVERSARY   Obv. Designer: Thomas D.
Rogers, Sr. **Rev. Designer:** John Mercanti

Date	Mintage	Proof	MS-65	Prf-65
1996D	31,230	—	150	—
1996P	—	(129,152)	—	72.50

**KM# 279 JACKIE ROBINSON 50TH
ANNIVERSARY Obv. Designer:** Alfred Maletsky
Rev. Designer: T. James Ferrell

Date	Mintage	Proof	MS-65	Prf-65
1997S	30,007	(110,495)	103	85.00

**KM# 278 U.S. BOTANIC GARDENS 175TH
ANNIVERSARY Designer:** Edgar Z. Steever

Date	Mintage	Proof	MS-65	Prf-65
1997P	57,272	(264,528)	47.50	46.00

**KM# 281 NATIONAL LAW ENFORCEMENT
OFFICERS MEMORIAL Designer:** Alfred
Maletsky

Date	Mintage	Proof	MS-65	Prf-65
1997P	28,575	(110,428)	190	165

**KM# 288 BLACK REVOLUTIONARY WAR
PATRIOTS Obv:** Crispus Attucks **Obv. Designer:**
John Mercanti **Rev. Designer:** Ed Dwight

Date	Mintage	Proof	MS-65	Prf-65
1998S	37,210	(75,070)	178	123

**KM# 287 ROBERT F. KENNEDY Obv.
Designer:** Thomas D. Rogers, Sr. **Rev. Designer:**
James M. Peed and Thomas D. Rogers, Sr.

Date	Mintage	Proof	MS-65	Prf-65
1998S	106,422	(99,020)	32.50	51.00

KM# 299 YELLOWSTONE Obv. Designer:
Edgar Z. Steever **Rev. Designer:** William C.
Cousins

Date	Mintage	Proof	MS-65	Prf-65
1999P	23,614	(128,646)	57.50	60.00

KM# 298 DOLLEY MADISON Obv. Designer: T.
James Ferrell **Rev. Designer:** Thomas D. Rogers,
Sr. **Designer:** Tiffany & Co.

Date	Mintage	Proof	MS-65	Prf-65
1999P	22,948	(158,247)	60.00	57.50

KM# 313 LEIF ERICSON Obv. Designer: John
Mercanti **Rev. Designer:** T. James Ferrell

Date	Mintage	Proof	MS-65	Prf-65
2000P	28,150	(58,612)	92.50	92.50
2000 Iceland	—	(15,947)	—	72.50

KM# 311 LIBRARY OF CONGRESS
BICENTENNIAL   Obv. Designer: Thomas D.
Rogers, Sr. **Rev. Designer:** John Mercanti

Date	Mintage	Proof	MS-65	Prf-65
2000P	52,771	(196,900)	45.00	45.00

KM# 324 CAPITOL VISITOR CENTER   Obv.
Designer: Marika Somogyi **Rev. Designer:** John
Mercanti

Date	Mintage	Proof	MS-65	Prf-65
2001P	66,636	(143,793)	41.50	46.00

KM# 325 AMERICAN INDIAN - BISON
Designer: James E. Fraser

Date	Mintage	Proof	MS-65	Prf-65
2001D	197,131	—	130	—
2001P	—	(272,869)	—	150

KM# 338   WEST POINT MILITARY
ACADEMY BICENTENNIAL   Obv. Designer: T.
James Ferrell **Rev. Designer:** John Mercanti

Date	Mintage	Proof	MS-65	Prf-65
2002W	103,201	(288,293)	32.50	36.00

KM# 336 WINTER OLYMPICS - SALT LAKE CITY Obv. Designer: John Mercanti **Rev. Designer:** Donna Weaver

Date	Mintage	Proof	MS-65	Prf-65
2002P	35,388	(142,873)	38.00	40.00

KM# 349 FIRST FLIGHT CENTENNIAL Obv: Orville and Wilbur Wright **Obv. Designer:** T. James Ferrell **Rev:** Wright Brothers airplane **Rev. Designer:** Norman E. Nemeth

Date	Mintage	Proof	MS-65	Prf-65
2003P	—	—	38.50	42.50

KM# 362 125TH ANNIVERSARY OF EDISON'S ELECTRIC LIGHT Obv. Designer: Donna Weaver **Rev. Designer:** John Mercanti

Date	Mintage	Proof	MS-65	Prf-65
2004P	—	—	43.50	46.00

KM# 363 LEWIS AND CLARK CORPS OF DISCOVERY BICENTENNIAL

Date	Mintage	Proof	MS-65	Prf-65
2004P	—	—	37.50	36.00

KM# 375 CHIEF JUSTICE JOHN MARSHALL, 250TH BIRTH ANNIVERSARY Obv. Designer: John Mercanti **Rev. Designer:** Donna Weaver

Date	Mintage	Proof	MS-65	Prf-65
2005P	—	—	40.00	41.50

KM# 376 U.S. MARINE CORPS, 230TH ANNIVERSARY

Date	Mintage	Proof	MS-65	Prf-65
2005P	—	—	85.00	90.00

KM# 388   BENJAMIN FRANKLIN, 300TH ANNIVERSARY OF BIRTH Obv: Bust 3/4 right, signature in oval below **Rev:** Continental Dollar of 1776 in center

Date	Mintage	Proof	MS-65	Prf-65
2006P	—	—	—	—

KM# 387   BENJAMIN FRANKLIN, 300TH ANNIVERSARY OF BIRTH Obv: Youthful Franklin flying kite **Obv. Designer:** Norman E. Nemeth **Rev:** Revolutionary era "Join or Die" snake cartoon illustration

Date	Mintage	Proof	MS-65	Prf-65
2006P	—	—	—	—

$5 (HALF EAGLE)

KM# 215 STATUE OF LIBERTY CENTENNIAL
Designer: Elizabeth Jones

Date	Mintage	Proof	MS-65	Prf-65
1986W	95,248	(404,013)	150	150

KM# 221 CONSTITUTION BICENTENNIAL
Designer: Marcel Jovine

Date	Mintage	Proof	MS-65	Prf-65
1987W	214,225	—	150	—
1987W	—	(651,659)	—	150

KM# 223 OLYMPICS Obv. Designer: Elizabeth Jones **Rev. Designer:** Marcel Jovine

Date	Mintage	Proof	MS-65	Prf-65
1988W	62,913	(281,456)	150	150

KM# 226 BICENTENNIAL OF THE CONGRESS
Obv. Designer: John Mercanti

Date	Mintage	Proof	MS-65	Prf-65
1989W	46,899	(164,690)	150	150

KM# 230 MOUNT RUSHMORE 50TH ANNIVERSARY Obv. Designer: John Mercanti **Rev. Designer:** Robert Lamb and William C. Cousins

Date	Mintage	Proof	MS-65	Prf-65
1991W	31,959	(111,991)	220	195

KM# 239 COLUMBUS QUINCENTENARY Obv.
Designer: T. James Ferrell **Rev. Designer:** Thomas D. Rogers, Sr.

Date	Mintage	Proof	MS-65	Prf-65
1992W	24,329	(79,730)	240	200

KM# 235 OLYMPICS Obv. Designer: James C.
Sharpe and T. James Ferrell **Rev. Designer:** James M. Peed

Date	Mintage	Proof	MS-65	Prf-65
1992W	27,732	(77,313)	200	180

KM# 242 JAMES MADISON AND BILL OF
RIGHTS Obv. Designer: Scott R. Blazek **Rev. Designer:** Joseph D. Peña

Date	Mintage	Proof	MS-65	Prf-65
1993W	—	(78,651)	240	215

KM# 245 WORLD WAR II 50TH ANNIVERSARY
Obv. Designer: Charles J. Madsen **Rev. Designer:** Edward S. Fisher

Date	Mintage	Proof	MS-65	Prf-65
1993W	23,089	(65,461)	250	240

KM# 248 WORLD CUP SOCCER Obv.
Designer: William J. Krawczewicz **Rev. Designer:** Dean McMullen

Date	Mintage	Proof	MS-65	Prf-65
1994W	22,464	(89,619)	215	185

KM# 256 CIVIL WAR Obv. Designer: Don
Troiani **Rev. Designer:** Alfred Maletsky

Date	Mintage	Proof	MS-65	Prf-65
1995W	12,735	(55,246)	660	435

KM# 261 OLYMPICS Obv: Torch runner

Date	Mintage	Proof	MS-65	Prf-65
1995W	14,675	(57,442)	550	450

KM# 265 OLYMPICS Obv: Stadium

Date	Mintage	Proof	MS-65	Prf-65
1995W	10,579	(43,124)	460	340

KM# 270 1996 ATLANTA OLYMPICS Obv:
Cauldron

Date	Mintage	Proof	MS-65	Prf-65
1996W	9,210	(38,555)	535	435

KM# 274 OLYMPICS Obv: Flag bearer

Date	Mintage	Proof	MS-65	Prf-65
1996W	9,174	(32,886)	535	435

KM# 277 SMITHSONIAN INSTITUTION 150TH
ANNIVERSARY Obv. Designer: Alfred Maletsky **Rev. Designer:** T. James Ferrell

Date	Mintage	Proof	MS-65	Prf-65
1996W	9,068	(21,772)	1,050	450

KM# 282 FRANKLIN DELANO ROOSEVELT
Obv. Designer: T. James Ferrell **Rev. Designer:**
James M. Peed and Thomas D. Rogers, Sr.

Date	Mintage	Proof	MS-65	Prf-65
1997W	11,894	(29,474)	400	400

KM# 280 JACKIE ROBINSON 50TH
ANNIVERSARY Obv. Designer: William C.
Cousins **Rev. Designer:** James M. Peed

Date	Mintage	Proof	MS-65	Prf-65
1997W	5,202	(24,546)	3,300	680

KM# 300 GEORGE WASHINGTON DEATH
BICENTENNIAL Designer: Laura G. Fraser

Date	Mintage	Proof	MS-65	Prf-65
1999W	22,511	(41,693)	360	360

KM# 326 CAPITOL VISITOR CENTER
Designer: Elizabeth Jones

Date	Mintage	Proof	MS-65	Prf-65
2001	6,761	(27,652)	735	375

KM# 337   2002 SALT LAKE CITY WINTER
OLYMPICS Designer: Donna Weaver

Date	Mintage	Proof	MS-65	Prf-65
2002	10,585	(32,877)	450	350

$10 (EAGLE)

KM# 211 LOS ANGELES XXIII OLYMPIAD
Weight: 16.7180 g. **Composition:** 0.9000 Gold,
0.4839 oz. AGW **Diameter:** 27mm. **Obv.**
Designer: James M. Peed and John Mercanti **Rev.**
Designer: John Mercanti

Date	Mintage	Proof	MS-65	Prf-65
1984W	75,886	(381,085)	275	275
1984P	33,309	—	—	275
1984D	34,533	—	—	290
1984S	48,551	—	—	275

KM# 312 LIBRARY OF CONGRESS Weight:
16.2590 g. **Composition:** Platinum-Gold-Alloy
Obv. Designer: John Mercanti **Rev. Designer:**
Thomas D. Rogers, Sr. **Notes:** Composition is 48
percent platinum, 48 percent gold, and 4 percent
alloy.

Date	Mintage	Proof	MS-65	Prf-65
2000W	6,683	—	1,800	—

KM# 350 FIRST FLIGHT CENTENNIAL Weight:
16.7180 g. **Composition:** 0.9000 Gold, .4839 oz.
AGW **Designer:** Donna Weaver

Date	Mintage	Proof	MS-65	Prf-65
2003P	—	—	470	470

MODERN COMMEMORATIVE COIN SETS

Olympic, 1983-1984

Date	Price
1983 & 1984 proof dollars	24.00
1983 & 1984 gold and silver uncirculated set: One 1983 and one 1984 uncirculated dollar and one 1984P uncirculated gold $10; KM209, 210, 211.	360
1983 & 1984S gold and silver proof set: One 1983 and one 1984 proof dollar and one 1984 proof gold $10; KM209, 210, 211.	360
1983 & 1984 6 coin set: One 1983 and one 1984 uncirculated and proof dollar, one uncirculated and one proof gold $10; KM209, 210, 211.	735
1983 collectors set: 1983 PDS uncirculated dollars; KM209.	35.00
1984 collectors set: 1984 PDS uncirculated dollars; KM210.	45.00

Statue of Liberty

Date	Price
1986 3 coin set: proof silver dollar, clad half dollar and gold $5; KM212, 214, 215.	175
1986 2 coin set: uncirculated silver dollar and clad half dollar; KM212, 214.	17.00
1986 2 coin set: proof silver dollar and clad half dollar; KM212, 214.	17.00
1986 3 coin set: uncirculated silver dollar, clad half dollar and gold $5; KM212, 214, 215.	175
1986 6 coin set: 1 each of the proof and uncirculated issues; KM212, 214, 215.	360

Constitution

Date	Price
1987 2 coin set: uncirculated silver dollar and gold $5; KM220, 221.	185
1987 2 coin set: proof silver dollar and gold $5; KM220, 221.	185
1987 4 coin set: 1 each of the proof and uncirculated issues; KM220, 221.	360

Olympic, 1988

Date	Price
1988 2 coin set: uncirculated silver dollar and gold $5; KM222, 223.	185
1988 2 coin set: Proof silver dollar and gold $5; KM222, 223.	195
1988 4 coin set: 1 each of proof and uncirculated issues; KM222, 223.	360

Congress

Date	Price
1989 2 coin set: uncirculated silver dollar and clad half dollar; KM224, 225.	22.00
1989 2 coin set: proof silver dollar and clad half dollar; KM224, 225.	23.00
1989 3 coin set: uncirculated silver dollar, clad half and gold $5; KM224, 225, 226.	195
1989 3 coin set: proof silver dollar, clad half and gold $5; KM224, 225, 226.	195
1989 6 coin set: 1 each of the proof and uncirculated issues; KM224, 225, 226.	380

Mt. Rushmore

Date	Price
1991 2 coin set: uncirculated half dollar and silver dollar; KM228, 229.	55.00
1991 2 coin set: proof half dollar and silver dollar; KM228, 229.	51.00
1991 3 coin set: uncirculated half dollar, silver dollar and gold $5; KM228, 229, 230.	275
1991 3 coin set: proof half dollar, silver dollar and gold $5; KM228, 229, 230.	275
1991 6 coin set: 1 each of proof and uncirculated issues; KM228, 229, 230.	505

Olympic, 1992

Date	Price
1992 2 coin set: uncirculated half dollar and silver dollar; KM233, 234.	30.00
1992 2 coin set: proof half dollar and silver dollar; KM233, 234.	32.50
1992 3 coin set: uncirculated half dollar, silver dollar and gold $5; KM233, 234, 235.	235
1992 3 coin set: proof half dollar, silver dollar and gold $5; KM233, 234, 235.	220
1992 6 coin set: 1 each of proof and uncirculated issues; KM233, 234, 235.	450

Columbus Quincentenary

Date	Price
1992 2 coin set: uncirculated half dollar and silver dollar; KM237, 238.	38.00
1992 2 coin set: proof half dollar and silver dollar; KM237, 238.	45.00
1992 3 coin set: uncirculated half dollar, silver dollar and gold $5; KM237, 238, 239.	285
1992 3 coin set: proof half dollar, silver dollar and gold $5; KM237, 238, 239.	275
1992 6 coin set: 1 each of proof and uncirculated issues; KM237, 238, 239.	575

Jefferson

Date	Price
1993 Jefferson: dollar, nickel and $2 note; KM249, 192.	125

Madison / Bill of Rights

Date	Price
1993 2 coin set: uncirculated half dollar and silver dollar; KM240, 241.	31.50
1993 2 coin set: proof half dollar and silver dollar; KM240, 241.	34.00
1993 3 coin set: uncirculated half dollar, silver dollar and gold $5; KM240, 241, 242.	275
1993 3 coin set: proof half dollar, silver dollar and gold $5; KM240, 241, 242.	250
1993 6 coin set: 1 each of proof and uncirculated issues; KM240, 241, 242.	540

World War II

Date	Price
1993 2 coin set: uncirculated half dollar and silver dollar; KM243, 244.	52.00
1993 2 coin set: proof half dollar and silver dollar; KM243, 244.	62.50
1993 3 coin set: uncirculated half dollar, silver dollar and gold $5; KM243, 244, 245.	310
1993 3 coin set: proof half dollar, silver dollar and gold $5; KM243, 244, 245.	300
1993 6 coin set: 1 each of proof and uncirculated issues; KM243, 244, 245.	625

World Cup

Date	Price
1994 2 coin set: uncirculated half dollar and silver dollar; KM246, 247.	35.00
1994 2 coin set: proof half dollar and silver dollar; KM246, 247.	41.50
1994 3 coin set: uncirculated half dollar, silver dollar and gold $5; KM246, 247, 248.	235
1994 3 coin set: proof half dollar, silver dollar and gold $5; KM246, 247, 248.	260
1994 6 coin set: 1 each of proof and uncirculated issues; KM246, 247, 248.	500

U.S. Veterans

Date	Price
1994 3 coin set: uncirculated POW, Vietnam, Women dollars; KM250, 251, 252.	240
1994 3 coin set: proof POW, Vietnam, Women dollars; KM250, 251, 252.	175

Olympic, 1995-96

Date	Price
1995 4 coin set: uncirculated basketball half, $1 gymnast & blind runner, $5 torch runner; KM257, 259, 260, 261.	540
1995 4 coin set: proof basketball half, $1 gymnast & blind runner, $5 torch runner; KM257, 259, 260, 261.	400
1995P 2 coin set: proof $1 gymnast & blind runner; KM259, 260.	120
1995P 2 coin set: proof $1 track & field, cycling; KM263, 264.	100.00
1995-96 4 coin set: proof halves, basketball, baseball, swimming, soccer; KM257, 262, 267, 271.	140
1995 & 96 8 coins in cherry wood case: proof silver dollars: blind runner, gymnast, cycling, track & field, wheelchair, tennis, rowing, high jump; KM259, 260, 263, 264, 268, 269, 272, 272A.	540
1995 & 96 16 coins in cherry wood case: bu and proof silver dollars: blind runner, gymnast, cycling, track & field, wheelchair, tennis, rowing, high jump; KM259, 260, 263, 264, 268, 269, 272, 272A.	2,500
1995 & 96 16 coins in cherry wood case: proof half dollars: basketball, baseball, swimming, soccer, KM257, 262, 267, 271. Proof silver dollars: blind runner, gymnast, cycling, track & field, wheelchair, tennis, rowing, high jump; KM259, 260, 263, 264, 268, 269, 272, 272A. Proof $5 gold: torch runner, stadium, cauldron, flag bearer, KM 261, 265, 270, 274.	2,250
1995 & 96 32 coins in cherry wood case: bu & proof half dollars: basketball, baseball, swimming, soccer, KM257, 262, 267, 271. BU & proof silver dollars: blind runner, gymnast, cycling, track & field, wheelchair, tennis, rowing, high jump, KM259, 260, 263, 264, 268, 269, 272, 272A. BU & proof $5 gold: torch runner, stadium, cauldron, flag bearer, KM261, 265, 270, 274.	5,900
1996P 2 coin set: proof $1 wheelchair & tennis; KM268, 269.	170
1996P 2 coin set: proof $1 rowing & high jump; KM272, 272A.	120

Civil War

Date	Price
1995 2 coin set: uncirculated half and dollar; KM254, 255.	100.00
1995 2 coin set: proof half and dollar; KM254, 255.	120
1995 3 coin set: uncirculated half, dollar and gold $5; KM254, 255, 256.	660
1995 3 coin set: proof half, dollar and gold $5; KM254, 255, 256.	500
1995 6 coin set: 1 each of proof and uncirculated issues; KM254, 255, 256.	1,220

Smithsonian

Date	Price
1996 2 coin set: proof dollar and $5 gold; KM276, 277.	440
1996 4 coin set: proof and B.U. ; KM276, 277.	1,500

Jackie Robinson

Date	Price
1997 2 coin set: proof dollar & $5 gold; KM279, 280.	700
1997 4 coin set: proof & BU; KM279, 280.	4,250
1997 legacy set.	650

Botanic Garden

Date	Price
1997 2 coin set: dollar, Jefferson nickel and $1 note; KM278, 192.	240

Franklin Delano Roosevelt

Date	Price
1997W 2 coin set: uncirculated and proof; KM282.	700

Kennedy

Date	Price
1998 2 coin set: proof; KM287.	75.00
1998 2 coin collectors set: Robert Kennedy dollar and John Kennedy half dollar; KM287, 202b. Matte finished.	345

Black Patriots

Date	Price
1998S 2 coin set: uncirculated and proof; KM288.	230

George Washington

Date	Price
1999 2 coin set: proof and uncirculated gold $5; KM300.	700

Dolley Madison

Date	Price
1999 2 coin set: proof and uncirculated silver dollars; KM298.	100.00

Yellowstone National Park

Date	Price
1999 2 coin set: proof and uncirculated silver dollars; KM299.	96.00

Millennium Coin & Currency

Date	Price
2000 2 coin set: uncirculated Sacagewea $1, silver Eagle & $1 note	70.00

Leif Ericson

Date	Price
2000 2 coin set: proof and uncirculated silver dollars; KM313.	85.00

Capitol Visitor Center

Date	Price
2001 3 coin set: proof half, silver dollar, gold $5; KM323, 324, 326.	380

American Buffalo

Date	Price
2001 2 coin set: 90% silver unc. & proof $1.; KM325.	270
2001 coin & currency set 90% unc. dollar & replicas of 1899 $5 silver cert.; KM325.	160

Winter Olympics - Salt Lake City

Date	Price
2002 2 coin set: proof 90% silver dollar KM336 & $5.00 Gold KM337	330
2002 4 coin set: 90% silver unc. & proof $1, KM336 & unc. & proof gold $5, KM337.	725

First Flight Centennial

Date	Price
2003 3-coin set includes proof gold ten dollar KM350, proof silver dollar KM349 & proof clad half dollar KM348	475

AMERICAN EAGLE BULLION COINS

SILVER DOLLAR

KM# 273 • 31.1010 g., 0.9993 **Silver**, 1 oz. , 40.6mm. • **Obv. Designer:** Adolph A. Weinman **Rev. Designer:** John Mercanti

Date	Mintage	Unc	Prf.
1986	5,393,005	20.00	—
1986S	(1,446,778)	—	32.00
1987	11,442,335	12.50	—
1987S	(904,732)	—	32.00
1988	5,004,646	16.50	—
1988S	(557,370)	—	60.00
1989	5,203,327	12.50	—
1989S	(617,694)	—	37.50
1990	5,840,210	16.50	—
1990S	(695,510)	—	35.00
1991	7,191,066	13.00	—
1991S	(511,924)	—	55.00
1992	5,540,068	15.50	—
1992S	(498,552)	—	50.00
1993	6,763,762	13.00	—
1993P	(403,625)	—	195
1994	4,227,319	16.50	—
1994P	(372,168)	—	250
1995	4,672,051	15.50	—
1995P	(395,400)	—	225
1995W 10th Anniversary	(30,125)	—	5,500
1996	3,603,386	47.50	—
1996P	(473,021)	—	70.00
1997	4,295,004	21.00	—
1997P	(429,682)	—	100.00
1998	4,847,549	13.00	—

Date	Mintage	Unc	Prf.
1998P	(452,319)	—	60.00
1999	7,408,640	13.00	—
1999P	(549,769)	—	65.00
2000P	(600,000)	—	32.00
2000	9,239,132	12.50	—
2001	9,001,711	12.50	—
2001W	(746,154)	—	32.00
2002	10,539,026	12.50	—
2002W	(647,342)	—	35.00
2003	8,495,008	12.50	—
2003W		—	32.50
2004	8,882,754	12.50	—
2004W	(783,219)	—	32.50
2005	8,891,025	12.00	—
2005W	823,000	—	33.00
2006		12.00	—
2006W	—	—	33.00

GOLD $5

KM# 216 • 3.3930 g., 0.9167 **Gold**, 0.1 oz., 16.5mm. • **Obv. Designer:** Augustus Saint-Gaudens **Rev. Designer:** Miley Busiek

Date	Mintage	Unc	Prf.
MCMLXXXVI (1986)	912,609	85.00	—
MCMLXXXVII (1987)	580,266	80.00	—
MCMLXXXVIII (1988)	159,500	200	—
MCMLXXXVIII (1988)P	(143,881)	—	80.00
MCMLXXXIX (1989)	264,790	85.00	—
MCMLXXXIX (1989)P	(82,924)	—	80.00
MCMXC (1990)	210,210	90.00	—
MCMXC (1990)P	(99,349)	—	80.00
MCMXCI (1991)	165,200	110	—
MCMXCI (1991)P	(70,344)	—	80.00
1992	209,300	95.00	—
1992P	(64,902)	—	80.00
1993	210,709	90.00	—
1993P	(58,649)	—	80.00
1994	206,380	90.00	—
1994W	(62,100)	—	80.00
1995	223,025	80.00	—
1995W	(62,650)	—	80.00
1996	401,964	80.00	—
1996W	(58,440)	—	80.00
1997	528,515	80.00	—
1997W	(35,000)	—	91.00
1998	1,344,520	70.00	—
1998W	(39,653)	—	80.00
1999	2,750,338	70.00	—
1999W	(48,426)	—	80.00
2000	569,153	85.00	—
2000W	(50,000)	—	90.00
2001	269,147	85.00	—
2001W	(37,547)	—	80.00
2002	230,027	85.00	—
2002W	(40,864)	—	80.00
2003	245,029	85.00	—
2003W	(40,634)	—	85.00
2004	250,016	85.00	—
2004W	(35,481)	—	90.00
2005	300,043	80.00	—
2005W	48,455	—	95.00
2006		75.00	—
2006W	—	—	80.00

GOLD $10

KM# 217 • 8.4830 g., 0.9167 **Gold**, 0.25 oz., 22mm. • **Obv. Designer:** Augustus Saint-Gaudens **Rev. Designer:** Miley Busiek

Date	Mintage	Unc	Prf.
MCMLXXXVI (1986)	726,031	175	—
MCMLXXXVII (1987)	269,255	175	—
MCMLXXXVIII (1988)	49,000	175	—
MCMLXXXVIII (1988)P	(98,028)	—	200
MCMLXXXIX (1989)	81,789	175	—
MCMLXXXIX (1989P)	(53,593)	—	200
MCMXC (1990)	41,000	175	—
MCMXC (1990)P	(62,674)	—	200
MCMXCI (1991)	36,100	425	—
MCMXCI (1991)P	(50,839)	—	200
1992	59,546	175	—
1992P	(46,290)	—	200
1993	71,864	175	—
1993P	(46,271)	—	200
1994	72,650	175	—
1994W	(47,600)	—	200
1995	83,752	175	—
1995W	(47,545)	—	200
1996	60,318	175	—
1996W	(39,190)	—	200
1997	108,805	175	—
1997W	(29,800)	—	200
1998	309,829	175	—
1998W	(29,733)	—	200
1999	564,232	175	—
1999W	(34,416)	—	200
2000	128,964	175	—
2000W	(36,000)	—	200
2001	71,280	175	—
2001W	(25,630)	—	200
2002	62,027	175	—
2002W	(29,242)	—	200
2003	74,029	175	—
2003W	(31,000)	—	200
2004	72,014	175	—
2004W	(29,127)	—	200
2005	72,015	175	—
2005W	34,637	—	200
2006	—	175	—
2006W	—	—	200

GOLD $25

KM# 218 • 16.9660 g., 0.9167 **Gold**, 0.5 oz., 27mm. • **Obv. Designer:** Augustus Saint-Gaudens **Rev. Designer:** Miley Busiek

Date	Mintage	Unc	Prf.
MCMLXXXVI (1986)	599,566	500	—
MCMLXXXVII (1987)	131,255	350	—
MCMLXXXVII (1987)P	(143,398)	—	400
MCMLXXXVIII (1988)	45,000	550	—

Date	Mintage	Unc	Prf.
MCMLXXXVIII (1988)P	(76,528)	—	400
MCMLXXXIX (1989)	44,829	650	—
MCMLXXXIX (1989)P	(44,264)	—	400
MCMXC (1990)	31,000	800	—
MCMXC (1990)P	(51,636)	—	400
MCMXCI (1991)	24,100	1,300	—
MCMXCI (1991)P	(53,125)	—	400
1992	54,404	500	—
1992P	(40,982)	—	400
1993	73,324	350	—
1993P	(43,319)	—	400
1994	62,400	350	—
1994W	(44,100)	—	400
1995	53,474	385	—
1995W	(45,511)	—	400
1996	39,287	525	—
1996W	(35,937)	—	400
1997	79,605	350	—
1997W	(26,350)	—	400
1998	169,029	350	—
1998W	(25,896)	—	400
1999	263,013	350	—
1999W	(30,452)	—	400
2000	79,287	350	—
2000W	(32,000)	—	400
2001	48,047	500	—
2001W	(23,261)	—	400
2002	70,027	350	—
2002W	(26,646)	—	400
2003	79,029	350	—
2003W	(29,000)	—	400
2004	98,040	350	—
2004W	(27,731)	—	400
2005	80,023	350	—
2005W	33,598	—	400
2006	—	345	—
2006W	—	—	400

Date	Mintage	Unc	Prf.
1996	189,148	715	—
1996W	(37,302)	—	725
1997	664,508	715	—
1997W	(28,000)	—	725
1998	1,468,530	710	—
1998W	(26,060)	—	725
1999	1,505,026	710	—
1999W	(31,446)	—	725
2000	433,319	715	—
2000W	(33,000)	—	725
2001	143,605	715	—
2001W	(24,580)	—	725
2002	222,029	715	—
2002W	(24,242)	—	725
2003	416,032	715	—
2003W	(29,000)	—	725
2004	417,019	715	—
2004W	(28,731)	—	725
2005	356,555	715	—
2005W	34,695	—	725
2006	—	710	—
2006W	—	—	725

PLATINUM $10

KM# 283 • 3.1100 g., 0.9995 **Platinum**, .1000 oz.
• **Obv. Designer:** John Mercanti **Rev. Designer:** Thomas D. Rogers Sr

Date	Mintage	Unc	Prf.
1997	70,250	150	—
1997W	(36,996)	—	150
1998	39,525	150	—
1999	55,955	145	—
2000	34,027	145	—
2001	52,017	145	—
2002	23,005	145	—
2003	22,007	145	—
2004	15,010	165	—
2005	14,013	170	—
2006	—	—	—

KM# 289 • 3.1100 g., 0.9995 **Platinum**, .1000 oz.
• **Obv. Designer:** John Mercanti

Date	Mintage	Unc	Prf.
1998W	(19,832)	—	150

KM# 301 • 3.1100 g., 0.9995 **Platinum**, .1000 oz.
• **Obv. Designer:** John Mercanti

Date	Mintage	Unc	Prf.
1999W	(19,123)	—	145

KM# 314 • 3.1100 g., 0.9995 **Platinum**, .1000 oz.
• **Obv. Designer:** John Mercanti

Date	Mintage	Unc	Prf.
2000W	(15,651)	—	145

KM# 327 • 3.1100 g., 0.9995 **Platinum**, .1000 oz.
• **Obv. Designer:** John Mercanti

Date	Mintage	Unc	Prf.
2001W	(12,193)	—	145

KM# 339 • 3.1100 g., 0.9995 **Platinum**, .1000 oz.
• **Obv. Designer:** John Mercanti

Date	Mintage	Unc	Prf.
2002W	(12,365)	—	145

GOLD $50

KM# 219 • 33.9310 g., 0.9167 **Gold**, 1 oz., 32.7mm. • **Obv. Designer:** Augustus Saint-Gaudens **Rev. Designer:** Miley Busiek

Date	Mintage	Unc	Prf.
MCMLXXXVI (1986)	1,362,650	715	—
MCMLXXXVI (1986)W	(446,290)	—	725
MCMLXXXVII (1987)	1,045,500	715	—
MCMLXXXVII (1987)W	(147,498)	—	725
MCMLXXXVIII (1988)	465,000	715	—
MCMLXXXVIII (1988)W	(87,133)	—	725
MCMLXXXIX (1989)	415,790	715	—
MCMLXXXIX (1989)W	(53,960)	—	725
MCMXC (1990)	373,210	715	—
MCMXC (1990)W	(62,401)	—	725
MCMXCI (1991)	243,100	715	—
MCMXCI (1991)W	(50,411)	—	725
1992	275,000	715	—
1992W	(44,835)	—	725
1993	480,192	715	—
1993W	(34,389)	—	725
1994	221,633	715	—
1994W	(36,300)	—	725
1995	200,636	715	—
1995W	(46,553)	—	725

KM# 351 • 3.1100 g., 0.9995 **Platinum**, .1000 oz.
• **Obv. Designer:** John Mercanti **Rev. Designer:**
Al Maletsky

Date	Mintage	Unc	Prf.
2003W	(8,161)	—	175

KM# 364 • 3.1100 g., 0.9995 **Platinum**, .1000 oz.
• **Obv. Designer:** John Mercanti

Date	Mintage	Unc	Prf.
2004W	(6,846)	—	350

KM# 377 • 3.1100 g., 0.9995 **Platinum**, 0.0999
oz. • **Obv. Designer:** John Mercanti **Rev.
Designer:** Donna Weaver

Date	Mintage	Unc	Prf.
2005W	8,000	—	210

PLATINUM $25

KM# 284 • 7.7857 g., 0.9995 **Platinum**, 0.2500
oz. • **Obv. Designer:** John Mercanti **Rev.
Designer:** Thomas D. Rogers Sr

Date	Mintage	Unc	Prf.
1997	27,100	365	—
1997W	(18,628)	—	365
1998	38,887	350	—
1999	39,734	350	—
2000	20,054	350	—
2001	21,815	365	—
2002	27,405	350	—
2003	25,207	365	—
2004	18,010	365	—
2005	12,013	365	—
2006	—	—	—

KM# 290 • 7.7857 g., 0.9995 **Platinum**, .2500 oz.
• **Obv. Designer:** John Mercanti

Date	Mintage	Unc	Prf.
1998W	(14,860)	—	350

KM# 302 • 7.7857 g., 0.9995 **Platinum**, .2500 oz.
• **Obv. Designer:** John Mercanti

Date	Mintage	Unc	Prf.
1999W	(13,514)	—	350

KM# 315 • 7.7857 g., 0.9995 **Platinum**, .2500 oz.
• **Obv. Designer:** John Mercanti

Date	Mintage	Unc	Prf.
2000W	(11,995)	—	350

KM# 328 • 7.7857 g., 0.9995 **Platinum**, .2500 oz.
• **Obv. Designer:** John Mercanti

Date	Mintage	Unc	Prf.
2001W	(8,858)	—	320

KM# 340 • 7.7857 g., 0.9995 **Platinum**, .2500 oz.
• **Obv. Designer:** John Mercanti

Date	Mintage	Unc	Prf.
2002W	(9,282)	—	320

KM# 352 • 7.7857 g., 0.9995 **Platinum**, .2500 oz.
• **Obv. Designer:** John Mercanti **Rev. Designer:**
Al Maletsky

Date	Mintage	Unc	Prf.
2003W	(6,045)	—	385

KM# 365 • 7.7857 g., 0.9995 **Platinum**, .2500 oz.
• **Obv. Designer:** John Mercanti

Date	Mintage	Unc	Prf.
2004W	(5,035)	—	950

PLATINUM $50

KM# 285 • 15.5520 g., 0.9995 **Platinum**, 0.5000
oz. • **Obv. Designer:** John Mercanti **Rev.
Designer:** Thomas D. Rogers Sr

Date	Mintage	Unc	Prf.
1997	20,500	660	—
1997W	(15,432)	—	660
1998	32,415	660	—
1999	32,309	660	—
2000	18,892	660	—
2001	12,815	660	—
2002	24,005	660	—
2003	17,409	660	—
2004	98,040	660	—
2005	9,013	660	—
2006	—	—	—

KM# 291 • 15.5520 g., 0.9995 **Platinum**, .5000
oz. • **Obv. Designer:** John Mercanti

Date	Mintage	Unc	Prf.
1998W	(13,821)	—	660

KM# 303 • 15.5520 g., 0.9995 **Platinum**, .5000
oz. • **Obv. Designer:** John Mercanti

Date	Mintage	Unc	Prf.
1999W	(11,098)	—	660

KM# 316 • 15.5520 g., 0.9995 **Platinum**, .5000
oz. • **Obv. Designer:** John Mercanti

Date	Mintage	Unc	Prf.
2000W	(11,049)	—	660

KM# 329 • 15.5520 g., 0.9995 **Platinum**, .5000
oz. • **Obv. Designer:** John Mercanti

Date	Mintage	Unc	Prf.
2001W	(8,268)	—	660

KM# 341 • 15.5520 g., 0.9995 **Platinum**, .5000
oz. • **Obv. Designer:** John Mercanti

Date	Mintage	Unc	Prf.
2002W	(8,772)	—	660

KM# 353 • 15.5520 g., 0.9995 **Platinum**, .5000
oz. • **Obv. Designer:** John Mercanti **Rev.
Designer:** Al Maletsky

Date	Mintage	Unc	Prf.
2003W	(6,181)	—	660

KM# 366 • 15.5520 g., 0.9995 **Platinum**, .5000
oz. • **Obv. Designer:** John Mercanti

Date	Mintage	Unc	Prf.
2004W	(4,886)	—	2,600

KM# 379 • 15.5520 g., 0.9995 **Platinum**, .5000
oz. • **Obv. Designer:** John Mercanti **Rev.
Designer:** Donna Weaver

Date	Mintage	Unc	Prf.
2005W Proof	5,720	—	735

PLATINUM $100

KM# 286 • 31.1050 g., 0.9995 **Platinum**, 1.000 oz. • **Obv. Designer:** John Mercanti **Rev. Designer:** Thomas D. Rogers Sr

Date	Mintage	Unc	Prf.
1997	56,000	1,275	—
1997W	(15,885)	—	1,275
1998	133,002	1,275	—
1999	56,707	1,275	—
2000	18,892	1,275	—
2001	14,070	1,275	—
2002	11,502	1,275	—
2003	8,007	1,275	—
2004	7,009	1,275	—
2005	6,310	1,400	—
2006	—	—	—

KM# 292 • 31.1050 g., 0.9995 **Platinum**, 1.000 oz. • **Obv. Designer:** John Mercanti

Date	Mintage	Unc	Prf.
1998W	(14,203)	—	1,275

KM# 304 • 31.1050 g., 0.9995 **Platinum**, 1.000 oz. • **Obv. Designer:** John Mercanti

Date	Mintage	Unc	Prf.
1999W	—	—	1,275

KM# 317 • 31.1050 g., 0.9995 **Platinum**, 1.000 oz. • **Obv. Designer:** John Mercanti

Date	Mintage	Unc	Prf.
2000W	—	—	1,275

KM# 330 • 31.1050 g., 0.9995 **Platinum**, 1.000 oz. • **Obv. Designer:** John Mercanti

Date	Mintage	Unc	Prf.
2001W	(8,990)	—	1,275

KM# 342 • 31.1050 g., 0.9995 **Platinum**, 1.000 oz. • **Obv. Designer:** John Mercanti

Date	Mintage	Unc	Prf.
2002W	(9,834)	—	1,275

KM# 354 • 31.1050 g., 0.9995 **Platinum**, 1.000 oz. • **Obv. Designer:** John Mercanti **Rev. Designer:** Al Maletsky

Date	Mintage	Unc	Prf.
2003W	(6,991)	—	1,275

KM# 367 • 31.1050 g., 0.9995 **Platinum**, 1.000 oz. • **Obv. Designer:** John Mercanti **Rev. Designer:** Donna Weaver

Date	Mintage	Unc	Prf.
2004W	(5,833)	—	4,500

KM# 380 • 31.1050 g., 0.9995 **Platinum**, 0.9995 oz. • **Obv. Designer:** John Mercanti **Rev. Designer:** Donna Weaver

Date	Mintage	Unc	Prf.
2005W	6,700	—	1,345

CANADA
CONFEDERATION

CIRCULATION COINAGE

CENT

KM# 1 Weight: 3.2400 g. **Composition:** Bronze

Date	Mintage	VG-8	F-12	VF-20	XF-40	MS-60	MS-63	Proof
1858	421,000	50.00	60.00	80.00	120	300	1,250	—
1859/8 Wide 9	Inc. above	25.00	35.00	60.00	90.00	250	1,350	—
1859 Narrow 9	9,579,000	2.25	3.00	5.00	7.00	35.00	175	—
1859 Double punched narrow 9 type I	Inc. above	175	250	350	540	1,150	3,000	—
1859 Double punched narrow 9 type II	Inc. above	35.00	70.00	95.00	150	325	1,600	—

KM# 7 Obv. Designer: Leonard C. Wyon **Edge:** Plain **Weight:** 3.2400 g. **Composition:** Bronze

Date	Mintage	VG-8	F-12	VF-20	XF-40	MS-60	MS-63	Proof
1876H	4,000,000	2.00	2.75	4.00	7.50	45.00	190	—
1881H	2,000,000	3.00	4.00	9.00	14.00	60.00	250	—
1882H	4,000,000	2.00	2.75	4.00	7.50	32.00	170	—
1884	2,500,000	2.25	3.00	5.00	8.50	60.00	225	—
1886	1,500,000	3.75	5.00	10.00	20.00	90.00	350	—
1887	1,500,000	2.75	4.00	6.00	11.00	55.00	215	—
1888	4,000,000	2.00	3.00	5.00	7.50	35.00	160	—
1890H	1,000,000	5.00	8.00	13.00	25.00	100.00	400	—
1891 Large date	1,452,000	5.50	9.00	13.50	30.00	125	420	—
1891 S.D.L.L.	Inc. above	50.00	75.00	110	160	620	2,150	—
1891 S.D.S.L.	Inc. above	35.00	50.00	65.00	95.00	225	650	—
1892	1,200,000	4.00	7.00	10.00	13.50	55.00	220	—
1893	2,000,000	2.50	3.00	5.00	7.50	35.00	125	—
1894	1,000,000	8.00	12.00	17.00	30.00	90.00	265	—
1895	1,200,000	4.00	7.00	10.00	16.00	55.00	225	—
1896	2,000,000	2.00	2.75	5.00	7.50	40.00	150	—
1897	1,500,000	2.50	4.00	5.00	9.00	45.00	165	—
1898H	1,000,000	5.00	7.00	12.00	18.00	75.00	250	—
1899	2,400,000	2.25	3.00	4.00	7.00	35.00	100.00	—
1900	1,000,000	5.00	9.00	15.00	22.00	85.00	400	—
1900H	2,600,000	2.00	2.50	4.00	5.50	30.00	75.00	—
1901	4,100,000	2.25	3.00	4.50	5.50	35.00	85.00	—

KM# 8 Obv. Designer: G. W. DeSaulles **Edge:** Plain **Weight:** 3.2400 g. **Composition:** Bronze

Date	Mintage	VG-8	F-12	VF-20	XF-40	MS-60	MS-63	Proof
1902	3,000,000	1.75	2.25	3.50	6.00	23.00	50.00	—
1903	4,000,000	1.75	2.25	3.00	6.00	25.00	55.00	—
1904	2,500,000	2.00	3.50	5.00	8.00	30.00	85.00	—

Date	Mintage	VG-8	F-12	VF-20	XF-40	MS-60	MS-63	Proof
1905	2,000,000	3.50	4.00	7.50	12.00	40.00	100.00	—
1906	4,100,000	1.75	2.25	3.00	6.00	30.00	125	—
1907	2,400,000	2.00	2.25	4.50	9.00	30.00	125	—
1907H	800,000	8.00	16.00	20.00	35.00	150	350	—
1908	2,401,506	2.00	3.50	5.00	8.00	30.00	90.00	150
1909	3,973,339	1.25	1.75	3.00	6.00	25.00	70.00	—
1910	5,146,487	1.25	1.50	2.00	5.00	26.00	70.00	—

KM# 15 Obv. Designer: E. B. MacKennal **Edge:** Plain **Weight:** 3.2400 g. **Composition:** Bronze

Date	Mintage	VG-8	F-12	VF-20	XF-40	MS-60	MS-63	Proof
1911	4,663,486	0.80	1.30	1.75	3.50	22.00	50.00	250

KM# 21 Obv. Designer: E. B. MacKennal **Edge:** Plain **Weight:** 3.2400 g. **Composition:** Bronze

Date	Mintage	VG-8	F-12	VF-20	XF-40	MS-60	MS-63	Proof
1912	5,107,642	0.75	1.50	2.25	3.50	21.00	55.00	—
1913	5,735,405	0.75	1.50	2.25	4.00	23.00	80.00	—
1914	3,405,958	1.00	1.50	2.50	4.00	30.00	95.00	—
1915	4,932,134	0.75	1.50	2.25	4.00	25.00	70.00	—
1916	11,022,367	0.50	0.65	1.25	3.00	16.00	50.00	—
1917	11,899,254	0.50	0.65	0.90	2.25	13.00	45.00	—
1918	12,970,798	0.50	0.65	0.90	2.25	12.00	45.00	—
1919	11,279,634	0.50	0.65	0.90	2.25	12.00	45.00	—
1920	6,762,247	0.60	0.75	1.00	2.25	15.00	55.00	—

Dot below date

KM# 28 Obv. Designer: E. B. MacKennal **Rev. Designer:** Fred Lewis **Edge:** Plain **Weight:** 3.2400 g. **Composition:** Bronze

Date	Mintage	VG-8	F-12	VF-20	XF-40	MS-60	MS-63	Proof
1920	15,483,923	0.20	0.50	1.00	2.00	11.00	35.00	—
1921	7,601,627	0.50	0.75	1.75	5.00	30.00	125	—
1922	1,243,635	13.00	16.00	21.00	35.00	175	650	—
1923	1,019,002	19.00	21.00	30.00	45.00	275	1,200	—
1924	1,593,195	5.00	6.50	8.50	15.00	100.00	375	—
1925	1,000,622	18.00	21.00	27.00	40.00	175	550	—
1926	2,143,372	3.50	4.50	7.00	11.00	90.00	325	—
1927	3,553,928	0.90	1.25	2.25	6.00	35.00	125	—
1928	9,144,860	0.15	0.30	0.65	1.50	15.00	55.00	—
1929	12,159,840	0.15	0.30	0.65	1.50	15.00	55.00	—
1930	2,538,613	1.35	1.80	4.50	8.50	45.00	125	—
1931	3,842,776	0.65	1.00	1.75	5.50	35.00	125	—
1932	21,316,190	0.15	0.20	0.50	1.50	14.00	45.00	—
1933	12,079,310	0.15	0.20	0.50	1.50	14.00	45.00	—
1934	7,042,358	0.20	0.30	0.75	1.50	14.00	45.00	—
1935	7,526,400	0.20	0.30	0.75	1.50	14.00	40.00	—
1936	8,768,769	0.15	0.30	0.75	1.50	9.00	30.00	—
1936 dot below date; Rare	678,823	—	—	—	—	—	—	—

Note: Only one possible business strike is known to exist. No other examples (or possible business strikes) have ever surfaced.

| 1936 dot below date, specimen, 3 known | — | — | — | — | — | — | — | — |

Note: At the David Akers auction of the John Jay Pittman collection (Part 1, 10-97), a gem specimen realized $121,000. At the David Akers auction of the John Jay Pittman collection (Part 3, 10-99), a near choice specimen realized $115,000.

Maple leaf

KM# 32   Obv. Designer: T. H. Paget **Rev. Designer:** George E. Kruger-Gray **Edge:** Plain **Weight:** 3.2400 g.
Composition: Bronze

Date	Mintage	VG-8	F-12	VF-20	XF-40	MS-60	MS-63	Proof
1937	10,040,231	0.40	0.50	0.75	1.00	3.00	9.00	—
1938	18,365,608	0.15	0.20	0.35	0.75	2.00	6.50	—
1939	21,600,319	0.15	0.20	0.35	0.70	1.75	5.00	—
1940	85,740,532	0.10	0.15	0.25	0.50	1.50	5.50	—
1941	56,336,011	0.10	0.15	0.25	0.50	6.00	50.00	—
1942	76,113,708	0.10	0.15	0.25	0.50	6.00	40.00	—
1943	89,111,969	0.10	0.15	0.25	0.45	2.50	25.00	—
1944	44,131,216	0.10	0.15	0.30	0.60	9.50	70.00	—
1945	77,268,591	0.10	0.15	0.20	0.30	1.50	14.00	—
1946	56,662,071	0.10	0.15	0.20	0.30	1.50	5.00	—
1947	31,093,901	0.10	0.15	0.20	0.30	1.50	6.00	—
1947 maple leaf	47,855,448	0.10	0.15	0.20	0.30	1.50	5.00	—

KM# 41   Obv: Modified legend **Obv. Designer:** T. H. Paget **Rev. Designer:** George E. Kruger-Gray **Edge:**
Plain **Weight:** 3.2400 g. **Composition:** Bronze

Date	Mintage	VG-8	F-12	VF-20	XF-40	MS-60	MS-63	Proof
1948	25,767,779	—	0.15	0.25	0.70	2.25	20.00	—
1949	33,128,933	—	0.10	0.15	0.25	1.25	6.00	—
1950	60,444,992	—	0.10	0.15	0.25	0.85	6.00	—
1951	80,430,379	—	0.10	0.15	0.20	0.85	8.00	—
1952	67,631,736	—	0.10	0.15	0.20	0.85	4.00	—

No strap

With strap

KM# 49   Obv: Elizabeth II effigy **Obv. Designer:** Mary Gillick **Rev. Designer:** George E. Kruger-Gray **Weight:**
3.2400 g. **Composition:** Bronze

Date	Mintage	VG-8	F-12	VF-20	XF-40	MS-60	MS-63	Proof
1953	67,806,016	0.10	0.15	0.20	0.25	0.65	1.50	—
Note: without strap								
1953	Inc. above	0.75	1.00	1.50	2.50	10.00	35.00	—
Note: with strap								
1954	22,181,760	0.10	0.15	0.25	0.40	1.00	4.00	—
Note: with strap								
1954 prooflike only	Inc. above	—	—	—	—	150	300	—
Note: without strap								
1955	56,403,193	—	0.10	0.15	0.20	0.35	1.00	—
Note: with strap								
1955	Inc. above	85.00	125	150	250	500	1,100	—
Note: without strap								
1956	78,658,535	—	—	—	0.10	0.50	0.90	—
1957	100,601,792	—	—	—	0.10	0.15	0.25	—
1958	59,385,679	—	—	—	0.10	0.15	0.25	—
1959	83,615,343	—	—	—	0.10	0.15	0.25	—
1960	75,772,775	—	—	—	0.10	0.15	0.25	—
1961	139,598,404	—	—	—	—	0.15	0.20	—
1962	227,244,069	—	—	—	—	0.10	0.20	—
1963	279,076,334	—	—	—	—	0.10	0.20	—
1964	484,655,322	—	—	—	—	0.10	0.20	—

KM# 59.1   Obv: Elizabeth II effigy **Obv. Designer:** Arnold Machin **Rev. Designer:** George E. Kruger-Gray
Edge: Plain **Weight:** 3.2400 g. **Composition:** Bronze

Date	Mintage	VG-8	F-12	VF-20	XF-40	MS-60	MS-63	Proof
1965	304,441,082	—	—	—	0.40	1.00	4.00	—
Note: sm. beads, pointed 5								
1965	Inc. above	—	—	—	—	0.15	0.20	—
Note: sm. beads, blunt 5								
1965	Inc. above	—	—	3.00	5.00	12.00	35.00	—
Note: lg. beads, pointed 5								
1965	Inc. above	—	—	—	0.10	0.15	0.20	—
Note: lg. beads, blunt 5								

Date	Mintage	VG-8	F-12	VF-20	XF-40	MS-60	MS-63	Proof
1966	184,151,087	—	—	—	—	0.10	0.20	—
1968	329,695,772	—	—	—	—	0.10	0.15	—
1969	335,240,929	—	—	—	—	0.10	0.15	—
1970	311,145,010	—	—	—	—	0.10	0.15	—
1971	298,228,936	—	—	—	—	0.10	0.15	—
1972	451,304,591	—	—	—	—	0.10	0.15	—
1973	457,059,852	—	—	—	—	0.10	0.15	—
1974	692,058,489	—	—	—	—	0.10	0.15	—
1975	642,318,000	—	—	—	—	0.10	0.15	—
1976	701,122,890	—	—	—	—	0.10	0.15	—
1977	453,762,670	—	—	—	—	0.10	0.15	—
1978	911,170,647	—	—	—	—	0.10	0.15	—

KM# 65 Subject: Confederation Centennial **Obv. Designer:** Arnold Machin **Rev:** Dove with wings spread **Rev. Designer:** Alex Coville **Composition:** Bronze

Date	Mintage	MS-60	MS-63	Proof
ND(1967)	345,140,645	0.10	0.20	1.00

KM# 59.2 Obv: Elizabeth II effigy. Smaller bust **Obv. Designer:** Arnold Machin **Rev. Designer:** George E. Kruger-Gray **Edge:** Plain **Weight:** 3.2400 g. **Composition:** Bronze

Date	Mintage	MS-60	MS-63	Proof
1979	754,394,064	0.10	0.15	—

KM# 127 Obv: Elizabeth II effigy **Obv. Designer:** Arnold Machin **Rev. Designer:** George E. Kruger-Gray **Edge:** Plain **Weight:** 2.8000 g. **Composition:** Bronze **Note:** Reduced weight.

Date	Mintage	MS-60	MS-63	Proof
1980	912,052,318	0.10	0.15	—
1981	1,209,468,500	0.10	0.15	—
1981 Proof	199,000	—	—	1.50

KM# 132 Obv: Elizabeth II effigy **Obv. Designer:** Arnold Machin **Rev. Designer:** George E. Kruger-Gray **Edge:** Plain **Weight:** 2.5000 g. **Composition:** Bronze **Shape:** Multi-sided **Note:** Reduced weight.

Date	Mintage	MS-60	MS-63	Proof
1982	911,001,000	0.10	0.15	—
1982 Proof	180,908	—	—	1.50
1983	975,510,000	0.10	0.15	—
1983 Proof	168,000	—	—	1.50
1984	838,225,000	0.10	0.15	—
1984 Proof	161,602	—	—	1.50
1985	771,772,500	10.00	19.00	—
Note: pointed 5				
1985	Inc. above	0.10	0.15	—
Note: blunt 5				
1985 Proof	157,037	—	—	1.50
Note: blunt 5				
1986	740,335,000	0.10	0.15	—
1986 Proof	175,745	—	—	1.50
1987	774,549,000	0.10	0.15	—
1987 Proof	179,004	—	—	1.50
1988	482,676,752	0.10	0.15	—
1988 Proof	175,259	—	—	1.50
1989	1,077,347,200	0.10	0.15	—
1989 Proof	170,928	—	—	1.50

KM# 181 Obv: Elizabeth II effigy **Obv. Designer:** Dora dePedery-Hunt **Rev. Designer:** George E. Kruger-Gray **Edge:** Plain **Weight:** 2.5000 g. **Composition:** Bronze

Date	Mintage	MS-60	MS-63	Proof
1990	218,035,000	0.10	0.15	—
1990 Proof	140,649	—	—	2.50
1991	831,001,000	0.10	0.15	—
1991 Proof	131,888	—	—	3.50
1993	752,034,000	0.10	0.15	—
1993 Proof	145,065	—	—	2.00
1994	639,516,000	0.10	0.15	—
1994 Proof	146,424	—	—	2.50
1995	624,983,000	0.10	0.15	—
1996	445,746,000	0.10	0.15	—
1996 Proof	—	—	—	2.50

KM# 204 Subject: Confederation 125 **Obv. Designer:** Dora dePedery-Hunt **Rev. Designer:** George E. Kruger-Gray **Composition:** Bronze

Date	Mintage	MS-60	MS-63	Proof
ND(1992)	673,512,000	0.10	0.15	—
ND(1992) Proof	147,061	—	—	2.50

Composition: Copper Plated Zinc

Date	Mintage	MS-60	MS-63	Proof
1996	445,746,000	0.10	0.15	2.50
1996 Proof	—	—	—	—

KM# 289 Edge: Round and plain **Composition:** Copper Plated Zinc

Date	Mintage	MS-60	MS-63	Proof
1997	549,868,000	0.10	0.15	—
1997 Proof	—	—	—	2.75
1998	999,578,000	0.10	0.15	—
1998 Proof	—	—	—	3.00
1998W	—	—	1.75	—
1999P	—	—	6.00	—
Note: Plated planchet, set only				
1999	1,089,625,000	0.10	0.15	—
1999W	—	—	—	—
1999 Proof	—	—	—	4.00
2000	771,908,206	0.10	0.15	—
2000 Proof	—	—	—	4.00
2000W	—	—	1.75	—
2001	919,358,000	—	0.10	—
2001 Proof	—	—	—	4.00
2003	92,219,775	—	0.10	—
2003 Proof	—	—	—	4.00
2003P	235,936,799	—	1.75	—

KM# 289a Composition: Bronze

Date	Mintage	MS-60	MS-63	Proof
1998		—	0.75	—

Note: In Specimen sets only

KM# 309 Subject: 90th Anniversary Royal Canadian Mint - 1908-1998 **Obv. Designer:** Dora dePedery-Hunt **Rev. Designer:** G. W. DeSaulles **Weight:** 5.6700 g. **Composition:** 0.9250 Copper-Plated Silver 0.1677 oz.

Date	Mintage	MS-63	Proof
ND(1998)	25,000	16.00	—
Note: Antique finish			
ND(1998) Proof	—	—	—

KM# 332 Subject: 90th Anniversary Royal Canadian Mint - 1908-1998 **Obv:** With "Canada" added to bust **Obv. Designer:** Dora dePedery-Hunt **Rev. Designer:** G. W. DeSaulles **Weight:** 5.6700 g. **Composition:** 0.9250 Silver .1677 oz. ASW

Date	Mintage	Proof
ND(2000) Proof	25,000	16.00
Note: Mirror finish		

KM# 445 Subject: Elizabeth II Golden Jubilee **Obv:** Queen, Jubilee commemorative dates 1952-2002 **Edge:** Plain **Composition:** Bronze-Plated Zinc

Date	Mintage	MS-63	Proof
ND(2002)	716,366,000	0.75	—
ND(2002)P	114,212,000	1.00	—
ND(2002) In proof sets only	32,642	—	2.50

KM# 445a Subject: Elizabeth II Golden Jubilee **Obv:** Queen, Jubilee commemorative dates 1952-2002 **Obv. Designer:** Dora dePedery-Hunt **Rev. Designer:** George E. Kruger-Gray **Composition:** 0.9250 Silver

Date	Mintage	MS-63	Proof
ND(2002) In sets only	100,000	—	3.00

KM# 468 Subject: 50th Anniversary of the Coronation of Elizabeth II **Obv:** 1953 effigy of the Queen, Jubilee commemorative dates 1952-2002 **Composition:** Copper

Date	Mintage	MS-63	Proof
ND(2003) In Coronation Proof sets only	—	2.50	

KM# 490 Obv: New effigy of Queen Elizabeth II **Obv. Designer:** Susanna Blunt **Edge:** Plain **Composition:** Bronze-Plated Zinc

Date	Mintage	MS-63	Proof
2003	56,877,144	0.25	—
2004	645,220,000	0.25	—
2004 Proof	—	—	2.50
2005	—	0.25	—
2006	—	0.25	—

3 CENTS

KM# 410 Subject: 1st Canadian Postage Stamp **Obv:** Queen's head right **Obv. Designer:** Dora dePedery-Hunt **Rev:** Partial stamp design **Rev. Designer:** Sandford Fleming **Edge:** Plain **Weight:** 3.1100 g. **Composition:** 0.9250 Gold Plated Silver .1600 oz. ASW AGW **Size:** 21.1 mm.

Date	Mintage	MS-63	Proof
2001 Proof	90,000	—	20.00

5 CENTS

Oval O's   Round O's

KM# 2 Designer: Leonard C. Wyon **Weight:** 1.1620 g. **Composition:** 0.9250 Silver 0.0346 oz. ASW

Date	Mintage	VG-8	F-12	VF-20	XF-40	MS-60	MS-63	Proof
1858 Small date	1,500,000	12.00	20.00	35.00	55.00	250	525	—
1858 Large date over small date	Inc. above	125	200	325	550	1,350	3,000	—
1870 Flat rim	2,800,000	13.50	22.50	40.00	60.00	250	650	—
1870 Wire rim	Inc. above	10.00	20.00	35.00	55.00	225	525	—
1871	1,400,000	13.50	22.50	40.00	70.00	275	600	—
1872H	2,000,000	9.00	16.00	35.00	55.00	250	750	—
1874H Plain 4	800,000	15.00	35.00	75.00	120	400	950	—
1874H Crosslet 4	Inc. above	14.00	30.00	60.00	120	450	1,100	—
1875H Large date	1,000,000	170	275	425	875	2,750	7,000	—
1875H Small date	Inc. above	90.00	175	285	500	1,750	4,550	—
1880H	3,000,000	5.00	8.00	18.00	40.00	250	600	—
1881H	1,500,000	6.00	10.00	20.00	45.00	265	650	—
1882H	1,000,000	8.00	15.00	25.00	55.00	275	700	—
1883H	600,000	15.00	30.00	70.00	150	750	2,000	—
1884	200,000	85.00	165	275	650	2,850	7,250	—
1885 Small 5	1,000,000	10.00	20.00	40.00	90.00	500	1,800	—
1885 Large 5	Inc. above	11.50	22.50	45.00	100.00	550	2,000	—
1885 Large 5 over small 5	Inc. above	50.00	100.00	175	450	2,850	2,750	—
1886 Small 6	1,700,000	7.00	15.00	25.00	50.00	300	900	—
1886 Large 6	Inc. above	9.00	16.00	28.00	60.00	350	1,000	—
1887	500,000	16.00	30.00	55.00	120	400	825	—
1888	1,000,000	5.00	9.00	18.00	35.00	165	425	—
1889	1,200,000	20.00	35.00	75.00	125	475	1,200	—
1890H	1,000,000	6.00	12.00	22.00	50.00	200	450	—
1891	1,800,000	5.00	8.00	15.00	30.00	150	385	—
1892	860,000	6.00	10.00	20.00	50.00	250	675	—

Date	Mintage	VG-8	F-12	VF-20	XF-40	MS-60	MS-63	Proof
1893	1,700,000	4.00	7.00	14.00	30.00	175	400	—
1894	500,000	12.00	25.00	50.00	100.00	300	1,100	—
1896	1,500,000	5.00	7.00	14.00	35.00	175	375	—
1897	1,319,283	4.50	6.50	13.50	30.00	150	325	—
1898	580,717	10.00	20.00	35.00	70.00	250	750	—
1899	3,000,000	4.50	6.50	12.00	25.00	115	300	—
1900 Oval 0's	1,800,000	4.50	6.50	12.00	25.00	115	325	—
1900 Round 0's	Inc. above	15.00	35.00	50.00	110	300	800	—
1901	2,000,000	4.50	6.50	12.00	35.00	150	400	—

KM# 9 Obv. Designer: G. W. DeSaulles **Rev. Designer:** Leonard C. Wyon **Weight:** 1.1620 g. **Composition:** 0.9250 Silver 0.0346 oz. ASW

Date	Mintage	VG-8	F-12	VF-20	XF-40	MS-60	MS-63	Proof
1902	2,120,000	2.25	3.00	4.00	7.00	35.00	55.00	—
1902	2,200,000	2.25	3.25	5.50	11.00	35.00	60.00	—
Note: lg. broad H								
1902	Inc. above	7.50	13.00	24.00	40.00	100.00	175	—
Note: sm. narrow H								

KM# 13 Weight: 1.1620 g. **Composition:** 0.9250 Silver 0.0346 oz. ASW

Date	Mintage	VG-8	F-12	VF-20	XF-40	MS-60	MS-63	Proof
1903	1,000,000	4.00	7.00	17.00	35.00	150	350	—
Note: 22 leaves								
1903H	2,640,000	1.75	3.00	7.00	16.00	100.00	300	—
Note: 21 leaves								
1904	2,400,000	2.75	4.50	7.00	23.00	175	500	—
1905	2,600,000	1.75	3.00	6.00	16.00	100.00	225	—
1906	3,100,000	2.25	3.00	6.00	13.00	85.00	225	—
1907	5,200,000	2.25	3.00	4.00	10.00	55.00	150	—
1908	1,220,524	6.00	10.00	23.00	35.00	100.00	175	—
1909	1,983,725	3.00	6.50	10.00	30.00	175	500	—
Note: round leaves								
1909	Inc. above	12.00	18.00	35.00	95.00	550	1,300	—
Note: pointed leaves								
1910	3,850,325	2.25	2.75	5.00	7.00	50.00	95.00	—
Note: pointed leaves								
1910	Inc. above	10.00	17.00	30.00	85.00	400	1,300	—
Note: round leaves								

KM# 16 Obv. Designer: E. B. MacKennal **Rev. Designer:** Leonard C. Wyon **Weight:** 1.1620 g. **Composition:** 0.9250 Silver 0.0346 oz. ASW

Date	Mintage	VG-8	F-12	VF-20	XF-40	MS-60	MS-63	Proof
1911	3,692,350	2.00	3.00	6.00	9.00	60.00	100.00	—

KM# 22 Obv. Designer: E. B. MacKennal **Rev. Designer:** Leonard C. Wyon **Weight:** 1.1620 g. **Composition:** 0.9250 Silver 0.0346 oz. ASW

Date	Mintage	VG-8	F-12	VF-20	XF-40	MS-60	MS-63	Proof
1912	5,863,170	2.00	3.00	5.00	9.00	50.00	150	—
1913	5,488,048	2.00	2.75	4.25	7.50	26.00	50.00	—
1914	4,202,179	2.00	3.00	5.00	9.00	50.00	125	—
1915	1,172,258	11.00	15.00	26.00	50.00	325	600	—
1916	2,481,675	2.75	5.00	9.00	20.00	75.00	250	—
1917	5,521,373	1.75	2.50	3.00	7.00	30.00	80.00	—
1918	6,052,298	1.75	2.50	3.00	6.50	30.00	65.00	—
1919	7,835,400	1.75	2.50	3.00	6.50	30.00	65.00	—

KM# 22a Obv. Designer: E. B. MacKennal **Rev. Designer:** Leonard C. Wyon **Weight:** 1.1664 g. **Composition:** 0.8000 Silver .0300 oz. ASW

Date	Mintage	VG-8	F-12	VF-20	XF-40	MS-60	MS-63	Proof
1920	10,649,851	1.75	2.50	3.00	6.50	26.00	50.00	—
1921	2,582,495	1,700	2,500	3,500	4,500	9,000	16,000	—

Note: Approximately 460 known; balance remelted. Stack's A.G. Carter Jr. Sale (12-89) choice BU, finest known, realized $57,200.

Near 6   Far 6

KM# 29   Obv. Designer: E. B. MacKennal **Rev. Designer:** W. H. J. Blakemore **Composition:** Nickel

Date	Mintage	VG-8	F-12	VF-20	XF-40	MS-60	MS-63	Proof
1922	4,794,119	0.20	0.75	1.75	7.00	45.00	95.00	—
1923	2,502,279	0.40	1.25	5.50	16.00	100.00	275	—
1924	3,105,839	0.25	1.00	3.75	10.00	85.00	200	—
1925	201,921	55.00	70.00	100.00	200	1,200	3,600	—
1926 near 6	938,162	2.25	4.00	16.00	60.00	375	1,300	—
1926 far 6	Inc. above	80.00	130	200	400	1,500	4,300	—
1927	5,285,627	0.20	0.65	2.75	10.00	60.00	125	—
1928	4,577,712	0.20	0.65	2.75	10.00	55.00	100.00	—
1929	5,611,911	0.20	0.65	2.75	10.00	60.00	150	—
1930	3,704,673	0.20	1.00	2.75	11.00	90.00	200	—
1931	5,100,830	0.20	1.00	3.25	18.00	175	475	—
1932	3,198,566	0.20	1.00	3.25	16.00	150	350	—
1933	2,597,867	0.40	1.50	6.00	18.00	175	650	—
1934	3,827,304	0.20	1.00	3.00	16.00	150	375	—
1935	3,900,000	0.20	1.00	2.75	11.00	95.00	250	—
1936	4,400,450	0.20	0.65	1.75	9.00	50.00	100.00	—

KM# 33   Obv. Designer: T. H. Paget **Rev. Designer:** George E. Kruger-Gray **Composition:** Nickel

Date	Mintage	VG-8	F-12	VF-20	XF-40	MS-60	MS-63	Proof
1937 dot	4,593,263	0.15	0.25	1.25	2.50	9.00	22.00	—
1938	3,898,974	0.20	0.90	2.00	7.00	50.00	150	—
1939	5,661,123	0.15	0.30	1.25	3.00	30.00	80.00	—
1940	13,920,197	0.15	0.20	0.75	2.25	18.00	55.00	—
1941	8,681,785	0.10	0.20	0.75	2.25	23.00	70.00	—
1942 round	6,847,544	0.15	0.20	0.75	1.75	18.00	35.00	—

KM# 39   Obv. Designer: T. H. Paget **Rev. Designer:** George E. Kruger-Gray **Composition:** Tombac **Shape:** 12-sided

Date	Mintage	VG-8	F-12	VF-20	XF-40	MS-60	MS-63	Proof
1942	3,396,234	0.40	0.65	1.25	1.75	3.00	14.00	—

KM# 40   Subject: Victory **Obv. Designer:** T. H. Paget **Rev. Designer:** Thomas Shingles **Composition:** Tombac

Date	Mintage	VG-8	F-12	VF-20	XF-40	MS-60	MS-63	Proof
1943	24,760,256	0.20	0.30	0.40	0.80	2.00	9.00	—
1944	8,000	—	—	—	—	—	—	—

Note: 1 known

KM# 40a Composition: Chrome Plated Steel

Date	Mintage	VG-8	F-12	VF-20	XF-40	MS-60	MS-63	Proof
1944	11,532,784	0.15	0.20	0.40	0.90	2.00	4.00	—
1945	18,893,216	0.15	0.20	0.40	0.80	2.00	4.00	—

Dot   Maple leaf

KM# 39a Obv. Designer: T. H. Paget **Rev. Designer:** George E. Kruger-Gray **Composition:** Nickel

Date	Mintage	VG-8	F-12	VF-20	XF-40	MS-60	MS-63	Proof
1946	6,952,684	0.15	0.20	0.50	2.00	8.00	30.00	—
1947	7,603,724	0.15	0.20	0.50	1.25	6.50	23.00	—
1947 dot	Inc. above	12.00	20.00	27.00	60.00	175	300	—
1947 maple leaf	9,595,124	0.15	0.20	0.45	1.25	6.00	21.00	—

KM# 42 Obv: Modified legend **Obv. Designer:** T. H. Paget **Rev. Designer:** George E. Kruger-Gray **Composition:** Nickel

Date	Mintage	VG-8	F-12	VF-20	XF-40	MS-60	MS-63	Proof
1948	1,810,789	0.40	0.50	1.00	3.00	12.00	30.00	—
1949	13,037,090	0.15	0.20	0.35	0.75	4.00	11.00	—
1950	11,970,521	0.15	0.20	0.35	0.75	4.00	11.00	—

KM# 42a Obv. Designer: T. H. Paget **Rev. Designer:** George E. Kruger-Gray **Composition:** Chromium And Nickel-Plated Steel

Date	Mintage	VG-8	F-12	VF-20	XF-40	MS-60	MS-63	Proof
1951	4,313,410	0.15	0.25	0.50	0.80	2.50	7.00	—
Note: Low relief; Second "A" in GRATIA points between denticles								
1951	Inc. above	400	525	700	1,000	1,900	3,100	—
Note: High relief; Second "A" in GRATIA points to a denticle								
1952	10,891,148	0.15	0.20	0.45	0.80	3.00	7.50	—

KM# 48 Subject: Nickel Bicentennial **Obv. Designer:** T. H. Paget **Rev. Designer:** Stephen Trenka **Composition:** Nickel **Shape:** 12-sided

Date	Mintage	VG-8	F-12	VF-20	XF-40	MS-60	MS-63	Proof
ND(1951)	9,028,507	0.15	0.20	0.25	0.45	1.75	5.50	—

KM# 50 Obv: Elizabeth II effigy **Obv. Designer:** Mary Gillick **Rev. Designer:** George E. Kruger-Gray **Composition:** Chromium And Nickel-Plated Steel **Shape:** 12-sided

Date	Mintage	VG-8	F-12	VF-20	XF-40	MS-60	MS-63	Proof
1953	16,635,552	0.15	0.20	0.40	0.90	3.00	4.50	—

Note: without strap

Date	Mintage	VG-8	F-12	VF-20	XF-40	MS-60	MS-63	Proof
1953	Inc. above	200	350	500	750	1,300	2,300	—
Note: without strap, near leaf								
1953	Inc. above	150	225	300	475	1,100	2,300	—
Note: with strap, far leaf								
1953	Inc. above	0.15	0.20	0.40	0.90	3.50	7.00	—
Note: with strap								
1954	6,998,662	0.15	0.25	0.50	1.00	4.00	8.00	—

KM# 50a Obv. Designer: Mary Gillick **Rev. Designer:** George E. Kruger-Gray **Composition:** Nickel

Date	Mintage	VG-8	F-12	VF-20	XF-40	MS-60	MS-63	Proof
1955	5,355,028	0.15	0.25	0.40	0.75	2.50	4.50	—
1956	9,399,854	—	0.20	0.30	0.45	2.25	3.50	—
1957	7,387,703	—	—	0.25	0.30	1.25	3.00	—
1958	7,607,521	—	—	0.25	0.30	1.25	3.00	—
1959	11,552,523	—	—	—	0.20	0.40	1.00	—
1960	37,157,433	—	—	—	0.15	0.50	1.00	—
1961	47,889,051	—	—	—	—	0.30	0.80	—
1962	46,307,305	—	—	—	—	0.30	0.80	—

KM# 57 Obv. Designer: Mary Gillick **Rev. Designer:** George E. Kruger-Gray **Composition:** Nickel **Shape:** Round

Date	Mintage	VG-8	F-12	VF-20	XF-40	MS-60	MS-63	Proof
1963	43,970,320	—	—	—	—	0.20	0.50	—
1964	78,075,068	—	—	—	—	0.20	0.50	—
1964	—	8.00	10.00	12.00	17.00	30.00	60.00	—
Note: extra water line								

KM# 60.1 Obv: Elizabeth II effigy **Obv. Designer:** Arnold Machin **Rev. Designer:** George E. Kruger-Gray **Composition:** Nickel

Date	Mintage	XF-40	MS-60	MS-63	Proof
1965	84,876,018	—	0.20	0.30	—
1966	27,976,648	—	0.20	0.30	—
1968	101,930,379	—	0.20	0.30	—
1969	27,830,229	—	0.20	0.30	—
1970	5,726,010	0.20	0.35	0.75	—
1971	27,312,609	—	0.20	0.30	—
1972	62,417,387	—	0.20	0.30	—
1973	53,507,435	—	0.20	0.30	—
1974	94,704,645	—	0.20	0.30	—
1975	138,882,000	—	0.20	0.30	—
1976	55,140,213	—	0.20	0.30	—
1977	89,120,791	—	0.20	0.30	—
1978	137,079,273	—	0.20	0.30	—

Date	Mintage	MS-60	MS-63	Proof
ND(1967)	36,876,574	0.20	0.40	1.00

KM# 60.2 Obv: Smaller bust **Obv. Designer:** Arnold Machin **Rev. Designer:** George E. Kruger-Gray **Composition:** Nickel

Date	Mintage	MS-60	MS-63	Proof
1979	186,295,825	0.20	0.30	—
1980	134,878,000	0.20	0.30	—
1981	99,107,900	0.20	0.30	—
1981 Proof	199,000	—	—	1.50

KM# 60.2a Obv. Designer: Arnold Machin **Rev. Designer:** George E. Kruger-Gray **Composition:** Copper-Nickel

Date	Mintage	MS-60	MS-63	Proof
1982	64,924,400	0.20	0.30	—
1982 Proof	180,908	—	—	1.50
1983	72,596,000	0.20	0.30	—
1983 Proof	168,000	—	—	1.50
1984	84,088,000	0.20	0.30	—
1984 Proof	161,602	—	—	1.50
1985	126,618,000	0.20	0.30	—
1985 Proof	157,037	—	—	1.50
1986	156,104,000	0.20	0.30	—
1986 Proof	175,745	—	—	1.50
1987	106,299,000	0.15	0.30	—
1987 Proof	179,004	—	—	1.50
1988	75,025,000	0.15	0.30	—
1988 Proof	175,259	—	—	1.50
1989	141,570,538	0.15	0.30	—
1989 Proof	170,928	—	—	1.50

KM# 66 Subject: Confederation Centennial **Obv. Designer:** Arnold Machin **Rev:** Snowshoe rabbit bounding left **Rev. Designer:** Alex Coville **Composition:** Nickel

KM# 182 Obv: Elizabeth II effigy **Obv. Designer:** Dora dePedery-Hunt **Rev. Designer:** George E. Kruger-Gray **Composition:** Copper-Nickel

Date	Mintage	MS-60	MS-63	Proof
1990	42,537,000	0.15	0.30	—
1990 Proof	140,649	—	—	2.50
1991	10,931,000	0.30	0.55	—
1991 Proof	131,888	—	—	7.00
1993	86,877,000	0.15	0.30	—
1993 Proof	143,065	—	—	2.50
1994	99,352,000	0.15	0.30	—
1994 Proof	146,424	—	—	3.00
1995	78,528,000	0.15	0.30	—
1995 Proof	50,000	—	—	2.50
1996 far 6	36,686,000	0.75	2.25	—
1996 near 6	Inc. above	0.70	2.25	—
1996 Proof	—	—	—	6.00
1997	27,354,000	0.15	0.30	—
1997 Proof	—	—	—	5.00
1998	156,873,000	0.15	0.30	—
1998W	—	—	1.50	—
1998 Proof	—	—	—	5.00
1999	124,861,000	0.15	0.30	—
1999W	—	—	—	—
1999 Proof	—	—	—	5.00
2000	108,514,000	0.15	0.30	—
2000W	—	—	1.50	—
2000 Proof	—	—	—	5.00
2001	166,672,000	0.15	0.30	—
2001 Proof	—	—	—	5.00
2003	—	0.15	0.30	—

KM# 205 Subject: Confederation 125 **Obv. Designer:** Dora dePedery-Hunt **Rev. Designer:** George E. Kruger-Gray **Composition:** Copper-Nickel

Date	Mintage	MS-60	MS-63	Proof
ND(1992)	53,732,000	0.15	0.30	—
ND(1992) Proof	147,061	—	—	4.00

KM# 182b Obv: Queen's head right **Obv. Designer:** Dora dePedery-Hunt **Rev:** Beaver **Rev. Designer:** George E. Kruger-Gray **Edge:** Plain **Weight:** 3.9000 g. **Composition:** Nickel Plated Steel **Size:** 21.2 mm.

Date	Mintage	MS-60	MS-63	Proof
1999 P	Est. 20,000	—	15.00	—
2000 P	Est. 2,300,000	1.50	3.50	—
2001 P	136,650	0.20	0.35	—
2003 P	31,388,921	—	0.35	—

KM# 182a Obv. Designer: Dora dePedery-Hunt **Rev. Designer:** George E. Kruger-Gray **Weight:** 5.3500 g. **Composition:** 0.9250 Silver 0.1591 oz. ASW

Date	Mintage	MS-63	Proof
1996 Proof	—	—	5.00
1997 Proof	—	—	5.00

Date	Mintage	MS-63	Proof
1998 Proof	—	—	5.00
1998O Proof	—	—	5.00
1999 Proof	—	—	5.00
2000 Proof	—	—	5.00
2001 Proof	—	—	5.00
2003 Proof	—	—	5.00

KM#310 Subject: 90th Anniversary Royal Canadian Mint **Obv. Designer:** Dora dePedery-Hunt **Rev. Designer:** W. H. J. Blackmore **Weight:** 1.1670 g. **Composition:** 0.9250 Silver .0347 oz. ASW

Date	Mintage	MS-63	Proof
ND(1998)	25,000	12.00	—
ND(1998) Proof	25,000	—	12.00

KM# 400 Subject: First French-Canadian Regiment **Obv:** Queen's portrait **Obv. Designer:** Dora dePedery-Hunt **Rev:** Regimental drums, sash and baton **Rev. Designer:** R. C. M. Staff **Edge:** Plain **Composition:** 0.9250 Silver **Size:** 21.2 mm.

Date	Mintage	MS-63	Proof
2000 Proof	—	—	9.00

KM# 413 Subject: Royal Military College **Obv:** Queen's head right **Rev:** Marching cadets and arch **Rev. Designer:** Gerald T. Locklin **Edge:** Plain **Weight:** 5.3500 g. **Composition:** 0.9250 Silver .1591 oz. ASW **Size:** 21.2 mm.

Date	Mintage	MS-63	Proof
2001 Proof	25,834	—	8.50

KM#453 Subject: Vimy Ridge - WWI **Obv:** Queen's head right **Rev:** Vimy Ridge Memorial, allegorical figure and dates 1917-2003 **Rev. Designer:** S. A. Allward **Composition:** 0.9250 Silver

Date	Mintage	MS-63	Proof
ND(2003) Proof	22,646	—	12.50

KM# 446 Subject: Elizabeth II Golden Jubilee **Obv:** Queen, Jubilee commemorative dates 1952-2002 **Obv. Designer:** Dora dePedery-Hunt **Rev. Designer:** George E. Kruger-Gray **Composition:** Copper-Nickel **Note:** Magnetic.

Date	Mintage	MS-63	Proof
ND(2002)P	134,362,000	0.75	—
ND(2002)P Proof	32,642	—	5.00

KM# 446a Subject: Elizabeth II Golden Jubilee **Obv:** Queen, Jubilee commemorative dates 1952-2002 **Composition:** 0.9250 Silver

Date	Mintage	MS-63	Proof
ND(2002) In proof sets only	100,000	—	11.50

KM# 469 Subject: 50th Anniversary of the Coronation of Elizabeth II **Obv:** 1953 effigy of the Queen, Jubilee commemorative dates 1952-2002 **Composition:** 0.9250 Silver

Date	Mintage	MS-63	Proof
ND(2003) In Coronation Proof sets only	30,000	11.50	—

KM# 491 Obv: New effigy of Queen Elizabeth II **Obv. Designer:** Susanna Blunt **Rev. Designer:** George E. Kruger-Gray **Composition:** Nickel Plated Steel **Note:** Magnetic.

Date	Mintage	MS-63	Proof
2003	61,392,180	1.50	—
2004	123,085,000	0.50	—
2005	—	0.50	—
2006	—	0.50	—

KM# 506 Obv: Queen Elizabeth II **Rev:** "Victory" design of the KM-40 reverse **Edge:** 12-sided plain **Weight:** 5.3500 g. **Composition:** 0.9250 Silver 0.1591 oz. ASW **Size:** 21.3 mm.

Date	Mintage	MS-63	Proof
ND(2004) Proof	20,000	—	11.50

KM# 491a Obv: Elizabeth II by Suanne Blunt **Rev:** Beaver **Edge:** Plain **Weight:** 5.3500 g. **Composition:** 0.9250 Silver 0.1591 oz. ASW **Size:** 21.1 mm.

Date	Mintage	MS-63	Proof
2004 Proof	—	—	3.00

10 CENTS

KM# 3 Obv: Victoria head left **Designer:** Leonard C. Wyon **Edge:** Reeded **Weight:** 2.3240 g. **Composition:** 0.9250 Silver 0.0691 oz. ASW

Date	Mintage	VG-8	F-12	VF-20	XF-40	MS-60	MS-63	Proof
1858/5		475	775	1,250	1,850	4,550	—	—
1858	1,250,000	20.00	35.00	65.00	100.00	325	850	—
1870 Narrow 0	1,600,000	18.00	30.00	75.00	125	375	900	—
1870 Wide 0	Inc. above	25.00	50.00	100.00	200	500	1,150	—
1871	800,000	22.00	40.00	90.00	175	500	1,800	—
1871H	1,870,000	22.00	40.00	95.00	200	550	1,250	—
1872H	1,000,000	90.00	150	300	550	1,750	3,350	—
1874H	600,000	12.00	22.00	45.00	100.00	350	900	—
1875H	1,000,000	200	375	650	1,350	4,500	9,500	—
1880H	1,500,000	12.00	22.00	45.00	85.00	300	800	—
1881H	950,000	17.50	30.00	60.00	110	375	1,000	—
1882H	1,000,000	17.50	30.00	60.00	110	385	1,100	—
1883H	300,000	45.00	85.00	185	325	900	2,000	—
1884	150,000	165	345	635	1,400	5,150	12,000	—
1885	400,000	40.00	75.00	185	425	1,700	4,500	—
1886 Small 6	800,000	20.00	40.00	85.00	185	800	2,250	—
1886 Large 6	Inc. above	30.00	50.00	100.00	215	925	2,150	—
1887	350,000	45.00	85.00	175	375	1,150	3,000	—
1888	500,000	10.00	22.00	45.00	85.00	300	800	—
1889	600,000	450	900	1,550	3,200	10,000	18,500	—
1890H	450,000	20.00	35.00	80.00	175	425	950	—
1891 21 leaves	800,000	20.00	35.00	85.00	175	450	1,150	—
1891 22 leaves	Inc. above	20.00	35.00	85.00	175	435	1,000	—
1892/1	520,000	120	220	425	675	2,350	3,250	—
1892	Inc. above	20.00	35.00	75.00	145	425	950	—
1893 Flat-top 3	500,000	30.00	55.00	110	200	675	1,750	—
1893 Round-top 3	Inc. above	500	975	1,800	3,200	8,000	17,500	—
1894	500,000	25.00	45.00	85.00	150	400	1,150	—
1896	650,000	12.00	22.00	40.00	75.00	275	650	—
1898	720,000	12.00	24.00	45.00	80.00	300	700	—
1899 Small 9's	1,200,000	8.50	16.00	35.00	75.00	210	575	—
1899 Large 9's	Inc. above	16.00	28.00	60.00	120	400	1,100	—
1900	1,100,000	8.50	18.00	40.00	85.00	225	650	—
1901	1,200,000	8.50	18.00	40.00	85.00	225	650	—

KM# 10 Obv: Edward VII bust right **Obv. Designer:** G. W. DeSaulles **Rev. Designer:** Leonard C. Wyon **Edge:** Reeded **Weight:** 2.3240 g. **Composition:** 0.9250 Silver 0.0691 oz. ASW

Date	Mintage	VG-8	F-12	VF-20	XF-40	MS-60	MS-63	Proof
1902	720,000	8.00	16.00	30.00	80.00	325	1,100	—
1902H	1,100,000	4.00	8.00	18.00	40.00	100.00	250	—
1903	500,000	14.00	30.00	75.00	200	1,000	2,100	—
1903H	1,320,000	7.00	16.00	30.00	65.00	250	550	—

Date	Mintage	VG-8	F-12	VF-20	XF-40	MS-60	MS-63	Proof
1904	1,000,000	11.00	24.00	45.00	100.00	325	700	—
1905	1,000,000	6.50	24.00	55.00	100.00	475	1,100	—
1906	1,700,000	6.50	12.00	30.00	60.00	275	750	—
1907	2,620,000	4.25	11.00	23.00	40.00	200	425	—
1908	776,666	8.00	24.00	55.00	95.00	200	400	—
1909	1,697,200	6.00	18.00	40.00	95.00	375	1,000	—
Note: "Victorian" leaves, similar to 1902-08 coins								
1909	Inc. above	10.00	27.00	55.00		125	500	1,300	—
Note: Broad leaves, similar to 1910-12 coins								
1910	4,468,331	4.00	8.00	18.00	35.00	125	300	—

KM# 17 **Obv. Designer:** E. B. MacKennal **Rev. Designer:** Leonard C. Wyon **Edge:** Reeded **Weight:** 2.3240 g. **Composition:** 0.9250 Silver 0.0691 oz. ASW

Date	Mintage	VG-8	F-12	VF-20	XF-40	MS-60	MS-63	Proof
1911	2,737,584	4.50	11.00	18.00	40.00	100.00	200	—

   Small leaves 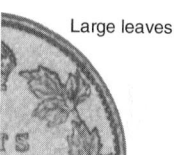 Large leaves

KM# 23 **Obv. Designer:** E. B. MacKennal **Rev. Designer:** Leonard C. Wyon **Edge:** Reeded **Weight:** 2.3240 g. **Composition:** 0.9250 Silver 0.0691 oz. ASW

Date	Mintage	VG-8	F-12	VF-20	XF-40	MS-60	MS-63	Proof
1912	3,235,557	1.75	4.25	9.00	30.00	175	500	—
1913	3,613,937	1.50	2.25	8.50	23.00	125	325	—
Note: sm. leaves								
1913	Inc. above	95.00	175	350	900	5,600	20,000	—
Note: lg. leaves								
1914	2,549,811	1.50	2.50	8.50	25.00	125	375	—
1915	688,057	6.00	15.00	30.00	100.00	325	650	—
1916	4,218,114	1.25	2.25	4.00	17.00	75.00	225	—
1917	5,011,988	1.00	1.50	3.00	10.00	50.00	95.00	—
1918	5,133,602	1.00	1.50	3.00	9.00	45.00	80.00	—
1919	7,877,722	1.00	1.50	3.00	9.00	45.00	80.00	—

KM# 23a **Obv. Designer:** Leonard C. Wyon **Edge:** Reeded **Weight:** 2.3328 g. **Composition:** 0.8000 Silver 0.0600 oz. ASW

Date	Mintage	VG-8	F-12	VF-20	XF-40	MS-60	MS-63	Proof
1920	6,305,345	1.00	1.50	3.00	12.00	50.00	125	—
1921	2,469,562	1.25	2.00	6.00	20.00	80.00	225	—
1928	2,458,602	1.00	1.75	4.00	12.00	55.00	125	—
1929	3,253,888	1.00	2.00	3.50	12.00	55.00	100.00	—
1930	1,831,043	1.00	2.50	4.50	14.00	60.00	125	—
1931	2,067,421	1.00	1.75	4.00	12.00	55.00	100.00	—
1932	1,154,317	1.50	2.50	9.00	23.00	90.00	225	—
1933	672,368	2.00	4.50	12.00	35.00	175	350	—
1934	409,067	3.00	6.00	22.00	60.00	250	500	—
1935	384,056	3.50	6.00	19.00	60.00	250	500	—
1936	2,460,871	1.00	1.25	3.00	9.00	45.00	80.00	—
1936 dot on rev. Specimen, 4 known	—	—	—	—	—	—	—	—

Note: At the David Akers sale of the John Jay Pittman collection, Part 1, 10-97, a gem specimen realized $120,000.

Maple leaf

KM# 34 **Obv. Designer:** T. H. Paget **Rev. Designer:** Emanuel Hahn **Edge:** Reeded **Weight:** 2.3328 g. **Composition:** 0.8000 Silver 0.0600 oz. ASW

Date	Mintage	VG-8	F-12	VF-20	XF-40	MS-60	MS-63	Proof
1937	2,500,095	0.55	1.00	2.00	3.75	12.00	18.00	—
1938	4,197,323	0.80	1.75	3.25	6.50	40.00	90.00	—
1939	5,501,748	0.65	1.25	2.50	5.00	30.00	65.00	—
1940	16,526,470	BV	0.55	1.50	3.00	15.00	30.00	—
1941	8,716,386	BV	1.25	2.50	6.00	25.00	90.00	—
1942	10,214,011	BV	0.55	1.25	4.00	20.00	45.00	—
1943	21,143,229	BV	0.55	1.25	4.00	11.00	30.00	—
1944	9,383,582	BV	0.55	1.50	4.50	15.00	40.00	—
1945	10,979,570	BV	0.55	1.25	4.00	11.00	23.00	—
1946	6,300,066	0.55	1.00	2.00	4.50	20.00	45.00	—
1947	4,431,926	0.60	1.25	2.50	6.00	20.00	45.00	—
1947	9,638,793	BV	0.55	1.50	3.00	10.00	15.00	—
Note: maple leaf								

KM# 43 Obv: Modified legend **Obv. Designer:** T. H. Paget **Rev. Designer:** Emanuel Hahn **Weight:** 2.3328 g. **Composition:** 0.8000 Silver 0.0600 oz. ASW

Date	Mintage	VG-8	F-12	VF-20	XF-40	MS-60	MS-63	Proof
1948	422,741	2.00	3.50	7.50	13.00	45.00	70.00	—
1949	11,336,172	—	0.60	0.85	2.00	9.00	13.00	—
1950	17,823,075	—	BV	0.65	1.50	5.00	12.00	—
1951	15,079,265	—	BV	0.55	1.50	4.00	11.00	—
1951	—	—	1.50	2.50	7.00	22.00	—	—
Note: Doubled die								
1952	10,474,455	—	BV	0.55	1.50	3.00	8.50	—

KM# 51 Obv: Elizabeth II effigy **Obv. Designer:** Mary Gillick **Rev. Designer:** Emanuel Hahn **Weight:** 2.3328 g. **Composition:** 0.8000 Silver 0.0600 oz. ASW

Date	Mintage	VG-8	F-12	VF-20	XF-40	MS-60	MS-63	Proof
1953	17,706,395	—	BV	0.80	1.25	3.00	6.00	—
Note: without straps								
1953	Inc. above	—	BV	0.80	1.25	3.00	8.00	—
Note: with straps								
1954	4,493,150	BV	0.60	1.00	2.25	5.00	16.00	—
1955	12,237,294	—	BV	0.60	0.75	3.00	7.00	—
1956	16,732,844	—	BV	0.60	0.75	2.00	5.00	—
1956	Inc. above	—	2.25	3.00	4.50	13.00	22.00	—
Note: dot below date								
1957	16,110,229	—	—	BV	0.65	1.50	2.25	—
1958	10,621,236	—	—	BV	0.65	1.50	2.25	—
1959	19,691,433	—	—	—	BV	1.25	2.00	—
1960	45,446,835	—	—	—	BV	1.00	1.50	—
1961	26,850,859	—	—	—	BV	0.75	1.50	—
1962	41,864,335	—	—	—	BV	0.55	1.50	—
1963	41,916,208	—	—	—	BV	0.55	1.00	—
1964	49,518,549	—	—	—	BV	0.55	1.00	—

KM# 61 Obv: Elizabeth II effigy **Obv. Designer:** Arnold Machin **Weight:** 2.3328 g. **Composition:** 0.8000 Silver 0.0600 oz. ASW

Date	Mintage	VG-8	F-12	VF-20	XF-40	MS-60	MS-63	Proof
1965	56,965,392	—	—	—	BV	0.55	1.00	—
1966	34,567,898	—	—	—	BV	0.55	1.00	—

KM# 67 Subject: Confederation Centennial **Rev:** Atlantic mackerel left **Rev. Designer:** Alex Colville **Weight:** 2.3328 g. **Composition:** 0.8000 Silver 0.0600 oz. ASW

Date	Mintage	VG-8	F-12	VF-20	XF-40	MS-60	MS-63	Proof
ND(1967)	62,998,215	—	—	—	BV	0.60	1.20	2.00

KM# 67a Subject: Confederation Centennial **Weight:** 2.3328 g. **Composition:** 0.5000 Silver 0.0372 oz. ASW

Date	Mintage	VG-8	F-12	VF-20	XF-40	MS-60	MS-63	Proof
ND(1967)	Inc. above	—	—	—	BV	0.50	1.00	—

Ottawa

KM# 72 Obv. Designer: Arnold Machin **Rev. Designer:** Emanuel Hahn **Weight:** 2.3328 g. **Composition:** 0.5000 Silver 0.0375 oz. ASW

Date	Mintage	VG-8	F-12	VF-20	XF-40	MS-60	MS-63	Proof
1968	70,460,000	—	—	—	BV	0.45	0.90	—
Note: Ottawa reeding								

Ottawa

KM# 72a Composition: Nickel

Date	Mintage	VG-8	F-12	VF-20	XF-40	MS-60	MS-63	Proof
1968	87,412,930	—	—	—	0.15	0.20	0.35	—
Note: Ottawa reeding								

Philadelphia

KM# 73 Obv. Designer: Arnold Machin **Rev. Designer:** Emanuel Hahn **Composition:** Nickel

Date	Mintage	VG-8	F-12	VF-20	XF-40	MS-60	MS-63	Proof
1968	85,170,000	—	—	—	0.15	0.25	0.35	—
Note: Philadelphia reeding								
1969	—	—	6,100	8,300	11,000	19,000	—	—
Note: lg. date, lg. ship, 10-20 known								

KM# 77.1 Obv. Designer: Arnold Machin **Rev:** Redesigned smaller ship **Rev. Designer:** Emanuel Hahn **Composition:** Nickel

Date	Mintage	VG-8	F-12	VF-20	XF-40	MS-60	MS-63	Proof
1969	55,833,929	—	—	—	0.15	0.25	0.35	—
1970	5,249,296	—	—	—	0.25	0.40	0.90	—
1971	41,016,968	—	—	—	0.15	0.20	0.35	—
1972	60,169,387	—	—	—	0.15	0.20	0.35	—
1973	167,715,435	—	—	—	0.15	0.20	0.35	—
1974	201,566,565	—	—	—	0.15	0.20	0.35	—
1975	207,680,000	—	—	—	0.15	0.20	0.35	—
1976	95,018,533	—	—	—	0.15	0.20	0.35	—
1977	128,452,206	—	—	—	0.15	0.20	0.35	—
1978	170,366,431	—	—	—	0.15	0.20	0.35	—

KM# 77.2 Obv: Smaller bust **Obv. Designer:** Arnold Machin **Rev. Designer:** Emanuel Hahn **Composition:** Nickel

Date	Mintage	VG-8	F-12	VF-20	XF-40	MS-60	MS-63	Proof
1979	237,321,321	—	—	—	0.15	0.20	0.35	—
1980	170,111,533	—	—	—	0.15	0.20	0.35	—
1981	123,912,900	—	—	—	0.15	0.20	0.35	—
1981 Proof	199,000	—	—	—	—	—	—	1.50
1982	93,475,000	—	—	—	0.15	0.20	0.35	—
1982 Proof	180,908	—	—	—	—	—	—	1.50
1983	111,065,000	—	—	—	0.15	0.20	0.35	—
1983 Proof	168,000	—	—	—	—	—	—	1.50
1984	121,690,000	—	—	—	0.15	0.20	0.35	—
1984 Proof	161,602	—	—	—	—	—	—	1.50
1985	143,025,000	—	—	—	0.15	0.20	0.35	—
1985 Proof	157,037	—	—	—	—	—	—	1.50
1986	168,620,000	—	—	—	0.15	0.20	0.35	—
1986 Proof	175,745	—	—	—	—	—	—	1.50
1987	147,309,000	—	—	—	0.15	0.20	0.35	—
1987 Proof	179,004	—	—	—	—	—	—	1.50
1988	162,998,558	—	—	—	0.15	0.20	0.35	—
1988 Proof	175,259	—	—	—	—	—	—	1.50
1989	199,104,414	—	—	—	0.15	0.20	0.35	—
1989 Proof	170,528	—	—	—	—	—	—	1.50

KM# 183 Obv: Elizabeth II effigy **Obv. Designer:** Dora dePedery-Hunt **Rev. Designer:** Emanuel Hahn **Composition:** Nickel

Date	Mintage	XF-40	MS-60	MS-63	Proof
1990	65,023,000	0.15	0.20	0.35	—
1990 Proof	140,649	—	—	—	2.50
1991	50,397,000	0.15	0.30	0.45	—
1991 Proof	131,888	—	—	—	4.00
1993	135,569,000	0.15	0.20	0.35	—
1993 Proof	143,065	—	—	—	2.00
1994	145,800,000	0.15	0.20	0.35	—
1994 Proof	146,424	—	—	—	2.50
1995	123,875,000	0.15	0.20	0.35	—
1995 Proof	50,000	—	—	—	2.50
1996	51,814,000	0.15	0.20	0.35	—
1996 Proof	—	—	—	—	2.50
1997	43,126,000	0.15	0.20	0.35	—
1997 Proof	—	—	—	—	2.50
1998	203,514,000	0.15	0.20	0.35	—
1998W	—	—	—	1.50	—
1998 Proof	—	—	—	—	2.50
1999	258,462,000	0.15	0.20	0.35	—
1999 Proof	—	—	—	—	2.50
2000	159,125,000	0.15	0.20	0.35	—
2000 Proof	—	—	—	—	2.50
2000W	—	—	—	1.50	—

KM# 183a Weight: 2.4000 g. **Composition:** 0.9250 Silver 0.0713 oz. ASW

Date	Mintage	MS-63	Proof
1996 Proof	—	—	5.50
1997 Proof	—	—	5.50
1998 Proof	—	—	4.00
1998O Proof	—	—	4.00
1999 Proof	—	—	5.00
2000 Proof	—	—	5.00
2001 Proof	—	—	5.00
2002 Proof	—	—	5.00
2003 Proof	—	—	5.00

KM# 206 Subject: Confederation 125 **Composition:** Nickel

Date	Mintage	VG-8	MS-60	MS-63	Proof
ND(1992)	174,476,000	—	0.25	0.35	—
ND(1992) Proof	147,061	—	—	—	3.00

KM# 299 Subject: John Cabot **Rev. Designer:** Donald H. Curley **Weight:** 2.4000 g. **Composition:** 0.9250 Silver .0714 oz. ASW

Date	Mintage	MS-63	Proof
ND(1997) Proof	49,848	—	17.50

KM# 311 Subject: 90th Anniversary Royal Canadian Mint **Weight:** 2.3200 g. **Composition:** 0.9250 Silver .0690 oz. ASW

Date	Mintage	MS-63	Proof
ND(1998) Matte	25,000	—	10.00
ND(1998) Proof	25,000	—	10.00

KM# 183b Obv: Queen's head right **Obv. Designer:** Dora dePedery-Hunt **Rev:** Sailboat **Rev. Designer:** Emanuel Hahn **Edge:** Reeded **Composition:** Nickel Plated Steel **Size:** 18 mm.

Date	Mintage	MS-63	Proof
1999 P	Est. 20,000	15.00	—
2000 P	Est. 200	600	—
2001 P	266,000,000	0.45	—
2003 P	162,398,000	0.20	—

KM# 409 Subject: First Canadian Credit Union **Obv:** Queen's head right **Rev:** Alphonse Desjardins' house, (founder of the first credit union in Canada) **Edge:** Reeded **Weight:** 2.4000 g. **Composition:** 0.9250 Silver .0714 oz. ASW **Size:** 18 mm.

Date	Mintage	MS-63	Proof
ND(2000) Proof	66,336	—	8.00

KM# 412 Subject: Year of the Volunteer **Obv:** Queen's head right **Rev:** Three portraits and radiant sun **Rev. Designer:** R. C. M. Staff **Edge:** Reeded **Weight:** 1.7700 g. **Composition:** Nickel Plated Steel **Size:** 18 mm.

Date	Mintage	MS-63	Proof
2001P Proof	—	—	8.50

KM# 412a Subject: Year of the Volunteer **Obv:** Queen's head right **Rev:** 3 conjoined busts above banner, radiant sun below **Edge:** Reeded **Weight:** 2.4000 g. **Composition:** 0.9250 Silver .0714 oz. ASW **Size:** 18 mm.

Date	Mintage	MS-63	Proof
2001P Proof	50,000	—	12.50

KM# 447 Subject: Elizabeth II Golden Jubilee **Obv:** Queen, Jubilee commemorative dates 1952-2002 **Composition:** Nickel Plated Steel

Date	Mintage	MS-63	Proof
ND(2002)P	251,278,000	1.00	—
ND(2002) Proof	32,642	—	2.50

KM# 447a Subject: Elizabeth II Golden Jubilee **Obv:** Queen, Jubilee commemorative dates 1952-2002 **Composition:** 0.9250 Silver

Date	Mintage	MS-63	Proof
ND(2002) In proof sets only	100,000	—	12.50

KM# 470 Subject: 50th Anniversary of the Coronation of Elizabeth II **Composition:** 0.9250 Silver

Date	Mintage	MS-63	Proof
ND(2003) In Coronation Proof sets only	30,000	12.00	—

KM# 492 Obv: New effigy of Queen Elizabeth II **Obv. Designer:** Susanna Blunt **Composition:** Nickel Plated Steel

Date	Mintage	MS-63	Proof
2003P	—	1.50	—
2004P	211,924,000	0.60	—
2005P	—	0.60	—
2006P	—	0.60	—

KM# 492a Obv: Elizabeth II by Suanne Blunt **Rev:** Sailboat **Edge:** Reeded **Weight:** 2.4000 g. **Composition:** 0.9250 Silver 0.0714 oz. ASW **Size:** 18 mm.

Date	Mintage	MS-63	Proof
2004 Proof	—	—	5.00

KM# 524 Subject: Golf, Championship of Canada, Centennial. **Weight:** 2.4000 g. **Composition:** 0.9250 Silver 0.0714 oz. ASW

Date	Mintage	MS-63	Proof
2004	—	12.50	—

20 CENTS

KM# 4 Weight: 4.6480 g. **Composition:** 0.9250 Silver 0.1382 oz. ASW

Date	Mintage	VG-8	F-12	VF-20	XF-40	MS-60	MS-63	Proof
1858	750,000	45.00	60.00	90.00	170	725	1,950	—

25 CENTS

KM# 5 Obv. Designer: Leonard C. Wyon **Weight:** 5.8100 g. **Composition:** 0.9250 Silver 0.1728 oz. ASW

Date	Mintage	VG-8	F-12	VF-20	XF-40	MS-60	MS-63	Proof
1870	900,000	14.00	30.00	75.00	150	550	1,500	—
1871	400,000	22.00	40.00	90.00	225	800	2,100	—
1871H	748,000	25.00	45.00	115	250	700	1,650	—
1872H	2,240,000	10.00	20.00	40.00	90.00	425	1,250	—
1872H	Inc. above	—	—	—	—	2,500	6,000	—
Note: Inverted A for V in Victoria								
1874H	1,600,000	10.00	20.00	40.00	90.00	375	1,100	—
1875H	1,000,000	275	550	1,350	2,750	10,000	17,500	—
1880H Narrow 0	400,000	40.00	85.00	220	400	1,150	2,750	—
1880H Wide 0	Inc. above	60.00	185	350	800	2,350	4,750	—
1880H Wide/narrow 0	Inc. above	100.00	225	400	950	2,800	—	—
1881H	820,000	20.00	45.00	90.00	250	1,000	2,300	—
1882H	600,000	20.00	45.00	110	265	1,000	2,150	—
1883H	960,000	16.00	32.00	70.00	150	500	1,250	—
1885	192,000	100.00	200	450	950	3,500	7,500	—
1886/3	540,000	35.00	80.00	150	375	1,500	3,200	—
1886	Inc. above	20.00	40.00	110	285	1,100	2,800	—
1887	100,000	85.00	225	450	1,000	4,250	8,000	—
1888	400,000	20.00	40.00	80.00	185	650	1,550	—
1889	66,324	100.00	250	500	1,000	3,500	8,500	—
1890H	200,000	25.00	50.00	125	275	950	2,250	—
1891	120,000	65.00	125	320	625	1,600	2,500	—
1892	510,000	15.00	25.00	65.00	175	675	1,600	—
1893	100,000	90.00	185	375	700	1,750	3,000	—
1894	220,000	20.00	40.00	90.00	250	700	1,600	—
1899	415,580	11.00	20.00	55.00	150	600	1,350	—
1900	1,320,000	11.00	20.00	45.00	100.00	525	1,200	—
1901	640,000	11.00	21.00	50.00	150	550	1,200	—

KM# 11 Obv. Designer: G. W. DeSaulles **Weight:** 5.8100 g. **Composition:** 0.9250 Silver 0.1728 oz. ASW

Date	Mintage	VG-8	F-12	VF-20	XF-40	MS-60	MS-63	Proof
1902	464,000	10.00	27.00	65.00	175	750	1,900	—
1902H	800,000	6.50	16.00	45.00	100.00	250	500	—

Date	Mintage	VG-8	F-12	VF-20	XF-40	MS-60	MS-63	Proof
1903	846,150	15.00	29.00	75.00	200	800	1,900	—
1904	400,000	20.00	55.00	150	350	1,600	5,000	—
1905	800,000	15.00	30.00	100.00	225	1,400	4,600	—
1906	1,237,843	8.00	21.00	55.00	150	500	1,700	—
Note: large crown								
1906 Rare	Inc. above	2,500	3,900	6,000	8,000	—	—	—
Note: small crown								
1907	2,088,000	6.50	16.00	55.00	125	425	1,200	—
1908	495,016	15.00	35.00	95.00	200	400	750	—
1909	1,335,929	13.00	26.00	70.00	175	600	1,700	—

KM# 11a   Weight: 5.8319 g. **Composition:** 0.9250 Silver 0.1734 oz. ASW

Date	Mintage	VG-8	F-12	VF-20	XF-40	MS-60	MS-63	Proof
1910	3,577,569	5.50	16.00	40.00	85.00	275	600	—

KM# 18   Obv. Designer: E. B. MacKennal **Weight:** 5.8319 g. **Composition:** 0.9250 Silver 0.1734 oz. ASW

Date	Mintage	VG-8	F-12	VF-20	XF-40	MS-60	MS-63	Proof
1911	1,721,341	6.50	18.00	35.00	85.00	250	425	—

KM# 24   Obv. Designer: E. B. MacKennal **Weight:** 5.8319 g. **Composition:** 0.9250 Silver 0.1734 oz. ASW

Date	Mintage	VG-8	F-12	VF-20	XF-40	MS-60	MS-63	Proof
1912	2,544,199	3.75	9.00	20.00	55.00	350	1,200	—
1913	2,213,595	3.25	8.50	17.00	50.00	300	950	—
1914	1,215,397	5.00	10.00	23.00	60.00	500	1,600	—
1915	242,382	16.00	45.00	150	425	2,200	6,100	—
1916	1,462,566	2.75	5.00	18.00	40.00	225	700	—
1917	3,365,644	1.85	4.50	11.00	30.00	125	225	—
1918	4,175,649	1.85	3.00	9.50	26.00	95.00	175	—
1919	5,852,262	1.85	3.00	9.50	25.00	95.00	175	—

Dot below wreath

KM# 24a   Obv. Designer: E. B. MacKennal **Weight:** 5.8319 g. **Composition:** 0.8000 Silver 0.1500 oz. ASW

Date	Mintage	VG-8	F-12	VF-20	XF-40	MS-60	MS-63	Proof
1920	1,975,278	2.50	4.50	12.00	30.00	150	400	—
1921	597,337	11.00	24.00	80.00	225	1,100	2,700	—
1927	468,096	27.00	50.00	100.00	225	750	1,600	—
1928	2,114,178	2.75	4.50	13.00	35.00	125	325	—
1929	2,690,562	1.75	4.00	13.00	35.00	125	325	—
1930	968,748	2.50	5.00	18.00	40.00	200	500	—
1931	537,815	2.50	5.50	20.00	50.00	200	500	—
1932	537,994	2.50	6.00	25.00	50.00	200	500	—
1933	421,282	3.00	6.50	28.00	65.00	175	325	—
1934	384,350	3.50	9.00	30.00	70.00	225	500	—
1935	537,772	3.50	7.50	22.00	50.00	150	325	—
1936	972,094	1.75	3.50	8.00	21.00	95.00	175	—
1936 dot	153,322	26.00	65.00	150	300	800	1,800	—
Note: David Akers John Jay Pittman sale Part Three, 10-99, nearly Choice Unc. realized $6,900; considered a possible specimen example								

Maple leaf after date

KM# 35 Obv. Designer: T. H. Paget **Rev. Designer:** Emanuel Hahn **Weight:** 5.8319 g. **Composition:** 0.8000 Silver 0.1500 oz. ASW

Date	Mintage	VG-8	F-12	VF-20	XF-40	MS-60	MS-63	Proof
1937	2,690,176	1.50	2.00	4.00	6.00	10.00	25.00	—
1938	3,149,245	1.50	3.00	5.00	10.00	40.00	125	—
1939	3,532,495	1.50	2.00	5.00	7.00	35.00	75.00	—
1940	9,583,650	—	BV	1.50	2.50	15.00	30.00	—
1941	6,654,672	—	BV	1.50	2.50	16.00	30.00	—
1942	6,935,871	—	BV	1.50	2.50	17.00	45.00	—
1943	13,559,575	—	BV	1.50	2.50	16.00	30.00	—
1944	7,216,237	—	BV	1.50	2.50	17.00	35.00	—
1945	5,296,495	—	BV	1.50	2.00	16.00	30.00	—
1946	2,210,810	BV	2.00	4.00	8.00	30.00	70.00	—
1947	1,524,554	BV	1.50	4.00	8.00	30.00	90.00	—
1947	Inc. above	30.00	40.00	70.00	150	250	500	—
Note: Dot after 7								
1947	4,393,938	BV	1.50	2.00	3.00	10.00	30.00	—
Note: Maple leaf								

KM# 44 Obv: Modified legend **Obv. Designer:** T. H. Paget **Rev. Designer:** Emanuel Hahn **Weight:** 5.8319 g. **Composition:** 0.8000 Silver 0.1500 oz. ASW

Date	Mintage	VG-8	F-12	VF-20	XF-40	MS-60	MS-63	Proof
1948	2,564,424	BV	1.50	3.00	9.00	35.00	70.00	—
1949	7,988,830	—	BV	1.50	2.00	5.50	18.00	—
1950	9,673,335	—	—	BV	1.50	4.50	14.00	—
1951	8,290,719	—	—	BV	1.50	4.50	10.00	—
1952	8,859,642	—	—	BV	1.50	4.50	10.00	—

KM# 52 Obv: Elizabeth II effigy **Obv. Designer:** Mary Gillick **Rev. Designer:** Emanuel Hahn **Weight:** 5.8319 g. **Composition:** 0.8000 Silver 0.1500 oz. ASW

Date	Mintage	VG-8	F-12	VF-20	XF-40	MS-60	MS-63	Proof
1953	10,546,769	—	—	BV	1.50	3.00	10.00	—
Note: without strap								
1953	Inc. above	—	—	BV	1.50	6.50	18.00	—
Note: with strap								
1954	2,318,891	BV	1.50	2.00	4.00	15.00	40.00	—
1955	9,552,505	—	—	BV	1.50	4.50	15.00	—
1956	11,269,353	—	—	BV	1.50	3.25	6.50	—
1957	12,770,190	—	—	—	BV	1.50	4.50	—
1958	9,336,910	—	—	—	BV	1.50	3.00	—
1959	13,503,461	—	—	—	BV	1.50	2.50	—
1960	22,835,327	—	—	—	BV	1.50	2.50	—
1961	18,164,368	—	—	—	BV	1.50	2.50	—
1962	29,559,266	—	—	—	BV	1.50	2.50	—
1963	21,180,652	—	—	—	—	BV	1.50	—
1964	36,479,343	—	—	—	—	BV	1.50	—

KM# 62   Obv: Elizabeth II effigy **Obv. Designer:** Arnold Machin **Rev. Designer:** Emanuel Hahn **Weight:** 5.8319 g. **Composition:** 0.8000 Silver 0.1500 oz. ASW

Date	Mintage	VG-8	F-12	VF-20	XF-40	MS-60	MS-63	Proof
1965	44,708,869	—	—	—	—	BV	1.50	—
1966	25,626,315	—	—	—	—	BV	1.50	—

KM# 68   Subject: Confederation Centennial **Rev:** Lynx striding left **Rev. Designer:** Alex Colville **Weight:** 5.8319 g. **Composition:** 0.8000 Silver 0.1500 oz. ASW

Date	Mintage	VG-8	F-12	VF-20	XF-40	MS-60	MS-63	Proof
ND(1967)	48,855,500	—	—	—	BV	1.50	2.00	—

KM# 68a   Subject: Confederation Centennial **Weight:** 5.8319 g. **Composition:** 0.5000 Silver 0.0937 oz. ASW

Date	Mintage	VG-8	F-12	VF-20	XF-40	MS-60	MS-63	Proof
ND(1967)	Inc. above	—	—	—	BV	1.00	1.75	—

KM# 62a   Obv: Elizabeth II effigy **Obv. Designer:** Machin **Weight:** 5.8319 g. **Composition:** 0.5000 Silver 0.0937 oz. ASW

Date	Mintage	VG-8	F-12	VF-20	XF-40	MS-60	MS-63	Proof
1968	71,464,000	—	—	—	BV	0.85	1.25	—

KM# 62b   Obv: Elizabeth II effigy **Obv. Designer:** Machin **Composition:** Nickel

Date	Mintage	VG-8	F-12	VF-20	XF-40	MS-60	MS-63	Proof
1968	88,686,931	—	—	—	0.30	0.45	0.75	—
1969	133,037,929	—	—	—	0.30	0.45	0.75	—
1970	10,302,010	—	—	—	0.30	1.00	2.00	—
1971	48,170,428	—	—	—	0.30	0.45	0.75	—
1972	43,743,387	—	—	—	0.30	0.45	0.75	—
1973	135,958,589	—	—	—	0.30	0.50	1.00	—
Note: Small bust								
1973	Inc. above	—	60.00	70.00	80.00	110	200	—
Note: Large bust								
1974	192,360,598	—	—	—	0.30	0.45	0.75	—
1975	141,148,000	—	—	—	0.30	0.45	0.75	—
1976	86,898,261	—	—	—	0.30	0.45	0.75	—
1977	99,634,555	—	—	—	0.30	0.45	0.75	—
1978	176,475,408	—	—	—	0.30	0.45	0.75	—

KM# 81.1   Subject: Royal Candian Mounted Police Centennial **Rev. Designer:** Paul Cedarberg **Composition:** Nickel **Note:** 120 beads.

Date	Mintage	VG-8	F-12	VF-20	XF-40	MS-60	MS-63	Proof
ND(1973)	134,958,587	—	—	—	0.30	0.55	1.00	—

KM# 81.2   Subject: RCMP Centennial **Composition:** Nickel **Note:** 132 beads.

Date	Mintage	VG-8	F-12	VF-20	XF-40	MS-60	MS-63	Proof
ND(1973)	Inc. above	40.00	55.00	70.00	85.00	100.00	200	—

KM# 74 Obv: Elizabeth II effigy, smaller bust **Obv. Designer:** Machin **Rev. Designer:** Emanuel Hahn **Composition:** Nickel

Date	Mintage	VG-8	F-12	VF-20	XF-40	MS-60	MS-63	Proof
1979	131,042,905	—	—	—	0.30	0.45	0.75	—
1980	76,178,000	—	—	—	0.30	0.45	0.75	—
1981	131,580,272	—	—	—	0.30	0.45	0.75	—
1981 Proof	199,000	—	—	—	—	—	—	2.00
1982	171,926,000	—	—	—	0.30	0.45	0.75	—
1982 Proof	180,908	—	—	—	—	—	—	2.00
1983	13,162,000	—	—	—	0.30	0.75	1.50	—
1983 Proof	168,000	—	—	—	—	—	—	3.00
1984	121,668,000	—	—	—	0.30	0.45	0.75	—
1984 Proof	161,602	—	—	—	—	—	—	2.00
1985	158,734,000	—	—	—	0.30	0.45	0.75	—
1985 Proof	157,037	—	—	—	—	—	—	2.00
1986	132,220,000	—	—	—	0.30	0.45	0.75	—
1986 Proof	175,745	—	—	—	—	—	—	2.00
1987	53,408,000	—	—	—	0.30	0.60	1.25	—
1987 Proof	179,004	—	—	—	—	—	—	2.00
1988	80,368,473	—	—	—	0.30	0.45	1.00	—
1988 Proof	175,259	—	—	—	—	—	—	2.00
1989	119,796,307	—	—	—	0.30	0.45	0.75	—
1989 Proof	170,928	—	—	—	—	—	—	2.00

KM# 184 Obv: Elizabeth II effigy **Obv. Designer:** Dora dePedery-Hunt **Rev. Designer:** Emanuel Hahn **Composition:** Nickel

Date	Mintage	VG-8	F-12	VF-20	XF-40	MS-60	MS-63	Proof
1990	31,258,000	—	—	—	0.30	0.45	0.90	—
1990 Proof	140,649	—	—	—	—	—	—	2.50
1991	459,000	—	—	2.00	3.50	6.00	12.00	—
1991 Proof	131,888	—	—	—	—	—	—	20.00
1993	73,758,000	—	—	—	0.25	0.35	0.70	—
1993 Proof	143,065	—	—	—	—	—	—	2.00
1994	77,670,000	—	—	—	0.25	0.35	0.70	—
1994 Proof	146,424	—	—	—	—	—	—	3.00
1995	89,210,000	—	—	—	0.25	0.35	0.70	—
1995 Proof	50,000	—	—	—	—	—	—	3.00
1996 Proof	—	—	—	—	—	—	—	6.00
1996	28,106,000	—	—	—	—	—	0.70	—
1997	—	—	—	—	—	—	0.70	—
1997 Proof	—	—	—	—	—	—	—	6.00
1998W	—	—	—	—	—	—	5.00	—
1999	258,888,000	—	—	—	—	—	0.75	—
1999 Proof	—	—	—	—	—	—	—	6.00
2000 Proof	—	—	—	—	—	—	—	6.00
2000	434,087,000	—	—	—	—	—	0.75	—
2000W	—	—	—	—	—	—	5.00	—
2001	64,182,000	—	—	—	—	—	4.00	—
2001 Proof	—	—	—	—	—	—	—	6.00

KM# 207 Subject: Confederation 125 **Obv. Designer:** Dora dePedery-Hunt **Rev. Designer:** Emanuel Hahn **Composition:** Nickel

Date	Mintage	VG-8	F-12	VF-20	XF-40	MS-60	MS-63	Proof
ND(1992)	442,986	—	—	—	—	—	12.50	—
ND(1992) Proof	147,061	—	—	—	—	—	—	20.00

KM# 203 Subject: 125th Anniversary of Confederation, New Brunswick **Rev:** Covered bridge in Newton **Rev. Designer:** Ronald Lambert **Composition:** Nickel

Date	Mintage	MS-60	MS-63	Proof
ND(1992)	12,174,000	0.35	0.70	—

KM# 203a Subject: 125th Anniversary of Confederation, New Brunswick **Weight:** 5.8319 g. **Composition:** 0.9250 Silver 0.1734 oz. ASW

Date	Mintage	MS-60	MS-63	Proof
ND(1992) Proof	149,579	—	—	5.50

KM# 212 Subject: 125th Anniversary of Confederation, North West Territories **Rev. Designer:** Beth McEachen **Composition:** Nickel

Date	Mintage	MS-60	MS-63	Proof
ND(1992)	12,582,000	0.35	0.70	—

KM# 212a Subject: 125th Anniversary of Confederation, North West Territories **Weight:** 5.8319 g. **Composition:** 0.9250 Silver 0.1734 oz. ASW

Date	Mintage	MS-60	MS-63	Proof
ND(1992) Proof	149,579	—	—	5.50

KM# 213 Subject: 125th Anniversary of Confederation, Newfoundland **Rev:** Fisherman rowing a dory **Rev. Designer:** Christopher Newhook **Composition:** Nickel

Date	Mintage	MS-60	MS-63	Proof
ND(1992)	11,405,000	0.35	0.70	—

KM# 213a Subject: 125th Anniversary of Confederation, Newfoundland **Weight:** 5.8319 g. **Composition:** 0.9250 Silver 0.1734 oz. ASW

Date	Mintage	MS-60	MS-63	Proof
ND(1992) Proof	149,579	—	—	5.50

KM# 214 Subject: 125th Anniversary of Confederation, Manitoba **Rev. Designer:** Muriel Hope **Composition:** Nickel

Date	Mintage	MS-60	MS-63	Proof
ND(1992)	11,349,000	0.35	0.70	—

KM# 214a Subject: 125th Anniversary of Confederation, Manitoba **Weight:** 5.8319 g. **Composition:** 0.9250 Silver 0.1734 oz. ASW

Date	Mintage	MS-60	MS-63	Proof
ND(1992) Proof	149,579	—	—	5.50

KM# 220 Subject: 125th Anniversary of Confederation, Yukon **Rev. Designer:** Libby Dulac **Composition:** Nickel

Date	Mintage	MS-60	MS-63	Proof
ND(1992)	10,388,000	0.35	0.70	—

KM# 220a Subject: 125th Anniversary of Confederation, Yukon **Weight:** 5.8319 g. **Composition:** 0.9250 Silver 0.1734 oz. ASW

Date	Mintage	MS-60	MS-63	Proof
ND(1992) Proof	149,579	—	—	5.50

KM# 221 Subject: 125th Anniversary of Confederation, Alberta **Rev:** Rock formations in the badlands near Drumhelter **Rev. Designer:** Mel Heath **Composition:** Nickel

Date	Mintage	MS-60	MS-63	Proof
ND(1992)	12,133,000	0.35	0.70	—

KM# 221a Subject: 125th Anniversary of Confederation, Alberta **Weight:** 5.8319 g. **Composition:** 0.9250 Silver 0.1734 oz. ASW

Date	Mintage	MS-60	MS-63	Proof
ND(1992) Proof	—	—	—	5.50

KM# 222 Subject: 125th Anniversary of Confederation, Prince Edward Island **Rev. Designer:** Nigel Roe **Composition:** Nickel

Date	Mintage	MS-60	MS-63	Proof
ND(1992)	13,001,000	0.35	0.70	—

KM# 222a Subject: 125th Anniversary of Confederation, Prince Edward Island **Weight:** 5.8319 g. **Composition:** 0.9250 Silver 0.1734 oz. ASW

Date	Mintage	MS-60	MS-63	Proof
ND(1992) Proof	149,579	—	—	5.50

KM# 223 Subject: 125th Anniversary of Confederation, Ontario **Rev:** Jack pine **Rev. Designer:** Greg Salmela **Composition:** Nickel

Date	Mintage	MS-60	MS-63	Proof
ND(1992)	14,263,000	0.35	0.70	—

KM# 223a Subject: 125th Anniversary of Confederation, Ontario **Weight:** 5.8319 g. **Composition:** 0.9250 Silver 0.1734 oz. ASW

Date	Mintage	MS-60	MS-63	Proof
ND(1992) Proof	149,579	—	—	5.50

KM# 231 Subject: 125th Anniversary of Confederation, Nova Scotia **Rev:** Lighthouse **Rev. Designer:** Bruce Wood **Composition:** Nickel

Date	Mintage	MS-60	MS-63	Proof
ND(1992)	13,600,000	0.35	0.70	—

KM# 231a Subject: 125th Anniversary of Confederation, Nova Scotia **Weight:** 5.8319 g. **Composition:** 0.9250 Silver 0.1734 oz. ASW

Date	Mintage	MS-60	MS-63	Proof
ND(1992) Proof	149,579	—	—	5.50

KM# 232 Subject: 125th Anniversary of Confederation, British Columbia **Rev. Designer:** Carla Herrera Egan **Composition:** Nickel

Date	Mintage	MS-60	MS-63	Proof
ND(1992)	14,001,000	0.35	0.70	—

KM# 232a Subject: 125th Anniversary of Confederation, British Columbia **Weight:** 5.8319 g. **Composition:** 0.9250 Silver 0.1734 oz. ASW

Date	Mintage	MS-60	MS-63	Proof
ND(1992) Proof	149,579	—	—	5.50

KM# 233 Subject: 125th Anniversary of Confederation, Saskatchewan **Rev. Designer:** Brian Cobb **Composition:** Nickel

Date	Mintage	MS-60	MS-63	Proof
ND(1992)	14,165,000	0.35	0.70	—

KM# 233a Subject: 125th Anniversary of Confederation, Saskatchewan **Weight:** 5.8319 g. **Composition:** 0.9250 Silver 0.1734 oz. ASW

Date	Mintage	MS-60	MS-63	Proof
ND(1992) Proof	149,579	—	—	5.50

KM# 234 Subject: 125th Anniversary of Confederation, Quebec **Rev. Designer:** Romualdas Bukauskas **Composition:** Nickel

Date	Mintage	MS-60	MS-63	Proof
ND(1992)	13,607,000	0.35	0.70	—

KM# 234a Subject: 125th Anniversary of Confederation, Quebec **Weight:** 5.8319 g. **Composition:** 0.9250 Silver 0.1734 oz. ASW

Date	Mintage	Proof
ND(1992) Proof	149,579	5.50

KM# 184a Weight: 5.9000 g. **Composition:** 0.9250 Silver 0.1754 oz. ASW

Date	Mintage	Proof
1996 Proof	—	6.50
1997 Proof	—	6.50
1998 Proof	—	5.50
1998O Proof	—	5.50
1999 Proof	—	5.50
2001 Proof	—	6.50
2003 Proof	—	6.50

KM# 184b Composition: Nickel Plated Steel

Date	Mintage	MS-60	MS-63	Proof
1999 P	Est. 20,000	—	20.00	—
2000 P	—	—	2,000	—
Note: 3-5 known				
2001 P	52,153,000	0.35	0.70	—
2002 P	—	—	0.50	—
2003 P	15,905,090	—	0.50	—

KM# 342 Subject: Millennium, January - A country unfolds **Rev:** Totem pole, portraits **Rev. Designer:** P. Ka-Kin Poon **Composition:** Nickel

Date	Mintage	MS-60	MS-63	Proof
1999	12,181,200	0.50	0.65	—

KM# 342a Subject: Millennium, January **Rev:** Totem pole, portraits **Weight:** 5.8319 g. **Composition:** 0.9250 Silver 0.1734 oz. ASW

Date	Mintage	Proof
1999 Proof	113,645	8.00

KM# 343 Subject: Millennium, February - Etched in stone **Rev:** Native petroglyphs **Rev. Designer:** L. Springer **Composition:** Nickel

Date	Mintage	MS-60	MS-63	Proof
1999	14,469,250	0.50	0.65	—

KM# 343a Subject: Millennium, February **Rev:** Native petroglyphs **Weight:** 5.8319 g. **Composition:** 0.9250 Silver 0.1734 oz. ASW

Date	Mintage	Proof
1999 Proof	113,645	8.00

KM# 344 Subject: Millennium, March - The log drive **Rev:** Lumberjack **Rev. Designer:** M. Lavoie **Composition:** Nickel

Date	Mintage	MS-60	MS-63	Proof
1999	15,033,500	0.50	0.65	—

KM# 344a Subject: Millennium, March **Rev:** Lumberjack **Weight:** 5.8319 g. **Composition:** 0.9250 Silver 0.1734 oz. ASW

Date	Mintage	Proof
1999 Proof	113,645	8.00

KM# 345 Subject: Millennium, April - Our Northern Heritage **Rev:** Owl, polar bear **Rev. Designer:** Ken Ojnak Ashevac **Composition:** Nickel

Date	Mintage	MS-60	MS-63	Proof
1999	15,446,000	0.50	0.65	—

KM# 345a Subject: Millennium, April **Rev:** Owl, polar bear **Weight:** 5.8319 g. **Composition:** 0.9250 Silver 0.1734 oz. ASW

Date	Mintage	Proof
1999 Proof	113,645	8.00

KM# 346 Subject: Millennium, May - The Voyageures **Rev:** Voyageurs in canoe **Rev. Designer:** S. Mineok **Composition:** Nickel

Date	Mintage	MS-60	MS-63	Proof
1999	15,566,100	0.50	0.65	—

KM# 346a Subject: Millennium, May **Rev:** Voyageurs in canoe **Weight:** 5.8319 g. **Composition:** 0.9250 Silver 0.1734 oz. ASW

Date	Mintage	Proof
1999 Proof	113,645	8.00

KM# 347 Subject: Millennium, June - from Coast to Coast **Rev:** 19th-century locomotive **Rev. Designer:** G. Ho **Composition:** Nickel

Date	Mintage	MS-60	MS-63	Proof
1999	20,432,750	0.50	0.65	—

KM# 347a Subject: Millennium, June **Rev:** 19th-century locomotive **Weight:** 5.8319 g. **Composition:** 0.9250 Silver 0.1734 oz. ASW

Date	Mintage	Proof
1999 Proof	113,645	8.00

KM# 348 Subject: Millennium, July - A Nation of people **Rev:** 6 stylized portraits **Rev. Designer:** M. H. Sarkany **Composition:** Nickel

Date	Mintage	MS-60	MS-63	Proof
1999	17,321,000	0.50	0.65	—

KM# 348a Subject: Millennium, July **Rev:** 6 stylized portraits **Weight:** 5.8319 g. **Composition:** 0.9250 Silver 0.1734 oz. ASW

Date	Mintage	Proof
1999 Proof	113,645	8.00

KM# 349 Subject: Millennium, August - the Pioneer Spirit **Rev:** Hay harvesting **Rev. Designer:** A. Botelho **Composition:** Nickel

Date	Mintage	MS-60	MS-63	Proof
1999	18,153,700	0.50	0.65	—

KM# 349a Subject: Millennium, August **Rev:** Hay harvesting **Weight:** 5.8319 g. **Composition:** 0.9250 Silver 0.1734 oz. ASW

Date	Mintage	Proof
1999 Proof	113,645	8.00

KM# 350 Subject: Millennium, September - Canada through a child's eye **Rev:** Childlike artwork **Rev. Designer:** Claudia Bertrand **Composition:** Nickel

Date	Mintage	MS-60	MS-63	Proof
1999	31,539,350	0.50	0.65	—

KM# 350a Subject: Millennium, September **Rev:** Childlike artwork **Weight:** 5.8319 g. **Composition:** 0.9250 Silver 0.1734 oz. ASW

Date	Mintage	Proof
1999 Proof	113,645	8.00

KM# 351 Subject: Millennium, October - tribute to the First Nations **Rev:** Aboriginal artwork **Rev. Designer:** J. E. Read **Composition:** Nickel

Date	Mintage	MS-60	MS-63	Proof
1999	32,136,650	0.50	0.65	—

KM# 351a Subject: Millennium, October **Rev:** Aboriginal artwork **Weight:** 5.8319 g. **Composition:** 0.9250 Silver 0.1734 oz. ASW

Date	Mintage	Proof
1999 Proof	113,645	8.00

KM# 352 Subject: Millennium, November - The airplane opens the North **Rev:** Bush plane with landing skis **Rev. Designer:** B. R. Brown **Composition:** Nickel

Date	Mintage	MS-60	MS-63	Proof
1999	27,162,800	0.50	0.65	—

KM# 352a Subject: Millennium, November **Rev:** Bush plane with landing skis **Weight:** 5.8319 g. **Composition:** 0.9250 Silver 0.1734 oz. ASW

Date	Mintage	Proof
1999 Proof	113,645	8.00

KM# 353 Subject: Millennium, December - This is Canada **Rev:** Eclectic geometric design **Rev. Designer:** J. L. P. Provencher **Composition:** Nickel

Date	Mintage	MS-63	Proof
1999	43,339,200	0.70	—

KM# 353a Subject: Millennium, December **Rev:** Eclectic geometric design **Weight:** 5.8319 g. **Composition:** 0.9250 Silver 0.1734 oz. ASW

Date	Mintage	Proof
1999 Proof	113,645	8.00

KM# 373 Subject: Health **Rev:** Ribbon and caduceus **Rev. Designer:** Anny Wassef **Composition:** Nickel

Date	Mintage	MS-60	MS-63	Proof
2000	35,470,900	0.50	0.65	—

KM# 373a Subject: Health **Rev:** Ribbon and caduceus **Composition:** 0.9250 Silver

Date	Mintage	MS-63	Proof
2000 Proof	76,956	—	8.00

KM# 374 Subject: Freedom **Rev:** 2 children and rising sun **Rev. Designer:** Kathy Vinish **Composition:** Nickel

Date	Mintage	MS-60	MS-63	Proof
2000	35,188,900	0.50	0.65	—

KM# 374a Subject: Freedom **Rev:** 2 children and rising sun **Composition:** 0.9250 Silver

Date	Mintage	Proof
2000 Proof	76,956	6.00

KM# 375 Subject: Family **Rev:** Circular native carvings **Rev. Designer:** Wade Stephen Baker **Composition:** Nickel

Date	Mintage	MS-60	MS-63	Proof
2000	35,107,700	0.50	0.65	—

KM# 375a Subject: Family **Rev:** Circular native carvings **Composition:** 0.9250 Silver

Date	Mintage	Proof
2000 Proof	76,956	6.00

KM# 376 Subject: Community **Rev:** Map on globe **Rev. Designer:** Michelle Thibodeau **Composition:** Nickel

Date	Mintage	MS-60	MS-63	Proof
2000	35,155,400	0.50	0.65	—

KM# 376a Subject: Community **Rev:** Map on globe **Composition:** 0.9250 Silver

Date	Mintage	Proof
2000 Proof	76,956	6.00

KM# 377 Subject: Harmony **Rev:** Maple leaf **Rev. Designer:** Haver Demirer **Composition:** Nickel

Date	Mintage	MS-60	MS-63	Proof
2000	35,184,200	0.50	0.65	—

KM# 377a Subject: Harmony **Rev:** Maple leaf **Composition:** 0.9250 Silver

Date	Mintage	Proof
2000 Proof	76,956	6.00

KM# 378 Subject: Wisdom **Rev:** Man with young child **Rev. Designer:** Cezar Serbanescu **Composition:** Nickel

Date	Mintage	MS-60	MS-63	Proof
2000	35,123,950	0.50	0.65	—

KM# 378a Subject: Wisdom **Rev:** Man with young child **Composition:** 0.9250 Silver

Date	Mintage	Proof
2000 Proof	76,956	6.00

KM# 379 Subject: Creativity **Rev:** Canoe full of children **Rev. Designer:** Kong Tat Hui **Composition:** Nickel

Date	Mintage	MS-60	MS-63	Proof
2000	35,316,770	0.50	0.65	—

KM# 379a Subject: Creativity **Rev:** Canoe full of children **Composition:** 0.9250 Silver

Date	Mintage	Proof
2000 Proof	76,956	6.00

KM# 380 Subject: Ingenuity **Rev:** Crescent-shaped city views **Rev. Designer:** John Jaciw **Composition:** Nickel

Date	Mintage	MS-60	MS-63	Proof
2000	36,078,360	0.50	0.65	—

KM# 380a Subject: Ingenuity **Rev:** Crescent-shaped city view **Composition:** 0.9250 Silver

Date	Mintage	Proof
2000 Proof	76,956	6.00

KM# 381 Subject: Achievement **Rev:** Rocket above jagged design **Rev. Designer:** Daryl Dorosz **Composition:** Nickel

Date	Mintage	MS-60	MS-63	Proof
2000	35,312,750	0.50	0.65	—

KM# 381a Subject: Achievement **Rev:** Rocket above jagged design **Composition:** 0.9250 Silver

Date	Mintage	Proof
2000 Proof	76,956	6.00

KM# 382 Subject: Natural legacy **Rev:** Environmental elements **Rev. Designer:** Randy Trantau **Composition:** Nickel

Date	Mintage	MS-60	MS-63	Proof
2000	36,236,900	0.50	0.65	—

KM# 382a Subject: Natural legacy **Rev:** Environmental elements **Composition:** 0.9250 Silver

Date	Mintage	Proof
2000 Proof	76,956	6.00

KM# 383 Subject: Celebration **Rev:** Fireworks, children behind flag **Rev. Designer:** Laura Paxton **Composition:** Nickel

Date	Mintage	MS-60	MS-63	Proof
2000	35,144,100	0.50	0.65	—

KM# 383a Subject: Celebration **Rev:** Fireworks, children behind flag **Composition:** 0.9250 Silver

Date	Mintage	Proof
2000 Proof	76,956	6.00

KM# 384.1 Subject: Pride **Obv:** Queen's portrait **Rev:** Large 2 in red with 3 small red maple leaves on large maple leaf **Rev. Designer:** Donald F. Warkentin **Edge:** Reeded **Composition:** Nickel **Size:** 23.9 mm. **Note:** Colorized version.

Date	Mintage	MS-63	Proof
2000	49,399	6.50	—

KM# 384.2 Subject: Pride **Rev:** Large 2 with three small maple leaves on large maple leaf **Rev. Designer:** Donald F. Warkentin **Composition:** Nickel

Date	Mintage	MS-60	MS-63	Proof
2000	50,666,800	0.50	0.65	—

KM# 384.2a Subject: Pride **Rev:** 2 with 3 small maple leaves on large maple leaf **Composition:** 0.9250 Silver

Date	Mintage	Proof
2000 Proof	76,956	6.00

KM# 419 Subject: Spirit of Canada **Obv:** Queen's head right **Rev:** Maple leaf at center, children holding hands below **Rev. Designer:** Silke Ware **Edge:** Reeded **Weight:** 5.0600 g. **Composition:** Nickel Plated Steel **Size:** 23.9 mm.

Date	Mintage	MS-63	Proof
2001	96,352	7.00	—

KM# 451 Subject: Canada Day **Obv:** Queen's portrait **Rev:** Human figures with large red maple leaf **Edge:** Reeded **Weight:** 4.4000 g. **Composition:** Nickel Plated Steel **Size:** 23.88 mm.

Date	Mintage	MS-63	Proof
2002	49,903	6.75	—

KM# 448 Subject: Elizabeth II Golden Jubilee **Composition:** Nickel Plated Steel **Note:** Double-dated 1952-2002.

Date	Mintage	MS-63	Proof
ND(2002)P	152,485,000	2.00	—
ND(2002) Proof	32,642	—	6.00

KM# 448a Subject: Elizabeth II Golden Jubilee **Obv:** Queen, Jubilee commemorative dates 1952-2002 **Composition:** 0.9250 Silver

Date	Mintage	MS-63	Proof
ND(2002) Proof	100,000	—	12.50

KM# 493 Obv: New effigy of Queen Elizabeth II **Obv. Designer:** Susanna Blunt **Composition:** Nickel Plated Steel

Date	Mintage	MS-63	Proof
2003P	66,861,633	3.00	—
2004P	159,465,000	1.00	—
2005P	—	1.00	—
2006P	—	1.00	—

KM# 471 Subject: 50th Anniversary of the Coronation of Elizabeth II **Obv:** 1953 effigy of the Queen, Jubilee commemorative dates 1952-2002 **Composition:** 0.9250 Silver

Date	Mintage	MS-63	Proof
ND(2003) In coronation proof sets only	30,000	12.50	—

KM# 474 Obv: Queen's head right **Rev:** Polar bear and red colored maple leaves **Composition:** 0.9250 Silver

Date	Mintage	MS-63	Proof
2003 Proof	—	—	7.50

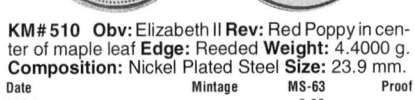

KM# 510 Obv: Elizabeth II **Rev:** Red Poppy in center of maple leaf **Edge:** Reeded **Weight:** 4.4000 g. **Composition:** Nickel Plated Steel **Size:** 23.9 mm.

Date	Mintage	MS-63	Proof
2004	—	8.00	—

KM# 510a Obv: Elizabeth II **Rev:** Gold-plated poppy in maple leaf **Edge:** Reeded **Composition:** 0.9250 Silver **Size:** 23.9 mm.

Date	Mintage	MS-63	Proof
2004 Proof	15,000	—	20.00

KM# 525 Subject: Celebration! Maple leaf, colorized **Composition:** Nickel Plated Steel

Date	Mintage	MS-63	Proof
2004	—	8.00	—

KM# 493a Obv: Elizabeth II by Suanne Blunt **Rev:** Caribou **Edge:** Reeded **Weight:** 5.9000 g. **Composition:** 0.9250 Silver 0.1755 oz. ASW **Size:** 23.6 mm.

Date	Mintage	MS-63	Proof
2004 Proof	—	—	6.50

KM# 529 Subject: WWII **Rev:** Three soldiers and flag **Composition:** Nickel Plated Steel

Date	Mintage	MS-63	Proof
2005	—	20.00	—

KM# 530 Subject: Alberta **Composition:** Nickel Plated Steel

Date	Mintage	MS-63	Proof
2005	—	8.50	—

KM# 531 Subject: Canada Day **Rev:** Beaver, colorized **Composition:** Nickel Plated Steel

Date	Mintage	MS-63	Proof
2005	—	8.50	—

KM# 532 Subject: Saskatchewan **Composition:** Nickel Plated Steel

Date	Mintage	MS-63	Proof
2005	—	8.50	—

KM# 533 Rev: Stuffed bear in Christmas stocking, colorized **Composition:** Nickel Plated Steel

Date	Mintage	MS-63	Proof
2005	—	8.50	—

KM# 535 Subject: Year of the Veteran **Rev:** Profile of young and old soldier **Composition:** Nickel Plated Steel

Date	Mintage	MS-63	Proof
2005	—	8.50	—

KM# 534 Subject: Toronto Maple Leafs **Rev:** Colorized team logo **Composition:** Nickel Plated Steel

Date	Mintage	MS-63	Proof
2006P	—	8.50	—

KM# 575 Subject: Montreal Canadiens **Rev:** Colorized logo **Composition:** Nickel Plated Steel

Date	Mintage	MS-63	Proof
2006P	—	8.50	—

KM# 576 Subject: Quebec Winter Carnival **Rev:** Snowman, colorized **Composition:** Nickel Plated Steel

Date	Mintage	MS-63	Proof
2006	—	8.50	—

50 CENTS

KM# 6 Obv. Designer: Leonard C. Wyon **Weight:** 11.6200 g. **Composition:** 0.9250 Silver .3456 oz. ASW

Date	Mintage	VG-8	F-12	VF-20	XF-40	MS-60	MS-63	Proof
1870	450,000	500	850	1,700	3,400	15,500	38,500	—
1870 LCW	Inc. above	45.00	75.00	165	375	3,500	10,000	—
1871	200,000	50.00	120	250	500	4,200	11,500	—
1871H	45,000	90.00	175	375	850	6,700	14,000	—
1872H	80,000	45.00	75.00	175	400	3,800	10,250	—
1872H Inverted A for V in Victoria	Inc. above	150	400	900	2,200	7,750	13,500	—
1881H	150,000	45.00	85.00	200	450	4,250	10,500	—
1888	60,000	175	300	600	1,100	5,600	13,500	—
1890H	20,000	650	1,250	2,000	4,000	12,250	22,500	—
1892	151,000	50.00	95.00	320	500	6,000	11,500	—
1894	29,036	250	450	950	2,100	9,000	17,500	—
1898	100,000	50.00	120	250	450	4,750	11,500	—

Date	Mintage	VG-8	F-12	VF-20	XF-40	MS-60	MS-63	Proof
1899	50,000	100.00	200	450	1,100	9,000	17,500	—
1900	118,000	45.00	75.00	165	375	4,000	10,500	—
1901	80,000	55.00	100.00	225	550	5,700	15,000	—

Victorian leaves

KM# 12 Obv. Designer: G. W. DeSaulles **Weight:** 11.6200 g. **Composition:** 0.9250 Silver .3456 oz. ASW

Date	Mintage	VG-8	F-12	VF-20	XF-40	MS-60	MS-63	Proof
1902	120,000	15.00	35.00	100.00	250	1,300	3,500	—
1903H	140,000	22.00	45.00	125	300	1,400	3,700	—
1904	60,000	150	200	400	900	3,300	9,500	—
1905	40,000	150	275	600	1,400	6,000	15,000	—
1906	350,000	12.00	35.00	95.00	250	1,300	3,500	—
1907	300,000	12.00	35.00	95.00	250	1,400	3,900	—
1908	128,119	21.00	65.00	175	375	1,000	2,000	—
1909	302,118	17.00	60.00	175	475	2,400	7,600	—
1910	649,521	15.00	40.00	150	350	1,500	4,000	—

Note: Victorian leaves

Edwardian leaves

KM# 12a Obv. Designer: G. W. DeSaulles **Weight:** 11.6638 g. **Composition:** 0.9250 Silver .3461 oz. ASW

Date	Mintage	VG-8	F-12	VF-20	XF-40	MS-60	MS-63	Proof
1910	Inc. above	8.00	29.00	85.00	250	1,200	3,300	—

Note: Edwardian leaves

KM# 19 Obv. Designer: E. B. MacKennal **Weight:** 11.6638 g. **Composition:** 0.9250 Silver .3461 oz. ASW

Date	Mintage	VG-8	F-12	VF-20	XF-40	MS-60	MS-63	Proof
1911	209,972	12.00	70.00	250	550	1,400	3,200	—

KM# 25 Obv: Modified legend Obv. Designer: E. B. MacKennal **Weight:** 11.6638 g. **Composition:** 0.9250 Silver .3461 oz. ASW

Date	Mintage	VG-8	F-12	VF-20	XF-40	MS-60	MS-63	Proof
1912	285,867	7.00	24.00	100.00	225	1,100	2,900	—
1913	265,889	6.00	24.00	150	300	1,400	4,800	—
1914	160,128	14.00	55.00	150	500	2,800	7,800	—
1916	459,070	5.50	14.00	55.00	175	650	2,100	—
1917	752,213	5.00	11.00	40.00	100.00	475	1,100	—
1918	754,989	5.00	10.00	30.00	90.00	400	1,000	—
1919	1,113,429	5.00	10.00	30.00	90.00	375	1,200	—

KM# 25a Obv. Designer: E. B. MacKennal **Weight:** 11.6638 g. **Composition:** 0.8000 Silver .3000 oz. ASW

Date	Mintage	VG-8	F-12	VF-20	XF-40	MS-60	MS-63	Proof
1920	584,691	5.00	13.00	35.00	125	500	1,200	—
1921	—	15,000	21,000	27,000	30,000	45,000	60,000	
Note: 75 to 100 known; David Akers John Jay Pittman sale, Part Three, 10-99, Gem Unc. realized $63,250								
1929	228,328	5.00	13.00	35.00	100.00	475	1,100	—
1931	57,581	11.00	29.00	80.00	225	800	1,800	—
1932	19,213	100.00	175	375	800	3,600	8,300	—
1934	39,539	15.00	30.00	80.00	225	650	1,300	—
1936	38,550	15.00	29.00	70.00	175	500	1,000	—

KM# 36 Obv. Designer: T. H. Paget **Rev. Designer:** George E. Kruger-Gray **Weight:** 11.6638 g. **Composition:** 0.8000 Silver .3000 oz. ASW

Date	Mintage	VG-8	F-12	VF-20	XF-40	MS-60	MS-63	Proof
1937	192,016	3.00	4.50	7.00	10.00	30.00	85.00	—
1938	192,018	3.00	5.50	10.00	25.00	90.00	400	—
1939	287,976	2.85	5.00	8.00	17.00	60.00	250	—
1940	1,996,566	BV	2.85	3.50	6.00	27.00	60.00	—
1941	1,714,874	BV	2.85	3.50	6.00	27.00	60.00	—
1942	1,974,164	BV	2.85	3.50	6.00	27.00	60.00	—
1943	3,109,583	BV	2.85	3.50	6.00	27.00	60.00	—
1944	2,460,205	BV	2.85	3.50	6.00	27.00	60.00	—
1945	1,959,528	BV	2.85	3.50	6.00	30.00	90.00	—
1946	950,235	BV	2.85	4.00	7.00	40.00	110	—
1946	Inc. above	15.00	28.00	45.00	150	1,100	2,800	—
Note: hoof in 6								
1947	424,885	BV	2.85	5.00	10.00	65.00	175	—
Note: straight 7								
1947	Inc. above	BV	2.85	6.00	15.00	75.00	200	—
Note: curved 7								
1947	38,433	18.00	23.00	30.00	60.00	150	275	—
Note: maple leaf, straight 7								
1947	Inc. above	1,000	1,300	1,700	2,200	3,900	7,000	—
Note: maple leaf, curved 7								

KM# 45 Obv: Modified legend **Obv. Designer:** T. H. Paget **Rev. Designer:** George E. Kruger-Gray **Weight:** 11.6638 g. **Composition:** 0.8000 Silver .3000 oz. ASW

Date	Mintage	VG-8	F-12	VF-20	XF-40	MS-60	MS-63	Proof
1948	37,784	45.00	55.00	70.00	95.00	150	225	—
1949	858,991	BV	2.85	3.50	7.00	25.00	100.00	—
1949	Inc. above	7.00	12.00	25.00	60.00	325	750	—
Note: hoof over 9								
1950	2,384,179	2.85	7.00	11.00	25.00	125	225	—
Note: no lines								
1950	Inc. above	—	BV	2.85	3.50	8.00	30.00	—

Date	Mintage	VG-8	F-12	VF-20	XF-40	MS-60	MS-63	Proof
Note: lines in 0								
1951	2,421,730	—	BV	2.85	3.25	6.00	26.00	—
1952	2,596,465	—	BV	2.85	3.25	6.00	18.00	—

KM# 53 Obv: Elizabeth II Effigy **Obv. Designer:** Mary Gillick **Weight:** 11.6638 g. **Composition:** 0.8000 Silver .3000 oz. ASW

Date	Mintage	VG-8	F-12	VF-20	XF-40	MS-60	MS-63	Proof
1953	1,630,429	—	—	BV	2.85	4.50	15.00	—
Note: small date								
1953	Inc. above	—	BV	2.85	4.00	15.00	35.00	—
Note: lg. date, straps								
1953	Inc. above	BV	2.85	3.50	9.00	50.00	150	—
Note: lg. date without straps								
1954	506,305	BV	2.85	3.50	7.00	18.00	35.00	—
1955	753,511	—	BV	2.85	3.50	10.00	30.00	—
1956	1,379,499	—	—	BV	2.85	4.50	14.00	—
1957	2,171,689	—	—	BV	2.85	3.50	10.00	—
1958	2,957,266	—	—	BV	2.85	3.25	8.50	—

KM# 56 Obv. Designer: Mary Gillick **Rev:** New shield **Rev. Designer:** Thomas Shingles **Weight:** 11.6638 g. **Composition:** 0.8000 Silver .3000 oz. ASW

Date	Mintage	VG-8	F-12	VF-20	XF-40	MS-60	MS-63	Proof
1959	3,095,535	—	—	—	BV	2.85	4.50	—
Note: horizontal shading								
1960	3,488,897	—	—	—	BV	2.85	3.50	—
1961	3,584,417	—	—	—	BV	2.85	3.25	—
1962	5,208,030	—	—	—	BV	2.85	3.25	—
1963	8,348,871	—	—	—	BV	2.85	3.25	—
1964	9,377,676	—	—	—	BV	2.85	3.25	—

KM# 63 Obv: Elizabeth II effigy **Obv. Designer:** Arnold Machin **Rev. Designer:** Thomas Shingles **Weight:** 11.6638 g. **Composition:** 0.8000 Silver .3000 oz. ASW

Date	Mintage	VG-8	F-12	VF-20	XF-40	MS-60	MS-63	Proof
1965	12,629,974	—	—	—	BV	2.85	3.25	—
1966	7,920,496	—	—	—	BV	2.85	3.25	—

KM# 69 Subject: Confederation Centennial **Rev:** Seated wolf howling **Rev. Designer:** Alex Colville **Weight:** 11.6638 g. **Composition:** 0.8000 Silver .3000 oz. ASW

Date	Mintage	XF-40	MS-60	MS-63	Proof
ND(1967)	4,211,392	2.85	3.25	6.50	9.00

KM# 75.1 Obv. Designer: Arnold Machin **Rev. Designer:** Thomas Shingles **Composition:** Nickel

Date	Mintage	XF-40	MS-60	MS-63	Proof
1968	3,966,932	0.50	0.65	1.00	—
1969	7,113,929	0.50	0.65	1.00	—
1970	2,429,526	0.50	0.65	1.00	—
1971	2,166,444	0.50	0.65	1.00	—
1972	2,515,632	0.50	0.65	1.00	—
1973	2,546,096	0.50	0.65	1.00	—
1974	3,436,650	0.50	0.65	1.00	—
1975	3,710,000	0.50	0.65	1.00	—
1976	2,940,719	0.50	0.65	1.00	—

KM# 75.2 Obv: Smaller bust **Obv. Designer:** Arnold Machin **Rev. Designer:** Thomas Shingles **Composition:** Nickel

Date	Mintage	MS-60	MS-63	Proof
1977	709,839	1.35	2.00	—

KM# 75.3 Obv. Designer: Arnold Machin **Rev:** Redesigned arms **Rev. Designer:** Thomas Shingles **Composition:** Nickel

Date	Mintage	MS-60	MS-63	Proof
1978	3,341,892	0.65	1.00	—
Note: square jewels				
1978	Inc. above	3.00	6.00	—
Note: round jewels				
1979	3,425,000	0.65	1.00	—
1980	1,574,000	0.65	1.00	—
1981	2,690,272	0.65	1.00	—
1981 Proof	199,000	—	—	3.00
1982	2,236,674	40.00	60.00	—
Note: small beads				
1982 Proof	180,908	—	—	3.00
Note: small beads				
1982	Inc. above	0.65	1.00	—
Note: large beads				
1983	1,177,000	0.65	1.00	—
1983 Proof	168,000	—	—	3.00
1984	1,502,989	0.65	1.00	—

Date	Mintage	MS-60	MS-63	Proof
1984 Proof	161,602	—	—	3.00
1985	2,188,374	0.65	1.00	—
1985 Proof	157,037	—	—	3.00
1986	781,400	1.00	1.25	—
1986 Proof	175,745	—	—	3.00
1987	373,000	1.00	1.25	—
1987 Proof	179,004	—	—	3.50
1988	220,000	1.00	1.25	—
1988 Proof	175,259	—	—	3.00
1989	266,419	1.00	1.25	—
1989 Proof	170,928	—	—	3.00

KM# 185 Obv: Elizabeth II effigy **Obv. Designer:** Dora dePedery-Hunt **Rev. Designer:** Thomas Shingles **Composition:** Nickel

Date	Mintage	XF-40	MS-60	MS-63	Proof
1990	207,000	0.50	1.00	1.25	—
1990 Proof	140,649	—	—	—	5.00
1991	490,000	0.50	0.85	1.00	—
1991 Proof	131,888	—	—	—	7.00
1993	393,000	0.50	0.85	1.00	—
1993 Proof	143,065	—	—	—	3.00
1994	987,000	0.50	0.75	1.00	—
1994 Proof	146,424	—	—	—	4.00
1995	626,000	0.50	0.75	1.00	—
1995 Proof	50,000	—	—	—	4.00
1996	458,000	0.50	0.65	1.00	—
1996 Proof	—	—	—	—	—

KM# 208 Subject: Confederation 125 **Obv. Designer:** Dora dePedery-Hunt **Rev. Designer:** Thomas Shingles **Composition:** Nickel

Date	Mintage	MS-60	MS-63	Proof
ND(1992)	445,000	0.75	1.00	—
ND(1992) Proof	147,061	—	—	5.00

KM# 261 Subject: Atlantic puffin **Rev. Designer:** Sheldon Beveridge **Weight:** 11.6638 g. **Composition:** 0.9250 Silver .3461 oz. ASW

Date	Mintage	MS-63	Proof
1995 Proof	—	—	22.00

KM# 262 Subject: Whooping crane **Rev. Designer:** Stan Witten **Weight:** 11.6638 g. **Composition:** 0.9250 Silver .3461 oz. ASW

Date	Mintage	MS-63	Proof
1995 Proof	—	—	22.00

KM# 263 Subject: Gray jays **Rev. Designer:** Sheldon Beveridge **Weight:** 11.6638 g. **Composition:** 0.9250 Silver .3461 oz. ASW

Date	Mintage	MS-63	Proof
1995 Proof	—	—	20.00

KM# 264 Subject: White-tailed ptarmigans **Rev. Designer:** Cosme Saffioti **Weight:** 11.6638 g. **Composition:** 0.9250 Silver .3461 oz. ASW

Date	Mintage	MS-63	Proof
1995 Proof	—	—	20.00

KM# 185a Weight: 11.6380 g. **Composition:** 0.9250 Silver .3461 oz. ASW

Date	Mintage	MS-63	Proof
1996 Proof	—	—	9.00

KM# 283 Subject: Moose calf **Rev. Designer:** Ago Aarand **Weight:** 11.6638 g. **Composition:** 0.9250 Silver .3461 oz. ASW

Date	Mintage	MS-63	Proof
1996 Proof	—	—	17.50

KM# 284 Subject: Wood ducklings **Rev. Designer:** Sheldon Beveridge **Weight:** 11.6638 g. **Composition:** 0.9250 Silver .3461 oz. ASW

Date	Mintage	MS-63	Proof
1996 Proof	—	—	17.50

KM# 285 Subject: Cougar kittens **Rev. Designer:** Stan Witten **Weight:** 11.6638 g. **Composition:** 0.9250 Silver .3461 oz. ASW

Date	Mintage	MS-63	Proof
1996 Proof	—	—	17.50

KM# 286 Subject: Black bear cubs **Rev. Designer:** Sheldon Beveridge **Weight:** 11.6638 g. **Composition:** 0.9250 Silver .3461 oz. ASW

Date	Mintage	MS-63	Proof
1996 Proof	—	—	17.50

KM# 290 Obv. Designer: Dora dePedery-Hunt **Rev:** Redesigned arms **Rev. Designer:** Cathy Bursey-Sabourin **Composition:** Nickel

Date	Mintage	XF-40	MS-60	MS-63	Proof
1997	387,000	0.50	0.65	1.00	—
1997 Proof	—	—	—	—	—
1998	308,000	0.50	0.65	1.00	—
1998 Proof	—	—	—	—	—
1998W	—	—	—	2.00	—
1999	496,000	0.50	0.65	1.00	—
1999 Proof	—	—	—	—	—
2000	559,000	0.50	0.65	1.00	—
2000 Proof	—	—	—	—	—
2000W	—	—	—	1.50	—
2003	—	—	—	1.00	—

KM# 292 Subject: Duck tolling retriever **Rev. Designer:** Stan Witten **Weight:** 11.6638 g. **Composition:** 0.9250 Silver .3461 oz. ASW

Date	Mintage	MS-63	Proof
1997 Proof	—	—	15.00

KM# 293 Subject: Labrador retriever **Rev. Designer:** Sheldon Beveridge **Weight:** 11.6638 g. **Composition:** 0.9250 Silver .3461 oz. ASW

Date	Mintage	MS-63	Proof
1997 Proof	—	—	15.00

KM# 294 Subject: Newfoundland **Rev. Designer:** William Woodruff **Weight:** 11.6638 g. **Composition:** 0.9250 Silver .3461 oz. ASW

Date	Mintage	MS-63	Proof
1997 Proof	—	—	15.00

KM# 295 Subject: Eskimo dog **Rev. Designer:** Cosme Saffioti **Weight:** 11.6638 g. **Composition:** 0.9250 Silver .3461 oz. ASW

Date	Mintage	MS-63	Proof
1997 Proof	—	—	15.00

KM# 290a Weight: 11.6380 g. **Composition:** 0.9250 Silver .3461 oz. ASW

Date	Mintage	MS-63	Proof
1997 Proof	—	—	10.00
1998 Proof	—	—	10.00
1999 Proof	—	—	10.00
2000 Proof	—	—	10.00
2001 Proof	—	—	10.00
2003 Proof	—	—	10.00

KM# 313 Subject: 90th Anniversary Royal Canadian Mint **Rev. Designer:** W. H. J. Blakemore **Weight:** 11.6638 g. **Composition:** 0.9250 Silver .3461 oz. ASW

Date	Mintage	MS-63	Proof
ND(1998) Matte	25,000	—	15.00
ND(1998) Proof	25,000	—	15.00

KM# 314 Subject: 110 years Canadian speed and figure skating **Rev. Designer:** Sheldon Beveridge **Weight:** 11.6638 g. **Composition:** 0.9250 Silver .3461 oz. ASW

Date	Mintage	MS-63	Proof
ND(1998) Proof	—	—	9.00

KM# 315 Subject: 100 years Canadian ski racing **Rev. Designer:** Ago Aarand **Weight:** 11.6638 g. **Composition:** 0.9250 Silver .3461 oz. ASW

Date	Mintage	MS-63	Proof
ND(1998) Proof	—	—	9.00

KM# 318 Subject: Killer whales **Rev. Designer:** William Woodruff **Weight:** 11.6638 g. **Composition:** 0.9250 Silver .3461 oz. ASW

Date	Mintage	MS-63	Proof
1998 Proof	—	—	15.00

KM# 319 Subject: Humpback whale **Rev. Designer:** Sheldon Beveridge **Weight:** 11.6638 g. **Composition:** 0.9250 Silver .3461 oz. ASW

Date	Mintage	MS-63	Proof
1998 Proof	—	—	15.00

KM# 320 Subject: Beluga whale **Rev. Designer:** Cosme Saffioti **Weight:** 11.6638 g. **Composition:** 0.9250 Silver .3461 oz. ASW

Date	Mintage	MS-63	Proof
1998 Proof	—	—	15.00

KM# 321 Subject: Blue whale **Rev. Designer:** Stan Witten **Weight:** 11.6638 g. **Composition:** 0.9250 Silver .3461 oz. ASW

Date	Mintage	MS-63	Proof
1998 Proof	—	—	15.00

KM# 327 Subject: 110 years Canadian soccer **Rev. Designer:** Stan Witten **Weight:** 11.6638 g. **Composition:** 0.9250 Silver .3461 oz. ASW

Date	Mintage	MS-63	Proof
ND(1998) Proof	—	—	9.00

KM# 328 Subject: 20 years Canadian auto racing **Rev. Designer:** Cosme Saffioti **Weight:** 11.6638 g. **Composition:** 0.9250 Silver .3461 oz. ASW

Date	Mintage	MS-63	Proof
ND(1998) Proof	—	—	9.00

KM# 290b Rev: Redesigned arms **Composition:** Nickel Plated Steel

Date	Mintage	MS-63	Proof
1999 P	Est. 20,000	15.00	—
2000 P	Est. 50	3,500	—
Note: Available only in RCM presentation coin clocks			
2001 P	389,000	1.25	—
2003 P	—	1.00	—

KM# 333 Subject: 1904 Canadian open **Rev. Designer:** William Woodruff **Weight:** 11.6638 g. **Composition:** 0.9250 Silver .3461 oz. ASW

Date	Mintage	MS-63	Proof
ND(1999) Proof	—	—	13.50

KM# 334 Subject: First U.S.-Canadian yacht race **Rev. Designer:** Stan Witten **Weight:** 11.6638 g. **Composition:** 0.9250 Silver .3461 oz. ASW

Date	Mintage	MS-63	Proof
ND(1999) Proof	—	—	9.00

KM# 335 Subject: Canadian cats, Cymric **Rev. Designer:** Susan Taylor **Weight:** 11.6638 g. **Composition:** 0.9250 Silver .3461 oz. ASW

Date	Mintage	MS-63	Proof
1999 Proof	—	—	17.50

KM# 336 Subject: Canadian cats, Tonkinese **Rev. Designer:** Susan Taylor **Weight:** 11.6638 g. **Composition:** 0.9250 Silver .3461 oz. ASW

Date	Mintage	MS-63	Proof
1999 Proof	—	—	17.50

KM# 337 Subject: Canadian cats, Cougar **Rev. Designer:** Susan Taylor **Weight:** 11.6638 g. **Composition:** 0.9250 Silver .3461 oz. ASW

Date	Mintage	MS-63	Proof
1999 Proof	—	—	15.00

KM# 338 Subject: Canadian cats, Lynx **Rev. Designer:** Susan Taylor **Weight:** 11.6638 g. **Composition:** 0.9250 Silver .3461 oz. ASW

Date	Mintage	MS-63	Proof
1999 Proof	—	—	15.00

KM# 371 Subject: Basketball **Obv:** Queen's portrait **Rev:** Basketball players **Rev. Designer:** Sheldon Beveridge **Edge:** Reeded **Weight:** 9.3600 g. **Composition:** 0.9250 Silver 0.2784 oz. ASW **Size:** 27.1 mm.

Date	Mintage	MS-63	Proof
ND(1999) Proof	—	—	9.00

KM# 372 Obv: Queen's portrait **Rev:** Football players **Rev. Designer:** Cosme Saffioti **Edge:** Reeded **Weight:** 9.3600 g. **Composition:** 0.9250 Silver 0.2784 oz. ASW **Size:** 27.1 mm.

Date	Mintage	MS-63	Proof
ND(1999) Proof	—	—	9.00

KM# 385 Subject: Ice hockey **Rev:** 4 hockey players **Rev. Designer:** Stanley Witten **Composition:** 0.9250 Silver

Date	Mintage	MS-63	Proof
ND(2000) Proof	—	—	12.00

KM# 386 Subject: Curling **Rev:** Motion study of a curler **Rev. Designer:** Cosme Saffioti **Composition:** 0.9250 Silver

Date	Mintage	MS-63	Proof
ND(2000) Proof	—	—	9.00

KM# 389 Rev: Great horned owl **Rev. Designer:** Susan Taylor **Weight:** 9.3500 g. **Composition:** 0.9250 Silver

Date	Mintage	MS-63	Proof
2000 Proof	—	—	17.50

KM# 390 Rev: Red-tailed hawk **Weight:** 9.3500 g. **Composition:** 0.9250 Silver

Date	Mintage	MS-63	Proof
2000 Proof	—	—	17.50

KM# 391 Rev: Osprey **Rev. Designer:** Susan Taylor **Weight:** 9.3500 g. **Composition:** 0.9250 Silver

Date	Mintage	MS-63	Proof
2000 Proof	—	—	17.50

KM# 392 Rev: Bald eagle **Rev. Designer:** William Woodruff **Weight:** 9.3500 g. **Composition:** 0.9250 Silver

Date	Mintage	MS-63	Proof
2000 Proof	—	—	17.50

KM# 393 Subject: Steeplechase **Rev. Designer:** Susan Taylor **Composition:** 0.9250 Silver

Date	Mintage	MS-63	Proof
2000 Proof	—	—	9.00

KM# 394 Subject: Bowling **Rev. Designer:** William Woodruff **Composition:** 0.9250 Silver

Date	Mintage	MS-63	Proof
2000 Proof	—	—	9.00

KM# 420 Subject: Festivals - Quebec, **Obv:** Queen's head right **Rev:** Snowman and Chateau Frontenac **Rev. Designer:** Sylvie Daigneault **Edge:** Reeded **Weight:** 9.3000 g. **Composition:** 0.9250 Silver .2766 oz. ASW **Size:** 27.13 mm.

Date	Mintage	MS-63	Proof
2001 Proof	58,123	—	11.50

KM# 421 Subject: Festivals - Nunavut, **Obv:** Queen's head right **Rev:** Dancer, dog sled and snowmobiles **Rev. Designer:** John Mardon **Edge:** Reeded **Weight:** 9.3000 g. **Composition:** 0.9250 Silver .2766 oz. ASW **Size:** 27.13 mm.

Date	Mintage	MS-63	Proof
2001 Proof	58,123	—	11.50

KM# 422 Subject: Festivals - Newfoundland, **Obv:** Queen's head right **Rev:** Sailor and musical people **Rev. Designer:** David Craig **Edge:** Reeded **Weight:** 9.3000 g. **Composition:** 0.9250 Silver .2766 oz. ASW **Size:** 27.13 mm.

Date	Mintage	MS-63	Proof
2001 Proof	58,123	—	11.50

KM# 423 Subject: Festivals - Prince Edward Island, **Obv:** Queen's head right **Rev:** Family, juggler and building **Rev. Designer:** Brenda Whiteway **Edge:** Reeded **Weight:** 9.3000 g. **Composition:** 0.9250 Silver .2766 oz. ASW **Size:** 27.13 mm.

Date	Mintage	MS-63	Proof
2001 Proof	58,123	—	11.50

KM# 424 Subject: Folklore - The Sled, **Obv:** Queen's head right **Rev:** Family scene **Rev. Designer:** Valentina Hotz-Entin **Edge:** Reeded **Weight:** 9.3000 g. **Composition:** 0.9250 Silver .2766 oz. ASW **Size:** 27.13 mm.

Date	Mintage	MS-63	Proof
2001 Proof	28,979	—	12.50

KM# 425 Subject: Folklore - The Maiden's Cave, **Obv:** Queen's head right **Rev:** Woman shouting **Rev. Designer:** Peter Kiss **Edge:** Reeded **Weight:** 9.3000 g. **Composition:** 0.9250 Silver .2766 oz. ASW **Size:** 27.13 mm.

Date	Mintage	MS-63	Proof
2001 Proof	28,979	—	12.50

KM# 426 Subject: Folklore - The Small Jumpers, **Obv:** Queen's head right **Rev:** Jumping children on seashore **Rev. Designer:** Miynki Tanobe **Edge:** Reeded **Weight:** 9.3000 g. **Composition:** 0.9250 Silver .2766 oz. ASW **Size:** 27.13 mm.

Date	Mintage	MS-63	Proof
2001 Proof	28,979	—	12.50

KM# 509 Obv: Queen Elizabeth II **Rev:** National arms **Edge:** Reeded **Weight:** 6.9000 g. **Composition:** Nickel Plated Steel **Size:** 27.13 mm.

Date	Mintage	MS-63	Proof
ND(2001) P	—	1.50	—

KM# 444 Subject: Queen's Golden Jubilee **Obv:** Bust of Queen Elizabeth II right and monogram **Rev:** Canadian arms **Rev. Designer:** Bursey Sabourin **Edge:** Reeded **Weight:** 6.8300 g. **Composition:** Nickel Plated Steel **Size:** 27 mm.

Date	Mintage	MS-63	Proof
ND(2002)P	1,440,000	2.00	—

KM# 461 Subject: Canadian Folklore and Legends, The Pig That Wouldn't Get Over the Stile **Rev. Designer:** Laura Jolicoeur **Composition:** 0.9250 Silver

Date	Mintage	MS-63	Proof
2002 Proof	19,267	—	13.50

KM# 458 Subject: Squamish Days Logger Sports **Rev. Designer:** Jose Osio **Composition:** 0.9250 Silver

Date	Mintage	MS-63	Proof
2002 Proof	59,998	—	12.00

KM# 456 Subject: Folklorama **Rev. Designer:** William Woodruff **Composition:** 0.9250 Silver

Date	Mintage	MS-63	Proof
2002 Proof	59,998	—	12.00

KM# 460 Subject: Canadian Folklore and Legends, The Ghost Ship **Rev. Designer:** Colette Boivin **Composition:** 0.9250 Silver

Date	Mintage	MS-63	Proof
2002 Proof	19,267	—	13.50

KM# 457 Subject: Calgary Stampede **Rev. Designer:** Stan Witten **Composition:** 0.9250 Silver

Date	Mintage	MS-63	Proof
2002 Proof	59,998	—	12.00

KM# 454 Subject: Annapolis Valley Apple Blossom Festival **Rev. Designer:** Bonnie Ross **Composition:** 0.9250 Silver

Date	Mintage	MS-63	Proof
2002 Proof	59,998	—	12.00

KM# 459 Subject: Canadian Folklore and Legends, **Obv:** Queen's head right **Rev:** The Shoemaker in Heaven **Rev. Designer:** Francine Gravel **Composition:** 0.9250 Silver

Date	Mintage	MS-63	Proof
2002 Proof	19,267	—	13.50

KM# 455 Subject: Stratford Festival **Obv:** Queen's head right **Rev:** Couple with building in background **Rev. Designer:** Laurie McGaw **Composition:** 0.9250 Silver

Date	Mintage	MS-63	Proof
2002 Proof	59,998	—	12.00

KM# 444a Subject: Elizabeth II Golden Jubilee **Obv:** Queen, Jubilee commemorative dates 1952-2002 **Composition:** 0.9250 Silver

Date	Mintage	MS-63	Proof
ND(2002) In proof sets only	100,000	—	17.50

KM# 444b Subject: Queen's Golden Jubilee **Obv:** Bust of Queen Elizabeth II right and monogram **Rev:** Canadian arms **Edge:** Reeded **Composition:** Gold Plated Silver **Size:** 27 mm. **Note:** Special 24 karat gold plated issue of KM#444.

Date	Mintage	MS-63	Proof
ND(2002) Proof	32,642	—	35.00

KM# 479 Subject: Great Northern Arts Festival **Composition:** 0.9250 Silver

Date	Mintage	MS-63	Proof
2003 Proof	—	—	16.50

KM# 476 Subject: Yukon International Storytelling Festival **Composition:** 0.9250 Silver

Date	Mintage	MS-63	Proof
2003 Proof	—	—	16.50

KM# 477 Subject: Festival Acadien de Caraquet **Obv:** Queen's head right **Rev:** Sailboat and couple **Composition:** 0.9250 Silver

Date	Mintage	MS-63	Proof
2003 Proof	—	—	16.50

KM# 478 Subject: Back to batoche **Composition:** 0.9250 Silver

Date	Mintage	MS-63	Proof
2003 Proof	—	—	16.50

KM# 475 Rev: Golden daffodil **Composition:** 0.9250 Silver

Date	Mintage	MS-63	Proof
2003 Proof	55,000	—	25.00

KM# 472 Subject: 50th Anniversary of the Coronation of Elizabeth II **Obv:** 1953 effigy of the Queen, Jubilee commemorative dates 1952-2002 **Composition:** 0.9250 Silver

Date	Mintage	MS-63	Proof
ND(2003) In coronation proof sets only	30,000	15.00	—

KM# 494 Obv: New effigy of Queen Elizabeth II **Obv. Designer:** Susanna Blunt **Rev. Designer:** Cathy Bursey-Sabourin **Composition:** Nickel Plated Steel

Date	MS-63	Proof
2003W	1.50	—
2004	1.50	—
2005	1.50	—
2006	1.50	—

KM# 606 Rev: Sulphur Butterfly, hologram **Composition:** Silver

Date	Mintage	MS-63	Proof
2004 Proof	—	—	35.00

KM# 494a Obv: Elizabeth II by Suanne Blunt **Rev:** Canadian coat of arms **Edge:** Reeded **Weight:** 11.6380 g. **Composition:** 0.9250 Silver 0.3461 oz. ASW **Size:** 27 mm.

Date	Mintage	MS-63	Proof
2004 Proof	—	—	10.00

KM# 536 Subject: Golden rose **Composition:** Silver With Partial Gold Plating

Date	Mintage	MS-63	Proof
2005 Proof	—	—	32.50

KM# 537 Subject: Great Spangled Fritillary butterfly, hologram **Composition:** Silver

Date	Mintage	MS-63	Proof
2005 Proof	—	—	35.00

KM# 538 Subject: Toronto Maple Leafs **Rev:** Darryl Sittler **Composition:** Silver

Date	Mintage	MS-63	Proof
2005	—	25.00	—

KM# 539 Subject: Toronto Maple Leafs **Rev:** Dave Keon **Composition:** Silver

Date	Mintage	MS-63	Proof
2005	—	25.00	—

KM# 540 Subject: Toronto Maple Leafs **Rev:** Jonny Bover **Composition:** Silver

Date	Mintage	MS-63	Proof
2005	—	25.00	—

KM# 541 Subject: Toronto Maple Leafs **Rev:** Tim Horton **Composition:** Silver

Date	Mintage	MS-63	Proof
2005	—	25.00	—

KM# 544 Subject: WWII - Battle of Scheldt **Rev:** Four soldiers walking down road **Composition:** Silver

Date	Mintage	MS-63	Proof
2005	—	22.50	—

KM# 545 Subject: WWII - Battle of the Atlantic **Rev:** Merchant ship sinking **Composition:** Silver

Date	Mintage	MS-63	Proof
2005	—	22.50	—

KM# 546 Subject: WWII - Conquest of Sicily **Rev:** Tank among town ruins **Composition:** Silver

Date	Mintage	MS-63	Proof
2005	—	22.50	—

KM# 547 Subject: WWII - Liberation of the Netherlands **Rev:** Soldiers in parade, one holding flag **Composition:** Silver

Date	Mintage	MS-63	Proof
2005	—	22.50	—

KM# 548 Subject: WWII - Raid of Dieppe **Rev:** Three soldiers comming off landing craft **Composition:** Silver

Date	Mintage	MS-63	Proof
2005	—	22.50	—

KM# 577 Subject: Montreal Canadiens **Rev:** Guy LaFleur **Composition:** Silver

Date	Mintage	MS-63	Proof
2005	—	25.00	—

KM# 578 Subject: Montreal Canadiens **Rev:** Jaque Plante **Composition:** Silver

Date	Mintage	MS-63	Proof
2005	—	25.00	—

KM# 579 Subject: Montreal Canadiens **Rev:** Jean Beliveau **Composition:** Silver

Date	Mintage	MS-63	Proof
2005	—	25.00	—

KM# 580 Subject: Montreal Canadiens **Rev:** Maurice Richard **Composition:** Silver

Date	Mintage	MS-63	Proof
2005	—	25.00	—

KM# 599 Subject: Monarch Butterfly, hologram **Composition:** Silver

Date	Mintage	MS-63	Proof
2005 Proof	—	—	35.00

DOLLAR

KM# 30 **Subject:** Silver Jubilee **Obv. Designer:** Percy Metcalfe **Rev. Designer:** Emanuel Hahn **Weight:** 23.3276 g. **Composition:** 0.8000 Silver 0.6000 oz. ASW

Date	Mintage	F-12	VF-20	XF-40	AU-50	MS-60	MS-63	Proof
1935	428,707	12.00	18.00	28.00	32.00	37.50	60.00	4,500

KM# 31 **Obv. Designer:** E. B. MacKennal **Rev:** Voyageur **Rev. Designer:** Emanuel Hahn **Weight:** 23.3276 g. **Composition:** 0.8000 Silver 0.6000 oz. ASW

Date	Mintage	F-12	VF-20	XF-40	AU-50	MS-60	MS-63	Proof
1936	339,600	12.50	14.50	16.50	21.50	35.00	75.00	5,000

Pointed 7   Blunt 7

Maple leaf

KM# 37 **Obv. Designer:** T. H. Paget **Rev:** Voyageur **Rev. Designer:** Emanuel Hahn **Weight:** 23.3276 g. **Composition:** 0.8000 Silver 0.6000 oz. ASW

Date	Mintage	F-12	VF-20	XF-40	AU-50	MS-60	MS-63	Proof
1937	207,406	9.00	10.00	12.00	22.00	25.00	65.00	—
1937 Mirror Proof	1,295	—	—	—	—	—	—	650
1937 Matte Proof	Inc. above	—	—	—	—	—	—	250
1938	90,304	25.00	35.00	45.00	55.00	70.00	175	6,000
1945	38,391	75.00	100.00	125	150	200	475	2,000
1946	93,055	15.00	25.00	35.00	45.00	95.00	225	1,800
1947		65.00	80.00	100.00	125	265	850	3,500
Note: pointed 7								
1947	65,595	45.00	60.00	80.00	95.00	125	250	4,500
Note: blunt 7								
1947	21,135	125	150	175	200	250	475	1,800
Note: maple leaf								

KM# 38 Subject: Royal Visit **Obv. Designer:** T. H. Paget **Rev. Designer:** Emanuel Hahn **Weight:** 23.3276 g.
Composition: 0.8000 Silver 0.6000 oz. ASW

Date	Mintage	F-12	VF-20	XF-40	AU-50	MS-60	MS-63	Proof
1939	1,363,816	5.75	6.25	7.50	9.00	11.50	20.00	—
1939	—	—	—	—	—	—	—	475
Note: Matte specimen								

KM# 46 Obv: Modified left legend **Obv. Designer:** T. H. Paget **Rev:** Voyageur **Rev. Designer:** Emanuel
Hahn **Weight:** 23.3276 g. **Composition:** 0.8000 Silver 0.6000 oz. ASW

Date	Mintage	F-12	VF-20	XF-40	AU-50	MS-60	MS-63	Proof
1948	18,780	500	600	650	750	850	1,200	3,000
1950	261,002	6.00	8.00	10.00	12.00	16.00	35.00	800
Note: with 3 water lines								
1950 Matte Proof	—	—	—	—	—	—	—	—
Note: with 4 water lines, 1 known								
1950	Inc. above	11.00	14.00	21.00	28.00	40.00	90.00	1,500
Note: arnprior with 2-1/2 water lines								
1951	416,395	BV	5.50	6.50	8.00	13.00	23.00	650
Note: with 3 water lines								
1951	Inc. above	35.00	50.00	60.00	70.00	125	275	2,000
Note: arnprior with 1-1/2 water lines								
1952	406,148	BV	5.50	6.50	8.00	10.00	23.00	1,000
Note: with 3 water lines								
1952	Inc. above	8.00	12.00	15.00	18.00	40.00	60.00	1,250
Note: short water lines, arnprior type								
1952	Inc. above	5.50	6.50	8.00	10.00	16.50	45.00	—
Note: without water lines								

KM# 47 Subject: Newfoundland **Obv. Designer:** T. H. Paget **Rev:** The Matthew, John Cabot's ship
Rev. Designer: Thomas Shingles **Weight:** 23.3276 g. **Composition:** 0.8000 Silver 0.6000 oz. ASW

Date	Mintage	F-12	VF-20	XF-40	AU-50	MS-60	MS-63	Proof
1949	672,218	10.00	13.00	16.50	18.50	22.50	27.50	—
1949 Specimen proof	—	—	—	—	—	—	—	1,200

KM# 54 Obv: Elizabeth II effigy **Obv. Designer:** Mary Gillick **Rev:** Voyageur **Rev. Designer:** Emanuel Hahn **Weight:** 23.3276 g. **Composition:** 0.8000 Silver 0.6000 oz. ASW **Note:** All genuine circulation strike 1955 Arnprior dollars have a die break running along the top of TI in the word GRATIA on the obverse.

Date	Mintage	F-12	VF-20	XF-40	AU-50	MS-60	MS-63	Proof
1953	1,074,578	—	—	BV	5.50	10.00	25.00	400
Note: without strap, wire rim								
1953	Inc. above	—	—	BV	5.50	10.00	25.00	—
Note: with strap, flat rim								
1954	246,606	5.50	6.50	8.00	10.00	16.00	35.00	—
1955	268,105	5.50	6.50	8.00	10.00	15.00	29.00	—
Note: with 3 water lines								
1955	Inc. above	45.00	65.00	90.00	100.00	125	175	—
Note: arnprior with 1-1/2 water lines* and die break								
1956	209,092	7.50	9.50	13.00	16.00	20.00	50.00	—
1957	496,389	—	—	BV	5.50	7.50	11.00	—
Note: with 3 water lines								
1957	Inc. above	BV	5.50	7.50	8.50	15.00	35.00	—
Note: with 1 water line								
1959	1,443,502	—	—	—	BV	5.50	11.00	—
1960	1,420,486	—	—	—	BV	5.50	11.00	—
1961	1,262,231	—	—	—	BV	5.50	7.00	—
1962	1,884,789	—	—	—	BV	5.50	7.00	—
1963	4,179,981	—	—	—	BV	5.50	7.00	—

KM# 55 Subject: British Columbia **Obv. Designer:** Mary Gillick **Rev. Designer:** Stephan Trenka **Weight:** 23.3276 g. **Composition:** 0.8000 Silver 0.6000 oz. ASW

Date	Mintage	F-12	VF-20	XF-40	AU-50	MS-60	MS-63	Proof
ND(1958)	3,039,630	—	BV	5.75	6.25	7.00	15.00	—

KM# 58 Subject: Charlottetown **Rev. Designer:** Dinko Voldanovic **Weight:** 23.3276 g. **Composition:** 0.8000 Silver 0.6000 oz. ASW

Date	Mintage	F-12	VF-20	XF-40	AU-50	MS-60	MS-63	Proof
ND(1964)	7,296,832	—	—	—	BV	5.75	8.00	—
ND(1964) Specimen proof	Inc. above	—	—	—	—	—	—	250

Small beads

Medium beads

Large beads

KM# 64.1 Obv: Elizabeth II effigy **Obv. Designer:** Arnold Machin **Rev:** Voyageur **Rev. Designer:** Emanual Hahn **Weight:** 23.3276 g. **Composition:** 0.8000 Silver 0.6000 oz. ASW

Date	Mintage	F-12	VF-20	XF-40	AU-50	MS-60	MS-63	Proof
1965	10,768,569	—	—	—	BV	5.50	6.50	—
Note: small beads, pointed 5								
1965	Inc. above	—	—	—	BV	5.50	6.50	—
Note: small beads, blunt 5								
1965	Inc. above	—	—	—	BV	5.50	6.50	—
Note: large beads, blunt 5								
1965	Inc. above	—	—	—	BV	5.50	6.50	—
Note: large beads, pointed 5								
1965	Inc. above	—	BV	7.00	9.00	12.00	35.00	—
Note: medium beads, pointed 5								
1966	9,912,178	—	—	—	BV	5.50	6.50	—
Note: large beads								
1966	485	—	—	1,200	1,500	1,800	2,200	—
Note: small beads								

Date	Mintage	MS-63	Proof
1968	—	5.00	—
Note: Small island			
1968	—	—	—
Note: No island			
1968	—	—	—
Note: Doubled die; exhibits extra water lines			
1969	4,809,313	1.25	—
1969	594,258	—	—
1972	2,676,041	1.50	—
1972	405,865	—	—

KM# 70 Subject: Confederation Centennial **Obv. Designer:** Arnold Machin **Rev:** Goose **Rev. Designer:** Alex Colville **Weight:** 23.3276 g. **Composition:** 0.8000 Silver 0.6000 oz. ASW

Date	Mintage	MS-63	Proof
ND(1967)	6,767,496	7.00	10.00

KM#76.1 Obv: Large bust **Obv. Designer:** Arnold Machin **Rev:** Voyageur **Rev. Designer:** Emanuel Hahn **Composition:** Nickel **Size:** 32 mm.

Date	Mintage	MS-63	Proof
1968	5,579,714	1.25	—
1968	1,408,143	—	—

KM# 78 Subject: Manitoba **Rev:** Pasque flower **Rev. Designer:** Raymond Taylor **Composition:** Nickel **Size:** 32 mm.

Date	Mintage	MS-63	Proof
1970	4,140,058	2.00	—
1970	645,869	—	—

KM# 79 Subject: British Columbia **Rev. Designer:** Thomas Shingles **Composition:** Nickel **Size:** 32 mm.

Date	Mintage	MS-63	Proof
1971	4,260,781	2.00	—
1971	468,729	—	—

KM# 80 Subject: British Columbia **Rev. Designer:** Patrick Brindley **Weight:** 23.3276 g. **Composition:** 0.5000 Silver 0.3750 oz. ASW **Size:** 36 mm.

Date	Mintage	MS-63	P/L	Spec.
1971	585,674	—	—	5.75

KM# 64.2a Obv: Smaller bust **Obv. Designer:** Arnold Machin **Rev:** Voyageur **Rev. Designer:** Emanuel Hahn **Weight:** 23.3276 g. **Composition:** 0.5000 Silver 0.3750 oz. ASW **Size:** 36 mm.

Date	Mintage	MS-63	P/L	Proof
1972 Proof	341,598	—	—	5.50
Note: Specimen $5.50.				

KM# 82 Subject: Prince Edward Island **Rev. Designer:** Terry Manning **Composition:** Nickel **Size:** 32 mm.

Date	Mintage	MS-63	Proof
1973	3,196,452	2.00	—
1973 (c)	466,881	—	—

KM# 83 Subject: Mountie **Rev. Designer:** Paul Cedarberg **Weight:** 23.3276 g. **Composition:** 0.5000 Silver 0.3750 oz. ASW **Size:** 36 mm.

Date	Mintage	MS-63	P/L	Spec.
1973	1,031,271	—	—	6.50

KM# 88 Subject: Winnipeg Centennial **Rev. Designer:** Paul Pederson and Patrick Brindley **Composition:** Nickel **Size:** 32 mm.

Date	Mintage	MS-63	Proof
1974	2,799,363	2.00	—
1974 (c)	363,786	—	—

KM# 88a Subject: Winnipeg Centennial **Rev. Designer:** Paul Pederson and Patrick Brindley **Composition:** 0.5000 Silver **Size:** 36 mm.

Date	Mintage	MS-63	P/L	Spec.
1974	728,947	—	—	5.75

KM# 76.2 Obv: Smaller bust **Obv. Designer:** Arnold Machin **Rev:** Voyageur **Rev. Designer:** Emanuel Hahn **Composition:** Nickel **Size:** 32 mm.

Date	Mintage	MS-63	Proof
1975	3,256,000	1.50	—
1975	322,325	—	—
1976	2,498,204	1.50	—
1976	274,106	—	—

KM# 76.3 Obv. Designer: Arnold Machin **Rev:** Voyageur **Rev. Designer:** Emanuel Hahn **Composition:** Nickel **Size:** 32 mm. **Note:** Only known in prooflike sets with 1976 obverse slightly modified.

Date	Mintage	MS-63	P/L	Proof
1975	Inc. above	—	3.00	—
Note: mule with 1976 obv.				

KM# 97 Subject: Calgary **Rev. Designer:** Donald D. Paterson **Weight:** 23.3276 g. **Composition:** 0.5000 Silver 0.3750 oz. ASW **Size:** 36 mm.

Date	Mintage	MS-63	P/L	Spec.
1975	930,956	—	—	5.75

KM# 106 Subject: Parliament Library **Rev. Designer:** Walter Ott and Patrick Brindley **Weight:** 23.3276 g. **Composition:** 0.5000 Silver 0.3750 oz. ASW **Size:** 36 mm.

Date	Mintage	MS-63	P/L	Spec.
1976	578,708	—	—	6.50
1976	Inc. above	—	—	15.00

Note: blue case VIP

KM# 117 Obv. Designer: Arnold Machin **Rev:** Voyageur modified **Rev. Designer:** Emanuel Hahn **Composition:** Nickel **Size:** 32 mm.

Date	Mintage	MS-63	Proof
1977	1,393,745	2.25	—

KM# 118 Subject: Silver Jubilee **Rev. Designer:** Raymond Lee **Weight:** 23.3276 g. **Composition:** 0.5000 Silver 0.3750 oz. ASW **Size:** 36 mm.

Date	Mintage	MS-63	P/L	Spec.
1977	744,848	—	—	5.50
1977	Inc. above	—	—	25.00

Note: red case VIP

KM# 120.1 Obv. Designer: Arnold Machin **Rev:** Voyageur **Rev. Designer:** Emanuel Hahn **Composition:** Nickel **Size:** 32 mm. **Note:** Modified design.

Date	Mintage	MS-63	Proof
1978	2,948,488	1.50	—
1979	2,954,842	1.50	—
1980	3,291,221	1.50	—
1981	2,778,900	1.50	—
1981 Proof	—	—	—
1982	1,098,500	1.50	—
1982 Proof	180,908	—	5.25
1983	2,267,525	1.50	—
1983 Proof	166,779	—	5.25
1984	1,223,486	1.50	—
1984 Proof	161,602	—	6.00
1985	3,104,092	1.50	—
1985 Proof	153,950	—	7.00
1986	3,089,225	2.00	—
1986 Proof	176,224	—	7.50
1987	287,330	3.50	—
1987 Proof	175,686	—	7.50

KM# 121 Subject: XI Commonwealth Games **Rev. Designer:** Raymond Taylor **Weight:** 23.3276 g. **Composition:** 0.5000 Silver 0.3750 oz. ASW **Size:** 36 mm.

Date	Mintage	MS-63	P/L	Spec.
1978	709,602	—	—	5.50

KM# 124 Subject: Griffon **Rev. Designer:** Walter Schluep **Weight:** 23.3276 g. **Composition:** 0.5000 Silver 0.3750 oz. ASW **Size:** 36 mm.

Date	Mintage	MS-63	P/L	Spec.
1979	826,695	—	—	8.50

KM# 128 Subject: Arctic Territories **Rev. Designer:** Donald D. Paterson **Weight:** 23.3276 g. **Composition:** 0.5000 Silver 0.3750 oz. ASW **Size:** 36 mm.

Date	Mintage	MS-63	P/L	Spec.
1980	539,617	—	—	17.50

KM# 130 Subject: Transcontinental Railroad **Rev. Designer:** Christopher Gorey **Weight:** 23.3276 g. **Composition:** 0.5000 Silver 0.3750 oz. ASW **Size:** 36 mm.

Date	Mintage	MS-63	P/L	Proof
1981	699,494	7.50	—	—
1981 Proof	—	—	—	13.50

KM# 133 Subject: Regina **Rev. Designer:** Huntley Brown **Weight:** 23.3276 g. **Composition:** 0.5000 Silver 0.3750 oz. ASW **Size:** 36 mm.

Date	Mintage	MS-63	P/L	Proof
1982	144,930	7.50	—	—
1982 Proof	758,958	—	—	6.00

KM# 134 Subject: Constitution **Rev. Designer:** Ago Aarand **Composition:** Nickel **Size:** 32 mm.

Date	Mintage	MS-63	P/L	Proof
1982	9,709,422	3.00	6.00	—

KM# 138 Subject: Edmonton University Games **Rev. Designer:** Carola Tietz **Weight:** 23.3276 g. **Composition:** 0.5000 Silver 0.3750 oz. ASW **Size:** 36 mm.

Date	Mintage	MS-63	P/L	Proof
1983	159,450	7.00	—	—
1983 Proof	506,847	—	—	6.00

KM# 140 Subject: Toronto Sesquicentennial **Rev. Designer:** D. J. Craig **Weight:** 23.3276 g. **Composition:** 0.5000 Silver 0.3750 oz. ASW **Size:** 36 mm.

Date	Mintage	MS-63	P/L	Proof
1984	133,610	7.50	—	—
1984 Proof	732,542	—	—	7.00

KM# 141 Subject: Jacques Cartier **Rev. Designer:** Hector Greville **Composition:** Nickel **Size:** 32 mm.

Date	Mintage	MS-63	P/L	Proof
1984	7,009,323	2.25	—	—
1984 Proof	87,760	—	—	6.00

KM# 120.2 Rev: Voyageur **Composition:** Nickel **Size:** 32 mm. **Note:** Modified design.

Date	Mintage	MS-63	P/L	Spec.
1985	—	1,900	—	—

Note: mule with New Zealand 50 cent, KM-37 obverse

KM# 143 Subject: National Parks / Moose **Rev. Designer:** Karel Rohlicek **Weight:** 23.3276 g. **Composition:** 0.5000 Silver 0.3750 oz. ASW **Size:** 36 mm.

Date	Mintage	MS-63	P/L	Proof
1985	163,314	7.50	—	—
1985 Proof	733,354	—	—	7.50

KM# 149 Subject: Vancouver **Rev. Designer:** Elliot John Morrison **Weight:** 23.3276 g. **Composition:** 0.5000 Silver 0.3750 oz. ASW **Size:** 36 mm.

Date	Mintage	MS-63	P/L	Proof
1986	125,949	8.00	—	—
1986 Proof	680,004	—	—	7.50

KM# 157 Obv: Elizabeth II effigy **Obv. Designer:** Arnold Machin **Rev:** Loon **Rev. Designer:** Robert R. Carmichael **Composition:** Aureate-Bronze Plated Nickel **Shape:** 11-sided

Date	Mintage	MS-63	Proof
1987	205,405,000	2.25	—
1987 Proof	178,120	—	8.00
1988	138,893,539	2.25	—
1988 Proof	175,259	—	6.75
1989	184,773,902	3.00	—
1989 Proof	170,928	—	6.75

KM# 154 Subject: John Davis **Rev. Designer:** Christopher Gorey **Weight:** 23.3276 g. **Composition:** 0.5000 Silver 0.3750 oz. ASW **Size:** 36 mm.

Date	Mintage	MS-63	P/L	Proof
1987	118,722	8.00	—	—
1987 Proof	602,374	—	—	9.00

KM# 161 Subject: Ironworks **Rev. Designer:** Robert R. Carmichael **Weight:** 23.3276 g. **Composition:** 0.5000 Silver 0.3750 oz. ASW **Size:** 36 mm.

Date	Mintage	MS-63	P/L	Proof
1988	106,872	8.00	—	—
1988 Proof	255,013	—	—	16.00

KM# 168 Subject: MacKenzie River **Rev. Designer:** John Mardon **Weight:** 23.3276 g. **Composition:** 0.5000 Silver 0.3750 oz. ASW **Size:** 36 mm.

Date	Mintage	MS-63	P/L	Proof
1989	99,774	8.00	—	—
1989 Proof	244,062	—	—	16.00

KM# 170 Subject: Henry Kelsey **Rev. Designer:** D. J. Craig **Weight:** 23.3276 g. **Composition:** 0.5000 Silver 0.3750 oz. ASW **Size:** 36 mm.

Date	Mintage	MS-63	P/L	Proof
1990	99,455	8.00	—	—
1990 Proof	254,959	—	—	18.00

KM# 186 Obv: Elizabeth II effigy **Obv. Designer:** Dora dePedery-Hunt **Rev:** Loon **Rev. Designer:** Robert R. Carmichael **Composition:** Aureate-Bronze Plated Nickel **Shape:** 11-sided

Date	Mintage	MS-63	Proof
1990	68,402,000	1.75	—
1990 Proof	140,649	—	7.00
1991	23,156,000	1.75	—
1991 Proof	—	—	13.00
1993	33,662,000	2.00	—
1993 Proof	—	—	6.00
1994	16,232,530	2.00	—
1994 Proof	—	—	7.00
1995	27,492,630	3.00	—
1995 Proof	—	—	7.00
1996	17,101,000	2.00	—
1996 Proof	—	—	7.50
1997	—	5.00	—
1997 Proof	—	—	8.00
1998	—	2.50	—
1998 Proof	—	—	10.00
1998W	—	—	—
1999	—	2.00	—
1999 Proof	—	—	8.00
2000	—	2.00	—
2000 Proof	—	—	8.00
2001	—	2.00	—
2001 Proof	—	—	8.00
2002	—	6.00	—
2002 Proof	—	—	—
2003	—	6.00	—
2003 Proof	100,000	—	12.00

KM# 179 Subject: S.S. Frontenac **Rev. Designer:** D. J. Craig **Weight:** 23.3276 g. **Composition:** 0.5000 Silver 0.3750 oz. ASW **Size:** 36 mm.

Date	Mintage	MS-63	P/L	Proof
1991	73,843	8.00	—	—
1991 Proof	195,424	—	—	24.00

KM# 210 Subject: Stagecoach service **Rev. Designer:** Karsten Smith **Weight:** 25.1750 g. **Composition:** 0.9250 Silver 0.7487 oz. ASW **Size:** 36 mm.

Date	Mintage	MS-63	P/L	Proof
1992	78,160	9.00	—	—
1992 Proof	187,612	—	—	13.00

KM# 209 Subject: Loon **Rev. Designer:** Robert R. Carmichael **Composition:** Aureate **Size:** 32 mm.

Date	Mintage	MS-63	Proof
ND(1992)	4,242,085	2.00	—
ND(1992) Proof	—	—	8.00

KM# 218 Subject: Parliament **Rev. Designer:** Rita Swanson **Composition:** Aureate **Size:** 26 mm.

Date	Mintage	MS-63	Proof
ND(1992)	23,915,00 0	2.25	—
ND(1992) Proof	24,227	—	9.00

KM# 235 Subject: Stanley Cup hockey **Rev. Designer:** Stewart Sherwood **Weight:** 25.1750 g. **Composition:** 0.9250 Silver 0.7487 oz. ASW **Size:** 36 mm.

Date	Mintage	MS-63	P/L	Proof
1993	88,150	9.00	—	—
1993 Proof	294,314	—	—	13.00

KM# 251 Subject: Last RCMP sled-dog patrol **Rev. Designer:** Ian Sparks **Weight:** 25.1750 g. **Composition:** 0.9250 Silver 0.7487 oz. ASW **Size:** 36 mm.

Date	Mintage	MS-63	P/L	Proof
1994	61,561	10.00	—	—
1994 Proof	170,374	—	—	24.50

KM# 248 Subject: War Memorial **Rev. Designer:** R. C. M. Staff **Composition:** Aureate **Size:** 26 mm.

Date	Mintage	MS-63	Proof
1994	20,004,830	2.25	—
1994 Proof	54,524	—	7.50

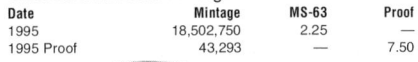

KM# 258 Subject: Peacekeeping Monument in Ottawa **Rev. Designer:** J. K. Harmon, R. G. Henriquez and C. H. Oberlander **Composition:** Aureate **Size:** 26 mm. **Note:** Mintage included with KM#186.

Date	Mintage	MS-63	Proof
1995	18,502,750	2.25	—
1995 Proof	43,293	—	7.50

KM# 259 Subject: Hudson Bay Co. **Rev. Designer:** Vincent McIndoe **Weight:** 25.1750 g. **Composition:** 0.9250 Silver 0.7487 oz. ASW **Size:** 36 mm.

Date	Mintage	MS-63	P/L	Proof
1995	61,819	10.00	—	—
1995 Proof	166,259	—	—	19.00

KM# 274 Subject: McIntosh Apple
Rev. Designer: Roger Hill **Weight:** 25.1750 g.
Composition: 0.9250 Silver 0.7487 oz. ASW **Size:**
36 mm.

Date	Mintage	MS-63	P/L	Proof
1996	58,834	10.00	—	—
1996 Proof	133,779	—	—	24.00

KM# 282 Subject: 25th Anniversary Hockey Victory **Rev:** The winning goal by Paul Aenderson. Based on a painting by Andre l'Archeveque. **Rev. Designer:** Walter Burden **Weight:** 25.1750 g. **Composition:** 0.9250 Silver 0.7487 oz. ASW **Size:** 36 mm.

Date	Mintage	MS-63	P/L	Proof
ND(1997)	155,252	10.00	—	—
ND(1997) Proof	184,965	—	—	24.00

KM# 291 Subject: Loon Dollar 10th Anniversary
Rev. Designer: Jean-Luc Grondin **Composition:**
Aureate **Size:** 26 mm.

Date	Mintage	MS-63	Proof
1997	—	—	—

KM# 296 Subject: Loon Dollar 10th Anniversary
Rev. Designer: Jean-Luc Grondin **Weight:**
25.1750 g. **Composition:** 0.9250 Silver 0.7487 oz.
ASW **Size:** 36 mm.

Date	Mintage	MS-63	P/L	Proof
1997 Proof	24,995	—	—	75.00

KM# 306 Subject: 120th Anniversary Royal Canadian Mounted Police **Rev. Designer:** Adeline Halvorson **Weight:** 25.1750 g. **Composition:** 0.9250 Silver 0.7487 oz. ASW **Size:** 36 mm. **Note:** Individually cased prooflikes, proofs or specimens are from broken-up prooflike or specimen sets.

Date	Mintage	MS-63	P/L	Proof
1998	79,777	—	11.00	—
1998 Proof	120,172	—	—	20.00

KM# 355 Subject: International Year of Old Persons **Rev. Designer:** S. Armstrong-Hodgson **Weight:** 25.1750 g. **Composition:** 0.9250 Silver 0.7487 oz. ASW **Size:** 36 mm.

Date	Mintage	MS-63	P/L	Proof
1999 Proof	24,976	—	—	40.00

KM# 356 Subject: Discovery of Queen Charlotte Isle **Rev. Designer:** D. J. Craig **Weight:** 25.1750 g. **Composition:** 0.9250 Silver 0.7487 oz. ASW **Size:** 36 mm.

Date	Mintage	MS-63	P/L	Proof
ND(1999)	67,655	—	11.00	—
ND(1999) Proof	126,435	—	—	22.50

KM# 401 Subject: Voyage of Discovery **Obv:** Queen's portrait **Rev:** Human and space shuttle **Rev. Designer:** D. F. Warkentine **Weight:** 25.1750 g. **Composition:** 0.9250 Silver 0.7487 oz. ASW **Size:** 36 mm.

Date	Mintage	MS-63	P/L	Proof
2000	60,100	—	11.00	—
2000 Proof	114,130	—	—	22.50

KM# 443 Subject: Queen's Golden Jubilee **Obv:** Queen's portrait with anniversary date **Rev:** Queen in her coach and a view of the coach **Edge:** Reeded **Weight:** 25.1750 g. **Composition:** 0.9250 Silver 0.7487 oz. ASW **Size:** 36 mm.

Date	Mintage	MS-63	P/L	Proof
ND(2000) Proof	125,000	—	—	20.00
ND(2002)	—	—	12.00	—
ND(2002) Proof	—	—	—	21.50

KM# 414 Subject: National Ballet **Obv:** Queen's head right **Rev:** Ballet dancers **Rev. Designer:** Scott McKowen **Edge:** Reeded **Weight:** 25.1750 g. **Composition:** 0.9250 Silver 0.7487 oz. ASW **Size:** 36 mm.

Date	Mintage	MS-63	P/L	Proof
2001	65,000	9.00	12.00	—
2001 Proof	225,000	—	—	21.50

KM# 434 Obv: Bust of Queen Elizabeth II right. **Rev:** Recycled 1911 pattern dollar design: denomination, country name and dates in crowned wreath. **Edge:** Reeded. **Weight:** 25.1750 g. **Composition:** 0.9250 Silver 0.7487 oz. ASW **Size:** 36 mm.

Date	Mintage	MS-63	P/L	Proof
ND(2001) Proof	25,000	—	—	55.00

KM# 186a Subject: Olympic Win **Composition:** Gold Plated

Date	Mintage	MS-63	Proof
2002 Proof	—	—	40.00

KM# 467 Subject: Elizabeth II Golden Jubilee **Obv:** Queen, Jubilee commemorative dates 1952-2002 **Composition:** Nickel

Date	Mintage	MS-63	Proof
ND(2002)	—	2.50	—
ND(2002) Proof	—	—	8.00

KM# 462 Obv: Commemorative dates 1952-2002 **Rev:** Family of Loons **Composition:** Aureate-Bronze Plated Nickel

Date	Mintage	MS-63	Proof
ND(2002) In Specimen Sets only	75,000	10.00	—

KM# 503 Subject: Queen Mother **Obv:** Queen's head right **Obv. Designer:** Dora de Pedery-Hunt **Rev:** Queen Mother facing **Weight:** 25.1750 g. **Composition:** 0.9250 Silver 0.7487 oz. ASW **Size:** 36 mm.

Date	Mintage	MS-63	Proof
2002 Proof	9,984	—	200

KM# 443a Subject: Queen's Golden Jubilee **Obv:** Queen's portrait with anniversary date **Rev:** Queen in her coach and a view of the coach **Edge:** Reeded **Composition:** Gold Plated Silver **Size:** 36 mm. **Note:** Special 24 karat gold plated issue of KM#443.

Date	Mintage	MS-63	Proof
ND(2002) Proof	32,642	—	40.00

KM# 450 Subject: Cobalt Mining Centennial **Obv:** Queen's portrait **Rev:** Mine tower and fox **Edge:** Reeded **Weight:** 25.1750 g. **Composition:** 0.9999 Silver 0.8093 oz. ASW **Size:** 36 mm.

Date	Mintage	MS-63	Proof
ND(2003)	75,000	20.00	—
ND(2003) Proof	125,000	—	28.00

KM# 480 Subject: Coronation of Queen Elizabeth II **Composition:** 0.9999 Silver

Date	Mintage	MS-63	Proof
2003 Proof	30,000	—	38.00

KM# 473 Subject: 50th Anniversary of the Coronation of Elizabeth II **Obv:** 1953 effigy of the Queen, Jubilee commemorative dates 1952-2002 **Rev:** Voyageur design similar to KM#54 **Composition:** 0.9999 Silver

Date	Mintage	MS-63	Proof
ND(2003) In coronation proof sets only	30,000	35.00	—

KM# 495 Obv: New effigy of Queen Elizabeth II **Obv. Designer:** Susanna Blunt **Rev. Designer:** Robert R. Carmichael **Composition:** Aureate-Bronze Plated Nickel

Date	Mintage	MS-63	Proof
2003	5,102,000	6.00	—
2004	3,409,000	3.00	—
2004 Proof	—	—	12.00
2005	—	3.00	—
2006	—	3.00	—

KM# 507 Obv: Queen Elizabeth II **Rev:** Loon **Edge:** Plain **Weight:** 6.9500 g. **Composition:** Aureate-Bronze Plated Nickel **Shape:** 11-sided **Size:** 26.5 mm.

Date	Mintage	MS-63	Proof
2004 Proof	—	—	12.50

KM# 512 Subject: First French Settlement in America **Obv:** Elizabeth II **Rev:** Sailing ship **Edge:** Reeded **Weight:** 25.1750 g. **Composition:** 0.9999 Silver 0.8093 oz. ASW **Size:** 36 mm.

Date	Mintage	MS-63	Proof
2004 Proof	10,400	—	42.50

KM# 513 Subject: Olympics **Obv:** Elizabeth II **Rev:** Maple leaf, Olympic flame and rings above loon **Edge:** Plain **Weight:** 6.9500 g. **Composition:** Aureate-Bronze Plated Nickel **Shape:** 11-sided **Size:** 26.5 mm.

Date	Mintage	MS-63	Proof
2004	—	12.50	—

KM# 513a Subject: Olympics **Obv:** Elizabeth II **Rev:** Multicolor maple leaf, Olympic flame and rings above loon **Edge:** Plain **Weight:** 9.3100 g. **Composition:** 0.9250 Silver 0.2769 oz. ASW **Shape:** 11-sided **Size:** 26.5 mm.

Date	Mintage	MS-63	Proof
2004 Proof	20,000	—	50.00

KM# 549 Subject: 40th Anniversary of National Flag **Composition:** Silver

Date	Mintage	MS-63	Proof
2005	—	22.50	—
2005 Proof	—	—	32.50

KM# 552 Subject: Terry Fox **Composition:** Aureate-Bronze Plated Nickel

Date	Mintage	MS-63	Proof
2005	—	3.50	—

KM# 553 Subject: Tuffed Puffin **Composition:** Aureate-Bronze Plated Nickel

Date	Mintage	MS-63	Proof
2005 In specimen sets only	—	30.00	—

KM# 549a Subject: 40th Anniversary of National Flag **Composition:** Silver With Partial Gold Plating

Date	Mintage	MS-63	Proof
2005	—	65.00	—

KM# 581 Rev: Loon and moon, teddy bear in stars **Composition:** Aureate-Bronze Plated Nickel

Date	Mintage	MS-63	Proof
2006	—	3.50	—

KM# 582 Subject: Snowy owl **Composition:** Aureate-Bronze Plated Nickel

Date	Mintage	MS-63	Proof
2006 In specimen sets only	40,000	30.00	—

KM# 583 Subject: Victoria Cross **Composition:** Silver

Date	Mintage	MS-63	Proof
2006	—	27.50	—
2006 Proof	—	—	35.00

KM# 583a Subject: Victoria Cross **Composition:** Silver With Partial Gold Plating

Date	Mintage	MS-63	Proof
2006 Proof	—	—	60.00

2 DOLLARS

KM# 270 Obv. Designer: Dora dePedery-Hunt **Rev:** Polar bear **Rev. Designer:** Brent Townsend **Composition:** Bi-Metallic **Size:** 28 mm.

Date	Mintage	MS-63	Proof
1996	375,483,000	3.25	10.00
1997	16,942,000	3.25	—
1998	4,926,000	3.25	—
1998W	—	3.25	—
1999	25,130,000	3.25	—
2000	29,847,000	3.25	—
2000W	—	3.25	—
2001	27,008,000	3.25	—
2002	11,910,000	3.25	—
2003	—	3.25	—

KM# 270b Rev: Polar bear **Composition:** Bi-Metallic Gold And Silver **Note:** Silver ring, .925; Gold plated silver center.

Date	Mintage	MS-63	P/L	Proof
1996 Proof	10,000	—	—	55.00
1998 Proof	—	—	—	—

KM# 270c Rev: Polar bear **Composition:** Bi-Metallic Gold And Silver **Note:** Silver ring; Gold plated silver center. 8.83g., .925 silver, .2626 ASW.

Date	Mintage	MS-63	Proof
1996 Proof	10,000	—	12.00
1997 Proof	—	—	10.00
1998O Proof	—	—	12.00
1999 Proof	—	—	12.00
2000 Proof	—	—	12.00
2001 Proof	—	—	12.00

KM# 270a Rev: Polar bear **Composition:** Bi-Metallic Gold And Silver **Size:** 32 mm. **Note:** Silver ring, 5.0958 g., .1638 ASW; Gold Center, 5.7456 g., .1847 AGW.

Date	Mintage	MS-63	P/L	Proof
1996 Proof	5,000	—	—	135

KM# 357 Subject: Nunavut **Rev. Designer:** G. Arnaktavyok **Composition:** Bi-Metallic

Date	Mintage	MS-63	P/L	Proof
1999	—	3.50	—	—

KM# 357a Subject: Nunavut **Obv:** Queen's head right. **Rev:** Drum dancer. **Edge:** Interrupted reeding. **Weight:** 8.5200 g. **Composition:** 0.9250 Gold Plated Silver **Size:** 28 mm.

Date	Mintage	MS-63	P/L	Proof
1999 Proof	—	—	—	15.00

KM# 357b Subject: Nunavut **Obv:** Queen's head right. **Rev:** Drum dancer. **Composition:** Gold

Date	Mintage	MS-63	P/L	Proof
1999 Proof	10,000	—	—	165

KM# 399 Subject: Knowledge **Rev:** Polar bear and 2 cubs **Rev. Designer:** Tony Bianco **Edge:** Reeded and plain sections **Composition:** Bi-Metallic **Size:** 28 mm.

Date	Mintage	MS-63	Proof
2000	—	3.50	—

KM# 399a Subject: Knowledge **Rev:** Polar bear and 2 cubs **Composition:** 0.9250 Gold Plated Silver

Date	Mintage	MS-63	P/L	Proof
2000 Proof	40,000	—	—	15.00

KM# 399b Subject: Knowledge **Rev:** Polar bear and two cubs right. **Weight:** 6.3100 g. **Composition:** 0.9160 Gold

Date	Mintage	MS-63	P/L	Proof
2000 Proof	—	—	—	165

KM# 449 Subject: Elizabeth II Golden Jubilee **Obv:** Queen, Jubilee commemorative dates 1952-2002 **Weight:** 7.3000 g. **Composition:** Bi-Metallic

Date	Mintage	MS-63	Proof
ND(2002)	27,008,000	4.00	—

KM# 449a Subject: Elizabeth II Golden Jubilee **Obv:** Queen, Jubilee commemorative dates 1952-2002 **Composition:** Bi-Metallic

Date	Mintage	MS-63	Proof
ND(2002) Proof	100,000	—	14.00

KM# 496 Obv: New effigy of Queen Elizabeth II **Obv. Designer:** Susanna Blunt **Rev. Designer:** Brent Townsend **Composition:** Bi-Metallic

Date	Mintage	MS-63	Proof
2003	—	3.50	—
2004	—	3.50	—
2005	—	3.50	—
2006	—	3.50	—

KM# 270d Subject: 100th Anniversary of the Cobalt Silver Strike **Composition:** Bi-Metallic

Date	Mintage	MS-63	Proof
2003 Proof	100,000	—	25.00

KM# 496a Obv: Elizabeth II by Suanne Blunt **Rev:** Polar Bear **Edge:** Segmented reeding **Weight:** 10.8414 g. **Composition:** 0.9250 Bi-Metallic Gold And Silver 0.3224 oz. **Size:** 28 mm.

Date	Mintage	MS-63	Proof
2004 Proof	—	—	25.00

KM# 584 Subject: 10th Anniversary of Polar Bear $2.00 **Composition:** Bi-Metallic

Date	Mintage	MS-63	Proof
2006 Proof	3,000	—	385

5 DOLLARS

KM# 26 Obv. Designer: E. B. MacKennal **Rev. Designer:** W. H. J. Blakemore **Weight:** 8.3592 g. **Composition:** 0.9000 Gold 0.2419 oz. AGW

Date	Mintage	F-12	VF-20	XF-40	AU-50	MS-60	MS-63
1912	165,680	BV	150	175	200	250	550
1913	98,832	BV	150	175	200	250	600
1914	31,122	175	275	350	425	650	2,000

KM# 84 Subject: 1976 Montreal Olympics **Rev:** Sailboat "Kingston" **Rev. Designer:** Georges Huel **Weight:** 24.3000 g. **Composition:** 0.9250 Silver 0.7227 oz. ASW **Size:** 38 mm. **Note:** Series I.

Date	Mintage	MS-63	Proof
1973	—	7.00	—
1973 Proof	165,203	—	7.50

KM# 85 Subject: 1976 Montreal Olympics **Rev:** North American map **Rev. Designer:** Georges Huel **Composition:** 0.9250 Silver 0.7227 oz. ASW **Note:** Series I.

Date	Mintage	MS-63	Proof
1973	—	7.00	—
1973 Proof	165,203	—	7.50

KM# 89 Subject: 1976 Montreal Olympics **Rev:** Olympic rings **Rev. Designer:** Anthony Mann **Weight:** 24.3000 g. **Composition:** 0.9250 Silver 0.7227 oz. ASW **Size:** 38 mm. **Note:** Series II.

Date	Mintage	MS-63	Proof
1974	—	7.00	—
1974 Proof	97,431	—	7.50

KM# 90 Subject: 1976 Montreal Olympics **Rev:** Athlete with torch **Rev. Designer:** Anthony Mann **Weight:** 24.3000 g. **Composition:** 0.9250 Silver 0.7227 oz. ASW **Size:** 38 mm. **Note:** Series II.

Date	Mintage	MS-63	Proof
1974	—	7.00	—
1974 Proof	97,431	—	7.50

KM# 91 Subject: 1976 Montreal Olympics **Rev:** Rowing **Rev. Designer:** Ken Danby **Weight:** 24.3000 g. **Composition:** 0.9250 Silver 0.7227 oz. ASW **Size:** 38 mm. **Note:** Series III.

Date	Mintage	MS-63	Proof
1974	—	7.00	—
1974 Proof	104,684	—	7.50

KM# 99 Subject: Montreal 1976 - 21st Summer Olympic Games **Rev:** Women's javelin event **Rev. Designer:** Leo Yerxa **Weight:** 24.3000 g. **Composition:** 0.9250 Silver 0.7227 oz. ASW **Size:** 38 mm. **Note:** Series IV.

Date	Mintage	MS-63	Proof
1975	—	7.00	—
1975 Proof	89,155	—	7.50

KM# 92 Subject: 1976 Montreal Olympics **Rev:** Canoeing **Rev. Designer:** Ken Danby **Weight:** 24.3000 g. **Composition:** 0.9250 Silver 0.7227 oz. ASW **Size:** 38 mm. **Note:** Series III.

Date	Mintage	MS-63	Proof
1974	—	7.00	—
1974 Proof	104,684	—	7.50

KM# 100 Subject: 1976 Montreal Olympics **Rev:** Swimmer **Rev. Designer:** Lynda Cooper **Weight:** 24.3000 g. **Composition:** 0.9250 Silver 0.7227 oz. ASW **Size:** 38 mm. **Note:** Series V.

Date	Mintage	MS-63	Proof
1975	—	7.00	—
1975 Proof	89,155	—	7.50

KM# 98 Subject: 1976 Montreal Olympics **Rev:** Marathon **Rev. Designer:** Leo Yerxa **Weight:** 24.3000 g. **Composition:** 0.9250 Silver 0.7227 oz. ASW **Size:** 38 mm. **Note:** Series IV.

Date	Mintage	MS-63	Proof
1975	—	7.00	—
1975 Proof	89,155	—	7.50

KM# 101 Subject: Montreal 1976 - 21st Summer Olympic Games **Rev:** Platform Diver **Rev. Designer:** Lynda Cooper **Weight:** 24.3000 g. **Composition:** 0.9250 Silver 0.7227 oz. ASW **Size:** 38 mm. **Note:** Series V.

Date	Mintage	MS-63	Proof
1975	—	7.00	—
1975 Proof	89,155	—	7.50

KM# 107 Subject: 1976 Montreal Olympics **Rev:** Fencing **Rev. Designer:** Shigeo Fukada **Weight:** 24.3000 g. **Composition:** 0.9250 Silver 0.7227 oz. ASW **Size:** 38 mm. **Note:** Series VI.

Date	Mintage	MS-63	Proof
1976	—	7.00	—
1976 Proof	82,302	—	7.50

KM# 108 Subject: 1976 Montreal Olympics **Obv. Legend:** Boxing **Rev. Designer:** Shigeo Fukada **Weight:** 24.3000 g. **Composition:** 0.9250 Silver 0.7227 oz. ASW **Size:** 38 mm. **Note:** Series VI.

Date	Mintage	MS-63	Proof
1976	—	7.00	—
1976 Proof	82,302	—	7.50

KM# 109 Subject: 1976 Montreal Olympics **Rev:** Olympic village **Rev. Designer:** Elliot John Morrison **Weight:** 24.3000 g. **Composition:** 0.9250 Silver 0.7227 oz. ASW **Size:** 38 mm. **Note:** Series VII.

Date	Mintage	MS-63	Proof
1976	—	7.00	—
1976 Proof	76,908	—	7.50

KM# 110 Subject: 1976 Montreal Olympics **Rev:** Olympic flame **Rev. Designer:** Elliott John Morrison **Weight:** 24.3000 g. **Composition:** 0.9250 Silver 0.7227 oz. ASW **Size:** 38 mm. **Note:** Series VII.

Date	Mintage	MS-63	Proof
1976	—	7.00	—
1976 Proof	79,102	—	7.50

KM# 316 Subject: Dr. Norman Bethune **Rev. Designer:** Harvey Chan **Weight:** 31.3900 g. **Composition:** 0.9999 Silver 1.0091 oz. ASW

Date	Mintage	MS-63	Proof
1998 Proof	61,000	—	35.00

KM# 398 Rev: Viking ship under sail **Rev. Designer:** Donald Curley **Composition:** Copper-Zinc-Nickel **Note:** Sold in sets with Norway 20 kroner, KM#465.

Date	Mintage	MS-63	Proof
1999 Proof	—	—	18.50

KM# 435 Subject: Guglielmo Marconi **Obv:** Bust of Queen Elizabeth II right **Rev:** Gold-plated cameo portrait of Marconi **Rev. Designer:** Cosme Saffioti **Edge:** Reeded **Weight:** 16.8600 g. **Composition:** 0.9250 Silver 0.5014 oz. ASW **Size:** 28.4 mm. **Note:** Only issued in two coin set with British 2 pounds KM#1014a.

Date	Mintage	MS-63	Proof
ND(2001) Proof	30,000	—	33.50

KM# 519 Obv: Elizabeth II **Rev:** National arms **Edge:** Reeded **Weight:** 8.3600 g. **Composition:** 0.9000 Gold 0.2419 oz. AGW **Size:** 21.6 mm.

Date	Mintage	MS-63	Proof
ND (2002) Proof	2,002	—	230

KM# 518 Subject: World Cup Soccer , Germany 2006 **Obv:** Elizabeth II and value **Rev:** Goalie on knees **Edge:** Reeded **Weight:** 31.3900 g. **Composition:** 0.9999 Silver 1.0091 oz. ASW **Size:** 38 mm.

Date	Mintage	MS-63	Proof
2003 Proof	50,000	—	32.50

KM# 514 Obv: Elizabeth II **Rev:** Moose **Edge:** Reeded **Weight:** 31.1200 g. **Composition:** 0.9999 Silver 1.0287 oz. ASW **Size:** 38 mm.

Date	Mintage	MS-63	Proof
2004 Proof	25,555	—	120

KM# 527 Subject: Golf, Championship of Canada, Centennial **Composition:** Silver

Date	Mintage	MS-63	Proof
2004 Proof	—	—	20.00

KM# 607 Rev: Maple leaf, winter colors **Composition:** Silver

Date	Mintage	MS-63	Proof
2004	—	35.00	—

KM# 554 Subject: Alberta **Composition:** 0.9999 Silver

Date	Mintage	MS-63	Proof
2005 Proof	—	—	42.50

KM# 555 Subject: Saskatchewan **Composition:** 0.9999 Silver

Date	Mintage	MS-63	Proof
2005 Proof	—	—	42.50

KM# 556 Subject: WWII Veterans **Rev:** Large V and three portraits **Composition:** Silver

Date	Mintage	MS-63	Proof
2005	—	35.00	—

KM# 557 Subject: Walrus and calf **Composition:** Silver

Date	Mintage	MS-63	Proof
2005 Proof	—	—	45.00

KM# 558 Subject: White tailed deer **Composition:** Silver

Date	Mintage	MS-63	Proof
2005 Proof	—	—	45.00

KM# 585 Subject: Peregrine Falcon **Composition:** 0.9999 Silver

Date	Mintage	MS-63	Proof
2006 Proof	—	—	50.00

KM# 586 Subject: Sable Island horse and foal **Composition:** 0.9999 Silver

Date	Mintage	MS-63	Proof
2006 Proof	—	—	50.00

8 DOLLARS

KM# 515 Obv: Elizabeth II **Rev:** Grizzly bear walking left **Edge:** Reeded **Weight:** 32.0000 g. **Composition:** 0.9999 Silver 1.0287 oz. ASW **Size:** 40 mm.

Date	Mintage	MS-63	Proof
2004 Proof	25,888	—	50.00

KM# 597 Subject: Canadian Pacific Railway, 120th Anniversary **Rev:** Railway bridge **Composition:** Silver

Date	Mintage	MS-63	Proof
2005 Proof	—	—	55.00

KM# 598 Subject: Canadian Pacific Railway, 120th Anniversary **Rev:** Chinese worker **Composition:** Silver

Date	Mintage	MS-63	Proof
2005 Proof	—	—	55.00

10 DOLLARS

KM# 27 Obv. Designer: E. B. MacKennal **Rev. Designer:** W. H. J. Blackmore **Weight:** 16.7185 g. **Composition:** 0.9000 Gold 0.4838 oz. AGW

Date	Mintage	F-12	VF-20	XF-40	AU-50	MS-60	MS-63
1912	74,759	BV	300	350	400	550	2,000
1913	149,232	BV	325	375	400	600	2,600
1914	140,068	BV	325	400	450	700	2,750

KM# 86.1 Subject: 1976 Montreal Olympics **Rev:** World map **Rev. Designer:** Georges Huel **Weight:** 48.6000 g. **Composition:** 0.9250 Silver 1.4454 oz. ASW **Size:** 45 mm. **Note:** Series I.

Date	Mintage	MS-63	Proof
1973	103,426	13.50	—
1973 Proof	165,203	—	14.00

KM# 87 Subject: 1976 Montreal Olympics **Rev:** Montreal skyline **Rev. Designer:** Georges Huel **Weight:** 48.6000 g. **Composition:** 0.9250 Silver 1.4454 oz. ASW **Size:** 87 mm. **Note:** Series I.

Date	Mintage	MS-63	Proof
1973	—	13.50	—
1973 Proof	165,203	—	14.00

KM# 86.2 Subject: 1976 Montreal Olympics **Rev:** World map **Rev. Designer:** Georges Huel **Weight:** 48.6000 g. **Composition:** 0.9250 Silver 1.4454 oz. ASW **Size:** 45 mm. **Note:** Series I.

Date	Mintage	MS-63	Proof
1974	320	275	—

   Note: Error: mule

KM# 93 Subject: 1976 Montreal Olympics **Rev:** Head of Zeus **Rev. Designer:** Anthony Mann **Weight:** 48.6000 g. **Composition:** 0.9250 Silver 1.4454 oz. ASW **Size:** 45 mm. **Note:** Series II.

Date	Mintage	MS-63	Proof
1974	—	13.50	—
1974 Proof	104,684	—	14.00

KM# 94 Subject: 1976 Montreal Olympics **Rev:** Temple of Zeus **Rev. Designer:** Anthony Mann **Weight:** 48.6000 g. **Composition:** 0.9250 Silver 1.4454 oz. ASW **Size:** 45 mm. **Note:** Series II.

Date	Mintage	MS-63	Proof
1974	—	13.50	—
1974 Proof	104,684	—	14.00

KM# 95 Subject: 1976 Montreal Olympics **Rev:** Cycling **Rev. Designer:** Ken Danby **Weight:** 48.6000 g. **Composition:** 0.9250 Silver 1.4454 oz. ASW **Size:** 45 mm. **Note:** Series III.

Date	Mintage	MS-63	Proof
1974	—	13.50	—
1974 Proof	97,431	—	14.00

KM# 96 Subject: 1976 Montreal Olympics **Rev:** Lacrosse **Rev. Designer:** Ken Danby **Weight:** 48.6000 g. **Composition:** 0.9250 Silver 1.4454 oz. ASW **Size:** 45 mm. **Note:** Series III.

Date	Mintage	MS-63	Proof
1974	—	13.50	—
1974 Proof	97,431	—	14.00

KM# 102 Subject: 1976 Montreal Olympics **Rev:** Men's hurdles **Rev. Designer:** Leo Yerxa **Weight:** 48.6000 g. **Composition:** 0.9250 Silver 1.4454 oz. ASW **Size:** 45 mm. **Note:** Series IV.

Date	Mintage	MS-63	Proof
1975	—	13.50	—
1975 Proof	82,302	—	14.00

KM# 103 Subject: Montreal 1976 - 21st Summer Olympic Games **Rev:** Women's shot put **Rev. Designer:** Leo Yerxa **Weight:** 48.6000 g. **Composition:** 0.9250 Silver 1.4454 oz. ASW **Size:** 45 mm. **Note:** Series IV.

Date	Mintage	MS-63	Proof
1975	—	13.50	—
1975 Proof	82,302	—	14.00

KM# 104 Subject: 1976 Montreal Olympics **Rev:** Sailing **Rev. Designer:** Lynda Cooper **Weight:** 48.6000 g. **Composition:** 0.9250 Silver 1.4454 oz. ASW **Size:** 45 mm. **Note:** Series V.

Date	Mintage	MS-63	Proof
1975	—	13.50	—
1975 Proof	89,155	—	14.00

KM# 105 Subject: 1976 Montreal Olympics **Rev:** Canoeing **Rev. Designer:** Lynda Cooper **Weight:** 48.6000 g. **Composition:** 0.9250 Silver 1.4454 oz. ASW **Size:** 45 mm. **Note:** Series V.

Date	Mintage	MS-63	Proof
1975	—	13.50	—
1975 Proof	89,155	—	14.00

KM# 111 Subject: 1976 Montreal Olympics **Rev:** Football **Rev. Designer:** Shigeo Fukada **Weight:** 48.6000 g. **Composition:** 0.9250 Silver 1.4454 oz. ASW **Size:** 45 mm. **Note:** Series VI.

Date	Mintage	MS-63	Proof
1976	—	13.50	—
1976 Proof	76,908	—	14.00

KM# 112 Subject: 1976 Montreal Olympics **Rev:** Field hockey **Rev. Designer:** Shigeo Fukada **Weight:** 48.6000 g. **Composition:** 0.9250 Silver 1.4454 oz. ASW **Size:** 45 mm. **Note:** Series VI.

Date	Mintage	MS-63	Proof
1976	—	13.50	—
1976 Proof	76,908	—	14.00

KM# 113 Subject: 1976 Montreal Olympics **Rev:** Olympic Stadium **Rev. Designer:** Elliott John Morrison **Weight:** 48.6000 g. **Composition:** 0.9250 Silver 1.4454 oz. ASW **Size:** 45 mm. **Note:** Series VII.

Date	Mintage	MS-63	Proof
1976	—	13.50	—
1976 Proof	79,102	—	14.00

KM# 114 Subject: 1976 Montreal Olympics **Rev:** Olympic Velodrome **Rev. Designer:** Elliott John Morrison **Weight:** 48.6000 g. **Composition:** 0.9250 Silver 1.4454 oz. ASW **Size:** 45 mm. **Note:** Series VII.

Date	Mintage	MS-63	Proof
1976	—	13.50	—
1976 Proof	79,102	—	14.00

KM# 520 Obv: Elizabeth II **Rev:** National arms **Edge:** Reeded **Weight:** 16.7200 g. **Composition:** 0.9000 Gold 0.4838 oz. AGW **Size:** 26.92 mm.

Date	Mintage	MS-63	Proof
ND (2002) Proof	2,002	—	465

KM# 559 Subject: Pope John Paul II **Composition:** 0.9999 Silver

Date	Mintage	MS-63	Proof
2005 Proof	—	—	45.00

15 DOLLARS

KM# 215 Subject: 1992 Olympics **Rev:** Coaching track **Rev. Designer:** Stewart Sherwood **Weight:** 33.6300 g. **Composition:** 0.9250 Silver 1.0000 oz. ASW **Size:** 39 mm.

Date	Mintage	MS-63	Proof
1992 Proof	275,000	—	28.00

Date	Mintage	MS-63	Proof
1992 Proof	275,000	—	28.00

KM# 304 Subject: Year of the Tiger **Rev. Designer:** Harvey Chain **Size:** 40 mm.

Date	Mintage	MS-63	Proof
1998 Proof	68,888	—	275
1998 Proof	68,888	—	275

KM# 331 Subject: Year of the Rabbitt **Rev. Designer:** Harvey Chain

Date	Mintage	MS-63	Proof
1999 Proof	—	—	35.00
1999 Proof	—	—	35.00

KM# 387 Subject: Year of the Dragon **Rev. Designer:** Harvey Chain

Date	Mintage	MS-63	Proof
2000 Proof	—	—	125
2000 Proof	—	—	125

KM# 216 Subject: 1992 Olympics **Rev:** High jump, rings, speed skating **Rev. Designer:** David Craig **Weight:** 33.6300 g. **Composition:** 0.9250 Silver 1.0000 oz. ASW

KM# 415 **Subject:** Year of the Snake **Obv:** Queen's head right **Rev:** Snake within circle of lunar

calendar signs **Rev. Designer:** Harvey Chain **Edge:** Reeded **Weight:** 33.6300 g. **Composition:** 0.9250 Silver 1 oz. ASW **Size:** 40 mm.

Date	Mintage	MS-63	Proof
2001 Proof	60,754	—	37.50
2001 Proof	60,754	—	37.50

KM# 463 Subject: Year of the Horse **Rev. Designer:** Harvey Chain **Composition:** 0.9250 Silver

Date	Mintage	MS-63	Proof
2002 Proof	59,395	—	60.00

KM# 481 Subject: Year of the Sheep **Rev. Designer:** Harvey Chain **Composition:** 0.9250 Silver **Size:** 40 mm.

Date	Mintage	MS-63	Proof
2003 Proof	68,888	—	60.00

KM# 610 Subject: Year of the Monkey **Composition:** Silver

Date	Mintage	MS-63	Proof
2004 Proof	—	—	85.00

KM# 560 Subject: Year of the Rooster **Composition:** Silver With Partial Gold Plating

Date	Mintage	MS-63	Proof
2005 Proof	—	—	75.00

KM# 587 Subject: Year of the Dog **Composition:** Silver With Partial Gold Plating

Date	Mintage	MS-63	Proof
2006 Proof	48,888	—	80.00

20 DOLLARS

Date	Mintage	MS-63	Proof
1985 Proof	Inc. above	—	175

Note: Plain edge

KM# 71 **Subject:** Centennial **Rev:** Arms **Weight:** 18.2733 g. **Composition:** 0.9000 Gold 0.5288 oz. AGW

Date	Mintage	MS-63	Proof
1967 Proof	337,688	—	310

KM# 146 **Subject:** 1988 Calgary Olympics **Rev:** Speed skater **Rev. Designer:** Friedrich Peter **Edge:** Lettered **Weight:** 33.6300 g. **Composition:** 0.9250 Silver 1.0000 oz. ASW **Size:** 40 mm.

Date	Mintage	MS-63	Proof
1985 Proof	354,222	—	21.50
1985 Proof	Inc. above	—	175

Note: Plain edge

KM# 145 **Subject:** 1988 Calgary Olympics **Rev:** Downhill skier **Rev. Designer:** Ian Stewart **Edge:** Lettered **Weight:** 33.6300 g. **Composition:** 0.9250 Silver 1.0000 oz. ASW **Size:** 40 mm.

Date	Mintage	MS-63	Proof
1985 Proof	406,360	—	21.50

KM# 147 Subject: 1988 Calgary Olympics **Rev:** Biathlon **Rev. Designer:** John Mardon **Edge:** Lettered **Weight:** 33.6300 g. **Composition:** 0.9250 Silver 1.0000 oz. ASW **Size:** 40 mm.

Date	Mintage	MS-63	Proof
1986 Proof	308,086	—	21.50
1986 Proof	Inc. above	—	175

Note: Plain edge

KM# 148 Subject: 1988 Calgary Olympics **Rev:** Hockey **Rev. Designer:** Ian Stewart **Edge:** Lettered **Weight:** 33.6300 g. **Composition:** 0.9250 Silver 1.0000 oz. ASW **Size:** 40 mm.

Date	Mintage	MS-63	Proof
1986 Proof	396,602	—	21.50
1986 Proof	Inc. above	—	175

Note: Plain edge

KM# 150 Subject: Calgary 1988 - 15th Winter Olympic Games **Rev:** Cross-country skier **Rev. Designer:** Ian Stewart **Edge:** Lettered **Weight:** 33.6300 g. **Composition:** 0.9250 Silver 1.0000 oz. ASW **Size:** 40 mm.

Date	Mintage	MS-63	Proof
1986 Proof	303,199	—	21.50

KM# 151 Subject: 1988 Calgary Olympics **Rev:** Free-style skier **Rev. Designer:** Walter Ott **Edge:** Lettered **Weight:** 33.6300 g. **Composition:** 0.9250 Silver 1.0000 oz. ASW **Size:** 40 mm.

Date	Mintage	MS-63	Proof
1986 Proof	294,322	—	21.50
1986 Proof	Inc. above	—	175

Note: Plain edge

KM# 155 Subject: Calgary 1988 - 15th Winter Olympic Games **Rev:** Figure skating pairs event **Rev. Designer:** Raymond Taylor **Edge:** Lettered **Weight:** 34.1070 g. **Composition:** 0.9250 Silver 1.0000 oz. ASW **Size:** 40 mm.

Date	Mintage	MS-63	Proof
1987 Proof	334,875	—	21.50

KM# 156 Subject: 1988 Calgary Olympics **Rev:** Curling **Rev. Designer:** Ian Stewart **Edge:** Lettered **Weight:** 34.1070 g. **Composition:** 0.9250 Silver 1.0000 oz. ASW **Size:** 40 mm.

Date	Mintage	MS-63	Proof
1987 Proof	286,457	—	21.50

KM# 159 Subject: 1988 Calgary Olympics **Rev:** Ski jumper **Rev. Designer:** Raymond Taylor **Edge:** Lettered **Weight:** 34.1070 g. **Composition:** 0.9250 Silver 1.0000 oz. ASW **Size:** 40 mm.

Date	Mintage	MS-63	Proof
1987 Proof	290,954	—	21.50

KM# 160 Subject: 1988 Calgary Olympics **Rev:** Bobsled **Rev. Designer:** John Mardon **Edge:** Lettered **Weight:** 34.1070 g. **Composition:** 0.9250 Silver 1.0000 oz. ASW **Size:** 40 mm.

Date	Mintage	MS-63	Proof
1987 Proof	274,326	—	21.50

KM# 172 Subject: Aviation **Rev:** Lancaster, Fauquier in cameo **Rev. Designer:** Robert R. Carmichael **Weight:** 31.1030 g. **Composition:** 0.9250 Silver 0.9743 oz. ASW **Size:** 38 mm.

Date	Mintage	MS-63	Proof
1990 Proof	43,596	—	100

KM# 173 Subject: Aviation **Rev:** Anson and Harvard, Air Marshal robert Leckie in cameo **Rev. Designer:** Geoff Bennett **Weight:** 31.1030 g. **Composition:** 0.9250 Silver 0.9743 oz. ASW **Size:** 38 mm.

Date	Mintage	MS-63	Proof
1990 Proof	41,844	—	35.00

KM# 196 Subject: Aviation **Rev:** Silver Dart, John A. D. McCurdy and F. W. "Casey" Baldwin in cameo **Rev. Designer:** George Velinger **Weight:** 31.1030 g. **Composition:** 0.9250 Silver 0.9743 oz. ASW **Size:** 38 mm.

Date	Mintage	MS-63	Proof
1991 Proof	28,791	—	30.00

KM# 197 Subject: Aviation **Rev:** de Haviland Beaver, Philip C. Garratt in cameo **Rev. Designer:** Peter Massman **Weight:** 31.1030 g. **Composition:** 0.9250 Silver 0.9742 oz. ASW **Size:** 38 mm.

Date	Mintage	MS-63	Proof
1991 Proof	29,399	—	30.00

KM# 224 Subject: Aviation **Rev:** Curtiss JN-4 Canick ("Jenny"), Sir Frank W. Baillie in cameo **Rev. Designer:** George Velinger **Weight:** 31.1030 g. **Composition:** 0.9250 Silver 0.9743 oz. ASW **Size:** 38 mm.

Date	Mintage	MS-63	Proof
1992 Proof	33,105	—	30.00

KM# 225 Subject: Aviation **Rev:** de Haviland Gypsy Moth, Murton A. Seymour in cameo **Rev. Designer:** John Mardon **Weight:** 31.1030 g. **Composition:** 0.9250 Silver 0.9743 oz. ASW **Size:** 38 mm.

Date	Mintage	MS-63	Proof
1992 Proof	32,537	—	30.00

KM# 236 Subject: Aviation **Rev:** Fairchild 71C float plane, James A. Richardson, Sr. in cameo **Rev. Designer:** Robert R. Carmichael **Weight:** 31.1030 g. **Composition:** 0.9250 Silver 0.0257 oz. ASW **Size:** 38 mm.

Date	Mintage	MS-63	Proof
1993 Proof	32,199	—	30.00

KM# 237 Subject: Aviation **Rev:** Lockheed 14, Zebulon Lewis Leigh in cameo **Rev. Designer:** Robert R. Carmichael **Weight:** 31.1030 g. **Composition:** 0.9250 Silver 0.9743 oz. ASW **Size:** 38 mm.

Date	Mintage	MS-63	Proof
1993 Proof	32,550	—	30.00

KM# 246 Subject: Aviation **Rev:** Curtiss HS-2L seaplane, Stewart Graham in cameo **Rev. Designer:** John Mardon **Weight:** 31.1030 g. **Composition:** 0.9250 Silver 0.9743 oz. ASW **Size:** 38 mm.

Date	Mintage	MS-63	Proof
1994 Proof	31,242	—	30.00

KM# 247 Subject: Aviation **Rev:** Vickers Vedette, Wilfred T. Reid in cameo **Rev. Designer:** Robert R. Carmichael **Weight:** 31.1030 g. **Composition:** 0.9250 Silver 0.9743 oz. ASW **Size:** 38 mm.

Date	Mintage	MS-63	Proof
1994 Proof	30,880	—	30.00

KM# 271 Subject: Aviation **Rev:** C-FEA1 Fleet Cannuck **Rev. Designer:** Robert Bradford **Weight:** 31.1030 g. **Composition:** 0.9250 Silver 0.9743 oz. ASW **Size:** 38 mm.

Date	Mintage	MS-63	Proof
1995 Proof	17,438	—	30.00

KM# 272 Subject: Aviation **Rev:** DHC-1 Chipmunk **Rev. Designer:** Robert Bradford **Weight:** 31.1030 g. **Composition:** 0.9250 Silver 0.9743 oz. ASW **Size:** 38 mm.

Date	Mintage	MS-63	Proof
1995 Proof	17,722	—	30.00

KM# 276 Subject: Aviation **Rev:** CF-100 Cannuck **Rev. Designer:** Jim Bruce **Weight:** 31.1030 g. **Composition:** 0.9250 Silver 0.9743 oz. ASW **Size:** 38 mm.

Date	Mintage	MS-63	Proof
1996 Proof	18,508	—	32.50

KM# 277 Subject: Aviation **Obv. Legend:** CF-105 Arrow **Rev. Designer:** Jim Bruce **Weight:** 31.1030 g. **Composition:** 0.9250 Silver 0.9743 oz. ASW **Size:** 38 mm.

Date	Mintage	MS-63	Proof
1996 Proof	27,163	—	65.00

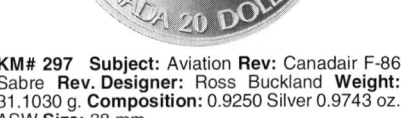

KM# 297 Subject: Aviation **Rev:** Canadair F-86 Sabre **Rev. Designer:** Ross Buckland **Weight:** 31.1030 g. **Composition:** 0.9250 Silver 0.9743 oz. ASW **Size:** 38 mm.

Date	Mintage	MS-63	Proof
1997 Proof	14,389	—	30.00

KM# 298 Subject: Aviation **Rev:** Canadair CT-114 Tutor **Rev. Designer:** Ross Buckland **Weight:** 31.1030 g. **Composition:** 0.9250 Silver 0.9743 oz. ASW **Size:** 38 mm.

Date	Mintage	MS-63	Proof
1997 Proof	15,669	—	30.00

KM# 329 Subject: Aviation **Rev:** CP-107 Argus
Weight: 31.1030 g. **Composition:** 0.9250 Silver
0.9743 oz. ASW **Size:** 38 mm.

Date	Mintage	MS-63	Proof
1998 Proof	50,000,000	—	37.50

KM# 330 Subject: Aviation **Rev:** CP-215 Water-
bomber **Rev. Designer:** Peter Mossman **Weight:**
31.1030 g. **Composition:** 0.9250 Silver 0.9743 oz.
ASW **Size:** 38 mm.

Date	Mintage	MS-63	Proof
1998 Proof	50,000,000	—	37.50

KM# 339 Subject: Aviation **Rev:** DHC-6 Twin Otter **Rev. Designer:** Neil Aird **Weight:** 31.1030 g.
Composition: 0.9250 Silver 0.9743 oz. ASW **Size:**
38 mm.

Date	Mintage	MS-63	Proof
1999 Proof	50,000,000	—	37.50

KM# 340 Subject: Aviation **Rev:** DHC-8 Dash 8
Weight: 31.1030 g. **Composition:** 0.9250 Silver
0.9743 oz. ASW **Size:** 38 mm.

Date	Mintage	MS-63	Proof
1999 Proof	50,000,000	—	37.50

KM# 395 Subject: First Canadian locomotive **Rev:**
Locomotive below multicolored cameo **Composition:** 0.9250 Silver **Size:** 38 mm.

Date	Mintage	MS-63	Proof
2000 Proof	—	—	40.00

KM# 396 Subject: First Canadian self-propelled
car **Rev:** Car below multicolored cameo **Composition:** 0.9250 Silver **Size:** 38 mm.

Date	Mintage	MS-63	Proof
2000 Proof	—	—	40.00

KM# 397 Subject: Bluenose sailboat **Rev:** Boat below multicolored cameo **Composition:** 0.9250 Silver **Size:** 38 mm.

Date	Mintage	MS-63	Proof
2000 Proof	—	—	150

KM# 411 Subject: First Canadian Steel Boiler Steam Locomotive **Obv:** Queen's head right **Rev:** Locomotive and cameo hologram **Rev. Designer:** Don Curely **Edge:** Reeded and plain sections **Weight:** 31.1035 g. **Composition:** 0.9250 Silver .9250 oz. ASW **Size:** 38 mm.

Date	Mintage	MS-63	Proof
2001 Proof	15,000	—	40.00

KM# 427 Subject: Transportation - The Marco Polo, **Obv:** Queen's head right **Rev:** Sailship with hologram cameo **Rev. Designer:** J. Franklin Wright **Edge:** Reeded and plain sections **Weight:** 31.1030 g. **Composition:** 0.9250 Silver .9250 oz. ASW **Size:** 38 mm.

Date	Mintage	MS-63	Proof
2001 Proof	15,000	—	40.00

KM# 428 Subject: Transportation - Russell Touring Car, **Obv:** Queen's head right **Rev:** Russell touring car with hologram cameo **Rev. Designer:** John Mardon **Edge:** Reeded and plain sections **Weight:** 31.1030 g. **Composition:** 0.9250 Silver .9250 oz. ASW **Size:** 38 mm.

Date	Mintage	MS-63	Proof
2001 Proof	15,000	—	40.00

KM# 464 Obv: Queen's head right **Rev:** Gray-Dort Model 25-SM with cameo hologram **Rev. Designer:** John Mardon **Composition:** 0.9250 Silver

Date	Mintage	MS-63	Proof
2002 Proof	Est. 15,000	—	45.00

KM# 465 Rev: Sailing ship William D. Lawrence **Rev. Designer:** Bonnie Ross **Composition:** 0.9250 Silver

Date	Mintage	MS-63	Proof
2002 Proof	15,000	—	45.00

KM# 484 Subject: Canadian National FA-1 diesel-electric locomotive **Composition:** 0.9250 Silver

Date	Mintage	MS-63	Proof
2003 Proof	15,000	—	45.00

KM# 485 Obv: Queens head right **Rev:** The Bricklin SV-1 **Composition:** Silver With Partial Gold Plating

Date	Mintage	MS-63	Proof
2003 Proof	Est. 15,000	—	50.00

KM# 482 Obv: Queens head right **Rev:** Niagara Falls hologram **Composition:** 0.9999 Silver

Date	Mintage	MS-63	Proof
2003 Proof	Est. 30,000	—	70.00

KM# 483 Subject: The HMCS Bras d'or (FHE-400) **Composition:** 0.9250 Silver

Date	Mintage	MS-63	Proof
2003 Proof	15,000	—	45.00

KM# 523 Subject: Canadian Rockies, colorized **Composition:** 0.9250 Silver

Date	Mintage	MS-63	Proof
2003 Proof	—	—	55.00

KM# 611 Rev: Iceburg, hologram **Composition:** Silver

Date	Mintage	MS-63	Proof
2004 Proof	—	—	60.00

KM# 561 Subject: Three-masted sailing ship, hologram **Weight:** 31.1050 g. **Composition:** 0.9999 Silver 1. oz. ASW

Date	Mintage	MS-63	Proof
2005 Proof	—	—	60.00

KM# 562 Subject: Northwest Territories Diamonds **Obv:** Elizabeth II **Rev:** Multicolor diamond hologram on landscape **Edge:** Reeded **Weight:** 31.3900 g. **Composition:** 0.9990 Silver **Size:** 38 mm.

Date	Mintage	MS-63	Proof
2005	25,000	—	45.00

KM# 563 Subject: Mingan Archepelago **Weight:** 31.1050 g. **Composition:** 0.9999 Silver 1. oz. ASW

Date	Mintage	MS-63	Proof
2005 Proof	—	—	62.50

KM# 564 Subject: Rainforests of the Pacific Northwest **Weight:** 31.1050 g. **Composition:** 0.9999 Silver 1. oz. ASW

Date	Mintage	MS-63	Proof
2005 Proof	—	—	60.00

KM# 565 Subject: Toronto Island National Park
Rev: Toronto Island Lighthouse **Composition:** Silver

Date	Mintage	MS-63	Proof
2005 Proof	—	—	62.50

KM# 588 Subject: Georgian Bay National Park
Weight: 31.1050 g. **Composition:** 0.9999 Silver
1. oz. ASW

Date	Mintage	MS-63	Proof
2006 Proof	—	—	65.00

KM# 589 Subject: Notre Dame Basilica, hologram
Composition: 0.9999 Silver

Date	Mintage	MS-63	Proof
2006 Proof	15,000	—	65.00

30 DOLLARS

KM# 590 Subject: Pacific Northwest Wood Carvings **Rev:** Welcome figure totem pole **Composition:** Silver

Date	Mintage	MS-63	Proof
2006 Proof	—	—	67.50

50 DOLLARS

KM# 543 Subject: WWII - Battle of Britain **Rev:** Fighter plane in sky **Composition:** Silver

Date	Mintage	MS-63	Proof
2005	—	22.50	—

KM# 566 Subject: WWII **Rev:** Large V and three portraits **Composition:** Gold

Date	Mintage	MS-63	Proof
2005 Proof	—	—	275

75 DOLLARS

KM# 567 Subject: Pope John Paul II **Composition:** 0.9999 Gold

Date	Mintage	MS-63	Proof
2005 Proof	—	—	425

100 DOLLARS

KM# 115 Subject: 1976 Montreal Olympics **Obv:** Beaded borders **Rev. Designer:** Dora dePedery-Hunt **Weight:** 13.3375 g. **Composition:** 0.5830 Gold 0.2500 oz. AGW **Size:** 27 mm.

Date	Mintage	MS-63	Proof
1976	650,000	150	—

KM# 116 Subject: 1976 Montreal Olympics **Obv:** Plain borders **Rev. Designer:** Dora dePedery-Hunt **Weight:** 16.9655 g. **Composition:** 0.9170 Gold 0.5000 oz. AGW **Size:** 25 mm.

Date	Mintage	MS-63	Proof
1976 Proof	337,342	—	300

KM# 119 Subject: Queen's silver jubilee **Rev:** Bouquet of provincial flowers **Rev. Designer:** Raymond Lee **Weight:** 16.9655 g. **Composition:** 0.9170 Gold 0.5000 oz. AGW

Date	Mintage	MS-63	Proof
ND(1977) Proof	180,396	—	300

KM# 122 Subject: Canadian unification **Rev:** Geese (representing the provinces) in flight formation **Rev. Designer:** Roger Savage **Weight:** 16.9655 g. **Composition:** 0.9170 Gold 0.5000 oz. AGW

Date	Mintage	MS-63	Proof
1978 Proof	200,000	—	310

KM# 126 Subject: International Year of the Child **Rev. Designer:** Carola Tietz **Weight:** 16.9655 g. **Composition:** 0.9170 Gold 0.5000 oz. AGW

Date	Mintage	MS-63	Proof
1979 Proof	250,000	—	300

KM# 129 Subject: Arctic Territories **Rev. Designer:** Arnaldo Marchetti **Weight:** 16.9655 g. **Composition:** 0.9170 Gold 0.5000 oz. AGW

Date	Mintage	MS-63	Proof
1980 Proof	300,000	—	300

KM# 131 Subject: National anthem **Rev. Designer:** Roger Savage **Weight:** 16.9655 g. **Composition:** 0.9170 Gold 0.5000 oz. AGW

Date	Mintage	MS-63	Proof
1981 Proof	102,000	—	300

KM# 137 Subject: New Constitution **Rev. Designer:** Friedrich Peter **Weight:** 16.9655 g. **Composition:** 0.9170 Gold 0.5000 oz. AGW

Date	Mintage	MS-63	Proof
1982 Proof	121,708	—	300

KM# 139 Subject: 400th Anniversary of St. John's, Newfoundland **Rev. Designer:** John Jaciw **Weight:** 16.9655 g. **Composition:** 0.9170 Gold 0.5000 oz. AGW

Date	Mintage	MS-63	Proof
ND(1983) Proof	83,128	—	300

KM# 142 Subject: Jacques Cartier **Rev. Designer:** Carola Tietz **Weight:** 16.9655 g. **Composition:** 0.9170 Gold 0.5000 oz. AGW

Date	Mintage	MS-63	Proof
ND(1984) Proof	67,662	—	300

KM# 144 Subject: National Parks **Rev:** Big-horn sheep **Rev. Designer:** Hector Greville **Weight:** 16.9655 g. **Composition:** 0.9170 Gold 0.5000 oz. AGW

Date	Mintage	MS-63	Proof
ND(1985) Proof	61,332	—	300

KM# 152 Subject: Peace **Rev. Designer:** Dora dePedery-Hunt **Weight:** 16.9655 g. **Composition:** 0.9170 Gold 0.5000 oz. AGW

Date	Mintage	MS-63	Proof
1986 Proof	76,409	—	300

KM# 158 Subject: 1988 Calgary Olympics **Rev:** Torch and logo **Rev. Designer:** Friedrich Peter **Edge:** Lettered in English and French **Weight:** 13.3375 g. **Composition:** 0.5830 Gold 0.2500 oz. AGW

Date	Mintage	MS-63	Proof
1987 Proof	142,750	—	150
Note: lettered edge			
1987 Proof	Inc. above	—	350
Note: plain edge			

KM# 162 Subject: Bowhead Whales, balaera mysticetus **Rev. Designer:** Robert R. Carmichael **Weight:** 13.3375 g. **Composition:** 0.5830 Gold 0.2500 oz. AGW

Date	Mintage	MS-63	Proof
1988 Proof	52,594	—	160

KM# 169 Subject: Sainte-Marie **Rev:** Huron Indian, Missionary and Mission building **Rev. Designer:** D. J. Craig **Weight:** 13.3375 g. **Composition:** 0.5830 Gold 0.2500 oz. AGW

Date	Mintage	MS-63	Proof
ND(1989) Proof	59,657	—	150

KM# 171 Subject: International Literacy Year
Rev. Designer: John Mardon **Weight:** 13.3375 g.
Composition: 0.5830 Gold 0.2500 oz. AGW

Date	Mintage	MS-63	Proof
1990 Proof	49,940	—	150

KM# 180 Subject: S.S. Empress of India
Rev. Designer: Karsten Smith **Weight:** 13.3375 g.
Composition: 0.5830 Gold 0.2500 oz. AGW

Date	Mintage	MS-63	Proof
1991 Proof	33,966	—	150

KM# 211 Subject: Montreal **Rev. Designer:**
Stewart Sherwood **Weight:** 13.3375 g. **Composition:** 0.5830 Gold 0.2500 oz. AGW

Date	Mintage	MS-63	Proof
1992 Proof	28,162	—	150

KM# 245 Subject: Antique Automobiles **Rev:** German Bene Victoria; Simmonds Steam Carriage;
French Panhard-Levassor's Daimler; American
Duryea. Canadian Featherston Haugh in center.
Rev. Designer: John Mardon **Weight:** 13.3375 g.
Composition: 0.5830 Gold 0.2500 oz. AGW

Date	Mintage	MS-63	Proof
1993 Proof	25,971	—	150

KM# 249 Subject: World War II Home Front
Rev. Designer: Paraskeva Clark **Weight:**
13.3375 g. **Composition:** 0.5830 Gold 0.2500 oz.
AGW

Date	Mintage	MS-63	Proof
1994 Proof	16,201	—	160

KM# 260 Subject: Louisbourg **Rev. Designer:**
Lewis Parker **Weight:** 13.3375 g. **Composition:**
0.5830 Gold 0.2500 oz. AGW

Date	Mintage	MS-63	Proof
1995 Proof	16,916	—	160

KM# 273 Subject: Klondike Gold Rush Centennial
Rev: Scene of Kate Carmack panning for gold
Rev. Designer: John Mantha **Weight:** 13.3375 g.
Composition: 0.5830 Gold 0.2500 oz. AGW

Date	Mintage	MS-63	Proof
ND(1996) Proof	17,973	—	160

KM# 287 Subject: Alexander Graham Bell
Rev. Designer: Donald H. Carley **Weight:** 13.3375 g.
Composition: 0.5830 Gold 0.2500 oz. AGW

Date	Mintage	MS-63	Proof
1997 Proof	14,775	—	160

KM# 307 Subject: Discovery of Insulin **Rev. Designer:** Robert R. Carmichael **Weight:** 13.3375 g. **Composition:** 0.5830 Gold 0.2500 oz. AGW

Date	Mintage	MS-63	Proof
1998 Proof	11,220	—	160

KM# 341 Subject: 50th Anniversary Newfoundland Unity With Canada **Rev. Designer:** Jackie Gale-Vaillancourt **Weight:** 13.3375 g. **Composition:** 0.5830 Gold 0.2500 oz. AGW

Date	Mintage	MS-63	Proof
1999 Proof	10,242	—	175

KM# 402 Subject: McClure's Arctic expedition **Obv:** Queen's portrait **Rev:** Six men pulling supply sled to an icebound ship **Rev. Designer:** John Mardon **Edge:** Reeded **Weight:** 13.3375 g. **Composition:** 0.5830 Gold 0.2500 oz. AGW **Size:** 27 mm.

Date	Mintage	MS-63	Proof
2000 Proof	9,767	—	175

KM# 416 Subject: Library of Parliament **Obv:** Queen's portrait **Rev:** Statue in domed building **Rev. Designer:** Robert R. Carmichael **Edge:** Reeded **Weight:** 13.3375 g. **Composition:** 0.5830 Gold 0.2500 oz. AGW **Size:** 27 mm.

Date	Mintage	MS-63	Proof
2001 Proof	8,080	—	185

KM# 486 Subject: 100th Anniversary of the Discovery of Marquis Wheat **Composition:** Gold

Date	Mintage	MS-63	Proof
2003 Proof	10,000	—	225

KM# 528 Subject: St. Lawrence Seaway, 50th Anniversary **Weight:** 13.3375 g. **Composition:** 0.5830 Gold 0.25 oz. AGW

Date	Mintage	MS-63	Proof
2004 Proof	—	—	235

KM# 616 Subject: Supreme Court **Rev:** Draped figure with sword **Composition:** Gold

Date	Mintage	MS-63	Proof
2005 Proof	—	—	275

KM# 591 Subject: 75th Anniversary, Hockey Classic between Royal Military College and U.S. Military Academy **Composition:** Gold

Date	Mintage	MS-63	Proof
2006 Proof	—	—	285

150 DOLLARS

KM# 388 Subject: Year of the Dragon **Rev. Designer:** Harvey Chan **Weight:** 13.6100 g. **Composition:** 0.7500 Gold .3282 oz. AGW

Date	Mintage	MS-63	Proof
2000 Proof	8,851	—	650

KM# 417 Subject: Year of the Snake **Obv:** Queen's head right **Rev:** Multicolor snake hologram **Edge:** Reeded **Weight:** 13.6100 g. **Composition:** 0.7500 Gold .3282 oz. AGW **Size:** 28 mm.

Date	Mintage	MS-63	Proof
2001 Proof	6,571	—	285

KM# 604 Rev: Year of the Horse, hologram **Composition:** Gold

Date	Mintage	MS-63	Proof
2002 Proof	6,843	—	320

KM# 487 Subject: Year of the Sheep **Rev. Designer:** Harvey Chan **Composition:** Gold

Date	Mintage	MS-63	Proof
2003 Proof	6,888	—	325

KM# 614 Rev: Year of the Monkey, hologram **Composition:** Gold

Date	Mintage	MS-63	Proof
2004 Proof	—	—	345

KM# 568 Subject: Year of the Rooster **Composition:** Gold

Date	Mintage	MS-63	Proof
2005 Proof	—	—	380

KM# 592 Subject: Year of the Dog, hologram **Composition:** Gold

Date	Mintage	MS-63	Proof
2006 Proof	4,888	—	385

175 DOLLARS

KM# 217 Subject: 1992 Olympics **Rev:** Passing the torch **Rev. Designer:** Stewart Sherwood **Edge:** Lettered **Weight:** 16.9700 g. **Composition:** 0.9170 Gold 0.5000 oz. AGW

Date	Mintage	MS-63	Proof
1992 Proof	22,092	—	300

200 DOLLARS

KM# 178 Subject: Canadian flag silver jubilee **Rev. Designer:** Stewart Sherwood **Weight:** 17.1350 g. **Composition:** 0.9170 Gold 0.5115 oz. AGW **Size:** 29 mm.

Date	Mintage	MS-63	Proof
1990 Proof	20,980	—	320

KM# 250 Subject: Interpretation of 1908 novel by Lucy Maud Montgomery, 1874-1942, Anne of Green Gables **Rev. Designer:** Phoebe Gilman **Weight:** 17.1350 g. **Composition:** 0.9170 Gold 0.5115 oz. AGW **Size:** 29 mm.

Date	Mintage	MS-63	Proof
1994 Proof	10,655	—	320

KM# 202 Subject: Hockey **Rev. Designer:** Stewart Sherwood **Weight:** 17.1350 g. **Composition:** 0.9170 Gold 0.5115 oz. AGW **Size:** 29 mm.

Date	Mintage	MS-63	Proof
1991 Proof	10,215	—	320

KM# 265 Subject: Maple-syrup production **Rev. Designer:** J. D. Mantha **Weight:** 17.1350 g. **Composition:** 0.9170 Gold 0.5115 oz. AGW **Size:** 29 mm.

Date	Mintage	MS-63	Proof
1995 Proof	6,579	—	320

KM# 230 Subject: Niagara Falls **Rev. Designer:** John Marden **Weight:** 17.1350 g. **Composition:** 0.9170 Gold 0.5115 oz. AGW **Size:** 29 mm.

Date	Mintage	MS-63	Proof
1992 Proof	9,465	—	320

KM# 275 Subject: Transcontinental Canadian Railway **Rev. Designer:** Suzanne Duranceau **Weight:** 17.1350 g. **Composition:** 0.9170 Gold 0.5115 oz. AGW **Size:** 29 mm.

Date	Mintage	MS-63	Proof
1996 Proof	8,047	—	320

KM# 244 Subject: Mounted police **Rev. Designer:** Stewart Sherwood **Weight:** 17.1350 g. **Composition:** 0.9170 Gold 0.5115 oz. AGW **Size:** 29 mm.

Date	Mintage	MS-63	Proof
1993 Proof	10,807	—	320

KM# 288 Subject: Haida mask **Rev. Designer:** Robert Davidson **Weight:** 17.1350 g. **Composition:** 0.9170 Gold 0.5115 oz. AGW **Size:** 29 mm.

Date	Mintage	MS-63	Proof
1997 Proof	11,610	—	450

KM# 317 Subject: Legendary white buffalo
Rev. Designer: Alex Janvier **Weight:** 17.1350 g.
Composition: 0.9170 Gold 0.5115 oz. AGW **Size:**
29 mm.

Date	Mintage	MS-63	Proof
1998 Proof	7,149	—	320

KM# 358 Subject: Mikmaq butterfly
Rev. Designer: Alan Syliboy **Weight:** 17.1350 g.
Composition: 0.9170 Gold 0.5115 oz. AGW **Size:**
29 mm.

Date	Mintage	MS-63	Proof
1999 Proof	6,510	—	320

KM# 403 Subject: Motherhood **Rev:** Inuit mother
with infant **Rev. Designer:** Germaine Arnaktauyak
Edge: Reeded **Weight:** 17.1350 g. **Composition:**
0.9170 Gold 0.5115 oz. AGW **Size:** 29 mm.

Date	Mintage	MS-63	Proof
2000 Proof	6,284	—	320

KM# 418 Subject: Cornelius D. Krieghoff's "The
Habitant farm" **Obv:** Queen's head right **Edge:**
Reeded **Weight:** 17.1350 g. **Composition:** 0.9170
Gold 0.5115 oz. AGW **Size:** 29 mm.

Date	Mintage	MS-63	Proof
2001 Proof	5,406	—	345

KM# 466 Subject: Thomas Thompson "The Jack
Pine" (1916-17) **Weight:** 17.1350 g. **Composition:**
0.9170 Gold .5115 oz. AGW

Date	Mintage	MS-63	Proof
2002 Proof	5,264	—	350

KM# 488 Subject: Fitzgerald's "Houses" (1929)
Weight: 17.1350 g. **Composition:** 0.9170 Gold
.5115 oz. AGW

Date	Mintage	MS-63	Proof
2003 Proof	10,000	—	360

KM# 516 Subject: "Fragments" **Obv:** Elizabeth II
Edge: Reeded **Weight:** 16.0000 g. **Composition:**
0.9167 Gold 0.4716 oz. AGW **Size:** 29 mm.

Date	Mintage	MS-63	Proof
2004 Proof	—	—	360

KM# 569 Subject: Fur traders **Composition:** Gold

Date	Mintage	MS-63	Proof
2005 Proof	—	—	420

KM# 593 Subject: 130th Anniversary, Supreme
Court **Composition:** Gold

Date	Mintage	MS-63	Proof
2006 Proof	—	—	420

KM# 594 Subject: Timber trade **Rev:** Lumber-
jacks felling tree **Composition:** Gold

Date	Mintage	MS-63	Proof
2006 Proof	—	—	420

300 DOLLARS

KM# 501 Obv: Triple cameo portraits of Queen Elizabeth II by Gillick, Machin and de Pedery-Hunt, each
in 14K gold, rose in center **Rev:** Dates "1952-2002"
and denomination in legend, rose in center **Weight:**
60.0000 g. **Composition:** Bi-Metallic Gold And Silver
Size: 50 mm. **Note:** Housed in anodized gold-colored
aluminum box with cherrywood stained siding

Date	Mintage	MS-63	Proof
ND(2002) Proof	993	—	1,150

KM# 517 Obv: Four coinage portraits of Elizabeth
II **Rev:** Canadian arms above value **Edge:** Plain
Weight: 60.0000 g. **Composition:** 0.5833 Gold
1.1252 oz. AGW **Size:** 50 mm.

Date	Mintage	MS-63	Proof
2004 Proof	1,000	—	1,200

KM# 570 Subject: Standard Time **Composition:**
Gold

Date	Mintage	MS-63	Proof
2005 Proof	—	—	1,200

KM# 596 Subject: Shinplaster **Rev:** Britannia
bust, spear over shoulder **Composition:** Gold

Date	Mintage	MS-63	Proof
2005 Proof	—	—	1,100

KM# 600 Subject: Welcome figure totem pole
Composition: Gold

Date	Mintage	MS-63	Proof
2005 Proof	—	—	1,150

KM# 595 Subject: The Shinplaster **Rev:** Seated
Britannia with shield **Composition:** Gold

Date	Mintage	MS-63	Proof
2006 Proof	—	—	1,250

350 DOLLARS

KM# 308 Subject: Flowers of Canada's Coat of Arms
Rev. Designer: Pierre Leduc **Weight:** 38.0500 g.
Composition: 0.9999 Gold 1.2233 oz. AGW

1998 Proof — 664 — 865

KM# 370 Subject: Lady's slipper **Rev. Designer:** Henry Purdy **Weight:** 38.0500 g. **Composition:** 0.9999 Gold 1.2233 oz. AGW

Date	Mintage	MS-63	Proof
1999 Proof	1,990	—	765

KM# 404 Subject: Pacific Dogwood **Obv:** Queen's portrait **Rev:** Three flowers **Rev. Designer:** Caren Heine **Edge:** Reeded **Weight:** 38.0500 g. **Composition:** 0.9999 Gold 1.2233 oz. AGW **Size:** 34 mm.

Date	Mintage	MS-63	Proof
2000 Proof	1,506	—	765

KM# 433 Subject: The Mayflower Flower **Obv:** Queen's portrait **Rev:** Two flowers **Rev. Designer:** Bonnie Ross **Edge:** Reeded **Weight:** 38.0500 g. **Composition:** 0.9999 Gold 1.2233 oz. AGW **Size:** 34 mm.

Date	Mintage	MS-63	Proof
2001 Proof	—	—	900

KM# 502 Subject: The Wild Rose **Obv:** Queen's portrait **Obv. Designer:** Dora de Pedery-Hunt **Rev:** Wild rose plant **Rev. Designer:** Dr. Andreas Kare Hellum **Weight:** 38.0500 g. **Composition:** 0.9999 Gold 1.2232 oz. AGW **Size:** 34 mm.

Date	Mintage	MS-63	Proof
2002 Proof	1,803	—	925

KM# 504 Subject: The White Trillium **Obv:** Queen's portrait **Obv. Designer:** Dora de Pedery-Hunt **Rev:** White Trillium **Weight:** 38.0500 g. **Composition:** 9999.0000 Gold 12232.1 oz. AGW **Size:** 34 mm.

Date	Mintage	MS-63	Proof
2003 Proof	3,003	—	925

KM# 601 Subject: Western Red Lilly **Composition:** Gold

Date	Mintage	MS-63	Proof
2005 Proof	—	—	975

KM# 626 Subject: Iris Vericolor **Obv:** Queen's portrait **Rev:** Iris **Weight:** 38.0500 g. **Composition:** 0.9999 Gold 1.2232 oz. AGW **Size:** 34 mm.

Date	Mintage	MS-63	Proof
2006 Proof	—	—	1,100

SOVEREIGN

KM# 14 Rev: St. George slaying dragon, mint mark below horse's rear hooves **Weight:** 7.9881 g. **Composition:** 0.9170 Gold .2354 oz. AGW

Date	Mintage	F-12	VF-20	XF-40	AU-50	MS-60	MS-63
1908C	636	1,250	1,850	2,350	2,600	2,850	4,000
1909C	16,273	150	200	245	285	500	1,600
1910C	28,012	BV	185	225	265	500	2,000

KM# 20 Rev: St. George slaying dragon, mint mark below horse's rear hooves **Weight:** 7.9881 g. **Composition:** 0.9170 Gold 0.2354 oz. AGW

Date	Mintage	F-12	VF-20	XF-40	AU-50	MS-60	MS-63
1911C	256,946	—	—	BV	135	155	180
1913C	3,715	550	700	950	1,200	1,500	3,000
1914C	14,871	175	225	285	300	525	950
1916C about 20 known	—	8,000	12,500	15,750	17,750	20,000	27,500
Note: Stacks' A.G. Carter Jr. Sale 12-89 Gem BU realized $82,500.							
1917C	58,845	—	—	BV	150	175	500
1918C	106,514	—	—	BV	150	175	750
1919C	135,889	—	—	BV	150	175	650

SILVER BULLION COINAGE

DOLLAR

KM# 617 Obv: Elizabeth II **Rev:** Maple leaf **Edge:** Reeded **Weight:** 1.5550 g. **Composition:** 0.9999 Silver 0.05 oz. ASW **Size:** 17 mm.

Date	Mintage	MS-63	Proof
2003	—	—	—

KM# 621 Obv: Elizabeth II **Rev:** Maple leaf and mint logo privy mark **Edge:** Reeded **Weight:** 1.5550 g. **Composition:** 0.9999 Silver 0.05 oz. ASW **Size:** 17 mm.

Date	Mintage	MS-63	Proof
2004 Proof	25,000	—	4.50

2 DOLLARS

KM# 618 Obv: Elizabeth II **Rev:** Maple leaf **Edge:** Reeded **Weight:** 3.1100 g. **Composition:** 0.9999 Silver 0.1 oz. ASW **Size:** 21 mm.

Date	Mintage	MS-63	Proof
2003	—	—	—

KM# 622 Obv: Elizabeth II **Rev:** Maple leaf and mint logo privy mark **Edge:** Reeded **Weight:** 3.1100 g. **Composition:** 0.9999 Silver 0.1 oz. ASW **Size:** 21 mm.

Date	Mintage	MS-63	Proof
2004 Proof	25,000	—	7.50

KM# 571   Rev: Lynx **Weight:** 3.1050 g. **Composition:** 0.9999 Silver .1000 oz. ASW

Date	Mintage	MS-63	Proof
2005 Proof	—	—	7.50

3 DOLLARS

KM# 619   Obv: Elizabeth II **Rev:** Maple leaf **Edge:** Reeded **Weight:** 7.7760 g. **Composition:** 0.9999 Silver 0.25 oz. ASW **Size:** 27 mm.

Date	Mintage	MS-63	Proof
2003	—	—	—

KM# 623   Obv: Elizabeth II **Rev:** Maple leaf and mint logo privy mark **Edge:** Reeded **Weight:** 7.7760 g. **Composition:** 0.9999 Silver 0.25 oz. ASW **Size:** 27 mm.

Date	Mintage	MS-63	Proof
2004 Proof	25,000	—	12.50

KM# 572   Rev: Lynx **Composition:** 0.9999 Silver .2500 oz. ASW

Date	Mintage	MS-63	Proof
2005 Proof	—	—	12.50

4 DOLLARS

KM# 620   Obv: Elizabeth II **Rev:** Maple leaf **Edge:** Reeded **Composition:** 0.9999 Silver 1.0000 oz. ASW **Size:** 34 mm.

Date	Mintage	MS-63	Proof
2003	—	30.00	—

KM# 624   Obv: Elizabeth II **Rev:** Maple leaf and mint logo privy mark **Edge:** Reeded **Weight:** 15.5500 g. **Composition:** 0.9999 Silver 0.4999 oz. ASW **Size:** 34 mm.

Date	Mintage	MS-63	Proof
2004 Proof	25,000	—	25.00

KM# 573   Rev: Lynx **Composition:** 0.9999 Silver .5000 oz. ASW

Date	Mintage	MS-63	Proof
2005 Proof	—	—	22.50

5 DOLLARS

KM# 163   Obv: Elizabeth II effigy **Obv. Designer:** Arnold Machin **Rev:** Maple leaf **Weight:** 31.1000 g. **Composition:** 0.9999 Silver 1.0000 oz. ASW

Date	Mintage	MS-63	Proof
1988	1,155,931	11.50	—
1989	3,332,200	10.00	—
1989 Proof	29,999	—	30.00

KM# 187   Obv: Elizabeth II effigy **Obv. Designer:** Dora de Pedery-Hunt **Rev:** Maple leaf **Weight:** 31.1000 g. **Composition:** 0.9999 Silver 1.0000 oz. ASW

Date	Mintage	MS-63	Proof
1990	1,708,800	11.00	—
1991	644,300	12.50	—
1992	343,800	12.50	—
1993	889,946	11.00	—
1994	1,133,900	11.50	—
1995	326,244	12.00	—
1996	250,445	32.50	—
1997	100,970	13.50	—
1998 Tiger privy mark	25,000	17.50	—
1998 Titanic privy mark	26,000	75.00	—
1998 R.C.M.P. privy mark	25,000	32.50	—
1998 90th Anniversary R.C.M. privy mark	13,025	17.50	—
1998	591,359	12.50	—
1999	1,229,442	12.00	—
1999 Rabbit privy mark	25,000	20.00	—
1999 "Y2K" privy mark	9,999	25.00	—
2000 Dragon privy mark	25,000	22.00	—
2000	403,652	12.00	—
2000 Expo Hanover privy mark	—	35.00	—
2001 Snake privy mark	25,000	22.00	—
2001	398,563	15.00	—
2002	576,196	15.00	—
2002 Horse privy mark	25,000	22.00	—
2003 Sheep privy mark	25,000	18.00	—
2003	—	15.00	—

KM# 363 **Rev:** Maple leaf **Weight:** 31.1000 g.
Composition: 0.9999 Silver 1 oz. ASW

Date	Mintage	MS-63	Proof
1999/2000	298,775	13.50	—

Note: Fireworks privy mark

KM# 436 **Obv:** Queen's portrait **Rev:** Three maple
leaves in autumn colors **Rev. Designer:** Debbie Adams **Edge:** Reeded **Weight:** 31.1035 g. **Composition:** 0.9999 Silver 0.9999 oz. ASW **Size:** 38 mm.

Date	Mintage	MS-63	Proof
2001	49,900	32.50	—

KM# 437 **Subject:** Multicolor Holographic Maple
Leaf **Obv:** Queen's portrait **Rev:** Radiant maple leaf
hologram with date privy mark **Edge:** Reeded
Weight: 31.1035 g. **Composition:** 0.9999 Silver
0.9999 oz. ASW **Size:** 38 mm.

Date	Mintage	MS-63	Proof
2001	29,906	75.00	—

KM# 505 **Obv:** Queen Elizabeth II **Rev:** Two maple
leaves in spring color (green) **Edge:** Reeded
Weight: 31.2800 g. **Composition:** 0.9999 Silver
1.0056 oz. ASW **Size:** 38 mm.

Date	Mintage	MS-63	Proof
2002 Proof	—	—	35.00

KM# 603 **Subject:** Loon, hologram **Composition:**
0.9999 Silver

Date	Mintage	MS-63	Proof
2002 Satin Proof	30,000	—	45.00

KM# 522 **Subject:** Colorized maple leaf **Weight:**
31.1050 g. **Composition:** 0.9999 Silver 0.9999 oz.
ASW

Date	Mintage	MS-63	Proof
2003	—	32.50	—

KM# 521 **Rev:** Maple leaf, summer colors **Composition:** 0.9999 Silver

Date	Mintage	MS-63	Proof
2003	—	35.00	—

KM# 508 Obv: Queen Elizabeth II **Rev:** Maple leaf **Edge:** Reeded **Weight:** 31.1200 g. **Composition:** 0.9999 Silver 1.0004 oz. ASW **Size:** 38 mm.

Date	Mintage	MS-63	Proof
2004	—	35.00	—

KM# 625 Obv: Elizabeth II **Rev:** Maple leaf and mint logo privy mark **Edge:** Reeded **Weight:** 31.1035 g. **Composition:** 0.9999 Silver 0.9999 oz. ASW **Size:** 38 mm.

Date	Mintage	MS-63	Proof
2004 Proof	25,000	—	35.00

KM# 550 Subject: Big Leaf Maple, colorized **Weight:** 31.1050 g. **Composition:** 0.9999 Silver 1. oz. ASW

Date	Mintage	MS-63	Proof
2005	25,000	35.00	—

KM# 574 Rev: Lynx **Composition:** 0.9999 Silver 1.0000 oz. ASW

Date	Mintage	MS-63	Proof
2005 Proof	—	—	35.00

50 DOLLARS

KM# 326 Subject: 10th Anniversary Silver Maple Leaf **Edge:** 10th ANNIVERSARY 10e ANNIVERSAIRE **Weight:** 311.0350 g. **Composition:** 0.9999 Silver 10.0000 oz. ASW

Date	Mintage	MS-63	Proof
1998 Proof	25,000	—	150

GOLD BULLION COINAGE

50 CENTS

KM# 526 Subject: Moose **Rev:** Moose head facing right **Weight:** 1.2700 g. **Composition:** 0.9999 Gold .0425 oz. AGW **Size:** 14 mm.

Date	Mintage	MS-63	Proof
2004 Proof	—	—	85.00

KM# 542 Subject: Voyageurs **Composition:** 0.9999 Gold .0425 oz. AGW

Date	Mintage	MS-63	Proof
2005 Proof	—	—	65.00

DOLLAR

KM# 238 Weight: 1.5551 g. **Composition:** 0.9999 Gold 0.05 oz. AGW

Date	Mintage	MS-63	Proof
1993	37,080	BV+37%	—
1994	78,860	BV+37%	—
1995	85,920	BV+37%	—
1996	56,520	BV+37%	—
1997	59,720	BV+37%	—
1998	44,260	BV+37%	—
1999	—	BV+46%	—
Note: Maple leaf with oval			
2000	—	—	—
Note: Maple leaf with oval			

KM# 365 Rev: Maple leaf hologram **Weight:** 1.5551 g. **Composition:** 0.9999 Gold 0.05 oz. AGW

Date	Mintage	MS-63	Proof
1999	500	75.00	—

2 DOLLARS

KM# 256 Rev: Maple leaf **Weight:** 2.0735 g. **Composition:** 0.9999 Gold 0.0666 oz. AGW

Date	Mintage	MS-63	Proof
1994	5,493	70.00	—

5 DOLLARS

KM# 135 Obv: Elizabeth II effigy **Obv. Designer:** Arnold Machin **Rev:** Maple leaf **Weight:** 3.1200 g. **Composition:** 0.9999 Gold .1000 oz. AGW

Date	Mintage	MS-63	Proof
1982	246,000	BV+14%	—
1983	304,000	BV+14%	—
1984	262,000	BV+14%	—
1985	398,000	BV+14%	—
1986	529,516	BV+14%	—
1987	459,000	BV+14%	—
1988	506,500	BV+14%	—
1989	539,000	BV+14%	—
1989 Proof	16,992	—	65.00

KM# 188 Obv: Elizabeth II effigy **Obv. Designer:** Dora dePedery-Hunt **Rev:** Maple leaf **Weight:** 3.1200 g. **Composition:** 0.9999 Gold 0.1000 oz. AGW

Date	Mintage	MS-63	Proof
1990	476,000	BV+14%	—
1991	322,000	BV+14%	—
1992	384,000	BV+14%	—
1993	248,630	BV+14%	—
1994	313,150	BV+14%	—
1995	294,890	BV+14%	—
1996	179,220	BV+14%	—
1997	188,540	BV+14%	—
1998	301,940	BV+14%	—
1999	—	BV+19%	—

Note: Maple leaf with oval "20 Years ANS" privy mark

2000	—	BV+19%	—

KM# 366 Rev: Maple leaf hologram **Weight:** 3.1200 g. **Composition:** 0.9999 Gold 0.1000 oz. AGW

Date	Mintage	MS-63	Proof
1999	500	150	—

KM# 439 Subject: Holographic Maple Leaves **Obv:** Queen's portrait **Rev:** Three maple leaves multicolor hologram **Edge:** Reeded **Weight:** 3.1310 g. **Composition:** 0.9999 Gold 0.1007 oz. AGW **Size:** 16 mm.

Date	Mintage	MS-63	Proof
2001 in sets only	600	150	—

10 DOLLARS

KM# 136 Obv: Elizabeth II effigy **Obv. Designer:** Arnold Machin **Rev:** Maple leaf **Weight:** 7.7850 g. **Composition:** 0.9999 Gold 0.2500 oz. AGW

Date	Mintage	MS-63	Proof
1982	184,000	BV+10%	—
1983	308,800	BV+10%	—
1984	242,400	BV+10%	—
1985	620,000	BV+10%	—
1986	915,200	BV+10%	—
1987	376,000	BV+10%	—
1988	436,000	BV+10%	—
1989	328,800	BV+10%	—
1989 Proof	6,998	—	160

KM# 189 Obv: Elizabeth II effigy **Obv. Designer:** Dora dePedery-Hunt **Rev:** Maple leaf **Weight:** 7.7850 g. **Composition:** 0.9999 Gold 0.2500 oz. AGW

Date	Mintage	MS-63	Proof
1990	253,600	BV+10%	—
1991	166,400	BV+10%	—
1992	179,600	BV+10%	—
1993	158,452	BV+10%	—
1994	148,792	BV+10%	—
1995	127,596	BV+10%	—
1996	89,148	BV+10%	—
1997	98,104	BV+10%	—
1998	85,472	BV+10%	—
1999	—	BV+15%	—

Note: Maple leaf with oval "20 Years ANS" privy mark

2000	—	BV+15%	—

Note: Maple leaf with oval "2000" privy mark

KM# 367 Rev: Maple leaf hologram **Weight:** 7.7850 g. **Composition:** 0.9999 Gold 0.2500 oz. AGW

Date	Mintage	MS-63	Proof
1999	—	200	—

KM# 440 Subject: Holographic Maples Leaves **Obv:** Queen's portrait **Rev:** Three maple leaves multicolor hologram **Edge:** Reeded **Weight:** 7.7970 g. **Composition:** 0.9999 Gold 0.2507 oz. AGW **Size:** 20 mm.

Date	Mintage	MS-63	Proof
2001	15,000	180	—

20 DOLLARS

KM# 153 Obv: Elizabeth II effigy **Obv. Designer:** Arnold Machin **Weight:** 15.5515 g. **Composition:** 0.9999 Gold 0.5000 oz. AGW **Size:** 32 mm.

Date	Mintage	MS-63	Proof
1986	529,200	BV+7%	—
1987	332,800	BV+7%	—
1988	538,400	BV+7%	—
1989	259,200	BV+7%	—
1989 Proof	6,998	—	300

KM# 190 Obv: Elizabeth II effigy **Obv. Designer:** Dora dePedery-Hunt **Rev:** Maple leaf **Weight:** 15.5515 g. **Composition:** 0.9999 Gold 0.5000 oz. AGW

Date	Mintage	MS-63	Proof
1990	174,400	BV+7%	—
1991	96,200	BV+7%	—
1992	108,000	BV+7%	—
1993	99,492	BV+7%	—
1994	104,766	BV+7%	—
1995	103,162	BV+7%	—
1996	66,246	BV+7%	—
1997	63,354	BV+7%	—
1998	65,366	BV+7%	—
1999	—	BV+12%	—
Note: Maple leaf with oval "20 Years ANS" privy mark			
2000	—	BV+12%	—

KM# 368 Rev: Maple leaf hologram **Weight:** 15.5515 g. **Composition:** 0.9999 Gold 0.5000 oz. AGW

Date	Mintage	MS-63	Proof
1999	500	675	—

KM# 441 Subject: Holographic Maples Leaves **Obv:** Queen's portrait **Rev:** Three maple leaves multicolor hologram **Edge:** Reeded **Weight:** 15.5840 g. **Composition:** 0.9999 Gold 0.501 oz. AGW **Size:** 25 mm.

Date	Mintage	MS-63	Proof
2001 in sets only	600	675	—

50 DOLLARS

KM# 125.1 Rev: Maple leaf flanked by .999 **Weight:** 31.1030 g. **Composition:** 0.9990 Gold 1.0000 oz. AGW

Date	Mintage	MS-63	Proof
1979	1,000,000	BV+4%	—
1980	1,251,500	BV+4%	—
1981	863,000	BV+4%	—
1982	883,000	BV+4%	—

KM# 125.2 Rev: Maple leaf flanked by .9999 **Weight:** 31.1030 g. **Composition:** 0.9999 Gold 1.0000 oz. AGW

Date	Mintage	MS-63	Proof
1983	843,000	BV+4%	—
1984	1,067,500	BV+4%	—
1985	1,908,000	BV+4%	—
1986	779,115	BV+4%	—
1987	978,000	BV+4%	—
1988	826,500	BV+4%	—
1989	856,000	BV+4%	—
1989 Proof	17,781	—	575

KM# 191 Obv: Elizabeth II effigy **Obv. Designer:** Dora dePedery-Hunt **Rev:** Maple leaf flanked by .9999 **Weight:** 31.1030 g. **Composition:** 0.9999 Gold 1.000 oz. AGW

Date	Mintage	MS-63	Proof
1990	815,000	BV+4%	—
1991	290,000	BV+4%	—
1992	368,900	BV+4%	—
1993	321,413	BV+4%	—
1994	180,357	BV+4%	—
1995	208,729	BV+4%	—
1996	143,682	BV+4%	—
1997	478,211	BV+4%	—
1998	593,704	BV+4%	—
1999	—	BV+7%	—
Note: Maple leaf with oval "20 Years ANS" privy mark			
2000	—	BV+7%	—
Note: Maple leaf with oval			

KM# 305 Rev: Mounted Mountie at gallop right **Rev. Designer:** Ago Aarand **Weight:** 31.1030 g. **Composition:** 0.9999 Gold 1 oz. AGW **Shape:** 10-sided

Date	Mintage	MS-63	Proof
1997	12,913	570	—

KM# 369 Rev: Maple leaf hologram **Weight:** 31.1030 g. **Composition:** 0.9999 Gold 1.000 oz. AGW

Date	Mintage	MS-63	Proof
2000	500	1,350	—

KM# 364 Rev: Maple leaf with fireworks privy mark **Weight:** 31.1030 g. **Composition:** 0.9999 Gold 1.0000 oz. AGW

Date	Mintage	MS-63	Proof
2000	—	775	—

KM# 442 Subject: Holographic Maples Leaves **Obv:** Queen's portrait **Rev:** Three maple leaves multicolor hologram **Edge:** Reeded **Weight:** 31.1500 g. **Composition:** 0.9999 Gold 1.0014 oz. AGW **Size:** 30 mm.

Date	Mintage	MS-63	Proof
2001 in sets only	600	1,350	—

PLATINUM BULLION COINAGE

DOLLAR

KM# 239 Rev: Maple leaf **Weight:** 1.5552 g. **Composition:** 0.9995 Platinum 0.0500 oz. APW

Date	Mintage	MS-63	Proof
1993	2,120	BV+35%	—
1994	4,260	BV+35%	—
1995	460	125	—
1996	1,640	BV+35%	—
1997	1,340	BV+35%	—
1998	2,000	BV+35%	—
1999	2,000	BV+35%	—

2 DOLLARS

KM# 257 Rev: Maple leaf **Weight:** 2.0735 g. **Composition:** 0.9995 Platinum 0.0666 oz. APW

Date	Mintage	MS-63	Proof
1994	1,470	225	—

5 DOLLARS

KM# 164 Obv. Designer: Arnold Machin **Rev:** Maple leaf **Weight:** 3.1203 g. **Composition:** 0.9995 Platinum 0.1000 oz. APW

Date	Mintage	MS-63	Proof
1988	74,000	BV+18%	—
1989	18,000	BV+18%	—
1989 Proof	11,999	—	120

KM# 192 Obv. Designer: dePedery-Hunt **Rev:** Maple leaf **Weight:** 3.1203 g. **Composition:** 0.9995 Platinum 0.1000 oz. APW

Date	Mintage	MS-63	Proof
1990	9,000	BV+18%	—
1991	13,000	BV+18%	—
1992	16,000	BV+18%	—
1993	14,020	BV+18%	—
1994	19,190	BV+18%	—
1995	8,940	BV+18%	—
1996	8,820	BV+18%	—
1997	7,050	BV+18%	—
1998	5,710	BV+18%	—
1999	2,000	BV+18%	—

10 DOLLARS

KM# 165 Obv. Designer: Machin **Rev:** Maple leaf **Weight:** 7.7857 g. **Composition:** 0.9995 Platinum 0.2500 oz. APW

Date	Mintage	MS-63	Proof
1988	93,600	BV+13%	—
1989	3,200	BV+13%	—
1989 Proof	1,999	—	275

KM# 193 Obv. Designer: dePedery-Hunt **Rev:** Maple leaf **Weight:** 7.7857 g. **Composition:** 0.9995 Platinum 0.2500 oz. APW

Date	Mintage	MS-63	Proof
1990	1,600	BV+13%	—
1991	7,200	BV+13%	—
1992	11,600	BV+13%	—
1993	8,048	BV+13%	—
1994	9,456	BV+13%	—
1995	6,524	BV+13%	—
1996	6,160	BV+13%	—
1997	4,552	BV+13%	—
1998	3,816	BV+13%	—
1999	2,000	BV+13%	—

20 DOLLARS

KM# 166 Obv. Designer: Machin **Rev:** Maple leaf **Weight:** 15.5519 g. **Composition:** 0.9995 Platinum 0.5000 oz. APW

Date	Mintage	MS-63	Proof
1988	23,600	BV+9%	—
1989	4,800	BV+9%	—
1989 Proof	1,999	—	525

KM# 194 Obv. Designer: dePedery-Hunt **Rev:** Maple leaf **Weight:** 15.5519 g. **Composition:** 0.9995 Platinum 0.5000 oz. APW

Date	Mintage	MS-63	Proof
1990	2,600	BV+9%	—
1991	5,600	BV+9%	—
1992	12,800	BV+9%	—
1993	6,022	BV+9%	—
1994	6,710	BV+9%	—
1995	6,308	BV+9%	—
1996	5,490	BV+9%	—
1997	3,990	BV+9%	—

Date	Mintage	MS-63	Proof
1998	5,486	BV+9%	—
1999	500	BV+15%	—

30 DOLLARS

KM# 174 Rev: Polar bear swimming **Rev. Designer:** Robert Bateman **Weight:** 3.1100 g. **Composition:** 0.9990 Platinum 0.1000 oz. APW

Date	Mintage	MS-63	Proof
1990 Proof	2,629	—	135

KM# 198 Rev: Snowy owl **Rev. Designer:** Glen Loates **Weight:** 3.1100 g. **Composition:** 0.9990 Platinum 0.1000 oz. APW

Date	Mintage	MS-63	Proof
1991 Proof	3,500	—	135

KM# 226 Rev: Cougar head and shoulders **Rev. Designer:** George McLean **Weight:** 3.1100 g. **Composition:** 0.9990 Platinum 0.1000 oz. APW

Date	Mintage	MS-63	Proof
1992 Proof	3,500	—	135

KM# 240 Rev: Arctic fox **Rev. Designer:** Claude D'Angelo **Weight:** 3.1100 g. **Composition:** 0.9990 Platinum 0.1000 oz. APW

Date	Mintage	MS-63	Proof
1993 Proof	3,500	—	140

KM# 252 Rev: Sea otter **Rev. Designer:** Ron S. Parker **Weight:** 3.1100 g. **Composition:** 0.9990 Platinum 0.1000 oz. APW

Date	Mintage	MS-63	Proof
1994 Proof	1,500	—	140

KM# 266 Rev: Canadian lynx **Rev. Designer:** Michael Dumas **Weight:** 3.1100 g. **Composition:** 0.9990 Platinum 0.1000 oz. APW

Date	Mintage	MS-63	Proof
1995 Proof	620	—	140

KM# 278 Rev: Falcon portrait **Rev. Designer:** Dwayne Harty **Weight:** 3.1100 g. **Composition:** 0.9990 Platinum 0.1000 oz. APW

Date	Mintage	MS-63	Proof
1996 Proof	489	—	140

KM# 300 Rev: Bison head **Rev. Designer:** Chris Bacon **Weight:** 3.1100 g. **Composition:** 0.9995 Platinum 0.1000 oz. APW

Date	Mintage	MS-63	Proof
1997 Proof	5,000	—	125

KM# 322 Rev: Grey wolf **Rev. Designer:** Kerr Burnett **Weight:** 3.1100 g. **Composition:** 0.9990 Platinum 0.1000 oz. APW

Date	Mintage	MS-63	Proof
ND(1998) Proof	2,000	—	140

KM# 359 Rev: Musk ox **Rev. Designer:** Mark Hobson **Weight:** 3.1100 g. **Composition:** 0.9995 Platinum 0.1000 oz. APW

Date	Mintage	MS-63	Proof
1999 Proof	1,500	—	140

KM# 405 Rev: Pronghorn antelope head **Rev. Designer:** Mark Hobson **Edge:** Reeded **Weight:** 3.1100 g. **Composition:** 0.9995 Platinum .1000 oz. APW **Size:** 16 mm.

Date	Mintage	MS-63	Proof
2000 Proof	600	—	140

KM# 429 Rev: Harlequin duck's head **Rev. Designer:** Cosme Saffioti and Susan Taylor **Edge:** Reeded **Weight:** 3.1100 g. **Composition:** 0.9995 Platinum .1000 oz. APW **Size:** 16 mm.

Date	Mintage	MS-63	Proof
2001 Proof	448	—	150

50 DOLLARS

KM# 167 Obv. Designer: Machin **Rev:** Maple leaf **Weight:** 31.1030 g. **Composition:** 0.9995 Platinum 1.0000 oz. APW

Date	Mintage	MS-63	Proof
1988	37,500	BV+4%	—
1989	10,000	BV+4%	—
1989 Proof	5,965	—	1,150

KM# 195 Obv. Designer: dePedery-Hunt **Rev:** Maple leaf **Weight:** 31.1030 g. **Composition:** 0.9995 Platinum 1.0000 oz. APW

Date	Mintage	MS-63	Proof
1990	15,100	BV+4%	—
1991	31,900	BV+4%	—
1992	40,500	BV+4%	—
1993	17,666	BV+4%	—
1994	36,245	BV+4%	—
1995	25,829	BV+4%	—
1996	62,273	BV+4%	—
1997	25,480	BV+4%	—
1998	10,403	BV+4%	—
1999	1,300	BV+10%	—

75 DOLLARS

KM# 175 Rev: Polar bear resting **Rev. Designer:** Robert Bateman **Weight:** 7.7760 g. **Composition:** 0.9990 Platinum 0.2500 oz. APW

Date	Mintage	MS-63	Proof
1990 Proof	2,629	—	300

KM# 199 Rev: Snowy owls perched on branch **Rev. Designer:** Glen Loates **Weight:** 7.7760 g. **Composition:** 0.9990 Platinum 0.2500 oz. APW

Date	Mintage	MS-63	Proof
1991 Proof	3,500	—	300

KM# 227 Rev: Cougar prowling **Rev. Designer:** George McLean **Weight:** 7.7760 g. **Composition:** 0.9990 Platinum 0.2500 oz. APW

Date	Mintage	MS-63	Proof
1992 Proof	3,500	—	320

KM# 241 Rev: Two Arctic foxes **Rev. Designer:** Claude D'Angelo **Weight:** 7.7760 g. **Composition:** 0.9990 Platinum 0.2500 oz. APW

Date	Mintage	MS-63	Proof
1993 Proof	3,500	—	320

KM# 253 Rev: Sea otter eating urchin **Rev. Designer:** Ron S. Parker **Weight:** 7.7760 g. **Composition:** 0.9990 Platinum 0.2500 oz. APW

Date	Mintage	MS-63	Proof
1994 Proof	1,500	—	320

KM# 267 Rev: Two lynx kittens **Rev. Designer:** Michael Dumas **Weight:** 7.7760 g. **Composition:** 0.9990 Platinum 0.2500 oz. APW

Date	Mintage	MS-63	Proof
1995 Proof	1,500	—	320

KM# 279 Rev: Peregrine falcon, diving falcon **Rev. Designer:** Dwayne Harty **Weight:** 7.7760 g. **Composition:** 0.9990 Platinum 0.2500 oz. APW

Date	Mintage	MS-63	Proof
1996 Proof	1,500	—	320

KM# 301 Rev: Two bison calves **Rev. Designer:** Chris Bacon **Weight:** 7.7760 g. **Composition:** 0.9990 Platinum 0.2500 oz. APW

Date	Mintage	MS-63	Proof
1997 Proof	1,500	—	320

KM# 323 Rev: Gray wolf **Rev. Designer:** Kerr Burnett **Weight:** 7.7760 g. **Composition:** 0.9990 Platinum 0.2500 oz. APW

Date	Mintage	MS-63	Proof
1998 Proof	1,000	—	320

KM# 360 Rev: Musk ox **Rev. Designer:** Mark Hobson **Weight:** 7.7760 g. **Composition:** 0.9990 Platinum 0.2500 oz. APW

Date	Mintage	MS-63	Proof
1999 Proof	500	—	325

KM# 406 Obv: Queen's portrait **Rev:** Standing pronghorn antelope **Rev. Designer:** Mark Hobson **Edge:** Reeded **Weight:** 7.7760 g. **Composition:** 0.9990 Platinum .2500 oz. APW **Size:** 20 mm.

Date	Mintage	MS-63	Proof
2000 Proof	600	—	325

KM# 430 Rev: Harlequin duck in flight **Rev. Designer:** Cosme Saffioti and Susan Taylor **Edge:** Reeded **Weight:** 7.7760 g. **Composition:** 0.9995 Platinum .2500 oz. APW **Size:** 20 mm.

Date	Mintage	MS-63	Proof
2001 Proof	448	—	375

150 DOLLARS

KM# 176 Rev: Polar bear walking **Rev. Designer:** Robert Bateman **Weight:** 15.5520 g. **Composition:** 0.9990 Platinum 0.5000 oz. APW

Date	Mintage	MS-63	Proof
1990 Proof	2,629	—	565

KM# 200 Rev: Snowy owl flying **Rev. Designer:** Glen Loates **Weight:** 15.5520 g. **Composition:** 0.9990 Platinum 0.5000 oz. APW

Date	Mintage	MS-63	Proof
1991 Proof	3,500	—	565

KM# 228 Rev: Cougar mother and cub **Rev. Designer:** George McLean **Weight:** 15.5520 g. **Composition:** 0.9990 Platinum 0.5000 oz. APW

Date	Mintage	MS-63	Proof
1992 Proof	3,500	—	575

KM# 242 Rev: Arctic fox by lake **Rev. Designer:** Claude D'Angelo **Weight:** 15.5520 g. **Composition:** 0.9990 Platinum 0.5000 oz. APW

Date	Mintage	MS-63	Proof
1993 Proof	3,500	—	575

KM# 254 Rev: Sea otter mother carrying pup **Rev. Designer:** Ron S. Parker **Weight:** 15.5520 g. **Composition:** 0.9990 Platinum 0.5000 oz. APW

Date	Mintage	MS-63	Proof
1994 Proof	—	—	600

KM# 268 Rev: Prowling lynx **Rev. Designer:** Michael Dumas **Weight:** 15.5520 g. **Composition:** 0.9990 Platinum 0.5000 oz. APW

Date	Mintage	MS-63	Proof
1995 Proof	226	—	575

KM# 280 Rev: Peregrine falcon - falcon on branch **Rev. Designer:** Dwayne Harty **Weight:** 15.5520 g. **Composition:** 0.9990 Platinum 0.5000 oz. APW

Date	Mintage	MS-63	Proof
1996 Proof	100	—	575

KM# 302 Rev: Bison bull **Rev. Designer:** Chris Bacon **Weight:** 15.5520 g. **Composition:** 0.9990 Platinum 0.5000 oz. APW

Date	Mintage	MS-63	Proof
1997 Proof	4,000	—	575

KM# 324 Rev: Two gray wolf cubs **Rev. Designer:** Kerr Burnett **Weight:** 15.5520 g. **Composition:** 0.9990 Platinum 0.5000 oz. APW

Date	Mintage	MS-63	Proof
1998 Proof	2,000	—	575

KM# 361 Rev: Musk ox **Rev. Designer:** Mark Hobson **Weight:** 15.5520 g. **Composition:** 0.9990 Platinum 0.5000 oz. APW

Date	Mintage	MS-63	Proof
1999 Proof	500	—	600

KM# 407 Rev: Two pronghorn antelope **Rev. Designer:** Mark Hobson **Edge:** Reeded **Weight:** 15.5500 g. **Composition:** 0.9990 Platinum .5000 oz. APW **Size:** 25 mm.

Date	Mintage	MS-63	Proof
2000 Proof	600	—	600

KM# 431 Rev: Two harlequin ducks **Rev. Designer:** Cosme Saffioti and Susan Taylor **Edge:** Reeded **Weight:** 15.5500 g. **Composition:** 0.9995 Platinum .5000 oz. APW **Size:** 25 mm.

Date	Mintage	MS-63	Proof
2001 Proof	448	—	700

300 DOLLARS

KM# 177 Rev: Polar bear mother and cub **Rev. Designer:** Robert Bateman **Weight:** 31.1035 g. **Composition:** 0.9990 Platinum 1.0000 oz. APW

Date	Mintage	MS-63	Proof
1990 Proof	2,629	—	1,150

KM# 201 Rev: Snowy owl with chicks **Rev. Designer:** Glen Loates **Weight:** 31.1035 g. **Composition:** 0.9990 Platinum 1.0000 oz. APW

Date	Mintage	MS-63	Proof
1991 Proof	3,500	—	1,150

KM# 229 Rev: Cougar resting in tree **Rev. Designer:** George McLean **Weight:** 31.1035 g. **Composition:** 0.9990 Platinum 1.0000 oz. APW

Date	Mintage	MS-63	Proof
1992 Proof	3,500	—	1,150

KM# 243 Rev: Mother fox and three kits **Rev. Designer:** Claude D'Angelo **Weight:** 31.1035 g. **Composition:** 0.9990 Platinum 1.0000 oz. APW

Date	Mintage	MS-63	Proof
1993 Proof	3,500	—	1,150

KM# 255 Rev: Two otters swimming **Rev. Designer:** Ron S. Parker **Weight:** 31.1035 g. **Composition:** 0.9990 Platinum 1.0000 oz. APW

Date	Mintage	MS-63	Proof
1994 Proof	—	—	1,150

KM# 269 Rev: Female lynx and three kittens **Rev. Designer:** Michael Dumas **Weight:** 31.1035 g. **Composition:** 0.9990 Platinum 1.0000 oz. APW

Date	Mintage	MS-63	Proof
1995 Proof	1,500	—	1,150

KM# 281 Rev: Peregrine falcon feeding nestlings **Rev. Designer:** Dwayne Harty **Weight:** 31.1035 g. **Composition:** 0.9990 Platinum 1.0000 oz. APW

Date	Mintage	MS-63	Proof
1996 Proof	1,500	—	1,150

KM# 303 Rev: Bison family **Rev. Designer:** Chris Bacon **Weight:** 31.1035 g. **Composition:** 0.9990 Platinum 1.0000 oz. APW

Date	Mintage	MS-63	Proof
1997 Proof	1,500	—	1,150

KM# 325 Rev: Gray wolf and two cubs **Rev. Designer:** Kerr Burnett **Weight:** 31.1035 g. **Composition:** 0.9990 Platinum 1.0000 oz. APW

Date	Mintage	MS-63	Proof
1998 Proof	—	—	1,150

KM# 362 Rev: Musk ox **Rev. Designer:** Mark Hobson **Weight:** 31.1035 g. **Composition:** 0.9990 Platinum 1.0000 oz. APW

Date	Mintage	MS-63	Proof
1999 Proof	500	—	1,150

KM# 408 Rev: Four pronghorn antelope **Rev. Designer:** Mark Hobson **Edge:** Reeded **Weight:** 31.1035 g. **Composition:** 0.9990 Platinum 1.0000 oz. APW **Size:** 30 mm.

Date	Mintage	MS-63	Proof
2000 Proof	600	—	1,150

KM# 432 Obv: Queen's head right **Rev:** Two standing harlequin ducks **Rev. Designer:** Cosme Saffioti and Susan Taylor **Edge:** Reeded **Weight:** 31.1035 g. **Composition:** 0.9995 Platinum 1.0000 oz. APW **Size:** 30 mm.

Date	Mintage	MS-63	Proof
2001 Proof	448	—	1,300

SETS

CUSTOM PROOF-LIKE SETS (CPL)

KM#	Date	Mintage	Identification	Issue Price	Mkt. Value
CPL1	1971 (7)	33,517	KM59.1 (2 pcs.), 60.1, 62b-75.1, 77.1 ,79	6.50	6.00
CPL2	1971 (7)	38,198	KM59.1 (2 pcs.), 60.1, 62b, 75.1-77.1	6.50	6.00
CPL3	1973 (7)	35,676	KM59.1 (2 pcs.), 60.1, 75.1, 77.1, 81.1 obv. 120 beads, 82	6.50	7.00
CPL4	1973 (7)	Inc. above	KM59.1 (2 pcs.), 60.1, 75.1, 77.1, 81.1 obv. 132 beads, 82	6.50	140
CPL5	1974 (7)	44,296	KM59.1 (2 pcs.), 60.1, 62b-75.1, 88	8.00	6.00
CPL6	1975 (7)	36,851	KM59.1 (2 pcs.), 60.1, 62b-75.1, 76.2, 77.1		
CPL7	1976 (7)	28,162	KM59.1 (2 pcs.), 60.1, 62b-75.1, 76.2, 77.1	8.00	6.00
CPL8	1977 (7)	44,198	KM59.1 (2 pcs.), 60.1, 62b-75.2, 77.1, 117	8.00	7.00
CPL9	1978 (7)	41,000	KM59.1 (2 pcs.), 60.1, 62b-75.3, 77.1, 120.1	8.15	5.50
CPL10	1979 (7)	31,174	KM59.2 (2 pcs.), 60.2, 74, 75.3, 77.2, 120.1	—	5.50
CPL11	1980 (7)	41,447	KM60.2, 74, 75.3, 77.2, 120.1, 127 (2 pcs.)	10.75	5.50
				10.75	6.00

MINT SETS

KM#	Date	Mintage	Identification	Issue Price	Mkt. Value
MS1	1973 (4)	Inc. above	KM84-85, 86.1, 87; Olympic Commemoratives, Series I	45.00	40.00
MS2	1974 (4)	Inc. above	KM89-90, 93-94; Olympic Commemoratives, Series II	48.00	40.00
MS3	1974 (4)	Inc. above	KM91-92, 95-96; Olympic Commemorative, Series III	48.00	40.00
MS4	1975 (4)	Inc. above	KM98-99, 102-103; Olympic Commemoratives, Series IV	48.00	40.00
MS5	1975 (4)	Inc. above	KM100-101, 104-105; Olympic Commemoratives, Series V	60.00	40.00
MS6	1976 (4)	Inc. above	KM107-108, 111-112; Olympic Commemoratives, Series VI	60.00	40.00
MS7	1976 (4)	Inc. above	KM109-110, 113-114; Olympic Commemoratives, Series VII	60.00	40.00
MS8	2001 (5)	600	KM438-442	1,996	2,450
MS12	2003 (7)	135,000	KM#289, 182b, 183b, 184b, 290, 186, 270	12.00	12.00
MS13	2003 (7)	75,000	KM#490-496	13.25	14.00

OLYMPIC COMMEMORATIVES (OCP)

KM#	Date	Mintage	Identification	Issue Price	Mkt. Value
OCP1	1973 (4)	Inc. above	KM84-87, Series I	78.50	45.00
OCP2	1974 (4)	Inc. above	KM89-90, 93-94, Series II	88.50	45.00
OCP3	1974 (4)	Inc. above	KM91-92, 95-96, Series III	88.50	45.00
OCP4	1975 (4)	Inc. above	KM98-99, 102-103, Series IV	88.50	45.00
OCP5	1975 (4)	Inc. above	KM100-101, 104-105, Series V	88.50	45.00
OCP6	1976 (4)	Inc. above	KM107-108, 111-112, Series VI	88.50	45.00
OCP7	1976 (4)	Inc. above	KM109-110, 113-114, Series VII	88.50	45.00

PROOF SETS

KM#	Date	Mintage	Identification	Issue Price	Mkt. Value
		100	X#Tn1a-Tn5a	—	40.00
		1,500	X#51-56	—	110
PS1	1981 (7)	199,000	KM60.2, 74, 75.3, 77.2, 120.1, 127, 130	36.00	17.50
PS2	1982 (7)	180,908	KM60.2a, 74, 75.3, 77.2, 120.1, 132-133	36.00	14.00
PS3	1983 (7)	166,779	KM60.2a, 74, 75.3, 77.2, 120.1, 132, 138	36.00	14.00
PS4	1984 (7)	161,602	KM60.2a, 74, 75.3, 77.2, 120.1, 132, 140	30.00	17.00
PS5	1985 (7)	157,037	KM60.2a, 74, 75.3, 77.2, 120.1, 132, 143	30.00	18.00
PS6	1986 (7)	175,745	KM60.2a, 74, 75.3, 77.2, 120.1, 132, 149	30.00	18.00
PS7	1987 (7)	179,004	KM60.2a, 74, 75.3, 77.2, 120.1, 132, 154	34.00	18.00
PS8	1988 (7)	175,259	KM60.2a, 74, 75.3, 77.2, 132, 157, 161	37.50	23.00
PS9	1989 (7)	170,928	KM60.2a, 74, 75.3, 77.2, 132, 157, 168	40.00	24.00
PS10	1989 (4)	6,823	KM125.2, 135-136, 153	1,190	1,100
PS11	1989 (4)	1,995	KM164-167	1,700	2,100
PS12	1989 (3)	2,550	KM125.2, 163, 167	1,530	1,775
PS13	1989 (3)	9,979	KM135, 163-164	165	225
PS14	1990 (7)	158,068	KM170, 181, 182, 183, 184, 185, 186	41.00	24.00
PS15	1990 (4)	2,629	KM174-177	1,720	2,100
PS16	1991 (7)	14,629	KM179, 181, 182, 183, 184, 185, 186	—	45.00
PS17	1991 (4)	873	KM198-201	1,760	2,200
PS18	1992 (13)	84,397	KM203a, 212a-214a, 218, 220a-223a, 231a-234a	—	60.00
PS19	1992 (7)	147,061	KM204-210	42.75	30.00
PS20	1992 (4)	3,500	KM226-229	1,680	2,200
PS21	1993 (7)	143,065	KM181, 182, 183, 184, 185, 186, 235	42.75	20.00
PS22	1993 (4)	3,500	KM240-243	1,329	2,100
PS23	1994 (7)	47,303	KM181-186, 248	47.50	28.00
PS24	1994 (7)	99,121	KM181, 182, 183, 184, 185, 186, 251	43.00	28.00
PS25	1994 (4)	1,500	KM252-255	915	2,200
PS26	1995 (7)	Inc. above	KM181, 182, 183, 184, 185, 186, 259	37.45	25.00
PS27	1995 (7)	50,000	KM181, 182, 183, 184, 185, 258-259	49.45	22.00
PS28	1995 (4)	Inc. above	KM261-264	42.00	60.00
PS29	1995 (4)	682	KM266-269	1,555	2,300
PS30	1995 (2)	Inc. above	KM261-262	22.00	21.00
PS31	1995 (2)	Inc. above	KM263-264	22.00	30.00
PS32	1996 (4)	423	KM278-281	1,555	2,300
PS33	1996 (7)	Inc. above	KM181a, 182a, 183a, 184a, 185a, 186, 274	49.00	35.00
PS34	1996 (4)	Inc. above	KM283-286	44.45	45.00
PS35	1997 (8)	Inc. above	KM182a, 183a, 184a, 209, 270c, 282, 289,	60.00	30.00
PS36	1997 (4)	Inc. above	KM292-295	44.45	35.00
PS37	1997 (4)	Inc. above	KM300-303	1,530	2,300
PS38	1998 (8)	Inc. above	KM182a, 183a, 184a, 186, 270b, 289, 290a, 306	59.45	50.00
PS39	1998 (5)	25,000	KM309-313	73.50	55.00
PS40	1998 (0)	61,000	KM316 w/China Y-727	72.50	30.00
PS41	1998 (4)	Inc. above	KM318-321	44.45	38.00
PS42	1998 (4)	1,000	KM322-325	1,552	2,300
PS43	1998 (5)	25,000	KM310-313, 332	73.50	30.00
PS44	1999 (8)	Inc. above	KM182a-184a, 186, 270c, 289, 290a,	59.45	60.00
PS45	1999 (4)	Inc. above	KM335-338	39.95	40.00
PS46	1999 (12)	Inc. above	KM342a-353a	99.45	75.00
PS47	1999 (4)	Inc. above	KM359-362	1,425	2,300
PS48	2000 (12)	—	KM373a, 374a, 375a, 376a, 377a, 378a, 379a, 380a, 381a, 382a, 383a, 384.2a	101	90.00
PS49	2000 (4)	—	KM389-392	44.00	40.00
PS50	2000 (4)	600	KM405-408	1,416	2,300
PS51	2001 (4)	—	KM429, 430, 431, 432	—	2,300
PS54	2002 (2)	—	KM#519, 520	750	725
PS57	2004 (8)	—	KM#490, 491a-494a, 495, 496a, 512	—	90.00
PS58	2004 (5)	25,000	KM#621-625	—	145

PROOF-LIKE DOLLARS

KM#	Date	Mintage	Identification	Issue Price	Mkt. Value
D1.1	1951 (0)	Inc. above	KM46, Canoe		175
D1.2	1951 (0)	Inc. above	KM46, Arnprior		700
D2.1	1952 (0)	Inc. above	KM46, water lines		1,200
D2.2	1952 (0)	Inc. above	KM46, without water lines	—	175
D3	1953 (1)	1,200	KM54, Canoe w/shoulder fold		325
D4	1954 (1)	5,300	KM54, Canoe	1.25	150
D5	1955 (1)	7,950	KM54, Canoe	1.25	125
D5a	1955 (1)	Inc. above	KM54, Arnprior	1.25	175
D6	1956 (0)	10,212	KM54, Canoe	1.25	70.00
D7	1957 (1)	16,241	KM54, Canoe	1.25	40.00
D8	1958 (1)	33,237	KM55, British Columbia	1.25	25.00
D9	1959 (1)	45,160	KM54, Canoe	1.25	15.00
D10	1960 (1)	82,728	KM54, Canoe	1.25	10.00
D11	1961 (1)	120,928	KM54, Canoe	1.25	7.50
D12	1962 (1)	248,901	KM54, Canoe	1.25	7.00
D13	1963 (1)	963,525	KM54, Canoe	1.25	6.00
D14	1964 (1)	2,862,441	KM58, Charlottetown	1.25	6.00
D15	1965 (1)	2,904,352	KM64.1, Canoe	—	6.00
D16	1966 (1)	672,514	KM64.1, Canoe	—	6.00
D17	1967 (1)	1,036,176	KM70, Confederation	—	7.50

PROOF-LIKE SETS (PL)

KM#	Date	Mintage	Identification	Issue Price	Mkt. Value
PL1	1953 (6)	1,200	KM49 w/o shoulder fold, 50-54	2.20	1,250
PL3	1954 (6)	3,000	KM49-54	2.50	450
PL4	1954 (6)	Inc. above	KM49 w/o shoulder fold, 50-54	2.50	1,100
PL5	1955 (6)	6,300	KM49, 50a, 51-54	2.50	375
PL6	1955 (6)	Inc. above	KM49, 50a, 51-54, Arnprior	2.50	500
PL7	1956 (6)	6,500	KM49, 50a, 51-54	2.50	225
PL8	1957 (6)	11,862	KM49, 50a, 51-54	2.50	150
PL9	1958 (6)	18,259	KM49, 50a, 51-53, 55	2.50	100.00
PL10	1959 (6)	31,577	KM49, 50a, 51, 52, 54, 56	2.50	45.00
PL11	1960 (6)	64,097	KM49, 50a, 51, 52, 54, 56	3.00	35.00
PL12	1961 (6)	98,373	KM49, 50a, 51, 52, 54, 56	3.00	16.00
PL13	1962 (6)	200,950	KM49, 50a, 51, 52, 54, 56	3.00	10.00
PL14	1963 (6)	673,006	KM49, 51, 52, 54, 56, 57	3.00	9.50
PL15	1964 (6)	1,653,162	KM49, 51, 52, 56-58	3.00	9.50
PL16	1965 (6)	2,904,352	KM59.1-60.1, 61-63, 64.1	4.00	9.50
PL17	1966 (6)	672,514	KM59.1-60.1, 61-63, 64.1	4.00	9.50
PL18	1967 (6)	961,887	KM65-70 (pliofilm flat pack)	4.00	12.00
PL18A	1967 (6)	70,583	KM65-70 and Silver Medal (red box)	12.00	16.00
PL18B	1967 (7)	337,688	KM65-71 (black box)	40.00	250
PL19	1968 (6)	521,641	KM59.1-60.1, 62b, 72a, 75.1-76.1	4.00	2.25
PL20	1969 (6)	326,203	KM59.1-60.1, 62b, 75.1-77.1	4.00	2.75
PL21	1970 (6)	349,120	KM59.1-60.1, 62b, 75.1, 77.1, 78	4.00	3.25
PL22	1971 (6)	253,311	KM59.1-60.1, 62b, 75.1, 77.1, 79	4.00	2.75
PL23	1972 (6)	224,275	KM59.1-60.1, 62b-77.1	4.00	2.75
PL24	1973 (6)	243,695	KM59.1-60.1, 62b-75.1 obv. 120 beads, 77.1, 81.1, 82	4.00	4.00
PL25	1973 (6)	Inc. above	KM59.1-60.1, 62b-75.1 obv. 132 beads, 77.1, 81.2, 82	4.00	150
PL26	1974 (6)	213,589	KM59.1-60.1, 62b-75.1, 77.1, 88	5.00	3.00
PL27.1	1975 (6)	197,372	KM59.1, 60.1, 62b-75.1, 76.2, 77.1	5.00	2.50
PL27.2	1975 (6)	Inc. above	KM59.1, 60.1, 62b-75.1, 76.3, 77.1	5.00	5.00
PL28	1976 (6)	171,737	KM59.1, 60.1, 62b-75.1, 76.2, 77.1	5.15	2.75
PL29	1977 (6)	225,307	KM59.1, 60.1, 62b, 75.2, 77.1, 117.1	5.15	2.75
PL30	1978 (6)	260,000	KM59.1-60.1, 62b, 75.3, 77.1, 120.1	5.25	2.75
PL31	1979 (6)	187,624	KM59.2-60.2, 74, 75.3, 77.2, 120.1	6.25	2.75
PL32	1980 (6)	410,842	KM60.2, 74, 75.3, 77.2, 120.1, 127	6.50	4.50
PL33	1981 (6)	186,250	KM60.2, 74, 75.3, 77.2, 120.1, 123	5.00	3.25
PL34	1982 (6)	203,287	KM60.2, 74, 75.3, 77.2, 120.1, 123	6.00	2.50
PL36	1983 (6)	190,838	KM60.2a, 74, 75.3, 77.2, 120.1, 132	5.00	5.00
PL36.1	1983 (6)	Inc. above	KM60.2a, 74, 75.3, 77.2, 120.1, 132; set in folder packaged by British Royal Mint Coin Club	—	5.00
PL37	1984 (6)	181,249	KM60.2a, 74, 75.3, 77.2, 120.1, 132	5.25	5.00
PL38	1985 (6)	173,924	KM60.2a, 74, 75.3, 77.2, 120.1, 132	5.25	6.00
PL39	1986 (6)	167,338	KM60.2a, 74, 75.3, 77.2, 120.1, 132	5.25	6.50
PL40	1987 (6)	212,136	KM60.2a, 74, 75.3, 77.2, 120.1, 132	5.25	5.00
PL41	1988 (6)	182,048	KM60.2a, 74, 75.3, 77.2, 132, 157	6.05	5.00
PL42	1989 (6)	173,622	KM60.2a, 74, 75.3, 77.2, 132, 157	6.60	8.00
PL43	1990 (6)	170,791	KM181-186	7.40	8.00
PL44	1991 (6)	147,814	KM181-186	7.40	25.00
PL45	1992 (6)	217,597	KM204-209	8.25	11.00
PL46	1993 (6)	171,680	KM181-186	8.25	4.00
PL47	1994 (6)	141,676	KM181-185, 258	8.50	5.50
PL48	1994 (6)	18,794	KM181-185, 258 (Oh Canada holder)	8.50	8.50
PL49	1995 (6)	143,892	KM181-186	6.95	6.00
PL50	1995 (6)	50,927	KM181-186 (Oh Canada holder)	14.65	8.50
PL51	1995 (6)	36,443	KM181-186 (Baby Gift holder)	—	9.00
PL52	1996 (6)	116,736	KM181-186	—	14.00
PL53	1996 (6)	29,747	KM181-186 (Baby Gift holder)	8.95	14.00
PL54	1996 (6)	Inc. above	KM181a-185a, 186	14.65	16.00
PL55	1996 (6)	Inc. above	KM181a-185a, 186 (Oh Canada holder)	—	12.00
PL56	1996 (6)	Inc. above	KM181a-185a, 186 (Baby Gift holder)	10.45	12.00
PL57	1997 (7)	Inc. above	KM182a-184a, 209, 270, 289-290	16.45	8.00
PL58	1997 (7)	Inc. above	KM182a-184a, 270, 289-291 (Oh Canada holder)	18.50	20.00
PL59	1997 (7)	Inc. above	KM182a-184a, 209, 270, 289-290 (Baby Gift holder)	10.45	9.50
PL60	1998 (7)	Inc. above	KM182-184, 186, 270, 289-290	16.45	10.00
PL61	1998 (7)	Inc. above	KM182-184, 186, 270, 289-290 (Oh Canada holder)	16.45	12.00
PL62	1998 (7)	Inc. above	KM182-184, 186, 270, 289-290 (Tiny Treasures holder)	16.95	12.00
PL63	1999 (12)	Inc. above	KM342-353	16.95	10.00
PL64	2000 (12)	—	KM373-384	—	10.00

SPECIMEN SETS (SS)

KM#	Date	Mintage	Identification	Issue Price	Mkt. Value
SS1	1858 (4)	Inc. above	KM1-4, Reeded edge	—	9,000
SS2	1858 (4)	Inc. above	KM1-4, Plain edge	—	6,000
SS3	1858 (8)	Inc. above	KM1-4; Double Set	—	15,000
SS4	1858 (8)	Inc. above	KM1 (overdate), 2-4; Double Set	—	15,000
SS5	1870 (4)	100	KM2, 3, 5, 6 (reeded edges)	—	28,500
SS6	1870 (8)	Inc. above	KM2, 3, 5, 6; Double Set (plain edges)	—	55,000
SS7	1872 (4)	Inc. above	KM2, 3, 5, 6	—	12,500
SS8	1875 (3)	Inc. above	KM2 (Large date), 3, 5	—	65,000
SS9	1880 (3)	Inc. above	KM2, 3, 5 (Narrow 0)	—	35,000
SS10	1881 (5)	Inc. above	KM7, 2, 3, 5, 6	—	26,500

KM#	Date	Mintage	Identification	Issue Price	Mkt. Value
SS11	1892 (2)	Inc. above	KM3, 5	—	10,000
SS12	1902 (5)	100	KM8-12	—	25,000
SS13	1902 (3)	Inc. above	KM9 (Large H), 10, 11	—	6,500
SS14	1903 (3)	Inc. above	KM10, 12, 13	—	7,000
SS15	1908 (5)	1,000	KM8, 10-13	—	2,200
SS16	1911 (5)	1,000	KM15-19	—	5,500
SS17	1911/12 (0)	5	KM15-20, 26-27	—	52,250
SS18	1921 (5)	Inc. above	KM22-25, 28	—	120,000
SS19	1922 (2)	Inc. above	KM28, 29	—	2,500
SS20	1923 (2)	Inc. above	KM28, 29	—	5,000
SS21	1924 (2)	Inc. above	KM28, 29	—	4,000
SS22	1925 (2)	Inc. above	KM28, 29	—	7,000
SS23	1926 (2)	Inc. above	KM28, 29 (Near 6)	—	5,000
SS24	1927 (3)	Inc. above	KM24a, 28, 29	—	8,000
SS25	1928 (4)	Inc. above	KM23a, 24a, 28, 29	—	12,000
SS26	1929 (5)	Inc. above	KM23a,-25a, 28, 29	—	22,500
SS27	1930 (4)	Inc. above	KM23a, 24a. 28, 29	—	16,000
SS28	1931 (5)	Inc. above	KM23a-25a, 28, 29	—	26,500
SS29	1932 (5)	Inc. above	KM23a-25a, 28, 29	—	20,000
SS30	1934 (5)	Inc. above	KM23-25, 28, 29	—	23,000
SS31	1936 (5)	Inc. above	KM23-25, 28, 29	—	12,000
SS32	1936 (6)	Inc. above	KM23a(dot), 24a(dot), 25a, 28(dot), 29, 30	—	400,000
SS33	1937 (6)	1,025	KM32-37, Matte Finish	—	750
SS34	1937 (4)	Inc. above	KM32-35, Mirror Fields	—	1,350
SS35	1937 (6)	75	KM32-37, Mirror Fields	—	3,900
SS36	1938 (6)	Inc. above	KM32-37	—	18,250
SS-A36	1939 (6)	Inc. above	KM32-35, 38, Matte Finish	—	—
SS-B36	1939 (6)	Inc. above	KM32-35, 38, Mirror Fields	—	1,000
SS-C36	1942 (2)	Inc. above	KM32, 33	—	1,000
SS-D36	1943 (2)	Inc. above	KM32, 40	—	1,000
SS-A37	1944 (2)	Inc. above	KM32, 40a	—	11,300
SS37	1944 (5)	3	KM32, 34-37, 40a	—	1,000
SS-A38	1945 (2)	Inc. above	KM32, 40a	—	4,650
SS38	1945 (6)	6	KM32, 34-37, 40a	—	4,000
SS39	1946 (6)	15	KM32, 34-37, 39a	—	8,500
SS40	1947 (6)	Inc. above	KM32, 34-37(7 curved), 37(7 pointed),	—	6,200
SS41	1947 (6)	Inc. above	KM32, 34-36(7 curved), 37(blunt 7), 39a	—	4,250
SS42	1947 (6)	Inc. above	KM32, 34-36(7 curved right), 37, 39a	—	6,000
SS43	1948 (6)	30	KM41-46	—	6,400
SS44	1949 (6)	20	KM41-45, 47	—	1,550
SS44A	1949 (2)	Inc. above	KM47	—	1,650
SS45	1950 (6)	12	KM41-46	—	3,175
SS46	1950 (6)	Inc. above	KM41-45, 46 (Arnprior)	—	2,725
SS47	1951 (7)	12	KM41, 48, 42a, 43-46 (w/water lines)	—	3,175
SS48	1952 (6)	2,317	KM41, 42a, 43-46 (water lines)	—	3,175
SS48A	1952 (6)	Inc. above	KM41, 42a, 43-46 (w/o water lines)	—	1,850
SS49	1953 (6)	28	KM49 w/o straps, 50-54	—	875
SS50	1953 (6)	Inc. above	KM49 w/ straps, 50-54	—	850
SS51	1964 (6)	Inc. above	KM49, 51, 52, 56-58	—	850
SS52	1965 (6)	Inc. above	KM59.1-60.1, 61-63, 64.1	—	
SS56	1971 (7)	66,860	KM59.1-60.1, 62b-75.1, 77.1, 79 (2 pcs.); Double Dollar Prestige Sets	12.00	9.50
SS57	1972 (7)	36,349	KM59.1,-60.1, 62b-75.1, 76.1 (2 pcs.), 77; Double Dollar Prestige Sets	12.00	18.00
SS58	1973 (7)	119,819	KM59.1-60.1, 75.1, 77.1, 81.1, 82, 83; Double Dollar Prestige Sets	12.00	10.00
SS59	1973 (7)	Inc. above	KM59.1-60.1, 75.1, 77.1, 81.2, 82, 83; Double Dollar Prestige Sets	—	150
SS60	1974 (7)	85,230	KM59.1-60.1, 62b-75.1, 77.1, 88, 88a; Double Dollar Prestige Sets	15.00	10.00
SS61	1975 (7)	97,263	KM59.1-60.1, 62b-75.1, 76.2, 77.1, 97; Double Dollar Prestige Sets	15.00	10.00
SS62	1976 (7)	87,744	KM59.1-60, 62b-75.1, 76.2, 77.1, 106; Double Dollar Prestige Sets	16.00	10.00
SS63	1977 (7)	142,577	KM59.1-60.1, 62b, 75.2, 77.1, 117.1, 118; Double Dollar Prestige Sets	16.50	10.00
SS64	1978 (7)	147,000	KM59.1-60.1, 62b, 75.3, 77.1, 120.1, 121; Double Dollar Prestige Sets	16.50	10.00
SS65	1979 (7)	155,698	KM59.2-60.2, 74, 75.3, 77.2, 120, 124; Double Dollar Prestige Sets	18.50	11.50
SS66	1980 (7)	162,875	KM60.2, 74-75.3, 77.2, 120, 127, 128; Double Dollar Prestige Sets	30.50	22.50
SS67	1981 (6)	71,300	KM60.2, 74, 75.3, 77.2, 120.1, 127; Regular Specimen Sets Resumed	10.00	5.50
SS68	1982 (6)	62,298	KM60.2a, 74, 75.3, 77.2, 120.1, 132; Regular Specimen Sets Resumed	11.50	5.50
SS69	1983 (6)	60,329	KM60.2a, 74, 75.3, 77.2, 120.1, 132; Regular Specimen Sets Resumed	12.75	5.50
SS70	1984 (6)	60,400	KM60.2a, 74, 75.3, 77.2, 120.1, 132; Regular Specimen Sets Resumed	10.00	5.50
SS71	1985 (6)	61,553	KM60.2a, 74, 75.3, 77.2, 120.1, 132; Regular Specimen Sets Resumed	10.00	6.00
SS72	1986 (6)	67,152	KM60.2a, 74, 75.3, 77.2, 120.1, 132; Regular Specimen Sets Resumed	10.00	6.00
SS72A	1987 (6)	75,194	KM60.2a, 74, 75.3, 77.2, 120.1, 132; Regular Specimen Sets Resumed	11.00	6.50

KM#	Date	Mintage	Identification	Issue Price	Mkt. Value
SS73	1988 (6)	70,205	KM60.2a, 74, 75.3, 77.2, 132, 157; Regular Specimen Sets Resumed	12.30	6.50
SS74	1989 (6)	75,306	KM60.2a, 74, 75.3, 77.2, 132, 157; Regular Specimen Sets Resumed	14.50	8.50
SS75	1990 (6)	76,611	KM181-186; Regular Specimen Sets Resumed	15.50	8.50
SS76	1991 (6)	68,552	KM181-186; Regular Specimen Sets Resumed	15.50	22.00
SS77	1992 (6)	78,328	KM204-209; Regular Specimen Sets Resumed	16.25	13.00
SS78	1993 (6)	77,351	KM181-186; Regular Specimen Sets Resumed	16.25	6.50
SS79	1994 (6)	77,349	KM181-186; Regular Specimen Sets Resumed	16.50	9.50
SS80	1995 (6)	Inc. above	KM181-186; Regular Specimen Sets Resumed	13.95	9.50
SS82	1996 (6)	Inc. above	KM181a-185a, 186; Regular Specimen Sets Resumed	18.95	12.00
SS83	1997 (7)	Inc. above	KM182a-184a, 270, 289-291; Regular Specimen Sets Resumed	19.95	25.00
SS84	1998 (7)	Inc. above	KM182-184, 186, 270, 289, 290; Regular Specimen Sets Resumed	19.95	11.00
SS85	1999 (7)	Inc. above	KM182-184, 186, 270, 289a, 290; Regular Specimen Sets Resumed	19.95	11.00
SS91	2003 (7)	75,000	KM#182-184, 186, 270, 289, 290	30.00	27.50

V.I.P. SPECIMEN SETS (VS)

KM#	Date	Mintage	Identification	Issue Price	Mkt. Value
VS1	1969 (0)	4		—	2,000
VS2	1970 (0)	100	KM59.1-60.1, 74.1-75.1, 77.1, 78	—	525
VS3	1971 (0)	69	KM59.1-60.1, 74.1-75.1, 77.1, 79(2 pcs.)	—	525
VS4	1972 (0)	25	KM59.1-60.1, 74.1-75.1, 76.1, (2 pcs.), 77.1	—	650
VS5	1973 (0)	26	KM59.1-60.1, 75.1, 77.1, 81.1, 82, 83	—	650
VS6	1974 (0)	72	KM59.1-60.1, 74.1-75.1, 77.1, 88, 88a	—	525
VS7	1975 (0)	94	KM59.1-60.1, 74.1-75.1, 76.2, 77.1, 97	—	525
VS8	1976 (0)	Inc. above	KM59.1-60.1, 74.1-75.1, 76.2, 77.1, 106	—	525

NEW BRUNSWICK
COLONIAL

HALFPENNY TOKEN

KM# 1   Composition: Copper

Date	Mintage	VG-8	F-12	VF-20	XF-40	MS-60	MS-63	Proof
1843	480,000	4.00	6.00	11.50	30.00	110	265	—
1843 Proof	—	—	—	—	—	—	—	750

KM# 3   Composition: Copper

Date	Mintage	VG-8	F-12	VF-20	XF-40	MS-60	MS-63	Proof
1854	864,000	4.00	6.00	11.50	30.00	100.00	265	—

KM# 3a   Composition: Bronze

Date	Mintage	VG-8	F-12	VF-20	XF-40	MS-60	MS-63	Proof
1854 Proof	—	—	—	—	—	—	—	400

1 PENNY TOKEN

KM# 2   Composition: Copper

Date	Mintage	VG-8	F-12	VF-20	XF-40	MS-60	MS-63	Proof
1843	480,000	3.75	7.50	15.00	45.00	165	325	—
1843 Proof	—	—	—	—	—	—	—	800

KM# 4 Composition: Copper

Date	Mintage	VG-8	F-12	VF-20	XF-40	MS-60	MS-63	Proof
1854	432,000	3.75	7.50	15.00	50.00	175	350	—

DECIMAL COINAGE

HALF CENT

KM# 5 Composition: Bronze

Date	Mintage	VG-8	F-12	VF-20	XF-40	MS-60	MS-63	Proof
1861	222,800	80.00	100.00	175	225	450	900	—
1861 Proof	—	—	—	—	—	—	—	2,200

CENT

KM# 6 Composition: Bronze

Date	Mintage	VG-8	F-12	VF-20	XF-40	MS-60	MS-63	Proof
1861	1,000,000	2.25	4.00	8.00	13.00	100.00	275	—
1861 Proof	—	—	—	—	—	—	—	450
1864 short 6	1,000,000	2.25	4.00	8.00	13.00	110	275	—
1864 long 6	Inc. above	2.25	4.00	8.00	13.00	110	275	—

5 CENTS

KM# 7 Weight: 1.1620 g. **Composition:** 0.9250 Silver .0346 oz. ASW

Date	Mintage	VG-8	F-12	VF-20	XF-40	MS-60	MS-63	Proof
1862	100,000	45.00	80.00	175	375	1,700	3,200	—
1862 Proof	—	—	—	—	—	—	—	3,500
1864 small 6	100,000	45.00	80.00	175	375	1,700	3,200	—
1864 large 6	Inc. above	45.00	80.00	175	375	1,700	3,200	—

10 CENTS

KM# 8   Weight: 2.3240 g. **Composition:** 0.9250 Silver .0691 oz. ASW

Date	Mintage	VG-8	F-12	VF-20	XF-40	MS-60	MS-63	Proof
1862	150,000	45.00	80.00	175	350	1,200	2,450	—
1862 recut 2	Inc. above	60.00	125	275	550	2,200	4,400	—
1862 Proof	—	—	—	—	—	—	—	2,850
1864	100,000	45.00	80.00	175	350	1,500	2,750	—

20 CENTS

KM# 9   Weight: 4.6480 g. **Composition:** 0.9250 Silver .1382 oz. ASW

Date	Mintage	VG-8	F-12	VF-20	XF-40	MS-60	MS-63	Proof
1862	150,000	19.00	35.00	80.00	225	1,050	2,500	—
1862 Proof	—	—	—	—	—	—	—	2,850
1864	150,000	19.00	35.00	80.00	225	1,050	2,500	—

NEWFOUNDLAND

CENT (Large)

KM# 1 Composition: Bronze

Date	Mintage	VG-8	F-12	VF-20	XF-40	MS-60	MS-63	Proof
1865	240,000	2.25	3.50	7.00	20.00	120	550	—
1872H	200,000	2.50	4.00	7.00	17.00	70.00	160	—
1872H Proof	—	—	—	—	—	—	—	800
1873	200,025	2.50	4.50	13.00	40.00	300	1,100	—
1873 Proof	—	—	—	—	—	—	—	3,000
1876H	200,000	2.50	7.00	15.00	40.00	300	1,100	—
1876H Proof, reported not confirmed	—	—	—	—	—	—	—	—
1880 round O, even date	400,000	2.25	3.50	7.00	20.00	90.00	300	—
1880 round O, low O	Inc. above	2.25	8.00	20.00	50.00	400	1,300	—
1880 oval 0	Inc. above	125	225	325	500	1,300	2,700	—
1880 oval O Proof	—	—	—	—	—	—	—	2,500
1885	40,000	25.00	50.00	75.00	125	500	1,800	—
1885 Proof	—	—	—	—	—	—	—	2,500
1888	50,000	30.00	50.00	80.00	175	750	3,000	—
1890	200,000	2.25	6.00	15.00	45.00	300	1,100	—
1894	200,000	2.25	5.00	10.00	25.00	140	700	—
1894 Proof	—	—	—	—	—	—	—	1,500
1896	200,000	2.25	3.50	7.00	18.00	120	350	—
1896 Proof	—	—	—	—	—	—	—	1,500

KM# 9 Obv. Designer: G.W. DeSaulles **Rev. Designer:** Horace Morehen **Composition:** Bronze

Date	Mintage	VG-8	F-12	VF-20	XF-40	MS-60	MS-63	Proof
1904H	100,000	4.00	8.00	20.00	37.50	300	700	—
1904H Proof	—	—	—	—	—	—	—	4,000
1907	200,000	1.50	2.50	4.00	20.00	220	650	—
1909	200,000	1.50	2.50	4.00	10.50	75.00	150	—
1909 Proof	—	—	—	—	—	—	—	400

KM# 16 Obv: George V bust facing left **Obv. Designer:** E.B. MacKennal **Rev:** Similar to KM#9 **Rev. Designer:** Horace Morehen **Composition:** Bronze

Date	Mintage	VG-8	F-12	VF-20	XF-40	MS-60	MS-63	Proof
1913	400,000	0.75	1.50	2.00	4.00	40.00	75.00	—
1917C	702,350	0.75	1.50	2.00	4.00	75.00	200	—
1917C Proof	—	—	—	—	—	—	—	800
1919C	300,000	0.80	1.60	2.25	5.00	125	300	—
1919C Proof	—	—	—	—	—	—	—	1,000
1920C	302,184	0.75	1.50	3.50	12.00	300	1,000	—
1929	300,000	0.75	1.50	2.00	4.00	55.00	100.00	—
1929C Proof	—	—	—	—	—	—	—	1,000
1936	300,000	0.75	1.25	1.75	3.00	28.00	75.00	—

CENT (Small)

KM# 18 Obv. Designer: Percy Metcalfe **Rev:** Pitcher plant **Rev. Designer:** Walter J. Newman **Composition:** Bronze

Date	Mintage	VG-8	F-12	VF-20	XF-40	MS-60	MS-63	Proof
1938	500,000	0.50	0.75	1.50	2.50	16.00	40.00	—
1938 Proof	—	—	—	—	—	—	—	1,000
1940	300,000	1.25	2.00	3.00	10.00	50.00	250	—
1940 re-engraved date	—	20.00	35.00	40.00	70.00	300	500	—
1940 Proof	—	—	—	—	—	—	—	1,000
1941C	827,662	0.35	0.45	0.70	1.50	20.00	120	—
1941C re-engraved date	—	9.00	13.00	20.00	35.00	100.00	400	—
1942	1,996,889	0.35	0.45	0.70	1.50	30.00	125	—
1943C	1,239,732	0.35	0.45	0.70	1.50	13.50	70.00	—
1944C	1,328,776	1.00	2.00	10.00	20.00	250	550	—
1947C	313,772	0.90	1.65	5.00	12.00	50.00	200	—
1947C Proof	—	—	—	—	—	—	—	2,000

5 CENTS

KM# 2 Weight: 1.1782 g. **Composition:** 0.9250 Silver .0350 oz. ASW

Date	Mintage	VG-8	F-12	VF-20	XF-40	MS-60	MS-63	Proof
1865	80,000	25.00	50.00	100.00	200	775	1,500	—
1865 Proof	—	—	—	—	—	—	—	4,000
1870	40,000	45.00	85.00	150	300	1,100	2,000	—
1870 Proof	—	—	—	—	—	—	—	4,000
1872H	40,000	22.00	45.00	85.00	175	600	1,400	—
1873	44,260	75.00	125	300	800	2,900	4,500	—
1873H	Inc. above	750	1,100	2,000	3,700	9,700	14,000	—
1873 Proof	—	—	—	—	—	—	—	10,000
1876H	20,000	80.00	125	225	425	1,200	2,750	—
1880	40,000	30.00	65.00	100.00	200	1,000	1,850	—
1880 Proof	—	—	—	—	—	—	—	5,000
1881	40,000	30.00	65.00	100.00	300	1,200	2,200	—
1881 Proof	—	—	—	—	—	—	—	5,000
1882H	60,000	15.00	27.00	50.00	125	800	1,500	—
1882H Proof	—	—	—	—	—	—	—	2,000
1885	16,000	125	200	325	700	2,400	4,500	—
1885 Proof	—	—	—	—	—	—	—	7,500
1888	40,000	40.00	75.00	150	375	1,900	3,200	—
1888 Proof	—	—	—	—	—	—	—	7,500
1890	160,000	6.00	12.00	30.00	85.00	800	1,500	—
1890 Proof	—	—	—	—	—	—	—	5,000
1894	160,000	6.50	12.50	30.00	75.00	800	1,500	—
1894 Proof	—	—	—	—	—	—	—	5,000
1896	400,000	4.00	8.00	20.00	50.00	700	1,350	—
1896 Proof	—	—	—	—	—	—	—	5,000

KM# 7 Designer: G.W. DeSaulles **Weight:** 1.1782 g. **Composition:** 0.9250 Silver .0350 oz. ASW

Date	Mintage	VG-8	F-12	VF-20	XF-40	MS-60	MS-63	Proof
1903	100,000	3.00	6.00	18.00	45.00	435	1,350	—
1903 Proof	—	—	—	—	—	—	—	2,000
1904H	100,000	2.00	5.00	14.00	35.00	160	285	—
1904H Proof	—	—	—	—	—	—	—	1,200
1908	400,000	3.00	6.00	11.50	30.00	260	750	—

KM# 13 Obv: George V bust facing left **Obv. Designer:** E.B. MacKennal **Rev:** Similar to KM#7 **Rev. Designer:** G.W. DeSaulles **Weight:** 1.1782 g. **Composition:** 0.9250 Silver .0350 oz. ASW

Date	Mintage	VG-8	F-12	VF-20	XF-40	MS-60	MS-63	Proof
1912	300,000	1.00	2.00	5.00	20.00	125	275	—
1912 Proof	—	—	—	—	—	—	—	2,000
1917C	300,319	1.00	2.00	4.00	25.00	250	650	—
1917C Proof	—	—	—	—	—	—	—	2,000
1919C	100,844	3.00	6.00	15.00	75.00	950	1,750	—
1919C Proof	—	—	—	—	—	—	—	2,000
1929	300,000	1.00	1.75	3.25	12.00	165	350	—

KM# 19   Obv. Designer: Percy Metcalfe **Rev. Designer:** G.W. DeSaulles **Weight:** 1.1782 g. **Composition:** 0.9250 Silver .0350 oz. ASW

Date	Mintage	VG-8	F-12	VF-20	XF-40	MS-60	MS-63	Proof
1938	100,000	0.85	1.00	1.50	4.00	70.00	225	—
1938 Proof	—	—	—	—	—	—	—	1,000
1940C	200,000	0.85	1.00	1.50	4.00	85.00	300	—
1940C Proof	—	—	—	—	—	—	—	2,000
1941C	621,641	0.65	1.00	1.50	2.50	15.00	35.00	—
1942C	298,348	0.85	1.00	2.00	2.50	17.50	40.00	—
1943C	351,666	0.60	0.90	1.25	2.50	15.00	30.00	—

KM# 19a   Obv. Designer: Percy Metcalfe **Rev. Designer:** G.W. DeSaulles **Weight:** 1.1664 g. **Composition:** 0.8000 Silver .0300 oz. ASW

Date	Mintage	VG-8	F-12	VF-20	XF-40	MS-60	MS-63	Proof
1944C	286,504	1.25	1.75	3.00	5.00	50.00	120	—
1945C	203,828	0.65	0.85	1.25	2.50	14.00	32.00	—
1946C	2,041	200	225	325	400	1,200	1,900	—
1946C Prooflike	—	—	—	—	—	—	2,500	—
1947C	38,400	2.00	3.00	5.00	10.00	65.00	125	—
1947C Prooflike	—	—	—	—	—	—	375	—

10 CENTS

KM# 3   Weight: 2.3564 g. **Composition:** 0.9250 Silver .0701 oz. ASW

Date	Mintage	VG-8	F-12	VF-20	XF-40	MS-60	MS-63	Proof
1865	80,000	15.00	30.00	75.00	180	1,100	2,250	—
1865 plain edge, Proof	—	—	—	—	—	—	—	5,500
1870	30,000	120	190	335	725	2,350	5,000	—
1870 Proof	—	—	—	—	—	—	—	10,000
1872H	40,000	13.50	20.00	50.00	135	800	1,700	—
1873 flat 3	23,614	35.00	70.00	175	425	2,200	4,500	—
1873 round 3	Inc. above	35.00	70.00	175	425	2,200	4,500	—
1873 Proof	—	—	—	—	—	—	—	12,000
1876H	10,000	35.00	70.00	150	350	1,400	2,500	—
1880/70	10,000	35.00	70.00	175	400	1,800	2,950	—
1880 Proof	—	—	—	—	—	—	—	7,500
1882H	20,000	30.00	55.00	150	475	2,200	4,500	—
1882H Proof	—	—	—	—	—	—	—	3,000
1885	8,000	65.00	125	225	550	2,200	4,250	—
1885 Proof	—	—	—	—	—	—	—	8,000
1888	30,000	35.00	70.00	200	700	2,500	4,200	—
1888 Proof	—	—	—	—	—	—	—	8,000
1890	100,000	5.50	11.50	35.00	100.00	1,100	1,550	—
1890 Proof	—	—	—	—	—	—	—	5,000
1894	100,000	5.50	11.50	25.00	90.00	700	1,550	—
1894 Proof	—	—	—	—	—	—	—	5,000
1896	230,000	5.00	10.00	25.00	90.00	700	1,500	—
1896 Proof	—	—	—	—	—	—	—	5,000

KM# 8   Designer: G.W. DeSaulles **Weight:** 2.3564 g. **Composition:** 0.9250 Silver .0701 oz. ASW

Date	Mintage	VG-8	F-12	VF-20	XF-40	MS-60	MS-63	Proof
1903	100,000	5.00	15.00	45.00	135	1,200	2,800	—
1903 Proof	—	—	—	—	—	—	—	2,500
1904H	100,000	2.50	6.50	20.00	60.00	200	350	—
1904H Proof	—	—	—	—	—	—	—	1,500

KM# 14   Obv. Designer: E.B. MacKennal **Rev. Designer:** G.W. DeSaulles **Weight:** 2.3564 g. **Composition:** 0.9250 Silver .0701 oz. ASW

Date	Mintage	VG-8	F-12	VF-20	XF-40	MS-60	MS-63	Proof
1912	150,000	0.85	1.75	6.00	25.00	165	300	—
1917C	250,805	0.75	1.50	7.50	30.00	400	1,500	—
1919C	54,342	1.20	2.50	6.00	25.00	175	350	—

KM# 20   Obv. Designer: Percy Metcalfe **Rev. Designer:** G.W. DeSaulles **Weight:** 2.3564 g. **Composition:** 0.9250 Silver .0701 oz. ASW

Date	Mintage	VG-8	F-12	VF-20	XF-40	MS-60	MS-63	Proof
1938	100,000	0.90	1.75	2.75	7.00	80.00	300	—
1938 Proof	—	—	—	—	—	—	—	2,000
1940	100,000	0.80	1.50	2.50	6.00	80.00	300	—
1940 Proof	—	—	—	—	—	—	—	2,500
1941C	483,630	0.75	1.50	2.20	3.50	27.00	125	—
1942C	293,736	0.75	1.50	2.20	3.50	30.00	130	—
1943C	104,706	0.75	1.50	2.50	3.50	60.00	200	—
1944C	151,471	2.50	3.50	10.00	20.00	200	800	—

KM# 20a   Obv. Designer: Percy Metcalfe **Rev. Designer:** G.W. DeSaulles **Weight:** 2.3328 g. **Composition:** 0.8000 Silver .0600 oz. ASW

Date	Mintage	VG-8	F-12	VF-20	XF-40	MS-60	MS-63	Proof
1945C	175,833	0.70	1.35	2.25	4.50	45.00	225	—
1946C	38,400	2.00	4.00	7.00	15.00	60.00	275	—
1946C Proof	—	—	—	—	—	—	—	750
1947C	61,988	1.50	3.00	4.50	9.00	65.00	275	—

20 CENTS

KM# 4   Weight: 4.7127 g. **Composition:** 0.9250 Silver .1401 oz. ASW

Date	Mintage	VG-8	F-12	VF-20	XF-40	MS-60	MS-63	Proof
1865	100,000	11.00	20.00	60.00	150	950	2,000	—
1865 plain edge, Proof	—	—	—	—	—	—	—	6,500
1865 reeded edge, Proof	—	—	—	—	—	—	—	10,000
1870	50,000	12.00	30.00	100.00	250	1,250	2,500	—
1870 plain edge, Proof	—	—	—	—	—	—	—	6,500
1870 reeded edge, Proof	—	—	—	—	—	—	—	6,500
1872H	90,000	7.00	14.00	40.00	140	750	1,800	—
1873	45,797	21.00	45.00	125	350	2,800	7,000	—
1873 Proof	—	—	—	—	—	—	—	12,000
1876H	50,000	15.00	30.00	80.00	200	1,350	2,700	—
1880/70	30,000	15.00	35.00	100.00	250	1,350	3,000	—
1880 Proof	—	—	—	—	—	—	—	8,000
1881	60,000	12.00	25.00	80.00	200	1,200	1,900	—
1881 Proof	—	—	—	—	—	—	—	8,000
1882H	100,000	5.00	12.00	35.00	140	1,000	1,900	—
1882H Proof	—	—	—	—	—	—	—	3,500
1885	40,000	14.00	30.00	80.00	225	1,900	3,500	—
1885 Proof	—	—	—	—	—	—	—	10,000
1888	75,000	6.00	15.00	45.00	150	900	2,200	—
1888 Proof	—	—	—	—	—	—	—	10,000
1890	100,000	6.00	15.00	45.00	150	700	1,600	—
1890 Proof	—	—	—	—	—	—	—	6,500
1894	100,000	15.00	30.00	100.00	300	1,200	—	—
1894 Proof	—	—	—	—	—	—	—	6,500
1896 small 96	125,000	5.00	10.00	30.00	100.00	700	1,800	—
1896 large 96	Inc. above	7.00	15.00	50.00	200	725	1,900	—
1896 large 96, Proof	—	—	—	—	—	—	—	6,500

Date	Mintage	VG-8	F-12	VF-20	XF-40	MS-60	MS-63	Proof
1899 hook 99	125,000	18.00	35.00	90.00	250	1,000	3,100	—
1899 large 99	Inc. above	5.00	8.00	30.00	125	700	1,900	—
1900	125,000	5.00	8.00	25.00	80.00	700	1,900	—
1900 Proof	—	—	—	—	—	—	—	6,500

KM# 10 Obv. Designer: G.W. DeSaulles **Rev. Designer:** W.H.J. Blakemore **Weight:** 4.7127 g. **Composition:** 0.9250 Silver .1401 oz. ASW

Date	Mintage	VG-8	F-12	VF-20	XF-40	MS-60	MS-63	Proof
1904H	75,000	10.00	20.00	55.00	275	2,500	6,000	—
1904H Proof	—	—	—	—	—	—	—	1,850

KM# 15 Obv: George V bust facing left **Obv. Designer:** E.B. MacKennal **Rev:** Similar to KM#10 **Rev. Designer:** W.H.J. Blakemore **Weight:** 4.7127 g. **Composition:** 0.9250 Silver .1401 oz. ASW

Date	Mintage	VG-8	F-12	VF-20	XF-40	MS-60	MS-63	Proof
1912	350,000	2.50	3.50	9.00	35.00	325	850	—
1912 Proof	—	—	—	—	—	—	—	2,500

25 CENTS

KM# 17 Obv. Designer: E.B. MacKennal **Rev. Designer:** W.H.J. Blakemore **Weight:** 5.8319 g. **Composition:** 0.9250 Silver .1734 oz. ASW

Date	Mintage	VG-8	F-12	VF-20	XF-40	MS-60	MS-63	Proof
1917C	464,779	2.00	3.00	5.00	9.00	145	300	—
1917C Proof	—	—	—	—	—	—	—	2,500
1919C	163,939	2.00	3.50	8.00	25.00	350	1,250	—
1919C Proof	—	—	—	—	—	—	—	2,500

50 CENTS

KM# 6 Weight: 11.7818 g. **Composition:** 0.9250 Silver .3504 oz. ASW

Date	Mintage	VG-8	F-12	VF-20	XF-40	MS-60	MS-63	Proof
1870	50,000	12.00	30.00	100.00	600	1,600	3,600	—
1870 plain edge, Proof	—	—	—	—	—	—	—	25,000
1870 reeded edge, Proof	—	—	—	—	—	—	—	25,000
1872H	48,000	10.00	20.00	50.00	225	1,600	3,600	—
1873	37,675	40.00	75.00	200	650	5,700	10,000	—

Date	Mintage	VG-8	F-12	VF-20	XF-40	MS-60	MS-63	Proof
1873 Proof	—	—	—	—	—	—	—	40,000
1874	80,000	25.00	45.00	125	550	4,300	8,000	—
1874 Proof	—	—	—	—	—	—	—	40,000
1876H	28,000	35.00	55.00	150	450	2,250	5,250	—
1880	24,000	30.00	60.00	175	600	4,000	9,500	—
1880 Proof	—	—	—	—	—	—	—	40,000
1881	50,000	20.00	35.00	135	400	2,250	5,250	—
1881 Proof	—	—	—	—	—	—	—	40,000
1882H	100,000	12.00	17.00	55.00	200	1,600	3,600	—
1882H Proof	—	—	—	—	—	—	—	8,000
1885	40,000	25.00	40.00	150	450	2,800	7,100	—
1885 Proof	—	—	—	—	—	—	—	40,000
1888	20,000	40.00	80.00	225	900	5,600	12,000	—
1888 Proof	—	—	—	—	—	—	—	40,000
1894	40,000	7.00	17.00	75.00	300	2,000	3,800	—
1896	60,000	7.00	15.00	65.00	225	1,600	3,600	—
1896 Proof	—	—	—	—	—	—	—	25,000
1898	76,607	7.00	12.00	60.00	200	1,700	3,600	—
1899 wide 9's	150,000	7.00	12.00	60.00	200	1,600	3,600	—
1899 narrow 9's	Inc. above	7.00	12.00	45.00	150	1,600	3,600	—
1900	150,000	7.00	12.00	45.00	175	1,600	3,600	—

KM# 11 Obv. Designer: G.W. DeSaulles **Rev. Designer:** W.H.J. Blakemore **Weight:** 11.7800 g. **Composition:** 0.9250 Silver .3504 oz. ASW

Date	Mintage	VG-8	F-12	VF-20	XF-40	MS-60	MS-63	Proof
1904H	140,000	3.75	6.00	14.00	35.00	275	850	—
1904H Proof	—	—	—	—	—	—	—	5,000
1907	100,000	3.50	6.00	14.50	45.00	350	1,000	—
1908	160,000	3.75	5.00	13.50	32.50	225	700	—
1909	200,000	3.75	5.00	13.50	35.00	300	800	—

KM# 12 Obv. Designer: E.B. MacKennal **Rev. Designer:** W.H.J. Blakemore **Weight:** 11.7800 g. **Composition:** 0.9250 Silver .3504 oz. ASW

Date	Mintage	VG-8	F-12	VF-20	XF-40	MS-60	MS-63	Proof
1911	200,000	3.50	4.50	7.50	20.00	200	550	—
1917C	375,560	3.50	4.50	7.50	16.50	145	350	—
1917C Proof	—	—	—	—	—	—	—	2,500
1918C	294,824	3.50	4.50	7.50	16.50	145	350	—
1919C	306,267	3.50	4.50	7.50	16.50	325	1,150	—
1919C Proof	—	—	—	—	—	—	—	2,500

2 DOLLARS

KM# 5 Weight: 3.3284 g. **Composition:** 0.9170 Gold .0981 oz. AGW

Date	Mintage	F-12	VF-20	XF-40	AU-50	MS-60	MS-63
1865	10,000	150	175	225	375	1,100	5,000
1865 plain edge, Specimen-63, $15,000.	Est. 10	—	—	—	—	—	—
1870	10,000	150	175	250	375	1,100	5,850
1870 reeded edge, Specimen-63 $20,000.	Est. 5	—	—	—	—	—	—
1872	6,050	150	275	325	600	2,100	8,650
1872 Specimen-63 $12,500.	Est. 10	—	—	—	—	—	—
1880	2,500	800	1,000	1,200	2,300	4,650	14,250
1880/70							
Note: Specimen. Bowers and Merena Norweb sale 11-96, specimen 64 realized $70,400.							
1881	10,000	125	150	200	325	1,200	5,400
1881 Specimen; Rare	—	—	—	—	—	—	—
1882H	25,000	125	150	200	225	425	1,600
1882H Specimen $4,250.	—	—	—	—	—	—	—
1885	10,000	125	150	200	225	425	1,800
1885 Specimen	—	—	—	—	—	—	—
Note: Bowers and Merena Norweb sale 11-96, specimen 66 realized $44,000							
1888	25,000	105	140	175	200	365	1,550
1888 Specimen; Rare	—	—	—	—	—	—	—

NOVA SCOTIA

STERLING COINAGE

HALFPENNY TOKEN

KM# 1a Composition: Copper

Date	Mintage	VG-8	F-12	VF-20	XF-40	MS-60	MS-63	Proof
1382 1382 (error)	—	500	700	1,650	—	—	—	—
1832/1382	—	6.00	15.00	50.00	100.00	—	—	—
1832 (imitation)	—	3.00	6.00	18.00	40.00	50.00	100.00	—

KM# 1 Composition: Copper

Date	Mintage	VG-8	F-12	VF-20	XF-40	MS-60	MS-63	Proof
1823	400,000	3.00	6.00	13.00	40.00	125	250	—
1823 without hyphen	Inc. above	5.00	10.00	20.00	50.00	170	350	—
1824	118,636	4.00	8.00	18.00	45.00	150	275	—
1832	800,000	3.00	5.00	7.50	21.00	80.00	175	—

KM# 3 Composition: Copper

Date	Mintage	VG-8	F-12	VF-20	XF-40	MS-60	MS-63	Proof
1840 small 0	300,000	3.50	10.00	15.00	35.00	125	250	—
1840 medium 0	Inc. above	2.50	9.00	14.00	30.00	125	250	—
1840 large 0	Inc. above	4.00	10.00	15.00	35.00	125	250	—
1843	300,000	3.00	6.00	16.00	40.00	125	250	—

KM# 5 Composition: Copper

Date	Mintage	VG-8	F-12	VF-20	XF-40	MS-60	MS-63	Proof
1856 without LCW	720,000	2.00	4.00	7.50	15.00	70.00	175	—
1856 without LCW, Proof	—	—	—	—	—	—	—	600
1856 without LCW, inverted A for V in PROVINCE, Proof	—	—	—	—	—	—	—	600

KM# 5a Composition: Bronze

Date	Mintage	VG-8	F-12	VF-20	XF-40	MS-60	MS-63	Proof
1856 with LCW, Proof	—	—	—	—	—	—	—	600

1 PENNY TOKEN

KM# 2 Composition: Copper

Date	Mintage	VG-8	F-12	VF-20	XF-40	MS-60	MS-63	Proof
1824	217,776	4.00	10.00	17.00	55.00	175	350	—
1832	200,000	4.00	8.00	15.00	35.00	125	250	—

KM# 2a Composition: Copper

Date	Mintage	VG-8	F-12	VF-20	XF-40	MS-60	MS-63	Proof
1832 (imitation)	—	3.75	7.50	22.50	42.50	—	—	—

KM# 4 Composition: Copper Size: 32 mm.

Date	Mintage	VG-8	F-12	VF-20	XF-40	MS-60	MS-63	Proof
1840	150,000	2.50	6.00	14.00	40.00	150	250	—
1843/0	150,000	12.00	20.00	40.00	80.00	175	—	—
1843	Inc. above	4.00	8.00	15.00	40.00	175	275	—

KM# 6 Composition: Copper

Date	Mintage	VG-8	F-12	VF-20	XF-40	MS-60	MS-63	Proof
1856 without LCW	360,000	2.50	5.00	8.50	19.00	110	200	—
1856 with LCW	Inc. above	2.50	5.00	8.00	25.00	100.00	175	—

KM# 6a Composition: Bronze

Date	Mintage	VG-8	F-12	VF-20	XF-40	MS-60	MS-63	Proof
1856 Proof	—	—	—	—	—	—	—	400

DECIMAL COINAGE

HALF CENT

KM# 7 Composition: Bronze

Date	Mintage	VG-8	F-12	VF-20	XF-40	MS-60	MS-63	Proof
1861	400,000	3.00	5.00	8.00	13.00	60.00	175	—
1864	400,000	3.00	5.00	8.00	13.00	55.00	175	—
1864 Proof	—	—	—	—	—	—	—	300

CENT

KM# 8.2 Composition: Bronze **Note:** Prev. KM#8. Small rosebud right of SCOTIA. The Royal Mint report records mintage of 1 million for 1862, which is considered incorrect.

Date	Mintage	VG-8	F-12	VF-20	XF-40	MS-60	MS-63	Proof
1861	800,000	2.00	3.00	5.00	11.00	250	215	—
1862	Est. 1,000,000	25.00	40.00	90.00	175	850	2,900	—
1864	800,000	2.00	3.00	5.00	11.00	250	225	—

PRINCE EDWARD ISLAND

DECIMAL COINAGE

CENT

KM# 4 Composition: Bronze

Date	Mintage	VG-8	F-12	VF-20	XF-40	MS-60	MS-63	Proof
1871	2,000,000	1.75	2.50	4.50	11.00	75.00	185	—
1871 Proof	—	—	—	—	—	—	—	2,000

CUT & COUNTERMARKED COINAGE

SHILLING

KM# 1   **Composition:** Silver **Note:** Countermark on center plug of Spanish or Spanish Colonial 8 Reales.

Date	Mintage	VG-8	F-12	VF-20	XF-40	MS-60	MS-63	Proof
ND	1,000	2,000	3,000	5,000	—	—	—	—

5 SHILLING

KM# 3   **Composition:** Silver **Note:** Countermark on holed Lima 8 Reales, KM#106.2.

Date	Mintage	VG-8	F-12	VF-20	XF-40	MS-60	MS-63	Proof
1809-11	1,000	1,000	1,750	3,000	—	—	—	—

KM# 2.1   **Composition:** Silver **Note:** Countermark on holed Mexico City 8 Reales, KM#109.

Date	Mintage	VG-8	F-12	VF-20	XF-40	MS-60	MS-63	Proof
1791-1808	—	800	1,350	2,250	—	—	—	—

KM# 2.2   **Composition:** Silver **Note:** Countermark on holed Mexico City 8 Reales, KM#110.

Date	Mintage	VG-8	F-12	VF-20	XF-40	MS-60	MS-63	Proof
ND	—	800	1,350	2,250	—	—	—	—

MEXICO

The United States of Mexico, located immediately south of the United States has an area of 759,529 sq. mi. (1,967,183 sq. km.) and an estimated population of 100 million. Capital: Mexico City. The economy is based on agriculture, manufacturing and mining. Oil, cotton, silver, coffee, and shrimp are exported.

Mexico was the site of highly advanced Indian civilizations 1,500 years before conquistador Hernando Cortes conquered the wealthy Aztec empire of Montezuma, 1519-21, and founded a Spanish colony, which lasted for nearly 300 years. During the Spanish period, Mexico, then called New Spain, stretched from Guatemala to the present states of Wyoming and California, its present northern boundary having been established by the secession of Texas during 1836 and the war of 1846-48 with the United States.

Independence from Spain was declared by Father Miguel Hidalgo on Sept. 16, 1810, (Mexican Independence Day) and was achieved by General Agustin de Iturbide in 1821. Iturbide became emperor in 1822 but was deposed when a republic was established a year later. For more than fifty years following the birth of the republic, the political scene of Mexico was characterized by turmoil, which saw two emperors (including the unfortunate Maximilian), several dictators and an average of one new government every nine months passing swiftly from obscurity to oblivion. The land, social, economic and labor reforms promulgated by the Reform Constitution of Feb. 5, 1917 established the basis for sustained economic development and participative democracy that have made Mexico one of the most politically stable countries of modern Latin America.

RULERS

Philip V, 1700-1746
Luis I, 1724
Ferdinand VI, 1746-59
Charles III, 1760-88
Charles IV, 1788-1808

MINT MARKS

Mo, Mxo – Mexico City Mint

Initials	Date	Name
L	1678-1703	Martin Lopez
J	1708-23	Jose E. de Leon
D	1724-27	?
R	1729-30	Nicolas de Roxas
G	1730	
F	1730-33	Felipe Rivas de Angulo
F	1733-84	Francisco de la Pena
M	1733-63	Manuel de la Pena
M	1754-70	Manuel Assorin
F	1762-70	Francisco de Rivera
M	1770-77	Manuel de Rivera
F	1777-1803	Francisco Arance Cobos
M	1784-1801	Mariano Rodriguez

COLONIAL

COB COINAGE

KM# 24 1/2 REAL
1.6900 g., 0.9310 Silver **Ruler:** Philip V **Obv:** Legend around crowned PHILIPVS monogram **Rev:** Legend around cross, lions and castles **Note:** Struck at Mexico City Mint, mint mark M, Mo.

Date	Mintage	Good	VG	F	VF	XF
ND(1701-28)	—	—	20.00	35.00	65.00	—
Date off flan						
1701 L	—	—	100	125	225	—
1702 L	—	—	100	125	225	—
1703 L	—	—	100	125	225	—
1704 L	—	—	100	125	225	—
1705 L	—	—	100	125	225	—
1706 J	—	—	100	125	225	—
1707 J	—	—	100	125	225	—
1708 J	—	—	100	125	175	—
1709 J	—	—	100	125	175	—
1710 J	—	—	100	125	175	—
1711 J	—	—	100	125	175	—
1712 J	—	—	100	125	175	—
1714 J	—	—	100	125	175	—
1715 J	—	—	100	125	175	—
1716 J	—	—	100	125	175	—
1717 J	—	—	100	125	175	—
1718 J	—	—	100	125	175	—
1719 J	—	—	100	125	175	—
1720 J	—	—	100	125	175	—
1721 J	—	—	100	125	175	—
1722 J	—	—	100	125	175	—
1723 J	—	—	100	125	175	—
1724 J	—	—	100	125	175	—
1724 D	—	—	100	125	175	—
1725 D	—	—	100	125	175	—
1726 D	—	—	100	125	175	—
1727 D	—	—	100	125	175	—
1728 D	—	—	100	125	175	—

KM# 24a 1/2 REAL
1.6900 g., 0.9160 Silver **Ruler:** Philip V **Obv:** Legend around crowned PHILIPVS monogram **Rev:** Legend around cross, lions and castles **Note:** Struck at Mexico City Mint, mint mark M, Mo.

Date	Mintage	Good	VG	F	VF	XF
ND(1729-33)	—	—	20.00	35.00	60.00	—
Date off flan						
1729 R	—	—	90.00	120	150	—

Date	Mintage	Good	VG	F	VF	XF
1730 R	—	—	90.00	120	150	—
1731 F	—	—	90.00	120	150	—
1732/1 F	—	—	90.00	120	150	—
1732 F	—	—	90.00	120	150	—
1733/2 F	—	—	90.00	120	150	—
1733 F	—	—	90.00	120	150	—

KM# 25 1/2 REAL
1.6900 g., 0.9310 Silver **Ruler:** Luis I **Obv:** Legend around crowned LVDOVICVS monogram **Rev:** Legend around cross, lions and castles **Note:** Struck at Mexico City Mint, mint mark M, Mo.

Date	Mintage	Good	VG	F	VF	XF
ND(1724-25)	—	—	125	200	250	—
Date off flan						
1724 D	—	—	325	450	550	—
1725 D	—	—	325	450	550	—

KM# 30 REAL
3.3800 g., 0.9310 Silver **Ruler:** Philip V **Obv:** Legend and date around crowned arms **Obv. Legend:** PHILIPVS V DEI G **Note:** Struck at Mexico City Mint, mint mark M, Mo.

Date	Mintage	Good	VG	F	VF	XF
ND(1701-28)	—	—	30.00	50.00	70.00	—
Date off flan						
1701 L	—	—	125	175	275	—
1702 L	—	—	125	175	275	—
1703 L	—	—	125	175	275	—
1704 L	—	—	125	175	275	—
1705 L	—	—	125	175	275	—
1706 J	—	—	125	175	275	—
1707 J	—	—	125	175	275	—
1708 J	—	—	125	175	275	—
1709 J	—	—	125	175	275	—
1710 J	—	—	125	175	275	—
1711 J	—	—	125	175	275	—
1712 J	—	—	125	175	275	—
1713 J	—	—	125	175	275	—
1714 J	—	—	125	175	275	—
1715 J	—	—	100	175	275	—
1716 J	—	—	100	175	275	—
1717 J	—	—	100	175	275	—
1718 J	—	—	100	175	275	—

Date	Mintage	Good	VG	F	VF	XF
1719 J	—	—	100	175	275	—
1720/19 J	—	—	100	175	275	—
1720 J	—	—	100	175	275	—
1721 J	—	—	100	175	275	—
1722 J	—	—	100	175	275	—
1723 J	—	—	100	175	275	—
1726 D	—	—	100	175	275	—
1727 D	—	—	100	175	275	—
1728 D	—	—	100	175	275	—

KM# 30a REAL
3.3800 g., 0.9160 Silver **Ruler:** Philip V **Obv:** Legend and date around crowned arms **Obv. Legend:** PHILIPVS V DEI G **Note:** Struck at Mexico City Mint, mint mark M, Mo.

Date	Mintage	Good	VG	F	VF	XF
ND(1729-32) Date off flan	—	—	25.00	40.00	65.00	—
1729 R	—	—	90.00	125	175	—
1730 R	—	—	90.00	125	175	—
1730 F	—	—	90.00	125	175	—
1730 G	—	—	90.00	125	175	—
1731 F	—	—	90.00	125	175	—
1732 F	—	—	90.00	125	175	—

KM# A31 REAL
3.3834 g., 0.9310 Silver .1013 oz. ASW **Ruler:** Luis I **Note:** A significant portion of the legend must be visibile for proper attribution. Struck at Mexico City Mint, mint mark M, Mo.

Date	Mintage	Good	VG	F	VF	XF
1724 D Rare	—	—	—	—	—	—
1725 D Rare	—	—	—	—	—	—

KM# 35 2 REALES
6.7700 g., 0.9310 Silver **Ruler:** Philip V **Obv:** Legend and date around crowned arms **Obv. Legend:** PHILIPVS V DEI G **Note:** Struck at Mexico City Mint, mint mark M, Mo.

Date	Mintage	Good	VG	F	VF	XF
ND(1701-28) Date off flan	—	—	45.00	65.00	100	—
1701 L	—	—	125	150	250	—
1702 L	—	—	125	150	250	—
1703 L	—	—	125	150	250	—
1704 L	—	—	125	150	250	—
1705 L	—	—	125	150	250	—
1706 J	—	—	125	150	250	—
1707 J	—	—	125	150	250	—
1708 J	—	—	125	150	250	—
1710 J	—	—	125	150	250	—
1711 J	—	—	125	150	250	—
1712 J	—	—	125	150	250	—
1713 J	—	—	125	150	250	—
1714 J	—	—	150	185	300	—
1715 J	—	—	150	185	300	—
1716 J	—	—	150	185	300	—
1717 J	—	—	150	185	300	—
1718 J	—	—	150	185	300	—
1719 J	—	—	150	185	300	—
1720 J	—	—	150	185	300	—
1721 J	—	—	150	185	300	—
1722 J	—	—	150	185	300	—
1723 J	—	—	150	185	300	—
1724 J	—	—	150	185	300	—
1726 D	—	—	150	185	300	—
1727 D	—	—	150	185	300	—
1728 D	—	—	150	185	300	—

KM# 35a 2 REALES
6.7700 g., 0.9160 Silver **Ruler:** Philip V **Obv:** Legend and date around crowned arms **Obv. Legend:** PHILIPVS V DEI G **Note:** Struck at Mexico City Mint, mint mark M, Mo.

Date	Mintage	Good	VG	F	VF	XF
ND(1729-32) Date off flan	—	—	40.00	60.00	90.00	—
1729 R	—	—	100	125	150	—
1730 R	—	—	100	125	150	—

Date	Mintage	Good	VG	F	VF	XF
1731 F	—	—	100	125	150	—
1731/0 F	—	—	100	125	150	—
1732 F	—	—	100	125	150	—

KM# 40 4 REALES
13.5400 g., 0.9310 Silver **Ruler:** Philip V **Obv:** Legend and date around crowned arms **Obv. Legend:** PHILIPVS V DEI G **Note:** Struck at Mexico City Mint, mint mark M, Mo.

Date	Mintage	Good	VG	F	VF	XF
1701 L	—	—	175	250	375	—
1702 L	—	—	175	250	375	—
1703 L	—	—	175	250	375	—
1704 L	—	—	175	250	375	—
1705 L	—	—	175	250	375	—
1706 J	—	—	175	250	375	—
1707 J	—	—	175	250	375	—
1708 J	—	—	175	250	375	—
1709 J	—	—	175	250	375	—
1710 J	—	—	175	250	375	—
1711 J	—	—	175	250	375	—
1712 J	—	—	175	250	375	—
1713 J	—	—	175	250	375	—
1714 J	—	—	175	250	375	—
1715 J	—	—	125	225	375	—
1716 J	—	—	200	300	500	—
1717 J	—	—	200	300	500	—
1718 J	—	—	200	300	500	—
1719 J	—	—	200	300	500	—
1720 J	—	—	200	300	500	—
1721 J	—	—	200	300	500	—
1722 J	—	—	200	300	500	—
1723 J	—	—	200	300	500	—
1726 D	—	—	200	300	500	—
1727 D	—	—	200	300	500	—
1728 D	—	—	200	300	500	—

KM# 40a 4 REALES

13.5400 g., 0.9160 Silver **Ruler:** Philip V **Obv:** Legend and date around crowned arms **Obv. Legend:** PHILIPVS V DEI G **Note:** Struck at Mexico City Mint, mint mark M, Mo.

Date	Mintage	Good	VG	F	VF	XF
ND(1729-33) Date off flan	—	—	50.00	70.00	100	—
1729 D	—	—	125	200	275	—
1730 R	—	—	125	200	275	—
1730 G	—	—	125	200	275	—
1731 F	—	—	125	200	275	—
1732/1 F	—	—	125	175	250	—

Date	Mintage	Good	VG	F	VF	XF
1732 F	—	—	125	175	250	—
1733/2 F	—	—	125	175	250	—

KM# 41 4 REALES
13.5400 g., 0.9160 Silver **Ruler:** Philip V **Obv:** Legend and date around crowned arms **Obv. Legend:** PHILIPVS V DEI G **Rev:** Legend around cross, lions and castles **Note:** Klippe. Similar to KM#40a. Struck at Mexico City Mint, mint mark M, Mo.

Date	Mintage	Good	VG	F	VF	XF
1733 F	—	—	450	600	750	—
1733 MF	—	—	450	600	750	—
1734/3 MF	—	—	450	600	750	—

KM# 42 4 REALES
13.5400 g., 0.9310 Silver **Ruler:** Luis I **Obv:** Legend around crowned arms **Obv. Legend:** LVDOVICUS I DEI G **Rev:** Legend around cross, lions and castles **Note:** A significant portion of the legend must be visible for proper attribution. Struck at Mexico City Mint, mint mark M, Mo.

Date	Mintage	Good	VG	F	VF	XF
1724 D Rare	—	—	—	—	—	—
1725 D Rare	—	—	—	—	—	—

KM# 46 8 REALES
27.0700 g., 0.9310 Silver **Ruler:** Charles II **Obv:** Legend and date around crowned arms **Obv. Legend:** CAROLVS II DEI G **Rev:** Legend around cross, lions and castles **Note:** Struck at Mexico City Mint, mint mark M, Mo.

Date	Mintage	Good	VG	F	VF	XF
1697 L	—	—	600	900	1,500	—
1701 L	—	—	700	1,000	1,700	—

Date	Mintage	Good	VG	F	VF	XF
1707 J	—	—	200	350	500	—
1708 J	—	—	200	350	500	—
1709 J	—	—	200	350	500	—
1710 J	—	—	200	350	500	—
1711 J	—	—	175	300	475	—
1712 J	—	—	175	300	475	—
1713 J	—	—	175	300	475	—
1714 J	—	—	175	300	475	—
1715 J	—	—	175	300	475	—
1716 J	—	—	375	575	800	—
1717 J	—	—	375	575	800	—
1718/7 J	—	—	375	575	800	—
1718 J	—	—	350	500	800	—
1719 J	—	—	350	500	800	—
1720 J	—	—	350	500	800	—
1721 J	—	—	350	500	800	—
1722 J	—	—	350	500	800	—
1723 J	—	—	350	500	800	—
1724 D	—	—	350	500	800	—
1725 D	—	—	350	500	800	—
1726 D	—	—	350	500	800	—
1727 D	—	—	350	500	800	—
1728 D	—	—	400	600	1,000	—

KM# 47a 8 REALES
27.0700 g., 0.9160 Silver **Ruler:** Philip V **Obv:** Legend and date around crowned arms **Obv. Legend:** PHILIPVS V DEI G **Rev:** Legend around cross, lions and castles **Note:** Struck at Mexico City Mint, mint mark M, Mo.

Date	Mintage	Good	VG	F	VF	XF
ND(1729-33) Date off flan	—	—	70.00	90.00	110	—
1729 R	—	—	150	250	400	—
1730 G/R	—	—	150	250	400	—
1730 R	—	—	150	250	400	—
1730 G	—	—	150	250	400	—
1730 F	—	—	150	250	400	—
1731/0 F	—	—	150	250	400	—
1731 F	—	—	150	250	400	—
1732/1 F	—	—	150	250	400	—
1732 F	—	—	150	250	400	—
1733/2 F	—	—	150	250	400	—
1733 F	—	—	150	250	400	—

KM# 47 8 REALES
27.0700 g., 0.9310 Silver **Ruler:** Philip V **Obv:** Legend and date around crowned arms **Obv. Legend:** PHILIPVS V DEI G **Rev:** Legend around cross, lions and castles **Note:** Struck at Mexico City Mint, mint mark M, Mo.

Date	Mintage	Good	VG	F	VF	XF
ND(1702-28) Date off flan	—	—	70.00	90.00	120	—
1702 L	—	—	200	350	500	—
1703 L	—	—	200	350	500	—
1704 L Rare	—	—	—	—	—	—
1705 L	—	—	200	350	600	—
1706 J	—	—	200	350	600	—

KM# 48 8 REALES
0.9160 g., Silver **Ruler:** Philip V **Note:** Klippe. Similar to KM#47a. Mint mark M, Mo.

Date	Mintage	Good	VG	F	VF	XF
ND(1733-34) Date off flan	—	—	150	200	300	—
1733 F	—	—	550	750	1,150	—
1733 MF	—	—	350	500	650	—
1734/3 MF	—	—	500	750	1,000	—
1734 MF	—	—	500	750	1,000	—

KM# 49   8 REALES
27.0700 g., 0.9310 Silver **Ruler:** Luis I **Obv:** Legend and date around crowned arms **Obv. Legend:** LVDOVICVS I DEI G **Rev:** Legend around cross, lions and castles **Note:** A significant portion of the legend must be visible for proper attribution. Struck at Mexico City Mint, mint mark M, Mo.

Date	Mintage	Good	VG	F	VF	XF
ND(1724-25) Date off flan; Rare	—	—	—	—	—	—
1724 D Rare	—	—	—	—	—	—
1725 D Rare	—	—	—	—	—	—

KM# 50   ESCUDO
3.3800 g., 0.9170 Gold **Ruler:** Charles II **Obv:** Legend and date around crowned arms **Obv. Legend:** CAROLVS II DEI G **Rev:** Legend around cross, lions and castles **Note:** Struck at Mexico City Mint, mint mark MXo.

Date	Mintage	VG	F	VF	XF	Unc
1701/0MXo L	—	—	3,000	4,000	5,000	—

KM# 51.1   ESCUDO
3.3800 g., 0.9170 Gold .0997 oz. AGW **Ruler:** Philip V **Obv:** Legend and date around crowned arms **Obv. Legend:** PHILIPVS V DEI G **Rev:** Legend around cross, lions and castles **Note:** Struck at Mexico City Mint, mint mark MXo.

Date	Mintage	VG	F	VF	XF	Unc
ND(1702-13) Date off flan	—	—	1,000	1,350	1,500	—
1702MXo L	—	—	1,500	2,500	3,500	—
1703/2MXo L	—	—	1,500	2,500	3,500	—
1704MXo L	—	—	1,500	2,500	3,500	—
1707MXo J	—	—	1,500	2,500	3,500	—
1708MXo J	—	—	1,500	2,500	3,500	—
1709MXo J	—	—	1,500	2,500	3,500	—
1710MXo J	—	—	1,500	2,500	3,500	—
1711MXo J	—	—	1,500	2,500	3,500	—
1712MXo J	—	—	1,500	2,500	3,500	—
1713MXo J	—	—	1,500	2,500	3,500	—

KM# 51.2   ESCUDO
3.3800 g., 0.9170 Gold .0997 oz. AGW **Ruler:** Philip V **Obv:** Legend and date around crowned arms **Obv. Legend:** PHILIPVS V DEI G **Rev:** Legend around cross, lions and castles **Note:** Struck at Mexico City Mint, mint mark Mo.

Date	Mintage	VG	F	VF	XF	Unc
ND(1702-13) Date off flan	—	—	1,200	1,500	1,750	—
1712Mo J	—	—	2,000	3,000	4,000	—
1714Mo J	—	—	1,400	2,000	3,000	—
1714Mo J J's 1's (J7J4J)	—	—	2,000	3,000	4,000	—
1715Mo J	—	—	2,000	3,000	4,000	—
1727Mo J Rare	—	—	—	—	—	—
1728Mo J Rare	—	—	—	—	—	—

Note: Die-struck counterfiets of 1731 F exist

KM# 52   2 ESCUDOS
6.7700 g., 0.9170 Gold .1996 oz. AGW **Ruler:** Philip V **Obv:** Legend and date around crowned arms **Obv. Legend:** CAROLVS II DEI G **Rev:** Legend around cross **Note:** Struck at Mexico City Mint, mint mark MXo.

Date	Mintage	VG	F	VF	XF	Unc
1701MXo L	—	—	4,000	2,200	6,000	—

KM# 53.1   2 ESCUDOS
6.7700 g., 0.9170 Gold .1996 oz. AGW **Ruler:** Philip V **Obv:** Legend and date around crowned arms **Obv. Legend:** PHILIPVS V DEI G **Rev:** Legend around cross **Note:** Struck at Mexico City Mint, mint mark MXo.

Date	Mintage	VG	F	VF	XF	Unc
ND(1704-13) Date off flan	—	—	1,200	1,500	1,750	—
1704MXo L	—	—	2,750	3,750	4,750	—
1708MXo J	—	—	2,750	3,750	4,750	—
1710MXo J	—	—	2,750	3,750	4,750	—
1711MXo J	—	—	2,750	3,750	4,750	—
1712MXo J	—	—	2,750	3,750	4,750	—
1713MXo J	—	—	2,750	3,750	4,750	—

KM# 53.2   2 ESCUDOS
6.7700 g., 0.9170 Gold .1996 oz. AGW **Ruler:** Philip V **Obv:** Legend and date around crowned arms **Obv. Legend:** PHILIPVS V DEI G **Rev:** Legend around cross **Note:** Struck counterfeits exist for 1731. Struck at Mexico City Mint, mint mark Mo.

Date	Mintage	VG	F	VF	XF	Unc
ND(1714-31) Date off flan	—	—	1,500	1,750	2,500	—
1714Mo J	—	—	—	2,500	3,500	—
1717Mo J Rare	—	—	—	—	—	—
1722Mo J Rare	—	—	—	—	—	—
1729Mo R Rare	—	—	—	—	—	—
1731Mo F Rare	—	—	—	—	—	—

KM# A54   2 ESCUDOS
6.7700 g., 0.9170 Gold .1996 oz. AGW **Ruler:** Luis I **Obv:** Legend and date around crowned arms **Obv. Legend:** LVDOVICVS I DEI G. **Rev:** Legend around cross **Note:** A significant portion of the legend must be visible for proper attribution. Struck at Mexico City Mint, mint mark MXo.

Date	Mintage	VG	F	VF	XF	Unc
NDMXo F Rare	—	—	—	—	—	—

KM# 55.1 4 ESCUDOS
13.5400 g., 0.9170 Gold .3992 oz. AGW **Ruler:** Philip V **Obv:** Legend and date around crowned arms **Obv. Legend:** PHILIPVS V DEI G **Rev:** Legend around cross **Note:** Struck at Mexico City Mint, mint mark MXo.

Date	Mintage	VG	F	VF	XF	Unc
ND(1705-13) Date off flan	—	—	2,500	3,000	4,000	—
1705MXo J	—	—	4,000	5,750	6,750	—
1706MXo L	—	—	4,000	5,750	6,750	—
1711MXo J	—	—	4,000	5,750	6,750	—
1712MXo J	—	—	4,000	5,750	6,750	—
1713MXo J	—	—	4,000	5,750	6,750	—

KM# 55.2 4 ESCUDOS
13.5400 g., 0.9170 Gold .3992 oz. AGW **Ruler:** Philip V **Obv:** Legend and date around crowned arms **Obv. Legend:** PHILIPVS V DEI G **Rev:** Legend around cross **Note:** Struck at Mexico City Mint, mint mark Mo.

Date	Mintage	VG	F	VF	XF	Unc
ND(1714-20) Date off flan	—	—	2,500	3,750	5,000	—
1714Mo J	—	—	—	5,750	7,500	—
1715Mo J	—	—	—	5,750	7,500	—
1720Mo J Rare	—	—	—	—	—	—

KM# 57.1 8 ESCUDOS
27.0700 g., 0.9170 Gold .7980 oz. AGW **Ruler:** Philip V **Obv:** Legend and date around crowned arms **Obv. Legend:** PHILIPVS V DEI G **Rev:** Legend around cross **Note:** Struck at Mexico City Mint, mint mark MXo.

Date	Mintage	VG	F	VF	XF	Unc
ND(1701-13) Date off flan	—	—	2,000	3,000	4,000	—
1701MXo L	—	—	6,000	7,500	9,000	—
1703MXo L	—	—	6,000	7,500	9,000	—
1706MXo J	—	—	6,000	7,500	9,000	—
1708MXo J	—	—	6,000	7,500	9,000	—
1709MXo J	—	—	6,000	7,500	9,000	—
1710MXo J	—	—	6,000	7,500	9,000	—
1711MXo J	—	—	3,500	4,000	5,750	—
1712MXo J	—	—	3,500	4,000	5,750	—
1713MXo J	—	—	3,500	4,000	5,750	—

KM# 57.2 8 ESCUDOS
27.0700 g., 0.9170 Gold .7980 oz. AGW **Ruler:** Philip V **Obv:** Legend and date around crowned arms **Obv. Legend:** PHILIPVS V DEI G **Rev:** Legend around cross **Note:** Struck at Mexico City Mint, mint mark Mo.

Date	Mintage	VG	F	VF	XF	Unc
ND(1714-32)Mo Date off flan	—	—	2,750	3,750	4,750	—
1714Mo J	—	—	5,000	6,000	7,500	—

Date	Mintage	VG	F	VF	XF	Unc
1714Mo Date over GRAT on obverse	—	—	6,000	7,500	9,000	—
1715Mo J Rare	—	—	—	—	—	—
1717/6Mo J Rare	—	—	—	—	—	—
1720/19Mo J Rare	—	—	—	—	—	—
1723Mo J Rare	—	—	—	—	—	—
1727/6Mo D Rare	—	—	—	—	—	—
1728/7Mo D Rare	—	—	—	—	—	—
1729Mo R Rare	—	—	—	—	—	—
1730Mo R Rare	—	—	—	—	—	—
1730Mo F Rare	—	—	—	—	—	—
1731Mo F Rare	—	—	—	—	—	—
1732Mo F Rare	—	—	—	—	—	—

KM# 57.3 8 ESCUDOS
27.0700 g., 0.9170 Gold .7980 oz. AGW **Obv:** Date around crowned arms **Obv. Legend:** PHILIPVS V DEI G **Rev:** Legend and date around cross **Note:** Struck at Mexico City Mint, mint mark Mo.

Date	Mintage	VG	F	VF	XF	Unc
1714Mo J Date on reverse	—	—	6,000	7,500	9,000	—

KM# 58 8 ESCUDOS
27.0700 g., 0.9170 Gold .7980 oz. AGW **Ruler:** Luis I **Obv:** Legend and date around crowned arms **Obv. Legend:** LVDOVICVS I DEI G **Rev:** Legend around cross **Note:** A significant portion of the legend must be visible for proper attribution. Struck at Mexico City Mint, mint mark Mo.

Date	Mintage	VG	F	VF	XF	Unc
ND(1724-25)Mo D Rare	—	—	—	—	—	—

ROYAL COINAGE

Struck on specially prepared round planchets using well centered dies in excellent condition to prove the quality of the minting to the Viceroy or even to the King.

KM# R24 1/2 REAL
1.6917 g., 0.9130 Silver .0506 oz. ASW **Ruler:** Philip V **Note:** Normally found holed. Struck at Mexico City Mint, mint mark Mo.

Date	Mintage	Good	VG	F	VF	XF
1715Mo J	—	—	250	500	750	—
1719Mo J	—	—	250	500	750	—
1721Mo J	—	—	250	500	750	—
1726Mo D	—	—	250	500	750	—
1727Mo D	—	—	250	500	750	—

KM# R24a 1/2 REAL
1.6917 g., 0.9170 Silver .0498 oz. ASW **Ruler:** Philip V **Note:** Normally found holed. Struck at Mexico City Mint, mark mark Mo.

Date	Mintage	Good	VG	F	VF	XF
1730Mo D	—	—	250	500	750	—

KM# R25 1/2 REAL
1.6917 g., 0.9310 Silver .0506 oz. ASW **Ruler:** Luis I **Note:** Struck at Mexico City Mint, mint mark Mo.

Date	Mintage	Good	VG	F	VF	XF
1724Mo D Rare	—	—	—	—	—	—

KM# R29 1/2 REAL
3.3834 g., 0.9310 Silver .1013 oz. ASW **Ruler:** Charles II **Obv. Legend:** CAROLVS II DEI G **Note:** Struck at Mexico City Mint, mint mark Mo.

Date	Mintage	Good	VG	F	VF	XF
1699Mo L Rare	—	—	—	—	—	—

KM# R30 REAL
3.3834 g., 0.9310 Silver .1013 oz. ASW **Ruler:** Philip V **Obv. Legend:** PHILIPVS V DEI G **Note:** Struck at Mexico City Mint, mint mark Mo.

Date	Mintage	Good	VG	F	VF	XF
1715Mo J Rare	—	—	—	—	—	—
1716Mo J Rare	—	—	—	—	—	—
1718Mo J Rare	—	—	—	—	—	—

KM# R35 2 REALES
6.7668 g., 0.9310 Silver .2026 oz. ASW **Ruler:** Philip V **Obv. Legend:** PHILIPVS V DEI G **Note:** Struck at Mexico City Mint, mint mark Mo.

Date	Mintage	Good	VG	F	VF	XF
1715Mo J Rare	—	—	—	—	—	—

KM# R35a 2 REALES
6.7668 g., 0.9170 Silver .1995 oz. ASW **Ruler:** Philip V **Note:** Struck at Mexico City Mint, mint mark Mo.

Date	Mintage	Good	VG	F	VF	XF
1730Mo R Rare	—	—	—	—	—	—

KM# R40 4 REALES
13.5337 g., 0.9310 Silver .4051 oz. ASW **Ruler:** Philip V
Obv. Legend: PHILIPVS V DEI G **Note:** Struck at Mexico
City Mint, mint mark Mo.

Date	Mintage	Good	VG	F	VF	XF
1716Mo J Rare	—	—	—	—	—	—
1719Mo J Rare	—	—	—	—	—	—
1721Mo J Rare	—	—	—	—	—	—
1722Mo J Rare	—	—	—	—	—	—
1723Mo J Rare	—	—	—	—	—	—

KM# R47 8 REALES
27.0674 g., 0.9310 Silver .8102 oz. ASW **Ruler:** Philip V
Obv. Legend: PHILIPVS V DEI G **Note:** Struck at Mexico
City Mint, mint mark Mo.

Date	Mintage	Good	VG	F	VF	XF
1702Mo L Rare	—	—	—	—	—	—
1703Mo L Rare	—	—	—	—	—	—
1705Mo J Rare	—	—	—	—	—	—
1706Mo J Rare	—	—	—	—	—	—
1709Mo J Rare	—	—	—	—	—	—
1711Mo J Rare	—	—	—	—	—	—
1714Mo J Rare	—	—	—	—	—	—
1715Mo J Rare	—	—	—	—	—	—
1716Mo J Rare	—	—	—	—	—	—
1717Mo J Rare	—	—	—	—	—	—
1719Mo J Rare	—	—	—	—	—	—
1721Mo J Rare	—	—	—	—	—	—
1722Mo J Rare	—	—	—	—	—	—
1723Mo J Rare	—	—	—	—	—	—
1724Mo D Rare	—	—	—	—	—	—
1725Mo D Rare	—	—	—	—	—	—
1726/5Mo D Rare	—	—	—	—	—	—
1726Mo D Rare	—	—	—	—	—	—
1727Mo D Rare	—	—	—	—	—	—

KM# R47a 8 REALES
27.0674 g., 0.9170 Silver .7980 oz. ASW **Note:** Struck at
Mexico City Mint, mint mark Mo.

Date	Mintage	Good	VG	F	VF	XF
1729 R Rare	—	—	—	—	—	—
1730 R/D Rare	—	—	—	—	—	—
1730 G Rare	—	—	—	—	—	—

KM# R49 8 REALES
27.0674 g., 0.9310 Silver .8102 oz. ASW **Ruler:** Luis I **Note:**
Struck at Mexico City Mint, mint mark Mo.

Date	Mintage	Good	VG	F	VF	XF
1724 D Rare	—	—	—	—	—	—
1725 D Rare	—	—	—	—	—	—

KM# R51.2 ESCUDO
3.3834 g., 0.9170 Gold .0997 oz. AGW **Note:** Struck at
Mexico City Mint, mint mark Mo.

Date	Mintage	Good	VG	F	VF	XF
1714Mo J Rare	—	—	—	—	—	—
1715Mo J Rare	—	—	—	—	—	—

KM# R53.1 2 ESCUDOS
6.7668 g., 0.9170 Gold .1995 oz. AGW **Note:** Struck at
Mexico City Mint, mint mark MXo.

Date	Mintage	Good	VG	F	VF	XF
1711MXo J Rare	—	—	—	—	—	—
1712MXo J Rare	—	—	—	—	—	—

KM# R55.1 4 ESCUDOS
13.5337 g., 0.9170 Gold .3990 oz. AGW **Note:** Struck at
Mexico City Mint, mint mark M, Mo.

Date	Mintage	Good	VG	F	VF	XF
1711 Rare	—	—	—	—	—	—

KM# R55.2 4 ESCUDOS
13.5337 g., 0.9170 Gold .3990 oz. AGW **Note:** Struck at
Mexico City Mint, mint mark M, Mo.

Date	Mintage	Good	VG	F	VF	XF
1714 Rare	—	—	—	—	—	—

KM# R56 8 ESCUDOS
27.0674 g., 0.9170 Gold .7980 oz. AGW **Note:** Fully struck
sample specimens referred to as "Royal" strikes are seldom
encountered. Struck at Mexico City Mint, mint mark MXo.

Date	Mintage	Good	VG	F	VF	XF
1695MXo L Rare	—	—	—	—	—	—
1698MXo L Rare	—	—	—	—	—	—

KM# R57.1 8 ESCUDOS
27.0674 g., 0.9170 Gold .7980 oz. AGW **Ruler:** Philip V
Note: Struck at Mexico City Mint, mint mark MXo.

Date	Mintage	Good	VG	F	VF	XF
1702MXo L Rare	—	—	—	—	—	—
1711MXo J Rare	—	—	—	—	—	—
1712MXo J Rare	—	—	—	—	—	—
1713MXo J Rare	—	—	—	—	—	—

KM# R57.3 8 ESCUDOS
27.0674 g., 0.9170 Gold .7980 oz. AGW **Note:** Struck at
Mexico City Mint, mint mark Mo.

Date	Mintage	Good	VG	F	VF	XF
1714Mo J Rare	—	—	—	—	—	—
1715Mo J Rare	—	—	—	—	—	—
1717Mo J Rare	—	—	—	—	—	—
1718Mo J Rare	—	—	—	—	—	—
1723Mo J Rare	—	—	—	—	—	—

MILLED COINAGE

16 Pilones = 1 Real; 8 Tiaco = 1 Real;
16 Reales = 1 Escudo

KM# 59 1/8 PILON (1/16 Real)
Copper **Obv:** Crowned F VII monogram **Rev:** Castles and
lions in wreath **Note:** Mint mark M, Mo.

Date	Mintage	VG	F	VF	XF	Unc
1814	—	10.00	20.00	45.00	120	—
1815	—	10.00	20.00	45.00	120	—

KM# 62 1/4 REAL
0.8458 g., 0.8960 Silver .0244 oz. ASW **Obv:** Castle **Rev:**
Lion **Note:** Mint mark M, Mo.

Date	Mintage	VG	F	VF	XF	Unc
1796	—	15.00	30.00	55.00	90.00	—
1797	—	15.00	30.00	55.00	90.00	—
1798	—	12.50	22.00	50.00	75.00	—
1799/8	—	12.50	22.00	50.00	75.00	—
1799	—	10.00	20.00	40.00	70.00	—
1800	—	10.00	25.00	55.00	90.00	—
1801/0	—	10.00	20.00	40.00	70.00	—
1801	—	10.00	20.00	40.00	70.00	—
1802	—	10.00	20.00	40.00	70.00	—
1803	—	10.00	20.00	40.00	70.00	—
1804	—	10.00	20.00	40.00	75.00	—
1805/4	—	12.50	25.00	55.00	85.00	—
1805	—	10.00	22.00	50.00	75.00	—
1806	—	10.00	22.00	50.00	80.00	—
1807/797	—	15.00	30.00	55.00	85.00	—
1807	—	12.50	25.00	50.00	80.00	—
1808	—	12.50	25.00	50.00	80.00	—
1809/8	—	12.50	25.00	50.00	80.00	—
1809	—	12.50	25.00	50.00	80.00	—
1810	—	12.50	25.00	50.00	75.00	—

Date	Mintage	VG	F	VF	XF	Unc
1811	—	12.50	25.00	50.00	75.00	—
1812	—	12.50	25.00	50.00	75.00	—
1813	—	10.00	20.00	40.00	70.00	—
1815	—	12.50	22.00	50.00	75.00	—
1816	—	10.00	20.00	40.00	70.00	—

KM# 63   1/4 TLACO (1/8 Real)
Copper **Obv:** Legend around crowned F. VII **Obv. Legend:** FERDIN. VII... **Note:** Mint mark M, Mo.

Date	Mintage	VG	F	VF	XF	Unc
1814	—	12.00	25.00	50.00	150	—
1815	—	12.00	25.00	50.00	150	—
1816	—	12.00	25.00	50.00	150	—

KM# 64   2/4 SENAL (1/4 Real)
Copper **Obv:** Legend around crowned F. VII **Obv. Legend:** FERDIN. VII... **Note:** Mint mark M, Mo.

Date	Mintage	VG	F	VF	XF	Unc
1814	—	12.00	25.00	50.00	150	—
1815/4	—	15.00	30.00	60.00	165	—
1815	—	12.00	25.00	50.00	150	—
1816	—	12.00	25.00	50.00	150	—
1821	—	20.00	40.00	75.00	200	—

KM# 65   1/2 REAL
1.6917 g., 0.9170 Silver .0498 oz. ASW **Ruler:** Philip V **Obv. Legend:** PHILIP. V. D. G. HISPAN. ET IND. REX **Note:** Mint mark M, Mo, MX.

Date	Mintage	VG	F	VF	XF	Unc
1732 Rare	—	—	—	—	—	—
1732 F	—	500	800	1,200	2,000	—
1733 MF (MX)	—	400	600	1,000	1,500	—
1733 F	—	200	325	550	800	—
1733/2 MF	—	300	400	600	800	—
1733 MF	—	300	400	600	800	—
1734/3 MF	—	12.00	25.00	45.00	85.00	—
1734 MF	—	12.00	25.00	45.00	85.00	—
1735/4 MF	—	10.00	20.00	45.00	85.00	—
1735 MF	—	10.00	20.00	45.00	85.00	—
1736/5 MF	—	10.00	20.00	45.00	85.00	—
1736 MF	—	10.00	20.00	45.00	85.00	—
1737/6 MF	—	10.00	20.00	45.00	85.00	—
1737 MF	—	10.00	20.00	45.00	85.00	—
1738/7 MF	—	10.00	20.00	45.00	85.00	—
1738 MF	—	10.00	20.00	45.00	85.00	—
1739 MF	—	10.00	20.00	45.00	85.00	—
1740/30 MF	—	8.00	18.00	40.00	75.00	—
1740 MF	—	8.00	18.00	40.00	75.00	—
1741 MF	—	8.00	18.00	40.00	75.00	—

KM# 66   1/2 REAL
1.6900 g., 0.9170 Silver .0498 oz. ASW **Obv. Legend:** PHS. V. D. G. HISP. ET IND. R **Note:** Struck at Mexico City Mint, mint mark M, Mo.

Date	Mintage	VG	F	VF	XF	Unc
1742 M	—	8.00	18.00	40.00	75.00	—
1743 M	—	8.00	18.00	40.00	75.00	—
1744/3 M	—	8.00	18.00	40.00	75.00	—
1744 M	—	8.00	18.00	40.00	75.00	—
1745 M Rare	—	—	—	—	—	—

Note: Legend variation: PHS. V. D. G. HISP. EST IND. R

1745 M	—	8.00	18.00	40.00	75.00	—
1746/5 M	—	8.00	18.00	40.00	75.00	—
1746 M	—	8.00	18.00	40.00	75.00	—
1747 M	—	8.00	18.00	40.00	75.00	—

KM# 67.1   1/2 REAL
1.6900 g., 0.9170 Silver .0498 oz. ASW **Obv:** Royal crown **Obv. Legend:** FRD. VI. D. G. HIPS. ET IND. R **Note:** Struck at Mexico City Mint, mint mark M, Mo.

Date	Mintage	VG	F	VF	XF	Unc
1747/6 M	—	—	—	—	—	—
1747 M	—	8.00	18.00	40.00	75.00	—
1748/7 M	—	8.00	18.00	40.00	75.00	—
1748 M	—	8.00	18.00	40.00	75.00	—
1749 M	—	8.00	18.00	40.00	75.00	—
1750 M	—	8.00	18.00	40.00	75.00	—
1751 M	—	10.00	20.00	45.00	85.00	—
1752 M	—	8.00	18.00	40.00	75.00	—
1753 M	—	8.00	18.00	40.00	75.00	—
1754 M	—	12.00	25.00	55.00	100	—
1755/6 M	—	12.00	25.00	55.00	100	—
1755 M	—	8.00	18.00	40.00	75.00	—
1756/5 M	—	8.00	18.00	40.00	75.00	—
1756 M	—	8.00	18.00	40.00	75.00	—
1757/6 M	—	8.00	18.00	40.00	75.00	—
1757 M	—	8.00	18.00	40.00	75.00	—

KM# 67.2   1/2 REAL
1.6917 g., 0.9170 Silver .0498 oz. ASW **Obv:** Different crown **Note:** Struck at Mexico City Mint, mint mark M, Mo.

Date	Mintage	VG	F	VF	XF	Unc
1757 M	—	8.00	18.00	40.00	75.00	—
1758/7 M	—	8.00	18.00	40.00	75.00	—
1758 M	—	8.00	18.00	40.00	75.00	—
1759 M	—	8.00	18.00	40.00	75.00	—
1760/59 M	—	8.00	18.00	40.00	75.00	—
1760 M	—	8.00	18.00	40.00	75.00	—

KM# 68   1/2 REAL
1.6900 g., 0.9170 Silver .0498 oz. ASW **Obv. Legend:** CAR. III. D. G. HISP. ET IND. R **Note:** Struck at Mexico City Mint, mint mark M, Mo.

Date	Mintage	VG	F	VF	XF	Unc
1760/59 M	—	8.00	18.00	40.00	75.00	—
1760 M	—	8.00	18.00	40.00	75.00	—
1761 M	—	8.00	18.00	40.00	75.00	—
1762 M	—	8.00	18.00	40.00	75.00	—
1763/2 M	—	8.00	18.00	40.00	75.00	—
1763 M	—	8.00	18.00	40.00	75.00	—
1764 M	—	8.00	18.00	40.00	75.00	—
1765/4 M	—	10.00	20.00	42.00	80.00	—
1765 M	—	8.00	18.00	40.00	75.00	—
1766 M	—	8.00	18.00	40.00	75.00	—
1767 M	—	10.00	20.00	45.00	85.00	—
1768/6 M	—	10.00	20.00	42.00	80.00	—
1768 M	—	8.00	18.00	40.00	75.00	—
1769 M	—	10.00	20.00	42.00	80.00	—
1770 M	—	10.00	20.00	42.00	80.00	—

Date	Mintage	VG	F	VF	XF	Unc
1770 F	—	15.00	30.00	60.00	100	—
1771 F	—	10.00	20.00	42.00	80.00	—

KM# 69.1 1/2 REAL
1.6900 g., 0.9030 Silver .0490 oz. ASW **Obv. Legend:**
CAROLUS. III. DEI. GRATIA **Rev:** Inverted FM and mint mark
Note: Struck at Mexico City Mint, mint mark Mo.

Date	Mintage	VG	F	VF	XF	Unc
1772Mo FM	—	5.00	12.00	27.00	65.00	—
1773Mo FM	—	4.50	10.00	25.00	55.00	—

KM# 69.2 1/2 REAL
1.6900 g., 0.9030 Silver .0491 oz. ASW **Obv. Legend:**
CAROLUS. III. DEI. GRATIA **Rev:** Normal initials and mint
mark **Note:** Struck at Mexico City Mint, mint mark Mo.

Date	Mintage	VG	F	VF	XF	Unc
1772Mo FF	—	9.00	18.00	35.00	80.00	—
1773Mo FM	—	4.50	10.00	25.00	60.00	—
1773Mo FM CAROLS (error)	—	75.00	150	250	400	—
1774Mo FM	—	4.50	10.00	25.00	55.00	—
1775Mo FM	—	4.50	10.00	25.00	55.00	—
1776Mo FM	—	4.50	10.00	25.00	55.00	—
1777/6Mo FM	—	10.00	18.00	35.00	75.00	—
1777Mo FM	—	7.00	15.00	30.00	65.00	—
1778Mo FF	—	4.50	10.00	25.00	55.00	—
1779Mo FF	—	4.50	10.00	25.00	55.00	—
1780/79Mo FF	—	6.00	12.50	30.00	75.00	—
1780Mo FF	—	4.50	10.00	25.00	55.00	—
1781Mo FF	—	4.50	10.00	25.00	55.00	—
1782/1Mo FF	—	6.00	12.50	30.00	75.00	—
1782Mo FF	—	4.50	10.00	25.00	55.00	—
1783Mo FF	—	4.50	10.00	25.00	55.00	—
1783Mo FM	—	125	300	450	—	—
1784Mo FF	—	4.50	10.00	25.00	55.00	—
1784Mo FM	—	7.00	15.00	35.00	80.00	—

KM# 69.2a 1/2 REAL
1.6917 g., 0.8960 Silver .0487 oz. ASW **Rev:** Normal initials
and mint mark **Note:** Struck at Mexico City Mint, mint mark M, Mo.

Date	Mintage	VG	F	VF	XF	Unc
1785/4 FM	—	7.00	15.00	35.00	80.00	—
1785 FM	—	5.00	12.00	27.00	60.00	—
1786 FM	—	4.50	10.00	25.00	55.00	—
1787 FM	—	4.50	10.00	25.00	55.00	—
1788 FM	—	4.50	10.00	25.00	55.00	—
1789 FM	—	8.00	16.00	40.00	100	—

KM# 70 1/2 REAL
1.6917 g., 0.8960 Silver .0487 oz. ASW **Obv:** Armored bust
of Charles III **Obv. Legend:** CAROLUS. IV... **Note:** Struck at
Mexico City Mint, mint mark M, Mo.

Date	Mintage	VG	F	VF	XF	Unc
1789 FM	—	12.00	25.00	50.00	100	—
1790 FM	—	12.00	25.00	50.00	100	—

KM# 71 1/2 REAL
1.6917 g., 0.8960 Silver .0487 oz. ASW **Obv:** Armored bust
of Charles III **Obv. Legend:** CAROLUS IIII... **Note:** Struck at
Mexico City Mint, mint mark M, Mo.

Date	Mintage	VG	F	VF	XF	Unc
1790 FM	—	12.00	25.00	50.00	100	—

KM# 72 1/2 REAL
1.6900 g., 0.9030 Silver .0490 oz. ASW **Obv:** Armored bust
of Charles IIII **Rev:** Pillars and arms **Note:** Mint mark M, Mo.

Date	Mintage	VG	F	VF	XF	Unc
1792 FM	—	6.00	12.00	25.00	50.00	—
1793 FM	—	6.00	12.00	25.00	50.00	—
1794/3 FM	—	7.50	15.00	30.00	75.00	—
1794 FM	—	5.00	10.00	22.00	45.00	—
1795 FM	—	4.00	10.00	22.00	45.00	—
1796 FM	—	4.00	10.00	22.00	45.00	—
1797 FM	—	4.00	10.00	22.00	45.00	—
1797/7 FM	—	5.00	11.50	25.00	50.00	—
1798 FM	—	4.00	10.00	22.00	45.00	—
1799 FM	—	4.00	10.00	22.00	45.00	—
1800/799 FM	—	5.00	11.50	25.00	50.00	—
1800 FM	—	4.00	10.00	22.00	45.00	—
1801 FM	—	7.50	15.00	30.00	80.00	—
1801 FT	—	4.00	10.00	22.00	45.00	—
1802 FT	—	4.00	10.00	22.00	45.00	—
1803 FT	—	5.00	11.50	25.00	50.00	—
1804 TH	—	4.00	10.00	22.00	45.00	—
1805 TH	—	4.00	10.00	22.00	45.00	—
1806 TH	—	4.00	10.00	22.00	45.00	—
1807/6 TH	—	5.00	11.50	25.00	50.00	—
1807 TH	—	4.00	10.00	22.00	45.00	—
1808/7 TH	—	5.00	11.50	25.00	50.00	—
1808 TH	—	4.00	10.00	22.00	45.00	—

KM# 73 1/2 REAL
1.6900 g., 0.9030 Silver .0490 oz. ASW **Obv:** Armored bust
of Ferdinand VII **Rev:** Pillars and arms **Note:** Mint mark M, Mo.

Date	Mintage	VG	F	VF	XF	Unc
1808 TH	—	3.50	8.00	20.00	35.00	—
1809 TH	—	3.50	8.00	20.00	35.00	—
1810 TH	—	5.00	10.00	22.00	45.00	—
1810 HJ	—	3.50	8.00	20.00	35.00	—
1811 HJ	—	3.50	8.00	20.00	35.00	—
1812/1 HJ	—	7.50	15.00	35.00	80.00	—
1812 HJ	—	3.50	8.00	20.00	35.00	—
1812 JJ	—	12.00	25.00	45.00	100	—
1813/2 JJ	—	12.00	25.00	45.00	100	—
1813 TH	—	3.50	8.00	20.00	35.00	—
1813 JJ	—	6.00	12.00	25.00	75.00	—
1813 HJ	—	7.50	15.00	35.00	90.00	—
1814/3 JJ	—	7.50	15.00	35.00	90.00	—
1814 JJ	—	5.00	10.00	22.00	45.00	—

KM# 74 1/2 REAL
1.6900 g., 0.9030 Silver .0490 oz. ASW **Obv:** Draped bust
of Ferdinand VII **Rev:** Pillars and arms **Note:** Mint mark M, Mo.

Date	Mintage	VG	F	VF	XF	Unc
1815 JJ	—	3.50	8.00	20.00	40.00	—
1816 JJ	—	3.50	8.00	20.00	40.00	—
1817/6 JJ	—	12.00	25.00	50.00	120	—
1817 JJ	—	3.50	8.00	28.00	45.00	—
1818/7 JJ	—	3.50	8.00	25.00	50.00	—
1818 JJ	—	3.50	8.00	25.00	50.00	—
1819/8 JJ	—	6.00	12.00	35.00	90.00	—
1819 JJ	—	3.50	8.00	20.00	40.00	—

Date	Mintage	VG	F	VF	XF	Unc
1820 JJ	—	3.50	8.00	25.00	50.00	—
1821 JJ	—	3.50	8.00	20.00	40.00	—

KM# 75.1 REAL
3.3834 g., 0.9170 Silver .0997 oz. ASW **Obv. Legend:**
PHILIP. V. D. G. HISPAN. ET IND. REX **Rev:** Pillars and
arms **Note:** Struck at Mexico City Mint, mint mark M, Mo, (MX).

Date	Mintage	VG	F	VF	XF	Unc
1732 Rare	—	—	—	—	—	—
1732 F	—	—	—	—	—	—
1733 F (MX)	—	150	350	425	750	—
1733 MF (MX)	—	150	350	425	750	—
1733 F Rare	—	—	—	—	—	—
1733 MF	—	100	200	300	500	—
1734/3 MF	—	15.00	30.00	65.00	150	—
1734 MF	—	12.00	25.00	60.00	140	—
1735 MF	—	12.00	25.00	60.00	140	—
1736 MF	—	12.00	25.00	60.00	140	—
1737 MF	—	12.00	25.00	60.00	140	—
1738 MF	—	12.00	25.00	60.00	140	—
1739 MF	—	12.00	25.00	60.00	140	—
1740 MF	—	12.00	25.00	60.00	140	—
1741 MF	—	12.00	25.00	60.00	140	—

KM# 75.2 REAL
3.3834 g., 0.9170 Silver .0997 oz. ASW **Obv. Legend:** PHS.
V. D. G. HISP. ET. IND. R **Note:** Struck at Mexico City Mint,
mint mark M, Mo.

Date	Mintage	VG	F	VF	XF	Unc
1742 M	—	10.00	20.00	50.00	120	—
1743 M	—	10.00	20.00	50.00	120	—
1744/3 M	—	10.00	20.00	50.00	120	—
1744 M	—	10.00	20.00	50.00	120	—
1745 M	—	8.00	18.00	50.00	120	—
1746/5 M	—	12.00	25.00	75.00	200	—
1746 M	—	10.00	20.00	55.00	125	—
1747 M	—	10.00	20.00	55.00	125	—

KM# 76.1 REAL
3.3800 g., 0.9170 Silver .0996 oz. ASW **Obv:** Royal crowns
Obv. Legend: FRD. VI. D. G. HISP. ET IND. R **Note:** Struck
at Mexico City Mint, mint mark M, Mo.

Date	Mintage	VG	F	VF	XF	Unc
1747 M	—	10.00	20.00	50.00	100	—
1748/7 M	—	10.00	20.00	50.00	100	—
1748 M	—	10.00	20.00	50.00	100	—
1749 M	—	10.00	20.00	50.00	100	—
1750/40 M	—	10.00	20.00	50.00	100	—
1750 M	—	10.00	20.00	50.00	100	—
1751 M	—	10.00	20.00	55.00	110	—
1752 M	—	10.00	20.00	50.00	100	—
1753 M	—	10.00	20.00	50.00	100	—
1754 M	—	10.00	20.00	55.00	110	—
1755/4 M	—	10.00	20.00	50.00	100	—
1755 M	—	10.00	20.00	50.00	100	—
1756 M	—	10.00	20.00	55.00	110	—
1757 M	—	10.00	20.00	55.00	110	—
1758/5 M	—	10.00	20.00	50.00	100	—
1758 M	—	10.00	20.00	50.00	100	—

KM# 76.2 REAL
3.3834 g., 0.9170 Silver .0997 oz. ASW **Obv:** Royal and Imperial
crowns **Note:** Struck at Mexico City Mint, mint mark M, Mo.

Date	Mintage	VG	F	VF	XF	Unc
1757 M	—	10.00	20.00	50.00	100	—
1758/7 M	—	10.00	20.00	50.00	100	—

Date	Mintage	VG	F	VF	XF	Unc
1758 M	—	10.00	20.00	50.00	100	—
1759 M	—	10.00	20.00	55.00	110	—
1760 M	—	15.00	30.00	70.00	140	—

KM# 77 REAL
3.3800 g., 0.9170 Silver .0996 oz. ASW **Obv. Legend:** CAR.
III. D. G. HISP. ET IND. R **Note:** Struck at Mexico City Mint,
mint mark M, Mo.

Date	Mintage	VG	F	VF	XF	Unc
1760 M	—	10.00	20.00	50.00	100	—
1761/0 M	—	10.00	20.00	55.00	125	—
1761 M	—	10.00	20.00	50.00	100	—
1762 M	—	10.00	20.00	50.00	100	—
1763/2 M	—	12.00	25.00	60.00	120	—
1763 M	—	10.00	20.00	50.00	100	—
1764 M	—	10.00	20.00	55.00	110	—
1765 M	—	10.00	20.00	55.00	110	—
1766 M	—	10.00	20.00	50.00	100	—
1767 M	—	10.00	20.00	55.00	110	—
1768 M	—	10.00	20.00	50.00	100	—
1769 M	—	10.00	20.00	50.00	100	—
1769/70 M	—	10.00	20.00	55.00	125	—
1770 M	—	10.00	20.00	55.00	125	—
1770 F	—	20.00	40.00	90.00	250	—
1771 F	—	20.00	40.00	90.00	250	—

KM# 78.1 REAL
3.3834 g., 0.9030 Silver .0982 oz. ASW **Obv. Legend:**
CAROLUS. III. DEI. GRATIA **Rev:** Inverted FM and mint mark
Note: Struck at Mexico City Mint, mint mark M, Mo.

Date	Mintage	VG	F	VF	XF	Unc
1772 FM	—	5.00	10.00	25.00	60.00	—
1773 FM	—	5.00	10.00	25.00	60.00	—

KM# 78.2 REAL
3.3800 g., 0.9030 Silver .0981 oz. ASW **Obv:** Draped bust
of Ferdinand VII **Obv. Legend:** CAROLUS. III. DEI. GRATIA
Rev. Legend: Normal initials and mint mark **Note:** Struck at
Mexico City Mint, mint mark M, Mo.

Date	Mintage	VG	F	VF	XF	Unc
1774 FM	—	5.00	10.00	25.00	60.00	—
1775/4 FM	—	6.00	12.00	28.00	75.00	—
1775 FM	—	5.00	10.00	25.00	60.00	—
1776 FM	—	5.00	10.00	25.00	60.00	—
1777 FM	—	5.00	10.00	25.00	60.00	—
1778 FF/M	—	6.00	12.00	28.00	75.00	—
1778 FF	—	5.00	10.00	25.00	60.00	—
1779 FF	—	5.00	10.00	25.00	60.00	—
1780 FF	—	5.00	10.00	25.00	60.00	—
1780 F F/M	—	5.00	10.00	25.00	60.00	—
1781 FF	—	5.00	10.00	25.00	60.00	—
1782 FF	—	5.00	10.00	25.00	60.00	—
1783 FF	—	5.00	10.00	25.00	60.00	—
1784 FF	—	5.00	10.00	25.00	60.00	—

KM# 78.2a REAL
3.3834 g., 0.8960 Silver .0975 oz. ASW **Rev:** Normal initials
and mint mark **Note:** Struck at Mexico City Mint, mint mark
M, Mo.

Date	Mintage	VG	F	VF	XF	Unc
1785 FF	—	6.00	12.00	28.00	75.00	—
1785 FM	—	6.00	12.00	28.00	75.00	—
1786 FM	—	6.00	12.00	28.00	75.00	—
1787 FF	—	15.00	30.00	60.00	125	—
1787 FM	—	12.00	25.00	50.00	100	—
1788 FF	—	50.00	100	200	—	—

Date	Mintage	VG	F	VF	XF	Unc
1788 FM	—	5.00	10.00	25.00	60.00	—
1789 FM	—	6.00	12.00	28.00	75.00	—

KM# 79 REAL
3.3800 g., 0.9030 Silver .0981 oz. ASW **Obv:** Armored bust of Charles III **Obv. Legend:** CAROLUS. IV... **Note:** Struck at Mexico City Mint, mint mark M, Mo.

Date	Mintage	VG	F	VF	XF	Unc
1789 FM	—	15.00	30.00	60.00	150	—
1790 FM	—	15.00	30.00	60.00	150	—

KM# 80 REAL
3.3800 g., 0.9030 Silver .0981 oz. ASW **Obv:** Armored bust of Charles III **Obv. Legend:** CAROLUS. IIII **Note:** Struck at Mexico City Mint, mint mark M, Mo.

Date	Mintage	VG	F	VF	XF	Unc
1790 FM	—	17.00	35.00	70.00	165	—

KM# 81 REAL
3.3834 g., 0.8960 Silver .0975 oz. ASW **Obv:** Armored bust of Charles IIII **Note:** Mint mark M, Mo.

Date	Mintage	VG	F	VF	XF	Unc
1792 FM	—	10.00	20.00	35.00	90.00	—
1793 FM	—	15.00	30.00	60.00	150	—
1794 FM	—	25.00	50.00	100	250	—
1795 FM	—	15.00	30.00	60.00	150	—
1796 FM	—	5.00	10.00	25.00	65.00	—
1797/6 FM	—	8.00	15.00	28.00	80.00	—
1797 FM	—	5.00	10.00	25.00	60.00	—
1798/7 FM	—	5.00	10.00	25.00	65.00	—
1798 FM	—	5.00	10.00	25.00	60.00	—
1799 FM	—	5.00	10.00	25.00	60.00	—
1800 FM	—	5.00	10.00	25.00	60.00	—
1801 FT/M	—	5.00	10.00	25.00	60.00	—
1801 FM	—	8.00	15.00	28.00	80.00	—
1801 FT	—	5.00	10.00	25.00	60.00	—
1802 FM	—	5.00	10.00	25.00	60.00	—
1802 FT	—	5.00	10.00	25.00	60.00	—
1802/1 FT	—	5.00	10.00	25.00	60.00	—
1802 FT/M	—	5.00	10.00	25.00	60.00	—
1803 FT	—	5.00	10.00	25.00	60.00	—
1804 TH	—	5.00	10.00	25.00	60.00	—
1805 TH	—	5.00	10.00	25.00	60.00	—
1806 TH	—	5.00	10.00	25.00	60.00	—
1807/6 TH	—	5.00	10.00	25.00	65.00	—
1807 TH	—	5.00	10.00	25.00	60.00	—
1808/7 TH	—	5.00	10.00	25.00	65.00	—
1808 FM	—	5.00	10.00	25.00	60.00	—

KM# 82 REAL
3.3800 g., 0.9030 Silver .0981 oz. ASW **Obv:** Armored bust of Ferdinand VII **Note:** Mint mark M, Mo.

Date	Mintage	VG	F	VF	XF	Unc
1809 TH	—	8.00	15.00	28.00	90.00	—
1810/09 TH	—	8.00	15.00	28.00	90.00	—
1810 TH	—	8.00	15.00	28.00	90.00	—
1811 TH	—	25.00	35.00	60.00	250	—
1811 HJ	—	8.00	15.00	28.00	90.00	—
1812 HJ	—	4.00	9.00	28.00	80.00	—
1812 JJ	—	10.00	20.00	40.00	120	—
1813 HJ	—	10.00	20.00	40.00	120	—
1813 JJ	—	50.00	100	150	250	—
1814 HJ	—	15.00	30.00	150	150	—
1814 JJ	—	50.00	100	175	300	—

KM# 83 REAL
3.3800 g., 0.9030 Silver .0981 oz. ASW **Obv:** Draped bust of Ferdinand VII **Note:** Mint mark M, Mo.

Date	Mintage	VG	F	VF	XF	Unc
1814 JJ	—	25.00	50.00	100	350	—
1815 HJ	—	15.00	30.00	60.00	150	—
1815 JJ	—	10.00	20.00	40.00	120	—
1816 JJ	—	5.00	10.00	25.00	70.00	—
1817 JJ	—	5.00	10.00	25.00	70.00	—
1818 JJ	—	30.00	60.00	125	500	—
1819 JJ	—	5.00	10.00	25.00	70.00	—
1820 JJ	—	5.00	10.00	25.00	70.00	—
1821/0 JJ	—	8.00	15.00	30.00	110	—
1821 JJ	—	5.00	10.00	25.00	50.00	—

KM# 84 2 REALES
6.7668 g., 0.9170 Silver .1995 oz. ASW **Obv. Legend:** PHILIP. V. D. G. HISPAN. ET IND. REX **Note:** Struck at Mexico City Mint, mint mark M, Mo, (MX).

Date	Mintage	VG	F	VF	XF	Unc
1732 Rare	—	—	—	—	—	—
1732 F	—	800	1,300	1,750	2,750	—
1733 F	—	600	800	1,350	2,250	—
1733 MF (MX)	—	350	600	1,000	1,650	—
1733 MF	—	600	900	1,500	2,500	—
1734/3 MF	—	20.00	40.00	85.00	170	—
1734 MF	—	20.00	40.00	85.00	170	—
1735/3 MF	—	15.00	30.00	75.00	150	—
1735/4 MF	—	15.00	30.00	75.00	150	—
1735 MF	—	15.00	30.00	75.00	150	—
1736/3 MF	—	18.00	35.00	80.00	160	—
1736/4 MF	—	18.00	35.00	80.00	160	—
1736/5 MF	—	18.00	35.00	80.00	160	—
1736 MF	—	18.00	35.00	80.00	160	—
1737/3 MF	—	18.00	35.00	80.00	160	—
1737 MF	—	18.00	35.00	80.00	160	—
1738/7 MF	—	18.00	35.00	80.00	160	—

Date	Mintage	VG	F	VF	XF	Unc
1738 MF	—	18.00	35.00	80.00	160	—
1739 MF	—	18.00	35.00	80.00	160	—
1740/30 MF	—	18.00	35.00	80.00	160	—
1740 MF	—	18.00	35.00	80.00	160	—
1741 MF	—	18.00	35.00	80.00	160	—

KM# 85 2 REALES
6.7700 g., 0.9170 Silver .1996 oz. ASW **Obv. Legend:** PHS.
V. D. G. HISP. ET IND. R **Note:** Struck at Mexico City Mint,
mint mark M, Mo.

Date	Mintage	F	VF	XF	Unc	BU
1742 M	—	30.00	75.00	125	—	—
1743/2 M	—	30.00	75.00	125	—	—
1743 M	—	30.00	75.00	125	—	—
1744/3 M	—	30.00	75.00	125	—	—
1744 M	—	30.00	75.00	125	—	—
1745/4 M	—	30.00	75.00	125	—	—
1745 M	—	30.00	75.00	125	—	—
1745 M HIP	—	400	—	—	—	—
1746/5 M	—	30.00	75.00	125	—	—
1746 M	—	30.00	75.00	125	—	—
1747 M	—	30.00	75.00	125	—	—
1750 M	—	450	650	1,000	—	—

KM# 86.1 2 REALES
6.7668 g., 0.9170 Silver .1995 oz. ASW **Obv:** Royal crowns
Obv. Legend: FRD. VI. D. G. HISP. ET IND. R **Note:** Struck
at Mexico City Mint, mint mark M, Mo.

Date	Mintage	VG	F	VF	XF	Unc
1747 M	—	16.00	32.00	78.00	135	—
1748/7 M	—	16.00	32.00	78.00	135	—
1748 M	—	15.00	30.00	75.00	125	—
1749 M	—	15.00	30.00	75.00	125	—
1750 M	—	15.00	30.00	75.00	125	—
1751/41 M	—	18.00	35.00	80.00	150	—
1751 M	—	15.00	30.00	75.00	125	—
1752 M	—	15.00	30.00	75.00	125	—
1753/2 M	—	18.00	35.00	80.00	150	—
1753 M	—	18.00	35.00	80.00	150	—
1754 M	—	18.00	35.00	80.00	150	—
1755/4 M	—	18.00	35.00	80.00	150	—
1755 M	—	18.00	35.00	80.00	150	—
1756/55 M	—	18.00	35.00	80.00	150	—
1756 M	—	18.00	35.00	80.00	140	—
1757/6 M	—	15.00	30.00	75.00	125	—
1757 M	—	18.00	35.00	80.00	150	—

KM# 86.2 2 REALES
6.7668 g., 0.9170 Silver .1995 oz. ASW **Obv:** Royal and Imperial
crowns **Note:** Struck at Mexico City Mint, mint mark M, Mo.

Date	Mintage	VG	F	VF	XF	Unc
1757 M	—	15.00	30.00	75.00	125	—
1758 M	—	15.00	30.00	75.00	125	—
1759/8 M	—	15.00	30.00	75.00	125	—
1759 M	—	20.00	40.00	90.00	175	—
1760 M	—	20.00	40.00	90.00	175	—

KM# 87 2 REALES
6.7700 g., 0.9170 Silver .1996 oz. ASW **Obv. Legend:** CAR.
III. D. G. HISP. ET IND. R **Note:** Struck at Mexico City Mint,
mint mark M, Mo.

Date	Mintage	VG	F	VF	XF	Unc
1760 M	—	15.00	30.00	75.00	125	—
1761 M	—	15.00	30.00	75.00	125	—
1762/1 M	—	15.00	30.00	75.00	125	—
1762 M	—	15.00	30.00	75.00	125	—
1763/2 M	—	15.00	30.00	75.00	125	—
1763 M	—	15.00	30.00	75.00	125	—
1764 M	—	15.00	30.00	75.00	125	—
1765 M	—	15.00	30.00	75.00	125	—
1766 M	—	12.00	35.00	80.00	160	—
1767 M	—	15.00	30.00	75.00	125	—
1768/6 M	—	15.00	30.00	75.00	125	—
1768 M	—	15.00	30.00	75.00	125	—
1769 M	—	15.00	30.00	75.00	125	—
1770 M	—	350	550	—	—	—
1770 F Rare	—	—	—	—	—	—
1771 F	—	15.00	30.00	75.00	125	—

KM# 88.1 2 REALES
6.7668 g., 0.9030 Silver .1964 oz. ASW **Obv. Legend:**
CAROLUS. III. DEI. GRATIA **Rev:** Inverted FM and mint mark
Note: Struck at Mexico City Mint, mint mark M, Mo.

Date	Mintage	VG	F	VF	XF	Unc
1772 FM	—	7.00	15.00	30.00	100	—
1773 FM	—	7.00	15.00	30.00	100	—

KM# 88.2 2 REALES
6.7700 g., 0.9030 Silver .1965 oz. ASW **Rev:** Normal initials
and mint mark **Note:** Struck at Mexico City Mint, mint mark
M, Mo.

Date	Mintage	VG	F	VF	XF	Unc
1773 FM	—	7.00	15.00	30.00	100	—
1774 FM	—	7.00	15.00	30.00	100	—
1775 FM	—	7.00	15.00	30.00	100	—
1776 FM	—	7.00	15.00	30.00	100	—
1777 FM	—	7.00	15.00	30.00	100	—
1778/7 FF	—	7.00	15.00	30.00	100	—
1778 FF	—	7.00	15.00	30.00	100	—
1779/8 FF	—	7.00	15.00	30.00	100	—
1779 FF	—	7.00	15.00	30.00	100	—
1780 FF	—	7.00	15.00	30.00	100	—
1781 FF	—	7.00	15.00	30.00	100	—
1782/1 FF	—	7.00	15.00	30.00	100	—
1782 FF	—	7.00	15.00	30.00	100	—
1783 FF	—	7.00	15.00	30.00	100	—
1784 FF	—	7.00	15.00	30.00	100	—

Date	Mintage	VG	F	VF	XF	Unc
1784 FF DEI GRTIA (error)	—	100	150	250	600	—
1784 FM	—	70.00	120	225	575	—

KM# 88.2a 2 REALES
6.7668 g., 0.8960 Silver .1949 oz. ASW **Note:** Struck at
Mexico City Mint, mint mark Mo.

Date	Mintage	VG	F	VF	XF	Unc
1785Mo FM	—	7.00	15.00	30.00	100	—
1786Mo FF	—	200	350	550	950	—
1786Mo FM	—	7.00	15.00	30.00	100	—
1787Mo FM	—	7.00	15.00	30.00	100	—
1788/98Mo FM	—	7.00	15.00	30.00	100	—
1788Mo FM	—	7.00	15.00	30.00	100	—
1789Mo FM	—	12.00	25.00	50.00	150	—

KM# 89 2 REALES
6.7700 g., 0.9030 Silver .1965 oz. ASW **Obv:** Armored bust
of Charles III **Obv. Legend:** CAROLUS. IV... **Note:** Struck at
Mexico City Mint, mint mark M, Mo.

Date	Mintage	VG	F	VF	XF	Unc
1789 FM	—	15.00	30.00	75.00	200	—
1790 FM	—	15.00	30.00	75.00	200	—

KM# 90 2 REALES
6.7700 g., 0.9030 Silver .1965 oz. ASW **Obv:** Armored bust
of Charles III **Obv. Legend:** CAROLUS. IIII... **Note:** Struck at
Mexico City Mint, mint mark M, Mo.

Date	Mintage	VG	F	VF	XF	Unc
1790 FM	—	17.00	35.00	80.00	200	—

KM# 91 2 REALES
6.7668 g., 0.8960 Silver .1949 oz. ASW **Obv:** Armored bust
of Carolus IIII **Note:** Mint mark M, Mo.

Date	Mintage	VG	F	VF	XF	Unc
1792 FM	—	15.00	30.00	60.00	200	—
1793 FM	—	15.00	30.00	60.00	200	—
1794/3 FM	—	50.00	100	200	450	—
1794 FM	—	40.00	75.00	150	400	—
1795 FM	—	7.00	15.00	30.00	85.00	—
1796 FM	—	7.00	15.00	30.00	85.00	—
1797 FM	—	7.00	15.00	30.00	85.00	—
1798 FM	—	7.00	15.00	30.00	85.00	—
1799/8 FM	—	7.00	15.00	32.00	90.00	—
1799 FM	—	7.00	15.00	30.00	85.00	—
1800 FM	—	7.00	15.00	30.00	85.00	—
1801 FT/M	—	7.00	15.00	30.00	85.00	—
1801 FT	—	7.00	15.00	30.00	85.00	—
1801 FM	—	20.00	40.00	75.00	250	—
1802 FT	—	7.00	15.00	30.00	85.00	—
1803 FT	—	7.00	15.00	30.00	85.00	—
1804/3 TH	—	7.00	15.00	30.00	85.00	—
1804 TH	—	7.00	15.00	30.00	85.00	—
1805 TH	—	7.00	15.00	30.00	85.00	—
1806/5 TH	—	7.00	15.00	32.00	90.00	—
1806 TH	—	7.00	15.00	30.00	85.00	—
1807/5 TH	—	7.00	15.00	32.00	90.00	—
1807/6 TH	—	15.00	30.00	60.00	200	—
1807 TH	—	7.00	15.00	30.00	85.00	—

Date	Mintage	VG	F	VF	XF	Unc
1808/7 TH	—	7.00	15.00	32.00	90.00	—
1808 TH	—	7.00	15.00	30.00	85.00	—

KM# 92 2 REALES
6.7700 g., 0.9030 Silver .1965 oz. ASW **Obv:** Armored bust
of Ferdinand VII **Note:** Mint mark M, Mo.

Date	Mintage	VG	F	VF	XF	Unc
1809 TH	—	15.00	30.00	75.00	200	—
181/00 TH	—	15.00	30.00	75.00	200	—
1810 TH	—	15.00	30.00	75.00	200	—
181/00 HJ/TH	—	15.00	30.00	75.00	200	—
181/00 HJ	—	15.00	30.00	75.00	200	—
1810 HJ	—	15.00	30.00	75.00	200	—
1811 TH	—	150	250	350	750	—
1811 HJ	—	15.00	30.00	75.00	200	—
1811 HJ/TH	—	40.00	80.00	150	300	—

KM# 93 2 REALES
6.7700 g., 0.9030 Silver .1965 oz. ASW **Obv:** Draped bust
of Ferdinand VII **Note:** Mint mark M, Mo.

Date	Mintage	VG	F	VF	XF	Unc
1812 TH	—	60.00	125	250	550	—
1812 HJ	—	40.00	100	200	500	—
1812 JJ	—	10.00	20.00	60.00	200	—
1813 TH	—	15.00	30.00	100	400	—
1813 JJ	—	20.00	60.00	125	350	—
1813 HJ	—	40.00	100	200	500	—
1814/2 JJ	—	15.00	30.00	100	400	—
1814 JJ	—	15.00	30.00	100	400	—
1815 JJ	—	6.00	12.00	28.00	85.00	—
1816 JJ	—	6.00	12.00	28.00	85.00	—
1817 JJ	—	6.00	12.00	28.00	85.00	—
1818 JJ	—	6.00	12.00	28.00	85.00	—
1819/8 JJ	—	5.50	12.00	30.00	85.00	—
1819 JJ	—	6.00	12.00	28.00	85.00	—
1820 JJ	—	175	—	—	—	—
1821/0 JJ	—	7.00	15.00	30.00	90.00	—
1821 JJ	—	6.00	12.00	28.00	85.00	—

KM# 94 4 REALES
13.5337 g., 0.9170 Silver .3990 oz. ASW **Obv. Legend:**
PHILLIP. V. D. G. HISPAN. ET IND. REX **Note:** Mint mark
M, Mo, MX.

Date	Mintage	VG	F	VF	XF	Unc
1732 Rare; Specimen	—	—	—	—	—	—
1732 F	—	2,000	3,000	5,000	10,000	—
1733/2 F	—	1,500	2,000	4,000	6,500	—
1733 MF	—	1,100	1,650	2,250	4,250	—
1733 MF (MX)	—	1,500	2,200	3,250	5,500	—
1733 MX/XM	—	1,500	2,200	3,250	5,500	—
1734/3 MF	—	150	300	600	1,200	—
1734 MF	—	150	300	600	1,200	—
1735/4 MF	—	100	175	300	600	—
1735 MF	—	100	175	300	600	—
1736 MF	—	100	175	300	600	—
1737 MF	—	100	175	300	600	—
1738/7 MF	—	100	175	300	600	—
1738 MF	—	100	175	300	600	—
1739 MF	—	100	175	300	600	—
1740/30 MF	—	100	200	325	625	—
1740 MF	—	100	175	300	600	—
1741 MF	—	100	175	300	600	—
1742/1 MF	—	100	175	300	600	—
1742/32 MF	—	100	175	300	600	—
1742 MF	—	100	175	300	600	—
1743 MF	—	100	175	300	600	—
1744/3 MF	—	100	200	325	625	—
1744 MF	—	100	175	300	600	—
1745 MF	—	100	175	300	600	—
1746 MF	—	100	175	300	600	—
1747 MF	—	150	275	400	650	—

KM# 95   4 REALES
13.5400 g., 0.9170 Silver .3992 oz. ASW **Obv. Legend:**
FERDND. VI. D. G. HISPAN. ET IND. REX **Note:** Struck at
Mexico City Mint, mint mark M, Mo.

Date	Mintage	VG	F	VF	XF	Unc
1747 MF	—	100	150	300	550	—
1748/7 MF	—	100	150	300	550	—
1748 MF	—	100	125	250	500	—
1749 MF	—	150	225	350	650	—
1750/40 MF	—	100	125	250	500	—
1751/41 MF	—	100	125	250	500	—
1751 MF	—	100	125	250	500	—
1752 MF	—	100	125	250	500	—
1753 MF	—	100	125	300	550	—
1754 MF	—	250	375	500	850	—
1755 MM	—	100	125	250	500	—
1756 MM	—	100	150	300	550	—
1757 MM	—	100	150	300	550	—
1758 MM	—	100	125	250	500	—
1759 MM	—	100	125	250	500	—
1760/59 MM	—	100	175	350	600	—
1760 MM	—	100	175	350	600	—

KM# 96   4 REALES
13.5400 g., 0.9170 Silver .3992 oz. ASW **Obv. Legend:**
CAROLVS. III. D. G. HISPAN. ET IND. REX **Note:** Struck at
Mexico City Mint, mint mark M, Mo.

Date	Mintage	VG	F	VF	XF	Unc
1760 MM	—	100	150	250	900	—
1761 MM	—	100	150	250	900	—
1761 MM Cross between H and I	—	100	150	250	900	—
1762 MM	—	75.00	125	250	500	—
1763/1 MM	—	100	150	300	600	—
1763 MM	—	100	150	300	600	—
1764 MM	—	400	600	1,000	2,000	—
1764 MF	—	350	500	1,000	2,000	—
1765 MF	—	350	500	1,000	2,000	—
1766 MF	—	250	350	550	1,250	—
1767 MF	—	100	150	300	600	—
1768 MF	—	75.00	125	250	500	—
1769 MF	—	75.00	125	250	500	—
1770 MF	—	75.00	125	250	500	—
1771 MF	—	125	200	325	700	—

KM# 97.1   4 REALES
13.5337 g., 0.9030 Silver .3929 oz. ASW **Obv. Legend:**
CAROLUS. III. DEI. GRATIA **Rev:** Inverted FM and mint mark
Note: Struck at Mexico City Mint, mint mark M, Mo.

Date	Mintage	VG	F	VF	XF	Unc
1772 FM	—	90.00	125	250	500	—
1773 FM	—	100	175	300	650	—

KM# 97.2   4 REALES
13.5400 g., 0.9030 Silver .3931 oz. ASW **Obv. Legend:**
CAROLUS. III. DEI. GRATIA **Rev:** Normal initials and mint
mark **Note:** Struck at Mexico City Mint, mint mark M, Mo.

Date	Mintage	VG	F	VF	XF	Unc
1774 FM	—	50.00	100	200	500	—
1775 FM	—	50.00	100	200	500	—
1776 FM	—	50.00	100	200	500	—
1777 FM	—	50.00	100	200	500	—
1778 FF	—	50.00	100	200	500	—

Date	Mintage	VG	F	VF	XF	Unc
1779 FF	—	50.00	100	200	500	—
1780 FF	—	50.00	100	200	500	—
1781 FF	—	50.00	100	200	500	—
1782 FF	—	50.00	100	200	500	—
1783 FF	—	50.00	100	200	500	—
1784 FF	—	50.00	100	200	500	—
1784 FM		100	200	350	600	—

KM# 97.2a   4 REALES
13.5337 g., 0.8960 Silver .3899 oz. ASW **Rev:** Normal initials and mint mark **Note:** Struck at Mexico City Mint, mint mark M, Mo.

Date	Mintage	VG	F	VF	XF	Unc
1785 FM	—	100	200	350	600	—
1786 FM	—	50.00	100	200	500	—
1787 FM	—	50.00	100	200	500	—
1788 FM	—	50.00	100	200	500	—
1789 FM	—	50.00	100	200	500	—

KM# 98   4 REALES
13.5400 g., 0.9030 Silver .3931 oz. ASW **Obv:** Armored bust of Charles III **Obv. Legend:** CAROLUS. IV... **Note:** Struck at Mexico City Mint, mint mark M, Mo.

Date	Mintage	VG	F	VF	XF	Unc
1789 FM	—	65.00	125	250	550	—
1790 FM	—	50.00	100	200	500	—

KM# 99   4 REALES
13.5400 g., 0.9030 Silver .3931 oz. ASW **Obv:** Armored bust of Charles III **Obv. Legend:** CAROLUS. IIII... **Note:** Struck at Mexico City Mint, mint mark M, Mo.

Date	Mintage	VG	F	VF	XF	Unc
1790 FM	—	65.00	125	250	550	—

KM# 100   4 REALES
13.5337 g., 0.8960 Silver .3899 oz. ASW **Obv:** Armored bust of Charles IIII **Rev:** Pillars, arms **Note:** Mint mark M, Mo.

Date	Mintage	VG	F	VF	XF	Unc
1792 FM	—	35.00	65.00	150	400	—
1793 FM	—	75.00	125	200	500	—
1794/3 FM	—	35.00	65.00	150	400	—
1794 FM	—	35.00	65.00	150	400	—
1795 FM	—	35.00	65.00	150	400	—
1796 FM	—	150	250	400	800	—
1797 FM	—	60.00	120	200	500	—
1798/7 FM	—	35.00	65.00	150	400	—
1798 FM	—	35.00	65.00	150	400	—
1799 FM	—	35.00	65.00	150	400	—
1800 FM	—	35.00	65.00	150	400	—
1801 FM	—	35.00	65.00	150	400	—
1801 FT	—	60.00	120	200	500	—
1802 FT	—	200	300	500	1,000	—
1803 FT	—	75.00	135	225	550	—

Date	Mintage	VG	F	VF	XF	Unc
1803 FM	—	200	300	500	1,000	—
1804 TH	—	40.00	75.00	175	450	—
1805 TH	—	35.00	65.00	150	400	—
1806 TH	—	35.00	65.00	150	400	—
1807 TH	—	35.00	65.00	150	400	—
1808/7 TH	—	40.00	75.00	175	450	—
1808 TH	—	40.00	75.00	175	450	—

KM# 101 4 REALES
13.5400 g., 0.9030 Silver .3931 oz. ASW **Obv:** Armored bust of Ferdinand VII **Note:** Mint mark M, Mo.

Date	Mintage	VG	F	VF	XF	Unc
1809 HJ	—	75.00	135	250	750	—
1810 HJ	—	75.00	135	250	750	—
1811 HJ	—	75.00	135	250	750	—
1812 HJ	—	400	650	900	1,850	—

KM# 102 4 REALES
13.5400 g., 0.9030 Silver .3931 oz. ASW **Obv:** Draped bust of Ferdinand VII **Note:** Mint mark M, Mo.

Date	Mintage	VG	F	VF	XF	Unc
1816 JJ	—	150	200	325	700	—
1817 JJ	—	250	400	500	1,000	—
1818/7 JJ	—	250	400	500	1,000	—
1819 JJ	—	175	250	325	700	—
1820 JJ	—	175	250	325	700	—
1821 JJ	—	75.00	135	250	650	—

KM# 103 8 REALES
27.0674 g., 0.9170 Silver .7980 oz. ASW **Obv. Legend:** PHILIP. V. D. G. HISPAN. ET IND. REX **Note:** Struck at Mexico City Mint, mint mark M, Mo, MX.

Date	Mintage	VG	F	VF	XF	Unc
1732 F	—	2,750	4,750	8,000	—	—
1733/2 F (MX)	—	3,000	5,250	9,000	—	—
1733 F	—	2,000	3,000	5,000	9,000	—
1733 F (MX) Rare	—	—	—	—	—	—
Note: Rare; Bonhams Patterson sale 7-96 VF 1733 F (MX) realized $11,710						
1733 MF Large crown; Rare	—	—	—	—	—	—
1733 MF (MX) Rare	—	—	—	—	—	—
1733 MF Small crown	—	700	1,500	2,500	4,250	—
1734/3 MF	—	100	150	275	575	—
1734 MF	—	100	150	250	450	—
1735 MF	—	100	150	250	450	—
1736/5 MF	—	100	150	275	575	—
1736 MF	—	100	150	250	450	—
1736 MF Small planchet	—	100	150	250	450	—
1737 MF	—	65.00	100	200	400	—
1738/6 MF	—	65.00	100	200	400	—
1738/7 MF	—	65.00	100	200	400	—
1738 MF	—	65.00	100	200	400	—
1739/6 MF 9 over inverted 6	—	65.00	100	200	400	—
1739 MF	—	65.00	100	200	400	—
1740/30 MF	—	100	150	275	500	—
1740/39 MF	—	100	150	275	500	—
1740 MF	—	65.00	100	200	400	—
1741/31 MF	—	65.00	100	200	400	—
1741 MF	—	65.00	100	200	400	—
1742/32 MF	—	75.00	125	220	500	—
1742/1 MF	—	65.00	100	200	400	—
1742 MF	—	65.00	100	200	400	—
1743/2 MF	—	65.00	100	200	400	—
1743 MF	—	65.00	100	200	400	—
1744/34 MF	—	65.00	100	200	400	—
1744/3 MF	—	65.00	100	200	400	—
1744 MF	—	65.00	100	200	400	—
1745/4 MF	—	65.00	100	200	425	—
1745 MF	—	65.00	100	200	400	—
1746/5 MF	—	100	150	275	575	—
1746 MF	—	65.00	100	200	400	—
1747 MF	—	65.00	100	200	400	—

Date	Mintage	VG	F	VF	XF	Unc
1754 MF	—	150	285	550	950	—
1755/4 MM	—	55.00	100	185	325	—
1755 MM	—	50.00	75.00	125	250	—
1756/5 MM	—	55.00	100	165	275	—
1756 MM	—	50.00	75.00	125	250	—
1757/6 MM	—	50.00	75.00	125	250	—
1757 MM	—	55.00	100	185	325	—
1758 MM	—	50.00	75.00	125	250	—
1759 MM	—	50.00	75.00	125	250	—
1760/59 MM	—	55.00	100	165	275	—
1760 MM	—	50.00	75.00	125	250	—

KM# 104.1 8 REALES
27.0674 g., 0.9170 Silver .7980 oz. ASW **Obv. Legend:**
FERDND. VI. D. G. HISPAN. ET IND. REX **Rev:** With Royal
crown on left pillar **Note:** Struck at Mexico City Mint, mint mark
M, Mo.

Date	Mintage	VG	F	VF	XF	Unc
1747 MF	—	55.00	100	175	300	—
1748/7 MF	—	60.00	120	250	450	—
1748 MF	—	50.00	75.00	125	250	—
1749 MF	—	50.00	75.00	125	250	—
1749/8 MF	—	50.00	75.00	125	250	—
1750 MF	—	50.00	75.00	125	250	—
1751/0 MF	—	55.00	100	165	275	—
1751 MF	—	50.00	75.00	125	250	—
1752/1 MF	—	55.00	100	165	275	—
1752 MF	—	50.00	75.00	125	250	—
1753/2 MF	—	50.00	75.00	125	250	—
1753 MF	—	55.00	100	165	275	—
1754/3 MF	—	55.00	100	185	325	—
1754 MF	—	50.00	75.00	125	250	—
1754 MM/MF	—	300	700	1,500	3,500	—
1754 MM	—	300	700	1,500	3,500	—

KM# 104.2 8 REALES
27.0674 g., 0.9170 Silver .7980 oz. ASW **Obv. Legend:**
FERDND. VI. D. G. HISPAN. ET IND. REX **Rev:** Imperial crown
on left pillar **Note:** Struck at Mexico City Mint, mint mark M, Mo.

Date	Mintage	VG	F	VF	XF	Unc
1754 MM	—	60.00	110	200	375	—
1754 MM/MF	—	75.00	125	250	500	—

KM# 105 8 REALES
27.0674 g., 0.9170 Silver .7980 oz. ASW **Obv. Legend:**
CAROLUS. III. D. G. HISPAN. ET IND. REX **Note:** Struck at
Mexico City Mint, mint mark M, Mo.

Date	Mintage	VG	F	VF	XF	Unc
1760/59 MM	—	450	700	—	—	—
Note: CAROLUS. III/Ferdin. Vi						
1760 MM	—	60.00	100	150	325	—
Note: CAROLUS. III/FERDIN. VI. recut die						
1760 MM	—	60.00	100	150	300	—
1761/50 MM	—	65.00	110	165	325	—
Note: Tip of cross between I and S in legend						
1761/51 MM	—	65.00	110	165	325	—
Note: Tip of cross between I and S in legend						
1761/0 MM	—	65.00	110	165	325	—
Note: Tip of cross between H and I in legend						
1761 MM	—	60.00	100	150	275	—
Note: Cross under I in legend						
1761 MM	—	60.00	100	150	275	—
Note: Tip of cross between H and I in legend						
1761 MM	—	65.00	110	165	325	—
Note: Tip of cross between I and S in legend						
1762/1 MM	—	70.00	120	175	450	—
Note: Tip of cross between H and I in legend						
1762/1 MM	—	70.00	120	175	450	—
1762 MM	—	60.00	100	150	275	—
Note: Tip of cross between H and I in legend						
1762 MM	—	50.00	75.00	125	250	—
Note: Tip of cross between I and S in legend						
1762 MF	—	500	750	1,250	2,300	—
1763/2 MM	—	300	450	750	1,350	—
1763 MM	—	450	650	1,150	2,250	—
1763/1 MF	—	50.00	75.00	125	250	—
1763/2 MF	—	50.00	75.00	125	250	—
1763 MF	—	50.00	75.00	125	250	—
1764 MF	—	50.00	75.00	125	250	—
Note: CAR/CRA						
1764 MF	—	50.00	75.00	125	250	—
1765 MF	—	50.00	75.00	125	250	—
1766/5 MF	—	75.00	150	225	575	—
1766 MF	—	50.00	75.00	125	250	—
1767/6 MF	—	50.00	75.00	125	250	—

Date	Mintage	VG	F	VF	XF	Unc
1767 MF	—	50.00	75.00	125	250	—
1768/7 MF	—	85.00	165	250	600	—
1768 MF	—	50.00	75.00	125	250	—
1769 MF	—	50.00	75.00	125	250	—
1770/60 MF	—	100	185	300	650	—
1770 MF	—	50.00	75.00	125	250	—
1770/60 FM	—	100	185	300	650	—
1770/69 FM	—	100	185	300	650	—
1770 FM/F	—	50.00	75.00	125	250	—
1770 FM	—	50.00	75.00	125	250	—
1771/0 FM	—	50.00	75.00	125	250	—
1771 FM	—	50.00	75.00	125	250	—

Date	Mintage	VG	F	VF	XF	Unc
1776 FM	—	25.00	45.00	75.00	150	—
1777/6 FM	—	35.00	65.00	180	300	—
1777 FM	—	25.00	45.00	75.00	150	—
1777 FF	—	35.00	50.00	100	250	—
1778 FM	—	—	—	—	—	—
Note: Superior Casterline sale 5-89 VF realized $17,600						
1778/7 FF	—	25.00	45.00	75.00	150	—
1778 FF	—	25.00	45.00	75.00	150	—
1779 FF	—	25.00	45.00	75.00	150	—
1780 FF	—	25.00	45.00	75.00	150	—
1781 FF	—	25.00	45.00	75.00	150	—
1782 FF	—	25.00	45.00	75.00	150	—
1783 FF	—	25.00	45.00	75.00	150	—
1783 FM	—	4,000	6,000	9,000	—	—
1784 FF	—	150	300	500	1,250	—
1784 FM	—	25.00	45.00	75.00	150	—

KM# 106.2a 8 REALES
27.0674 g., 0.8960 Silver .7797 oz. ASW **Obv. Legend:** CAROLUS.III.DEI.GRATIA **Rev:** Normal initials and mint mark **Note:** Struck at Mexico City Mint, mint mark M, Mo.

Date	Mintage	VG	F	VF	XF	Unc
1785 FM	—	25.00	45.00	75.00	150	—
1786/5 FM	—	50.00	100	200	400	—
1786 FM	—	25.00	45.00	75.00	150	—
1787/6 FM	—	100	250	450	1,200	—
1787 FM	—	25.00	45.00	75.00	150	—
1788 FM	—	25.00	45.00	75.00	150	—
1789 FM	—	50.00	100	150	225	—

KM# 106.1 8 REALES
27.0674 g., 0.9030 Silver .7858 oz. ASW **Obv. Legend:** CAROLUS. III. DEI. GRATIA **Rev:** Inverted initials and mint mark **Note:** Two varieties exist, one with inverted initials "F.M." (left), and one with normal presentation (right). Struck at Mexico City Mint, mint mark M, Mo.

Date	Mintage	VG	F	VF	XF	Unc
1772 FM	—	25.00	50.00	120	250	—
1772 FM Inverted	—	150	350	750	1,250	—
1773 FM	—	25.00	50.00	100	175	—

KM# 107 8 REALES
27.0674 g., 0.9030 Silver .7858 oz. ASW **Obv:** Armored bust of Charles III **Obv. Legend:** CAROLUS. IV... **Note:** Struck at Mexico City Mint, mint mark M, Mo.

Date	Mintage	VG	F	VF	XF	Unc
1789 FM	—	40.00	65.00	120	250	—
1790 FM	—	30.00	50.00	100	200	—

KM# 106.2 8 REALES
27.0674 g., 0.9030 Silver .7858 oz. ASW **Obv. Legend:** CAROLUS. III. DEI. GRATIA **Rev:** Normal initials and mint mark **Note:** Struck at Mexico City Mint, mint mark M, Mo.

Date	Mintage	VG	F	VF	XF	Unc
1773 FM	—	25.00	50.00	80.00	160	—
1774 FM	—	25.00	45.00	75.00	150	—
1775 FM	—	25.00	45.00	75.00	150	—

Date	Mintage	VG	F	VF	XF	Unc
1800 FM	—	20.00	35.00	50.00	100	—
1801/0 FT/FM	—	20.00	35.00	50.00	100	—
1801/791 FM	—	35.00	60.00	100	250	—
1801/0 FM	—	35.00	60.00	100	250	—
1801 FM	—	20.00	40.00	100	250	—
1801 FT/M	—	35.00	60.00	100	250	—
1801 FT	—	20.00	35.00	50.00	100	—
1802/1 FT	—	35.00	60.00	100	250	—
1802 FT	—	20.00	35.00	50.00	100	—
1802 FT/M	—	20.00	35.00	50.00	100	—
1803 FT	—	20.00	35.00	50.00	110	—
1803 FT/M	—	20.00	35.00	50.00	100	—
1803 TH	—	75.00	150	250	500	—
1804/3 TH	—	35.00	60.00	100	250	—
1804 TH	—	20.00	35.00	50.00	100	—
Note: CARLUS (error)						
1805/4 TH	—	40.00	80.00	125	275	—
1805 TH	—	20.00	35.00	50.00	100	—
Note: Narrow date						
1805 TH	—	20.00	35.00	50.00	100	—
Note: Wide date						
1806 TH	—	20.00	35.00	50.00	100	—
1807/6 TH	—	150	250	350	700	—
1807 TH	—	20.00	35.00	50.00	100	—
1808/7 TH	—	20.00	35.00	50.00	100	—
1808 TH	—	20.00	35.00	50.00	100	—

KM# 108 8 REALES
27.0674 g., 0.9030 Silver .7858 oz. ASW **Obv:** Armored bust of Charles III **Obv. Legend:** CAROLUS. IIII **Note:** Struck at Mexico City Mint, mint mark M, Mo.

Date	Mintage	VG	F	VF	XF	Unc
1790 FM	—	30.00	50.00	100	200	—

KM# 109 8 REALES
27.0674 g., 0.8960 Silver .7797 oz. ASW **Obv:** Armored bust of Charles IIII **Note:** Mint mark M, Mo.

Date	Mintage	VG	F	VF	XF	Unc
1791 FM	—	20.00	35.00	50.00	100	—
1792 FM	—	20.00	35.00	50.00	100	—
1793 FM	—	20.00	35.00	50.00	100	—
1794 FM	—	20.00	35.00	50.00	100	—
1795/4 FM	—	20.00	35.00	50.00	100	—
1795 FM	—	20.00	35.00	50.00	100	—
1796 FM	—	20.00	35.00	50.00	100	—
1797 FM	—	20.00	35.00	50.00	100	—
1798 FM	—	20.00	35.00	50.00	100	—
1799 FM	—	20.00	35.00	50.00	100	—
1800/700 FM	—	20.00	35.00	50.00	100	—

KM# 110 8 REALES
27.0674 g., 0.8960 Silver .7797 oz. ASW **Obv:** Armored bust of Ferdinand VII **Note:** Mint mark M, Mo.

Date	Mintage	VG	F	VF	XF	Unc
1808 TH	—	25.00	40.00	75.00	145	—
1809/8 TH	—	25.00	40.00	75.00	145	—
1809 TH	—	20.00	35.00	55.00	120	—
1809 HJ	—	25.00	40.00	75.00	145	—
1809 HJ/TH	—	20.00	35.00	55.00	120	—
1810/09 HJ	—	25.00	40.00	75.00	145	—
1810 TH	—	75.00	150	300	600	—
1810 HJ/TH	—	25.00	40.00	75.00	145	—
1810 HJ	—	25.00	40.00	75.00	145	—
1811/0 HJ	—	20.00	35.00	55.00	120	—
1811 HJ	—	20.00	35.00	55.00	120	—
1811 HJ/TH	—	20.00	35.00	50.00	100	—

KM# 111 8 REALES
27.0700 g., 0.9030 Silver .7859 oz. ASW **Obv:** Draped bust
of Ferdinand VII **Note:** Mint mark M, Mo.

Date	Mintage	VG	F	VF	XF	Unc
1811 HJ	—	20.00	40.00	60.00	125	—
1812 HJ	—	50.00	75.00	125	250	—
1812 JJ/HJ	—	20.00	35.00	50.00	100	—
1812 JJ	—	20.00	35.00	50.00	100	—
1813 HJ	—	50.00	75.00	125	250	—
1813 JJ	—	20.00	35.00	50.00	100	—
1814/3 HJ	—	1,200	2,500	5,000	—	—
1814/3 JJ	—	20.00	35.00	50.00	100	—
1814 JJ	—	20.00	35.00	50.00	100	—
1815/4 JJ	—	20.00	35.00	50.00	100	—
1815 JJ	—	20.00	35.00	50.00	100	—
1816/5 JJ	—	20.00	35.00	50.00	90.00	—
1816 JJ	—	20.00	35.00	50.00	90.00	—
1817 JJ	—	20.00	35.00	50.00	90.00	—
1818 JJ	—	20.00	35.00	50.00	90.00	—
1819 JJ	—	20.00	35.00	50.00	90.00	—
1820 JJ	—	20.00	35.00	50.00	90.00	—
1821 JJ	—	20.00	35.00	50.00	90.00	—

KM# 112 1/2 ESCUDO
1.6917 g., 0.8750 Gold .0476 oz. AGW **Obv. Legend:** FERD.
VII. D. G. HISP. ET IND **Note:** Mint mark M, Mo.

Date	Mintage	VG	F	VF	XF	Unc
1814 JJ	—	100	150	225	375	—
1815/4 JJ	—	150	200	250	400	—
1815 JJ	—	150	200	250	400	—
1816 JJ	—	100	150	225	375	—
1817 JJ	—	150	200	250	400	—
1818 JJ	—	150	200	250	400	—
1819 JJ	—	150	200	250	400	—
1820 JJ	—	200	300	400	550	—

KM# 113 ESCUDO
3.3834 g., 0.9170 Gold .0997 oz. AGW **Obv. Legend:**
PHILIP. V. D. G. HISP. ET IND. REX **Note:** Struck at
Mexico City Mint, mint mark M, Mo.

Date	Mintage	VG	F	VF	XF	Unc
1732 F	—	1,000	2,000	3,000	4,000	—
1733/2 F	—	1,000	2,000	3,000	4,000	—
1734/3 MF	—	150	250	400	850	—

Date	Mintage	VG	F	VF	XF	Unc
1735/4 MF	—	150	250	400	850	—
1735 MF	—	150	250	400	850	—
1736/5 MF	—	150	250	400	850	—
1736 MF	—	150	250	400	850	—
1737 MF	—	200	300	600	1,200	—
1738/7 MF	—	200	300	600	1,200	—
1738 MF	—	200	300	600	1,200	—
1739 MF	—	200	300	600	1,200	—
1740/30 MF	—	200	300	600	1,200	—
1741 MF	—	200	300	600	1,200	—
1742 MF	—	200	300	600	1,200	—
1743/2 MF	—	150	275	450	800	—
1743 MF	—	150	250	400	700	—
1744/3 MF	—	150	250	400	700	—
1744 MF	—	150	250	400	700	—
1745 MF	—	150	250	400	700	—
1746/5 MF	—	150	250	400	700	—
1747 MF Rare	—	—	—	—	—	—

KM# 114 ESCUDO
3.3834 g., 0.9170 Gold .0997 oz. AGW **Obv:** Long bust **Obv.
Legend:** FERD. VI. D. G. HISPAN. ET IND. REX **Note:** Struck
at Mexico City Mint, mint mark M, Mo.

Date	Mintage	VG	F	VF	XF	Unc
1747 MF	—	1,650	3,000	5,000	7,500	—

KM# 115.1 ESCUDO
3.3834 g., 0.9170 Gold .0997 oz. AGW **Obv:** Short bust **Obv.
Legend:** FERD. VI. D. G. HISPAN. ET IND. REX **Note:** Struck
at Mexico City Mint, mint mark M, Mo.

Date	Mintage	VG	F	VF	XF	Unc
1748 MF	—	250	350	550	950	—
1749 MF	—	300	450	700	1,150	—
1750 MF	—	150	250	400	800	—
1751 MF	—	150	250	400	800	—

KM# 115.2 ESCUDO
3.3834 g., 0.9170 Gold .0997 oz. AGW **Obv:** Short bust **Obv.
Legend:** FERD. VI. D. G. HISPAN. ET IND. REX **Rev:**
Without 1 S flanking arms **Note:** Struck at Mexico City Mint,
mint mark M, Mo.

Date	Mintage	VG	F	VF	XF	Unc
1752 MF	—	125	225	375	750	—
1753/2 MF	—	150	250	400	800	—
1753 MF	—	150	250	400	800	—
1754 MF	—	150	250	400	800	—
1755 MM	—	150	250	400	800	—
1756 MM	—	150	250	400	800	—

KM# A116 ESCUDO
3.3834 g., 0.9170 Gold .0997 oz. AGW **Obv:** Armored bust
Note: Struck at Mexico City Mint, mint mark M, Mo.

Date	Mintage	VG	F	VF	XF	Unc
1757 MM	—	150	250	400	800	—
1759 MM	—	150	250	400	800	—

KM# 116 ESCUDO
3.3834 g., 0.9170 Gold .0997 oz. AGW **Obv. Legend:**
CAROLVS. III. D. G. HISPAN. ET IND. REX **Rev. Legend:**
NOMINA MAGNA SEQUOR **Note:** Struck at Mexico City Mint,
mint mark M, Mo.

Date	Mintage	VG	F	VF	XF	Unc
1760 MM	—	400	800	1,500	2,500	—
1761/0 MM	—	400	800	1,500	2,500	—
1761 MM	—	400	800	1,500	2,500	—

KM# 117   ESCUDO
3.3834 g., 0.9170 Gold .0997 oz. AGW **Obv:** Large bust
Obv. Legend: CAR. III. D. G. HISP. ET IND. R **Rev. Legend:**
IN. UTROQ. FELIX **Note:** Mint mark M, Mo.

Date	Mintage	VG	F	VF	XF	Unc
1762 MM	—	250	375	600	1,000	—
1763 MM	—	275	425	700	1,100	—
1764 MM	—	250	375	600	1,000	—
1765 MF	—	250	375	600	1,000	—
1766 MF	—	250	375	600	1,000	—
1767 MF	—	250	375	600	1,000	—
1768 MF	—	250	375	600	1,000	—
1769 MF	—	250	375	600	1,000	—
1770 MF	—	250	375	600	1,000	—
1771 MF	—	250	375	600	1,000	—

KM# 118.1   ESCUDO
3.3834 g., 0.9010 Gold .0980 oz. AGW **Obv:** Large bust
Obv. Legend: CAROL. III. D. G. HISPAN. ET IND. R **Rev:**
Initials and mint mark upright **Rev. Legend:** FELIX. A. D **Note:**
Mint mark M, Mo.

Date	Mintage	VG	F	VF	XF	Unc
1772 MF	—	125	150	275	475	—
1772 FM	—	125	150	275	475	—
1773 FM	—	125	150	275	475	—

KM# 118.1a   ESCUDO
3.3834 g., 0.8750 Gold .0952 oz. AGW **Obv:** Large bust
Obv. Legend: CAROL. III. D. G. HISPAN. ET IND. R **Rev:**
Initial letters and mint mark upright **Rev. Legend:** FELIX. A.
D **Note:** Mint mark M, Mo.

Date	Mintage	VG	F	VF	XF	Unc
1788 FM	—	125	150	275	475	—

KM# 118.2   ESCUDO
3.3834 g., 0.9010 Gold .0980 oz. AGW **Obv:** Large bust
Obv. Legend: CAROL. III. D. G. HISPAN. ET IND. R **Rev:**
Initials and mint mark inverted **Rev. Legend:** FELIX. A. D
Note: Mint mark M, Mo.

Date	Mintage	VG	F	VF	XF	Unc
1773 FM	—	125	150	275	475	—
1774 FM	—	125	150	275	475	—
1775 FM	—	125	150	275	475	—
1776 FM	—	125	150	275	475	—
1777 FM	—	125	150	275	475	—
1778 FF	—	125	150	275	475	—
1779 FF	—	125	150	275	475	—
1780 FF	—	125	150	275	475	—
1781 FF	—	125	150	275	475	—
1782 FF	—	125	150	275	475	—
1783/2 FF	—	125	150	275	475	—
1783 FF	—	125	150	275	475	—
1784/3 FF	—	125	150	275	475	—
1784/3 FM/F	—	125	150	275	475	—

KM# 118.2a   ESCUDO
3.3800 g., 0.8750 Gold .0950 oz. AGW **Obv:** Large bust
Obv. Legend: CAROL. III. D. G. HISPAN. ET IND. R. **Rev:**

Initials and mint mark inverted **Rev. Legend:** FELIX. A. D.
Note: Mint mark M, Mo.

Date	Mintage	VG	F	VF	XF	Unc
1785 FM	—	125	150	275	475	—
1786 FM	—	125	150	275	475	—
1787 FM	—	125	150	275	475	—
1788 FM	—	125	150	275	475	—

KM# 119   ESCUDO
3.3834 g., 0.8750 Gold .0952 oz. AGW **Obv:** Bust of Charles
III **Obv. Legend:** CAROL. IIII. D. G... **Rev:** Initial letters and
mint mark upright **Rev. Legend:** FELIX. A. D **Note:** Mint mark
M, Mo.

Date	Mintage	VG	F	VF	XF	Unc
1789 FM	—	300	550	1,000	2,000	—
1790 FM	—	300	550	1,000	2,000	—

KM# 120   ESCUDO
3.3834 g., 0.8750 Gold .0952 oz. AGW **Obv:** Armored bust
of Charles IV **Obv. Legend:** CAROL. IIII. D. G... **Rev:** Initial
letters and mint mark upright **Rev. Legend:** FELIX. A. D **Note:**
Mint mark M, Mo.

Date	Mintage	VG	F	VF	XF	Unc
1792 MF	—	125	165	235	345	—
1793 FM	—	125	165	235	345	—
1794 FM	—	125	165	235	345	—
1795 FM	—	125	165	235	345	—
1796 FM	—	125	165	235	345	—
1797 FM	—	125	165	235	345	—
1798 FM	—	125	165	235	345	—
1799 FM	—	125	165	235	345	—
1800 FM	—	125	165	235	345	—
1801 FM	—	125	165	235	345	—
1801 FT	—	125	165	235	345	—
1802 FT	—	125	165	235	345	—
1803 FT	—	125	165	235	345	—
1804/3 TH	—	125	165	235	345	—
1804 TH	—	125	165	235	345	—
1805 TH	—	125	165	235	345	—
1806/5 TH	—	125	165	235	345	—
1806 TH	—	125	165	235	345	—
1807 TH	—	125	165	235	345	—
1808 TH	—	125	165	235	345	—

KM# 121   ESCUDO
3.3834 g., 0.8750 Gold .0952 oz. AGW **Obv:** Armored bust
of Ferdinand VII **Obv. Legend:** FERDIN. VII. D. G... **Rev:**
Initial letters and mint mark upright **Rev. Legend:** FELIX. A.
D **Note:** Mint mark M, Mo.

Date	Mintage	VG	F	VF	XF	Unc
1809 HJ/TH	—	125	165	235	400	—
1809 HJ	—	125	165	235	400	—
1811/0 HJ	—	125	165	235	400	—
1812 HJ	—	150	250	300	500	—

KM# 122 ESCUDO
3.3834 g., 0.8750 Gold .0952 oz. AGW **Obv:** Undraped bust of Ferdinand VII **Obv. Legend:** FERDIN. VII. D. G... **Rev:** Initial letters and mint mark upright **Rev. Legend:** FELIX. A. D **Note:** Mint mark M, Mo.

Date	Mintage	VG	F	VF	XF	Unc
1814 HJ	—	150	250	300	500	—
1815 HJ	—	150	250	300	500	—
1815 JJ	—	150	250	300	500	—
1816 JJ	—	175	275	325	550	—
1817 JJ	—	150	250	300	500	—
1818 JJ	—	150	250	300	500	—
1819 JJ	—	150	250	300	500	—
1820 JJ	—	150	250	300	500	—

KM# 124 2 ESCUDOS
6.7660 g., 0.9170 Gold .1995 oz. AGW **Obv. Legend:** PHILIP. V. D. G. HISPAN. ET IND. REX **Rev. Legend:** INITIUM SAPIENTIAE TIMOR DOMINI **Note:** Mint mark M, Mo.

Date	Mintage	VG	F	VF	XF	Unc
1732 F	—	1,000	1,500	2,000	3,000	—
1733 F	—	750	1,000	1,500	2,500	—
1734/3 MF	—	400	500	900	1,400	—
1735 MF	—	400	500	900	1,400	—
1736/5 MF	—	400	500	900	1,400	—
1736 MF	—	400	500	900	1,400	—
1737 MF	—	400	500	900	1,400	—
1738/7 MF	—	400	500	900	1,400	—
1739 MF	—	400	500	900	1,400	—
1740/30 MF	—	400	500	900	1,400	—
1741 MF	—	400	500	900	1,400	—
1742 MF	—	400	500	900	1,400	—
1743 MF	—	400	500	900	1,400	—
1744/2 MF	—	400	500	900	1,400	—
1744 MF	—	400	500	900	1,400	—
1745 MF	—	400	500	900	1,400	—
1746/5 MF	—	400	500	900	1,400	—
1747 MF	—	400	500	900	1,400	—

KM# 125 2 ESCUDOS
6.7660 g., 0.9170 Gold .1995 oz. AGW **Obv:** Large bust **Obv. Legend:** FERD. VI. D. G... **Rev. Legend:** INITIUM... **Note:** Mint mark M, Mo.

Date	Mintage	VG	F	VF	XF	Unc
1747 MF	—	3,000	5,500	9,000	15,000	—

KM# 126.1 2 ESCUDOS
6.7660 g., 0.9170 Gold .1995 oz. AGW **Obv:** Small young bust **Obv. Legend:** FERD. VI. D. G... **Rev. Legend:** NOMINA MAGNA SEQUOR **Note:** Mint mark M, Mo.

Date	Mintage	VG	F	VF	XF	Unc
1748 MF	—	450	750	1,500	3,000	—
1749/8 MF	—	450	750	1,500	3,000	—
1750 MF	—	400	700	1,400	2,850	—
1751 MF	—	400	700	1,400	2,850	—

KM# 126.2 2 ESCUDOS
6.7660 g., 0.9170 Gold .1995 oz. AGW **Obv:** Small young bust **Obv. Legend:** FERD. VI. D. G... **Rev:** Without 2 S by arms **Rev. Legend:** NOMINA MAGNA SEQUOR **Note:** Mint mark M, Mo.

Date	Mintage	VG	F	VF	XF	Unc
1752 MF	—	400	700	1,400	2,850	—
1753 MF	—	400	700	1,400	2,850	—
1754 MF	—	600	850	1,750	3,500	—
1755 MM	—	400	700	1,400	2,850	—
1756 MM	—	600	850	1,750	3,500	—

KM# 127 2 ESCUDOS
6.7660 g., 0.9170 Gold .1995 oz. AGW **Obv:** Armored bust **Obv. Legend:** FERDND. VI. D. G... **Rev:** Without 2 S by arms **Rev. Legend:** NOMINA MAGNA SEQUOR **Note:** Mint mark M, Mo.

Date	Mintage	VG	F	VF	XF	Unc
1757 MM	—	450	750	1,500	3,000	—
1759 MM	—	450	750	1,500	3,000	—

KM# 128 2 ESCUDOS
6.7660 g., 0.9170 Gold .1995 oz. AGW **Obv:** Young bust **Obv. Legend:** CAROLVS. III. D. G... **Rev:** Without 2 S by arms **Rev. Legend:** NOMINA MAGNA SEQUOR **Note:** Mint mark M, Mo.

Date	Mintage	VG	F	VF	XF	Unc
1760 MM	—	550	1,000	2,000	4,000	—
1761 MM	—	550	1,000	2,000	4,000	—

KM# 129   2 ESCUDOS
6.7668 g., 0.9170 Gold .1995 oz. AGW **Obv:** Large young bust **Obv. Legend:** CAROLUS. III. D. G... **Rev:** Without 2 S by arms **Rev. Legend:** IN. UTROQ. FELIX. AUSPICE. DEO **Note:** Mint mark M, Mo.

Date	Mintage	VG	F	VF	XF	Unc
1762 MF	—	500	900	1,850	3,750	—
1763 MF	—	500	900	1,850	3,750	—
1764/3 MF	—	500	900	1,850	3,750	—
1765 MF	—	500	900	1,850	3,750	—
1766 MF	—	500	900	1,850	3,750	—
1767 MF	—	500	900	1,850	3,750	—
1768 MF	—	500	900	1,850	3,750	—
1769 MF	—	500	900	1,850	3,750	—
1770 MF	—	500	900	1,850	3,750	—
1771 MF	—	500	900	1,850	3,750	—

KM# 130.1   2 ESCUDOS
6.7668 g., 0.9010 Gold .1960 oz. AGW **Obv:** Older bust **Obv. Legend:** CAROLUS. III. D. G... **Rev:** Initials and mint mark upright **Rev. Legend:** IN. UTROQ. FELIX. AUSPICE. DEO **Note:** Mint mark M, Mo.

Date	Mintage	VG	F	VF	XF	Unc
1772 FM	—	200	375	550	1,000	—
1773 FM	—	200	375	550	1,000	—

KM# 130.1a   2 ESCUDOS
6.7668 g., 0.8750 Gold .1904 oz. AGW **Obv:** Older bust **Obv. Legend:** CAROLUS. III. D. G... **Rev:** Initials and mint mark upright **Rev. Legend:** IN. UTROQ. FELIX. AUSPICE. DEO **Note:** Mint mark M, Mo.

Date	Mintage	VG	F	VF	XF	Unc
1788 FM	—	175	300	450	900	—

KM# 130.2   2 ESCUDOS
6.7668 g., 0.9010 Gold .1960 oz. AGW **Obv:** Older bust **Obv. Legend:** CAROLUS. III. D. G... **Rev:** Initials and mint mark inverted **Rev. Legend:** IN. UTROQ. FELIX. AUSPICE. DEO **Note:** Mint mark M, Mo.

Date	Mintage	VG	F	VF	XF	Unc
1773 FM	—	200	375	550	1,000	—
1774 FM	—	200	375	550	1,000	—
1775 FM	—	200	375	550	1,000	—
1776 FM	—	200	375	550	1,000	—
1777 FM	—	175	300	450	900	—
1778 FF	—	175	300	450	900	—
1779 FF	—	175	300	450	900	—
1780 FF	—	175	300	450	900	—
1781 FM/M	—	175	300	450	900	—
1781 FF	—	175	300	450	900	—
1782 FF	—	175	300	450	900	—
1783 FF	—	175	300	450	900	—
1784 FF	—	175	300	450	900	—
1784 FM/F	—	175	300	450	900	—

KM# 130.2a   2 ESCUDOS
6.7668 g., 0.8750 Gold .1904 oz. AGW **Obv:** Older bust **Obv. Legend:** CAROLUS. III. D. G... **Rev:** Initials and mint mark inverted **Rev. Legend:** IN. UTROQ. FELIX. AUSPICE. DEO **Note:** Mint mark M, Mo.

Date	Mintage	VG	F	VF	XF	Unc
1785 FM	—	175	300	450	900	—
1786 FM	—	175	300	450	900	—
1787 FM	—	175	300	450	900	—
1788 FM	—	175	300	450	900	—

KM# 131   2 ESCUDOS
6.7668 g., 0.8750 Gold .1904 oz. AGW **Obv:** Bust of Charles III **Obv. Legend:** CAROL. IV. D. G... **Rev:** Initials and mint mark upright **Rev. Legend:** IN. UTROQ. FELIX. AUSPICE. DEO **Note:** Mint mark M, Mo.

Date	Mintage	VG	F	VF	XF	Unc
1789 FM	—	650	1,200	2,000	3,500	—
1790 FM	—	650	1,200	2,000	3,500	—

KM# 132   2 ESCUDOS
6.7668 g., 0.8750 Gold .1904 oz. AGW **Obv:** Armored bust of Charles IV **Obv. Legend:** CAROL. IIII. D. G... **Rev:** Initials and mint mark upright **Rev. Legend:** IN. UTROQ. FELIX. AUSPICE. DEO **Note:** Mint mark M, Mo.

Date	Mintage	VG	F	VF	XF	Unc
1791 FM Mo	—	300	375	600	950	—
over inverted						
Mo						
1792 FM	—	125	225	350	575	—
1793 FM	—	125	225	350	575	—
1794 FM	—	125	225	350	575	—
1795 FM	—	125	225	350	575	—
1796 FM	—	125	225	350	575	—
1797 FM	—	125	225	350	575	—
1798 FM	—	125	225	350	575	—
1799 FM	—	125	225	350	575	—
1800 FM	—	125	225	350	575	—
1801 FT	—	125	225	350	575	—
1802 FT	—	125	225	350	575	—
1803 FT	—	125	225	350	575	—
1804 TH	—	125	225	350	575	—
1805 TH	—	125	225	350	575	—
1806/5 TH	—	125	225	350	575	—
1807 TH	—	125	225	350	575	—
1808 TH	—	125	225	350	575	—

KM# 134   2 ESCUDOS
6.7668 g., 0.8750 Gold .1904 oz. AGW **Obv:** Undraped bust of Ferdinand VII **Obv. Legend:** FERDIN. VII. D. G... **Rev:** Initials and mint mark upright **Rev. Legend:** IN. UTROQ. FELIX. AUSPICE. DEO **Note:** Mint mark M, Mo.

Date	Mintage	VG	F	VF	XF	Unc
1814 JJ	—	250	425	700	1,200	—
1815 JJ	—	250	425	700	1,200	—
1816 JJ	—	250	425	700	1,200	—
1817 JJ	—	250	425	700	1,200	—
1818 JJ	—	250	425	700	1,200	—
1819 JJ	—	250	425	700	1,200	—
1820 JJ	—	250	425	700	1,200	—
1821 JJ	—	250	425	700	1,200	—

KM# 135   4 ESCUDOS
13.5337 g., 0.9170 Gold .3990 oz. AGW **Obv. Legend:**
PHILIP. V. D. G. HISPAN. ET IND. REX **Rev. Legend:**
INITIUM SAPIENTIAE TIMOR DOMINI **Note:** Mint mark M,
Mo.

Date	Mintage	VG	F	VF	XF	Unc
1732 Rare	—	—	—	—	—	—
1732 F Rare	—	—	—	—	—	—
1733 F Rare	—	—	—	—	—	—
1734/3 F	—	1,000	1,500	2,800	4,500	—
1734 MF	—	850	1,350	2,500	4,250	—
1735 MF	—	850	1,350	2,500	4,500	—
1736 MF	—	850	1,350	2,500	4,500	—
1737 MF	—	750	1,250	2,400	4,000	—
1738/7 MF	—	750	1,250	2,400	4,000	—
1738 MF	—	750	1,250	2,400	4,000	—
1739 MF	—	750	1,250	2,400	4,000	—
1740/30 MF	—	750	1,250	2,400	4,000	—
1740 MF	—	750	1,250	2,400	4,000	—
1741 MF	—	750	1,250	2,400	4,000	—
1742/32 MF	—	750	1,250	2,400	4,000	—
1743 MF	—	750	1,250	2,400	4,000	—
1744 MD	—	750	1,250	2,400	4,000	—
1745 MF	—	750	1,250	2,400	4,000	—
1746 MF	—	750	1,250	2,400	4,000	—
1747 MF	—	750	1,250	2,400	4,000	—
1746/5 MF	—	750	1,250	2,400	4,000	—

KM# 136   4 ESCUDOS
13.5337 g., 0.9170 Gold .3990 oz. AGW **Obv:** Large bust
Obv. Legend: FERDND. VI. D. G... **Rev. Legend:** INITIUM
SAPIENTIAE TIMOR DOMINI **Note:** Mint mark M, Mo.

Date	Mintage	VG	F	VF	XF	Unc
1747 MF	—	7,500	13,500	20,000	30,000	—

KM# 137   4 ESCUDOS
13.5337 g., 0.9170 Gold .3990 oz. AGW **Obv:** Small bust
Obv. Legend: FERDND. VI. D. G... **Rev:** 4S divided by arms
Rev. Legend: NOMINA MAGNA... **Note:** Mint mark M, Mo.

Date	Mintage	VG	F	VF	XF	Unc
1748 MF	—	1,500	3,000	5,000	8,000	—
1749 MF	—	1,500	3,000	5,000	8,000	—
1750/48 MF	—	1,500	3,000	5,000	8,000	—
1750 MF	—	1,500	3,000	5,000	8,000	—
1751 MF	—	1,500	3,000	5,000	8,000	—

KM# 138   4 ESCUDOS
13.5337 g., 0.9170 Gold .3990 oz. AGW **Obv:** Small bust
Obv. Legend: FERDND. VI. D. G... **Rev:** Without value **Rev.
Legend:** NOMINA MAGNA... **Note:** Mint mark M, Mo.

Date	Mintage	VG	F	VF	XF	Unc
1752 MF	—	1,000	2,000	3,500	6,000	—
1753 MF	—	1,000	2,000	3,500	6,000	—
1754 MF	—	1,000	2,000	3,500	6,000	—
1755 MM	—	1,000	2,000	3,500	6,000	—
1756 MM	—	1,000	2,000	3,500	6,000	—

KM# 139   4 ESCUDOS
13.5337 g., 0.9170 Gold .3990 oz. AGW **Obv:** Large full bust
Obv. Legend: FERDND. VI. D. G... **Rev:** Without value **Rev.
Legend:** NOMINA MAGNA... **Note:** Mint mark M, Mo.

Date	Mintage	VG	F	VF	XF	Unc
1757 MM	—	1,250	2,500	4,000	6,500	—
1759 MM	—	1,250	2,500	4,000	6,500	—

KM# 140   4 ESCUDOS
13.5337 g., 0.9170 Gold .3990 oz. AGW **Obv:** Young bust
Obv. Legend: CAROLVS. III. D. G... **Rev:** Without value **Rev.
Legend:** NOMINA MAGNA SEQUOR **Note:** Mint mark M, Mo.

Date	Mintage	VG	F	VF	XF	Unc
1760 MM	—	3,500	6,500	10,000	20,000	—
1761 MM	—	3,500	6,500	10,000	20,000	—

KM# 141   4 ESCUDOS
13.5337 g., 0.9170 Gold .3990 oz. AGW **Obv:** Large young
bust **Obv. Legend:** CAROLUS. III. D. G... **Rev:** Without value
Rev. Legend: IN. UTROQ. FELIX. AUSPICE. DEO **Note:**
Mint mark M, Mo.

Date	Mintage	VG	F	VF	XF	Unc
1762 MF	—	2,500	4,500	7,500	15,000	—
1763 MF	—	2,500	4,500	7,500	15,000	—
1764 MF	—	2,500	4,500	7,500	15,000	—
1765 MF	—	2,500	4,500	7,500	15,000	—
1766/5 MF	—	2,500	4,500	7,500	15,000	—
1767 MF	—	2,500	4,500	7,500	15,000	—
1768 MF	—	2,500	4,500	7,500	15,000	—
1769 MF	—	2,500	4,500	7,500	15,000	—
1770 MF	—	2,500	4,500	7,500	15,000	—
1771 MF	—	2,500	4,500	7,500	15,000	—

KM# 142.1   4 ESCUDOS
13.5337 g., 0.9010 Gold .3920 oz. AGW **Obv:** Large young
bust **Obv. Legend:** CAROL. III. D. G... **Rev:** Initials and mint
mark upright **Rev. Legend:** IN. UTROQ. FELIX. AUSPICE.
DEO **Note:** Mint mark M, Mo.

Date	Mintage	VG	F	VF	XF	Unc
1772 FM	—	400	650	1,000	2,000	—
1773 FM	—	400	650	1,000	2,000	—

KM# 142.1a   4 ESCUDOS
13.5337 g., 0.8750 Gold .3807 oz. AGW **Obv:** Large young
bust **Obv. Legend:** CAROL. III. D. G... **Rev:** Initials and mint
mark upright **Rev. Legend:** IN. UTROQ. FELIX. AUSPICE.
DEO **Note:** Mint mark M, Mo.

Date	Mintage	VG	F	VF	XF	Unc
1788 FM	—	400	650	1,000	2,000	—

KM# 142.2   4 ESCUDOS
13.5337 g., 0.9010 Gold .3920 oz. AGW **Obv:** Large young
bust **Obv. Legend:** CAROL. III. D. G... **Rev:** Initials and mint
mark inverted **Rev. Legend:** IN. UTROQ. FELIX. AUSPICE.
DEO **Note:** Mint mark M, Mo.

Date	Mintage	VG	F	VF	XF	Unc
1773 FM	—	400	600	900	1,850	—
1774 FM	—	400	600	900	1,850	—
1775 FM	—	400	600	900	1,850	—
1776 FM	—	400	600	900	1,850	—
1777 FM	—	400	600	900	1,850	—
1778 FF	—	400	600	900	1,850	—
1779 FF	—	400	600	900	1,850	—
1780 FF	—	400	600	900	1,850	—
1781 FF	—	400	600	900	1,850	—
1782 FF	—	400	600	900	1,850	—
1783 FF	—	400	600	900	1,850	—
1784 FF	—	400	600	900	1,850	—
1784/3 FM/F	—	400	600	900	1,850	—

KM# 142.2a   4 ESCUDOS
13.5337 g., 0.8750 Gold .3807 oz. AGW **Obv:** Large young
bust **Obv. Legend:** CAROL. III. D. G... **Rev:** Initials and mint
mark inverted **Rev. Legend:** IN. UTROQ. FELIX. AUSPICE.
DEO **Note:** Mint mark M, Mo.

Date	Mintage	VG	F	VF	XF	Unc
1785 FM	—	400	600	900	1,850	—
1786 FM/F	—	400	600	900	1,850	—
1786 FM	—	400	600	900	1,850	—
1787 FM	—	400	600	900	1,850	—
1788 FM	—	400	600	900	1,850	—

KM# 143.1   4 ESCUDOS
13.5337 g., 0.8750 Gold .3807 oz. AGW **Obv:** Bust of
Charles III **Obv. Legend:** CAROL. IV. D. G **Rev:** Initials and
mint mark upright **Rev. Legend:** IN. UTROQ. FELIX.
AUSPICE. DEO **Note:** Mint mark M, Mo.

Date	Mintage	VG	F	VF	XF	Unc
1789 FM	—	500	700	1,100	2,150	—
1790 FM	—	500	700	1,100	2,150	—

KM# 143.2   4 ESCUDOS
13.5337 g., 0.8750 Gold .3807 oz. AGW **Obv:** Bust of
Charles III **Obv. Legend:** CAROL. IIII D. G... **Rev:** Initials and
mint mark upright **Rev. Legend:** IN. UTROQ. FELIX.
AUSPICE. DEO **Note:** Mint mark M, Mo.

Date	Mintage	VG	F	VF	XF	Unc
1790 FM	—	600	1,000	1,800	3,000	—

KM# 144   4 ESCUDOS
13.5337 g., 0.8750 Gold .3807 oz. AGW **Obv:** Armored bust
of Charles IIII **Obv. Legend:** CAROL. IIII D. G... **Rev:** Initials
and mint mark upright **Rev. Legend:** IN. UTROQ. FELIX.
AUSPICE. DEO **Note:** Mint mark M, Mo.

Date	Mintage	VG	F	VF	XF	Unc
1792 FM	—	300	500	750	1,500	—
1793 FM	—	300	500	750	1,500	—
1794/3 FM	—	300	500	750	1,500	—
1795 FM	—	300	500	750	1,500	—
1796 FM	—	300	500	750	1,500	—
1797 FM	—	300	500	750	1,500	—
1798/7 FM	—	300	500	750	1,500	—
1798 FM	—	300	500	750	1,500	—
1799 FM	—	300	500	750	1,500	—
1800 FM	—	300	500	750	1,500	—
1801 FM	—	300	500	750	1,500	—
1801 FT	—	300	500	750	1,500	—
1802 FT	—	300	500	750	1,500	—
1803 FT	—	300	500	750	1,500	—
1804/3 TH	—	300	500	750	1,500	—
1804 TH	—	300	500	750	1,500	—
1805 TH	—	300	500	750	1,500	—
1806/5 TH	—	300	500	750	1,500	—
1807 TH	—	300	500	750	1,500	—
1808/0 TH	—	300	500	750	1,500	—
1808 TH	—	300	500	750	1,500	—

KM# 145   4 ESCUDOS
13.5337 g., 0.8750 Gold .3807 oz. AGW **Obv:** Armored bust
of Ferdinand VII **Obv. Legend:** FERDIN. VII D. G... **Rev:**
Initials and mint mark upright **Rev. Legend:** IN. UTROQ.
FELIX. AUSPICE. DEO **Note:** Mint mark M, Mo.

Date	Mintage	VG	F	VF	XF	Unc
1810 HJ	—	350	500	850	1,700	—
1811 FM	—	350	500	850	1,700	—
1812 HJ	—	350	500	850	1,700	—

KM# 146   4 ESCUDOS
13.5337 g., 0.8750 Gold .3807 oz. AGW **Obv:** Undraped
bust of Ferdinand VII **Obv. Legend:** FERDIN. VII D. G... **Rev:**
Initials and mint mark upright **Rev. Legend:** IN. UTROQ.
FELIX. AUSPICE. DEO **Note:** Mint mark M, Mo.

Date	Mintage	VG	F	VF	XF	Unc
1814 HJ	—	400	700	1,200	2,700	—
1815 HJ	—	400	700	1,200	2,700	—
1815 JJ	—	400	700	1,200	2,700	—
1816 JJ	—	400	700	1,200	2,700	—
1817 JJ	—	400	700	1,200	2,700	—
1818 JJ	—	400	700	1,200	2,700	—
1819 JJ	—	400	700	1,200	2,700	—
1820 JJ	—	400	700	1,200	2,700	—

KM# 149   8 ESCUDOS
27.0674 g., 0.9170 Gold .7980 oz. AGW **Obv:** Young bust
Obv. Legend: FERDND. VI. D. G... **Rev. Legend:** INITIUM
SAPIENTIAE TIMOR DOMINI **Note:** Mint mark M, Mo.

Date	Mintage	VG	F	VF	XF	Unc
1747 MF	—	9,000	15,000	22,000	35,000	—

KM# 148   8 ESCUDOS
27.0674 g., 0.9170 Gold .7980 oz. AGW **Obv. Legend:**
PHILIP. V. D. G. HISPAN. ET IND. REX **Rev. Legend:**
INITIUM SAPIENTIAE TIMOR DOMINI **Note:** Mint mark M,
Mo.

Date	Mintage	VG	F	VF	XF	Unc
1732 Rare	—	—	—	—	—	—
1732 F Rare	—	—	—	—	—	—
1733 F Rare	—	—	—	—	—	—
1734 MF	—	1,000	1,650	2,750	4,850	—
1734 MF/F	—	1,000	1,650	2,750	4,850	—
1735 MF	—	1,000	1,500	2,500	4,500	—
1736 MF	—	1,000	1,500	2,500	4,500	—
1737 MF	—	1,000	1,500	2,500	4,500	—
1738/7 MF	—	1,000	1,500	2,500	4,500	—
1738 MF	—	1,000	1,500	2,500	4,500	—
1739 MF	—	1,000	1,500	2,500	4,500	—
1740 MF	—	1,000	1,500	2,500	4,500	—
1740/30 MF	—	1,000	1,500	2,500	4,500	—
1741 MF	—	1,000	1,500	2,500	4,500	—
1742 MF	—	1,000	1,500	2,500	4,500	—
1743 MF	—	1,000	1,500	2,500	4,500	—
1744 MF	—	1,000	1,500	2,500	4,500	—
1744/3 MF	—	1,000	1,500	2,500	4,500	—
1745 MF	—	1,000	1,500	2,500	4,500	—
1745/4 MF	—	1,000	1,500	2,500	4,500	—
1746 MF	—	1,000	1,500	2,500	4,500	—
1746/5 MF	—	1,000	1,500	2,500	4,500	—
1747 MF	—	1,100	1,750	2,850	5,000	—

KM# 150   8 ESCUDOS
27.0674 g., 0.9170 Gold .7980 oz. AGW **Obv:** Small bust
Obv. Legend: FERDND. VI. D. G... **Rev. Legend:** NOMINA
MAGNA SEQUOR **Note:** Mint mark M, Mo.

Date	Mintage	VG	F	VF	XF	Unc
1748 MF	—	1,200	2,000	3,500	6,000	—
1749/8 MF	—	1,200	2,000	3,500	6,000	—
1749 MF	—	1,200	2,000	3,500	6,000	—
1750 MF	—	1,200	2,000	3,500	6,000	—
1751/0 MF	—	1,500	2,000	3,500	6,000	—
1751 MF	—	1,200	2,000	3,500	6,000	—

KM# 151   8 ESCUDOS
27.0674 g., 0.9170 Gold .7980 oz. AGW **Obv:** Large bust
Obv. Legend: FERDND. VI. D. G... **Rev:** Without 8 S divided
by arms **Rev. Legend:** NOMINA MAGNA SEQUOR **Note:**
Mint mark M, Mo.

Date	Mintage	VG	F	VF	XF	Unc
1752 MF	—	1,200	2,000	3,500	6,000	—
1753 MF	—	1,200	2,000	3,500	6,000	—
1754 MF	—	1,200	2,000	3,500	6,000	—
1755 MM	—	1,200	2,000	3,500	6,000	—
1756 MM	—	1,200	2,000	3,500	6,000	—

KM# 153   8 ESCUDOS
27.0674 g., 0.9170 Gold .7980 oz. AGW **Obv:** Young bust
with Order of the Golden Fleece at date **Obv. Legend:**
CAROLVS. III. D. G... **Rev:** Without 8 S divided by arms **Rev.**
Legend: NOMINA MAGNA SEQUOR **Note:** Mint mark M, Mo.

Date	Mintage	VG	F	VF	XF	Unc
1760 MM	—	1,750	3,000	5,000	9,000	—
1761/0 MM	—	2,000	3,500	5,500	10,000	—
1761 MM	—	2,000	3,500	5,500	10,000	—

KM# 152   8 ESCUDOS
27.0674 g., 0.9170 Gold .7980 oz. AGW **Obv:** Medium, full
bust **Obv. Legend:** FERDND. VI. D. G... **Rev:** Without 8 S
divided by arms **Rev. Legend:** NOMINA MAGNA SEQUOR
Note: Mint mark M, Mo.

Date	Mintage	VG	F	VF	XF	Unc
1757 MM	—	1,200	2,000	3,500	6,000	—
1758 MM	—	1,200	2,000	3,500	6,000	—
1759 MM	—	1,200	2,000	3,500	6,000	—

KM# 154   8 ESCUDOS
27.0674 g., 0.9170 Gold .7980 oz. AGW **Obv:** Young bust
with Order of the Golden Fleece on chest **Obv. Legend:**
CAROLVS. III. D. G... **Rev:** Without 8 S divided by arms **Rev.**
Legend: NOMINA MAGNA SEQUOR **Note:** Mint mark M, Mo.

Date	Mintage	VG	F	VF	XF	Unc
1761 MM	—	1,750	3,000	5,250	9,500	—

KM# 155   8 ESCUDOS
27.0674 g., 0.9170 Gold .7980 oz. AGW **Obv:** Large bust
Obv. Legend: CAROLUS. III. D. G... **Rev:** Without 8 S divided
by arms **Rev. Legend:** IN. UTROQ. FELIX. AUSPICE **Note:**
Mint mark M, Mo.

Date	Mintage	VG	F	VF	XF	Unc
1762 MM	—	1,600	2,750	4,500	8,500	—
1763 MM	—	1,600	2,750	4,500	8,500	—
1764 MF	—	1,750	3,000	5,000	9,000	—
1764/2 MF	—	1,750	3,000	5,000	9,000	—
1764 MM	—	1,750	3,000	5,000	9,000	—
1765/4 MF	—	1,750	3,000	5,000	9,000	—
1765/4 MM	—	1,750	3,000	5,000	9,000	—
1765 MF	—	1,750	3,000	5,000	9,000	—
1765 MM	—	1,500	2,500	4,000	7,500	—
1766 MF	—	1,500	2,500	4,000	7,500	—
1767/6 MF	—	1,500	2,500	4,000	7,500	—
1767 MF	—	1,500	2,500	4,000	7,500	—
1768/7 MF	—	1,500	2,500	4,000	7,500	—

Date	Mintage	VG	F	VF	XF	Unc
1768 MF	—	1,500	2,500	4,000	7,500	—
1769 MF	—	1,500	2,500	4,000	7,500	—
1770 MF	—	1,500	2,500	4,000	7,500	—
1771 MF	—	1,750	3,000	5,000	9,000	—

Date	Mintage	VG	F	VF	XF	Unc
1776 FM	—	500	700	1,100	1,650	—
1777/6 FM	—	500	700	1,100	1,650	—
1777 FM	—	500	700	1,100	1,650	—
1778 FF	—	500	700	1,100	1,650	—
1779 FF	—	500	700	1,100	1,650	—
1780 FF	—	500	700	1,100	1,650	—
1781 FF	—	500	700	1,100	1,650	—
1782 FF	—	500	700	1,100	1,650	—
1783 FF	—	500	700	1,100	1,650	—
1784 FF	—	500	700	1,100	1,650	—
1784 FM/F	—	500	700	1,100	1,650	—
1784 FM	—	500	700	1,100	1,650	—
1785 FM	—	500	700	1,100	1,650	—

KM# 156.1   8 ESCUDOS
27.0674 g., 0.9010 Gold .7840 oz. AGW   **Obv:** Mature bust
Obv. Legend: CAROL. III. D. G... **Rev:** Initials and mint mark
upright **Rev. Legend:** ... AUSPICE. DEO **Note:** Mint mark M,
Mo.

Date	Mintage	VG	F	VF	XF	Unc
1772 FM	—	500	750	1,250	2,000	—
1773 FM	—	550	850	1,350	2,250	—

KM# 156.1a   8 ESCUDOS
27.0674 g., 0.8750 Gold .7615 oz. AGW   **Obv:** Mature bust **Obv.
Legend:** CAROL. III. D. G... **Rev:** Initials and mint mark upright
Rev. Legend: ... AUSPICE. DEO **Note:** Mint mark M, Mo.

Date	Mintage	VG	F	VF	XF	Unc
1788 FM	—	500	700	1,100	1,650	—

KM# 156.2a   8 ESCUDOS
27.0674 g., 0.8750 Gold .7615 oz. AGW   **Obv:** Mature bust
Obv. Legend: CAROL. III. D. G... **Rev:** Initials and mint mark
inverted **Rev. Legend:** ... AUSPICE. DEO **Note:** Mint mark
M, Mo.

Date	Mintage	VG	F	VF	XF	Unc
1786 FM	—	500	700	1,100	1,650	—
1787 FM	—	500	700	1,100	1,650	—
1788 FM	—	500	700	1,100	1,650	—

KM# 156.2   8 ESCUDOS
27.0674 g., 0.9010 Gold .7840 oz. AGW   **Obv:** Mature bust
Obv. Legend: CAROL. III. D. G... **Rev:** Initials and mint mark
inverted **Rev. Legend:** ... AUSPICE. DEO **Note:** Mint mark
M, Mo.

Date	Mintage	VG	F	VF	XF	Unc
1773 FM	—	500	700	1,100	1,650	—
1774 FM	—	500	700	1,100	1,650	—
1775 FM	—	500	700	1,100	1,650	—

KM# 157   8 ESCUDOS
27.0674 g., 0.8750 Gold .7615 oz. AGW   **Obv:** Bust of Charles
III **Obv. Legend:** CAROL. IV. D. G... **Rev:** Arms, Order chain
Rev. Legend: IN UTROQ... A. D **Note:** Mint mark M, Mo.

Date	Mintage	VG	F	VF	XF	Unc
1789 FM	—	500	700	1,150	2,000	—
1790 FM	—	500	700	1,150	2,000	—

Date	Mintage	VG	F	VF	XF	Unc
1801 FT	—	350	450	625	1,000	—
1802 FT	—	350	450	625	1,000	—
1803 FT	—	350	450	625	1,000	—
1804/3 TH	—	400	500	700	1,150	—
1804 TH	—	350	450	625	1,000	—
1805 TH	—	350	450	625	1,000	—
1806 TH	—	350	450	625	1,000	—
1807/6 TH	—	400	500	700	1,150	—
1807 TH Mo over inverted Mo	—	400	500	700	1,150	—
1808/7 TH	—	450	600	800	1,250	—
1807 TH	—	350	450	625	1,000	—
1808 TH	—	450	600	800	1,250	—

KM# 158   8 ESCUDOS
27.0674 g., 0.8750 oz. AGW **Obv:** Bust of Charles III **Obv. Legend:** CAROL. IIII. D. G... **Rev:** Arms, Order chain **Rev. Legend:** IN UTROQ... A. D **Note:** Mint mark M, Mo.

Date	Mintage	VG	F	VF	XF	Unc
1790 FM	—	500	700	1,150	2,000	—

KM# 160   8 ESCUDOS
27.0674 g., 0.8750 Gold .7615 oz. AGW **Obv:** Armored bust of Ferdinand VII **Obv. Legend:** FERDIN. VII. D. G... **Rev:** Arms, Order chain **Rev. Legend:** IN UTROQ. FELIX **Note:** Mint mark M, Mo.

Date	Mintage	VG	F	VF	XF	Unc
1808 TH	—	400	500	750	1,250	—
1809 HJ	—	400	500	750	1,350	—
1810 HJ	—	375	475	700	1,200	—
1811/0 HJ	—	425	525	800	1,350	—
1811 HJ H/T	—	425	525	800	1,350	—
1811 HJ	—	425	525	800	1,350	—
1811 JJ	—	375	475	700	1,200	—
1812 JJ	—	375	475	700	1,200	—

KM# 159   8 ESCUDOS
27.0674 g., 0.8750 Gold .7615 oz. AGW **Obv:** Armored bust of Charles IIII **Obv. Legend:** CAROL. IIII. D. G... **Rev:** Arms, Order chain **Rev. Legend:** IN UTROQ. FELIX **Note:** Mint mark M, Mo.

Date	Mintage	VG	F	VF	XF	Unc
1791 FM	—	350	450	625	1,000	—
1792 FM	—	350	450	625	1,000	—
1793 FM	—	350	450	625	1,000	—
1794 FM	—	350	450	625	1,000	—
1795 FM	—	350	450	625	1,000	—
1796/5 FM	—	400	500	700	1,150	—
1796 FM	—	350	450	625	1,000	—
1797 FM	—	350	450	625	1,000	—
1797 FM EPLIX	—	400	500	700	1,150	—
1798 FM	—	350	450	625	1,000	—
1799 FM	—	350	450	625	1,000	—
1800 FM	—	350	450	625	1,000	—
1801/0 FT	—	400	500	700	1,150	—
1801 FM	—	350	450	625	1,000	—

KM# 161   8 ESCUDOS
27.0674 g., 0.8750 Gold .7615 oz. AGW **Obv:** Undraped bust of Ferdinand VII **Obv. Legend:** FERDIN. VII. D. G... **Rev:** Arms, Order chain **Rev. Legend:** IN UTROQ. FELIX **Note:** Mint mark M, Mo.

Date	Mintage	VG	F	VF	XF	Unc
1814 JJ	—	360	465	650	1,000	—
1815/4 JJ	—	400	500	700	1,150	—
1815/4 HJ	—	400	500	700	1,150	—
1815 JJ	—	360	465	650	1,000	—
1815 HJ	—	360	465	650	1,000	—
1816 JJ	—	360	465	650	1,000	—
1817 JJ	—	400	500	700	1,150	—
1818/7 JJ	—	360	465	675	1,100	—
1818 JJ	—	360	465	675	1,100	—
1819 JJ	—	360	465	675	1,100	—
1820 JJ	—	360	465	675	1,100	—
1821 JJ	—	400	500	750	1,300	—

PROCLAMATION MEDALLIC COINAGE

The Q used in the following listings refer to Standard Catalog of Mexican Coins, Paper Money, Stocks, Bonds, and Medals by Krause Publications, Inc., ©1981.

KM# Q22   1/2 REAL
1.6000 g., Silver **Issuer:** Mexico City **Obv. Legend:** A CARLOS IV REY DE ESPANA Y DE LAS YNDIAS **Rev. Legend:** PROCLAMADO EN MEXICO ANO DE 1789

Date	Mintage	F	VF	XF	Unc	BU
1789	—	20.00	28.50	40.00	—	—

KM# Q22a   1/2 REAL
Bronze **Issuer:** Mexico City **Obv. Legend:** A CARLOS IV REY DE ESPANA Y DE LAS YNDIAS **Rev. Legend:** PROCLAMADO EN MEXICO ANO DE 1789

Date	Mintage	F	VF	XF	Unc	BU
1789	—	22.50	35.00	50.00	—	—

KM# Q23   1/2 REAL
Silver **Issuer:** Mexico City **Obv:** Crowned arms in double-lined circle **Obv. Legend:** A CARLOS IV REY DE ESPANA Y DE LAS YNDIAS **Rev. Legend:** PROCLAMADO EN MEXICO ANO DE 1789

Date	Mintage	F	VF	XF	Unc	BU
1789	—	20.00	28.50	40.00	—	—

KM# Q23a   1/2 REAL
Bronze **Issuer:** Mexico City **Obv:** Crowned arms in double-lined circle **Obv. Legend:** A CARLOS IV REY DE ESPANA Y DE LAS YNDIAS **Rev. Legend:** PROCLAMADO EN MEXICO ANO DE 1789

Date	Mintage	F	VF	XF	Unc	BU
1789	—	22.50	35.00	50.00	—	—

KM# Q24   REAL
Silver **Issuer:** Mexico City **Obv. Legend:** A CARLOS IV REY DE ESPANA Y DE LAS YNDIAS **Rev. Legend:** PROCLAMADO EN MEXICO ANO DE 1789

Date	Mintage	F	VF	XF	Unc	BU
1789	—	20.00	28.50	40.00	—	—

KM# Q24a   REAL
Bronze **Issuer:** Mexico City **Obv. Legend:** A CARLOS IV REY DE ESPANA Y DE LAS YNDIAS **Rev. Legend:** PROCLAMADO EN MEXICO ANO DE 1789

Date	Mintage	F	VF	XF	Unc	BU
1789	—	22.50	35.00	50.00	—	—

KM# Q-A24   REAL
Silver **Issuer:** Mexico City **Obv:** Crowned arms in double-lined circle **Obv. Legend:** A CARLOS IV REY DE ESPANA Y DE LAS YNDIAS **Rev. Legend:** PROCLAMADO EN MEXICO ANO DE 1789

Date	Mintage	F	VF	XF	Unc	BU
1789	—	20.00	28.50	40.00	—	—

KM# Q-A24a   REAL
Copper **Issuer:** Mexico City **Obv:** Crowned arms in double-lined circle **Obv. Legend:** A CARLOS IV REY DE ESPANA Y DE LAS YNDIAS **Rev. Legend:** PROCLAMADO EN MEXICO ANO DE 1789

Date	Mintage	F	VF	XF	Unc	BU
1789	—	22.50	35.00	50.00	—	—

KM# Q8   REAL
Silver **Issuer:** Chiapa **Obv:** Crowned arms between pillars, IR below **Obv. Legend:** FERNANDO VII REY DE ESPANA Y DE SUS INDIAS **Rev:** Legend in 5 lines within wreath **Rev. Legend:** PROCLA/MADO/ENCIUD/R. DECHIAPPA/1808

Date	Mintage	F	VF	XF	Unc	BU
1808	—	20.00	32.50	47.50	75.00	—

KM# Q25   2 REALES
6.7000 g., Silver **Issuer:** Mexico City **Obv. Legend:** A CARLOS IV REY DE ESPANA Y DE LAS YNDIAS **Rev. Legend:** PROCLAMADO EN MEXICO ANO DE 1789

Date	Mintage	F	VF	XF	Unc	BU
1789	—	35.00	50.00	75.00	—	—

KM# Q25a   2 REALES
6.7000 g., Bronze **Issuer:** Mexico City **Obv. Legend:** A CARLOS IV REY DE ESPANA Y DE LAS YNDIAS **Rev. Legend:** PROCLAMADO EN MEXICO ANO DE 1789

Date	Mintage	F	VF	XF	Unc	BU
1789	—	30.00	45.00	60.00	—	—

KM# Q64   2 REALES
Silver **Issuer:** Queretaro **Obv. Legend:** FERNANDO VII REY DE ESPANA

Date	Mintage	F	VF	XF	Unc	BU
1808	—	20.00	37.50	67.50	100	—

KM# Q10   2 REALES
Silver **Issuer:** Chiapa **Obv. Legend:** FERNANDO VII REY DE ESPANA Y DE SUS INDIAS

Date	Mintage	F	VF	XF	Unc	BU
1808	—	37.50	57.50	78.50	115	—

KM# Q27   4 REALES
13.6000 g., Silver **Issuer:** Mexico City **Obv. Legend:** A CARLOS IV REY DE ESPANA Y DE LAS YNDIAS **Rev. Legend:** PROCLAMADO EN MEXICO ANO DE 1789

Date	Mintage	F	VF	XF	Unc	BU
1789	—	100	150	225	—	—

KM# Q27a   4 REALES
13.6000 g., Bronze **Issuer:** Mexico City **Obv. Legend:** A CARLOS IV REY DE ESPANA Y DE LAS YNDIAS **Rev. Legend:** PROCLAMADO EN MEXICO ANO DE 1789

Date	Mintage	F	VF	XF	Unc	BU
1789	—	70.00	100	150	—	—

KM# Q-A66   4 REALES
Silver **Issuer:** Queretaro **Obv. Legend:** FERNANDO VII REY DE ESPANA

Date	Mintage	F	VF	XF	Unc	BU
1808	—	85.00	135	200	325	—

KM# Q28   8 REALES
27.0000 g., Silver **Issuer:** Mexico City **Obv. Legend:** A CARLOS IV REY DE ESPANA Y DE LAS YNDIAS **Rev. Legend:** PROCLAMADO EN MEXICO ANO DE 1789

Date	Mintage	F	VF	XF	Unc	BU
1789	—	200	275	400	—	—

KM# Q28a   8 REALES
27.0000 g., Bronze **Issuer:** Mexico City **Obv. Legend:** A CARLOS IV REY DE ESPANA Y DE LAS YNDIAS **Rev. Legend:** PROCLAMADO EN MEXICO ANO DE 1789

Date	Mintage	F	VF	XF	Unc	BU
1789	—	70.00	100	150	—	—

KM# Q68   8 REALES
Silver **Issuer:** Queretaro **Obv. Legend:** FERNANDO VII REY DE ESPANA

Date	Mintage	F	VF	XF	Unc	BU
1808	—	185	350	475	625	—

EMPIRE OF ITURBIDE

RULERS
Augustin I Iturbide, 1822-1823
MINT MARKS
Mo - Mexico City
ASSAYERS' INITIALS
JA - Jose Garcia Ansaldo, 1812-1833
JM - Joaquin Davila Madrid, 1809-1833

MILLED COINAGE

16 Reales = 1 Escudo

KM# 299   1/8 REAL
Copper **Ruler:** Augustin I Iturbide **Rev. Inscription:** DE LA
PROVINCIA DE NUEVA VISCAYA

Date	Mintage	Good	VG	F	VF	XF
1821D	—	22.50	50.00	85.00	150	—
1822D	—	7.50	13.50	28.50	60.00	—
1823D	—	7.50	12.50	25.00	50.00	—

KM# 300   1/4 REAL
Copper **Ruler:** Augustin I Iturbide **Rev. Inscription:** DE LA
PROVINCIA DE NUEVA VISCAYA

Date	Mintage	Good	VG	F	VF	XF
1822D	—	160	275	400	550	—

KM# 301   1/2 REAL
0.9030 Silver **Ruler:** Augustin I Iturbide

Date	Mintage	F	VF	XF	Unc	BU
1822Mo JM	—	20.00	40.00	80.00	300	—
1823Mo JM	—	15.00	30.00	60.00	250	—

KM# 302   REAL
0.9030 Silver **Ruler:** Augustin I Iturbide

Date	Mintage	VG	F	VF	XF	Unc
1822Mo JM	—	100	175	350	550	900

KM# 303   2 REALES
6.7667 g., 0.9030 Silver **Ruler:** Augustin I Iturbide

Date	Mintage	F	VF	XF	Unc	BU
1822Mo JM	—	50.00	100	350	1,000	—
1823Mo JM	—	40.00	80.00	250	850	—

KM# 304   8 REALES
27.0674 g., 0.9030 Silver **Ruler:** Augustin I Iturbide

Date	Mintage	F	VF	XF	Unc	BU
1822Mo JM	—	75.00	150	300	950	—
1822Mo JM	—	—	—	—	—	—
Proof, 3 known						

Note: Ponterio & Associates Sale #86, 04-97, choice AU
Proof realized $12,650.

KM# 305   8 REALES
0.9030 Silver **Ruler:** Augustin I Iturbide **Obv:** Bust similar to
8 Escudos, KM#131 **Rev:** Similar to KM#304

Date	Mintage	F	VF	XF	Unc	BU
1822Mo JM Rare	—	—	—	—	—	—

KM# 306.1   8 REALES
0.9030 Silver **Ruler:** Augustin I Iturbide **Obv:** Legend divided
Rev: 8 R.J.M. at upper left of eagle **Note:** Type I.

Date	Mintage	F	VF	XF	Unc	BU
1822Mo JM	—	90.00	170	450	1,300	—

KM# 306.2   8 REALES
0.9030 Silver **Ruler:** Augustin I Iturbide **Obv:** Legend divided
Rev: Cross on crown **Note:** Type I.

Date	Mintage	F	VF	XF	Unc	BU
1822Mo JM	—	650	1,000	—	—	—

KM# 307 8 REALES
0.9030 Silver **Ruler:** Augustin I Iturbide **Obv:** Similar to KM#306 **Rev:** Similar to KM#310 **Note:** Type II.

Date	Mintage	F	VF	XF	Unc	BU
1822Mo JM	—	150	350	650	2,250	—

KM# 308 8 REALES
0.9030 Silver **Ruler:** Augustin I Iturbide **Obv:** Continous legend with long smooth truncation **Rev:** Similar to KM#306 **Note:** Type III.

Date	Mintage	F	VF	XF	Unc	BU
1822Mo JM	—	175	500	950	2,250	—

Note: Variety with long, straight truncation is valued at $5,000 in uncirculated condition

KM# 309 8 REALES
0.9030 Silver **Ruler:** Augustin I Iturbide **Obv:** Similar to KM#308 **Rev:** Similar to KM#310 **Note:** Type IV.

Date	Mintage	F	VF	XF	Unc	BU
1822Mo JM	—	50.00	120	250	850	—

KM# 310 8 REALES
0.9030 Silver **Ruler:** Augustin I Iturbide **Obv:** Continuous legend with short irregular truncation **Rev:** 8 R.J.M. below eagle **Note:** Type V.

Date	Mintage	F	VF	XF	Unc	BU
1822Mo JM	—	50.00	120	225	900	—
1823Mo JM	—	50.00	120	225	900	—

KM# 311 8 REALES
0.9030 Silver **Ruler:** Augustin I Iturbide **Obv:** Bust with long truncation **Rev:** Similar to KM#310 **Note:** Type VI.

Date	Mintage	F	VF	XF	Unc	BU
1822Mo JM Rare	—	—	—	—	—	—

KM# 312 4 SCUDOS
13.5334 g., 0.8750 Gold **Ruler:** Augustin I Iturbide **Obv:** Bust **Rev:** Eagle in shield

Date	Mintage	F	VF	XF	Unc	BU
1823Mo JM	—	1,000	1,750	2,850	5,500	—

KM# 313.1   8 SCUDOS
27.0674 g., 0.8750 Gold   **Ruler:** Augustin I Iturbide **Obv.**
Legend: AUGUSTINUS

Date	Mintage	F	VF	XF	Unc	BU
1822Mo JM	—	1,200	2,000	3,750	—	—

Note: Superior Casterline sale 5-89 choice AU realized
$11,000

KM# 313.2   8 SCUDOS
0.8750 Gold   **Ruler:** Augustin I Iturbide **Obv:** Error in legend
Obv. Legend: AUGSTINUS

Date	Mintage	F	VF	XF	Unc	BU
1822Mo JM	—	1,250	2,250	4,200	—	—

KM# 314   8 SCUDOS
0.8750 Gold   **Ruler:** Augustin I Iturbide **Obv:** Large bust **Rev:**
Eagle in shield

Date	Mintage	F	VF	XF	Unc	BU
1823Mo JM	—	1,000	1,800	3,250	6,000	—

REPUBLIC
First

MINT MARKS
A, AS - Alamos
CE - Real de Catorce
CA,CH - Chihuahua
C, Cn, Gn(error) - Culiacan
D, Do - Durango
EoMo - Estado de Mexico
Ga - Guadalajara
GC - Guadalupe y Calvo
G, Go - Guanajuato
H, Ho - Hermosillo
M, Mo - Mexico City
O, OA - Oaxaca
SLP, PI, P, I/P - San Luis Potosi
Z, Zs – Zacatecas

ASSAYERS INITIALS

ALAMOS MINT

PG	1862-68	Pascual Gaxiola
DL, L	1866-79	Domingo Larraguibel
AM	1872-74	Antonio Moreno
ML, L	1878-95	Manuel Larraguibel

REAL DE CATORCE MINT

ML	1863	Mariano Cristobal Ramirez

CHIHUAHUA MINT

MR	1831-34	Mariano Cristobal Ramirez
AM	1833-39	Jose Antonio Mucharraz
MJ	1832	Jose Mariano Jimenez
RG	1839-56	Rodrigo Garcia
JC	1856-65	Joaquin Campa
BA	1858	Bruno Arriada
FP	1866	Francisco Potts
JC	1866-1868	Jose Maria Gomez del Campo
MM, M	1868-95	Manuel Merino
AV	1873-80	Antonio Valero
EA	1877	Eduardo Avila
JM	1877	Jacobo Mucharraz
GR	1877	Guadalupe Rocha
MG	1880-82	Manuel Gameros

CULIACAN MINT

CE	1846-70	Clemente Espinosa de los Monteros
C	1870	???
PV	1860-61	Pablo Viruega
MP, P	1871-76	Manuel Onofre Parodi
GP	1876	Celso Gaxiola & Manuel Onofre Parodi
CG, G	1876-78	Celso Gaxiola
JD, D	1878-82	Juan Dominguez
AM, M	1882-1899	Antonio Moreno
F	1870	Fernando Ferrari
JQ, Q	1899-1903	Jesus S. Quiroz

DURANGO MINT

RL	1825-1832	???
RM	1830-48	Ramon Mascarenas
OMC	1840	Octavio Martinez de Castro
CM	1848-76	Clemente Moron
JMR	1849-52	Jose Maria Ramirez
CP, P	1853-64, 1867-73	Carlos Leon de la Pena
LT	1864-65	???
JMP, P	1877	Carlos Miguel de la Palma
PE, E	1878	Pedro Espejo
TB, B	1878-80	Trinidad Barrera
JP	1880-94	J. Miguel Palma
MC, C,	1882-90	Manuel M. Canseco or Melchor Calderon
JB	1885	Jocobo Blanco
ND, D	1892-95	Norberto Dominguez

ESTADO DE MEXICO MINT

L	1828-30	Luis Valazquez de la Cadena
F	1828-30	Francisco Parodi

GUADALAJARA MINT

FS	1818-35	Francisco Suarez
JM	1830-32	???
JG	1836-39, 1842-67	Juan de Dios Guzman
MC	1839-46	Manuel Cueras
JM	1867-69	Jesus P. Manzano
IC, C	1869-77	Ignacio Canizo y Soto
MC	1874-75	Manuel Contreras
JA, A	1877-81	Julio Arancivia
FS, S	1880-82	Fernando Sayago
TB, B	1883-84	Trinidad Barrera
AH, H	1884-85	Antonio Hernandez y Prado
JS, S	1885-95	Jose S. Schiafino

GUADALUPE Y CALVO MINT

MP	1844-52	Manuel Onofre Parodi

GUANAJUATO MINT

JJ	1825-26	Jose Mariano Jimenez
MJ, MR, JM, PG, PJ, PF		???
PM	1841-48, 1853-61	Patrick Murphy
YF	1862-68	Yldefonso Flores
YE	1862-63	Ynocencio Espinoza
FR	1870-78	Faustino Ramirez
SB, RR		???
RS	1891-1900	Rosendo Sandoval

HERMOSILLO MINT

PP	1835-36	Pedro Peimbert
FM	1871-76	Florencio Monteverde
MP	1866	Manuel Onofre Parodi
PR	1866-75	Pablo Rubio
R	1874-75	Pablo Rubio
GR	1877	Guadalupe Rocha
AF, F	1876-77	Alejandro Fourcade
JA, A	1877-83	Jesus Acosta
FM, M	1883-86	Fernando Mendez
FG, G	1886-95	Fausto Gaxiola

MEXICO CITY MINT

Because of the great number of assayers for this mint (Mexico City is a much larger mint than any of the others)there is much confusion as to which initial stands for which assayer at any one time. Therefore we feel that it would be of no value to list the assayers.

OAXACA MINT

AE	1859-91	Agustin Endner
E	1889-90	Agustin Endner
FR	1861-64	Francisco de la Rosa
EN	1890	Eduardo Navarro Luna
N	1890	Eduardo Navarro Luna

POTOSI MINT

JS	1827-42	Juan Sanabria
AM	1838, 1843-49	Jose Antonio Mucharraz
PS	1842-43, 1848-49, 1857-61, 1867-70	Pompaso Sanabria
S	1869-70	Pomposo Sanabria
MC	1849-59	Mariano Catano
RO	1859-65	Romualdo Obregon
MH, H	1870-85	Manuel Herrera Razo
O	1870-73	Juan R. Ochoa
CA, G	1867-70	Carlos Aguirre Gomez
BE, E	1879-81	Blas Escontria
LC, C	1885-86	Luis Cuevas
MR, R	1886-93	Mariano Reyes

ZACATECAS MINT

A	1825-29	Adalco
Z	1825-26	Mariano Zaldivar
V	1824-31	Jose Mariano Vela
O	1829-67	Manuel Ochoa
M	1831-67	Manuel Miner
VL	1860-66	Vicente Larranaga
JS	1867-68, 1876-86	J.S. de Santa Ana
YH	1868-74	Ygnacio Hierro
JA	1874-76	Juan H. Acuna
FZ	1886-1905	Francisco de P. Zarate

Die Varieties
Similar basic designs were utilized by all the Mexican mints, but many variations are noticeable, particularly in the eagle, cactus and sprays.

1835 Durango, 8 Escudos
Illustration enlarged.
A large winged eagle was portrayed on the earlier coinage of the new republic.

1849 Mexico City, 8 Escudos
Illustration enlarged.
The later eagle featured undersized wings.

1844 Durango, 8 Escudos
Illustration enlarged.

The early renditions of the hand held Liberty cap over open book were massive in the gold escudo series.

1864 Durango, 8 Escudos

Illustration enlarged.

A finer, more petite style was adopted later on in the gold escudo series.

PROFILE EAGLE COINAGE

The first coins of the Republic were of the distinctive Profile Eagle style, sometimes called the "Hooked Neck Eagle". They were struck first in Mexico City in 1823 in denominations of eight reales and eight escudos. In 1824, they were produced at the Durango and Guanajuato mints in addition to Mexico City. Denominations included the one half, one, two and eight reales. No gold escudos of this design were struck in 1824. In 1825, only the eight reales were struck briefly at the Guanajuato mint.

NOTE: For a more extensive examination of Profile Eagle Coinage, please refer to Hookneck - El Aguilade Perfil by Clyde Hubbard and David O Harrow.

KM# 369 1/2 REAL
1.6900 g., 0.9030 Silver .0490 oz. ASW **Obv:** Full breast Profile eagle **Rev:** Cap and rays **Note:** Die varieties exist.

Date	Mintage	F	VF	XF	Unc	BU
1824Mo JM	—	45.00	75.00	150	600	—

KM# 371.1 REAL
3.3800 g., 0.9030 Silver .081 oz. ASW **Obv:** Thin Profile eagle **Rev:** Superscript S reversed

Date	Mintage	F	VF	XF	Unc	BU
1824Do RL	—	3,750	7,500	10,000	15,000	—

KM# 371.2 REAL
3.3800 g., 0.9030 Silver .081 oz. ASW **Obv:** Thin Profile eagle **Rev:** Superscript S normal

Date	Mintage	F	VF	XF	Unc	BU
1824Do RL 3 known	—	—	—	—	—	—

Mint mark: Do

KM# 373.1 2 REALES
6.7600 g., 0.9030 Silver .1962 oz. ASW **Obv:** Profile eagle **Rev:** Cap and rays **Note:** Die varieties exist.

Date	Mintage	F	VF	XF	Unc	BU
1824Do RL	—	50.00	125	850	2,200	—

KM# 373.2 2 REALES
6.7600 g., 0.9030 Silver .1962 oz. ASW **Obv:** Thin Profile eagle **Rev:** Type I, dot before 2R in legend

Date	Mintage	F	VF	XF	Unc	BU
1824D RL	—	100	200	1,000	3,000	—

KM# 373.3 2 REALES
6.7600 g., 0.9030 Silver .1962 oz. ASW **Obv:** Thin Profile eagle **Rev:** Type II, no dot before 2R in legend

Date	Mintage	F	VF	XF	Unc	BU
1824D RL	—	100	200	1,000	3,000	—

KM# 373.4 2 REALES
Obv: Profile eagle **Note:** Varieties exist.

Date	Mintage	F	VF	XF	Unc	BU
1824Mo JM	—	30.00	70.00	450	2,000	—

Note: No coins are known with visible feather details on the eagle's breast

1825/4 JJ overdate

NOTE: Most examples of this overdate exhibit the results of a warped obverse die.

NOTE: Other easily identified die varieties are the 1824 w/the missing superscript "s" for granos and the 1825 w/a dash under the "I" of MEXICANA resulting from a die chip, but these die varieties are not rare.

NOTE: Guanajuato eight reales are characterized by flat strikes on large, thin planchets. Visible feather details on the eagle's breast and legible Libertads on the cap are the exception.

Tight snake loop at eagle's beak.

Open snake loop at eagle's beak.

The Standard or Republic Edge

The Colonial or Circle & Rectangle

The standard Flat-Topped Three

Typical Submissive
Snake Obverse

Typical Folded
Snake Obverse

NOTE: Legible Libertads on the Cap are common on Durango eight reales.

Med. Libertad   Small Libertad   Large Libertad
Cap Reverse   Cap Reverse   Cap Reverse

NOTE: The three styles of obverses and the three styles of reverses were combined to make six distinct varieties of coins.

KM# 376.1 8 REALES
27.0700 g., 0.9030 Silver .7859 oz. ASW **Obv:** Thin profile eagle, defiant snake **Rev:** Medium Libertad

Date	Mintage	F	VF	XF	Unc	BU
1824Do RL	—	500	1,200	4,500	7,000	—

Note: Five die varieties are known, all are rare

KM# 376.2   8 REALES
27.0700 g., 0.9030 Silver .7859 oz. ASW **Obv:** Thin profile
eagle, defiant snake **Rev:** Small Libertad

Date	Mintage	F	VF	XF	Unc	BU
1824Do RL	—	300	400	1,600	3,500	—

Note: Eleven die varieties are known, some are rare

KM# 376.3   8 REALES
27.0700 g., 0.9030 Silver .7859 oz. ASW **Obv:** Thin profile
eagle, submissive snake **Rev:** Small Libertad

Date	Mintage	F	VF	XF	Unc	BU
1824Do RL	—	200	350	1,250	2,750	—

Note: Seven die varieties are known, some are rare

KM# 376.4   8 REALES
27.0700 g., 0.9030 Silver .7859 oz. ASW **Obv:** Thin profile
eagle, submissive snake **Rev:** Large Libertad

Date	Mintage	F	VF	XF	Unc	BU
1824Do RL	—	200	350	1,250	2,750	—

Note: Twelve die varieties known, some are rare

KM# 376.5   8 REALES
27.0700 g., 0.9030 Silver .7859 oz. ASW **Obv:** Thin profile
eagle, folded snake **Rev:** Small Libertad

Date	Mintage	F	VF	XF	Unc	BU
1824Do RL	—	200	350	1,200	2,500	—

Note: Only one die variety is known

KM# 376.6   8 REALES
27.0700 g., 0.9030 Silver .7859 oz. ASW **Obv:** Thin profile
eagle, folded snake **Rev:** Large Libertad

Date	Mintage	F	VF	XF	Unc	BU
1824Do RL	—	200	400	1,500	3,000	—

Note: Eleven die varieties known, some are rare

KM# A376.2   8 REALES
27.0700 g., 0.9030 Silver .7859 oz. ASW **Obv:** Full breast
profile eagle **Edge:** Standard or Republic

Date	Mintage	F	VF	XF	Unc	BU
1823Mo JM	—	150	300	800	4,500	—
1824Mo JM	—	125	250	700	4,000	—

KM# A376.1   8 REALES
27.0700 g., 0.9030 Silver .7859 oz. ASW **Obv:** Full breast
profile eagle

Date	Mintage	F	VF	XF	Unc	BU
1824Go JM	—	250	400	1,100	3,500	—
1825/4Go JJ	—	600	1,200	2,750	7,000	—
1825Go JJ	—	500	750	1,400	5,500	—

KM# A376.3   8 REALES
27.0700 g., 0.9030 Silver .7859 oz. ASW **Obv:** Full breast
profile eagle **Edge:** Colonial or circle and rectangle

Date	Mintage	F	VF	XF	Unc	BU
1823Mo JM Rare	—	—	—	—	—	—

The Round-Topped Three

KM# A376.4   8 REALES
27.0700 g., 0.9030 Silver .7859 oz. ASW **Obv:** Full breast
profile eagle **Rev:** Round topped three **Edge:** Standard or
Republic

Date	Mintage	F	VF	XF	Unc	BU
1823Mo JM	—	2,000	4,000	6,000	8,000	—

Note: Many die varieties exist. Illustrations of one of the die differences is the size of the snake loop at the eagle's beak. This
difference is not apparent except on the 1824 Mo 8 Reales

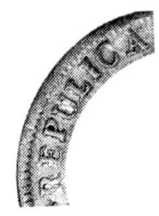

KM# A376.5   8 REALES
27.0700 g., 0.9030 Silver .7859 oz. ASW **Obv:** REPULICA
(error)

Date	Mintage	F	VF	XF	Unc	BU
1824Mo JM	—	6,000	9,000	11,000	—	—

Note: Legible Libertads on the cap are not as prevalent on
the Mexico City 8 Reales as on the Durango 8 Reales. They
are much more numerous than on the Guanajuato 8 Reales

Type I Obverse/Reverse

NOTE: The cap on the reverse of the curved tail Type
points to the "A" of LIBERTAD.

KM# 382.1 8 ESCUDOS
27.0700 g., 0.8750 Gold .7616 oz. AGW **Obv:** Profile eagle, snakes tail curved **Rev:** Cap points to "A" of LIBERTAD

Date	Mintage	F	VF	XF	Unc	BU
1823Mo JM	—	6,000	9,000	12,500	20,000	—

Type II Obverse/Reverse

NOTE: The cap on the reverse of the looped tail Type points to the "T" of LIBERTAD.

KM# 382.2 8 ESCUDOS
27.0700 g., 0.8750 Gold .7616 oz. AGW **Obv:** Profile eagle, snake's tail looped **Rev:** Cap points to "T" of LIBERTAD

Date	Mintage	F	VF	XF	Unc	BU
1823Mo JM	—	5,000	8,000	12,000	18,000	—

Note: The quality of the strikes of Type I coins is almost always superior to that of the Type II. Details of the eagle feathers, cactus and lettering on the open book are better on most Type I coins but the Type II coins are scarcer. Type I coins outnumber Type II coins by about two to one

STATE COINAGE

KM# 316 1/16 REAL (Medio Octavo)
4.7500 g., Copper, 21 mm. **Obv. Legend:** DEPARTMENTO DE JALISCO **Edge:** Oblique reeding

Date	Mintage	Good	VG	F	VF	XF
1860	—	3.00	8.00	17.50	55.00	—

KM# 317 1/16 REAL (Medio Octavo)
4.7500 g., Copper, 21 mm. **Obv. Legend:** ESTADO LIBRE DE JALISCO **Edge:** Oblique reeding

Date	Mintage	Good	VG	F	VF	XF
1861	—	2.50	6.00	13.50	32.50	—

KM# 320 1/8 REAL (Octavo Real)
Copper **Rev. Legend:** LIBERTAD **Edge:** Oblique reeding **Note:** Size varies 17-18mm. Weight varies 2.5-4 g. These pieces were frequently struck over 1/8 Real, dated 1821-23 of Nueva Vizcaya. All known examples struck over these coins are believed to be contemporary counterfeits.

Date	Mintage	Good	VG	F	VF	XF
1824D	—	5.00	12.50	35.00	85.00	—
1828D	—	150	250	400	1,000	—

KM# 338 1/8 REAL (Octavo Real)
4.0000 g., Brass, 21 mm. **Obv. Legend:** ESTo LIBe FEDo DE ZACATECAS **Edge:** Oblique reeding

Date	Mintage	Good	VG	F	VF	XF
1825	—	3.00	5.50	12.00	25.00	—
1827	—	3.00	5.50	12.00	25.00	—
1827 Inverted A for V in OCTAVO	—	12.00	20.00	40.00	100	—
1827 OCTAVA (error)	—	15.00	25.00	50.00	120	—
1827 Inverted 1	—	12.00	20.00	40.00	100	—
1829 Rare	—	—	—	—	—	—
1830	—	2.75	5.00	8.00	20.00	—
1831	—	4.50	6.75	13.50	27.50	—
1832	—	2.75	5.00	8.00	20.00	—
1833	—	2.75	5.00	8.00	20.00	—
1835	—	3.50	6.00	10.00	25.00	—
1846	—	3.50	6.00	10.00	25.00	—
1851	—	38.00	70.00	115	220	—
1852	—	3.50	6.00	10.00	25.00	—
1858	—	2.75	5.00	8.00	20.00	—
1859	—	2.75	5.00	8.00	20.00	—
1862	—	2.75	5.00	8.00	20.00	—
1863 Reversed 6 in date	—	2.75	5.00	8.00	20.00	—

KM# 329 1/8 REAL (Octavo Real)
4.8000 g., Copper, 21 mm. **Obv. Legend:** ESTADO LIBRE DE JALISCO **Edge:** Oblique reeding

Date	Mintage	Good	VG	F	VF	XF
1828	—	3.00	5.00	8.00	22.50	—
1831	—	62.50	100	185	275	—
1832/28	—	4.50	6.50	11.00	27.50	—
1832	—	4.50	6.00	10.00	25.00	—
1833	—	3.50	5.50	9.00	23.50	—
1834	—	37.50	80.00	150	235	—

KM# 321 1/8 REAL (Octavo Real)
3.3000 g., Copper **Rev:** Date **Rev. Legend:** OCTo. DE. R. DE DO **Edge:** Oblique reeding **Note:** Size varies 18-19mm.

Date	Mintage	Good	VG	F	VF	XF
1828D	—	7.50	18.50	40.00	115	—

KM# 335 1/8 REAL (Octavo Real)
Copper **Obv. Legend:** ESTADO DE OCCIDENTE **Edge:** Oblique reeding **Note:** Size varies: 17-18mm, weight varies: 2-3 g. The C before date on reverse may be a mint mark standing for Concepcion de Alamos.

Date	Mintage	Good	VG	F	VF	XF
1828 Reverse S	—	35.00	65.00	120	—	—
1829	—	30.00	60.00	110	—	—

KM# 336 1/8 REAL (Octavo Real)
Copper, 21 mm. **Obv. Legend:** ESTADO LIBRE DE SAN
LUIS POTOSI **Edge:** Oblique reeding **Note:** Weight varies
(1829-31) 4.5-5.5 g; (1859) 4-4.5 g.

Date	Mintage	Good	VG	F	VF	XF
1829	—	6.00	11.00	26.50	62.50	—
1830	—	8.50	15.00	30.00	70.00	—
1831	—	6.00	9.50	18.50	47.50	—
1859	—	5.00	8.00	16.50	45.00	—
1865/1	—	—	—	—	—	—
Reported, not confirmed						

KM# 326 1/8 REAL (Octavo Real)
3.5000 g., Copper, 21 mm. **Obv. Legend:** ESTADO LIBRE
DE GUANAJUATO **Edge:** Ornamented with incuse dots

Date	Mintage	Good	VG	F	VF	XF
1829	—	3.00	5.00	10.00	26.50	—
1829 error w/ GUANJUATO	—	4.00	6.50	12.50	28.50	—
1830	—	8.00	13.50	28.50	62.50	—

KM# 318 1/8 REAL (Octavo Real)
3.5400 g., Copper, 20 mm. **Obv. Legend:** ESTADO
SOBERANO DE CHIHUAHUA **Edge:** Plain

Date	Mintage	Good	VG	F	VF	XF
1833	—	350	750	—	—	—
1834	—	350	750	—	—	—
1835/3	—	350	750	—	—	—

KM# 322 1/8 REAL (Octavo Real)
3.5000 g., Copper, 20 mm. **Obv. Legend:** ESTADO DE
DURANGO

Date	Mintage	Good	VG	F	VF	XF
1833 Rare	—	—	—	—	—	—

KM# 339 1/8 REAL (Octavo Real)
4.0000 g., Copper, 21 mm. **Obv. Legend:** DEPARTMENTO
DE ZACATECAS **Edge:** Oblique reeding

Date	Mintage	Good	VG	F	VF	XF
1836	—	5.00	8.50	17.50	40.00	—
1845	—	7.50	12.50	22.50	50.00	—
1846	—	8.50	10.00	20.00	45.00	—

KM# 323 1/8 REAL (Octavo Real)
3.5000 g., Copper **Obv. Legend:** REPUBLICA MEXICANA
Note: Size varies: 19-23mm.

Date	Mintage	Good	VG	F	VF	XF
1842/33	—	12.50	22.50	42.50	115	—
1842	—	8.50	15.00	32.50	100	—

KM# 324 1/8 REAL (Octavo Real)
Copper, 19 mm. **Obv. Legend:** REPUBLICA MEXICANA
Rev. Legend: DEPARTAMENTO DE DURANGO **Edge:**
Ornamented with arc and dot pattern **Note:** Weight varies:
3.5-3.8 g.

Date	Mintage	Good	VG	F	VF	XF
1845	—	22.50	55.00	115	250	—
1846 Rare	—	—	—	—	—	—
1847	—	3.50	7.50	17.50	37.50	—

KM# 325 1/8 REAL (Octavo Real)
Copper, 19 mm. **Obv. Legend:** REPUBLICA MEXICANA
Rev. Legend: ESTADO DE DURANGO **Edge:** Ornamented
with arc and dot pattern **Note:** Weight varies: 3.5-3.8 g.

Date	Mintage	Good	VG	F	VF	XF
1851	—	3.50	8.00	12.50	33.50	—
1852/1	—	3.50	6.50	11.00	33.50	—
1852	—	3.00	5.00	8.00	30.00	—
1854	—	7.00	13.50	28.50	62.50	—

KM# 319 1/8 REAL (Octavo Real)
3.5400 g., Copper, 20 mm. **Obv. Legend:** ESTADO DE
CHIHUAHUA **Edge:** Plain

Date	Mintage	Good	VG	F	VF	XF
1855	—	5.00	8.50	25.00	75.00	—

KM# 327 1/8 REAL (Octavo Real)
7.2000 g., Brass, 29 mm. **Obv. Legend:** ESTADO LIBRE
DE GUANAJUATO **Edge:** Plain

Date	Mintage	Good	VG	F	VF	XF
1856	—	7.50	12.00	20.00	75.00	—

KM# 330   1/8 REAL (Octavo Real)
9.5000 g., Copper, 28 mm. **Obv. Legend:** ESTADO LIBRE
DE JALISCO **Edge:** Oblique reeding

Date	Mintage	Good	VG	F	VF	XF
1856	—	3.00	6.00	9.00	18.50	—
1857	—	3.00	6.00	9.00	18.50	—
1858	—	3.00	6.00	9.00	18.50	—
1861	—	75.00	135	200	300	—
1862/1	—	4.00	7.00	10.00	22.50	—
1862	—	4.00	7.00	10.00	22.50	—

KM# 328   1/8 REAL (Octavo Real)
Brass, 25 mm. **Obv. Legend:** ESTADO LIBRE DE
GUANAJUATO **Edge:** Plain **Note:** Weight varies: 7.1-7.2 g.

Date	Mintage	Good	VG	F	VF	XF
1856	—	4.00	7.50	12.50	35.00	—
1857	—	3.50	6.00	10.00	30.00	—

KM# 328a   1/8 REAL (Octavo Real)
Copper, 25 mm. **Obv. Legend:** ESTADO LIBRE DE
GUANAJUATO **Edge:** Plain **Note:** Weight varies: 7.1-7.2 g.

Date	Mintage	Good	VG	F	VF	XF
1857	—	7.00	16.50	32.50	55.00	—

KM# 331   1/8 REAL (Octavo Real)
9.5000 g., Copper, 28 mm. **Obv. Legend:** DEPARTMENTO
DE JALISCO **Edge:** Oblique reeding

Date	Mintage	Good	VG	F	VF	XF
1858	—	4.00	7.00	13.50	28.50	—
1859	—	3.00	5.75	8.00	20.00	—
1860/59	—	3.25	6.00	9.00	22.50	—
1860	—	3.25	6.00	9.00	22.50	—
1862	—	4.00	8.00	17.50	37.50	—

KM# 337   1/8 REAL (Octavo Real)
6.7000 g., Copper, 28 mm. **Obv. Legend:** ESTO LIBE Y
SOBO DE SONORA **Edge:** Reeded

Date	Mintage	Good	VG	F	VF	XF
1859 Rare	—	—	—	—	—	—

KM# 366   1/4 REAL (Un Quarto/Una Quartilla)
8.0000 g., Brass **Obv. Legend:** ESTO LIBE FEDO DE
ZACATECAS **Edge:** Oblique reeding **Note:** Size varies: 28-29mm.

Date	Mintage	Good	VG	F	VF	XF
1824 Rare	—	—	—	—	—	—
1825	—	2.50	5.00	10.00	20.00	—
1826	—	75.00	130	220	325	—
1827/17	—	2.50	5.00	9.00	20.00	—
1829	—	2.50	5.00	9.00	20.00	—
1830	—	2.50	5.00	8.50	20.00	—
1831	—	40.00	85.00	140	220	—
1832	—	2.50	5.00	9.00	20.00	—
1833	—	2.50	5.00	9.00	20.00	—
1834 Rare	—	—	—	—	—	—
1835	—	2.50	5.00	9.00	20.00	—
1846	—	2.50	5.00	8.50	20.00	—
1847	—	2.50	5.00	8.50	20.00	—
1852	—	2.50	5.00	8.50	20.00	—
1853	—	2.50	5.00	8.50	20.00	—
1855	—	4.50	10.00	25.00	65.00	—
1858	—	2.50	5.00	8.50	20.00	—
1859	—	2.50	5.00	8.50	20.00	—
1860	—	75.00	125	200	310	—
1862/57	—	2.50	5.00	8.50	20.00	—
1862/59/7	—	8.00	18.00	37.50	75.00	—
1862	—	2.50	5.00	8.00	20.00	—
1863/2	—	2.50	5.00	8.00	20.00	—
1863	—	2.50	5.00	8.00	20.00	—
1864	—	4.00	11.00	25.00	60.00	—

KM# 359   1/4 REAL (Un Quarto/Una Quartilla)
Copper **Obv. Legend:** ESTADO LIBRE DE SAN LUIS
POTOSI **Rev. Legend:** MEXICO LIBRE **Edge:** Oblique
reeding **Note:** Size varies: 25-31mm, weight varies: (1828-
32) 9-10 g.; (1859-60) 8-9 g.

Date	Mintage	Good	VG	F	VF	XF
1828	—	2.00	3.50	8.00	17.50	—
1829	—	3.00	4.50	8.50	18.50	—
1830	—	2.00	3.50	7.00	15.00	—
1832	—	3.25	5.00	9.00	20.00	—
1859 Large LIBRE	—	2.50	4.00	7.50	16.50	—
1859 Small LIBRE	—	2.50	4.00	7.50	16.50	—
1860	—	2.50	4.00	7.00	16.50	—

KM# 351   1/4 REAL (Un Quarto/Una Quartilla)
7.0000 g., Copper, 27 mm. **Obv. Legend:** ESTADO LIBRE
DE GUANAJUATO **Edge:** Ornamented with incuse dots

Date	Mintage	Good	VG	F	VF	XF
1828	—	3.75	8.00	18.50	40.00	—
1828 Error with GUANJUATO	—	4.00	9.00	20.00	42.50	—
1829	—	5.50	12.00	22.50	47.50	—

KM# 353 1/4 REAL (Un Quarto/Una Quartilla)
9.3500 g., Copper, 28 mm. **Obv:** Oblique reeding **Obv.**
Legend: ESTADO LIBRE DE JALISCO

Date	Mintage	Good	VG	F	VF	XF
1828	—	3.75	7.00	15.00	37.50	—
1829/8	—	3.00	6.00	13.00	33.00	—
1829	—	3.00	6.00	13.00	33.00	—
1830/20	—	3.00	5.00	10.00	28.50	—
1830/29	—	3.00	5.00	10.00	28.50	—
1830	—	3.00	5.00	10.00	28.50	—
1831 Rare	—	—	—	—	—	—
1832/20	—	3.00	5.00	10.00	28.50	—
1832/28	—	3.00	5.00	10.00	28.50	—
1832	—	2.50	5.00	9.00	27.50	—
1833/2	—	3.00	5.00	9.00	27.50	—
1834	—	2.50	5.00	9.00	27.50	—
1835/3	—	3.00	5.00	9.00	27.50	—
1835	—	2.50	5.00	9.00	27.50	—
1836 Rare	—	—	—	—	—	—

KM# 364 1/4 REAL (Un Quarto/Una Quartilla)
Copper **Obv. Legend:** EST. D. SONORA UNA CUART
Edge: Oblique reeding **Note:** Size varies: 21-22mm. Weight
varies: 2.3-5.5 g.

Date	Mintage	Good	VG	F	VF	XF
1831 L.S. Rare	—	—	—	—	—	—
1832 L.S.	—	2.75	5.50	15.00	50.00	—
1833/2 L.S.	—	2.00	4.00	12.50	37.50	—
1833 L.S.	—	2.00	4.00	12.50	37.50	—
1834 L.S.	—	2.00	4.00	12.50	37.50	—
1835/3 L.S.	—	2.50	5.50	15.00	40.00	—
1835 L.S.	—	2.00	4.00	12.50	37.50	—
1836 L.S.	—	2.00	4.00	12.50	37.50	—

KM# 340 1/4 REAL (Un Quarto/Una Quartilla)
Copper, 27 mm. **Obv. Legend:** ESTADO SOBERANO DE
CHIHUAHUA **Edge:** Herringbone pattern

Date	Mintage	Good	VG	F	VF	XF
1833	—	7.50	16.50	37.50	85.00	—
1834	—	6.50	13.50	28.00	55.00	—
1835	—	5.00	10.00	22.00	50.00	—
1835 Plain edge	—	5.00	8.00	12.00	50.00	—

KM# 354 1/4 REAL (Un Quarto/Una Quartilla)
9.3500 g., Copper, 28 mm. **Obv. Legend:** DEPARTMENTO
DE JALISCO **Edge:** Oblique reeding

Date	Mintage	Good	VG	F	VF	XF
1836 Rare	—	—	—	—	—	—

KM# 367 1/4 REAL (Un Quarto/Una Quartilla)
8.0000 g., Brass **Obv. Legend:** DEPARTMENTO DE
ZACATECAS **Edge:** Oblique reeding **Note:** Size varies: 28-
29mm.

Date	Mintage	Good	VG	F	VF	XF
1836	—	4.00	8.50	13.50	25.00	—
1845 Rare	—	—	—	—	—	—
1846	—	3.50	6.75	9.00	20.00	—

KM# 345 1/4 REAL (Un Quarto/Una Quartilla)
7.0000 g., Copper, 27 mm. **Obv. Legend:** REPUBLICA
MEXICANA **Rev:** DURANGO above in wreath

Date	Mintage	Good	VG	F	VF	XF
1845 Rare	—	—	—	—	—	—

KM# 341 1/4 REAL (Un Quarto/Una Quartilla)
7.0800 g., Copper, 27 mm. **Obv. Legend:** ESTADO LIBRE
DE CHIHUAHUA **Edge:** Plain

Date	Mintage	Good	VG	F	VF	XF
1846 With fraction bar	—	3.50	6.00	12.00	37.50	—
1846 Without fraction bar	—	5.00	8.50	15.00	45.00	—

KM# 363 1/4 REAL (Un Quarto/Una Quartilla)
27.0000 g., Copper, 27 mm. **Obv. Legend:** ESTADO LIBRE
Y SOBERANO DE SINALOA **Edge:** Reeded

Date	Mintage	Good	VG	F	VF	XF
1847	—	3.50	5.50	12.00	23.50	—
1848	—	3.50	5.50	11.00	22.00	—
1859	—	3.00	4.50	7.50	16.50	—
1861	—	1.75	3.00	4.00	10.00	—
1862	—	1.75	3.00	4.00	11.00	—
1863	—	2.50	4.00	5.00	11.00	—
1864/3	—	2.50	4.00	5.00	11.00	—
1864	—	1.75	3.00	4.75	10.00	—
1865	—	3.00	5.50	8.50	18.50	—
1866/5	7,401,000	2.50	3.50	5.00	11.00	—
1866	Inc. above	1.75	3.00	4.00	10.00	—

KM# 363a 1/4 REAL (Un Quarto/Una Quartilla)
7.0000 g., Brass, 27 mm. **Obv. Legend:** ESTADO LIBRE Y
SOBERANO DE SINALOA **Edge:** Reeded

Date	Mintage	Good	VG	F	VF	XF
1847	—	5.00	10.00	18.50	40.00	—

KM# 342 1/4 REAL (Un Quarto/Una Quartilla)
7.0800 g., Copper, 27 mm. **Obv. Legend:** ESTADO DE
CHIHUAHUA **Edge:** Plain

Date	Mintage	Good	VG	F	VF	XF
1855	—	2.50	5.75	13.50	40.00	—
1856	—	2.50	5.75	13.50	40.00	—

KM# 343 1/4 REAL (Un Quarto/Una Quartilla)
7.0800 g., Copper, 27 mm. **Obv. Legend:** DEPARTMENTO
DE CHIHUAHUA **Edge:** Plain

Date	Mintage	Good	VG	F	VF	XF
1855	—	3.00	5.75	13.00	36.50	—
1855 DE (reversed D)	—	4.50	8.50	17.50	40.00	—

KM# 352 1/4 REAL (Un Quarto/Una Quartilla)
14.0000 g., Copper, 32 mm. **Obv. Legend:** EST. LIB. DE
GUANAXUATO **Rev. Legend:** OMNIA VINCIT LABOR
Edge: Plain

Date	Mintage	Good	VG	F	VF	XF
1856	—	7.50	18.50	37.50	65.00	—
1857	—	6.50	13.50	27.50	48.00	—

KM# 352a 1/4 REAL (Un Quarto/Una Quartilla)
14.0000 g., Brass, 32 mm. **Obv. Legend:** EST. LIB. DE
GUANAXUATO **Rev. Legend:** OMNIA VINCIT LABOR
Edge: Plain

Date	Mintage	Good	VG	F	VF	XF
1856	—	3.25	6.75	13.50	30.00	—
1857	—	3.25	6.75	13.50	30.00	—

KM# 346 1/4 REAL (Un Quarto/Una Quartilla)
7.5000 g., Copper, 27 mm. **Obv. Legend:** REPUBLICA
MEXICANA **Rev:** Date, value **Rev. Legend:** DURANGO
Edge: Ornamented with arc and dot pattern

Date	Mintage	Good	VG	F	VF	XF
1858 Rare	—	—	—	—	—	—

KM# 347 1/4 REAL (Un Quarto/Una Quartilla)
7.5000 g., Copper, 27 mm. **Obv. Legend:** ESTADO DE
DURANGO **Rev. Legend:** CONSTITUCION **Edge:**
Ornamented wiht arc and dot pattern **Note:** Brass examples
have been reported, but not confirmed.

Date	Mintage	Good	VG	F	VF	XF
1858	—	4.00	8.50	22.00	50.00	—

KM# 355 1/4 REAL (Un Quarto/Una Quartilla)
19.0000 g., Copper, 32 mm. **Obv. Legend:** ESTADO LIBRE
DE JALISCO **Edge:** Oblique reeding

Date	Mintage	Good	VG	F	VF	XF
1858	—	3.00	5.50	10.00	22.50	—
1861	—	3.50	7.50	15.00	30.00	—
1862	—	3.00	5.50	10.00	22.50	—

KM# 356 1/4 REAL (Un Quarto/Una Quartilla)
19.0000 g., Copper, 32 mm. **Obv. Legend:**
DEPARTMENTO DE JALISCO **Edge:** Oblique reeding

Date	Mintage	Good	VG	F	VF	XF
1858	—	2.75	5.00	8.50	18.50	—
1859/8	—	2.75	5.00	8.50	18.50	—
1859	—	2.75	5.00	8.50	18.50	—
1860	—	2.75	5.00	8.50	18.50	—

KM# 365 1/4 REAL (Un Quarto/Una Quartilla)
14.3000 g., Copper, 32 mm. **Obv. Legend:** ESTO. LIBE. Y
SOBO. DE SONORA **Edge:** Reeded

Date	Mintage	Good	VG	F	VF	XF
1859	—	2.00	5.00	8.00	20.00	—
1861/59	—	2.75	6.50	11.00	25.00	—
1861	—	2.00	5.00	8.00	20.00	—
1862	—	2.00	5.00	8.00	20.00	—
1863/2	—	5.00	12.50	25.00	55.00	—

KM# 344 1/4 REAL (Un Quarto/Una Quartilla)
Copper, 28 mm. **Obv. Legend:** E. CHIHA LIBERTAD **Edge:** Plain **Note:** Weight varies 11-11.5 g.

Date	Mintage	Good	VG	F	VF	XF
1860	—	2.00	4.00	11.00	25.00	—
1861	—	2.00	4.00	11.00	25.00	—
1865/1	—	2.50	5.50	13.50	30.00	—
1865	—	6.00	14.00	28.50	65.00	—
1866/5	—	5.00	9.50	25.00	60.00	—
1866 Coin rotation	—	2.00	4.00	11.00	25.00	—
1866 Medal rotation	—	2.00	4.00	11.00	25.00	—

KM# 348 1/4 REAL (Un Quarto/Una Quartilla)
Copper, 27 mm. **Obv. Legend:** DEPARTMENTO DE DURANGO **Rev. Legend:** LIBERTAD EN EL ORDEN **Edge:** Ornamented wiht arc and dot pattern **Note:** Weight varies: 7-7.5 g.

Date	Mintage	Good	VG	F	VF	XF
1860	—	2.25	6.00	15.00	38.50	—
1866	—	3.00	7.50	16.50	42.50	—

KM# 360 1/4 REAL (Un Quarto/Una Quartilla)
Copper **Obv. Legend:** ESTADO LIBRE DE SAN LUIS POTOSI **Rev. Legend:** REPUBLICA MEXICANA **Edge:** Oblique reeding **Note:** Size varies: 25-31mm.

Date	Mintage	Good	VG	F	VF	XF
1862	1,367	2.50	4.00	7.00	15.00	—
1862 LIBR	Inc. above	3.25	5.00	8.00	16.50	—

KM# 349 1/4 REAL (Un Quarto/Una Quartilla)
7.0000 g., Copper **Obv. Legend:** ESTADO DE DURANGO **Rev. Legend:** INDEPENDENCIA Y LIBERTAD **Edge:** Ornamented wiht arc and dot pattern **Note:** Size varies: 26-27mm.

Date	Mintage	Good	VG	F	VF	XF
1866	—	3.75	8.50	22.00	50.00	—

KM# 361 1/4 REAL (Un Quarto/Una Quartilla)
Copper **Obv. Legend:** ESTADO LIBRE Y SOBERANO DE S.L. POTOSI **Rev. Legend:** LIBERTAD Y REFORMA **Edge:** Reeded or plain **Note:** Size varies: 27-28mm. Weight varies: 9-10 g.

Date	Mintage	Good	VG	F	VF	XF
1867	3,177,000	2.50	3.75	6.50	15.00	—
1867 AFG	Inc. above	2.50	3.75	6.50	15.00	—

Note: AFG are the coin designer/engraver initials

KM# 362 1/4 REAL (Un Quarto/Una Quartilla)
Copper **Obv. Legend:** ESTADO LIBRE Y SOBERANO DE S.L. POTOSI **Rev. Legend:** LIBERTAD Y REFORMA **Edge:** Plain

Date	Mintage	Good	VG	F	VF	XF
1867	Inc. above	2.50	3.75	6.50	15.00	—
1867 AFG	Inc. above	2.50	3.75	6.50	15.00	—

Note: AFG are the coin designer/engraver initials

KM# 350 1/4 REAL (Un Quarto/Una Quartilla)
7.5000 g., Copper, 27 mm. **Obv. Legend:** ESTADO DE DURANGO **Rev. Legend:** SUFRAGIO LIBRE **Edge:** Ornamented with arc and dot pattern **Note:** Brass examples have been reported, but not confirmed.

Date	Mintage	Good	VG	F	VF	XF
1872	—	2.00	3.75	8.50	18.50	—

FEDERAL COINAGE

KM# 315 1/16 REAL (Medio Octavo)
1.7500 g., Copper, 17 mm. **Obv. Legend:** REPUBLICA MEXICANA **Edge:** Ornamented with small incuse rectangles

Date	Mintage	VG	F	VF	XF	Unc
1831	—	10.00	20.00	50.00	100	—
1832/1	—	12.00	22.00	55.00	125	—
1832	—	10.00	20.00	50.00	100	—
1833	—	10.00	20.00	50.00	100	—

KM# 315a 1/16 REAL (Medio Octavo)
1.7500 g., Brass, 17 mm. **Obv. Legend:** REPUBLICA MEXICANA **Edge:** Ornamented with small incuse rectangles

Date	Mintage	VG	F	VF	XF	Unc
1832	—	13.50	22.50	60.00	165	—
1833	—	10.00	17.50	50.00	135	—
1835	—	400	800	1,250	2,500	—

KM# 333 1/8 REAL (Octavo Real)
3.5000 g., Copper, 21 mm. **Obv. Legend:** REPUBLICA
MEXICANA **Edge:** Ornamented wiht small incuse rectangles

Date	Mintage	Good	VG	F	VF	XF
1829	—	7.50	12.00	25.00	55.00	—
1830	—	1.00	2.00	6.00	20.00	—
1831	—	1.50	3.50	7.00	25.00	—
1832	—	1.50	3.50	7.00	25.00	—
1833/2	—	1.50	3.50	7.00	25.00	—
1833	—	1.50	2.75	6.00	20.00	—
1834	—	1.50	2.75	6.00	20.00	—
1835/4	—	1.75	3.50	7.00	25.00	—
1835	—	1.50	2.75	6.00	20.00	—

KM# 332 1/8 REAL (Octavo Real)
7.0000 g., Copper, 27 mm. **Obv. Legend:** REPUBLICA
MEXICANA **Edge:** Ornamented with small incuse rectangles

Date	Mintage	VG	F	VF	XF	Unc
1829	—	450	900	1,500	2,500	—

KM# 334 1/8 REAL (Octavo Real)
14.0000 g., Copper **Obv. Legend:** LIBERTAD **Edge:**
Lettered (1841-41); Plain (1850-61) **Edge Lettering:**
REPUBLICA MEXICANA **Note:** Size varies: 29-30mm.

Date	Mintage	Good	VG	F	VF	XF
1841	—	6.00	15.00	30.00	75.00	—
1842	—	2.50	5.00	10.00	30.00	—
1850	—	12.50	20.00	30.00	80.00	—
1861	—	5.00	12.00	25.00	70.00	—

KM# 357 1/4 REAL (Un Quarto/Una Quartilla)
14.0000 g., Copper, 33 mm. **Obv. Legend:** REPUBLICA
MEXICANA **Edge:** Ornamented with small incuse rectangles

Date	Mintage	VG	F	VF	XF	Unc
1829	—	8.00	30.00	75.00	250	—

KM# 358 1/4 REAL (Un Quarto/Una Quartilla)
7.0000 g., Copper, 27 mm. **Obv. Legend:** REPUBLICA
MEXICANA **Edge:** Ornamented with small incuse rectangles
Note: Reduced size.

Date	Mintage	VG	F	VF	XF	Unc
1829	—	12.00	25.00	50.00	150	—
1830	—	1.50	2.75	5.00	10.00	—
1831	—	1.50	2.75	5.00	10.00	—
1832	—	5.50	10.00	20.00	35.00	—
1833	—	1.50	2.75	5.00	10.00	—
1834/3	—	1.75	3.00	6.00	12.00	—
1834	—	1.50	2.75	5.00	10.00	—
1835	—	1.50	2.75	5.00	10.00	—
1836	—	1.50	2.75	5.00	10.00	—
1837	—	6.50	13.50	22.50	45.00	—

KM# 358a.1 1/4 REAL (Un Quarto/Una Quartilla)
7.0000 g., Brass, 27 mm. **Countermark:** JM **Obv. Legend:**
REPUBLICA MEXICANA **Edge:** Ornamented with small
incuse rectangles **Note:** Reduced size.

Date	Mintage	VG	F	VF	XF	Unc
1831	—	8.00	13.50	27.50	50.00	—

KM# 358a.2 1/4 REAL (Un Quarto/Una Quartilla)
7.0000 g., Brass, 27 mm. **Obv. Legend:** REPUBLICA
MEXICANA **Edge:** Ornamented with small incuse rectangles
Note: Without countermark.

Date	Mintage	VG	F	VF	XF	Unc
1831	—	—	—	—	—	—

KM# 368 1/4 REAL (Un Quarto/Una Quartilla)
0.8450 g., 0.9030 Silver .0245 oz. ASW **Note:** Mint mark CA.

Date	Mintage	VG	F	VF	XF	Unc
1843CA RG	—	75.00	125	300	500	—

KM# 368.1 1/4 REAL (Un Quarto/Una Quartilla)
0.8450 g., 0.9030 Silver .0245 oz. ASW **Note:** Mint mark C.

Date	Mintage	VG	F	VF	XF	Unc
1855C LR	—	50.00	100	200	400	—

KM# 368.2 1/4 REAL (Un Quarto/Una Quartilla)
0.8450 g., 0.9030 Silver .0245 oz. ASW **Note:** Struck at
Durango Mint, mint mark Do.

Date	Mintage	VG	F	VF	XF	Unc
1842Do LR	—	12.00	20.00	40.00	125	—
1843Do	—	20.00	25.00	60.00	150	—

KM# 368.3 1/4 REAL (Un Quarto/Una Quartilla)
0.8450 g., 0.9030 Silver .0245 oz. ASW **Note:** Mint mark Ga.

Date	Mintage	VG	F	VF	XF	Unc
1842Ga JG	—	2.50	5.50	8.00	20.00	—
1843/2Ga JG	—	—	—	—	—	—
1843Ga JG	—	6.00	9.00	12.50	30.00	—
1843Ga MC	—	4.00	6.50	9.00	25.00	—
1844Ga MC	—	4.00	6.50	9.00	25.00	—
1844Ga LR	—	2.50	5.00	7.50	15.00	—
1845Ga LR	—	2.50	4.50	7.50	15.00	—
1846Ga LR	—	5.00	8.00	10.00	25.00	—
1847Ga LR	—	4.00	6.50	9.00	25.00	—
1848Ga LR Rare	—	—	—	—	—	—
1850Ga LR Rare	—	—	—	—	—	—
1851Ga LR	—	6.00	10.00	20.00	50.00	—
1852Ga LR	—	50.00	100	135	200	—
1854/3Ga LR	—	50.00	100	135	200	—
1854Ga LR	—	5.00	10.00	12.50	30.00	—
1855Ga LR	—	5.00	8.00	10.00	30.00	—
1857Ga LR	—	6.50	10.00	15.00	27.50	—
1862Ga LR	—	5.50	10.00	15.00	30.00	—

KM# 368.4 1/4 REAL (Un Quarto/Una Quartilla)
0.8450 g., 0.9030 Silver .0245 oz. ASW **Note:** Mint mark GC.

Date	Mintage	VG	F	VF	XF	Unc
1844GC LR	—	50.00	75.00	125	300	—

KM# 368.5 1/4 REAL (Un Quarto/Una Quartilla)
0.8450 g., 0.9030 Silver .0245 oz. ASW **Note:** Mint mark Go.

Date	Mintage	VG	F	VF	XF	Unc
1842Go PM	—	4.00	6.00	10.00	20.00	—
1842Go LR	—	2.00	4.00	8.00	15.00	—
1843/2Go LR	—	4.00	6.00	10.00	20.00	—
1843Go LR	—	2.00	4.00	8.00	15.00	—
1844/3Go LR	—	—	—	—	—	—
1844Go LR	—	2.00	4.00	8.00	15.00	—
1845Go LR	—	8.00	15.00	30.00	60.00	—
1846/5Go LR	—	—	—	—	—	—
1846Go LR	—	4.00	6.00	10.00	20.00	—
1847Go LR	—	2.00	4.00	8.00	15.00	—
1848/7Go LR	—	2.00	4.00	8.00	15.00	—
1848Go LR	—	2.00	4.00	8.00	15.00	—
1849/7Go LR	—	8.00	15.00	30.00	60.00	—
1849Go LR	—	2.00	4.00	8.00	15.00	—
1850Go LR	—	2.00	4.00	8.00	15.00	—
1851Go LR	—	2.00	4.00	8.00	15.00	—
1852Go LR	—	2.00	4.00	8.00	15.00	—
1853Go LR	—	2.00	4.00	8.00	15.00	—
1855Go LR	—	4.00	8.00	15.00	30.00	—
1856/4Go LR	—	—	—	—	—	—
1856Go LR	—	5.00	10.00	20.00	35.00	—
1862/1Go LR	—	3.00	5.00	10.00	20.00	—
1862Go LR	—	2.00	4.00	8.00	15.00	—
1863Go	—	2.00	4.00	8.00	15.00	—

KM# 368.6 1/4 REAL (Un Quarto/Una Quartilla)
0.8450 g., 0.9030 Silver .0245 oz. ASW **Note:** Mint mark Mo.

Date	Mintage	VG	F	VF	XF	Unc
1842Mo LR	—	2.00	4.00	8.00	15.00	—
1843Mo LR	—	2.00	4.00	8.00	15.00	—
1844/3Mo LR	—	8.00	12.00	20.00	40.00	—
1844Mo LR	—	4.00	6.00	10.00	20.00	—
1845Mo LR	—	4.00	6.00	10.00	20.00	—
1846Mo LR	—	2.00	4.00	8.00	15.00	—
1850Mo LR	—	5.00	10.00	20.00	35.00	—
1858Mo LR	—	4.00	8.00	15.00	30.00	—
1859Mo LR	—	4.00	6.00	10.00	20.00	—
1860Mo LR	—	4.00	6.00	10.00	20.00	—
1861Mo LR	—	4.00	6.00	10.00	20.00	—
1862Mo LR	—	4.00	6.00	10.00	20.00	—
1863/53Mo LR	—	—	—	—	—	—
1863Mo LR	—	4.00	6.00	10.00	20.00	—

KM# 368.7 1/4 REAL (Un Quarto/Una Quartilla)
0.8450 g., 0.9030 Silver .0245 oz. ASW **Note:** Mint mark SLP, PI, P, I/P.

Date	Mintage	VG	F	VF	XF	Unc
1842S.L.Pi	—	2.00	4.00	8.00	15.00	—
1843/2S.L.Pi	—	4.00	6.00	10.00	20.00	—
1843S.L.Pi	—	2.00	4.00	8.00	15.00	—
1844S.L.Pi	—	2.00	4.00	8.00	15.00	—
1845/3S.L.Pi	—	4.00	6.00	10.00	25.00	—
1845/4S.L.Pi	—	4.00	6.00	10.00	25.00	—
1845S.L.Pi	—	2.00	4.00	8.00	15.00	—
1847/5S.L.Pi	—	4.00	6.00	10.00	20.00	—
1847S.L.Pi	—	2.00	4.00	8.00	15.00	—
1851/47S.L.Pi	—	4.00	8.00	15.00	30.00	—
1854S.L.Pi	—	125	200	275	400	—
1856S.L.Pi	—	4.00	8.00	15.00	30.00	—
1857S.L.Pi	—	5.00	10.00	20.00	35.00	—
1862/57S.L.Pi	—	10.00	20.00	40.00	85.00	—

KM# 368.8 1/4 REAL (Un Quarto/Una Quartilla)
0.8450 g., 0.9030 Silver .0245 oz. ASW **Note:** Mint mark Zs.

Date	Mintage	VG	F	VF	XF	Unc
1842/1Zs LR	—	4.00	8.00	15.00	30.00	—
1842Zs LR	—	4.00	6.00	10.00	20.00	—

KM# 370 1/2 REAL
1.6900 g., 0.9030 Silver .0490 oz. ASW **Obv:** Hook-necked eagle

Date	Mintage	F	VF	XF	Unc	BU
1862A PG Rare	—	—	—	—	—	—

KM# 370.1 1/2 REAL
1.6900 g., 0.9030 Silver .0490 oz. ASW **Obv:** Facing eagle

Date	Mintage	F	VF	XF	Unc	BU
1844 Ca RG	—	75.00	125	175	275	—
1845 Ca RG	—	75.00	125	150	250	—

KM# 370.2 1/2 REAL
1.6900 g., 0.9030 Silver .0490 oz. ASW **Obv:** Facing eagle
Note: Mint mark C, Co.

Date	Mintage	F	VF	XF	Unc	BU
1846 CE	—	30.00	50.00	75.00	150	—
1848/7 CE	—	15.00	25.00	45.00	90.00	—
1849/8 CE	—	15.00	25.00	45.00	90.00	—
1849 CE	—	—	—	—	—	—
1852 CE	—	12.50	20.00	40.00	80.00	—
1853/1 CE	—	12.50	20.00	40.00	80.00	—
1854 CE	—	20.00	35.00	50.00	100	—
1856 CE	—	12.50	20.00	40.00	80.00	—
1857/6 CE	—	20.00	35.00	50.00	100	—
1857 CE	—	15.00	25.00	45.00	90.00	—
1858 CE Error 1 for 1/2	—	12.50	20.00	40.00	80.00	—
1860/59 PV	—	20.00	35.00	50.00	100	—
1860 PV	—	12.50	20.00	40.00	80.00	—
1861 PV	—	12.50	20.00	40.00	80.00	—
1863 CE Error 1 for 1/2	—	15.00	25.00	45.00	90.00	—
1867 CE	—	12.50	20.00	40.00	80.00	—
1869 6/5 CE Error 1 for 1/2	—	12.50	20.00	40.00	80.00	—

KM# 370.3 1/2 REAL
1.6900 g., 0.9030 Silver .0490 oz. ASW **Obv:** Facing eagle
Note: Mint mark D, Do.

Date	Mintage	F	VF	XF	Unc	BU
1832 RM	—	125	225	350	600	—
1832 RM/L	—	—	—	—	—	—
1833/2 RM/L	—	75.00	100	150	225	—
1833/1 RM/L	—	12.50	20.00	40.00	80.00	—
1833 RM	—	25.00	40.00	75.00	150	—
1834/1 RM	—	25.00	40.00	75.00	150	—
1834 RM	—	12.50	20.00	40.00	80.00	—
1837/1 RM	—	12.50	30.00	60.00	200	—
1837/4 RM	—	12.50	30.00	60.00	200	—
1837/6 RM	—	12.50	30.00	60.00	200	—
1841/33 RM	—	15.00	30.00	60.00	250	—
1842/32 RM	—	12.50	20.00	40.00	80.00	—
1842 RM	—	12.50	20.00	40.00	80.00	—
1842 8R RM Error	—	12.50	20.00	40.00	80.00	—
1842 1/2/8R RM	—	12.50	20.00	40.00	80.00	—
1843/33 RM	—	15.00	25.00	50.00	100	—
1843 RM	—	15.00	25.00	50.00	100	—
1845/31 RM	—	12.50	20.00	40.00	80.00	—
1845/34 RM	—	12.50	20.00	40.00	80.00	—
1845/35 RM	—	12.50	20.00	40.00	80.00	—
1845 RM	—	15.00	25.00	50.00	100	—
1846 RM	—	30.00	50.00	80.00	200	—
1848/5 RM	—	35.00	55.00	110	250	—
1848/36 RM	—	25.00	40.00	75.00	200	—
1849 JMR	—	25.00	40.00	75.00	200	—
1850 RM Rare	—	—	—	—	—	—
1850 JMR	—	25.00	40.00	75.00	200	—
1851 JMR	—	20.00	35.00	50.00	100	—
1852/1 JMR	—	65.00	125	250	600	—
1852 JMR	—	30.00	50.00	80.00	200	—
1853 CP	—	12.50	20.00	40.00	80.00	—
1854 CP	—	25.00	40.00	75.00	200	—
1855 CP	—	25.00	40.00	60.00	150	—
1856/5 CP	—	20.00	35.00	50.00	100	—
1857 CP	—	20.00	35.00	50.00	100	—
1858/7 CP	—	20.00	35.00	50.00	100	—
1859 CP	—	20.00	35.00	50.00	100	—
1860/59 CP	—	40.00	65.00	135	300	—
1861 CP	—	125	250	400	700	—
1862 CP	—	25.00	40.00	60.00	125	—
1864 LT	—	100	300	500	1,000	—
1869 CP	—	40.00	65.00	125	275	—

KM# 370.4 1/2 REAL
1.6900 g., 0.9030 Silver .0490 oz. ASW **Obv:** Facing eagle

Date	Mintage	F	VF	XF	Unc	BU
1829EoMo LF	—	175	300	500	1,400	—

KM# 370.5 1/2 REAL
1.6900 g., 0.9030 Silver .0490 oz. ASW **Obv:** Facing eagle

Date	Mintage	F	VF	XF	Unc	BU
1825Ga FS	—	25.00	40.00	75.00	200	—
1826Ga FS	—	10.00	15.00	35.00	80.00	—
1828/7Ga FS	—	12.50	20.00	40.00	90.00	—
1829Ga FS	—	7.50	15.00	30.00	70.00	—
1830/29Ga FS	—	40.00	60.00	100	200	—
1831Ga LP Rare						
1832Ga FS	—	10.00	20.00	35.00	80.00	—
1834/3Ga FS	—	65.00	100	175	250	—
1834Ga FS	—	10.00	20.00	35.00	80.00	—
1835/4/3Ga FS/LP	—	15.00	25.00	40.00	90.00	—
1837/6Ga JG	—	100	250	500	1,000	—
1838/7Ga JG	—	15.00	25.00	40.00	90.00	—
1839/8Ga JG/FS	—	35.00	75.00	150	250	—
1839Ga MC	—	10.00	20.00	35.00	80.00	—
1840/39Ga MC/JG	—	—	—	—	—	—
1840Ga MC	—	15.00	25.00	40.00	90.00	—
1841Ga MC	—	20.00	35.00	50.00	100	—
1842/1Ga JG	—	15.00	25.00	40.00	90.00	—
1842Ga JG	—	10.00	20.00	35.00	80.00	—
1843/2Ga JG	—	15.00	30.00	50.00	100	—
1843Ga JG	—	10.00	20.00	35.00	80.00	—
1843Ga MC/JG	—	10.00	20.00	35.00	80.00	—
1843Ga MC	—	10.00	20.00	35.00	80.00	—
1844Ga MC	—	10.00	20.00	35.00	80.00	—
1845Ga MC	—	10.00	20.00	35.00	80.00	—
1845Ga JG	—	10.00	20.00	35.00	80.00	—
1846Ga MC	—	10.00	20.00	35.00	80.00	—
1846Ga JG	—	10.00	20.00	35.00	80.00	—
1847Ga JG	—	10.00	20.00	35.00	80.00	—
1848/7Ga JG	—	10.00	20.00	35.00	80.00	—
1849Ga JG	—	10.00	20.00	35.00	80.00	—
1850/49Ga JG	—	—	—	—	—	—
1850Ga JG	—	10.00	20.00	35.00	80.00	—
1851/0Ga JG	—	10.00	20.00	35.00	80.00	—
1852Ga JG	—	10.00	20.00	35.00	80.00	—
1853Ga JG	—	10.00	20.00	35.00	80.00	—
1854Ga JG	—	10.00	20.00	35.00	80.00	—
1855/4Ga JG	—	10.00	20.00	35.00	80.00	—
1855Ga JG	—	10.00	20.00	35.00	80.00	—
1856Ga JG	—	10.00	20.00	35.00	80.00	—
1857Ga JG	—	10.00	20.00	35.00	80.00	—
1858/7Ga JG	—	10.00	20.00	35.00	80.00	—
1858Ga JG	—	10.00	20.00	35.00	80.00	—
1859/7Ga JG	—	10.00	20.00	35.00	80.00	—
1860/59Ga JG	—	10.00	20.00	35.00	80.00	—
1861Ga JG	—	5.00	12.50	25.00	60.00	—
1862/1Ga JG	—	15.00	25.00	40.00	90.00	—

KM# 370.6 1/2 REAL
1.6900 g., 0.9030 Silver .0490 oz. ASW **Obv:** Facing eagle

Date	Mintage	F	VF	XF	Unc	BU
1844GC MP	—	50.00	100	150	350	—
1845GC MP	—	25.00	50.00	100	200	—
1846GC MP	—	25.00	50.00	100	200	—
1847GC MP	—	25.00	50.00	100	300	—
1848GC MP	—	20.00	40.00	75.00	150	—
1849GC MP	—	25.00	50.00	100	200	—
1850GC MP	—	30.00	60.00	125	250	—
1851GC MP	—	25.00	50.00	100	200	—

KM# 370.7 1/2 REAL
1.6900 g., 0.9030 Silver .0490 oz. ASW **Obv:** Facing eagle
Note: Varieties exist.

Date	Mintage	F	VF	XF	Unc	BU
1826Go MJ	—	125	250	400	1,000	—
1827/6Go MJ	—	7.50	15.00	30.00	75.00	—
1828/7Go MJ	—	7.50	15.00	30.00	75.00	—
1828Go MJ Denomination 2/1	—	—	—	—	—	—
1828Go JG	—	—	—	—	—	—
1828Go MR	—	50.00	100	150	250	—
1829/8Go MJ	—	5.00	10.00	25.00	50.00	—
1829Go MJ	—	5.00	10.00	25.00	50.00	—
1829Go MJ Reversed N in MEXICANA	—	5.00	10.00	25.00	50.00	—
1830Go MJ	—	5.00	10.00	25.00	50.00	—
1831/29Go MJ	—	15.00	30.00	60.00	150	—
1831Go MJ	—	10.00	20.00	40.00	80.00	—
1832/1Go MJ	—	7.50	15.00	30.00	75.00	—
1832Go MJ	—	7.50	15.00	30.00	75.00	—

Date	Mintage	F	VF	XF	Unc	BU
1833Go MJ Round top 3	—	10.00	20.00	40.00	80.00	—
1833Go MJ Flat top 3	—	10.00	20.00	40.00	80.00	—
1834Go PJ	—	5.00	10.00	25.00	50.00	—
1835Go PJ	—	5.00	10.00	25.00	50.00	—
1836/5Go PJ	—	7.50	15.00	30.00	75.00	—
1836Go PJ	—	5.00	10.00	25.00	50.00	—
1837Go PJ	—	5.00	10.00	25.00	50.00	—
1838/7Go PJ	—	5.00	10.00	25.00	50.00	—
1839Go PJ	—	5.00	10.00	25.00	50.00	—
1839Go PJ Error: REPUBLIGA	—	5.00	10.00	25.00	50.00	—
1840/39Go PJ	—	7.50	10.00	25.00	75.00	—
1840Go PJ Straight J	—	5.00	10.00	25.00	50.00	—
1840Go PJ Curved J	—	5.00	10.00	25.00	50.00	—
1841/31Go PJ	—	5.00	10.00	25.00	50.00	—
1841Go PJ	—	5.00	10.00	25.00	50.00	—
1842/1Go PJ	—	5.00	10.00	25.00	50.00	—
1842/1Go PM	—	5.00	10.00	25.00	50.00	—
1842Go PM/J	—	5.00	10.00	25.00	50.00	—
1842Go PJ	—	5.00	10.00	25.00	50.00	—
1842Go PM	—	5.00	10.00	25.00	50.00	—
1843/33Go PM 1/2 over 8	—	5.00	10.00	25.00	50.00	—
1843Go PM Convex wings	—	5.00	10.00	25.00	50.00	—
1843Go PM Concave wings	—	5.00	10.00	25.00	50.00	—
1844/3Go PM	—	5.00	10.00	25.00	50.00	—
1844Go PM	—	10.00	20.00	40.00	90.00	—
1845/4Go PM	—	5.00	10.00	25.00	50.00	—
1845Go PM	—	5.00	10.00	25.00	50.00	—
1846/5Go PM	—	5.00	10.00	25.00	50.00	—
1846Go PM	—	5.00	10.00	25.00	50.00	—
1847/6Go PM	—	7.50	15.00	30.00	60.00	—
1847Go PM	—	7.50	15.00	30.00	60.00	—
1848/35Go PM	—	5.00	10.00	25.00	50.00	—
1848Go PM	—	5.00	10.00	25.00	50.00	—
1848Go PF/M	—	5.00	10.00	25.00	50.00	—
1849/39Go PF	—	5.00	10.00	25.00	50.00	—
1849Go PF	—	5.00	10.00	25.00	50.00	—
1849Go PF Error: MEXCANA	—	5.00	10.00	25.00	50.00	—
1850Go PF	—	5.00	10.00	25.00	50.00	—
1851Go PF	—	5.00	10.00	25.00	50.00	—
1852/1Go PF	—	2.50	7.50	17.50	40.00	—
1852Go PF	—	5.00	10.00	25.00	50.00	—
1853Go PF/R	—	5.00	10.00	25.00	50.00	—
1853Go PF	—	5.00	10.00	25.00	50.00	—
1854Go PF	—	5.00	10.00	25.00	50.00	—
1855Go PF	—	5.00	10.00	25.00	50.00	—
1856/4Go PF	—	5.00	10.00	25.00	50.00	—
1856/5Go PF	—	5.00	10.00	25.00	50.00	—
1856Go PF	—	5.00	10.00	25.00	50.00	—
1857/6Go PF	—	5.00	10.00	25.00	50.00	—
1857Go PF	—	5.00	10.00	25.00	50.00	—
1858/7Go PF	—	7.50	15.00	30.00	60.00	—
1858Go PF	—	5.00	10.00	25.00	50.00	—
1859Go PF	—	5.00	10.00	25.00	50.00	—
1860Go PF Small 1/2	—	5.00	10.00	25.00	50.00	—
1860Go PF Large 1/2	—	5.00	10.00	25.00	50.00	—
1860/59Go PF	—	5.00	10.00	25.00	50.00	—
1861Go PF Small 1/2	—	5.00	10.00	25.00	50.00	—
1861Go PF Large 1/2	—	5.00	10.00	25.00	50.00	—
1862/1Go YE	—	5.00	10.00	25.00	50.00	—
1862Go YE	—	2.50	7.50	17.50	40.00	—
1862Go YF	—	5.00	10.00	25.00	50.00	—
1867Go YF	—	2.50	7.50	17.50	40.00	—
1868Go YF	—	2.50	7.50	17.50	40.00	—

KM# 370.8 1/2 REAL
1.6900 g., 0.9030 Silver .0490 oz. ASW **Obv:** Facing eagle

Date	Mintage	F	VF	XF	Unc	BU
1839Ho PP Unique						
1862Ho FM	—	500	650	1,000	—	—
1867Ho PR/FM Inverted 6, and 7/1	—	100	175	250	500	—

KM# 370.9 1/2 REAL
1.6900 g., 0.9030 Silver .0490 oz. ASW **Obv:** Facing eagle

Date	Mintage	F	VF	XF	Unc	BU
1825Mo JM Short top 5	—	10.00	20.00	40.00	80.00	—
1825Mo JM Long top 5	—	10.00	20.00	40.00	80.00	—
1826/5Mo JM	—	10.00	20.00	40.00	80.00	—
1826Mo JM	—	5.00	10.00	20.00	60.00	—
1827/6Mo JM	—	5.00	10.00	20.00	60.00	—
1827Mo JM	—	5.00	10.00	20.00	60.00	—
1828/7Mo JM	—	7.50	15.00	25.00	85.00	—
1828Mo JM	—	10.00	20.00	40.00	90.00	—
1829Mo JM	—	7.50	15.00	25.00	75.00	—
1830Mo JM	—	5.00	10.00	20.00	60.00	—
1831Mo JM	—	5.00	10.00	20.00	60.00	—
1832Mo JM	—	7.50	12.50	27.50	60.00	—
1833Mo MJ	—	7.50	12.50	27.50	60.00	—
1834Mo ML	—	5.00	10.00	20.00	60.00	—
1835Mo ML	—	5.00	10.00	20.00	60.00	—
1836/5Mo ML/MF	—	7.50	15.00	25.00	65.00	—
1836Mo ML	—	7.50	15.00	25.00	65.00	—
1838Mo ML	—	5.00	10.00	20.00	60.00	—
1839/8Mo ML	—	5.00	10.00	25.00	65.00	—
1839Mo ML	—	5.00	10.00	20.00	50.00	—
1840Mo ML	—	5.00	10.00	20.00	50.00	—
1841Mo ML	—	5.00	10.00	20.00	50.00	—
1842Mo ML	—	5.00	10.00	20.00	50.00	—
1842Mo MM	—	5.00	10.00	20.00	50.00	—
1843Mo MM	—	10.00	20.00	40.00	80.00	—
1844Mo MF	—	5.00	10.00	20.00	50.00	—
1845/4Mo MF	—	5.00	10.00	25.00	60.00	—
1845Mo MF	—	5.00	10.00	20.00	50.00	—
1846Mo MF	—	5.00	10.00	20.00	50.00	—
1847Mo RC	—	10.00	20.00	40.00	80.00	—
1847Mo RC R/M	—	10.00	20.00	40.00	80.00	—
1848/7Mo GC/RC	—	5.00	10.00	20.00	50.00	—
1849Mo GC	—	5.00	10.00	20.00	50.00	—
1850Mo GC	—	5.00	10.00	20.00	50.00	—
1851Mo GC	—	5.00	10.00	20.00	50.00	—
1852Mo GC	—	5.00	10.00	20.00	50.00	—
1853Mo GC	—	5.00	10.00	20.00	50.00	—
1854Mo GC	—	5.00	10.00	20.00	50.00	—
1855Mo GC	—	5.00	10.00	20.00	50.00	—
1855Mo GF/GC	—	7.50	12.50	25.00	65.00	—
1856/5Mo GF	—	7.50	12.50	25.00	65.00	—
1857Mo GF	—	5.00	10.00	20.00	50.00	—
1858Mo FH	—	3.00	5.00	12.50	40.00	—
1858Mo FH F/G	—	5.00	10.00	20.00	50.00	—
1858/9Mo FH	—	5.00	10.00	20.00	50.00	—
1859Mo FH	—	3.00	6.00	15.00	50.00	—
1860Mo FH/GC	—	5.00	10.00	20.00	50.00	—
1860Mo FH	—	3.00	6.00	15.00	50.00	—
1860Mo TH	—	25.00	50.00	100	200	—
1860/59Mo FH	—	7.50	12.50	25.00	65.00	—
1861Mo CH	—	3.00	6.00	15.00	45.00	—
1862/52Mo CH	—	5.00	10.00	20.00	50.00	—
1862Mo CH	—	3.00	6.00	15.00	45.00	—
1863/55Mo TH/GC	—	5.00	10.00	20.00	50.00	—
1863Mo CH/GC	—	5.00	10.00	20.00	50.00	—
1863Mo CH	—	3.00	6.00	15.00	45.00	—

KM# 370.10 1/2 REAL
1.6900 g., 0.9030 Silver .0490 oz. ASW **Obv:** Facing eagle

Date	Mintage	F	VF	XF	Unc	BU
1831 Pi JS	—	7.50	12.50	25.00	65.00	—
1841/36 Pi JS	—	20.00	40.00	75.00	125	—
1842/1 Pi PS	—	20.00	40.00	75.00	125	—
1842/1 Pi PS P/J	—	60.00	80.00	150	300	—
1842 Pi PS/PJ	—	50.00	75.00	125	250	—
1842 PS	—	60.00	80.00	150	300	—
1842 Pi JS	—	20.00	40.00	75.00	125	—
1843/2 Pi PS	—	17.50	25.00	40.00	80.00	—
1843 Pi PS	—	15.00	25.00	35.00	70.00	—
1843 Pi AM	—	10.00	15.00	25.00	60.00	—
1844 Pi AM	—	10.00	15.00	30.00	65.00	—
1845 Pi AM	—	250	375	500	1,500	—
1846/5 Pi AM	—	40.00	75.00	125	200	—
1847/6 Pi AM	—	15.00	25.00	40.00	80.00	—
1848 Pi AM	—	15.00	25.00	40.00	80.00	—
1849 Pi MC/AM	—	15.00	25.00	40.00	80.00	—
1849 Pi MC	—	12.50	20.00	35.00	70.00	—
1850/49 Pi MC	—	—	—	—	—	—
1850 Pi MC	—	10.00	15.00	25.00	60.00	—

Date	Mintage	F	VF	XF	Unc	BU
1850P MC	—	—	—	—	—	—
1851 Pi MC	—	10.00	15.00	25.00	60.00	—
1852 Pi MC	—	10.00	20.00	30.00	65.00	—
1853 Pi MC	—	7.50	12.50	20.00	60.00	—
1854 Pi MC	—	7.50	12.50	20.00	60.00	—
1855 Pi MC	—	15.00	20.00	35.00	70.00	—
1856 Pi MC	—	15.00	25.00	50.00	100	—
1856PI (no I)	—	—	—	—	—	—
1857 Pi MC	—	7.50	12.50	20.00	60.00	—
1857 Pi PS	—	10.00	15.00	30.00	65.00	—
1858 Pi MC	—	12.50	20.00	35.00	70.00	—
1858 Pi PS	—	12.50	20.00	35.00	70.00	—
1859 Pi MC Rare	—	—	—	—	—	—
1860/59 Pi PS	—	125	200	600	—	—
1861 Pi RO	—	10.00	15.00	30.00	60.00	—
1862/1 Pi RO	—	15.00	25.00	50.00	125	—
1862 Pi RO	—	15.00	25.00	50.00	125	—
1863/2 Pi RO	—	15.00	25.00	45.00	100	—

KM# 370.11 1/2 REAL
1.6900 g., 0.9030 Silver .0490 oz. ASW **Obv:** Facing eagle
Note: Mint mark Z, Zs.

Date	Mintage	F	VF	XF	Unc	BU
1826 AZ	—	5.00	10.00	20.00	60.00	—
1826 AO	—	5.00	10.00	20.00	60.00	—
1827 AO	—	5.00	10.00	20.00	60.00	—
1828/7 AO	—	5.00	10.00	20.00	60.00	—
1829 AO	—	5.00	10.00	20.00	60.00	—
1830 OV	—	5.00	10.00	20.00	60.00	—
1831 OV	—	25.00	50.00	75.00	150	—
1831 OM	—	5.00	10.00	20.00	60.00	—
1832 OM	—	5.00	10.00	20.00	60.00	—
1833 OM	—	5.00	10.00	20.00	60.00	—
1834 OM	—	5.00	10.00	20.00	60.00	—
1835/4 OM	—	5.00	10.00	20.00	60.00	—
1835 OM	—	5.00	10.00	20.00	60.00	—
1836 OM	—	5.00	10.00	20.00	60.00	—
1837 OM	—	10.00	20.00	40.00	80.00	—
1838 OM	—	5.00	10.00	20.00	60.00	—
1839 OM	—	7.50	15.00	30.00	65.00	—
1840 OM	—	10.00	25.00	45.00	90.00	—
1841 OM	—	10.00	25.00	45.00	90.00	—
1842/1 OM	—	5.00	10.00	20.00	60.00	—
1842 OM	—	5.00	10.00	20.00	60.00	—
1843 OM	—	40.00	75.00	115	250	—
1844 OM	—	5.00	10.00	20.00	60.00	—
1845 OM	—	5.00	10.00	20.00	60.00	—
1846 OM	—	7.50	15.00	30.00	65.00	—
1847 OM	—	5.00	10.00	20.00	50.00	—
1848 OM	—	5.00	10.00	20.00	50.00	—
1849 OM	—	5.00	10.00	20.00	50.00	—
1850 OM	—	5.00	10.00	20.00	50.00	—
1851 OM	—	5.00	10.00	20.00	50.00	—
1852 OM	—	5.00	10.00	20.00	50.00	—
1853 OM	—	5.00	10.00	20.00	50.00	—
1854/3 OM	—	5.00	10.00	20.00	50.00	—
1854 OM	—	5.00	10.00	20.00	50.00	—
1855/3 OM	—	7.50	15.00	30.00	65.00	—
1855 OM	—	5.00	10.00	20.00	50.00	—
1856 OM	—	5.00	10.00	20.00	50.00	—
1857 MO	—	5.00	10.00	20.00	50.00	—
1858 MO	—	5.00	10.00	20.00	50.00	—
1859 MO	—	6.00	8.50	17.50	35.00	—
1859 VL	—	6.00	8.50	17.50	40.00	—
1860/50 VL Inverted A for V	—	5.00	10.00	20.00	50.00	—
1860/59 VL Inverted A for V	—	5.00	10.00	20.00	50.00	—
1860 MO	—	5.00	10.00	20.00	50.00	—
1860 VL	—	5.00	10.00	20.00	50.00	—
1861/0 VL Inverted A for V	—	7.50	15.00	30.00	65.00	—
1861 VL Inverted A for V	—	5.00	10.00	20.00	50.00	—
1862 VL Inverted A for V	—	5.00	10.00	20.00	50.00	—
1863/1 VL Inverted A for V	—	7.50	15.00	30.00	65.00	—
1863 VL Inverted A for V	—	5.00	10.00	20.00	50.00	—
1869 YH	—	5.00	10.00	20.00	50.00	—

KM# 372 REAL
3.3800 g., 0.9030 Silver .0981 oz. ASW

Date	Mintage	F	VF	XF	Unc	BU
1844 Ca RG	—	500	1,000	1,500	2,750	—
1845 Ca RG	—	500	1,000	1,500	2,750	—
1855 Ca RG	—	100	150	225	450	—

KM# 372.1 REAL
3.3800 g., 0.9030 Silver .0981 oz. ASW

Date	Mintage	F	VF	XF	Unc	BU
1846C CE	—	12.50	25.00	40.00	110	—
1848C CE	—	12.50	25.00	40.00	110	—
1850C CE	—	12.50	25.00	40.00	110	—
1851/0C CE	—	12.50	25.00	40.00	110	—
1852/1C CE	—	7.50	15.00	30.00	100	—
1853/2C CE	—	7.50	15.00	30.00	100	—
1854C CE	—	7.50	15.00	30.00	100	—
1856C CE	—	40.00	65.00	100	225	—
1857/4C CE	—	10.00	20.00	35.00	100	—
1857/6C CE	—	10.00	20.00	35.00	100	—
1858C CE	—	5.00	7.50	15.00	100	—
1859C CE	—	—	—	—	—	—
1860C PV	—	5.00	7.50	15.00	100	—
1861C PV	—	5.00	7.50	15.00	100	—
1863C CE 3 known	—	—	—	1,650	2,250	—
1869C CE	—	—	7.50	15.00	100	—

KM# 372.2 REAL
3.3800 g., 0.9030 Silver .0981 oz. ASW

Date	Mintage	F	VF	XF	Unc	BU
1832/1Do RM	—	5.00	10.00	20.00	90.00	—
1832Do RM/RL	—	10.00	15.00	30.00	100	—
1832Do RM	—	5.00	10.00	20.00	100	—
1834/24Do RM/RL	—	15.00	25.00	50.00	150	—
1834/3Do RM/RL	—	15.00	25.00	50.00	150	—
1834Do RM	—	10.00	20.00	40.00	110	—
1836/4Do RM	—	5.00	7.50	15.00	100	—
1836Do RM	—	5.00	7.50	15.00	100	—
1837Do RM 3/2	—	12.50	20.00	40.00	110	—
1837Do RM	—	12.50	20.00	40.00	110	—
1841Do RM	—	7.50	15.00	30.00	100	—
1842/32Do RM	—	10.00	20.00	40.00	110	—
1842Do RM	—	7.50	15.00	30.00	100	—
1843Do RM	—	5.00	7.50	15.00	100	—
1844/34Do RM	—	15.00	25.00	45.00	125	—
1845Do RM	—	5.00	7.50	15.00	100	—
1846Do RM	—	7.50	15.00	30.00	100	—
1847Do RM	—	10.00	15.00	35.00	100	—
1848/31Do RM	—	10.00	15.00	35.00	100	—
1848/33Do RM	—	10.00	15.00	35.00	100	—
1848/5Do RM	—	10.00	15.00	35.00	100	—
1848Do RM	—	7.50	12.50	20.00	100	—
1849/8Do CM	—	10.00	15.00	30.00	100	—
1850Do JMR	—	20.00	40.00	75.00	175	—
1851Do JMR	—	20.00	40.00	75.00	175	—
1852Do JMR	—	20.00	40.00	75.00	175	—
1853Do CP	—	12.50	20.00	35.00	100	—
1854/1Do CP	—	10.00	15.00	25.00	100	—
1854Do CP	—	7.50	12.50	20.00	100	—
1855Do CP	—	10.00	15.00	25.00	100	—
1856Do CP	—	12.50	20.00	35.00	100	—
1857Do CP	—	12.50	20.00	35.00	100	—
1858Do CP	—	12.50	20.00	35.00	100	—
1859Do CP	—	7.50	12.50	20.00	100	—
1860/59Do CP	—	10.00	15.00	25.00	100	—
1861Do CP	—	15.00	25.00	40.00	110	—
1862/1Do CP	—	225	300	450	1,250	—
1864Do LT	—	15.00	25.00	40.00	110	—

KM# 372.3 REAL
3.3800 g., 0.9030 Silver .0981 oz. ASW

Date	Mintage	F	VF	XF	Unc	BU
1828EoMo LF	—	200	300	450	1,500	—

KM# 372.4 REAL
3.3800 g., 0.9030 Silver .0981 oz. ASW

Date	Mintage	F	VF	XF	Unc	BU
1826Ga FS	—	15.00	30.00	50.00	125	—
1828/7Ga FS	—	15.00	30.00	50.00	125	—
1829/8/7Ga FS	—	—	—	—	—	—
1829Ga FS	—	15.00	30.00	50.00	125	—
1830Ga FS	—	250	425	600	—	—
1831Ga LP	—	15.00	30.00	50.00	125	—
1831Ga LP/FS	—	300	450	600	—	—
1832Ga FS	—	250	350	500	—	—

Date	Mintage	F	VF	XF	Unc	BU
1833/2Ga G FS	—	100	150	275	550	—
1833Ga FS	—	75.00	125	225	500	—
1834/3Ga FS	—	75.00	125	225	500	—
1835Ga FS	—	—	—	—	—	—
1837/6Ga JG/FS	—	12.50	20.00	35.00	100	—
1838/7Ga JG/FS	—	100	200	400	—	—
1839Ga JG	—	250	350	500	—	—
1840Ga JG	—	12.50	20.00	35.00	100	—
1840Ga MC	—	7.50	12.50	25.00	70.00	—
1841Ga MC	—	50.00	75.00	125	250	—
1842/0Ga JG/MC	—	10.00	15.00	30.00	100	—
1842Ga JG	—	7.50	12.50	20.00	100	—
1843Ga JG	—	150	200	300	750	—
1843Ga MC	—	5.00	7.50	15.00	100	—
1844Ga MC	—	7.50	12.50	20.00	100	—
1845Ga MC	—	10.00	15.00	25.00	100	—
1845Ga JG	—	5.00	7.50	15.00	100	—
1846Ga JG	—	12.50	20.00	35.00	100	—
1847/6Ga JG	—	10.00	15.00	25.00	100	—
1847Ga JG	—	10.00	15.00	25.00	100	—
1848Ga JG	—	400	550	700	—	—
1849Ga JG	—	7.50	12.50	20.00	100	—
1850Ga JG	—	175	275	400	—	—
1851Ga JG	—	10.00	15.00	25.00	100	—
1852Ga JG	—	10.00	15.00	25.00	100	—
1853/2Ga JG	—	10.00	15.00	25.00	100	—
1854Ga JG	—	10.00	15.00	25.00	100	—
1855Ga JG	—	15.00	25.00	40.00	100	—
1856Ga JG	—	7.50	12.50	20.00	100	—
1857/6Ga JG	—	12.50	20.00	35.00	100	—
1858/7Ga JG	—	15.00	25.00	40.00	110	—
1859/8Ga JG	—	25.00	50.00	75.00	150	—
1860/59Ga JG	—	30.00	60.00	90.00	225	—
1861/0Ga JG	—	20.00	30.00	50.00	125	—
1861Ga JG	—	25.00	50.00	100	250	—
1862Ga JG	—	7.50	12.50	20.00	100	—

KM# 372.5 REAL
3.3800 g., 0.9030 Silver .0981 oz. ASW

Date	Mintage	F	VF	XF	Unc	BU
1844GC MP	—	40.00	60.00	100	250	—
1845GC MP	—	40.00	60.00	100	250	—
1846GC MP	—	40.00	60.00	100	250	—
1847GC MP	—	40.00	60.00	100	250	—
1848GC MP	—	40.00	60.00	100	250	—
1849/7GC MP	—	40.00	60.00	100	250	—
1849/8GC MP	—	40.00	60.00	100	250	—
1849GC MP	—	40.00	60.00	100	250	—
1850GC MP	—	40.00	60.00	100	250	—
1851GC MP	—	40.00	60.00	100	250	—

KM# 372.6 REAL
3.3800 g., 0.9030 Silver .0981 oz. ASW

Date	Mintage	F	VF	XF	Unc	BU
1826/5Go JJ	—	5.00	7.50	15.00	85.00	—
1826Go MJ	—	4.00	6.00	15.00	85.00	—
1827Go MJ	—	4.00	6.00	15.00	65.00	—
1827Go JM	—	10.00	15.00	25.00	75.00	—
1828/7Go MR	—	4.00	6.00	15.00	85.00	—
1828Go MJ	—	4.00	6.00	15.00	85.00	—
Note: Straight J, small 8						
1828Go MJ	—	4.00	6.00	15.00	85.00	—
Note: Full J, large 8						
1828G MR/JJ	—	4.00	6.00	15.00	85.00	—
1828Go MR	—	4.00	6.00	15.00	85.00	—
1829/8Go MG Small eagle	—	4.00	6.00	15.00	85.00	—
1829Go MJ Small eagle	—	4.00	6.00	15.00	85.00	—
1829Go MJ Large eagle	—	4.00	6.00	15.00	85.00	—
1830Go MJ Small initials	—	4.00	6.00	15.00	85.00	—
1830Go MJ Medium initials	—	4.00	6.00	15.00	85.00	—
1830Go MJ Large initials	—	4.00	6.00	15.00	85.00	—
1830Go MJ	—	4.00	6.00	15.00	85.00	—

Date	Mintage	F	VF	XF	Unc	BU
Note: Reversed N in MEXICANA						
1830GC MJ 3/2	—	4.00	6.00	15.00	85.00	—
1831/0Go MJ	—	4.00	6.00	15.00	85.00	—
Note: Reversed N in MEXICANA						
1831Go MJ	—	4.00	6.00	15.00	85.00	—
1832/1Go MJ	—	15.00	30.00	50.00	125	—
1832Go MJ	—	15.00	30.00	50.00	125	—
1833Go MJ Top of 3 round	—	4.00	6.00	15.00	85.00	—
1833Go MJ Top of 3 flat	—	4.00	6.00	15.00	85.00	—
1834Go PJ	—	4.00	6.00	15.00	85.00	—
1835Go PJ	—	7.50	12.50	20.00	85.00	—
1836Go PJ	—	4.00	6.00	15.00	85.00	—
1837Go PJ	—	15.00	30.00	50.00	125	—
1838/7Go PJ	—	10.00	20.00	35.00	85.00	—
1839Go PJ	—	4.00	6.00	15.00	85.00	—
1840/39Go PJ	—	4.00	6.00	15.00	85.00	—
1840Go PJ	—	4.00	6.00	15.00	85.00	—
1841/31Go PJ	—	10.00	20.00	35.00	85.00	—
1841Go PJ	—	4.00	6.00	15.00	85.00	—
1842Go PJ	—	4.00	6.00	15.00	85.00	—
1842Go PM	—	4.00	6.00	15.00	85.00	—
1843Go PM Convex wings	—	4.00	6.00	15.00	85.00	—
1843Go PM Concave wings	—	4.00	6.00	15.00	85.00	—
1844Go PM	—	4.00	6.00	15.00	85.00	—
1845/4Go PM	—	4.00	6.00	15.00	85.00	—
1845Go PM	—	4.00	6.00	15.00	85.00	—
1846/5Go PM	—	7.50	12.50	20.00	85.00	—
1846Go PM	—	4.00	6.00	15.00	85.00	—
1847/6Go PM	—	4.00	6.00	15.00	85.00	—
1847Go PM	—	4.00	6.00	15.00	85.00	—
1848Go PM	—	4.00	6.00	15.00	85.00	—
1849Go PF	—	10.00	20.00	35.00	85.00	—
1850Go PF	—	4.00	6.00	15.00	85.00	—
1851Go PF	—	10.00	20.00	35.00	100	—
1853/2Go PF	—	7.50	12.50	20.00	75.00	—
1853Go PF	—	4.00	6.00	15.00	75.00	—
1853Go PF/M 5/4	—	7.50	12.50	20.00	75.00	—
1854/3Go PF	—	4.00	6.00	15.00	75.00	—
1854Go PF Large eagle	—	4.00	6.00	15.00	75.00	—
1854Go PF Small eagle	—	4.00	6.00	15.00	75.00	—
1855/3Go PF	—	4.00	6.00	15.00	75.00	—
1855/4Go PF	—	4.00	6.00	15.00	75.00	—
1855Go PF	—	4.00	6.00	15.00	75.00	—
1856/5Go PF	—	4.00	6.00	15.00	75.00	—
1856Go PF	—	4.00	6.00	15.00	75.00	—
1857/6Go PF	—	4.00	6.00	15.00	75.00	—
1857Go PF	—	4.00	6.00	15.00	75.00	—
1858Go PF	—	4.00	6.00	15.00	75.00	—
1859Go PF	—	4.00	6.00	15.00	75.00	—
1860/50Go PF	—	4.00	6.00	15.00	75.00	—
1860Go PF	—	4.00	6.00	15.00	75.00	—
1861Go PF	—	4.00	6.00	15.00	75.00	—
1862Go YE	—	4.00	6.00	15.00	75.00	—
1862/1Go YF	—	7.50	12.50	20.00	75.00	—
1862Go YF	—	4.00	6.00	15.00	75.00	—
1867Go YF	—	4.00	6.00	15.00	75.00	—
1868/7Go YF	—	4.00	6.00	15.00	75.00	—

KM# 372.7 REAL
3.3800 g., 0.9030 Silver .0981 oz. ASW

Date	Mintage	F	VF	XF	Unc	BU
1867Ho PR	—	38.50	75.00	120	250	—
Note: Small 7/1						
1867Ho PR	—	38.50	75.00	120	250	—
Note: Large 7/ small 7						
1868Ho PR	—	38.50	75.00	120	250	—

KM# 372.8 REAL
3.3800 g., 0.9030 Silver .0981 oz. ASW

Date	Mintage	F	VF	XF	Unc	BU
1825Mo JM	—	10.00	20.00	40.00	110	—
1826Mo JM	—	7.50	15.00	30.00	100	—
1827/6Mo JM	—	7.50	15.00	30.00	75.00	—
1827Mo JM	—	5.00	10.00	20.00	70.00	—
1828Mo JM	—	7.50	15.00	30.00	100	—
1830/29Mo JM	—	5.00	10.00	20.00	100	—
1830Mo JM	—	5.00	12.50	25.00	100	—
1831Mo JM	—	100	200	300	750	—
1832Mo JM	—	5.00	10.00	20.00	100	—
1833/2Mo MJ	—	5.00	10.00	20.00	100	—
1850Mo GC	—	5.00	10.00	20.00	100	—

Date	Mintage	F	VF	XF	Unc	BU
1852Mo GC	—	275	425	575	—	—
1854Mo GC	—	10.00	20.00	40.00	100	—
1855Mo GF	—	5.00	10.00	20.00	80.00	—
1856Mo GF	—	5.00	10.00	20.00	80.00	—
1857Mo GF	—	5.00	10.00	20.00	80.00	—
1858Mo FH	—	5.00	10.00	20.00	80.00	—
1859Mo FH	—	5.00	10.00	20.00	80.00	—
1861Mo CH	—	5.00	10.00	20.00	80.00	—
1862Mo CH	—	5.00	10.00	20.00	80.00	—
1863/2Mo CH	—	7.50	12.50	25.00	80.00	—

KM# 372.9 REAL
3.3800 g., 0.9030 Silver .0981 oz. ASW

Date	Mintage	F	VF	XF	Unc	BU
1831 Pi JS	—	5.00	10.00	20.00	125	—
1837 Pi JS	—	600	750	1,000	—	—
1838/7 Pi JS	—	250	300	375	—	—
1838 Pi JS	—	20.00	35.00	60.00	125	—
1840/39 Pi JS	—	7.50	15.00	30.00	125	—
1840 Pi JS	—	7.50	15.00	30.00	125	—
1841 Pi JS	—	7.50	15.00	30.00	125	—
1842 Pi JS	—	15.00	30.00	55.00	150	—
1842 Pi PS	—	5.00	10.00	20.00	125	—
1843 Pi PS	—	12.50	20.00	35.00	125	—
1843 Pi AM	—	40.00	60.00	80.00	150	—
1844 Pi AM	—	40.00	60.00	80.00	150	—
1845 Pi AM	—	7.50	15.00	30.00	125	—
1846/5 Pi AM	—	7.50	15.00	30.00	125	—
1847/6 Pi AM	—	7.50	15.00	30.00	125	—
1847 Pi AM	—	7.50	15.00	30.00	125	—
1848/7 Pi AM	—	7.50	15.00	30.00	125	—
1849 Pi PS	—	7.50	15.00	30.00	125	—
1849/8 Pi SP	—	60.00	100	150	—	—
1849 Pi SP	—	15.00	25.00	40.00	125	—
1850 Pi MC	—	5.00	10.00	20.00	125	—
1851/0 Pi MC	—	7.50	15.00	30.00	125	—
1851 Pi MC	—	7.50	15.00	30.00	125	—
1852/1/0 Pi MC	—	10.00	20.00	35.00	125	—
1852 Pi MC	—	7.50	15.00	30.00	125	—
1853/1 Pi MC	—	12.50	20.00	35.00	125	—
1853 Pi MC	—	10.00	20.00	35.00	125	—
1854/2 Pi MO	—	30.00	60.00	100	—	—
1854/3 Pi MC	—	20.00	40.00	60.00	150	—
1855/4 Pi MC	—	20.00	40.00	60.00	150	—
1855 Pi MC	—	15.00	25.00	45.00	125	—
1856 Pi MC	—	15.00	25.00	45.00	125	—
1857 Pi PS	—	20.00	35.00	55.00	135	—
1857 Pi MC	—	20.00	40.00	60.00	150	—
1858 Pi MC	—	12.50	20.00	35.00	125	—
1859 Pi PS	—	10.00	15.00	30.00	125	—
1860/59 Pi PS	—	10.00	15.00	30.00	125	—
1861 Pi PS	—	7.50	12.50	20.00	125	—
1861 Pi RO	—	12.50	20.00	35.00	125	—
1862/1 Pi RO	—	12.50	20.00	35.00	90.00	—
1862 Pi RO	—	7.50	12.50	20.00	125	—

KM# 372.10 REAL
3.3800 g., 0.9030 Silver .0981 oz. ASW

Date	Mintage	F	VF	XF	Unc	BU
1826Zs AZ	—	5.00	12.50	35.00	120	—
1826Zs AO	—	5.00	12.50	35.00	120	—
1827Zs AO	—	5.00	12.50	35.00	120	—
1828/7Zs AO	—	5.00	12.50	35.00	120	—
1828Zs AO	—	5.00	12.50	35.00	120	—
1828Zs AO Inverted V for A	—	5.00	12.50	35.00	120	—
1829Zs AO	—	5.00	12.50	35.00	120	—
1830Zs ZsOV	—	5.00	12.50	35.00	120	—
1830Zs ZOV	—	5.00	12.50	35.00	120	—
1831Zs OV	—	5.00	12.50	35.00	120	—
1831Zs OM	—	5.00	12.50	30.00	120	—
1832Zs OM	—	5.00	12.50	30.00	120	—
1833/2Zs OM	—	5.00	12.50	30.00	120	—
1833/2Zs OM/V	—	5.00	12.50	30.00	120	—
1833Zs OM	—	5.00	12.50	30.00	120	—
1834/3Zs OM	—	5.00	12.50	30.00	120	—
1834Zs OM	—	5.00	12.50	30.00	120	—
1835/4Zs OM	—	20.00	35.00	60.00	150	—
1835Zs OM	—	4.00	8.00	20.00	65.00	—
1836/5Zs OM	—	4.00	8.00	20.00	85.00	—
1836Zs OM	—	4.00	8.00	20.00	85.00	—

Date	Mintage	F	VF	XF	Unc	BU
1837Zs OM	—	4.00	8.00	20.00	85.00	—
1838Zs OM	—	4.00	8.00	20.00	85.00	—
1839Zs OM	—	4.00	8.00	20.00	85.00	—
1840Zs OM	—	4.00	8.00	20.00	85.00	—
1841Zs OM	—	20.00	40.00	60.00	150	—
1842/1Zs OM	—	4.00	8.00	20.00	85.00	—
1842Zs OM	—	4.00	8.00	20.00	85.00	—
1843Zs OM	—	4.00	8.00	20.00	85.00	—
1844Zs OM	—	4.00	8.00	20.00	85.00	—
1845/4Zs OM	—	5.00	12.50	30.00	100	—
1845Zs OM	—	4.00	8.00	20.00	85.00	—
1846Zs OM	—	4.00	8.00	20.00	85.00	—

Note: Old font and obverse

Date	Mintage	F	VF	XF	Unc	BU
1846Zs OM	—	4.00	8.00	20.00	85.00	—

Note: New font and obverse

Date	Mintage	F	VF	XF	Unc	BU
1847Zs OM	—	4.00	8.00	20.00	85.00	—
1848Zs OM	—	4.00	8.00	20.00	85.00	—
1849Zs OM	—	10.00	25.00	50.00	125	—
1850Zs OM	—	4.00	6.00	15.00	85.00	—
1851Zs OM	—	4.00	6.00	15.00	85.00	—
1852Zs OM	—	4.00	6.00	15.00	85.00	—
1853Zs OM	—	4.00	6.00	15.00	85.00	—
1854/2Zs OM	—	4.00	6.00	15.00	85.00	—
1854/3Zs OM	—	4.00	6.00	15.00	85.00	—
1854Zs OM	—	4.00	6.00	15.00	85.00	—
1855/4Zs OM	—	4.00	6.00	15.00	85.00	—
1855Zs OM	—	4.00	6.00	15.00	85.00	—
1855Zs MO	—	4.00	6.00	15.00	85.00	—
1856Zs MO	—	4.00	6.00	15.00	85.00	—
1856Zs MO/OM	—	4.00	6.00	15.00	85.00	—
1857Zs MO	—	4.00	6.00	15.00	85.00	—
1858Zs MO	—	4.00	6.00	15.00	85.00	—
1859Zs MO	—	4.00	6.00	15.00	75.00	—
1860 MO	—	250	—	—	—	—
1860Zs VL	—	4.00	6.00	15.00	75.00	—
1860Zs VL Inverted A for V	—	4.00	6.00	15.00	75.00	—
1861Zs VL	—	4.00	6.00	15.00	75.00	—
1861Zs VL Inverted A for V	—	4.00	6.00	15.00	75.00	—
1862Zs VL	—	5.00	12.50	30.00	100	—
1868Zs JS	—	25.00	45.00	90.00	175	—
1869Zs YH	—	4.00	8.00	20.00	75.00	—

KM# 374 2 REALES
6.7600 g., 0.9030 Silver .1962 oz. ASW **Obv:** Facing eagle
Edge: Reeded

Date	Mintage	F	VF	XF	Unc	BU
1872A AM	15,000	50.00	115	225	550	—

KM# 374.1 2 REALES
6.7600 g., 0.9030 Silver .1962 oz. ASW **Obv:** Facing eagle
Edge: Reeded

Date	Mintage	F	VF	XF	Unc	BU
1863 Ce ML	—	125	200	325	675	—

KM# 374.2 2 REALES
6.7600 g., 0.9030 Silver .1962 oz. ASW **Obv:** Facing eagle
Edge: Reeded

Date	Mintage	F	VF	XF	Unc	BU
1832 Ca MR	—	30.00	60.00	100	200	—
1833 Ca MR	—	30.00	60.00	125	500	—
1834 Ca MR	—	35.00	75.00	125	500	—
1834 Ca AM	—	35.00	75.00	125	500	—
1835 Ca AM	—	35.00	75.00	125	500	—
1836 Ca AM	—	20.00	40.00	80.00	200	—
1844 Ca AM Rare	—	—	—	—	—	—
1844 Ca RG Unique	—	—	—	—	—	—
1845 Ca RG	—	20.00	40.00	80.00	200	—
1855 Ca RG	—	20.00	40.00	80.00	200	—

KM# 374.3 2 REALES
6.7600 g., 0.9030 Silver .1962 oz. ASW **Obv:** Facing eagle
Edge: Reeded

Date	Mintage	F	VF	XF	Unc	BU
1846/1146C CE	—	25.00	50.00	100	225	—
1847C CE	—	12.50	20.00	40.00	200	—
1848C CE	—	12.50	20.00	40.00	200	—
1850C CE	—	25.00	50.00	75.00	200	—
1851C CE	—	12.50	20.00	40.00	200	—
1852/1C CE	—	12.50	20.00	40.00	200	—
1853/2C CE	—	12.50	20.00	40.00	200	—
1854C CE	—	15.00	30.00	50.00	200	—
1856C CE	—	20.00	35.00	70.00	200	—
1857C CE	—	12.50	20.00	40.00	200	—
1860C PV	—	12.50	20.00	40.00	200	—
1861C PV	—	12.50	20.00	40.00	200	—
1869C CE	—	12.50	20.00	40.00	200	—

KM# 374.4 2 REALES
6.7600 g., 0.9030 Silver .1962 oz. ASW **Obv:** Facing eagle
Edge: Reeded

Date	Mintage	F	VF	XF	Unc	BU
1826Do RL	—	20.00	40.00	60.00	200	—
1832Do RM	—	20.00	40.00	60.00	200	—

Note: Style of pre-1832

Date	Mintage	F	VF	XF	Unc	BU
1832Do RM	—	20.00	40.00	60.00	200	—

Note: Style of post-1832

Date	Mintage	F	VF	XF	Unc	BU
1834/2Do RM	—	20.00	40.00	60.00	200	—
1834/3Do RM	—	20.00	40.00	60.00	200	—
1835/4Do RM/RL	—	200	300	500	—	—
1841/31Do RM	—	50.00	75.00	125	250	—
1841Do RM	—	50.00	75.00	125	250	—
1842/32Do RM	—	12.50	20.00	40.00	200	—
1843Do RM/RL	—	12.50	20.00	40.00	200	—
1844Do RM	—	35.00	50.00	80.00	200	—
1845/34Do RM/RL	—	12.50	20.00	40.00	200	—
1846/36Do RM	—	100	150	200	350	—
1848/36Do RM	—	12.50	20.00	40.00	200	—
1848/37Do RM	—	12.50	20.00	40.00	200	—
1848/7Do RM	—	12.50	20.00	40.00	200	—
1848Do RM	—	12.50	20.00	40.00	200	—
1849Do CM/RM	—	12.50	20.00	40.00	200	—
1849Do CM	—	12.50	20.00	40.00	200	—
1851Do JMR/RL	—	12.50	20.00	40.00	200	—
1852Do JMR	—	12.50	20.00	40.00	200	—
1854Do CP/CR	—	30.00	50.00	80.00	200	—
1855Do CP	—	250	350	500	—	—
1856Do CP	—	100	150	250	500	—
1858Do CP	—	12.50	20.00	40.00	200	—
1859/8Do CP	—	12.50	20.00	40.00	200	—
1861Do CP	—	12.50	20.00	40.00	200	—

KM# 374.5 2 REALES
6.7600 g., 0.9030 Silver .1962 oz. ASW **Obv:** Facing eagle
Edge: Reeded

Date	Mintage	F	VF	XF	Unc	BU
1828EoMo LF	—	325	525	900	2,500	—

KM# 374.6 2 REALES
6.7600 g., 0.9030 Silver .1962 oz. ASW **Obv:** Facing eagle
Edge: Reeded

Date	Mintage	F	VF	XF	Unc	BU
1825Ga FS	—	20.00	40.00	80.00	200	—
1826Ga FS	—	20.00	40.00	80.00	200	—
1828/7Ga FS	—	100	150	225	400	—
1829Ga FS Rare	—	—	—	—	—	—
1832/0Ga FS/LP	—	100	150	225	350	—
1832Ga FS	—	12.50	20.00	40.00	200	—
1833/2Ga FS/LP	—	12.50	20.00	40.00	200	—
1834/27Ga FS Rare	—	—	—	—	—	—
1834Ga FS	—	12.50	20.00	40.00	200	—
1835Ga FS	—	2,100	—	—	—	—
1837Ga JG	—	12.50	20.00	40.00	200	—
1838Ga JG	—	12.50	20.00	40.00	200	—
1840/30Ga MC	—	12.50	20.00	40.00	200	—
1841Ga MC	—	30.00	50.00	200	500	—
1842/32Ga JG/MC	—	35.00	50.00	100	200	—
1842Ga JG	—	20.00	40.00	80.00	200	—
1843Ga JG	—	12.50	20.00	40.00	200	—
1843Ga MC/JG	—	12.50	20.00	40.00	200	—
1844Ga MC	—	12.50	20.00	40.00	200	—
1845/3Ga MC/JG	—	12.50	20.00	40.00	200	—
1845/4Ga MC/JG	—	12.50	20.00	40.00	200	—
1845Ga JG	—	12.50	20.00	40.00	200	—
1846Ga JG	—	12.50	20.00	40.00	200	—
1847/6Ga JG	—	25.00	40.00	80.00	200	—
1848/7Ga JG	—	12.50	20.00	40.00	200	—
1849Ga JG	—	12.50	20.00	40.00	200	—
1850/40Ga JG	—	12.50	20.00	40.00	200	—
1851Ga JG	—	250	350	500	—	—
1852Ga JG	—	12.50	20.00	40.00	200	—
1853/1Ga JG	—	12.50	20.00	40.00	200	—
1854/3Ga JG	—	250	350	500	—	—
1855Ga JG	—	35.00	50.00	80.00	200	—
1856Ga JG	—	12.50	20.00	40.00	200	—
1857Ga JG	—	250	350	500	—	—

Date	Mintage	F	VF	XF	Unc	BU
1859/8Ga JG	—	12.50	20.00	40.00	200	—
1859Ga JG	—	12.50	20.00	40.00	200	—
1862/1Ga JG	—	12.50	20.00	40.00	200	—

KM# 374.7 2 REALES
6.7600 g., 0.9030 Silver .1962 oz. ASW **Obv:** Facing eagle
Edge: Reeded

Date	Mintage	F	VF	XF	Unc	BU
1844GC MP	—	40.00	60.00	125	275	—
1845GC MP	—	40.00	60.00	125	275	—
1846GC MP	—	50.00	100	150	300	—
1847GC MP	—	35.00	50.00	100	250	—
1848GC MP	—	50.00	100	150	300	—
1849GC MP	—	50.00	100	150	300	—
1850GC MP	—	125	250	—	—	—
1851/0GC MP	—	50.00	100	150	300	—
1851GC MP	—	50.00	100	150	300	—

KM# 374.8 2 REALES
6.7600 g., 0.9030 Silver .1962 oz. ASW **Obv:** Facing eagle
Edge: Reeded **Note:** Varieties exist.

Date	Mintage	F	VF	XF	Unc	BU
1825Go JJ	—	7.50	15.00	30.00	150	—
1826/5Go JJ	—	7.50	15.00	30.00	150	—
1826Go JJ	—	7.50	10.00	25.00	150	—
1826Go MJ	—	7.50	10.00	25.00	150	—
1827/6Go MJ	—	7.50	10.00	25.00	150	—
1827Go MJ	—	7.50	10.00	25.00	150	—
1828/7Go MR	—	7.50	15.00	30.00	150	—
1828Go MJ	—	7.50	10.00	20.00	150	—
1828Go JM	—	7.50	10.00	20.00	150	—
1829Go MJ	—	7.50	10.00	20.00	150	—
1831Go MJ	—	7.50	10.00	20.00	150	—
1832Go MJ	—	7.50	10.00	20.00	150	—
1833Go MJ	—	7.50	10.00	20.00	150	—
1834Go PJ	—	7.50	10.00	20.00	150	—
1835/4Go PJ	—	7.50	15.00	30.00	150	—
1835Go PJ	—	7.50	10.00	20.00	150	—
1836Go PJ	—	7.50	10.00	20.00	150	—
1837/6Go PJ	—	7.50	10.00	20.00	150	—
1837Go PJ	—	7.50	10.00	20.00	150	—
1838/7Go PJ	—	7.50	10.00	20.00	150	—
1838Go PJ	—	7.50	10.00	20.00	150	—
1839/8Go PJ	—	7.50	15.00	30.00	150	—
1839Go PJ	—	7.50	10.00	20.00	150	—
1840Go PJ	—	7.50	10.00	20.00	150	—
1841Go PJ	—	7.50	10.00	20.00	150	—
1842Go PJ	—	7.50	10.00	20.00	150	—
1842Go PM/PJ	—	7.50	10.00	20.00	150	—
1842Go PM	—	7.50	10.00	20.00	150	—
1843/2Go PM	—	7.50	10.00	20.00	150	—

Note: Concave wings, thin rays, small letters

1843Go PM	—	7.50	10.00	20.00	150	—

Note: Convex wings, thick rays, large letters

1844Go PM	—	7.50	10.00	20.00	150	—
1845/4Go PM	—	7.50	10.00	20.00	150	—
1845Go PM	—	7.50	10.00	20.00	150	—
1846/5Go PM	—	10.00	15.00	35.00	150	—
1846Go PM	—	7.50	10.00	20.00	150	—
1847Go PM	—	7.50	10.00	20.00	150	—
1848/7Go PM	—	7.50	15.00	30.00	150	—
1848Go PM	—	7.50	15.00	30.00	150	—
1848Go PF	—	100	150	250	500	—
1849/8Go PF/PM	—	7.50	10.00	20.00	150	—
1849Go PF	—	7.50	10.00	20.00	150	—
1850/40Go PF	—	7.50	10.00	20.00	150	—
1850Go PF	—	7.50	10.00	20.00	150	—
1851Go PF	—	7.50	10.00	20.00	150	—
1852/1Go PF	—	7.50	10.00	20.00	150	—
1852Go PF	—	7.50	10.00	20.00	150	—
1853Go PF	—	7.50	10.00	20.00	150	—
1854/3Go PF	—	7.50	10.00	20.00	150	—
1854Go PF	—	7.50	10.00	20.00	150	—

Note: Old font and obverse

1854Go PF	—	7.50	10.00	20.00	150	—

Note: New font and obverse

1855Go PF	—	7.50	10.00	20.00	150	—
1855Go PF	—	7.50	10.00	20.00	150	—

Note: Star in G of mint mark

1856/5Go PF	—	10.00	15.00	35.00	150	—
1856Go PF	—	10.00	15.00	25.00	150	—

Date	Mintage	F	VF	XF	Unc	BU
1857/6Go PF	—	7.50	10.00	20.00	150	—
1857Go PF	—	7.50	10.00	20.00	150	—
1858/7Go PF	—	7.50	10.00	20.00	150	—
1858Go PF	—	7.50	10.00	20.00	150	—
1859/7Go PF	—	7.50	10.00	20.00	150	—
1859Go PF	—	7.50	10.00	20.00	150	—
1860/7Go PF	—	7.50	10.00	20.00	150	—
1860/50Go PF	—	7.50	10.00	20.00	150	—
1860/59Go PF	—	7.50	10.00	20.00	150	—
1860Go PF	—	7.50	10.00	20.00	150	—
1861/51Go PF	—	7.50	10.00	20.00	150	—
1861/57Go PF	—	7.50	10.00	20.00	150	—
1861/0Go PF	—	7.50	10.00	20.00	150	—
1861Go PF	—	7.50	10.00	20.00	150	—
1862/1Go YE	—	7.50	10.00	20.00	125	—
1862Go YE	—	7.50	10.00	20.00	125	—
1862/57Go YE	—	7.50	10.00	20.00	125	—
1862Go YE/PF	—	7.50	10.00	20.00	125	—
1862Go YF	—	7.50	10.00	20.00	125	—
1863/52Go YF	—	7.50	10.00	20.00	125	—
1863Go YF	—	7.50	10.00	20.00	125	—
1867/57Go YF	—	7.50	10.00	20.00	125	—
1868/57Go YF	—	10.00	15.00	25.00	125	—

KM# 374.9 2 REALES
6.7600 g., 0.9030 Silver .1962 oz. ASW **Obv:** Facing eagle
Edge: Reeded

Date	Mintage	F	VF	XF	Unc	BU
1861Ho FM	—	200	300	400	650	—
1862/52Ho FM/C. CE	—	250	350	500	—	—
1867/1Ho PR/FM	—	75.00	150	250	500	—

KM# 374.10 2 REALES
6.7600 g., 0.9030 Silver .1962 oz. ASW **Obv:** Facing eagle
Edge: Reeded **Note:** Varieties exist.

Date	Mintage	F	VF	XF	Unc	BU
1825Mo JM	—	10.00	15.00	30.00	175	—
1826Mo JM	—	10.00	15.00	30.00	175	—
1827Mo JM	—	10.00	15.00	30.00	175	—
1828Mo JM	—	10.00	15.00	30.00	175	—
1829/8Mo JM	—	10.00	15.00	30.00	175	—
1829Mo JM	—	10.00	15.00	30.00	175	—
1830Mo JM	—	40.00	60.00	125	250	—
1831Mo JM	—	10.00	15.00	30.00	175	—
1832Mo JM	—	100	200	400	—	—
1833/2Mo MJ/JM	—	10.00	15.00	30.00	175	—
1834Mo ML	—	50.00	100	200	400	—
1836Mo MF	—	10.00	15.00	30.00	175	—
1837Mo ML	—	10.00	15.00	30.00	175	—
1840/7Mo ML	—	150	225	350	—	—
1840Mo ML	—	150	225	350	—	—
1841Mo ML	—	15.00	40.00	100	250	—
1842 ML Rare	—	—	—	—	—	—
1847Mo RC Narrow date	—	10.00	15.00	30.00	175	—
1847Mo RC Wide date	—	10.00	15.00	30.00	175	—
1848Mo GC	—	10.00	15.00	30.00	175	—
1849Mo GC	—	10.00	15.00	30.00	175	—
1850Mo GC	—	10.00	15.00	30.00	175	—
1851Mo GC	—	40.00	60.00	125	250	—
1852Mo GC	—	10.00	15.00	30.00	175	—
1853Mo GC	—	10.00	15.00	30.00	175	—
1854/44Mo GC	—	10.00	15.00	30.00	175	—
1855Mo GC	—	10.00	15.00	30.00	175	—
1855Mo GF/GC	—	10.00	15.00	30.00	175	—
1855Mo GF	—	10.00	15.00	30.00	175	—
1856/5Mo GF/GC	—	10.00	15.00	30.00	175	—
1857Mo GF	—	10.00	15.00	30.00	175	—
1858Mo FH	—	7.50	12.50	25.00	150	—
1858Mo FH/GF	—	7.50	12.50	25.00	150	—

Date	Mintage	F	VF	XF	Unc	BU
1859Mo FH	—	7.50	12.50	25.00	150	—
1860Mo FH	—	7.50	12.50	25.00	150	—
1860Mo TH	—	7.50	12.50	25.00	150	—
1861Mo CH	—	7.50	12.50	25.00	150	—
1862Mo CH	—	7.50	12.50	25.00	150	—
1863Mo CH	—	7.50	12.50	25.00	150	—
1863Mo TH	—	7.50	12.50	25.00	150	—
1867Mo CH	—	7.50	12.50	25.00	150	—
1868Mo CH	—	10.00	15.00	30.00	150	—
1868Mo PH	—	7.50	12.50	25.00	150	—

KM# 374.11 2 REALES
6.7600 g., 0.9030 Silver .1962 oz. ASW **Obv:** Facing eagle
Edge: Reeded

Date	Mintage	F	VF	XF	Unc	BU
1829 Pi JS	—	10.00	15.00	30.00	200	—
1830/20 Pi JS	—	20.00	30.00	60.00	200	—
1837 Pi JS	—	10.00	15.00	30.00	200	—
1841 Pi JS	—	10.00	15.00	30.00	200	—
1842/1 Pi JS	—	10.00	15.00	30.00	200	—
1842 Pi JS	—	10.00	15.00	30.00	200	—
1842 Pi PS	—	20.00	35.00	60.00	200	—
1843 Pi PS	—	12.50	20.00	40.00	200	—
1843 Pi AM	—	10.00	15.00	30.00	200	—
1844 Pi AM	—	10.00	15.00	30.00	200	—
1845 Pi AM	—	10.00	15.00	30.00	200	—
1846 Pi AM	—	10.00	15.00	30.00	200	—
1849 Pi MC	—	10.00	15.00	30.00	200	—
1850 Pi MC	—	10.00	15.00	30.00	200	—
1856 Pi MC	—	40.00	60.00	125	250	—
1857 Pi MC	—	—	—	—	—	—
1858 Pi MC	—	12.50	20.00	40.00	200	—
1859 Pi MC	—	50.00	70.00	100	200	—
1861 Pi PS	—	10.00	15.00	30.00	200	—
1862 Pi RO	—	12.50	20.00	40.00	200	—
1863 Pi RO	—	100	250	350	500	—
1868 Pi PS	—	10.00	15.00	30.00	200	—
1869/8 Pi PS	—	10.00	15.00	30.00	200	—
1869 Pi PS	—	10.00	15.00	30.00	200	—

KM# 374.12 2 REALES
6.7600 g., 0.9030 Silver .1962 oz. ASW **Obv:** Facing eagle
Edge: Reeded **Note:** Varieties exist.

Date	Mintage	F	VF	XF	Unc	BU
1825Zs AZ	—	10.00	15.00	30.00	150	—
1826Zs AV	—	7.50	10.00	25.00	150	—
Note: A is inverted V						
1826Zs AZ	—	7.50	10.00	25.00	150	—
Note: A is inverted V						
1826Zs AO	—	10.00	15.00	30.00	150	—
1827Zs AO	—	6.00	8.00	12.00	150	—
Note: A is inverted V						
1827Zs AO	—	6.00	8.00	12.00	150	—
1828/7Zs AO	—	15.00	30.00	60.00	175	—
1828Zs AO	—	7.50	10.00	25.00	100	—
1828Zs AO	—	7.50	10.00	25.00	150	—
Note: A is inverted V						
1829Zs AO	—	7.50	10.00	25.00	150	—
1829Zs OV	—	7.50	10.00	25.00	150	—
1830Zs OV	—	7.50	10.00	25.00	150	—
1831Zs OV	—	7.50	10.00	25.00	150	—
1831Zs OM/OV	—	7.50	10.00	25.00	150	—
1831Zs OM	—	7.50	10.00	25.00	150	—
1832/1Zs OM	—	15.00	30.00	60.00	150	—
1832Zs OM	—	7.50	10.00	25.00	150	—
1833/27Zs OM	—	7.50	10.00	25.00	150	—
1833/2Zs OM	—	7.50	10.00	25.00	150	—
1833Zs OM	—	7.50	10.00	25.00	150	—
1834Zs OM	—	40.00	60.00	125	200	—
1835Zs OM	—	7.50	10.00	25.00	150	—
1836Zs OM	—	7.50	10.00	25.00	150	—
1837Zs OM	—	7.50	10.00	25.00	150	—
1838Zs OM	—	15.00	30.00	60.00	150	—
1839Zs OM	—	7.50	10.00	20.00	150	—
1840Zs OM	—	7.50	10.00	20.00	150	—
1841/0Zs OM	—	7.50	10.00	20.00	150	—
1841Zs OM	—	7.50	10.00	20.00	150	—
1842Zs OM Narrow date	—	7.50	10.00	20.00	150	—
1842Zs OM Wide date	—	7.50	10.00	20.00	150	—
1843Zs OM	—	7.50	10.00	20.00	150	—

Date	Mintage	F	VF	XF	Unc	BU
1844Zs OM	—	7.50	10.00	20.00	150	—
1845Zs OM	—	7.50	10.00	20.00	150	—
Note: Small letters with leaves						
1845Zs OM	—	7.50	10.00	20.00	150	—
Note: Large letters with leaves						
1846Zs OM	—	7.50	10.00	20.00	150	—
1847Zs OM	—	7.50	10.00	20.00	150	—
1848Zs OM	—	7.50	10.00	20.00	150	—
1849Zs OM	—	7.50	10.00	20.00	150	—
1850Zs OM	—	7.50	10.00	20.00	150	—
1851Zs OM	—	7.50	10.00	20.00	150	—
1852Zs OM	—	7.50	10.00	20.00	150	—
1853Zs OM	—	7.50	10.00	20.00	150	—
1854/3Zs OM	—	7.50	10.00	20.00	150	—
1854Zs OM	—	7.50	10.00	20.00	150	—
1855/4Zs OM	—	7.50	10.00	20.00	150	—
1855Zs OM	—	7.50	10.00	20.00	150	—
1855Zs MO	—	7.50	10.00	20.00	150	—
1856/5Zs MO	—	7.50	10.00	20.00	150	—
1856Zs MO	—	7.50	10.00	20.00	150	—
1857Zs MO	—	7.50	10.00	20.00	150	—
1858Zs MO	—	7.50	10.00	20.00	150	—
1859Zs MO	—	7.50	10.00	20.00	150	—
1860/59Zs MO	—	7.50	10.00	20.00	150	—
1860Zs MO	—	7.50	10.00	20.00	100	—
1860Zs VL	—	7.50	10.00	20.00	150	—
1861Zs VL	—	7.50	10.00	20.00	150	—
1862Zs VL	—	7.50	10.00	20.00	100	—
1863Zs MO	—	12.50	20.00	40.00	150	—
1863Zs VL	—	7.50	10.00	20.00	150	—
1864Zs MO	—	7.50	10.00	20.00	150	—
1864Zs VL	—	7.50	10.00	20.00	150	—
1865Zs MO	—	7.50	10.00	20.00	150	—
1867Zs JS	—	7.50	10.00	20.00	150	—
1868Zs JS	—	10.00	15.00	35.00	150	—
1868Zs YH	—	7.50	10.00	20.00	150	—
1869Zs YH	—	7.50	10.00	20.00	150	—
1870Zs YH	—	7.50	10.00	20.00	150	—

KM# 375 4 REALES
13.5400 g., 0.9030 Silver .3925 oz. ASW **Obv:** Facing eagle

Date	Mintage	F	VF	XF	Unc	BU
1863 Ce ML Large C	—	200	500	850	4,000	—
1863 Ce ML Small C	—	225	650	1,500	6,000	—

KM# 375.1 4 REALES
13.5400 g., 0.9030 Silver .3925 oz. ASW **Obv:** Facing eagle

Date	Mintage	F	VF	XF	Unc	BU
1846C CE	—	400	550	900	—	—
1850C CE	—	75.00	125	250	700	—
1852C CE	—	200	300	500	1,250	—
1857C CE Rare	—	—	—	—	—	—
1858C CE	—	100	200	350	1,000	—
1860C PV	—	25.00	50.00	125	650	—

KM# 375.2 4 REALES
13.5400 g., 0.9030 Silver .3925 oz. ASW **Obv:** Facing eagle

Date	Mintage	F	VF	XF	Unc	BU
1843Ga MC	—	20.00	40.00	80.00	600	—
1844/3Ga MC	—	30.00	60.00	125	600	—
1844Ga MC	—	20.00	40.00	80.00	600	—
1845Ga MC	—	20.00	40.00	80.00	600	—
1845Ga JG	—	20.00	40.00	80.00	600	—
1846Ga JG	—	20.00	40.00	80.00	600	—
1847Ga JG	—	40.00	80.00	150	600	—
1848/7Ga JG	—	40.00	80.00	150	600	—

Date	Mintage	F	VF	XF	Unc	BU
1849Ga JG	—	40.00	80.00	150	600	—
1850Ga JG	—	65.00	125	250	650	—
1852Ga JG Rare	—	—	—	—	—	—
1854Ga JG Rare	—	—	—	—	—	—
1855Ga JG	—	100	200	400	1,250	—
1856Ga JG Rare	—	—	—	—	—	—
1857/6Ga JG	—	65.00	125	250	700	—
1858Ga JG	—	125	250	450	1,250	—
1859/8Ga JG	—	125	250	450	1,250	—
1860Ga JG	—	850	1,450	—	—	—
1863/2Ga JG	—	150	300	1,250	7,500	—
1863Ga JG	—	150	300	1,250	7,500	—

KM# 375.3   4 REALES
13.5400 g., 0.9030 Silver .3925 oz. ASW **Obv:** Facing eagle

Date	Mintage	F	VF	XF	Unc	BU
1844GC MP	—	3,000	5,000	6,000	—	—
1845GC MP	—	3,000	4,000	5,000	9,000	—
1846GC MP	—	1,700	2,800	—	—	—
1847GC MP	—	1,500	2,500	—	—	—
1849GC MP	—	2,000	3,000	—	—	—
1850GC MP	—	500	1,000	—	—	—

KM# 375.4   4 REALES
13.5400 g., 0.9030 Silver .3925 oz. ASW **Obv:** Facing eagle
Note: Varieties exist. Some 1862 dates appear to be 1869 because of weak dies.

Date	Mintage	F	VF	XF	Unc	BU
1835Go PJ	—	12.50	25.00	60.00	600	—
1836/5Go PJ	—	15.00	30.00	75.00	600	—
1836Go PJ	—	15.00	30.00	75.00	600	—
1837Go PJ	—	12.50	25.00	60.00	600	—
1838/7Go PJ	—	15.00	30.00	75.00	600	—
1838Go PJ	—	12.50	30.00	75.00	600	—
1839Go PJ	—	12.50	25.00	60.00	600	—
1840/30Go PJ	—	20.00	50.00	100	600	—
1840 PJ	—	20.00	50.00	100	600	—
1841/30 PJ	—	200	325	600	1,500	—
1841/31Go PJ	—	150	250	450	1,250	—
1842Go PJ Rare	—	—	—	—	—	—
1842Go PM	—	15.00	30.00	75.00	400	—
1843/2Go PM	—	12.50	25.00	60.00	400	—

Note: Eagle with convex wings, thick rays

1843Go PM	—	12.50	25.00	60.00	400	—

Note: Eagle with concave wings, thin rays

1844/3Go PM	—	15.00	30.00	75.00	600	—
1844Go PM	—	20.00	50.00	100	600	—
1845/4Go PM	—	20.00	50.00	100	600	—
1845Go PM	—	20.00	50.00	100	600	—
1846/5Go PM	—	15.00	30.00	75.00	600	—
1846Go PM	—	15.00	30.00	75.00	600	—
1847/6Go PM	—	15.00	30.00	75.00	600	—
1847Go PM	—	15.00	30.00	75.00	600	—
1848/7Go PM	—	20.00	50.00	100	600	—
1848Go PM	—	20.00	50.00	100	600	—
1849Go PF	—	20.00	50.00	100	600	—
1850Go PF	—	12.50	25.00	60.00	600	—
1851Go PF	—	12.50	25.00	60.00	600	—
1852Go PF	—	15.00	30.00	75.00	600	—
1852Go PF 5/4	—	20.00	50.00	100	600	—
1853Go PF	—	15.00	30.00	75.00	600	—
1854Go PF Large eagle	—	15.00	30.00	75.00	600	—
1854Go PF Small eagle	—	15.00	30.00	75.00	600	—
1855/4Go PF	—	15.00	30.00	75.00	600	—
1855Go PF	—	12.50	25.00	60.00	600	—
1856Go PF	—	12.50	25.00	60.00	600	—

Date	Mintage	F	VF	XF	Unc	BU
1857Go PF	—	20.00	50.00	100	600	—
1858Go PF	—	20.00	50.00	100	600	—
1859Go PF	—	20.00	50.00	100	600	—
1860/59Go PF	—	15.00	30.00	75.00	600	—
1860Go PF	—	15.00	30.00	75.00	600	—
1861/51Go PF	—	15.00	30.00	75.00	600	—
1861Go PF	—	20.00	50.00	100	600	—
1862/1Go YE	—	15.00	30.00	75.00	600	—
1862/1Go YF	—	15.00	30.00	75.00	600	—
1862Go YE/PF	—	15.00	30.00	75.00	600	—
1862Go YE	—	15.00	30.00	75.00	600	—
1862Go YF	—	15.00	30.00	75.00	600	—
1863/53Go YF	—	15.00	30.00	75.00	600	—
1863Go YF/PF	—	15.00	30.00	75.00	600	—
1863Go YF	—	15.00	30.00	75.00	600	—
1867/57Go YF/PF	—	15.00	30.00	75.00	600	—
1868/58Go YF/PF	—	15.00	30.00	75.00	600	—
1870Go FR	—	15.00	30.00	75.00	600	—

KM# 375.5   4 REALES
13.5400 g., 0.9030 Silver .3925 oz. ASW **Obv:** Facing eagle

Date	Mintage	F	VF	XF	Unc	BU
1861Ho FM	—	200	350	500	2,500	—
1867/1Ho PR/FM	—	150	275	400	2,500	—

KM# 375.6   4 REALES
13.5400 g., 0.9030 Silver .3925 oz. ASW **Obv:** Facing eagle

Date	Mintage	F	VF	XF	Unc	BU
1827/6Mo JM	—	200	400	800	—	—
1850Mo GC Rare	—	—	—	—	—	—
1852Mo GC Rare	—	—	—	—	—	—
1854Mo GC Rare	—	—	—	—	—	—
1855Mo GF/GC	—	50.00	100	200	1,250	—
1855Mo GF	—	100	200	350	1,500	—
1856Mo GF/GC	—	50.00	125	400	1,200	—
1856Mo GF Rare	—	—	—	—	—	—
1859Mo FH	—	20.00	50.00	150	1,000	—
1861Mo CH	—	15.00	35.00	125	1,000	—
1862Mo CH	—	20.00	50.00	150	1,000	—
1863/2Mo CH	—	20.00	50.00	150	1,000	—
1863Mo CH	—	75.00	150	300	1,500	—
1867Mo CH	—	20.00	50.00	150	1,000	—
1868Mo CH/PH	—	30.00	75.00	150	1,000	—
1868Mo CH	—	20.00	50.00	150	1,000	—
1868Mo PH	—	30.00	75.00	200	1,250	—

KM# 375.7   4 REALES
13.5400 g., 0.9030 Silver .3925 oz. ASW **Obv:** Facing eagle

Date	Mintage	F	VF	XF	Unc	BU
1861O FR	—	225	450	750	2,750	—

Note: Ornamental edge

1861O FR	—	300	550	850	2,850	—

Note: Herringbone edge

1861O FR	—	200	400	700	—	—

Note: Obliquely reeded edge

KM# 375.8   4 REALES
13.5400 g., 0.9030 Silver .3925 oz. ASW **Obv:** Facing eagle

Date	Mintage	F	VF	XF	Unc	BU
1837 Pi JS	—	200	350	—	—	—
1838 Pi JS	—	150	250	400	650	—
1842 Pi PS	—	50.00	100	200	650	—
1843/2 Pi PS	—	50.00	100	200	650	—
1843/2 Pi PS	—	50.00	100	200	650	—

Note: 3 cut from 8 punch

1843 Pi AM	—	30.00	75.00	150	650	—
1843 Pi PS	—	50.00	100	200	650	—
1844 Pi AM	—	30.00	75.00	150	650	—
1845/4 Pi AM	—	20.00	50.00	100	650	—

Date	Mintage	F	VF	XF	Unc	BU
1845 Pi AM	—	20.00	50.00	100	650	—
1846 Pi AM	—	20.00	50.00	100	650	—
1847 Pi AM	—	75.00	150	250	700	—
1848 Pi AM Rare	—	—	—	—	—	—
1849 Pi MC/AM	—	20.00	50.00	100	650	—
1849 Pi MC	—	20.00	50.00	100	650	—
1849 Pi PS	—	20.00	50.00	100	650	—
1850 Pi MC	—	20.00	50.00	100	650	—
1851 Pi MC	—	20.00	50.00	100	650	—
1852 Pi MC	—	20.00	50.00	100	650	—
1853 Pi MC	—	20.00	50.00	100	650	—
1854 Pi MC	—	100	200	400	1,100	—
1855 Pi MC	—	175	300	750	2,000	—
1856 Pi MC	—	250	400	700	—	—
1857 Pi MC Rare	—	—	—	—	—	—
1857 Pi PS Rare	—	—	—	—	—	—
1858 Pi MC	—	100	200	400	1,000	—
1859 Pi MC	—	2,000	3,000	—	—	—
1860 Pi PS	—	300	450	700	—	—
1861 Pi PS	—	30.00	75.00	150	650	—
1861 Pi RO/PS	—	30.00	75.00	150	650	—
1861 Pi RO	—	50.00	100	200	650	—
1862 Pi RO	—	30.00	75.00	150	650	—
1863 Pi RO	—	30.00	75.00	150	650	—
1864 Pi RO	—	1,600	2,600	—	—	—
1868 Pi PS	—	30.00	75.00	150	650	—
1869/8 Pi PS	—	30.00	75.00	150	650	—
1869 Pi PS	—	30.00	75.00	150	650	—

KM# 375.9   4 REALES
13.5400 g., 0.9030 Silver .3925 oz. ASW **Obv:** Facing eagle

Date	Mintage	F	VF	XF	Unc	BU
1830Zs OM	—	20.00	50.00	100	600	—
1831Zs OM	—	15.00	30.00	75.00	600	—
1832/1Zs OM	—	20.00	50.00	100	600	—
1832Zs OM	—	20.00	50.00	100	600	—
1833/2Zs OM	—	20.00	50.00	100	600	—
1833/27Zs OM	—	15.00	30.00	75.00	600	—
1833Zs OM	—	15.00	30.00	75.00	600	—
1834/3Zs OM	—	20.00	50.00	100	600	—
1834Zs OM	—	15.00	30.00	75.00	600	—
1835Zs OM	—	15.00	30.00	75.00	600	—
1836Zs OM	—	15.00	30.00	75.00	600	—
1837/5Zs OM	—	20.00	50.00	100	600	—
1837/6Zs OM	—	20.00	50.00	100	600	—
1837Zs OM	—	20.00	50.00	100	600	—
1838/7Zs OM	—	15.00	30.00	75.00	600	—
1839Zs OM	—	250	375	500	—	—
1840Zs OM	—	500	1,300	—	—	—
1841Zs OM	—	15.00	30.00	75.00	600	—
1842Zs OM Small letters	—	15.00	40.00	85.00	600	—
1842Zs OM Large letters	—	15.00	30.00	75.00	600	—
1843Zs OM	—	15.00	30.00	75.00	600	—
1844Zs OM	—	20.00	50.00	100	600	—
1845Zs OM	—	20.00	50.00	100	600	—
1846/5Zs OM	—	25.00	60.00	125	600	—
1846Zs OM	—	20.00	50.00	100	600	—
1847Zs OM	—	15.00	30.00	75.00	600	—
1848/6Zs OM	—	50.00	75.00	125	600	—
1848Zs OM	—	20.00	50.00	100	600	—
1849Zs OM	—	20.00	50.00	100	600	—
1850Zs OM	—	20.00	50.00	100	600	—
1851Zs OM	—	15.00	30.00	75.00	600	—
1852Zs OM	—	15.00	30.00	75.00	600	—
1853Zs OM	—	20.00	50.00	100	600	—
1854/3Zs OM	—	30.00	75.00	150	600	—
1855/4Zs OM	—	20.00	50.00	100	600	—
1855Zs OM	—	15.00	30.00	75.00	600	—
1856Zs OM	—	15.00	30.00	75.00	600	—
1856Zs MO	—	20.00	50.00	100	600	—
1857/5Zs MO	—	20.00	50.00	100	600	—
1857Zs O/M	—	20.00	50.00	100	600	—
1857Zs MO	—	15.00	30.00	75.00	600	—
1858Zs MO	—	20.00	50.00	100	600	—
1859Zs MO	—	15.00	30.00	75.00	600	—
1860/59Zs MO	—	20.00	50.00	100	600	—
1860Zs MO	—	15.00	30.00	75.00	600	—
1860Zs VL	—	20.00	50.00	100	600	—
1861/0Zs VL	—	20.00	50.00	100	600	—
1861Zs VL	—	15.00	30.00	75.00	600	—

Date	Mintage	F	VF	XF	Unc	BU
1861Zs VL 6/5	—	20.00	50.00	100	600	—
1862/1Zs VL	—	20.00	50.00	100	600	—
1862Zs VL	—	20.00	50.00	100	600	—
1863Zs VL	—	20.00	50.00	100	600	—
1863Zs MO	—	20.00	50.00	100	600	—
1864Zs VL	—	15.00	30.00	75.00	600	—
1868Zs JS	—	20.00	50.00	100	600	—
1868Zs YH	—	15.00	30.00	75.00	600	—
1869Zs YH	—	15.00	30.00	75.00	600	—
1870Zs YH	—	15.00	30.00	75.00	600	—

KM# 377   8 REALES
27.0700 g., 0.9030 Silver .7859 oz. ASW **Obv:** Facing eagle
Note: Mint mark A, As. Varieties exist.

Date	Mintage	F	VF	XF	Unc	BU
1864 PG	—	750	1,250	2,000	—	—
1865/4 PG Rare	—	—	—	—	—	—
1865 PG	—	500	750	1,000	—	—
1866/5 PG Rare	—	—	—	—	—	—
1866 PG	—	1,250	2,250	—	—	—
1866 DL Rare	—	—	—	—	—	—
1867 DL	—	1,150	2,150	—	—	—
1868 DL	—	50.00	90.00	150	300	—
1869/8 DL	—	50.00	90.00	150	—	—
1869 DL	—	50.00	80.00	120	300	—
1870 DL	—	30.00	60.00	120	300	—
1871 DL	—	20.00	35.00	75.00	200	—
1872 AM/DL	—	25.00	50.00	100	300	—
1872 AM	—	25.00	50.00	100	250	—
1873 AM	509,000	15.00	25.00	50.00	150	—
1874/3 As DL	—	25.00	50.00	100	250	—
1874 DL	—	15.00	25.00	50.00	150	—
1875A DL 7/7	—	40.00	80.00	120	300	—
1875A DL	—	15.00	25.00	50.00	150	—
1875 As DL	—	30.00	60.00	110	250	—
1876 DL	—	15.00	25.00	50.00	150	—
1877 DL	515,000	15.00	25.00	50.00	150	—
1878 DL	513,000	15.00	25.00	50.00	150	—
1879 DL	—	20.00	35.00	75.00	175	—
1879 ML	—	30.00	60.00	125	350	—
1880 ML	—	12.00	15.00	30.00	140	—
1881 ML	966,000	12.00	15.00	30.00	140	—
1882 ML	480,000	12.00	15.00	30.00	140	—
1883 ML	464,000	12.00	15.00	30.00	140	—
1884 ML	—	12.00	15.00	30.00	140	—
1885 ML	280,000	12.00	15.00	30.00	140	—
1886 ML	857,000	12.00	15.00	25.00	110	—
1886/0As/Cn ML/JD	Inc. above	15.00	20.00	35.00	160	—
1887 ML	650,000	12.00	15.00	25.00	110	—
1888/7 ML	508,000	30.00	60.00	100	400	—
1888 ML	Inc. above	12.00	15.00	25.00	110	—
1889 ML	427,000	12.00	15.00	25.00	110	—
1890 ML	450,000	12.00	15.00	25.00	110	—
1891 ML	533,000	12.00	15.00	25.00	110	—

Date	Mintage	F	VF	XF	Unc	BU
1892/0 ML	—	20.00	30.00	60.00	160	—
1892 ML	465,000	12.00	15.00	25.00	110	—
1893 ML	734,000	10.00	12.00	22.00	85.00	—
1894 ML	725,000	10.00	12.00	22.00	85.00	—
1895 ML	477,000	10.00	12.00	22.00	85.00	—

KM# 377.1   8 REALES
27.0700 g., 0.9030 Silver .7859 oz. ASW **Obv:** Facing eagle

Date	Mintage	F	VF	XF	Unc	BU
1863 Ce ME	—	425	700	1,350	3,000	—
1863 Ce /Pl ML/ MC	—	425	750	1,500	3,250	—

KM# 377.2   8 REALES
27.0700 g., 0.9030 Silver .7859 oz. ASW **Obv:** Facing eagle
Note: Varieties exist.

Date	Mintage	F	VF	XF	Unc	BU
1831 Ca MR	—	1,000	1,750	2,250	3,250	—
1832 Ca MR	—	125	200	300	600	—
1833 Ca MR	—	250	550	1,000	—	—
1834 Ca MR	—	300	600	1,150	—	—
1834 Ca AM	—	350	500	700	—	—
1835 Ca AM	—	150	250	475	900	—
1836 Ca AM	—	100	200	300	600	—
1837 Ca AM	—	550	1,150	—	—	—
1838 Ca AM	—	100	200	300	600	—
1839 Ca RG	—	750	1,250	2,500	—	—
1840 Ca RG	—	300	500	800	1,500	—
Note: 1 dot after date						
1840 Ca RG	—	300	500	800	1,500	—
Note: 3 dots after date						
1841 Ca RG	—	50.00	100	150	300	—
1842 Ca RG	—	25.00	40.00	75.00	150	—

Date	Mintage	F	VF	XF	Unc	BU
1843 Ca RG	—	40.00	80.00	125	250	—
1844/1 Ca RG	—	35.00	70.00	100	200	—
1844 Ca RG	—	25.00	40.00	75.00	160	—
1845 Ca RG	—	25.00	40.00	75.00	160	—
1846 Ca RG	—	30.00	60.00	100	250	—
1847 Ca RG	—	40.00	80.00	125	250	—
1848 Ca RG	—	35.00	70.00	125	250	—
1849 Ca RG	—	30.00	60.00	100	200	—
1850/40 Ca RG	—	40.00	80.00	125	250	—
1850 Ca RG	—	30.00	60.00	100	200	—
1851/41 Ca RG	—	100	200	300	500	—
1851 Ca RG	—	150	250	400	750	—
1852/42 Ca RG	—	150	250	400	750	—
1852 Ca RG	—	150	250	400	750	—
1853/43 Ca RG	—	150	250	400	750	—
1853 Ca RG	—	150	250	350	700	—
1854/44 Ca RG	—	100	200	300	500	—
1854 Ca RG	—	50.00	100	150	300	—
1855/45 Ca RG	—	100	200	350	650	—
1855 Ca RG	—	50.00	100	150	300	—
1856/45 Ca RG	—	275	450	750	1,250	—
1856/5 Ca RG	—	400	700	1,500	3,500	—
1857 Ca JC/RG	—	40.00	80.00	125	250	—
1857 Ca JC	—	50.00	100	150	250	—
1858 Ca JC	—	35.00	70.00	125	250	—
1858 Ca BA	—	2,000	3,500	—	—	—
1859 Ca JC	—	40.00	80.00	125	250	—
1860 Ca JC	—	20.00	40.00	90.00	175	—
1861 Ca JC	—	15.00	25.00	55.00	125	—
1862 Ca JC	—	15.00	25.00	55.00	125	—
1863 Ca JC	—	20.00	35.00	75.00	150	—
1864 Ca JC	—	20.00	35.00	75.00	150	—
1865 Ca JC	—	100	200	350	600	—
1865 Ca FP	—	1,350	2,150	3,250	—	—
1866 Ca JC	—	750	1,150	2,250	—	—
1866 Ca FP	—	1,000	2,000	3,250	5,000	—
1866 Ca JG	—	850	1,650	2,750	4,250	—
1867 Ca JG	—	100	200	350	600	—
1868 Ca JG	—	75.00	150	250	400	—
1868 Ca MM	—	65.00	125	200	350	—
1869 Ca MM	—	20.00	35.00	65.00	135	—
1870 Ca MM	—	20.00	35.00	65.00	135	—
1871/0 Ca MM	—	15.00	25.00	55.00	125	—
1871 Ca MM	—	15.00	25.00	55.00	125	—
1871 Ca MM	—	20.00	35.00	65.00	135	—
Note: First M over inverted M						
1873 Ca MM	—	20.00	35.00	65.00	135	—
1873 Ca MM/T	—	15.00	25.00	55.00	125	—
1874 Ca MM	—	12.00	15.00	30.00	100	—
1875 Ca MM	—	12.00	15.00	30.00	100	—
1876 Ca MM	—	12.00	15.00	30.00	100	—
1877 Ca EA	472,000	20.00	40.00	85.00	200	—
1877 Ca GR	Inc. above	25.00	45.00	65.00	150	—
1877 Ca JM	Inc. above	12.00	15.00	30.00	100	—
1877 Ca AV	Inc. above	100	200	350	750	—
1878 Ca AV	439,000	12.00	15.00	25.00	80.00	—
1879 Ca AV	—	12.00	15.00	25.00	80.00	—
1880 Ca AV	—	200	350	600	1,250	—
1880 Ca PM	—	500	800	1,250	2,500	—
1880 Ca MG	—	12.00	15.00	25.00	100	—
Note: Normal initials						
1880 Ca MG	—	12.00	15.00	25.00	100	—
Note: Tall initials						
1880 Ca MM	—	12.00	15.00	25.00	100	—
1881 Ca MG	1,085,000	10.00	12.00	20.00	65.00	—
1882 Ca MG	779,000	10.00	12.00	20.00	65.00	—
1882 Ca MM	Inc. above	10.00	12.00	20.00	65.00	—
1882 Ca MM	Inc. above	20.00	45.00	100	175	—
Note: M sideways						
1883 Ca MM	818,000	—	—	—	—	—
Note: Sideways M						
1883/2 Ca MM/G	—	12.00	15.00	30.00	80.00	—
1883 Ca MM	Inc. above	10.00	12.00	20.00	65.00	—
1884/3 Ca MM	—	12.00	15.00	30.00	90.00	—
1884 Ca MM	—	10.00	12.00	20.00	65.00	—
1885/4 Ca MM	1,345,000	15.00	25.00	55.00	125	—
1885/6 Ca MM	Inc. above	15.00	25.00	55.00	125	—
1885 Ca MM	Inc. above	10.00	12.00	20.00	65.00	—
1886 Ca MM	2,483,000	10.00	12.00	20.00	65.00	—

Date	Mintage	F	VF	XF	Unc	BU
1887 Ca MM	2,625,000	10.00	12.00	20.00	65.00	—
1888/7 Ca MM	2,434,000	15.00	25.00	65.00	135	—
1888 Ca MM	Inc. above	10.00	12.00	20.00	65.00	—
1889 Ca MM	2,681,000	10.00	12.00	20.00	65.00	—
1890/89 Ca MM	—	15.00	25.00	55.00	125	—
1890 Ca MM	2,137,000	10.00	12.00	20.00	65.00	—
1891/0 Ca MM	2,268,000	15.00	25.00	55.00	135	—
1891 Ca MM	Inc. above	10.00	12.00	20.00	80.00	—
1892 Ca MM	2,527,000	10.00	12.00	20.00	65.00	—
1893 Ca MM	2,632,000	10.00	12.00	20.00	65.00	—
1894 Ca MM	2,642,000	10.00	12.00	20.00	65.00	—
1895 Ca MM	1,112,000	10.00	12.00	20.00	65.00	—

KM# 377.3 8 REALES
27.0700 g., 0.9030 Silver .7859 oz. ASW **Obv:** Facing eagle
Note: Mint mark C, Cn. Varieties exist.

Date	Mintage	F	VF	XF	Unc	BU
1846 CE	—	150	300	800	1,500	—
1846 CE	—	175	385	900	1,650	—
Note: Dot after G						
1846 CE	—	125	265	750	1,450	—
Note: No dot after G						
1847 CE	—	400	700	1,500	—	—
1848 CE	—	125	250	450	1,000	—
1849 CE	—	75.00	125	200	400	—
1850 CE	—	75.00	125	200	400	—
1851 CE	—	125	250	450	1,000	—
1852/1 CE	—	100	150	250	500	—
1852 CE	—	100	200	300	600	—
1853/0 CE	—	200	350	700	1,300	—
1853/2/0	—	200	400	750	1,400	—
1853 CE	—	100	175	300	600	—
Note: Thick rays						
1853 CE	—	200	350	650	—	—
Note: Error: MEXIGANA						
1854 CE	—	750	1,250	—	—	—
1854 CE	—	175	350	750	1,200	—
Note: Large eagle and hat						
1855/6 CE	—	40.00	60.00	100	200	—
1855 CE	—	25.00	40.00	75.00	150	—
1856 CE	—	50.00	100	175	350	—
1857 CE	—	20.00	35.00	75.00	150	—
1858 CE	—	30.00	40.00	75.00	150	—
1859 CE	—	20.00	35.00	75.00	150	—
1860/9 PV/CV	—	50.00	70.00	100	200	—
1860/9 PV/E	—	50.00	70.00	100	200	—
1860 CE	—	25.00	40.00	75.00	150	—
1860 PV	—	40.00	60.00	90.00	175	—
1861/0 CE	—	50.00	80.00	120	250	—
1861 PV/CE	—	75.00	125	200	350	—
1861 CE	—	20.00	35.00	60.00	150	—
1862 CE	—	20.00	35.00	60.00	150	—
1863/2 CE	—	30.00	50.00	75.00	200	—

Date	Mintage	F	VF	XF	Unc	BU
1863 CE	—	20.00	30.00	60.00	150	—
1864 CE	—	30.00	60.00	100	300	—
1865 CE	—	125	200	325	650	—
1866 CE	—	400	750	1,250	2,250	—
1867 CE	—	125	200	350	700	—
1868/7 CE	—	30.00	40.00	75.00	150	—
1868/8	—	50.00	100	150	300	—
1868 CE	—	30.00	40.00	75.00	150	—
1869 CE	—	30.00	40.00	75.00	175	—
1870 CE	—	50.00	100	150	350	—
1873 MP	—	50.00	100	150	300	—
1874/3 MP	—	30.00	40.00	75.00	150	—
1874C MP	—	20.00	30.00	45.00	100	—
1874 CN MP	—	125	200	300	600	—
1875 MP	—	12.00	15.00	22.00	80.00	—
1876 GP	—	12.00	15.00	30.00	90.00	—
1876 CG	—	12.00	15.00	22.00	80.00	—
1877 CG	339,000	12.00	15.00	22.00	80.00	—
1877Gn CG Error	—	65.00	125	200	400	—
1877 JA	Inc. above	35.00	75.00	125	250	—
1878/7 CG	483,000	35.00	75.00	125	250	—
1878 CG	Inc. above	15.00	25.00	35.00	125	—
1878 JD/CG	—	25.00	35.00	50.00	150	—
1878 JD	Inc. above	15.00	20.00	30.00	125	—
1878 JD	Inc. above	20.00	30.00	40.00	150	—
Note: D over retrograde D						
1879 JD	—	12.00	15.00	30.00	135	—
1880/70 JD	—	15.00	20.00	30.00	90.00	—
1880 JD	—	12.00	15.00	22.00	120	—
1881/0 JD	1,032,000	15.00	20.00	30.00	90.00	—
1881C JD	Inc. above	12.00	15.00	22.00	80.00	—
1881Cn JD	Inc. above	40.00	60.00	90.00	150	—
1882 JD	397,000	12.00	15.00	22.00	80.00	—
1882 AM	Inc. above	12.00	15.00	22.00	80.00	—
1883 AM	333,000	12.00	15.00	22.00	125	—
1884 AM	—	12.00	15.00	22.00	80.00	—
1885/6 AM	227,000	20.00	30.00	45.00	110	—
1885C AM	Inc. above	35.00	70.00	150	350	—
1885Cn AM	Inc. above	12.00	15.00	22.00	80.00	—
1885Gn AM Error	Inc. above	25.00	50.00	100	275	—
1886 AM	571,000	12.00	15.00	22.00	80.00	—
1887 AM	732,000	12.00	15.00	22.00	80.00	—
1888 AM	768,000	12.00	15.00	22.00	80.00	—
1889 AM	1,075,000	12.00	15.00	22.00	80.00	—
1890 AM	874,000	10.00	12.00	20.00	65.00	—
1891 AM	777,000	10.00	12.00	20.00	65.00	—
1892 AM	681,000	10.00	12.00	20.00	65.00	—
1893 AM	1,144,000	10.00	12.00	20.00	65.00	—
1894 AM	2,118,000	10.00	12.00	20.00	65.00	—
1895 AM	1,834,000	10.00	12.00	20.00	65.00	—
1896 AM	2,134,000	10.00	12.00	20.00	65.00	—
1897 AM	1,580,000	10.00	12.00	20.00	65.00	—

KM# 377.4 8 REALES
27.0700 g., 0.9030 Silver .7859 oz. ASW **Obv:** Facing eagle
Note: Varieties exist.

Date	Mintage	F	VF	XF	Unc	BU
1825Do RL	—	30.00	65.00	150	375	—
1826Do RL	—	40.00	85.00	200	475	—
1827/6Do RL	—	35.00	60.00	85.00	200	—
1827/8Do RL	—	150	275	500	—	—
1827Do RL	—	30.00	50.00	90.00	200	—
1828/7Do RL	—	35.00	60.00	90.00	200	—
1828Do RL	—	25.00	50.00	80.00	175	—
1829Do RL	—	25.00	50.00	80.00	175	—
1830Do RM	—	25.00	50.00	90.00	200	—
Note: B on eagle's claw						
1831Do RM	—	20.00	30.00	60.00	150	—
Note: B on eagle's claw						
1832Do RM	—	35.00	60.00	120	300	—
Note: Mexican dies, B on eagle's claw						
1832/1Do RM/RL	—	25.00	35.00	75.00	165	—
Note: French dies						
1833/2Do RM/RL	—	20.00	35.00	75.00	165	—
1833Do RM	—	15.00	30.00	60.00	150	—
1834/3/2Do RM/RL	—	20.00	35.00	75.00	165	—
1834Do RM	—	15.00	25.00	50.00	150	—
1835/4Do RM/RL	—	20.00	35.00	65.00	150	—
1835Do RM	—	20.00	35.00	65.00	150	—
1836/1Do RM	—	20.00	35.00	65.00	150	—

Date	Mintage	F	VF	XF	Unc	BU
1836/4Do RM	—	20.00	35.00	65.00	150	—
1836/5/4Do RM/RL	—	75.00	150	250	500	—
1836Do RM	—	20.00	30.00	55.00	150	—
1836Do RM	—	20.00	30.00	55.00	150	—
Note: M on snake						
1837/1Do RM	—	20.00	30.00	55.00	150	—
1837Do RM	—	20.00	30.00	55.00	150	—
1838/1Do RM	—	20.00	30.00	60.00	165	—
1838/7Do RM	—	20.00	30.00	60.00	165	—
1838Do RM	—	20.00	30.00	55.00	150	—
1839/1Do RM/RL	—	20.00	30.00	55.00	150	—
1839/1Do RM	—	20.00	30.00	55.00	150	—
1839Do RM	—	20.00	30.00	55.00	150	—
1840/38/31Do RM	—	20.00	30.00	55.00	150	—
1840/39Do RM	—	20.00	30.00	55.00	150	—
1840Do RM	—	20.00	30.00	55.00	150	—
1841/31Do RM	—	65.00	125	275	450	—
1841/39Do RM/L	—	25.00	50.00	85.00	200	—
1841/39Do RM	—	25.00	50.00	85.00	200	—
1842/31Do RM	—	125	250	400	750	—
Note: B below cactus						
1842/31Do RM	—	40.00	80.00	125	250	—
1842/32Do RM	—	40.00	80.00	125	250	—
1842Do RM	—	20.00	30.00	55.00	150	—
Note: Eagle of 1832-41						
1842Do RM	—	20.00	30.00	55.00	150	—
Note: Pre-1832 eagle resumed						
1842Do RM	—	40.00	80.00	125	250	—
1843/33Do RM	—	50.00	90.00	150	250	—
1843Do RM	—	50.00	90.00	150	250	—
1844/34Do RM	—	100	200	300	500	—
1844/35Do RM	—	100	200	300	500	—
1844/43Do RM	—	60.00	120	220	425	—
1845/31Do RM	—	100	200	300	500	—
1845/34Do RM	—	35.00	75.00	125	250	—
1845/35Do RM	—	35.00	75.00	125	250	—
1845Do RM	—	20.00	30.00	55.00	150	—
1846/31Do RM	—	20.00	30.00	55.00	150	—
1846/36Do RM	—	20.00	30.00	55.00	150	—
1846Do RM	—	20.00	30.00	55.00	150	—
1847Do RM	—	25.00	50.00	80.00	185	—
1848/7Do RM	—	125	250	400	750	—
1848/7Do CM/RM	—	100	200	350	700	—
1848Do CM/RM	—	100	200	350	700	—
1848Do RM	—	100	200	300	600	—
1848Do CM	—	50.00	100	200	400	—
1849/39Do CM	—	100	200	350	700	—
1849Do CM	—	65.00	125	250	550	—
1849Do JMR/CM Oval 0	—	200	400	450	800	—
1849Do JMR Oval 0	—	200	325	450	800	—
1849Do JMR Round 0	—	200	400	600	1,000	—
1850Do JMR	—	100	150	250	500	—
1851/0Do JMR	—	65.00	125	225	475	—
1851Do JMR	—	100	150	250	500	—
1852Do CP/JMR	—	450	800	1,500	—	—
1852Do CP	—	750	1,200	2,250	—	—
1852Do JMR	—	175	250	375	650	—
1853Do CP/JMR	—	125	235	350	600	—
1853Do CP	—	200	350	600	1,200	—
1854Do CP	—	25.00	35.00	65.00	300	—
1855Do CP	—	50.00	100	175	350	—
Note: Eagle type of 1854						
1855Do CP	—	50.00	100	175	350	—
Note: Eagle type of 1856						
1856Do CP	—	50.00	100	175	350	—
1857Do CP	—	35.00	65.00	125	250	—
1858/7Do CP	—	25.00	35.00	70.00	165	—
1858Do CP	—	20.00	30.00	60.00	165	—
1859Do CP	—	20.00	30.00	60.00	165	—
1860/59Do CP	—	30.00	50.00	100	200	—
1860Do CP	—	20.00	30.00	60.00	165	—
1861/0Do CP	—	20.00	30.00	60.00	165	—
1861Do CP	—	20.00	30.00	50.00	125	—
1862/1Do CP	—	25.00	35.00	60.00	125	—
1862Do CP	—	20.00	30.00	60.00	175	—
1863/1Do CP	—	30.00	60.00	90.00	200	—
1863/2Do CP	—	25.00	50.00	75.00	175	—

Date	Mintage	F	VF	XF	Unc	BU
1863/53Do CP	—	30.00	60.00	90.00	200	—
1863Do CP	—	25.00	50.00	75.00	175	—
1864Do CP	—	100	150	250	500	—
1864Do LT	—	25.00	40.00	80.00	175	—
1864Do LT/T	—	25.00	40.00	80.00	175	—
1864Do LT/CP	—	50.00	100	175	350	—
1865Do LT Rare	—	—	—	—	—	—
1866/4Do CM	—	2,750	5,500	—	—	—
1866Do CM	—	1,750	3,250	5,500	8,000	—
1867Do CM	—	3,500	—	—	—	—
1867/6Do CP	—	200	400	600	1,200	—
1867Do CP	—	175	300	500	1,000	—
1867Do CP/CM	—	125	250	400	900	—
1867Do CP/LT	—	200	400	650	1,250	—
1868Do CP	—	25.00	40.00	80.00	175	—
1869Do CP	—	20.00	30.00	50.00	135	—
1870/69Do CP	—	20.00	30.00	50.00	125	—
1870/9Do CP	—	20.00	30.00	50.00	125	—
1870Do CP	—	20.00	30.00	50.00	125	—
1873Do CP	—	125	225	325	600	—
1873Do CM	—	30.00	50.00	100	200	—
1874/3Do CM	—	12.00	15.00	22.00	100	—
1874Do CM	—	10.00	15.00	22.00	80.00	—
1874Do JH	—	1,150	1,750	2,750	—	—
1875Do CM	—	10.00	15.00	22.00	80.00	—
1875Do JH	—	80.00	150	250	450	—
1876Do CM	—	10.00	15.00	22.00	80.00	—
1877Do CM	431,000	1,450	2,500	—	—	—
1877Do CP	Inc. above	10.00	15.00	22.00	80.00	—
1877Do JMP	Inc. above	750	1,250	2,000	—	—
1878Do PE	409,000	15.00	25.00	40.00	100	—
1878Do TB	Inc. above	10.00	15.00	25.00	90.00	—
1879Do TB	—	10.00	15.00	22.00	80.00	—
1880/70Do TB	—	60.00	100	175	350	—
1880/70Do TB/JP	—	150	250	375	650	—
1880/70Do JP	—	15.00	25.00	40.00	100	—
1880Do TB	—	150	250	375	650	—
1880Do JP	—	10.00	15.00	22.00	80.00	—
1881Do JP	928,000	10.00	15.00	25.00	90.00	—
1882Do JP	414,000	10.00	15.00	22.00	80.00	—
1882Do MC/JP	Inc. above	30.00	60.00	100	200	—
1882Do MC	Inc. above	25.00	50.00	75.00	150	—
1883/73Do MC	452,000	15.00	25.00	40.00	90.00	—
1883Do MC	Inc. above	10.00	15.00	22.00	80.00	—
1884/3Do MC	—	15.00	25.00	40.00	90.00	—
1884Do MC	—	10.00	15.00	22.00	80.00	—
1885Do MC	547,000	10.00	12.00	20.00	70.00	—
1885Do JB	Inc. above	25.00	35.00	50.00	125	—
1886/5Do MC	—	15.00	25.00	40.00	100	—
1886/3Do MC	955,000	15.00	25.00	40.00	100	—
1886Do MC	Inc. above	10.00	12.00	20.00	70.00	—
1887Do MC	1,004,000	10.00	12.00	20.00	70.00	—
1888/7Do MC	—	65.00	125	250	450	—
1888Do MC	996,000	10.00	12.00	20.00	70.00	—
1889Do MC	874,000	10.00	12.00	20.00	70.00	—
1890Do MC	1,119,000	10.00	12.00	20.00	70.00	—
1890Do JP	Inc. above	10.00	12.00	20.00	70.00	—
1891Do JP	1,487,000	10.00	12.00	20.00	70.00	—
1892Do JP	1,597,000	10.00	12.00	20.00	70.00	—
1892Do ND	Inc. above	25.00	50.00	100	200	—
1893Do ND	1,617,000	10.00	12.00	20.00	70.00	—
1894Do ND	1,537,000	10.00	12.00	20.00	70.00	—
1895/3Do ND	761,000	15.00	25.00	40.00	100	—
1895Do ND	Inc. above	10.00	12.00	20.00	70.00	—
1895Do ND/P	—	15.00	25.00	40.00	100	—

KM# 377.5 8 REALES
27.0700 g., 0.9030 Silver .7859 oz. ASW **Obv:** Facing eagle

Date	Mintage	F	VF	XF	Unc	BU
1828EoMo LF/ LP	—	350	850	2,150	—	—
1828EoMo LF	—	350	850	2,150	5,500	—
1829EoMo LF	—	300	750	1,850	4,500	—
1830/20EoMo LF	—	1,250	2,750	4,250	—	—
1830EoMo LF	—	1,000	2,000	3,250	6,000	—

KM# 377.6 8 REALES
27.0700 g., 0.9030 Silver .7859 oz. ASW **Obv:** Facing eagle
Note: Varieties exist.

Date	Mintage	F	VF	XF	Unc	BU
1825Ga FS	—	150	275	475	1,000	—
1826/5Ga FS	—	125	250	450	1,000	—
1826Ga FS	—	125	250	450	1,000	—
1827/87Ga FS	—	125	250	450	1,000	—
1827Ga FS	—	125	250	450	1,000	—
1287Ga FS Error	—	8,500	9,500	—	—	—
1828Ga FS	—	200	375	550	1,200	—
1829/8Ga FS	—	200	375	550	1,200	—
1829Ga FS	—	175	325	475	950	—
1830/29Ga FS	—	100	175	300	600	—
1830Ga FS	—	100	175	300	600	—
1830Ga LP/FS	—	800	1,450	—	—	—

Note: The 1830 LP/FS is currently only known with a Philippine countermark.

Date	Mintage	F	VF	XF	Unc	BU
1831Ga LP	—	200	400	600	1,200	—
1831Ga FS/LP	—	300	500	750	1,500	—
1831Ga FS	—	125	275	400	—	—
1832/1Ga FS	—	50.00	100	175	300	—
1832/1Ga FS/LP	—	50.00	100	175	300	—
1832Ga FS/LP	—	75.00	100	285	550	—
1832Ga FS	—	25.00	50.00	100	225	—
1833/2/1Ga FS/LP	—	45.00	75.00	125	250	—
1833/2Ga FS	—	25.00	50.00	100	225	—
1834/2Ga FS	—	60.00	125	200	350	—
1834/3Ga FS	—	60.00	125	200	350	—

Date	Mintage	F	VF	XF	Unc	BU
1834/0Ga FS	—	50.00	100	150	300	—
1834Ga FS	—	50.00	100	150	300	—
1835Ga FS	—	25.00	50.00	100	225	—
1836/5Ga FS	—	175	350	—	—	—
1836/1Ga JG/FS	—	40.00	80.00	125	250	—
1836Ga FS	—	275	450	750	—	—
1836Ga JG/FS	—	25.00	50.00	100	225	—
1836Ga JG	—	25.00	50.00	100	225	—
1837/6Ga JG/FS	—	50.00	100	175	300	—
1837/6Ga JG	—	45.00	90.00	160	285	—
1837Ga JG	—	40.00	80.00	125	250	—
1838/7Ga JG	—	100	175	300	550	—
1838Ga JG	—	100	150	275	500	—
1839Ga MC	—	100	200	350	600	—
1839Ga MC/JG	—	100	200	300	550	—
1839Ga JG	—	60.00	125	200	350	—
1840/30Ga MC	—	50.00	75.00	150	275	—
1840Ga MC	—	30.00	60.00	125	250	—
1841Ga MC	—	30.00	60.00	125	250	—
1842/1Ga JG/MG	—	100	150	250	450	—
1842/1Ga JG/MC	—	100	150	250	450	—
1842Ga JG	—	25.00	50.00	100	225	—
1842Ga JG/MG	—	25.00	50.00	100	225	—
1843/2Ga MC/JG	—	25.00	50.00	100	225	—
1843Ga MC/JG	—	25.00	50.00	100	225	—
1843Ga JG	—	400	600	900	1,650	—
1843Ga MC	—	50.00	100	150	300	—
1844Ga MC	—	50.00	100	150	300	—
1845Ga MC	—	75.00	150	300	700	—
1845Ga JG	—	500	850	1,250	1,850	—
1846Ga JG	—	40.00	80.00	150	300	—
1847Ga JG	—	100	150	225	400	—
1848/7Ga JG	—	55.00	85.00	125	250	—
1848Ga JG	—	50.00	75.00	100	225	—
1849Ga JG	—	90.00	100	125	325	—
1849/39Ga JG	—	250	500	—	—	—
1850Ga JG	—	50.00	100	150	300	—
1851Ga JG	—	125	200	350	650	—
1852Ga JG	—	100	150	250	450	—
1853/2Ga JG	—	125	175	250	475	—
1853Ga JG	—	90.00	125	175	300	—
1854/3Ga JG	—	65.00	90.00	125	250	—
1854Ga JG	—	50.00	75.00	110	225	—
1855/4Ga JG	—	50.00	100	150	275	—
1855Ga JG	—	25.00	50.00	100	225	—
1856/4Ga JG	—	60.00	125	175	300	—
1856/5Ga 56	—	60.00	125	175	300	—
1856Ga JG	—	50.00	100	150	275	—
1857Ga JG	—	50.00	100	225	450	—
1858Ga JG	—	100	150	300	500	—
1859/7Ga JG	—	25.00	50.00	110	225	—
1859/8Ga JG	—	25.00	50.00	100	200	—
1859Ga JG	—	20.00	40.00	80.00	175	—
1860Ga JG Without dot	—	350	750	1,200	2,250	—
1860Ga JG	—	2,000	3,250	4,500	—	—

Note: Dot in loop of snake's tail, base alloy

Date	Mintage	F	VF	XF	Unc	BU
1861Ga JG	—	2,200	5,750	—	—	—
1862Ga JG	—	850	1,350	2,750	4,500	—
1863/52Ga JG	—	—	—	—	—	—
1863/59Ga JG	—	45.00	50.00	85.00	145	—
1863/2Ga JG	—	30.00	50.00	90.00	175	—
1863/4Ga JG	—	40.00	75.00	150	250	—
1863Ga JG	—	25.00	45.00	75.00	150	—
1863Ga FV Rare	—	—	—	—	—	—
1867Ga JM Rare	—	—	—	—	—	—
1868/7Ga JM	—	50.00	75.00	125	200	—
1868Ga JM	—	50.00	75.00	125	200	—
1869Ga JM	—	50.00	75.00	125	200	—
1869Ga IC	—	75.00	125	200	375	—
1870/60Ga IC	—	60.00	90.00	150	275	—
1870Ga IC	—	60.00	90.00	150	275	—
1873Ga IC	—	15.00	25.00	50.00	125	—
1874Ga IC	—	10.00	15.00	22.00	90.00	—
1874Ga MC	—	25.00	50.00	100	200	—
1875Ga IC	—	15.00	30.00	60.00	125	—
1875Ga MC	—	10.00	15.00	22.00	90.00	—
1876Ga IC	559,000	15.00	30.00	50.00	100	—
1876Ga MC	Inc. above	125	175	250	375	—

Date	Mintage	F	VF	XF	Unc	BU
1877Ga IC	928,000	10.00	15.00	22.00	90.00	—
1877/6Ga JA	—	10.00	15.00	22.00	90.00	—
1877Ga JA	Inc. above	10.00	15.00	22.00	90.00	—
1878Ga JA	764,000	10.00	15.00	22.00	90.00	—
1879Ga JA	—	10.00	15.00	22.00	90.00	—
1880/70Ga FS	—	15.00	25.00	50.00	125	—
1880Ga JA	—	10.00	15.00	22.00	90.00	—
1880Ga FS	—	10.00	15.00	22.00	90.00	—
1881Ga FS	1,300,000	10.00	15.00	22.00	90.00	—
1882/1Ga FS	537,000	15.00	25.00	50.00	125	—
1882Ga FS	Inc. above	10.00	15.00	22.00	90.00	—
1882Ga TB/FS	Inc. above	50.00	100	175	300	—
1882Ga TB	Inc. above	50.00	100	175	300	—
1883Ga TB	561,000	15.00	25.00	40.00	125	—
1884Ga TB	—	10.00	12.00	20.00	85.00	—
1884Ga AH	—	10.00	12.00	20.00	85.00	—
1885Ga AH	443,000	10.00	12.00	20.00	90.00	—
1885Ga JS	Inc. above	30.00	60.00	100	200	—
1886Ga JS/H	—	10.00	12.00	20.00	85.00	—
1886Ga JS	1,038,999	10.00	12.00	20.00	85.00	—
1887Ga JS	878,000	10.00	12.00	20.00	85.00	—
1888Ga JS	1,159,000	10.00	12.00	20.00	85.00	—
1889Ga JS	1,583,000	10.00	12.00	20.00	85.00	—
1890Ga JS	1,658,000	10.00	12.00	20.00	85.00	—
1891Ga JS	1,507,000	10.00	12.00	20.00	85.00	—
1892/1Ga JS	1,627,000	15.00	25.00	50.00	125	—
1892Ga JS	Inc. above	10.00	12.00	20.00	80.00	—
1893Ga JS	1,952,000	10.00	12.00	20.00	80.00	—
1894Ga JS	2,045,999	10.00	12.00	20.00	80.00	—
1895/3Ga JS	—	12.00	20.00	35.00	100	—
1895Ga JS	1,146,000	10.00	12.00	20.00	65.00	—

KM# 377.7 8 REALES
27.0700 g., 0.9030 Silver .7859 oz. ASW Obv: Facing eagle

Date	Mintage	F	VF	XF	Unc	BU
1844GC MP	—	350	500	1,000	2,000	—
1844GC MP	—	400	600	1,200	2,250	—
Note: Error, reversed S in Ds, Gs						
1845GC MP	—	125	200	325	700	—
Note: Eagle's tail square						
1845GC MP	—	175	350	650	1,200	—
Note: Eagle's tail round						
1846GC MP	—	175	350	750	1,650	—
Note: Eagle's tail square						
1846GC MP	—	125	200	350	750	—
Note: Eagle's tail round						
1847GC MP	—	150	250	400	800	—
1848GC MP	—	175	300	500	900	—
1849GC MP	—	175	300	525	1,000	—
1850GC MP	—	175	300	575	1,100	—
1851GC MP	—	300	500	900	1,600	—
1852GC MP	—	350	600	1,250	2,500	—

KM# 377.8 8 REALES
27.0700 g., 0.9030 Silver .7859 oz. ASW Obv: Facing eagle
Note: Varieties exist.

Date	Mintage	F	VF	XF	Unc	BU
1825Go JJ	—	40.00	70.00	150	300	—
1825G JJ	—	1,250	1,650	—	—	—
Note: Error mint mark G						
1826Go JJ	—	40.00	80.00	175	350	—
Note: Straight J's						
1826Go JJ	—	30.00	60.00	125	250	—
Note: Full J's						
1826Go MJ	—	250	450	850	—	—
1827Go MJ	—	40.00	75.00	125	250	—
1827Go MJ/JJ	—	—	—	—	—	—
1827Go MR	—	100	200	350	600	—
1828Go MJ	—	—	—	—	—	—
Note: Error mint mark Goo						
1828Go MJ	—	30.00	60.00	125	250	—
1828/7Go MR	—	150	300	600	1,200	—
1828Go MR	—	150	300	600	1,200	—
1829Go MJ	—	20.00	35.00	55.00	165	—
1830Go MJ	—	20.00	30.00	55.00	165	—
Note: Oblong beading and narrow J						
1830Go MJ	—	20.00	30.00	55.00	165	—
Note: Regular beading and wide J						
1831Go MJ	—	12.00	20.00	40.00	150	—
Note: Colon after date						
1831Go MJ	—	12.00	20.00	40.00	150	—
Note: 2 stars after date						
1832Go MJ	—	12.00	20.00	40.00	150	—
1832Go MJ	—	20.00	35.00	65.00	175	—
Note: 1 of date over inverted 1						
1833Go MJ/1	—	20.00	35.00	65.00	175	—
1833Go MJ	—	12.00	20.00	40.00	150	—
1833Go JM	—	400	750	1,250	2,500	—
1834Go PJ	—	12.00	20.00	40.00	150	—
1835Go PJ	—	12.00	20.00	40.00	150	—
Note: Star on cap						
1835Go PJ	—	12.00	20.00	40.00	150	—
Note: Dot on cap						
1836Go PJ	—	12.00	20.00	40.00	150	—
1837Go PJ	—	12.00	20.00	40.00	150	—
1838Go PJ	—	12.00	20.00	40.00	150	—
1839Go PJ/JJ	—	12.00	20.00	40.00	150	—
1839Go PJ	—	12.00	20.00	40.00	150	—
1840/30Go PJ	—	20.00	30.00	50.00	150	—
1840Go PJ	—	12.00	20.00	35.00	125	—
1841/31Go PJ	—	12.00	20.00	35.00	125	—
1841Go PJ	—	12.00	20.00	35.00	125	—
1842/1Go PM	—	20.00	30.00	50.00	125	—
1842/31Go PM/PJ	—	25.00	35.00	60.00	150	—
1842Go PJ	—	20.00	30.00	50.00	125	—
1842Go PM/PJ	—	12.00	20.00	35.00	125	—
1842Go PM	—	12.00	20.00	35.00	125	—
1843Go PM	—	12.00	20.00	35.00	125	—
Note: Dot after date						

Date	Mintage	F	VF	XF	Unc	BU
1843Go PM	—	12.00	20.00	35.00	125	—
Note: Triangle of dots after date						
1844Go PM	—	12.00	20.00	35.00	125	—
1845Go PM	—	12.00	20.00	35.00	125	—
1846/5Go PM	—	20.00	30.00	50.00	150	—
Note: Eagle type of 1845						
1846Go PM	—	15.00	25.00	40.00	135	—
Note: Early type of 1847						
1847Go PM Narrow date	—	12.00	20.00	35.00	125	—
1847Go PM Wide date	—	12.00	20.00	35.00	125	—
1848/7Go PM	—	20.00	35.00	65.00	150	—
1848Go PM	—	20.00	35.00	65.00	150	—
1848Go PF	—	12.00	20.00	35.00	125	—
1849Go PF	—	12.00	20.00	35.00	125	—
1850Go PF	—	12.00	20.00	35.00	125	—
1851/0Go PF	—	20.00	30.00	50.00	150	—
1851Go PF	—	12.00	20.00	35.00	125	—
1852/1Go PF	—	20.00	30.00	50.00	150	—
1852Go PF	—	12.00	20.00	35.00	125	—
1853/2Go PF	—	20.00	30.00	50.00	150	—
1853Go PF	—	12.00	20.00	35.00	125	—
1854Go PF	—	12.00	20.00	35.00	125	—
1855Go PF Large letters	—	12.00	20.00	35.00	125	—
1855Go PF Small letters	—	12.00	20.00	35.00	125	—
1856/5Go PF	—	20.00	30.00	50.00	150	—
1856Go PF	—	12.00	20.00	35.00	125	—
1857/5Go PF	—	20.00	30.00	50.00	150	—
1857/6Go PF	—	20.00	35.00	70.00	200	—
1857Go PF	—	12.00	15.00	20.00	75.00	—
1858/7Go PI	—	12.00	20.00	35.00	125	—
1858Go PF	—	12.00	20.00	35.00	125	—
1859/7Go PF	—	12.00	20.00	35.00	125	—
1859/8Go PF	—	20.00	30.00	50.00	150	—
1859Go PF	—	12.00	20.00	35.00	125	—
1860/50Go PF	—	20.00	30.00	50.00	150	—
1860/59Go PF	—	12.00	18.00	25.00	85.00	—
1860Go PF	—	12.00	15.00	20.00	75.00	—
1861/51Go PF	—	15.00	20.00	30.00	100	—
1861/0Go PF	—	12.00	15.00	20.00	75.00	—
1861Go PF	—	12.00	15.00	20.00	75.00	—
186/52Go YE	—	—	—	—	—	—
1862Go YE/PF	—	12.00	15.00	20.00	75.00	—
1862Go YE	—	12.00	15.00	20.00	75.00	—
1862Go YF	—	12.00	15.00	20.00	75.00	—
1862Go YF/PF	—	12.00	15.00	20.00	75.00	—
1863/53Go YF	—	12.00	18.00	25.00	75.00	—
1863/54Go YF	—	15.00	20.00	30.00	100	—
1863Go YE Rare	—	—	—	—	—	—
1863Go YF	—	12.00	15.00	20.00	75.00	—
1867/57Go YF	—	15.00	20.00	30.00	100	—
1867Go YF	—	12.00	15.00	20.00	75.00	—
1868/58Go YF	—	15.00	20.00	30.00	100	—
1868/7Go YF	—	15.00	20.00	30.00	100	—
1868Go YF	—	12.00	15.00	20.00	75.00	—
1870/60Go FR	—	20.00	30.00	50.00	150	—
1870Go FR	—	1,800	3,000	5,000	7,500	—
1870Go FR/YF	—	20.00	35.00	70.00	200	—
1870Go FR	—	12.00	15.00	20.00	75.00	—
1873Go FR	—	12.00	15.00	20.00	75.00	—
1874/3Go FR	—	15.00	20.00	30.00	85.00	—
1874Go FR	—	15.00	25.00	35.00	100	—
1875/3Go FR	—	15.00	20.00	30.00	85.00	—
1875/6Go FR	—	15.00	20.00	30.00	85.00	—
1875Go FR	—	12.00	15.00	20.00	75.00	—
Note: Small circle with dot on eagle						
1876/5Go FR	—	15.00	20.00	30.00	85.00	—
1876Go FR	—	12.00	15.00	20.00	60.00	—
1877Go FR	2,477,000	12.00	15.00	20.00	60.00	—
1878/7Go FR	2,273,000	15.00	20.00	30.00	75.00	—
1878/7Go SM	—	15.00	20.00	30.00	75.00	—
1878Go FR	Inc. above	12.00	15.00	20.00	65.00	—
1878Go SM, S/F	—	15.00	20.00	25.00	70.00	—
1878Go SM	—	12.00	15.00	20.00	65.00	—
1879/7Go SM	—	15.00	20.00	30.00	75.00	—
1879/8Go SM	—	15.00	20.00	30.00	75.00	—
1879/8Go SM/FR	—	15.00	20.00	30.00	75.00	—
1879Go SM	—	12.00	15.00	20.00	65.00	—
1879Go SM/FR	—	15.00	20.00	30.00	75.00	—
1880/70Go SB	—	15.00	20.00	30.00	75.00	—

Date	Mintage	F	VF	XF	Unc	BU
1880Go SB/SM	—	12.00	15.00	20.00	65.00	—
1880Go SB	—	12.00	15.00	20.00	65.00	—
1881/71Go SB	3,974,000	15.00	20.00	30.00	75.00	—
1881/0Go SB	Inc. above	15.00	20.00	30.00	75.00	—
1881Go SB	Inc. above	12.00	15.00	20.00	65.00	—
1882Go SB	2,015,000	12.00	15.00	20.00	75.00	—
1883Go SB	2,100,000	35.00	75.00	125	250	—
1883Go BR	Inc. above	12.00	15.00	20.00	65.00	—
1883Go BR/SR	—	12.00	15.00	20.00	65.00	—
1883Go BR/SB	Inc. above	12.00	15.00	20.00	65.00	—
1884/73Go BR	—	20.00	30.00	40.00	100	—
1884/74Go BR	—	20.00	30.00	40.00	100	—
1884/3Go BR	—	20.00	30.00	60.00	150	—
1884Go BR	—	12.00	15.00	20.00	65.00	—
1884/74Go RR	—	50.00	100	175	350	—
1884Go RR	—	25.00	50.00	100	250	—
1885/75Go RR	2,363,000	15.00	20.00	30.00	75.00	—
1885Go RR	Inc. above	12.00	15.00	20.00	65.00	—
1886/75Go RR	4,127,000	15.00	20.00	25.00	70.00	—
1886/76Go RR	Inc. above	12.00	15.00	20.00	65.00	—
1886/5Go RR/BR	Inc. above	12.00	15.00	20.00	65.00	—
1886Go RR	Inc. above	12.00	15.00	20.00	65.00	—
1887Go RR	4,205,000	10.00	15.00	20.00	65.00	—
1888Go RR	3,985,000	10.00	15.00	20.00	65.00	—
1889Go RR	3,646,000	10.00	15.00	20.00	65.00	—
1890Go RR	3,615,000	10.00	15.00	20.00	65.00	—
1891Go RS/R	—	10.00	15.00	20.00	65.00	—
1891Go RS	3,197,000	10.00	15.00	20.00	65.00	—
1892/0Go RS	—	10.00	15.00	20.00	65.00	—
1892Go RS	3,672,000	10.00	15.00	20.00	65.00	—
1893Go RS	3,854,000	10.00	15.00	20.00	65.00	—
1894Go RS	4,127,000	10.00	15.00	20.00	65.00	—
1895/1Go RS	3,768,000	15.00	20.00	25.00	75.00	—
1895/3Go RS	Inc. above	15.00	20.00	25.00	75.00	—
1895Go RS	Inc. above	10.00	15.00	20.00	65.00	—
1896/1Go As RS/ML	5,229,000	15.00	20.00	25.00	75.00	—
1896/1Go RS	Inc. above	12.00	15.00	20.00	65.00	—
1896Go/Ga RS	Inc. above	—	—	—	—	—
1896Go RS	Inc. above	10.00	12.00	18.00	60.00	—
1897Go RS	4,344,000	10.00	12.00	18.00	60.00	—

KM# 377.9 8 REALES
27.0700 g., 0.9030 Silver .7859 oz. ASW **Obv:** Facing eagle
Note: Varieties exist.

Date	Mintage	F	VF	XF	Unc	BU
1835Ho PP Rare	—	—	—	—	—	—
1836Ho PP Rare	—	—	—	—	—	—
1839Ho PR Unique	—	—	—	—	—	—
1861Ho FM Reeded edge	—	4,500	7,500	—	—	—
1862Ho FM Rare	—	—	—	—	—	—
Note: Plain edge, snakes tail left, long ray over *8R						
1862Ho FM	—	1,550	2,700	—	—	—
Note: Plain edge, snake's tail left						
1862Ho FM	—	1,650	2,750	—	—	—
Note: Reeded edge, snakes tail right						
1863Ho FM	—	150	300	800	—	—
1864Ho FM	—	850	1,650	2,750	—	—
1864Ho PR/FM	—	1,200	2,200	—	—	—
1864Ho PR	—	650	1,250	2,150	3,350	—
1865Ho FM	—	250	500	950	1,850	—
1866Ho FM	—	1,150	2,150	3,500	5,500	—
1866Ho MP	—	950	1,750	3,000	4,650	—

Date	Mintage	F	VF	XF	Unc	BU
1867Ho PR	—	100	175	275	500	—
1868Ho PR	—	20.00	35.00	65.00	175	—
1869Ho PR	—	40.00	60.00	125	250	—
1870Ho PR	—	100	175	275	550	—
1871/0Ho PR	—	50.00	75.00	125	250	—
1871Ho PR	—	30.00	50.00	90.00	200	—
1872/1Ho PR	—	35.00	60.00	90.00	200	—
1872Ho PR	—	30.00	50.00	75.00	175	—
1873Ho PR	351,000	30.00	50.00	85.00	150	—
1874Ho PR	—	15.00	20.00	40.00	125	—
1875Ho PR	—	15.00	20.00	40.00	125	—
1876Ho AF	—	15.00	20.00	40.00	125	—
1877Ho AF	410,000	20.00	30.00	50.00	150	—
1877Ho GR	Inc. above	100	150	225	400	—
1877Ho JA	Inc. above	25.00	50.00	85.00	175	—
1878Ho JA	451,000	15.00	20.00	40.00	120	—
1879Ho JA	—	15.00	20.00	40.00	120	—
1880Ho JA	—	15.00	20.00	40.00	120	—
1881Ho JA	586,000	15.00	20.00	40.00	120	—
1882Ho JA	240,000	25.00	40.00	65.00	125	—
Note: O above H						
1882Ho JA	Inc. above	25.00	40.00	65.00	125	—
Note: O after H						
1883/2Ho JA	204,000	200	350	500	1,000	—
1883/2Ho FM/JA	Inc. above	25.00	40.00	75.00	150	—
1883Ho FM/JA	—	27.00	45.00	85.00	165	—
1883Ho FM	Inc. above	20.00	30.00	60.00	125	—
1883Ho JA	Inc. above	275	450	800	1,500	—
1884/3Ho FM	—	20.00	25.00	50.00	125	—
1884Ho FM	—	15.00	20.00	40.00	120	—
1885Ho FM	132,000	15.00	20.00	40.00	120	—
1886Ho FM	225,000	20.00	30.00	45.00	125	—
1886Ho FG	Inc. above	20.00	30.00	45.00	125	—
1887/6Ho FG	—	20.00	35.00	65.00	150	—
1887Ho FG	150,000	20.00	35.00	65.00	150	—
1888Ho FG	364,000	12.00	18.00	25.00	100	—
1889Ho FG	490,000	12.00	18.00	25.00	100	—
1890Ho FG	565,000	12.00	18.00	25.00	100	—
1891Ho FG	738,000	12.00	18.00	25.00	100	—
1892Ho FG	643,000	12.00	18.00	25.00	100	—
1893Ho FG	518,000	12.00	18.00	25.00	100	—
1894Ho FG	504,000	12.00	18.00	25.00	100	—
1895Ho FG	320,000	12.00	18.00	25.00	100	—

KM# 377.10 8 REALES
27.0700 g., 0.9030 Silver .7859 oz. ASW **Obv:** Facing eagle
Note: Varieties exist. 1874 CP is a die struck counterfeit.

Date	Mintage	F	VF	XF	Unc	BU
1824Mo JM Round tail	—	75.00	125	250	500	—
1824Mo JM Square tail	—	75.00	125	250	500	—
1825Mo JM	—	25.00	40.00	75.00	200	—
1826/5Mo JM	—	25.00	40.00	75.00	200	—
1826Mo JM	—	20.00	30.00	55.00	165	—
1827Mo JM	—	25.00	35.00	60.00	175	—

Date	Mintage	F	VF	XF	Unc	BU
Note: Medal alignment						
1827Mo JM	—	25.00	35.00	60.00	175	—
Note: Coin alignment						
1828Mo JM	—	30.00	60.00	100	250	—
1829Mo JM	—	20.00	30.00	90.00	220	—
1830/20Mo JM	—	35.00	5.00	150	300	—
1830Mo JM	—	30.00	50.00	90.00	220	—
1831Mo JM	—	30.00	50.00	100	240	—
1832/1Mo JM	—	25.00	40.00	65.00	180	—
1832Mo JM	—	20.00	30.00	55.00	165	—
1833Mo MJ	—	25.00	40.00	80.00	200	—
1833Mo ML	—	450	650	950	2,000	—
1834/3Mo ML	—	25.00	35.00	60.00	175	—
1834Mo ML	—	20.00	30.00	55.00	165	—
1835Mo ML Narrow date	—	20.00	30.00	55.00	165	—
1835Mo ML Wide date	—	20.00	30.00	55.00	165	—
1836Mo ML	—	50.00	100	150	325	—
1836Mo ML/MF	—	50.00	100	150	325	—
1836Mo MF	—	30.00	50.00	90.00	220	—
1836Mo MF/ML	—	35.00	60.00	100	240	—
1837/6Mo ML	—	30.00	50.00	80.00	200	—
1837/6Mo MM	—	30.00	50.00	80.00	200	—
1837/6Mo MM/ML	—	30.00	50.00	80.00	200	—
1837/6Mo MM/MF	—	30.00	50.00	80.00	200	—
1837Mo ML	—	30.00	50.00	80.00	200	—
1837Mo MM	—	75.00	125	175	325	—
1838Mo MM	—	30.00	50.00	80.00	200	—
1838Mo ML	—	20.00	35.00	60.00	180	—
1838Mo ML/MM	—	20.00	35.00	60.00	180	—
1839Mo ML Narrow date	—	15.00	25.00	50.00	165	—
1839Mo ML Wide date	—	15.00	25.00	50.00	165	—
1840Mo ML	—	15.00	25.00	50.00	165	—
1841Mo ML	—	15.00	25.00	45.00	150	—
1842Mo ML	—	15.00	25.00	45.00	150	—
1842Mo MM	—	15.00	25.00	45.00	150	—
1843Mo MM	—	15.00	25.00	45.00	150	—
1844Mo MF/MM	—	—	—	—	—	—
1844Mo MF	—	15.00	25.00	45.00	150	—
1845/4Mo MF	—	15.00	25.00	45.00	150	—
1845Mo MF	—	15.00	25.00	45.00	150	—
1846/5Mo MF	—	15.00	25.00	50.00	165	—
1846Mo MF	—	15.00	25.00	50.00	165	—
1847/6Mo MF	—	2,000	3,550	—	—	—
1847Mo MF	—	1,650	3,000	5,000	7,500	—
1847Mo RC	—	20.00	30.00	55.00	165	—
1847Mo RC/MF	—	15.00	25.00	45.00	150	—
1848Mo GC	—	15.00	25.00	45.00	150	—
1849/8Mo GC	—	20.00	35.00	60.00	180	—
1849Mo GC	—	15.00	25.00	45.00	150	—
1850/40Mo GC	—	25.00	50.00	100	240	—
1850/49Mo GC	—	25.00	50.00	100	240	—
1850Mo GC	—	20.00	40.00	75.00	200	—
1851Mo GC	—	20.00	40.00	60.00	175	—
1852Mo GC	—	20.00	40.00	75.00	200	—
1853Mo GC	—	15.00	25.00	50.00	160	—
1854Mo GC	—	12.00	15.00	30.00	125	—
1855Mo GC	—	20.00	35.00	65.00	180	—
1855Mo GF	—	12.00	15.00	30.00	125	—
1855Mo GF/GC	—	12.00	15.00	30.00	125	—
1856/4Mo GF	—	15.00	25.00	45.00	145	—
1856/5Mo GF	—	15.00	25.00	45.00	145	—
1856Mo GF	—	12.00	15.00	30.00	125	—
1857Mo GF	—	10.00	15.00	30.00	125	—
1858/7Mo FH/GF	—	10.00	15.00	30.00	125	—
1858Mo FH Narrow date	—	10.00	15.00	30.00	125	—
1858Mo FH Wide date	—	10.00	15.00	30.00	125	—
1859Mo FH	—	10.00	15.00	30.00	125	—
1859/8Mo FH	—	25.00	50.00	100	240	—
1860/59Mo FH	—	15.00	20.00	30.00	125	—
1860Mo FH	—	10.00	15.00	30.00	125	—
1860Mo TH	—	12.00	18.00	40.00	145	—
1861Mo TH	—	12.00	18.00	40.00	145	—
1861Mo CH	—	10.00	15.00	20.00	75.00	—
1862Mo CH	—	10.00	15.00	20.00	75.00	—
1863Mo CH	—	10.00	15.00	20.00	75.00	—
1863Mo CH/TH	—	10.00	15.00	20.00	75.00	—
1863Mo TH	—	10.00	15.00	20.00	75.00	—

Date	Mintage	F	VF	XF	Unc	BU
1867Mo CH	—	10.00	15.00	20.00	65.00	—
1867Mo CH/TH	—	20.00	45.00	70.00	185	—
1868Mo CH	—	10.00	15.00	20.00	65.00	—
1868Mo PH	—	10.00	15.00	20.00	65.00	—
1868Mo CH/PH	—	10.00	15.00	20.00	65.00	—
1868Mo PH Narrow date	—	10.00	15.00	20.00	65.00	—
1868Mo PH Wide date	—	10.00	15.00	20.00	65.00	—
1869Mo CH	—	10.00	15.00	20.00	65.00	—
1873Mo MH	—	10.00	15.00	20.00	65.00	—
1873Mo MH/HH	—	12.00	18.00	25.00	75.00	—
1874/69Mo MH	—	20.00	45.00	70.00	185	—
1874Mo MH	—	12.00	18.00	25.00	75.00	—
1874Mo BH/MH	—	12.00	18.00	25.00	75.00	—
1874Mo BH	—	12.00	18.00	25.00	85.00	—
1875Mo BH	—	10.00	15.00	20.00	65.00	—
1876/4Mo BH	—	12.00	18.00	25.00	75.00	—
1876/5Mo BH	—	12.00	18.00	25.00	75.00	—
1876Mo BH	—	10.00	15.00	20.00	65.00	—
1877Mo MH	898,000	10.00	15.00	20.00	65.00	—
1877Mo MH/BH	Inc. above	12.00	18.00	25.00	75.00	—
1878Mo MH	2,154,000	10.00	15.00	20.00	65.00	—
1879/8Mo MH	—	10.00	15.00	20.00	75.00	—
1879Mo MH	—	10.00	15.00	20.00	65.00	—
1880/79Mo MH	—	15.00	20.00	30.00	75.00	—
1880Mo MH	—	10.00	15.00	20.00	75.00	—
1881Mo MH	5,712,000	10.00	15.00	20.00	65.00	—
1882/1Mo MH	2,746,000	12.00	18.00	25.00	75.00	—
1882Mo MH	Inc. above	10.00	15.00	20.00	65.00	—
1883/2Mo MH	2,726,000	12.00	18.00	25.00	85.00	—
1883Mo MH Narrow date	Inc. above	10.00	15.00	20.00	65.00	—
1883Mo MH Wide date	—	10.00	15.00	20.00	65.00	—
1884/3Mo MH	—	15.00	20.00	30.00	75.00	—
1884Mo MH	—	10.00	15.00	20.00	65.00	—
1885Mo MH	3,649,000	10.00	15.00	20.00	65.00	—
1886Mo MH	7,558,000	10.00	12.00	18.00	60.00	—
1887Mo MH	7,681,000	10.00	12.00	18.00	60.00	—
1888Mo MH Narrow date	7,179,000	10.00	12.00	18.00	60.00	—
1888Mo MH Wide date	—	10.00	12.00	18.00	60.00	—
1889Mo MH	7,332,000	10.00	15.00	20.00	65.00	—
1890Mo MH Narrow date	7,412,000	10.00	12.00	18.00	60.00	—
1890Mo AM Wide date	—	10.00	12.00	18.00	60.00	—
1890Mo AM	Inc. above	10.00	12.00	18.00	60.00	—
1891Mo AM	8,076,000	10.00	12.00	18.00	60.00	—
1892Mo AM	9,392,000	10.00	12.00	18.00	60.00	—
1893Mo AM	10,773,000	10.00	12.00	18.00	55.00	—
1894Mo AM	12,394,000	10.00	12.00	18.00	45.00	—
1895Mo AM	10,474,000	10.00	12.00	18.00	45.00	—
1895Mo AB	Inc. above	10.00	12.00	18.00	60.00	—
1896Mo AB	9,327,000	10.00	12.00	18.00	60.00	—
1896Mo AM	Inc. above	10.00	12.00	18.00	60.00	—
1897Mo AM	8,621,000	10.00	12.00	18.00	60.00	—

Date	Mintage	F	VF	XF	Unc	BU
1859 AE	—	500	900	1,750	—	—
Note: A in O of mint mark						
1860 AE	—	200	450	800	—	—
Note: A in O of mint mark						
1861O FR	—	125	250	550	1,350	—
1861 Oa FR	—	150	350	700	—	—
1862O FR	—	40.00	80.00	200	375	—
1862 Oa FR	—	65.00	125	250	450	—
1863O FR	—	30.00	60.00	100	250	—
1863O AE	—	30.00	60.00	100	250	—
1863 Oa AE	—	100	150	250	450	—
Note: A in O of mint mark						
1863 Oa AE	—	1,000	1,750	2,750	—	—
Note: A above O in mint mark						
1864 FR	—	25.00	50.00	75.00	200	—
1865 AE	—	1,850	3,000	—	—	—
1867 AE	—	40.00	80.00	150	400	—
1868 AE	—	40.00	80.00	150	400	—
1869 AE	—	30.00	60.00	100	250	—
1873 AE	—	200	300	550	1,350	—
1874 AE	142,000	15.00	30.00	50.00	200	—
1875/4 AE	131,000	25.00	50.00	75.00	200	—
1875 AE	Inc. above	15.00	30.00	40.00	135	—
1876 AE	140,000	20.00	35.00	55.00	200	—
1877 AE	139,000	20.00	30.00	50.00	200	—
1878 AE	125,000	20.00	30.00	50.00	200	—
1879 AE	153,000	20.00	30.00	50.00	200	—
1880 AE	143,000	15.00	30.00	45.00	150	—
1881 AE	134,000	20.00	35.00	60.00	150	—
1882 AE	100,000	20.00	35.00	60.00	150	—
1883 AE	122,000	15.00	30.00	45.00	150	—
1884 AE	142,000	15.00	30.00	50.00	150	—
1885 AE	158,000	15.00	25.00	40.00	135	—
1886 AE	120,000	15.00	30.00	45.00	150	—
1887/6 AE	115,000	25.00	50.00	80.00	200	—
1887 AE	Inc. above	15.00	25.00	40.00	135	—
1888 AE	145,000	15.00	25.00	40.00	135	—
1889 AE	150,000	20.00	30.00	60.00	175	—
1890 AE	181,000	20.00	30.00	60.00	175	—
1891 EN	160,000	15.00	25.00	40.00	135	—
1892 EN	120,000	15.00	25.00	40.00	135	—
1893 EN	66,000	45.00	75.00	115	300	—

KM# 377.12 8 REALES
27.0700 g., 0.9030 Silver .7859 oz. ASW **Obv:** Facing eagle
Note: Varieties exist.

Date	Mintage	F	VF	XF	Unc	BU
1827 Pi JS	—	3,800	—	—	—	—
1827 Pi SA	—	6,000	9,000	—	—	—
1828/7 Pi JS	—	275	425	650	1,250	—
1828 Pi JS	—	225	375	550	1,100	—
1829 Pi JS	—	35.00	65.00	125	250	—
1830 Pi JS	—	30.00	50.00	100	200	—

KM# 377.11 8 REALES
27.0700 g., 0.9030 Silver .7859 oz. ASW **Obv:** Facing eagle
Note: Mint mark O, Oa. Varieties exist.

Date	Mintage	F	VF	XF	Unc	BU
1858O AE	—	2,500	4,000	—	—	—
1858 Oa AE Unique	—	—	—	—	—	—

Date	Mintage	F	VF	XF	Unc	BU
1831/0 Pi JS	—	35.00	75.00	200	350	—
1831 Pi JS	—	25.00	35.00	75.00	200	—
1832/22 Pi JS	—	25.00	35.00	65.00	165	—
18/032 Pi JS	—	40.00	80.00	175	300	—
1832 Pi JS	—	25.00	35.00	65.00	165	—
1833/2 Pi JS	—	30.00	45.00	80.00	250	—
1833 Pi JS Narrow date	—	20.00	30.00	50.00	150	—
1833 Pi JS Wide date	—	20.00	30.00	50.00	150	—
1834/3 Pi JS	—	35.00	65.00	125	300	—
1834 Pi JS	—	15.00	25.00	50.00	150	—
1835/4 Pi JS	—	60.00	125	250	500	—
1835 Pi JS	—	20.00	30.00	65.00	175	—
Note: Denomination as 8R						
1835 Pi JS	—	15.00	25.00	50.00	150	—
Note: Denomination as 8Rs						
1836 Pi JS	—	20.00	30.00	55.00	150	—
1837 Pi JS	—	30.00	50.00	85.00	200	—
1838 Pi JS	—	20.00	30.00	55.00	150	—
1839 Pi JS	—	20.00	40.00	70.00	150	—
1840 Pi JS	—	20.00	30.00	60.00	150	—
1841 Pi JS	—	25.00	40.00	85.00	200	—
1841iP JS Error	—	200	350	550	—	—
1842/1 Pi JS	—	40.00	65.00	125	300	—
1842/1 Pi JS/PS	—	35.00	55.00	90.00	200	—
1842 Pi JS	—	30.00	50.00	80.00	175	—
Note: Eagle type of 1843						
1842 Pi PS	—	30.00	50.00	80.00	175	—
1842 Pi PS/JS	—	30.00	50.00	80.00	175	—
Note: Eagle type of 1841						
1843/2 Pi PS Round top 3	—	50.00	75.00	150	300	—
1843 Pi PS Flat top 3	—	60.00	100	200	475	—
1843 Pi AM Round top 3	—	20.00	30.00	55.00	150	—
1843 Pi AM Flat top 3	—	20.00	30.00	55.00	150	—
1844 Pi AM	—	20.00	30.00	55.00	150	—
1845/4 Pi AM	—	35.00	55.00	120	250	—
1845 Pi AM	—	25.00	50.00	100	225	—
1846/5 Pi AM	—	40.00	65.00	125	300	—
1846 Pi AM	—	15.00	25.00	50.00	150	—
1847 Pi AM	—	30.00	50.00	85.00	175	—
1848/7 Pi AM	—	30.00	60.00	100	200	—
1848 Pi AM	—	30.00	50.00	85.00	175	—
1849/8 Pi PS/AM	—	950	1,750	—	—	—
1849 Pi PS	—	950	1,750	—	—	—
1849 Pi MC/PS	—	60.00	125	250	500	—
1849 Pi AM	—	1,850	3,250	5,000	—	—
1849 Pi MC	—	60.00	125	250	500	—
1850 Pi MC	—	40.00	80.00	150	300	—
1851 Pi MC	—	75.00	150	275	550	—
1852 Pi MC	—	75.00	125	200	400	—
1853 Pi MC	—	150	275	400	850	—
1854 Pi MC	—	100	150	250	500	—
1855 Pi MC	—	100	150	250	500	—
1856 Pi MC	—	65.00	100	200	400	—
1857 Pi MC	—	400	700	1,250	—	—
1857 Pi PS/MC	—	150	250	450	1,000	—
1857 Pi PS	—	125	200	350	650	—
1858 Pi MC/PS	—	250	400	650	1,200	—
1858 Pi MC	—	250	400	650	1,200	—
1858 Pi PS	—	650	1,150	1,750	—	—
1859/8 Pi MC/PS	—	3,650	5,750	—	—	—
1859 Pi MC/PS	—	900	1,750	—	—	—
1859 Pi MC	—	2,000	3,500	5,000	—	—
1859 Pi PS/MC	—	800	1,500	2,500	—	—
1860 Pi FC Rare	—	—	—	—	—	—
1860 Pi FE Rare	—	—	—	—	—	—
1860 Pi MC	—	1,750	2,750	6,000	—	—
1860 Pi PS/FE	—	500	1,000	—	—	—
1860 Pi RO Rare	—	—	—	—	—	—
Note: Spink America Gerber sale 6-96 cleaned VF or better realized $33,000						
1860 Pi PS	—	400	600	900	1,750	—
1861 Pi PS	—	30.00	60.00	90.00	175	—

Date	Mintage	F	VF	XF	Unc	BU
1861 Pi RO	—	25.00	35.00	55.00	125	—
1862/1 Pi RO	—	20.00	25.00	50.00	125	—
1862 Pi RO	—	15.00	20.00	40.00	100	—
1862 Pi RO	—	15.00	20.00	40.00	100	—
Note: Oval O in RO						
1862 Pi RO	—	20.00	30.00	50.00	125	—
Note: Round O in RO, 6 is an inverted 9						
1863/2 Pi RO	—	25.00	35.00	65.00	150	—
1863 Pi RO	—	15.00	20.00	40.00	125	—
1863	—	25.00	35.00	55.00	125	—
Note: 6 over inverted 6						
1863 Pi FC	—	2,750	4,750	—	—	—
1864 Pi RO Rare	—	—	—	—	—	—
1867 Pi CA	—	300	500	—	—	—
1867 Pi LR	—	250	400	650	—	—
1867 Pi PS/CA	—	850	—	—	—	—
1867 Pi PS	—	30.00	60.00	125	275	—
1868/7 Pi PS	—	30.00	60.00	125	250	—
1868 Pi PS	—	20.00	30.00	50.00	125	—
1869/8 Pi PS	—	20.00	25.00	45.00	125	—
1869 Pi PS	—	15.00	20.00	40.00	125	—
1870/69 Pi PS	—	750	1,450	3,500	—	—
1870 Pi PS	—	650	1,250	2,500	—	—
1873 Pi MH	—	18.00	25.00	45.00	150	—
1874/3 Pi MH	—	25.00	50.00	120	250	—
1874 Pi MH	—	10.00	12.00	22.00	120	—
1875 Pi MH	—	10.00	12.00	22.00	100	—
1876/5 Pi MH	—	18.00	25.00	45.00	150	—
1876 Pi MH	—	10.00	12.00	22.00	100	—
1877/6 Pi MH	—	165	325	550	—	—
1877 Pi MH	1,018,000	10.00	12.00	22.00	120	—
1878 Pi MH	1,046,000	15.00	30.00	100	225	—
1879/8 Pi MH	—	15.00	20.00	30.00	125	—
1879 Pi MH	—	10.00	12.00	22.00	100	—
1879 Pi BE	—	25.00	50.00	75.00	150	—
1879 Pi MH	—	30.00	50.00	100	200	—
1880 Pi MR	—	250	375	750	—	—
1880 Pi MH/R	—	10.00	12.00	22.00	100	—
1880 Pi MH	—	10.00	12.00	22.00	100	—
1881 Pi MH/R	—	10.00	12.00	22.00	100	—
1881 Pi MH	2,100,000	10.00	12.00	22.00	100	—
1882/1 Pi MH	1,602,000	15.00	20.00	30.00	125	—
1882 Pi MH	Inc. above	10.00	12.00	22.00	100	—
1883/2 Pi MH	—	15.00	20.00	30.00	125	—
1883 Pi MH	1,545,000	10.00	12.00	22.00	100	—
1884/3 Pi MH	—	15.00	20.00	30.00	125	—
1884 Pi MH/MM	—	12.00	15.00	22.00	90.00	—
1884 Pi MH	—	10.00	12.00	20.00	80.00	—
1885/4 Pi MH	1,736,000	15.00	20.00	30.00	125	—
1885/8 Pi MH	Inc. above	15.00	20.00	30.00	125	—
1885 Pi MH	Inc. above	10.00	12.00	20.00	80.00	—
1885 Pi LC	Inc. above	12.00	18.00	25.00	100	—
1886 Pi LC	3,347,000	10.00	12.00	20.00	80.00	—
1886 Pi MR	Inc. above	10.00	12.00	20.00	80.00	—
1887 Pi MR	2,922,000	10.00	12.00	20.00	80.00	—
1888/7 Pi MR	—	15.00	20.00	30.00	125	—
1888 Pi MR	2,438,000	10.00	12.00	20.00	70.00	—
1889 Pi MR	2,103,000	10.00	12.00	20.00	80.00	—
1890 Pi MR	1,562,000	10.00	12.00	20.00	70.00	—
1891 Pi MR	1,184,000	10.00	12.00	20.00	70.00	—
1892 Pi MR	1,336,000	10.00	12.00	20.00	70.00	—
1893 Pi MR	530,000	10.00	12.00	20.00	80.00	—

KM# 377.13   8 REALES
27.0700 g., 0.9030 Silver .7859 oz. ASW **Obv:** Facing eagle
Note: Varieties exist.

Date	Mintage	F	VF	XF	Unc	BU
1825Zs AZ	—	25.00	35.00	65.00	175	—
1826/5Zs AZ	—	25.00	45.00	85.00	200	—
1826Zs AZ	—	100	200	400	800	—
1826Zs AV	—	175	350	600	1,500	—
1826/5Zs AO/AZ	—	300	600	1,000	2,000	—
1826Zs AO	—	200	350	750	2,000	—
1827Zs AO/AZ	—	35.00	50.00	125	250	—
1827Zs AO	—	25.00	45.00	85.00	200	—
1828Zs AO	—	15.00	20.00	45.00	165	—
1829Zs AO	—	15.00	20.00	45.00	165	—
1829Zs OV	—	50.00	90.00	150	300	—
1830Zs OV	—	15.00	20.00	45.00	165	—
1831Zs OV	—	25.00	50.00	90.00	200	—

Date	Mintage	F	VF	XF	Unc	BU
1831Zs OM	—	15.00	25.00	55.00	165	—
1832/1Zs OM	—	20.00	25.00	45.00	165	—
1832Zs OM	—	15.00	20.00	40.00	150	—
1833/2Zs OM	—	20.00	30.00	45.00	165	—
1833Zs OM/MM	—	15.00	25.00	40.00	150	—
1833Zs OM	—	15.00	20.00	35.00	150	—
1834Zs OM	—	15.00	20.00	35.00	150	—
1835Zs OM	—	15.00	20.00	40.00	150	—
1836/4Zs OM	—	20.00	30.00	50.00	165	—
1836/5Zs OM	—	20.00	30.00	50.00	165	—
1836Zs OM	—	15.00	20.00	35.00	150	—
1837Zs OM	—	15.00	20.00	35.00	150	—
1838/7Zs OM	—	20.00	30.00	45.00	165	—
1838Zs OM	—	15.00	20.00	35.00	150	—
1839Zs OM	—	15.00	20.00	35.00	150	—
1840Zs OM	—	15.00	20.00	35.00	150	—
1841Zs OM	—	15.00	20.00	35.00	150	—
1842Zs OM	—	15.00	20.00	35.00	150	—
Note: Eagle type of 1841						
1842Zs OM	—	15.00	20.00	35.00	150	—
Note: Eagle type of 1843						
1843Zs OM	—	15.00	20.00	35.00	150	—
1844Zs OM	—	15.00	20.00	35.00	150	—
1845Zs OM	—	15.00	20.00	35.00	150	—
1846Zs OM	—	15.00	20.00	35.00	150	—
1847Zs OM	—	15.00	20.00	35.00	150	—
1848/7Zs OM	—	20.00	30.00	45.00	165	—
1848Zs OM	—	15.00	20.00	35.00	150	—
1849Zs OM	—	15.00	20.00	35.00	150	—
1850Zs OM	—	15.00	20.00	35.00	150	—
1851Zs OM	—	15.00	20.00	35.00	150	—
1852Zs OM	—	15.00	20.00	35.00	150	—
1853Zs OM	—	30.00	45.00	75.00	200	—
1854/3Zs OM	—	20.00	30.00	60.00	175	—
1854Zs OM	—	15.00	25.00	45.00	165	—
1855Zs OM	—	20.00	30.00	60.00	175	—
1855Zs MO	—	30.00	60.00	90.00	200	—
1856/5Zs MO	—	20.00	30.00	45.00	165	—
1856Zs MO	—	15.00	20.00	35.00	150	—
1857/5Zs MO	—	20.00	30.00	45.00	165	—
1857Zs MO	—	15.00	20.00	35.00	150	—
1858/7Zs MO	—	15.00	20.00	35.00	150	—
1858Zs MO	—	15.00	20.00	35.00	150	—
1859/8Zs MO	—	15.00	20.00	35.00	150	—
1859Zs MO	—	15.00	20.00	35.00	150	—
1859Zs VL/MO	—	25.00	50.00	75.00	175	—
1859Zs VL	—	20.00	40.00	60.00	165	—
1860/50Zs MO	—	10.00	12.00	20.00	80.00	—
1860/59Zs MO	—	10.00	12.00	20.00	80.00	—
1860Zs MO	—	10.00	12.00	20.00	80.00	—
1860Zs VL/MO	—	10.00	12.00	20.00	80.00	—
1860Zs VL	—	10.00	12.00	20.00	80.00	—
1861/0Zs VL/MO	—	10.00	12.00	20.00	80.00	—
1861Zs VL	—	10.00	12.00	20.00	80.00	—
1861/0Zs VL	—	10.00	12.00	20.00	80.00	—
1862/1Zs VL	—	15.00	20.00	35.00	100	—
1862Zs VL	—	10.00	12.00	20.00	80.00	—
1863Zs VL	—	10.00	12.00	20.00	80.00	—
1863Zs MO	—	10.00	12.00	20.00	80.00	—
1864/3Zs VL	—	15.00	20.00	35.00	100	—
1864Zs VL	—	10.00	12.00	20.00	80.00	—
1864Zs MO	—	15.00	20.00	35.00	100	—
1865/4Zs MO	—	200	450	800	1,550	—
1865Zs MO	—	150	300	600	1,250	—
1866Zs VL	—	—	—	—	—	—
Note: Contemporary counterfeit						
1867Zs JS Rare	—	—	—	—	—	—
1868Zs JS	—	10.00	12.00	20.00	80.00	—
1868Zs YH	—	10.00	12.00	20.00	80.00	—
1869Zs YH	—	10.00	12.00	20.00	80.00	—
1870Zs YH Rare	—	—	—	—	—	—
1873Zs YH	—	10.00	12.00	20.00	80.00	—
1874Zs YH	—	10.00	12.00	20.00	80.00	—
1874Zs JA/YA	—	10.00	12.00	20.00	80.00	—
1874Zs JA	—	10.00	12.00	20.00	80.00	—
1875Zs JA	—	10.00	12.00	20.00	80.00	—
1876Zs JA	—	10.00	12.00	20.00	80.00	—
1876Zs JS	—	10.00	12.00	20.00	80.00	—
1877Zs JS	2,700,000	10.00	12.00	20.00	80.00	—

Date	Mintage	F	VF	XF	Unc	BU
1878Zs JS	2,310,000	10.00	12.00	20.00	80.00	—
1879/8Zs JS	—	15.00	20.00	35.00	100	—
1879Zs JS	—	10.00	12.00	20.00	80.00	—
1880Zs JS	—	10.00	12.00	20.00	80.00	—
1881Zs JS	5,592,000	10.00	12.00	20.00	80.00	—
1882/1Zs JS	2,485,000	15.00	20.00	35.00	100	—
1882Zs JS Straight J	Inc. above	10.00	12.00	20.00	65.00	—
1882Zs JS Full J	Inc. above	10.00	12.00	20.00	65.00	—
1883/2Zs JS	2,563,000	15.00	20.00	35.00	100	—
1883Zs JS	Inc. above	10.00	12.00	20.00	80.00	—
1884Zs JS	—	10.00	12.00	20.00	80.00	—
1885Zs JS	2,252,000	10.00	12.00	20.00	65.00	—
1886/5Zs JS	5,303,000	15.00	20.00	35.00	100	—
1886/8Zs JS	Inc. above	15.00	20.00	35.00	100	—
1886Zs JS	Inc. above	10.00	12.00	20.00	65.00	—
1886Zs FZ	Inc. above	10.00	12.00	20.00	65.00	—
1887Zs FZ	4,733,000	10.00	12.00	20.00	65.00	—
1887Z FZ	Inc. above	20.00	30.00	50.00	100	—
1888/7Zs FZ	5,132,000	12.00	15.00	25.00	80.00	—
1888Zs FZ	Inc. above	10.00	12.00	20.00	65.00	—
1889Zs FZ	4,344,000	10.00	12.00	20.00	65.00	—
1890Zs FZ	3,887,000	10.00	12.00	20.00	65.00	—
1891Zs FZ	4,114,000	10.00	12.00	20.00	65.00	—
1892/1Zs FZ	4,238,000	12.00	15.00	25.00	80.00	—
1892Zs FZ Narrow date	Inc. above	10.00	12.00	20.00	65.00	—
1892Zs FZ Wide date	—	10.00	12.00	20.00	65.00	—
1893Zs FZ	3,872,000	10.00	12.00	20.00	65.00	—
1894Zs FZ	3,081,000	10.00	12.00	20.00	65.00	—
1895Zs FZ	4,718,000	10.00	12.00	20.00	65.00	—
1896Zs FZ	4,226,000	10.00	12.00	20.00	55.00	—
1897Zs FZ	4,877,000	10.00	12.00	20.00	55.00	—

KM# 378   1/2 ESCUDO
1.6900 g., 0.8750 Gold .0475 oz. AGW **Obv:** Facing eagle

Date	Mintage	VG	F	VF	XF	Unc
1848C CE	—	35.00	50.00	75.00	150	—
1853C CE	—	35.00	50.00	75.00	150	—
1854C CE Revised eagle	—	35.00	50.00	75.00	150	—
Note: Dates 1854-1870 of this type display the revised eagle						
1856C CE	—	50.00	100	150	250	—
1857C CE	—	35.00	50.00	75.00	150	—
1859C CE	—	35.00	50.00	75.00	150	—
1860C CE	—	35.00	50.00	75.00	150	—
1862C CE	—	35.00	50.00	75.00	125	—
1863C CE	—	35.00	50.00	75.00	125	—
1866C CE	—	35.00	50.00	75.00	125	—
1867C CE	—	35.00	50.00	75.00	125	—
1870C CE	—	75.00	150	275	450	—

KM# 378.1   1/2 ESCUDO
1.6900 g., 0.8750 Gold .0475 oz. AGW **Obv:** Facing eagle

Date	Mintage	VG	F	VF	XF	Unc
1833Do RM/RL	—	35.00	50.00	75.00	150	—
1834/1Do RM	—	35.00	50.00	75.00	150	—
1834/3Do RM	—	35.00	50.00	75.00	150	—
1835/2Do RM	—	35.00	50.00	75.00	150	—
1835/3Do RM	—	35.00	50.00	75.00	150	—
1835/4Do RM	—	35.00	50.00	75.00	150	—
1836/4Do RM	—	35.00	50.00	75.00	150	—
1837Do RM	—	35.00	50.00	75.00	150	—
1838Do RM	—	40.00	60.00	100	175	—
1843Do RM	—	40.00	60.00	100	175	—
1844/33Do RM	—	40.00	60.00	100	175	—
1844/33Do R,/RL	—	65.00	125	275	450	—
1845Do CM	—	40.00	60.00	100	175	—
1846Do RM	—	40.00	60.00	100	175	—
1848Do RM	—	40.00	60.00	100	175	—
1850/33Do JMR	—	40.00	60.00	100	175	—
1851Do JMR	—	40.00	60.00	100	200	—
1852Do JMR	—	40.00	60.00	100	175	—

Date	Mintage	VG	F	VF	XF	Unc
1853/33Do CP	—	75.00	150	300	500	—
1853Do CP	—	35.00	50.00	75.00	150	—
1854Do CP	—	35.00	50.00	75.00	150	—
1855Do CP	—	35.00	50.00	75.00	150	—
1859Do CP	—	35.00	50.00	75.00	150	—
1861Do CP	—	35.00	50.00	75.00	150	—
1862Do CP	—	35.00	50.00	75.00	150	—
1864Do LT	—	75.00	125	250	400	—

KM# 378.2 1/2 ESCUDO
1.6900 g., 0.8750 Gold .0475 oz. AGW **Obv:** Facing eagle

Date	Mintage	VG	F	VF	XF	Unc
1825Ga FS	—	40.00	60.00	100	175	—
1829Ga FS	—	40.00	60.00	100	175	—
1831Ga FS	—	40.00	60.00	100	175	—
1834Ga FS	—	40.00	60.00	100	175	—
1835Ga FS	—	40.00	60.00	100	175	—
1837Ga JG	—	40.00	60.00	100	175	—
1838Ga JG	—	40.00	60.00	100	175	—
1839Ga JG	—	—	—	—	—	—
1842Ga JG	—	—	—	—	—	—
1847Ga JG	—	40.00	60.00	100	175	—
1850Ga JG	—	35.00	50.00	75.00	150	—
1852Ga JG	—	35.00	50.00	75.00	150	—
1859Ga JG	—	40.00	60.00	100	175	—
1861Ga JG	—	35.00	50.00	75.00	150	—

KM# 378.3 1/2 ESCUDO
1.6900 g., 0.8750 Gold .0475 oz. AGW **Obv:** Facing eagle

Date	Mintage	VG	F	VF	XF	Unc
1846GC MP	—	50.00	75.00	100	175	—
1847GC MP	—	50.00	75.00	100	175	—
1848/7GC MP	—	50.00	75.00	100	200	—
1850GC MP	—	50.00	75.00	100	175	—
1851GC MP	—	50.00	75.00	100	175	—
Revised eagle						

KM# 378.4 1/2 ESCUDO
1.6900 g., 0.8750 Gold .0475 oz. AGW **Obv:** Facing eagle

Date	Mintage	VG	F	VF	XF	Unc
1845Go PM	—	30.00	40.00	65.00	125	—
1849Go PF	—	30.00	40.00	65.00	125	—
1851/41Go PF	—	30.00	40.00	65.00	125	—
1851Go PF	—	30.00	40.00	65.00	125	—
1852Go PF	—	30.00	40.00	65.00	125	—
1853Go PF	—	30.00	40.00	65.00	125	—
1855Go PF	—	30.00	50.00	80.00	150	—
1857Go PF	—	30.00	40.00	65.00	125	—
1858/7Go PF	—	30.00	40.00	65.00	125	—
1859Go PF	—	30.00	40.00	65.00	125	—
1860Go PF	—	30.00	40.00	65.00	125	—
1861Go PF	—	30.00	40.00	65.00	125	—
1862/1Go YE	—	30.00	40.00	65.00	125	—
1863Go PF	—	30.00	50.00	80.00	150	—
1863Go YF	—	30.00	40.00	65.00	125	—

KM# 378.5 1/2 ESCUDO
1.6900 g., 0.8750 Gold .0475 oz. AGW **Obv:** Facing eagle

Date	Mintage	VG	F	VF	XF	Unc
1825/1Mo JM	—	50.00	75.00	125	200	—
1825/4Mo JM	—	50.00	75.00	125	200	—
1825Mo JM	—	30.00	40.00	80.00	150	—
1827/6Mo JM	—	30.00	40.00	80.00	150	—
1827Mo JM	—	30.00	40.00	80.00	150	—
1829Mo JM	—	30.00	40.00	80.00	150	—

Date	Mintage	VG	F	VF	XF	Unc
1831/0Mo JM	—	30.00	40.00	80.00	150	—
1831Mo JM	—	30.00	40.00	60.00	125	—
1832Mo	—	30.00	40.00	60.00	125	—
1833Mo MJ Olive and oak branches reversed	—	30.00	50.00	90.00	175	—
1834Mo ML	—	30.00	40.00	60.00	125	—
1835Mo ML	—	30.00	40.00	80.00	150	—
1838Mo ML	—	30.00	50.00	90.00	175	—
1839Mo ML	—	30.00	50.00	90.00	175	—
1840Mo ML	—	30.00	40.00	60.00	125	—
1841Mo ML	—	30.00	40.00	60.00	125	—
1842Mo ML	—	30.00	40.00	80.00	150	—
1842Mo MM	—	30.00	40.00	80.00	150	—
1843Mo MM	—	30.00	40.00	60.00	125	—
1844Mo MF	—	30.00	40.00	60.00	125	—
1845Mo MF	—	30.00	40.00	60.00	125	—
1846/5Mo MF	—	30.00	40.00	60.00	125	—
1846Mo MF	—	30.00	40.00	60.00	125	—
1848Mo GC	—	30.00	40.00	60.00	125	—
1850Mo GC	—	30.00	40.00	60.00	125	—
1851Mo GC	—	30.00	40.00	60.00	125	—
1852Mo GC	—	30.00	40.00	60.00	125	—
1853Mo GC	—	30.00	40.00	60.00	125	—
1854Mo GC	—	30.00	40.00	60.00	125	—
1855Mo GF	—	30.00	40.00	60.00	125	—
1856/4Mo GF	—	30.00	40.00	60.00	125	—
1857Mo GF	—	30.00	40.00	60.00	125	—
1858/7Mo FH/GF	—	35.00	50.00	75.00	150	—
1858Mo FH	—	30.00	40.00	60.00	125	—
1859Mo FH	—	30.00	40.00	60.00	125	—
1860/59Mo FH	—	30.00	40.00	60.00	125	—
1861Mo CH/FH	—	30.00	40.00	80.00	150	—
1862Mo CH	—	30.00	40.00	60.00	125	—
1863/57Mo CH/GF	—	30.00	40.00	60.00	125	—
1868/58Mo PH	—	30.00	40.00	80.00	150	—
1869/59Mo CH	—	30.00	40.00	80.00	150	—

KM# 378.6 1/2 ESCUDO
1.6900 g., 0.8750 Gold .0475 oz. AGW **Obv:** Facing eagle

Date	Mintage	VG	F	VF	XF	Unc
1860Zs VL	—	35.00	50.00	75.00	150	—
1862/1Zs VL	—	35.00	50.00	75.00	150	—
1862Zs VL	—	30.00	40.00	65.00	125	—

KM# 379 ESCUDO
3.3800 g., 0.8750 Gold .0950 oz. AGW **Obv:** Facing eagle

Date	Mintage	VG	F	VF	XF	Unc
1846C CE	—	75.00	100	200	350	—
1847C CE	—	50.00	75.00	125	175	—
1848C CE	—	50.00	75.00	125	175	—
1849/8C CE	—	60.00	100	150	225	—
1850C CE	—	50.00	75.00	125	175	—
1851C CE	—	60.00	100	150	225	—
1853/1C CE	—	60.00	100	150	225	—
1854C CE	—	50.00	75.00	125	175	—
1856/5/4C CE	—	60.00	100	150	225	—
1856C CE	—	50.00	75.00	125	175	—
1857/1C CE	—	60.00	100	150	225	—
1857C CE	—	50.00	75.00	125	175	—
1861C PV	—	50.00	75.00	125	175	—
1862C CE	—	50.00	75.00	125	175	—
1863C CE	—	50.00	75.00	125	175	—
1866C CE	—	50.00	75.00	125	175	—
1870C CE	—	50.00	75.00	125	175	—

KM# 379.1 ESCUDO
3.3800 g., 0.8750 Gold .0950 oz. AGW **Obv:** Facing eagle

Date	Mintage	VG	F	VF	XF	Unc
1832Do R.L.	—	—	—	—	—	—
1833/2Do RM/R.L.	—	75.00	125	200	300	—
1834Do RM	—	60.00	100	150	200	—
1835Do RM	—	—	—	—	—	—
1836Do RM/RL	—	60.00	100	150	200	—
1838Do RM	—	60.00	100	150	200	—
1846/38Do RM	—	75.00	125	200	300	—
1850Do JMR	—	75.00	125	175	225	—
1851/31Do JMR	—	75.00	125	200	300	—
1851Do JMR	—	75.00	125	175	225	—
1853Do CP	—	75.00	125	175	225	—
1854/34Do CP	—	75.00	125	175	225	—
1854/44Do CP/RP	—	75.00	125	175	225	—
1855Do CP	—	75.00	125	175	225	—
1859Do CP	—	75.00	125	175	225	—
1861Do CP	—	75.00	125	175	225	—
1864Do LT/CP Rare	—	—	—	—	—	—

KM# 379.2 ESCUDO
3.3800 g., 0.8750 Gold .0950 oz. AGW **Obv:** Facing eagle

Date	Mintage	VG	F	VF	XF	Unc
1825Ga FS	—	60.00	90.00	125	200	—
1826Ga FS	—	60.00	90.00	125	200	—
1829Ga FS	—	—	—	—	—	—
1831Ga FS	—	60.00	90.00	125	200	—
1834Ga FS	—	60.00	90.00	125	200	—
1835Ga JG	—	60.00	90.00	125	200	—
1842Ga JG/MC	—	60.00	90.00	125	200	—
1843Ga MC	—	60.00	90.00	125	200	—
1847Ga JG	—	60.00	90.00	125	200	—
1848/7Ga JG	—	60.00	90.00	125	200	—
1849Ga JG	—	60.00	90.00	125	200	—
1850/40Ga JG	—	65.00	125	225	325	—
1850Ga JG	—	60.00	90.00	125	200	—
1852/1Ga JG	—	60.00	90.00	125	200	—
1856Ga JG	—	60.00	90.00	125	200	—
1857Ga JG	—	60.00	90.00	125	200	—
1859/7Ga JG	—	60.00	90.00	125	200	—
1860/59Ga JG	—	65.00	100	175	275	—
1860Ga	—	60.00	90.00	125	200	—

KM# 379.3 ESCUDO
3.3800 g., 0.8750 Gold .0950 oz. AGW **Obv:** Facing eagle

Date	Mintage	VG	F	VF	XF	Unc
1844GC MP	—	75.00	100	175	250	—
1845GC MP	—	75.00	100	175	250	—
1846GC MP	—	75.00	100	175	250	—
1847GC MP	—	75.00	100	175	250	—
1848GC MP	—	75.00	100	175	250	—
1849GC MP	—	75.00	100	175	250	—
1850GC MP	—	75.00	100	175	250	—
1851GC MP Revised eagle	—	75.00	100	175	250	—

KM# 379.4 ESCUDO
3.3800 g., 0.8750 Gold .0950 oz. AGW **Obv:** Facing eagle

Date	Mintage	VG	F	VF	XF	Unc
1845Go PM	—	60.00	75.00	125	200	—
1849Go PF	—	60.00	75.00	125	200	—
1851Go PF	—	60.00	75.00	125	200	—
1853Go PF	—	60.00	75.00	125	200	—
1860Go PF	—	75.00	125	200	300	—
1862Go PE	—	60.00	75.00	125	200	—

KM# 379.5 ESCUDO
3.3800 g., 0.8750 Gold .0950 oz. AGW **Obv:** Facing eagle

Date	Mintage	VG	F	VF	XF	Unc
1825Mo JM	—	50.00	70.00	100	150	—
1827/6Mo JM	—	50.00	70.00	100	150	—
1827Mo JM	—	50.00	70.00	100	150	—
1830/29Mo JM	—	50.00	70.00	100	150	—
1831Mo JM	—	50.00	70.00	100	150	—
1832Mo JM	—	50.00	70.00	125	175	—
1833Mo MJ	—	50.00	70.00	100	150	—
1834Mo ML	—	50.00	70.00	125	175	—
1841Mo ML	—	50.00	70.00	125	175	—
1843Mo MM	—	50.00	70.00	100	150	—
1845Mo MF	—	50.00	70.00	100	150	—
1846/5Mo MF	—	50.00	70.00	100	150	—
1848Mo GC	—	50.00	70.00	125	175	—
1850Mo GC	—	50.00	70.00	125	175	—
1856/4Mo GF	—	50.00	70.00	100	150	—
1856/5Mo GF	—	50.00	70.00	100	150	—
1856Mo GF	—	50.00	70.00	100	150	—
1858Mo FH	—	50.00	70.00	125	175	—
1859Mo FH	—	50.00	70.00	100	150	—
1860Mo TH	—	50.00	70.00	125	175	—
1861Mo CH	—	50.00	70.00	100	150	—
1862Mo CH	—	50.00	70.00	125	175	—
1863Mo TH	—	50.00	70.00	100	150	—
1869Mo CH	—	50.00	70.00	100	150	—

KM# 379.6 ESCUDO
3.3800 g., 0.8750 Gold .0950 oz. AGW **Obv:** Facing eagle
Note: Struck at Zacatecas Mint, mint mark Zs.

Date	Mintage	VG	F	VF	XF	Unc
1853Zs OM	—	100	125	200	300	—
1860/59Zs VL V is inverted A	—	75.00	100	200	350	—
1860Zs VL	—	75.00	100	150	200	—
1862Zs VL	—	75.00	100	150	200	—

KM# 380 2 ESCUDOS
6.7700 g., 0.8750 Gold .1904 oz. AGW **Obv:** Facing eagle

Date	Mintage	VG	F	VF	XF	Unc
1846C CE	—	100	150	225	325	—
1847C CE	—	100	150	225	325	—
1848C CE	—	100	150	225	325	—
1852C CE	—	100	150	225	325	—
1854C CE	—	100	175	250	375	—
1856/4C CE	—	100	175	250	375	—
1857C CE	—	100	150	225	325	—

KM# 380.1 2 ESCUDOS
6.7700 g., 0.8750 Gold .1904 oz. AGW **Obv:** Facing eagle

Date	Mintage	VG	F	VF	XF	Unc
1833Do RM	—	300	450	700	1,200	—
1837/4Do RM	—	—	—	—	—	—
1837Do RM	—	—	—	—	—	—
1844Do RM	—	275	400	600	1,000	—

KM# 380.2 2 ESCUDOS
6.7700 g., 0.8750 Gold .1904 oz. AGW **Obv:** Facing eagle

Date	Mintage	VG	F	VF	XF	Unc
1828EoMo LF	—	700	1,000	1,750	2,500	—

KM# 380.3 2 ESCUDOS
6.7700 g., 0.8750 Gold .1904 oz. AGW **Obv:** Facing eagle

Date	Mintage	VG	F	VF	XF	Unc
1835Ga FS	—	100	150	225	325	—
1836/5Ga JG	—	125	200	400	500	—
1839/5Ga JG	—	—	—	—	—	—
1839Ga JG	—	100	150	200	285	—
1840Ga MC	—	100	150	200	285	—
1841Ga MC	—	100	150	250	400	—
1847/6Ga JG	—	100	150	225	300	—
1848/7Ga JG	—	100	150	225	300	—
1850/40Ga JG	—	100	150	200	285	—
1851Ga JG	—	100	150	200	285	—
1852Ga JG	—	100	150	225	325	—
1853Ga JG	—	100	150	200	285	—
1854/2Ga JG	—	—	—	—	—	—
1858Ga JG	—	100	150	200	285	—
1859/8Ga JG	—	100	150	225	300	—
1859Ga JG	—	100	150	200	285	—
1860/50Ga JG	—	100	150	225	300	—
1860Ga JG	—	100	150	225	300	—
1861/59Ga JG	—	100	150	200	285	—
1861/0Ga JG	—	100	150	200	285	—
1863/1Ga JG	—	100	150	200	285	—
1870Ga IC	—	100	150	200	285	—

KM# 380.4 2 ESCUDOS
6.7700 g., 0.8750 Gold .1904 oz. AGW **Obv:** Facing eagle

Date	Mintage	VG	F	VF	XF	Unc
1844GC MP	—	150	200	275	400	—
1845GC MP	—	750	1,250	2,000	3,000	—
1846GC MP	—	750	1,250	2,000	3,000	—
1847GC MP	—	125	175	350	500	—
1848GC MP	—	150	200	350	450	—
1849GC MP	—	150	200	300	400	—
1850GC MP	—	150	200	300	400	—

KM# 380.5 2 ESCUDOS
6.7700 g., 0.8750 Gold .1904 oz. AGW **Obv:** Facing eagle

Date	Mintage	VG	F	VF	XF	Unc
1845Go PM	—	100	150	250	400	—
1849Go PF	—	100	150	250	400	—
1853Go PF	—	100	150	250	400	—
1856Go PF	—	100	150	250	400	—
1859Go PF	—	100	150	250	400	—
1860/59Go PF	—	100	150	250	400	—
1860Go PF	—	100	150	250	400	—
1862Go YE	—	100	150	250	400	—

KM# 380.6 2 ESCUDOS
6.7700 g., 0.8750 Gold .1904 oz. AGW **Obv:** Facing eagle

Date	Mintage	VG	F	VF	XF	Unc
1861Ho FM	—	500	1,000	1,500	2,000	—

KM# 380.7 2 ESCUDOS
6.7700 g., 0.8750 Gold .1904 oz. AGW **Obv:** Facing eagle

Date	Mintage	VG	F	VF	XF	Unc
1825Mo JM	—	100	150	200	285	—
1827/6Mo JM	—	100	150	200	285	—
1827Mo JM	—	100	150	200	285	—
1830/29Mo JM	—	100	150	200	285	—
1831Mo JM	—	100	150	200	285	—
1833Mo ML	—	100	150	200	285	—
1841Mo ML	—	100	150	200	285	—
1844Mo MF	—	100	150	200	285	—
1845Mo MF	—	100	150	200	285	—
1846Mo MF	—	125	200	400	600	—
1848Mo GC	—	100	150	200	285	—
1850Mo GC	—	100	150	200	285	—
1856/5Mo GF	—	100	150	200	285	—
1856Mo GF	—	100	150	200	285	—
1858Mo FH	—	100	150	200	285	—
1859Mo FH	—	100	150	200	285	—
1861Mo TH	—	100	150	200	285	—
1861Mo CH	—	100	150	200	300	—
1862Mo CH	—	100	150	200	300	—
1863Mo TH	—	100	150	200	300	—
1868Mo PH	—	100	150	200	300	—
1869Mo CH	—	100	150	200	300	—

KM# 380.8 2 ESCUDOS
6.7700 g., 0.8750 Gold .1904 oz. AGW **Obv:** Facing eagle

Date	Mintage	VG	F	VF	XF	Unc
1860Zs VL	—	150	300	600	1,200	—
1862Zs VL	—	250	500	800	1,200	—
1864Zs MO	—	150	300	600	1,200	—

KM# 381 4 ESCUDOS
13.5400 g., 0.8750 Gold .3809 oz. AGW **Obv:** Facing eagle

Date	Mintage	VG	F	VF	XF	Unc
1846C CE	—	1,200	1,700	—	—	—
1847C CE	—	400	650	850	1,350	—
1848C CE	—	600	900	1,250	1,850	—

KM# 381.1 4 ESCUDOS
13.5400 g., 0.8750 Gold .3809 oz. AGW **Obv:** Facing eagle

Date	Mintage	VG	F	VF	XF	Unc
1832Do RM/LR Rare	—	—	—	—	—	—
1832Do RM	—	600	900	1,250	1,850	—
1833Do RM/RL Rare	—	—	—	—	—	—
1852Do JMR Rare	—	—	—	—	—	—

KM# 381.2 4 ESCUDOS
13.5400 g., 0.8750 Gold .3809 oz. AGW **Obv:** Facing eagle

Date	Mintage	VG	F	VF	XF	Unc
1844Ga MC	—	500	750	1,000	1,600	—
1844Ga JG	—	400	650	850	1,350	—

KM# 381.3 4 ESCUDOS
13.5400 g., 0.8750 Gold .3809 oz. AGW **Obv:** Facing eagle

Date	Mintage	VG	F	VF	XF	Unc
1844GC MP	—	400	650	850	1,350	—
1845GC MP	—	350	500	700	1,000	—
1846GC MP	—	400	650	850	1,350	—
1848GC MP	—	400	650	850	1,350	—
1850GC MP	—	500	750	1,000	1,600	—

KM# 381.4 4 ESCUDOS
13.5400 g., 0.8750 Gold .3809 oz. AGW **Obv:** Facing eagle

Date	Mintage	VG	F	VF	XF	Unc
1829/8Go MJ	—	200	300	450	850	—
1829Go JM	—	200	300	450	850	—
1829Go MJ	—	200	300	450	850	—

Date	Mintage	VG	F	VF	XF	Unc
1831Go MJ	—	200	300	450	850	—
1832Go MJ	—	200	300	450	850	—
1833Go MJ	—	200	300	500	900	—
1834Go PJ	—	250	450	650	1,000	—
1835Go PJ	—	250	450	650	1,000	—
1836Go PJ	—	200	300	500	900	—
1837Go PJ	—	200	300	500	900	—
1838Go PJ	—	200	300	500	900	—
1839Go PJ	—	250	450	650	1,000	—
1840Go PJ	—	200	300	500	900	—
1841Go PJ	—	250	450	650	1,000	—
1845Go PM	—	200	300	500	900	—
1847/5Go YE	—	250	450	650	1,000	—
1847Go PM	—	250	450	650	1,000	—
1849Go PF	—	250	450	650	1,000	—
1851Go PF	—	250	450	650	1,000	—
1852Go PF	—	200	300	500	900	—
1855Go PF	—	200	300	500	900	—
1857/5Go PF	—	200	300	500	900	—
1858/7Go PF	—	200	300	500	900	—
1858Go PF	—	200	300	500	900	—
1859/7Go PF	—	250	450	650	1,000	—
1860Go PF	—	275	475	750	1,200	—
1862Go YE	—	200	300	500	900	—
1863Go YF	—	200	300	500	900	—

KM# 381.5 4 ESCUDOS
13.5400 g., 0.8750 Gold .3809 oz. AGW **Obv:** Facing eagle

Date	Mintage	VG	F	VF	XF	Unc
1861Ho FM	—	1,000	1,500	2,500	3,750	—

KM# 381.6 4 ESCUDOS
13.5400 g., 0.8750 Gold .3809 oz. AGW **Obv:** Facing eagle

Date	Mintage	VG	F	VF	XF	Unc
1825Mo JM	—	200	300	525	950	—
1827/6Mo JM	—	200	300	500	900	—
1829Mo JM	—	200	350	650	1,000	—
1831Mo JM	—	200	350	650	1,000	—
1832Mo JM	—	275	475	750	1,200	—
1844Mo MF	—	200	350	650	1,000	—
1850Mo GC	—	200	350	650	1,000	—
1856Mo GF	—	200	300	500	900	—
1857/6Mo GF	—	200	300	500	900	—
1857Mo GF	—	200	300	500	900	—
1858Mo FH	—	200	350	650	1,000	—
1859/8Mo FH	—	200	350	650	1,000	—
1861Mo CH	—	400	800	1,200	1,750	—
1863Mo CH	—	200	350	650	1,000	—
1868Mo PH	—	200	300	500	900	—
1869Mo CH	—	200	300	500	900	—

KM# 381.7 4 ESCUDOS
13.5400 g., 0.8750 Gold .3809 oz. AGW **Obv:** Facing eagle
Note: Mint mark O, Oa.

Date	Mintage	VG	F	VF	XF	Unc
1861O FR	—	1,500	2,500	4,000	6,500	—

KM# 381.8   4 ESCUDOS
13.5400 g., 0.8750 Gold .3809 oz. AGW   **Obv:** Facing eagle

Date	Mintage	VG	F	VF	XF	Unc
1860Zs VL Rare	—	—	—	—	—	—
1862Zs VL	—	750	1,250	2,250	3,750	—

KM# 383   8 ESCUDOS
27.0700 g., 0.8750 Gold .7616 oz. AGW   **Obv:** Facing eagle

Date	Mintage	F	VF	XF	Unc	BU
1864A PG	—	650	1,250	2,250	—	—
1866A DL	—	—	—	7,500	—	—
1868/7A DL	—	1,500	2,250	3,250	—	—
1869A DL	—	650	1,250	2,250	—	—
1870A DL	—	1,500	2,250	3,250	—	—
1872A AM Rare	—	—	—	—	—	—

KM# 383.1   8 ESCUDOS
27.0700 g., 0.8750 Gold .7616 oz. AGW   **Obv:** Facing eagle

Date	Mintage	F	VF	XF	Unc	BU
1841 Ca RG	—	400	750	1,250	1,750	—
1842 Ca RG	—	350	500	1,000	1,500	—
1843 Ca RG	—	350	500	1,000	1,500	—
1844 Ca RG	—	350	500	1,000	1,500	—

Date	Mintage	F	VF	XF	Unc	BU
1845 Ca RG	—	350	500	1,000	1,500	—
1846 Ca RG	—	500	1,250	1,500	2,000	—
1847 Ca RG	—	1,000	2,500	—	—	—
1848 Ca RG	—	350	500	1,000	1,500	—
1849 Ca RG	—	350	500	1,000	1,500	—
1850/40 Ca RG	—	350	500	1,000	1,500	—
1851/41 Ca RG	—	50.00	500	1,000	1,500	—
1852/42 Ca RG	—	350	500	1,000	1,500	—
1853/43 Ca RG	—	350	500	1,000	1,500	—
1854/44 Ca RG	—	350	500	1,000	1,500	—
1855/43 Ca RG	—	350	500	1,000	1,500	—
1856/46 Ca RG	—	400	650	1,250	1,750	—
1857 Ca JC/RG	—	325	475	750	1,250	—
1858 Ca JC	—	325	475	750	1,250	—
1858 Ca BA/RG	—	325	475	750	1,250	—
1859 Ca JC/RG	—	325	475	750	1,250	—
1860 Ca JC/RG	—	350	500	1,000	1,500	—
1861 Ca JC	—	350	475	750	1,250	—
1862 Ca JC	—	350	475	750	1,250	—
1863 Ca JC	—	500	1,000	1,750	2,250	—
1864 Ca JC	—	400	750	1,250	1,750	—
1865 Ca JC	—	750	1,500	2,500	3,500	—
1866 Ca JC	—	350	500	1,000	1,500	—
1866 Ca FP	—	600	1,250	2,000	2,500	—
1866 Ca JG	—	350	500	1,000	1,500	—
1867 Ca JG	—	350	475	750	1,250	—
1868 Ca JG Concave wings	—	350	475	750	1,250	—
1869 Ca MM Regular eagle	—	350	475	750	1,250	—
1870/60 Ca MM	—	350	475	750	1,250	—
1871/61 Ca MM	—	350	475	750	1,250	—

KM# 383.2   8 ESCUDOS
27.0700 g., 0.8750 Gold .7616 oz. AGW   **Obv:** Facing eagle

Date	Mintage	F	VF	XF	Unc	BU
1846C CE	—	350	500	1,000	1,750	—
1847C CE	—	350	500	800	1,250	—
1848C CE	—	350	500	1,000	1,750	—
1849C CE	—	325	450	700	1,250	—
1850C CE	—	325	450	700	1,250	—
1851C CE	—	350	500	800	1,250	—
1852C CE	—	350	500	800	1,250	—
1853/1C CE	—	325	450	700	1,250	—
1854C CE	—	325	450	700	1,250	—
1855/4C CE	—	350	500	1,000	1,750	—
1855C CE	—	350	500	800	1,250	—
1856C CE	—	325	450	700	1,250	—
1857C CE	—	325	450	700	1,250	—
1857C CE	—	—	—	—	—	—
Note: Without periods after C's						
1858C CE	—	325	450	700	1,250	—
1859C CE	—	325	450	700	1,250	—
1860/58C CE	—	350	500	800	1,250	—
1860C CE	—	350	500	800	1,250	—
1860C PV	—	325	450	700	1,250	—
1861C PV	—	350	500	800	1,250	—

Date	Mintage	F	VF	XF	Unc	BU
1861C CE	—	350	500	800	1,250	—
1862C CE	—	350	500	800	1,250	—
1863C CE	—	350	500	800	1,250	—
1864C CE	—	325	450	700	1,250	—
1865C CE	—	350	500	800	1,250	—
1866/5C CE	—	325	450	700	1,250	—
1866C CE	—	325	450	700	1,250	—
1867C CB Error	—	325	450	700	1,250	—
1867C CE/CB	—	325	450	700	1,250	—
1868C CB Error	—	350	500	800	1,250	—
1869C CE	—	350	500	800	1,250	—
1870C CE	—	350	500	800	1,250	—

Date	Mintage	F	VF	XF	Unc	BU
Note: Mexican style eagle						
1858Do CP	—	350	500	800	1,250	—
1859Do CP	—	350	500	800	1,250	—
1860/59Do CP	—	450	700	1,250	2,200	—
1861/0Do CP	—	400	600	1,000	1,750	—
1862/52Do CP	—	350	500	800	1,250	—
1862/1Do CP	—	350	500	800	1,250	—
1862Do CP	—	350	500	800	1,250	—
1863/53Do CP	—	350	500	800	1,250	—
1864Do LT	—	350	500	800	1,250	—
1865/4Do LT	—	500	1,000	1,650	2,750	—
1866/4Do CM	—	1,250	2,000	2,500	—	—
1866Do CM	—	400	600	1,000	1,750	—
1867/56Do CP	—	400	600	1,000	1,750	—
1867/4Do CP	—	350	500	800	1,250	—
1868/4Do CP/LT	—	—	—	—	—	—
1869Do CP	—	500	1,250	1,750	2,750	—
1870Do CP	—	400	600	1,000	1,750	—

KM# 383.3 8 ESCUDOS
27.0700 g., 0.8750 Gold .7616 oz. AGW **Obv:** Facing eagle

Date	Mintage	F	VF	XF	Unc	BU
1832Do RM	—	850	1,750	2,000	3,000	—
1833Do RM/RL	—	350	500	800	1,250	—
1834Do RM	—	350	500	800	1,250	—
1835Do RM	—	350	500	800	1,250	—
1836Do RM/RL	—	350	500	800	1,250	—
1836Do RM	—	350	500	800	1,250	—
Note: M on snake						
1837Do RM	—	350	500	800	1,250	—
1838/6Do RM	—	350	500	800	1,250	—
1838Do RM	—	350	500	800	1,250	—
1839Do RM	—	325	450	700	1,250	—
1840/30Do RM/RL	—	400	600	1,000	1,750	—
1841/30Do RM	—	550	750	1,250	2,000	—
1841/31Do RM	—	350	500	800	1,250	—
1841/34Do RM	—	350	500	800	1,250	—
1841Do RM/RL	—	350	500	800	1,250	—
1842/32Do RM	—	350	500	800	1,250	—
1843/33Do RM	—	550	750	1,250	2,000	—
1843/1Do RM	—	350	500	800	1,250	—
1843Do RM	—	350	500	800	1,250	—
1844/34Do RM/RL	—	500	1,000	1,500	2,500	—
1844Do RM	—	450	800	1,250	2,000	—
1845/36Do RM	—	400	600	1,000	1,750	—
1845Do RM	—	400	600	1,000	1,750	—
1846Do RM	—	350	500	800	1,250	—
1847/37Do RM	—	350	500	800	1,250	—
1848/37Do RM	—	—	—	—	—	—
1848Do CM	—	350	500	800	1,250	—
1849/39Do CM	—	350	500	800	1,250	—
1849Do J.M.R. Rare	—	—	—	—	—	—
1850Do .JMR.	—	400	750	1,250	2,000	—
1851Do JMR	—	400	750	1,250	2,000	—
1852/1Do JMR	—	450	800	1,250	2,000	—
1852Do CP	—	450	800	1,250	2,000	—
1853Do CP	—	450	800	1,250	2,000	—
1854Do CP	—	400	600	1,000	1,750	—
1855/4Do CP	—	350	500	800	1,250	—
1855Do CP	—	350	500	800	1,250	—
1856Do CP	—	400	600	1,000	1,750	—
1857Do CP	—	350	500	800	1,250	—
Note: French style eagle, 1832-57						
1857Do CP	—	350	500	800	1,250	—

KM# 383.4 8 ESCUDOS
27.0700 g., 0.8750 Gold .7616 oz. AGW **Obv:** Facing eagle

Date	Mintage	F	VF	XF	Unc	BU
1828EoMo LF	—	3,500	5,500	8,500	—	—
1829EoMo LF	—	3,500	5,500	8,500	—	—

KM# 383.5 8 ESCUDOS
27.0700 g., 0.8750 Gold .7616 oz. AGW **Obv:** Facing eagle

Date	Mintage	F	VF	XF	Unc	BU
1825Ga FS	—	500	1,000	1,250	1,750	—
1826Ga FS	—	500	1,000	1,250	1,750	—
1830Ga FS	—	500	1,000	1,250	1,750	—
1836Ga FS	—	750	1,500	2,000	3,000	—
1836Ga JG	—	1,000	2,500	3,500	—	—
1837Ga JG	—	1,000	2,500	3,500	—	—
1840Ga MC	—	750	1,500	2,000	3,000	—
1841/31Ga MC	—	1,000	2,500	—	—	—
1841Ga MC	—	850	1,650	2,250	—	—
1842Ga JG	—	—	—	—	—	—

Date	Mintage	F	VF	XF	Unc	BU
1843Ga MC	—	—	—	—	—	—
1845Ga MC	—	400	850	1,100	1,650	—
1847Ga JG	—	2,250	—	—	—	—
1849Ga JG	—	500	1,000	1,250	1,750	—
1850Ga JG	—	400	850	1,100	1,650	—
1851Ga JG	—	400	850	1,100	1,650	—
1852/1Ga JG	—	500	1,000	1,250	1,750	—
1855Ga JG	—	1,000	2,500	3,500	—	—
1856Ga JG	—	400	850	1,100	1,650	—
1857Ga JG	—	400	850	1,100	1,650	—
1861/0Ga JG	—	500	1,000	1,250	1,750	—
1861Ga JG	—	400	700	1,200	1,750	—
1863/1Ga JG	—	◦ 500	1,000	1,250	1,750	—
1866Ga JG	—	400	850	1,100	1,650	—

Date	Mintage	F	VF	XF	Unc	BU
1832Go MJ	—	500	1,250	1,750	2,500	—
1833Go MJ	—	350	500	700	1,000	—
1834Go PJ	—	350	500	700	1,000	—
1835Go PJ	—	350	500	700	1,000	—
1836Go PJ	—	400	650	900	1,250	—
1837Go PJ	—	400	650	900	1,250	—
1838/7Go PJ	—	350	500	700	1,000	—
1838Go PJ	—	350	500	800	1,200	—
1839/8Go PJ	—	350	500	700	1,000	—
1839Go PJ	—	350	500	800	1,200	—
Note: Regular eagle						
1840Go PJ	—	350	500	700	1,000	—
Note: Concave wings						
1841Go PJ	—	350	500	700	1,000	—
1842Go PJ	—	325	400	500	900	—
1842Go PM	—	350	500	700	1,000	—
1843Go PM	—	350	500	700	1,000	—
Note: Small eagle						
1844/3Go PM	—	400	650	900	1,250	—
1844Go PM	—	350	500	700	1,000	—
1845Go PM	—	350	500	700	1,000	—
1846/5Go PM	—	350	500	800	1,200	—
1846Go PM	—	350	500	700	1,000	—
1847Go PM	—	400	650	900	1,250	—
1848/7Go PM	—	350	500	700	1,000	—
1848Go PM	—	350	500	700	1,000	—
1848Go PF	—	350	500	700	1,000	—
1849Go PF	—	325	400	500	900	—
1850Go PF	—	325	400	500	900	—
1851Go PF	—	375	500	700	1,000	—
1852Go PF	—	375	500	700	1,000	—
1853Go PF	—	325	400	500	900	—
1854Go PF	—	350	500	700	1,000	—
Note: Eagle of 1853						
1854Go PF	—	350	500	700	1,000	—
Note: Eagle of 1855						
1855/4Go PF	—	400	650	900	1,250	—
1855Go PF	—	350	500	700	1,000	—
1856Go PF	—	350	500	700	1,000	—
1857Go PF	—	350	500	700	1,000	—
1858Go PF	—	350	500	700	1,000	—
1859Go PF	—	325	400	500	800	—
1860/50Go PF	—	325	400	500	900	—
1860/59Go PF	—	400	650	900	1,250	—
1860Go PF	—	375	500	700	1,100	—
1861/0Go PF	—	325	400	500	800	—
1861Go PF	—	325	400	500	800	—
1862/1Go YE	—	350	500	700	1,000	—
1862Go YE	—	350	500	700	1,000	—
1862Go YF	—	—	—	—	—	—
1863/53Go YF	—	350	500	700	1,000	—
1863Go PF	—	350	500	700	1,000	—
1867/57Go YF/PF	—	350	500	700	1,000	—
1867Go YF	—	350	500	700	1,000	—
1868/58Go YF	—	350	500	700	1,000	—
1870Go FR	—	325	400	500	900	—

KM# 383.6   8 ESCUDOS
27.0700 g., 0.8750 Gold .7616 oz. AGW   **Obv:** Facing eagle

Date	Mintage	F	VF	XF	Unc	BU
1844GC MP	—	550	750	1,250	2,000	—
1845GC MP	—	550	750	1,250	2,000	—
Note: Eagle's tail square						
1845GC MP	—	550	750	1,250	2,000	—
Note: Eagle's tail round						
1846GC MP	—	450	650	1,000	1,750	—
Note: Eagle's tail square						
1846GC MP	—	450	650	1,000	1,750	—
Note: Eagle's tail round						
1847GC MP	—	450	650	1,000	1,750	—
1848GC MP	—	550	750	1,250	2,000	—
1849GC MP	—	550	750	1,250	2,000	—
1850GC MP	—	450	650	1,000	1,750	—
1851GC MP	—	450	650	1,000	1,750	—
1852GC MP	—	550	750	1,250	2,000	—

KM# 383.7   8 ESCUDOS
27.0700 g., 0.8750 Gold .7616 oz. AGW   **Obv:** Facing eagle

Date	Mintage	F	VF	XF	Unc	BU
1828Go MJ	—	700	1,750	2,250	3,000	—
1829Go MJ	—	600	1,500	2,000	2,750	—
1830Go MJ	—	350	500	750	1,000	—
1831Go MJ	—	600	1,500	2,000	2,750	—

KM# 383.8   8 ESCUDOS
27.0700 g., 0.8750 Gold .7616 oz. AGW   **Obv:** Facing eagle

Date	Mintage	F	VF	XF	Unc	BU
1863Ho FM	—	400	650	1,000	2,000	—
1864Ho FM	—	600	1,250	1,750	2,750	—
1864Ho PR/FM	—	400	650	1,000	2,000	—
1865Ho FM/PR	—	500	800	1,250	2,500	—
1867/57Ho PR	—	400	650	1,000	2,000	—
1868Ho PR	—	500	800	1,250	2,500	—
1868Ho PR/FM	—	500	800	1,250	2,500	—
1869Ho PR/FM	—	400	650	1,000	2,000	—
1869Ho PR	—	400	650	1,000	2,000	—
1870Ho PR	—	400	650	1,000	2,000	—
1871/0Ho PR	—	500	800	1,250	2,500	—
1871Ho PR	—	500	800	1,250	2,500	—
1872/1Ho PR	—	600	1,250	1,750	2,750	—
1873Ho PR	—	400	650	1,000	2,000	—

Date	Mintage	F	VF	XF	Unc	BU
1854/3Mo GC	—	325	400	500	900	—
1855Mo GF	—	325	400	500	900	—
1856/5Mo GF	—	325	400	500	900	—
1856Mo GF	—	325	400	500	900	—
1857Mo GF	—	325	400	500	900	—
1858Mo FH	—	325	400	500	900	—
1859Mo FH	—	400	750	1,000	1,500	—
1860Mo FH	—	325	400	500	900	—
1860Mo TH	—	325	400	500	900	—
1861/51Mo CH	—	325	400	500	900	—
1862Mo CH	—	325	400	500	900	—
1863/53Mo CH	—	325	400	500	900	—
1863/53Mo TH	—	325	400	500	900	—
1867Mo CH	—	325	400	500	900	—
1868Mo CH	—	325	400	500	900	—
1868Mo PH	—	325	400	500	900	—
1869Mo CH	—	325	400	500	900	—

KM# 383.9 8 ESCUDOS
27.0700 g., 0.8750 Gold .7616 oz. AGW **Obv:** Facing eagle
Note: Formerly reported 1825/3 JM is merely a reworked 5.

Date	Mintage	F	VF	XF	Unc	BU
1824Mo JM	—	500	1,000	1,250	2,000	—
Note: Large book reverse						
1825Mo JM	—	325	400	500	1,000	—
Note: Small book reverse						
1826/5Mo JM	—	700	1,750	2,250	3,000	—
1827Mo JM	—	350	500	700	1,000	—
1828Mo JM	—	350	500	700	1,000	—
1829Mo JM	—	350	500	700	1,000	—
1830Mo JM	—	350	500	700	1,000	—
1831Mo JM	—	350	500	700	1,000	—
1832/1Mo JM	—	350	500	700	1,000	—
1832Mo JM	—	350	500	700	1,000	—
1833Mo MJ	—	400	750	1,000	1,500	—
1833Mo ML	—	325	400	500	900	—
1834Mo ML	—	400	750	1,000	1,500	—
1835/4Mo ML	—	500	1,000	1,250	2,000	—
1836Mo ML	—	325	400	500	900	—
1836Mo MF	—	500	700	1,200	2,000	—
1837/6Mo ML	—	325	400	500	900	—
1838Mo ML	—	325	400	500	900	—
1839Mo ML	—	325	400	500	900	—
1840Mo ML	—	325	400	500	900	—
1841Mo ML	—	325	400	500	900	—
1842/1Mo ML	—	—	—	—	—	—
1842Mo ML	—	325	400	500	900	—
1842Mo MM	—	—	—	—	—	—
1843Mo MM	—	325	400	500	900	—
1844Mo MF	—	325	400	500	900	—
1845Mo MF	—	325	400	500	900	—
1846Mo MF	—	500	1,000	1,250	2,000	—
1847Mo MF	—	950	2,250	—	—	—
1847Mo RC	—	325	500	800	1,250	—
1848Mo GC	—	325	400	500	900	—
1849Mo GC	—	325	400	500	900	—
1850Mo GC	—	325	400	500	900	—
1851Mo GC	—	325	400	500	900	—
1852Mo GC	—	325	400	500	900	—
1853Mo GC	—	325	400	500	900	—
1854/44Mo GC	—	325	400	500	900	—

KM# 383.10 8 ESCUDOS
27.0700 g., 0.8750 Gold .7616 oz. AGW **Obv:** Facing eagle

Date	Mintage	F	VF	XF	Unc	BU
1858 Oa AE	—	2,000	3,000	4,000	6,000	—
1859O AE	—	1,000	2,500	3,750	5,500	—
1860O AE	—	1,000	2,500	3,750	5,500	—
1861O FR	—	450	850	1,250	2,750	—
1862O FR	—	450	850	1,250	2,750	—
1863O FR	—	450	850	1,250	2,750	—
1864O FR	—	450	850	1,250	2,750	—
1867O AE	—	450	850	1,250	2,750	—
1868O AE	—	450	850	1,250	2,750	—
1869O AE	—	450	850	1,250	2,750	—

KM# 383.11 8 ESCUDOS
27.0700 g., 0.8750 Gold .7616 oz. AGW **Obv:** Facing eagle

Date	Mintage	F	VF	XF	Unc	BU
1858Zs MO	—	400	750	1,000	2,000	—
1859Zs MO	—	325	400	500	900	—
1860/59Zs VL/MO	—	2,000	3,000	4,000	—	—
1860/9Zs MO	—	400	750	1,000	2,000	—
1860Zs MO	—	375	500	700	1,000	—
1861/0Zs VL	—	375	500	700	1,000	—
1861Zs VL	—	375	500	700	1,000	—
1862Zs VL	—	375	500	700	1,100	—
1863Zs VL	—	375	525	750	1,150	—
1863Zs MO	—	375	500	700	1,000	—

Date	Mintage	F	VF	XF	Unc	BU
1864Zs MO	—	750	1,000	1,500	3,000	—
1865Zs MO	—	375	500	700	1,000	—
1865Zs MP	—	—	—	—	—	—
Note: Contemporary counterfeit						
1868Zs JS	—	400	600	800	1,250	—
1868Zs YH	—	400	600	800	1,250	—
1869Zs YH	—	400	600	800	1,250	—
1870Zs YH	—	400	600	800	1,250	—
1871Zs YH	—	400	600	800	1,250	—

EMPIRE OF MAXIMILIAN

RULER
Maximilian, Emperor, 1864-1867
MINT MARKS
Refer To Republic Coinage
MONETARY SYSTEM
100 Centavos = 1 Peso (8 Reales)

MILLED COINAGE

16 Pilones=1 Real; 8 Tiaco=1 Real;
16 Reales=1Escudo

KM# 384   CENTAVO
Copper **Ruler:** Maximilian

Date	Mintage	F	VF	XF	Unc	BU
1864M	—	40.00	75.00	225	1,100	—

KM# 385   5 CENTAVOS
1.3537 g., 0.9030 Silver .0393 oz. ASW **Ruler:** Maximilian

Date	Mintage	F	VF	XF	Unc	BU
1864G	90,000	17.50	35.00	75.00	320	—
1865G	—	20.00	30.00	55.00	285	—
1866G	—	75.00	150	300	1,800	—

KM# 385.1   5 CENTAVOS
1.3537 g., 0.9030 Silver .0393 oz. ASW **Ruler:** Maximilian

Date	Mintage	F	VF	XF	Unc	BU
1864M	—	12.50	20.00	55.00	285	—
1866/4M	—	25.00	40.00	75.00	385	—
1866M	—	20.00	35.00	65.00	375	—

KM# 385.2   5 CENTAVOS
1.3537 g., 0.9030 Silver .0393 oz. ASW **Ruler:** Maximilian

Date	Mintage	F	VF	XF	Unc	BU
1864P	—	150	400	1,500	2,500	—

KM# 385.3   5 CENTAVOS
1.3537 g., 0.9030 Silver .0393 oz. ASW **Ruler:** Maximilian

Date	Mintage	F	VF	XF	Unc	BU
1865Z	—	25.00	45.00	150	425	—

KM# 386   10 CENTAVOS
2.7073 g., 0.9030 Silver .0786 oz. ASW **Ruler:** Maximilian

Date	Mintage	F	VF	XF	Unc	BU
1864G	45,000	20.00	45.00	90.00	325	—
1865G	—	30.00	60.00	110	375	—

KM# 386.1   10 CENTAVOS
2.7073 g., 0.9030 Silver .0786 oz. ASW **Ruler:** Maximilian
Note: Struck at Mexico City Mint, mint mark M.

Date	Mintage	F	VF	XF	Unc	BU
1864M	—	15.00	25.00	55.00	285	—
1866/4M	—	25.00	35.00	70.00	320	—
1866/5M	—	25.00	40.00	85.00	375	—
1866M	—	25.00	35.00	75.00	375	—

KM# 386.2   10 CENTAVOS
2.7073 g., 0.9030 Silver .0786 oz. ASW **Ruler:** Maximilian

Date	Mintage	F	VF	XF	Unc	BU
1864P	—	70.00	150	300	600	—

KM# 386.3   10 CENTAVOS
2.7073 g., 0.9030 Silver .0786 oz. ASW **Ruler:** Maximilian

Date	Mintage	F	VF	XF	Unc	BU
1865Z	—	25.00	55.00	165	475	—

KM# 387   50 CENTAVOS
13.5365 g., 0.9030 Silver .3929 oz. ASW **Ruler:** Maximilian

Date	Mintage	F	VF	XF	Unc	BU
1866Mo	31,000	40.00	95.00	200	600	—

KM# 388   PESO
27.0700 g., 0.9030 Silver .7857 oz. ASW **Ruler:** Maximilian

Date	Mintage	F	VF	XF	Unc	BU
1866Go	—	300	400	900	3,500	—

KM# 388.1 PESO
27.0700 g., 0.9030 Silver .7857 oz. ASW **Ruler:** Maximilian

Date	Mintage	F	VF	XF	Unc	BU
1866Mo	2,148,000	30.00	45.00	125	375	—
1867Mo	1,238,000	40.00	65.00	175	425	—

KM# 388.2 PESO
27.0700 g., 0.9030 Silver .7857 oz. ASW **Ruler:** Maximilian

Date	Mintage	F	VF	XF	Unc	BU
1866 Pi	—	45.00	90.00	275	725	—

KM# 389 20 PESOS
33.8400 g., 0.8750 Gold .9520 oz. AGW **Ruler:** Maximilian

Date	Mintage	F	VF	XF	Unc	BU
1866Mo	8,274	500	900	1,350	2,500	—

REPUBLIC
Second

MINT MARKS
A, AS - Alamos
CE - Real de Catorce
CA,CH - Chihuahua
C, Cn, Gn(error) - Culiacan
D, Do - Durango
EoMo - Estado de Mexico
Ga - Guadalajara
GC - Guadalupe y Calvo
G, Go - Guanajuato
H, Ho - Hermosillo
M, Mo - Mexico City
O, OA - Oaxaca
SLP, PI, P, I/P - San Luis Potosi
Z, Zs – Zacatecas

ASSAYERS INITIALS

CULIACAN MINT

Initials	Years	Mint Officials
JQ, Q	1899-1903	Jesus S. Quiroz
FV, V	1903	Francisco Valdez
MH, H	1904	Merced Hernandez
RP, P	1904-05	Ramon Ponce de Leon

MEXICO CITY MINT
Because of the great number of assayers for this mint (Mexico City is a much larger mint than any of the others) there is much confusion as to which initial stands for which assayer at any one time. Therefore we feel that it would be of no value to list the assayers.

ZACATECAS MINT

Initials	Years	Mint Officials
FZ	1886-1905	Francisco de P. Zarate
FM	1904-05	Francisco Mateos

DECIMAL COINAGE

100 Centavos = 1 Peso

KM# 390 CENTAVO
Copper, 25 mm. **Obv:** Seated Liberty **Rev:** Thick wreath.

Date	Mintage	F	VF	XF	Unc	BU
1863Mo	—	15.00	30.00	75.00	500	—

Note: Round top 3, reeded edge

1863Mo	—	15.00	30.00	75.00	500	—

Note: Round top 3, plain edge

1863Mo	—	12.00	28.00	70.00	500	—

Note: Flat top 3, reeded edge

KM# 390.1 CENTAVO
Copper, 26.5 mm. **Obv:** Seated Liberty **Rev:** Thin wreath

Date	Mintage	F	VF	XF	Unc	BU
1863SLP	1,024,999	15.00	30.00	60.00	400	—

KM# 391 CENTAVO
Copper **Obv:** Standing eagle **Edge:** Reeded.

Date	Mintage	F	VF	XF	Unc	BU
1875 As Rare	—	—	—	—	—	—
1876 As	50,000	100	200	300	650	—
1880 As	—	25.00	50.00	125	400	—
1881 As	—	30.00	60.00	125	350	—

KM# 391.1 CENTAVO
Copper **Obv:** Standing eagle **Edge:** Plain

Date	Mintage	F	VF	XF	Unc	BU
1874Cn	266,000	12.50	17.50	35.00	250	—
1875/4Cn	153,000	15.00	20.00	45.00	250	—
1875Cn	Inc. above	10.00	15.00	25.00	250	—
1876Cn	154,000	5.00	8.00	15.00	200	—
1877/6Cn	993,000	7.50	11.50	17.50	200	—
1877Cn	Inc. above	6.00	9.00	15.00	200	—
1880Cn	142,000	7.50	10.00	12.50	200	—
1881Cn	167,000	7.50	10.00	25.00	200	—
1897Cn Large N in mint mark	300,000	2.50	5.00	12.00	50.00	—
1897Cn Small N in mint mark	Inc. above	2.50	5.00	9.00	45.00	—

KM# 391.2 CENTAVO
Copper **Obv:** Standing eagle

Date	Mintage	F	VF	XF	Unc	BU
1879Do	110,000	10.00	17.50	35.00	150	—
1880Do	69,000	40.00	90.00	175	500	—
1891Do	—	8.00	11.00	30.00	150	—
1891Do/Mo	—	8.00	11.00	30.00	150	—

KM# 391.3 CENTAVO
Copper **Obv:** Standing eagle

Date	Mintage	F	VF	XF	Unc	BU
1872Ga	263,000	15.00	30.00	60.00	200	—
1873Ga	333,000	6.00	9.00	25.00	150	—
1874Ga	76,000	15.00	25.00	50.00	175	—
1875Ga	—	10.00	15.00	30.00	150	—
1876Ga	303,000	3.00	6.00	17.50	150	—
1877Ga	108,000	4.00	6.00	20.00	150	—
1878Ga	543,000	4.00	6.00	15.00	150	—
1881/71Ga	975,000	7.00	9.00	20.00	175	—
1881Ga	Inc. above	7.00	9.00	20.00	175	—
1889Ga/Mo	—	3.50	5.00	25.00	125	—
1890Ga	—	4.00	7.50	20.00	100	—

KM# 391.4 CENTAVO
Copper **Obv:** Standing eagle

Date	Mintage	F	VF	XF	Unc	BU
1874Go	—	20.00	40.00	80.00	250	—
1875Go	190,000	11.50	20.00	60.00	200	—
1876Go	—	125	200	350	750	—
1877Go Rare	—	—	—	—	—	—
1878Go	576,000	8.00	11.00	30.00	175	—
1880Go	890,000	6.00	10.00	25.00	175	—

KM# 391.5 CENTAVO
Copper **Obv:** Standing eagle

Date	Mintage	F	VF	XF	Unc	BU
1875Ho	3,500	450	—	—	—	—
1876Ho	8,508	50.00	100	225	500	—
1880Ho Short H, round O	102,000	7.50	15.00	35.00	150	—
1880Ho Tall H, oval O	Inc. above	7.50	15.00	35.00	150	—
1881Ho	459,000	5.00	10.00	25.00	150	—

KM# 391.6 CENTAVO
Copper **Obv:** Standing eagle **Note:** Varieties exist.

Date	Mintage	F	VF	XF	Unc	BU
1869Mo	1,874,000	7.50	25.00	60.00	200	—
1870/69Mo	1,200,000	10.00	25.00	60.00	225	—
1870Mo	Inc. above	8.00	20.00	50.00	200	—
1871Mo	918,000	8.00	15.00	40.00	200	—
1872/1Mo	1,625,000	6.50	10.00	30.00	200	—
1872Mo	Inc. above	6.00	9.00	25.00	200	—
1873Mo	1,605,000	4.00	7.50	20.00	200	—
1874/3Mo	1,700,000	5.00	7.00	15.00	100	—
1874Mo	Inc. above	3.00	5.50	15.00	100	—
1874Mo	Inc. above	5.00	10.00	25.00	200	—
1875Mo	1,495,000	6.00	8.00	30.00	100	—
1876Mo	1,600,000	3.00	5.50	12.50	100	—

Date	Mintage	F	VF	XF	Unc	BU
1877Mo	1,270,000	3.00	5.50	13.50	100	—
1878/5Mo	1,900,000	7.50	11.00	22.50	125	—
1878/6Mo	Inc. above	7.50	11.00	22.50	125	—
1878/7Mo	Inc. above	7.50	11.00	20.00	125	—
1878Mo	Inc. above	6.00	9.00	13.50	100	—
1879/8Mo	1,505,000	4.50	6.50	13.50	100	—
1879Mo	Inc. above	3.00	5.50	12.50	75.00	—
1880/70Mo	1,130,000	5.50	7.50	15.00	100	—
1880/72Mo	Inc. above	20.00	50.00	100	250	—
1880/79Mo	Inc. above	15.00	35.00	75.00	175	—
1880Mo	Inc. above	4.25	6.00	12.50	75.00	—
1881Mo	1,060,000	4.50	7.00	15.00	75.00	—
1886Mo	12,687,000	1.50	2.00	10.00	40.00	—
1887Mo	7,292,000	1.50	2.00	10.00	35.00	—
1888/78Mo	9,984,000	2.50	3.00	10.00	30.00	—
1888/7Mo	Inc. above	2.50	3.00	10.00	30.00	—
1888Mo	Inc. above	1.50	2.00	10.00	30.00	—
1889Mo	19,970,000	2.00	3.00	10.00	30.00	—
1890/89Mo	18,726,000	2.50	3.00	12.00	40.00	—
1890/990Mo	Inc. above	2.50	3.00	12.00	40.00	—
1890Mo	Inc. above	1.50	2.00	10.00	30.00	—
1891Mo	14,544,000	1.50	2.00	10.00	30.00	—
1892Mo	12,908,000	1.50	2.00	10.00	30.00	—
1893/2Mo	5,078,000	2.50	3.00	12.00	35.00	—
1893Mo	Inc. above	1.50	2.00	10.00	30.00	—
1894/3Mo	1,896,000	3.00	6.00	15.00	50.00	—
1894Mo	Inc. above	2.00	3.00	12.00	35.00	—
1895/3Mo	3,453,000	3.00	4.50	12.50	35.00	—
1895/85Mo	Inc. above	3.00	6.00	15.00	50.00	—
1895Mo	Inc. above	2.00	3.00	10.00	30.00	—
1896Mo	3,075,000	2.00	3.00	10.00	30.00	—
1897Mo	4,150,000	1.50	2.00	10.00	30.00	—

KM# 391.7 CENTAVO
Copper **Obv:** Standing eagle

Date	Mintage	F	VF	XF	Unc	BU
1872 Oa	16,000	300	500	1,200	—	—
1873 Oa	11,000	350	600	—	—	—
1874 Oa	4,835	450	—	—	—	—
1875 Oa	2,860	500	—	—	—	—

KM# 391.8 CENTAVO
Copper **Obv:** Standing eagle

Date	Mintage	F	VF	XF	Unc	BU
1871 Pi Rare	—	—	—	—	—	—
1877 Pi	249,000	15.00	50.00	200	—	—
1878 Pi	751,000	12.50	25.00	50.00	200	—
1878 Pp error mintmark - rare	—	—	—	—	—	—
1891Pi/Mo	—	10.00	50.00	150	300	—
1891 Pi	—	8.00	25.00	125	250	—

KM# 391.9 CENTAVO
Copper **Obv:** Standing eagle **Note:** Struck at Zacatecas Mint, mint mark Zs.

Date	Mintage	F	VF	XF	Unc	BU
1872Zs	55,000	22.50	30.00	100	300	—
1873Zs	1,460,000	4.00	8.00	25.00	150	—
1874/3Zs	685,000	5.50	11.00	30.00	250	—
1874Zs	Inc. above	4.00	8.00	25.00	200	—

Date	Mintage	F	VF	XF	Unc	BU
1875/4Zs	200,000	8.50	17.00	45.00	250	—
1875Zs	Inc. above	7.00	14.00	35.00	200	—
1876Zs	—	5.00	10.00	25.00	200	—
1877Zs	—	50.00	125	300	750	—
1878Zs	—	4.50	9.00	25.00	200	—
1880Zs	100,000	5.00	10.00	30.00	200	—
1881Zs	1,200,000	4.25	8.00	25.00	150	—

KM# 392 CENTAVO
Copper-Nickel

Date	Mintage	F	VF	XF	Unc	BU
1882Mo	99,955,000	7.50	12.50	17.50	35.00	—
1883Mo	Inc. above	0.50	0.75	1.00	1.50	—

KM# 393 CENTAVO
Copper **Obv:** Restyled eagle **Note:** Varieties exist.

Date	Mintage	F	VF	XF	Unc	BU
1898Mo	1,529,000	4.00	6.00	15.00	50.00	—

KM# 394 CENTAVO
Copper **Note:** Reduced size. Varieties exist.

Date	Mintage	F	VF	XF	Unc	BU
1901C	220,000	15.00	22.50	35.00	65.00	—
1902C	320,000	15.00	22.50	50.00	90.00	—
1903C	536,000	7.50	12.50	20.00	50.00	—
1904/3C	148,000	35.00	50.00	75.00	125	—
1905C	110,000	100	150	250	550	—

KM# 394.1 CENTAVO
Copper **Note:** Reduced size. Varieties exist.

Date	Mintage	F	VF	XF	Unc	BU
1899M	51,000	150	175	300	800	—
1900M Wide date	4,010,000	2.50	4.00	8.00	28.00	—
1900M Narrow date	Inc. above	2.50	4.00	8.00	28.00	—
1901M	1,494,000	3.00	8.00	17.50	50.00	—
1902/899M	2,090,000	30.00	60.00	100	175	—
1902M	Inc. above	2.25	4.00	10.00	40.00	—
1903M	8,400,000	1.50	3.00	7.00	20.00	—
1904/3M	10,250,000	1.50	10.00	20.00	55.00	—
1904M	Inc. above	1.50	3.00	8.00	25.00	—
1905M	3,643,000	2.25	4.00	10.00	40.00	—

KM# 395 2 CENTAVOS
Copper-Nickel

Date	Mintage	F	VF	XF	Unc	BU
1882	50,023,000	2.00	3.00	7.50	15.00	—
1883/2	Inc. above	2.00	3.00	7.50	15.00	—
1883	Inc. above	0.50	0.75	1.00	2.50	—

KM# 396 5 CENTAVOS
1.3530 g., 0.9030 Silver .0392 oz. ASW **Obv:** Facing eagle
Rev: Denomination in wreath

Date	Mintage	F	VF	XF	Unc	BU
1868 Ca	—	40.00	65.00	125	450	—
1869 Ca	30,000	25.00	40.00	100	400	—
1870/69 Ca	—	35.00	55.00	120	425	—
1870 Ca	35,000	30.00	50.00	100	400	—

KM# 396.1 5 CENTAVOS
1.3530 g., 0.9030 Silver .0392 oz. ASW **Obv:** Facing eagle
Rev: Deonomination in wreath

Date	Mintage	F	VF	XF	Unc	BU
1863SLP	—	37.50	135	350	1,200	—

KM# 397 5 CENTAVOS
1.3530 g., 0.9030 Silver .0392 oz. ASW **Obv:** Facing eagle
Rev: Cap and rays **Note:** Varieties exist.

Date	Mintage	F	VF	XF	Unc	BU
1867/3Mo	—	22.50	50.00	125	425	—
1867Mo	—	18.50	42.50	100	400	—
1868/7Mo	—	22.50	50.00	150	500	—
1868Mo	—	18.50	42.50	100	400	—

KM# 397.1 5 CENTAVOS
1.3530 g., 0.9030 Silver .0392 oz. ASW **Obv:** Facing eagle
Rev: Cap and rays

Date	Mintage	F	VF	XF	Unc	BU
1868/7P	34,000	25.00	50.00	125	450	—
1868P	Inc. above	20.00	45.00	100	400	—
1869P	14,000	200	300	600	—	—

KM# 398 5 CENTAVOS
1.3530 g., 0.9030 Silver .0392 oz. ASW **Obv:** Standing eagle
Rev: Denomination in wreath

Date	Mintage	F	VF	XF	Unc	BU
1874 As DL	—	10.00	20.00	40.00	150	—
1875 As DL	—	10.00	20.00	40.00	150	—
1876 As L	—	22.00	45.00	70.00	160	—
1878 As L Mule, gold peso reverse	—	250	350	650	—	—
1879 As L Mule, gold peso obverse	—	40.00	65.00	120	275	—
1880 As L Mule, gold peso obverse	12,000	55.00	85.00	165	325	—
1886 As L	43,000	12.00	25.00	50.00	165	—
1886 As L Mule, gold peso obverse	Inc. above	55.00	85.00	165	300	—
1887 As L	20,000	25.00	50.00	75.00	165	—
1888 As L	32,000	12.00	25.00	50.00	125	—
1889 As L	16,000	25.00	50.00	100	200	—
1890 As L	30,000	25.00	50.00	85.00	175	—
1891 As L	8,000	65.00	125	200	400	—
1892 As L	13,000	20.00	40.00	60.00	125	—
1893 As L	24,000	10.00	20.00	45.00	90.00	—
1895 As L	20,000	10.00	20.00	45.00	90.00	—

KM# 398.1 5 CENTAVOS
1.3530 g., 0.9030 Silver .0392 oz. ASW **Obv:** Standing eagle
Rev: Denomination in wreath **Note:** Mint mark: *Ca or Ch*.

Date	Mintage	F	VF	XF	Unc	BU
1871* M	14,000	20.00	40.00	100	250	—
1873* M Crude date	—	100	150	250	500	—
1874* M Crude date	—	25.00	50.00	75.00	150	—
1886* M	25,000	7.50	15.00	30.00	100	—
1887* M	37,000	7.50	15.00	30.00	100	—
1887* Ca/MoM	Inc. above	10.00	20.00	40.00	125	—
1888* M	145,000	1.50	3.00	6.00	25.00	—
1889* M	44,000	5.00	10.00	20.00	50.00	—
1890* M	102,000	1.50	3.00	6.00	25.00	—
1891* M	164,000	1.50	3.00	6.00	25.00	—
1892* M	85,000	1.50	3.00	6.00	25.00	—
1892* M 9/ inverted 9	Inc. above	2.00	4.00	7.50	30.00	—
1893* M	133,000	1.50	3.00	6.00	25.00	—
1894* M	108,000	1.50	3.00	6.00	25.00	—
1895* M	74,000	2.00	4.00	7.50	30.00	—

KM# 398.2   5 CENTAVOS
1.3530 g., 0.9030 Silver .0392 oz. ASW **Obv:** Standing eagle **Rev:** Denomination in wreath

Date	Mintage	F	VF	XF	Unc	BU
1871Cn P	—	125	200	350	—	—
1873Cn P	4,992	50.00	100	200	400	—
1874Cn P	—	25.00	50.00	100	200	—
1875Cn P Rare	—	—	—	—	—	—
1876Cn P	—	25.00	50.00	100	200	—
1886Cn M	10,000	25.00	50.00	100	200	—
1887Cn M	10,000	25.00	50.00	100	200	—
1888Cn M	119,000	1.50	3.00	6.00	30.00	—
1889Cn M	66,000	4.00	7.50	15.00	50.00	—
1890Cn M	180,000	1.50	3.00	6.00	25.00	—
1890/9Cn M	—	2.00	4.00	8.00	40.00	—
1890Cn D Error	Inc. above	125	175	250	—	—
1891Cn M	87,000	2.00	4.00	7.50	25.00	—
1894Cn M	24,000	4.00	7.50	15.00	40.00	—
1896Cn M	16,000	7.50	12.50	25.00	75.00	—
1897Cn M	223,000	1.50	2.50	5.00	20.00	—

KM# 398.3   5 CENTAVOS
1.3530 g., 0.9030 Silver .0392 oz. ASW **Obv:** Standing eagle **Rev:** Denomination in wreath

Date	Mintage	F	VF	XF	Unc	BU
1874Do M	—	100	150	225	500	—
1877Do P	4,795	75.00	125	225	450	—
1878/7Do E/P	4,300	200	300	450	—	—
1879Do B	—	125	200	350	—	—
1880Do B Rare	—	—	—	—	—	—
1881Do P	3,020	300	500	800	—	—
1887Do C	42,000	5.00	8.00	17.50	60.00	—
1888/9Do C	91,000	6.00	10.00	20.00	70.00	—
1888Do C	Inc. above	4.00	7.50	15.00	55.00	—
1889Do C	49,000	3.50	6.00	12.50	50.00	—
1890Do C	136,000	4.00	7.50	15.00	55.00	—
1890Do P	Inc. above	5.00	8.00	17.50	60.00	—
1891/0Do P	48,000	3.50	6.00	12.50	50.00	—
1891Do P	Inc. above	3.00	5.00	10.00	45.00	—
1894Do D	38,000	3.50	6.00	12.50	50.00	—

KM# 398.4   5 CENTAVOS
1.3530 g., 0.9030 Silver .0392 oz. ASW **Obv:** Standing eagle **Rev:** Denomination in wreath

Date	Mintage	F	VF	XF	Unc	BU
1877Ga A	—	15.00	30.00	60.00	150	—
1881Ga S	156,000	4.00	7.50	15.00	60.00	—
1886Ga S	87,000	2.00	4.00	7.50	25.00	—
1888Ga S Large G	262,000	2.00	4.00	10.00	30.00	—
1888Ga S Small G	Inc. above	2.00	4.00	10.00	30.00	—
1889Ga S	178,000	1.50	3.00	7.50	25.00	—
1890Ga S	68,000	4.00	7.50	12.50	35.00	—
1891Ga S	50,000	4.00	6.50	10.00	35.00	—
1892Ga S	78,000	2.00	4.00	7.50	25.00	—
1893Ga S	44,000	4.00	7.50	15.00	45.00	—

KM# 398.5   5 CENTAVOS
1.3530 g., 0.9030 Silver .0392 oz. ASW **Obv:** Standing eagle **Rev:** Denomination in wreath

Date	Mintage	F	VF	XF	Unc	BU
1869Go S	80,000	15.00	30.00	75.00	175	—
1871Go S	100,000	5.00	10.00	25.00	75.00	—
1872Go S	30,000	30.00	60.00	125	250	—
1873Go S	40,000	30.00	60.00	125	250	—
1874Go S	—	7.00	12.00	25.00	75.00	—
1875Go S	—	8.00	15.00	30.00	75.00	—
1876Go S	—	8.00	15.00	30.00	75.00	—
1877Go S	—	7.00	12.00	20.00	75.00	—
1878/7Go S	20,000	8.00	15.00	25.00	75.00	—
1879Go S	—	8.00	15.00	25.00	75.00	—
1880Go S	55,000	15.00	30.00	60.00	200	—
1881/0Go S	160,000	5.00	8.00	17.50	60.00	—
1881Go S	Inc. above	4.00	6.00	12.00	45.00	—
1886Go S	230,000	1.50	3.00	6.00	30.00	—
1887Go R/S	—	1.50	3.00	6.00	30.00	—
1887Go R	230,000	1.50	2.50	5.00	30.00	—
1888Go R	320,000	1.50	2.50	5.00	20.00	—
1889Go R	60,000	4.00	6.00	12.00	45.00	—
1890/5Go R/S	—	1.50	3.00	6.00	30.00	—
1890Go R	250,000	1.50	2.50	5.00	20.00	—
1891/0Go R	168,000	1.80	3.00	6.00	30.00	—
1891Go R	Inc. above	1.50	2.50	5.00	20.00	—
1892Go R	138,000	1.50	3.00	6.00	25.00	—
1893Go R	200,000	1.25	2.50	5.00	20.00	—
1894Go R	200,000	1.25	2.50	5.00	20.00	—
1896Go R	525,000	1.25	2.00	4.00	15.00	—
1896Go R/S	—	1.50	3.00	6.00	25.00	—
1897Go R	596,000	1.50	2.00	4.00	15.00	—
1898Go R	—					

KM# 398.6   5 CENTAVOS
1.3530 g., 0.9030 Silver .0392 oz. ASW **Obv:** Standing eagle **Rev:** Denomination in wreath

Date	Mintage	F	VF	XF	Unc	BU
1874/69Ho R	—	125	225	350	—	—
1874Ho R	—	100	200	325	—	—
1878/7Ho A Rare	22,000	—	—	—	—	—
1878Ho A	Inc. above	20.00	40.00	80.00	175	—
1878Ho A Mule, gold peso obverse	Inc. above	40.00	80.00	150	300	—
1880Ho A	43,000	7.50	15.00	30.00	75.00	—
1886Ho A	44,000	5.00	10.00	20.00	75.00	—
1887Ho G	20,000	5.00	10.00	20.00	75.00	—
1888Ho G	12,000	7.50	15.00	30.00	85.00	—
1889Ho G	67,000	3.00	6.00	12.50	40.00	—
1890Ho G	50,000	3.00	6.00	12.50	40.00	—
1891Ho G	46,000	3.00	6.00	12.50	40.00	—
1893Ho G	84,000	2.50	5.00	10.00	30.00	—
1894Ho G	68,000	2.00	4.00	10.00	30.00	—

KM# 398.7   5 CENTAVOS
1.3530 g., 0.9030 Silver .0392 oz. ASW **Obv:** Standing eagle **Rev:** Denomination in wreath **Note:** Struck at Mexico City Mint, mint mark Mo. Varieties exist.

Date	Mintage	F	VF	XF	Unc	BU
1869/8Mo C	40,000	8.00	15.00	40.00	120	—
1870Mo C	140,000	4.00	7.00	20.00	60.00	—
1871Mo C	103,000	9.00	20.00	40.00	100	—
1871Mo M	Inc. above	7.50	12.50	25.00	60.00	—
1872Mo M	266,000	5.00	8.00	20.00	55.00	—
1873Mo M	20,000	40.00	60.00	100	225	—
1874/69Mo M	—	7.50	15.00	30.00	75.00	—
1874Mo M	—	4.00	7.00	17.50	50.00	—
1874/3Mo B	—	5.00	8.00	22.50	55.00	—
1874Mo B	—	5.00	8.00	22.50	55.00	—
1875Mo B	—	4.00	7.00	15.00	50.00	—
1875Mo B/M	—	6.00	9.00	17.50	60.00	—
1876/5Mo B	—	4.00	7.00	15.00	50.00	—
1876Mo B	—	4.00	7.00	12.50	50.00	—
1877/6Mo M	80,000	4.00	7.00	15.00	60.00	—
1877Mo M	Inc. above	4.00	7.00	12.50	60.00	—
1878/7Mo M	100,000	4.00	7.00	15.00	55.00	—
1878Mo M	Inc. above	2.50	5.00	12.50	45.00	—
1879/8Mo M	—	8.00	12.50	22.50	55.00	—
1879Mo M	—	4.50	7.00	15.00	50.00	—

Date	Mintage	F	VF	XF	Unc	BU
1879Mo M 9/inverted 9	—	10.00	15.00	25.00	75.00	—
1880/76Mo M/B	—	5.00	7.50	15.00	50.00	—
1880/76Mo M	—	5.00	7.50	15.00	50.00	—
1880Mo M	—	4.00	6.00	12.00	40.00	—
1881/0Mo M	180,000	4.00	6.00	10.00	35.00	—
1881Mo M	Inc. above	3.00	4.50	9.00	35.00	—
1886/0Mo M	398,000	2.00	2.75	7.50	25.00	—
1886/1Mo M	Inc. above	2.00	2.75	7.50	25.00	—
1886Mo M	Inc. above	1.75	2.25	6.00	20.00	—
1887Mo m	720,000	1.75	2.00	5.00	20.00	—
1887Mo M/m	Inc. above	1.75	2.00	6.00	20.00	—
1888/7Mo M	1,360,000	2.25	2.50	6.00	20.00	—
1888Mo M	Inc. above	1.75	2.00	5.00	20.00	—
1889/8Mo M	1,242,000	2.25	2.50	6.00	20.00	—
1889Mo M	Inc. above	1.75	2.00	5.00	20.00	—
1890/00Mo M	1,694,000	1.75	2.75	6.00	20.00	—
1890Mo M	Inc. above	1.50	2.00	5.00	20.00	—
1891Mo M	1,030,000	1.75	2.00	5.00	20.00	—
1892Mo M	1,400,000	1.75	2.00	5.00	20.00	—
1892Mo M 9/inverted 9	Inc. above	2.00	2.75	7.50	20.00	—
1893Mo M	220,000	1.75	2.00	5.00	15.00	—
1894Mo M	320,000	1.75	2.00	5.00	15.00	—
1895Mo M	78,000	3.00	5.00	8.00	25.00	—
1896Mo B	80,000	1.75	2.00	5.00	20.00	—
1897Mo B	160,000	1.75	2.00	5.00	15.00	—

KM# 398.8 5 CENTAVOS
1.3530 g., 0.9030 Silver .0392 oz. ASW **Obv:** Standing eagle **Rev:** Denomination in wreath

Date	Mintage	F	VF	XF	Unc	BU
1890 Oa E Rare	48,000	—	—	—	—	—
1890 Oa N	Inc. above	65.00	125	200	350	—

KM# 398.9 5 CENTAVOS
1.3530 g., 0.9030 Silver .0392 oz. ASW **Obv:** Standing eagle **Rev:** Denomination in wreath **Note:** Varieties exist.

Date	Mintage	F	VF	XF	Unc	BU
1869 Pi S	—	300	400	500	—	—
1870 Pi G/MoC Rare	20,000	150	250	400	—	—
1870 Pi O	Inc. above	200	300	450	—	—
1871 Pi O Rare	5,400	—	—	—	—	—
1872 Pi O	—	75.00	100	175	400	—
1873 Pi Rare	5,000	—	—	—	—	—
1874 Pi H	—	30.00	50.00	100	225	—
1875 Pi H	—	7.50	12.50	30.00	75.00	—
1876 Pi H	—	10.00	20.00	45.00	100	—
1877 Pi H	—	7.50	12.50	20.00	60.00	—
1878/7 Pi H Rare	—	—	—	—	—	—
1878 Pi H	—	60.00	90.00	150	300	—
1879 H	—	200	400	—	—	—
1880 Pi H Rare	6,200	—	—	—	—	—
1881 Pi H Rare	4,500	—	—	—	—	—
1886 Pi R	33,000	12.50	25.00	50.00	125	—
1887/0 Pi R	169,000	4.00	7.50	15.00	45.00	—
1887 Pi R	Inc. above	3.00	5.00	10.00	32.00	—
1888 Pi R	210,000	2.00	4.00	9.00	30.00	—
1889/7 Pi R	197,000	2.50	5.00	10.00	32.00	—
1889 Pi R	Inc. above	2.00	4.00	9.00	30.00	—
1890 Pi R	221,000	2.00	3.00	6.00	25.00	—
1891/89 Pi R/B	176,000	2.00	4.00	8.00	25.00	—
1891 Pi R	Inc. above	2.00	3.00	6.00	20.00	—
1892/89 Pi R	182,000	2.00	4.00	8.00	25.00	—
1892/0 Pi R	Inc. above	2.00	4.00	8.00	25.00	—
1892 Pi R	Inc. above	2.00	3.00	6.00	20.00	—
1893 Pi R	41,000	5.00	10.00	20.00	60.00	—

KM# 398.10 5 CENTAVOS
1.3530 g., 0.9030 Silver .0392 oz. ASW **Obv:** Standing eagle **Rev:** Denomination in wreath

Date	Mintage	F	VF	XF	Unc	BU
1870Zs H	40,000	12.50	25.00	50.00	125	—
1871Zs H	40,000	12.50	25.00	50.00	125	—
1872Zs H	40,000	12.50	25.00	50.00	125	—
1873/2Zs H	20,000	35.00	65.00	125	275	—

Date	Mintage	F	VF	XF	Unc	BU
1873Zs H	Inc. above	25.00	50.00	100	250	—
1874Zs H	—	7.50	12.50	25.00	75.00	—
1874Zs A	—	40.00	75.00	150	300	—
1875Zs A	—	7.50	12.50	25.00	75.00	—
1876Zs A	—	50.00	75.00	150	500	—
1876/5Zs S	—	15.00	30.00	60.00	150	—
1876Zs S	—	12.50	25.00	50.00	125	—
1877Zs S	—	3.00	6.00	12.00	40.00	—
1878Zs S	60,000	3.00	6.00	12.00	40.00	—
1879/8Zs S	—	3.00	6.00	15.00	50.00	—
1879Zs S	—	3.00	6.00	12.00	40.00	—
1880/79Zs S	130,000	6.00	10.00	20.00	60.00	—
1880Zs S	Inc. above	5.00	8.00	16.00	45.00	—
1881Zs S	210,000	2.50	5.00	10.00	35.00	—
1886/4Zs S	360,000	6.00	10.00	20.00	60.00	—
1886Zs S	Inc. above	2.00	3.00	6.00		—
1886Zs Z	Inc. above	5.00	10.00	25.00	65.00	—
1887Zs Z	400,000	2.00	3.00	6.00	25.00	—
1888/7Zs Z	500,000	2.00	3.00	6.00	25.00	—
1888Zs Z	Inc. above	2.00	3.00	6.00	25.00	—
1889Zs Z	520,000	2.00	3.00	6.00	25.00	—
1889Zs Z 9/inverted 9	Inc. above	2.00	3.00	6.00	25.00	—
1889Zs Z/MoM	Inc. above	2.00	3.00	6.00	25.00	—
1890Zs Z	580,000	1.75	2.50	5.00	20.00	—
1890Zs Z/MoM	Inc. above	2.00	3.00	6.00	25.00	—
1890Zs ZsZ 9/8	—	2.00	3.00	6.00	25.00	—
1890Zs ZsZ 0/9 Z/M	—	2.00	3.00	6.00	25.00	—
1891Zs Z	420,000	1.75	2.50	5.00	20.00	—
1892Zs Z	346,000	1.75	2.50	5.00	20.00	—
1893Zs Z	258,000	1.75	2.50	5.00	20.00	—
1894Zs Z	228,000	1.75	2.50	5.00	20.00	—
1894Zs ZoZ Error	Inc. above	2.00	4.00	8.00	30.00	—
1895Zs Z	260,000	1.75	2.50	5.00	20.00	—
1895Zs Z	260,000	1.75	2.50	5.00	20.00	—
1895/4Zs ZsZ	—	2.00	3.00	6.00	25.00	—
1896Zs Z	200,000	1.75	2.50	5.00	20.00	—
1896Zs 6/inverted 6	Inc. above	2.00	3.00	6.00	25.00	—
1897/6Zs Z	200,000	2.00	3.00	6.00	25.00	—
1897Zs Z	Inc. above	1.75	2.50	5.00	20.00	—

KM# 399 5 CENTAVOS
Copper-Nickel

Date	Mintage	F	VF	XF	Unc	BU
1882	Inc. above	0.50	1.00	2.50	7.50	—
1883	Inc. above	25.00	50.00	80.00	250	—

KM# 400 5 CENTAVOS
0.9030 Silver **Obv:** Restyled eagle **Note:** Varieties exist.

Date	Mintage	F	VF	XF	Unc	BU
1898Cn M	44,000	1.75	4.00	8.00	20.00	—
1899Cn M	111,000	5.50	8.50	20.00	50.00	—
1899Cn Q	Inc. above	1.75	2.50	4.50	15.00	—
1900/800Cn Q	239,000	3.50	5.00	12.50	30.00	—
1900Cn Q	Inc. above	1.75	3.00	6.00	16.50	—
Note: Round Q, single tail						
1900Cn Q	Inc. above	1.75	3.00	6.00	16.50	—
Note: Narrow C, oval Q						
1900Cn Q	Inc. above	1.75	3.00	6.00	16.50	—
Note: Wide C, oval Q						
1901Cn Q	148,000	1.75	2.50	4.50	15.00	—
1902Cn Q	262,000	1.75	3.00	6.00	16.50	—
Note: Narrow C, heavy serifs						
1902Cn Q	Inc. above	1.75	3.00	6.00	16.50	—
Note: Wide C, light serifs						
1903/1Cn Q	331,000	2.00	3.00	6.00	16.50	20.00

Date	Mintage	F	VF	XF	Unc	BU
1903Cn Q	Inc. above	1.75	2.50	4.50	15.00	18.00
1903/1898Cn V	Inc. above	3.50	4.50	9.00	22.50	—
1903Cn V	Inc. above	1.75	2.50	4.50	15.00	—
1904Cn H	352,000	1.75	2.25	5.00	16.50	—
1904Cn H 0/9	—	1.75	2.50	5.00	16.50	—
1904Cn H/C	—	1.75	2.50	5.00	16.50	—

KM# 400.1 5 CENTAVOS
0.9030 Silver **Obv:** Restyled eagle **Note:** Varieties exist.

Date	Mintage	F	VF	XF	Unc	BU
1898Go R Mule, gold peso obverse	180,000	7.50	15.00	30.00	75.00	—
1899Go R	260,000	1.75	2.50	4.50	15.00	—
1900Go R	200,000	1.75	2.50	4.50	15.00	—

KM# 400.2 5 CENTAVOS
0.9030 Silver **Obv:** Restyled eagle

Date	Mintage	F	VF	XF	Unc	BU
1898Mo M	80,000	2.00	4.00	7.00	25.00	—
1899Mo M	168,000	1.75	2.50	4.50	15.00	—
1900/800Mo M	300,000	4.50	6.50	10.00	30.00	—
1900Mo M	Inc. above	1.75	2.50	4.50	15.00	—
1901Mo M	100,000	1.75	2.50	4.50	15.00	—
1902Mo M	144,000	1.25	2.00	3.75	12.00	—
1902/1Mo MoM	—	1.75	3.00	7.00	16.50	—
1903Mo M	500,000	1.25	2.00	3.75	12.00	—
1904/804Mo M	1,090,000	1.75	3.50	8.50	16.50	18.50
1904/94Mo M	Inc. above	1.75	3.75	9.00	16.50	18.50
1904Mo M	Inc. above	1.75	3.00	6.00	15.00	—
1905Mo M	344,000	1.75	3.00	7.00	16.50	—

KM# 400.3 5 CENTAVOS
0.9030 Silver **Obv:** Restyled eagle

Date	Mintage	F	VF	XF	Unc	BU
1898Zs Z	100,000	1.75	2.25	4.50	12.50	—
1899Zs Z	50,000	2.00	3.00	7.00	20.00	—
1900Zs Z	55,000	1.75	2.50	5.00	16.50	—
1901Zs Z	40,000	1.75	2.50	5.00	16.50	—
1902/1Zs Z	34,000	2.00	4.50	9.00	22.50	—
1902Zs Z	Inc. above	1.75	3.75	7.50	18.50	—
1903Zs Z	217,000	1.25	2.00	5.00	12.50	—
1904Zs Z	191,000	1.75	2.50	5.00	12.50	—
1904Zs M	Inc. above	1.75	2.50	6.00	16.50	—
1905Zs M	46,000	2.00	4.50	9.00	22.50	—
1905Zs M Repullica - Rare	Inc. above					

KM# 401.1 10 CENTAVOS
2.7070 g., 0.9030 Silver .0785 oz. ASW **Obv:** Eagle **Rev:** Value within wreath **Note:** Previous KM#401.

Date	Mintage	F	VF	XF	Unc	BU
1868/7 Ca	—	30.00	60.00	150	550	—
1868 Ca	—	30.00	60.00	150	550	—
1869 Ca	15,000	25.00	50.00	125	600	—
1870 Ca	17,000	22.50	45.00	100	550	—

KM# 401.2 10 CENTAVOS
2.7070 g., 0.9030 Silver .0785 oz. ASW **Obv:** Eagle **Rev:** Value within wreath

Date	Mintage	F	VF	XF	Unc	BU
1863SLP	—	75.00	150	275	900	—

KM# 402 10 CENTAVOS
2.7070 g., 0.9030 Silver .0785 oz. ASW **Obv:** Eagle **Rev:** Cap and rays

Date	Mintage	F	VF	XF	Unc	BU
1867/3Mo	—	50.00	100	200	550	—
1867Mo	—	20.00	50.00	150	450	—
1868/7Mo	—	20.00	50.00	175	500	—
1868Mo	—	20.00	55.00	175	500	—

KM# 402.1 10 CENTAVOS
2.7070 g., 0.9030 Silver .0785 oz. ASW **Obv:** Eagle **Rev:** Cap and rays

Date	Mintage	F	VF	XF	Unc	BU
1868/7P	38,000	45.00	90.00	175	650	—
1868P	Inc. above	20.00	40.00	100	550	—
1869/7P	4,900	55.00	125	250	800	—

KM# 403 10 CENTAVOS
2.7070 g., 0.9030 Silver .0785 oz. ASW **Obv:** Eagle **Rev:** Value within wreath **Note:** Varieties exist.

Date	Mintage	F	VF	XF	Unc	BU
1874 As DL	—	20.00	40.00	80.00	175	—
1875 As L	—	5.00	10.00	25.00	90.00	—
1876 As L	—	10.00	18.00	40.00	110	—
1878/7 As L	—	10.00	18.00	45.00	120	—
1878 As L	—	5.00	10.00	30.00	100	—
1879 As L	—	10.00	18.00	40.00	110	—
1880 As L	13,000	10.00	18.00	40.00	110	—
1882 As L	22,000	10.00	18.00	40.00	110	—
1883 As L	8,520	25.00	50.00	100	225	—
1884 As L	—	7.50	12.50	35.00	100	—
1885 As L	15,000	7.50	12.50	35.00	100	—
1886 As L	45,000	7.50	12.50	35.00	100	—
1887 As L	15,000	7.50	12.50	35.00	100	—
1888 As L	38,000	7.50	12.50	35.00	100	—
1889 As L	20,000	7.50	12.50	35.00	100	—
1890 As L	40,000	7.50	12.50	35.00	100	—
1891 As L	38,000	7.50	12.50	35.00	100	—
1892 As L	57,000	5.00	10.00	25.00	90.00	—
1893 As L	70,000	10.00	18.00	40.00	110	—

Note: An 1891 As L over 1889 HoG exists which was evidently produced at the Alamos Mint using dies sent from the Hermosillo Mint.

KM# 403.1 10 CENTAVOS
2.7070 g., 0.9030 Silver .0785 oz. ASW **Obv:** Eagle **Rev:** Value within wreath **Note:** Mint mark CH, Ca. Varieties exist.

Date	Mintage	F	VF	XF	Unc	BU
1871 M	8,150	15.00	30.00	60.00	150	—
1873 M Crude date	—	35.00	75.00	125	175	—
1874 M	—	10.00	17.50	35.00	100	—
1880/70 G	7,620	20.00	40.00	80.00	175	—
1880 G/g	Inc. above	15.00	25.00	50.00	125	—
1881 Rare	340	—	—	—	—	—
1883 M	9,000	10.00	20.00	40.00	125	—
1884/73	—	5.00	30.00	60.00	150	—
1884 M	—	10.00	20.00	40.00	125	—
1886 M	45,000	7.50	12.50	30.00	100	—
1887/3 M/G	96,000	5.00	10.00	20.00	75.00	—
1887 M/G	—	2.00	4.00	8.00	75.00	—
1887 M	Inc. above	2.00	4.00	8.00	75.00	—
1888 M/G	—	2.00	4.00	8.00	75.00	—
1888 M	299,000	1.50	2.50	5.00	75.00	—
1888 Ca/Mo	Inc. above	1.50	2.50	5.00	75.00	—
1889/8 M	115,000	2.00	4.00	8.00	75.00	—
1889 M Small 89 (5 Centavo font)	Inc. above	2.00	4.00	8.00	75.00	—
1890/80 M	140,000	2.00	4.00	8.00	75.00	—
1890/89 M	Inc. above	2.00	4.00	8.00	75.00	—
1890 M	Inc. above	1.50	3.00	7.00	75.00	—
1891 M	163,000	1.50	3.00	7.00	75.00	—
1892 M	169,000	1.50	3.00	7.00	75.00	—
1892 M 9/inverted 9	Inc. above	2.00	4.00	8.00	75.00	—
1893 M	246,000	1.50	3.00	7.00	75.00	—
1894 M	163,000	1.50	3.00	7.00	75.00	—
1895 M	127,000	1.50	3.00	7.00	75.00	—

KM# 403.2 10 CENTAVOS
2.7070 g., 0.9030 Silver .0785 oz. ASW **Obv:** Eagle **Rev:** Value within wreath

Date	Mintage	F	VF	XF	Unc	BU
1871Cn P Rare	—	—	—	—	—	—
1873Cn P	8,732	20.00	50.00	100	225	—
1881Cn D	9,440	75.00	175	325	500	—
1882Cn D	12,000	75.00	125	200	400	—
1885Cn M Mule, gold 2-1/2 peso obverse	18,000	25.00	50.00	100	200	—
1886Cn M Mule, gold 2-1/2 peso obverse	13,000	50.00	100	150	300	—
1887Cn M	11,000	20.00	40.00	75.00	175	—
1888Cn M	56,000	5.00	10.00	25.00	125	—
1889Cn M	42,000	5.00	10.00	20.00	75.00	—
1890Cn M	132,000	2.00	4.00	7.50	75.00	—
1891Cn M	84,000	5.00	10.00	20.00	75.00	—

Date	Mintage	F	VF	XF	Unc	BU
1892/1Cn M	37,000	4.00	8.00	15.00	75.00	—
1892Cn M	Inc. above	2.50	5.00	10.00	75.00	—
1894Cn M	43,000	2.50	5.00	10.00	75.00	—
1895Cn M	23,000	2.50	5.00	10.00	60.00	—
1896Cn M	121,000	1.50	2.50	5.00	50.00	—

KM# 403.3   10 CENTAVOS
2.7070 g., 0.9030 Silver .0785 oz. ASW **Obv:** Eagle **Rev:**
Value within wreath

Date	Mintage	F	VF	XF	Unc	BU
1878Do E	2,500	100	175	300	600	—
1879Do B Rare	—	—	—	—	—	—
1880/70Do B Rare	—	—	—	—	—	—
1880/79Do B Rare	—	—	—	—	—	—
1884Do C	—	30.00	60.00	100	225	—
1886Do C	13,000	75.00	150	300	500	—
1887Do C	81,000	4.00	8.00	15.00	100	—
1888Do C	31,000	6.00	12.00	30.00	100	—
1889Do C	55,000	4.00	8.00	15.00	100	—
1890Do C	50,000	4.00	8.00	15.00	100	—
1891Do P	139,000	2.00	4.00	8.00	80.00	—
1892Do P	212,000	2.00	4.00	8.00	80.00	—
1892Do D	Inc. above	2.00	4.00	8.00	80.00	—
1893Do D	258,000	2.00	4.00	8.00	80.00	—
1893Do D/C	Inc. above	2.50	5.00	10.00	80.00	—
1894Do D	184,000	1.50	3.00	6.00	80.00	—
1894Do D/C	Inc. above	2.00	4.00	8.00	80.00	—
1895Do D	142,000	1.50	3.00	6.00	80.00	—

KM# 403.4   10 CENTAVOS
2.7070 g., 0.9030 Silver .0785 oz. ASW **Obv:** Eagle **Rev:**
Value within wreath **Note:** Varieties exist.

Date	Mintage	F	VF	XF	Unc	BU
1871Ga C	4,734	75.00	125	200	500	—
1873/1Ga C	25,000	10.00	15.00	35.00	150	—
1873Ga C	Inc. above	10.00	15.00	35.00	150	—
1874Ga C	—	10.00	15.00	35.00	150	—
1877Ga A	—	10.00	15.00	30.00	150	—
1881Ga S	115,000	5.00	10.00	25.00	150	—
1883Ga B	90,000	4.00	8.00	15.00	90.00	—
1884Ga B	—	5.00	10.00	20.00	90.00	—
1884Ga B/S	—	6.00	12.50	25.00	90.00	—
1884Ga H	—	3.00	5.00	10.00	90.00	—
1885Ga H	93,000	3.00	5.00	10.00	90.00	—
1886Ga S	151,000	2.50	4.00	9.00	90.00	—
1887Ga S	162,000	1.50	3.00	6.00	90.00	—
1888Ga S	225,000	1.50	3.00	6.00	90.00	—
1888Ga GaS/HoG	Inc. above	1.50	3.00	6.00	90.00	—
1889Ga S	310,000	1.50	3.00	6.00	40.00	—
1890Ga S	303,000	1.50	3.00	6.00	40.00	—
1891Ga S	199,000	5.00	10.00	20.00	45.00	—
1892Ga S	329,000	1.50	3.00	6.00	40.00	—
1893Ga S	225,000	1.50	3.00	6.00	40.00	—
1894Ga S	243,000	3.00	6.00	12.00	40.00	—
1895Ga S	80,000	1.50	3.00	6.00	40.00	—

KM# 403.5   10 CENTAVOS
2.7070 g., 0.9030 Silver .0785 oz. ASW **Obv:** Eagle **Rev:**
Value within wreath **Note:** Varieties exist.

Date	Mintage	F	VF	XF	Unc	BU
1869Go S	7,000	20.00	40.00	80.00	200	—
1871/0Go S	60,000	15.00	25.00	50.00	125	—
1872Go S	60,000	15.00	25.00	50.00	125	—
1873Go S	50,000	15.00	25.00	50.00	125	—
1874Go S	—	15.00	25.00	50.00	125	—
1875Go S	—	250	350	500	800	—
1876Go S	—	10.00	20.00	40.00	100	—
1877Go S	—	80.00	120	200	400	—
1878/7Go S	10,000	10.00	20.00	45.00	110	—
1878Go S	Inc. above	7.50	12.00	20.00	75.00	—
1879Go S	—	7.50	12.00	20.00	75.00	—
1880Go S	—	100	200	300	450	—
1881/71Go S	100,000	3.00	5.00	10.00	75.00	—
1881/0Go S	Inc. above	3.50	5.00	10.00	75.00	—
1881Go S	Inc. above	3.00	5.00	10.00	75.00	—
1882/1Go S	40,000	3.00	6.00	12.00	75.00	—
1883Go B	—	3.00	5.00	10.00	75.00	—
1884Go B	—	1.50	3.00	6.00	75.00	—
1884Go S	—	6.00	12.50	25.00	90.00	—
1885Go R	100,000	1.50	3.00	6.00	75.00	—
1886Go R	95,000	3.00	5.00	10.00	75.00	—
1887Go R	330,000	2.50	5.00	10.00	75.00	—
1888Go R	270,000	1.50	3.00	6.00	75.00	—

Date	Mintage	F	VF	XF	Unc	BU
1889Go R	205,000	2.00	4.00	8.00	75.00	—
1889Go GoR/HoG	Inc. above	3.00	5.00	10.00	75.00	—
1890Go R	270,000	1.50	3.00	6.00	35.00	—
1890Go GoR/Cn M	Inc. above	1.50	3.00	6.00	35.00	—
1891Go R	523,000	1.50	3.00	6.00	35.00	—
1891Go R/G	—	1.50	3.00	6.00	35.00	—
1891Go GoR/HoG	Inc. above	1.50	3.00	6.00	35.00	—
1892Go R	440,000	1.50	3.00	6.00	35.00	—
1893/1Go R	389,000	3.00	5.00	10.00	35.00	—
1893Go R	Inc. above	1.50	3.00	6.00	35.00	—
1894Go R	400,000	1.50	2.50	5.00	35.00	—
1895Go R	355,000	1.50	2.50	5.00	35.00	—
1896Go R	190,000	1.50	2.50	5.00	35.00	—
1897Go R	205,000	1.50	2.50	5.00	35.00	—

KM# 403.6   10 CENTAVOS
2.7070 g., 0.9030 Silver .0785 oz. ASW **Obv:** Eagle **Rev:**
Value within wreath

Date	Mintage	F	VF	XF	Unc	BU
1874Ho R	—	30.00	60.00	100	200	—
1876Ho F	3,140	200	300	450	750	—
1878Ho A	—	5.00	10.00	15.00	85.00	—
1879Ho A	—	25.00	50.00	90.00	175	—
1880Ho A	—	3.00	6.00	12.50	85.00	—
1881Ho A	28,000	4.00	7.00	15.00	85.00	—
1882/1Ho A	25,000	5.00	10.00	20.00	85.00	—
1882/1Ho a	Inc. above	6.00	12.50	25.00	85.00	—
1882Ho A	Inc. above	4.00	7.00	15.00	85.00	—
1883Ho	7,000	65.00	100	200	400	—
1884Ho A	—	35.00	75.00	150	300	—
1884/3Ho M	—	10.00	20.00	40.00	90.00	—
1884Ho M	—	7.50	15.00	30.00	85.00	—
1885Ho M	21,000	12.50	25.00	50.00	100	—
1886Ho M Rare	10,000	—	—	—	—	—
1886Ho G	Inc. above	7.50	12.50	25.00	85.00	—
1887Ho G	—	25.00	50.00	75.00	150	—
1888Ho G	25,000	6.00	12.50	25.00	85.00	—
1889Ho G	42,000	3.00	6.00	10.00	85.00	—
1890Ho G	48,000	3.00	6.00	10.00	85.00	—
1891/80Ho G	136,000	3.00	6.00	10.00	85.00	—
1891/0Ho G	Inc. above	3.00	6.00	10.00	85.00	—
1891Ho G	Inc. above	3.00	6.00	10.00	85.00	—
1892Ho G	67,000	3.00	6.00	10.00	85.00	—
1893Ho G	67,000	3.00	6.00	10.00	85.00	—

KM# 403.7   10 CENTAVOS
2.7070 g., 0.9020 Silver .0785 oz. ASW **Obv:** Eagle **Rev:**
Value within wreath **Note:** Varieties exist.

Date	Mintage	F	VF	XF	Unc	BU
1869/8Mo C	30,000	10.00	20.00	40.00	100	—
1869Mo C	Inc. above	8.00	17.50	35.00	90.00	—
1870Mo C	110,000	3.00	7.50	15.00	50.00	—
1871Mo C	84,000	50.00	75.00	125	250	—
1871Mo M	Inc. above	12.00	17.50	45.00	125	—
1872/69Mo M	198,000	10.00	20.00	35.00	100	—
1872Mo M	Inc. above	3.00	7.50	15.00	65.00	—
1873Mo M	40,000	10.00	15.00	30.00	75.00	—
1874Mo M	—	5.00	10.00	20.00	65.00	—
1874Mo M/C	—	5.00	10.00	20.00	65.00	—
1874/64Mo B	—	5.00	10.00	20.00	65.00	—
1874Mo B/M	—	20.00	40.00	60.00	125	—
1874Mo B	—	5.00	10.00	15.00	65.00	—
1875Mo B	—	20.00	40.00	60.00	125	—
1876/5Mo B	—	3.00	5.00	9.00	65.00	—
1876/5Mo B/M	—	3.00	5.00	9.00	65.00	—
1877/6Mo M	—	3.00	5.00	9.00	65.00	—
1877/6Mo M/B	—	3.00	5.00	9.00	65.00	—
1877Mo M	—	3.00	5.00	9.00	65.00	—
1878/7Mo M	100,000	3.00	5.00	9.00	65.00	—
1878Mo M	Inc. above	3.00	5.00	9.00	65.00	—
1879/69Mo M	—	3.00	5.00	9.00	65.00	—
1879Mo M/C	—	3.00	5.00	9.00	65.00	—
1880/79Mo M	—	3.00	5.00	9.00	65.00	—

Date	Mintage	F	VF	XF	Unc	BU
1881/0Mo M	510,000	3.00	5.00	9.00	35.00	—
1881Mo M	Inc. above	3.00	5.00	9.00	35.00	—
1882/1Mo M	550,000	3.00	5.00	9.00	35.00	—
1882Mo M	Inc. above	3.00	5.00	9.00	35.00	—
1883/2Mo M	250,000	3.00	5.00	9.00	35.00	—
1884Mo M	—	3.00	5.00	9.00	35.00	—
1885Mo M	470,000	3.00	5.00	9.00	35.00	—
1886Mo M	603,000	3.00	5.00	9.00	35.00	—
1887Mo M	580,000	3.00	5.00	9.00	35.00	—
1888/7Mo MoM	710,000	3.00	5.00	9.00	35.00	—
1888Mo MoM	Inc. above	3.00	5.00	9.00	35.00	—
1888Mo MOM	Inc. above	3.00	5.00	9.00	35.00	—
1889/8Mo M	622,000	3.00	5.00	9.00	35.00	—
1889Mo M	Inc. above	3.00	5.00	9.00	35.00	—
1890/89Mo M	815,000	3.00	5.00	9.00	35.00	—
1890Mo M	Inc. above	3.00	5.00	9.00	35.00	—
1891Mo M	859,000	1.50	2.50	7.00	25.00	—
1892Mo M	1,030,000	1.50	2.50	7.00	25.00	—
1893Mo M	310,000	1.50	2.50	7.00	25.00	—
1893Mo M/C	Inc. above	1.50	2.50	7.00	25.00	—
1893Mo Mo/Ho M/G	—	1.50	2.50	7.00	25.00	—
1894/3Mo M	—	5.00	10.00	20.00	60.00	—
1894Mo M	350,000	5.00	10.00	20.00	60.00	—
1895Mo M	320,000	1.50	2.50	7.00	25.00	—
1896Mo B/G	340,000	1.50	2.50	7.00	25.00	—
1896Mo M	Inc. above	35.00	70.00	100	150	—
1897Mo M	170,000	1.50	2.50	5.00	20.00	—

KM# 403.8   10 CENTAVOS
2.7070 g., 0.9030 Silver .0785 oz. ASW   **Obv:** Eagle **Rev:** Value within wreath

Date	Mintage	F	VF	XF	Unc	BU
1889 Oa E	21,000	200	400	600	—	—
1890 Oa E	31,000	100	150	250	500	—
1890 Oa N Rare	Inc. above	—	—	—	—	—

KM# 403.9   10 CENTAVOS
2.7070 g., 0.9030 Silver .0785 oz. ASW   **Obv:** Eagle **Rev:** Value within wreath **Note:** Varieties exist.

Date	Mintage	F	VF	XF	Unc	BU
1869/8 Pi S Rare	4,000	—	—	—	—	—
1870/69 Pi O Rare	18,000	—	—	—	—	—
1870 Pi G	Inc. above	125	200	325	600	—
1871 Pi O	21,000	50.00	100	150	300	—
1872 Pi O	16,000	150	225	350	650	—
1873 Pi O Rare	4,750	—	—	—	—	—
1874 Pi H	—	25.00	50.00	100	200	—
1875 Pi H	—	75.00	125	200	400	—
1876 Pi H	—	75.00	125	200	400	—
1877 Pi H	—	75.00	125	200	400	—
1878 Pi H	—	250	500	750	—	—
1879 Pi H	—	—	—	—	—	—
1880 Pi H	—	150	250	350	—	—
1881 Pi H	7,600	250	350	500	—	—
1882 Pi H Rare	4,000	—	—	—	—	—
1883 Pi H	—	125	200	300	500	—
1884 Pi H	—	25.00	50.00	100	200	—
1885 Pi H	51,000	25.00	50.00	100	200	—
1885 Pi C Rare	Inc. above	—	—	—	—	—
1886 Pi C	52,000	15.00	30.00	60.00	150	—
1886 Pi R	Inc. above	5.00	10.00	20.00	65.00	—
1887 Pi R	118,000	2.50	5.00	10.00	50.00	—
1888 Pi R	136,000	2.50	5.00	10.00	50.00	—
1889/8 Pi R/G	—	7.50	12.50	20.00	60.00	—
1889/7 Pi R	131,000	7.50	12.50	20.00	60.00	—
1890 Pi R	204,000	1.50	3.00	7.50	40.00	—
1891/89 Pi R	163,000	2.50	5.00	10.00	40.00	—
1891 Pi R	Inc. above	1.50	3.50	6.00	30.00	—
1892/0 Pi R	200,000	2.00	4.00	8.00	40.00	—
1892 Pi R	Inc. above	1.50	2.50	5.00	40.00	—
1892 Pi R/G	—	2.00	4.00	8.00	40.00	—
1893 Pi R	48,000	7.50	10.00	17.50	60.00	—
1893 Pi R/G	—	1.50	10.00	17.50	60.00	—

KM# 403.10   10 CENTAVOS
2.7070 g., 0.9030 Silver .0785 oz. ASW   **Obv:** Eagle **Rev:** Value within wreath **Note:** Varieties exist.

Date	Mintage	F	VF	XF	Unc	BU
1870Zs H	20,000	100	150	200	400	—
1871/0Zs H	10,000	—	—	—	—	—
1871Zs H	Inc. above	—	—	—	—	—
1872Zs H	10,000	150	200	275	500	—
1873Zs H	10,000	250	350	600	—	—
1874/3Zs H	—	50.00	75.00	150	300	—
1874Zs A	—	200	300	500	—	—
1875Zs A	—	5.00	10.00	25.00	100	—
1876Zs A	—	5.00	10.00	25.00	100	—
1876Zs S	—	100	200	300	500	—
1877Zs S Small S	—	7.50	12.50	25.00	100	—
1877Zs S Regular S	—	7.50	12.50	25.00	100	—
1878/7Zs S	30,000	5.00	10.00	20.00	80.00	—
1878Zs S	Inc. above	5.00	10.00	20.00	80.00	—
1879Zs S	—	5.00	10.00	20.00	80.00	—
1880Zs S	—	5.00	10.00	20.00	80.00	—
1881/0Zs S	120,000	3.00	6.00	12.50	50.00	—
1881Zs S	Inc. above	3.00	6.00	12.50	50.00	—
1882/1Zs S	64,000	12.50	25.00	50.00	125	—
1882Zs S	Inc. above	12.50	25.00	50.00	125	—
1883/73Zs S	102,000	2.00	4.00	8.00	50.00	—
1883Zs S	Inc. above	2.00	4.00	8.00	50.00	—
1884/3Zs S	—	2.00	4.00	8.00	50.00	—
1884Zs S	—	2.00	4.00	8.00	50.00	—
1885Zs S	297,000	1.50	2.50	5.00	50.00	—
1885Zs S Small S in mint mark	Inc. above	2.50	4.00	8.00	50.00	—
1885Zs Z Without assayers initials (error)	Inc. above	3.50	7.50	15.00	65.00	—
1886Zs S	274,000	1.50	2.50	5.00	30.00	—
1886Zs Z	Inc. above	12.50	25.00	50.00	125	—
1887Zs Z	233,000	1.50	2.50	5.00	30.00	—
1887Zs Z Z (Error)	Inc. above	3.50	10.00	25.00	100	—
1888Zs Z	270,000	1.50	2.50	5.00	30.00	—
1888Zs Z Z (Error)	Inc. above	3.50	10.00	25.00	100	—
1889/7Zs Z/S	240,000	4.00	8.00	12.50	40.00	—
1889Zs ZS	Inc. above	1.50	4.00	8.00	30.00	—
1889Zs Z/G	—	1.50	4.00	8.00	30.00	—
1889Zs Z	Inc. above	1.50	2.50	5.00	30.00	—
1890Zs ZsZ	410,000	1.50	2.50	5.00	30.00	—
1890Zs Z Z (Error)	Inc. above	3.75	10.00	25.00	100	—
1891Zs Z	1,105,000	1.50	2.50	5.00	30.00	—
1891Zs ZsZ Double s	Inc. above	2.00	4.00	7.00	30.00	—
1892Zs Z	1,102,000	1.50	2.50	5.00	30.00	—
1892Zs Z/G	—	2.00	4.00	7.00	30.00	—
1893/2Zs Z	—	2.00	4.00	8.00	40.00	—
1893Zs Z	1,010,999	1.50	2.50	5.00	25.00	—
1894Zs Z	892,000	1.50	2.50	5.00	30.00	—
1895Zs Z	920,000	1.50	2.50	5.00	30.00	—
1895Zs Z 9/5	—	2.00	4.00	7.00	30.00	—
1896/5Zs ZsZ	700,000	1.50	2.50	5.00	30.00	—
1896Zs ZsZ	Inc. above	1.50	2.50	5.00	30.00	—
1896Zs Z Z (Error)	Inc. above	3.75	10.00	25.00	100	—
1896/5Zs Z/G	—	1.50	2.50	5.00	30.00	—
1896Zs Z/G	—	1.50	2.50	5.00	30.00	—
1897/6Zs ZsZ	900,000	2.00	5.00	10.00	30.00	—
1897/6Zs Z Z (Error)	Inc. above	3.75	10.00	25.00	100	—
1897Zs Z	Inc. above	1.50	2.50	5.00	30.00	—

KM# 404   10 CENTAVOS
2.7070 g., 0.9030 Silver .0785 oz. ASW   **Obv:** Restyled eagle **Note:** Varieties exist.

Date	Mintage	F	VF	XF	Unc	BU
1898Cn M	9,870	50.00	100	200	500	—
1899Cn Q Round Q, single tail	80,000	5.00	7.50	25.00	100	—
1899Cn Q Oval Q, double tail	Inc. above	5.00	7.50	25.00	100	—
1900Cn Q	160,000	1.50	2.50	5.00	20.00	—

Date	Mintage	F	VF	XF	Unc	BU
1901Cn Q	235,000	1.50	2.50	5.00	18.00	20.00
1902Cn Q	186,000	1.50	2.50	5.00	20.00	—
1903Cn Q	256,000	1.50	2.50	6.00	20.00	—
1903Cn V	Inc. above	1.50	2.50	5.00	15.00	—
1904Cn H	307,000	1.50	2.50	5.00	15.00	—

KM# 404.1 10 CENTAVOS
2.7070 g., 0.9030 Silver .0785 oz. ASW **Obv:** Restyled eagle

Date	Mintage	F	VF	XF	Unc	BU
1898Go R	435,000	1.50	2.50	5.00	20.00	—
1899Go R	270,000	1.50	2.50	5.00	25.00	—
1900Go R	130,000	7.50	12.50	25.00	60.00	—

KM# 404.2 10 CENTAVOS
2.7070 g., 0.9030 Silver .0785 oz. ASW **Obv:** Restyled eagle

Date	Mintage	F	VF	XF	Unc	BU
1898Mo M	130,000	1.50	2.50	5.00	20.00	—
1899Mo M	190,000	1.50	2.50	5.00	20.00	—
1900Mo M	311,000	1.50	2.50	5.00	20.00	—
1901Mo M	80,000	2.50	3.50	7.00	22.50	—
1902Mo M	181,000	1.50	2.50	6.00	20.00	—
1903Mo M	581,000	1.50	2.50	6.00	20.00	—
1904Mo M	1,266,000	1.25	2.00	4.50	18.00	—
1904Mo MM (Error)	Inc. above	2.50	5.00	10.00	25.00	—
1905Mo M	266,000	2.00	3.75	7.50	20.00	—

KM# 404.3 10 CENTAVOS
2.7070 g., 0.9020 Silver .0785 oz. ASW **Obv:** Restyled eagle

Date	Mintage	F	VF	XF	Unc	BU
1898Zs Z	240,000	1.50	2.50	7.50	20.00	—
1899Zs Z	105,000	1.50	3.00	10.00	22.00	—
1900Zs Z	219,000	7.50	10.00	20.00	45.00	—
1901Zs Z	70,000	2.50	5.00	10.00	25.00	—
1902Zs Z	120,000	2.50	5.00	10.00	25.00	—
1903Zs Z	228,000	1.50	3.00	9.00	18.00	20.00
1904Zs Z	368,000	1.50	3.00	9.00	18.00	20.00
1904Zs M	Inc. above	1.50	3.00	9.00	22.00	25.00
1905Zs M	66,000	7.50	20.00	50.00	200	—

KM# 405 20 CENTAVOS
5.4150 g., 0.9030 Silver .1572 oz. ASW **Obv:** Restyled eagle

Date	Mintage	F	VF	XF	Unc	BU
1898Cn M	114,000	5.00	12.50	35.00	140	—
1899Cn M	44,000	12.00	20.00	45.00	225	—
1899Cn Q	Inc. above	20.00	35.00	100	250	—
1900Cn Q	68,000	6.50	12.50	35.00	140	—
1901Cn Q	185,000	5.00	10.00	30.00	120	—
1902/802Cn Q	98,000	6.00	10.00	30.00	120	—
1902Cn Q	Inc. above	4.00	9.00	30.00	120	—
1903Cn Q	93,000	4.00	9.00	30.00	120	—
1904/3Cn H	258,000	—	—	—	—	—
1904Cn H	Inc. above	5.00	10.00	30.00	120	—

KM# 405.1 20 CENTAVOS
5.4150 g., 0.9027 Silver .1572 oz. ASW **Obv:** Restyled eagle

Date	Mintage	F	VF	XF	Unc	BU
1898Go R	135,000	4.00	8.00	20.00	100	—
1899Go R	215,000	4.00	8.00	20.00	100	—
1900/800Go R	38,000	10.00	20.00	60.00	250	—

KM# 405.2 20 CENTAVOS

5.4150 g., 0.9030 Silver .1572 oz. ASW **Obv:** Restyled eagle
Note: Varieties exist.

Date	Mintage	F	VF	XF	Unc	BU
1898Mo M	150,000	4.00	8.00	20.00	90.00	—
1899Mo M	425,000	4.00	8.00	20.00	90.00	—
1900/800Mo M	295,000	4.00	8.00	20.00	90.00	—
1901Mo M	110,000	4.00	8.00	20.00	90.00	—
1902Mo M	120,000	4.00	8.00	20.00	90.00	—
1903Mo M	213,000	4.00	8.00	20.00	90.00	—
1904Mo M	276,000	4.00	8.00	20.00	90.00	—
1905Mo M	117,000	6.50	20.00	50.00	150	—

KM# 405.3 20 CENTAVOS
5.4150 g., 0.9027 Silver .1572 oz. ASW **Obv:** Restyled eagle

Date	Mintage	F	VF	XF	Unc	BU
1898Zs Z	195,000	5.00	10.00	20.00	100	—
1899Zs Z	210,000	5.00	10.00	20.00	100	—
1900/800Zs Z	97,000	5.00	10.00	20.00	100	—
1901Zs Z	Inc. above	5.00	10.00	20.00	100	—
1901/0Zs Z	130,000	25.00	50.00	100	250	—
1902Zs Z	105,000	5.00	10.00	20.00	100	—
1903Zs Z	143,000	5.00	10.00	20.00	100	—
1904Zs Z	246,000	5.00	10.00	20.00	100	—
1904Zs M	Inc. above	5.00	10.00	50.00	300	—
1905Zs M	59,000	10.00	70.00	50.00	400	—

KM# 406 25 CENTAVOS
6.7680 g., 0.9030 Silver .1965 oz. ASW **Note:** Mint mark A, As.

Date	Mintage	F	VF	XF	Unc	BU
1874 L	—	20.00	40.00	90.00	200	—
1875 L	—	15.00	30.00	70.00	200	—
1876 L	—	30.00	50.00	100	200	—
1877 L	11,000	200	300	500	—	—
1877.	Inc. above	10.00	25.00	60.00	200	—
1878 L	25,000	10.00	25.00	60.00	200	—
1879 L	—	10.00	25.00	60.00	200	—
1880 L	—	10.00	25.00	60.00	200	—
1880. L	—	10.00	25.00	60.00	200	—
1881 L	8,800	500	700	—	—	—
1882 L	7,777	15.00	35.00	80.00	200	—
1883 L	28,000	10.00	25.00	60.00	200	—
1884 L	—	10.00	25.00	60.00	200	—
1885 L	—	20.00	40.00	90.00	200	—
1886 L	46,000	15.00	30.00	70.00	200	—
1887 L	12,000	12.50	27.50	65.00	200	—
1888 L	20,000	12.50	27.50	65.00	200	—
1889 L	14,000	12.50	27.50	65.00	200	—
1890 L	23,000	10.00	25.00	60.00	200	—

KM# 406.1 25 CENTAVOS
6.7680 g., 0.9030 Silver .1965 oz. ASW **Note:** Mint mark CA, CH, Ca.

Date	Mintage	F	VF	XF	Unc	BU
1871 M	18,000	25.00	50.00	100	200	—
1872 M Very crude date	24,000	50.00	100	150	300	—
1883 M	12,000	10.00	25.00	50.00	175	—
1885/3 M	35,000	10.00	25.00	50.00	175	—
1885 M	Inc. above	10.00	25.00	50.00	175	—
1886 M	22,000	10.00	25.00	50.00	175	—
1887/6 M	26,000	10.00	15.00	30.00	175	—
1887 M	Inc. above	10.00	15.00	30.00	175	—
1888 M	14,000	10.00	25.00	50.00	175	—
1889 M	50,000	10.00	15.00	30.00	175	—

KM# 406.2 25 CENTAVOS
6.7680 g., 0.9030 Silver .1965 oz. ASW

Date	Mintage	F	VF	XF	Unc	BU
1871Cn P	—	250	500	750	—	—
1872Cn P	2,780	300	550	800	—	—
1873Cn P	20,000	100	150	250	500	—
1874Cn P	—	20.00	50.00	125	250	—
1875Cn P	—	250	500	750	—	—
1876Cn P Rare	—	—	—	—	—	—

Date	Mintage	F	VF	XF	Unc	BU
1878/7Cn D/S	—	100	150	250	500	—
1878Cn Cn/Go D/S	—	100	150	250	500	—
1878Cn D	—	100	150	250	500	—
1879Cn D	—	15.00	35.00	70.00	175	—
1880Cn D	—	250	500	750	—	—
1881/0Cn D	18,000	15.00	30.00	60.00	175	—
1882Cn D	—	200	350	600	—	—
1882Cn M Rare	—	—	—	—	—	—
1883Cn M	15,000	50.00	100	150	300	—
1884Cn M	—	20.00	40.00	80.00	175	—
1885/4Cn M	19,000	20.00	40.00	80.00	175	—
1886Cn M	22,000	12.50	20.00	50.00	175	—
1887Cn M	32,000	12.50	20.00	50.00	175	—
1888Cn M	86,000	7.50	15.00	30.00	175	—
1888Cn M Cn/Mo	—	—	—	—	—	—
1889Cn M	50,000	10.00	25.00	50.00	175	—
1890Cn M 9/8	—	7.50	17.50	40.00	175	—
1890Cn M	91,000	7.50	17.50	40.00	175	—
1892/0Cn M	16,000	20.00	40.00	80.00	200	—
1892Cn M	Inc. above	20.00	40.00	80.00	200	—

KM# 406.3 25 CENTAVOS
6.7680 g., 0.9030 Silver .1965 oz. ASW

Date	Mintage	F	VF	XF	Unc	BU
1873Do P Rare	892	—	—	—	—	—
1877Do P	—	25.00	50.00	100	200	—
1878/7Do E	—	250	500	750	—	—
1878Do B Rare	—	—	—	—	—	—
1879Do B	—	50.00	75.00	125	250	—
1880Do B Rare	—	—	—	—	—	—
1882Do C	17,000	25.00	50.00	100	225	—
1884/3Do C	—	25.00	50.00	100	200	—
1885Do C	15,000	20.00	40.00	80.00	200	—
1885Do C/S	—	20.00	40.00	80.00	200	—
1886Do C	33,000	15.00	30.00	60.00	200	—
1887Do C	27,000	10.00	20.00	50.00	200	—
1888Do C	25,000	10.00	20.00	50.00	200	—
1889Do C	29,000	10.00	20.00	50.00	200	—
1890Do C	68,000	7.50	15.00	40.00	200	—

KM# 406.4 25 CENTAVOS
6.7680 g., 0.9030 Silver .1965 oz. ASW

Date	Mintage	F	VF	XF	Unc	BU
1880Ga A	38,000	25.00	50.00	100	200	—
1881/0Ga S	39,000	25.00	50.00	100	200	—
1881Ga S	Inc. above	25.00	50.00	100	200	—
1882Ga S	18,000	25.00	50.00	100	200	—
1883/2Ga B/S	—	50.00	100	150	300	—
1884Ga B	—	20.00	40.00	80.00	150	—
1889Ga S	30,000	20.00	40.00	80.00	150	—

KM# 406.5 25 CENTAVOS
6.7680 g., 0.9030 Silver .1965 oz. ASW **Note:** Varieties exist.

Date	Mintage	F	VF	XF	Unc	BU
1870Go S	128,000	10.00	20.00	50.00	125	—
1871Go S	172,000	10.00	20.00	50.00	125	—
1872/1Go S	178,000	10.00	20.00	50.00	125	—
1872Go S	Inc. above	10.00	20.00	50.00	125	—
1873Go S	120,000	10.00	20.00	50.00	125	—
1874Go S	—	15.00	30.00	60.00	150	—
1875/4Go S	—	15.00	30.00	60.00	150	—
1875Go S	—	10.00	20.00	50.00	125	—
1876Go S	—	20.00	40.00	80.00	175	—
1877Go S	124,000	10.00	20.00	50.00	125	—
1878Go S	146,000	10.00	20.00	50.00	125	—
1879Go S	—	10.00	20.00	50.00	125	—
1880Go S	—	20.00	40.00	80.00	175	—
1881Go S	408,000	7.50	17.50	45.00	125	—
1882Go S	204,000	7.50	17.50	45.00	125	—
1883Go B	168,000	7.50	17.50	45.00	125	—
1884/69Go B	—	7.50	17.50	45.00	125	—
1884/3Go B	—	7.50	17.50	45.00	125	—
1884/3Go B/R	—	7.50	17.50	45.00	125	—
1884Go B	—	7.50	17.50	45.00	125	—
1885/65Go R	300,000	7.50	17.50	45.00	125	—
1885/69Go R	Inc. above	7.50	17.50	45.00	125	—
1885Go R	Inc. above	7.50	17.50	45.00	125	—
1886/66Go R	322,000	7.50	17.50	45.00	125	—
1886/69Go R/S	Inc. above	7.50	17.50	45.00	125	—
1886/5/69Go R	Inc. above	7.50	15.00	45.00	125	—
1886Go R	Inc. above	7.50	15.00	45.00	125	—
1887Go R	254,000	7.50	15.00	45.00	125	—

Date	Mintage	F	VF	XF	Unc	BU
1887Go/Cn R/D	Inc. above	7.50	15.00	45.00	125	—
1888Go R	312,000	7.50	15.00	45.00	125	—
1889/8Go R	304,000	7.50	15.00	45.00	125	—
1889/8Go/Cn R/D	Inc. above	7.50	15.00	45.00	125	—
1889Go R	Inc. above	7.50	15.00	45.00	125	—
1890Go R	236,000	7.50	15.00	45.00	125	—

KM# 406.6 25 CENTAVOS
6.7680 g., 0.9030 Silver .1965 oz. ASW **Note:** Varieties exist.

Date	Mintage	F	VF	XF	Unc	BU
1874/64Ho R	Inc. above	10.00	20.00	40.00	125	—
1874/69Ho R	—	10.00	20.00	40.00	125	—
1874Ho R	23,000	10.00	20.00	40.00	125	—
1875Ho R Rare	—	—	—	—	—	—
1876/4Ho F/R	34,000	10.00	20.00	50.00	150	—
1876Ho F/R	Inc. above	10.00	25.00	60.00	150	—
1876Ho F	Inc. above	10.00	25.00	55.00	135	—
1877Ho F	—	10.00	20.00	50.00	125	—
1878Ho A	23,000	10.00	20.00	50.00	125	—
1879Ho A	—	10.00	20.00	50.00	125	—
1880Ho A	—	15.00	30.00	60.00	125	—
1881Ho A	19,000	15.00	30.00	60.00	125	—
1882Ho A	8,120	20.00	40.00	80.00	150	—
1883Ho M	2,000	100	200	300	600	—
1884Ho M	—	12.50	25.00	50.00	150	—
1885Ho M	—	10.00	20.00	50.00	125	—
1886Ho G	6,400	30.00	60.00	125	250	—
1887Ho G	12,000	10.00	20.00	40.00	125	—
1888Ho G	20,000	10.00	20.00	40.00	125	—
1889Ho G	28,000	10.00	20.00	40.00	125	—
1890/80Ho G	18,000	25.00	50.00	100	125	—
1890Ho G	Inc. above	25.00	50.00	100	125	—

KM# 406.7 25 CENTAVOS
6.7680 g., 0.9027 Silver .1965 oz. ASW **Note:** Varieties exist.

Date	Mintage	F	VF	XF	Unc	BU
1869Mo C	76,000	10.00	25.00	50.00	125	—
1870/69Mo C	—	6.00	12.00	30.00	125	—
1870/9Mo C	136,000	6.00	12.00	30.00	125	—
1870Mo C	Inc. above	6.00	12.00	30.00	125	—
1871Mo M	138,000	6.00	12.00	30.00	125	—
1872Mo M	220,000	6.00	12.00	30.00	125	—
1873/1Mo M	48,000	10.00	25.00	50.00	125	—
1873Mo M	Inc. above	10.00	25.00	50.00	125	—
1874/69Mo B/M	—	10.00	25.00	50.00	125	—
1874/3Mo M	—	10.00	25.00	50.00	125	—
1874/3Mo B	—	10.00	25.00	50.00	125	—
1874/3Mo B/M	—	10.00	25.00	50.00	125	—
1874Mo M	—	6.00	12.00	30.00	125	—
1874Mo B/M	—	10.00	25.00	50.00	125	—
1875Mo B	—	6.00	12.00	30.00	125	—
1876/5Mo B	—	7.50	15.00	40.00	125	—
1876Mo B	—	6.00	12.00	30.00	125	—
1877Mo M	56,000	10.00	25.00	50.00	125	—
1878/1Mo M	120,000	10.00	25.00	50.00	125	—
1878/7Mo M	Inc. above	10.00	25.00	50.00	125	—
1878Mo M	—	6.00	12.00	30.00	125	—
1879Mo M	—	10.00	20.00	40.00	125	—
1880Mo M	—	7.50	15.00	35.00	125	—
1881/0Mo M	300,000	10.00	25.00	50.00	125	—
1881Mo M	Inc. above	10.00	25.00	50.00	125	—
1882Mo M	212,000	7.50	15.00	35.00	125	—
1883Mo M	108,000	7.50	15.00	35.00	125	—
1884/3Mo M	—	10.00	25.00	50.00	125	—
1884Mo M	—	10.00	20.00	40.00	125	—
1885Mo M	216,000	10.00	20.00	40.00	125	—
1886/5Mo M	436,000	7.50	15.00	35.00	125	—
1886Mo M	Inc. above	7.50	15.00	35.00	125	—
1887Mo M	376,000	7.50	15.00	35.00	125	—
1888Mo M	192,000	7.50	15.00	35.00	125	—

Date	Mintage	F	VF	XF	Unc	BU
1889Mo M	132,000	7.50	15.00	35.00	125	—
1890Mo M	60,000	10.00	20.00	40.00	125	—

KM# 406.8 25 CENTAVOS
6.7680 g., 0.9030 Silver .1965 oz. ASW **Note:** Varieties exist.

Date	Mintage	F	VF	XF	Unc	BU
1869 Pi S	—	25.00	75.00	150	300	—
1870 Pi G	50,000	10.00	30.00	75.00	150	—
1870 Pi O	Inc. above	15.00	35.00	85.00	175	—
1871 Pi O	30,000	10.00	30.00	75.00	150	—
1872 Pi O	46,000	10.00	30.00	75.00	150	—
1873 Pi O	13,000	15.00	40.00	90.00	175	—
1874 Pi H	—	15.00	40.00	90.00	200	—
1875 Pi H	—	10.00	20.00	60.00	150	—
1876/5 Pi H	—	15.00	30.00	80.00	175	—
1876 Pi H	—	10.00	25.00	65.00	150	—
1877 Pi H	19,000	10.00	25.00	65.00	150	—
1878 Pi H	—	15.00	30.00	60.00	150	—
1879/8 Pi H	—	10.00	25.00	60.00	150	—
1879 Pi H	—	10.00	25.00	60.00	150	—
1879 Pi E	—	100	200	300	600	—
1880 Pi H	—	20.00	40.00	100	200	—
1880 Pi H/M	—	20.00	40.00	100	200	—
1881 Pi H	50,000	20.00	40.00	80.00	175	—
1881 Pi E Rare	Inc. above	—	—	—	—	—
1882 Pi H	20,000	10.00	20.00	60.00	150	—
1883 Pi H	17,000	10.00	25.00	65.00	150	—
1884 Pi H	—	10.00	25.00	65.00	150	—
1885/4 Pi H	—	10.00	20.00	60.00	150	—
1885 Pi H	43,000	10.00	20.00	60.00	150	—
1886 Pi C	78,000	10.00	25.00	65.00	150	—
1886 Pi R	Inc. above	7.50	20.00	50.00	150	—
1886 Pi R 6/ inverted 6	Inc. above	7.50	20.00	50.00	150	—
1887Pi/ZsR	92,000	7.50	20.00	50.00	150	—
1887Pi/ZsB	Inc. above	100	150	300	500	—
1887 Pi R	—	7.50	20.00	50.00	150	—
1888 Pi R	106,000	7.50	20.00	50.00	150	—
1888Pi/ZsR	Inc. above	10.00	20.00	50.00	150	—
1888 Pi R/B	Inc. above	10.00	20.00	50.00	150	—
1889 Pi R	115,000	7.50	15.00	40.00	150	—
1889Pi/ZsR	Inc. above	10.00	20.00	50.00	150	—
1889 Pi R/B	Inc. above	10.00	20.00	50.00	150	—
1890 Pi R	64,000	10.00	20.00	50.00	150	—
1890Pi/ZsR/B	Inc. above	7.50	15.00	40.00	150	—
1890 Pi R/B	Inc. above	10.00	20.00	50.00	150	—

KM# 406.9 25 CENTAVOS
6.7680 g., 0.9030 Silver .1965 oz. ASW **Note:** Varieties exist.

Date	Mintage	F	VF	XF	Unc	BU
1870Zs H	152,000	6.00	15.00	50.00	125	—
1871Zs H	250,000	6.00	15.00	50.00	125	—
1872Zs H	260,000	6.00	15.00	50.00	125	—
1872Zs H	—	—	—	—	—	—
1873Zs H	132,000	6.00	15.00	50.00	125	—
1874Zs H	—	10.00	20.00	60.00	125	—
1874Zs A	—	10.00	20.00	60.00	125	—
1875Zs A	—	7.00	20.00	60.00	125	—
1876Zs A	—	6.00	15.00	50.00	125	—
1876Zs S	—	6.00	15.00	50.00	125	—
1877Zs S	350,000	6.00	15.00	50.00	125	—
1878Zs S	252,000	6.00	15.00	50.00	125	—
1878/1Zs S	—	7.00	20.00	60.00	125	—
1878/7Zs S	—	7.00	20.00	60.00	125	—
1879Zs S	—	6.00	15.00	50.00	125	—
1880Zs S	—	6.00	15.00	50.00	125	—
1881/0Zs S	570,000	6.00	15.00	50.00	125	—
1881Zs S	Inc. above	6.00	15.00	50.00	125	—
1882/1Zs S	300,000	10.00	17.50	55.00	125	—
1882Zs S	Inc. above	6.00	15.00	50.00	125	—
1883/2Zs S	193,000	10.00	17.50	55.00	125	—
1883Zs S	Inc. above	6.00	15.00	50.00	125	—
1884/3Zs S	—	10.00	17.50	55.00	125	—
1884Zs S	—	6.00	15.00	50.00	125	—
1885Zs S	309,000	6.00	15.00	50.00	125	—
1886/2Zs S	—	10.00	17.50	55.00	125	—
1886/5Zs S	613,000	6.00	15.00	50.00	125	—
1886Zs S	Inc. above	6.00	15.00	50.00	125	—
1886Zs Z	Inc. above	6.00	15.00	55.00	125	—
1887Zs Z	389,000	6.00	15.00	50.00	125	—
1888Zs Z	408,000	6.00	15.00	50.00	125	—

Date	Mintage	F	VF	XF	Unc	BU
1889Zs Z	400,000	6.00	15.00	50.00	125	—
1890Zs Z	269,000	6.00	15.00	50.00	125	—

KM# 407 50 CENTAVOS
13.5360 g., 0.9030 Silver .3930 oz. ASW **Rev:** Balance scale
Note: Mint mark A, As.

Date	Mintage	F	VF	XF	Unc	BU
1875 L	—	12.00	25.00	70.00	400	—
1876/5 L	—	25.00	50.00	120	450	—
1876 L	—	12.00	25.00	70.00	400	—
1876. L	—	—	—	—	—	—
1877 L	26,000	15.00	30.00	85.00	450	—
1878 L	—	12.00	25.00	70.00	400	—
1879 L	—	25.00	50.00	120	450	—
1880 L	57,000	12.00	25.00	70.00	400	—
1881 L	18,000	15.00	30.00	80.00	450	—
1884 L	6,286	65.00	120	250	650	—
1885As/HoL	21,000	15.00	35.00	90.00	450	—
1888 L	—	4,000	5,000	7,000	—	—

KM# 407.1 50 CENTAVOS
13.5360 g., 0.9030 Silver .3930 oz. ASW **Rev:** Balance scale
Note: Mint mark Ca, CHa.

Date	Mintage	F	VF	XF	Unc	BU
1883 M	12,000	30.00	60.00	125	500	—
1884 M	—	25.00	50.00	125	500	—
1885 M	13,000	15.00	35.00	90.00	400	—
1886 M	18,000	20.00	40.00	100	450	—
1887 M	26,000	25.00	65.00	150	500	—

KM# 407.2 50 CENTAVOS
13.5360 g., 0.9030 Silver .3930 oz. ASW **Rev:** Balance scale

Date	Mintage	F	VF	XF	Unc	BU
1871Cn P	—	400	550	750	1,500	—
1873Cn P	—	400	550	750	1,500	—
1874Cn P	—	200	300	500	1,000	—
1875/4Cn P	—	20.00	40.00	75.00	450	—
1875Cn P	—	12.00	25.00	50.00	450	—
1876Cn P	—	15.00	30.00	60.00	450	—
1877/6Cn G	—	15.00	30.00	60.00	450	—
1877Cn G	—	12.00	25.00	50.00	450	—
1878Cn G	18,000	20.00	40.00	75.00	450	—
1878Cn/Mo D	Inc. above	30.00	60.00	100	450	—
1878Cn D	Inc. above	15.00	35.00	75.00	450	—
1879Cn D	—	12.00	25.00	50.00	450	—
1879Cn D/G	—	12.00	25.00	50.00	450	—
1880/8Cn D	—	15.00	30.00	60.00	450	—
1880Cn D	—	15.00	30.00	60.00	450	—
1881/0Cn D	188,000	15.00	30.00	60.00	450	—
1881Cn D	Inc. above	15.00	30.00	60.00	450	—
1881Cn G	Inc. above	125	175	275	550	—
1882Cn D	—	175	300	500	2,000	—
1882Gn G	—	100	250	300	1,000	—
1883 D	19,000	25.00	50.00	100	500	—
1885/3Cn M/H	9,254	30.00	60.00	100	500	—
1886Cn M/G	7,030	50.00	100	300	1,500	—
1886Cn M	Inc. above	40.00	80.00	150	800	—
1887Cn M	76,000	20.00	40.00	100	450	—
1888Cn M	—	4,000	6,000	—	—	—
1892Cn M	8,200	40.00	80.00	150	650	—

KM# 407.3   50 CENTAVOS
13.5360 g., 0.9030 Silver .3930 oz. ASW **Rev:** Balance scale

Date	Mintage	F	VF	XF	Unc	BU
1871Do P Rare	591	—	—	—	—	—
1873Do P	4,010	150	250	500	1,250	—
1873Do M/P	Inc. above	150	250	500	1,250	—
1874Do M	—	20.00	40.00	175	750	—
1875Do M	—	20.00	40.00	80.00	350	—
1875Do H	—	150	250	450	1,000	—
1876/5Do M	—	35.00	70.00	150	500	—
1876Do M	—	35.00	70.00	150	500	—
1877Do P	2,000	30.00	45.00	150	1,250	—
1878Do B Rare	—	—	—	—	—	—
1879Do B Rare	—	—	—	—	—	—
1880Do P	—	30.00	60.00	125	500	—
1881Do P	10,000	40.00	80.00	150	550	—
1882Do C	8,957	30.00	75.00	200	800	—
1884/2Do C	—	20.00	50.00	125	600	—
1884Do C	—	—	—	—	—	—
1885Do B	—	15.00	40.00	100	500	—
1885Do B/P	—	15.00	40.00	100	500	—
1886Do C	16,000	15.00	40.00	100	500	—
1887Do/Mo C	28,000	15.00	40.00	100	500	—
1887Do C	—	15.00	40.00	100	500	—

KM# 407.4   50 CENTAVOS
13.5360 g., 0.9030 Silver .3930 oz. ASW **Rev:** Balance scale
Note: Struck at Guanajuato Mint, mitn mark Go. Varieties exist.

Date	Mintage	F	VF	XF	Unc	BU
1869Go S	—	15.00	35.00	75.00	550	—
1870Go S	166,000	12.00	25.00	50.00	450	—
1871Go S	148,000	12.00	25.00	50.00	450	—
1872/1Go S	144,000	15.00	30.00	60.00	500	—
1872Go S	Inc. above	12.00	25.00	50.00	450	—
1873Go S	50,000	12.00	25.00	50.00	450	—
1874Go S	—	12.00	25.00	50.00	450	—
1875Go S	—	15.00	35.00	75.00	450	—
1876/5Go S	—	12.00	25.00	50.00	450	—
1877Go S	76,000	12.00	25.00	60.00	450	—
1878Go S	37,000	15.00	30.00	75.00	550	—
1879/8Go S	—	15.00	30.00	60.00	500	—
1879Go S	—	12.00	25.00	50.00	450	—
1880Go S	—	12.00	25.00	50.00	450	—
1881/79Go S	32,000	15.00	30.00	60.00	500	—
1881Go S	Inc. above	12.00	25.00	50.00	450	—
1882Go S	18,000	12.00	25.00	50.00	450	—
1883/2Go B/S	—	15.00	30.00	60.00	500	—
1883Go B	—	12.00	25.00	50.00	450	—
1883Go S Rare	—	—	—	—	—	—
1884Go B/S	—	15.00	30.00	60.00	500	—
1885/4Go R/B	—	15.00	30.00	60.00	500	—
1885Go R	53,000	12.00	25.00	50.00	450	—
1886/5Go R/B	59,000	15.00	30.00	60.00	500	—
1886/5Go R/S	Inc. above	20.00	40.00	75.00	500	—
1886Go R	Inc. above	20.00	40.00	75.00	450	—
1887Go R	18,000	20.00	40.00	75.00	550	—
1888Go R 1 known; Rare	—	—	—	—	—	—

KM# 407.5   50 CENTAVOS
13.5360 g., 0.9030 Silver .3930 oz. ASW **Rev:** Balance scale
Note: Varieties exist.

Date	Mintage	F	VF	XF	Unc	BU
1874Ho R	—	20.00	40.00	100	600	—
1875/4Ho R	—	20.00	50.00	125	600	—
1875Ho R	—	20.00	50.00	125	600	—
1876/5Ho F/R	—	15.00	35.00	100	550	—
1876Ho F	—	15.00	35.00	100	550	—
1877Ho F	—	50.00	75.00	150	650	—

Date	Mintage	F	VF	XF	Unc	BU
1880/70Ho A	—	15.00	35.00	100	550	—
1880Ho A	—	15.00	35.00	100	550	—
1881Ho A	13,000	15.00	35.00	100	550	—
1882Ho A	—	75.00	150	250	750	—
1888Ho G	—	2,000	3,000	6,000	—	—
1894Ho G	59,000	15.00	30.00	100	450	—
1895Ho G	8,000	250	350	700	1,500	—

KM# 407.6   50 CENTAVOS
13.5360 g., 0.9027 Silver .3930 oz. ASW **Rev:** Balance scale

Date	Mintage	F	VF	XF	Unc	BU
1869Mo C	46,000	15.00	35.00	95.00	600	—
1870Mo C	52,000	15.00	30.00	90.00	550	—
1871Mo C	14,000	40.00	75.00	150	650	—
1871Mo M/C	Inc. above	35.00	75.00	150	600	—
1872/1Mo M	60,000	35.00	75.00	150	550	—
1872Mo M	Inc. above	35.00	75.00	150	550	—
1873Mo M	6,000	35.00	75.00	150	600	—
1874/3Mo M	—	200	400	600	1,250	—
1874/2Mo B	—	15.00	30.00	75.00	500	—
1874/2Mo B/M	—	15.00	30.00	75.00	500	—
1874/3Mo B/M	—	15.00	30.00	75.00	500	—
1874Mo B	—	15.00	30.00	75.00	500	—
1875Mo B	—	15.00	30.00	75.00	550	—
1876/5Mo B	—	15.00	30.00	75.00	500	—
1876Mo B	—	12.00	25.00	75.00	500	—
1877/2Mo M	—	20.00	40.00	100	550	—
1877Mo M	—	15.00	30.00	90.00	500	—
1878/7Mo M	8,000	25.00	50.00	125	600	—
1878Mo M	Inc. above	15.00	35.00	100	550	—
1879Mo M	—	25.00	50.00	125	550	—
1880Mo M	—	100	150	250	750	—
1881Mo M	16,000	25.00	50.00	125	600	—
1881/0Mo M	—	30.00	50.00	125	600	—
1882/1Mo M	2,000	30.00	60.00	150	750	—
1883/2Mo M	4,000	150	225	350	1,000	—
1884Mo M	—	150	225	350	1,000	—
1885Mo M	12,000	30.00	60.00	150	600	—
1886/5Mo M	66,000	15.00	35.00	90.00	475	—
1886Mo M	Inc. above	12.00	25.00	75.00	450	—
1887/6Mo M	88,000	15.00	35.00	90.00	475	—
1887Mo M	Inc. above	15.00	35.00	75.00	475	—
1888Mo M	—	3,000	4,000	6,000	—	—

KM# 407.7   50 CENTAVOS
13.5360 g., 0.9030 Silver .3930 oz. ASW **Rev:** Balance scale

Date	Mintage	F	VF	XF	Unc	BU
1870 Pi G	Inc. above	20.00	40.00	100	450	—
1870/780 Pi G	50,000	25.00	45.00	110	500	—
1870 Pi O	Inc. above	20.00	40.00	100	450	—
1871 Pi O	—	15.00	30.00	80.00	400	—
1871 Pi O/G	64,000	15.00	30.00	80.00	400	—
1872 Pi O	52,000	15.00	30.00	80.00	400	—
1872 Pi O/G	Inc. above	15.00	30.00	80.00	400	—
1873 Pi O	32,000	20.00	40.00	100	450	—
1873 Pi H	Inc. above	25.00	50.00	125	550	—
1874 Pi H/O	—	15.00	30.00	80.00	400	—
1875/3 Pi H	—	15.00	30.00	80.00	400	—
1875 Pi H	—	15.00	30.00	80.00	400	—
1876 Pi H	—	30.00	60.00	150	700	—
1877 Pi H	34,000	20.00	40.00	100	450	—
1878 Pi H	9,700	20.00	40.00	100	450	—
1879/7 Pi H	—	15.00	35.00	90.00	400	—
1879 Pi H	—	15.00	35.00	90.00	400	—
1880 Pi H	—	20.00	40.00	100	450	—
1881 Pi H	28,000	20.00	40.00	100	450	—
1882 Pi H	22,000	15.00	30.00	80.00	400	—
1883 Pi H 8/8	29,000	50.00	100	200	750	—
1883 Pi H	Inc. above	15.00	30.00	80.00	400	—

Date	Mintage	F	VF	XF	Unc	BU
1884 Pi H	—	50.00	100	175	600	—
1885/3 Pi H	—	20.00	40.00	100	450	—
1885/0 Pi H	45,000	20.00	40.00	100	450	—
1885/4 Pi H	Inc. above	20.00	40.00	100	450	—
1885 Pi H	Inc. above	25.00	50.00	125	450	—
1885 Pi C	Inc. above	15.00	30.00	80.00	400	—
1886/1 Pi R	92,000	50.00	100	175	600	—
1886/1 Pi C	—	25.00	40.00	100	450	—
1886 Pi C	Inc. above	15.00	30.00	80.00	400	—
1886 Pi R	Inc. above	15.00	30.00	80.00	400	—
1887 Pi R	Inc. above	15.00	30.00	90.00	450	—

KM# 407.8 50 CENTAVOS
13.5360 g., 0.9030 Silver .3930 oz. ASW **Rev:** Balance scale
Note: Varieties exist.

Date	Mintage	F	VF	XF	Unc	BU
1870Zs H	86,000	12.00	25.00	60.00	450	—
1871Zs H	146,000	12.00	25.00	50.00	400	—
1872Zs H	132,000	12.00	25.00	50.00	400	—
1873Zs H	56,000	12.00	25.00	50.00	400	—
1874Zs H	—	12.00	25.00	50.00	400	—
1874Zs A Rare	—	—	—	—	—	—
1875Zs A	—	12.00	25.00	50.00	400	—
1876/5Zs A	—	15.00	30.00	60.00	450	—
1876Zs A	—	12.00	25.00	50.00	400	—
1876Zs S	—	100	200	350	750	—
1877Zs S	100,000	12.00	25.00	50.00	400	—
1878/7Zs S	254,000	15.00	30.00	60.00	450	—
1878Zs S	Inc. above	15.00	30.00	60.00	400	—
1879Zs S	—	12.00	25.00	50.00	400	—
1880Zs S	—	12.00	25.00	50.00	400	—
1881Zs S	201,000	12.00	25.00	50.00	400	—
1882/1Zs S	2,000	50.00	100	250	650	—
1882Zs S	Inc. above	50.00	100	250	650	—
1883Zs/Za S	31,000	30.00	60.00	100	450	—
1883Zs S	Inc. above	25.00	50.00	100	450	—
1884/3Zs S	—	15.00	30.00	60.00	450	—
1884Zs S	—	12.00	25.00	50.00	450	—
1885/4Zs S	2,000	25.00	50.00	125	450	—
1885Zs S	Inc. above	25.00	50.00	125	450	—
1886Zs Z	2,000	150	275	400	1,000	—
1887Zs Z	63,000	30.00	60.00	125	450	—

KM# 408 PESO
27.0730 g., 0.9030 Silver .7860 oz. ASW **Rev:** Balance scale

Date	Mintage	F	VF	XF	Unc	BU
1872CH M	Inc. above	17.50	25.00	50.00	250	—
1872CH P/M	747,000	750	1,500	3,500	—	—
1872CH P	Inc. above	350	700	1,500	—	—
1872/1CH M	Inc. above	25.00	40.00	75.00	400	—
1873CH M	320,000	20.00	30.00	60.00	265	—
1873CH M/P	Inc. above	25.00	40.00	75.00	350	—

KM# 408.1 PESO
27.0730 g., 0.9030 Silver .7860 oz. ASW **Rev:** Balance scale

Date	Mintage	F	VF	XF	Unc	BU
1870Cn E	—	40.00	80.00	150	500	—
1871/11Cn P	478,000	25.00	45.00	100	450	—
1871Cn P	Inc. above	20.00	40.00	75.00	300	—
1872/1Cn P	—	20.00	40.00	75.00	300	—
1872Cn P	209,000	20.00	40.00	75.00	300	—
1873Cn P narrow date	527,000	20.00	40.00	75.00	300	—
1873Cn P wide date	Inc. above	20.00	40.00	75.00	300	—

KM# 408.2 PESO
27.0730 g., 0.9027 Silver .7860 oz. ASW **Rev:** Balance scale

Date	Mintage	F	VF	XF	Unc	BU
1870Do P	—	50.00	100	175	450	—
1871Do P	427,000	25.00	50.00	75.00	300	—
1872Do P	296,000	20.00	40.00	75.00	350	—
1872Do PT	Inc. above	100	175	250	850	—
1873Do P	203,000	25.00	45.00	85.00	350	—

KM# 408.3 PESO
27.0730 g., 0.9030 Silver .7860 oz. ASW **Rev:** Balance scale

Date	Mintage	F	VF	XF	Unc	BU
1870Ga C	—	650	850	—	—	—
1871Ga C	829,000	25.00	65.00	135	600	—
1872Ga C	485,000	40.00	90.00	175	650	—
1873/2Ga C	277,000	40.00	90.00	175	700	—
1873Ga C	Inc. above	25.00	65.00	135	600	—

KM# 408.4 PESO
27.0730 g., 0.9027 Silver .7860 oz. ASW **Rev:** Balance scale

Date	Mintage	F	VF	XF	Unc	BU
1871/0Go S	3,946,000	30.00	50.00	90.00	350	—
1871/3Go S	Inc. above	20.00	35.00	70.00	275	—
1871Go S	Inc. above	12.00	20.00	40.00	220	—

Date	Mintage	F	VF	XF	Unc	BU
1872Go S	4,067,000	12.00	20.00	40.00	250	—
1873/2Go S	1,560,000	15.00	25.00	50.00	250	—
1873Go S	Inc. above	12.00	20.00	45.00	250	—
1873Go/Mo/S/M	Inc. above	12.00	20.00	45.00	250	—

KM# 408.5 PESO
27.0730 g., 0.9030 Silver .7860 oz. ASW **Rev:** Balance scale

Date	Mintage	F	VF	XF	Unc	BU
1869Mo C	—	35.00	65.00	135	600	—
1870/69Mo C	5,115,000	15.00	25.00	55.00	275	—
1870Mo C	Inc. above	12.00	20.00	40.00	250	—
1870Mo M/C	Inc. above	18.00	30.00	60.00	275	—
1870Mo M	Inc. above	18.00	30.00	60.00	275	—
1871/0Mo M	6,974,000	15.00	25.00	55.00	275	—
1871Mo M	Inc. above	12.00	20.00	40.00	250	—
1872/1Mo M	—	15.00	25.00	50.00	275	—
1872/1Mo M/C	4,801,000	15.00	25.00	50.00	275	—
1872Mo M	Inc. above	12.00	20.00	40.00	250	—
1873Mo M	1,765,000	12.00	20.00	40.00	250	—

Note: The 1869 C with large LEY on the scroll is a pattern

KM# 408.6 PESO
27.0730 g., 0.9030 Silver .7860 oz. ASW **Rev:** Balance scale

Date	Mintage	F	VF	XF	Unc	BU
1869 Oa E	—	275	400	600	2,000	—
1870 Oa E Small A	Inc. above	15.00	30.00	75.00	400	—
1870Oa E Large A	Inc. above	100	150	300	900	—
1871/69 Oa E	140,000	30.00	50.00	125	550	—
1871 Oa E Small A	Inc. above	15.00	30.00	60.00	300	—
1871 Oa E Large A	Inc. above	15.00	30.00	75.00	400	—
1872 Oa E Small A	180,000	15.00	30.00	75.00	400	—
1872 Oa E Large A	Inc. above	50.00	100	200	450	—
1873 Oa E	105,000	15.00	30.00	75.00	350	—

KM# 408.7 PESO
27.0730 g., 0.9030 Silver .7860 oz. ASW **Rev:** Balance scale
Note: Varieties exist.

Date	Mintage	F	VF	XF	Unc	BU
1870 Pi S	1,967,000	200	350	500	1,000	—
1870 Pi S/A	Inc. above	200	350	550	1,200	—
1870 Pi G	Inc. above	25.00	40.00	75.00	550	—
1870 Pi H Contemporary counterfeits	Inc. above	—	—	—	—	—
1870 Pi O/G	Inc. above	25.00	40.00	75.00	550	—
1870 Pi O	Inc. above	20.00	30.00	100	400	—
1871/69 Pi O	2,103,000	75.00	100	200	500	—
1871 Pi O/G	Inc. above	15.00	30.00	60.00	500	—
1871 Pi O	—	15.00	30.00	60.00	500	—
1872 Pi O	1,873,000	15.00	30.00	60.00	500	—
1873 Pi O	893,000	15.00	30.00	60.00	500	—
1873 Pi H	Inc. above	15.00	30.00	60.00	500	—

KM# 408.8 PESO
27.0730 g., 0.9030 Silver .7860 oz. ASW **Rev:** Balance scale
Note: Varieties exist.

Date	Mintage	F	VF	XF	Unc	BU
1870Zs H	4,519,000	12.00	30.00	40.00	220	—
1871Zs H	4,459,000	12.00	20.00	40.00	220	—
1872Zs H	4,039,000	12.00	20.00	40.00	220	—

Date	Mintage	F	VF	XF	Unc	BU
1873/1Zs H	Inc. above	12.00	20.00	40.00	220	—
1873Zs H	1,782,000	12.00	20.00	40.00	220	—

KM# 409 PESO
27.0730 g., 0.9030 Silver .7860 oz. ASW **Rev:** Liberty cap

Date	Mintage	F	VF	XF	Unc	BU
1898Cn AM	1,720,000	10.00	15.00	25.00	65.00	—
1898Cn/MoAM	Inc. above	15.00	30.00	90.00	150	—
1899Cn AM	1,722,000	25.00	50.00	90.00	175	—
1899Cn JQ	Inc. above	10.00	15.00	50.00	125	—
1900Cn JQ	1,804,000	10.00	15.00	25.00	75.00	—
1901Cn JQ	1,473,000	10.00	15.00	25.00	75.00	—
1902Cn JQ	1,194,000	10.00	15.00	45.00	125	—
1903Cn JQ	1,514,000	10.00	15.00	30.00	85.00	—
1903Cn FV	Inc. above	25.00	50.00	100	225	—
1904Cn MH	1,554,000	10.00	15.00	25.00	75.00	—
1904Cn RP	Inc. above	50.00	100	150	350	—
1905Cn RP	598,000	25.00	50.00	100	250	—

KM# 409.1 PESO
27.0730 g., 0.9030 Silver .7860 oz. ASW **Rev:** Liberty cap
Note: Varieties exist.

Date	Mintage	F	VF	XF	Unc	BU
1898Go RS	4,256,000	11.50	16.00	35.00	75.00	—
1898Go/MoRS	Inc. above	20.00	30.00	60.00	125	—
1899Go RS	3,207,000	11.50	16.00	30.00	75.00	—
1900Go RS	1,489,000	25.00	50.00	100	250	—

KM# 409.2 PESO
27.0730 g., 0.9027 Silver .7860 oz. ASW **Rev:** Liberty cap
Note: Varieties exist.

Date	Mintage	F	VF	XF	Unc	BU
1898Mo AM Original strike - reverse with 139 beads	10,156,000	10.00	12.50	18.50	60.00	—
1898Mo AM Restrike (1949) - reverse with 134 beads	10,250,000	10.00	12.50	16.50	40.00	—
1899Mo AM	7,930,000	11.50	13.50	20.00	70.00	—
1900Mo AM	8,226,000	11.50	13.50	20.00	70.00	—
1901Mo AM	14,505,000	10.00	12.50	20.00	70.00	—
1902/1Mo AM	16,224,000	150	300	500	950	—
1902Mo AM	Inc. above	10.00	12.50	20.00	70.00	—
1903Mo AM	22,396,000	10.00	12.50	20.00	70.00	—
1903Mo MA (Error)	Inc. above	1,500	2,500	3,500	7,500	—
1904Mo AM	14,935,000	10.00	12.50	20.00	70.00	—
1905Mo AM	3,557,000	15.00	25.00	55.00	125	—
1908Mo AM	7,575,000	11.50	13.50	20.00	60.00	—
1908Mo GV	Inc. above	11.50	13.50	18.50	40.00	—
1909Mo GV	2,924,000	11.50	13.50	18.50	40.00	—

KM# 409.3 PESO
27.0730 g., 0.9030 Silver .7860 oz. ASW **Rev:** Liberty cap
Note: Struck at Zacatecas Mint, mint mark Zs. Varieties exist.

Date	Mintage	F	VF	XF	Unc	BU
1898Zs FZ	5,714,000	11.50	13.50	20.00	60.00	—
1899Zs FZ	5,618,000	11.50	13.50	20.00	65.00	—
1900Zs FZ	5,357,000	11.50	13.50	20.00	65.00	—

Date	Mintage	F	VF	XF	Unc	BU
1901Zs FZ	Inc. above	11.50	13.50	20.00	55.00	—
1901Zs AZ	5,706,000	4,000	6,500	10,000	—	—
1902Zs FZ	7,134,000	11.50	13.50	20.00	55.00	—
1903/2Zs FZ	3,080,000	12.50	15.00	50.00	125	—
1903Zs FZ	Inc. above	11.50	13.50	20.00	65.00	—
1904Zs FZ	2,423,000	11.50	15.00	25.00	85.00	—
1904Zs FM	Inc. above	11.50	15.00	25.00	75.00	—
1905Zs FM	995,000	20.00	40.00	60.00	150	—

KM# 410 PESO
1.6920 g., 0.8750 Gold .0476 oz. AGW

Date	Mintage	F	VF	XF	Unc	BU
1888AsL/MoM Rare	—	—	—	—	—	—
1888 As L Rare	—	—	—	—	—	—

KM# 410.1 PESO
1.6920 g., 0.8750 Gold .0476 oz. AGW

Date	Mintage	F	VF	XF	Unc	BU
1888Ca/MoM Rare	104	—	—	—	—	—

KM# 410.2 PESO
1.6920 g., 0.8750 Gold .0476 oz. AGW

Date	Mintage	F	VF	XF	Unc	BU
1873Cn P	1,221	75.00	100	150	250	—
1875Cn P	—	85.00	125	150	250	—
1878Cn G	248	100	175	225	475	—
1879Cn D	—	100	150	175	285	—
1881/0Cn D	338	100	150	175	285	—
1882Cn D	340	100	150	175	285	—
1883Cn D	—	100	150	175	285	—
1884Cn M	—	100	150	175	285	—
1886/4Cn M	277	100	150	225	450	—
1888/7Cn M	2,586	100	175	225	450	—
1888Cn M	Inc. above	65.00	100	150	265	—
1889Cn M Rare	—	—	—	—	—	—
1891/89Cn M	969	75.00	100	150	265	—
1892Cn M	780	75.00	100	150	265	—
1893Cn M	498	85.00	125	150	265	—
1894Cn M	493	80.00	125	150	265	—
1895Cn M	1,143	65.00	100	150	250	—
1896/5Cn M	1,028	65.00	100	150	250	—
1897Cn M	785	65.00	100	150	250	—
1898Cn M	3,521	65.00	100	150	225	—
1898Cn/MoM	Inc. above	65.00	100	150	250	—
1899Cn Q	2,000	65.00	100	150	225	—
1901Cn Q	Inc. above	65.00	100	150	225	—
1901/0Cn Q	2,350	65.00	100	150	225	—
1902Cn Q	2,480	65.00	100	150	225	—
1902Cn/MoQ/C	Inc. above	65.00	100	150	225	—
1904Cn H	3,614	65.00	100	150	225	—
1904Cn/Mo/ H	Inc. above	65.00	100	150	250	—
1905Cn P	1,000	—	—	—	—	—

Note: Reported, not confirmed

KM# 410.3 PESO
1.6920 g., 0.8750 Gold .0476 oz. AGW

Date	Mintage	F	VF	XF	Unc	BU
1870Go S	—	100	125	150	265	—
1871Go S	500	100	175	225	475	—
1888Go R	210	125	200	250	550	—
1890Go R	1,916	75.00	100	150	265	—
1892Go R	533	100	150	175	350	—
1894Go R	180	150	200	250	550	—

Date	Mintage	F	VF	XF	Unc	BU
1895Go R	676	100	150	175	325	—
1896/5Go R	4,671	65.00	100	150	250	—
1897/6Go R	4,280	65.00	100	150	250	—
1897Go R	Inc. above	65.00	100	150	250	—
1898Go R Regular obverse	5,193	65.00	100	150	250	—
1898Go R Mule, 5 Centavos obverse, normal reverse	Inc. above	75.00	100	150	250	—
1899Go R	2,748	65.00	100	150	250	—
1900/800Go R	864	75.00	125	150	285	—

KM# 410.4 PESO
1.6920 g., 0.8750 Gold .0476 oz. AGW

Date	Mintage	F	VF	XF	Unc	BU
1875Ho R Rare	310	—	—	—	—	—
1876Ho F Rare	—	—	—	—	—	—
1888Ho G/MoM Rare	—	—	—	—	—	—

KM# 410.5 PESO
1.6920 g., 0.8750 Gold .0476 oz. AGW

Date	Mintage	F	VF	XF	Unc	BU
1870Mo C	2,540	45.00	65.00	95.00	185	—
1871Mo M/C	1,000	55.00	100	150	250	—
1872Mo M/C	3,000	45.00	65.00	95.00	185	—
1873/1Mo M	2,900	45.00	65.00	95.00	185	—
1873Mo M	Inc. above	45.00	65.00	95.00	185	—
1874Mo M	—	45.00	65.00	95.00	185	—
1875Mo B/M	—	45.00	65.00	95.00	185	—
1876/5Mo B/M	—	45.00	65.00	95.00	185	—
1877Mo M	—	45.00	65.00	95.00	185	—
1878Mo M	2,000	45.00	65.00	95.00	185	—
1879Mo M	—	45.00	65.00	95.00	185	—
1880/70Mo M	—	45.00	65.00	95.00	185	—
1881/71Mo M	1,000	45.00	65.00	95.00	185	—
1882/72Mo M	—	45.00	65.00	95.00	185	—
1883/72Mo M	1,000	45.00	65.00	95.00	185	—
1884Mo M	—	45.00	65.00	95.00	185	—
1885/71Mo M	—	45.00	65.00	95.00	185	—
1885Mo M	—	45.00	65.00	95.00	185	—
1886Mo M	1,700	45.00	65.00	95.00	185	—
1887Mo M	2,200	45.00	65.00	95.00	185	—
1888Mo M	1,000	45.00	65.00	95.00	185	—
1889Mo M	500	100	150	200	285	—
1890Mo M	570	100	150	200	285	—
1891Mo M	746	100	150	200	285	—
1892/0Mo M	2,895	45.00	65.00	95.00	185	—
1893Mo M	5,917	45.00	65.00	95.00	185	—
1894/3MMo	—	45.00	65.00	95.00	185	—
1894Mo M	6,244	45.00	65.00	95.00	185	—
1895Mo M	8,994	45.00	65.00	95.00	185	—
1895Mo B	Inc. above	45.00	65.00	95.00	185	—
1896Mo B	7,166	45.00	65.00	95.00	185	—
1896Mo M	Inc. above	45.00	65.00	95.00	185	—
1897Mo M	5,131	45.00	65.00	95.00	185	—
1898/7Mo M	5,368	45.00	65.00	95.00	185	—
1899Mo M	9,515	45.00	65.00	95.00	185	—
1900/800Mo M	9,301	45.00	65.00	95.00	185	—
1900/880Mo M	Inc. above	45.00	65.00	95.00	185	—
1900/890Mo M	Inc. above	45.00	65.00	95.00	185	—
1900Mo M	Inc. above	45.00	65.00	95.00	185	—
1901Mo M Small date	Inc. above	45.00	65.00	95.00	185	—
1901/801Mo M Large date	8,293	45.00	65.00	95.00	185	—
1902Mo M Large date	11,000	45.00	65.00	95.00	185	—
1902Mo M Small date	Inc. above	45.00	65.00	95.00	185	—
1903Mo M Large date	10,000	45.00	65.00	95.00	185	—
1903Mo M Small date	Inc. above	55.00	85.00	125	200	—

Date	Mintage	F	VF	XF	Unc	BU
1904Mo M	9,845	45.00	65.00	95.00	185	—
1905Mo M	3,429	45.00	65.00	95.00	185	—

KM# 410.6 PESO
1.6920 g., 0.8750 Gold .0476 oz. AGW

Date	Mintage	F	VF	XF	Unc	BU
1872Zs H	2,024	125	150	175	275	—
1875/3Zs A	—	125	150	200	325	—
1878Zs S	—	125	150	175	275	—
1888Zs Z	280	175	225	325	700	—
1889Zs Z	492	150	175	225	450	—
1890Zs Z	738	150	175	225	450	—

KM# 411 2-1/2 PESOS
4.2300 g., 0.8750 Gold .1190 oz. AGW

Date	Mintage	F	VF	XF	Unc	BU
1888As/MoL Rare	—	—	—	—	—	—

KM# 411.1 2-1/2 PESOS
4.2300 g., 0.8750 Gold .1190 oz. AGW

Date	Mintage	F	VF	XF	Unc	BU
1893Cn M	141	1,500	2,000	2,500	3,500	—

KM# 411.2 2-1/2 PESOS
4.2300 g., 0.8750 Gold .1190 oz. AGW

Date	Mintage	F	VF	XF	Unc	BU
1888Do C Rare	—	—	—	—	—	—

KM# 411.3 2-1/2 PESOS
4.2300 g., 0.8750 Gold .1190 oz. AGW

Date	Mintage	F	VF	XF	Unc	BU
1871Go S	600	1,250	2,000	2,500	3,250	—
1888Go/MoR	110	1,750	2,250	2,750	3,500	—

KM# 411.4 2-1/2 PESOS
4.2300 g., 0.8750 Gold .1190 oz. AGW

Date	Mintage	F	VF	XF	Unc	BU
1874Ho R Rare	—	—	—	—	—	—
1888Ho G Rare	—	—	—	—	—	—

KM# 411.5 2-1/2 PESOS
4.2300 g., 0.8750 Gold .1190 oz. AGW

Date	Mintage	F	VF	XF	Unc	BU
1870Mo C	820	150	250	350	750	—
1872Mo M/C	800	150	250	350	750	—
1873/2Mo M	—	200	350	750	1,350	—
1874Mo M	—	200	350	750	1,350	—
1874Mo B/M	—	200	350	750	1,350	—
1875Mo B	—	200	350	750	1,350	—

Date	Mintage	F	VF	XF	Unc	BU
1876Mo B	—	250	500	1,000	1,600	—
1877Mo M	—	200	350	750	1,350	—
1878Mo M	400	200	350	750	1,350	—
1879Mo M	—	200	350	750	1,350	—
1880/79Mo M	—	200	350	750	1,350	—
1881Mo M	400	200	350	750	1,350	—
1882Mo M	—	200	350	750	1,350	—
1883/73Mo M	400	200	350	750	1,350	—
1884Mo M	—	250	500	1,000	1,600	—
1885Mo M	—	200	350	750	1,350	—
1886Mo M	400	200	350	750	1,350	—
1887Mo M	400	200	350	750	1,350	—
1888Mo M	540	200	350	750	1,350	—
1889Mo M	240	150	300	525	950	—
1890Mo M	420	200	350	750	1,350	—
1891Mo M	188	200	350	750	1,350	—
1892Mo M	240	200	350	750	1,350	—

KM# 411.6 2-1/2 PESOS
4.2300 g., 0.8750 Gold .1190 oz. AGW

Date	Mintage	F	VF	XF	Unc	BU
1872Zs H	1,300	200	350	500	1,200	—
1873Zs H	—	175	325	450	850	—
1875/3Zs A	—	200	350	750	1,350	—
1877Zs S	—	200	350	750	1,350	—
1878Zs S	300	200	350	750	1,350	—
1888Zs/MoS	80	300	500	1,000	1,800	—
1889Zs/Mo Z	184	250	450	950	1,600	—
1890Zs Z	326	200	350	750	1,350	—

KM# 412 5 PESOS
8.4600 g., 0.8750 Gold .2380 oz. AGW

Date	Mintage	F	VF	XF	Unc	BU
1875 As L	—	—	—	—	—	—
1878 As L	383	900	1,700	3,000	4,500	—

KM# 412.1 5 PESOS
8.4600 g., 0.8750 Gold .2380 oz. AGW

Date	Mintage	F	VF	XF	Unc	BU
1888 Ca M Rare	120	—	—	—	—	—

KM# 412.2 5 PESOS
8.4600 g., 0.8750 Gold .2380 oz. AGW

Date	Mintage	F	VF	XF	Unc	BU
1873Cn P	—	300	600	1,000	1,500	—
1874Cn P	—	—	—	—	—	—
1875Cn P	—	300	500	700	1,250	—

Date	Mintage	F	VF	XF	Unc	BU
1876Cn P	—	300	500	700	1,250	—
1877Cn G	—	300	500	700	1,250	—
1882Cn Rare	174	—	—	—	—	—
1888Cn M	—	500	1,000	1,350	2,000	—
1890Cn M	435	250	500	750	1,250	—
1891Cn M	1,390	250	400	500	1,000	—
1894Cn M	484	250	500	750	1,600	—
1895Cn M	142	500	750	1,500	2,500	—
1900Cn Q	1,536	165	300	400	900	—
1903Cn Q	1,000	165	300	400	750	—

Date	Mintage	F	VF	XF	Unc	BU
1875Mo B	—	200	400	550	950	—
1876/5Mo B/M	—	200	400	550	1,000	—
1877Mo M	—	250	450	750	1,250	—
1878/7Mo M	400	200	400	550	1,250	—
1878Mo M	Inc. above	200	400	550	1,250	—
1879/8Mo M	—	200	400	550	1,250	—
1880Mo M	—	200	400	550	1,250	—
1881Mo M	—	200	400	550	1,250	—
1882Mo M	200	250	450	750	1,250	—
1883Mo M	200	250	450	750	1,250	—
1884Mo M	—	250	450	750	1,250	—
1886Mo M	200	250	450	750	1,250	—
1887Mo M	200	250	450	750	1,250	—
1888Mo M	250	200	400	550	1,250	—
1889Mo M	190	250	450	750	1,250	—
1890Mo M	149	250	450	750	1,250	—
1891Mo M	156	250	450	750	1,250	—
1892Mo M	214	250	450	750	1,250	—
1893Mo M	1,058	200	400	500	800	—
1897Mo M	370	200	400	550	1,000	—
1898Mo M	376	200	400	550	1,000	—
1900Mo M	1,014	165	300	400	650	—
1901Mo M	1,071	165	300	400	650	—
1902Mo M	1,478	165	300	400	650	—
1903Mo M	1,162	165	300	400	650	—
1904Mo M	1,415	165	300	400	650	—
1905Mo M	563	200	400	550	1,500	—

KM# 412.3 5 PESOS
8.4600 g., 0.8750 Gold .2380 oz. AGW

Date	Mintage	F	VF	XF	Unc	BU
1873/2Do P	—	700	1,250	1,800	3,000	—
1877Do P	—	700	1,250	1,800	3,000	—
1878Do E	—	700	1,250	1,800	3,000	—
1879/7Do B	—	700	1,250	1,800	3,000	—
1879Do B	—	700	1,250	1,800	3,000	—

KM# 412.4 5 PESOS
8.4600 g., 0.8750 Gold .2380 oz. AGW

Date	Mintage	F	VF	XF	Unc	BU
1871Go S	1,600	400	800	1,250	2,500	—
1887Go R	140	600	1,200	1,500	2,750	—
1888Go R Rare	65	—	—	—	—	—
1893Go R Rare	16	—	—	—	—	—

KM# 412.5 5 PESOS
8.4600 g., 0.8750 Gold .2380 oz. AGW

Date	Mintage	F	VF	XF	Unc	BU
1874Ho R	—	1,750	2,500	3,000	4,500	—
1877Ho R	990	750	1,250	2,000	3,000	—
1877Ho A	Inc. above	650	1,100	1,750	2,750	—
1888Ho G Rare	—	—	—	—	—	—

KM# 412.6 5 PESOS
8.4600 g., 0.8750 Gold .2380 oz. AGW

Date	Mintage	F	VF	XF	Unc	BU
1870Mo C	550	200	400	550	900	—
1871/69Mo M	1,600	165	300	400	650	—
1871Mo M	Inc. above	165	300	400	650	—
1872Mo M	1,600	165	300	400	650	—
1873/2Mo M	—	200	400	550	850	—
1874Mo M	—	200	400	550	850	—
1875/3Mo B/M	—	200	400	550	950	—

KM# 412.7 5 PESOS
8.4600 g., 0.8750 Gold .2380 oz. AGW

Date	Mintage	F	VF	XF	Unc	BU
1874Zs A	—	250	500	750	1,500	—
1875Zs A	—	200	400	500	1,000	—
1877Zs S/A	—	200	400	550	1,000	—
1878/7Zs S/A	—	200	400	550	1,000	—
1883Zs S	—	165	300	450	700	—
1888Zs Z	70	1,000	1,500	2,000	3,000	—
1889Zs Z	373	200	300	500	850	—
1892Zs Z	1,229	165	300	450	700	—

KM# 413 10 PESOS
16.9200 g., 0.8750 Gold .4760 oz. AGW **Rev:** Balance scale

Date	Mintage	F	VF	XF	Unc	BU
1874 As DL Rare	—	—	—	—	—	—
1875 As L	642	600	1,250	2,500	3,500	—
1878 As L	977	500	1,000	2,000	3,000	—
1879 As L	1,078	500	1,000	2,000	3,000	—
1880 As L	2,629	500	1,000	2,000	3,000	—
1881 As L	2,574	500	1,000	2,000	3,000	—
1882 As L	3,403	500	1,000	2,000	3,000	—
1883 As L	3,597	500	1,000	2,000	3,000	—
1884 As L Rare	—	—	—	—	—	—
1885 As L	4,562	500	1,000	2,000	3,000	—
1886 As L	4,643	500	1,000	2,000	3,000	—
1887 As L	3,667	500	1,000	2,000	3,000	—
1888 As L	4,521	500	1,000	2,000	3,000	—
1889 As L	5,615	500	1,000	2,000	3,000	—
1890 As L	4,920	500	1,000	2,000	3,000	—
1891 As L	568	500	1,000	2,000	3,000	—

Date	Mintage	F	VF	XF	Unc	BU
1892 As L	—	—	—	—	—	—
1893 As L	817	500	1,000	2,000	3,000	—
1894/3 As L	1,658	—	—	—	—	—
1894 As L	Inc. above	500	1,000	2,000	3,000	—
1895 As L	1,237	500	1,000	2,000	3,000	—

Date	Mintage	F	VF	XF	Unc	BU
1881/79Do P	2,617	350	550	900	1,450	—
1882Do P Rare	1,528	—	—	—	—	—
1882Do C	Inc. above	350	550	900	1,450	—
1883Do C	793	450	750	1,250	2,000	—
1884Do C	108	450	750	1,250	2,000	—

KM# 413.1   10 PESOS
16.9200 g., 0.8750 Gold .4760 oz. AGW **Rev:** Balance scale

Date	Mintage	F	VF	XF	Unc	BU
1888 Ca M	175	—	—	7,500	—	—

KM# 413.2   10 PESOS
16.9200 g., 0.8750 Gold .4760 oz. AGW **Rev:** Balance scale

Date	Mintage	F	VF	XF	Unc	BU
1881Cn D	—	400	600	1,000	1,750	—
1882Cn D	874	400	600	1,000	1,750	—
1882Cn E	Inc. above	400	600	1,000	1,750	—
1883Cn D	221	—	—	—	—	—
1883Cn M	Inc. above	400	600	1,000	1,750	—
1884Cn D	—	400	600	1,000	1,750	—
1884Cn M	—	400	600	1,000	1,750	—
1885Cn M	1,235	400	600	1,000	1,750	—
1886Cn M	981	400	600	1,000	1,750	—
1887Cn M	2,289	400	600	1,000	1,750	—
1888Cn M	767	400	600	1,000	1,750	—
1889Cn M	859	400	600	1,000	1,750	—
1890Cn M	1,427	400	600	1,000	1,750	—
1891Cn M	670	400	600	1,000	1,750	—
1892Cn M	379	400	600	1,000	1,750	—
1893Cn M	1,806	400	600	1,000	1,750	—
1895Cn M	179	500	1,000	1,500	2,500	—
1903Cn Q	774	400	600	1,000	1,750	—

KM# 413.3   10 PESOS
16.9200 g., 0.8750 Gold .4760 oz. AGW **Rev:** Balance scale

Date	Mintage	F	VF	XF	Unc	BU
1872Do P	1,755	350	500	800	1,250	—
1873/2Do P	1,091	350	550	900	1,450	—
1873/2Do M/P	Inc. above	350	550	900	1,450	—
1874Do M	—	350	550	900	1,450	—
1875Do M	—	350	550	900	1,450	—
1876Do M	—	450	750	1,250	2,000	—
1877Do P	—	350	550	900	1,450	—
1878Do E	582	350	550	900	1,450	—
1879/8Do B	—	350	550	900	1,450	—
1879Do B	—	350	550	900	1,450	—
1880Do P	2,030	350	550	900	1,450	—

KM# 413.4   10 PESOS
16.9200 g., 0.8750 Gold .4760 oz. AGW **Rev:** Balance scale

Date	Mintage	F	VF	XF	Unc	BU
1870Ga C	490	500	800	1,000	1,550	—
1871Ga C	1,910	400	800	1,500	2,250	—
1872Ga C	780	500	1,000	2,000	2,500	—
1873Ga C	422	500	1,000	2,000	3,000	—
1874/3Ga C	477	500	1,000	2,000	3,000	—
1875Ga C	710	500	1,000	2,000	3,000	—
1878Ga A	183	600	1,200	2,500	3,500	—
1879Ga A	200	600	1,200	2,500	3,500	—
1880Ga S	404	500	1,000	2,000	3,000	—
1881Ga S	239	600	1,200	2,500	3,500	—
1891Ga S	196	600	1,200	2,500	3,500	—

KM# 413.5   10 PESOS
16.9200 g., 0.8750 Gold .4760 oz. AGW **Rev:** Balance scale

Date	Mintage	F	VF	XF	Unc	BU
1872Go S	1,400	2,000	4,000	6,500	10,000	—
1887Go R Rare	80	—	—	—	—	—

Note: Stack's Rio Grande Sale 6-93, P/L AU realized, $12,650

Date	Mintage	F	VF	XF	Unc	BU
1888Go R Rare	68	—	—	—	—	—

KM# 413.6   10 PESOS
16.9200 g., 0.8750 Gold .4760 oz. AGW **Rev:** Balance scale

Date	Mintage	F	VF	XF	Unc	BU
1874Ho R Rare	—	—	—	—	—	—
1876Ho F Rare	357	—	—	—	—	—
1878Ho A	814	1,750	3,000	3,500	5,500	—
1879Ho A	—	1,000	2,000	2,500	4,000	—
1880Ho A	—	1,000	2,000	2,500	4,000	—
1881Ho A Rare	—	—	—	—	—	—

KM# 413.7 10 PESOS
16.9200 g., 0.8750 Gold .4760 oz. AGW **Rev:** Balance scale

Date	Mintage	F	VF	XF	Unc	BU
1870Mo C	480	500	900	1,200	2,000	—
1872/1Mo M/C	2,100	350	550	900	1,350	—
1873Mo M	—	400	600	950	1,450	—
1874/3Mo M	—	400	600	950	1,450	—
1875Mo B/M	—	400	600	950	1,450	—
1876Mo B Rare	—	—	—	—	—	—
1878Mo M	300	400	600	950	1,450	—
1879Mo M	—	—	—	—	—	—
1881Mo M	100	500	1,000	1,600	2,500	—
1882Mo M	—	400	600	950	1,450	—
1883Mo M	100	600	1,000	1,600	2,500	—
1884Mo M	—	600	1,000	1,600	2,500	—
1885Mo M	—	400	600	950	1,450	—
1886Mo M	100	600	1,000	1,600	2,500	—
1887Mo M	100	600	1,000	1,625	2,750	—
1888Mo M	144	450	750	1,200	2,500	—
1889Mo M	88	600	1,000	1,600	2,500	—
1890Mo M	137	600	1,000	1,600	2,500	—
1891Mo M	133	600	1,000	1,600	2,500	—
1892Mo M	45	600	1,000	1,600	2,500	—
1893Mo M	1,361	350	550	900	1,350	—
1897Mo M	239	400	600	950	1,450	—
1898/7Mo M	244	425	625	1,000	1,750	—
1900Mo M	733	400	600	950	1,450	—
1901Mo M	562	350	500	800	1,250	—
1902Mo M	719	350	500	800	1,250	—
1903Mo M	713	350	500	800	1,250	—
1904Mo M	694	350	500	800	1,250	—
1905Mo M	401	400	600	950	1,500	—

KM# 413.8 10 PESOS
16.9200 g., 0.8750 Gold .4760 oz. AGW **Rev:** Balance scale

Date	Mintage	F	VF	XF	Unc	BU
1870 Oa E	4,614	400	600	900	1,350	—
1871 Oa E	2,705	400	600	900	1,350	—
1872 Oa E	5,897	400	600	900	1,350	—
1873 Oa E	3,537	400	600	950	1,500	—
1874 Oa E	2,205	400	600	1,200	1,800	—
1875 Oa E	312	450	750	1,400	2,250	—
1876 Oa E	766	450	750	1,400	2,250	—
1877 Oa E	463	450	750	1,400	2,250	—
1878 Oa E	229	450	750	1,400	2,250	—
1879 Oa E	210	450	750	1,400	2,250	—
1880 Oa E	238	450	750	1,400	2,250	—
1881 Oa E	961	400	600	1,200	2,000	—
1882 Oa E	170	600	1,000	1,500	2,500	—
1883 Oa E	111	600	1,000	1,500	2,500	—
1884 Oa E	325	450	750	1,400	2,250	—
1885 Oa E	370	450	750	1,400	2,250	—
1886 Oa E	400	450	750	1,400	2,250	—
1887 Oa E	—	700	1,250	2,250	4,000	—
1888 Oa E	—	—	—	—	—	—

KM# 413.9 10 PESOS
16.9200 g., 0.8750 Gold .4760 oz. AGW **Rev:** Balance scale

Date	Mintage	F	VF	XF	Unc	BU
1871Zs H	2,000	350	500	800	1,250	—
1872Zs H	3,092	300	500	750	1,150	—
1873Zs H	936	400	600	950	1,450	—
1874Zs H	—	400	600	950	1,450	—
1875/3Zs A	—	400	600	1,000	1,750	—
1876/5Zs S	—	400	600	1,000	1,750	—
1877Zs S/H	506	400	600	1,000	1,750	—
1878Zs S	711	400	600	1,000	1,750	—
1879/8Zs S	—	450	750	1,400	2,250	—
1879Zs S	—	450	750	1,400	2,250	—
1880Zs S	2,089	350	550	950	1,450	—
1881Zs S	736	400	600	1,000	1,750	—
1882Zs S	1,599	350	550	950	1,450	—
1883/2Zs S	256	400	600	1,000	1,750	—
1884/3Zs S	—	350	550	950	1,600	—
1884Zs S	—	350	550	950	1,600	—
1885Zs S	1,588	350	550	950	1,450	—
1886Zs S	5,364	350	550	950	1,450	—
1887Zs Z	2,330	350	550	950	1,450	—
1888Zs Z	4,810	350	550	950	1,450	—
1889Zs Z	6,154	300	500	750	1,250	—
1890Zs Z	1,321	350	550	950	1,450	—
1891Zs Z	1,930	350	550	950	1,450	—
1892Zs Z	1,882	350	550	950	1,450	—
1893Zs Z	2,899	350	550	950	1,450	—
1894Zs Z	2,501	350	550	950	1,450	—
1895Zs Z	1,217	350	550	950	1,450	—

KM# 414 20 PESOS
33.8400 g., 0.8750 Gold .9520 oz. AGW **Rev:** Balance scale

Date	Mintage	F	VF	XF	Unc	BU
1876 As L Rare	276	—	—	—	—	—
1877 As L Rare	166	—	—	—	—	—
1878 As L	—	—	—	—	—	—
1888 As L Rare	—	—	—	—	—	—

KM# 414.1 20 PESOS
33.8400 g., 0.8750 Gold .9520 oz. AGW **Rev:** Balance scale
Note: Mint mark CH, Ca.

Date	Mintage	F	VF	XF	Unc	BU
1872CH M	995	BV	700	1,000	2,500	—
1873CH M	950	BV	700	1,000	2,500	—
1874CH M	1,116	BV	675	950	2,500	—
1875CH M	750	BV	700	1,000	2,500	—
1876CH M	600	BV	800	1,250	2,750	—
1877CH Rare	55	—	—	—	—	—
1882CH M	1,758	BV	675	950	2,500	—
1883CH M	161	650	1,000	1,500	3,000	—
1884CH M	496	BV	700	1,000	2,500	—

Date	Mintage	F	VF	XF	Unc	BU
1885CH M	122	650	1,000	1,500	3,000	—
1887 Ca M	550	BV	700	1,000	2,500	—
1888 Ca M	351	BV	700	1,000	2,500	—
1889 Ca M	464	BV	700	1,000	2,500	—
1890 Ca M	1,209	BV	675	950	2,500	—
1891 Ca M	2,004	BV	650	900	2,250	—
1893 Ca M	418	BV	700	950	2,500	—
1895 Ca M	133	650	1,000	1,500	3,000	—

KM# 414.2   20 PESOS
33.8400 g., 0.8750 Gold .9520 oz. AGW **Rev:** Balance scale

Date	Mintage	F	VF	XF	Unc	BU
1870Cn E	3,749	BV	675	950	2,000	—
1871Cn P	3,046	BV	675	950	2,000	—
1872Cn P	972	BV	675	950	2,000	—
1873Cn P	1,317	BV	675	950	2,000	—
1874Cn P	—	BV	675	950	2,000	—
1875Cn P	—	600	1,200	1,800	2,500	—
1876Cn P	—	BV	675	950	2,000	—
1876Cn G	—	BV	675	950	2,000	—
1877Cn G	167	600	1,000	1,500	3,000	—
1878Cn Rare	842	—	—	—	—	—
1881/0Cn D	2,039	—	—	—	—	—
1881Cn D	Inc. above	BV	675	950	2,000	—
1882/1Cn D	736	BV	675	950	2,000	—
1883Cn M	1,836	BV	675	950	2,000	—
1884Cn M	—	BV	675	950	2,000	—
1885Cn M	544	BV	675	950	2,000	—
1886Cn M	882	BV	675	950	2,000	—
1887Cn M	837	BV	675	950	2,000	—
1888Cn M	473	BV	675	950	2,000	—
1889Cn M	1,376	BV	675	950	2,000	—
1890Cn M	—	BV	675	950	2,000	—
1891Cn M	237	BV	900	1,200	2,250	—
1892Cn M	526	BV	675	950	2,000	—
1893Cn M	2,062	BV	675	950	2,000	—
1894Cn M	4,516	BV	675	950	2,000	—
1895Cn M	3,193	BV	675	950	2,000	—
1896Cn M	4,072	BV	675	950	2,000	—
1897/6Cn M	959	BV	675	950	2,000	—
1897Cn M	Inc. above	BV	675	950	2,000	—
1898Cn M	1,660	BV	675	950	2,000	—
1899Cn M	1,243	BV	675	950	2,000	—
1899Cn Q	Inc. above	BV	900	1,200	2,250	—
1900Cn Q	1,558	BV	675	950	2,000	—
1901Cn Q	Inc. above	BV	675	950	2,000	—
1901/0Cn Q	1,496	—	—	—	—	—
1902Cn Q	1,059	BV	675	950	2,000	—
1903Cn Q	1,121	BV	675	950	2,000	—
1904Cn H	4,646	BV	675	950	2,000	—
1905Cn P	1,738	BV	900	1,200	2,250	—

KM# 414.3   20 PESOS
33.8400 g., 0.8750 Gold .9520 oz. AGW **Rev:** Balance scale

Date	Mintage	F	VF	XF	Unc	BU
1870Do P	416	1,000	1,500	2,000	2,500	—
1871/0Do P	1,073	1,000	1,750	2,250	2,750	—
1871Do P	Inc. above	1,000	1,500	2,000	2,500	—
1872/1Do PT	—	1,500	3,000	4,500	7,000	—
1876Do M	—	1,000	1,500	2,000	2,500	—

Date	Mintage	F	VF	XF	Unc	BU
1877Do P	94	1,500	2,250	2,750	3,250	—
1878Do Rare	258	—	—	—	—	—

KM# 414.4   20 PESOS
33.8400 g., 0.8750 Gold .9520 oz. AGW **Rev:** Balance scale

Date	Mintage	F	VF	XF	Unc	BU
1870Go S	3,250	BV	650	900	1,500	—
1871Go S	20,000	BV	650	900	1,500	—
1872Go S	18,000	BV	650	900	1,500	—
1873Go S	7,000	BV	650	900	1,500	—
1874Go S	—	BV	650	900	1,500	—
1875Go S	—	BV	650	900	1,500	—
1876Go S	—	BV	650	900	1,500	—
1876Go M/S	—	—	—	—	—	—
1877Go M/S Rare	15,000	—	—	—	—	—
1877Go R	Inc. above	BV	650	900	1,500	—
1877Go S Rare	Inc. above	—	—	—	—	—
1878/7Go M/S	13,000	675	1,250	2,000	2,800	—
1878Go M	Inc. above	675	1,250	2,000	2,800	—
1878Go S	Inc. above	BV	650	900	1,500	—
1879Go S	8,202	BV	800	1,200	2,300	—
1880Go S	7,375	BV	650	900	1,500	—
1881Go S	4,909	BV	650	900	1,500	—
1882Go S	4,020	BV	650	900	1,500	—
1883/2Go B	3,705	BV	750	1,150	2,250	—
1883Go B	Inc. above	BV	650	900	1,500	—
1884Go B	1,798	BV	650	900	1,500	—
1885Go R	2,660	BV	650	900	1,500	—
1886Go R	1,090	550	800	1,250	2,500	—
1887Go R	1,009	550	800	1,250	2,500	—
1888Go R	1,011	550	800	1,250	2,500	—
1889Go R	956	550	800	1,250	2,500	—
1890Go R	879	550	800	1,250	2,500	—
1891Go R	818	550	800	1,250	2,500	—
1892Go R	730	550	800	1,250	2,500	—
1893Go R	3,343	BV	650	1,000	2,000	—
1894/3Go R	6,734	BV	650	900	1,500	—
1894Go R	Inc. above	BV	650	900	1,500	—
1895/3Go R	7,118	BV	650	900	1,500	—
1895Go R	Inc. above	BV	650	900	1,500	—
1896Go R	9,219	BV	650	900	1,500	—
1897/6Go R	6,781	BV	650	900	1,500	—
1897Go R	Inc. above	BV	650	900	1,500	—
1898Go R	7,710	BV	650	900	1,500	—
1899Go R	8,527	BV	650	900	1,500	—
1900Go R	4,512	550	800	1,250	2,350	—

KM# 414.5 20 PESOS
33.8400 g., 0.8750 Gold .9520 oz. AGW **Rev:** Balance scale

Date	Mintage	F	VF	XF	Unc	BU
1874Ho R Rare	—	—	—	—	—	—
1875Ho R Rare	—	—	—	—	—	—
1876Ho F Rare	—	—	—	—	—	—
1888Ho g Rare	—	—	—	—	—	—

KM# 414.6 20 PESOS
33.8400 g., 0.8750 Gold .9520 oz. AGW **Rev:** Balance scale

Date	Mintage	F	VF	XF	Unc	BU
1870Mo C	14,000	BV	600	850	1,450	—
1871Mo M	21,000	BV	600	850	1,450	—
1872/1Mo M	11,000	BV	600	850	1,600	—
1872Mo M	Inc. above	BV	600	850	1,450	—
1873Mo M	5,600	BV	600	850	1,450	—
1874/2Mo M	—	BV	600	850	1,450	—
1874/2Mo B	—	BV	700	1,000	1,600	—
1875Mo B	—	BV	650	900	1,500	—
1876Mo B	—	BV	650	900	1,500	—
1876Mo M Reported, not confirmed	—	—	—	—	—	—
1877Mo M	2,000	BV	700	1,100	2,000	—
1878Mo M	7,000	BV	650	900	1,500	—
1879Mo M	—	BV	650	900	1,750	—
1880Mo M	—	BV	650	900	1,750	—
1881/0Mo M	11,000	BV	600	850	1,450	—
1881Mo M	Inc. above	BV	600	850	1,450	—
1882/1Mo M	5,800	BV	600	850	1,450	—
1882Mo M	Inc. above	BV	600	850	1,450	—
1883/1Mo M	4,000	BV	600	850	1,450	—
1883Mo M	Inc. above	BV	600	850	1,450	—
1884/3Mo M	—	BV	650	900	1,500	—
1884Mo M	—	BV	650	900	1,500	—
1885Mo M	6,000	BV	650	900	1,750	—
1886Mo M	10,000	BV	600	850	1,450	—
1887Mo M	12,000	600	800	1,500	2,500	—
1888Mo M	7,300	BV	600	850	1,450	—
1889Mo M	6,477	BV	600	900	1,650	—

Date	Mintage	F	VF	XF	Unc	BU
1890Mo M	7,852	BV	600	850	1,500	—
1891/0Mo M	8,725	BV	600	850	1,500	—
1891Mo M	Inc. above	BV	600	850	1,500	—
1892Mo M	11,000	BV	600	850	1,450	—
1893Mo M	15,000	BV	600	850	1,450	—
1894Mo M	14,000	BV	600	850	1,450	—
1895Mo M	13,000	BV	600	850	1,450	—
1896Mo B	14,000	BV	600	850	1,450	—
1897/6Mo M	12,000	BV	600	850	1,450	—
1897Mo M	Inc. above	BV	600	850	1,450	—
1898Mo M	20,000	BV	600	850	1,450	—
1899Mo M	23,000	BV	600	850	1,450	—
1900Mo M	21,000	BV	600	850	1,450	—
1901Mo M	29,000	BV	600	850	1,450	—
1902Mo M	38,000	BV	600	850	1,450	—
1903/2Mo M	31,000	BV	600	850	1,450	—
1903Mo M	Inc. above	BV	600	850	1,450	—
1904Mo M	52,000	BV	600	850	1,450	—
1905Mo M	9,757	BV	600	850	1,450	—

KM# 414.7 20 PESOS
33.8400 g., 0.8750 Gold .9520 oz. AGW **Rev:** Balance scale

Date	Mintage	F	VF	XF	Unc	BU
1870 Oa E	1,131	750	1,500	2,500	5,000	—
1871 Oa E	1,591	750	1,500	2,500	5,000	—
1872 Oa E	255	1,000	1,750	3,000	7,000	—
1888 Oa E	170	2,000	3,000	5,000	—	—

KM# 414.8 20 PESOS
33.8400 g., 0.8750 Gold .9520 oz. AGW **Rev:** Balance scale

Date	Mintage	F	VF	XF	Unc	BU
1871Zs H	1,000	3,500	6,500	7,000	9,000	—
1875Zs A	—	4,000	6,000	7,500	9,500	—
1878Zs S	441	4,000	6,000	7,500	9,500	—
1888Zs Z Rare	50	—	—	—	—	—
1889Zs Z	640	3,500	5,500	7,000	9,000	—

UNITED STATES

DECIMAL COINAGE

100 Centavos = 1 Peso

KM# 415 CENTAVO
Bronze, 20 mm. **Note:** Struck at Mexico City Mint, mint mark Mo.

Date	Mintage	F	VF	XF	Unc	BU
1905 Narrow date	6,040,000	4.00	6.50	14.00	90.00	—
1905 Wide date	—	4.00	6.50	14.00	90.00	—
1906 Narrow date	Est. 67,505,000	0.50	0.75	1.25	14.00	—

Note: 50,000,000 pcs. were struck at the Birmingham Mint

Date	Mintage	F	VF	XF	Unc	BU
1906 Wide date	Inc. above	0.75	1.50	2.50	20.00	—
1910 Narrow date	8,700,000	2.00	3.00	6.50	85.00	—
1910 Wide date	—	2.00	3.00	6.50	85.00	—
1911 Narrow date	16,450,000	0.60	1.00	2.75	22.50	—
1911 Wide date	Inc. above	0.75	1.00	4.00	32.00	—
1912	12,650,000	1.00	1.35	3.25	32.00	—
1913	12,850,000	0.75	1.25	3.00	35.00	—
1914 Narrow date	17,350,000	0.75	1.00	3.00	13.50	18.00
1914 Wide date	Inc. above	0.75	1.00	3.00	13.50	18.00
1915	2,277,000	11.00	25.00	67.50	250	—
1916	500,000	45.00	80.00	170	1,200	—
1920	1,433,000	22.00	50.00	110	400	—
1921	3,470,000	5.50	15.50	47.00	275	—
1922	1,880,000	9.00	17.00	50.00	250	—
1923	4,800,000	0.75	1.25	1.75	13.50	—
1924/3	2,000,000	65.00	170	285	525	—
1924	Inc. above	4.50	11.00	22.00	235	275
1925	1,550,000	4.50	10.00	25.00	220	—
1926	5,000,000	1.00	2.00	4.00	26.00	30.00
1927/6	6,000,000	30.00	45.00	70.00	150	—
1927	Inc. above	0.75	1.25	4.50	36.00	—
1928	5,000,000	0.75	1.00	3.25	16.50	25.00
1929	4,500,000	0.75	1.00	1.75	17.00	25.00
1930	7,000,000	0.75	1.00	2.50	19.00	—
1933	10,000,000	0.25	0.35	1.75	16.50	—
1934	7,500,000	0.25	0.95	3.25	30.00	—
1935	12,400,000	0.15	0.25	0.40	11.50	—
1936	20,100,000	0.15	0.20	0.30	8.00	—
1937	20,000,000	0.15	0.25	0.35	3.25	5.00
1938	10,000,000	0.10	0.15	0.30	2.00	2.75
1939	30,000,000	0.10	0.20	0.30	1.00	1.50
1940	10,000,000	0.20	0.30	0.60	5.50	7.50
1941	15,800,000	0.15	0.25	0.35	2.00	3.00
1942	30,400,000	0.15	0.20	0.30	1.25	2.00
1943	4,310,000	0.30	0.50	0.75	8.00	10.00
1944	5,645,000	0.15	0.25	0.50	6.00	7.50
1945	26,375,000	0.10	0.15	0.25	1.00	1.25
1946	42,135,000	—	0.15	0.20	0.60	1.00
1947	13,445,000	—	0.10	0.15	0.80	1.25
1948	20,040,000	0.10	0.15	0.30	1.10	2.00
1949	6,235,000	0.10	0.15	0.30	1.25	2.00

Note: Varieties exist.

KM# 416   CENTAVO
Bronze, 16 mm. **Note:** Zapata issue. Struck at Mexico City Mint, mint mark Mo. Reduced size.

Date	Mintage	F	VF	XF	Unc	BU
1915	179,000	18.00	30.00	50.00	75.00	—

KM# 417   CENTAVO
Brass, 16 mm. **Note:** Struck at Mexico City Mint, mint mark Mo.

Date	Mintage	F	VF	XF	Unc	BU
1950	12,815,000	—	0.15	0.35	1.65	2.00
1951	25,740,000	—	0.15	0.35	0.65	1.00
1952	24,610,000	—	0.10	0.25	0.40	0.75
1953	21,160,000	—	0.10	0.25	0.40	0.85
1954	25,675,000	—	0.10	0.15	0.85	1.20
1955	9,820,000	—	0.15	0.25	0.85	1.50
1956	11,285,000	—	0.15	0.25	0.80	1.25
1957	9,805,000	—	0.15	0.25	0.85	1.35
1958	12,155,000	—	0.10	0.25	0.45	0.75
1959	11,875,000	—	0.10	0.25	0.75	1.25
1960	10,360,000	—	0.10	0.15	0.40	0.65
1961	6,385,000	—	0.10	0.15	0.45	0.85
1962	4,850,000	—	0.10	0.15	0.55	0.90
1963	7,775,000	—	0.10	0.15	0.25	0.45
1964	4,280,000	—	0.10	0.15	0.20	0.30

Date	Mintage	F	VF	XF	Unc	BU
1965	2,255,000	—	0.10	0.15	0.25	0.40
1966	1,760,000	—	0.10	0.25	0.60	0.75
1967	1,290,000	—	0.10	0.15	0.40	0.60
1968	1,000,000	—	0.10	0.20	0.85	1.25
1969	1,000,000	—	0.10	0.15	0.65	0.85

KM# 418   CENTAVO
Brass, 13 mm. **Note:** Reduced size.

Date	Mintage	F	VF	XF	Unc	BU
1970	1,000,000	—	0.20	0.40	1.45	1.75
1972	1,000,000	—	0.20	0.45	2.50	3.25
1972/2	—	—	0.50	1.25	3.50	5.00
1973	1,000,000	—	1.65	2.75	8.50	12.00

KM# 419   2 CENTAVOS
Bronze, 25 mm. **Note:** Struck at Mexico City Mint, mint mark Mo.

Date	Mintage	F	VF	XF	Unc	BU
1905	50,000	150	300	500	1,200	1,350
1906 Inverted 6	9,998,000	30.00	55.00	120	375	—
1906 Wide date	Inc. above	5.00	11.00	23.00	80.00	—
1906 Narrow date	Inc. above	6.50	14.00	28.00	85.00	—

Note: 5,000,000 pieces were struck at the Birmingham Mint

1920	1,325,000	6.50	17.50	35.00	350	—
1921	4,275,000	2.50	4.75	10.00	90.00	—
1922	—	225	550	1,350	4,000	—
1924	750,000	8.50	22.50	55.00	450	—
1925	3,650,000	2.50	3.50	7.50	38.00	—
1926	4,750,000	1.00	2.25	5.50	35.00	—
1927	7,250,000	0.60	1.00	4.50	22.00	—
1928	3,250,000	0.75	1.50	4.75	30.00	—
1929	250,000	65.00	180	500	1,000	—
1935	1,250,000	4.25	9.25	22.50	200	—
1939	5,000,000	0.60	0.90	2.25	20.00	22.00
1941	3,550,000	0.45	0.60	1.25	18.00	20.00

KM# 420   2 CENTAVOS
Bronze, 20 mm. **Note:** Zapata issue. Struck at Mexico City Mint, mint mark Mo. Reduced size.

Date	Mintage	F	VF	XF	Unc	BU
1915	487,000	7.50	9.00	17.50	75.00	—

KM# 421   5 CENTAVOS
Nickel   **Note:** Struck at Mexico City Mint, mint mark Mo. Varieties exist.

Date	Mintage	F	VF	XF	Unc	BU
1905	1,420,000	7.00	10.00	25.00	300	375
1906/5	10,615,000	13.00	30.00	70.00	375	—
1906	Inc. above	0.75	1.35	3.25	55.00	75.00

Date	Mintage	F	VF	XF	Unc	BU
1907	4,000,000	1.25	4.00	12.00	350	—
1909	2,052,000	3.25	10.00	48.00	360	—
1910	6,181,000	1.30	3.50	6.00	78.00	115
1911 Narrow date	4,487,000	1.00	3.00	5.00	85.00	125
1911 Wide date	Inc. above	2.50	5.00	9.00	110	160
1912 Small mint mark	420,000	90.00	100	230	725	—
1912 Large mint mark	Inc. above	70.00	95.00	175	575	—
1913	2,035,000	1.75	4.25	9.00	100	150

Note: Wide and narrow dates exist for 1913

1914	2,000,000	1.00	2.00	3.50	70.00	95.00

Note: 5,000,000 pieces appear to have been struck at the Birmingham Mint in 1914 and all of 1909-1911. The Mexican Mint report does not mention receiving the 1914 dated coins

KM# 422   5 CENTAVOS
Bronze

Date	Mintage	F	VF	XF	Unc	BU
1914Mo	2,500,000	10.00	23.00	50.00	240	—
1915Mo	11,424,000	3.00	5.00	20.00	145	—
1916Mo	2,860,000	15.00	35.00	150	645	—
1917Mo	800,000	75.00	195	375	825	—
1918Mo	1,332,000	35.00	90.00	200	625	—
1919Mo	400,000	115	225	360	925	—
1920Mo	5,920,000	3.00	8.00	40.00	265	—
1921Mo	2,080,000	10.00	24.00	75.00	275	—
1924Mo	780,000	40.00	95.00	260	625	—
1925Mo	4,040,000	5.50	11.00	47.50	200	—
1926Mo	3,160,000	5.50	11.00	48.00	300	—
1927Mo	3,600,000	4.00	7.00	30.00	215	250
1928Mo Large date	1,740,000	11.00	18.00	65.00	250	—
1928Mo Small date	Inc. above	30.00	45.00	95.00	385	—
1929Mo	2,400,000	5.50	11.00	48.00	195	—
1930Mo	2,600,000	5.00	8.00	27.50	210	—

Note: Large oval O in date

1930Mo	Inc. above	60.00	125	250	565	—

Note: Small square O in date

1931Mo	—	475	750	1,150	3,000	—
1933Mo	8,000,000	1.50	2.25	3.50	27.50	35.00
1934Mo	10,000,000	1.25	1.75	2.75	25.00	40.00
1935Mo	21,980,000	0.75	1.20	2.50	22.50	30.00

KM# 423   5 CENTAVOS
Copper-Nickel

Date	Mintage	F	VF	XF	Unc	BU
1936M	46,700,000	—	0.65	1.25	6.50	7.50
1937M	49,060,000	—	0.50	1.00	6.00	7.00
1938M	3,340,000	—	4.00	10.00	75.00	250
1940M	22,800,000	—	0.75	1.25	8.00	10.00
1942M	7,100,000	—	1.50	3.00	35.00	45.00

KM# 424   5 CENTAVOS
Bronze **Rev:** "Josefa" Ortiz de Dominguez

Date	Mintage	F	VF	XF	Unc	BU
1942Mo	900,000	—	25.00	75.00	375	550
1943Mo	54,660,000	—	0.50	0.75	2.50	3.50
1944Mo	53,463,000	—	0.25	0.35	0.75	1.00
1945Mo	44,262,000	—	0.25	0.35	0.75	1.25
1946Mo	49,054,000	—	0.50	1.00	2.00	3.00
1951Mo	50,758,000	—	0.75	0.90	3.00	5.00
1952Mo	17,674,000	—	1.50	2.50	9.50	11.50
1953Mo	31,568,000	—	1.25	2.00	6.00	9.00
1954Mo	58,680,000	—	0.40	1.00	2.75	4.00
1955Mo	31,114,000	—	2.00	3.00	11.00	14.00

KM# 425   5 CENTAVOS
Copper-Nickel **Rev:** Josefa

Date	Mintage	F	VF	XF	Unc	BU
1950Mo	5,700,000	—	0.75	1.50	6.00	7.00

Note: 5,600,000 pieces struck at Connecticut melted

KM# 426   5 CENTAVOS
Brass **Rev:** Josefa

Date	Mintage	F	VF	XF	Unc	BU
1954Mo Dot	—	—	10.00	45.00	300	375
1954Mo Without dot	—	—	15.00	30.00	250	290
1955Mo	12,136,000	—	0.75	1.50	9.00	12.50
1956Mo	60,216,000	—	0.20	0.30	0.75	1.25
1957Mo	55,288,000	—	0.15	0.20	0.90	1.50
1958Mo	104,624,000	—	0.15	0.20	0.60	1.00
1959Mo	106,000,000	—	0.15	0.25	0.75	1.25
1960Mo	99,144,000	—	0.10	0.15	0.50	0.75
1961Mo	61,136,000	—	0.10	0.15	0.50	0.75
1962Mo	47,232,000	—	0.10	0.15	0.25	0.35
1963Mo	156,680,000	—	—	0.15	0.25	0.40
1964Mo	71,168,000	—	—	0.15	0.20	0.40
1965Mo	155,720,000	—	—	0.15	0.25	0.35
1966Mo	124,944,000	—	—	0.15	0.40	0.65
1967Mo	118,816,000	—	—	0.15	0.25	0.40
1968Mo	189,588,000	—	—	0.15	0.50	0.75
1969Mo	210,492,000	—	—	0.15	0.55	0.80

KM# 426a   5 CENTAVOS
Copper-Nickel **Rev:** Josefa

Date	Mintage	F	VF	XF	Unc	BU
1960Mo	—	—	250	300	350	—
1962Mo	19	—	250	300	350	—
1965Mo	—	—	250	300	350	—

KM# 427   5 CENTAVOS
Brass, 18 mm. **Rev:** Josefa **Note:** Due to some minor alloy
variations this type is often encountered with a bronze-color
toning. Reduced size.

Date	Mintage	F	VF	XF	Unc	BU
1970	163,368,000	—	0.10	0.15	0.35	0.45
1971	198,844,000	—	0.10	0.15	0.25	0.30
1972	225,000,000	—	0.10	0.15	0.25	0.30
1973 Flat top 3	595,070,000	—	0.10	0.15	0.25	0.40
1973 Round top 3	Inc. above	—	0.10	0.15	0.20	0.30
1974	401,584,000	—	0.10	0.15	0.30	0.40
1975	342,308,000	—	0.10	0.15	0.25	0.35
1976	367,524,000	—	0.10	0.15	0.40	0.60

KM# 428   10 CENTAVOS
2.5000 g., 0.8000 Silver .0643 oz. ASW **Note:** Struck at
Mexico City Mint, mint mark Mo.

Date	Mintage	F	VF	XF	Unc	BU
1905	3,920,000	—	6.00	8.00	40.00	50.00
1906	8,410,000	—	5.50	7.50	27.00	35.00
1907/6	5,950,000	—	50.00	135	275	350
1907	Inc. above	—	5.50	6.25	35.00	42.50
1909	2,620,000	—	8.50	13.00	70.00	85.00
1910/00	3,450,000	—	10.00	40.00	75.00	85.00
1910	Inc. above	—	7.00	15.00	25.00	30.00
1911 Narrow date	2,550,000	—	11.00	17.00	88.00	125
1911 Wide date	Inc. above	—	7.50	10.00	42.00	60.00
1912	1,350,000	—	10.00	18.00	130	160
1912 Low 2	Inc. above	—	10.00	18.00	115	140
1913/2	1,990,000	—	10.00	25.00	40.00	70.00
1913	Inc. above	—	7.00	10.00	33.00	40.00
1914	3,110,000	—	5.50	7.00	15.00	20.00

Note: Wide and narrow dates exist for 1914

KM# 429   10 CENTAVOS
1.8125 g., 0.8000 Silver .0466 oz. ASW, 15 mm. **Note:**
Struck at Mexico City Mint, mint mark Mo. Reduced size.

Date	Mintage	F	VF	XF	Unc	BU
1919	8,360,000	—	10.00	15.00	85.00	110

KM# 430   10 CENTAVOS
Bronze **Note:** Struck at Mexico City Mint, mint mark Mo.

Date	Mintage	F	VF	XF	Unc	BU
1919	1,232,000	—	25.00	70.00	450	525
1920	6,612,000	—	15.00	50.00	400	475
1921	2,255,000	—	35.00	80.00	650	800
1935	5,970,000	—	14.00	30.00	120	175

KM# 431   10 CENTAVOS
1.6600 g., 0.7200 Silver .0384 oz. ASW **Note:** Struck at
Mexico City Mint, mint mark Mo.

Date	Mintage	F	VF	XF	Unc	BU
1925/15	5,350,000	—	30.00	75.00	125	175
1925/3	Inc. above	—	20.00	40.00	125	150
1925	Inc. above	—	2.00	5.00	40.00	45.00
1926/16	2,650,000	—	30.00	75.00	125	175
1926	Inc. above	—	3.50	7.50	65.00	85.00
1927	2,810,000	—	2.25	3.00	17.50	22.50
1928	5,270,000	—	2.00	2.75	13.50	16.50
1930	2,000,000	—	3.75	5.00	18.75	25.00
1933	5,000,000	—	1.50	3.00	10.00	11.50
1934	8,000,000	—	1.75	2.50	8.00	10.00
1935	3,500,000	—	2.75	5.00	11.00	12.50

KM# 432   10 CENTAVOS
Copper-Nickel **Note:** Struck at Mexico City Mint, mint mark
Mo.

Date	Mintage	F	VF	XF	Unc	BU
1936	33,030,000	—	0.75	2.50	9.00	10.00
1937	3,000,000	—	8.00	45.00	215	250
1938	3,650,000	1.25	2.00	7.00	60.00	75.00
1939	6,920,000	—	1.00	3.50	27.50	30.00
1940	12,300,000	—	0.40	1.25	5.00	6.00
1942	14,380,000	—	0.60	1.50	7.00	9.00
1945	9,558,000	—	0.40	0.70	3.50	4.00
1946	46,230,000	—	0.40	0.60	2.50	3.00

KM# 433   10 CENTAVOS
Bronze **Rev:** Benito Juarez **Note:** Mint mark Mo.

Date	Mintage	F	VF	XF	Unc	BU
1955	1,818,000	—	0.75	3.25	23.00	30.00
1956	5,255,000	—	0.75	3.25	23.00	28.00
1957	11,925,000	—	0.20	0.40	5.50	8.00
1959	26,140,000	—	0.30	0.45	0.75	1.25
1966	5,873,000	—	0.15	0.25	0.60	1.75
1967	32,318,000	—	0.10	0.15	0.30	0.40

KM# 434.4   10 CENTAVOS
Copper-Nickel **Rev:** Five full, plus one partial row, sharp
stem and narrow date **Note:** Variety IV

Date	Mintage	F	VF	XF	Unc	BU
1974	—	—	—	—	1.50	2.50
1979	—	—	—	—	1.50	2.50

Sharp stem

KM# 434.1   10 CENTAVOS
Copper-Nickel **Rev:** Five full rows of kernels, sharp stem,
wide date **Note:** Variety I

Date	Mintage	F	VF	XF	Unc	BU
1974	6,000,000	—	—	0.35	0.75	1.00
1975	5,550,000	—	0.10	0.35	0.75	1.00
1976	7,680,000	—	0.10	0.20	0.30	0.40
1977	144,650,000	—	1.25	2.25	3.00	3.50
1978	271,870,000	—	—	1.00	1.50	2.25
1979	375,660,000	—	—	0.50	1.00	1.75
1980/79	21,290,000	—	2.45	3.75	6.00	7.00
1980	Inc. above	—	1.50	2.00	4.50	5.50

Blunt stem

KM# 434.2 10 CENTAVOS
Copper-Nickel **Rev:** Five full, plus one partial row at left, blunt stem, narrow date **Note:** Variety II

Date	Mintage	F	VF	XF	Unc	BU
1974	Inc. above	—	—	0.10	0.20	0.30
1977	Inc. above	—	0.15	0.50	1.25	2.25
1978	Inc. above	—	—	0.10	0.30	0.40
1979	Inc. above	—	0.15	0.35	0.85	1.50
1980	Inc. above	—	—	0.10	0.20	0.30

KM# 434.3 10 CENTAVOS
Copper-Nickel **Rev:** Five full, plus one partial row, blunt stem and wide date **Note:** Variety III

Date	Mintage	F	VF	XF	Unc	BU
1980/79	—	—	—	—	5.00	6.00

KM# 435 20 CENTAVOS
5.0000 g., 0.8000 Silver .1286 oz. ASW **Note:** Struck at Mexico City Mint, mint mark Mo.

Date	Mintage	F	VF	XF	Unc	BU
1905	2,565,000	—	12.00	20.00	145	175
1906	6,860,000	—	9.00	16.50	60.00	80.00
1907 Straight 7	4,000,000	—	11.50	20.00	70.00	100
1907 Curved 7	5,435,000	—	7.50	13.50	65.00	90.00
1908	350,000	50.00	90.00	225	1,500	—
1910	1,135,000	—	11.00	16.00	80.00	95.00
1911	1,150,000	12.00	15.00	35.00	125	150
1912	625,000	20.00	40.00	70.00	335	375
1913	1,000,000	—	14.50	30.00	95.00	115
1914	1,500,000	—	10.00	21.50	62.50	75.00

KM# 436 20 CENTAVOS
3.6250 g., 0.8000 Silver .0932 oz. ASW, 19 mm. **Note:** Mint mark Mo. Reduced size.

Date	Mintage	F	VF	XF	Unc	BU
1919	4,155,000	—	30.00	55.00	190	225

KM# 437 20 CENTAVOS
Bronze **Note:** Struck at Mexico City Mint, mint mark Mo.

Date	Mintage	F	VF	XF	Unc	BU
1920	4,835,000	—	45.00	140	650	750
1935	20,000,000	—	6.00	10.00	80.00	125

KM# 438 20 CENTAVOS
3.3333 g., 0.7200 Silver .0772 oz. ASW **Note:** Struck at Mexico City Mint, mint mark Mo.

Date	Mintage	F	VF	XF	Unc	BU
1920	3,710,000	—	6.00	17.50	165	200
1921	6,160,000	—	6.00	14.00	100	145
1925	1,450,000	—	12.00	20.00	125	150
1926/5	1,465,000	—	20.00	65.00	325	375
1926	Inc. above	—	3.25	7.50	80.00	110
1927	1,405,000	—	3.50	8.00	85.00	115
1928	3,630,000	—	4.00	5.25	14.50	19.50
1930	1,000,000	—	5.00	8.00	25.00	35.00
1933	2,500,000	—	2.25	3.00	10.00	11.50
1934	2,500,000	—	2.25	4.00	11.00	12.50
1935	2,460,000	—	2.25	4.00	11.00	12.50
1937	10,000,000	—	1.75	2.25	4.00	5.00
1939	8,800,000	—	1.75	2.25	4.00	5.00
1940	3,000,000	—	1.75	2.25	3.50	5.00
1941	5,740,000	—	1.50	2.25	3.00	4.00
1942	12,460,000	—	1.50	2.25	3.25	3.75
1943	3,955,000	—	2.00	2.50	3.50	4.25

KM# 439 20 CENTAVOS
Bronze **Note:** Struck at Mexico City Mint, mint mark Mo.

Date	Mintage	F	VF	XF	Unc	BU
1943	46,350,000	—	1.25	3.00	18.00	25.00
1944	83,650,000	—	0.40	0.65	8.00	10.00
1945	26,801,000	—	1.25	3.50	9.50	12.00
1946	25,695,000	—	1.10	2.25	6.00	8.25
1951	11,385,000	—	3.00	8.75	90.00	110
1952	6,560,000	—	3.00	5.00	25.00	32.00
1953	26,948,000	—	0.35	0.80	8.25	12.00
1954	40,108,000	—	0.35	0.80	8.00	11.50
1955	16,950,000	—	2.75	7.00	60.00	75.00

KM# 440 20 CENTAVOS
Bronze **Note:** Struck at Mexico City Mint, mint mark Mo.

Date	Mintage	F	VF	XF	Unc	BU
1955 Inc. KM#439	Inc. above	—	0.75	1.75	17.00	22.00
1956	22,431,000	—	0.30	0.35	3.00	4.00
1957	13,455,000	—	0.45	1.25	9.00	12.00
1959	6,017,000	—	4.50	9.00	75.00	100
1960	39,756,000	—	0.15	0.25	0.75	1.00
1963	14,869,000	—	0.25	0.35	0.80	1.00
1964	28,654,000	—	0.25	0.40	0.90	1.25
1965	74,162,000	—	0.20	0.35	0.80	1.00
1966	43,745,000	—	0.15	0.25	0.75	1.00
1967	46,487,000	—	0.20	0.50	1.00	1.25
1968	15,477,000	—	0.30	0.55	1.35	1.65
1969	63,647,000	—	0.20	0.35	0.80	1.00
1970	76,287,000	—	0.15	0.20	0.90	1.30
1971	49,892,000	—	0.30	0.50	1.25	1.50

KM# 441 20 CENTAVOS
Bronze

Date	Mintage	F	VF	XF	Unc	BU
1971 Inc. KM#440	Inc. above	—	0.20	0.35	1.85	2.35
1973	78,398,000	—	0.25	0.35	0.95	1.50
1974	34,200,000	—	0.20	0.35	1.25	1.75

KM# 442 20 CENTAVOS
Copper-Nickel **Rev:** Francisco Madero

Date	Mintage	F	VF	XF	Unc	BU
1974	112,000,000	—	0.10	0.15	0.25	0.30
1975	611,000,000	—	0.10	0.15	0.30	0.35
1976	394,000,000	—	0.10	0.15	0.35	0.45
1977	394,350,000	—	0.10	0.15	0.40	0.45
1978	527,950,000	—	0.10	0.15	0.25	0.30
1979	524,615,000	—	0.10	0.15	0.25	0.30
1979	—	—	1.25	2.00	4.00	8.00

Note: Doubled die obv. small letters

| 1979 | — | — | 1.25 | 2.00 | 4.00 | 8.00 |

Note: Doubled die obv. large letters

1980	326,500,000	—	0.15	0.20	0.30	0.40
1981 Open 8	106,205,000	—	0.30	0.50	1.00	2.00
1981 Closed 8, high date	248,500,000	—	0.30	0.50	1.00	2.00
1981 Closed 8, low date	—	—	1.00	1.50	3.50	4.25
1981/1982	—	—	40.00	75.00	175	195

Note: The 1981/1982 overdate is often mistaken as 1982/1981

| 1982 | 286,855,000 | — | 0.40 | 0.60 | 0.90 | 1.10 |

Date	Mintage	F	VF	XF	Unc	BU
1983 Round top 3	100,930,000	—	0.25	0.40	1.75	2.25
1983 Flat top 3	Inc. above	—	0.25	0.50	1.25	1.75
1983 Proof	998	Value: 15.00				

KM# 491 20 CENTAVOS
Bronze **Subject:** Olmec Culture

Date	Mintage	F	VF	XF	Unc	BU
1983	260,000,000	—	0.20	0.25	1.25	1.75
1983 Proof	53	Value: 185				
1984	180,320,000	—	0.20	0.35	1.85	2.25

KM# 443 25 CENTAVOS
3.3330 g., 0.3000 Silver .0321 oz. ASW **Note:** Struck at Mexico City Mint, mint mark Mo.

Date	Mintage	F	VF	XF	Unc	BU
1950	77,060,000	—	0.50	0.75	1.60	2.00
1951	41,172,000	—	0.50	0.75	1.60	2.00
1952	29,264,000	—	0.75	1.10	1.75	2.25
1953	38,144,000	—	0.60	0.70	1.50	2.00

KM# 444 25 CENTAVOS
Copper-Nickel **Rev:** Francisco Madero

Date	Mintage	F	VF	XF	Unc	BU
1964	20,686,000	—	—	0.15	0.20	0.30
1966 Closed beak	180,000	—	0.65	1.00	2.25	2.50
1966 Open beak	Inc. above	—	1.75	3.50	10.00	13.50

KM# 445 50 CENTAVOS
12.5000 g., 0.8000 Silver .3215 oz. ASW **Note:** Struck at Mexico City Mint, mint mark Mo.

Date	Mintage	F	VF	XF	Unc	BU
1905	2,446,000	12.50	20.00	30.00	150	225
1906 Open 9	16,966,000	—	6.00	10.00	40.00	60.00
1906 Closed 9	Inc. above	—	5.00	9.00	35.00	50.00
1907 Straight 7	18,920,000	—	5.00	9.00	25.00	28.50
1907 Curved 7	14,841,000	—	5.25	9.00	25.00	32.00
1908	488,000	—	80.00	190	545	650
1912	3,736,000	—	11.00	14.00	45.00	60.00
1913/07	10,510,000	—	40.00	90.00	240	275
1913/2	Inc. above	—	20.00	27.50	65.00	85.00
1913	Inc. above	—	5.50	8.50	27.50	35.00
1914	7,710,000	—	6.75	13.50	32.00	45.00
1916 Narrow date	480,000	—	60.00	85.00	200	290
1916 Wide date	Inc. above	—	60.00	85.00	200	290

Date	Mintage	F	VF	XF	Unc	BU
1917	37,112,000	—	6.00	9.50	20.00	22.50
1918	1,320,000	—	70.00	135	250	335

Date	Mintage	F	VF	XF	Unc	BU
1950	13,570,000	—	1.50	1.85	3.00	4.50
1951	3,650,000	—	2.00	2.50	3.75	5.75

KM# 446 50 CENTAVOS
9.0625 g., 0.8000 Silver .2331 oz. ASW, 27 mm. **Note:**
Struck at Mexico City Mint, mint mark Mo. Reduced size.

Date	Mintage	F	VF	XF	Unc	BU
1918/7	2,760,000	—	525	675	1,250	—
1918	Inc. above	—	17.50	55.00	300	385
1919	29,670,000	—	9.50	22.50	95.00	125

KM# 447 50 CENTAVOS
8.3333 g., 0.7200 Silver .1929 oz. ASW **Obv:** Eagle with
snake **Rev:** Value below radiant sun **Note:** Struck at Mexico
City Mint, mint mark Mo.

Date	Mintage	F	VF	XF	Unc	BU
1919	10,200,000	—	10.00	20.00	90.00	110
1920	27,166,000	—	8.00	14.00	70.00	80.00
1921	21,864,000	—	8.00	14.00	85.00	100
1925	3,280,000	—	17.50	30.00	125	160
1937	20,000,000	—	4.25	5.50	7.50	8.50
1938	100,000	—	50.00	85.00	225	300
1939	10,440,000	—	6.00	8.00	15.00	18.50
1942	800,000	—	6.00	9.00	16.00	20.00
1943	41,512,000	—	3.00	4.25	5.50	6.50
1944	55,806,000	—	3.00	4.25	5.50	6.50
1945	56,766,000	—	3.00	4.25	5.50	6.50

KM# 448 50 CENTAVOS
7.9730 g., 0.4200 Silver .1076 oz. ASW **Note:** Struck at
Mexico City Mint, mint mark Mo.

Date	Mintage	F	VF	XF	Unc	BU
1935	70,800,000	—	2.50	3.25	5.50	7.00

KM# 449 50 CENTAVOS
6.6600 g., 0.3000 Silver .0642 oz. ASW **Rev:** Cuauhtemoc
Note: Struck at Mexico City Mint, mint mark Mo.

KM# 450 50 CENTAVOS
Bronze **Note:** Struck at Mexico City Mint, mint mark Mo.

Date	Mintage	F	VF	XF	Unc	BU
1955	3,502,000	—	1.50	3.00	29.00	35.00
1956	34,643,000	—	0.75	1.50	3.75	4.50
1957	9,675,000	—	1.00	2.00	6.50	7.50
1959	4,540,000	—	0.50	0.75	2.00	2.75

KM# 451 50 CENTAVOS
Copper-Nickel

Date	Mintage	F	VF	XF	Unc	BU
1964	43,806,000	—	0.15	0.20	0.40	0.60
1965	14,326,000	—	0.20	0.25	0.45	0.65
1966	1,726,000	—	0.20	0.40	1.30	1.75
1967	55,144,000	—	0.20	0.30	0.65	1.00
1968	80,438,000	—	0.15	0.30	0.65	0.90
1969	87,640,000	—	0.20	0.35	0.80	1.00

KM# 452 50 CENTAVOS
Copper-Nickel **Obv:** Stylized eagle **Note:** Coins dated 1975
and 1976 exist with and without dots in centers of three circles
on plumage on reverse. Edge varieties exist.

Date	Mintage	F	VF	XF	Unc	BU
1970	76,236,000	—	0.15	0.20	0.80	1.00
1971	125,288,000	—	0.15	0.20	0.90	1.30
1972	16,000,000	—	1.25	2.00	3.00	4.75
1975 Dots	177,958,000	—	0.60	1.25	3.50	6.00
1975 No dots	Inc. above	—	0.15	0.20	0.75	1.00
1976 Dots	37,480,000	—	0.75	1.25	5.00	6.00
1976 No dots	Inc. above	—	0.15	0.20	0.50	0.75
1977	12,410,000	—	6.50	10.00	32.50	42.50
1978	85,400,000	—	0.15	0.25	0.50	0.75
1979 Round 2nd 9 in date	229,000,000	—	0.15	0.25	0.50	0.65
1979 Square 9's in date	Inc. above	—	0.20	0.40	1.60	2.00
1980 Narrow date, square 9	89,978,000	—	0.45	0.75	1.75	2.50
1980 Wide date, round 9	178,188,000	—	0.20	0.25	1.00	1.15
1981 Rectangular 9, narrow date	142,212,000	—	0.50	0.75	1.75	2.50
1981 Round 9, wide date	Inc. above	—	0.30	0.50	1.25	1.75
1982	45,474,000	—	0.20	0.40	1.00	1.25

Date	Mintage	F	VF	XF	Unc	BU
1983	90,318,000	—	0.50	0.75	2.00	2.50
1983 Proof	998	Value: 35.00				

Date	Mintage	F	VF	XF	Unc	BU
1918	3,050,000	—	35.00	125	1,350	2,100
1919	6,151,000	—	20.00	50.00	900	1,600

KM# 492   50 CENTAVOS
Stainless Steel **Subject:** Palenque Culture **Obv:** Stylized eagle **Rev:** Cuauhtemoc

Date	Mintage	F	VF	XF	Unc	BU
1983	99,540,000	—	—	0.30	1.50	2.50
1983 Proof	53	Value: 195				

KM# 455   PESO
16.6600 g., 0.7200 Silver .3856 oz. ASW **Note:** Struck at Mexico City Mint, mint mark Mo.

Date	Mintage	F	VF	XF	Unc	BU
1920/10	8,830,000	—	50.00	90.00	325	—
1920	Inc. above	—	8.00	25.00	185	300
1921	5,480,000	—	8.00	25.00	155	200
1922	33,620,000	—	BV	5.00	20.00	26.00
1923	35,280,000	—	BV	5.00	20.00	28.00
1924	33,060,000	—	BV	5.00	20.00	26.00
1925	9,160,000	—	4.50	10.00	60.00	75.00
1926	28,840,000	—	BV	5.00	20.00	25.00
1927	5,060,000	—	7.00	10.00	70.00	85.00
1932 Open 9	50,770,000	—	BV	4.00	5.00	7.00
1932 Closed 9	Inc. above	—	BV	4.00	5.00	7.00
1933/2	43,920,000	—	15.00	25.00	85.00	—
1933	Inc. above	—	BV	4.25	5.50	7.50
1934	22,070,000	—	BV	4.50	9.00	10.50
1935	8,050,000	—	4.50	6.00	11.50	13.50
1938	30,000,000	—	—	BV	5.00	6.50
1940	20,000,000	—	—	BV	6.00	7.50
1943	47,662,000	—	—	BV	4.50	6.00
1944	39,522,000	—	—	BV	5.00	6.50
1945	37,300,000	—	—	BV	5.00	6.50

KM# 453   PESO
27.0700 g., 0.9030 Silver .7859 oz. ASW **Subject:** Caballito **Designer:** Charles Pillet **Note:** Struck at Mexico City Mint, mint mark Mo.

Date	Mintage	F	VF	XF	Unc	BU
1910	3,814,000	—	45.00	50.00	160	250
1911	1,227,000	—	45.00	75.00	200	275
Note: Long lower left ray on reverse						
1911	Inc. above	—	145	210	600	800
Note: Short lower left ray on reverse						
1912	322,000	—	100	210	365	500
1913/2	2,880,000	—	45.00	75.00	270	400
1913	Inc. above	—	45.00	70.00	175	250
Note: 1913 coins exist with even and unevenly spaced date						
1914	120,000	—	600	950	2,800	—

KM# 456   PESO
14.0000 g., 0.5000 Silver .2250 oz. ASW **Rev:** Jose Morelos y Pavon **Note:** Struck at Mexico City Mint, mint mark Mo.

Date	Mintage	F	VF	XF	Unc	BU
1947	61,460,000	—	BV	2.50	4.50	5.50
1948	22,915,000	—	2.50	3.50	5.50	6.50
1949	4,000,000	—	—	1,200	1,600	2,500
Note: Not released for circulation						
1949 Proof	—	Value: 4,000				

KM# 454   PESO
18.1300 g., 0.8000 Silver .4663 oz. ASW **Note:** Struck at Mexico City Mint, mint mark Mo.

KM# 457 PESO
13.3300 g., 0.3000 Silver .1285 oz. ASW **Rev:** Jose Morelos y Pavon **Note:** Struck at Mexico City Mint, mint mark Mo.

Date	Mintage	F	VF	XF	Unc	BU
1950	3,287,000	—	2.50	4.00	7.00	8.50

KM# 458 PESO
16.0000 g., 0.1000 Silver .0514 oz. ASW **Subject:** 100th Anniversary of Constitution **Obv. Designer:** Manuel L. Negrete **Edge Lettering:** INDEPENDENCIA Y LIBERTAD **Note:** Struck at Mexico City Mint, mint mark Mo.

Date	Mintage	F	VF	XF	Unc	BU
1957	500,000	—	3.50	5.00	12.50	15.00

KM# 459 PESO
16.0000 g., 0.1000 Silver .0514 oz. ASW **Subject:** 100th Anniversary of Constitution **Rev:** Jose Morelos y Pavon **Edge Lettering:** INDEPENDENCIA Y LIBERTAD **Note:** Mint mark Mo.

Date	Mintage	F	VF	XF	Unc	BU
1957	28,273,000	—	0.65	1.00	2.50	10.00
1958	41,899,000	—	BV	0.75	1.65	2.00

Date	Mintage	F	VF	XF	Unc	BU
1959	27,369,000	—	1.25	2.00	5.50	8.00
1960	26,259,000	—	0.65	1.10	3.25	4.50
1961	52,601,000	—	BV	0.90	2.25	3.00
1962	61,094,000	—	BV	0.75	1.75	2.25
1963	26,394,000	—	BV	0.75	1.75	2.00
1964	15,615,000	—	BV	0.75	2.00	2.40
1965	5,004,000	—	—	0.75	1.85	2.00
1966	30,998,000	—	—	0.65	1.35	1.85
1967	9,308,000	—	—	0.85	2.75	3.50

Tall date   Short date

KM# 460 PESO
Copper-Nickel **Rev:** Jose Morelos y Pavon

Date	Mintage	F	VF	XF	Unc	BU
1970 Narrow date	102,715,000	—	0.25	0.65	0.80	
1970 Wide date	Inc. above	—	1.25	2.50	7.50	9.00
1971	426,222,000	—	0.20	0.25	0.55	0.75
1972	120,000,000	—	0.20	0.25	0.40	0.65
1974	63,700,000	—	0.20	0.25	0.65	0.90
1975 Tall narrow date	205,979,000	—	0.25	0.45	1.00	1.35
1975 Short wide date	Inc. above	—	0.30	0.40	0.75	1.00
1976	94,489,000	—	0.15	0.20	0.50	0.75
1977 Thick date close to rim	94,364,000	—	0.25	0.45	1.00	1.25
1977 Thin date, space between sideburns and collar	Inc. above	—	1.00	2.00	6.50	13.50
1978 Closed 8	208,300,000	—	0.20	0.30	1.00	1.50
1978 Open 8	55,140,000	—	0.75	1.75	12.00	15.00
1979 Thin date	117,884,000	—	0.20	0.30	1.15	1.50
1979 Thick date	Inc. above	—	0.20	0.30	1.25	1.75
1980 Closed 8	318,800,000	—	0.25	0.35	1.00	1.25
1980 Open 8	23,865,000	—	0.75	1.50	8.00	12.00
1981 Closed 8	413,349,000	—	0.20	0.30	0.75	0.90
1981 Open 8	58,616,000	—	0.50	1.25	6.50	8.00
1982 Closed 8	235,000,000	—	0.25	0.75	2.25	2.50
1982 Open 8	—	—	0.75	1.50	8.00	12.00
1983 Wide date	100,000,000	—	0.30	0.45	3.00	3.50
1983 Narrow date	Inc. above	—	0.30	0.45	3.00	3.50
1983 Proof	1,051,000	Value: 38.00				

KM# 496 PESO
Stainless Steel **Rev:** Jose Morelos y Pavon

Date	Mintage	F	VF	XF	Unc	BU
1984	722,802,000	—	0.10	0.25	0.65	1.00
1985	985,000,000	—	0.10	0.25	0.50	0.75
1986	740,000,000	—	0.10	0.25	0.50	0.75
1987	250,000,000	—	—	0.25	0.50	0.80
1987 Proof; 2 known	—	Value: 1,000				

KM# 461   2 PESOS
1.6666 g., 0.9000 Gold .0482 oz. AGW   **Note:** Struck at
Mexico City Mint, mint mark Mo.

Date	Mintage	F	VF	XF	Unc	BU
1919	1,670,000	—	BV	35.00	65.00	—
1920/10	—	BV	35.00	55.00	100	—
1920	4,282,000	—	BV	35.00	50.00	—
1944	10,000	BV	35.00	50.00	70.00	—
1945	Est. 140,000	—	—	—	BV+20 %	—
1946	168,000	BV	35.00	50.00	75.00	—
1947	25,000	BV	35.00	50.00	75.00	—
1948 No specimens known	45,000	—	—	—	—	—

Note: During 1951-1972 a total of 4,590,493 pieces were
restruck, most likely dated 1945. In 1996 matte restrikes
were produced

KM# 462   2 PESOS
26.6667 g., 0.9000 Silver .7717 oz. ASW   **Subject:**
Centennial of Independence **Designer:** Emilio del Moral
Note: Struck at Mexico City Mint, mint mark Mo.

Date	Mintage	F	VF	XF	Unc	BU
1921	1,278,000	—	40.00	55.00	325	450

KM# 463   2-1/2 PESOS
2.0833 g., 0.9000 Gold .0602 oz. AGW   **Note:** Struck at
Mexico City Mint, mint mark Mo.

Date	Mintage	F	VF	XF	Unc	BU
1918	1,704,000	—	BV	40.00	80.00	—
1919	984,000	—	BV	40.00	80.00	—
1920/10	607,000	—	BV	55.00	130	—
1920	Inc. above	—	BV	40.00	65.00	—
1944	20,000	—	BV	40.00	55.00	—
1945	Est. 180,000	—	—	—	BV+18 %	—
1946	163,000	—	BV	40.00	55.00	—
1947	24,000	200	265	325	425	—
1948	63,000	—	BV	40.00	70.00	—

Note: During 1951-1972 a total of 5,025,087 pieces were
restruck, most likely dated 1945. In 1996 matte restrikes
were produced

KM# 464   5 PESOS
4.1666 g., 0.9000 Gold .1205 oz. AGW   **Note:** Struck at
Mexico City Mint, mint mark Mo.

Date	Mintage	F	VF	XF	Unc	BU
1905	18,000	120	175	245	570	—
1906	4,638,000	—	—	BV	85.00	—
1907	1,088,000	—	—	BV	90.00	—
1910	100,000	—	—	BV	120	—
1918/7	609,000	—	—	BV	200	—
1918	Inc. above	—	—	BV	265	—
1919	506,000	—	—	BV	100	—
1920	2,385,000	—	—	BV	100	—
1955	Est. 48,000	—	—	—	BV+11%	—

Note: During 1955-1972 a total of 1,767,645 pieces were
restruck, most likely dated 1955. In 1996 matte restrikes
were produced

KM# 465   5 PESOS
30.0000 g., 0.9000 Silver .8681 oz. ASW   **Rev:** Head of
Cuauhtemoc left **Note:** Struck at Mexico City Mint, mint mark Mo.

Date	Mintage	F	VF	XF	Unc	BU
1947	5,110,000	—	—	BV	9.00	11.00
1948	26,740,000	—	—	BV	8.50	10.00

KM# 466   5 PESOS
27.7800 g., 0.7200 Silver .06431 oz. ASW   **Subject:** Opening
of Southern Railroad **Edge Lettering:** COMERCIO -
AGRICULTURA - INDUSTRIA **Designer:** Manuel L. Negrete
Note: Struck at Mexico City Mint, mint mark Mo.

Date	Mintage	F	VF	XF	Unc	BU
1950	200,000	—	22.50	40.00	50.00	55.00

Note: It is recorded that 100,000 pieces were melted to be used for the 1968 Mexican Olympic 25 Pesos

KM# 467   5 PESOS
27.7800 g., 0.7200 Silver .6431 oz. ASW **Rev:** Miguel Hidalgo y Costilla **Edge Lettering:** COMERCIO - AGRICULTURA - INDUSTRIA **Note:** Struck at Mexico City Mint, mint mark Mo.

Date	Mintage	F	VF	XF	Unc	BU
1951	4,958,000	—	—	BV	7.00	9.00
1952	9,595,000	—	—	BV	6.75	8.00
1953	20,376,000	—	—	BV	6.75	8.00
1954	30,000	—	30.00	60.00	70.00	85.00

KM# 468   5 PESOS
27.7800 g., 0.7200 Silver .6431 oz. ASW **Subject:** Bicentennial of Hidalgo's Birth **Edge Lettering:** COMERCIO - AGRICULTURA - INDUSTRIA **Designer:** Manuel L. Negrete **Note:** Struck at Mexico City Mint, mint mark Mo.

Date	Mintage	F	VF	XF	Unc	BU
1953	1,000,000	—	BV	6.50	9.50	12.50

KM# 469   5 PESOS
18.0500 g., 0.7200 Silver .4170 oz. ASW **Note:** Struck at Mexico City Mint, mint mark Mo.

Date	Mintage	F	VF	XF	Unc	BU
1955	4,271,000	—	BV	4.25	5.00	7.00
1956	4,596,000	—	BV	4.25	5.00	7.00
1957	3,464,000	—	BV	4.25	5.00	7.00

KM# 470   5 PESOS
18.0500 g., 0.7200 Silver .4170 oz. ASW **Subject:** 100th Anniversary of Constitution **Edge Lettering:** INDEPENDENCIA Y LIBERTAD **Designer:** Manuel L. Negrete **Note:** Struck at Mexico City Mint, mint mark Mo.

Date	Mintage	F	VF	XF	Unc	BU
1957	200,000	—	5.50	7.50	13.50	15.50

KM# 471   5 PESOS
18.0500 g., 0.7200 Silver .6431 oz. ASW **Subject:** Centennial of Carranza's Birth **Edge:** Plain **Designer:** Manuel L. Negrete **Note:** Struck at Mexico City Mint, mint mark Mo.

Date	Mintage	F	VF	XF	Unc	BU
1959	1,000,000	—	—	BV	7.00	9.00

Small date   Large date

KM# 472 5 PESOS
Copper-Nickel **Rev:** Vicente Guerrero **Edge Lettering:**
INDEPENDENCIA Y LIBERTAD **Note:** Small date, large date
varieties.

Date	Mintage	F	VF	XF	Unc	BU
1971	28,457,000	—	0.50	0.95	2.50	3.25
1972	75,000,000	—	0.60	1.25	2.00	2.50
1973	19,405,000	—	1.25	2.00	4.50	5.50
1974	34,500,000	—	0.50	0.80	1.75	2.25
1976 Small date	26,121,000	—	0.75	1.45	3.25	4.00
1976 Large date	121,550,000	—	0.35	0.50	1.50	1.75
1977	102,000,000	—	0.35	0.50	1.50	1.75
1978	25,700,000	—	1.00	1.50	4.50	6.25

KM# 485 5 PESOS
Copper-Nickel **Subject:** Quetzalcoatl **Edge Lettering:**
LIBERTAD Y INDEPENDENCIA **Note:** Inverted and normal
edge legend varieties exist for the 1980 and 1981 dates.

Date	Mintage	F	VF	XF	Unc	BU
1980	266,899,999	—	0.25	0.50	1.75	2.25
1981	30,500,000	—	0.45	0.65	2.75	3.25
1982	20,000,000	—	1.50	2.35	4.25	5.25
1982 Proof	1,051	Value: 18.00				
1983 Proof; 7 known	—	Value: 1,200				
1984	16,300,000	—	1.25	2.00	4.75	6.00
1985	76,900,000	—	2.00	3.25	4.25	5.00

KM# 502 5 PESOS
Brass **Subject:** Quetzalcoatl **Note:** Circulation coinage.

Date	Mintage	F	VF	XF	Unc	BU
1985	30,000,000	—	—	0.15	0.35	0.50
1987	81,900,000	—	8.00	9.50	12.50	15.00
1988	76,600,000	—	—	0.10	0.25	0.35
1988 Proof; 2 known	—	Value: 600				

KM# 473 10 PESOS
8.3333 g., 0.9000 Gold .2411 oz. AGW **Rev:** Miguel Hidalgo
Note: Struck at Mexico City Mint, mint mark Mo.

Date	Mintage	F	VF	XF	Unc	BU
1905	39,000	—	BV	155	225	—
1906	2,949,000	—	BV	150	175	—
1907	1,589,000	—	BV	150	175	—
1908	890,000	—	BV	150	175	—
1910	451,000	—	BV	150	175	—
1916	26,000	—	BV	175	350	—
1917	1,967,000	—	BV	150	175	—
1919	266,000	—	BV	150	200	—
1920	12,000	BV	BV	425	650	—
1959	Est. 50,000	—	—	— BV+7%	—	

Note: *During 1961-1972 a total of 954,983 pieces were
restruck, most likely dated 1959. In 1996 matte restrikes
were produced

KM# 474 10 PESOS
28.8800 g., 0.9000 Silver .8357 oz. ASW **Rev:** Miguel
Hidalgo **Note:** Struck at Mexico City Mint, mint mark Mo.

Date	Mintage	F	VF	XF	Unc	BU
1955	585,000	—	—	BV	9.00	12.00
1956	3,535,000	—	—	BV	8.50	11.00

KM# 475 10 PESOS
28.8800 g., 0.9000 Silver .8357 oz. ASW **Subject:** 100th
Anniversary of Constutution **Edge Lettering:**
INDEPENDENCIA Y LIBERTAD **Designer:** Manuel L.
Negrete **Note:** Struck at Mexico City Mint, mint mark Mo.

Date	Mintage	F	VF	XF	Unc	BU
1957	100,000	—	12.50	27.50	45.00	50.00

KM# 476 10 PESOS
28.8800 g., 0.9000 Silver .8357 oz. ASW **Subject:** 150th Anniversary - War of Independence **Designer:** Manuel L. Negrete **Note:** Struck at Mexico City Mint, mint mark Mo.

Date	Mintage	F	VF	XF	Unc	BU
1960	1,000,000	—	—	BV	9.00	12.50

KM# 477.1 10 PESOS
Copper-Nickel **Rev:** Miguel Hidalgo **Shape:** 7-sided **Note:** Thin flan - 1.6mm

Date	Mintage	F	VF	XF	Unc	BU
1974	3,900,000	—	0.50	1.00	3.00	4.00
1974 Proof		Value: 625				
1975	1,000,000	—	2.25	3.25	7.50	8.50
1976	74,500,000	—	0.25	0.75	1.75	2.25
1977	79,620,000	—	0.50	1.00	2.00	3.00

KM# 477.2 10 PESOS
Copper-Nickel **Rev:** Miguel Hidalgo **Shape:** 7-sided **Note:** Thick flan - 2.3mm

Date	Mintage	F	VF	XF	Unc	BU
1978	124,850,000	—	0.50	0.75	2.50	2.75
1979	57,200,000	—	0.50	0.75	2.25	2.50
1980	55,200,000	—	0.50	0.75	2.50	3.75
1981	222,768,000	—	0.40	0.60	2.25	2.65
1982	151,770,000	—	0.50	0.80	2.50	3.50
1982 Proof	1,051	Value: 40.00				
1983 Proof; 3 known	—	Value: 1,800				
1985	58,000,000	—	1.25	1.75	5.75	7.50

KM# 512 10 PESOS
Stainless Steel **Rev:** Miguel Hidalgo **Note:** Date varieties exist.

Date	Mintage	F	VF	XF	Unc	BU
1985	257,000,000	—	—	0.15	0.50	0.75
1986	392,000,000	—	—	0.15	0.50	1.50

Date	Mintage	F	VF	XF	Unc	BU
1987	305,000,000	—	—	0.15	0.35	0.50
1988	500,300,000	—	—	0.15	0.25	0.35
1989	—	—	0.20	0.25	0.75	1.50
1990	—	—	—	0.25	0.75	1.25
1990 Proof; 2 known	—	Value: 550				

KM# 478 20 PESOS
16.6666 g., 0.9000 Gold .4823 oz. AGW **Note:** Struck at Mexico City Mint, mint mark Mo.

Date	Mintage	F	VF	XF	Unc	BU
1917	852,000	—	—	BV	300	—
1918	2,831,000	—	—	BV	300	—
1919	1,094,000	—	—	BV	300	—
1920/10	462,000	—	—	BV	300	—
1920	Inc. above	—	—	BV	300	—
1921/11	922,000	—	—	BV	300	—
1921/10	—	—	—	—	—	—
1921	Inc. above	—	—	BV	300	—
1959	Est. 13,000	—	—	—	—	—

Note: During 1960-1971 a total of 1,158,414 pieces were restruck, most likely dated 1959. In 1996 matte restrikes were produced

KM# 486 20 PESOS
Copper-Nickel

Date	Mintage	F	VF	XF	Unc	BU
1980	84,900,000	—	0.50	0.85	2.25	3.00
1981	250,573,000	—	0.60	0.80	2.25	3.25
1982	236,892,000	—	1.00	1.75	2.50	3.50
1982 Proof	1,051	Value: 45.00				
1983 Proof; 3 known	—	Value: 575				
1984	55,000,000	—	1.00	1.50	2.50	4.75

KM# 508 20 PESOS
Brass **Rev:** Guadalupe Victoria, First President

Date	Mintage	F	VF	XF	Unc	BU
1985 Wide date	25,000,000	—	0.10	0.20	1.00	1.25
1985 Narrow date	Inc. above	—	0.10	0.25	1.50	2.00
1986	10,000,000	—	1.00	1.75	5.00	5.50
1988	355,200,000	—	0.10	0.20	0.45	0.75
1989	—	—	0.15	0.30	1.50	2.00
1990	—	—	0.15	0.30	1.50	2.50
1990 Proof; 3 known	—	Value: 575				

Snake's tongue straight

KM# 479.1   25 PESOS
22.5000 g., 0.7200 Silver .5209 oz. ASW **Obv:** Snake with straight tongue **Designer:** Lorenzo Rafael **Note:** Type I, Rings aligned.

Date	Mintage	F	VF	XF	Unc	BU
1968	27,182,000	—	BV	5.00	5.50	6.50

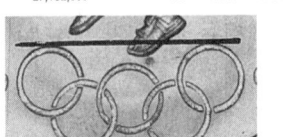

KM# 479.2   25 PESOS
22.5000 g., 0.7200 Silver .5209 oz. ASW **Subject:** Summer Olympics - Mexico City **Note:** Type II, center ring low.

Date	Mintage	F	VF	XF	Unc	BU
1968	Inc. above	—	5.00	5.50	8.50	10.00

Snake's tongue curved

KM# 479.3   25 PESOS
22.5000 g., 0.7200 Silver .5209 oz. ASW **Subject:** Summer Olympics - Mexico City **Note:** Snake with long curved or normal tongue. Type III, center rings low.

Date	Mintage	F	VF	XF	Unc	BU
1968	Inc. above	—	5.25	6.25	9.50	11.00

KM# 480   25 PESOS
22.5000 g., 0.7200 Silver .5209 oz. ASW **Rev:** Benito Juarez

Date	Mintage	F	VF	XF	Unc	BU
1972	2,000,000	—	—	BV	5.50	7.50

KM# 514   25 PESOS
8.4060 g., 0.9250 Silver .2450 oz. ASW **Subject:** 1986 World Cup Soccer Games

Date	Mintage	F	VF	XF	Unc	BU
1985 Proof	234,000	Value: 12.00				

KM# 497   25 PESOS
7.7760 g., 0.7200 Silver .1800 oz. ASW **Subject:** 1986 World Cup Soccer Games

Date	Mintage	F	VF	XF	Unc	BU
1985	354,000	—	—	—	—	7.50

KM# 503   25 PESOS
8.4060 g., 0.9250 Silver .2450 oz. ASW **Subject:** 1986 World Cup Soccer Games **Rev:** Pre-Columbian hieroglyphs, ojo de buey, and soccer ball

Date	Mintage	F	VF	XF	Unc	BU
1985 Proof	277,000	Value: 12.00				

KM# 519 25 PESOS
8.4060 g., 0.9250 Silver .2450 oz. ASW **Subject:** 1986 World Cup Soccer Games

Date	Mintage	F	VF	XF	Unc	BU
1986 Proof	—	Value: 12.00				

KM# 497a 25 PESOS
8.4060 g., 0.9250 Silver .2450 oz. ASW **Subject:** 1986 World Cup Soccer Games **Rev:** Without fineness statement

Date	Mintage	F	VF	XF	Unc	BU
1986 Proof	—	Value: 12.00				

KM# 481 50 PESOS
41.6666 g., 0.9000 Gold 1.2057 oz. AGW **Subject:** Centennial of Independence **Edge:** Reeded **Designer:** Emilio del Meral **Note:** During 1949-1972 a total of 3,975,654 pieces were restruck, most likely dated 1947. In 1996 matte restrikes were produced. Struck at Mexico City Mint, mint mark Mo.

Date	Mintage	F	VF	XF	Unc	BU
1921	180,000	—	—	BV	750	—
1922	463,000	—	—	BV	750	—
1923	432,000	—	—	BV	750	—
1924	439,000	—	—	BV	750	—
1925	716,000	—	—	BV	750	—
1926	600,000	—	—	BV	750	—
1927	606,000	—	—	BV	750	—
1928	538,000	—	—	BV	750	—
1929	458,000	—	—	BV	750	—
1930	372,000	—	—	BV	750	—
1931	137,000	—	—	BV	750	—
1944	593,000	—	—	BV	750	—
1945	1,012,000	—	—	BV	750	—
1946	1,588,000	—	—	BV	750	—
1947	309,000	—	—	—	BV+3%	—
1947 Specimen	—	—	—	—	—	—

Note: Value, $6,500

KM# 482 50 PESOS
41.6666 g., 0.9000 Gold 1.2057 oz. AGW

Date	Mintage	F	VF	XF	Unc	BU
1943	89,000	—	—	—	BV	725

KM# 490 50 PESOS
Copper-Nickel **Subject:** Coyolxauhqui **Edge:** Reeded **Note:** Doubled die examples of 1982 and 1983 dates exist.

Date	Mintage	F	VF	XF	Unc	BU
1982	222,890,000	—	1.00	2.50	5.00	6.00
1983	45,000,000	—	1.50	3.00	6.00	6.50
1983 Proof	1,051	Value: 40.00				
1984	73,537,000	—	1.00	1.35	3.50	4.00
1984 Proof; 4 known	—	Value: 750				

KM# 495 50 PESOS
Copper-Nickel **Subject:** Benito Juarez **Edge:** Reeded

Date	Mintage	F	VF	XF	Unc	BU
1984	94,216,000	—	0.65	1.25	2.70	3.00
1985	296,000,000	—	0.25	0.45	1.25	2.00
1986	50,000,000	—	6.00	10.00	12.00	14.00
1987	210,000,000	—	0.25	0.45	1.00	1.25
1988	80,200,000	—	6.25	9.00	13.50	15.50

KM# 495a 50 PESOS
Stainless Steel **Subject:** Benito Juarez **Edge:** Plain

Date	Mintage	F	VF	XF	Unc	BU
1988	353,300,000	—	—	0.20	1.25	1.75
1990	—	—	—	0.30	1.00	2.00
1992	—	—	—	0.25	1.00	2.75

KM# 498 50 PESOS
15.5520 g., 0.7200 Silver .3601 oz. ASW **Subject:** 1986
World Cup Soccer Games

Date	Mintage	F	VF	XF	Unc	BU
1985	347,000	—	—	—	—	6.50

KM# 523 50 PESOS
16.8310 g., 0.9250 Silver .5000 oz. ASW **Subject:** 1986
World Cup Soccer Games

Date	Mintage	F	VF	XF	Unc	BU
1986 Proof	190,000	Value: 20.00				

KM# 498a 50 PESOS
16.8310 g., 0.9250 Silver .5000 oz. ASW **Subject:** 1986
World Cup Soccer Games **Rev:** Without fineness statement

Date	Mintage	F	VF	XF	Unc	BU
1986 Proof	10,000	Value: 20.00				

KM# 504 50 PESOS
16.8310 g., 0.9250 Silver .5000 oz. ASW **Subject:** 1986
World Cup Soccer Games **Rev:** Pre-Columbia athlete playing
pot-a-poke, or tlachco, the forerunners of soccer; without
fineness statement

Date	Mintage	F	VF	XF	Unc	BU
1985 Proof	347,000	Value: 20.00				

KM# 532 50 PESOS
15.5500 g., 0.9990 Silver .5000 oz. ASW **Subject:** 50th
Anniversary - Nationalization of Oil Industry

Date	Mintage	F	VF	XF	Unc	BU
ND(1988)	30,000	—	—	—	20.00	22.00

KM# 515 50 PESOS
16.8310 g., 0.9250 Silver .5000 oz. ASW **Subject:** 1986
World Cup Soccer Games

Date	Mintage	F	VF	XF	Unc	BU
1985 Proof	234,000	Value: 20.00				

Low 7's

KM# 483.1 100 PESOS
27.7700 g., 0.7200 Silver .6429 oz. ASW **Rev:** Jose Morelos
y Pavon **Edge:** Reeded

Date	Mintage	F	VF	XF	Unc	BU
1977	5,225,000	—	—	BV	6.50	10.00

Note: Low 7's, sloping right shoulder round left shoulder
with no clothing folds

1977	Inc. above	—	—	BV	6.50	10.50

Note: High 7's, sloping right shoulder, round right shoulder
with no clothing folds

High 7's

KM# 483.2 100 PESOS
27.7700 g., 0.7200 Silver .6429 oz. ASW **Rev:** Jose Morelos
y Pavon

Date	Mintage	F	VF	XF	Unc	BU
1977	—	—	—	—	BV	6.25	7.00

Note: Date in line, higher right shoulder, left shoulder with
clothing folds. Mintage inc. KM#483.1

1978	9,879,000	—	—	BV	6.50	8.50
1979	784,000	—	—	BV	6.50	8.50
1979 Proof	—	Value: 650				

KM# 493 100 PESOS
Aluminum-Bronze **Rev:** Venustiano Carranza

Date	Mintage	F	VF	XF	Unc	BU
1984	227,809,000	—	0.45	0.60	2.50	4.00
1985	377,423,000	—	0.30	0.50	2.00	3.00
1986	43,000,000	—	1.00	2.50	4.75	7.50
1987	165,000,000	—	0.60	1.25	2.25	3.00
1988	433,100,000	—	0.30	0.50	2.00	2.75
1989	—	—	0.35	0.65	2.00	2.75
1990	—	—	0.15	0.40	1.50	2.50
1990 Proof; 1 known	—	Value: 650				
1991	—	—	0.15	0.25	1.00	2.50
1992	—	—	0.30	0.75	1.75	3.00

KM# 499 100 PESOS
31.1030 g., 0.7200 Silver .7201 oz. ASW **Subject:** 1986
World Cup Soccer Games

Date	Mintage	F	VF	XF	Unc	BU
1985	302,000	—	—	—	—	15.00

KM# 499a   100 PESOS
32.6250 g., 0.9250 Silver 1.0000 oz. ASW **Subject:** 1986
World Cup Soccer Games **Rev:** Without fineness statement

Date	Mintage	F	VF	XF	Unc	BU
1985 Proof	9,006	Value: 30.00				

KM# 505   100 PESOS
32.6250 g., 0.9250 Silver 1.0000 oz. ASW **Subject:** 1986
World Cup Soccer Games **Rev:** Defensive player shown
heading the ball away from the net, without fineness statement

Date	Mintage	F	VF	XF	Unc	BU
1985 Proof	9,006	Value: 30.00				

KM# 521   100 PESOS
32.6250 g., 0.9250 Silver 1.0000 oz. ASW **Subject:** 1986
World Cup Soccer Games **Rev:** Without fineness statement

Date	Mintage	F	VF	XF	Unc	BU
1986 Proof	208,000	Value: 30.00				

KM# 524   100 PESOS
32.6250 g., 0.9250 Silver 1.0000 oz. ASW **Subject:** 1986
World Cup Soccer Games **Rev:** Without fineness statement

Date	Mintage	F	VF	XF	Unc	BU
1986 Proof	190,000	Value: 30.00				

KM# 537   100 PESOS
32.6250 g., 0.9250 Silver 1.0000 oz. ASW **Subject:** World
Wildlife Fund **Rev:** Monarch butterflies

Date	Mintage	F	VF	XF	Unc	BU
1987 Proof	Est. 30,000	Value: 50.00				

KM# 533 100 PESOS
31.1030 g., 0.9990 Silver 1.0000 oz. ASW **Subject:** 50th Anniversary - Nationalization of Oil Industry

Date	Mintage	F	VF	XF	Unc	BU
1988	10,000	—	—	—	28.00	40.00

KM# 539 100 PESOS
33.6250 g., 0.9250 Silver 1.0000 oz. ASW **Subject:** Save the Children

Date	Mintage	F	VF	XF	Unc	BU
1991 Proof	30,000	Value: 45.00				

KM# 540 100 PESOS
27.0000 g., 0.9250 Silver .8029 oz. ASW **Subject:** Ibero - American Series **Rev:** Pillars

Date	Mintage	F	VF	XF	Unc	BU
1991 Proof	50,000	Value: 55.00				
1992 Proof	75,000	Value: 45.00				

KM# 566 100 PESOS
31.1035 g., 0.9990 Silver 1.0000 oz. ASW **Subject:** Save the Vaquita Porpoise **Obv:** Eagle with snake

Date	Mintage	F	VF	XF	Unc	BU
1992 Proof	—	Value: 45.00				

KM# 509 200 PESOS
Copper-Nickel **Subject:** 175th Anniversary of Independence **Rev:** Independence monument, heads of Allende, Hidalgo, Morelos and Guerrero

Date	Mintage	F	VF	XF	Unc	BU
1985	75,000,000	—	—	0.25	3.00	4.00

KM# 510 200 PESOS
Copper-Nickel **Subject:** 75th Anniversary of 1910 Revolution **Rev:** Heads of Pancho Villa, Emiliano Zapata, Venustiano Carranza and Francisco Madero

Date	Mintage	F	VF	XF	Unc	BU
1985	98,590,000	—	—	0.25	3.25	4.50

KM# 525 200 PESOS
Copper-Nickel **Subject:** 1986 World Cup Soccer Games **Edge:** Reeded

Date	Mintage	F	VF	XF	Unc	BU
1986	50,000,000	—	—	1.00	3.50	4.50

KM# 526 200 PESOS
62.2060 g., 0.9990 Silver 2.0000 oz. ASW **Subject:** 1986 World Cup Soccer Games

Date	Mintage	F	VF	XF	Unc	BU
1986	50,000	—	—	—	40.00	50.00

KM# 500.1 250 PESOS
8.6400 g., 0.9000 Gold .2500 oz. AGW **Subject:** 1986 World Cup Soccer Games

Date	Mintage	F	VF	XF	Unc	BU
1985	100,000	—	—	—	—	150
1986	—	—	—	—	—	150

KM# 500.2 250 PESOS
8.6400 g., 0.9000 Gold .2500 oz. AGW **Subject:** 1986 World Cup Soccer Games **Rev:** Without fineness statement

Date	Mintage	F	VF	XF	Unc	BU
1985 Proof	4,506	Value: 150				
1986 Proof	—	Value: 160				

KM# 506.1 250 PESOS
8.6400 g., 0.9000 Gold .2500 oz. AGW **Subject:** 1986 World Cup Soccer Games

Date	Mintage	F	VF	XF	Unc	BU
1985	88,000	—	—	—	—	150

KM# 506.2 250 PESOS
8.6400 g., 0.9000 Gold .2500 oz. AGW **Subject:** 1986 World Cup Soccer Games **Rev:** Without fineness statement

Date	Mintage	F	VF	XF	Unc	BU
1985 Proof	Est. 80,000	Value: 150				

KM# 507.2 500 PESOS
17.2800 g., 0.9000 Gold .5000 oz. AGW **Subject:** 1986 World Cup Soccer Games **Obv:** Eagle facing left with snake in beak **Rev:** Without fineness statement

Date	Mintage	F	VF	XF	Unc	BU
1985 Proof	—	Value: 300				

KM# 511 500 PESOS
33.4500 g., 0.9250 Silver 1.0000 oz. ASW **Subject:** 75th Anniversary of 1910 Revolution **Obv:** Eagle facing left with snake in beak

Date	Mintage	F	VF	XF	Unc	BU
1985 Proof	40,000	Value: 35.00				

KM# 501.1 500 PESOS
17.2800 g., 0.9000 Gold .5000 oz. AGW **Subject:** 1986 World Cup Soccer Games **Obv:** Eagle facing left with snake in beak

Date	Mintage	F	VF	XF	Unc	BU
1985	102,000	—	—	—	—	300
1986	—	—	—	—	—	300

KM# 501.2 500 PESOS
17.2800 g., 0.9000 Gold .5000 oz. AGW **Subject:** 1986 World Cup Soccer Games **Obv:** Eagle facing left with snake in beak **Rev:** Without fineness statement

Date	Mintage	F	VF	XF	Unc	BU
1985 Proof	5,506	Value: 300				
1986 Proof	—	Value: 300				

KM# 507.1 500 PESOS
17.2800 g., 0.9000 Gold .5000 oz. AGW **Subject:** 1986 World Cup Soccer Games **Obv:** Eagle facing left with snake in beak

Date	Mintage	F	VF	XF	Unc	BU
1985	—	—	—	—	—	300

KM# 529 500 PESOS
Copper-Nickel **Rev:** Francisco Madero

Date	Mintage	F	VF	XF	Unc	BU
1986	20,000,000	—	—	1.00	3.25	3.50
1987	180,000,000	—	—	0.75	2.25	2.50
1988	230,000,000	—	—	0.50	2.25	2.50
1988 Proof; 2 known	—	Value: 650				
1989	—	—	—	0.75	2.25	3.00
1992	—	—	—	1.00	2.25	3.50

KM# 534 500 PESOS
17.2800 g., 0.9000 Gold .5000 oz. AGW **Subject:** 50th Anniversary - Nationalization of Oil Industry **Rev:** Monument **Note:** Similar to 5000 Pesos, KM#531.

Date	Mintage	F	VF	XF	Unc	BU
1988	—	—	—	—	—	300

KM# 513 1000 PESOS
17.2800 g., 0.9000 Gold .5000 oz. AGW **Subject:** 175th Anniversary of Independence

Date	Mintage	F	VF	XF	Unc	BU
1985 Proof	—	Value: 325				

KM# 527 1000 PESOS
31.1030 g., 0.9990 Gold 1.0000 oz. AGW **Subject:** 1986 World Cup Soccer Games

Date	Mintage	F	VF	XF	Unc	BU
1986	—	—	—	—	—	600

KM# 536 1000 PESOS
Aluminum-Bronze **Note:** Juana de Asbaje

Date	Mintage	F	VF	XF	Unc	BU
1988	229,300,000	—	0.85	2.00	4.25	5.75
1989	—	—	0.85	2.00	4.25	5.75

Date	Mintage	F	VF	XF	Unc	BU
1990	—	—	0.85	2.00	4.00	5.50
1990 Proof; 2 known	—	Value: 550				
1991	—	—	1.00	2.00	3.00	7.00
1992	—	—	1.00	2.00	3.00	7.00

KM# 535 1000 PESOS
34.5590 g., 0.9000 Gold 1.0000 oz. AGW **Subject:** 50th Anniversary - Nationalization of Oil Industry **Rev:** Portrait of Cardenas **Note:** Similar to 5000 Pesos, KM#531.

Date	Mintage	F	VF	XF	Unc	BU
1988 Proof	—	Value: 600				

KM# 528 2000 PESOS
62.2000 g., 0.9990 Gold 2.0000 oz. AGW **Subject:** 1986 World Cup Soccer Games

Date	Mintage	F	VF	XF	Unc	BU
1986	—	—	—	—	—	1,200

KM# 531 5000 PESOS
Copper-Nickel **Subject:** 50th Anniversary - Nationalization of Oil Industry

Date	Mintage	F	VF	XF	Unc	BU
ND(1988)	50,000,000	—	—	4.75	7.75	10.00

REFORM COINAGE

1 New Peso = 1000 Old Pesos

KM# 546 5 CENTAVOS
Stainless Steel

Date	Mintage	F	VF	XF	Unc	BU
1992	136,800,000	—	—	0.15	0.20	0.25
1993	234,000,000	—	—	0.15	0.20	0.25
1994	125,000,000	—	—	0.15	0.20	0.25
1995	195,000,000	—	—	0.15	0.20	0.25

Date	Mintage	F	VF	XF	Unc	BU
1995 Proof	6,981	Value: 0.50				
1996	104,831,000	—	—	0.15	0.20	0.25
1997	153,675,000	—	—	0.15	0.20	0.25
1998	64,417,000	—	—	0.15	0.20	0.25
1999	9,949,000	—	—	0.15	0.20	0.25
2000Mo	10,871,000	—	—	0.15	0.20	0.25
2001Mo	34,811,000	—	—	0.15	0.20	0.25
2002Mo	14,901,000	—	—	0.15	0.20	0.25

KM# 547   10 CENTAVOS
Stainless Steel

Date	Mintage	F	VF	XF	Unc	BU
1992	121,250,000	—	—	0.20	0.30	0.35
1993	755,000,000	—	—	0.20	0.25	0.30
1994	557,000,000	—	—	0.20	0.25	0.30
1995	560,000,000	—	—	0.20	0.25	0.30
1995 Proof	6,981	Value: 0.50				
1996	594,216,000	—	—	0.20	0.25	0.30
1997	581,622,000	—	—	0.20	0.25	0.30
1998	602,667,000	—	—	0.20	0.25	0.30
1999	488,346,000	—	—	0.20	0.25	0.30
2000	577,546,000	—	—	0.20	0.30	0.35
2001	618,061,000	—	—	0.20	0.25	0.30
2002	463,968,000	—	—	0.20	0.25	0.30
2003Mo	378,938,000	—	—	0.20	0.25	0.30

KM# 548   20 CENTAVOS
Aluminum-Bronze   **Shape:** 12-sided

Date	Mintage	F	VF	XF	Unc	BU
1992	95,000,000	—	—	0.25	0.35	0.40
1993	95,000,000	—	—	0.25	0.35	0.40
1994	105,000,000	—	—	0.25	0.35	0.40
1995	180,000,000	—	—	0.25	0.35	0.40
1995 Proof	6,981	Value: 0.75				
1996	54,896,000	—	—	0.25	0.35	0.40
1997	178,807,000	—	—	0.25	0.35	0.40
1998	223,847,000	—	—	0.25	0.35	0.40
1999	233,753,000	—	—	0.25	0.35	0.40
2000	223,973,000	—	—	0.25	0.35	0.40
2001	234,360,000	—	—	0.25	0.35	0.40
2002Mo	229,256,000	—	—	0.25	0.35	0.40
2003Mo	149,518,000	—	—	0.25	0.35	0.40

KM# 549   50 CENTAVOS
Aluminum-Bronze   **Shape:** Scalloped

Date	Mintage	F	VF	XF	Unc	BU
1992	120,150,000	—	—	0.45	0.85	1.00
1993	330,000,000	—	—	0.45	0.75	1.00
1994	100,000,000	—	—	0.45	0.75	1.00
1995	60,000,000	—	—	0.45	0.75	1.00
1995 Proof	6,981	Value: 0.90				
1996	69,956,000	—	—	0.45	0.75	1.00
1997	129,029,000	—	—	0.45	0.75	1.00
1998	223,605,000	—	—	0.45	0.75	1.00
1999	89,516,000	—	—	0.45	0.75	1.00
2000	135,112,000	—	—	0.45	0.75	1.00
2001	199,006,000	—	—	0.45	0.75	1.00

Date	Mintage	F	VF	XF	Unc	BU
2002	94,552,000	—	—	0.45	0.75	1.00
2003Mo	124,522,000	—	—	0.45	0.75	1.00

KM# 550   NUEVO PESO
Bi-Metallic Aluminumn-Bronze center in Stainless Steel ring

Date	Mintage	F	VF	XF	Unc	BU
1992	144,000,000	—	—	0.60	1.50	2.25
1993	329,860,000	—	—	0.60	1.50	2.25
1994	221,000,000	—	—	0.60	1.50	2.25
1995 Small date	125,000,000	—	—	0.60	1.50	2.25
1995 Large date	Inc. above	—	—	0.60	1.50	2.25
1995 Proof	6,981	Value: 2.75				

KM# 603   PESO
Bi-Metallic Stainless-steel ring in Aluminum Bronze center
Note: Similar to KM#550 but without N.

Date	Mintage	F	VF	XF	Unc	BU
1996Mo	169,510,000	—	—	—	1.25	2.25
1997Mo	222,870,000	—	—	—	1.25	2.25
1998Mo	261,942,000	—	—	—	1.25	2.25
1999Mo	99,168,000	—	—	—	1.25	2.25
2000Mo	158,379,000	—	—	—	1.25	2.25
2001Mo	208,576,000	—	—	—	1.25	2.25
2002Mo	119,541,000	—	—	—	1.25	2.25
2003Mo	169,320,000	—	—	—	1.25	2.25

KM# 551   2 NUEVOS PESOS
Bi-Metallic Aluminumn-Bronze center in Stainless Steel ring

Date	Mintage	F	VF	XF	Unc	BU
1992	60,000,000	—	—	1.00	2.35	2.50
1993	77,000,000	—	—	1.00	2.35	2.50
1994	44,000,000	—	—	1.00	2.35	2.50
1995	20,000,000	—	—	1.00	2.35	2.50
1995 Proof	6,981	Value: 4.50				

KM# 604   2 PESOS
Bi-Metallic Aluminumn-Bronze center in Stainless Steel ring
Note: Similar to KM#551, but denomination without N.

Date	Mintage	F	VF	XF	Unc	BU
1996Mo	24,902,000	—	—	—	2.35	2.50
1997Mo	34,560,000	—	—	—	2.35	2.50
1998Mo	104,138,000	—	—	—	2.35	2.50
1999Mo	34,713,000	—	—	—	2.35	2.50
2000Mo	69,322,000	—	—	—	2.35	2.50
2001Mo	74,563,000	—	—	—	2.35	2.50
2002Mo	74,547,000	—	—	—	2.35	2.50
2003Mo	39,814,000	—	—	—	2.35	2.50

KM# 552 5 NUEVOS PESOS
Bi-Metallic Aluminumn-Bronze center in Stainless Steel ring

Date	Mintage	F	VF	XF	Unc	BU
1992	70,000,000	—	—	2.00	4.00	4.50
1993	168,240,00 0	—	—	2.00	4.00	4.50
1994	58,000,000	—	—	2.00	4.00	4.50
1995 Proof	6,981	Value: 25.00				

KM# 588 5 NUEVOS PESOS
27.0000 g., 0.9250 Silver .8030 oz. ASW **Subject:**
Environmental Protection **Rev:** Pacific Ridley Sea Turtle

Date	Mintage	F	VF	XF	Unc	BU
1994 Proof	20,000	Value: 50.00				

KM# 652 5 NUEVOS PESOS
31.1710 g., 0.9990 Silver 1.0012 oz. ASW, 40 mm. **Series:**
Endangered Wildlife **Subject:** Aguila Real **Obv:** National
arms past and present **Rev:** Eagle on branch

Date	Mintage	F	VF	XF	Unc	BU
2000	50,000	—	—	—	30.00	—

KM# 655 5 NUEVOS PESOS
31.1710 g., 0.9990 Silver 1.0012 oz. ASW, 40 mm. **Series:**
Endangered Wildlife **Subject:** Cocodrilo de Rio **Obv:** National
arms past and present **Rev:** Crocodile

Date	Mintage	F	VF	XF	Unc	BU
2000	50,000	—	—	—	30.00	—

KM# 656 5 NUEVOS PESOS
31.1710 g., 0.9990 Silver 1.0012 oz. ASW, 40 mm. **Series:**
Endangered Wildlife **Subject:** Nutria de Rio **Obv:** National
arms past and present **Rev:** Nutria

Date	Mintage	F	VF	XF	Unc	BU
2000	50,000	—	—	—	30.00	—

KM# 657 5 NUEVOS PESOS
31.1710 g., 0.9990 Silver 1.0012 oz. ASW, 40 mm. **Series:**
Endangered Wildlife - Berrendo **Obv:** National arms past and
present **Rev:** Peninsula antelope, giant cardon cactus in back

Date	Mintage	F	VF	XF	Unc	BU
2000	50,000	—	—	—	30.00	—

KM# 658 5 NUEVOS PESOS
31.1710 g., 0.9990 Silver 1.0012 oz. ASW, 40 mm. **Series:** Endangered Wildlife **Obv:** National arms past and present **Rev:** Jaguar resting

Date	Mintage	F	VF	XF	Unc	BU
2001	50,000	—	—	—	30.00	—

KM# 653 5 NUEVOS PESOS
31.1710 g., 0.9990 Silver 1.0012 oz. ASW, 40 mm. **Subject:** Aguila Arpia **Obv:** National arms past and present **Rev:** Harpie Eagle

Date	Mintage	F	VF	XF	Unc	BU
2001	50,000	—	—	—	30.00	—

KM# 659 5 NUEVOS PESOS
31.1710 g., 0.9990 Silver 1.0012 oz. ASW, 40 mm. **Series:** Endangered Wildlife **Obv:** National arms past and present **Rev:** Black-tailed Prairie dog

Date	Mintage	F	VF	XF	Unc	BU
2001	50,000	—	—	—	30.00	—

KM# 654 5 NUEVOS PESOS
31.1710 g., 0.9990 Silver 1.0012 oz. ASW, 40 mm. **Series:** Endangered Wildlife **Subject:** Oso Negro **Obv:** National arms past and present **Rev:** Black bear

Date	Mintage	F	VF	XF	Unc	BU
2001	50,000	—	—	—	30.00	—

KM# 660 5 NUEVOS PESOS
31.1710 g., 0.9990 Silver 1.0012 oz. ASW, 40 mm. **Series:** Endangered Wildlife **Obv:** National arms past and present **Rev:** Volcano Rabbit

Date	Mintage	F	VF	XF	Unc	BU
2001	50,000	—	—	—	30.00	—

KM# 651 5 NUEVOS PESOS
31.1710 g., 0.9990 Silver 1.0012 oz. ASW, 40 mm. **Series:** Endangered Wildlife **Obv:** National arms past and present **Rev:** West Indian Manati **Edge:** Reeded

Date	Mintage	F	VF	XF	Unc	BU
2001	50,000	—	—	—	30.00	—

KM# 629 5 PESOS
27.0000 g., 0.9250 Silver .8030 oz. ASW **Subject:** Jarabe Tapatio **Obv:** Mexican emblem within circle of arms **Rev:** Two dancers

Date	Mintage	F	VF	XF	Unc	BU
1997 Proof	20,000	Value: 275				
1998 Proof	—	Value: 275				

KM# 605 5 PESOS
Bi-Metallic Aluminumn-Bronze center in Stainless Steel ring **Note:** Similar to KM#552 but deonomination without N.

Date	Mintage	F	VF	XF	Unc	BU
1997Mo	39,468,000	—	—	3.00	4.00	5.00
1998Mo	103,729,000	—	—	3.00	4.00	5.00
1999Mo	59,427,000	—	—	3.00	4.00	5.00
2000Mo	20,869,000	—	—	3.00	4.00	5.00
2001Mo	79,169,000	—	—	3.00	4.00	5.00
2002Mo	34,754,000	—	—	3.00	4.00	5.00
2003Mo	54,676,000	—	—	3.00	4.00	5.00

KM# 627 5 PESOS
31.1035 g., 0.9990 Silver 1.0000 oz. ASW **Subject:** World Wildlife Fund **Obv:** Mexican eagle **Rev:** Wolf with pup

Date	Mintage	F	VF	XF	Unc	BU
1998 Proof	Est. 15,000	Value: 75.00				

KM# 630 5 PESOS
31.1800 g., 0.9990 Silver 1.0025 oz. ASW **Subject:** Millennium Series **Obv:** Current national eagle within circle of obsolete versions **Rev:** Butterfly, dates **Rev. Designer:** Francisco Ortega Romero

Date	Mintage	F	VF	XF	Unc	BU
1999-2000 Proof	75,000	Value: 40.00				

KM# 631 5 PESOS
31.1800 g., 0.9990 Silver 1.0025 oz. ASW **Subject:** Millennium Series **Obv:** Current national eagle within circle of obsolete versions **Rev:** Stylized dove/hand of peace **Rev. Designer:** Omar Jiminez Torres

Date	Mintage	F	VF	XF	Unc	BU
1999-2000 Proof	75,000	Value: 40.00				

KM# 632 5 PESOS
31.1800 g., 0.9990 Silver 1.0025 oz. ASW **Subject:** Millennium Series **Obv:** Current national eagle within circle of obsolete versions **Rev:** Olga Maria Vega de Ochoa

Date	Mintage	F	VF	XF	Unc	BU
1999-2000 Proof	75,000	Value: 40.00				

KM# 635   5 PESOS
19.6000 g., 0.9250 Silver .6411 oz. ASW **Subject:**
Millennium Series **Obv:** Current national eagle within circle
of obsolete versions **Rev:** Naval training ship Cuauhtemoc

Date	Mintage	F	VF	XF	Unc	BU
1999	—		Value: 35.00			

KM# 640   5 PESOS
31.1030 g., 0.9990 Silver .9990 oz. ASW, 40 mm. **Subject:**
UNICEF **Obv:** National arms **Rev:** Two children flying kite
Edge: Reeded

Date	Mintage	F	VF	XF	Unc	BU
1999 Proof	—		Value: 45.00			

KM# 670   5 PESOS
27.0000 g., 0.9250 Silver 0.803 oz. ASW, 40 mm. **Series:**
Ibero-America **Obv:** Mexican arms within circle of other
national arms **Rev:** Cowboy trick riding two horses **Edge:**
Reeded

Date	Mintage	F	VF	XF	Unc	BU
2000 Proof	—		Value: 45.00			

KM# 678   5 PESOS
27.0000 g., 0.9250 Silver 0.803 oz. ASW, 40 mm. **Subject:**
Ibero-America: Acapulco Galleon **Obv:** Mexican arms
encircled by ten coats of arms **Rev:** Spanish galleon with
Pacific Ocean background and trading scene in foreground
Edge: Reeded

Date	Mintage	F	VF	XF	Unc	BU
2003Mo Proof	5,000		Value: 65.00			

KM# 553   10 NUEVOS PESOS
Bi-Metallic 0.925 Silver center, .1667 oz. ASW within
Aluminumn-Bronze ring

Date	Mintage	F	VF	XF	Unc	BU
1992	20,000,000	—	—	—	7.50	8.50
1993	47,981,000	—	—	—	7.50	8.50
1994	15,000,000	—	—	—	7.50	8.50
1995	15,000,000	—	—	—	7.50	8.50
1995 Proof	6,981		Value: 15.00			

KM# 606   10 PESOS
Bi-Metallic 0.925 Silver .1667 ASW center within Aluminumn-
Bronze ring **Note:** Similar to KM#553, but denomination
without N.

Date	Mintage	F	VF	XF	Unc	BU
1996 Reported not confirmed	—	—	—	—	—	—

KM# 616   10 PESOS
Bi-Metallic Copper-Nickel-Brass center within Brass ring
Obv: National emblem **Rev:** Aztec design

Date	Mintage	F	VF	XF	Unc	BU
1997	44,837,000	—	—	—	5.00	6.50
1998	203,735,000	—	—	—	5.00	6.50
1998		—	—	—	5.00	6.50
Note: Small date, date on brass ring						
1998	—	—	—	—	5.00	6.50
Note: Large date, date partially on copper-nickel center						
1999	29,842,000	—	—	—	5.00	6.50
2000		—	—	—	5.00	6.50
2002	44,721,000	—	—	—	5.00	6.50

KM# 633 10 PESOS
62.0300 g., 0.9990 Silver 1.9923 oz. ASW **Subject:**
Millennium Series **Obv:** Current national eagle within circle
of obsolete versions **Rev:** Old and modern buildings, dates

Date	Mintage	F	VF	XF	Unc	BU
1999-2000 Proof	75,000	Value: 45.00				

KM# 636 10 PESOS
Bi-Metallic Copper-Nickel center in Brass ring **Subject:**
Millennium Series **Rev:** Aztec carving

Date	Mintage	F	VF	XF	Unc	BU
2000Mo	24,839,000	—	—	—	5.00	6.50
2001Mo	44,768,000	—	—	—	5.00	6.50
2002Mo	—	—	—	—	5.00	6.50
2003Mo	—	—	—	—	5.00	6.50
2004Mo	—	—	—	—	5.00	6.50
2005Mo	—	—	—	—	5.00	6.50

KM# 686 10 PESOS
31.1040 g., 0.9990 Silver 0.999 oz. ASW, 40 mm. **Obv:**
Mexican arms **Rev:** Sinaloa arms **Edge:** Reeded **Note:**
Mexican States: Sinaloa

Date	Mintage	F	VF	XF	Unc	BU
2004Mo Proof	10,000	Value: 55.00				

KM# 561 20 NUEVOS PESOS
Bi-Metallic 0.925 Silver 16.9g, (.2500 oz. ASW) center within
Aluminumn-Bronze ring

Date	Mintage	F	VF	XF	Unc	BU
1993	25,000,000	—	—	—	12.00	13.00
1994	5,000,000	—	—	—	12.00	13.00
1995	5,000,000	—	—	—	12.00	13.00

KM# 641 20 PESOS
6.2210 g., 0.9990 Gold .1998 oz. AGW, 21.9 mm. **Subject:**
UNICEF **Obv:** National arms **Rev:** Child playing with lasso
Edge: Reeded

Date	Mintage	F	VF	XF	Unc	BU
1999 Proof	—	Value: 275				

KM# 637   20 PESOS
Bi-Metallic Copper-Nickel center within Brass ring **Subject:**
Xiuhtecuhtli **Rev:** Aztec with torch

Date	Mintage	F	VF	XF	Unc	BU
2000	14,890,000	—	—	—	15.00	17.50
2001	2,478,000	—	—	—	15.00	17.50

KM# 638   20 PESOS
Bi-Metallic Copper-Nickel center within Brass ring **Rev:**
Octavio Paz

Date	Mintage	F	VF	XF	Unc	BU
2000	14,943,000	—	—	—	15.00	17.50
2001	2,515,000	—	—	—	15.00	17.50

KM# 571   50 NUEVOS PESOS
Bi-Metallic 0.925 Silver .5000 ASW center within Brass ring
Subject: Nino Heroes

Date	Mintage	F	VF	XF	Unc	BU
1993	2,000,000	—	—	—	25.00	28.00
1994	1,500,000	—	—	—	25.00	28.00
1995	1,500,000	—	—	—	25.00	28.00

KM# 608   50 PESOS
Bi-Metallic 0.925 Sllver .5000 ASW center within Brass ring
Note: Similar to 50 New Pesos, KM#571 without "N" before
denomination.

Date	Mintage	F	VF	XF	Unc	BU
1996 Reported not confirmed	—	—	—	—	—	—

KM# 712   100 PESOS
33.8253 g., Bi-Metallic .925 Silver ring in Brass ring, 39.9 mm.
Obv: Mexican arms **Rev:** Chiapas state arms **Edge:**
Segmented reeding

Date	Mintage	F	VF	XF	Unc	BU
2005Mo	—	—	—	—	45.00	—

KM# 713   100 PESOS
33.8253 g., Bi-Metallic .925 Silver ring in Brass ring, 39.9 mm.
Obv: Mexican arms **Rev:** Federal District arms **Edge:**
Segmented reeding

Date	Mintage	F	VF	XF	Unc	BU
2005Mo	—	—	—	—	45.00	—

KM# 714   100 PESOS
33.8253 g., Bi-Metallic .925 Silver ring in Brass ring,
39.9 mm. **Obv:** Mexican arms **Rev:** Durango arms **Edge:**
Segmented reeding

Date	Mintage	F	VF	XF	Unc	BU
2005Mo	—	—	—	—	45.00	—

KM# 715 100 PESOS
33.8253 g., Bi-Metallic .925 Silver ring in Brass ring, 39.9 mm.
Obv: Mexican arms **Rev:** Guanajuato arms **Edge:**
Segmented reeding

Date	Mintage	F	VF	XF	Unc	BU
2005Mo	—	—	—	—	45.00	—

KM# 716 100 PESOS
33.8253 g., Bi-Metallic .925 Silver ring in Brass ring, 39.9 mm.
Obv: Mexican arms **Rev:** Guerrero state arms **Edge:**
Segmented reeding

Date	Mintage	F	VF	XF	Unc	BU
2005Mo	—	—	—	—	45.00	—

KM# 717 100 PESOS
33.8253 g., Bi-Metallic .925 Silver ring in Brass ring, 39.9 mm.
Obv: Mexican arms **Rev:** Hidalgo state arms **Edge:**
Segmented reeding

Date	Mintage	F	VF	XF	Unc	BU
2005Mo	—	—	—	—	45.00	—

KM# 757 100 PESOS
Bi-Metallic **Subject:** Baja California **Rev:** Ram's head

Date	Mintage	F	VF	XF	Unc	BU
2005	—	—	—	—	—	18.00

KM# 760 100 PESOS
Bi-Metallic **Subject:** Estado de Campeche **Rev:** Jade Mask

Date	Mintage	F	VF	XF	Unc	BU
2006	—	—	—	—	—	18.00

KM# 762 100 PESOS
Bi-Metallic **Subject:** Estado de Baja California Sur **Rev:**
Deer, sunset and cactus, map superimposed

Date	Mintage	F	VF	XF	Unc	BU
2006	—	—	—	—	—	18.00

KM# 764 100 PESOS
Bi-Metallic **Subject:** Benito Juarez Garcia **Rev:** Bust facing

Date	Mintage	F	VF	XF	Unc	BU
2006	—	—	—	—	—	18.00

SILVER BULLION COINAGE

Libertad Series

KM# 542 1/20 ONZA (1/20 Troy Ounce of Silver)
1.5551 g., 0.9990 Silver .0500 oz. ASW **Rev:** Winged Victory

Date	Mintage	F	VF	XF	Unc	BU
1991	50,017	—	—	—	—	4.50
1992	295,783	—	—	—	—	4.50

Date	Mintage	F	VF	XF	Unc	BU
1992 Proof	5,000	Value: 10.00				
1993	100,000	—	—	—	—	4.50
1993 Proof	—	Value: 10.00				
1994	90,100	—	—	—	—	4.50
1994 Proof	10,000	Value: 10.00				
1995	50,000	—	—	—	—	4.50
1995 Proof	2,000	Value: 10.00				

KM# 609 1/20 ONZA (1/20 Troy Ounce of Silver)
1.5551 g., 0.9990 Silver .0500 oz. ASW **Obv:** Mexican eagle
Rev: Winged Victory

Date	Mintage	F	VF	XF	Unc	BU
1996	50,000	—	—	—	—	10.00
1996 Proof	1,000	Value: 15.00				
1997	20,000	—	—	—	—	10.00
1997 Proof	800	Value: 15.00				
1998	6,400	—	—	—	—	10.00
1998 Proof	300	Value: 18.50				
1999	8,001	—	—	—	—	12.00
1999 Proof	600	Value: 16.50				
2000	57,500	—	—	—	—	12.00
2000 Proof	900	Value: 16.50				
2001	25,000	—	—	—	—	12.00
2001 Proof	1,500	Value: 15.00				
2002	45,000	—	—	—	—	8.00
2002 Proof	2,800	Value: 13.00				
2003	—	—	—	—	—	8.00
2003 Proof	—	Value: 13.00				
2004	—	—	—	—	—	8.00
2004 Proof	—	Value: 13.00				
2005	—	—	—	—	—	8.00
2005 Proof	—	Value: 12.00				

KM# 543 1/10 ONZA (1/10 Troy Ounce of Silver)
3.1103 g., 0.9990 Silver .1000 oz. ASW **Obv:** Mexican eagle
Rev: Winged Victory

Date	Mintage	F	VF	XF	Unc	BU
1991	50,017	—	—	—	—	5.50
1992	299,983	—	—	—	—	5.50
1992 Proof	5,000	Value: 12.00				
1993	100,000	—	—	—	—	5.50
1993 Proof	—	Value: 12.00				
1994	90,100	—	—	—	—	5.50
1994 Proof	10,000	Value: 12.00				
1995	50,000	—	—	—	—	5.50
1995 Proof	2,000	Value: 12.00				

KM# 610 1/10 ONZA (1/10 Troy Ounce of Silver)
3.1103 g., 0.9990 Silver .1000 oz. ASW **Obv:** Mexican eagle
Rev: Winged Victory

Date	Mintage	F	VF	XF	Unc	BU
1996	50,000	—	—	—	—	12.00
1996 Proof	1,000	Value: 17.50				
1997	20,000	—	—	—	—	12.00
1997 Proof	800	Value: 17.50				
1998	6,400	—	—	—	—	12.00
1998 Proof	300	Value: 22.50				
1999	8,000	—	—	—	—	14.00

Date	Mintage	F	VF	XF	Unc	BU
1999 Proof	600	Value: 20.00				
2000	27,500	—	—	—	—	14.00
2000 Proof	1,000	Value: 20.00				
2001	25,000	—	—	—	—	14.00
2001 Proof	1,500	Value: 18.00				
2002	35,000	—	—	—	—	10.00
2002 Proof	2,800	Value: 15.00				
2003	—	—	—	—	—	10.00
2003 Proof	—	Value: 15.00				
2004	—	—	—	—	—	10.00
2004 Proof	—	Value: 15.00				
2005	—	—	—	—	—	10.00
2005 Proof	—	Value: 14.00				

KM# 544   1/4 ONZA (1/4 Troy Ounce of Silver)
7.7758 g., 0.9990 Silver .2500 oz. ASW **Obv:** Mexican eagle
Rev: Winged Victory

Date	Mintage	F	VF	XF	Unc	BU
1991	50,017	—	—	—	—	7.50
1992	104,000	—	—	—	—	7.50
1992 Proof	5,000	Value: 15.00				
1993	86,500	—	—	—	—	7.50
1993 Proof	—	Value: 15.00				
1994	90,100	—	—	—	—	7.50
1994 Proof	15,000	Value: 15.00				
1995	50,000	—	—	—	—	7.50
1995 Proof	2,000	Value: 15.00				

KM# 611   1/4 ONZA (1/4 Troy Ounce of Silver)
7.7758 g., 0.9990 Silver .2500 oz. ASW **Obv:** Mexican eagle
Rev: Winged Victory

Date	Mintage	F	VF	XF	Unc	BU
1996	50,000	—	—	—	—	15.00
1996 Proof	1,000	Value: 20.00				
1997	20,000	—	—	—	—	15.00
1997 Proof	800	Value: 20.00				
1998	6,400	—	—	—	—	15.00
1998 Proof	300	Value: 32.50				
1999	7,000	—	—	—	—	18.00
1999 Proof	600	Value: 25.00				
2000	21,000	—	—	—	—	18.00
2000 Proof	700	Value: 25.00				
2001	25,000	—	—	—	—	18.00
2001 Proof	1,000	Value: 22.00				
2002	35,000	—	—	—	—	13.00
2002 Proof	2,800	Value: 20.00				
2003	—	—	—	—	—	13.00
2003 Proof	—	Value: 20.00				
2004	—	—	—	—	—	13.00
2004 Proof	—	Value: 20.00				
2005	—	—	—	—	—	13.00
2005 Proof	—	Value: 18.00				

KM# 545   1/2 ONZA (1/2 Troy Ounce of Silver)
15.5517 g., 0.9990 Silver .5000 oz. ASW **Obv:** Mexican
eagle **Rev:** Winged Victory

Date	Mintage	F	VF	XF	Unc	BU
1991	50,618	—	—	—	—	9.00
1992	119,000	—	—	—	—	9.00
1992 Proof	5,000	Value: 17.50				
1993	71,500	—	—	—	—	9.00
1993 Proof	—	Value: 17.50				
1994	90,100	—	—	—	—	9.00
1994 Proof	15,000	Value: 17.50				
1995	50,000	—	—	—	—	9.00
1995 Proof	2,000	Value: 17.50				

KM# 612   1/2 ONZA (1/2 Troy Ounce of Silver)
15.5517 g., 0.9990 Silver .5000 oz. ASW **Obv:** Mexican
eagle **Rev:** Winged Victory

Date	Mintage	F	VF	XF	Unc	BU
1996	50,000	—	—	—	—	20.00
1996 Proof	1,000	Value: 30.00				
1997	20,000	—	—	—	—	20.00
1997 Proof	800	Value: 30.00				
1998	6,400	—	—	—	—	22.00
1998 Proof	300	Value: 45.00				
1999	7,000	—	—	—	—	22.00
1999 Proof	600	Value: 35.00				
2000	20,000	—	—	—	—	22.00
2000 Proof	700	Value: 35.00				
2001	20,000	—	—	—	—	22.00
2001 Proof	1,000	Value: 30.00				
2002	35,000	—	—	—	—	18.00
2002 Proof	2,800	Value: 25.00				
2003	—	—	—	—	—	18.00
2003 Proof	—	Value: 25.00				
2004	—	—	—	—	—	18.00
2004 Proof	—	Value: 25.00				
2005	—	—	—	—	—	18.00
2005 Proof	—	Value: 22.00				

KM# 494.1 ONZA (Troy Ounce of Silver)
31.1000 g., 0.9990 Silver 1.0000 oz. ASW **Subject:** Libertad

Date	Mintage	F	VF	XF	Unc	BU
1982	1,049,680	—	—	—	BV	12.50
1983	1,001,768	—	—	—	BV	12.50
1983 Proof	998	Value: 200				
1984	1,014,000	—	—	—	BV	12.50
1985	2,017,000	—	—	—	BV	12.50
1986	1,699,426	—	—	—	BV	12.50
1986 Proof	30,006	Value: 25.00				
1987	500,000	—	—	—	BV	35.00
1987 Proof	12,000	Value: 30.00				
1987 Proof doubled date	Inc. above	Value: 40.00				
1988	1,500,500	—	—	—	BV	35.00
1989	1,396,500	—	—	—	BV	20.00
1989 Proof	10,000	Value: 50.00				

KM# 494.2 ONZA (Troy Ounce of Silver)
31.1000 g., 0.9990 Silver 1.0000 oz. ASW **Edge:** Reeded

Date	Mintage	F	VF	XF	Unc	BU
1988 Proof	10,000	Value: 55.00				
1990	1,200,000	—	—	—	BV	12.50
1990 Proof	10,000	Value: 45.00				
1991	1,650,518	—	—	—	BV	15.00

KM# 494.5 ONZA (Troy Ounce of Silver)
31.1000 g., 0.9990 Silver 1.0000 oz. ASW **Subject:** Libertad **Obv:** KM#494.3 **Rev:** KM#494.2 **Edge:** Reeded edge **Note:** Mule

Date	Mintage	F	VF	XF	Unc	BU
1991 Proof	10,000	Value: 40.00				

KM# 494.3 ONZA (Troy Ounce of Silver)
31.1000 g., 0.9990 Silver 1.0000 oz. ASW **Subject:** Libertad **Obv:** Eight dots below eagle's left talons **Rev:** Revised design and lettering **Edge:** Reeded edge

Date	Mintage	F	VF	XF	Unc	BU
1991	Inc. above	—	—	—	BV	22.00
1992	2,458,000	—	—	—	BV	12.50
1992 Proof	10,000	Value: 40.00				

KM# 494.4 ONZA (Troy Ounce of Silver)
31.1000 g., 0.9990 Silver 1.0000 oz. ASW **Subject:** Libertad **Obv:** Seven dots below eagle's left talons, dull claws on right talon, thick letters **Rev:** Revised design and lettering **Edge:** Reeded edge **Note:** Mule

Date	Mintage	F	VF	XF	Unc	BU
1993	1,000,000	—	—	—	BV	14.00
1993 Proof	—	Value: 35.00				
1994	400,000	—	—	—	BV	18.00
1994 Proof	10,000	Value: 35.00				
1995	500,000	—	—	—	BV	16.00
1995 Proof	2,000	Value: 35.00				

KM# 613 ONZA (Troy Ounce of Silver)
33.6250 g., 0.9250 Silver 1.0000 oz. ASW **Obv:** Mexican eagle **Rev:** Winged Victory

Date	Mintage	F	VF	XF	Unc	BU
1996	300,000	—	—	—	—	16.00
1996 Proof	2,000	Value: 40.00				
1997	100,000	—	—	—	—	16.50
1997 Proof	1,500	Value: 42.00				
1998	67,000	—	—	—	—	40.00
1998 Proof	500	Value: 80.00				
1999	95,000	—	—	—	—	20.00
1999 Proof	600	Value: 50.00				

Date	Mintage	F	VF	XF	Unc	BU
1998	7,000	—	—	—	—	30.00
1998 Proof	400	Value: 100				
1999	5,000	—	—	—	—	50.00
1999 Proof	280	Value: 175				
2000	7,500	—	—	—	—	50.00
2000 Proof	500	Value: 60.00				
2001	1,700	—	—	—	—	50.00
2001 Proof	500	Value: 60.00				
2002	8,700	—	—	—	—	45.00
2002 Proof	1,000	Value: 55.00				
2003	—	—	—	—	—	45.00
2003 Proof	—	Value: 55.00				
2004	—	—	—	—	—	40.00
2004 Proof	—	Value: 50.00				
2005	—	—	—	—	—	40.00
2005 Proof	—	Value: 50.00				

KM# 639   ONZA (Troy Ounce of Silver)
31.1000 g., 0.9990 Silver 1.0000 oz. ASW **Subject:** Libertad
Obv: Modern Mexican eagle within circle of obsolete versions
Edge: Reeded edge **Note:** Mule

Date	Mintage	F	VF	XF	Unc	BU
2000	340,000	—	—	—	—	20.00
2000 Proof	1,600	Value: 50.00				
2001	650,000	—	—	—	—	20.00
2001 Proof	2,000	Value: 50.00				
2002	850,000	—	—	—	—	18.00
2002 Proof	3,800	Value: 50.00				
2003Mo	—	—	—	—	—	18.00
2003Mo Proof	—	Value: 50.00				
2004Mo	—	—	—	—	—	18.00
2004Mo Proof	—	Value: 45.00				
2005	—	—	—	—	—	18.00
2005 Proof	—	Value: 45.00				

KM# 614   2 ONZAS (2 Troy Ounces of Silver)
62.2070 g., 0.9990 Silver 2.0000 oz. ASW **Subject:** Libertad
Obv: Mexican eagle within circle of obsolete versions **Rev:**
Winged Victory

Date	Mintage	F	VF	XF	Unc	BU
1996	50,000	—	—	—	—	28.50
1996 Proof	1,200	Value: 47.50				
1997	15,000	—	—	—	—	28.50
1997 Proof	1,300	Value: 50.00				

KM# 615   5 ONZAS (5 Troy Ounces of Silver)
155.5175 g., 0.9990 Silver 5.0000 oz. ASW **Subject:**
Libertad **Obv:** Mexican eagle within circle of obsolete versions
Rev: Winged Victory

Date	Mintage	F	VF	XF	Unc	BU
1996	20,000	—	—	—	—	110
1996 Proof	1,200	Value: 200				
1997	10,000	—	—	—	—	110
1997 Proof	1,300	Value: 200				
1998	3,500	—	—	—	—	220
1998 Proof	400	Value: 400				
1999	2,800	—	—	—	—	100
1999 Proof	100	Value: 500				
2000	4,000	—	—	—	—	100
2000 Proof	500	Value: 200				
2001	4,000	—	—	—	—	95.00
2001 Proof	600	Value: 200				
2002	5,200	—	—	—	—	95.00
2002 Proof	1,000	Value: 200				
2003	—	—	—	—	—	85.00
2003 Proof	—	Value: 110				
2004	—	—	—	—	—	85.00
2004 Proof	—	Value: 110				
2005	—	—	—	—	—	85.00
2005 Proof	—	Value: 110				

KM# 677   KILO (32.15 Troy Ounces of Silver)
999.9775 g., 0.9990 Silver 32.1178 oz. ASW, 110 mm.
Subject: Collector Bullion **Obv:** Current Mexican emblem within circle of obsolete versions **Rev:** Winged Victory statue **Edge:** Reeded

Date	Mintage	F	VF	XF	Unc	BU
2002Mo Prooflike	1,100	—	—	—	—	750
2003Mo Proof	3,000	Value: 650				
2004Mo Prooflike	—	—	—	—	—	650
2005Mo Proof	—	Value: 675				

GOLD BULLION COINAGE

KM# 530   1/20 ONZA (1/20 Ounce of Pure Gold)
1.7500 g., 0.9000 Gold .0500 oz. AGW **Obv:** Winged Victory **Rev:** Calendar stone

Date	Mintage	F	VF	XF	Unc	BU
1987	—	—	—	—	—	275
1988	—	—	—	—	—	—

KM# 589   1/20 ONZA (1/20 Ounce of Pure Gold)
1.5551 g., 0.9990 Gold .05 oz. AGW **Obv:** Winged Victory **Rev:** Eagle and snake

Date	Mintage	F	VF	XF	Unc	BU
1991	10,000	—	—	—	—	BV+30%
1992	65,225	—	—	—	—	BV+30%
1993	10,000	—	—	—	—	BV+30%
1994	10,000	—	—	—	—	BV+30%

KM# 642   1/20 ONZA (1/20 Ounce of Pure Gold)
1.5551 g., 0.9990 Gold .05 oz. AGW **Obv:** Winged Victory **Rev:** Teocuitlatl and an indian working

Date	Mintage	F	VF	XF	Unc	BU
2000 Proof	—	Value: 50.00				

KM# 671   1/20 ONZA (1/20 Ounce of Pure Gold)
1.5551 g., 0.9990 Gold .05 oz. AGW, 16 mm. **Obv:** Mexican arms **Rev:** Winged Victory facing left **Edge:** Reeded **Note:** Design similar to KM#609. Value estimates do not include the high taxes and surcharges added to the issue prices by the Mexican Government.

Date	Mintage	F	VF	XF	Unc	BU
2000	5,300	—	—	—	BV+30%	—
2002Mo	5,000	—	—	—	BV+30%	—
2004Mo	—	—	—	—	BV+30%	—
2005Mo	—	—	—	—	BV+30%	—
2006Mo	—	—	—	—	BV+30%	—

KM# 628   1/15 ONZA (1/15 Ounce of Pure Gold)
0.9990 Gold .0755 oz. AGW **Obv:** Winged Victory above legend

Date	Mintage	F	VF	XF	Unc	BU
1987	—	—	—	—	—	275

KM# 541   1/10 ONZA (1/10 Ounce of Pure Gold)
3.1103 g., 0.9990 Gold .1000 oz. AGW

Date	Mintage	F	VF	XF	Unc	BU
1991	10,000	—	—	—	—	BV+20%
1992	50,777	—	—	—	—	BV+20%
1993	10,000	—	—	—	—	BV+20%
1994	10,000	—	—	—	—	BV+20%

KM# 672   1/10 ONZA (1/10 Ounce of Pure Gold)
3.1103 g., 0.9990 Gold 0.0999 oz. AGW, 20 mm. **Obv:** Mexican arms **Rev:** Winged Victory facing left **Edge:** Reeded **Note:** Design similar to KM#610. Value estimates do not include the high taxes and surcharges added to the issue prices by the Mexican Government.

Date	Mintage	F	VF	XF	Unc	BU
2000	3,500	—	—	—	BV+20%	—
2002Mo	5,000	—	—	—	BV+20%	—
2004Mo	—	—	—	—	BV+20%	—
2005Mo	—	—	—	—	BV+20%	—

KM# 487   1/4 ONZA (1/4 Ounce of Pure Gold)
8.6396 g., 0.9000 Gold .2500 oz. AGW **Note:** Similar to KM#488.

Date	Mintage	F	VF	XF	Unc	BU
1981	313,000	—	—	—	—	BV+11%
1982	—	—	—	—	—	BV+11%

KM# 590   1/4 ONZA (1/4 Ounce of Pure Gold)
7.7758 g., 0.9990 Gold .2500 oz. AGW **Obv:** Winged Victory above legend **Rev:** Eagle and snake

Date	Mintage	F	VF	XF	Unc	BU
1991	10,000	—	—	—	—	BV+11%
1992	28,106	—	—	—	—	BV+11%
1993	2,500	—	—	—	—	BV+11%
1994	2,500	—	—	—	—	BV+11%

KM# 673   1/4 ONZA (1/4 Ounce of Pure Gold)
7.7758 g., 0.9990 Gold .25 oz. AGW, 26.9 mm. **Obv:** Mexican arms **Rev:** Winged Victory facing left **Edge:** Reeded **Note:** Design similar to KM#611. Value estimates do not include the high taxes and surcharges added to the issue prices by the Mexican Government.

Date	Mintage	F	VF	XF	Unc	BU
2000	2,500	—	—	—	BV+12%	—
2002Mo	—	—	—	—	BV+12%	—
2004Mo	—	—	—	—	BV+12%	—
2005Mo	—	—	—	—	BV+12%	—

KM# 488   1/2 ONZA (1/2 Ounce of Pure Gold)
17.2792 g., 0.9000 Gold .5000 oz. AGW

Date	Mintage	F	VF	XF	Unc	BU
1981	193,000	—	—	—	—	BV+8%
1982	—	—	—	—	—	BV+8%
1989 Proof	704	Value: 500				

KM# 591   1/2 ONZA (1/2 Ounce of Pure Gold)
15.5517 g., 0.9990 Gold .5000 oz. AGW **Obv:** Winged Victory above legend **Rev:** Eagle and snake

Date	Mintage	F	VF	XF	Unc	BU
1991	10,000	—	—	—	—	BV+8%
1992	25,220	—	—	—	—	BV+8%
1993	2,500	—	—	—	—	BV+8%
1994	2,500	—	—	—	—	BV+8%

KM# 674   1/2 ONZA (1/2 Ounce of Pure Gold)
15.5517 g., 0.9990 Gold 0.4995 oz. AGW, 32.9 mm. **Obv:** Mexican arms **Rev:** Winged Victory facing left **Edge:** Reeded **Note:** Design similar to KM#612. Value estimates do not include the high taxes and surcharges added to the issue prices by the Mexican Government.

Date	Mintage	F	VF	XF	Unc	BU
2000	1,500	—	—	—	BV+8%	—
2002Mo	—	—	—	—	BV+8%	—
2004Mo	—	—	—	—	BV+8%	—
2005Mo	—	—	—	—	BV+8%	—
2006Mo	—	—	—	—	BV+8%	—

KM# 489   ONZA (Ounce of Pure Gold)
34.5585 g., 0.9000 Gold 1.0000 oz. AGW **Note:** Similar to KM#488.

Date	Mintage	F	VF	XF	Unc	BU
1981	596,000	—	—	—	—	BV+3%
1985	—	—	—	—	—	BV+3%
1988	—	—	—	—	—	BV+3%

KM# 592   ONZA (Ounce of Pure Gold)
31.1035 g., 0.9990 Gold 1.0000 oz. AGW **Obv:** Winged Victory above legend **Rev:** Eagle and snake

Date	Mintage	F	VF	XF	Unc	BU
1991	109,193	—	—	—	—	BV+3%
1992	46,281	—	—	—	—	BV+3%

Date	Mintage	F	VF	XF	Unc	BU
1993	10,000	—	—	—	—	BV+3%
1994	1,000	—	—	—	—	BV+3%

KM# 675 ONZA (Ounce of Pure Gold)
31.1035 g., 0.9990 Gold 0.999 oz. AGW, 40 mm. **Obv:** Mexican arms **Rev:** Winged Victory facing left **Edge:** Reeded **Note:** Design similar to KM#639. Value estimates do not include the high taxes and surcharges added to the issue prices by the Mexican Government.

Date	Mintage	F	VF	XF	Unc	BU
2000	2,730	—	—	—	BV+3%	—
2002Mo		—	—	—	BV+3%	—
2004Mo		—	—	—	BV+3%	—
2005Mo		—	—	—	BV+3%	—
2006Mo		—	—	—	BV+3%	—

PLATINUM BULLION COINAGE

KM# 538 1/4 ONZA (1/4 Ounce)
7.7775 g., 0.9990 Platinum .2500 oz. APW

Date	Mintage	F	VF	XF	Unc	BU
1989	704	Value: 365				

BULLION COINAGE

Pre-Columbian • Azteca Series

KM# 644 NUEVO PESO
7.7700 g., 0.9990 Silver .2496 oz. ASW, 26.8 mm. **Subject:** Eagle Warrior **Obv:** National arms **Rev:** Eagle warrior **Edge:** Reeded

Date	Mintage	F	VF	XF	Unc	BU
1993Mo	1,500	—	—	—	—	10.00
1993 Proof	900	Value: 20.00				

KM# 645 2 NUEVOS PESOS
15.4200 g., 0.9990 Silver .4953 oz. ASW, 32.9 mm. **Subject:** Eagle Warrior **Obv:** National arms **Rev:** Eagle warrior **Edge:** Reeded

Date	Mintage	F	VF	XF	Unc	BU
1993Mo	1,500	—	—	—	—	10.00
1993 Proof	800	Value: 22.00				

KM# 646 5 NUEVOS PESOS
31.0500 g., 0.9990 Silver .9973 oz. ASW, 40 mm. **Subject:** Eagle Warrior **Obv:** National arms **Rev:** Eagle warrior **Edge:** Reeded

Date	Mintage	F	VF	XF	Unc	BU
1993	2,000	—	—	—	—	16.00
1993 Proof	1,000	Value: 45.00				

KM# 647 5 NUEVOS PESOS
31.0000 g., 0.9990 Silver .9957 oz. ASW, 40 mm. **Subject:** Xochipilli **Obv:** National arms **Rev:** Seated figure sculpture **Edge:** Reeded

Date	Mintage	F	VF	XF	Unc	BU
1993	2,000	—	—	—	—	15.00
1993 Proof	800	Value: 52.00				

KM# 648   5 NUEVOS PESOS
31.0000 g., 0.9990 Silver .9957 oz. ASW, 40 mm. **Subject:**
Brasco Efigie **Obv:** National arms **Rev:** Sculpture **Edge:**
Reeded

Date	Mintage	F	VF	XF	Unc	BU
1993	2,000	—	—	—	—	15.00
1993 Proof	500	Value: 40.00				

KM# 649   5 NUEVOS PESOS
31.0000 g., 0.9990 Silver .9957 oz. ASW, 40 mm. **Subject:**
Huchucteotl **Obv:** National arms **Rev:** Aztec sculpture **Edge:**
Reeded

Date	Mintage	F	VF	XF	Unc	BU
1993	5,000	—	—	—	—	15.00
1993 Proof	800	Value: 45.00				

KM# 650   10 NUEVOS PESOS
155.3100 g., 0.9990 Silver 4.9883 oz. ASW, 64 mm.
Subject: Piedra de Tizoc **Obv:** National arms **Rev:** Warrior
capturing woman **Edge:** Reeded **Note:** Illustration reduced.

Date	Mintage	F	VF	XF	Unc	BU
1992 Proof	—	Value: 150				
1993	1,000	—	—	—	—	60.00
1993 Proof	1,000	Value: 85.00				

KM# 554   25 PESOS
7.7758 g., 0.9990 Silver .2500 oz. ASW **Rev:** Eagle warrior

Date	Mintage	F	VF	XF	Unc	BU
1992	50,000	—	—	—	10.00	—
1992 Proof	3,000	Value: 15.00				

KM# 555 50 PESOS
15.5517 g., 0.9990 Silver .5000 oz. ASW **Rev:** Eagle warrior

Date	Mintage	F	VF	XF	Unc	BU
1992	50,000	—	—	—	16.00	—
1992 Proof	3,000	Value: 24.00				

KM# 556 100 PESOS
31.1035 g., 0.9990 Silver 1.0000 oz. ASW **Rev:** Eagle warrior

Date	Mintage	F	VF	XF	Unc	BU
1992	205,000	—	—	—	16.00	—
1992	4,000	Value: 42.00				

KM# 562 100 PESOS
31.1035 g., 0.9990 Silver 1.0000 oz. ASW **Rev:** Xochipilli - The God of Joy, Music and Dance

Date	Mintage	F	VF	XF	Unc	BU
1992 Proof	4,000	Value: 42.00				

KM# 563 100 PESOS
31.1035 g., 0.9990 Silver 1.0000 oz. ASW **Rev:** Brasero Efigie - The God of Rain

Date	Mintage	F	VF	XF	Unc	BU
1992 Proof	4,000	Value: 40.00				

KM# 564 100 PESOS
31.1035 g., 0.9990 Silver 1.0000 oz. ASW **Rev:** Huehueteotl - The God of Fire

Date	Mintage	F	VF	XF	Unc	BU
1992 Proof	4,000	Value: 42.00				

KM# 558 250 PESOS
7.7758 g., 0.9990 Gold .2500 oz. AGW **Subject:** Native Culture **Rev:** Sculpture of jaguar head

Date	Mintage	F	VF	XF	Unc	BU
1992	10,000	—	—	—	150	—
1992 Proof	2,000	Value: 275				

KM# 559   500 PESOS
15.5517 g., 0.9990 Gold .5000 oz. AGW **Subject:** Native
Culture - Sculpture of Jaguar Head

Date	Mintage	F	VF	XF	Unc	BU
1992	10,000	—	—	—	300	—
1992 Proof	2,000	Value: 470				

KM# 560   1000 PESOS
31.1035 g., 0.9990 Gold 1.0000 oz. AGW **Subject:** Native
Culture **Rev:** Sculpture of jaguar head

Date	Mintage	F	VF	XF	Unc	BU
1992	17,850	—	—	—	600	—
1992 Proof	2,000	Value: 625				

KM# 557   10000 PESOS
155.5175 g., 0.9990 Silver 5.0000 oz. ASW, 64 mm.
Subject: Pieora De Tizoc **Rev:** Native warriors taking female
captive **Note:** Illustration reduced.

Date	Mintage	F	VF	XF	Unc	BU
1992	51,900	—	—	—	—	60.00
1992 Proof	3,300	Value: 150				

Pre-Columbian • Central Veracruz Series

KM# 567   NUEVO PESO
7.7601 g., 0.9990 Silver .2498 oz. ASW **Subject:** Bajo
relieve de el Tajin

Date	Mintage	F	VF	XF	Unc	BU
1993	100,000	—	—	—	—	8.75
1993 Proof	3,300	Value: 20.00				

KM# 568   2 NUEVOS PESOS
15.5516 g., 0.9990 Silver .4995 oz. ASW **Subject:** Bajo
relieve de el Tajin

Date	Mintage	F	VF	XF	Unc	BU
1993	100,000	—	—	—	—	12.00
1993 Proof	3,000	Value: 20.00				

KM# 569   5 NUEVOS PESOS
31.1035 g., 0.9990 Silver .9991 oz. ASW **Subject:** Bajo
relieve de el Tajin **Obv:** Mexican eagle

Date	Mintage	F	VF	XF	Unc	BU
1993	100,000	—	—	—	—	15.00
1993 Proof	3,000	Value: 42.00				

KM# 582 5 NUEVOS PESOS
31.1035 g., 0.9990 Silver .9991 oz. ASW **Subject:** Palma Con Cocodrilo **Obv:** National emblem **Rev:** Aerial view of crocodile

Date	Mintage	F	VF	XF	Unc	BU
1993	4,500	—	—	—	—	15.00
1993 Proof	2,650	Value: 42.00				

KM# 583 5 NUEVOS PESOS
31.1035 g., 0.9990 Silver .9991 oz. ASW **Subject:** Anciano Con Brasero **Rev:** Kneeling figure sculpture

Date	Mintage	F	VF	XF	Unc	BU
1993	2,650	—	—	—	—	15.00
1993 Proof	1,500	Value: 42.00				

KM# 584 5 NUEVOS PESOS
31.1035 g., 0.9990 Silver .9991 oz. ASW **Subject:** Carita Sonriente **Rev:** Sculptured head

Date	Mintage	F	VF	XF	Unc	BU
1993	4,500	—	—	—	—	15.00
1993 Proof	3,300	Value: 42.00				

KM# 570 10 NUEVOS PESOS
Center Weight: 115.5175 g. **Center Composition:** 0.9990 Silver 4.9956 oz. ASW , 64 mm. **Subject:** Piramide Del El Tajin **Note:** Illustration reduced.

Date	Mintage	F	VF	XF	Unc	BU
1993	50,000	—	—	—	—	60.00
1993 Proof	3,100	Value: 85.00				

KM# 585 25 NUEVOS PESOS
7.7758 g., 0.9990 Gold .2500 oz. AGW **Subject:** Hacha Ceremonial **Note:** Similar to 100 New Pesos, KM#587.

Date	Mintage	F	VF	XF	Unc	BU
1993	15,500	—	—	—	150	—
1993 Proof	800	Value: 275				

KM# 586 50 NUEVOS PESOS
15.5517 g., 0.9990 Gold .5000 oz. AGW **Subject:** Hacha Ceremonial **Note:** Similar to 100 New Pesos, KM#587.

Date	Mintage	F	VF	XF	Unc	BU
1993	15,500	—	—	—	300	—
1993 Proof	500	Value: 475				

KM# 587 100 NUEVOS PESOS
31.1035 g., 0.9990 Gold 1.0000 oz. AGW **Subject:** Hacha Ceremonial

Date	Mintage	F	VF	XF	Unc	BU
1993	7,150	—	—	—	600	—
1993 Proof	500	Value: 600				

Pre-Columbian • Mayan Series

KM# 572   NUEVO PESO
7.7601 g., 0.9990 Silver .2498 oz. ASW **Subject:** Chaac
Mool

Date	Mintage	F	VF	XF	Unc	BU
1994 Matte	30,000	—	—	—	—	10.00
1994 Proof	2,500	Value: 20.00				

KM# 573   2 NUEVOS PESOS
15.5516 g., 0.9990 Silver .4995 oz. ASW **Subject:** Chaac
Mool

Date	Mintage	F	VF	XF	Unc	BU
1994 Matte	30,000	—	—	—	—	12.00
1994 Proof	2,500	Value: 20.00				

KM# 574   5 NUEVOS PESOS
31.1035 g., 0.9990 Silver .9991 oz. ASW **Subject:** Chaac
Mool **Rev:** Reclining Sculpture

Date	Mintage	F	VF	XF	Unc	BU
1994 Matte	50,000	—	—	—	—	15.00
1994 Proof	3,000	Value: 42.00				

KM# 575   5 NUEVOS PESOS
31.1035 g., 0.9990 Silver .9991 oz. ASW **Subject:** Chaac
Mool **Rev:** Tomb of Palenque Memorial Stone

Date	Mintage	F	VF	XF	Unc	BU
1994	4,500	—	—	—	—	15.00
1994 Proof	2,800	Value: 42.00				

KM# 577   5 NUEVOS PESOS
31.1035 g., 0.9990 Silver .9991 oz. ASW **Subject:** Mascaron
Del Dios Chaac **Rev:** Elaborately carved wall segment

Date	Mintage	F	VF	XF	Unc	BU
1994	4,500	—	—	—	—	15.00
1994 Proof	2,500	Value: 42.00				

KM# 578   5 NUEVOS PESOS
31.1035 g., 0.9990 Silver .9991 oz. ASW **Subject:** Dintel 26
Rev: Two seated figures wall carving

Date	Mintage	F	VF	XF	Unc	BU
1994	4,500	—	—	—	—	15.00
1994 Proof	2,600	Value: 42.00				

KM# 676   10 NUEVOS PESOS
155.5175 g., 0.9990 Silver 4.995 oz. ASW, 65 mm. **Subject:**
Piramid Del Castillo **Obv:** National emblem above metal
content statement **Rev:** Pyramid above two line inscription
Rev. Inscription: PIRAMIDE DEL CASTILLO / CHICHEN-
ITZA **Edge:** Reeded

Date	Mintage	F	VF	XF	Unc	BU
1993Mo Proof	—	Value: 325				

KM# 593   PESO
7.7750 g., 0.9990 Silver .2500 oz. ASW **Subject:** Senor De Las Limas **Note:** Similar to 5 Pesos, KM#595.

Date	Mintage	F	VF	XF	Unc	BU
1996	4,000	—	—	—	—	10.00
1996 Proof	2,200	Value: 20.00				
1998 Matte	2,400	—	—	—	—	12.00

KM# 576   10 NUEVOS PESOS
Center Weight: 115.5175 g. **Center Composition:** 0.9990 Silver 4.9956 oz. ASW , 64 mm. **Subject:** Piramide del Castillo **Note:** Illustration reduced.

Date	Mintage	F	VF	XF	Unc	BU
1994	20,000	—	—	—	—	60.00
1994 Proof	2,100	Value: 85.00				

KM# 579   25 NUEVOS PESOS
7.7758 g., 0.9990 Gold .2500 oz. AGW **Subject:** Personaje de Jaina **Rev:** Seated figure

Date	Mintage	F	VF	XF	Unc	BU
1994	2,000	—	—	—	150	—
1994 Proof	500	Value: 275				

KM# 580   50 NUEVOS PESOS
15.5517 g., 0.9990 Gold .5000 oz. AGW **Subject:** Personaje de Jaina **Rev:** Seated figure

Date	Mintage	F	VF	XF	Unc	BU
1994	1,000	—	—	—	300	—
1994 Proof	500	Value: 475				

KM# 594   2 PESOS
15.5517 g., 0.9990 Silver .5000 oz. ASW **Subject:** Senor De Las Limas **Note:** Similar to 5 Pesos, KM#595.

Date	Mintage	F	VF	XF	Unc	BU
1996	4,000	—	—	—	—	12.00
1996 Proof	2,200	Value: 20.00				
1998 Matte	2,400	—	—	—	—	15.00

KM# 581   100 NUEVOS PESOS
31.1035 g., 0.9990 Gold 1.0000 oz. AGW **Subject:** Personaje de Jaina

Date	Mintage	F	VF	XF	Unc	BU
1994	1,000	—	—	—	600	—
1994 Proof	500	Value: 600				

KM# 595   5 PESOS
31.1035 g., 0.9990 Silver 1.0000 oz. ASW **Subject:** Senor De Las Limas

Date	Mintage	F	VF	XF	Unc	BU
1996	4,000	—	—	—	—	15.00
1996 Proof	3,000	Value: 42.00				
1998 Matte	3,400	—	—	—	—	15.00

KM# 598 5 PESOS
31.1035 g., 0.9990 Silver 1.0000 oz. ASW **Subject:** Hacha
Ceremonial

Date	Mintage	F	VF	XF	Unc	BU
1996	4,500	—	—	—	—	15.00
1996 Proof	2,700	Value: 42.00				
1998 Matte	2,000	—	—	—	—	15.00

KM# 596 5 PESOS
31.1035 g., 0.9990 Silver 1.0000 oz. ASW **Subject:** Hombre
Jaguar

Date	Mintage	F	VF	XF	Unc	BU
1996	1,500	—	—	—	—	15.00
1996 Proof	2,800	Value: 42.00				
1998 Matte	6,000	—	—	—	—	15.00
1998 Proof	4,800	Value: 42.00				

KM# 597 5 PESOS
31.1035 g., 0.9990 Silver 1.0000 oz. ASW **Subject:** El
Luchador

Date	Mintage	F	VF	XF	Unc	BU
1996	4,500	—	—	—	—	15.00
1996 Proof	2,700	Value: 42.00				
1998 Matte	2,000	—	—	—	—	15.00

KM# 599 10 PESOS
Center Weight: 1555.5175 g. **Center Composition:** 0.9990
Silver 5.0000 oz. ASW , 64 mm. **Subject:** Cabeza Olmeca
Note: Illustration reduced.

Date	Mintage	F	VF	XF	Unc	BU
1996	2,000	—	—	—	—	60.00
1996 Proof	2,750	Value: 85.00				
1998 Matte	2,150	—	—	—	—	60.00

KM# 600 25 PESOS
7.7758 g., 0.9990 Gold .2500 oz. AGW **Subject:** Sacerdote
Note: Similar to 100 Pesos, KM#602.

Date	Mintage	F	VF	XF	Unc	BU
1996	500	—	—	—	150	—
1996 Proof	750	Value: 275				

KM# 601 50 PESOS
15.5517 g., 0.9990 Gold .5000 oz. AGW **Subject:** Sacerdote
Note: Similar to 100 Pesos, KM#602.

Date	Mintage	F	VF	XF	Unc	BU
1996	500	—	—	—	300	—
1996 Proof	500	Value: 475				

KM# 602 100 PESOS
31.1035 g., 0.9990 Gold 1.0000 oz. AGW **Subject:** Sacerdote

Date	Mintage	F	VF	XF	Unc	BU
1996	500	—	—	—	600	—
1996 Proof	500	Value: 600				

Pre-Columbian • Teotihuacan Series

KM# 617 PESO
7.7759 g., 0.9990 Silver .2500 oz. ASW **Subject:** Disco De La Muerte **Obv:** Mexican eagle

Date	Mintage	F	VF	XF	Unc	BU
1997	3,000	—	—	—	—	9.00
1997 Proof	1,600	Value: 17.50				
1998 Matte	2,400	—	—	—	—	10.00
1998 Proof	500	Value: 20.00				

KM# 618 2 PESOS
15.5517 g., 0.9990 Silver .5000 oz. ASW **Subject:** Disco De La Muerte **Obv:** Mexican eagle

Date	Mintage	F	VF	XF	Unc	BU
1997	3,000	—	—	—	—	10.00
1997 Proof	1,600	Value: 20.00				
1998	2,400	—	—	—	—	10.00
1998 Proof	500	Value: 20.00				

KM# 619 5 PESOS
31.1035 g., 0.9990 Silver 1.0000 oz. ASW **Subject:** Teotihuacan - Disco de la Muerte **Obv:** Eagle and snake

Date	Mintage	F	VF	XF	Unc	BU
1997	3,500	—	—	—	—	15.00
1997 Proof	Est. 1,800	Value: 42.00				
1998	3,400	—	—	—	—	15.00
1998 Proof	500	Value: 50.00				

KM# 620 5 PESOS
31.1035 g., 0.9990 Silver 1.0000 oz. ASW **Subject:** Teotihuacan - Mascara **Obv:** Eagle and snake

Date	Mintage	F	VF	XF	Unc	BU
1997	4,500	—	—	—	—	15.00
1997 Proof	Est. 1,800	Value: 42.00				
1998	2,000	—	—	—	—	15.00
1998 Proof	500	Value: 50.00				

KM# 621   5 PESOS
31.1035 g., 0.9990 Silver 1.0000 oz. ASW **Subject:**
Teotihuacan - Vasija **Obv:** Eagle and snake

Date	Mintage	F	VF	XF	Unc	BU
1997	4,500	—	—	—	—	15.00
1997 Proof	Est. 1,800	Value: 42.00				
1998 Matte	2,000	—	—	—	—	15.00
1998 Proof	500	Value: 50.00				

KM# 622   5 PESOS
31.1035 g., 0.9990 Silver 1.0000 oz. ASW **Subject:**
Teotihuacan - Jugador de Pelota **Obv:** Eagle and snake

Date	Mintage	F	VF	XF	Unc	BU
1997	4,500	—	—	—	—	15.00
1997 Proof	Est. 1,800	Value: 42.00				
1998 Matte	2,000	—	—	—	—	15.00
1998 Proof	500	Value: 50.00				

KM# 623   10 PESOS
1555.5175 g., 0.9990 Silver 5.0000 oz. ASW, 64 mm.
Subject: Piramide Del Sol **Obv:** Mexican eagle **Note:**
Illustration reduced.

Date	Mintage	F	VF	XF	Unc	BU
1997	1,500	—	—	—	—	60.00
1997 Proof	2,100	Value: 85.00				
1998 Matte	2,150	—	—	—	—	60.00

KM# 624   25 PESOS
7.7758 g., 0.9990 Gold .2500 oz. AGW **Subject:** Serpiente
Emplumada **Obv:** Mexican eagle **Note:** Similar to 100 Pesos,
KM#626.

Date	Mintage	F	VF	XF	Unc	BU
1997	500	—	—	—	150	—
1997 Proof	200	Value: 275				

KM# 625   50 PESOS
15.5517 g., 0.9990 Gold .5000 oz. AGW **Subject:** Serpiente
Emplumada **Obv:** Mexican eagle **Note:** Similar to 100 Pesos,
KM#626.

Date	Mintage	F	VF	XF	Unc	BU
1997	500	—	—	—	300	—
1997 Proof	200	Value: 475				

KM# 626   100 PESOS
31.1035 g., 0.9990 Gold 1.0000 oz. AGW **Subject:**
Teotihuacan - Serpiente Emplumada **Obv:** Eagle and snake

Date	Mintage	F	VF	XF	Unc	BU
1997	500	—	—	—	600	—
1997 Proof	Est. 200	Value: 600				

Pre-Columbian • Tolteca Series

KM# 661   PESO
7.7759 g., 0.9990 Silver .2500 oz. ASW, 27 mm. **Subject:**
Jaguar **Obv:** National emblem **Rev:** Jaguar carving **Edge:**
Reeded

Date	Mintage	F	VF	XF	Unc	BU
1998	6,000	—	—	—	—	9.00
1998 Proof	4,800	Value: 15.00				

KM# 662   2 PESOS
15.5517 g., 0.9990 Silver .5000 oz. ASW, 33 mm. **Subject:**
Jaguar **Obv:** National emblem **Rev:** Jaguar carving **Edge:**
Reeded

Date	Mintage	F	VF	XF	Unc	BU
1998	6,000	—	—	—	—	10.00
1998 Proof	4,800	Value: 20.00				

KM# 663   5 PESOS
31.1035 g., 0.9990 Silver 1.0000 oz. ASW, 40 mm. **Subject:**
Jaguar **Obv:** National emblem **Rev:** Jaguar carving **Edge:**
Reeded

Date	Mintage	F	VF	XF	Unc	BU
1998	6,000	—	—	—	—	15.00
1998 Proof	4,800	Value: 42.00				

KM# 664 5 PESOS
31.1035 g., 0.9990 Silver 1.0000 oz. ASW, 40 mm. **Obv:**
National emblem **Rev:** Sacerdote sculpture **Edge:** Reeded

Date	Mintage	F	VF	XF	Unc	BU
1998	5,000	—	—	—	—	15.00
1998 Proof	4,800	Value: 42.00				

KM# 666 5 PESOS
31.1035 g., 0.9990 Silver 1.0000 oz. ASW, 40 mm. **Subject:**
Serpiente con Craneo **Obv:** National emblem **Rev:** Large
sculpture **Edge:** Reeded

Date	Mintage	F	VF	XF	Unc	BU
1998	5,000	—	—	—	—	15.00
1998 Proof	4,800	Value: 42.00				

KM# 634 10 PESOS
155.7300 g., 0.9990 Silver 5.0018 oz. ASW **Subject:**
Atlantes **Obv:** National arms **Rev:** Three carved statues

Date	Mintage	F	VF	XF	Unc	BU
1998	3,500	—	—	—	—	60.00
1998 Proof	4,200	Value: 85.00				

KM# 667 25 PESOS
7.7759 g., 0.9990 Gold 0.2498 oz. AGW, 23 mm. **Subject:**
Aguila **Obv:** Mexican arms **Rev:** Eagle sculpture **Edge:**
Reeded

Date	Mintage	F	VF	XF	Unc	BU
1998	300	—	—	—	150	—
1998 Proof	300	Value: 270				

KM# 668 50 PESOS
15.5517 g., 0.9990 Gold 0.4995 oz. AGW, 29 mm. **Subject:**
Aguila **Obv:** Mexican arms **Rev:** Eagle sculpture **Edge:**
Reeded

Date	Mintage	F	VF	XF	Unc	BU
1998	300	—	—	—	300	—
1998 Proof	300	Value: 475				

KM# 665 5 PESOS
31.1035 g., 0.9990 Silver 1.0000 oz. ASW, 40 mm. **Subject:**
Quetzalcoatl **Obv:** National emblem **Rev:** Quetzalcoatl
sculpture **Edge:** Reeded

Date	Mintage	F	VF	XF	Unc	BU
1998	5,000	—	—	—	—	15.00
1998 Proof	4,800	Value: 42.00				

KM# 669 100 PESOS
31.1035 g., 0.9990 Gold 0.999 oz. AGW, 34.5 mm. **Subject:**
Aguila **Obv:** Mexican arms **Rev:** Eagle sculpture **Edge:**
Reeded

Date	Mintage	F	VF	XF	Unc	BU
1998	300	—	—	—	600	—
1998 Proof	300	Value: 600				

MEDALLIC SILVER BULLION COINAGE

KM# M49a ONZA
33.6250 g., 0.9250 Silver 1.0000 oz. ASW **Obv:** Mint mark above coin press

Date	Mintage	F	VF	XF	Unc	BU
1949	1,000,000	—	12.00	13.50	17.50	27.50

KM# M49b.3 ONZA
33.6250 g., 0.9250 Silver 1.0000 oz. ASW **Obv:** Close spacing between DE MONEDA **Rev:** Left scale pan points to U in UNA **Note:** Type III

Date	Mintage	F	VF	XF	Unc	BU
1979	4,508,000	—	—	BV	11.00	12.50

KM# M49b.1 ONZA
33.6250 g., 0.9250 Silver 1.0000 oz. ASW **Obv:** Wide spacing between DE MONEDA **Rev:** Mint mark below balance scale **Note:** Type I

Date	Mintage	F	VF	XF	Unc	BU
1978	280,000	—	—	BV	11.50	13.50

KM# M49b.2 ONZA
33.6250 g., 0.9250 Silver 1.0000 oz. ASW **Obv:** Close spacing between DE MONEDA **Rev:** Mint mark below balance scale **Note:** Type II

Date	Mintage	F	VF	XF	Unc	BU
1978	Inc. above	—	—	BV	11.50	13.50

KM# M49b.4 ONZA
33.6250 g., 0.9250 Silver 1.0000 oz. ASW **Obv:** Close spacing between DE MONEDA **Rev:** Left scale pan points between U and N of UNA **Note:** Type IV

Date	Mintage	F	VF	XF	Unc	BU
1979	Inc. above	—	—	BV	11.00	12.50

KM# M49b.5   ONZA
33.6250 g., 0.9250 Silver 1.0000 oz. ASW   **Obv:** Close
spacing between DE MONEDA **Rev:** Left scale pan points
between U and N of UNA **Note:** Type V

Date	Mintage	F	VF	XF	Unc	BU
1980	6,104,000	—	—	BV	11.00	12.50
1980/70	Inc. above	—	—	BV	11.00	14.50

MILLED GOLD COINAGE

KM# M91a   10 PESOS
8.3333 g., 0.9000 Gold .2411 oz. AGW   **Subject:** 200th
Anniversary - Birth of Hidalgo

Date	Mintage	F	VF	XF	Unc	BU
1953	—	—	—	—	BV	125

KM# M123a   10 PESOS
8.3333 g., 0.9000 Gold .2411 oz. AGW   **Subject:** Centennial
of Constitution

Date	Mintage	F	VF	XF	Unc	BU
1957	Est. 73,000	—	—	—	BV	125

Note: Mintage includes #M122a

KM# M92a   20 PESOS
16.6666 g., 0.9000 Gold .4823 oz. AGW   **Subject:** 200th
Anniversary - Birth of Hidalgo

Date	Mintage	F	VF	XF	Unc	BU
1953	—	—	—	—	BV	225

KM# M122a   50 PESOS
41.6666 g., 0.9000 Gold 1.2057 oz. AGW   **Subject:**
Centennial of Constitution

Date	Mintage	F	VF	XF	Unc	BU
1957 Inc. M123a	—	—	—	—	BV	600

BANK SETS

Hard Case Sets unless otherwise noted.

KM#	Date	Mintage	Identification	Issue Price	Mkt Val
BS1	1972 (6)	—	KM#418, 427, 452, 460, 472, 480	—	30.00
BS2	1973 (5)	—	KM#418, 427 (2), 441, 472	—	20.00
BS3	1974 (7)	—	KM#427, 434.4, 441, 442, 460, 472, 477.1	—	30.00
BS4	1975 (7)	—	KM#427, 434.1, 442, 452, 460 (2), 477.1	—	20.00
BS5	1976 (9)	—	KM#427, 434.1, 442, 452 (2), 460, 472(2), 477.1	—	15.00
BS6	1977 (9)	—	KM#434.1, 434.2, 442, 452, 460 (2), 472, 477.1, 483.1	—	35.00
BS7	1977 (9)	—	KM#434.1, 434.2, 442, 452, 460 (2), 472, 477.1, 483.2 Type II for 3-ring binder	—	—
BS8	1978 (9)	500	KM#434.1, 434.2, 442, 452, 460 (2), 472, 477.2, 483.2, Type I, flat pack	—	35.00
BS9	1978 (9)	—	KM#434.1, 434.2, 442, 452, 460 (2), 472, 477.2, 483.2 Type II for 3-ring binder,	—	15.00
BS10	1979 (9)	—	KM#434.1, 434.4, 442, 452 (2), 460 (2), 477.2, 483.2 Type I flat pack	11.00	25.00
BS11	1979 (8)	—	KM#434.1, 434.2, 442, 452 (2), 460, 477.2, 483.2 Type II for 3-ring binder	11.00	15.00
BS12	1980 (9)	—	KM#434.2, 442, 452 (2), 460 (2), 485, 486, 477.2	4.20	25.00

KM#	Date	Mintage	Identification	Issue Price	Mkt Val
BS13	1981 (9)	—	KM#442 (2), 452 (2), 460 (2), 477.2, 485, 486	4.20	25.00
BS14	1982 (7)	—	KM#442, 452, 460, 477.2, 485, 486, 490	—	20.00
BS15	1983 (11)	—	KM#442 (2), 452 (2), 460 (2), 490, 491 (2), 492 (2)	—	20.00
BS16	1983 (11)	—	KM#442 (2), 452 (2), 460 (2), 490, 491 (2), 492 (2) 3-ring plastic page	—	12.50
BS17	1984 (8)	—	KM#485, 486, 490, 491, 493, 495 (2), 496,	—	25.00
BS22	1988 (8)	—	KM#493, 495a, 502, 508, 512, 529, 531, 536	—	20.00
BS18	1985 (12)	—	KM#477.2, 485, 493 (2), 495 (2), 496, 502, 508, 509, 510, 512	—	30.00
BS19	1985 (12)	—	KM#477.2, 485, 493 (2), 495 (2), 496, 502, 508, 509, 510, 512 3-ring plastic page	—	20.00
BS20	1986 (7)	—	KM#493, 495, 496, 508, 512, 525, 529 3-ring plastic page	—	20.00
BS21	1987 (9)	—	KM#493, 495 (2), 496, 502 (2), 512, 529 (2)	—	20.00
BS23	1989 (10)	—	KM#493 (3), 508 (3), 512, 529, 536 (2)	—	20.00
BS24	1990 (8)	—	KM#493 (2), 495a, 509 (2), 512, 536 (2)	—	20.00
BS25	1991 (4)	—	KM#493 (2), 536 (2)	—	15.00
BS26	1992 (5)	—	KM#493 (2), 495a, 529, 536	—	15.00
BS27	1992 (8)	—	KM#546-553	—	30.00
BS28	1993 (7)	—	KM#546-552	—	18.00
BS29	1993 (3)	—	KM#553, 561, 571	—	35.00
BS30	1994 (7)	—	KM#546-552	—	18.00
BS31	1994 (3)	—	KM#553, 561, 571	—	35.00
BS32	1995 (9)	—	KM#546-551, 553, 561, 571	—	45.00
BS33	1996 (6)	—	KM#546-549, 603, 604	12.00	30.00
BS34	1997 (8)	—	KM#546-549, 603-605, 616	—	30.00
BS35	1998 (8)	—	KM#546-549, 603-605, 616	—	30.00
BS36	1999 (8)	—	KM#546-549, 603-605, 616	—	35.00
BS37	2000 (7)	—	KM#547-549, 603-605, 636 Set in folder	—	30.00
BS38	2001 (10)	—	KM#546-549, 603-605, 636-638 Set in folder	—	30.00
BS39	2002 (8)	—	KM#546-549, 603-605, 616 Set in folder	—	30.00
BS40	2003 (6)	—	KM#547-549, 603-605 Set in folder	—	30.00

PROOF SETS

KM#	Date	Mintage	Identification	Issue Price	Mkt Val
XPS2	1988Mo (5)	—	X#MB45-MB49	—	300
XPS3	1988Mo (5)	—	X#MB57-MB61	—	—
PS1	1982/1983 (8)	998	KM442, 452, 460, 485, 477.2, 486, 490, 494.1	495	285
PS2	1982/1983 (8)	—	KM460, 477.2, 485, 486, 490, 491, 492, PnB169 (in white box with Mo. in gold)	—	—
PS3	1982/1983 (7)	23	KM460, 477.2, 485, 486, 490, 491, 492 (in white box with Mo in gold)	—	500
PS4	1982/1983 (7)	17	KM460, 477.2, 485, 486, 490, 491, 492 (in white box)	—	500
PS5	1982/1983 (7)	8	KM460, 477.2, 485, 486, 490, 491, 492 (in white box)	—	500
PS6	1983 (7)	3	KM460, 477.2, 485, 486, 490, 491, 492	—	—
PS10	1985 (3)	—	KM503-505 (in blue box)	—	60.00
PS11	1985 (2)	—	KM511, 513	—	350

KM#	Date	Mintage	Identification	Issue Price	Mkt Val
PS7	1985/1986 (12)	—	KM497a-499a, 503-505, 514-515, 519, 521, 523-524	—	250
PS8	1985 (4)	—	KM500.2-501.2, 506.2, 507.2	—	700
PS9	1985 (3)	—	KM499a, 514, 515 (in blue box)	—	60.00
XPS1	1987Mo (2)	—	X#MB34, 35	—	—
PS12	1989 (3)	704	KM488, 494.1, 538, Rainbow	730	850
PS13	1992 (5)	5,000	KM494.3, 542-545	—	87.50
PS14	1993 (5)	5,000	KM494.4, 542-545	—	87.50
PS15	1994 (5)	5,000	KM494.4, 542-545	—	85.00
PS16	1995 (7)	—	KM546-550, 552, 553, 555	45.00	48.00

CHIHUAHUA

The Chihuahua Mint was established by a decree of October 8, 1810 as a temporary mint. Their first coins were cast 8 Reales using Mexico City coins as patterns and obliterating/changing the mint mark and moneyer initials. Two c/m were placed on the obverse - on the left, a T designating receipt by the Royal Treasurer, crowned pillars of Hercules on the right with pomegranate beneath, the comptrollers symbol.

In 1814, standard dies were made available, thus machine struck 8 Reales were produced until 1822. Only the one denomination was made at Chihuahua.

Mint mark: CA.

WAR OF INDEPENDENCE

ROYALIST COINAGE

KM# 123   8 REALES
Cast Silver **Ruler:** Ferdinand VII **Countermark:** T at left, pillars at right, pomegranate below **Obv:** Imaginary bust of Ferdinand VII **Obv. Legend:** FERDIN. VII. DEI. GRATIA

Date	Mintage	Good	VG	F	VF	XF
1810CA RP Rare	—	—	—	—	—	—
1811CA RP	—	45.00	60.00	100	150	—
1812CA RP	—	30.00	40.00	60.00	90.00	—
1813CA RP	—	30.00	40.00	60.00	90.00	—

KM# 111.1   8 REALES
27.0700 g., 0.9030 Silver .7860 oz. ASW **Ruler:**
Ferdinand VII **Obv:** Draped bust of Ferdinand VII **Obv.**
Legend: FERDIN. VII. DEI. GRATIA **Rev:** Similar to KM#123

Date	Mintage	VG	F	VF	XF	Unc
1815CA RP	—	200	275	350	500	—
1816CA RP	—	80.00	125	150	275	—
1817CA RP	—	100	150	185	275	—
1818CA RP	—	100	150	185	275	—
1819/8 RP	—	125	175	250	350	—
1819CA RP	—	125	175	250	350	—
1820CA RP	—	200	275	350	500	—
1821CA RP	—	200	275	350	500	—
1822CA RP	—	400	600	800	1,100	—

Note: KM#111.1 is normally found struck over earlier cast 8
Reales, KM#123 and Monclova (MVA) 1812 cast countermark 8 Reales, KM#202 and Zacatecas 8 Reales, KM#190

DURANGO

The Durango mint was authorized as a temporary mint
on the same day as the Chihuahua Mint, October 8, 1810. The
mint opened in 1811 and made coins of 6 denominations
between 1811 and 1822.
Mint mark: D.

WAR OF INDEPENDENCE

ROYALIST COINAGE

KM# 60   1/8 REAL
Copper **Ruler:** Ferdinand VII **Obv:** Crown above double F7
monogram **Rev:** EN DURANGO, value, date

Date	Mintage	VG	F	VF	XF	Unc
1812D	—	32.50	75.00	125	250	—
1813D Rare	—	—	—	—	—	—
1814D Rare	—	—	—	—	—	—

KM# 61   1/8 REAL
Copper **Ruler:** Ferdinand VII **Obv:** Crown above double F7
monogram **Rev:** Spray added above date

Date	Mintage	VG	F	VF	XF	Unc
1814D	—	15.00	30.00	50.00	90.00	—
1815D	—	18.00	35.00	60.00	100	—

Date	Mintage	VG	F	VF	XF	Unc
1816D	—	18.00	35.00	60.00	100	—
1817D	—	15.00	30.00	50.00	90.00	—
1818D	—	15.00	30.00	50.00	90.00	—
1818D OCTAVO DD REAL (error)	—	45.00	80.00	125	225	—

KM# 74.1   1/2 REAL
1.6900 g., 0.9030 Silver .0491 oz. ASW **Ruler:** Ferdinand VII
Obv: Draped bust of Ferdinand VII

Date	Mintage	VG	F	VF	XF	Unc
1813D RM	—	250	450	750	1,800	—
1814D MZ	—	250	450	750	1,850	—
1816D MZ	—	250	450	750	1,850	—

KM# 83.1   REAL
3.3800 g., 0.9030 Silver .0981 oz. ASW **Ruler:** Ferdinand VII
Obv: Draped bust of Ferdinand VII

Date	Mintage	VG	F	VF	XF	Unc
1813D RM	—	250	450	650	1,650	—
1814D MZ	—	250	450	650	1,650	—
1815D MZ	—	250	450	650	1,650	—

KM# 92.2   2 REALES
6.7700 g., 0.9030 Silver .1966 oz. ASW **Ruler:** Ferdinand VII
Obv: Armored bust of Ferdinand VII **Rev. Legend:** MON
PROV DE DURANGO...

Date	Mintage	VG	F	VF	XF	Unc
1811D RM	—	375	450	850	1,750	—

KM# 92.3   2 REALES
6.7700 g., 0.9030 Silver .1966 oz. ASW **Ruler:** Ferdinand VII
Obv: Armored bust of Ferdinand VII **Rev. Legend:** HISPAN
ET IND REX...

Date	Mintage	VG	F	VF	XF	Unc
1812 RM	—	250	400	750	1,650	—

KM# 93.1   2 REALES
6.7700 g., 0.9030 Silver .1966 oz. ASW **Ruler:** Ferdinand VII
Obv: Draped bust of Ferdinand VII

Date	Mintage	VG	F	VF	XF	Unc
1812D RM	—	250	400	750	1,650	—
1813D RM	—	300	600	1,000	2,750	—
1813D MZ	—	300	600	1,000	2,750	—
1814D MZ	—	300	600	1,000	2,750	—
1815D MZ	—	300	600	1,000	2,750	—
1816D MZ	—	300	600	1,000	2,750	—
1817D MZ	—	300	600	1,000	2,750	—

KM# 102.1   4 REALES
13.5400 g., 0.9030 Silver .3931 oz. ASW **Ruler:**
Ferdinand VII **Obv:** Draped bust of Ferdinand VII

Date	Mintage	VG	F	VF	XF	Unc
1814D MZ	—	550	1,000	1,650	4,500	—
1816D MZ	—	450	900	1,400	4,000	—
1817D MZ	—	450	900	1,400	4,000	—

Date	Mintage	VG	F	VF	XF	Unc
1819D CG	—	30.00	60.00	100	250	—
1820D CG	—	30.00	60.00	100	250	—
1821D CG	—	30.00	40.00	80.00	200	—
1822D CG	—	30.00	50.00	90.00	240	—

Note: Occasionally these are found struck over cast Chihuahua 8 reales and are very rare in general, specimens dated prior to 1816 are rather crudely struck

GUADALAJARA

The Guadalajara Mint made its first coins in 1812 and the mint operated until April 30, 1815. It was to reopen in 1818 and continue operations until 1822. It was the only Royalist mint to strike gold coins, both 4 and 8 Escudos. In addition to these it struck the standard 5 denominations in silver.
Mint mark: GA.

WAR OF INDEPENDENCE

ROYALIST COINAGE

KM# 74.2 1/2 REAL
1.6900 g., 0.9030 Silver .0491 oz. ASW **Ruler:** Ferdinand VII
Obv: Draped bust of Ferdinand VII

Date	Mintage	VG	F	VF	XF	Unc
1812GA MR	—	—	—	—	—	—
Rare						
1814GA MR	—	40.00	100	200	300	—
1815GA MR	—	200	350	500	1,000	—

KM# 110.1 8 REALES
27.0700 g., 0.9030 Silver .7860 oz. ASW **Ruler:** Ferdinand VII **Obv:** Armored bust of Ferdinand VII

Date	Mintage	VG	F	VF	XF	Unc
1811D RM	—	600	1,000	1,750	5,000	—
1812D RM	—	350	650	1,000	3,500	—
1814D MZ	—	350	650	1,000	3,500	—

KM# 83.2 REAL
3.3800 g., 0.9030 Silver .0981 oz. ASW **Ruler:** Ferdinand VII
Obv: Draped bust of Ferdinand VII

Date	Mintage	VG	F	VF	XF	Unc
1813GA MR	—	300	500	800	—	—
1814GA MR	—	150	200	350	650	—
1815GA MR	—	300	500	800	—	—

KM# 93.2 2 REALES
6.7700 g., 0.9030 Silver .1966 oz. ASW **Ruler:** Ferdinand VII
Obv: Draped bust of Ferdinand VII

Date	Mintage	VG	F	VF	XF	Unc
1812GA MR	—	300	500	800	2,500	—
1814/2GA MR	—	75.00	125	250	600	—
1814GA MR	—	75.00	125	250	600	—
1815/4GA MR	—	425	725	1,100	3,600	—
1815GA MR	—	400	700	1,000	3,500	—
1821GA FS	—	200	250	350	900	—

KM# 111.2 8 REALES
27.0700 g., 0.9030 Silver .7860 oz. ASW **Ruler:** Ferdinand VII **Obv:** Draped bust of Ferdinand VII

Date	Mintage	VG	F	VF	XF	Unc
1812D RM	—	125	175	275	800	—
1813D RM	—	150	200	325	850	—
1813D MZ	—	125	175	275	750	—
1814/2D MZ	—	150	200	300	750	—
1814D MZ	—	150	200	300	750	—
1815D MZ	—	75.00	125	225	600	—
1816D MZ	—	50.00	75.00	125	325	—
1817D MZ	—	30.00	50.00	90.00	250	—
1818D MZ	—	50.00	75.00	125	350	—
1818D RM	—	50.00	75.00	125	325	—
1818D CG/RM	—	100	125	150	350	—
1818D CG	—	50.00	75.00	125	325	—
1819D CG/RM	—	50.00	100	150	300	—

KM# 102.2   4 REALES
13.5400 g., 0.9030 Silver .3931 oz. ASW **Ruler:**
Ferdinand VII **Obv:** Draped small bust of Ferdinand VII

Date	Mintage	VG	F	VF	XF	Unc
1814GA MR	—	40.00	65.00	150	250	—
1815GA MR	—	80.00	150	300	500	—

KM# 102.3   4 REALES
13.5400 g., 0.9030 Silver .3931 oz. ASW **Ruler:**
Ferdinand VII **Obv:** Large bust

Date	Mintage	VG	F	VF	XF	Unc
1814GA MR	—	50.00	100	200	400	—

KM# 102.4   4 REALES
13.5400 g., 0.9030 Silver .3931 oz. ASW **Ruler:**
Ferdinand VII **Obv:** Large bust with berries in laurel

Date	Mintage	VG	F	VF	XF	Unc
1814GA MR	—	60.00	120	250	450	—

KM# 111.3   8 REALES
27.0700 g., 0.9030 Silver .7860 oz. ASW **Ruler:**
Ferdinand VII **Obv:** Draped bust of Ferdinand VII

Date	Mintage	VG	F	VF	XF	Unc
1812GA MR	—	2,000	3,500	5,000	7,000	—
1813/2GA MR	—	60.00	100	150	400	—
1813GA MR	—	60.00	100	150	400	—
1814GA MR	—	20.00	35.00	60.00	180	—
Note: Several bust varieties exist for the 1814 issue						
1815GA MR	—	150	200	350	750	—
1818GA FS	—	30.00	50.00	75.00	200	—
1821/18GA FS	—	30.00	50.00	75.00	200	—
1821GA FS	—	25.00	35.00	60.00	165	—
1821/2GA FS	—	30.00	50.00	75.00	200	—
1822/1GA FS	—	30.00	50.00	75.00	200	—
1822GA FS	—	30.00	50.00	75.00	200	—

Note: Die varieties exist. Early dates are also encountered struck over other types

KM# 147   4 ESCUDOS
13.5400 g., 0.8750 Gold .3809 oz. AGW **Ruler:**
Ferdinand VII **Obv:** Uniformed bust of Ferdinand VII

Date	Mintage	VG	F	VF	XF	Unc
1812GA MR Rare	—	—	—	—	—	—

KM# 162   8 ESCUDOS
27.0700 g., 0.8750 Gold .7616 oz. AGW **Ruler:**
Ferdinand VII **Obv:** Large uniformed bust of Ferdinand VII

Date	Mintage	VG	F	VF	XF	Unc
1812GA MR Rare	—	—	—	—	—	—
1813GA MR	—	5,250	8,250	12,500	21,000	—

GUANAJUATO

The Guanajuato Mint was authorized December 24, 1812 and started production shortly thereafter; closing for unknown reasons on May 15, 1813. The mint was reopened in April, 1821 by the insurgents, who struck coins of the old royal Spanish design to pay their army, even after independence, well into 1822.

Only the 2 and 8 Reales coins were made.
Mint mark: Go.

WAR OF INDEPENDENCE

ROYALIST COINAGE

KM# 93.3   2 REALES
6.7700 g., 0.9030 Silver .1966 oz. ASW **Ruler:** Ferdinand VII
Obv: Draped bust of Ferdinand VII

Date	Mintage	VG	F	VF	XF	Unc
1821Go JM	—	35.00	65.00	100	185	—
1822Go JM	—	30.00	50.00	75.00	145	—

KM# 163   8 ESCUDOS
27.0700 g., 0.8750 Gold .7616 oz. AGW **Ruler:**
Ferdinand VII **Obv:** Small uniformed bust of Ferdinand VII

Date	Mintage	VG	F	VF	XF	Unc
1813GA MR	—	10,000	16,000	30,000	45,000	—

Note: Spink America Gerber sale 6-96 VF or better realized $46,200

KM# 161.1   8 ESCUDOS
27.0700 g., 0.8750 Gold .7616 oz. AGW **Ruler:**
Ferdinand VII **Obv:** Undraped bust of Ferdinand VII

Date	Mintage	VG	F	VF	XF	Unc
1821GA FS	—	1,200	2,000	4,000	6,500	—

KM# 164   8 ESCUDOS
27.0700 g., 0.8750 Gold .7616 oz. AGW **Ruler:**
Ferdinand VII **Obv:** Draped bust of Ferdinand VII

Date	Mintage	VG	F	VF	XF	Unc
1821GA FS	—	5,000	7,500	14,000	23,000	—

KM# 111.4   8 REALES
27.0700 g., 0.9030 Silver .7860 oz. ASW **Ruler:**
Ferdinand VII **Obv:** Draped bust of Ferdinand VII

Date	Mintage	VG	F	VF	XF	Unc
1812Go JJ	—	3,000	5,000	—	—	—
1813Go JJ	—	125	175	275	600	—
1821Go JM	—	25.00	50.00	75.00	200	—
1822Go JM	—	20.00	35.00	60.00	185	—

NUEVA GALICIA

(Later became Jalisco State)

In early colonial times, Nueva Galicia was an extensive province which substantially combined later provinces of Zacatecas and Jalisco. These are states of Mexico today although the name was revived during the War of Independence. The only issue was 2 Reales of rather enigmatic origin. No decrees or other authorization to strike this coin has yet been located or reported.

WAR OF INDEPENDENCE

INSURGENT COINAGE

KM# 218 2 REALES
0.9030 Silver **Obv:** N. G. in center, date **Obv. Legend:** PROVYCIONAL... **Rev:** 2R in center **Rev. Legend:** ... A. JUNIANA...

Date	Mintage	Good	VG	F	VF	XF
1813	—	1,000	2,500	4,500	—	—

Note: Excellent struck counterfeits exist

NUEVA VISCAYA

(Later became Durango State)

This 8 Reales, intended for the province of Nueva Viscaya, was minted in the newly-opened Durango Mint during February and March of 1811, before the regular coinage of Durango was started.

WAR OF INDEPENDENCE

ROYALIST COINAGE

KM# 181 8 REALES
27.0700 g., 0.9030 Silver .7860 oz. ASW **Ruler:** Ferdinand VII **Obv:** Arms of Durango **Obv. Legend:** MON. PROV. DE NUEV. VIZCAYA **Rev:** Royal arms

Date	Mintage	Good	VG	F	VF	XF
1811 RM	—	1,000	2,250	2,850	5,500	—

Note: Several varieties exist.

OAXACA

The city of Oaxaca was in the midst of a coin shortage when it became apparent the city would be taken by the Insurgents. Royalist forces under Lt. Gen. Saravia had coins made. They were cast in a blacksmith shop. 1/2, 1, and 8 Reales were made only briefly in 1812 before the Royalists surrendered the city.

WAR OF INDEPENDENCE

ROYALIST COINAGE

KM# 166 1/2 REAL
0.9030 Silver **Ruler:** Ferdinand VII **Obv:** Cross separating castle, lion, Fo, 7o **Rev:** Legend around shield **Rev. Legend:** PROV. D. OAXACA

Date	Mintage	Good	VG	F	VF	XF
1812	—	1,000	1,500	2,500	3,500	—

KM# 167 REAL
0.9030 Silver **Ruler:** Ferdinand VII **Obv:** Cross separating castle, lion, Fo, 7o **Rev:** Legend around shield **Rev. Legend:** PROV. D. OAXACA

Date	Mintage	Good	VG	F	VF	XF
1812	—	350	650	1,200	2,500	—

KM# 168 8 REALES
0.9030 Silver **Obv:** Cross seperating castle, lion, Fo, 7o **Rev:** Shield, authorization mark above **Note:** These issues usually display a second mark 'O' between the crowned pillars on the obverse. Varieties of large and small lion in shield also exist.

Date	Mintage	Good	VG	F	VF	XF
1812 "A"	—	1,300	1,900	3,300	5,000	—
1812 "B"	—	1,300	1,900	3,300	5,000	—
1812 "C"	—	1,300	1,900	3,300	5,000	—
1812 "D"	—	1,300	1,900	3,300	5,000	—
1812 "K"	—	1,300	1,900	3,300	5,000	—
1812 "L"	—	1,300	1,900	3,300	5,000	—
1812 "Mo"	—	1,300	1,900	3,300	5,000	—

Date	Mintage	Good	VG	F	VF	XF
1812 "N"	—	1,300	1,900	3,300	5,000	—
1812 "O"	—	1,300	1,900	3,300	5,000	—
1812 "R"	—	1,300	1,900	3,300	5,000	—
1812 "V"	—	1,300	1,900	3,300	5,000	—
1812 "Z"	—	1,300	1,900	3,300	5,000	—

INSURGENT COINAGE

Oaxaca was the hub of Insurgent activity in the south where coinage started in July 1811 and continued until October 1814. The Oaxaca issues represent episodic strikings, usually under dire circumstances by various individuals. Coins were commonly made of copper due to urgency and were intended to be redeemed at face value in gold or silver once silver was available to the Insurgents. Some were later made in silver, but most appear to be of more recent origin, to satisfy collectors.

KM# 219 1/2 REAL
Struck Copper **Issuer:** SUD, Under General Morelos **Obv:** Bow, arrow, SUD **Rev:** Morelos monogram Mo, date

Date	Mintage	Good	VG	F	VF	XF
1811	—	6.75	11.50	20.00	35.00	—
1812	—	6.75	11.50	20.00	35.00	—
1813	—	5.50	9.00	17.50	30.00	—
1814	—	9.00	16.50	25.00	40.00	—

Note: Uniface strikes exist of #219

KM# 220.1 1/2 REAL
Struck Silver **Issuer:** SUD, Under General Morelos **Obv:** Bow, arrow, SUD **Rev:** Morelos monogram Mo, date

Date	Mintage	Good	VG	F	VF	XF
1811	—	—	—	—	—	—
1812	—	—	—	—	—	—
1813	—	—	—	—	—	—

KM# 220.2 1/2 REAL
Struck Silver **Issuer:** SUD, Under General Morelos **Obv:** Bow, arrow, SUD **Rev:** Morelos monogram Mo, date

Date	Mintage	Good	VG	F	VF	XF
1811	—	—	—	—	—	—
1812	—	—	—	—	—	—
1813	—	25.00	50.00	100	150	—

Note: Use caution as silver specimens appear questionable and may be considered spurious

KM# 221 1/2 REAL
Struck Silver **Issuer:** SUD, Under General Morelos **Obv:** Bow, arrow **Obv. Legend:** PROVICIONAL DE OAXACA **Rev:** Lion **Rev. Legend:** AMERICA MORELOS

Date	Mintage	Good	VG	F	VF	XF
1812	—	35.00	60.00	100	150	—
1813	—	35.00	60.00	100	150	—

KM# 221a 1/2 REAL
Struck Copper **Issuer:** SUD, Under General Morelos **Obv:** Bow, arrow **Obv. Legend:** PROVICIONAL DE OAXACA **Rev:** Lion **Rev. Legend:** AMERICA MORELOS

Date	Mintage	Good	VG	F	VF	XF
1812	—	27.50	42.50	70.00	100	—
1813	—	20.00	35.00	60.00	85.00	—

KM# A222 1/2 REAL
Struck Copper **Issuer:** SUD, Under General Morelos **Obv:** Similar to KM#220 **Rev:** Similar to KM#221 but with 1/2 at left of lion **Rev. Legend:** AMERICA MORELOS

Date	Mintage	Good	VG	F	VF	XF
1813	—	27.50	42.50	70.00	100	—

KM# 243 1/2 REAL
Struck Copper **Issuer:** Tierra Caliente (Hot Country), Under General Morelos **Obv:** Bow, T.C., SUD **Rev:** Morelos monogram, value, date

Date	Mintage	Good	VG	F	VF	XF
1813	—	37.50	70.00	125	200	—

KM# 222 REAL
Struck Copper **Issuer:** SUD, Under General Morelos **Obv:** Bow, arrow, SUD **Rev:** Morelos monogram, 1 R., date

Date	Mintage	Good	VG	F	VF	XF
1811	—	4.75	9.00	18.00	38.00	—
1812	—	3.75	7.00	14.00	30.00	—
1813	—	3.75	7.00	14.00	30.00	—

KM# 222a REAL
Struck Silver **Issuer:** SUD, Under General Morelos **Obv:** Bow, arrow, SUD **Rev:** Morelos monogram, 1 R., date

Date	Mintage	Good	VG	F	VF	XF
1812	—	—	—	—	—	—
1813	—	—	—	—	—	—

KM# 223 REAL
Cast Silver **Issuer:** SUD, Under General Morelos **Obv:** Bow, arrow, SUD with floral ornaments **Rev:** Morelos monogram, 1 R., date

Date	Mintage	Good	VG	F	VF	XF
1812	—	—	—	—	—	—
1813	—	27.50	60.00	115	160	—

Note: Use caution as many silver specimens appear questionable and may be considered spurious

KM# 224 REAL
Struck Copper **Issuer:** SUD, Under General Morelos **Obv:** Bow, arrow/SUD **Rev:** Lion **Rev. Legend:** AMERICA MORELOS

Date	Mintage	Good	VG	F	VF	XF
1813	—	27.50	42.50	75.00	110	—

KM# 225   REAL
Silver **Issuer:** SUD, Under General Morelos **Obv:** Bow,
arrow/SUD **Rev:** Lion **Rev. Legend:** AMERICA MORELOS

Date	Mintage	Good	VG	F	VF	XF
1813 Rare	—	—	—	—	—	—

KM# 244   REAL
Struck Copper **Issuer:** Tierra Caliente (Hot Country), Under
General Morelos **Obv:** Bow, T.C., SUD **Rev:** Morelos
monogram, value, date

Date	Mintage	Good	VG	F	VF	XF
1813	—	13.50	25.00	50.00	80.00	—

KM# 226.1   2 REALES
Struck Copper **Issuer:** SUD, Under General Morelos **Obv:**
Bow, arrow/SUD **Rev:** Morelos monogram, .2.R., date

Date	Mintage	Good	VG	F	VF	XF
1811	—	12.50	25.00	55.00	100	—
1811 inverted 2	—	15.00	30.00	60.00	120	—
1812	—	2.50	4.00	6.50	12.00	—
1813	—	3.00	5.00	8.00	15.00	—
1814	—	13.50	28.00	65.00	120	—

KM# 226.1a   2 REALES
Struck Silver **Issuer:** SUD, Under General Morelos **Obv:**
Bow, arrow/SUD **Rev:** Morelos monogram, .2.R., date

Date	Mintage	Good	VG	F	VF	XF
1812	—	175	300	500	750	—

KM# 229   2 REALES
Cast Silver **Issuer:** SUD, Under General Morelos **Obv:** Bow,
arrow, SUD **Rev:** Morelos monogram, value, date in center
with ornamentation around

Date	Mintage	Good	VG	F	VF	XF
1812	—	60.00	100	150	225	—
1812 Filled in D in SUD	—	60.00	100	150	225	—

Note: Use caution as many silver specimens appear questionable and may be considered spurious

KM# 245   2 REALES
Struck Copper **Issuer:** Tierra Caliente (Hot Country), Under
General Morelos **Obv:** Bow, T.C., SUD **Rev:** Morelos
monogram, value, date

Date	Mintage	Good	VG	F	VF	XF
1813	—	9.00	22.50	35.00	50.00	—

KM# 227   2 REALES
Struck Silver **Issuer:** SUD, Under General Morelos **Obv:**
Bow, arrow **Obv. Legend:** SUD-OXA **Rev:** Morelos
monogram, value, date

Date	Mintage	Good	VG	F	VF	XF
1813	—	60.00	100	200	300	—
1814	—	60.00	100	200	300	—

KM# 228   2 REALES
Struck Silver **Issuer:** SUD, Under General Morelos **Obv:**
Bow, arrow **Obv. Legend:** SUD. OAXACA **Rev:** Morelos
monogram, value, date

Date	Mintage	Good	VG	F	VF	XF
1814	—	60.00	100	200	325	—

KM# 226.2   2 REALES
Struck Silver **Issuer:** SUD, Under General Morelos **Obv:**
Three large stars added **Rev:** Morelos monogram, .2.R., date

Date	Mintage	Good	VG	F	VF	XF
1814	—	10.00	20.00	40.00	60.00	—

KM# 246   2 REALES
Struck Copper **Issuer:** Tierra Caliente (Hot Country), Under
General Morelos **Obv:** Bow, T.C., SUD **Rev:** Morelos
monogram, value, date

Date	Mintage	Good	VG	F	VF	XF
1814	—	22.50	50.00	100	175	—

KM# 234   8 REALES
Copper **Issuer:** SUD, Under General Morelos **Obv:** Bow,
arrow, SUD in floral ornamentation **Obv. Legend:** SUD-OXA
Rev: Morelos monogram, .8.R., date surrounded by ornate
flowery fields

Date	Mintage	Good	VG	F	VF	XF
1811	—	75.00	125	150	225	—
1812	—	4.00	6.00	10.00	20.00	—
1813	—	4.00	6.00	10.00	20.00	—
1814	—	10.00	15.00	25.00	50.00	—

KM# 233.2   8 REALES
Copper **Issuer:** SUD, Under General Morelos **Obv:** Bow,
arrow, SUD **Rev:** Morelos monogram, 8 R, date, plain fields

Date	Mintage	Good	VG	F	VF	XF
1812	—	6.00	8.00	12.00	15.00	—
1813	—	6.00	8.00	12.00	15.00	—
1814	—	10.00	12.00	15.00	20.00	—

Note: Similar to KM#233.4 but lines below bow slant left

KM# 235   8 REALES
Cast Silver **Issuer:** SUD, Under General Morelos **Obv:** Bow,
arrow, SUD in floral ornamentation **Rev:** Morelos monogram,
value, date surrounded by ornate flowery fields

Date	Mintage	Good	VG	F	VF	XF
1811	—	—	—	—	—	—
1812	—	75.00	125	200	350	—
1813	—	60.00	100	175	300	—
1814	—	—	—	—	—	—

Note: Most silver specimens available in today's market are
considered spurious

KM# 234a   8 REALES
Struck Silver **Issuer:** SUD, under General Morelos **Obv:**
Bow, arrow, SUD in floral ornamentation **Rev:** Morelos
monogram, .8.R., date surrounded by ornate flowery fields

Date	Mintage	Good	VG	F	VF	XF
1811	—	—	—	2,500	4,000	—
1812	—	—	—	1,200	2,000	—

KM# 233.1   8 REALES
Copper **Issuer:** SUD, Under General Morelos **Obv:** Bow,
arrow, SUD **Rev:** Morelos monogram, 8.R., date, plain fields

Date	Mintage	Good	VG	F	VF	XF
1812	—	15.00	30.00	60.00	90.00	—

KM# 233.1a   8 REALES
Struck Silver **Issuer:** SUD, Under General Morelos **Obv:** Bow,
arrow, SUD **Rev:** Morelos monogram, 8.R., date, plain fields

Date	Mintage	Good	VG	F	VF	XF
1812	—	100	150	250	450	—

KM# 233.5a   8 REALES
Silver **Issuer:** SUD, Under General Morelos **Obv:** 8 dots below
bow, SUD, plain fields **Rev:** Morelos monogram, 8.R., date

Date	Mintage	Good	VG	F	VF	XF
1812	—	—	—	1,200	2,000	—

KM# 236   8 REALES
0.9030 Struck Silver **Issuer:** SUD, Under General Morelos
Obv: M monogram **Obv. Legend:** PROV. D. OAXACA **Rev:**
Lion shield with or without bow above

Date	Mintage	Good	VG	F	VF	XF
1812 Rare	—	—	—	—	—	—

KM# 237   8 REALES
0.9030 Sterling Silver **Issuer:** SUD, Under General Morelos
Obv: M monogram, without legend **Rev:** Lion shield with or
without bow above

Date	Mintage	Good	VG	F	VF	XF
1813 Rare	—	—	—	—	—	—

KM# 238   8 REALES
0.9030 Struck Silver **Issuer:** SUD, Under General Morelos
Obv: Bow/M/SUD **Rev:** PROV. DE. ... arms

Date	Mintage	Good	VG	F	VF	XF
1813 Rare	—	—	—	—	—	—

KM# 233.2a 8 REALES
Silver **Issuer:** SUD, Under General Morelos **Obv:** bow, arrow, SUD **Rev:** Morelos monogram, 8R, date, plain fields

Date	Mintage	Good	VG	F	VF	XF
1813	—	—	—	1,200	2,000	—

KM# 233.3 8 REALES
Struck Copper **Issuer:** SUD, Under General Morelos **Obv:** Bow, arrow, SUD, with left slant lines below bow **Rev:** Morelos monogram, 8.R., date, plain fields

Date	Mintage	Good	VG	F	VF	XF
1813	—	10.00	17.50	30.00	50.00	—

KM# 233.4 8 REALES
Struck Copper **Issuer:** SUD, Under General Morelos **Obv:** Bow, arrow, SUD, with right slant lines below bow **Rev:** Morelos monogram, 8.R., date, plain fields

Date	Mintage	Good	VG	F	VF	XF
1813	—	10.00	17.50	30.00	50.00	—

PUEBLA
WAR OF INDEPENDENCE
INSURGENT COINAGE

KM# 250 1/2 REAL
Copper **Issuer:** Zacatlan, struck by General Osorno **Obv:** Osorno monogram, ZACATLAN, date **Rev:** Crossed arrows, wreath, value

Date	Mintage	Good	VG	F	VF	XF
1813 Rare	—	—	—	—	—	—

KM# 251 REAL
Copper **Issuer:** Zacatlan, struck by General Osorno **Obv:** Osorno monogram, ZACATLAN, date **Rev:** Crossed arrows, wreath, value

Date	Mintage	Good	VG	F	VF	XF
1813	—	100	150	225	450	—

KM# 252 2 REALES
Copper **Issuer:** Zacatlan, struck by General Osorno **Obv:** Osorno monogram, ZACATLAN, date **Rev:** Crossed arrows, wreath, value

Date	Mintage	Good	VG	F	VF	XF
1813	—	125	175	275	500	—

REAL DEL CATORCE
(City in San Luis Potosi)

Real del Catorce is an important mining center in the Province of San Luis Potosi. In 1811 an 8 Reales coin was issued under very primitive conditions while the city was still in Royalist hands. Few survive.

WAR OF INDEPENDENCE
ROYALIST COINAGE

KM# 169 8 REALES
0.9030 Silver **Ruler:** Ferdinand VII **Obv. Legend:** EL R. D. CATORC. POR FERNA. VII **Rev. Legend:** MONEDA. PROVISIONAL. VALE. 8R

Date	Mintage	VG	F	VF	XF	Unc
1811	—	7,000	15,000	35,000	65,000	—

Note: Spink America Gerber Sale 6-96 VF or XF realized $63,800

SAN FERNANDO DE BEXAR
WAR OF INDEPENDENCE
TOKEN COINAGE

KM# Tn1 1/2 REAL (Jola)
Copper **Ruler:** Ferdinand VII **Note:** Prev. KM#170.

Date	Mintage	Good	VG	F	VF	XF
1818	8,000	—	—	—	25,000	30,000

KM# Tn2 1/2 REAL (Jola)
Copper **Ruler:** Ferdinand VII **Note:** Prev. KM#171.

Date	Mintage	Good	VG	F	VF	XF
1818	Inc. above	—	—	—	22,500	27,500

SAN LUIS POTOSI

Sierra de Pinos

WAR OF INDEPENDENCE

ROYALIST COINAGE

KM# A172   1/4 REAL
Copper   **Ruler:** Ferdinand VII **Issuer:** Sierra de Pinos, Villa

Date	Mintage	Good	VG	F	VF	XF
1814	—	75.00	125	200	350	—

KM# A172a   1/4 REAL
Silver   **Ruler:** Ferdinand VII

Date	Mintage	Good	VG	F	VF	XF
1814 Rare	—	—	—	—	—	—

SOMBRERETE

(Under Royalist Vargas)

The Sombrerete Mint opened on October 8, 1810 in an area that boasted some of the richest mines in Mexico. The mint operated only until July 16, 1811, only to reopen in 1812 and finally close for good at the end of the year. Mines Administrator Fernando Vargas, was also in charge of the coining, all coins bear his name.

WAR OF INDEPENDENCE

ROYALIST COINAGE

KM# 172   1/2 REAL
0.9030 Silver   **Ruler:** Ferdinand VII **Obv:** Legend around crowned globes **Obv. Legend:** FERDIN. VII.
SOMBRERETE... **Rev:** Legend above lys in oval, sprays, date below **Rev. Legend:** VARGAS

Date	Mintage	Good	VG	F	VF	XF
1811	—	45.00	70.00	150	250	—
1812	—	50.00	90.00	175	275	—

KM# 173   REAL
0.9030 Silver   **Ruler:** Ferdinand VII **Obv:** Legend around crowned globes **Obv. Legend:** FERDIN. VII.
SOMBRERETE... **Rev:** Legend above lys in oval with denomination flanking, sprays, date below **Rev. Legend:** VARGAS

Date	Mintage	Good	VG	F	VF	XF
1811	—	45.00	70.00	150	250	—

Note: For 1811, denomination reads as '1R' or 'R1'

1812	—	50.00	90.00	175	275	—

KM# 175   4 REALES
0.9030 Silver   **Ruler:** Ferdinand VII **Obv:** Crowned Royal arms **Obv. Legend:** R. CAXA. DE. SOMBRERETE **Rev:** Large legend **Rev. Legend:** VARGAS/1811 **Note:** Prev. KM#172.

Date	Mintage	Good	VG	F	VF	XF
1812	—	50.00	100	200	450	—

KM# 176   8 REALES
0.9030 Silver   **Ruler:** Ferdinand VII **Countermark:** VARGAS, date, S **Obv:** Royal arms **Obv. Legend:** R. CAXA. DE SOMBRERETE **Rev:** Several countermarks between crowned pillars

Date	Mintage	Good	VG	F	VF	XF
1810	—	1,000	1,750	2,750	4,000	—
1811	—	225	325	450	600	—

MEXICO • VALLADOLID MICHOACAN 553

KM# 177   8 REALES
0.9030 Silver **Ruler:** Ferdinand VII **Obv:** Crowned Royal arms **Obv. Legend:** R. CAXA. DE SOMBRETE **Rev. Legend:** VARGAS/date/3, S between crowned pillars

Date	Mintage	Good	VG	F	VF	XF
1811	—	125	185	245	500	—
1812	—	125	175	225	475	—

VALLADOLID MICHOACAN

WAR OF INDEPENDENCE

ROYALIST COINAGE

KM# 178   8 REALES
0.9030 Silver **Ruler:** Ferdinand VII **Obv:** Royal arms in wreath, value at sides **Rev:** PROVISIONAL/DE VALLADOLID/1813

Date	Mintage	Good	VG	F	VF	XF
1813 Rare	—	—	—	—	—	—

KM# 179   8 REALES
0.9030 Silver **Ruler:** Ferdinand VII **Obv:** Bust **Obv. Legend:** FERDIN. VII. **Rev:** Arms, pillars, P. D. V. in legend

Date	Mintage	Good	VG	F	VF	XF
1813 Rare	—	—	—	—	—	—

Note: Spink America Gerber sale 6-96 good realized $23,100

VERACRUZ

In Zongolica, in the province of Veracruz, 2 priests and a lawyer decided to raise an army to fight for independence. Due to isolation from other Insurgent forces, they decided to make their own coins. Records show that they intended to mint coins of 1/2, 1, 2, 4, and 8 Reales, but specimens are extant of only the three higher denominations.

WAR OF INDEPENDENCE

INSURGENT COINAGE

KM# 253   2 REALES
0.9030 Silver **Issuer:** Zongolica **Obv:** Bow and arrow **Obv. Legend:** VIVA FERNANDO VII Y AMERICA **Rev:** Value, crossed palm branch, sword, date **Rev. Legend:** ZONGOLICA

Date	Mintage	Good	VG	F	VF	XF
1812	—	85.00	175	300	500	—

KM# 255   8 REALES
0.9030 Silver **Issuer:** Zongolica **Obv:** Bow and arrow **Obv. Legend:** VIVA FERNANDO VII Y AMERICA **Rev:** Value, crossed palm branch, sword, date **Rev. Legend:** ZONGOLICA **Note:** Similar to 2 Reales, KM#253.

Date	Mintage	Good	VG	F	VF	XF
1812 Rare	—	—	—	—	—	—

Note: Spink America Gerber sale 6-96 VF to XF realized $57,200

WAR OF INDEPENDENCE

INSURGENT COUNTERMARKED COINAGE
General Vicente Guerrero

The countermark of an eagle facing left within a pearled oval has been attributed by some authors as that of General Vicente Guerrero, a leader of the insurgents in the south, 1816-1821.

KM# 276   1/2 REAL
Silver **Issuer:** General Vicente Guerrero **Countermark:** Eagle **Note:** Countermark on Mexico City KM#72.

CM Date	Host Date	Good	VG	F	VF	XF
ND	ND	40.00	60.00	80.00	175	—

KM# 277   REAL
Silver **Issuer:** General Vicente Guerrero **Countermark:** Eagle **Note:** Countermark on Mexico City KM#78.

CM Date	Host Date	Good	VG	F	VF	XF
ND	1772 FM	35.00	50.00	75.00	165	—

KM# 278.1   2 REALES
Silver **Issuer:** General Vicente Guerrero **Countermark:** Eagle **Note:** Countermark on Mexico City KM#88.

CM Date	Host Date	Good	VG	F	VF	XF
ND	1784 FM	40.00	60.00	100	225	—
ND	1798	40.00	60.00	100	225	—

KM# 278.2   2 REALES
Silver **Issuer:** General Vicente Guerrero **Countermark:** Eagle **Note:** Countermark on Mexico City KM#91.

CM Date	Host Date	Good	VG	F	VF	XF
ND	1807 PJ	30.00	50.00	80.00	200	—

KM# 279   8 REALES
Silver **Issuer:** General Vicente Guerrero **Countermark:**
Eagle **Note:** Countermark on Zacatecas KM#191.

CM Date	Host Date	Good	VG	F	VF	XF
ND	1811	100	150	200	350	—

INSURGENT COUNTERMARKED COINAGE

KM# 286   8 REALES
Silver **Issuer:** Unknown, presumed insurgent **Countermark:**
ZMY **Note:** Countermark on Zacatecas KM#191.

CM Date	Host Date	Good	VG	F	VF	XF
ND	1812	100	150	200	350	—

INSURGENT COUNTERMARKED COINAGE

Congress of Chilpanzingo

Type A: Hand holding bow and arrow between quiver with arrows, sword and bow.

Type B: Crowned eagle on bridge.

KM# 256.1   1/2 REAL
Silver **Issuer:** Congress of Chilpanzingo **Countermark:**
Type A hand holding bow and arrow between quiver with
arrows, sword and bow **Note:** Countermark on cast Mexico
City KM#72.

CM Date	Host Date	Good	VG	F	VF	XF
ND	1812	42.50	70.00	90.00	120	—

KM# 256.2   1/2 REAL
Silver **Issuer:** Congress of Chilpanzingo **Countermark:**
Type A hand holding bow and arrow between quiver with
arrows, sword and bow **Note:** Countermark on Zacatecas
KM#181.

CM Date	Host Date	Good	VG	F	VF	XF
ND	1811	50.00	75.00	100	125	—

KM# A257   REAL
Cast Silver **Issuer:** Congress of Chilpanzingo **Countermark:**
Type A hand holding bow and arrow between quiver with
arrows, sword and bow **Note:** Countermark on cast Mexico
City KM#81.

CM Date	Host Date	Good	VG	F	VF	XF
ND	1803	18.50	30.00	50.00	80.00	—

KM# 257.1   2 REALES
Silver **Issuer:** Congress of Chilpanzingo **Countermark:**
Type B crowned eagle on bridge **Note:** Countermark on 1/4
cut of 8 Reales.

CM Date	Host Date	Good	VG	F	VF	XF
	ND Unique	—	—	—	—	—

KM# 257.2   2 REALES
Silver **Issuer:** Congress of Chilpanzingo **Countermark:**
Type B crowned eagle on bridge **Note:** Countermark on
Zacatecas KM#186.

CM Date	Host Date	Good	VG	F	VF	XF
ND	1811 Unique	—	—	—	—	—

KM# 258.1   8 REALES
Silver **Issuer:** Congress of Chilpanzingo **Countermark:**
Type A hand holding bow and arrow between quiver with
arrows, sword and bow **Note:** Countermark on cast Mexico
City KM#109.

CM Date	Host Date	Good	VG	F	VF	XF
ND	1805	45.00	65.00	85.00	125	—

Note: A countermark appears on coins dated 1805 TH

KM# 258.2   8 REALES
Silver **Issuer:** Congress of Chilpanzingo **Countermark:**
Type A hand holding bow and arrow between quiver with
arrows, sword and bow **Note:** Countermark on cast Mexico
City KM#110.

CM Date	Host Date	Good	VG	F	VF	XF
ND	1810 HJ	50.00	75.00	100	150	—

KM# 258.3   8 REALES
Silver **Issuer:** Congress of Chilpanzingo **Countermark:**
Type A hand holding bow and arrow between quiver with
arrows, sword and bow **Note:** Countermark on cast Mexico
City KM#111.

CM Date	Host Date	Good	VG	F	VF	XF
ND	1811 HJ	45.00	65.00	85.00	125	—
ND	1812 HJ	100	125	175	275	—

KM# 259.1   8 REALES
Silver **Issuer:** Congress of Chilpanzingo **Countermark:**
Type B crowned eagle on bridge **Note:** Countermark on
Chihuahua KM#111.1.

CM Date	Host Date	Good	VG	F	VF	XF
ND	1816 RP	200	250	300	350	—

KM# 259.2   8 REALES
Silver **Issuer:** Congress of Chilpanzingo **Countermark:**
Type B crowned eagle on bridge **Note:** Countermark on cast
Mexico City KM#111.

CM Date	Host Date	Good	VG	F	VF	XF
ND	1811 HJ	130	140	150	175	—

KM# 259.3   8 REALES
Silver **Issuer:** Congress of Chilpanzingo **Countermark:**
Type B crowned eagle on bridge **Note:** Countermark on
Valladolid KM#178.

CM Date	Host Date	Good	VG	F	VF	XF
ND	1813	1,000	2,000	3,000	5,000	—

KM# 259.4   8 REALES
Silver **Issuer:** Congress of Chilpanzingo **Countermark:**
Type B crowned eagle on bridge **Note:** Countermark on
Zacatecas KM#190.

CM Date	Host Date	Good	VG	F	VF	XF
ND	1810	400	500	600	750	—

INSURGENT COUNTERMARKED COINAGE

Don Jose Maria De Linares

KM# 263.1   8 REALES
Silver **Issuer:** Don Jose Maria De Linares **Countermark:**
LINA/RES* **Note:** Countermark on Mexico City KM#110.

CM Date	Host Date	Good	VG	F	VF	XF
ND	1808 TH	250	300	375	500	—

KM# 263.2   8 REALES
Silver **Issuer:** Don Jose Maria De Linares **Countermark:**
LINA/RES * **Note:** Countermark on Zacatecas KM#190.

CM Date	Host Date	Good	VG	F	VF	XF
ND	1811	300	375	450	575	—

KM# 263.3   8 REALES
Silver **Issuer:** Don Jose Maria De Linares **Countermark:**
LINA/RES* **Note:** Countermark on Zacatecas KM#191.

CM Date	Host Date	Good	VG	F	VF	XF
ND	1812	250	300	375	500	—

INSURGENT COUNTERMARKED COINAGE

Ensaie

KM# 260.3 8 REALES
Silver **Issuer:** Ensaie **Countermark:** Eagle over ENSAIE, crude sling below **Note:** Countermark on Zacatecas KM#190.

CM Date	Host Date	Good	VG	F	VF	XF
ND	1810	—	—	—	—	—
ND	1811	100	150	200	300	—

KM# 260.4 8 REALES
Silver **Issuer:** Ensaie **Countermark:** Eagle over ENSAIE, crude sling below **Note:** Countermark on Zacatecas KM#191.

CM Date	Host Date	Good	VG	F	VF	XF
ND	1810	500	700	900	1,200	—
ND	1811	250	300	375	500	—
ND	1812	200	250	285	400	—

KM# 260.1 8 REALES
Silver **Issuer:** Ensaie **Countermark:** Eagle over ENSAIE, crude sling below **Note:** Countermark on Mexico City KM#110.

CM Date	Host Date	Good	VG	F	VF	XF
ND	1811 HJ	150	200	275	350	—

KM# 260.2 8 REALES
Silver **Issuer:** Ensaie **Countermark:** Eagle over ENSAIE, crude sling below **Note:** Countermark on Zacatecas KM#189.

CM Date	Host Date	Good	VG	F	VF	XF
ND	1811	200	400	600	800	—

INSURGENT COUNTERMARKED COINAGE

Jose Maria Liceaga

J.M.L. with banner on cross, crossed olive branches.

(J.M.L./V., D.s, S.M., S.Y.S.L., Ve, A.P., s.r.a., Sea, P.G., S., S.M., El)

KM# A260 1/2 REAL
Silver **Issuer:** Jose Maria Liceaga **Countermark:** JML/SM with banner on cross, crossed olive branches **Note:** Countermark on cast Mexico City 1/2 Real.

CM Date	Host Date	Good	VG	F	VF	XF
ND	ND	100	150	200	275	—

KM# 261.6 2 REALES
Silver **Issuer:** Jose Maria Liceaga **Countermark:** J.M.L./V. with banner on cross, crossed olive branches **Note:** Countermark on Zacatecas KM#187.

CM Date	Host Date	Good	VG	F	VF	XF
ND	1811	200	225	250	300	—

KM# 261.7 2 REALES
Silver **Issuer:** Jose Maria Liceaga **Countermark:** J.M.L./DS with banner on cross, crossed olive branches **Note:** Countermark on Zacatecas KM#187.

CM Date	Host Date	Good	VG	F	VF	XF
ND	1811	200	235	275	325	—

KM# 261.8 2 REALES
Silver **Issuer:** Jose Maria Liceaga **Countermark:** J.M.L./ S.M. with banner on cross, crossed olive branches **Note:** Countermark on Zacatecas KM#187.

CM Date	Host Date	Good	VG	F	VF	XF
ND	1811	200	235	275	325	—

KM# 261.9 2 REALES
Silver **Issuer:** Jose Maria Liceaga **Countermark:** J.M.L./ S.Y. with banner on cross, crossed olive branches **Note:** Countermark on Zacatecas KM#187.

CM Date	Host Date	Good	VG	F	VF	XF
ND	1811	200	235	275	325	—

KM# 261.1 2 REALES
Silver **Issuer:** Jose Maria Liceaga **Countermark:** J.M.L./Ve with banner on cross, crossed olive branches **Note:** Countermark on 1/4 cut of 8 Reales.

CM Date	Host Date	Good	VG	F	VF	XF
ND	ND	175	225	300	—	—

KM# 261.2 2 REALES
Silver **Issuer:** Jose Maria Liceaga **Countermark:** J.M.L./V with banner on cross, crossed olive branchs **Note:** Countermark on Zacatecas KM#186.

CM Date	Host Date	Good	VG	F	VF	XF
ND	1811	200	225	250	300	—

KM# 261.3 2 REALES
Silver **Issuer:** Jose Maria Liceaga **Countermark:** J.M.L./DS

with banner on cross, crossed olive branches **Note:**
Countermark on Zacatecas KM#186.

CM Date	Host Date	Good	VG	F	VF	XF
ND	1811	200	235	275	325	—

KM# 261.4 2 REALES
Silver **Issuer:** Jose Maria Liceaga **Countermark:** J.M.L./
S.M. with banner on cross, crossed olive branches **Note:**
Countermark on Zacatecas KM#186.

CM Date	Host Date	Good	VG	F	VF	XF
ND	1811	200	235	275	325	—

KM# 261.5 2 REALES
Silver **Issuer:** Jose Maria Liceaga **Countermark:** J.M.L./
S.Y. with banner on cross, crossed olive branches **Note:**
Countermark on Zacatecas KM#186.

CM Date	Host Date	Good	VG	F	VF	XF
ND	1811	200	235	275	325	—

KM# 262.1 8 REALES
Silver **Issuer:** Jose Maria Liceaga **Countermark:** J.M.L./
D.S. with banner on cross, crossed olive branches **Note:**
Countermark on Zacatecas KM#190.

CM Date	Host Date	Good	VG	F	VF	XF
ND	1811	250	325	425	550	—

KM# 262.4 8 REALES
Silver **Issuer:** Jose Maria Liceaga **Countermark:** J.M.L./
S.F. with banner on cross, crossed olive branches **Note:**
Countermark on Zacatecas KM#190.

CM Date	Host Date	Good	VG	F	VF	XF
ND	1811	200	275	375	525	—

KM# 262.2 8 REALES
Silver **Issuer:** Jose Maria Liceaga **Countermark:** J.M.L./E
with banner on cross, crossed olive branches **Note:**
Countermark on Zacatecas KM#190.

CM Date	Host Date	Good	VG	F	VF	XF
ND	1811	225	300	400	550	—

KM# 262.3 8 REALES
Silver **Issuer:** Jose Maria Liceaga **Countermark:** J.M.L./
P.G. with banner on cross, crossed olive branches **Note:**
Countermark on Durango KM#111.2.

CM Date	Host Date	Good	VG	F	VF	XF
ND	1813 RM	200	275	375	525	—

KM# 262.5 8 REALES
Silver **Issuer:** Jose Maria Liceaga **Countermark:** J.M.L./
S.M. with banner on cross, crossed olive branches **Note:**
Countermark on Zacatecas KM#190.

CM Date	Host Date	Good	VG	F	VF	XF
ND	1811	200	275	375	525	—

KM# 262.10 8 REALES
Silver **Issuer:** Jose Maria Liceaga, J.M.L. with banner on
cross, crossed olive branches. (J.M.L./V. D.s., S.M.,
S.Y.S.L.,Ve, A.P., s.r.a., Sea, P.G., S., S.M., E.)
Countermark: J.M.L./S.M. **Note:** Countermark on Zacatecas
KM#190.

CM Date	Host Date	Good	VG	F	VF	XF
ND	1811	—	—	—	—	—

KM# 262.6 8 REALES
Silver **Issuer:** Jose Maria Liceaga **Countermark:** J.M.L./
V.E. with banner on cross, cross olive branches **Note:**
Countermark on Zacatecas KM#190.

CM Date	Host Date	Good	VG	F	VF	XF
ND	1811	200	275	375	525	—

KM# 262.12 8 REALES
Silver **Issuer:** Jose Maria Liceaga, Banner on cross, crossed
olive branches **Countermark:** J.M.L. / P.G. **Note:**
Countermark on Guanajuato 8 Reales, KM#111.4.

CM Date	Host Date	Good	VG	F	VF	XF
ND	ND1813	150	250	425	—	—

KM# 262.7 8 REALES
Silver **Issuer:** Jose Maria Liceaga, J.M.L with banner on cross, crossed olive branches. (J.M.L./V., D.s, S.M., S.Y.S.L., Ve, A.P., s.r.a., Sea, P.G., S., S.M., E.) **Countermark:** J.M.L./ D.S. **Note:** Countermark on Zacatecas KM#190.

CM Date	Host Date	Good	VG	F	VF	XF
ND	1811	—	—	—	—	—

KM# 262.9 8 REALES
Silver **Issuer:** Jose Maria Liceaga, J.M.L. with banner on cross, crossed olive branches. (J.M.L./V. D.s., S.M., S.Y.S.L.,Ve, A.P., s.r.a., Sea, P.G., S., S.M., E.) **Countermark:** J.M.L./S.F. **Note:** Countermark on Zacatecas KM#190.

CM Date	Host Date	Good	VG	F	VF	XF
ND	1811	—	—	—	—	—

KM# 262.11 8 REALES
Silver **Issuer:** Jose Maria Liceaga, J.M.L. with banner on cross, crossed olive branches. (J.M.L./V. D.s., S.M., S.Y.S.L.,Ve, A.P., s.r.a., Sea, P.G., S., S.M., E.) **Countermark:** J.M.L./V.E. **Note:** Countermark on Zacatecas KM#190.

CM Date	Host Date	Good	VG	F	VF	XF
ND	1811	—	—	—	—	—

KM# 262.8 8 REALES
Silver **Issuer:** Jose Maria Liceaga
,J.M.L. with banner on cross, crossed olive branches. (J.M.L./ V. D.s., S.M., S.Y.S.L.,Ve, A.P., s.r.a., Sea, P.G., S., S.M., E.) **Countermark:** J.M.L./E **Note:** Countermark on Zacatecas KM#190.

CM Date	Host Date	Good	VG	F	VF	XF
ND	1811	—	—	—	—	—

L.V.S. - Labor Vincit Semper

Some authorities believe L.V.S. is for La Villa de Sombrerete.

KM# 264.1 8 REALES
Cast Silver **Issuer:** Labor Vincit Semper, Some authorities believe L.V.S. is for "La Villa de Sombrerete" **Countermark:** L.V.S. **Note:** Countermark on Chihuahua KM#123.

CM Date	Host Date	Good	VG	F	VF	XF
ND	1811 RP	275	350	450	550	—
ND	1812 RP	200	250	300	375	—

KM# 264.2 8 REALES
Silver **Issuer:** Labor Vincit Semper, Some authorities believe L.V.S. is for Sombrerete" **Countermark:** L.V.S. **Note:** Countermark on Chihuahua KM#111.1 overstruck on KM#123.

CM Date	Host Date	Good	VG	F	VF	XF
ND	1816 RP	250	300	325	375	—
ND	1817 RP	250	300	325	375	—

CM Date	Host Date	Good	VG	F	VF	XF
ND	1818 RP	250	300	325	375	—
ND	1819 RP	400	450	500	600	—
ND	1820 RP	450	500	550	650	—

KM# 264.3 8 REALES
Silver **Issuer:** Labor Vincit Semper, Some authorities believe L.V.S. is for "La Villa de Sombrerete" **Countermark:** L.V.S. **Note:** Countermark on Guadalajara KM#111.3.

CM Date	Host Date	Good	VG	F	VF	XF
ND	1817	185	220	250	310	—

KM# 264.4 8 REALES
Silver **Issuer:** Labor Vincit Semper, Some authorities believe L.V.S. is for "La Villa de Sombrerete" **Countermark:** L.V.S. **Note:** Countermark on Nueva Vizcaya KM#165.

CM Date	Host Date	Good	VG	F	VF	XF
ND	1811 RM	1,150	3,150	5,250	8,250	—

KM# 264.5 8 REALES
Silver **Issuer:** Labor Vincit Semper, Some authorities believe L.V.S. is for "La Villa de Sombrerete" **Countermark:** L.V.S. **Note:** Countermark on Sombrerete KM#177.

CM Date	Host Date	Good	VG	F	VF	XF
ND	1811	300	350	450	550	—
ND	1812	300	350	450	550	—

KM# 264.6 8 REALES
Silver **Issuer:** Labor Vincit Semper, Some authorities believe L.V.S. is for "La Villa de Sombrerete" **Countermark:** L.V.S. **Note:** Countermark on Zacatecas KM#190.

CM Date	Host Date	Good	VG	F	VF	XF
ND	1811	350	400	450	550	—

KM# 264.7 8 REALES
Silver **Issuer:** Labor Vincit Semper, Some authorities believe L.V.S. is for "La Villa de Sombrerete" **Countermark:** L.V.S. **Note:** Countermark on Zacatecas KM#192.

CM Date	Host Date	Good	VG	F	VF	XF
ND	1813	350	400	450	550	—

Morelos

Morelos monogram

Type A: Stars above and below monogram in circle.

Type B: Dots above and below monogram in oval.

Type C: Monogram in rectangle.

Note: Many specimens of Type C available in todays market are considered spurious.

KM# A265   2 REALES
Copper **Issuer:** Morelos **Countermark:** Type A stars above
and below monogram in circle **Note:** Countermark on Oaxaca
Sud, KM#226.1.

CM Date	Host Date	Good	VG	F	VF	XF
ND	1812	—	—	—	—	—

KM# 265.1   8 REALES
Silver **Issuer:** Morelos **Countermark:** Type A star above
and below monogram in circle **Note:** Countermark on Mexico
City KM#109.

CM Date	Host Date	Good	VG	F	VF	XF
ND	1797 FM	45.00	50.00	60.00	85.00	—
ND	1798 FM	45.00	50.00	60.00	85.00	—
ND	1800 FM	45.00	50.00	60.00	85.00	—
ND	1807 TH	45.00	50.00	60.00	85.00	—

KM# 265.2   8 REALES
Silver **Issuer:** Morelos **Countermark:** Type A stars above
and below monogram in circle **Note:** Countermark on Mexico
City KM#110.

CM Date	Host Date	Good	VG	F	VF	XF
ND	1809 TH	55.00	65.00	85.00	120	—
ND	1811 HJ	55.00	65.00	85.00	120	—

KM# 265.3   8 REALES
Silver **Issuer:** Morelos **Countermark:** Type A stars above
and below monogram in circle **Note:** Countermark on Mexico
City KM#111.

CM Date	Host Date	Good	VG	F	VF	XF
ND	1812 JJ	50.00	60.00	75.00	110	—

KM# 265.5   8 REALES
Cast Silver **Issuer:** Morelos **Countermark:** Type A stars
above and below monogram in circle **Note:** Countermark on
Supreme National Congress KM#206.

CM Date	Host Date	Good	VG	F	VF	XF
ND	1811	200	250	375	600	—

KM# 266.1   8 REALES
Silver **Issuer:** Morelos **Countermark:** Type B dots above
and below monogram in oval **Note:** Countermark on
Guatamala 8 Reales, C#67.

CM Date	Host Date	Good	VG	F	VF	XF
ND	1810 M Rare	—	—	—	—	—

KM# 266.2   8 REALES
Silver **Issuer:** Morelos **Countermark:** Type B dots above
and below monogram in oval **Note:** Countermark on Mexico
City KM#110.

CM Date	Host Date	Good	VG	F	VF	XF
ND	1809 TH	45.00	55.00	65.00	90.00	—

KM# 267.1   8 REALES
Silver **Issuer:** Morelos **Countermark:** Type C monogram in
rectangle **Note:** Countermark on Zacatecas KM#189. Many
specimens of Type C available in today's market are
considered spurious.

CM Date	Host Date	Good	VG	F	VF	XF
ND	1811	300	350	425	650	—

KM# 265.4   8 REALES
Copper **Issuer:** Morelos **Countermark:** Type A stars above
and below monogram in circle **Note:** Countermark on Oaxaca
Sud KM#233.2.

CM Date	Host Date	Good	VG	F	VF	XF
ND	1812	12.50	17.50	25.00	40.00	—
ND	1813	12.50	17.50	25.00	40.00	—
ND	1814	12.50	17.50	25.00	40.00	—

KM# 265.6   8 REALES
Silver **Issuer:** Morelos **Countermark:** Type A stars above
and below monogram in circle **Note:** Countermark on
Zacatecas KM#190.

CM Date	Host Date	Good	VG	F	VF	XF
ND	1811	375	625	900	—	—

KM# 265.7   8 REALES
Silver **Issuer:** Morelos **Countermark:** Type A stars above
and below monogram in circle **Note:** Countermark on
Zacatecas KM#191.

CM Date	Host Date	Good	VG	F	VF	XF
ND	1811	200	250	375	600	—

KM# 267.2   8 REALES
Silver **Issuer:** Morelos **Countermark:** Type C: monogram
in rectangle **Note:** Countermark Type C on Zacatecas
KM#190. Many specimens of Type C available in today's
market are considered spurious.

CM Date	Host Date	Good	VG	F	VF	XF
ND	1811	300	350	425	650	—

Norte

Issued by the Supreme National Congress and
the Army of the North.

Countermark: Eagle on cactus; star to left; NORTE
below.

KM# 268   1/2 REAL
Silver **Issuer:** Supreme National Congress and the Army of
the North **Countermark:** Eagle on cactus; star to left; NORTE
below **Note:** Countermark on Zacatecas KM#180.

CM Date	Host Date	Good	VG	F	VF	XF
ND	1811	250	300	375	450	—

KM# 269   2 REALES
Silver **Issuer:** Supreme National Congress and the Army of
the North **Countermark:** Eagle on cactus; star to left; NORTE
below **Note:** Countermark on Zacatecas KM#187.

CM Date	Host Date	Good	VG	F	VF	XF
ND	1811	225	275	325	400	—

KM# A269   2 REALES
Silver **Issuer:** Supreme National Congress and the Army of
the North **Countermark:** Eagle on cactus; star to left; NORTE
below **Note:** Countermark on Zacatecas KM#188.

CM Date	Host Date	Good	VG	F	VF	XF
ND	1812	—	—	—	—	—

KM# B269   4 REALES
Silver **Issuer:** Supreme National Congress and the Army of
the North **Countermark:** Eagle on cactus; star to left; NORTE
below **Note:** Countermark on Sombrerete KM#175.

CM Date	Host Date	Good	VG	F	VF	XF
ND	1812	100	150	200	275	—

KM# 270.4   8 REALES
Silver **Issuer:** Supreme National Congress and the Army of
the North **Countermark:** Eagle on cactus; star to left; NORTE
below **Note:** Countermark on Zacatecas KM#191.

CM Date	Host Date	Good	VG	F	VF	XF
ND	1811	200	300	400	550	—
ND	1811	200	300	400	550	—
ND	1812	200	300	400	550	—

KM# 270.1   8 REALES
Silver **Issuer:** Supreme National Congress and the Army of
the North **Countermark:** Eagle on cactus; star to left; NORTE
below **Note:** Countermark on Chihuahua KM#111.1.

CM Date	Host Date	Good	VG	F	VF	XF
ND	1813 RP	250	350	450	550	—

KM# 270.2   8 REALES
Silver **Issuer:** Supreme National Congress and the Army of
the North **Countermark:** Eagle on cactus; star to left; NORTE
below **Note:** Countermark on Guanajuato KM#111.4.

CM Date	Host Date	Good	VG	F	VF	XF
ND	1813 JM	400	550	700	800	—

KM# 270.3   8 REALES
Silver **Issuer:** Supreme National Congress and the Army of
the North **Countermark:** Eagle on cactus; star to left; NORTE
below **Note:** Countermark on Zacatecas KM#190.

CM Date	Host Date	Good	VG	F	VF	XF
ND	1811	300	400	500	650	—

Osorno

Countermark: Osorno monogram. (Jose Francisco Osorno)

KM# 271.1 1/2 REAL
Silver **Issuer:** Jose Francisco Osorno **Countermark:** Osorno monogram **Note:** Countermark on Mexico City KM#72.

CM Date	Host Date	Good	VG	F	VF	XF
ND	1798 FM	65.00	100	150	200	—
ND	1802 FT	65.00	100	150	200	—
ND	1806	65.00	100	150	200	—

KM# 271.2 1/2 REAL
Silver **Issuer:** Jose Francisco Osorno **Countermark:** Osorno monogram **Note:** Countermark on Mexico City KM#73.

CM Date	Host Date	Good	VG	F	VF	XF
ND	1809 TH	65.00	100	150	200	—

KM# 272.1 REAL
Silver **Issuer:** Jose Francisco Osorno **Countermark:** Osorno monogram **Note:** Countermark on Mexico City KM#81.

CM Date	Host Date	Good	VG	F	VF	XF
ND	1803 FT	65.00	100	150	200	—

KM# 272.2 REAL
Silver **Issuer:** Jose Francisco Osorno **Countermark:** Osorno monogram **Note:** Countermark on Potosi KM#70.

CM Date	Host Date	Good	VG	F	VF	XF
ND	ND	75.00	115	175	250	—

KM# 272.3 REAL
Silver **Issuer:** Jose Francisco Osorno **Countermark:** Osorno monogram **Note:** Countermark on Guatemala KM#54.

CM Date	Host Date	Good	VG	F	VF	XF
ND	1804	75.00	115	175	250	—

KM# A272.1 2 REALES
Silver **Issuer:** Jose Francisco Osorno **Countermark:** Osorno monogram **Note:** Countermark on Mexico City KM#88.2.

CM Date	Host Date	Good	VG	F	VF	XF
ND	1788 FM	75.00	125	175	250	—

KM# A272.2 2 REALES
Silver **Issuer:** Jose Francisco Osorno **Countermark:** Osorno monogram **Note:** Countermark on Mexico City KM#91.

CM Date	Host Date	Good	VG	F	VF	XF
ND	1808 TH	75.00	125	175	250	—

KM# A272.3 2 REALES
Silver **Issuer:** Jose Francisco Osorno **Countermark:** Osorno monogram **Note:** Countermark on Mexico City KM#92.

CM Date	Host Date	Good	VG	F	VF	XF
ND	1809 TH	75.00	125	175	250	—

KM# A272.4 2 REALES
Silver **Issuer:** Jose Francisco Osorno **Countermark:** Osorno monogram **Note:** Countermark on Zacatlian KM#252.

CM Date	Host Date	Good	VG	F	VF	XF
ND	1813	150	200	300	400	—

KM# 273.1 4 REALES
Silver **Issuer:** Jose Francisco Osorno **Countermark:** Osorno monogram **Note:** Countermark on Mexico City KM#97.2.

CM Date	Host Date	Good	VG	F	VF	XF
ND	1782 FF	85.00	150	200	275	—

KM# 273.2 4 REALES
Silver **Issuer:** Jose Francisco Osorno **Countermark:** Osorno monogram **Note:** Countermark on Mexico City KM#100.

CM Date	Host Date	Good	VG	F	VF	XF
ND	1799 FM	85.00	150	200	275	—

KM# 274.1 8 REALES
Silver **Issuer:** Jose Francisco Osorno **Countermark:** Osorno
monogram **Note:** Countermark on Lima 8 Reales, C#101.

CM Date	Host Date	Good	VG	F	VF	XF
ND	1811 JP	200	225	250	300	—

KM# 274.2 8 REALES
Silver **Issuer:** Jose Francisco Osorno **Countermark:** Osorno
monogram **Note:** Countermark on Mexico City KM#110.

CM Date	Host Date	Good	VG	F	VF	XF
ND	1809 TH	125	150	225	300	—
ND	1810 HJ	125	150	225	300	—
ND	1811 HJ	125	150	225	300	—

VILLA / GRAN

(Julian Villagran)

KM# 298 2 REALES
Cast Silver , Julian Villagran **Countermark:** VILLA/GRAN
Note: Countermark on cast Mexico City KM#91.

CM Date	Host Date	Good	VG	F	VF	XF
ND	1799 FM	150	200	250	350	—
ND	1802 FT	150	200	250	350	—

KM# 275 8 REALES
Cast Silver **Issuer:** Julian Villagran **Countermark:** VILLA/
GRAN **Note:** Countermark on cast Mexico City KM#109.

CM Date	Host Date	Good	VG	F	VF	XF
ND	1796 FM	200	250	300	400	—
ND	1806 TH	200	250	300	400	—

Multiple Countermarks

Many combinations of Royalist and Insurgent
countermarks are usually found on the cast copies
produced by Chihuahua and Mexico City and on the
other crude provisional issues of this period. Struck
Mexico City coins were used to make molds for casting necessity issues and countermarked afterwards
to show issuing authority. Some were marked again
by either both or separate opposing friendly forces
to authorize circulation in their areas of occupation.
Some countermarks are only obtainable with com-
panion markings.

KM# 289 2 REALES
Silver **Issuer:** C.M.S. and S.C.M. **Countermark:** C.M.S.
(Comandancia Militar Suriana) and eagle with S.C.M.
(Soberano Congreso Mexicano) **Note:** Countermark on
Mexico City KM#91.

CM Date	Host Date	Good	VG	F	VF	XF
ND	ND	—	—	—	—	—

KM# 295 2 REALES
Silver **Issuer:** Militar del Sur and Soberano Congreso
Mexicano **Countermark:** M.d.S. and eagle with S.C.M **Note:**
Countermark on Mexico City KM#91.

CM Date	Host Date	Good	VG	F	VF	XF
ND	ND	150	250	450	—	—

KM# 296 2 REALES
Silver **Issuer:** Jose Francisco Osorno and Julian Villagran
Countermark: Osorno monogram and VILLA/GRAN **Note:**
Countermark on cast Mexico City KM#110.

CM Date	Host Date	Good	VG	F	VF	XF
ND	1809 TH	—	—	—	—	—

KM# A286 2 REALES
Silver **Issuer:** Jose Maria Liceaga and VTIL **Countermark:**
J.M.L./D.S. AND VTIL **Note:** Countermark on Zacatecas
KM#186.

CM Date	Host Date	Good	VG	F	VF	XF
ND	1811	75.00	125	175	250	—

KM# B286 2 REALES
Silver **Issuer:** Jose Maria Liceaga and VTIL **Countermark:**
J.M.L./V.E. and VTIL **Note:** Countermark on Zacatecas
KM#186.

CM Date	Host Date	Good	VG	F	VF	XF
ND	1810	75.00	125	175	250	—
ND	1811	75.00	125	175	250	—

KM# 285.2 8 REALES
Silver **Issuer:** Chilpanzingo and Morelos **Countermark:**
Chilpanzingo Type A and Morelos monogram Type A **Note:**
Countermark on cast Mexico City KM#110.

CM Date	Host Date	Good	VG	F	VF	XF
ND	1810 HJ	35.00	45.00	60.00	140	—
ND	1811 HJ	35.00	45.00	60.00	140	—

KM# C286 8 REALES
Silver **Issuer:** Chilpanzingo and Morelos and LVS
Countermark: Chilpanzingo Type A, Morelos Type A and
LVS monogram on cast Mexico City KM#110

CM Date	Host Date	Good	VG	F	VF	XF
ND	1809 HJ	50.00	75.00	125	275	—

KM# A298 8 REALES
Silver **Issuer:** S.J.N.G. and VTIL **Countermark:** S.J.N.G
and VTIL on Zacatecas KM#191

CM Date	Host Date	Good	VG	F	VF	XF
ND	ND	35.00	50.00	75.00	200	—

KM# A297 8 REALES
Silver **Issuer:** Chilpanzingo and ENSAIE **Countermark:**
Chilpanzingo Type B and ENSAIE **Note:** Countermark on
Zacatecas KM#189.

CM Date	Host Date	Good	VG	F	VF	XF
ND	ND	175	250	350	—	—

KM# 297 8 REALES
Silver **Issuer:** Chilpanzingo and LVA **Countermark:**
Chilpanzingo Type A and LVA **Note:** Countermark on Mexico
City KM#109.

CM Date	Host Date	Good	VG	F	VF	XF
ND	1805 TH	45.00	75.00	145	250	—

KM# 281 8 REALES
Silver **Issuer:** Chilpanzingo and LVS **Countermark:**
Chilpanzingo Type A and script LVS **Note:** Countermark on
cast Mexico City KM#110.

CM Date	Host Date	Good	VG	F	VF	XF
ND	1809 HJ	45.00	65.00	135	250	—

KM# 288.2 8 REALES
Silver **Issuer:** Chilpanzingo and Suprema Junta Nacional
Gubernativa **Countermark:** Chilpanzingo Type B **Note:**
Countermark on Zacatecas KM#190. Prev. KM#288.

CM Date	Host Date	Good	VG	F	VF	XF
ND	1811	—	—	—	—	—

KM# 290.2   8 REALES
Silver **Issuer:** ENSAIE and VTIL **Countermark:** ENSAIE
and VTIL **Note:** Countermark on Zacatecas KM#190. Prev.
KM#290.

CM Date	Host Date	Good	VG	F	VF	XF
ND	1811	100	175	275	350	—

KM# 291   8 REALES
Silver **Issuer:** Jose Maria Liceaga and VTIL **Countermark:**
J.M.L./D.S. and VTIL **Note:** Countermark on Mexico City
KM#110.

CM Date	Host Date	Good	VG	F	VF	XF
ND	1810 HJ	85.00	150	250	400	—

KM# 282   8 REALES
Silver **Issuer:** La Comandancia Militar and Morelos
Countermark: L.C.M and Morelos monogram Type A **Note:**
Countermark on cast Mexico City KM#109.

CM Date	Host Date	Good	VG	F	VF	XF
ND	1792 FM	—	—	—	—	—

KM# 283   8 REALES
Silver **Issuer:** Morelos and Morelos **Countermark:** Morelos
Type A and C **Note:** Countermark on cast Mexico City
KM#109.

CM Date	Host Date	Good	VG	F	VF	XF
ND	1806 TH	—	—	—	—	—

KM# 284   8 REALES
Silver **Issuer:** Chilpanzingo and Morelos **Countermark:**
Chilpanzingo Type A and Morelos monogram Type A **Note:**
Countermark on cast Mexico City KM#109.

CM Date	Host Date	Good	VG	F	VF	XF
ND	1806 TH	35.00	50.00	100	200	—
ND	1807 TH	35.00	50.00	100	200	—

KM# 285.1   8 REALES
Silver **Issuer:** Chilpanzingo and Morelos **Countermark:**
Chilpanzingo Type A and Morelos monogram Type A **Note:**
Countermark on struck Mexico City KM#110.

CM Date	Host Date	Good	VG	F	VF	XF
ND	1809 TH	45.00	65.00	135	250	—

KM# 285.3   8 REALES
Silver **Issuer:** Chilpanzingo and Morelos **Countermark:**
Chilpanzingo Type A and Morelos monogram Type A **Note:**
Countermark on cast Mexico City KM#111.

CM Date	Host Date	Good	VG	F	VF	XF
ND	1811 HJ	75.00	120	175	275	—

KM# A290   8 REALES
Silver **Issuer:** ENSAIE and Jose Maria Liceaga
Countermark: ENSAIE and J.M.L. **Note:** Countermark on
Zacatecas KM#190.

CM Date	Host Date	Good	VG	F	VF	XF
ND	1811	100	175	275	350	—

KM# 294   8 REALES
Silver **Issuer:** L.V.A. and Morelos **Countermark:** Script LVA
and Morelos monogram Type A **Note:** Countermark on cast
Mexico City KM#110.

CM Date	Host Date	Good	VG	F	VF	XF
ND	ND HJ	45.00	75.00	135	250	—

KM# 288.1   8 REALES
Silver **Issuer:** Chilpanzingo and Suprema Junta Nacional
Gubernativa **Countermark:** Chilpanzingo Type B and
S.J.N.G **Note:** Countermark on Zacatecas KM#189.

CM Date	Host Date	Good	VG	F	VF	XF
ND	1811	—	—	—	—	—

KM# 290.1   8 REALES
Silver **Issuer:** ENSAIE and VTIL **Countermark:** ENSAIE
and VTIL **Note:** Countermark on Zacatecas KM#189.

CM Date	Host Date	Good	VG	F	VF	XF
ND	1811	100	175	275	350	—

KM# 280.1   8 REALES
Silver **Issuer:** Chilpanzingo and Crown and flag
Countermark: Chilpanzingo Type B and Crown and flag
Note: Countermark on Zacatecas KM#189.

CM Date	Host Date	Good	VG	F	VF	XF
ND	1811	—	—	—	—	—

KM# 280.2 8 REALES
Silver **Issuer:** Chilpanzingo and crown and flag
Countermark: Chilpanzingo Type B and crown and flag **Note:**
Countermark on Zacatecas KM#190.

CM Date	Host Date	Good	VG	F	VF	XF
ND	1811	—	—	—	—	—

KM# 287 8 REALES
Silver **Issuer:** Chilpanzingo - Provisional De Valladolid
Countermark: Chilpanzingo Type B and P.D.V **Note:**
Countermark on Valladolid KM#178.

CM Date	Host Date	Good	VG	F	VF	XF
ND	1813	—	—	—	—	—

ZACATECAS

The city of Zacatecas, in a rich mining region has provided silver for the world since mid-1500. On November 14,
1810 a mint began production for the Royalist cause. Zacatecas was the most prolific during the War of Independence.
Four of the 5 standard silver denominations were made here,
4 Reales were not. The first, a local type showing mountains
of silver on the coins were made only in 1810 and 1811. Some
1811 coins were made by the Insurgents who took the city on
April 15, 1811, later retaken by the Royalists on May 21, 1811.
Zacatecas struck the standard Ferdinand VII bust type until
1922.
Mint marks: Z, ZS, Zs.

WAR OF INDEPENDENCE

ROYALIST COINAGE

KM# 180 1/2 REAL
0.9030 Silver **Ruler:** Ferdinand VII **Obv:** Local arms with
flowers and castles **Rev:** Mountain **Note:** Mint marks: Z, ZS,
Zs.

Date	Mintage	Good	VG	F	VF	XF
1810	—	75.00	125	200	400	—
1811	—	30.00	50.00	90.00	175	—

Note: Date aligned with legend

KM# 181 1/2 REAL
0.9030 Silver **Ruler:** Ferdinand VII **Obv:** Royal arms **Rev:**
Mountain **Rev. Legend:** MONEDA PROVISIÓNAL DE
ZACATECAS **Note:** Mint marks: Z, ZS, Zs.

Date	Mintage	Good	VG	F	VF	XF
1811	—	30.00	50.00	90.00	175	—

KM# 182 1/2 REAL
0.9030 Silver **Ruler:** Ferdinand VII **Obv:** Provincial bust **Obv.
Legend:** FERDIN. VII **Rev:** Mountain **Rev. Legend:** MONEDA
PROVISIONAL DE ZACATECAS **Note:** Mint marks: Z, ZS, Zs.

Date	Mintage	Good	VG	F	VF	XF
1811	—	30.00	40.00	65.00	135	—
1812	—	25.00	35.00	60.00	120	—

KM# 73.1 1/2 REAL
1.6900 g., 0.9030 Silver .0491 oz. ASW **Ruler:** Ferdinand VII
Obv: Armored bust of Ferdinand VII **Rev:** Crowned arms,
pillars **Note:** Mint marks: Z, ZS, Zs.

Date	Mintage	Good	VG	F	VF	XF
1813 AG	—	20.00	40.00	60.00	100	—
1813 FP	—	25.00	45.00	85.00	175	—
1814 AG	—	15.00	30.00	60.00	100	—
1815 AG	—	12.50	25.00	40.00	60.00	—
1816 AG	—	10.00	15.00	25.00	50.00	—
1817 AG	—	10.00	15.00	25.00	50.00	—
1818 AG	—	10.00	15.00	25.00	50.00	—
1819 AG	—	10.00	15.00	25.00	50.00	—

KM# 74.3 1/2 REAL
1.6900 g., 0.9030 Silver .0491 oz. ASW **Ruler:** Ferdinand VII
Obv: Draped bust Ferdinand VII **Rev:** Crowned arms, pillars
Note: Mint marks: Z, ZS, Zs.

Date	Mintage	VG	F	VF	XF	Unc
1819 AG	—	8.00	12.00	25.00	50.00	—
1820 AG	—	8.00	12.00	25.00	50.00	—
1820 RG	—	5.00	10.00	20.00	45.00	—
1821 AG	—	150	250	450	850	—
1821 RG	—	5.00	10.00	20.00	45.00	—

KM# 183 REAL
0.9030 Silver **Ruler:** Ferdinand VII **Obv:** Local arms with
flowers and castles **Rev:** Mountain **Note:** Mint marks: Z, ZS, Zs.

Date	Mintage	Good	VG	F	VF	XF
1810	—	100	150	300	500	—
1811	—	20.00	40.00	75.00	150	—

Note: Date aligned with legend

KM# 184 REAL
0.9030 Silver **Ruler:** Ferdinand VII **Obv:** Royal arms **Rev:**
Mountain **Rev. Legend:** MONEDA PROVISIÓNAL DE
ZACATECAS **Note:** Mint marks: Z, ZS, Zs.

Date	Mintage	Good	VG	F	VF	XF
1811	—	15.00	30.00	60.00	135	—

KM# 185 REAL
0.9030 Silver **Ruler:** Ferdinand VII **Obv:** Provincial bust **Obv.
Legend:** FERDIN. VII. **Rev:** Crowned arms, pillars **Rev.
Legend:** MONEDA PROVISIONAL DE ZACATECAS **Note:**
Mint marks: Z, ZS, Zs.

Date	Mintage	Good	VG	F	VF	XF
1811	—	50.00	85.00	120	200	—
1812	—	40.00	70.00	100	175	—

KM# 82.1   REAL
3.3800 g., 0.9030 Silver .0981 oz. ASW **Ruler:** Ferdinand VII
Obv: Armored bust of Ferdinand VII **Obv. Legend:** FERDIN.
VII. **Rev:** Crowned arms, pillars **Note:** Mint marks: Z, ZS, Zs.

Date	Mintage	Good	VG	F	VF	XF
1813 FP	—	50.00	100	150	250	—
1814 FP	—	20.00	35.00	50.00	85.00	—
1814 AG	—	20.00	35.00	50.00	85.00	—
1815 AG	—	20.00	35.00	50.00	85.00	—
1816 AG	—	10.00	20.00	30.00	65.00	—
1817 AG	—	6.50	12.50	20.00	45.00	—
1818 AG	—	6.50	12.50	20.00	45.00	—
1819 AG	—	5.00	9.00	15.00	35.00	—

KM# 83.3   REAL
3.3800 g., 0.9030 Silver .0981 oz. ASW **Ruler:** Ferdinand VII
Obv: Draped bust of Ferdinand VII **Obv. Legend:** FERDIN.
VII. **Rev:** Crowned arms, pillars **Note:** Mint marks: Z, ZS, Zs.

Date	Mintage	VG	F	VF	XF	Unc
1820 AG	—	5.00	10.00	20.00	60.00	—
1820 RG	—	5.00	10.00	20.00	60.00	—
1821 AG	—	15.00	30.00	45.00	90.00	—
1821 AZ	—	10.00	20.00	40.00	85.00	—
1821 RG	—	6.00	12.00	25.00	65.00	—
1822 AZ	—	6.00	12.00	25.00	65.00	—
1822 RG	—	15.00	30.00	45.00	90.00	—

KM# 186   2 REALES
0.9030 Silver **Ruler:** Ferdinand VII **Obv:** Local arms with
flowers and castles **Rev:** Mountain **Note:** Mint marks: Z, ZS,
Zs.

Date	Mintage	Good	VG	F	VF	XF
1810 Rare	—	—	—	—	—	—
1811	—	25.00	40.00	70.00	120	—

Note: Date aligned with legend

KM# 187   2 REALES
0.9030 Silver **Ruler:** Ferdinand VII **Obv:** Royal arms **Rev:**
Mountain above L. V. O **Rev. Legend:** MONEDA
PROVISIONAL DE ZACATECAS **Note:** Mint marks: Z, ZS, Zs.

Date	Mintage	Good	VG	F	VF	XF
1811	—	15.00	30.00	60.00	100	—

KM# 188   2 REALES
0.9030 Silver **Ruler:** Ferdinand VII **Obv:** Armored bust **Obv.**
Legend: FERDIN. VII **Rev:** Crowned arms, pillars **Rev.**
Legend: MONEDA PROVISIONAL DE ZACATECAS **Note:**
Mint marks: Z, ZS, Zs.

Date	Mintage	Good	VG	F	VF	XF
1811	—	35.00	65.00	135	225	—
1812	—	30.00	60.00	125	200	—

KM# 92.1   2 REALES
6.7700 g., 0.9030 Silver .1966 oz. ASW **Ruler:** Ferdinand VII
Obv: Large armored bust of Ferdinand VII **Obv. Legend:**
FERDIN. VII **Rev:** Crowned arms, pillars **Note:** Mint marks:
Z, ZS, Zs.

Date	Mintage	Good	VG	F	VF	XF
1813 FP	—	35.00	50.00	75.00	125	—
1814 FP	—	35.00	50.00	75.00	125	—
1814 AG	—	35.00	50.00	75.00	125	—
1815 AG	—	6.50	12.50	25.00	55.00	—
1816 AG	—	6.50	12.50	25.00	55.00	—
1817 AG	—	6.50	12.50	25.00	55.00	—
1818 AG	—	6.50	12.50	25.00	55.00	—

KM# 93.4   2 REALES
6.7700 g., 0.9030 Silver .1966 oz. ASW **Ruler:** Ferdinand VII
Obv: Draped bust of Ferdinand VII **Obv. Legend:** FERDIN.
VII **Rev:** Crowned arms, pillars **Note:** Mint marks: Z, ZS, Zs.

Date	Mintage	VG	F	VF	XF	Unc
1818 AG	—	6.50	12.50	25.00	50.00	—
1819 AG	—	10.00	20.00	40.00	85.00	—
1819 AG Reversed 'S' in HISPAN	—	10.00	20.00	40.00	85.00	—
1820 AG	—	10.00	20.00	40.00	85.00	—
1820 RG	—	10.00	20.00	40.00	85.00	—
1821 AG	—	10.00	20.00	40.00	85.00	—
1821 AZ/RG	—	10.00	20.00	40.00	85.00	—
1821 AZ	—	10.00	20.00	40.00	85.00	—
1821 RG	—	10.00	20.00	40.00	85.00	—
1822 AG	—	10.00	20.00	40.00	85.00	—
1822 RG	—	10.00	20.00	40.00	85.00	—

KM# A92 2 REALES
6.7700 g., 0.9030 Silver .1966 oz. ASW **Ruler:** Ferdinand VII
Obv: Small armored bust of Ferdinand VII **Obv. Legend:**
FERDIN. VII **Rev:** Crowned arms, pillars **Note:** Mint marks:
Z, ZS, Zs.

Date	Mintage	Good	VG	F	VF	XF
1819 AG	—	45.00	100	200	400	—

KM# 189 8 REALES
0.9030 Silver **Ruler:** Ferdinand VII **Obv:** Local arm with flowers
and castles **Rev:** Mountain above L.V.O. **Note:** Mint Zacatecas.

Date	Mintage	Good	VG	F	VF	XF
1810	—	300	500	750	1,250	—
1811	—	100	150	225	350	—

Note: Date aligned with legend. Also exists with incomplete
date

KM# 190 8 REALES
0.9030 Silver **Ruler:** Ferdinand VII **Obv:** Royal arms **Obv.
Legend:** FERDIN. VII. DEI... **Rev:** Mountain above L. V. O
Rev. Legend: MONEDA PROVISIONAL DE ZACATECAS

Date	Mintage	Good	VG	F	VF	XF
1811	—	65.00	100	135	220	—

Note: Date aligned with legend

KM# 191 8 REALES
0.9030 Silver **Ruler:** Ferdinand VII **Obv:** Armored bust of
Ferdinand VII **Obv. Legend:** FERDIN. VII. 8.R. DEI... **Rev:**
Crowned arms, pillars **Rev. Legend:** MONEDA
PROVISIONAL DE ZACATECAS

Date	Mintage	Good	VG	F	VF	XF
1811	—	45.00	75.00	145	275	—
1812	—	50.00	85.00	160	300	—

KM# 192 8 REALES
0.9030 Silver **Ruler:** Ferdinand VII **Obv:** Draped bust of
Ferdinand VII **Obv. Legend:** FERDIN. VII. DEI... **Rev:**
Crowned arms, pillars **Rev. Legend:** MONEDA
PROVISIONAL DE ZACATECAS

Date	Mintage	Good	VG	F	VF	XF
1812	—	75.00	150	275	450	—

KM# 111.5 8 REALES
27.0700 g., 0.9030 Silver .7860 oz. ASW **Ruler:**
Ferdinand VII **Obv:** Draped bust of Ferdinand VII **Obv.
Legend:** FERDIN. VII. DEI. GRATIA **Rev:** Crowned arms,
pillars **Rev. Legend:** HISPAN. ET IND. REX **Note:** Mint mark:
Zs. Several bust types exist for the 1821 issues.

Date	Mintage	VG	F	VF	XF	Unc
1813 FP	—	75.00	125	175	275	—
1814 FP	—	150	250	350	450	—

Date	Mintage	VG	F	VF	XF	Unc
1814 AG	—	100	150	200	300	—
1814 AG D over horizontal D in IND	—	125	175	225	325	—
1814 AG/FP	—	100	150	200	300	—
1815 AG	—	50.00	100	150	250	—
1816 AG	—	35.00	50.00	65.00	125	—
1817 AG	—	35.00	50.00	65.00	125	—
1818 AG	—	30.00	40.00	50.00	100	—
1819 AG	—	30.00	40.00	50.00	100	—
1819 AG 'GRATIA' error	—	100	200	300	400	—
1820 AG 18/11 error	—	100	200	300	400	—
1820 AG	—	30.00	40.00	50.00	100	—
1820 RG	—	30.00	40.00	50.00	100	—
1821/81 RG	—	75.00	150	225	300	—
1821 RG	—	15.00	25.00	35.00	65.00	—
1821 AZ/RG	—	50.00	100	150	200	—
1821 AZ	—	50.00	100	150	200	—
1822 RG	—	40.00	60.00	100	175	—

KM# 111.6   8 REALES
27.0700 g., 0.9030 Silver .7860 oz. ASW **Ruler:**
Ferdinand VII **Obv:** Draped bust of Ferdinand VII **Obv.**
Legend: FERDIN. VII. DEI. GRATIA **Rev:** Crown with lower
rear arc **Rev. Legend:** HISAV. ET IND. REX

Date	Mintage	VG	F	VF	XF	Unc
1821 Zs	—	160	320	550	750	—

ROYALIST COUNTERMARKED COINAGE

LCM - La Comandancia Militar

Crown and Flag

This countermark exists in 15 various sizes.

KM# 193.1   2 REALES
0.9030 Silver **Issuer:** La Comandancia Militar **Countermark:**
LCM **Note:** Countermark on Mexico KM#92.

CM Date	Host Date	Good	VG	F	VF	XF
ND	1809 TH	85.00	165	250	400	—

KM# 193.2   2 REALES
0.9030 Silver **Issuer:** La Comandancia Militar, (The LCM
countermark exists in 15 various sizes) **Countermark:** LCM
Note: Countermark on Mexico KM#186.

CM Date	Host Date	Good	VG	F	VF	XF
ND	1811	85.00	165	250	400	—

KM# 194.1   8 REALES
Cast Silver **Issuer:** La Comandancia Militar, (The LCM
countermark exists in 15 various sizes) **Countermark:** LCM
Note: Countermark on Chihuahua KM#123.

CM Date	Host Date	Good	VG	F	VF	XF
ND	1811 RP	100	200	300	450	—
ND	1812 RP	100	200	300	450	—

KM# 194.2   8 REALES
0.9030 Silver **Issuer:** La Comandancia Militar, The LCM
countermark exists in 15 different sizes **Countermark:** LCM
Note: Countermark on Chihuahua KM#111.1 struck over
KM#123.

CM Date	Host Date	Good	VG	F	VF	XF
ND	1815 RP	200	275	400	550	—
ND	1817 RP	125	175	225	300	—
ND	1820 RP	125	175	225	300	—
ND	1821 RP	125	175	225	300	—

KM# 194.3   8 REALES
0.9030 Silver **Issuer:** La Comandancia Militar, The LCM
countermark exists in 15 different sizes **Countermark:** LCM
Note: Countermark on Durango KM#111.2.

CM Date	Host Date	Good	VG	F	VF	XF
ND	1812 RM	70.00	125	190	250	—
ND	1821 CG	70.00	125	190	250	—

KM# 194.4   8 REALES
0.9030 Silver **Issuer:** La Comandancia Militar, The LCM
countermark exists in 15 different sizes **Countermark:** LCM
Note: Countermark on Guadalajara KM#111.3.

CM Date	Host Date	Good	VG	F	VF	XF
ND	1813 MR	150	225	300	475	—

KM# 194.5   8 REALES
0.9030 Silver **Issuer:** La Comandancia Militar, The LCM
countermark exists in 15 different sizes **Countermark:** LCM
Note: Countermark on Guanajuato KM#111.4.

CM Date	Host Date	Good	VG	F	VF	XF
ND	1813 JJ	225	350	475	650	—

KM# 194.6 8 REALES
0.9030 Silver **Issuer:** La Comandancia Militar, The LCM
countermark exists in 15 different sizes **Countermark:** LCM
Note: Countermark on Nueva Viscaya KM#165.

CM Date	Host Date	Good	VG	F	VF	XF
ND	1811 RM	—	—	—	—	—
	Rare					

KM# 194.7 8 REALES
0.9030 Silver **Issuer:** La Comandancia Militar, The LCM
countermark exists in 15 different sizes **Countermark:** LCM
Note: Countermark on Mexico KM#111.

CM Date	Host Date	Good	VG	F	VF	XF
ND	1811 HJ	125	225	350	600	—
ND	1812 JJ	110	135	190	325	—
ND	1817 JJ	50.00	65.00	85.00	125	—
ND	1818 JJ	50.00	65.00	85.00	125	—
ND	1820 JJ	—	—	—	—	—

KM# 194.8 8 REALES
0.9030 Silver **Issuer:** La Comandancia Militar, The LCM
countermark exists in 15 different sizes **Countermark:** LCM
Note: Countermark on Sombrerete KM#176.

CM Date	Host Date	Good	VG	F	VF	XF
ND	1811 Rare	—	—	—	—	—
ND	1812 Rare	—	—	—	—	—

KM# 194.9 8 REALES
0.9030 Silver **Issuer:** La Comandancia Militar, The LCM
countermark exists in 15 different sizes **Countermark:** LCM
Note: Countermark on Zacatecas KM#190.

CM Date	Host Date	Good	VG	F	VF	XF
ND	1811	225	350	450	—	—

KM# 194.10 8 REALES
0.9030 Silver **Issuer:** La Comandancia Militar, The LCM
countermark exists in 15 different sizes **Countermark:** LCM
Note: Countermark on Zacatecas KM#111.5.

CM Date	Host Date	Good	VG	F	VF	XF
ND	1813 FP	—	—	—	—	—
ND	1814 AG	—	—	—	—	—
ND	1822 RG	—	—	—	—	—

LCV - Las Cajas de Veracruz

The Royal Treasury of the City of Veracruz

KM# 195 7 REALES
Silver **Issuer:** Las Cajas de Veracruz, The Royal Treasury
of the City of Veracruz **Countermark:** LCV **Note:**
Countermark and 7 on underweight 8 Reales.

CM Date	Host Date	Good	VG	F	VF	XF
ND	ND Rare	—	—	—	—	—

Note: Most examples are counterfeit

KM# 196 7-1/4 REALES
Silver **Issuer:** Las Cajas de Veracruz, The Royal Treasury
of the City of Veracruz **Countermark:** LCV **Note:**
Countermark and 7-1/4 on underweight 8 Reales.

CM Date	Host Date	Good	VG	F	VF	XF
ND	ND Rare	—	—	—	—	—

Note: Most examples are counterfeit

KM# 197 7-1/2 REALES
Silver **Issuer:** Las Cajas de Veracruz, The Royal Treasury
of the City of Veracruz **Countermark:** LCV **Note:**
Countermark and 7-1/2 on underweight 8 Reales.

CM Date	Host Date	Good	VG	F	VF	XF
ND	ND Rare	—	—	—	—	—

Note: Most examples are counterfeit

KM# 198   7-3/4 REALES
Silver **Issuer:** Las Cajas de Veracruz, The Royal Treasury
of the City of Veracruz **Countermark:** LCV **Note:**
Countermark and 7-3/4 on underweight 8 Reales.

CM Date	Host Date	Good	VG	F	VF	XF
ND	ND	300	375	450	600	—

Note: Many examples are counterfeit

KM# A198   8 REALES
Cast Silver **Issuer:** Las Cajas de Veracruz, The Royal
Treasury of the City of Veracruz **Countermark:** LCV **Note:**
Countermark on Chihuahua KM#123.

CM Date	Host Date	Good	VG	F	VF	XF
ND	1811 RP	150	250	400	500	—

KM# 199   8 REALES
Silver **Issuer:** Las Cajas de Veracruz, The Royal Treasury
of the City of Veracruz **Countermark:** LCV **Note:**
Countermark on Zacatecas KM#191.

CM Date	Host Date	Good	VG	F	VF	XF
ND	1811	175	225	275	350	—
ND	1812	175	225	275	350	—

MS (Monogram) - Manuel Salcedo

KM# 200   8 REALES
Silver **Issuer:** Manuel Salcedo **Countermark:** MS
monogram **Note:** Countermark on Mexico KM#110.

CM Date	Host Date	Good	VG	F	VF	XF
ND	1809 TH	150	250	400	500	—
ND	1810 HJ	150	250	400	500	—
ND	1811 HJ	150	250	400	500	—

MVA - Monclova

KM# 202.3   8 REALES
Silver **Issuer:** Monclova, MVA **Countermark:** MVA/1812
Note: Countermark on cast Mexico KM#110.

CM Date	Host Date	Good	VG	F	VF	XF
1812	1809 HJ	100	150	250	350	—
1812	1809 TH	100	150	250	350	—
1812	1810 HJ	100	150	250	350	—

KM# 201 8 REALES
Silver **Issuer:** Monclova, MVA **Countermark:** MVA/1811
Note: Countermark on Chihuahua KM#111.1; struck over
cast Mexico KM#110.

CM Date	Host Date	Good	VG	F	VF	XF
ND	1809	250	450	700	1,000	—
ND	1816 RP	250	450	700	1,000	—
ND	1821 RP	250	450	700	1,000	—

KM# 202.5 8 REALES
Silver **Issuer:** Monclova, MVA **Countermark:** MVA/1812
Note: Countermark on Zacatecas KM#189.

CM Date	Host Date	Good	VG	F	VF	XF
1812	1813	300	350	450	550	—

KM# 202.1 8 REALES
Silver **Issuer:** Monclova, MVA **Countermark:** MVA/1812
Note: Countermark on Chihuahua KM#111.1; struck over
cast Mexico KM#109.

CM Date	Host Date	Good	VG	F	VF	XF
1812	1810	125	175	250	350	—

KM# 202.2 8 REALES
Silver **Issuer:** Monclova, MVA **Countermark:** MVA/1812
Note: Countermark on cast Mexico KM#109.

CM Date	Host Date	Good	VG	F	VF	XF
1812	1798 FM	100	150	250	350	—
1812	1802 FT	100	150	250	350	—

INSURGENT COINAGE

American Congress

KM# 216 REAL
0.9030 Silver **Issuer:** American Congress **Obv:** Eagle on
cactus **Obv. Legend:** CONGRESO AMERICANO **Rev:** F. 7
on spread mantle **Rev. Legend:** DEPOSIT D.L. AUCTORI J

Date	Mintage	Good	VG	F	VF	XF
ND(1813)	—	35.00	75.00	120	200	—

KM# 217 REAL
0.9030 Silver **Issuer:** American Congress **Obv:** Eagle on
cactus **Obv. Legend:** CONGR. AMER. **Rev:** F. 7 on spread
mantle **Rev. Legend:** DEPOS. D. L. AUT. D.

Date	Mintage	Good	VG	F	VF	XF
ND(1813)	—	35.00	75.00	120	200	—

National Congress

KM# 209 1/2 REAL
Struck Copper **Issuer:** National Congress **Obv:** Eagle on
bridge **Obv. Legend:** VICE FERD. VII DEI GRATIA ET **Rev:**
Value, bow quiver, etc **Rev. Legend:** S. P. CONG. NAT. IND.

Date	Mintage	Good	VG	F	VF	XF
1811	—	45.00	85.00	150	200	—
1812	—	27.50	60.00	100	150	—
1813	—	27.50	60.00	100	150	—
1814	—	45.00	85.00	150	200	—

KM# 210 1/2 REAL
0.9030 Silver **Issuer:** National Congress **Obv:** Eagle on
bridge **Obv. Legend:** VICE FERD. VII DEI GRATIA ET **Rev:**
Value, bow quiver, etc **Rev. Legend:** S. P. CONG. NAT. IND.

Date	Mintage	Good	VG	F	VF	XF
1812	—	27.50	60.00	100	150	—
1813	—	45.00	90.00	175	275	—

Note: 1812 exists with the date reading inwards and out-
wards

KM# 211 REAL
0.9030 Silver **Issuer:** National Congress **Obv:** Eagle on
bridge **Obv. Legend:** VICE FERD. VII DEI GRATIA ET **Rev:**
Value, bow quiver, etc **Rev. Legend:** S. P. CONG. NAT. IND.

Date	Mintage	Good	VG	F	VF	XF
1812	—	22.50	45.00	80.00	125	—
1813	—	22.50	45.00	80.00	125	—

Note: 1812 exists with the date reading either inward or
outward

KM# 212   2 REALES
Struck Copper   **Issuer:** National Congress **Obv:** Eagle on
bridge **Obv. Legend:** VICE FERD. VII DEI GRATIA ET **Rev:**
Value, bow quiver, etc **Rev. Legend:** S. P. CONG. NAT. IND.

Date	Mintage	Good	VG	F	VF	XF
1812	—	100	150	200	275	—
1813	—	23.50	50.00	75.00	120	—
1814	—	32.50	75.00	110	165	—

KM# A213   2 REALES
Struck Silver   **Issuer:** National Congress **Obv:** Eagle on
bridge **Obv. Legend:** VICE FERD. VII DEI GRATIA ET **Rev:**
Value, bow, quiver, etc **Rev. Legend:** S. P. CONG. NAT.
IND.

Date	Mintage	Good	VG	F	VF	XF
1813	—	950	1,750	3,000	4,850	—

KM# 213   2 REALES
0.9030 Silver   **Issuer:** National Congress **Obv:** Eagle on
bridge in shield, denomination at sides **Obv. Legend:** VICE
FERD. VII DEI GRATIA ET **Rev:** Canon, quiver, arm, etc

Date	Mintage	Good	VG	F	VF	XF
1813	—	75.00	155	265	375	—

Note: These dies were believed to be intended for the striking of 2 Escudos

KM# 214   4 REALES
0.9030 Silver **Issuer:** National Congress **Obv:** Eagle on bridge
Obv. Legend: VICE FERD. VII DEI GRATIA ET **Rev:** Value,
bow, quiver, etc **Rev. Legend:** S. P. CONG. NAT. IND.

Date	Mintage	Good	VG	F	VF	XF
1813	—	600	1,200	2,450	4,400	—

KM# 215.1   8 REALES
0.9030 Silver   **Issuer:** National Congress **Obv:** Small
crowned eagle **Obv. Legend:** VICE FERD. VII DEI GRATIA
ET **Rev:** Value, bow, quiver, etc **Rev. Legend:** S. P. CONG.
NAT. IND.

Date	Mintage	Good	VG	F	VF	XF
1812Mo	—	600	1,150	2,350	4,250	—

KM# 215.2   8 REALES
0.9030 Silver   **Issuer:** National Congress **Obv:** Large
crowned eagle **Obv. Legend:** VICE FERD. VII DEI GRATIA
ET **Rev:** Value, bow, quiver, etc **Rev. Legend:** S. P. CONG.
NAT. IND.

Date	Mintage	Good	VG	F	VF	XF
1813Mo	—	600	1,150	2,350	4,250	—

Supreme National Congress of America

PDV - Provisional de Valladolid

VTIL - Util = useful

(Refer to Multiple countermarks)

KM# 203   1/2 REAL
Struck Copper   **Issuer:** Supreme National Congress of
America **Obv:** Eagle on bridge **Obv. Legend:** FERDIN. VII
DEI GRATIA **Rev:** Value, bow, quiver, etc **Rev. Legend:** S.
P. CONG. NAT. IND. GUV.T.

Date	Mintage	Good	VG	F	VF	XF
1811	—	27.50	45.00	60.00	100	—
1812	—	27.50	45.00	60.00	100	—
1813	—	27.50	45.00	60.00	100	—
1814	—	27.50	45.00	60.00	100	—

KM# 204   REAL
Struck Copper   **Issuer:** Supreme National Congress of
America **Obv:** Eagle on bridge **Obv. Legend:** FERDIN. VII
DEI GRATIA **Rev:** Value, bow, quiver, etc **Rev. Legend:** S.
P. CONG. NAT. IND. GUV.T.

Date	Mintage	Good	VG	F	VF	XF
1811	—	45.00	75.00	125	200	—

KM# 205   2 REALES
Struck Copper   **Issuer:** Supreme National Congress of
America **Obv:** Eagle on bridge **Obv. Legend:** FERDIN. VII
DEI GRATIA **Rev:** Value, bow, quiver, etc

Date	Mintage	Good	VG	F	VF	XF
1812	—	225	325	475	750	—

KM# 206   8 REALES
Cast Silver **Issuer:** Supreme National Congress of America
Obv: Eagle on bridge **Obv. Legend:** FERDIN. VII DEI
GRATIA **Rev:** Value, bow, quiver, etc

Date	Mintage	Good	VG	F	VF	XF
1811	—	150	250	350	500	—
1812	—	150	250	350	500	—

KM# 207   8 REALES
Struck Silver **Issuer:** Supreme National Congress of America
Obv: Eagle on bridge **Obv. Legend:** FERDIN. VII DEI
GRATIA **Rev:** Value, bow, quiver, etc

Date	Mintage	Good	VG	F	VF	XF
1811	—	—	—	—	—	—
1812	—	300	600	1,000	1,500	—

KM# 208   8 REALES
Struck Copper **Issuer:** Supreme National Congress of
America **Obv:** Eagle on bridge **Obv. Legend:** FERDIN. VII...
Rev: Bow, sword and quiver **Rev. Legend:** PROVICIONAL
POR LA SUPREMA JUNTA DE AMERICA

Date	Mintage	Good	VG	F	VF	XF
1811	—	100	150	225	450	—
1812	—	100	150	225	450	—

MEXICO-REVOLUTIONARY

AGUASCALIENTES

Aguascalientes is a state in central Mexico. Its coin issues, struck by authority of Pancho Villa, represent his deepest penetration into the Mexican heartland. Lack of silver made it necessary to make all denominations in copper.

FRANCISCO PANCHO VILLA

REVOLUTIONARY COINAGE

KM# 601   CENTAVO
Copper

Date	Mintage	VG	F	VF	XF	Unc
1915	—	30.00	45.00	70.00	100	—
Note: Large date, reeded edge						
1915	—	250	350	450	—	—
Note: Large date, plain edge						
1915	—	30.00	40.00	60.00	90.00	—
Note: Small date, reeded edge						
1915	—	30.00	50.00	75.00	115	—
Note: Small date, plain edge						

KM# 601a   CENTAVO
Silver

Date	Mintage	F	VF	XF	Unc	BU
1915 Large date	50	—	400	650	—	—
1915 Small date	Inc. above	—	400	650	—	—

KM# 602.1   2 CENTAVOS
Copper

Date	Mintage	VG	F	VF	XF	Unc
1915	—	40.00	100	200	350	—
Note: Round front 2, plain edge						

KM# 602.2   2 CENTAVOS
Copper

Date	Mintage	VG	F	VF	XF	Unc
1915	—	35.00	60.00	85.00	200	—
Note: Square front 2, reeded edge						
1915 Plain edge	—	50.00	90.00	200	300	—
Note: Square front 2						

KM# 602a   2 CENTAVOS
Silver

Date	Mintage	F	VF	XF	Unc	BU
1915	50	—	700	1,200	—	—

KM# 603   5 CENTAVOS
Copper

Date	Mintage	VG	F	VF	XF	Unc
1915 Plain edge; Rare	—	—	—	—	—	—
1915 Reeded edge	—	10.00	20.00	30.00	45.00	—

KM# 604.1   5 CENTAVOS
Copper   **Rev:** Vertically shaded 5

Date	Mintage	VG	F	VF	XF	Unc
1915	—	20.00	30.00	40.00	60.00	—
Note: Reeded edge						
1915	—	100	150	225	325	—
Note: Plain edge						

KM# 604.2   5 CENTAVOS
Copper   **Rev:** Horizontally shaded 5

Date	Mintage	VG	F	VF	XF	Unc
1915	—	25.00	30.00	50.00	95.00	—
Note: Reeded edge						
1915	—	30.00	40.00	60.00	100	—
Note: Plain edge						

KM# 604a   5 CENTAVOS
Silver

Date	Mintage	F	VF	XF	Unc	BU
1915	50	—	2,500	3,500	—	—

KM# 606   20 CENTAVOS
Copper   **Obv:** Blunt winged eagle   **Rev:** With wavy-bottomed 2

Date	Mintage	VG	F	VF	XF	Unc
1915 Reeded edge	—	10.00	15.00	30.00	60.00	—

KM# 605 20 CENTAVOS
Copper, 29.7 mm. **Obv:** Blunt winged eagle **Rev:** With flat-bottomed 2

Date	Mintage	VG	F	VF	XF	Unc
1915 Reeded edge	—	10.00	15.00	30.00	60.00	—

KM# 605a 20 CENTAVOS
Silver **Obv:** Blunt winged eagle **Rev:** With flat-bottomed 2
Note: Piedfort.

Date	Mintage	F	VF	XF	Unc	BU
1915	50	—	3,000	3,800	—	—

Note: Plain edge

KM# 600 20 CENTAVOS
Copper **Obv:** Pointed winged eagle **Rev:** With wavy-bottomed 2 **Edge:** Reeded

Date	Mintage	VG	F	VF	XF	Unc
1915	—	15.00	20.00	35.00	60.00	—

KM# 600a 20 CENTAVOS
Silver **Obv:** Pointed winged eagle **Rev:** With wavy-bottomed 2

Date	Mintage	VG	F	VF	XF	Unc
1915	—	1,000	1,500	2,000	3,000	—

Note: Varieties exist with both plain and milled edges and many variations in the shading of the numerals

CHIHUAHUA

Chihuahua is a northern state of Mexico bordering the U.S. It was the arena that introduced Pancho Villa to the world. Villa, an outlaw, was given a title when asked by Madero to participate in maintaining order during Madero's presidency. After Madero's death in February 1913, Villa became a persuasive leader. Chihuahua was where he made his first coins - the Parral series. The *Army of the North* pesos also came from this state. This coin helped Villa recruit soldiers because of his ability to pay in silver while others were paying in worthless paper money.

HIDALGO DEL PARRAL
Fuerzas Constitucionalistas

REVOLUTIONARY COINAGE

KM# 607 2 CENTAVOS
Copper

Date	Mintage	VG	F	VF	XF	Unc
1913	—	5.00	10.00	15.00	25.00	—

KM# 607a 2 CENTAVOS
Brass

Date	Mintage	VG	F	VF	XF	Unc
1913	—	95.00	150	200	350	—

KM# 608 50 CENTAVOS
Silver **Edge:** Reeded

Date	Mintage	VG	F	VF	XF	Unc
1913	—	15.00	30.00	50.00	75.00	—

KM# 609 50 CENTAVOS
Silver **Edge:** Plain

Date	Mintage	VG	F	VF	XF	Unc
1913	—	50.00	70.00	95.00	125	—

KM# 609a 50 CENTAVOS
Copper **Edge:** Plain

Date	Mintage	VG	F	VF	XF	Unc
1913 rare	—	125	225	375	450	—

KM# 610 PESO
Silver **Rev:** 1 through PESO and ball, BOLITA

Date	Mintage	VG	F	VF	XF	Unc
1913	—	1,200	1,800	2,500	3,000	—

KM# 611 PESO
Silver **Obv:** Similar to KM#610 **Rev:** 1 above PESO **Note:** Well struck counterfeits of this coin exist with the dot at the end of the word Peso even with the bottom of the O. On legitimate pieces the dot is slightly higher.

Date	Mintage	VG	F	VF	XF	Unc
1913	—	35.00	40.00	55.00	135	—

CONSTITUTIONALIST ARMY
Ejercito Constitucionalista

REVOLUTIONARY COINAGE

KM# 612   5 CENTAVOS
Copper   **Rev:** Small rosettes at date

Date	Mintage	VG	F	VF	XF	Unc
1914	—	25.00	35.00	60.00	95.00	—

KM# 613   5 CENTAVOS
Copper   **Rev:** Large ornamental spear heads at date **Note:** Numerous varieties exist.

Date	Mintage	VG	F	VF	XF	Unc
1914	—	1.00	2.50	4.00	10.00	—
1915	—	1.00	2.50	4.00	10.00	—

KM# 613a   5 CENTAVOS
Brass   **Rev:** Large ornamental spear heads at date **Note:** Numerous varieties exist.

Date	Mintage	VG	F	VF	XF	Unc
1914	—	2.00	3.00	8.00	10.00	—
1915	—	2.00	3.00	8.00	10.00	—

KM# 613b   5 CENTAVOS
Cast Copper   **Rev:** Large ornamental spear heads at date

Date	Mintage	VG	F	VF	XF	Unc
1914	—	75.00	150	250	350	—

KM# 614   5 CENTAVOS
Copper   **Rev:** Double lined V

Date	Mintage	VG	F	VF	XF	Unc
1915 MS	—	150	250	325	500	—
1915 SS Unique	—	—	—	—	—	—

KM# 614a   5 CENTAVOS
Copper   **Rev:** Solid V

Date	Mintage	VG	F	VF	XF	Unc
1915 Rare	—	—	—	—	—	—

KM# 614b   5 CENTAVOS
Copper   **Obv:** KM#614 **Rev:** Reverse of KM#613 **Note:** Mule.

Date	Mintage	VG	F	VF	XF	Unc
1915	—	—	350	—	—	—

KM# 614c   5 CENTAVOS
Copper   **Obv:** KM#614 **Rev:** Obverse of KM#612 **Note:** Mule.

Date	Mintage	VG	F	VF	XF	Unc
1915 Rare	—	—	—	—	—	—

KM# 615   10 CENTAVOS
Copper

Date	Mintage	VG	F	VF	XF	Unc
1915	—	1.25	2.50	3.50	5.00	—

KM# 615a   10 CENTAVOS
Brass

Date	Mintage	VG	F	VF	XF	Unc
1915	—	1.75	5.00	15.00	20.00	—

Note: Many varieties exist

ARMY OF THE NORTH
Ejercito Del Norte

REVOLUTIONARY COINAGE

KM# 619   PESO
Silver

Date	Mintage	VG	F	VF	XF	Unc
1915	—	20.00	30.00	40.00	100	—

KM# 619a   PESO
Copper

Date	Mintage	VG	F	VF	XF	Unc
1915	—	500	1,000	1,500	2,200	—

KM# 619b   PESO
Brass   **Note:** Uniface obverse

Date	Mintage	VG	F	VF	XF	Unc
1915 Rare	—	—	—	—	—	—

DURANGO

A state in north central Mexico. Another area of operation for Pancho Villa. The *Muera Huerta* peso originates in this state. The coins were made in Cuencame under the orders of Generals Cemceros and Contreras.

CUENCAME
Muera Huerta (Death to Huerta)

REVOLUTIONARY COINAGE

KM# 620 PESO
Silver **Rev:** 1914 below UN PESO with three stars at each side

Date	Mintage	VG	F	VF	XF	Unc
1914	—	800	1,400	2,000	4,000	—

KM# 621 PESO
Silver **Obv:** Continuous border **Rev:** Continuous border

Date	Mintage	VG	F	VF	XF	Unc
1914	—	75.00	100	150	250	550

KM# 621a PESO
Copper **Obv:** Continuous border **Rev:** Continuous border
Note: Varieties exist.

Date	Mintage	VG	F	VF	XF	Unc
1914	—	300	500	750	1,500	—

KM# 621b PESO
Brass

Date	Mintage	VG	F	VF	XF	Unc
1914	—	—	800	1,000	2,000	

KM# 622 PESO
Silver **Obv:** Dot and dash border **Rev:** Continuous border
Note: The so-called 20 Pesos gold Muera Huerta pieces are modern fantasies. Refer to Unusual World Coins, 4th edition, ©2005, KP Books, Inc.

Date	Mintage	VG	F	VF	XF	Unc
1914	—	60.00	100	150	225	500

ESTADO DE DURANGO

REVOLUTIONARY COINAGE

KM# 625 CENTAVO
Copper

Date	Mintage	VG	F	VF	XF	Unc
1914	—	2.00	4.00	8.00	12.00	—

KM# 625a CENTAVO
Brass

Date	Mintage	VG	F	VF	XF	Unc
1914	—	75.00	150	300	400	—

KM# 625b CENTAVO
Lead

Date	Mintage	VG	F	VF	XF	Unc
1914	—	20.00	40.00	65.00	90.00	—

KM# 625c CENTAVO
Copper **Obv:** Obverse of KM#625 **Rev:** Obverse of KM#625

Date	Mintage	VG	F	VF	XF	Unc
1914	—	25.00	50.00	80.00	125	—

KM# 624 CENTAVO
Cast Lead **Rev:** Retrograde N

Date	Mintage	VG	F	VF	XF	Unc
1914	—	45.00	75.00	100	200	—

KM# 626   CENTAVO
Copper

Date	Mintage	VG	F	VF	XF	Unc
1914	—	15.00	20.00	35.00	45.00	—

KM# 626a   CENTAVO
Brass

Date	Mintage	VG	F	VF	XF	Unc
1914	—	75.00	100	200	350	—

KM# 626b   CENTAVO
Lead

Date	Mintage	VG	F	VF	XF	Unc
1914	—	20.00	25.00	40.00	60.00	—

Note: Varieties in size exist

KM# 627   CENTAVO
Copper   **Obv:** Three stars below date **Rev:** Retrograde N

Date	Mintage	VG	F	VF	XF	Unc
1914	—	6.00	10.00	15.00	20.00	—

KM# 627a   CENTAVO
Lead   **Obv:** Three stars below date **Rev:** Retrograde N

Date	Mintage	VG	F	VF	XF	Unc
1914	—	20.00	30.00	40.00	50.00	—

KM# 628   CENTAVO
Aluminum   **Obv:** Eagle on cactus

Date	Mintage	VG	F	VF	XF	Unc
1914	—	0.65	1.00	2.00	3.00	6.00

KM# 629   5 CENTAVOS
Copper   **Obv. Legend:** ESTADO DE DURANGO **Rev:** Large 5

Date	Mintage	VG	F	VF	XF	Unc
1914	—	2.00	3.00	5.00	10.00	—

KM# 630   5 CENTAVOS
Copper   **Obv. Legend:** E. DE DURANGO **Rev:** Thin 5

Date	Mintage	VG	F	VF	XF	Unc
1914	—	125	275	375	600	—

KM# 631   5 CENTAVOS
Copper   **Obv. Legend:** E. DE DURANGO **Rev:** Thick 5

Date	Mintage	VG	F	VF	XF	Unc
1914	—	1.25	3.00	5.00	11.00	—

KM# 631a   5 CENTAVOS
Brass   **Obv. Legend:** E. DE DURANGO **Rev:** Thick 5

Date	Mintage	VG	F	VF	XF	Unc
1914	—	30.00	40.00	50.00	85.00	—

KM# 631b   5 CENTAVOS
Lead   **Obv. Legend:** E. DE DURANGO **Rev:** Thick 5

Date	Mintage	VG	F	VF	XF	Unc
1914	—	45.00	70.00	100	180	—

KM# 632   5 CENTAVOS
Copper   **Obv. Legend:** E. DE DURANGO **Rev:** Denomination V

Date	Mintage	VG	F	VF	XF	Unc
1914	—	4.00	8.00	15.00	35.00	—

KM# 632a   5 CENTAVOS
Lead   **Obv. Legend:** E. DE DURANGO **Rev:** Denomination V

Date	Mintage	VG	F	VF	XF	Unc
1914	—	50.00	75.00	100	150	—

KM# 633   5 CENTAVOS
Lead   **Obv:** Three stars below 1914 **Rev:** 5 CVS

Date	Mintage	VG	F	VF	XF	Unc
1914	—	—	500	1,000	—	—

KM# 634   5 CENTAVOS
Brass

Date	Mintage	VG	F	VF	XF	Unc
1914	—	0.50	1.00	2.00	3.50	—

KM# 634a   5 CENTAVOS
Copper   **Note:** There are numerous varieties of these general types of the Durango 1 and 5 Centavo pieces.

Date	Mintage	VG	F	VF	XF	Unc
1914	—	75.00	125	175	250	—

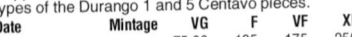

GUERRERO

Guerrero is a state on the southwestern coast of Mexico. It was one of the areas of operation of Zapata and his forces in the south of Mexico. The Zapata forces operated seven different mints in this state. The date ranges were from 1914 to 1917 and denominations from 2 Centavos to 2 Pesos. Some were cast but most were struck and the rarest coin of the group is the Suriana 1915 2 Pesos.

EMILIANO ZAPATA
(General Salgado)

REVOLUTIONARY COINAGE

KM# 638   2 CENTAVOS
Copper

Date	Mintage	VG	F	VF	XF	Unc
1915	—	75.00	125	175	250	—

KM# 635   3 CENTAVOS
Copper

Date	Mintage	VG	F	VF	XF	Unc
1915	—	500	1,000	1,500	2,000	—

KM# 636   5 CENTAVOS
Copper

Date	Mintage	VG	F	VF	XF	Unc
1915GRO	—	800	1,200	2,000	3,000	—

KM# 637.1   10 CENTAVOS
Copper   **Obv:** Snake head ends at L in REPUBLICA

Date	Mintage	VG	F	VF	XF	Unc
1915GRO	—	600	800	1,000	1,500	—

KM# 637.2   10 CENTAVOS
Copper   **Obv:** Snake head ends at C in REPUBLICA

Date	Mintage	VG	F	VF	XF	Unc
1915GRO	—	3.00	5.00	8.00	15.00	—

KM# 637.2a   10 CENTAVOS
Brass   **Obv:** Snake head ends at C in REPUBLICA

Date	Mintage	VG	F	VF	XF	Unc
1915GRO	—	8.00	15.00	25.00	50.00	—

KM# 637.2b   10 CENTAVOS
Lead   **Obv:** Snake head ends at C in REPUBLICA

Date	Mintage	VG	F	VF	XF	Unc
1915GRO	—	50.00	75.00	175	275	—

KM# 637.3   10 CENTAVOS
Copper   **Obv:** Snake head ends before A in REPUBLICA   **Rev:** Dot after date

Date	Mintage	VG	F	VF	XF	Unc
1915GRO	—	3.00	5.00	8.00	15.00	—

KM# 637.3a   10 CENTAVOS
Brass   **Obv:** Snake head ends before A in REPUBLICA   **Rev:** Dot after date

Date	Mintage	VG	F	VF	XF	Unc
1915GRO	—	8.00	15.00	25.00	50.00	—

KM# 639   25 CENTAVOS
Silver   **Obv:** Cap and rays

Date	Mintage	VG	F	VF	XF	Unc
1915	—	100	200	400	500	—

KM# 640   50 CENTAVOS
Silver   **Obv:** Cap and rays

Date	Mintage	VG	F	VF	XF	Unc
1915	—	900	1,500	2,100	3,000	—

KM# 641a   PESO (UN)
Copper

Date	Mintage	Good	VG	F	VF	XF
1914	—	—	100	150	225	900

KM# 642   PESO (UN)
0.3000 g., 1.0000 Gold-Silver   **Obv:** Star before and after UN PESO   **Rev:** Cap and rays

Date	Mintage	VG	F	VF	XF	Unc
1914	—	50.00	75.00	100	150	—
1915	—	600	1,000	1,500	1,800	—

KM# 641   PESO (UN)
0.3000 g., 1.0000 Gold-Silver **Obv:** Star before UN PESO
Rev: Cap and rays **Note:** Many die varieties exist.

Date	Mintage	VG	F	VF	XF	Unc
1914	—	15.00	25.00	35.00	65.00	—

KM# 643   2 PESOS (Dos)
0.5950 g., 1.0000 Gold-Silver **Rev:** Sun and mountains **Note:** Many varieties exist.

Date	Mintage	VG	F	VF	XF	Unc
1914GRO	—	12.00	20.00	32.00	60.00	—

KM# 643a   2 PESOS (Dos)
Copper

Date	Mintage	Good	VG	F	VF	XF
1914	—	—	—	900	1,000	1,300

KM# 644   2 PESOS (Dos)
0.5950 g., 1.0000 Gold-Silver **Rev:** Sun and mountains

Date	Mintage	VG	F	VF	XF	Unc
1915GRO	—	65.00	85.00	160	200	—

KM# 644a   2 PESOS (Dos)
Copper **Rev:** Sun and mountains

Date	Mintage	VG	F	VF	XF	Unc
1915GRO	—	400	600	800	1,000	—

ATLIXTAC

REVOLUTIONARY COINAGE

KM# 645   10 CENTAVOS
Copper

Date	Mintage	VG	F	VF	XF	Unc
1915	—	3.00	5.00	8.00	15.00	—

KM# 646   10 CENTAVOS
Copper **Obv:** Stars in legend

Date	Mintage	VG	F	VF	XF	Unc
1915	—	3.00	5.00	8.00	15.00	—

CACAHUATEPEC

REVOLUTIONARY COINAGE

KM# 648   5 CENTAVOS
Copper

Date	Mintage	VG	F	VF	XF	Unc
1917	—	12.00	25.00	40.00	75.00	—

KM# 649   20 CENTAVOS
Silver **Rev:** Cap and rays above denomination

Date	Mintage	VG	F	VF	XF	Unc
1917	—	75.00	125	300	350	—

KM# 650   50 CENTAVOS
Silver **Rev:** Cap and rays above denomination

Date	Mintage	VG	F	VF	XF	Unc
1917	—	10.00	30.00	45.00	90.00	—

KM# 651   PESO (UN)
Silver **Rev:** Cap and rays

Date	Mintage	VG	F	VF	XF	Unc
1917 L.V. Go	—	1,250	2,250	3,500	5,000	—

CACALOTEPEC

REVOLUTIONARY COINAGE

KM# 652   20 CENTAVOS
Silver **Rev:** Cap and rays above denomination

Date	Mintage	VG	F	VF	XF	Unc
1917	—	1,000	1,800	3,000	4,000	—

CAMPO MORADO

REVOLUTIONARY COINAGE

KM# 653   5 CENTAVOS
Copper

Date	Mintage	VG	F	VF	XF	Unc
1915 C.M.	—	9.00	15.00	22.50	35.00	—

KM# 654   10 CENTAVOS
Copper

Date	Mintage	VG	F	VF	XF	Unc
1915 C.M. GRO	—	6.00	10.00	17.50	27.50	—

KM# 655   20 CENTAVOS
Copper

Date	Mintage	VG	F	VF	XF	Unc
1915 C.M. GRO	—	15.00	25.00	35.00	50.00	—

KM# 656   50 CENTAVOS
Copper **Obv:** UN PESO effaced below eagle

Date	Mintage	VG	F	VF	XF	Unc
1915 C.M. GRO	—	12.00	20.00	30.00	60.00	—

KM# 657   50 CENTAVOS
Copper **Note:** Regular obverse.

Date	Mintage	VG	F	VF	XF	Unc
1915 C.M. GRO	—	6.00	10.00	15.00	25.00	—

KM# 657a   50 CENTAVOS
Base Silver **Note:** Regular obverse.

Date	Mintage	VG	F	VF	XF	Unc
1915 C.M. GRO	—	165	275	400	575	—

KM# 658   PESO (UN)
0.3000 g., 1.0000 Gold-Silver **Obv:** Date below eagle

Date	Mintage	VG	F	VF	XF	Unc
1914 Co Mo Gro	—	450	500	800	1,000	—

KM# 658a   PESO (UN)
Brass **Obv:** Date below eagle

Date	Mintage	VG	F	VF	XF	Unc
1914 Co Mo Gro	—	—	—	—	—	—
Unique						

KM# 659   PESO (UN)
0.3000 g., 1.0000 Gold-Silver   **Rev:** Date below Liberty cap

Date	Mintage	VG	F	VF	XF	Unc
1914 CAMPO Mo	—	15.00	30.00	45.00	60.00	—

KM# 660   2 PESOS (Dos)
0.5950 g., 1.0000 Gold-Silver   **Rev:** Sun over mountains

Date	Mintage	VG	F	VF	XF	Unc
1915 Co. Mo.	—	12.00	20.00	30.00	50.00	—

KM# 660a   2 PESOS (Dos)
Copper   **Rev:** Sun over mountains

Date	Mintage	VG	F	VF	XF	Unc
1915 Co. Mo.	—	—	600	800	1,000	—

KM# 661   2 PESOS (Dos)
0.5950 g., 1.0000 Gold-Silver   **Rev:** Star before and after Co. Mo

Date	Mintage	VG	F	VF	XF	Unc
1915 Co. Mo.	—	1,500	2,000	5,000	7,000	—

KM# 662   2 PESOS (Dos)
0.5950 g., 1.0000 Gold-Silver   **Rev:** Cap and rays

Date	Mintage	VG	F	VF	XF	Unc
1915 C. M. GRO	—	20.00	30.00	45.00	85.00	—

KM# 662a.1   2 PESOS (Dos)
Copper   **Rev:** Cap and rays

Date	Mintage	VG	F	VF	XF	Unc
1915 C. M. GRO	—	—	—	—	1,200	—

KM# 662a.2   2 PESOS (Dos)
Copper   **Obv:** Star between spray and R in REPUBLICA   **Rev:** Cap and rays

Date	Mintage	VG	F	VF	XF	Unc
1915 C. M. GRO Unique	—	—	—	—	—	—

CHILPANCINGO

REVOLUTIONARY COINAGE

KM# 663   10 CENTAVOS
Cast Silver   **Rev:** Sun above denomination

Date	Mintage	VG	F	VF	XF	Unc
1914	—	700	1,000	1,200	1,500	—

Note: Many counterfeits exist

KM# 664   20 CENTAVOS
Cast Silver   **Rev:** Sun above denomination

Date	Mintage	VG	F	VF	XF	Unc
1914	—	700	1,000	1,200	1,500	—

Note: Many counterfeits exist

SURIANA

REVOLUTIONARY COINAGE

KM# 665   2 PESOS (Dos)
1.0000 Gold-Silver .595 oz.   **Rev:** Sun over mountains

Date	Mintage	VG	F	VF	XF	Unc
1915 Rare	—	—	—	18,000	25,000	—

Note: Spink America Gerber sale part 2, 6-96 VF realized $16,500

TAXCO

REVOLUTIONARY COINAGE

KM# 667   2 CENTAVOS
Copper   **Obv. Legend:** EDO.DE.GRO

Date	Mintage	VG	F	VF	XF	Unc
1915 O/T	—	25.00	40.00	60.00	90.00	—

KM# 668   5 CENTAVOS
Copper

Date	Mintage	VG	F	VF	XF	Unc
1915	—	9.00	15.00	25.00	35.00	—

KM# 669   10 CENTAVOS
Copper

Date	Mintage	VG	F	VF	XF	Unc
1915	—	9.00	20.00	35.00	50.00	—

KM# 670   50 CENTAVOS
Copper   **Obv:** Legend in large letters

Date	Mintage	VG	F	VF	XF	Unc
1915	—	15.00	25.00	50.00	65.00	—

KM# 671   50 CENTAVOS
Silver   **Rev:** Sun above denomination

Date	Mintage	VG	F	VF	XF	Unc
1915	—	20.00	30.00	40.00	70.00	—

KM# 672   PESO (UN)
11.5000 g., 0.3000 Gold-Silver   **Obv:** Star before UN PESO
Rev: Star before G

Date	Mintage	VG	F	VF	XF	Unc
1915	—	12.00	20.00	30.00	45.00	—

KM# 672a   PESO (UN)
Brass   **Obv:** Star before UN PESO **Rev:** Star before G

Date	Mintage	VG	F	VF	XF	Unc
1915	—	200	300	450	600	—

KM# 672b   PESO (UN)
Lead   **Obv:** Star before UN PESO **Rev:** Star before G

Date	Mintage	VG	F	VF	XF	Unc
1915	—	50.00	100	200	350	—

KM# 672c   PESO (UN)
Copper   **Obv:** Star before UN PESO **Rev:** Star before G

Date	Mintage	VG	F	VF	XF	Unc
1915	—	200	300	400	650	—

KM# 673   PESO (UN)
0.3000 g., 1.0000 Gold-Silver   **Obv:** Star before UN PESO
Rev: Without star before G

Date	Mintage	VG	F	VF	XF	Unc
1915	—	250	400	500	800	—

KM# 674   PESO (UN)
0.3000 g., 1.0000 Gold-Silver   **Obv:** Without star before UN
PESO **Rev:** Without star before G

Date	Mintage	VG	F	VF	XF	Unc
1915	—	100	200	300	500	—

JALISCO

Jalisco is a state on the west coast of Mexico. The few coins made for this state show that the *Army of the North* did not restrict their operations to the northern border states. The coins were made in Guadalajara under the watchful eye of General Dieguez, commander of this segment of Villa's forces.

GUADALAJARA

REVOLUTIONARY COINAGE

KM# 675 CENTAVO
Copper **Obv:** Cap and rays

Date	Mintage	VG	F	VF	XF	Unc
1915	—	9.50	15.00	20.00	30.00	—

KM# 675a CENTAVO
Brass **Obv:** Cap and rays

Date	Mintage	VG	F	VF	XF	Unc
1915	—	—	—	300	450	—

KM# A676 CENTAVO
Copper **Obv:** Cap and rays **Rev:** Retrograde **Note:** Varieties exist.

Date	Mintage	VG	F	VF	XF	Unc
1915	—	75.00	200	500	800	—

KM# 676.1 2 CENTAVOS
Copper **Obv:** Cap and rays

Date	Mintage	VG	F	VF	XF	Unc
1915	—	10.00	18.00	20.00	35.00	—

Note: Varieties exist.

KM# 676.2 2 CENTAVOS
Copper **Obv:** Retrograde date, smaller Liberty cap and shorter rays

Date	Mintage	VG	F	VF	XF	Unc
1915	—	200	300	400	550	—

KM# 677 5 CENTAVOS
Copper **Obv:** Cap and rays

Date	Mintage	VG	F	VF	XF	Unc
1915	—	6.50	12.00	15.00	25.00	—

KM# 677a 5 CENTAVOS
Brass **Obv:** Cap and rays

Date	Mintage	VG	F	VF	XF	Unc
1915 rare	—	—	—	—	—	—

KM# 678 10 CENTAVOS
Copper **Obv:** Cap and rays above denomination **Rev:** Arms

Date	Mintage	VG	F	VF	XF	Unc
1915	—	—	—	3,000	5,000	—

KM# A678 PESO
Copper

Date	Mintage	VG	F	VF	XF	Unc
1915	—	—	—	—	15,000	—

MEXICO, ESTADO DE

Estado de Mexico is a state in central Mexico that surrounds the Federal District on three sides. The issues by the Zapata forces in this state have two distinctions – the Amecameca pieces are the crudest and the Toluca cardboard piece is the most unusual. General Tenorio authorized the crude incuse Amecameca pieces.

AMECAMECA

REVOLUTIONARY COINAGE

KM# 679 5 CENTAVOS
Brass **Obv. Legend:** EJERCITO CONVENCIONISTA

Date	Mintage	VG	F	VF	XF	Unc
ND unique	—	—	—	—	—	—

KM# 680 5 CENTAVOS
Brass **Obv:** Eagle above RM **Note:** Hand stamped.

Date	Mintage	VG	F	VF	XF	Unc
ND	—	200	300	500	600	—

KM# 681a 10 CENTAVOS
Copper **Obv:** Eagle above RM **Note:** Hand stamped.

Date	Mintage	VG	F	VF	XF	Unc
ND	—	75.00	125	225	350	—

KM# 681 10 CENTAVOS
Brass **Obv:** Eagle above RM **Note:** Hand stamped. Varieties exist.

Date	Mintage	VG	F	VF	XF	Unc
ND	—	60.00	90.00	150	200	—

KM# 682 20 CENTAVOS
Brass **Obv:** Eagle above RM **Note:** Hand stamped. Varieties exist.

Date	Mintage	VG	F	VF	XF	Unc
ND	—	15.00	22.50	35.00	60.00	—

KM# 682a 20 CENTAVOS
Copper **Obv:** Eagle above RM **Note:** Hand stamped.

Date	Mintage	VG	F	VF	XF	Unc
ND	—	25.00	50.00	175	250	—

KM# 683 20 CENTAVOS
Copper **Obv:** Eagle over A. D. J.

Date	Mintage	VG	F	VF	XF	Unc
ND	—	7.50	12.50	20.00	35.00	—

KM# 683a 20 CENTAVOS
Brass **Obv:** Eagle over A. D. J.

Date	Mintage	VG	F	VF	XF	Unc
ND	—	—	—	200	350	—

KM# 684 25 CENTAVOS
Brass **Obv. Legend:** EJERCITO CONVENCIONISTA

Date	Mintage	VG	F	VF	XF	Unc
ND unique	—	—	—	—	—	—

KM# 685 25 CENTAVOS
Copper **Obv:** Eagle over sprays **Note:** Hand stamped. Many modern counterfeits exist in all metals.

Date	Mintage	VG	F	VF	XF	Unc
ND	—	15.00	20.00	30.00	40.00	—

KM# 685a 25 CENTAVOS
Brass **Obv:** Eagle over sprays **Note:** Hand stamped.

Date	Mintage	VG	F	VF	XF	Unc
ND	—	—	—	50.00	100	—

KM# 685b 25 CENTAVOS
Silver **Obv:** Eagle over sprays **Note:** Hand stamped.

Date	Mintage	VG	F	VF	XF	Unc
ND	—	—	—	175	250	—

KM# 686 50 CENTAVOS
Copper **Obv:** Eagle over sprays **Note:** Hand stamped.

Date	Mintage	VG	F	VF	XF	Unc
ND	—	8.00	10.00	18.00	30.00	—

KM# 686a 50 CENTAVOS
Brass **Obv:** Eagle over sprays **Note:** Hand stamped.

Date	Mintage	VG	F	VF	XF	Unc
ND	—	75.00	100	150	200	—

Note: Stem of "¢" above the 5

KM# 687 50 CENTAVOS
Copper **Note:** Contemporary counterfeit, hand engraved.

Date	Mintage	VG	F	VF	XF	Unc
ND	—	12.00	30.00	50.00	80.00	—

Note: "¢" clears top of 5

TENANCINGO, TOWN
(Distrito Federal Mexico)

REVOLUTIONARY COINAGE

KM# 688.1 2 CENTAVOS
Copper **Rev:** Without TM below deonomination

Date	Mintage	VG	F	VF	XF	Unc
1915	—	—	—	800	2,000	—

KM# 688.2 2 CENTAVOS
Copper **Rev:** With TM below deonomination

Date	Mintage	VG	F	VF	XF	Unc
1915	—	—	400	800	2,000	—

KM# 689.1 5 CENTAVOS
Copper **Rev:** Lined C

Date	Mintage	VG	F	VF	XF	Unc
1915	—	10.00	20.00	30.00	50.00	—

KM# 689.2 5 CENTAVOS
Copper **Rev:** Solid C

Date	Mintage	VG	F	VF	XF	Unc
1915	—	100	200	400	500	—

KM# 690.1 10 CENTAVOS
Copper **Rev:** Without dot in C

Date	Mintage	VG	F	VF	XF	Unc
1916	—	10.00	20.00	40.00	60.00	—

KM# 690.2 10 CENTAVOS
Copper **Rev:** Dot in C

Date	Mintage	VG	F	VF	XF	Unc
1916	—	100	200	400	500	—

KM# 691 20 CENTAVOS
Copper

Date	Mintage	VG	F	VF	XF	Unc
1915	—	25.00	40.00	55.00	75.00	—

TOLUCA, CITY
(Distrito Federal Mexico)

KM# 692.1 5 CENTAVOS
Grey Cardboard **Obv:** Without dot after TOLUCA

Date	Mintage	VG	F	VF	XF	Unc
1915	—	15.00	30.00	50.00	75.00	—

KM# 692.2 5 CENTAVOS
Grey Cardboard **Obv:** Dot after TOLUCA

Date	Mintage	VG	F	VF	XF	Unc
1915	—	15.00	30.00	50.00	75.00	—

KM# 693.1 20 CENTAVOS
Copper **Countermark:** 20 within C **Note:** Countermark on
1 Centavo, KM#415. Varieties exist.

CM Date	Host Date	Good	VG	F	VF	XF
ND(1915)	ND	—	20.00	30.00	45.00	60.00

KM# 693.2 20 CENTAVOS
Copper **Countermark:** 20 within C **Note:** Countermark on
1 Centavo, KM#394.1.

CM Date	Host Date	Good	VG	F	VF	XF
ND(1915)	1904	—	200	400	800	1,000

KM# 694 40 CENTAVOS
Copper **Countermark:** 40 within C **Note:** Countermark on
2 Centavos, KM#419. Varieties exist.

CM Date	Host Date	Good	VG	F	VF	XF
ND(1915)	ND	—	25.00	40.00	60.00	80.00

MORELOS

Morelos is a state in south central Mexico, adjoining the
federal district on the south. It was the headquarters of Emiliano Zapata. His personal quarters were at Tlatizapan in Morelos. The Morelos coins from 2 Centavos to 1 Peso were all
copper except one type of 1 Peso in silver. The two operating
Zapatista mints in Morelos were Atlihuayan and Tlaltizapan.

EMILIANO ZAPATA
(Zapatista)

KM# 695 2 CENTAVOS
Copper **Obv. Legend:** E.L. DE MORELOS

Date	Mintage	VG	F	VF	XF	Unc
1915	—	1,000	1,400	1,800	2,250	—

KM# 696   5 CENTAVOS
Copper   **Rev. Legend:** E. DE MOR. 1915

Date	Mintage	VG	F	VF	XF	Unc
1915	—	300	500	1,000	3,500	—

KM# 697   10 CENTAVOS
Copper

Date	Mintage	VG	F	VF	XF	Unc
1915	—	12.00	20.00	30.00	40.00	—

KM# 698   10 CENTAVOS
Copper   **Rev:** Date effaced from die

Date	Mintage	VG	F	VF	XF	Unc
ND	—	12.00	20.00	35.00	55.00	—

KM# 699   10 CENTAVOS
Copper   **Rev. Legend:** E. DE MOR

Date	Mintage	VG	F	VF	XF	Unc
1915	—	1,000	2,000	2,500	3,000	—

KM# 700   10 CENTAVOS
Copper   **Rev. Legend:** MOR

Date	Mintage	VG	F	VF	XF	Unc
1916	—	5.00	20.00	30.00	50.00	—

KM# 701   20 CENTAVOS
Copper

Date	Mintage	VG	F	VF	XF	Unc
1915	—	9.00	15.00	25.00	35.00	—

KM# 702   50 CENTAVOS
Copper   **Obv:** MOR beneath eagle   **Rev:** 50C monogram

Date	Mintage	VG	F	VF	XF	Unc
1915	—	300	500	900	1,300	—

KM# 703a   50 CENTAVOS
Brass   **Obv:** Sprays beneath eagle   **Rev:** 50C monogram

Date	Mintage	VG	F	VF	XF	Unc
1915	—	100	200	400	600	—

KM# 706   50 CENTAVOS
Copper   **Obv:** Sprays beneath eagle   **Rev. Legend:**
REFORMA LIBERTAD JUSTICIA Y LEY

Date	Mintage	VG	F	VF	XF	Unc
1915	—	350	500	800	1,000	—

KM# 703   50 CENTAVOS
Copper   **Obv:** Sprays beneath eagle   **Rev:** 50C monogram
Note: This coin exists with a silver and also a brass wash.

Date	Mintage	VG	F	VF	XF	Unc
1915	—	12.50	17.50	30.00	42.00	—

KM# 704   50 CENTAVOS
Copper   **Obv:** MORELOS below eagle

Date	Mintage	VG	F	VF	XF	Unc
1916	—	12.50	20.00	30.00	50.00	—

KM# 708 PESO (UN)
Silver **Rev:** Cap and rays

Date	Mintage	VG	F	VF	XF	Unc
1916	—	450	750	1,000	1,500	—

KM# 708a PESO (UN)
Copper **Rev:** Cap and rays

Date	Mintage	VG	F	VF	XF	Unc
1916	—	450	750	1,000	1,500	—

OAXACA

Oaxaca is one of the southern states in Mexico. The coins issued in this state represent the most prolific series of the Revolution. Most of the coins bear the portrait of Benito Juarez, have corded or plain edges and were issued by a provisional government in the state. The exceptions are the rectangular 1 and 3 Centavos pieces that begin the series.

PROVISIONAL GOVERNMENT

KM# 709 CENTAVO (UN)
Copper **Note:** Rectangular flan.

Date	Mintage	VG	F	VF	XF	Unc
1915	—	60.00	90.00	200	300	—

KM# 710 CENTAVO (UN)
Copper **Obv:** Bust of Juarez left

Date	Mintage	VG	F	VF	XF	Unc
1915	—	12.00	17.50	25.00	40.00	—

KM# 710a CENTAVO (UN)
Brass **Obv:** Bust of Juarez left

Date	Mintage	VG	F	VF	XF	Unc
1915	—	50.00	100	200	300	—

KM# 711 3 CENTAVOS (Tres)
Copper **Rev. Legend:** PROVISIO... **Note:** Rectangular flan.

Date	Mintage	VG	F	VF	XF	Unc
1915	—	60.00	150	200	300	—

KM# 712 3 CENTAVOS (Tres)
Copper **Rev. Legend:** PROVISI... **Note:** Rectangular flan.

Date	Mintage	VG	F	VF	XF	Unc
1915	—	1,000	2,000	3,000	6,000	—

KM# 713.1 3 CENTAVOS (Tres)
Copper **Obv:** Bust of Juarez left **Rev:** Without TM below denomination

Date	Mintage	VG	F	VF	XF	Unc
1915	—	3.00	5.00	12.00	25.00	—

KM# 713.2 3 CENTAVOS (Tres)
Copper **Rev:** Without TM below denomination **Edge:** Plain

Date	Mintage	VG	F	VF	XF	Unc
1915	—	—	—	70.00	100	—

KM# 713.3 3 CENTAVOS (Tres)
Copper **Rev:** With TM below denomination

Date	Mintage	VG	F	VF	XF	Unc
1915	—	100	200	400	500	—

KM# 714 3 CENTAVOS (Tres)
Copper **Rev:** Small 3

Date	Mintage	VG	F	VF	XF	Unc
1915	—	6.00	10.00	15.00	30.00	—

KM# 715 5 CENTAVOS
Copper **Note:** JAN. 15 1915. incuse lettering

Date	Mintage	VG	F	VF	XF	Unc
1915 Rare	—	—	—	—	—	—

KM# 716 5 CENTAVOS
Copper **Obv:** Facing bust of Juarez

Date	Mintage	VG	F	VF	XF	Unc
1915	—	—	—	—	8,000	—

KM# 717 5 CENTAVOS
Copper Obv: Second bust, low relief with long, pointed truncation

Date	Mintage	VG	F	VF	XF	Unc
1915	—	1.50	3.00	4.50	10.00	—

KM# 722 10 CENTAVOS
Copper Obv: Second bust, low relief with long, pointed truncation

Date	Mintage	VG	F	VF	XF	Unc
1915	—	1.50	2.50	5.00	10.00	—

KM# 723 10 CENTAVOS
Copper Note: Obverse and reverse legend retrograde.

Date	Mintage	VG	F	VF	XF	Unc
1915 Rare	—	—	—	—	—	—

KM# 718 5 CENTAVOS
Copper Obv: Fifth bust, heavy with short unfinished lapels

Date	Mintage	VG	F	VF	XF	Unc
1915	—	1.50	2.50	4.00	10.00	—

KM# 724 10 CENTAVOS
Copper Obv: Fourth bust, bold, unfinished truncation using 1 Peso obverse die of KM#740

Date	Mintage	VG	F	VF	XF	Unc
1915	—	3.00	5.00	7.00	10.00	—

KM# 725 10 CENTAVOS
Copper Obv: Fifth bust, heavy with short unfinished lapels centered high

Date	Mintage	VG	F	VF	XF	Unc
1915	—	1.50	2.50	4.00	10.00	—

KM# 719 5 CENTAVOS
Copper Obv: Sixth bust, curved bottom

Date	Mintage	VG	F	VF	XF	Unc
1915	—	1.50	2.50	4.00	10.00	—

KM# 726 10 CENTAVOS
Copper Obv: Sixth bust, curved bottom

Date	Mintage	VG	F	VF	XF	Unc
1915	—	1.50	2.50	4.00	10.00	—

KM# 720 5 CENTAVOS
Copper Obv: Seventh bust, short truncation with closed lapels

Date	Mintage	VG	F	VF	XF	Unc
1915	—	1.50	3.00	4.50	10.00	—

KM# 721 5 CENTAVOS
Copper Obv: Eighth bust, short curved truncation

Date	Mintage	VG	F	VF	XF	Unc
1915	—	1.50	2.50	5.00	10.00	—

KM# 727.1 10 CENTAVOS
Copper Obv: Seventh bust, short truncation with closed lapels

Date	Mintage	VG	F	VF	XF	Unc
1915	—	1.50	2.50	4.00	10.00	—

KM# 727.2   10 CENTAVOS
Copper **Obv:** T below bow, M below 1st leaf **Note:** At present, only four pieces of this type are known. All are VF or better.

Date	Mintage	VG	F	VF	XF	Unc
1915	—	—	—	400	550	—

KM# 727.3   10 CENTAVOS
Copper **Obv:** Counterstamp GV on seventh bust, short truncation with closed lapels **Rev:** Similar to KM#727.1 **Note:** This counterstamp appears on several different type host 10 cent coins.

Date	Mintage	VG	F	VF	XF	Unc
1915	—	100	200	300	400	—

Note: Letters GV correspond to General Garcia Vigil

KM# 728   20 CENTAVOS
Silver **Obv:** Second bust, low relief with long pointed truncation

Date	Mintage	VG	F	VF	XF	Unc
1915	—	500	750	1,200	1,500	—

KM# 728a   20 CENTAVOS
Copper **Obv:** Second bust, low relief with long pointed truncation

Date	Mintage	VG	F	VF	XF	Unc
1915 Rare	—	—	—	—	—	—

KM# 729.1   20 CENTAVOS
Copper **Obv:** Fourth bust, unfinished truncation using 1 Peso obverse die

Date	Mintage	VG	F	VF	XF	Unc
1915	—	1.50	3.00	4.50	10.00	—

KM# 729.2   20 CENTAVOS
Copper **Counterstamp:** Liberty cap **Obv:** Counterstamp liberty cap and rays on fourth bust, bold unfinished truncation using 1 Peso obverse die

Date	Mintage	VG	F	VF	XF	Unc
1915	—	100	150	300	350	—

KM# 730   20 CENTAVOS
Copper **Obv:** 5th bust, heavy with short unfinished lapels using 20 Pesos obverse die

Date	Mintage	VG	F	VF	XF	Unc
1915	—	5.00	7.00	10.00	15.00	—

KM# 731.1   20 CENTAVOS
Copper **Obv:** Sixth bust, curved bottom

Date	Mintage	VG	F	VF	XF	Unc
1915	—	1.50	2.50	5.00	10.00	—

KM# 731.2   20 CENTAVOS
Copper **Note:** Similar to KM#731.1 but with fourth bust.

Date	Mintage	VG	F	VF	XF	Unc
1915 Unique	—	—	—	—	—	—

KM# 732   20 CENTAVOS
Copper **Obv:** Sixth bust

Date	Mintage	VG	F	VF	XF	Unc
1915	—	1.50	2.50	4.00	10.00	—

KM# 733   20 CENTAVOS
Copper **Obv:** 7th bust, short truncation with closed lapels

Date	Mintage	VG	F	VF	XF	Unc
1915	—	1.50	3.00	4.50	10.00	—

KM# 734   50 CENTAVOS
Silver **Obv:** Fifth bust, heavy, with short unfinished lapels, centered high

Date	Mintage	VG	F	VF	XF	Unc
1915	—	10.00	20.00	40.00	85.00	—

KM# 735 50 CENTAVOS
Silver **Obv:** Sixth bust, curved bottom

Date	Mintage	VG	F	VF	XF	Unc
1915	—	8.00	12.00	20.00	35.00	—

KM# 736 50 CENTAVOS
Silver **Obv:** Seventh bust, short truncation with closed lapels

Date	Mintage	VG	F	VF	XF	Unc
1915	—	6.00	9.00	15.00	25.00	—

KM# 737 50 CENTAVOS
Silver **Obv:** Eighth bust, short truncation with pronounced curve

Date	Mintage	VG	F	VF	XF	Unc
1915	—	6.50	10.00	16.00	30.00	—

KM# 739 50 CENTAVOS
Billon **Obv:** Ninth bust, high nearly straight truncation

Date	Mintage	VG	F	VF	XF	Unc
1915	—	—	—	—	3,000	—

KM# 739a 50 CENTAVOS
Copper **Obv:** Ninth bust, high nearly straight truncation

Date	Mintage	VG	F	VF	XF	Unc
1915	—	—	—	—	—	—

KM# 740.1 PESO (UN)
Silver **Obv:** Fourth bust, with heavy unfinished truncation

Date	Mintage	VG	F	VF	XF	Unc
1915	—	3.00	5.00	10.00	20.00	—

KM# 740.2 PESO (UN)
Silver **Obv:** Fourth bust, with heavy unfinished truncation
Rev: TM below bow on wreath

Date	Mintage	VG	F	VF	XF	Unc
1915	—	150	300	400	600	—

KM# 741 PESO (UN)
Silver **Obv:** Fifth bust, heavy, with short unfinished lapels, centered high

Date	Mintage	VG	F	VF	XF	Unc
1915	—	6.00	9.00	20.00	25.00	—

KM# 742 PESO (UN)
Silver **Obv:** Sixth bust, curved bottom line

Date	Mintage	VG	F	VF	XF	Unc
1915	—	6.00	9.00	20.00	25.00	—

KM# 742a PESO (UN)
Copper **Obv:** Sixth bust, curved bottom line

Date	Mintage	VG	F	VF	XF	Unc
1915	—	—	—	—	500	—

KM# 743 PESO (UN)
Silver **Obv:** Seventh bust, short truncation with closed lapels

Date	Mintage	VG	F	VF	XF	Unc
1915	—	8.00	10.00	15.00	20.00	—

KM# 743a PESO (UN)
Silver **Obv:** Seventh bust, short truncation with closed lapels
Rev: TM below bow on wreath

Date	Mintage	VG	F	VF	XF	Unc
1915	—	35.00	75.00	150	200	—

KM# 744 2 PESOS (Dos)
Silver **Obv:** Fourth bust, using 1 Peso obverse die

Date	Mintage	VG	F	VF	XF	Unc
1915	—	12.00	20.00	30.00	50.00	—

KM# 744a 2 PESOS (Dos)
Copper **Obv:** Fourth bust, using 1 Peso obverse die

Date	Mintage	VG	F	VF	XF	Unc
1915 Rare	—	—	—	—	—	—

KM# 745   2 PESOS (Dos)
, 22 mm.   **Obv:** Fifth bust **Rev:** Curved bottomed 2 over
PESOS **Note:** 0.9020 Silver, 0.0100 Gold.

Date	Mintage	VG	F	VF	XF	Unc
1915	—	12.00	20.00	30.00	50.00	—

KM# 745a   2 PESOS (Dos)
Copper **Obv:** Fifth bust **Rev:** Curved bottomed 2 over PESOS

Date	Mintage	VG	F	VF	XF	Unc
1915	—	50.00	75.00	110	160	—

KM# A746   2 PESOS (Dos)
Copper   **Obv:** Seventh bust, short truncation with closed
lapels

Date	Mintage	VG	F	VF	XF	Unc
1915 Unique	—	—	—	—	—	—

KM# 746   2 PESOS (Dos)
Silver **Obv:** Sixth bust **Rev:** 2 PESOS

Date	Mintage	VG	F	VF	XF	Unc
1915	—	10.00	15.00	30.00	55.00	—

KM# A747   2 PESOS (Dos)
Silver **Obv:** Sixth bust **Rev:** Dos PESOS **Note:** Obverse die
is free hand engraved.

Date	Mintage	VG	F	VF	XF	Unc
1915	—	—	—	185	275	—

KM# 746a   2 PESOS (Dos)
Copper **Obv:** Sixth bust **Rev:** 2 PESOS

Date	Mintage	Good	VG	F	VF	XF
1915	—	—	150	200	600	900

KM# 747.1   2 PESOS (Dos)
Silver **Obv:** Sixth bust **Rev:** DOS PESOS

Date	Mintage	VG	F	VF	XF	Unc
1915	—	10.00	15.00	30.00	60.00	—

KM# 747.2   2 PESOS (Dos)
Silver **Obv:** Sixth bust, dot after date **Rev:** DOS PESOS

Date	Mintage	VG	F	VF	XF	Unc
1915	—	10.00	20.00	30.00	60.00	—

KM# 747.3   2 PESOS (Dos)
Silver **Obv:** Sixth bust, dot after date, periods after L and S
Rev: DOS PESOS

Date	Mintage	VG	F	VF	XF	Unc
1915	—	10.00	20.00	30.00	60.00	—

KM# 748   2 PESOS (Dos)
0.9020 Silver, 22 mm.   **Obv:** Seventh bust, short truncation
with closed lapels

Date	Mintage	VG	F	VF	XF	Unc
1915	—	12.00	20.00	40.00	60.00	—

KM# 749   2 PESOS (Dos)
Silver **Obv:** Tenth, small nude bust

Date	Mintage	VG	F	VF	XF	Unc
1915 Unique	—	—	—	—	2,500	—

KM# 750   5 PESOS
0.1750 Gold **Obv:** Third bust, heavy, with short unfinished
lapels

Date	Mintage	VG	F	VF	XF	Unc
1915	—	150	200	275	375	—

KM# 750a   5 PESOS
Copper **Obv:** Third bust, heavy, with short unfinished lapels

Date	Mintage	VG	F	VF	XF	Unc
1915 Unique	—	—	—	—	—	—

KM# 751 5 PESOS
0.9020 Silver **Obv:** Seventh bust, short truncation with closed
lapels

Date	Mintage	VG	F	VF	XF	Unc
1915	—	50.00	100	200	250	—

KM# 751a 5 PESOS
Copper **Obv:** Seventh bust, short truncation with closed
lapels

Date	Mintage	VG	F	VF	XF	Unc
1915	—	125	200	300	800	—

KM# A752 10 PESOS
0.1500 Gold **Obv:** Fourth bust

Date	Mintage	VG	F	VF	XF	Unc
1915 Rare	—	—	—	—	—	—

KM# 752 10 PESOS
0.1750 Gold **Obv:** Fifth bust

Date	Mintage	VG	F	VF	XF	Unc
1915	—	200	275	375	500	—

KM# 752a 10 PESOS
Copper **Obv:** Fifth bust

Date	Mintage	VG	F	VF	XF	Unc
1915	—	500	1,000	1,500	3,000	—

KM# A753 20 PESOS
0.1500 Gold **Obv:** Fourth bust

Date	Mintage	VG	F	VF	XF	Unc
1915 Unique	—	—	—	—	—	—

KM# 753 20 PESOS
0.1750 Gold **Obv:** Fifth bust, heavy, with short unfinished
lapels, centered high

Date	Mintage	VG	F	VF	XF	Unc
1915	—	400	500	700	800	—

KM# 754 20 PESOS
0.1750 Gold **Obv:** Seventh bust, short truncation with closed
lapels

Date	Mintage	VG	F	VF	XF	Unc
1915	—	200	300	400	625	—

KM# 755 60 PESOS
0.8590 Gold **Edge:** Reeded

Date	Mintage	F	VF	XF	Unc	BU
1916 Rare	—	—	8,000	15,000	22,000	—

KM# 755a 60 PESOS
Silver **Edge:** Reeded

Date	Mintage	F	VF	XF	Unc	BU
1916	—	—	—	—	1,800	—

KM# 755b 60 PESOS
Copper **Edge:** Plain

Date	Mintage	F	VF	XF	Unc	BU
1916	—	—	—	1,000	1,800	—

PUEBLA

A state of central Mexico. Puebla was a state that occasionally saw Zapata forces active within its boundaries. Also active, and an issuer of coins, was the Madero brigade who issued coins with their name two years after Madero's death. The state issue of 2, 5, 10 and 20 Centavos saw limited circulation and recent hoards have been found of some values.

CHICONCUAUTLA
Madero Brigade

REVOLUTIONARY COINAGE

KM# 756 10 CENTAVOS
Copper

Date	Mintage	VG	F	VF	XF	Unc
1915	—	7.50	12.50	17.50	25.00	—

KM# 758   20 CENTAVOS
Copper **Rev:** TRANSITORIO without rosettes

Date	Mintage	VG	F	VF	XF	Unc
1915	—	2.50	4.00	6.50	12.00	—

KM# 757   20 CENTAVOS
Copper **Rev:** TRANSITORIO between rosettes **Note:**
Varieties exist.

Date	Mintage	VG	F	VF	XF	Unc
1915	—	2.50	4.00	6.50	12.00	—

TETELA DEL ORO Y OCAMPO

REVOLUTIONARY COINAGE

KM# 759   2 CENTAVOS
Copper

Date	Mintage	VG	F	VF	XF	Unc
1915	—	12.50	20.00	28.00	45.00	—
1915 Restrikes	—	—	1.00	1.50	2.00	—

KM# 760   2 CENTAVOS
Copper **Rev. Legend:** E. DE PU.

Date	Mintage	VG	F	VF	XF	Unc
1915	—	15.00	25.00	35.00	75.00	—

KM# 761   2 CENTAVOS
Copper **Rev. Legend:** E. DE PUE.

Date	Mintage	VG	F	VF	XF	Unc
1915	—	9.00	15.00	22.50	35.00	—

KM# 762   5 CENTAVOS
Copper

Date	Mintage	VG	F	VF	XF	Unc
1915	—	50.00	100	150	250	—

KM# 764   20 CENTAVOS
Copper

Date	Mintage	VG	F	VF	XF	Unc
1915	—	50.00	100	150	225	—

KM#	Date	Mintage	Identification	Mkt Val
TS1	1915	—	10 Centavos. Copper. Uniface, KM#763.	475
TS2	1915	—	10 Centavos. Brass. Uniface, KM#763.	750
TS3	1915	—	10 Centavos. Copper. KM#761. Eagle.	1,600

SINALOA

A state along the west coast of Mexico. The cast pieces of this state have been attributed to two people - Generals Rafael Buelna and Juan Carrasco. The cap and rays 8 Reales is usually attributed to General Buelna and the rest of the series to Carrasco. Because of their crude nature it is questionable whether separate series or mints can be determined.

BUELNA / CARRASCO

CAST & COUNTERMARKED COINAGE
Revolutionary

These are all crude sand cast coins using regular coins to prepare the mold. Prices below give a range for how much of the original coin from which the mold was prepared is visible.

KM# 765   20 CENTAVOS
Cast Silver **Note:** Sand molded using regular 20 Centavos.

CM Date	Host Date	Good	VG	F	VF	XF
ND(ca.1915)	ND(1898-1905)	200	300	—	—	—

KM# 766 50 CENTAVOS
Cast Silver **Note:** Sand molded using regular 50 Centavos, KM#445.

Date	Mintage	Good	VG	F	VF	XF
ND(1905-1918)	—	200	300	—	—	—

KM# 767 50 CENTAVOS
Cast Silver **Countermark:** G.C. **Obv:** With additional countermark **Note:** Sand molded using regular 50 Centavos, KM#445.

CM Date	Host Date	Good	VG	F	VF	XF
ND	ND(1905-1918)	100	150	200	300	—

KM# 768.1 PESO
Cast Silver **Note:** Sand molded using regular 8 Reales, KM#377.

CM Date	Host Date	Good	VG	F	VF	XF
ND(ca.1915)	ND(1824-97)	17.50	35.00	45.00	55.00	—

KM# 768.2 PESO
Cast Silver **Countermark:** G.C. **Obv:** With additional countermark **Note:** Sand molded using regular 8 Reales, KM#377.

KM# 769 PESO
Cast Silver **Note:** Sand molded using regular Peso, KM#409.

CM Date	Host Date	Good	VG	F	VF	XF
ND	ND(1898-1909)	10.00	20.00	30.00	40.00	—

KM# 770 PESO
Cast Silver **Countermark:** G.C **Obv:** With additional countermark **Note:** Sand molded using regular Peso, KM#409.

CM Date	Host Date	Good	VG	F	VF	XF
ND(ca.1915)	ND(1898-1909)	30.00	60.00	140	175	—

CM Date	Host Date	Good	VG	F	VF	XF
ND(ca.1915)	ND(1824-97)	25.00	45.00	100	150	—

Bibliography

Boyd, Julian P. (Editor). *The Papers of Thomas Jefferson*. Vol. 7. New Jersey: Princeton University Press, 1953.

Bowers, Q. David. *The History of United States Coinage as Illustrated by the Garrett Collection*. Los Angeles: Bowers & Ruddy Galleries, 1979.

Breen, Walter. *Walter Breen's Complete Encyclopedia of U.S. and Colonial Coins*. New York: F.C.I. Press, Doubleday, 1988.

Bressett, Ken, and Kosoff, A. *Official A.N.A. Grading Standard for United States Coins*. Fourth Edition. Colorado Springs, Colo.: American Numismatic Association, 1991.

Brown, Martin R., and Dunn, John W. *A Guide to the Grading of United States Coins*. Fourth and Fifth Editions. Racine, Wis.: Whitman Publishing Co., 1964 and 1969.

Bullowa, David M. *Numismatic Notes and Monographs No. 83: The Commemorative Coinage of the United States 1892-1938*. New York, N.Y.: American Numismatic Society, 1938.

Evans, George G. *Illustrated History of the United States Mint*. Revised Edition. Philadelphia: George G. Evans, 1892.

Fitzpatrick, John E. (Editor). *The Writings of George Washington*. Vol. 28. Washington: U.S. Government Printing Office, 1938.

Heath, Dr. George. *The Numismatist*, September 1888 and February 1892.

Hepburn, A. Barton. *A History of Currency in the United States*. Revised Edition. New York: Sentry Press, 1967.

Krause, Chester L., and Mishler, Clifford. Colin R. Bruce II (Senior Editor). *The Standard Catalog of World Gold Coins*. Fourth Edition. Iola, Wis.: Krause Publications, 2000.

Krueger, Kurt R. "Grading: Bestial Pandemonium Unleashed." *The Numismatist*, January 1976. Colorado Springs, Colo.: American Numismatic Association, 1975.

Ruddy, James F. *Photograde*. Wolfeboro, N.H.: Bowers and Merena Galleries In., 1983.

Sheldon, William H. *Early American Cents*. New York: Harper & Row. 1949.

Syrett, Harold C. *The Papers of Alexander Hamilton*. Vol. 7. New York: Columbia University Press, 1963.

Taxay, Don. *The U.S. Mint and Coinage: An Illustrated History From 1776 to the Present*. Second Edition. New York: Arco Publishing Co., 1969.

U.S. Congress. Senate. *International Monetary Conference*. 1878. Senate Ex. Doc. 58. 45th Congress, Third Session. Washington, 1879.

U.S. Congress. Senate. *Coinage Laws of the United States 1792 to 1894 with an Appendix of Statistics Relating to Coins and Currency*. Fourth Edition. Washington, D.C.: Government Printing Office, 1894.

Van Allen, Leroy C., and Mallis, A. George. *Comprehensive Catalog and Encyclopedia of U.S. Morgan and Peace Silver Dollars*. New York: F.C.I. Press, 1976.

Willem, John M. *The United States Trade Dollar: America's Only Unwanted, Unhonored Coin*. New York: By the author, 1959; reprint edition, Racine, Wis.: Western Publishing Co., 1965.

Yeoman, R.S. *A Guidebook of United States Coins*. 45th Edition. Racine, Wis.: Western Publishing Co., 1991.

Enhance Your Collection With Help From Reliable References